Consumer Behaviour
INCLUDES ONLY BUYING TRENDS

Dinesh Kumar

Formerly Associate Professor (Marketing)
at Birla Institute of Management Technology (BIMTECH)

OXFORD
UNIVERSITY PRESS

Oxford University Press is a department of the University of Oxford.
It furthers the University's objective of excellence in research, scholarship,
and education by publishing worldwide. Oxford is a registered trade mark of
Oxford University Press in the UK and in certain other countries.

Published in India by
Oxford University Press
YMCA Library Building, 1 Jai Singh Road, New Delhi 110001, India

© Oxford University Press 2015

The moral rights of the author/s have been asserted.

First published in 2015

All rights reserved. No part of this publication may be reproduced, stored in
a retrieval system, or transmitted, in any form or by any means, without the
prior permission in writing of Oxford University Press, or as expressly permitted
by law, by licence, or under terms agreed with the appropriate reprographics
rights organization. Enquiries concerning reproduction outside the scope of the
above should be sent to the Rights Department, Oxford University Press, at the
address above.

You must not circulate this work in any other form
and you must impose this same condition on any acquirer.

ISBN-13: 978-0-19-809592-7
ISBN-10: 0-19-809592-9

Typeset in Garamond
by MacroTex Solutions, Chennai
Printed in India by Magic International (P) Ltd., Greater Noida

Third-party website addresses mentioned in this book are provided
by Oxford University Press in good faith and for information only.
Oxford University Press disclaims any responsibility for the material contained therein.

Preface

I often ask my students what they think consumer behaviour and what goes on in their minds when they buy products and brands. It should not be a difficult question since they have been consumers from the time they were born. With more than twenty years of consuming experience, they should be able to answer the question well enough.

However, more often than not, they struggle for an answer. 'What do you mean what goes on in our minds when we buy Coke or coffee? Nothing goes on in there—we just buy it when we feel like it', they say. However that's not true; many thoughts come into consumers' mind as they go about choosing and buying stuff. Very often we are unaware of why we begin to desire objects, and we can barely answer the question what makes us visit a shop and select one brand out of the many that are displayed on a retailer's shelf. Indeed, that is what makes the study of consumer behaviour so difficult yet exciting.

The study of consumer behaviour involves understanding the thinking of people to determine the thrill of discovering new products or a discount coupon, the joy of going out and shopping with friends, the satisfaction of owning and displaying new things. This path takes us to study not only psychology but also a variety of other subjects such as economics, society, family, culture, communication theories, ethics, and even anthropology. Anthropology? Yes, indeed. A case study in the book shows how a study of anthropology helped Intel design a school computer!

With such a vast canvas, consumer behaviour is like a widescreen movie in which many activities or events are going on at the same time. This book is a result of observing people buying a variety of products for years and questioning them about them.

ABOUT THE BOOK

Though there are a number of books available on the subject of consumer behaviour, this book has been written considering the many new developments in this exciting field. The era of the connected consumer has brought in tremendous change in human behaviour, and the data analysis provides unimagined tools to companies to analyse this behaviour with remarkable accuracy. In every chapter, these find a mention through numerous examples or exhibits. While Chapter 3, *Consumer Decision-making models*, for instance, covers the online model consisting of consumer decision journey (CDJ), modern consumer behavior has been described in detail in Chapter 16 on *Online Buying Behaviour*.

This book is a leap forward from the existing books available on the subject in many ways. First, it takes into account the latest research on the subject—topics such as online consumer behaviour and use of data analytics are arguably the future of this subject. Secondly, theory can be taught better if supported with adequate exhibits and case studies. In every chapter, a large number of examples have been used to help build readers' interest.

Third, the book is written from an Indian perspective. A detailed discussion on Indian market segmentation and Indian culture describes Indian traditions providing an insight into the mind of an Indian consumer as opposed to other books that may have American and European cases and examples.

PEDAGOGICAL FEATURES

Several pedagogical innovations have been used in the book. It would be correct to assume that students like to discuss cases and examples of brands that they know of as opposed to the ones with hypothetical situations. Therefore, real-life brands have been used and the questions are designed on them to interest and engage students. The large number of cases and examples will make the book invaluable for classroom teaching. The key features of this book are as follows:

Readable, authoritative, and comprehensive text The book has a style that is authoritative and easy to read. Concepts have been explained point-wise and they are supported with numerous examples, which makes it more comprehensible for students to understand.

Indian and global perspective Though the book is written in the Indian context, examples and case studies from other countries have also been included in the right measure, which add a global perspective to the book.

Theory and practical applications Much of consumer behaviour is theory, but care has been taken to add practical orientations through real-life case studies. Readers will therefore be able to relate to the theories with actual happenings in the world.

References from the respected journals Large number of papers and books has been cited while explaining concepts for drawing on references. This is for students to get inspired to read more text on consumer behaviour.

Case studies The book encompasses 36 opening and closing case studies, discussing real-life examples. The applications have been developed for the specific purpose of illustrating concepts. Teachers are suggested to use them to enhance the learning process of the students.

Situations from real life 'CB in Action' boxes included in all chapters are mini research situations from real life with a 'What would you do?' question. Instructors can use these exercises in class and involve students in fun learning activities. These will stimulate students to think of solutions to real-life problems.

Insight boxes Apart from these, chapters also encompass insight boxes, which provide global, research, and ethical issues. These can be used as discussion points in the class while offering students ideas for undertaking research.

Chapter-end exercises Concept-review questions, critical thinking questions, and a suggestive list of projects and assignments have been included to help in classroom teaching. These exercises would encourage students to discuss and review concepts and, undertake projects that will help them understand various consumer behaviour situations.

ONLINE RESOURCES

The following resources are available to support the faculty and students using this text:

For Faculty
- Instructor's manual
- PowerPoint slides

For Students
- Flash cards

COVERAGE AND STRUCTURE

Though the book has been specifically developed from an Indian perspective, it also provides a global outlook of consumer behaviour. Cases from India as well as other countries have been included to support the various concepts in all the chapters. For instance, the chapter-end case study on Grameen Bank of Bangladesh in Chapter 12 on *Consumer Influence and Diffusion of Innovation* provides a remarkable study on the way innovations spread through social movements. Similarly, Celtel's spread in Zambia; the chapter-end case study of Chapter 17 on *Consumer Engagement and Equity* provides an idea to the reader about ways to create value in a competitive market through loyalty and engagement.

The book has been divided into six parts.

Part I, Overview of Consumer Behaviour provides an outline of the subject including evolution of consumers, consumer decision-making models, and how it is used in consumer analysis, segmentation, and strategy. A discussion on study of the Indian population and market segments is a unique feature of this section.

This part explains in detail nature of business-to-business (B2B) buying behaviour and its difference with consumer retail buying. This is supported with a case study on Rolls Royce highlighting B2B relationships and how sensors in machines provide continuous data to manufacturers to help provide service before a fault is reported and another showing the dark side of B2B selling behavior where pharmaceutical companies influence doctors to prescribe their medicines, often unnecessary, just to increase their sales.

Part II, Consumer as an Individual is devoted to understanding the effect of personality, motivation, perception, and attitude on the buying behaviour. It provides explanation on how brands impart personality to appeal to the target audience and use a particular marketing approach to motivate consumers to purchase a certain product. This section uses examples on the approach used by the liquor brands such as Absolut, Smirnoff, and Bacardi to give a personality to their brands and match it with their target market to make it easier for students to understand the concepts. It includes perception and neuroscience, which show that the human brain forms impressions even before a person is aware of them. This section further explains how people learn to use products, efforts made by companies to teach people to consume and understand their attitudes towards buying a product.

Part III, Influences on Consumer Behaviour offers insights into the influence of families, class, and culture on the consumption behavior or purchase decisions of customers. It explains concepts using examples of Indian family, class, and culture.

Part IV, Modifying Consumer Behaviour, discusses innovations and innovative ideas/approaches companies use in manufacturing, co-creation of new ideas and products by consumers and producers. It further discusses strategies for designing marketing communications and messages to persuade consumers to try and purchase products. The text supports these strategies with examples such as innovation strategy of P&G and creation of brand Benetton with some of the most compelling images in advertising history.

Part V, Measuring and Analysing Consumer Behaviour elaborates discussion on the consumer research process and approaches used by companies to build long-term loyalties with customers. It includes a case study on how Tommy Hilfiger was able to improve its sales through market research.

Part VI, Modern Consumer explains online consumer behaviour and consumer engagement in times of exploding social media usage in which the power of brands is shifting from companies to consumers. It covers in detail online consumer behavior along with the future of shopping and omni-channel marketing. Though ethical insights form parts of various chapters, a chapter on ethics and social responsibility looks at these issues in detail.

I hope the book engages readers in the same way that it engaged me while writing it. Like my earlier book, *Marketing Channels* (OUP, 2012), I have kept the style readable and light. I hope you enjoy reading this book as well.

Any book can be improved through interaction with users. I therefore, eagerly look forward to receiving your comments and suggestions at mmindchd@gmail.com for which I will be extremely grateful.

Dinesh Kumar

Acknowledgements

Many people have helped me in writing this book and I would like to thank all of them.

I would like to thank Dr H. Chaturvedi, Director, Birla Institute of Management Technology (BIMTECH), Greater Noida who encouraged and supported me when I started writing my books. It was at BIMTECH where I worked as Associate Professor in 2009 that I started writing my first book, *Marketing Channels* (OUP, 2012). My special thanks are due to Prof. N. N. Sharma, Associate Professor, India Centre for Public Policy (ICPP), BIMTECH who encouraged me at every step. Since I had to shift to Chandigarh after a stint at BIMTECH, I miss the discussions I had with him and my other colleagues.

I am grateful to all my colleagues who always had a word of encouragement for me. Special thanks are due to the Dr Babita Dosajh, Associate Professor, Amity Global Business School, Chandigarh, a trusted friend and colleague, who has always encouraged me in my work.

I would also like to thank to Mr Anmol Dar, Managing Director, Superbrands, for allowing us to reproduce ads and visuals in our book.

I am extremely grateful to my family, Punam and Karan, who have been pillars of support in all my endeavours.

Dinesh Kumar

Brief Contents

Preface iii
Detailed Contents ix
List of Exhibits and Case Studies xv
Features of the Book xviii

PART I: OVERVIEW OF CONSUMER BEHAVIOUR — 1

1. Introduction to Consumer Behaviour — 3
2. Consumer Analysis, Segmentation, and Strategy — 27
3. Consumer Decision-making Models — 63
4. Business-to-business Buying Behaviour — 95

PART II: CONSUMER AS AN INDIVIDUAL — 133

5. Personality and the Consumer — 135
6. Consumer Motivation — 178
7. Consumer Perception — 211
8. Consumer Learning — 261
9. Consumer Attitudes and Change — 300

PART III: INFLUENCES ON CONSUMER BEHAVIOUR — 339

10. Family and Social Class — 341
11. Culture and Consumer Behaviour — 375

PART IV: MODIFYING CONSUMER BEHAVIOUR — 419

12. Consumer Influence and Diffusion of Innovation — 421
13. Communications and Consumer Behaviour — 465

PART V: MEASURING AND ANALYSING CONSUMER BEHAVIOUR — 513

14. Consumer Research Process — 515
15. Consumption and Post-purchase Behaviour — 560

PART VI: MODERN CONSUMER — 599

16. Online Buying Behaviour — 601
17. Consumer Engagement and Equity — 643
18. Ethics and Social Responsibility — 674

Index 703
About the author 707

Detailed Contents

Preface iii
Brief Contents vii
List of Exhibits and Case Studies xv
Features of the Book xviii

PART I: OVERVIEW OF CONSUMER BEHAVIOUR — 1

1. Introduction to Consumer Behaviour — 3
Introduction — 5
  Ubiquitous Consumer Culture 5
  Consumer Behaviour 6
  Emergence of Marketing Concept 8
Consumers and Society — 10
  McDonaldization of Society 10
  Aesthetic Attitude 11
  Individualization and Self-expression 12
  Enjoyable and Pleasurable 14
  Customer Value and Satisfaction 15
  Consumption as a Basis of Existence 16
  Study of Irrational Behaviour 16
  Limitations of Consumer Psychology 17
  Consumer Behaviour in Economic Uncertainty 18
Consumer Behaviour in the Future — 21

2. Consumer Analysis, Segmentation, and Strategy — 27
Introduction — 29
De-massifying Markets — 30
Market Segmentation — 30
  Need for Segmentation 33
Bases of Segmentation — 34
  Geographic Segmentation 35
  Demographic Segmentation 36
  Sociocultural Segmentation 37
  Psychographic or Lifestyle Segmentation 38
  Benefit Segmentation 40
  Psychological Segmentation 41
  Use-related Segmentation 42
  Hybrid Segmentation 42
  Clustering Techniques 44
  Indian Market Segmentation 48
  Criticism of Segmentation 51
  Counter-segmentation 52
Using Segmentation Effectively — 53
  Microtargeting 55
  Mass Customization 55
Towards a New Era — 56

3. Consumer Decision-making Models — 63
Introduction — 65
  Levels of Consumer Decision-making 65
Human Mind—A Black Box — 66
  Economic Man 68
  Consumer Decision-making Process 68
  Critique of the Economic Man 72
Analytical Models of Consumer Behaviour — 72
  Nicosia Model 73
  Howard–Sheth Model 76
  Engel–Blackwell–Miniard Model 79
  Evaluation of Models 82
Consumer Decision Journey — 84
Prescriptive Cognitive Models — 85
  Theory of Reasoned Action 85
  Theory of Planned Behaviour 86
Humanistic Models — 87
  Theory of Trying 88
  Goal-directed Behaviour 89

4. Business-to-business Buying Behaviour — 95
Introduction — 97
Players in Business Market — 98
  Supply Chain Market 98
  Business User Markets 98
Characteristics of B2B Markets — 99
Differences Between B2B and B2C — 101
Understanding B2B Transactions — 103
  B2B Buying Drivers 103
  Types of B2B Products 105
  B2B Services 107
B2B Purchase Process — 107
B2B Segments — 108
  Demographics 109

Operating Variables 109
　　Purchasing Approaches 110
　　Situational Factors 110
　　Buyers' Personal Characteristics 111
　Understanding B2B Buying Behaviour　112
　　Individual Determinants 112
　　Organizational Determinants 113
　　Institutional Buying 115

　Buying Situations and Buying Behaviour　116
　　Buying Situations 116
　　Buying Centre 117
　Role of B2B Brands　118
　　Customer Satisfaction in B2B Markets 121
　B2B E-Marketplace　122
　B2B Relationships　122
　　Managing B2B Relationships 124

PART II: CONSUMER AS AN INDIVIDUAL　133

5. Personality and the Consumer　135
　Introduction　136
　　Nature of Personality 137
　Theories of Personality　137
　　Freudian Theory of Personality 138
　　Neo-Freudian Theory 140
　　Trait Theory 143
　Personality and Consumer Behaviour　145
　　Consumer Personality and Brand Personality 146
　　Consumer Innovativeness 146
　　Consumer Dogmatism 147
　　Social Character 148
　Cognitive Personality Factors　150
　　Materialism 150
　　Fixation, Impulsive, and Compulsive Consumption 151
　　Consumer Ethnocentrism 152
　　Cosmopolitanism 153
　Brand Personality　154
　　Brand Personification 154
　　Advertising Elements 157
　　Anthropomorphism 158
　　Product Personality and Gender 159
　　Product Personality and Geography 162
　　Personality and Colour 163
　　Colour Differentiation 163
　Self and Self-Image　164
　　One or Multiple Selves 166
　　Extended Self 167
　　Altering the Self 167
　　Virtual Personality 169

6. Consumer Motivation　178
　Introduction　180
　　Consumer Motivation 181
　Needs, Goals, and Motives　182

　　Nature and Function of Goals 184
　　Characteristics of Needs 184
　　Success and Failure Influence Goals 185
　Maslow's Hierarchy of Needs　185
　　Marketing Applications of Need Hierarchy 186
　　Product Design and Need Hierarchy 188
　　Self-Determination Theory 191
　Motives　192
　　Arousal of Motives 193
　　Components of Motivation 194
　Discovering Motives　196
　　Motivational Dimensions 196
　　Motivation Research 196
　　Analytic Hierarchy Process 198
　　Zaltman Metaphor Elicitation Technique 199
　　Avatar-based Marketing 200
　　Maximum Difference Scaling 203

7. Consumer Perception　211
　Introduction　213
　Perception　214
　　Perception and Marketing 215
　　Advertising and Perception 215
　Hedonic Consumption　216
　　Imagery in Marketing 217
　Sensory Marketing　220
　　Vision 220
　　Smell 221
　　Touch 222
　　Taste 222
　　Sound 223
　Stages of Perception　224
　　Exposure 224
　　Methods to Increase Exposure 226
　　Attention 227
　　Perceptual Interpretation 228

Perceptual Inference 230
   Semiotics 230
   Perceptual Distortion 231
   Perceptual Categorization 232
Retention 234
Perception Levels 236
   Weber's Law 236
   Subliminal Perception 236
   Brain Scanning 237
   Measuring Brain Activity 237
   Mirror Neurons 240
How Customers Think 240
   Perceptual Organization 241
   Gestalt Psychology 241
   Experiential Marketing 244
   Individual Characteristics 244
   Situational Characteristics 245
Altering Perceptions 245
   Customer-perceived Value 246
   Customer Perception and Product Strategy 247
Perceptual Mapping 249
   Benefits of Perceptual Mapping 249
   Perceptual Mapping Methods 251
Measuring Brand Image 251

8. Consumer Learning 261
Introduction 263
Consumer Learning 264
   Nature of Learning 264
   Learning Process 265
   Elements of Consumer Learning 266
   Getting Consumers Involved 267
   From Passive to Active Learning 268
   Central and Peripheral Routes 270
Behavioural Learning 272
   Classical Conditioning 272
   Instrumental or Operant Conditioning 274
   Observational or Vicarious Learning 276
Cognitive Learning—Information Processing 278

Memory Stages 281
Sensory Store 281
Storage, Retention, and Retrieval 282
Cognitive Processes 283
Marketing Implications of Behavioural Learning 285
   Shaping 285
   Habits 285
   Repetition 286
   Dangers of Repetition 286
   Stimulus Generalization 288
   Stimulus Discrimination 291
Measuring Learning 292
Brand Loyalty 293

9. Consumer Attitudes and Change 300
Introduction 302
Defining Attitude 302
   Nature of Attitude 304
   Functions of Attitudes 304
   Applications in Marketing 305
Models of Consumer Attitudes 305
   Tri-component Model of Attitudes 307
   Multi-attribute Attitude Model 308
   Theory of Reasoned Action 309
   Attitude towards the Ad 310
   Attitude towards the Store 312
   Theory of Trying to Consume 314
   Theory of Planned Behaviour 314
Attitude Formation 314
   Role of Experience 315
   Role of Personality 315
   Role of Society 315
Attitude and Behaviour 316
Changing Attitudes 317
   Resolving Conflicting Attitudes 326
   Altering Attitude Components 327
   Changing Consumer Beliefs about Competitors 328

PART III: INFLUENCES ON CONSUMER BEHAVIOUR 339

10. Family and Social Class 341
Introduction 342
Role of Family 343
   Functions of Family 344
   Indian Family Structures 344
   Changing Indian Family 345
   Family Buying Behaviour in India 346

Decision-makers in the Family 346
   Consumer Socialization 348
   Reverse Socialization 349
   Children as Consumers 350
   Marketing to Youth 351
   Marketing to Couples and Adults 352
   Seniors Market 355

xii Detailed Contents

    Family Life Cycle   356
    Family Decision-making   357
  Social Class   360
    Indian Social Class Segments   361
    Status Consumption   363
    Brand Awareness   363
    Value Orientation   364
    Measuring Social Class   364
    Subjective Method   365
    Reputational Method   365
    Objective Method   365
  Social Class Profiles   366
    Geodemographic Clustering of
    Markets   367
    Benefits of Geodemographic Clusters   367

11. Culture and Consumer Behaviour   375
Introduction   377
Meaning of Culture   377
    Characteristics of Culture   378
    Interaction of Culture and Consumer
    Behaviour   379
Hofstede's Cultural Dimensions   380
    Individualism   381
    Power Distance   383
    Masculinity   385
    Uncertainty Avoidance   385
    Long-term Orientation   385
Values   386
    Terminal and Instrumental Values   386
    Schwartz's Model of Universal Human
    Values   387

    Indian Core Values   388
Indian Cultural and Value Dimensions   389
    Individual and Family   390
    Modernity Through Conformity   391
    Success and Growth   391
    Age and Youthfulness   392
    Happiness and Adaptability   393
    Religion and Spirituality   393
    Rituals and Customs   394
    Traditions   394
    Languages   396
    Symbols and Signs   397
Measuring Culture   398
Contradictions in Indian Culture   399
    Demographics   399
    Modernity vs Traditionalism   399
    Bling vs Spirituality   400
    Decency vs Obscenity   400
    Violence vs Compassion   400
Cross-cultural Consumer Behaviour   402
    Strategic Decisions   402
    Products   403
    Global Influences on Indian Consumers   404
Subcultural Influences   405
    Country of Origin Effects   406
    Age Subcultures   407
    Geographic Subcultures   408
    Religious Subcultures   408
Multinational Strategies   408
    Global Strategy   409
    Local Strategy   411
    Glocal Strategy   411

PART IV: MODIFYING CONSUMER BEHAVIOUR   419

12. Consumer Influence and Diffusion of Innovation   421
Introduction   423
    Innovation and its Sources   423
    Need for Innovation   424
    Importance of New Products   427
Types of Innovation   429
    Firm-oriented Innovation   429
    Market-oriented Innovation   429
    Product-oriented Innovation   430
    Service Innovation   431
    Process Innovation   432
    Disruptive Innovation   432
Innovation Value Chain   433

Diffusion Process   434
    Spread of Innovations   435
    Product Characteristics   435
    Social Characteristics   436
    Characteristics of People   437
    Adopter Categories   438
    Importance of Critical Mass   440
Models of Innovation Diffusion   440
Reference Groups   442
    Brand Communities   444
    Social Movements   444
    Tribes and Tribal Marketing   445
    Making Brands 'Cool'   445
    Kitty Parties   447

Aspiration Groups 448
Negative Reference Groups 448
Consumer Activism on the Internet 449
Diffusion through Word of Mouth 449
Importance of Buzz 449
Social Networking 450
Guerrilla Marketing 451
Viral Marketing 451
Role of Opinion Leaders 451
Hurdles in Diffusion 452
Crossing the Chasm 453
Consumer Influence 455
Four Gears Model 455
Consumers as Innovators 456

13. Communications and Consumer Behaviour 465
Introduction 467
Marketing Communication 468
Semiotic System 468
Communication Models 469
Shannon–Weaver Model of Communication 469
Aida Model 471
Fogg's Behaviour Model for Persuasive Design 472
Communications Strategy 473
Understanding Customers 475
Customers are People 476
Understanding Customer Scenarios 476
Integrating Customer Experience 479
Consumer Processing and Evaluation 480
Message Strategy 482
Elaboration Likelihood Model 483
Types of Messages 484
Message Appeals 487
Message as Art Form 491
Media Strategy 491
Types of Media 491
Fragmentation of Media 492
Above- and Below-the-line
Campaigns 495
WOM Techniques 498
Consumer Imagery and Brand Personality 500
Communications and Brand Srategy 500
Dealing with Negative Publicity 501

PART V: MEASURING AND ANALYSING CONSUMER BEHAVIOUR 513

14. Consumer Research Process 515
Introduction 518
Importance of Consumer Research 518
Types of Consumer Research 520
Overview of the Consumer Research Process 523
Defining the Research Problem and Objectives of Research 523
Developing a Research Plan 523
Searching for and Evaluating Secondary Data 524
Designing a Primary Research Study 525
Sampling Methods 525
Collecting Primary Data 527
Analysing Data 528
Presenting Findings 529
Qualitative Research 530
Discovering Hidden Needs 531
Depth Interviews 535
Laddering 535
Focus Groups 536
Projective Techniques 536
Metaphor Analysis 539
Mystery Shopping 540
Quantitative Research 540
Quantitative Data Collection Methods 540
Measurement Scales 541
Observation 545
Surveys 546
Experimentation 547
Modern Research 548
Data Mining 548
Data Analytics 548
Real-time Experience Tracking 549
Advertising Analytics 550
Social Media Analysis 550
Uses of Big Data 552
Limitations of Consumer Research 552

15. Consumption and Post-Purchase Behaviour 560
Introduction 562
Types of Purchase Decisions 562
Purchase Continuum 563
Consumer Satisfaction 565
Theories of Customer Satisfaction 566

Detailed Contents

    Measuring Satisfaction   567
    Satisfaction in Services—Servqual Model   567
    Kano Model   568
    Customer Satisfaction Index Models   569
    Strategies for Satisfaction   570
    Unhappy Customers and Decreasing Satisfaction   571
Customer Loyalty   573
    Integrated Experience across Touchpoints   573
    Enhancing Customer Experience   575
    Benefits of Consumer Loyalty   575
    Types of Loyalty   577
    Measuring Loyalty   578
Loyalty Strategy   583
    Reducing Customer Effort   584
Loyalty Programmes   586
    Consumer Loyalty and Profits   588
    E-loyalty   590

PART VI: MODERN CONSUMER   599

16. Online Buying Behaviour   601
Introduction   603
    Online Shopping in India   604
    Composition of India's E-Commerce   606
Understanding the Online Shopper   607
    Age and Online Buying   607
    Online Segmentation   607
    Profile of the Online Shopper   608
    Reasons for Buying Online   608
    Reasons for Not Buying Online   609
    Expectations of Online Shoppers   610
Media Consumption   611
    Media Usage—Interactions During the Purchase Process   612
    Consumer Decision Journey   613
Framework for Online Consumer Behaviour   615
    Consumer and Environmental Characteristics   615
    Product or Service Characteristics   616
    Medium Characteristics   619
    Online Merchants   620
Digital Value Creation—Infinite Possibility   621
    Web Equity   623
Using Social Media   626
    Social Behaviour of Consumers   626
    Omnichannel Marketing   629
    Building Customer Loyalty   629
    Online Communities   630
    Data Mining and Analytics   631
Transforming the Business   633
    Future of Online Consumer Behaviour   633

17. Consumer Engagement and Equity   643
Introduction   645
    Evolving Consumer Behaviour   647
    Era of Consumer Engagement   647
    Rethinking the 4Ps   649
    Customer Engagement   649
    Enhancing Customer Experience   652
    Brands Squeezed Dry   655
    Becoming Customer-centric   655
Customer Engagement Value   657
    Brand Engagement   658
    Customer Equity Management   658
    Customer Value   660
Customer Lifetime Value   661
Customer Referral Value   662
    Building Customer Equity   664
    Dialogue Marketing   665

18. Ethics and Social Responsibility   674
Introduction   676
Ethics   677
    Pursuit of Low Prices and Ethical Considerations   679
Ethical Issues in Marketing   680
    Intended Consequences   682
    Unintended Consequences   683
Ethical Consumption   686
    Factors Impeding Ethical Consumption   687
    Sins of Greenwashing   689
Globalization and Ethics   691
    Consumer Protection   692
Corporate Social Responsibility—The Basis   693
    Definition and Scope   694
    Legal Provisions Relating to CSR in India   695

Index   703
About the author   707

List of Exhibits and Case Studies

Chapter 1
Case Study:	Importance of Observing Consumers	3
Case Study:	Advertising and Behaviour	25

Chapter 2
Case Study:	L'Oréal—Serving Many Segments	27
Exhibit 2.1:	Superbrands—Bata	32
Exhibit 2.2:	Geographic Segmentation by Dainik Bhaskar	36
Exhibit 2.3:	Targeting Children	38
Exhibit 2.4:	Status Bathroom	41
Exhibit 2.5:	Modifying Products for Different Segments	56
Case Study:	Putting Segmentation to Use	60

Chapter 3
Case Study:	Nudging Consumers Towards Choices	63
Exhibit 3.1:	Tanishq and the Consumer Decision-making Process	69
Exhibit 3.2:	Creating Need in the Market: Archies and Acquaguard	70
Exhibit 3.3:	Building Brand Loyalty	74
Exhibit 3.4:	Apollo Hospitals	78
Case Study:	Why Customers Hire Milkshakes	93

Chapter 4
Case Study:	Rolls-Royce: The Long Arm of B2B Relationships	95
Exhibit 4.1:	Steel Superbrands	119
Exhibit 4.2:	Amadeus: Building a B2B Brand	121
Case Study:	Dark Side of B2B Selling Behaviour	130

Chapter 5
Case Study:	Woodland: Creating an Outdoors Personality	135
Exhibit 5.1:	Monte Carlo: Projecting a Young Brand	141
Exhibit 5.2:	Eurochamp: A Higher Calling	148
Exhibit 5.3:	Superbrands—Brands and Personality	155
Exhibit 5.4:	How Brands Try to Extend Gender Usage	161
Case Study:	Getting High	175

Chapter 6
Case Study:	Handwashing—Motivating New Habit Formation	178
Exhibit 6.1:	Fulfilling Needs	182
Exhibit 6.2:	Creating an Image	189
Exhibit 6.3:	Using Emotions	199
Case Study:	Repositioning Brands to Match Real Motives	208

Chapter 7
Case Study:	Selling a Mean Machine	211
Exhibit 7.1:	Barbie—Changing Perceptions	214
Exhibit 7.2:	Taj Hotels: More than a Luxury Brand	223
Exhibit 7.3:	Umbrella Brands	233
Case Study:	Dilemma of Luxury Brands	257

Chapter 8
Case Study:	Marketing a Stone	261
Exhibit 8.1:	Educating Customers	267
Exhibit 8.2:	Good Knight's Line Extensions	289
Case Study:	Private Labels—The Growing Trend	298

Chapter 9
Case Study:	Creating Brandtopias	300
Exhibit 9.1:	Blue Star: The Expert	303
Exhibit 9.2:	Measuring Attitudes towards Film Stars	309
Exhibit 9.3:	Companies with a Cause	321
Case Study:	Wearing Your Attitude	333

Chapter 10
Case Study:	Tomorrow's Customers Today	341
Exhibit 10.1:	LIC for Senior Citizens	355
Case Study:	Elusive Middle Class	371

Chapter 11
Case Study:	Creating Madeleine Objects	375
Exhibit 11.1:	Time out	392
Exhibit 11.2:	Star Network's Strategy	403
Case Study:	Satisfying Needs or Encouraging Racial Bias?	416

Chapter 12
Case Study:	P&G—Creativity of Edison and Speed of Ford	421

Case Study:	Spread of Social Movements—Grameen Bank and BRAC	462

Chapter 13
Case Study:	Nokia's Communication Strategy	465
Exhibit 13.1:	Communication Strategy of Axe	477
Exhibit 13.2:	Message Appeals According to Ogilvy	487
Exhibit 13.3:	Cadbury's—Handling Negative Publicity	502
Case Study:	Making of Brand Benetton	508

Chapter 14
Case Study:	Tommy Hilfiger—Using Market Research for Higher Margins	515
Exhibit 14.1:	Using Ethnographic Research—A PC for Students and Teachers	534
Case Study:	Future of Market Research	557

Chapter 15
Case Study:	Loyalty Beyond Reason	560
Exhibit 15.1:	LIC Offers Integrated Experiences	574
Case Study:	Loyalty or Profits?	595

Chapter 16
Case Study:	Is Traditional Marketing Dead?	601
Exhibit 16.1:	Adding Tangibility to Online Trades	618
Case Study:	How Online Behaviour Changes Everything	639

Chapter 17
Case Study:	Future of Shopping	643
Case Study:	Optimizing Customer Equity at Celtel	670

Chapter 18
Case Study:	Hunger Games	674
Case Study:	Rana Plaza Disaster	700

Features of the Book

Boxed Exhibits

Interesting exhibits as well as Marketing Insights, Global Insights, Ethical Insights, and CB in Action have been included in the chapters to help students understand various marketing strategies used by companies.

Case Studies

36 case studies have been provided in the book to consolidate one's understanding of the concepts discussed in the chapter.

Figures/Images

Numerous marketing communications along with their explanations are interspersed in the text to illustrate approaches used by marketers.

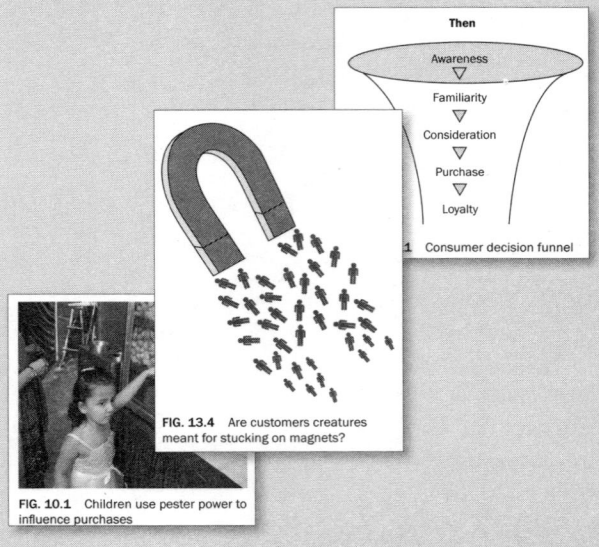

KEY TERMS

16 personality factors model (16PF) Measures personality on 16 factors and captures individual differences for each factor to provide a comprehensive description of personality

Anthropomorphism The process of prescribing human characteristics to non-human objects

Brand personality The set of human characteristics associated with a brand

Consumer ethnocent... and a resultant desire... products and brands...

Consumer fixation... becomes obsessed o...

Consumer innovative... ed by new products... consumers to try and...

Key Terms

Key terms are provided at the end of every chapter to serve as a quick review guide of important topics covered in the chapter.

Concept-review Questions

1. What is consumer motivation? Why is it important in the study of consumer behaviour?
2. Distinguish between needs, goals, motives, and desires. Show how these lead to drives that ultimately...

7. Critically exam... will sell philosop... often as being m... themselves'. How... ZMET a...

Critical Thinking Questions

Implementing systems for satisfying needs of B2B buyers is hugely expensive, as in the case of Rolls-Royce discussed in this chapter. Given the high cost of capital, can companies really implement such...

2. Companies have t... with their B2B partn... underhand dealings. I... of this. Can paymen... corrup...

Projects and Assignments

1. Conduct a survey of your classmates. Ask them to list out the brands that they like to buy. Then ask them to list why they prefer those brands. After the survey, find out how many brands are bought by them due to family or class influences and how many are their personal choices.

whether there is a... and consumption o...

3. Study the awareness... India among your c... targeted ads such a... Coffee Day. Using t...

Chapter-end Exercises

Each chapter provides concept-review questions, critical thinking questions, and project assignments for classroom discussion to enhance learning.

CHAPTER SIXTEEN
Online Buying Behaviour

CHAPTER SEVENTEEN
Consumer Engagement and Equity

CHAPTER EIGHTEEN
Ethics and Social Responsibility

Section on Modern Consumer

Online consumer behavior, consumer engagement, and future of shopping in times of exploding social media usage have been covered in detail.

Companion Online Resources for Instructors and Students

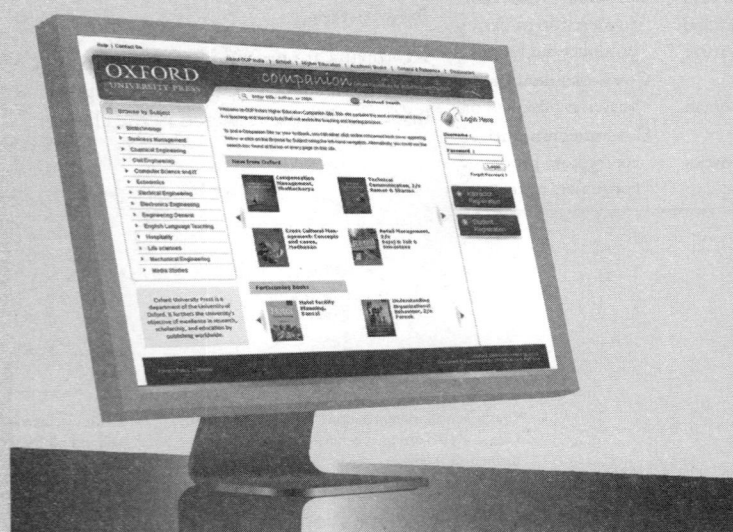

Visit www.oupinheonline.com to access both teaching and learning solutions online.

The following resources are available to support the faculty and students using this book:

For Faculty

- Instructor's manual
- PowerPoint slides

For Students

- Flash cards

Steps to Register

Step 1: Getting Started

- Go to www.oupinheonline.com

Step 2: Browse quickly by:

- BASIC SEARCH
  - → Author
  - → Title
  - → ISBN
- ADVANCED SEARCH
  - ▷ Subjects
  - ▷ Recent titles

Step 3: Select Title

Select title for which you are looking for resources.

Step 4: Search Results with Resources available

Operations Research, 1/e
S.R. Yadav & A.K. Malik

Select resources by chapter

Student Resources

Instructor Resources

Click here

Step 5: To download Results

Download All

Step 6: Login to download

The page you wish to access is password-protected.
Please login to access the resources

User Name :
Password :

Login

Forgot Password? | New Student? Register | New Instructor? Register

New Instructor? Register

Step 7: Registration Form

Please fill correct details and *marked fields are mandatory

Instructor Registration

Personal Details

User Name * : (Enter a valid email address as your User Name e.g. support@gmail.com)

Username should be email ID

Password * :
Confirm Password * :
Security Question * : --Select--
Security Answer * :
Salutation * : --Select--
Name * :
Designation * :
Department * :
Mobile * :
Alternative Email Id :

Please fill correct Mobile no. to get SMS after verification

Institute Details

Institute Name * : (Please enter full Institute Name.)
University * : --Select--
Address * : (Please enter complete address of the institute.)
Country * : --Select--
State :
City * :

Course Taught

SNo.	Course	Sem/Year	Enrolment
1		--Select--	
2		--Select--	
3		--Select--	
4		--Select--	
5		--Select--	

Submit

SUBMIT

Step 8: Message after completing the registration form

Thank you for registering with us. We shall revert to you within 48 hours after verifying the details provided by you. Once validated please login using your username and the password and access the resources.

Step 9: Verification

You will receive a confirmation on your mobile & email ID.

For any further query please write to us at HEMarketing.in@oup.com with your mobile number

Step 10: Visit us again after validation

- Go to www.oupinheonline.com
- Login from Member Login

Member Login

User Name :

Password :

Login

Forgot Password?

Step 11: My Subscriptions

My Subscriptions

Valid Subscriptions

Operations Research, 1/e
Yadav & Malik
Valid Till :
16 Oct 2015

You can view Subscriptions in your account

- Click on the title
- Select Chapter or "Select All"
- Click on "Download All"
- Click on "I Accept"
- A zip file will be downloaded on your system. You may use this along with the textbook.

PART ONE

Overview of Consumer Behaviour

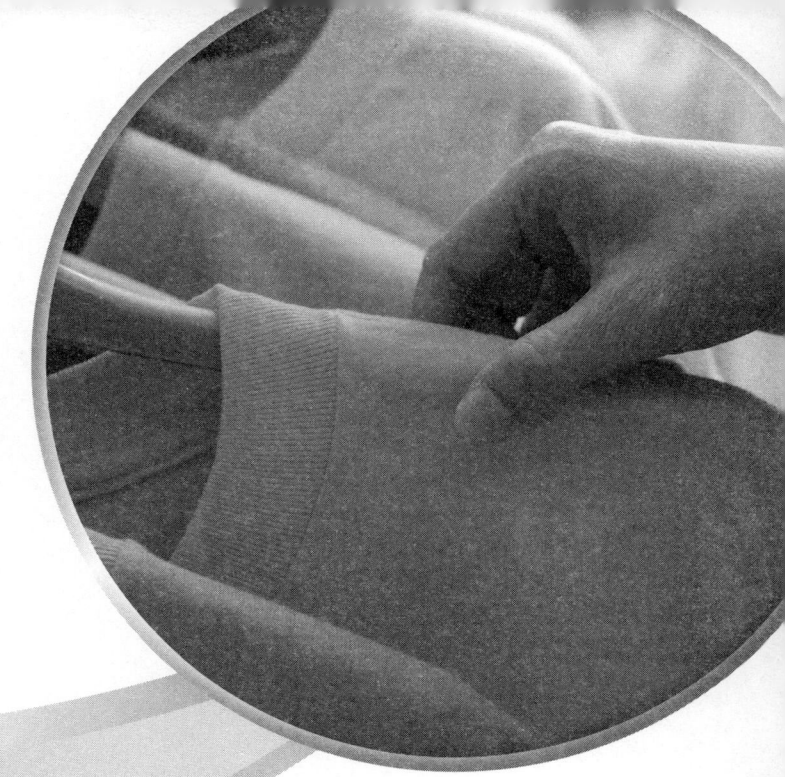

CHAPTER 1:
Introduction to Consumer Behaviour

CHAPTER 2:
Consumer Analysis, Segmentation, and Strategy

CHAPTER 3:
Consumer Decision-making Models

CHAPTER 4:
Business-to-business Buying Behaviour

CHAPTER ONE

Introduction to Consumer Behaviour

LEARNING OBJECTIVES

This chapter introduces the study of consumer behaviour. Drawing from many disciplines, it is an interesting study of human sociology and psychology.

After studying this chapter, the reader will be able to
- learn about the importance and nature of the study of consumer behaviour
- understand the evolution of the marketing concept
- appreciate how consumers have changed over the years and how society has been impacted
- learn about the importance and limitations of consumer psychology
- understand consumer behaviour in times of economic uncertainty, and how marketing is evolving to serve the modern and connected customer.

CASE STUDY

Importance of Observing Consumers

Businesses have a lot to gain by studying consumer behaviour. Insights gained by merely observing consumers reveal many aspects of behaviour, which may easily be missed out otherwise. This case study describes how a restaurant discovered some shocking truths by just observing consumers. Without such insight, the restaurant had come to a completely erroneous diagnosis of the problem.

A restaurant in New York found that it was getting bad reviews from its customers. The service was seen as slow, even though there had been no increase in business compared to how it was ten years ago. Ironically, the restaurant had more staff and had cut down on its menu items. Despite this change, comments on the restaurant's review sites listed the complaints such as slow service and long waiting period for a table.

A consultant hired to find the root causes of the complaints and suggest solutions first came up with the usual suggestions—the staff could be too slow, the workers needed training to be fast and efficient, the kitchen processes were slow—all of which would add up to slow service, delays in clearing tables, and long waiting time for customers. These observations, however, did not take into account consumer behaviour, and were common suggestions that could be obtained from just about anyone. Even the customers themselves, if asked, would highlight these very defects.

Yet, this diagnosis was wrong. The consultants then decided to find out how the staff was serving customers earlier. They found a few old tapes in the old surveillance system. By watching these, they

4 Consumer Behaviour

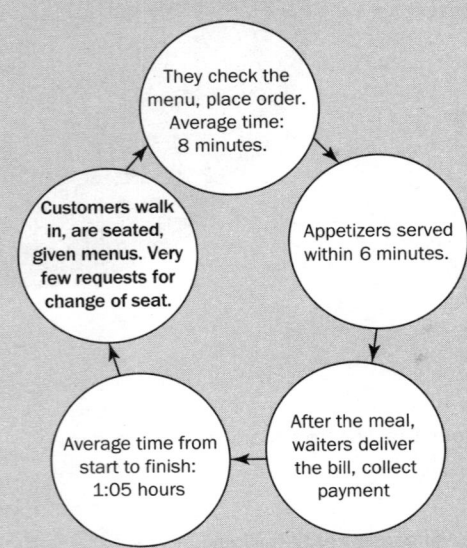

FIG. 1.1 Activities in 2004

1 July 2004. The restaurant had been very busy that day. The activities are summarized in Figs 1.1 and 1.2.

When we compare these two scenarios, we come to a conclusion about the efficiency of the staff and of the restaurant. The solutions do not lie in training and motivation as was earlier believed but in understanding the needs of the modern consumer.

The case study highlights the importance of consumer behaviour research. Seen superficially, market processes look simple and rational. When we dig deeper, we discover the real forces that underlie those processes. Marketing cannot be understood without digging into the minds and actions of consumers.

While reading this chapter, try to answer the following questions:

1. How is consumer behaviour changing over the years? How have modern lifestyles changed the way business is done?
2. How has society changed over the years? Have marketing activities resulted in any societal changes?
3. How can companies track and find out consumer needs?

discovered a completely different set of problems entirely contributing to delayed service.

The findings were amazing as they gave insights into consumer behaviour that would not have been possible to get otherwise. The old footage was dated

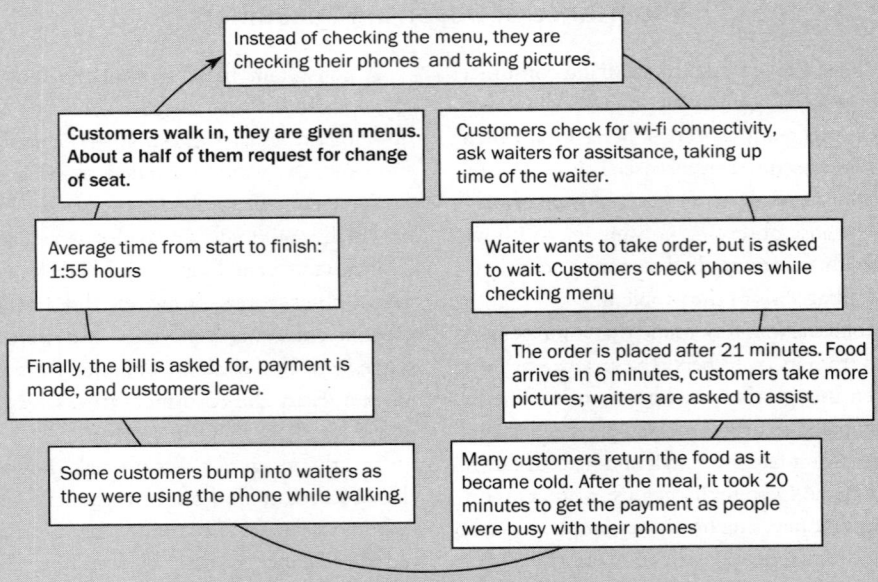

FIG. 1.2 Activities in 2014

4. How do companies need to change to cater to the modern and connected customer? In the case discussed here, what could the restaurant have done to improve efficiency?

Source:
'Restaurant watches video footage on customers and uncovers shocking truth', San Francisco Globe, July 12, 2014, http://sfglobe.com/?id=1658&src=share_fb_new_1658, last accessed on 21 October 2014.

INTRODUCTION

Consider the following situations:

- You are in a store with a shopping list. You are drawn to a sign that tells you something is free. You check out the product and find that a gift is being given free with something. You buy that product even though you do not need either the product or the free gift.
- You walk into a fast food restaurant for a quick snack. While waiting, you see the brightly displayed menu and notice that a combo meal works out cheaper than the items purchased separately. You order a combo meal thinking you got a bargain even though you ended up eating more than you had actually planned and also paid more in the process.
- You are walking down a shopping street. Suddenly, the warm fragrance of brewing coffee tells you that you are near a coffee shop. You are drawn inside the shop even though you did not have any intention of having coffee earlier.

If you have experienced any of these situations, you can be forgiven because companies have mapped consumer behaviour into their offerings in their quest for luring customers to buy more. Consumers mostly make choices on the way products are packaged or displayed; they let go of their rational instincts when they make purchase decisions. Consumer behaviour delves deep into human psychology to device methods that influence these decisions. Through forceful offers and advertisements, companies try to reach out to customers and do not want to miss a single opportunity to be able to communicate with them. This has led to a consumer culture that crosses geographic and political boundaries.

Ubiquitous Consumer Culture

Consumer culture has become ubiquitous in modern societies. Almost everything we do, see, or experience is connected in some way or another to us, as consumers. There are two views on this aspect. First, consumer culture is seen as entirely controlling, with every single thought and movement analysed by corporations using modern technology that makes it possible to track a person's every move. Or, it is seen as entirely liberating—consumption is seen as the ultimate experience or *nirvana* that anyone can achieve. Consuming a chocolate or buying a new car is seen as the ultimate experience anyone can possibly have.

This behaviour affects society and culture as well. A look at movies makes it clear as to how the consumer culture has come to dominate our thinking. Brosh (2000) writes of a modern adaptation of the famous novel, *Pride and Prejudice*, by Jane Austen. As movies represent the existing culture, the script writers took the liberty of changing the backdrop of the movie to a more modern one. In the movie, the first scene is not a conversation in the Bennet home as in the book. Instead, the movie opens with a scene in which women are shopping.

When the movie was adapted for the modern times, the producers wanted it to appeal to the modern viewer. The book opens with a conversation in a drawing room, but this would not appeal to today's generation. The producers chose shopping as a backdrop in the opening scene, since consumer culture has come to represent modern culture. Consumption of goods has been placed at the centre of all human endeavour. Descartes' famous quote, 'I think, therefore I am', has been replaced firmly in modern societies with, 'I consume, therefore I am'.

Due to modern methods of production, markets are flooded with goods. Consequently, the basis of marketing has changed not to sell what is needed, but on increasing consumption to absorb the heightened rates of production. Brosh explains, 'The economy and culture shifted drastically. A culture that valued thrift and hard work was being replaced by a culture that valued a rising standard of living and the consumption that enabled it'.

Stimulating field The study of consumer behaviour involves peering into the minds of people to discover what goes on there as they choose products and services. During this process, we discover many influences on the individual purchase decision—besides the felt need, would the product make a suitable impression or would it match one's personality and lifestyle? These are but two of the many thought processes that go on in the consumer's mind.

Discovering these influences draws us into a variety of disciplines. That is why consumer behaviour is one of the most stimulating, complex, and intellectually challenging areas. Free markets cannot force people to consume something or the other; they rely on the judgment and free will of consumers. This makes the task of marketing extremely difficult. We need to know how people make decisions, what impresses them, what does not, and how their mind works.

Enriches from different disciplines To learn about people, the field of consumer behaviour draws from and welcomes insights from several disciplines, including economics, psychology, culture, mathematics, social sciences, political science, communications, anthropology, the creative arts, and modern technology. As Anderson, Meethan, and Miles (2002) explain, consumer behaviour combines intriguing perspectives, creative leaps, and freedom of imagination, yet grounds it in real action.

This book combines perspectives from all these fields. It begins an exciting journey into deciphering human behaviour as people buy and consume things.

Consumer Behaviour

Consumer behaviour is defined as the study of individuals, groups, or organizations and the processes they use to select, secure, and dispose of products, services, experiences, or ideas to satisfy needs and the impact these processes have on the consumer and society.

This definition has several elements covered in it which are explained individually. A reading of this section helps to understand the many disciplines that are covered in our study of consumer behaviour.

Individuals Consumer behaviour is concerned with what goes on inside the heads of individuals when they see a product or service, make a selection, or decide to buy. Since buying is usually spontaneous and the entire process happens in the mind, a deep study of psychology is needed. Apart from advertising, we also see how colour, sounds, and smells affect the buying behaviour.

We delve not only in psychology, personality, learning, and motivation, but also in neuroscience, which deals with scanning brains of consumers with advanced machines. The latest trend is the use of big data analysis, which is the study of data trails left behind by consumers as they scout the Internet with their computers or mobile devices.

Groups People usually like to buy what other people have, who they consider similar to themselves. They also buy in groups, seeking opinions from each other. This part of our study borrows from sociology. Readers must have noticed that people with similar traits have a common appearance, clothes, and accessories. Young people like to frequent certain outlets, prefer similar brands and go to similar shops, while older people frequent other outlets. When we consider customers as groups having similar needs and behaviour, we are actually talking about segmentation, targeting, and positioning (STP), which are three important concepts in marketing strategy. Brands are built by applying these concepts.

Organizations Business-to-consumer (B2C) buying is the visible face of marketing. However, extensive buying is done by businesses not for their own consumption, but using the raw materials, components, semi-finished goods, and services to produce other things. Such buying is called organizational, or business-to-business (B2B) buying. Our study includes how businesses buy from other businesses, the elements and behaviour exhibited by organizations while making choices and placing orders.

Select The process of selection initiates the question—when confronted with choices, how do individuals or organizations choose one option over the others? We analyse the processes and factors that are active in the background while making selections.

Secure After the selection, the consumer pays for the product and makes the purchase. This is the process of securing goods and services. Going beyond buying, it includes post-purchase behaviour of using and storing, showing off or talking about the purchases, and posting comments on social media sites or reviews. Such word-of-mouth publicity is invaluable for companies. This behaviour is analysed in various consumer models and are explained in detail in this book.

Dispose of A neglected area of consumer behaviour is the disposal of waste materials, by-products, or the products themselves once they have served their purpose. The job is left to poor people who collect what can be sold, reused, or recycled. Material that cannot be reused or recycled is dumped in landfills and rivers, or left to litter the environment. Such practices threaten the ecosystem in both rich and poor countries alike. Some countries have implemented laws and practices of scientific management of waste, thus helping reduce what goes in landfills. In other countries, notably in India too, cities and towns are reduced to polluting garbage heaps. The study of ethics in consumer behaviour looks at the unintended consequences of consumption. If such concerns that are harming of the environment are not addressed, the planet itself will be threatened.

Products The first 'P' of marketing, it is not simply what is produced by company. Products are purchased because they fulfil needs. Theodore Levitt used to tell his students, 'People don't want to buy a quarter-inch drill. They want a quarter-inch hole!' As explained in chapter-end case study in Chapter 3, consumers 'hire' products for what they do for them. A milk shake, for instance, is not just a shake. It fulfils the need to get some nourishment or feel good about oneself, or a means to pass time on the subway.

The study of consumer behaviour helps us go beyond the physical aspects of products and focus, instead, on the needs that consumers use them for. It is insights like these that help savvy companies get ahead and survive long term in an ever changing market. Charles Revson, the founder of Revlon, had shown the difference between product and needs through his famous quote, 'In the factory we make cosmetics; in the store we sell hope'.

Services The understanding that a product does something for consumers rather than something they buy leads us to explore the world of services. There are no pure products, every product has a service attached to it. A host of companies offer services either to enhance existing products or add value to them. Thus, we see a transformation of the society. Many household chores such as knitting or sewing have been replaced by readymade garments. Cooking has been made easy by means of processed foods. At the same time, certain services like beauty parlours and gyms, which did not exist some years back, have sprouted all over the country to cater to customer needs.

Experiences Another transformation that has taken place is that increasingly, companies focus on creating experiences for customers. This is not limited to restaurants and holiday resorts. Today, companies do not rely on retailers alone, but spend huge sums of money in creating branded stores where people like to visit. The ambience, the displays, the sales people, the sights, smells and sounds—all are used to deliver a pleasurable experience. Consumer behaviour research finds that it is easier to make people part with their money in stores that deliver an experience that they expect.

Ideas Perhaps the greatest contribution to the study of consumer behaviour is to find ways to make people adapt to ideas. These ideas are about consuming new products and services, but are not limited just to consumption. Ideas such as washing hands before eating, administering polio drops to children, protecting the environment, and so on, are easier to implement if we know the behavioural drivers and resistance to change. Two such ideas, the ushering in of microfinance by Grameen Bank in Bangladesh for the poor and inculcating the habit of washing of hands are presented as case studies in this book.

The emphasis on consumer behaviour arises from the marketing concept, which places emphasis not on production or selling, but on meeting customer needs. This resulted in the emergence of the marketing concept.

Emergence of Marketing Concept

In this section, we look at how the marketing concept evolved over time. Marketing and selling have been going on since time immemorial. Even in the Stone Age, presumably, people gave away what they had in excess in exchange of some favour. If a group had killed an animal for food, they would give away the unconsumed meat to others, otherwise, it would rot. Another group who were good in making tools would give them away to the first group as they would have no use for the extra tools that they had. This marked the birth of the barter system, or the basis of exchange that exists to this day. No selling was required; it was simply fulfilling the needs of others.

With the invention of money, the exchange was made easier. It also encouraged specialization—people created what they did best and sold the excess of what they had. Those who were good at making their products became richer than others. They started looking for ways to increase their production because they had the expertise to do so. Trade routes allowed them to send products wherever they commanded good prices.

The industrial revolution of the 19th century saw the birth of factories and an emphasis on mechanical ways of increasing production. The emphasis was to increase production and there was a ready market for factory-made goods. This orientation is called the production concept. The emphasis was on producing large quantities of goods, productivity, and efficiency, while reducing cost as well. Consumers' tastes did not matter. Markets expanded, and goods were exported through better means of transport.

Excess production gradually started posing problems. What was a factory to do with goods that could not be sold either at home or abroad? The answer was to employ sales people who would convince more people to buy the goods. The emphasis now came upon selling since supplies were much in excess. Known as the selling concept, it refers to aggressive selling of goods or services, rather than on whether or not they are actually needed. There was oversupply and reluctant consumers, who had to be shown, convinced, and cajoled or threatened with fear to buy the products. Though some companies have outlived the selling concept, it is still being followed, as aggressive sales people, telemarketing calls, and spamming are widely prevalent. Such companies call potential customers at all hours and harangue them to make them buy a variety of products that they otherwise would not buy, simply because of excess capacities.

As customers turned away from these aggressive selling techniques, some companies, at least, realized that this was not the way to go forward. There was a limit to what could be sold, despite all the sales people who could be employed. Instead of pushing customers to buy things that they did not want, why not make things that people demanded? This led to the birth of the study of consumer needs. The marketing concept, as this was called, led to a change in thinking that marketing was not simply selling things, but fulfilling human needs and thereby making a profit out of it.

Coinciding with the marketing concept was the spread of mass media and better means of communication. Newspapers and radio carried information and advertising. Television did what was hitherto unimaginable—it carried moving pictures and sound instantaneously to homes. This gave the rise to branding, and companies such as P&G and Coca Cola built huge brands by linking their brands to lifestyles. The TV soap opera was invented to get people glued to their sets and advertising slipped in during the programmes, influencing millions of people to use and adopt brands.

The mass media was also a means of social change. Through advertising and public relations (PR), companies could change ideas about the lives they lived. Girls were made to change their opinions to buy diamonds or begin to smoke, as case studies in this book describe. Could this tremendous power be used to change society itself for its betterment? Thus was born the societal marketing concept, which applies the tools of marketing to change people's ideas for long-term betterment. Principles of consumer behaviour are now being used to introduce ideas to help society.

CONSUMERS AND SOCIETY

The study of consumer behaviour has several positive outcomes on the society. As we discover and fulfil human needs, it helps us derive the following benefits:

- It fosters productivity and efficiency, and leads to better standard of living.
- It promotes an aesthetic attitude.
- It encourages individualism and self-expression.
- It is enjoyable and pleasurable.

These themes are discussed here.

The consumer culture engages humanity in meaningful work. Productivity and efficiency are encouraged. The study of consumer behaviour not only introduces efficiency and productivity in businesses but in the society as a whole. This process is referred to as McDonaldization of the society (Fig. 1.3).

McDonaldization of Society

The changes in society as we move towards a consumer culture is described as the McDonaldization of society. Ritzer (2007), in his book of the same name, defines McDonaldization as 'the process by which the principles of the fast-food restaurant are coming to dominate more and more sectors of American society as well as the rest of the world'. These principles are efficiency, predictability, calculability, and control.

Efficiency McDonald's has brought efficiency into operations of a wide variety of businesses and services. Restaurants have created systems to get customers in and out as quickly as possible. These processes are now being followed by department stores, malls, theatres, and so on, reducing waiting time of customers. Work processes have been simplified and broken down, and automation has been introduced across sectors, to deliver products and services efficiently.

Predictability When people visit McDonald's anywhere in the world, they know what to expect. They get the same experience—employees are trained to take orders and deliver food effortlessly, and the stores have the same ambience. Other companies have realized the importance of predictability—customers like to buy products knowing they will not be short-changed, and like what they get. Other businesses have standardized their business processes so that they too are able to deliver products and services with the same amount of predictability each time.

FIG. 1.3 Consumer society introduces enjoyment in life

Calculability Businesses have learnt to quantify everything. This helps in establishing standards and also in ranking products and services. Not only are students ranked and compared by their grade point average (GPA) but colleges across the country are ranked and various parameters are quantified that help students make informed choices. Television shows are graded on TRPs to determine which ones command high advertising rates in comparison to others.

Control Work is broken down into a series of steps that can be controlled by non-human technologies. At McDonald's, it means controlling processes so that consumers get exactly what they ordered every time. Such systems are seen at clinics and hospitals, airplanes, and a host of businesses. Automation in universities, hospitals, and supermarkets help deliver standardized products and services to the delight of customers.

Taken together, these principles constitute the rationality of modern life. Companies and organizations consolidate their activities on these principles, contributing to the universal McDonaldization of society. In India, after the country liberalized and opened its doors to foreign food chains, it has resulted in the improvement not only of restaurants, but of homes and public spaces as well. We look for rationality and efficiency in education, work life, and leisure, spreading the impact of better methods. This has also contributed to better standard of living.

Aesthetic Attitude

Better products for consumers give rise to better design. McQuilten (2011) writes that design has become an aesthetic discipline. Fashion design, industrial design, product design, and commercial design make up our contemporary environment. Computer technologies create virtual designs that mimic reality. Design has become the basis of production and consumption.

Design is the visible face of consumption, which serves the purpose of helping consumers to express themselves. Sparke (2013) writes that the designs of new products are so novel—mobile phones, vehicles, consumer goods, that they take on an iconic significance in people's lives. Their symbolic and visual impact is so powerful that people start thinking of them as extensions of their own personality. The smooth and aerodynamic forms of products have become visual markers of modernity. Indeed, many companies have been built on the basis of superior design.

Further, as marketing is concerned with providing progressively better products to consumers, technology from unrelated areas has moved into the homes of customers. Many of the products and materials that we use, for instance, have been developed for defence or space research and not as consumer goods.

A pleasing design influences consumption, and this had led to an appreciation of aesthetics that goes much beyond products. People no longer accept shoddy work and home places. The face and style of restaurants have changed. Even cheap restaurants have better interiors and facilities than in the past. Consumers now expect and demand better hygiene and pleasing ambience from businesses. Routine life becomes more pleasing visually as society adopts design as a basis of its existence.

Featherstone (2007) calls this a 'celebration of the aesthetic potential of mass culture and the aestheticized perceptions of the people who stroll through the urban spaces of the large cities… in this aestheticized commodity world the curiosity and memory of the stroller is fed by the ever-changing landscape in which objects appear divorced from their context and subject to mysterious connections which are read on the surface of things. The everyday life of the big cities becomes aestheticized'.

GLOBAL INSIGHT
Design, Aesthetics, and Products

Many companies have built their reputation and revenues based on better design and have captured the hearts of consumers. Some of these are described here.

Airbnb Airbnb is a home and apartment rental service. The key to its success is their user experience design, where listings are placed like a beautiful travel magazine.

Nike The sportswear company markets well-designed and comfortable shoes. To replace the EVA foam and nylon used in shoes, it is partnering with NASA, the US State Department, and USAID to research the textiles of the future. Internally, Nike has synthesized and compiled nearly eight years' worth of their findings on sustainable materials into a graphic app called Making, which enables any designer, anywhere, to create apparel that has less of a carbon footprint.

Philips Philips built a flatter and friendlier LED bulb that caught on in markets. The company is now introducing mood lighting through its Philips Hue lighting system.

Starbucks Starbucks decided to build concept stores that fit into the neighbourhood. The flagship Starbucks store in Mumbai, for instance, is built on Indian ethnic theme that appeals to local customers.

Apple Steve Jobs hired Jerry Manock in 1977 and set up the Apple industrial design centre. Jobs was notoriously obsessed with design and style, and the company's products stand testimony to that. The secret is that the entire organization is structured to appreciate and support design.

3M One of the most innovative companies in the world, it places a great importance on design. 'Design is far more than just making things look good. Design helps solve a myriad of challenges, from enhancing usability to communicating function. Elegance and simplicity must coexist to go beyond meeting the customer's needs. By embracing this philosophy, we seamlessly infuse emotion into functionality,' says the company's website.

Sources:
http://news.starbucks.com/news/starbucks-opens-spectacular-flagship-store-in-mumbai-honoring-the-dynamic-c.
http://solutions.3m.com/innovation/en_US/stories/design-at-heart.
http://www.fastcompany.com/3026684/most-innovative-companies-2014/the-worlds-top-10-most-innovative-companies-in-design.
www.apple.com.
All last accessed on 25 July 2014.

Individualization and Self-expression

An emphasis on consumer behaviour encourages individualism and self-expression. The Indian consumer has changed, which can be seen in changing lifestyles. This is reflected in three main segments—women, men, and youth.

Changing Indian Consumer

Indians are getting more materialistic—they are traditionally thought of as spiritual people who reject worldly goods. However, this has changed. According to research published by *Harvard Business Review* (2006), about half of India's urban population had adopted a 'work hard get rich' ethos by 1996, while another nine per cent had done so by 2006. As younger people enter the workforce, people get motivated by personal ambition and they put in more hours per week at work.

Rise of Consumerism

Consumerism is an ideology that encourages the acquisition of goods and services in greater proportions. Traditionally, Indians have avoided luxury, but over time, life's pleasures have gained importance. The desire for electronics and consumer goods has shot up. Though children's education has always been of primary importance, Indians are spending more on travel and entertainment. The trend is not limited to the young, nor is it limited only to large cities. The market for consumer goods, computers, laptops, and mobile phones has grown tremendously. Since many of the consumers are first-time users, it signifies an exploding market. There is great income disparity, with about one-third Indians living at $1 a day or less. As the middle and lower income groups get opportunities to make more money, it could well fuel consumerism in the long run.

Indian Brands

Foreign goods were once well sought after in the country. With the opening up of the economy, people were able to buy and experience a host of coveted brands. With time, they have become discerning customers who realize that not all foreign goods are suited for the country. Many foreign brands have had to struggle in the country. Others have 'Indianized' their products with prices affordable for the average Indian customer. Indian brands such as Tata, Godrej, and Bajaj are still preferred, despite the availability of foreign brands. However, there are contradictions in our society. Companies that can understand complexities of behaviour are likely to succeed in the country.

Changing Women

Women constitute half of humanity. Traditional societies limit women to closed and constrained spaces, but the consumer society values them as consumers. As active consumers, they buy or influence buying of most of the goods for their families. Advertising is, therefore, directed mostly at female consumers. Free markets define womanhood as a celebration, with the prime objective of looking good and having fun through consumption. Cyndie Lauper's popular song, 'Girls just want to have fun' symbolizes the freedom and fun associated with girls in free societies.

The entire industries of fashion and cosmetics are meant for women. Marketing encourages women to buy, buy, and buy. They are the ultimate consumers, with films and advertising promoting an image of beauty and romance to be followed and pursued. Every pimple and every perceived defect have industries finding cures for them that are then marketed aggressively; women follow the idea of beauty projected in the media and must shop in order to imitate the ideal that they have absorbed from films, advertising, and television.

While doing so, women turn themselves into commoditized versions of femininity and also become objects to be consumed. Ironically, women were demeaned to become objects to be owned and used by the very culture that encouraged their freedom.

Consuming Men

Advertising of motor cycles and after-shave lotions has traditionally been directed at men. Modern marketing tries to break barriers between the sexes as far as consumption goes. Men have been made to consume products that would have been considered 'female' at one time. Today, nobody laughs or calls them sissies as they go to beauty parlours, use cosmetics, or try to look good.

Earlier, men were encouraged to adopt a 'macho' image and movies too projected that image. In a major cultural shift catalyzed by advertising, men are projected as caring fathers, doing things that would have been inconceivable some decades back. For instance, they are shown in ads as shopping for groceries, looking after children, and even doing the laundry, accompanied by products that they could buy.

Changing Youngsters—Selling Lifestyles

Lifestyle refers to the typical way of life of an individual, group, or culture. It is a combination of intangible factors such as consumer demographics and intangible factors which include psychological aspects of an individual such as personal values, preferences, and outlook.

Young consumers constitute the biggest size of the market and, therefore, attract companies to them. Not only is this segment a growing market but is also a barometer of social change. The notion of lifestyle marketing owes its origin to marketing to the youth segment. As young people are impressionable, advertising tries to get them in the habit of using their products. The latest in fashion, cosmetics, and mobile phones are created for them. The common theme in all advertising messages highlights the symbolic meaning and emotional role of products and their consumption.

Consumption for the youth is not only a means to fulfil needs but has become life-enhancing and expressive. Fashion brands, for instance, used to put their labels on the inside of shirts and coats where they could not be seen, but now the labels and brands are aggressively embroidered across clothes where they can be seen by others. Youngsters use consumption to express themselves, and even to rebel. Television has emerged as the most influential medium, driving social change and promoting a way of life. Advertising increases the significance of cultural aspects, as opposed to economic aspects of life.

There are two consequences to this change. First, the consuming desire among youngsters sometimes remains unfulfilled as they are not earning, leading to problems both socially and behaviourally. Many crimes among youngsters have been shown to be a result of unfulfilled desires. Second, many questionable products are sold in the garb of lifestyle enhancement. Consequently, youngsters develop habits which cause immense harm not only to them but to society as a whole.

Apart from obesity, young people take to habits of smoking and consuming alcohol, which have long-term effects. The average age at which a person starts drinking alcohol has been gradually decreasing in India and in many other countries, giving rise to alcoholism and other diseases. Though advertising of these products is banned in India, a subtle lifestyle marketing has succeeded in making young people consume them at progressively younger ages.

Enjoyable and Pleasurable

Consumers do like to fulfil their needs, but today's consumers want experiences. We live in the 'experience economy', first described by Pine and Gilmore (1998). This kind of economy has evolved following the agrarian, industrial, and the service economy. The authors say that businesses must orchestrate memorable events for their customers, and that memory itself becomes the product. 'An experience occurs when a company intentionally uses services as the stage, and goods as props, to engage individual customers in a way that creates a memorable event', they write (see Fig. 1.4).

Companies wishing to engage their customers across a host of touchpoints extending from the physical to the virtual world try to deliver unique experiences. Solis, writes in his book, *The End of Business as Usual* (2012) that 'engagement presents brands with opportunities to shape and steer experiences to earn relevance and influence the decisions of connected customers'.

FIG. 1.4 Companies are offering experiences to customers

These experiences bring joy and happiness to consumers. Buying, consuming, and showing off products is fun and gives a hedonic feeling. Hedonic consumption refers to the sense of enjoyment and pleasure that the consumer obtains from the buying, consuming, and owning experience. Shopping is a hedonic experience too, done with family or friends. As a consequence, retailers fulfill a multi-sensory, fantasy, and emotive aspects of one's experience with products. Retailers try to introduce the thrill of consumption through images, taste, sound, and smell. Shopping is also done to throw-off stress, escape from negative moods, and to relax. Malls ensure thrills of grand spaces with compelling images and activities so that people are able to obtain different thrilling experiences.

All these kinds of motivation are discovered when we delve into consumer psychology. It gives us an unusual insight into the minds of customers, as the chapter-opening case study illustrates. The object of studying consumer behaviour is to create customer value and satisfaction for building long-term relations with customers.

Customer Value and Satisfaction

The purpose of marketing is to provide customer satisfaction and, thereby, create customer value, leading to customer loyalty. Loyal customers are those who re-buy products and services provided by a company. They will do so only if they are satisfied customers and will not shift to a competitor's offerings. Companies, thus, try to build long-term relationships with their customers. This is accomplished by delivering high customer value and exceeding customer's expectations.

These concepts are important because of the following:

- Satisfied customers are more likely to continue to buy from a company, dissatisfied customers will look for alternative suppliers.
- Satisfied customers tell others about their experiences and make recommendations, dissatisfied engage in negative word-of-mouth publicity.

Kotler and Keller (2012) define customer perceived value (CPV) as the difference between the customer's evaluation of all the benefits and all the costs of an offering and the perceived alternatives. Customer value (CV) is the perceived monetary value of the bundle of economic, functional, and psychological benefits customers expect from a product or service. Customer value is enhanced by providing services, quality of personnel, and brand image. It is the difference between what a customer gets from a product and what he or she has to sacrifice in order to get it. Customer lifetime value (CLV) is the total combined customer lifetime values of all of a company's customers.

The key to retention of customers is customer relationship marketing (CRM), the process of managing detailed information about individual customers and managing all customer touchpoints to maximize loyalty. Customer relationship management often requires building a customer database and using data mining to detect trends, segments, and individual needs.

Consumption as a Basis of Existence

The study of consumer behaviour goes beyond individuals and groups to society as a whole. Marketing and advertising do change the way we live. They also impact our way of thinking. In earlier times, society was defined by social class, with noblemen and *maharajas* consuming things that others could not afford. Today, consumption is defined by lifestyle, and not limited to birth or class. Shopping is a social and emotional experience, compared to merely satisfying needs as in the past.

Before humans could work, they had to have food, shelter, and clothing. Consumption, being the servant of needs, had to be justified in terms of something else. Survival was the purpose of consumption, and once needs were met, there was no point in consuming more. Indulging in excess consumption was looked down upon as gluttony and intemperance. Thorstein Veblen called this 'conspicuous' or 'ostentatious' consumption. Excess consumption was nothing but vainglory and self-conceit.

Ironically, the distinctive mark of the modern society is excess consumption. For example, buying a small car serves its purpose of getting around and is also environment-friendly, but the use of small trucks, called SUVs was promoted as being the smarter option. In similar ways, our consumption habits are progressively turning bigger and bigger. Studying consumer behaviour helps us to influence what people believe about products and consumption.

Society no longer draws limits to consumption. In the consumer society, consumption is the purpose of existence. It is self-propelling. Needs are traditionally seen as a state of tension that decrease or wither away once the needs are fulfilled. In the consumer society, on the contrary, the needs and the tension must be kept alive. Marketing tries to do this and to make the needs stronger. As Bauman (2001) writes, 'consumer society proclaims the impossibility of gratification and measures its progress by ever-rising demand'. Can such behaviour be termed as 'rational'?

Study of Irrational Behaviour

A major assumption that we make in our study is that people are rational beings, who make consumption decisions for their self-interest. Economics helps us understand that people like to maximize their utility while allocating scarce resources across things to consume. This not only sounds logical, but provides a basis of our study. If purchase decisions are not rational but random, there would be no way to assess behaviour.

However, when we delve into psychology, we find that this assumption is not quite true; humans are anything but rational. Ariely (2009) writes that if humans were comic book characters, we would be more closely related to Homer Simpson than to Superman. In other words, humans do silly things and are certainly not rational beings. Our decisions are made on emotional and irrational basis, as was proved during the crash of 2008. 'Belief in the ultimate rationality of humans, organizations, and markets crumbled, and the attendant dangers to business and public policy were fully exposed,' writes Ariely.

Though economists admit that people behave irrationally from time to time, economic theory is based on the assumption of rationality even today. Behavioural economics goes beyond economics and examines the decisions people make in the real world. Our study of emotions and personality tries to unravel the irrational decisions made by consumers. Excess consumption is a manifestation of irrational behaviour.

Consumer psychology has its limitations too. New products, for instance, are launched, keeping consumer behaviour in mind. Despite this, after extensive research, a majority of products fail. Schneider and Hall (2011) write that even P&G stumbles with new products. 'Less than three per cent of new consumer packaged goods exceed first-year sales of $50 million—considered the benchmark of a highly successful launch', they write. Thus, it is important to keep the limitations of consumer psychology into mind.

Limitations of Consumer Psychology

Pham (2013) writes that the way consumer psychologists plan and conduct their research has several shortcomings—problems that could be called 'the seven sins of consumer psychology', which are as follows:

Narrow scope Consumer behaviour is normally understood as a series of stages from desire to acquisition. Most consumer psychology focuses on the initial stage of the consumption process—the acquisition stage, which includes attitudes, persuasion, search consideration, decision-making, and choice. However, acquisition is only a small subset of all consumption-related activities, and large areas of consumer behaviour such as needs and wants, usage, consumption and disposal, remain unaddressed.

Narrow lenses Consumer psychology takes a narrow and mechanistic view of the consumer. 'If we do X to consumers, process P will be triggered, and then outcome Y will take place.' However, consumer behaviour is more a set of concentric circles, each circle representing a different type of lens on consumer behaviour. At the centre is the mechanical core, consisting of attention, memory and inference-making. Outside this mechanical core is the affective layer that consists of feelings, moods, emotions, and affective preferences, which affect the inner core. This is surrounded by the motivational circle, with consumers' goals, motives, needs, and values, which exert influence on the inner affective and the mechanical circles. The next circle has socio-relational context. Social influences, family, and social roles exert influence on the inner circles. Finally, consumption behaviour takes place within a cultural context that is shaped by language, norms, and history.

Narrow epistemology Consumer behaviour is seen as a relation between theoretical constructs which are connected to explain a phenomenon. This is faulty. Many believe that consumer behaviour can be studied better by observation and descriptive studies. Our opening case on the New York restaurant highlights the importance of observation. No amount of statistical analysis could have discovered consumer behaviour better than an observation of the old surveillance tapes.

Disregard for psychological content Consumer research relies on an exclusive emphasis on analysing psychological processes, as opposed to understanding the mental contents on which these processes operate. Psychological processes such as thinking, feeling, or judging may be universal, but the contents of consumers' thoughts, feelings, and judgments are much more variable. Consumption behaviour cannot be explained without reference to the content of consumers' motives, feelings, actions, beliefs, and thoughts. Thus, consumer behaviour would gain by studying the psychological contents of consumption behaviour. Dichter has shown that behind consumption objects lies a symbolic meaning that is deeply rooted in our unconscious motives. He showed that if one is to generate genuine insights about consumer behaviour, one needs to pay close attention to matters of content.

Overgeneralization Consumer behaviour studies suffer from the tendency to overgeneralize from available evidence. We seek to form theories from data patterns, forgetting the situational factors. Very often, results cannot be replicated, which is the basis of scientific research. Consumer research is, therefore, not scientific. 'We tend to walk around with oversimplified theories that we use and promulgate indiscriminately', writes Pham.

Research by convenience Consumer research conducted and published in India has an over-reliance on convenience samples taken from students that is supposedly about consumers in general. Many research papers attempt to explain the obvious. An over-reliance on statistical analysis hides the wide variety of behaviour that can be observed. Internationally, the body of consumer behaviour research is centered on North American consumers. The research-by-convenience extends to the convenience of the instruments used; most consumer research diminishes the findings to statistical analysis. Such research has limited or no relevance to companies, since it tends to exaggerate the strength of the observed effects.

Hypothetical studies Most consumer studies do not actually show us anything meaningful about consumer behaviour since consumers are not rational and do not act in straight cause and effect manner. Questionnaires and surveys are based on answers given by consumers even though the answers may be wrong. Very often, consumers themselves are not aware of the basis of their decisions.

Consumer behaviour and psychology are also in a state of flux because of two powerful reasons. One is the economic turmoil and uncertainty that we live in. The second is the emergence of the connected consumer. These two trends are described here.

Consumer Behaviour in Economic Uncertainty

We live in times of economic uncertainty. Periods of boom are followed by contraction of economies, which then see loss of business confidence, loss of jobs, and lacklustre growth. All these have an impact on consumer behaviour. At the aggregate economic level, recessions are marked by a widespread decrease in consumer spending.

When growth rates are good, people like to spend on their hobbies and leisure. High-end clubs and restaurants find favour with people. Markets spring up to serve them. Consumers look for gadgets and technology, and do not mind spending extra for enriching or fun experiences and premium products. They also do not mind paying extra for socially conscious consumption, and do not mind buying environment friendly products, which usually carry an expensive tag.

Recessions make people sober up. In times of slowing growth and uncertainty, some consumer trends are slowed or halted. The world has seen economic uncertainty since 2008. The developed world is now witnessing flat growth, while developing economies struggle. Flatters and Willmott (2009) have identified eight trends that are substantially affected by recession. These are divided into dominant, advancing, slowed, or arrested trends.

Dominant Trends
The following are the dominant trends:

Demand for simplicity People crave for simplicity during economic decline. Recession accelerates the desire for simplicity and consumers look for means to simplify choice making. They tend to trust brands and value, look for opinions and advice, and choose user-friendly technologies.

Focus on corporate governance The second dominant trend is that customers do not tolerate mistakes of companies during recessions.

Advancing Trends

Discretionary thrift and mercurial consumption are the advancing trends.

Discretionary thrift Thrift becomes fashionable. Even affluent consumers start economizing. This is because conspicuous consumption is seen as avoidable when many people suffer from hardships. The more affluent consumers show mounting dissatisfaction with excessive consumption. Many desire a more wholesome and less wasteful life. Recycling, using goods for a longer period, and following traditional values gain importance.

Mercurial consumption While consumers become agile and fickle during booms enjoying the many brands on offer, during recession, they begin showing loyal behaviour. They also look for value, discarding expensive options.

Slowed Trends

The following are the slowed trends:

Green consumerism Though consumers have embraced green products and services in the past, they find few takers during hard times. Consumers tend to bypass expensive alternatives that claim to be environment-friendly, preferring convenient choices instead.

Decline of deference Public respect for institutions and government decline during recession. The government is seen as doing little to rectify the situation.

Arrested Trends

We can consider ethical consumerism and extreme experience seeking as arrested trends.

Ethical consumerism Ethical consumerism or ethical consumption is practiced through 'positive buying'. This means that people favour 'ethical products' or products, which have not caused harm to anyone during their production and supply. It is based on the concept of 'rupee voting' and includes buying fair-trade products, locally sourced produce, and eggs laid by cage-free hens. Ethical consumerism takes a backseat during a recession.

Extreme-experience seeking Periods of economic growth see the rise of extreme experiences, such as bungee jumping, river rafting, and similar pursuits. Exotic experiences that are expensive, frivolous, risky, or environmentally destructive, such as driving a race car or even recreational air travel, suffer from the recession-driven mood of seriousness.

A surprising outcome of consumer behaviour during a recession is that people start buying cosmetics and products that help them look good. This is called the lipstick effect.

Lipstick effect Economic declines have psychological consequences. For example, recent recessions have been linked to dwindling optimism among college students about their employment prospects and a decline in life satisfaction and well-being.

It is said that hemlines and heels rise and fall with the state of the stock market. A study conducted by Hill, et al. (2012) shows that sales of cosmetics and appearance enhancing products tend to do well during recessions. Sales figures from L'Oreal showed that during 2008, it registered a sales growth of 5.3 per cent, even while the rest of the economy was suffering. The notion that women may spend relatively more money on attractiveness-enhancing products during times of economic recession is referred to as the lipstick effect.

The study correlated economic conditions with consumer spending. The researchers found that economic decline leads to shifts in consumer spending priorities. Dire economic forecast leads people to reallocate money from electronics and furniture towards purchasing products that enhance appearance, such as cosmetics and clothing. The study found that when jeans, perfume, and high-heeled boots were advertised as serving a mate attraction function, it increased women's desirability for those products. However, when the same products were advertised as serving a non-mating function, the lipstick effect was suppressed. This shows that women allocate resources to products that can help attract a mate in times of recession.

The lipstick effect is explained by studying mating psychology. Since males with resources decrease during hard times, women have to look more attractive. The study analysed data for over 20 years and found that higher unemployment was associated with decreased spending on products unrelated to appearance such as furniture, electronics, and leisure or hobby products, but was associated with increased spending on appearance-enhancing products such as cosmetics and clothing. These findings demonstrate the lipstick effect, showing that women seek to boost beauty, specifically in times of economic recession.

Elliot (2008) gives further evidence, saying that employment in the US cosmetics sector went up in the recessions of 1990 and 2001 while jobs in the rest of manufacturing were being shed. In Japan, spending on clothes fell by 25 per cent since 1997, but sales of accessories were up by 10 per cent. In Europe, personal products outperformed the broader market by an average of 100 per cent in each of the three recessions of the early 1980s, early 1990s, and early 2000s.

Connected consumer The second major trend affecting consumer behaviour is the emergence of the connected consumer. Many assumptions in marketing are being challenged because of this shift in behaviour.

Marketing faces a considerable challenge to serve today's connected consumer. Customers have access to technology like smartphones, and this has changed the way people behave and interact with one another. Today's customers can search for information and access companies and websites through apps even while they are on the move. Companies now have to opt for omni-channel marketing, that is, they must integrate consumer experience across physical and online channels (see Fig. 1.5). The new consumer behaviour, while offering great opportunities for brands and companies, also poses a threat in terms of increasing competition, integrating various channels including social media, the emergence of demanding and aware individuals, and their diminishing attention spans that makes communications and engagement increasingly difficult.

FIG. 1.5 Companies now have to opt for omni-channel marketing, that is, they must integrate consumer experience across physical and online channels

Rigby (2011) writes that retailers will have to integrate digital and physical arenas which complement each other instead of competing, increasing sales and lowering costs. However, if customers see this as intrusion, they will turn away.

CONSUMER BEHAVIOUR IN THE FUTURE

How will consumer behaviour change in the future? Though crystal gazing is a self-defeating exercise, several trends are discernible which could well shape consumer expectations of the future. Barkworth (2014) analyses the small cultural shifts that point to the emerging behaviour of consumers. The top six global trends identified by Barkworth are as follows:

Multiplicity Consumers expect products and services to involve all their senses and involve them in new experiences through a range of touchpoints. There is a growing desire for multiplicity and experiences are expected to offer more. It is no longer enough to immerse the viewer in an experience, and people are rejecting the idea of passive on-looking. They are now looking for active participation.

Hyper efficiency Consumers will look for smarter and more efficient ways to satisfy their needs. Since modern life is marked by limited space and limited resources, people want sleeker and quicker products. With a growing awareness of how limited resources are, innovations are creating valuable assets out of the otherwise unused resources, and a new wave of 'serious games' and collaborative digital platforms are smartly mobilizing our collective intelligence and imagination.

The new industrial revolution Digital and technological advances help people to new creative forms and a new appreciation of the digital as a thing of beauty. Technological advances are enabling people to make the transition from users to creators. Digital has become a source of inspiration and the means to create. The rise of 3D printing is hailing a new era for industry. Soon everyone will be a manufacturer, able to create what they want, when they want it.

Escape Consumers are exhibiting an increasing desire to let go, to let loose, and indulge in freedom or sheer hedonistic joy. A form of escapism, we are seeing the desire to indulge. In a turbulent world, there is a craving for silliness and outright frivolity. People are seeking occasions that allow them to let go of all responsibilities and inhibitions, and embrace outlandish hedonism.

Mindfulness Increasingly, people are making their leisure time more about self-development. This intensity can also come from a very different angle, in the form of mindfulness. In a world full of buzz and surface interactions, people are seeking more depth and meaning. Leisure is becoming as much about self-development as pleasure-seeking, and there is a growing sense of earnestness, consideration and thoughtfulness. Some people may crave time away from the Internet, and are severing their connection to technology.

Super-personalized Communications, products, and experiences can now be personalized, thanks to new technologies. Advances in technology mean that companies can cater to individual consumers and give them what they want—sometimes without even being asked.

These trends are discussed in detail in the later chapters of the book.

CONCLUSION

We stand at a very exciting period in the evolution of marketing. Many of the concepts that we are familiar with need a re-look, prompting some to ask the question, 'Is marketing dead?' While we do face a digital disruption, we can safely wager that marketing is facing a transformation as it adjusts to new realities. Human behaviour has always been unpredictable, and this makes the task of marketing both difficult and interesting. In fact, it is unpredictability and irrationality of customers that make the study of consumer behaviour intriguing. We look for ways to unravel the mysteries of the human mind as we try to decipher what goes on inside it when the consumer looks for and selects a brand to buy.

The themes described in this chapter are discussed in detail in the book, with ample case studies and insights.

SUMMARY

Consumer behaviour, which is the study of people as they select and buy goods and services, is one of the most stimulating, complex, and intellectually challenging areas. The field draws from and welcomes insights from a variety of disciplines. This chapter introduces consumer behaviour, describes its importance and the consequences of the rise of the consumer society.

The marketing concept evolved from production and selling concepts of the past. It focuses on fulfilling consumer needs. For modern society, consumption has become the basis of existence. The distinctive mark of the modern society is excess consumption, which leads us to the idea that human behaviour is mostly irrational. The after-effects of the consumer society are very harmful and also threaten the planet.

On the positive side, the consumer society fosters productivity and efficiency, leads to better standard of life, promotes an aesthetic attitude, encourages individualism and self-expression, and emphasizes enjoyment and pleasure. The McDonaldization of society has brought in efficiency, predictability, calculability, and control to our lives. The change is obvious in the life of the Indian consumer: people are getting more materialistic, there is rise of consumerism in society, and Indian brands have evolved to compete with well-known foreign names.

Understanding consumer behaviour helps us to deliver customer satisfaction and value, which help in building relations with customers. However, it has some limitations as well. The seven limitations are as follows:

- It has a narrow scope.
- It views consumer behaviour from narrow lenses.
- It has a narrow epistemology.
- It disregards psychological content.
- It tends to overgeneralize.
- It relies on research by convenience.
- Most studies are hypothetical.

Consumer behaviour is also impacted by economic conditions. Economic uncertainty tends to sober consumers, in which some trends become dominant while others are subdued. Consumers tend to seek simplicity and become thrifty, while green and ethical consumerism slows down. Consumer behaviour of the future will be governed by six trends—multiplicity, hyper efficiency, a new industrial revolution, escape, mindfulness, and super personalized communications and products.

KEY TERMS

Consumerism Consumerism is an ideology that encourages the acquisition of goods and services in ever-greater amounts

Consumer behaviour The study of individuals, groups, or organizations and the processes they use to select, secure, and dispose of products, services, experiences, or ideas to satisfy needs and the impacts that these processes have on the consumer and society

Customer lifetime value (CLV) The total combined customer lifetime values of all of a company's customers

Customer perceived value (CPV) The difference between the customer's evaluation of all the benefits and all the costs of an offering and the perceived alternatives

Customer relationship marketing (CRM) The process of managing detailed information about individual customers and managing all customer touchpoints to maximize loyalty

Customer value (CV) The perceived monetary value of the bundle of economic, functional, and psychological benefits customers expect from a product or a service

Hedonic consumption The sense of enjoyment and pleasure that the consumer gets from the buying, consuming, and owning experience

Lifestyle The typical way of life of an individual, group, or culture

Lipstick effect The notion that women spend relatively more money on attractiveness-enhancing products during times of economic recession

Marketing concept Goal-oriented, integrated philosophy practiced by producers of goods and services that focuses on satisfying the needs of consumers

McDonaldization The process by which the principles of the fast-food restaurant are coming to dominate more and more sectors of American society as well as the rest of the world. These principles are efficiency, predictability, calculability, and control.

Production concept The thinking that placed emphasis was on producing large quantities of goods, productivity, and efficiency while also reducing cost

Selling concept The philosophy that places emphasis on aggressive selling of goods or services, whether they are actually needed or not

Societal marketing concept Application of marketing tools to change people's ideas for their long term betterment

EXERCISES

Concept-review Questions

1. What is consumer behaviour? What are the elements covered in it?
2. Discuss the importance of consumer behaviour. Why is it necessary for marketing practitioners to study it?
3. Why is it said that consumer behaviour is one of the most stimulating, complex, and intellectually challenging areas? What makes it so?
4. What is the marketing concept? Discuss its evolution over the years.
5. How is the marketing concept related to consumer behaviour? In what ways has one contributed to the development of the other?
6. Describe the positive and negative impacts of unbridled consumption on society.
7. What are the limitations of consumer psychology and consumer behaviour research?
8. Compare and contrast consumer behaviour in times of boom and depression.
9. Do you think consumer behaviour is getting impacted because of the connected customer? Identify the ways in which consumer behaviour is changing.
10. Describe how consumer behaviour has changed over the years. What can you say about the future?

Critical Thinking Questions

1. Do you agree with the statement made in the text about Descartes' famous quote, 'I think, therefore I am', has been replaced firmly in modern societies with, 'I consume, therefore I am'? Do we judge people by what they are or by what they own and consume? What are the consequences of such thinking?
2. Take a look at the ads running on television currently. Describe how women are portrayed in these ads. Are women portrayed as consumers in their own right or as serving others or portrayed as commodities? Do you agree with the statement that women have become objects to be owned and used by the very culture that encouraged their freedom?
3. Consumer behaviour research is often criticized as being too narrow and hypothetical. Why is this so? Decide your position whether consumer behaviour is quantitative or qualitative, and develop your argument.
4. Targeting young people by selling lifestyles often results in unfulfilled desires, leading to problems, both socially and behaviourally. It also leads to youth adopting harmful lifestyles. Is this ethical? What can be done to avoid the charge that marketing is ruining lives?

Projects and Assignments

1. Compare the remakes of old movies. Some of the movies you can view are *Agneepath*, *Don*, *Karz*, and *Devdas*. You could also choose some Hollywood remakes. Compare today's remakes with the earlier ones and make notes on differences in consumer behaviour you see in them. Do you see any differences in the way the movies have been set up or the way that consumer culture is evident in these movies?
2. Interview your friends of the basis of their buying an expensive dress, car, or mobile phone. Identify the factors that contributed to the purchase decision. How many of these were rational and how many were irrational? What conclusions can you draw about consumer behaviour from this exercise?
3. Think of a hypothetical consumer in 2030. How do you think would he/she be doing the purchasing and using newer technologies? In what ways would his/her consuming behaviour be different from a shopper today?
4. Interview your parents about the things they consumed and how they bought them. Dig out old magazines and take a look at the ads. Contrast it with consumer behaviour today and the present-day ads. How are they different? Would you agree to the sentiment echoed by many old-timers that the good old days were better? Give reasons for your answer.

REFERENCES

Anderson, Alison, Kevin Meethan, and R. Steven Miles, *Changing Consumer: Markets and Meanings*, Routledge, London, 2002.

Ariely, Dan, 'The end of rational economics', *Harvard Business Review*, July 2009.

Barkworth, Hazel, 'Six trends that will shape consumer behaviour this year', Forbes CMO Network, April, 2014: http://www.forbes.com/sites/onmarketing/2014/02/04/six-trends-that-will-shape-consumer-behavior-this-year/, last accessed on 23 October 2014.

Barr, Stewart, *Environment and Society: Sustainability, Policy and the Citizen*, Ashgate Publishing Ltd, Hampshire, 2008.

Bauman, Zygmunt, 'Consuming life', *Journal of Consumer Culture*, No. 9, pp. 9–29, 2001.

Brosh, Liora, 'Consuming women: The representation of women in the 1940 adaptation of pride and prejudice', *Quarterly Review of Film and Video*, 17:2, pp. 147–159, 2000.

Elliott, L., 'Into the red: 'Lipstick effect' reveals the true face of the recession', *The Guardian*, December, 22, 2008. Available at: http://www.theguardian.com/business/2008/dec/22/recession-cosmetics-lipstick, last accessed on 24 July 2014.

Featherstone, Mike, *Consumer Culture and Postmodernism*, 2/e, Sage Publications, London, 2007.

Flatters, Paul and Michael Willmott, 'Understanding the postrecession Consumer', *Harvard Business Review*, July 2009.

Gopal, Ashok and Rajesh Srinivasan, 'The new Indian consumer', *Harvard Business Review*, October 2006.

Hewlett, Sylvia Ann, Laura Sherbin, and Karen Sumberg, 'How gen Y & boomers will reshape your agenda', *Harvard Business Review*, July 2009.

Hill, S. E., Rodeheffer, C. D., Griskevicius, V., Durante, K., and White, A. E., 'Boosting beauty in an economic decline: Mating, spending, and the lipstick effect'. *Journal of Personality and Social Psychology*, Vol 103, No. 2, August 2012, pp. 275–91, 2012.

Kotler, Philip and Kevin Lane Keller, *A Framework for Marketing Management*, 5/e, Prentice Hall, New Jersey, 2012.

McQuilten, Grace, *Art in Consumer Culture: Mis-design*, Ashgate Publishing Ltd, Surrey, 2011.

Pham, Michel Tuan, 'The seven sins of consumer psychology', *Journal of Consumer Psychology*, Volume 23, Issue 4, October 2013, pp. 411–423, 2011.

Pine, B. Joseph and James H. Gilmore, 'Welcome to the experience economy', *Harvard Business Review*, June 1998.

Rigby, Darrell, 'The future of shopping', *Harvard Business Review*, December 2011.

Ritzer George, *The McDonaldization of Society*, 5/e, Pine Forge Press, Los Angeles, 2007.

Schneider, Joan and Julie Hall, 'Why most product launches fail', *Harvard Business Review*, April 2011.

Solis, Brian, *The End of Business as Usual*, John Wiley & Sons, New Jersey, 2012.

Sparke, Penny, *An Introduction to Design and Culture: 1900 to the Present*, 3/e, Routledge, New York, 2013.

CASE STUDY

Advertising and Behaviour

Advertising is a powerful method to influence consumer behaviour. Every day, people are bombarded with advertising messages. It is estimated that the average adult is exposed to about 300 ads per day. Advertising is seen in private and public places, not only in TV, print, and online, but also in the least likely of places, such as school textbooks and notebooks, hospitals, and even in non-profit agencies.

Advertising increases the information that consumers have and allows them to make better choices. However, it also raises questions about manipulation of vulnerable groups and also excessive commercialism that it fosters. That is because ads sell much more than products—they sell values, images, love, and sexuality. People define their self-worth and self-image by comparing themselves to images in the media. L'Oréal's famous advertising slogan, 'Because I'm worth it' has gone beyond being an advertising slogan to reflect the values and beliefs of a large section of consumers. People get influenced by advertising—young women try to follow the ideal of beauty projected by advertising and develop eating disorders. Children contribute by pushing their 'pester power'.

Young people and adolescents are particularly vulnerable to marketing messages. Since they are in the process of learning values and defining their self-concept, they pick up a lot from what they see in ads. Peer pressure multiplies the power of media; the dominant cultural messages that they see are imbibed and internalized. Mass communication introduces a peer pressure that erodes private and individual values and standards.

Teenagers learn their modes of behaviour and consumption from ads. They follow the stereotypes projected. Advertising creates a mythical and beautiful world which helps them escape reality. It is a perfect world, without problems, in which you get a stream of products designed just for you. In this world, people talk only about products and the services they consume. The goals of humanity are now to buy and consume, and corporations cater to these goals happily. However, the impact on society is often ignored. Take a look at how some of our values have changed.

Women

Women are shown almost exclusively as housewives or sex objects. A housewife is seen cooking and cleaning in most advertisements. She feels guilt for not being more beautiful, for not being a better wife and mother. Companies help her by providing machines that make her life easy and products to look beautiful. She is thin, generally tall, and long-legged, and, above all, young. All 'beautiful' women in advertisements conform to this norm. Women try to imitate that idea of beauty, and tend to feel ashamed and guilty if they fail. Their desirability and lovability are contingent upon physical perfection. A smooth skin, white teeth, no wrinkles or pimples, slim waists, and a sexy outlook is what one has to acquire to be acceptable. These images do not reflect reality; yet, people are aspiring to these biologically impossible ideals. The media sells desire; since the ideals are not close to reality, it would not be wrong to say that the media perpetuates a market for frustration and disappointment (see Fig. 1.6).

Swinson (2011) writes that people who are unhappy about their bodies develop eating disorders,

FIG. 1.6 Indian advertising places women in traditional roles

turn to diet pills or steroids, or try cosmetic surgery and Botox injections. One study found that one in four people is depressed about their body; another found that almost a third of women say they would sacrifice a year of life to achieve the ideal body weight and shape.

Such advertising keeps the diet industry going strong; perhaps at a substantial cost in terms of the mental and physical health of many young women. Girls actively want to look like Barbie dolls. Websites like http://www.humanbarbie.org/gallery.html show a large number of girls who have been able to get Barbie bodies and looks. *The Independent* (2013) reports that Ukraine's Valeria Lukyanova, who is a human Barbie doll, lives on a diet or liquids. Lunch in her case, is a glass of freshly squeezed celery and carrot juice, mixed together with a trio of Indian chutneys. Her aim is to subsist on air and light alone.

Children

Advertising targeted to young children is particularly worrisome to parents because children lack the ability to resist commercial messages. Some countries have passed laws designed to limit or regulate advertising aimed at children. For example, while airing of TV ads selling toys to children are banned in Greece between 7 a.m. and 10 p.m., Sweden and Norway ban all advertising aimed at children under the age of 12.

Pine and Nash (2002) studied requests made by children to Father Christmas. They found that children who watched more commercial television were found to request a greater number of items from Father Christmas. These children also requested more branded items than children who watched less. A positive correlation was found between watching television alone and number of requests, showing that lone viewing renders children more susceptible to advertising. A comparison group of children from Sweden, where advertising to children is not permitted, asked for significantly fewer items. They concluded that children who watched more TV, and especially those who watch alone, may be socialized to become consumers from a very early age.

Companies defend their marketing messages as it constitutes their freedom of speech. They also say that advertising occurs within a social context and they are merely providing products and services that society demands, directly or indirectly. The problems, however, are twofold. First, since marketing plays with consumer psychology, it has the power to manipulate thoughts of people—should this power not be used responsibly? Second, marketing has forced commercialism of almost everything on the planet. It penetrates almost every sphere of potential customers, including private spaces: think of spam e-mail and SMS messages, posts on your social media sites, and ads that open up on your computer screen hindering your work. Companies also gather private information about consumers without their knowledge or consent.

Questions for Discussion

1. What effects do marketing activities have on society in general and consumers in particular? Does marketing reflect the existing values of society or does it change them?
2. Do you think that the use of consumer psychology in marketing has got out of hand? Should there be limits to what companies can portray in their marketing messages?
3. Look at advertising critically. Do you think the present volume of advertising is socially beneficial? Which ads are discriminatory or encourage questionable behaviour?
4. Should freedom of expression of companies not be restricted so as to ban commercial messages from public and private spheres that are not marketplaces?

Sources:

'Life in plastic, it's fantastic: Meet Ukraine's real-life Barbie girl', *The Independent*, 10 February, 2013, http://www.independent.co.uk/news/world/europe/life-in-plastic-its-fantastic-meet-ukraines-reallife-barbie-girl-8488914.html, last accessed on 23 October 2014.

Pine, Karen J. and Avril Nash, 'Dear Santa: The effects of television advertising on young children', *International Journal of Behavioral Development*, Vol. 26, No. 6, pp. 529–539, 2002.

Swinson, Jo, 'False beauty in advertising and the pressure to look 'good'', CNN, August 10, 2011, http://edition.cnn.com/2011/OPINION/08/08/swinson.airbrushing.ads/, last accessed on 23 October 2014.

CHAPTER TWO

Consumer Analysis, Segmentation, and Strategy

LEARNING OBJECTIVES

This chapter explains how consumers are grouped together based on their common characteristics, as a way of devising the most effective marketing programmes for them. Consumer analysis and segmentation are an integral part of designing marketing strategy.

After studying this chapter, the reader would be able to

- define and explain market segmentation, target markets, and product differentiation
- understand the criteria used for segmenting consumers
- understand the role of market segmentation in making marketing strategies
- evaluate alternative approaches for pursuing segmentation strategies, like counter-segmentation
- evaluate microtargeting and mass customization

CASE STUDY

L'Oréal—Serving Many Segments

Managers think of markets as composed of different people with different needs, called segments, rather than thinking of them as homogenous entities. Large companies, with a portfolio of products and brands, would find it difficult to manage their brands without segmentation. This case study shows how a large company, L'Oréal, uses its various brands and products to serve different segments, on the basis of culture, product usage, age, as well as digital segmentation.

L'Oréal is a leading cosmetics brand, but what is less known is that, it is a group with 23 global brands with sales of over £20 billion in 2011. It operates in 130 countries and has over 66,000 employees. Its mission is to 'make beauty universal'.

The company has a broad line and is also active in luxury products with well-known brands such as Yves Saint-Laurent and Giorgio Armani. It has a wide range of cosmetics products with brands such as Garnier and Maybelline, and a professional range that is sold only in salons. In addition, it has a range of Active Cosmetics that offers products such as nutritional supplements and health products. Each product line targets distinct market segments.

The brands cater to different segments and are also exclusive to each distribution channel: professional products brands to hair salons; consumer products brands to retail stores including drug stores and food stores; luxury products brands to specialty stores and department stores; and active cosmetics brands to dispensing dermatologists and pharmacies. Each brand is positioned according to a segmentation based on price and image positioning, and there is a distinct market strategy for each segment.

Selling such a wide range involves targeting and meeting the needs of different types of consumers. For instance, a brand like Garnier can be sold off the shelves of stores, but products of The Body Shop are sold in exclusive, branded stores. Similarly, while the Active Cosmetics brands target different segments of customers who want personal advice, the fashion brands have entirely different upscale strategies. The company follows a segmentation strategy in the following ways:

Customer needs and behaviour To sell its range of products, the company segments the market on the basis of consumer needs and behaviour. Brands such as Garnier and Maybelline cater to shoppers looking for quick solutions, whereas the L'Oréal professional range is offered in salons caters to consumers looking for beauty services. Active Cosmetics brands such as Vichy and La Roche-Posay available in pharmacies, and are positioned to consumers who look to solve beauty problems and need to seek professional advice as well.

National and cultural segmentation Many companies want to homogenize brands to make them acceptable across a range of cultures, but L'Oréal's products seek to embody cultural segmentation by highlighting their country of origin through various brands. For instance, though L'Oréal is a French company, it also owns brands that are associated with the country of their origin: Italian (Giorgio Armani), Japanese (Shu Uemura), and American (Maybelline). L'Oréal has developed a winning formula: a growing portfolio of international brands. Many people using these brands think that they are local brands rather than owned by the French giant. For instance, many people think that Maybelline New York with its distinctive 'urban American chic' is an American brand. As per a Trefis report (2012), in India, the company has adopted a dual pricing strategy aimed to make its hair care range more affordable. Premium segments are covered by retaining the premium price tag and image for its skin care and cosmetics products.

Cosmetics usage The company tracks the way cosmetics are used and serves segments on the basis of cosmetics usage. While some brands convey leisure and luxury, L'Oréal realized that the growing number of women in the workforce and rising urbanization had created a class of women who wanted to look good, but lacked time to groom themselves. So it developed nail enamel that dried in one minute and repositioned its Great Finish nail enamel by changing its name to Express Finish. This targeted working urban women. The company uses the same approach with its other brands.

Age segmentation L'Oréal targets the young as well as older customers by analysing their needs. It relaunched its Helena Rubinstein skin care and cosmetics brand as a product for the 21st century 20- to 30-year-old woman who wanted wild colours, in urban centres such as New York, Paris, London, and Tokyo. For older women, it operates Laclinic Beauty Institute, an aesthetic medicine centre, with a centre for aesthetic dentistry and a plastic, reconstructive, and aesthetic surgery department. The company is also targeting younger people by developing mobile apps. It believes that this generation wants to make the most of its leisure time. Customers are provided with company and product information via these apps freeing up shopping time for those of them who are tech-savvy. Its Instant Beauty app in France allows users to scan L'Oréal products to obtain information, consumer reviews, recommendations from friends, and add products to a shopping list.

Digital segmentation L'Oréal has given a digital push to all its brands. It evaluates online conversations by reviewing blogs, social media channels, chat rooms, and online editorials for conversations about L'Oréal brands as part of its marketing and PR strategy. The company aims to achieve a 360° perspective for its brands through this method.

Using these segmentation strategies, the company is able to manage a very large and complex operation, while also maintaining the identities of its brands. Further, the company is able to understand and serve a large number of customers with varied needs by segmenting markets.

While reading this chapter, try to answer the following questions:
1. How do companies segment markets and provide products to serve specific needs of those segments?
2. What is the basis of segmenting markets?
3. How are clustering techniques used?
4. Is segmentation really necessary? Should companies serve large markets or slice them into very thin slices?

Sources:

Baker, Rosie, 'L'Oréal plots digital drive', *Marketing Week*, 9 March 2011, http://www.marketingweek.co.uk/loreal-plots-digital-drive/3024216.article, last accessed on 27 March 2012.

Baker, Rosie and Lucy Handley, 'L'Oréal looks to ramp up geo-location marketing', *Marketing Week*, 22 November 2011, http://www.marketingweek.co.uk/loreal-looks-to-ramp-up-geo-location-marketing/3032105.article, last accessed on 27 March 2012.

Businessweek, 28 June, 1999, http://www.businessweek.com/1999/99_26/b3635016.htm, last accessed on 27 March 2012.

Trefis (2012), 'L'Oréal targets "masstige" segment in India with dual pricing strategy', 10 July, http://www.trefis.com/stock/lrlcy/articles/130297/loreal-targets-masstige-segment-in-india-with-dual-pricing-strategy/2012-07-10, last accessed on 8 August 2013.

www.loreal.com, last accessed on 14 March 2012.

INTRODUCTION

At the core of segmentation strategy is the question of whether companies should make standardized products for entire markets or specialized products for certain selected segments. There was a time when products were made for individuals. Shoes, clothes, and a range of products were handcrafted. In the era of mass marketing, companies produced standardized goods and sold them using mass media to communicate to customers. This was also the age of mass production, when large factories produced huge quantities of goods and thus achieved economies of scale.

This changed consumer behaviour perceptibly. Families bought products that were good enough for all their members. Soaps, creams, and oils that suited the entire household were bought. A 1940s advertisement for a popular soap, Hamam (Fig. 2.1), projects the soap as 'toilet soap' or simply, a soap for bathing. Everyone in a particular family used it and presumably no harm came out of the habit.

Contrast it with the situation today. Now, families are likely to purchase separate soaps for different members. Soaps are available for bathing and handwash, for fighting germs, for males and females, for babies, and so on. For the more discerning, there are fairness soaps and soaps especially for oily and dry skins.

FIG. 2.1 1940s advertisement for Hamam soap

Source: http://www.ebay.in/itm/HAMAM-501-SOAPS-2-SIDED-Porcelain-Enamel-Sign-c1940s-/180585701465#ht_5045wt_905, last accessed on 30 March 2012

The situation is similar for practically all products. The one-size-fits-all approach seems to be a thing of the past as companies continue to slice markets into very thin segments. Rust, Moorman, and Bhalla (2010) point out that the phenomenon is aided by technology. 'Never before have companies had such powerful technologies for interacting directly with customers, collecting and mining information about them, and tailoring their offerings accordingly', they write.

As a consequence, according to *Businessweek* (2004), companies are 'standing mass marketing on its head by shifting emphasis from selling to the vast, anonymous crowd to selling to millions of particular consumers'.

Politicians have traditionally segmented the population by highlighting individual differences of caste, state, and religion. A leader like Mahatma Gandhi, on the other hand, was able to appeal to all sections of society as he did not differentiate between people. Whether companies should segment markets or sell to the mass market, is a matter of debate.

DE-MASSIFYING MARKETS

The idea of segmentation is based on the understanding that there are different types of people. Toffler (1981) calls it de-massifying markets. 'The mass market has split into ever-multiplying, ever-changing sets of mini-markets that demand a continually expanding range of options, models, types, sizes, colours, and customizations', he writes. Companies need to discover whether similar people with similar needs can be grouped into segments so that their needs can be met.

Dealing with market segments also helps companies to understand their customers better. In his classic article, *Marketing Myopia*, Levitt (1960) gives examples of several industries which got wiped out because they only kept track of their businesses and did not focus on customer needs. 'Without a very sophisticated eye on the customer, most new products might have been wrong, their sales methods useless', he wrote. Marketing, he further said, has to be preoccupied with the product and 'the whole cluster of things associated with creating, delivering, and, finally, consuming it'. Only when managers concentrate on precise market segments, can they really do all this.

Once segments have been identified, the products offered must meet the separate needs. Therefore, product differentiation is tied to segmentation. In his book, *The Marketing Imagination*, Levitt (1983) writes that differentiation represents an imaginative response to the existence of potential customers in such a way as to give them compelling reasons to want to do business with the company. To differentiate an offering effectively requires knowing what drives and attracts customers.

Market Segmentation

Market segmentation refers to grouping of customers with similar characteristics and needs.

McDonald and Dunbar (2004) define a market segment as a group of customers within a market who share a similar level of interest in the same, or comparable, set of needs.

There are two ways of segmenting markets: on the basis of products or on the basis of customers. For the purpose of this chapter, we concentrate on consumer segmentation.

FIG. 2.2 Market—one big loaf or thin slices

Instead of thinking of the market as one mass or big loaf with different people and varied needs, segmentation helps managers to think of markets as a sliced loaf of bread (Fig. 2.2). Each slice is an identifiable segment, which has common characteristics and needs, and displays similar responses to marketing actions.

An accurate definition of segmentation was given in 1956 by Wendell R. Smith in his seminal paper, 'Market segmentation involves viewing a heterogeneous market as a number of smaller homogeneous markets, in response to differing preferences, attributable to the desires of customers for more precise satisfactions of their varying wants'.

Smith wrote that smaller homogeneous markets are visualized in response to differing product preferences among important market segments. His view was also economic—he explained different market segments as having different demand curves with reference to matters such as price sensitivity, colour, material, or package size. Like differentiation, segmentation often involves substantial use of advertising and promotion, to inform consumers of the availability of goods or services produced for, or presented as, meeting their needs with precision.

Another seminal paper is by Yankelovich (1964), who wrote that managers must have a method of analysis that helps them focus sharply on new opportunities.

Members of particular segments are identified by one or more 'people' characteristics, such as demographic, sociographic, or personality variables. Once subgroups have been identified, marketers can supposedly improve their marketing efforts by more closely approximating the needs of each subgroup. For example, by discovering the needs of the time-pressed, urban, working woman, L'Oréal was able to offer a quick-drying nail enamel that precisely met her needs (see chapter-opening case study). Such insights can only be obtained by being closely in touch with the selected segments.

Levitt (1983) has explained the concept thus: 'Segmentation requires knowing how customers differ from one another and how those differences can be clustered into commercially meaningful segments. To think segments means you have to think about what drives customers, customer groups, and the choices that are or might be available to them. To think segments means to think beyond what's obviously out there to see'.

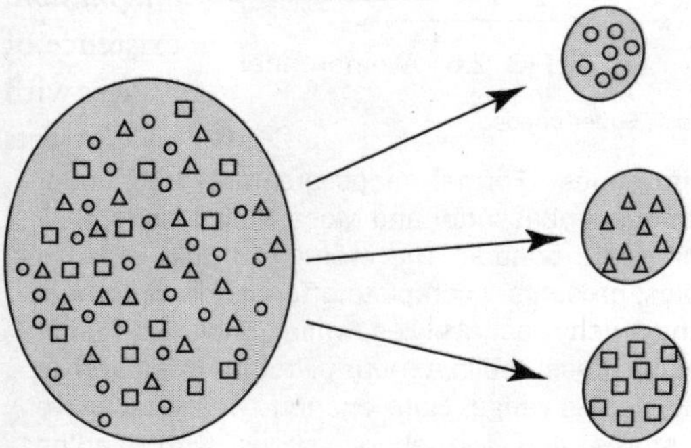

This is explained in Fig. 2.3. Markets consist of all kinds of people, shown in different shapes in the circle on the left. Segmentation refers to grouping of customers on the basis of some commonality, similarity, or kinship. So managers tend to cluster customers with common needs. Once clustered, they are able to spot the specific needs and offer products accordingly.

Companies use segmentation in various ways. How Bata uses segmentation is shown in Exhibit 2.1 on Superbrands.

FIG. 2.3 Markets divided into consumer segments

EXHIBIT 2.1 Superbrands—Bata

Bata is a Czech brand but is well known in India. It is as an integral part of the Indian culture. Bata is a multinational company and one of the world's largest retailers of footwear and accessories (see Fig. 2.4).

FIG. 2.4 Bata showroom

Courtesy: Superbrands

Incorporated as Bata Shoe Company Private Limited in 1931, the company was set up initially as a small division in Konnagar (near Kolkata) in 1932. It went public in 1973 when it changed its name to Bata India Limited. According to its website, Bata India has now established itself as India's largest footwear retailer with a retail network of over 1200 stores. This gives it a reach that no other footwear company can match. The company also operates a large non-retail distribution network through its urban wholesale division and caters to millions of customers through over 30,000 dealers.

The company serves several segments through various brands, distribution channels, and promotions.

Women A range 'Malini Ramani for Bata' is a unique concept of designer wear for the masses. The collection includes a wide variety of bright metallic wedge-heeled Kolhapuri chappals, which went on to become a fad amongst the young and fashion-conscious. Simultaneously, Bata also adopted several trendy innovations to its current range such as Marie Claire and Naturalizer to fulfil the needs of an evolving customer. In 2011, it launched a new collection of ladies footwear by Marie Claire in a glamorous fashion event with Miss Universe, Ms Ximena Navarrette and international fashion designer, Ms Sanjana Jon Available in wedges, kitten heels, gladiators, ballerinas, and pumps in an attractive variety of leather, denim, mesh, soft uppers, metallic, and ethnic hues, the Marie Claire collection was showcased in the fashion show (see Fig. 2.5).

FIG. 2.5 Marie claire

Courtesy: Superbrands

Youth The youth is targeted through its brand of North Star and specialty outdoor brand Weinbrenner. The designs have been inspired by global trends with special emphasis on casual styles (Fig. 2.6).

FIG. 2.6 Weinbrenner

Courtesy: Superbrands

Formal shoes Formal shoes are marketed under its famous Ambassador and Mocassino brands. New offerings are popular. The premium brand of Hush Puppies, presents a complete offering for customers looking for city casual styles, while Scholl and Comfit are being presented in a youthful range. To expand its Hush Puppies range, Bata opened twenty exclusive new stores and five shop-in-shops with leading department stores.

(Contd)

EXHIBIT 2.1 (Contd)

> **Mass market** Sandak, Batalite, and Sunshine labels continue to attract millions with their trendy and lightweight all-weather footwear.
>
> **Online shoppers** The company has introduced The Bata Home Delivery Service under which customers can place orders for any Bata footwear, which they are unable to find at a Bata store near them and have it home delivered through courier. Along with home delivery, Bata's website provides consumers the option to browse its extensive range of footwear and shop online.
>
> **School children** Bata organizes contests for its target market of school children. In one such contest, it offered consumers a chance to win a Bata School Buddy freebie on purchase of products worth ₹599 from its Back to School collection.
>
> *Source*: Superbrands 2012

Need for Segmentation

Market segmentation essentially represents the adjustment of market offerings to consumer or user requirements. Smith (1956) wrote that exploitation of market segments provides for greater maximization of consumer satisfaction, tends to build a more secure market position, and leads to greater overall stability.

There are many reasons why market segmentation is used extensively as a strategy. Faced with a choice of products, consumers look for products that meet their specific or individual needs. Markets want products that are pre-sold by producers and are recognized by consumers as meeting their precise needs.

Market segmentation produces significant benefits. It results in the concentration of marketing energy by concentrating on the subdivision to gain a competitive advantage. It is analogous to the military principle of 'concentration of force', where, rather than attacking on all fronts, battalions concentrate on capturing enemy divisions one by one.

Companies must use their knowledge of segmentation to assess strengths and vulnerabilities, to plan product lines, to determine advertising and selling strategy, and to set precise marketing objectives.

Market segmentation is not an end in itself. It should lead to identifying target markets and assessing the profitability of serving those markets, positioning products, and developing a marketing mix to appeal to each segment in the chosen position (Fig. 2.7).

Specifically, segmentation analysis helps to achieve the following aims:

- Direct promotional efforts to the most potentially profitable segments of the market
- Design a product line that meets the specific demands of the market
- Catch the major trends in a swiftly changing market and thus take advantage of them
- Create appeals that are most effective in advertising and thus become more efficient
- Choose advertising media that are more likely to be seen by targeted segments
- Correct the timing of advertising and promotion so that they are used at times when selling resistance is least
- Understand demographic market information and know customers better
- Design effective and cost-efficient marketing strategies

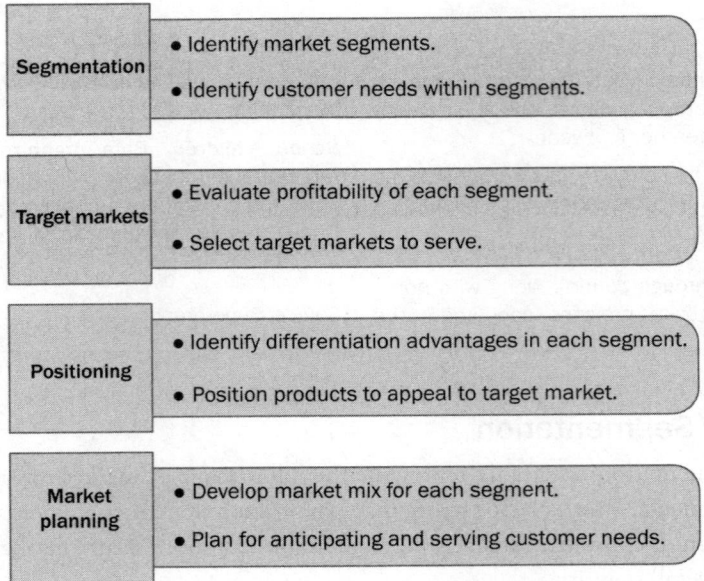

FIG. 2.7 Market segmentation helps identify target markets and position products

- Achieve accurate positioning of products with customers and for effective competitive analysis
- Achieve reduction of competition and establish a niche

Segmentation results in financial benefits for companies. To achieve this, the bases of segmentation must be understood and the actual segmentation itself must be carefully done.

BASES OF SEGMENTATION

In choosing segments, companies have to keep the following criteria in mind. Kotler, et al. (2009) suggested that effective segments must have the following five qualities:

Measurable The segment should be measurable, that is, its size, purchasing power, and characteristics of the segments should be measurable.

Substantial The segment must be sufficiently large to provide revenues and profits.

Accessible The buyers in the segment must be reached through appropriate promotional and distribution channels. They should be servable, that is, there should be target-group specific advertising media that the target audience likes to use.

Differentiable The segments should be conceptually distinguishable and respond differently to different marketing mixes. If two segments respond identically to a particular offer, they do not constitute separate segments.

Actionable Effective programmes should be formulated for attracting and serving the segments.

Companies segment markets traditionally on a number of variables. The bases of segmentation are summarized in Table 2.1.

TABLE 2.1 Bases of segmenting consumer markets

Basis of segmentation	Segmentation variables
Geographic (Physical location of the customer)	**Region:** North, South, West, East, and Central India **States:** Markets are segmented on the basis of districts or states **Size/Density:** Metros, small towns, rural areas **Climate/Season:** Cold to hot temperate, humid, rainy
Demographic (Population and its characteristics)	**Age:** Youth, older people **Sex:** Male, female **Religion/Caste:** India has six major religions. Segmentation is also done on the basis of caste **Marital status:** Single, married, divorced, widowed **Income:** Lower, middle class, rich **Education/Literacy:** Illiterate, basic literate, school, college, higher education **Occupation:** Unskilled, skilled, white collar
Psychographic or lifestyle segmentation	**Social status:** Peer group pressure **Economic:** Value or economy customers **Lifestyles:** Based on activities, interests, and opinions (AIOs)
Socio-cultural segmentation	**Culture:** Regional, Indian, Western **Subculture:** North Indian, Gujarati, Rajasthani, South Indian, etc **Religion:** Hindu, Muslim, Christian, Sikh, Buddhist, Jain, etc **Social class:** Lower, middle, upper **Family life cycle:** Single, married/living together, full nest, empty nest
Use-/Profit-related segmentation	**Use-related:** Heavy users, occasional purchasers **Profit-related:** Profitable and less profitable customers **Occasions:** Births, marriages, anniversaries, special occasions, festivals **Behavioural:** User status, usage rate, loyalty status, buyer-readiness stage, and attitude
Hybrid segmentation	Combination of any of the aforementioned techniques **Geodemographic:** Nielsen PRIZM **Socio-economic:** SEC criteria **Demographic/Psychographic:** SBI VALS
Benefit segmentation	**Functional benefits:** Social and emotional benefits Value for money Convenience
Psychological segmentation	**Personal needs and motivation:** Personality Perception Learning Attitudes

Geographic Segmentation

Companies often find it easy to use market segments based on the way a country is organized—they can cater to the specific requirements of consumers within a state that will usually have a similar culture, language, and climate. India is organized into 28 states and 7 union territories, 593 districts and 5493 subdistricts, according to Census 2001 (see Table 2.2). It is convenient to use this organization to implement marketing and promotion programmes. Distribution is also made easier by looking at each state separately. Large companies vary their products and packaging so that they appeal to customers within a state. Please see Exhibit 2.2.

TABLE 2.2 Administrative divisions in India

Item	Number	Item	Number
No. of states	28	No. of urban agglomerations and towns	4,378
No. of union territories	7	No. of urban agglomerations	384
No. of districts	593	No. of towns	5,161
No. of subdistricts	5,463	No. of inhabited villages	593,732
No. of CD blocks (As per map profile)	6,374	No. of uninhabited villages	44,856

Source: Census of India 2011, ORGI, reprinted with permission

EXHIBIT 2.2 Geographic Segmentation by Dainik Bhaskar

In this exciting milieu, where some 300 dailies across the country compete for the consumer's attention, newspapers published by the Dainik Bhaskar Group in four languages—Dainik Bhaskar in Hindi, Divya Bhaskar in Gujarati, Divya Marathi in Marathi and DNA in English—form the morning's information source for 19 million readers (see Fig. 2.8). This huge readership makes the Dainik Bhaskar Group the largest newspaper group in India (Source: IRS Q4, 2011 AIR). Dainik Bhaskar, by itself, spread across eleven states rolls out 36 editions and is read by 14.60 million people. With 9.63 million urban readers, it is also the largest urban newspaper in India (Source IRS Q4, 2011).

The Dainik Bhaskar Group's strength lies in empowering regional markets in Tier II and III towns. It takes pride in being the non-metro urban newspaper in the heart of India—a region so immense that it dwarfs several countries and with purchasing power and growth potential of a number of others. In this vast market the Dainik Bhaskar Group reaches out to 38% of the population and 38% of the national market potential. It does this through a multi-media convergence with radio, event marketing, print, short code and Internet as its arrow heads.

FIG. 2.8 Dainik Bhaskar in different Indian Languages

Courtesy: Superbrands

Source: Superbrands 2012

Smaller companies who either lack resources or do not wish to expand for other reasons, will find that confining their operations to certain states helps them to know and serve their customers better. Indeed, there are many products that are available in certain states and are not marketed in others. For example, brands such as Anchor toothpaste and Dyna soap are only available in a few states of India.

Demographic Segmentation

Demographic figures reveal invaluable data with respect to the population. Data with regard to population shows us the number of people in India classified according to age and sex (Table 2.3). Such data is available for each state. Further, the data shows the percentage of population in broad age groups (Fig. 2.9), which helps managers to estimate the size of markets and the number of

TABLE 2.3 India's demographic data

Age group	Persons	Males	Females
6 years and below	163,819,614	84,999,203	78,820,411
Proportion to total population (%)	15.9	16.0	15.9
7 to 14 years	199,791,198	104,488,119	95,303,079
Proportion to total population (%)	19.4	19.6	19.2
15 to 59 years	585,638,723	303,400,561	282,238,162
Proportion to total population (%)	56.9	57.0	56.9
60 years and above	76,622,321	37,768,327	38,853,994
Proportion to total population (%)	7.5	7.1	7.8
Age not stated	2,738,472	1,500,562	1,237,910
Proportion to total population (%)	0.3	0.3	0.3

Source: Census of India 2011, ORGI, reprinted with permission

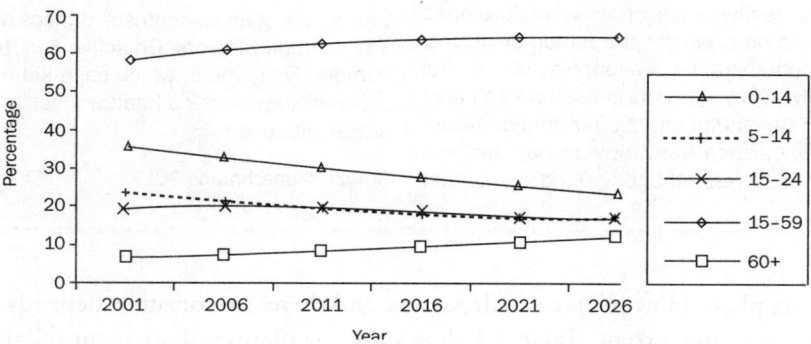

FIG. 2.9 Age-wise distribution of Indian population

Source: Census of India 2011, ORGI, reprinted with permission

their targeted consumers within each age group. Exhibit 2.3 on Cartoon network shows how children are targeted as a separate category.

The population pyramid (Fig. 2.11) is another useful tool that gives age-wise percentage of population. From this, we can estimate the percentage of population within certain age groups. This data helps us know the macro trends taking place in society. A bulge in the bottom layer shows that the proportion of people in the younger age group is over 50 per cent in India today. Companies marketing products for specific age groups can assess how much demand is likely to arise in the future for their age-specific products. (See Table 2.3).

Sociocultural Segmentation

Sociocultural data shows how people live. This impacts their consumption patterns, and companies do well to take social and cultural factors into account when devising products and

> ### EXHIBIT 2.3 Targeting Children
>
> It is not unusual for a channel to promote its shows and characters on-air via promos, bugs, tickers or contests. But what Cartoon Network does better than the rest is bridge the gap between kids and reel cartoons, by organising events where kids can meet their favourite characters and interact with them.
>
> Over the years, Cartoon Network has nurtured these on-ground events into brands themselves that kids across the country eagerly await. One such event is *Toon Cricket*–Cartoon Network's most successful annual on-ground property. With over ten years of cricket matches between the channel's most popular characters such as Tom and Jerry, Scooby Doo, The Powerpuff Girls, Dexter, Johnny Bravo, Ben 10 and others, it attracts thousands of families into stadiums across the country. Please see Fig. 2.10.
>
> Each year, a new surprise element is added that helps to pump up the energy and excitement. In 2010, an augmented reality application was developed where kids could be a part of the match decisions, download live photographs, wallpapers, etc. In the following year five lucky kids were chosen via a contest to be a part of Ben's Ultimate 11 Team and feature on the channel. Cartoon Network 'Fun Day Out' and 'Go Active Fun Run' were other onground events that made headlines. 'Fun Day Out' is a multicity event that is packed with character performances, meets and greets, games, contests, dances and tons of fun. The Cartoon Network 'Go Active Fun Run' was a non-competitive game in which each kid teamed up with a parent to promote a healthy lifestyle through a pro-social initiative.
>
>
>
> **FIG. 2.10** Popular characters from Cartoon Network
>
> *Courtesy*: Superbrands
>
> *Source*: Superbrands 2012

marketing plans. How people eat, dress, live, and therefore consume, depends on culture and religion to a large extent. Table 2.4 shows the population of six main religions in India. It shows the propensity to consume certain products, for example, non-vegetarian foods. Since attitudes towards food are dictated by religion, chains like McDonalds have had to modify their menus to be acceptable to people in different countries.

Further, the extent to which society is westernized, or the influence of subcultures and even of social classes, dictate what kind of products are consumed. Companies keep track of such trends while offering products, opening retail outlets, and providing services. Branded clothes have become popular in India but companies hoping to sell high-priced Western ladies' wear find that the market segment is very small. Similarly, companies producing wine also find that they are catering to a small segment because wine drinking is not a cultural phenomenon in the country.

Psychographic or Lifestyle Segmentation

Psychographics or lifestyles are defined as the study and classification of people according to their attitudes, aspirations, and other psychological criteria. Psychographic variables are any attributes relating to personality, values, attitudes, interests, or lifestyles. They are also called Activities, Interests, and Opinions (AIO), and reflect a lifestyle that reveals the attitudes and values of a

Consumer Analysis, Segmentation, and Strategy | 39

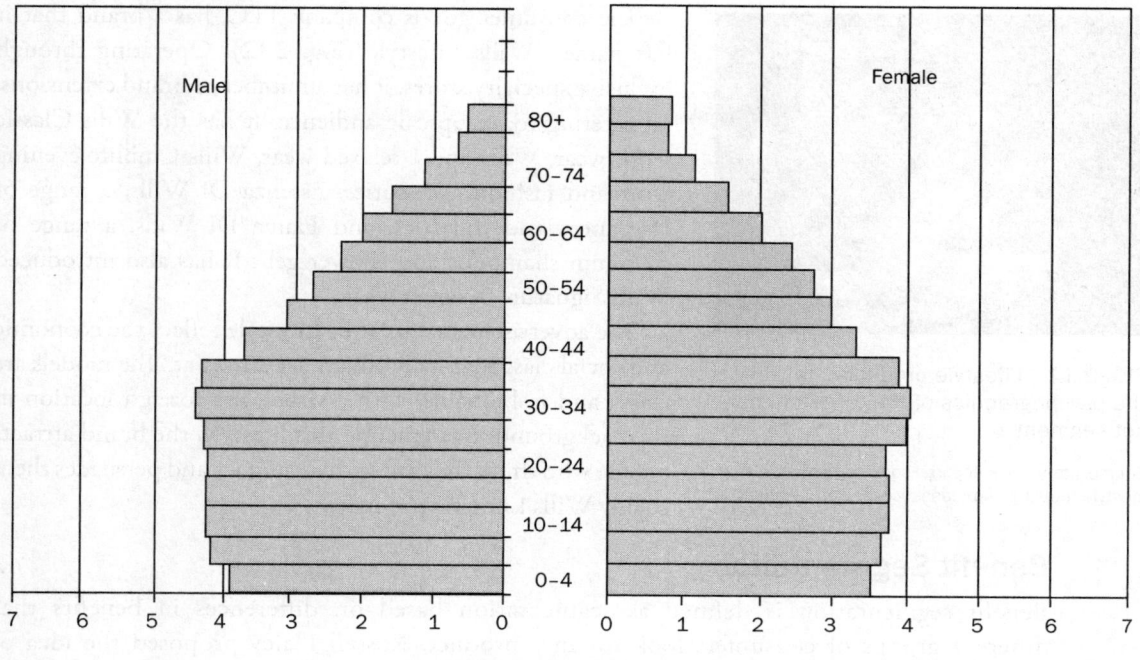

FIG. 2.11 Population pyramid

Source: Census of India 2011, ORGI, reprinted with permission

TABLE 2.4 Composition of religions in India's population

Religion	Number	Percentage
Hindus	827,578,868	80.5
Muslims	138,188,240	13.4
Christians	24,080,016	2.3
Sikhs	19,215,730	1.9
Buddhists	7,955,207	0.8
Jains	4,225,053	0.4
Other religions and persuasions	6,639,626	0.6

Source: Census of India 2011, ORGI, reprinted with permission

person or a group. Companies use lifestyle segmentation in advertisements, projecting a lifestyle that their target group has, or is aspiring to have. The look of the model and the setting attempt to create the perception that the brand is suited to the members of the targeted class or segment.

FIG. 2.12 Lifestyle products that reflect the psychographics of the targeted market segment

Source: http://www.itcportal.com/itc-business/fmcg/lifestyle-retailing.aspx, last accessed on 3 April 2012

The consumer goods company, ITC, has a brand that it has named Wills Lifestyle (Fig. 2.12). Operating through exclusive specialty stores, it has a number of brand extensions, all catering to an upscale audience. It has the Wills Classic work wear, Wills Sport relaxed wear, Wills Clublife evening wear and fashion accessories, Essenza Di Wills, a range of fragrances and toiletries, and Fiama Di Wills, a range of premium shampoos and shower gels. It has also introduced Wills Signature designer wear.

The advertisements of Wills Lifestyle reflect the economic and social class that its products are aimed at. The models are classy and fashionable, with a visual of a foreign location in the background. By depicting this lifestyle, the brand attracts people who think they are in this category and persuades them to buy Wills Lifestyle products.

Benefit Segmentation

Benefit segmentation is defined as segmentation based on differences in benefits that different groups of consumers look for in a product. Russell Haley proposed the idea of benefit segmentation in 1968. He wrote that the benefits that people seek in consuming a given product are the basic reasons for the existence of true market segments. He illustrated the concept by dividing the consumers of toothpaste into four segments on the basis of the different benefits each offers. *The Worriers* buy a toothpaste brand for preventing tooth decay, the *Sociables* for the brightness of their teeth, the *Sensory* segment buys it for flavour and appearance of the product, and the *Independent* segment buys it for no reason but to switch brands for variety.

Clearly, companies doing benefit segmentation must not only identify benefits, but also understand the markets. By doing such an analysis, managers can estimate the size of the market by combining it with demographic data, decide on the tone and copy of advertising, decide on media environments, and also decide on the product, and packaging to be offered. The marketing implications are many: once these benefit segments are understood, new product opportunities and effective ways of positioning can be devised, along with compatible point-of-purchase materials, and selection of sales promotion likely to appeal to the target segment.

Merely classifying consumers on the basis of benefits is not enough. Haley further writes that once people are classified into segments, each segment is contrasted with all the others in terms of demography, volumes, perceptions, media habits, its personality, lifestyle, etc. 'In this way,' writes Haley, 'a reasonably deep understanding of the people who make up each segment can be obtained. By capitalising on this understanding, it is possible to reach them, to talk to them in their own terms, and to present a product in the most favourable light possible'.

Haley also identified the types of market segments that are found in all product categories. These help in devising products and advertising messages that would most likely appeal to the segments being targeted.

- *Status seeker*: A consumer who is very concerned with the prestige of the brand (Exhibit 2.4)
- *Swinger*: A customer who likes to be modern and up-to-date in all activities, including brand selection
- *Conservative*: A customer who sticks to large, successful companies and popular brands
- *Rational man*: A customer who looks for economy, value, and durability
- *Inner-directed man*: A customer who is especially concerned with his self-concept, who thinks of himself as independent, honest, and as endowed with a sense of humour
- *Hedonist*: A customer who is concerned primarily with sensory benefits

It is easy to see how brands exploit these market segments by offering products. Advertisements of popular products can be classified on the basis of the aforementioned segments.

Psychological Segmentation

Psychological segmentation focuses on the individual. It tries to discover an individual's personality, and uses self-image and self-esteem, thereby attaching products to a person's extended self. It uses a person's inner motivation, attitude, emotions, and perception to market products. It assumes that the economic model of rational behaviour does not apply to individuals, but that consumers make decisions relatively automatically, influenced by their social and physical context, with the unconscious playing a large part.

EXHIBIT 2.4 Status Bathroom

Status seekers spend a lot of money on their homes. The next big trend that is emerging from this rapid evolution is coordinated bath spaces. These amalgamate the design language of various products such as bath fittings, sanitary ware, wellness products, and even accessories. Today, bathrooms are becoming bath suites. This change in mindset and aesthetics has spawned a whole new genre of bathrooms that now marry convenience, functionality, luxury, technology, colour, and shape into a magical world. Builders, architects, and home owners are now realizing that a good bathroom enhances not only the desirability but also the value of a property.

The Indian bath and bath fittings industry is becoming more fashion-led rather than function-led, as it was all these years.

Jaquar has attained leadership in the bath fittings space and is rushing towards a position of eminence in the bathing solutions space quickly (Fig. 2.13). With the company's presence in Europe, the Asia-Pacific region, the Middle East, and Africa, the new-look Jaquar gives the customer the status he is so keen to acquire.

FIG. 2.13 Jaguar sanitary ware
Courtesy: Superbrands

Source: Superbrands 2012

Psychological segmentation attempts to discover these inner traits and to position products accordingly.

Use-related Segmentation

There are three aspects of use-related segmentation: on the basis of heavy or low usage, how the product is consumed, and on the basis of loyalty.

The first classifies consumers on the basis of quantities purchased by them, that is, *heavy* or *low usage*. Dik Twedt (1965) gave the 'heavy half theory', which says that in most product categories, one-half of customers account for around 80 per cent of the consumption. He found that one household from the heavy half bought as much as nine households in the light half. By using this theory, companies can concentrate on the most valuable customers. They can differentiate between customers who place large, medium, or light orders, which in turn is helpful for assigning appropriate sales staff for different types of customers. For instance, consumer goods companies will have separate sales staff to deal with large customers like Big Bazaar and another set of people to sell to small *kirana* shops.

The second aspect of analysing use-related segmentation is to discover how the product is being used by the target customers. This paves the way for providing *additional benefits* as expected by customers, to either modify current products, or place new offerings in the market. Seybold (2001) has discussed the idea of customer scenario, that is, the broad context in which a customer uses products. How this idea can be used by companies is discussed in the chapter-end case study on National Semiconductor.

The third aspect of use-related segmentation is *brand loyalty*. Companies segment on the basis of those customers who are loyal and those who are not. For loyal customers, companies devise special deals and discounts, along with a reward point plan. Such relationship plans help retain loyal customers and encourage them to make additional purchases.

Hybrid Segmentation

Hybrid segmentation combines any of the aforementioned segmentation techniques, since a single basis of segmentation is often not enough to decipher segments. For instance, merely using demographic segmentation will give an idea of the size of the targeted segment but little else. Similarly, using the psychological or psychographic approach might tell you what type of person will use a particular product but nothing more. By combining two or more techniques, you can understand your segments much better.

The following are the hybrid segmentation techniques:

- Demographic–psychographic
- Geodemographic—clustering techniques such as Nielsen PRIZM, ACORN, and values and lifestyle system (VALS)
- Yankelovich mindbase segmentation

Demographic—psychographic segmentation The attempt in demographic–psychographic segmentation is to match demographic profiles with lifestyles. Demographics identify the different observable characteristics of a population. Within this, there are groups, for example, of doctors, accountants, single people, teens, or women executives. Through psychographics,

CB IN ACTION Analysing Segments

This exercise requires you to discover how segmentation is used in real life. Select one or two product categories such as shampoos, cars, restaurants, televisions, and apparel. Then list all the brands available in each category. A visit to the supermarket shows, for instance, that shampoo brands consist of Sunsilk, Clinic Plus, Dove, Pantene, Head & Shoulders, Garnier Fructis, Vatika, and a few others.

Now analyse each brand to see which consumer segment it targets. A look at brand advertisements, a visit to the brand website, and looking at social media pages of the brands will give you a good idea of the segments that are being targeted by the company. List your analysis as in Table 2.5:

Doing this exercise for different product categories will show how segments are located and served by companies.

TABLE 2.5 Products and segmentation

Brand	Geographic	Demographic	Socio-cultural	Psychographic	Benefit	Psychological	Use-related
Sunsilk							
Clinic Plus							
Dove							
Pantene							
Head & Shoulders							
Garnier							
Vatika							

we understand the identifiable characteristics of people, related to psychological factors such as attitudes, values, lifestyles, motivations, and needs.

This form of hybrid segmentation works on the basis that it is easy to reach customers by understanding what they have in common, and what motivates them to buy. Both demography and psychographics help to understand the psychology of the buyer, used for marketing products.

Geodemographic segmentation Geodemographic studies are based on the premise that consumers who reside within geographic clusters such as PIN codes or neighbourhoods, also share demographic and lifestyle similarities. The assumption of geodemographic segmentation is, 'You are where you live'. Geodemographic segmentation combines geographic, demographic, and socio-economic data, and consists of clustering small geographic areas into relatively homogeneous market segments. The assumption is that people with similar incomes, preferences, and consumption patterns tend to cluster together, illustrated by the saying, 'birds of a feather flock together'. The main advantages of geodemographic segmentation are as follows:

- It has the ability to link different sets of data.
- It does not rely on one-dimensional classifiers but is multifaceted.
- It is easy to use since it is linked to the postcode system.
- It provides data for 'above-the-line' and 'below-the-line' marketing activities, such as direct mailers and door-to-door campaigns.

Clustering Techniques

There are many clustering techniques available. The most famous of these are Nielsen PRIZM in the US and A Class of Residential Neighbourhoods (ACORN) in the UK. These are described here.

PRIZM

The potential rating index by zip markets (PRIZM) model classifies every US household in terms of 66 demographic and behaviour types or segments and describes 'consumers' likes, dislikes, lifestyles and purchase behaviour,' according to the company. It was developed by Claritas, which was later acquired by the Nielsen Company. The 66-segment model uses the following demographic drivers: age, income, presence of children, marital status, homeownership, and urbanization.

The final 66 segments are arranged to make up two standard sets of groups: Social and Lifestage. The social classification uses a geographical base and the lifestage classification uses a demographic base. By classifying the segments on these two parameters, it is possible to discover market behaviour of the segments quite accurately.

Though the segments are made based on US society and many of them are not applicable to India, it gives an indication as to how markets are segmented. Different countries will have different criteria as their social and demographic data are different. Moreover, data on households is not available in such detail to slice such thin layers of Indian consumers. (See Tables 2.6 and 2.7).

ACORN

ACORN (a classification of residential neighbourhoods) is a geodemographic segmentation of the UK's population. It segments consumer households into five categories, 17 groups, and 56 types. By analysing significant social factors and population behaviour, it provides precise information and an understanding of the different types of people in every part of the UK.

TABLE 2.6 PRIZM social groups

Income	Urban	Small Towns	Rural
High	Rich and famous	Town elites	Landed gentry
Middle	Young professionals	Salaried class	Traders, small business owners
Low	Low salaried, retired elders	Daily wagers	Young and rustic, casual labour

TABLE 2.7 PRIZM life-stage groups

Income	Young	Family	Mature
High	Mid-life success	Accumulated wealth	Affluent empty nesters
Middle	Young achievers	Mainstream families	Cautious couples
Low	Striving singles	Sustaining families	Sustaining seniors

VALS

Another way of segmentation is the values, attitudes, and lifestyle system (VALS), which was developed in 1978 by SRI International, (now Strategic Business Insights or SBI). It is a way of viewing people on the basis of their attitudes, needs, values, beliefs, and demographics. VALS segments US adults into eight distinct types (Fig. 2.14), or mindsets, using a set of psychological traits and key demographics.

The basic principle of VALS is that people express their personalities through their market behaviour. It reflects a pattern that explains the relationship between personality traits and consumer behaviour. VALS not only distinguishes differences in motivation, it also captures the psychological and material constraints on consumption.

The horizontal dimension represents the individual's primary motivation. The vertical dimension represents resources that a person has, based on education and income. The thinkers and believers are motivated by the pursuit of ideals, but the former have more resources. Similarly, achievers and strivers are motivated by personal achievement, whereas the experiencers and makers are more interested in self-expression.

It illustrates the eight types on two critical concepts for understanding consumers: primary motivation and resources. Their combination determines how a person will express himself or herself in the marketplace as a consumer.

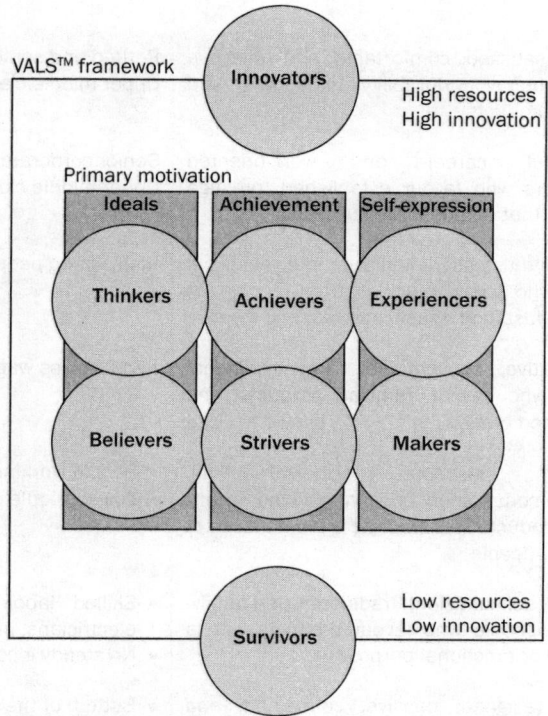

FIG. 2.14 VALS segments

Source: Adapted from http://www.strategicbusinessinsights.com/vals/ustypes.shtml, last accessed on 4 April 2014

The VALS system can be seen as a set of pigeonholes in which consumers are classified and placed. By studying the motivation and resources of households, they can be classified in each of the eight segments.

Though the VALS segments are described for US markets, the eight segments are applicable in other countries too, but the percentage of people in each segment will vary from country to country. Rich countries are likely to have more people in upper segments while poor countries will have more people in lower segments. Table 2.8 explains the VALS segments and also attempts to classify Indian consumers in these segments. Combining this with the SEC classification in India (discussed later in this chapter), one can arrive at accurate figures of each segment.

The VALS segments are shown in detail in Table 2.8. The terminology used in India and the segment equivalent in this country are also explained.

TABLE 2.8 VALS segments and their applicability in Indian context

VALS segments	Characteristics	Indian equivalent
Innovators	Successful, sophisticated, active, people who take charge, whose purchases reflect cultivated tastes for upscale, niche-oriented products	Business owners Land owners Very senior corporate executives
Thinkers	Mature, satisfied, comfortable, and reflective people who favour durability, functionality, and value in products	Retired and senior salary earners Upper middle class
Achievers	Successful, career- and work-oriented consumers who favour established, prestige products that demonstrate success	Senior corporate executives Upper middle class
Experiencers	Young, enthusiastic, impulsive, and rebellious people who spend much of their income on clothing, fast food, music, movies, and video	Rich, young people with prosperous parents or jobs
Believers	Conservative, conventional, and traditional people who favour familiar products and established brands	Middle-class wage earners
Strivers	Uncertain, insecure, approval-seeking, resource-constrained consumers who favour stylish products that emulate the purchases of wealthier people	• People working on contractual jobs • Lower middle class
Makers	Practical, self-sufficient, traditional, and family-oriented people who favour products with a practical or functional purpose	• Skilled labour, consisting of carpenters, electricians, plumbers and the like • No steady income
Survivors	Elderly, resigned, passive, concerned, and resource-constrained consumers who are cautious and loyal to brands	• Bottom of the pyramid consumers • Unskilled labour, no steady jobs

TABLE 2.9 Profile and marketing implications of Yankelovich mindbase segments

Yankelovich mindbase segment and motto	Lifestyle	Marketing implications
Segment 1—Up and comer 'I am expressive.' Motto: *Carpe diem*—seize the day	• I live life to the fullest • I am active and engaged • I live in the now • The future is limitless • I can be or do anything	• Young people, fashionable, actively support hot styles • Look for products that help them to express themselves, or match their personality
Segment 2—Young materialist 'I am driven.' Motto: Nothing ventured, nothing gained	• I want to succeed personally and professionally • I am at the top in whatever I do, whether in career or family	• Young adults • Trendy, lover gadgets • Look for products that reflect their success and achievement
Segment 3—Stressed by life 'I am at capacity.' Motto: Time is of the essence	• I am very busy and look for control and simplification • I want to devote time to my hobbies and family	• Executives and business owners, usually in their 30s • Look for convenience and products/stores that help save time
Segment 4—New traditionalist 'I am rock steady.' Motto: Do the right thing	• I lead a contented life • I am dependable and generous	• Older people with savings, age around 45 • Look for quality products and good value • Make thoughtful decisions
Segment 5—Family limited 'I am down-to-earth.' Motto: Easy on down the road	• I cruise down life's path at my own pace • I want to enhance my life, treat myself to novel experiences and products	• Like to buy things to feel good • Look for unique products and like to enjoy life
Segment 6—Detached introverts 'I am sophisticated.' Motto: Sense and sensibility	• I am intelligent, confident, and sensitive • I have high expectations	• Age approaching 50 • Demanding as customers • Know what they want • Look for quality, convenience, and service
Segment 7—Renaissance elders 'I measure twice.' Motto: An ounce of prevention	• I am mature and on the path to self actualization • I live a healthy, active life and want my future to be secure and highly rewarding	• Older, retired people, above 60 • Look for health and financial security • Like to buy products that help them look like good citizens
Segment 8—Retired from life 'I am devoted.' Motto: Home is where my heart is	• I am traditional and look for comforts of home • I am spiritual and content	• Older people, age above 65 • Stick to proven products and brands • Like traditional products

> **CB IN ACTION** Yankelovich Mindbase Segmentation
>
> Yankelovich mindbase segmentation is a lifestyle segmentation technique. It lists eight types of people based on their lifestyles as described in this chapter. When you observe people, you will find that they fall in one category or the other.
>
> A fun activity that gives insights into consumer behaviour, is to have a group of friends analyse each other on the basis of segments proposed by Yankelovich. First ask your friends to describe their personality based on characteristics described in Table 2.9. Then as a group activity, describe each friend on the basis of the eight segments and explain the reasons why you think your friend falls in that particular category. See whether your observation matches with the personal observations of your friends.
>
> What kinds of products are suitable for each segment?

Yankelovich Mindbase

Yankelovich mindbase is based on lifestyles. It segments the population into eight core behavioural segments, with 32 subgroups, that distinguish consumers by their values, lifestyles, and motivations. These are summed up in Table 2.9.

Indian Market Segmentation

In a series of articles published in *Mint*, Indicus Analytics has provided the bases for market segments in India. It classifies the Indian consumer into 33 distinct segments on the basis of socio-economic categories (SEC). Marketing companies know that consumers' expenditure on goods depends on several factors, such as income, education, occupation, family size, family type, and regional and community influences. The segments in the figure show SEC classification on the vertical axis—SEC A is the category with the most income, whereas SEC E has the least income. On the horizontal axis, the market is classified on the basis of age. For example, the categories G1 to G5 represent the bottom-of-the-pyramid consumers, while A1 to A5 represent the most prosperous. Of these, SEC A4 and A5 represent the most affluent segments. While drawing up marketing strategy, companies can decide to target one or many segments.

The socio-economic profile of consumers is used to differentiate between segments. The broad characteristics of five categories, SEC A to E, are described here (see Table. 2.10). The unit of segmentation is the household and there are two parameters used—the occupation of the chief wage earner and the educational level of adult members. Education is generally a defining characteristic determining earning capacity, though businessmen or skilled workers with lower educational levels may do just as well, if not better, than professionals. Further, segmentation on the basis of life stages gives finer and more useful cuts. However, these five segments can be used at the outset to get a broad picture of consumer segments across the cities of India.

SEC A This is made up of the most affluent households, where the chief wage earner is a businessman, professional, executive or manager, and adult members have studied up to the graduate or postgraduate level. These comprise around 11 per cent of all urban households. More

Consumer Analysis, Segmentation, and Strategy

TABLE 2.10 Socio-economic classification calculated by Indicus Analytics

Education	SEC classification	Chief wage earner	Life-stage subsegments
High	SEC A	Graduate/PG businessman/Professional	A1–A5
	SEC B	School-educated businessman	B1–B5
	SEC C	School-educated skilled worker	C1–C5
	SEC D	Primary-educated skilled worker	D1–D5
Low	SEC E	Unskilled worker	E1–E5

ETHICAL INSIGHT
Segmentation: The Ethical Question

Segmentation has many uses. It helps to precisely serve the needs of a selected set of consumers. It requires companies to understand the target customers in terms of lifestyles and psychology. This, however, raises ethical concerns as to whether companies are using segmentation techniques to take advantage of vulnerable or disadvantaged sections of society.

Martin Lindstrom (2011) argues in his book, *Brandwashed*, that advertising often convinces us to buy things by exploiting our hopes and fears. He gives the example of Axe which targets the 'Insecure Novice'—the guy who cannot make friends with girls. The advertising of the company has followed the theme of 'nerd-sprays-Axe, nerd-gets-girl' that has helped it become a hugely successful brand. The question is: should advertisers play on the latent fears and vulnerability of the target market?

The fact is that companies across the globe have used segmentation techniques to target unsuspecting people to get them hooked to products that are sometimes harmful. This is how they do it, according to *Brandwashed*.

Targeting the unborn A company sent candy to doctors to give away to pregnant mothers, since what they eat affects the foetal brain and what the baby will later want to eat. Later, the company launched a coffee product that tasted just like the candy, and it became hugely successful with kids. Lindstrom reports that mothers would even give agitated newborn babies the coffee to quickly calm them down.

Inappropriate products Companies target padded bikini tops at children and 'push up' bras to young girls. A parent wrote, 'The push up bra is effectively a sex tool, designed to push the breasts up and out, putting them front and centre where they're more accessible to the eye (and everything else). How is this okay for a second-grader?' Another example of targeting vulnerable sections was by Tesco which launched a toy called the Peekaboo Pole Dancing Kit, marketed to girls under 10. According to *The Telegraph* (2006), the Tesco Direct site exhorted young girls to 'Unleash the sex kitten inside...'

Targeting vulnerable groups Children and youngsters are vulnerable groups. Tobacco companies send birthday presents to teens when they turn 18, which include vouchers for cigarettes. They send these packages every month, and it was seen that after the third pack, the teens were usually hooked. Beauty products and 'first-time hair removers' are targeted at 10-to-15-year-olds. Lindstrom says that marketers are increasingly aiming beauty products at kids. Many 6–15 year old girls, even in India, use lipstick and lip gloss.

Pester power Some products are targeted at children to increase what Lindstrom calls 'pester power'—the way kids force their parents to buy stuff. Children making embarrassing public scenes and sneaking items into their parents' shopping carts are common sights in India as well. Advertisers try hard to trigger a desire in the child to encourage such behaviour.

Encouraging unhealthy habits Alcohol in the form of 'alcopops'—sweet, flavoured, coloured, soda-like alcoholic beverages—are supposedly intended for adults, but are easily available to youngsters because

(Contd)

ETHICAL INSIGHT (Contd)

of lax regulation. It is increasingly being marketed to teenage girls. *Headlines Today* (2013) found that 13-year-old girls are the most popular consumers of such products. *The Times of India* (2012) reports that the age at which an average person begins drinking hard liquor has dropped from 28 years a decade ago to 18 now, an indication that a sizeable number of school students is consuming alcohol. Many studies have shown that drinking at such a young age is likely to develop into alcohol addiction or alcohol abuse. *Time* (2013) reports that a long-term study conducted at University of Heidelberg showed that the age at which a person starts drinking is a good predictor of whether or not he or she will develop an addiction. It was found that a person who starts drinking between age 11 and 14 has a 16 per cent chance of becoming an alcoholic 10 years later.

A backlash against such marketing has long existed in the West. Activism by consumer groups has called the companies into question. The objective of One Million Moms (http://onemillionmoms.com/) is to stop the exploitation of children, especially by the entertainment media and fights against the 'immorality, violence, vulgarity, and profanity the entertainment media is throwing at your children.'

The question is: should companies be doing such things? How can we protect vulnerable and weak groups from the advertising onslaught?

Sources:
Chatterjee, Nandini, 'Alcohol addiction trickles down to youngsters still in school', The Times of India, 27 July 2012.
CNN Wire , 'Abercrombie criticized for selling push-up tops to little girls', 27 March 2011, http://edition.cnn.com/2011/BUSINESS/03/26/abercrombie.bikini.controversy/index.html, last accessed on 29 July 2013.
Headlines Today, 'Gurgaon pubs under scanner after school kids were caught drinking', 17 July, http://indiatoday.intoday.in/video/gurgaon-pubs-gurgaon-police-bar-owners-alcohol-hookah-students/1/291788.html, last accessed on 29 July 2013.
Lindstrom, Martin, *Brandwashed: Tricks Companies Use to Manipulate Our Minds and Persuade Us to Buy*, Crown Business, New York, 2011.
Szalavitz, Maia, 'If drinking starts at puberty, it's more likely to lead to alcohol problems', *Time*, 24 May 2013, http://healthland.time.com/2013/05/24/if-drinking-starts-at-puberty-its-more-likely-to-lead-to-alcohol-problems/#ixzz2aaKuDOjE, last accessed on 29 July 2013.

than half the chief wage earners in this segment have been educated at a level higher than school. Their earning capacity is among the highest in cities.

SEC B This category has chief wage earners who are either school-educated businessmen or skilled workers with a college degree or diploma. This segment accounts for around 17 per cent of urban Indian households.

SEC C The chief wage earners in this segment are skilled workers and are mainly school-educated, though a few adults in these households may have had some college-level training. The income level is therefore, less than the previous two categories. This segment consists of 21% of Indian households.

SEC D This segment has low-income households where the chief wage earners could be skilled workers. In such families, school may be the highest educational level reached. This SEC may also comprise households with unskilled workers where some adults have college-level education. About 25% of the households fall under this category.

SEC E This segment has the lowest level of income; the chief wage earners are unskilled workers and the educational level of adults does not exceed schooling. This is the largest segment in Indian cities, and is comprised mostly of migrants from villages or much smaller towns. This segment constitutes about 26% of the Indian households.

More than half the urban households fall into the lowest two segments—numbering around 160 million people. However, in the 12 districts of Amritsar, Gandhinagar, Ludhiana, Kolhapur, Rupnagar, Mumbai, Jalandhar, Valsad, Patiala, Gurdaspur, Jabalpur, and Sangrur, these two segments make up less than 40 per cent of the urban population. Seven of the 12 are in Punjab, reflecting the general level of prosperity in that state.

Punjab and Gujarat also report higher levels of SEC B and C households, representing the middle class. The five districts with the highest share of urban population in these two segments are Gandhinagar, Rupnagar, Amritsar, Jalandhar, and Ludhiana.

Top-end households comprising SEC A, where spending is the highest, are found in higher proportion in the urban areas of Delhi, Mumbai, Bangalore, Chennai, and Kolkata. On average, SEC A accounts for 11.6% of the total population. The five districts where the proportion of SEC A is the highest (more than 16.5 per cent) are Gurdaspur, Ernakulam, Chennai, Kolhapur, and Patiala. Little wonder then, that smaller towns show the spending patterns of the upwardly mobile.

Criticism of Segmentation

Though segmentation is a powerful tool for understanding how markets work, there is a growing body of thought that questions it. Lewis and Bridger (2000) write that 'the reality of new consumers is that they defy categorisation—which is why segmentation, that foundation stone of market research for more than 70 years, so often fails when applied to them'.

Segmentation is at best a psychological phenomenon, where managers try to place customers into neat little boxes based on their characteristics, habits, or personality. Based on these, they make assumptions as to what such people should or should not consume. However, the marketplace is dynamic, and people cannot really be classified into types. Some of the criticisms of segmentation are as follows:

Customers cannot be classified into neat little piles Segmentation exists in the mind of the manager, because humans defy classification. Moreover, we do not know who buys what and for what purpose.

Leads to fragmentation of society By treating the individual as its focus, market segmentation leads to fragmentation. Political parties in India, for instance, play on caste and religious segmentation and the result has been fissures in society. Different groups seethe with discontent, often resulting in disruptions. Similarly, market segmentation by firms highlights individual differences, leading to further segmentation of society.

Very thin layers By analysing consumers on various parameters, companies are able to identify consumer needs accurately, but in the process are left with a very thin slice. Serving such small segments is often not profitable.

Exploitative By targeting people based on personality and psychology, market segmentation exploits their weaknesses and emotions. Often, this leads to harmful behaviour. One such harmful behaviour is compulsive consumption. Obesity, burgeoning credit card debt, and disruptive behaviour are the result of segmenting and targeting vulnerable people.

As a result, some companies choose to go the opposite way. Instead of slicing the bread thinly, they combine two or more slices and offer mass-produced goods at cheaper prices. Discount stores, for example, stock numerous product lines by little-known brands, a product for every need, at the lowest prices, besides offering excellent quality for the price. This phenomenon is called counter-segmentation.

Counter-segmentation

On realizing that too much segmentation results in the loss of some benefits and cost advantages, some companies combine segments to achieve larger segments.

Counter-segmentation is defined as combining market segments to appeal to a broad range of consumers. The assumption is that consumers will be happy with fewer choices because it means lower prices.

Kapferer (2008) notes that the hypersegmentation of shampoos according to new hair needs, leads the customer to take into account more needs in his/her choosing process. He gives the example of Procter & Gamble, which eliminated 15 to 25 per cent of the product extensions that were not achieving a sufficient turnover within 18 months. All-in-one products are offered on the same principle of simplification, and the resultant benefit is economy of scale.

Counter-segmentation may offer absolutely no choice and products are generally only available in a single version with no variety. The advantage is that such products will be cheaper: a common diaper, whatever the weight or the gender of the baby, in contrast to Phases (boy or girl) by Pampers, will be 40 per cent cheaper than the branded product.

Quelch and Kenny (1994) make an interesting observation that 'people do not eat or drink more, wash their hair more, or brush their teeth more frequently simply because they have more products from which to choose'.

Managers will do well to consider these aspects before venturing into market segmentation. Not all segmentation achieves the desired results (see the case of Airtel discussed in Research Insight box). The challenge is to use segmentation effectively.

 CB IN ACTION   Segmentation or Counter-segmentation?

As this chapter shows, there are compelling reasons for segmentation and equally compelling reasons for counter-segmentation. Have a debate in your class on this issue. Ask half the class to debate on one side of the issue and the other half on the opposite side. They should read some current literature, look at some examples of companies that have done segmentation in contrast to others who have trimmed their product lines, and also cover the ethical issues (see box on Ethical Insight).

At the end of the debate, see which side has the better argument. The instructor should conclude the discussion. The debate will not only be an interesting one, but will help you understand the concept of segmentation.

USING SEGMENTATION EFFECTIVELY

Market segmentation is a powerful tool, but it is not used effectively at times by managers. The choice of segments is not based on analysis but on the manager's perceptions and inclination. Another mistake is to limit segmentation only to creating advertisements.

Consequently, we find advertisements targeting one or the other segment, but the benefits gained by their brands are minimal. One of the failures in recent history has been that of Tata Nano, which targeted millions of people going around on scooters, but failed to get them to buy the car designed for them, at least in the volumes expected. Many other companies have burnt their fingers by overestimating 'The Great Indian Middle Class'. Companies have in the past tried (unsuccessfully) to sell cigarettes specially branded for women. Changing lifestyles in India caused many companies to market premium products but the empty malls dotting the country point to quite a different story indeed.

Lewis and Bridger in their book, *The Soul of the New Consumer* (2000) point out that segmentation is a deconstructive procedure that involves placing consumers in pigeonholes, but this technique can overlook subtle and unexpected variations. Another reason that segmentation fails is that it ignores the fact that women buy cigars for men and men purchase make-up for women.

They write that 'by attempting to chop so disparate a population as new consumers into chunks that somehow seem to go together, segmentation runs the risk of producing one dimensional thinking about a highly multi-dimensional phenomenon'.

There are two aspects to this. The first is using segmentation on the basis of a manager's perception. Condom makers, for instance, have traditionally targeted males. An interesting example was reported by *The Economist* (2012). It described a Chinese condom maker, Safedom, which went against the traditional wisdom of targeting condoms at men. While Western brands firmly target men, with macho names to match, Safedom sells condoms with brand names such as 'Beautiful Girl' and 'Green Lemon,' emphasizing female health benefits. In a country where condoms are provided free by the government, Safedom has garnered 8 per cent of the market, selling a billion condoms in China in 2012.

The second aspect is the use of advertisements. Many companies make the mistake of creating advertisements that appeal to the target segment, without making any changes to product offerings. Yankelovich and Meer (2006) say that though segmentation is useful in guiding companies in tailoring products and services for consumer groups most likely to purchase them, it has been used merely to serve the needs of advertising. Companies use segmentation to create advertising 'which it serves mainly by populating commercials with characters that viewers can identify with—the marketing equivalent of central casting'.

Indeed, we see many instances of advertising in the Indian media of products targeted at particular segments but without any discernible product differentiation. For instance, the fact that young people dominate Indian demography has pushed many companies to target them. Such advertisements have smart, young people in humorous situations. However, neither the product attributes nor services are specific to the targeted audience. Movies targeted specifically at young viewers are usually flops, and a visit to cafés shows that there are many school and college students who like to spend their time, but not money, at such outlets. The Research Insight box

RESEARCH INSIGHT
Targeting the Young or the Old?

Companies often make a wrong selection of their market segments. Guided by perception of societal changes or personal liking, companies choose segments. In India, for example, companies are targeting the youth market. They look at the growing population of young people earning high salaries and hope to get a share of the wallet of this highly visible and supposedly affluent class. Young people are in fact, the toast of advertisers. However, is this segment really as profitable as it is hoped? Some companies have found out just the opposite.

The leading telecom service provider, Airtel, started a campaign in August 2011, drawing on a teenager's ability to make friends and the importance he or she accords to the exercise. The commercial used music and lyrics with the theme—*Har ek friend zaroori hota hai* (you need friends of all types)—to communicate the message.

In the process, Bharti Airtel, India's largest telecom services company both by revenue and subscribers, attempted to do two things: target a population, mostly in the 18–20 age-group, that is increasingly taking to data services faster than any other demographic, and telling them that the service provider is the best option they have.

According to the company, this was a thematic campaign, without any product proposition per se, but looking to push brand preference.

The insight of every friend being important came after numerous conversations with youngsters. In the TV commercial, the film uses a series of visuals to show the different types of friends that young people have—an all-weather friend, a casual friend, a friend you are comfortable with, or a friend you don't get along with so well. It is this slice-of-life advertising that has endeared itself to many, point out industry experts. Apart from the TV commercial, digital and outdoor campaigns were also launched.

The advertisement with subtitles was also launched on YouTube and was an instant hit. The digital campaign invited people to create different friend types and tag their companions appropriately. The person who tagged the most number of friends was supposed to win a trip to Las Vegas.

Apart from the popularity of the ad, did Airtel achieve greater sales? The TRAI report for the quarter ending September 2011 said that the wireless subscriber base had gone up from 851.70 million in June 2011 to 873.61 million in September 2011, representing an increase of 2.57 per cent. In the same period, the net addition for Bharti Airtel was a subscriber base of 172.78 million in September 2011, up from 169.19 million in the previous quarter. This represents a rate of growth of 2.13 per cent.

The market share of Bharti in wireless actually fell from 19.86 percent in June 2011 to 19.78 percent in September 2011, even though the advertisement was being telecast during that period.

One would have expected that the market share would be steady, if not increasing, during the time that the popular ad was being shown. However the fall in market share, even by a small percentage, shows that the company could not garner even the industry growth rate during the period.

Many companies make similar mistakes. Restaurants targeting young customers have also found that the real money lies elsewhere. *The Economic Times* (2012) reports that many restaurants which earlier targeted the young, are now offering special loyalty cards and the comforts of blankets and shawls, besides reaching out to old-age homes, to woo elders with enough spare time and money.

The young and lively restaurant formats or the youthful cafés found that their target customers did not have high discretionary incomes. Instead, they discovered that their elderly guests actively operated Facebook and Twitter accounts and were members of online forums. Restaurants such as McDonald's, Mainland China, Little Italy, Subway, and Punjab Grill estimate that consumers in the 60+ age group account for up to 15 per cent of their sales.

Correcting the earlier ideas of segmentation and targeting, McDonald's is now developing a menu specifically targeted at the older age group and reaching out to old-age homes. Mainland China has introduced some off-the-menu dishes: steamed butter noodles (for easy chewing) and special steamed fish for senior citizens, and also offers complimentary dessert to them.

Another restaurant, Little Italy, offers reading glasses and is also introducing grab bars or rods

(Contd)

RESEARCH INSIGHT (Contd)

to help older people maintain their balance in washrooms. The Barbeque Nation chain is training its staff in emergency medical assistance, like helping a customer who has suffered a sudden heart attack. It says that this kind of service would be most beneficial for this age group.

Such eat-out joints are tweaking their offerings because senior citizens have more disposable income than the young. While their frequency of eating out may not be as high, senior citizens are typically more profitable consumers. They tend to not only have more spare money but also spare time. Moreover, restaurants find that older people are more loyal.

Should companies target the young consumer or the older customer who has more spending power?

Sources:
Mukherjee, Writankar and Sarah Jacob, 'Restaurants such as McDonald's and Subway add senior citizens to their business platter', *The Economic Times*, 23 March 2012.
Pinto, Viveat Susan, 'Airtel: Playing up friendship', *Business Standard*, 26 August 2011.
TRAI, July–September 2011, New Delhi, 'The Indian telecom services performance indicators', http://www.trai.gov.in/WriteReadData/trai/upload/Reports/57/Indicator%20Report%20-Sep-11.pdf, last accessed on 30 March 2012.

describes the case of Airtel, which created a highly popular advertisement targeting the young, but failed to get additional market share.

Microtargeting

Technology allows very precise segmentation simply because precise information is available. Today it is possible to track the purchase habits of individual customers. Companies also use data mining to keep track of customers as they surf the Internet. Microtargeting allows very narrow segmentation, up to the level of individuals.

Microtargeting is narrowing the segment size to the point of customizing products and marketing programmes for specific individuals. It involves the use of local and direct marketing datamining techniques that involve predictive market segmentation. Microtargeting is used by political parties to connect with individual voters. They use direct communication methods, such as direct mailers, phone calls, home visits, email, SMS, and so on, to build support for fundraising or votes. Microtargeting uses personalized, tailored messages to subgroups on the basis of unique information about that subgroup.

Companies have to slice segments very thin to achieve microtargeting, since it requires sophisticated information management techniques. This leads us to mass customization, or manufacturing products tailormade for individuals (see Exhibit 2.5 on Sintex).

Mass Customization

Information technology allows companies to interact with their customers on a one-to-one basis, to find out individual needs. This has led to co-creating products that perfectly suit the needs of those individual consumers. Now technology is going a step further.

The Economist (2011) reports of a technology that may well make mass production history—the technology of 3D printing. It says that 'three-dimensional printing makes it as cheap to create single items as it is to produce thousands and thus undermines economies of scale. It may have as profound an impact on the world as the coming of the factory did.'

> **EXHIBIT 2.5 Modifying Products for Different Segments**
>
> Sintex is a manufacturer of plastic water tanks and building materials. This exhibit shows how it is, targeting different social segments in the urban and rural areas, enabling the company to capitalize on unattended pockets of demand and effectively compete at all price points. Separately, it has, under the Renotuf brand introduced a new range of tanks using blow-moulding technology. The company has also launched aesthetically-designed and attractively coloured tanks to increase rural penetration. Fig. 2.15 shows some type of water tanks available.
>
> For large consumers, it has very big underground water tanks—in capacities that range from 1000 litres to 100,000 litres—for high-end bungalows and other such residences and institutional applications comprising malls, commercial spaces, and the hospitality infrastructure. In association with IMMT, Odisha, the company has developed tanks with filters especially for villages in Karnataka, where the water has very high iron content; the filter removes up to 98% of iron, reinforcing the company's capability to customize tanks for special needs, thus fuelling local market growth.
>
>
>
> **FIG. 2.15** Sintex water tanks

The technology allows making individualized products on the computer and then 'printing' them out just as one would print out a document. A 3D printer called a fabricator, or a 'faber' builds up the object gradually, one layer at a time, till the entire product is done. The surprising thing is that the object works as well, if not better, than the original product. Consumers can thus 'print' out whatever they require. The manufacturer sends the blueprints of parts or panels of cars, bicycles or airplanes by email and customers can simply print out the individualized product at his end, provided he has the equipment.

The technology results in individualized products, saves cost and reduces waste. 'Mass production could, in short, give way to mass customization for all kinds of products, from shoes to spectacles to kitchenware,' says the report. In this way, it is a disruptive technology. How it will impact manufacturing is not clear yet but it is obvious that we stand on the threshold of a new era of mass customization. Will it lead to even more finely-divided market segments?

TOWARDS A NEW ERA

Mass customization opens the way for co-creating value with the consumer. Prahalad and Ramaswamy (2004) describe the process as co-creating. The customer is no longer isolated from the manufacturing process, but an active participant in the design or manufacturing process. In this way the system becomes a 'consumer-to-business-to-consumer' (C2B2C) pattern of economic activity. The roles of the consumer and company converge towards a unique co-creation experience, or an 'experience of one.'

The four building blocks of co-creation are dialogue, access, risk assessment, and transparency (DART). Combining these four building blocks can lead to new business models and functionalities designed to enable compelling co-creation experiences. The authors further say that this will help move the managers from 'company think' to 'consumer think'. For the former, a digital camera, for example, is merely the vessel of value. For customers, it is a combination of the aspirations, frustrations, and wishes of the heterogeneous group of consumers who experience their product or service. Misled by company think, companies do not think of the latter, but clutter the marketplace with products that are feature-rich but experience poor.

The new technology and the resultant shift in thinking towards the consumer promises a brave new era of enhancing customer experience. When and how it happens, however, remains to be seen.

CONCLUSION

Market segmentation is a powerful tool required to group customers on the basis of their common characteristics and needs. However, the job does not stop at grouping customers or creating advertisements for them that they like. A segmentation strategy consists of analysing consumers, no doubt, but also serving them in ways that mass markets cannot. Saul J. Berman (2011) writes in the HBR Blog Network that traditional segmentation approaches are at best correlative—they take an identifiable characteristic and match it with a likely behaviour. However, today's relevant segments are not only industry-specific, they are probably company-specific as well. These segments change constantly, requiring revision and correction with new data on consumers.

Technology has aided consumer analysis right down to the individual level. Today we are witnessing the development of a new technology that could deliver personalized products, making mass customization a reality. On the other hand, we also live in a period of intense economic uncertainty. There is no doubt that the proportion of younger population will increase, but they also face the prospect of higher unemployment. High inflation and cost of living means that older workers will have to work longer to be able to have an affordable retired life.

These two trends could push market segmentation in opposite directions. In the future, companies might find delivering individualized products profitable, but at the same time there will be a large number of customers who might want cheaper products even if they are mass produced.

SUMMARY

Segmentation is the opposite of mass production and mass marketing. Rather than view the market as one mass, companies group customers on the basis of common needs and view these groups as homogenous segments. Each customer segment can be provided with goods and services that will most appropriately fulfil customer needs. Each segment must be measurable, substantial, accessible, differentiable, and actionable.

There are several bases for segmenting customers. These are demographic, geographic, psychographic, psychological, socio-cultural, use-related, or benefit segmentation. Companies also combine these variables to evolve hybrid segmentation techniques, like PRIZM and VALS.

Indian market segmentation is usually done on the basis of socio-economic classification (SEC). The Indicus Analytics classifies the Indian consumer into 33 distinct segments, for which detailed data is available.

Though segmentation is a powerful tool, it attracts criticism as well. Critics say that modern consumers defy categorization, segmentation leads to fragmentation of society, it is exploitative, and sometimes companies divide consumers into very thin layers that are not profitable to serve. Thus, some companies opt for counter-segmentation, or combining segments to appeal to a broader range of customers.

The challenge is to use segmentation effectively. Sometimes managers overestimate the size of segments, or they are not able to discern the spending patterns of the target segments. An understanding of target segments with relevant products is necessary to use the strategy effectively. Yet, many companies stop at merely making commercials showing characters that viewers identify with, but the products do not have any discernible additional benefits or differentiation. Such activities do not serve market segments.

The chapter also discusses new trends in segmentation. Microtargeting occurs when segments are narrowed to individual consumers. The market is also moving towards mass customization through the use of information technology and 3D printing technology. This allows customers to customize products and 'print' them out at their own homes, if they have the equipment. This technology may well end the era of mass production and usher in the era of C2B2C, or co-creation with the customer.

KEY TERMS

ACORN A classification of residential neighbourhoods (ACORN) based on a geodemographic segmentation of the UK's population

Benefit segmentation Classification of customers based on the differences in specific benefits that different groups of consumers look for in a product or service

C2B2C Consumer-to-business-to-consumer, or the involvement of the consumer with companies for co-creating products

Counter-segmentation A strategy of combining market segments to appeal to a broad range of consumers

Demographic segmentation Market segmentation based on differences in demographic factors of different groups of consumers

Geographic segmentation Collecting and analysing information according to the physical location of the customer

Hybrid segmentation Combination of any of the aforementioned techniques or market segmentation for better understanding of customers

Market segment A market segment is a group of customers within a market who share a similar level of interest in the same, or comparable, set of needs

Market segmentation Grouping of customers with similar characteristics and needs

Microtargeting Very narrow segmentation, down to the level of individual customers

PRIZM Nielsen-PRIZM (Potential rating index by ZIP markets) is a set of geodemographic segments for the United States, developed by Claritas, now part of Nielsen

Psychographic segmentation Classifying customers on the basis of social class or lifestyle

Psychological or behavioural segmentation The separation of consumers into categories based on psychological characteristics, such as personality, perception, learning, and attitudes

Socio-cultural segmentation Classification of customers on the basis of sociological and cultural variables, such as social class, family life cycle, religion, race, nationality, values, beliefs, and customs.

Socio-economic criteria (SEC) Criteria to segment customers on the basis of their socio-economic profile

Use-related segmentation A form of segmentation that categorizes consumers in terms of heavy or light usage of products or services, or their contribution to the company's profits.

Values, attitudes, and lifestyles (VALS) A psychographic segmentation, classifying customers on the basis of psychological and sociological factors, developed by SRI International, now Strategic Business Insights (SBI)

Yankelovich mindbase A system of classifying consumers by their values, lifestyles, and motivations, used in the US

EXERCISES

Concept-review Questions

1. What is market segmentation? Using how many different criteria can markets be segmented?
2. What are the benefits of market segmentation? Describe each with an example.
3. Discuss the qualities that market segments must have in order to be useful for companies.
4. Describe demographic segmentation. What data does it use?
5. Describe the VALS, ACORN, and PRIZM segmentation techniques. Which one would you prefer and why?
6. What are the ethical considerations that companies must keep in mind while using segmentation techniques? Is it correct to exploit consumers on psychological basis?
7. Describe the SEC classification of Indian markets and explain their characteristics.
8. What is the criticism against segmentation? Do you agree with the points raised by critics?
9. Discuss the ways in which segmentation can be used effectively.
10. Discuss the mistakes that companies make while segmenting markets. How can they be overcome?

Critical Thinking Questions

1. Comment on the strategy of selling family soap as opposed to differentiated soap for different segments. Which would result in greater profits?
2. Does segmentation lead to fragmentation of society? Do you see any harm in fragmenting markets?
3. Discuss how people can be classified on the basis of their personality. Do you agree with the statement that personality dictates consumption? What type of personality would be consuming what brands?
4. This chapter describes several hybrid segmentation techniques. Discuss which one would be most suitable for Indian markets and also explain the reasons for your choice.
5. Discuss the cases or products for which counter-segmentation strategy must be used.
6. Society is being pushed in opposite directions: microtargeting on the one hand and the demand for cheap, mass produced goods on the other. How can companies reconcile these two opposite trends?

Projects and Assignments

1. Select certain products that you normally use. Discuss their segmentation strategies and how the company uses segmentation to focus on the target customers.
2. Using your class as a sample, group your peers on the basis of VALS and socio-cultural segmentation. Discuss with them whether your classification is correct.
3. Take examples of products in FMCG, white goods and personal products and discuss which type of segmentation strategy would be best suited for each of the products.
4. Attempt a VALS classification of the Indian consumer. Estimate the percentage of population that would fall in each category of the classification.

REFERENCES

Berman, Saul J., 'Learning how to make market segmentation work again', *HBR Blog Network*, 15 March 2011.

Haley, Russel I., (1968), 'Benefit segmentation: A decision-oriented research tool', *Journal of Marketing*, Vol. 32, July, pp.30–35. Reprinted in *Marketing Management*, Vol. 4, No. 1, Summer 1995, pp. 59–62.

http://blogs.hbr.org/cs/2011/03/how_to_make_market_segmentation_work.html, last accessed on 2 April 2012.

http://www.censusindia.gov.in/Census_Data_2001/, last accessed on 2 April 2012.

http://www.itcportal.com/itc-business/fmcg/lifestyle-retailing.aspx, last accessed on 3 April 2012.

http://www.tetrad.com/pub/documents/PRIZMfactsheet.pdf, last accessed on 4 April 2012.

Kapferer, Jean-Noël, *New Strategic Brand Management: Creating and Sustaining Brand Equity Long Term*, 4th ed., Kogan Page, London and Philadelphia, 2008, p. 226.

Kotler, Philip, K.L. Keller,, A. Koshy, and M. Jha, (2009), *Marketing Management: A South Asian Perspective*, 13th ed., Pearson Education, New Delhi.

Levitt, Theodore, 'Marketing myopia', *Harvard Business Review*, Volume 82, Issue 7–8, 1960, pp. 138–49.

Levitt, Theodore, *The Marketing Imagination*, The Free Press, New York/London, 1983.

Lewis, David and Darren Bridger, (2000), *The Soul of the New Consumer*, Nicholas Brealey Publishing, London, pp. 73–77.

McDonald, Malcolm and Ian Dunbar, (2004), *Market Segmentation*, Elsevier Butterworth–Heineman, Oxford, p. 241.

Mukherjee, Writankar and Sarah Jacob, 'Restaurants such as McDonald's and Subway add senior citizens to their business platter', *The Economic Times*, 23 March 2012.

Population Projections for India and States 2001–2026: *Report of The Technical Group On Population Projections* Constituted by the National Commission on Population, New Delhi, May 2006.

Prahalad C.K. and Venkat Ramaswamy, *The Future of Competition*, Harvard Business School Publishing, Boston, 2004.

'Print me a Stradivarius', *The Economist*, 12 February 2011.

Quelch, John A. and David Kenny, 'Extend profits, not product lines', *Harvard Business Review*, September–October, 1994.

'Reds in Bed', *The Economist*, 7 January 2012.

Rust, Ronald T., Christine Moorman, and Gaurav Bhalla, 'Rethinking marketing', *Harvard Business Review*, January–February 2010.

Seybold, Patricia B., 'Get inside the lives of your customers', *Harvard Business Review*, May 2001, pp. 81–89.

Smith, W. (1956). 'Product differentiation and market segmentation as alternative marketing strategies'. *Journal of Marketing*, Vol. 21, No. 1, July, 1956, pp. 3–8.

Toffler, Alvin, *The Third Wave*, Bantam Books, New York, 1981, p. 231.

Trefis Team (2012), 'L'Oréal targets 'masstige' segment in India with dualpricing strategy', 10 July, http://www.trefis.com/stock/lrlcy/articles/130297/loreal-targets-masstige-segment-in-india-with-dual-pricing-strategy/2012-07-10, last accessed on 16 July 2013.

Twedt, Dik Warren (1965), 'How can the advertising dollar work harder?', Journal of Marketing, Vol. 29, No. 2, April 1965, pp. 60–62.

Waaser, E., M. Dahneke, M. Pekkarinen, and M. Weissel, 'Smarter segmentation for your sales force', *Harvard Business Review*, March 2004.

Yankelovich, B.D., 'New criteria for market segmentation', *Harvard Business Review*, 42 (2), 1964, pp. 83–90.

Yankelovich, Daniel and David Meer, 'Rediscovering Market Segmentation', *Harvard Business Review*, February, 2006, Vol. 84, No. 2, pp. 122–31.

CASE STUDY
Putting Segmentation to Use

It is not enough to think of customers as belonging to different segments. Having identified segments, companies must go about serving those customers. A deeper understanding of customers is required. Instead of merely creating advertisements that show the targeted segment, companies have to understand the deeper context in which products are purchased and used. This case study shows how a company reap benefits by understanding how the products were being used by the targeted customer segment.

Seybold (2001) writes that over the years, companies have collected huge amounts of data and divided buyers into very fine segments but have missed out on the big picture: 'The context in which customers select, buy, and use products and services.' To understand consumer behaviour, she writes that they should 'see how those products and services fit into the real lives of customers. She calls this *customer scenario*, the broad context in which a customer uses products.

To explain this, she gives the example of two customers, having the same characteristics as age, income, education and therefore belonging to the same segment, who are buying refrigerators. The first wants a quick replacement for an old one that stopped working, the second customer wants one for his new home.

Though they belong to the same market segment, the scenarios of both customers are different, and when the company or the salesperson treats both customers the same, they lose out on big opportunities. By understanding their scenarios, companies can deal with them for their benefit. To the first customer, the company can offer expedited delivery and charge for it. To the second customer, the company can offer a plan to sell customized appliances for his new home and also offer a cross-selling plan that helps him buy other products that he needs.

It is by understanding customer scenarios that the company finds 'creative ways to expand its reach into the lives of buyers, helping them save time, use products and services more effectively, and fulfil supplementary needs that may not involve the company's offerings at all'.

This thinking was applied by National Semi-conductor (now part of Texas Instruments), the leading supplier of analogue and digital microchips, to deepen relationships and get increased business from its clients. It realized that a critical customer segment of its products was that of design engineers. When they designed products, they chose components at the beginning of the product development cycle, which resulted in large, multimillion dollar sales. The logical step was to provide information to them, and the company designed a website that gave all the information about the company products, which the design engineers used. However, by going a step further and understanding the scenarios within which the engineers worked, the company could ensure that they used National parts for development of their products.

National went about understanding the needs of its market segment deeply, finding out the scenarios in which the engineers worked. It found that the design engineers needed information on parts, no doubt, but could the company become part of the design process itself? Understanding the design scenario, National developed a set of online easy-to-use tools which provided the engineers a platform to design products. The system, called Webench, generated designs along with complete parts list, specifications, prices, cost–benefit analysis, and a bill of materials to develop a prototype.

The software let the engineers to refine the design, run real-time simulations, save all the iterations and share them with colleagues. Once the design was finalised, the system generated a bill of materials listing all the parts required, including those manufactured by National. The site linked to distributors and carried current prices so that parts could be ordered easily.

As it went along, National realized another aspect of consumer behaviour. Though the design engineers liked the software, they were hesitant to pay for using it. So the company decided to make the simulation available for free. As Seybold writes, 'Instead of nickel-and-diming customers...the company could reap bigger rewards down the line: large orders for National's parts.'

Understanding its segment carefully helped not only the customers but also generated large orders for National. Design engineers used Webench to design 20,000 units of power supplied in the first year of operation alone. By the year 2000, there were 31,000 users on the site, which was generating 3000 orders or referrals to distributors every day.

New opportunities emerged. The engineers wanted thermal simulations, so the company created WebTHERM, again allowing the engineers to use it for free. The software allowed users to see the thermal behaviour of an electronic printed circuit board. Today, the Webench website lists architect tools, circuit simulation, designer tools, and various other tools that engineers can use for free and generate large orders for the company. Understanding the customer scenarios, the company provides one-stop design centre with links to supply chain partners.

This case shows that identifying customer segments is not enough. A company has to go further and develop deep understanding as to how the segment is using its products and anticipate its needs. Only then can any company hope to reap benefit from its identified segments.

Questions for Discussion

1. Write down what you learnt from this case. What steps must a company take after identifying customer segments?
2. What do you understand by the term 'customer scenario'? How could National use this for serving its customer segments?
3. National Semiconductors could work closely with its segment as it knew what the design engineers wanted. What aspects of consumer behaviour was it able to discover and use effectively?
4. Comment on how other companies can develop deep understanding of their segments and reap greater benefits and loyalty in return.

Sources:
Seybold, Patricia B., 'Get inside the lives of your customers', Harvard Business Review, May 2001, pp. 81–89.
www.ti.com, last accessed on 27 March 2014.

CHAPTER THREE

Consumer Decision-making Models

LEARNING OBJECTIVES

How do consumers make purchase decisions? In an attempt to understand the 'black box' that is the human mind, researchers have approached the problem in different ways. This chapter describes the models and theories that explain purchase behaviour.

After studying this chapter, the reader would be able to understand

- economic models of consumer behaviour
- analytical and prescriptive cognitive models
- the humanistic approach consisting of the theory of trying
- modern consumer behaviour models called the consumer decision journey

CASE STUDY

Nudging Consumers Towards Choices

Consumer decision-making models analyse the effect of various factors that come into play when people make choices. An understanding of these can help companies nudge customers into making choices that are profitable for the companies. More importantly, consumers can be influenced to make choices that are beneficial for society.

In their book *Nudge*, Thaler and Sunstein (2008) write that 'choice architecture'—the way that choices are structured and placed before consumers—can lead to both good and bad choices. Companies can design environments to influence decisions through defaults, which are the building blocks of this architecture. While some customers make active decisions, others rely on what is presented to them and do not want to be bothered about making choices at all.

They give the example of organ donations. In Germany, people have to actively make a choice to opt for organ donation. Only 12 per cent of Germans have joined the donor pool. In Austria, by contrast, all citizens are part of the donor pool by default and can easily opt out. The figures are stark: 99.98 per cent of Austrians have continued to stay in the donor pool with very few people opting out. This shows that consumers can be made to take decisions based on how choices are presented to them.

Goldstein, et al. (2008) write that companies use a combination of forced choice and adaptive defaults to help customers make their purchases. At a basic level, defaults serve as manufacturer recommendations, and people are happy with what they get by accepting them. When people install a software package, for instance, they accept the terms and conditions by clicking 'next' and accept defaults, very often without reading what they are. They just want to get the job done without bothering to make active choices.

Most companies use these techniques to set defaults to help the customers, but they also set defaults that are beneficial for them. Airlines may have a full range of meals on offer but present the passengers with limited choices for operational reasons. However, sometimes it is more nefarious: consumers are persuaded to purchase unwanted warranties, to subscribe to unwanted mailing lists, or to accept provisions leading to loss of privacy.

Consumer decision models help us understand how decisions are made, and companies can then set defaults, so that outcomes are either beneficial for the company or the consumer. In doing so, two types of defaults are used: mass defaults and personalized defaults.

Mass defaults apply to all customers of a product or service, without taking individual preferences into account. These consist of the following:

Benign defaults These represent a company's best guess about which product or service configurations would be most acceptable to most customers, or would pose the least risk to the firm and the customer.

Random defaults Customers are assigned arbitrarily to one of several default configurations.

Hidden options The default is presented as a customer's only choice, although alternatives exist, but these are hidden or hard to find. A company may, for instance, push a premium product as a default even though a cheaper alternative exists, but is hard to find.

Personalized defaults reflect individual differences, and can be tailored to meet customers' needs. These consist of the following:

Smart defaults When companies apply defaults on the basis of what is known about an individual customer or segment to customize settings, it is known as a smart default. Demographic or geographic variables are taken into consideration while designing choice architecture.

Persistent defaults Travel and hospitality companies automatically assign seats or rooms to customers who have previously chosen them, using a persistent default.

Adaptive defaults These are dynamic defaults that update themselves based on the current or real-time decisions that a customer makes. This is particularly helpful in online environments, where a customer is helped along as he/she clicks on choices.

Defaults are ways of nudging customers towards choices that they otherwise would not make. They come from an understanding of the consumer decision-making process. Various models are used to understand the factors that affect purchase behaviour. These models form the basis for not only designing products, services, and offerings, but also for how these are sold and presented to the customer to draw out the best response. Understanding these models helps in designing marketing communications, store design, online options, and a host of applications that are only limited by the imagination of managers.

While reading this chapter, try to answer the following questions:

1. What are the factors that come into play when consumers make purchase decisions?
2. How do consumer models help in understanding behaviour?
3. What behavioural influences are considered by different models? What are their practical implications?
4. Has consumer behaviour changed because of online search and interaction with brands?

Sources:

Goldstein, Daniel G., Eric J. Johnson, Andreas Herrmann, and Mark Heitmann, 'Nudge your customers toward better choices', *Harvard Business Review*, December 2008, pp. 99–105.

Thaler, Richard H. and Cass R. Sunstein, *Nudge: Improving Decisions About Health, Wealth, and Happiness*, Yale University Press, New Haven, 2008.

INTRODUCTION

In the movie, *What Women Want*, Mel Gibson plays a chauvinistic advertising executive who falls in the bathtub while holding an electric shaver. The fluke accident gives him the ability to hear what women think and what they think left him, and the movie goers, surprised and delighted.

The thought would have crossed many marketing managers that how wonderful it would be if they could hear what consumers thought. However in reality, this is extremely difficult, if not impossible. The best products sometimes fail, whereas many silly ones sell in great numbers. As Galbraith (1999) notes, 'We view the production of some of the most frivolous goods with pride. We regard the production of some of the most significant and civilizing services with regret'.

Not understanding consumer behaviour results in companies committing costly mistakes. Even the most successful companies err because of their inability to read customers' thoughts. Usually, companies think in terms of segmentation and customer profiles. Hackos (2007) writes that customer profiles represent the best guesses about who might be buying a company's products. 'Though companies espouse the importance of knowing the customer, they are often content to speculate about the customer or to take customer profiles at face value', she writes.

Consumer models integrate various behavioural factors that influence decision-making. *Economic models* explain that most people like to maximize their satisfaction or utility at least cost. *Cognitive models* take into account consumer learning, intelligence, and experience. While emotions are combined in *humanistic models*, a multiplicity of touchpoints is taken into consideration in the *consumer decision journey model*.

Significantly, consumer models shift the focus from products and markets to consumers. Consumers have needs and 'hire' products to fulfil those needs. If companies understand why consumers hire products, they can expand their markets, as the chapter-end case study shows. To gain insights into purchase behaviour, it is important to understand consumer models and the levels of consumer decision-making that take place.

Levels of Consumer Decision-making

The need therefore, is to peek inside consumer's heads. Several models of consumer decision-making have been proposed. They can be classified as follows:

Economic models These are quantitative models that assume man is a rational being who seeks to maximize utility.

Cognitive models These models assume that human beings process information that they are exposed to and take their own decisions. The models rely on a person's perception, learning, memory, thinking, emotion, and motivation. Cognitive models can be further classified as follows:

- *Analytical*: Consumer decision models and the theory of buyer behaviour
- *Prescriptive*: The theory of reasoned action and the theory of planned behaviour

Humanistic or emotional approach Since emotions play an important role in buying, this approach considers emotions and moods. The theory of trying includes emotions and personal motivations in buyer behaviour.

Consumer behaviour models These are a combination of economic and psychological models, like consumer decision journey.

All these models try to discover what goes on within consumer's mind when faced with choices. They study humans as economic, cognitive, and emotional beings, and attempts are being made to build models that describe how human beings make buying decisions. Some books describe a passive decision-making model as well. It says that consumers merely respond to the sales and promotional efforts of companies. It assumes that consumers can be manipulated by aggressive salesmen and that they are guided to choices by promotion, somewhat in the manner of sheep being herded by their owner. However, the assumption that people lack cognitive skills of their own and are manipulated by companies has been rejected, and is not covered in this book.

As consumers interact with companies through various touchpoints, a contemporary model, which describes the consumer decision journey, is also discussed. All the models attempt to discover what goes on inside a consumer's mind—a seemingly impenetrable black box.

HUMAN MIND—A BLACK BOX

If you ask someone, 'Why did you buy brand X?' and follow the answer with a series of further 'whys' you may have a conversation like this:

Q: 'Why did you buy brand X?'   A: 'Oh, I wanted to try something new.'

Q: 'Great. But why did you want to try something new?'   A: 'For variety.'

Q: 'Why did you want variety?'   A: 'No reason, just like that.'

The preceding conversation, or a similar one, will inevitably lead to the final answer that consumers themselves do not know why they buy most things. Indeed, decision-making is done in their minds, which is likened to a sealed black box and it is difficult, if not impossible, to peer inside and discover the processes that take place there. Neuroscience has tried to delve into the human brain, and while it has discovered what excites the brain, we are still far from answering questions such as the following:

- How people make their purchase decisions
- What makes them buy brand X and not Y
- How they are influenced to make choices

These questions have troubled the minds of the marketing managers for a long time. How nice it would be if we could only know what goes on in the minds of people as they gaze at large displays and arrays of enticing goods!

Models of consumer decision-making attempt just that. All models are structured around the basic model given in Fig. 3.1. The black box represents the consumer's mind. When marketing stimuli are given, it triggers a process inside this box. The output of the model is the consumer action whether to buy a product or not.

FIG. 3.1 Impenetrable human mind represented by a black box

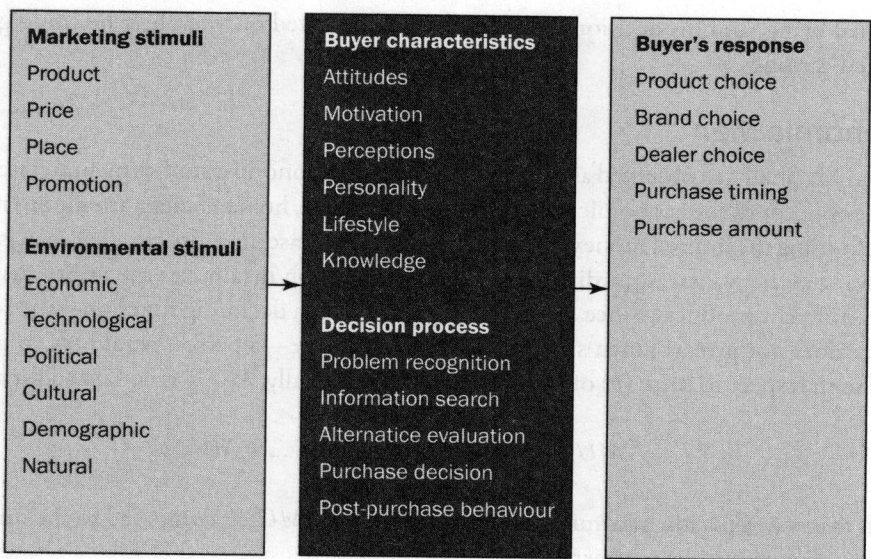

FIG. 3.2 Elaborating the black box

The 'black box' is a construct in psychology used to explain the unexplained. Since we cannot look inside a customer's mind, we can't understand what happens as a person makes choices. We can observe the external factors but not the thought process. In the model, input consists of environmental factors and marketing messages (stimuli), and output consists of purchase behaviour.

Two components are thought to affect buying behaviour: buyer characteristics and the decision process itself. This is elaborated in Fig. 3.2. The first is psychological and the second is cognitive, in which a consumer recognizes a problem and then goes about trying to solve it. The steps involved in the decision-making process will be explained later, but it is important to understand here that consumers may not go through all the steps in the decision process. There are three types of consumer decisions:

Routine response The consumer does not search for information or alternatives but undertakes a habitual path. For products such as bread, eggs, or salt, the consumer just goes to the nearest store and replenishes his stock. Information search or alternative evaluation does not happen in routine response.

Limited problem-solving In this case, the consumer has experienced the product and knows what he/she wants but has not fully made up his/her mind. Replacing a television set falls in this category: the consumer has the criteria for selection, but still wants to explore other brands.

Extensive problem-solving When the consumer has no criteria and starts searching afresh, it is called extensive problem-solving. In this case, the customer will go through all the stages of the decision process.

Different models have elaborated on the black box in different ways. The earliest attempt to decipher the model was with the rise of economics as a subject. Man was seen as an economic, rational being, and his decisions were believed to be based on what best he could get out of his limited earnings.

Economic Man

Alfred Marshall had observed as early as 1927 that 'the economist studies mental states'. According to the concept of the economic man, or *homo economicus*, human beings attempt to maximize the benefit using the limited money that they possess. This reasoning assumes that man is rational and knows what he wants. According to economists, a person maximizes the utility that he/she gets from different products. Since marginal utility (MU) is a declining function—the second cup of coffee does not give as much satisfaction as the first one—a person would try to maximize the MU with respect to price (p) of each product. Theoretically, MU/p is equalized for all products.

$$MU_1/p_1 = MU_2/p_2 = MU_3/p_3, ... = MU_n/p_n$$

In this way, a person maximizes the marginal utility (MU) as compared to the price (p), where 1, 2, ..., n represent the number of products.

The underlying assumptions of this model are that people know how much utility they are deriving from each product, and that they are aware of all available choices. They evaluate the choices and take a rational decision, as depicted in the consumer decision-making process.

Consumer Decision-making Process

People make calculated decisions and only buy as much of a particular product as gives them incremental utility. The decision process in a consumer's mind takes place in the following sequence:

- Recognize a problem or need
- Search for information
- Look for alternatives that satisfy that need
- Decide what to buy based on utility derived
- Evaluate the product or service

This simple consumer decision-making model is shown in Fig. 3.3 and is also illustrated in Exhibit 3.1.

Recognizing the Problem

The first step is when a person recognizes a problem or the need for something. This step is not as simple as is made out in most books. There are two aspects to it: first, a person feels a need, such as the need for food, or clothes. The second aspect is more important: a person does not feel the need, but a need is created in him/her.

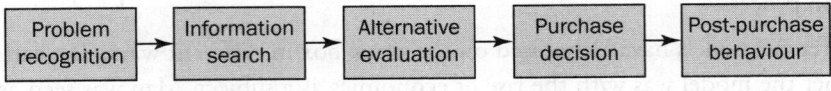

FIG. 3.3 Consumer decision-making process

Consumer Decision-making Models

EXHIBIT 3.1 Tanishq and the Consumer Decision-making Process

Indians are the largest purchasers of gold in the world. The market has traditionally been dominated by jewellers, large and small. Customer relationships are cemented over many years. Family-owned firms establish stores in towns and cities from where people buy gold ornaments, sometimes dealing with the same jeweller for generations. Very often, the jeweller is referred to as a 'family jeweller' in much the same way as people would refer to a trusted doctor.

There are a number of reasons for this. Many families buy gold ornaments over a period of time and see an investment in gold as the only safe haven. Others invest in gold ornaments as a cache to be used when their children get married. A dowry for a daughter is the most common reason for accumulating gold ornaments. Jewellers understood this and would often make recommendations based on the buyer's budget. Trust would be built by offering discounts and the promise to buy back the jewellery at good prices, should the need arise.

Now organized retail is seeking to change these habits. The market for jewellery, estimated to be about $25 billion a year, is a strong incentive for organized chains to hope for a slice of the pie. However, these shops are efficient, business-like operations that do not offer customer relationships, apart from a loyalty card. Have these chains been able to change consumer behaviour and break into the stronghold of traditional retailers?

There are signs that they are succeeding, though after a long struggle. Tata's Tanishq brand was the first to try its hand at jewellery retailing, starting in 1996. It took more than a decade for it to take off. *The Economist* reports that difficulties in breaking into the market resulted in the project being 'almost abandoned'. Today, other organized players, such as Gitanjali Gems and Reliance Jewels have entered the market. Family jewellery businesses are also expanding into regional chains.

Consumer behaviour has changed, and so has the consumer decision-making process. Among the perceptible changes are the following:

- Youngsters with disposable income of their own, want everyday jewellery that they can wear to office
- Change in tastes, away from heavy gold jewellery to smart trinkets
- Brands inspire trust and have transparent valuation methods

Another change is that women are buying jewellery more to adorn themselves rather than as a saving fund for daughters. Youngsters want trendy designs and cheaper jewellery to wear everyday rather than the heavy sets bought for them by their parents. There is also a question of trust—large chains are seen as more reliable than unfamiliar small vendors. Besides, Tanishq has added an online store that offers discounted jewellery.

People who stick to smaller shops perceive branded jewellery to be much more expensive than what they can buy from smaller stores. The absence of haggling in branded stores also limits their appeal. Another problem is that big ticket purchases in jewellery are often paid for in cash to avoid income tax problems. Retail chains, where all dealings are accounted for, lose out on that count.

Be that as it may, consumer preferences are changing perceptibly. There is a shift away from gold jewellery to other precious metals and stones. Women are willing to pay more for well-crafted jewellery that looks good to wear for everyday use and avoid buying heavy or gaudy gold chains that can only be worn on formal occasions.

- Analyse this situation in terms of problem recognition, information search, information evaluation, purchase decision, and post-purchase behaviour.

Sources:
Annual Report of Titan Industries Limited, 2012–13.
'Jewellers in India: Chains of gold', *The Economist*, 12 May 2012,

Very often, marketing communications have to generate the need, or at least make a person aware that a problem exists. For instance, people may not bother about their skin colour, but marketing communications play a role in generating the awareness that skin colour is important. Similarly, deodorants have not been used in the past in India, but companies urge people to recognize the need for getting rid of body odour—a need that is not 'recognized' by the person but created by the advertiser. In this way, many needs that are not recognized by consumers on their own are created by advertisers. Please see Exhibit 3.2 that shows how marketers have been responsible for creating needs in the market.

Search for Information

Search for information, also called pre-purchase search, involves the following decisions by the customer:

- Which product will serve my needs best?
- Which brand will be the most suitable for me?
- Which store should I buy it from?
- Should I buy it on the Internet?
- Should I pay in cash or should I buy on credit?
- Should I use a credit card?
- Should I buy on instalments?

Since there are many ways in which a consumer can interact with a company, the pre-purchase search becomes a complex process, especially if it is a high-involvement product. Product attributes (style, price, and alternative offerings), situational factors (deals and promotions), and

---

 EXHIBIT 3.2 Creating Need in the Market: Archies and Acquaguard

Archies has been instrumental in single-handedly creating needs and bringing in concepts such as Valentine's Day, Father's Day, and Mother's Day. These days are celebrated globally but were new to India. The company has also created its own occasions such as Friendship Day, celebrated on the first Sunday of August and Daughter's Day, celebrated on the last Sunday of September. In a country where the bias is so unabashedly towards a male child, the latter is a particularly significant contribution.

Similarly, the success of Aquaguard has created marketing history.

Aquaguard, a pioneer in water purifiers entered the country when water purifiers were simply not used. Indians used tap water, and it was pretty good in most urban places. However, the growing country was also polluting its water resources. Eureka Forbes realized the need for pure drinking water in homes and offices and introduced Aquaguard (see Fig. 3.4).

The company has won a series of products that have won laurels: the first water purifier to be certified by the trinity comprising the Indian Medical Association, CE, and ISI; and the first purifier to have a continuous EMS (electronic monitoring system) to monitor the quality of water, a built-in voltage stabilizer, auto filling and a nano silver-based carbon block.

Today, Aquaguard has a 4000 plus strong sales force supported by over 5800 service technicians and more than 1100 service centres across India.

FIG. 3.4 Communications from Aquaguard

Courtesy: Superbrands

Source: Superbrands 2012

the characteristics of the consumer—all of these play a role in the search process. The consumer may also interact with friends and seek information online.

Alternative Evaluation

Once consumers have the information about all the brands available, they shortlist the ones that serve their purpose, based on the criteria they have. The brands are classified into sets, such as 'evoked set' consisting of brands the consumer considers when making the purchase decision, 'inept set', comprising those brands he/she excludes because of lack of affordability, suitability, quality, or price, etc., and 'inert set' comprising brands the consumer is indifferent to.

Purchase Decision

The final purchase decision will depend on some customer criteria, based on product attributes, need for status, or performance. The customer may seek others' opinions and also read product reviews online. The customer may follow a few heuristics, like the following, before arriving at the final decision:

Look for the cheapest product Some customers look for deals and value, and are happy to buy the cheapest product on offer as long as their functional needs are fulfilled.

Choose products suited to one's lifestyle Customers tend to choose products that match their lifestyle. While rich people will buy the most expensive gadgets, the middle class may find such products 'too flashy' for their lifestyle.

Depend on their past experience with the brand One decision rule is past experience with the brand. For instance, if there was a fly in the soup served to a customer in a restaurant, he/she will tend to avoid that restaurant even if it was a one-off event.

Exhibit brand loyalty Many customers stick to a brand out of habit and do not want to undertake a fresh search for every purchase.

However, it is not always that these decision rules are followed. The importance of impulse purchase or the play of emotions while buying products cannot be ruled out. Companies look for such selling opportunities. They invest in very pleasing point-of-purchase material, salesmen who entice, or offer last-minute discounts, in order to sway customers, no matter how much research they may have carried out before making up their minds.

Post-purchase Behaviour

The purchase decision does not end with the purchase. How a customer stores or experiences a product becomes important. Companies try to maintain a long-term relationship with their customers and try to get repeat business from them or referrals from their friends. Post-purchase behaviour becomes important because of several reasons:

Customer equity Companies try to exceed customer expectations so that they can get repeat business in an effort to increase customer lifetime value.

Cognitive dissonance Sometimes customers feel that they should have purchased an alternate brand the moment they have made their decision. This is called cognitive dissonance—when there is a discrepancy between the decision-making process and the final choice of the brand. A positive outcome is that customers will try to persuade friends to buy the same brand, to reduce cognitive dissonance.

> **CB IN ACTION** Understanding the Decision-making Process
>
> This exercise requires you to work in pairs. Take a non-routine product that your friend has bought in the recent past, such as a car or a cell phone. Now interview your friend as to how he/she went through the consumer decision-making process. Understand consumer behaviour at different stages of the process, and try to find the answers to the following questions:
>
> 1. How did your friend become aware of the need for the product?
> 2. How was the information search accomplished? Analyse the sources from where information was sought and how it influenced the decision.
> 3. What alternatives were considered? What were the criteria on which they were evaluated?
> 4. What were the factors that influenced the final purchase decision? How was it arrived at?
> 5. Analyse the post-purchase behaviour of your friend. Was there any cognitive dissonance, and how was it resolved?

Advocacy Present-day customers will advocate products or share experiences on online forums and social media sites. This can have both harmful as well as beneficial effects. Companies try to create opinion leaders who advocate their products.

Both the economic rationale and the consumer decision-making model described assume people are rational and follow rules to arrive at purchase decisions. Such reasoning ignores the fact that people are not always rational, and that shopping very often does not have well-reasoned objectives, but is indulged in for sheer pleasure. Further, utility is not measurable, and making calculated decisions is not always possible. The model of the rational man has therefore been criticized by many economists.

Critique of the Economic Man

Scitovsky (1992) points out in his book, *The Joyless Economy* that the economic representation of the consumer as someone whose tastes are set, who knows what he/she wants, and who goes about buying things rationally, is quite inadequate. The idea kept economists from recognizing that the most important motive force of consuming behaviour is 'man's yearning for novelty, his desire to know the unknown'. He further writes that the yearning for new things and ideas is the source of all progress, all civilization, and to ignore it as a source of satisfaction is surely wrong.

Samuelson (1947) wrote that 'it is a hypothesis which places definite restrictions upon demand functions and price–quantity data; these could be refuted or verified under ideal observational conditions'. Amartya Sen (1977) too reflects the same idea, writing that 'a dubious tribute can be paid to the economic man... If he shines at all, he shines in comparison—in contrast—with the dominant image of the rational fool'.

ANALYTICAL MODELS OF CONSUMER BEHAVIOUR

Though people are not the 'self-seeking individualists' of the utility theory, it nevertheless gives an understanding of consumer motivation. Subsequent models tried to overcome the limitations of the economic rationale. Some of the analytical models of consumer behaviour are the Nicosia model, Howard—Sheth model, and the Engel—Blackwell—Miniard model.

The Nicosia model links the consumer's attributes and the firm that tries to influence those attributes through advertising messages. It connects the firm and the consumer with a closed loop of experience and learning.

The Nicosia model shows the interplay of the purchase decision as internal to the consumer and the way it connects to the firm's attributes. Both seek information from each other and learn from their experiences.

Nicosia Model

The model given by Nicosia (1976) connects the firm's communication efforts and the consumers' characteristics. As the firm communicates with consumers through its advertising, it affects consumers' attitudes. Gradually, it leads to a reaction in the form of search, evaluation, and decision to purchase.

The purchase behaviour serves as feedback for the firm to modify its advertising and marketing efforts.

- It considers not only consumption but storage as well. The way a person keeps his/her car, for instance, is an important factor in designing a marketing strategy for cars.
- The consumer's experience is also part of the model, which modifies the consumer's attitudes towards products and brands.
- The motivation, search and evaluation are linked not only to consumer learning but also to the company.

The Nicosia model is divided into four major fields as shown in Fig. 3.5.

Field 1—Consumer Attitudes

This field connects the firm's marketing communications with consumer attitudes, both forming separate subfields. Marketing communications impact consumer memory, attitude, and

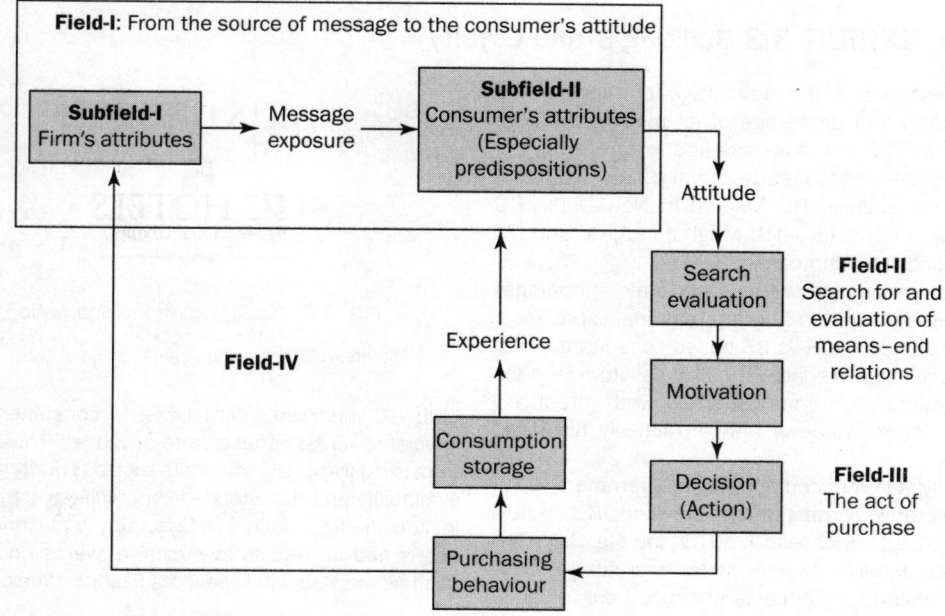

FIG. 3.5 Nicosia model

Source: Nicosia, F., *Consumer Decision Processes, Marketing and Advertising Implications*, Prentice Hall, Englewood Cliffs, 1966

behaviour, which are represented by the second subfield, that is, the consumer's personality and predispositions. There is an interplay between the two subfields when the consumer sees a market communication of the company and even the product itself.

Field 2—Search and Evaluation

The second field consists of the consumer's search and evaluation. Consumers are motivated by their needs, and they look for products to satisfy them. All brands will be on their radar, so a company will look for ways to motivate consumers to purchase its brands. The field includes attitude, motivation, search, evaluation, as well as the purchase itself. This model is not limited only to consumption but also considers storage, since many products are bought to display one's status and prestige to others. For example, a larger car is bought as a stature-enhancing device—including the way it is parked and driven around. The purchasing behaviour forms a closed loop with the firm's attributes and is a learning experience for the firm as well. Please see Exhibit 3.3.

Field 3—Act of Purchase

The model considers the act of buying and consumption. Where the consumer shops, and how he/she shops, yield insights into consumer behaviour.

Field 4—Feedback

The consumer's action serves as feedback to both the firm and to the consumer itself. The firm can modify its marketing programme based on this feedback, whereas the customer will store his/her experience with the product in memory. If he/she is happy, he/she will develop brand loyalty, but if unhappy with the purchase, he/she will probably look for alternative products and brands.

 EXHIBIT 3.3 Building Brand Loyalty

Wills Lifestyle has the advantage of tapping into the goodwill and properties of its parent company. Catering to high-end business and leisure travellers Wills Lifestyle has already opened four boutique stores—one each in ITC Maurya in New Delhi, ITC Gardenia in Bengaluru, ITC Mughal in Agra, and ITC Grand Central in Mumbai.

To enhance the store appeal and make shopping at a Wills Lifestyle store a truly international experience, the brand hired FRCH—a US based consultant which specializes in retail space. The brands' store façades and interiors are complemented with creatively designed store windows and attractively displayed products.

Finally, it introduced a loyalty programme through a collaborative arrangement between ITC Hotels and Wills Lifestyle called Club ITC (see Fig. 3.6). The consumer benefits through faster accruals, a wider array of redemption options, enhanced convenience and recognition of being part of an exclusive set. As

FIG. 3.6 Club ITC: An Amalgamation

Courtesy: Superbrands

Club ITC members, Wills Lifestyle consumers enjoy special rewards, benefits, and privileges. These range from exclusive in-store benefits such as priority garment availability and doorstep delivery to lifestyle privileges in fine dining, exotic holidays, stay at luxurious ITC hotels and invitations to exclusive events and shows such as the Wills Lifestyle India Fashion Week.

Source: Superbrands 2012

GLOBAL INSIGHT
Malls and the Experience of Buying

Consumer behaviour models explain why people buy. The Nicosia model shows how a firm's attributes and individual attributes, like experience, play a part in consumer attitude, which then impacts search, evaluation, and the purchase process. This exhibit explains what retail companies are doing to bring back experience into shopping.

Shopping has traditionally been multidimensional—the shopping street is a place that offers people a chance to hang out, to browse the shops in a leisurely fashion, and go for a walk. Now global shopping malls—hit by the economic slowdown, online buying, and decreasing footfalls—are doing just that. They are bringing back the experience into shopping.

In online buying, the experience that people had in the shopping street is sought to be replicated by the online search for bargains. Not surprisingly, physical stores are feeling the heat and trying to win back customers. They seek to bring back the fun and experience of shopping street to get customers into their stores.

Clifford (2012) reports how Glimcher Realty Trust, which owns and manages shopping malls in the US, is trying to make the malls Internet-proof by leasing out space to businesses that do more than sell merchandise. It takes the unconventional approach by finding tenants such as laser salons, and trainers conducting hairstyling and clay modelling lessons for shoppers.

The company figures that while people can buy clothes online, they can't enjoy shopping in the traditional way that might have included going out to lunch with friends, having a glass of wine, or a salad. So the idea was to bring back the fun in shopping. Consumers could get their hair done, or engage in fun activities such as making pottery, soap, or a cake, in an effort to enrich their mall shopping experience. Developers are now slowly adding more service-oriented elements to malls such as follows:

Make meaning A membership store where people make crafts, cakes, and other things
Drybar A salon in which stylists don't use scissors, but blow-dryers, to give shoppers hair blown into beachy waves
Blissful yoga A service that offers yoga lessons
Industrie denim A jeans store that enables women to study their rear view with a 'booty cam.'
Lego store A store that offers Lego-construction classes

The rationale is that opening a shopping mall would not guarantee success and organizations have to look for game-changing approaches. The aforementioned services offer opportunities for consumers to do something meaningful. They come back more often, since they have more reasons to visit the mall. Concept stores offering these experiences help in pushing up sales in other shops in the mall as well.

How does the addition of experience affect a person's attitude and thereby the search, buying, and evaluation process for brands and in retail?

Sources:
Clifford, Stephanie, 'Malls' new pitch: Come for the experience', *The New York Times*, 17 July 2012.
http://www.retailinasia.com/article/retail/merchandising-marketing/2013/03/taking-stock-bringing-back-personal-touch-shopping-ex, last accessed on 7 March 2014.
https://portal.motorolasolutions.com/web/Portal/resources/docs/ngem/pdf/Retail_Mobile_Loyalty_WP_0810-web.pdf, last accessed on 7 March 2014.

The Nicosia model is an improvement over the rationale offered by the economic man. However, it does not consider the internal factors or what goes on in the mind of the customer while selecting products and making purchases. As we will study in subsequent chapters, the consumer's culture, personality, and psychology play a great role in consumer choice. Sometimes, a consumer is restrained by his/her cultural background, brand loyalty, and countless other internal factors.

Tuck (1976) writes that at best, the Nicosia model describes the consumer decision process as it *might* happen, but there is no evidence that the process takes place in the manner of a flow chart. As a consequence, the model has 'never been seriously used in the making of marketing decisions'.

Other theories focus on the consumer's purchase decision as a combination of personality variables, social class, culture, time pressure, and financial status. These variables were considered in the Howard–Sheth model as exogenous variables impacting the consumer in many ways. This model is more complicated, as it takes into account internal factors such as perception and consumer learning as well.

Howard–Sheth Model

The consumer behaviour model created by Howard and Sheth (1969) in their 'Theory of buyer behaviour' includes a number of variables connected with precision, showing how people buy. The model integrates social, psychological, and marketing influences on consumers. Foxall (1990) says that it provides 'a sophisticated integration of the various social, psychological, and marketing influences on consumer choice into a coherent sequence of information processing'. A simplified Howard–Sheth model of buyer behaviour is given in Fig. 3.7.

Consumers interpret marketing stimuli through intervening variables, called hypothetical constructs, which are further classified as perceptual and learning constructs. The model also considers exogenous variables, such as personality, social class, financial status, and culture, which act as inhibitors. The strength of the Howard–Sheth model is that it combines a number of variables in the choice process.

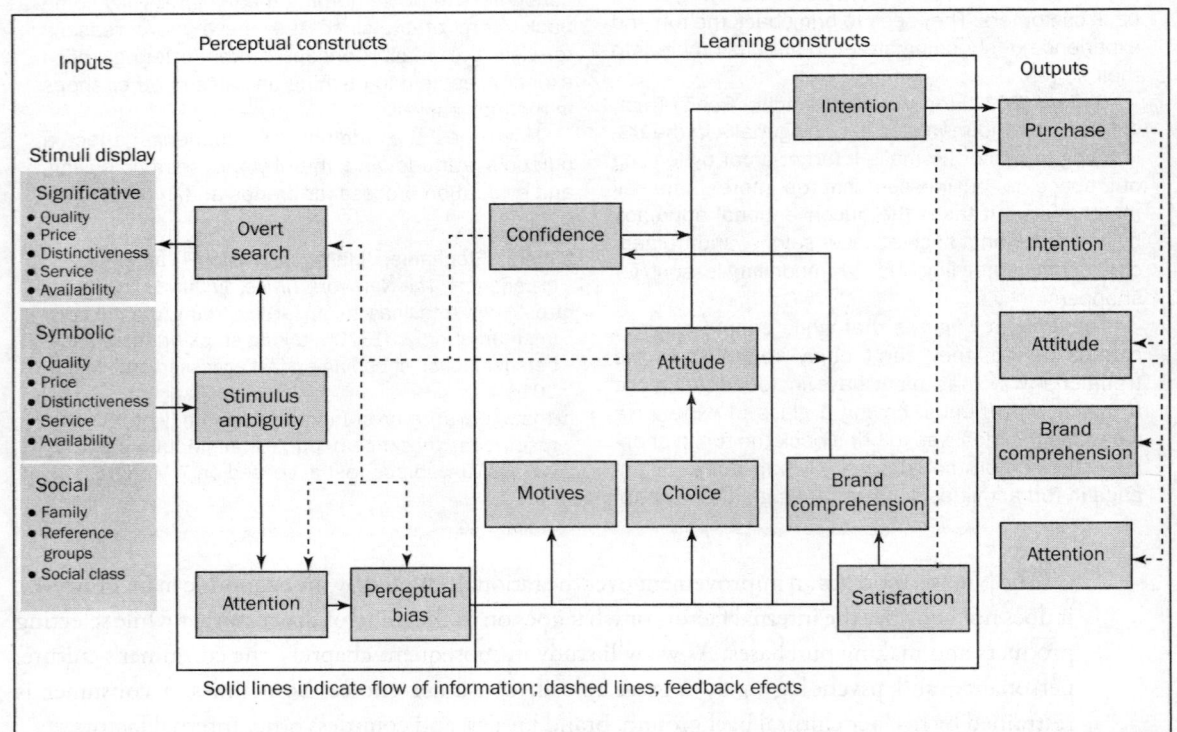

FIG. 3.7 Howard–Sheth model of consumer behaviour

Source: Adapted from Howard and Sheth (1969)

The model starts with the consumer's exposure to several marketing stimuli. The first are product attributes such as quality, colour, and prices, which are called *significative stimuli*. The advertising and other messages that a consumer is subject to are called *symbolic stimuli*. The influence of family and other reference groups is considered as *social stimuli*.

A consumer receives all these stimuli that are processed through intervening variables called *hypothetical constructs*. These are classified in two categories—*perceptual* and *learning*. Perceptual constructs are as follows

- *sensitivity to information* or how the consumer is impacted by the information
- *perceptual bias* or distortion of the information received due to the consumers' perceptions
- *search for information* wherein consumers actively seek information on products they want to consume

Learning constructs control, filter, and process the information that is received by the consumer. They are as follows:

- *motive* or an impelling action that guides consumers to fulfil their needs
- *evoked set* or the consumers' assessment of the consumption choices available, and their ability to fulfil their needs
- *decision mediators* or mental rules or heuristics of the consumer for assessing purchase alternatives
- *predispositions* or preferences towards certain brands
- *inhibitors* or limiting factors such as availability of money or time that restrict the choices
- *satisfaction* or post-purchase assessment that guides future purchase decisions

How Apollo hospitals use these perceptual and learning constructs is shown in Exhibit 3.4.

Learning constructs explain buyer learning, or how the consumer seeks information on new products and considers future purchases. A consumer already has experience of existing brands either directly or indirectly. For new products, he/she has to seek information and learn about them. The learning constructs make new products familiar.

The output column of the model on the extreme right represents the buyers' response. These steps are similar to the AIDA (attention, interest, desire, and action) model as these show the steps to purchase and are as follows:

- *Attention*: Whether the consumer is interested in the stimuli
- *Comprehension*: If the interest has led to understanding of the information
- *Attitudes*: Favourable or unfavourable evaluation of the product by the consumer
- *Intention*: Whether the buyer intends to buy the product
- *Purchase*: The actual purchase behaviour

The model considers exogenous variables as well, such as personality, social class, financial status, and culture, which act as inhibitors. These are not well defined and are not included in Fig. 3.7.

The strength of the Howard–Sheth model is that it combines a number of variables in the choice process. It is an integrated model that incorporates the most number of steps to explain the consumer behaviour. This model has been extensively used in marketing for explaining brand choice.

EXHIBIT 3.4 Apollo Hospitals

Apollo Hospitals started in 1983 with the goal of 'Our mission is to bring healthcare of international standards within the reach of every individual. We are committed to the achievement and maintenance of excellence in education, research and health care for the benefit of humanity'. Today, Apollo Group is one of the largest integrated health-care groups in the region. The group ensures its position of strength at every touchpoint of the health-care delivery chain.

According to the company's website, its presence encompasses over 10,000 beds across 61 hospitals, more than 1500 pharmacies, over 100 primary care and diagnostic clinics, 115 telemedicine units across nine countries, health insurance services, global projects consultancy, 15 academic institutions, and a Research Foundation with a focus on global clinical trials, epidemiological studies, and stem-cell and genetic research.

Apollo Hospitals serves customers across all touchpoints (Fig. 3.8). The company uses sophisticated diagnostic and treatment technologies—it introduced the country's first 320-slice CT scanner and the first CyberKnife. Apollo Hospitals also launched insurance services in a joint venture with Munich Insurance. A further extension to its brand franchise came in the form of tele-clinics reaching into the hinterland. Apollo Tele-clinics deploys telemedicine to take super specialist quality health care to rural and remote parts of India. It extended this facility internationally and now provides a fully functional pan-African network.

Complete coverage, complete protection, complete healthcare.
The Apollo Circle of Life.
A vision that believes in first class infrastructure at every touchpoint of the delivery chain

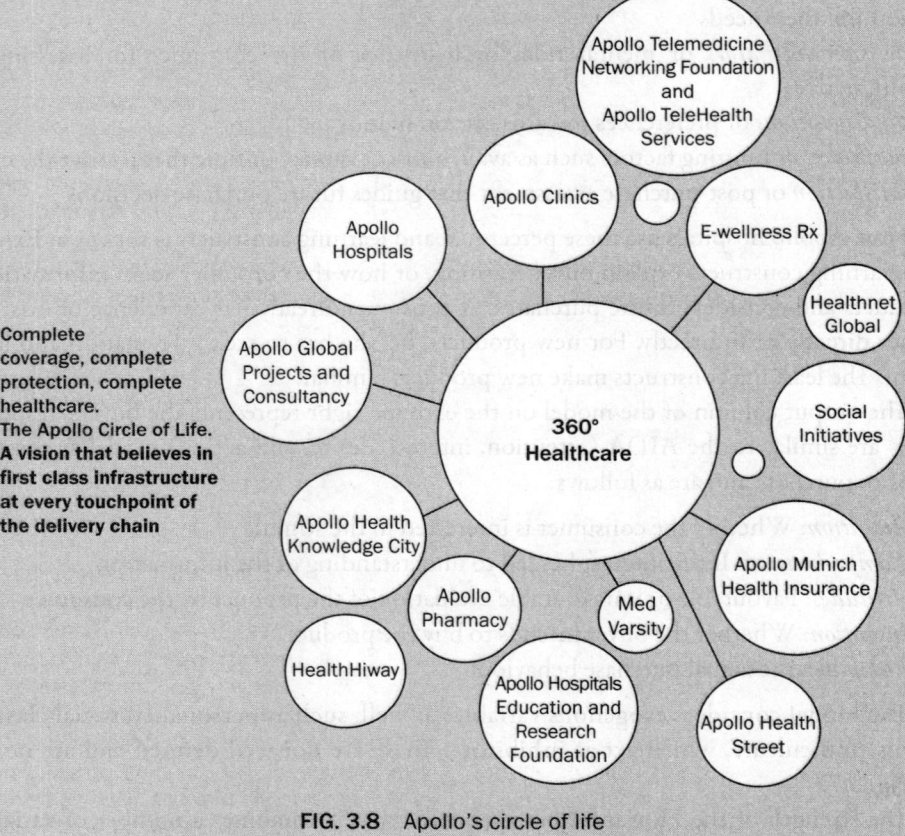

FIG. 3.8 Apollo's circle of life

Courtesy: Superbrands

(Contd)

EXHIBIT 3.4 (Contd)

> The company has also set up the Apollo Institute of Robotic Surgery. The facility offers the Da Vinci Si surgical system, which is an advanced platform for minimally invasive surgery. It introduced Day Surgery, a contemporary, state-of-the-art facility designed for those requiring short-stay, surgically-induced hospitalization with an offer that allows them to return home the same day.
>
> The group also introduced Apollo Sugar Clinics, designed for diabetes management. Customized mobile applications enable the patient to send their sugar count and blood pressure readings to the doctor in cases where regular monitoring is required.
>
> The Apollo Hospitals Education and Research Foundation (AHERF) is the single largest SMO (site management organization) in India that conducts trials and supports clinical research training, basic and epidemiological research, stem cells research, bio-banking and research services, integrative medicine programmes, and customization and validation and development of the healthcare technology.
>
> By offering complete health care, Apollo is using all elements of consumer behaviour models. It understands what customers want, and also develops their confidence by investing in a wide array of medical services. These comprehensive services are designed to alter perceptual and learning constructs (Howard–Sheth model) of consumers.
>
> *Source*: Superbrands 2012

Hunt and Pappas (1972) say that the unique contribution of the theory of buyer behaviour at the time of its publication was the way in which the variables were combined. One important aspect is that attitude influences purchase through intentions. Loudon and Bitta (1993) write that 'the model recognizes explicitly for the first time different types of consumer problem-solving and information search behaviours. It also recognizes that outcomes of consumers are more than just purchases.'

They also point out the following limitations of the model: it does not make sharp distinctions between exogenous and other variables; some of the variables are not well defined and are difficult to measure; it has limited generality since it does not explain family decision-making; and it is quite complex and difficult for a beginner to comprehend.

Further, though the model combines perceptual and learning constructs, we do not know how exactly a consumer's mind works. The Engel–Blackwell–Miniard model includes perceptual and learning constructs by integrating memory and the decision process to explain consumer buying.

Engel–Blackwell–Miniard Model

Another model is the Engel–Blackwell–Miniard model (1990), originally developed by Engel, Kollat, and Blackwell in 1968, and has been revised and updated in 1990. This model is somewhat similar to the Howard–Sheth model, but is structured around the consumer decision process starting with need recognition, followed by a search of information both internally and externally, evaluation of alternatives, purchase, and post-purchase satisfaction or dissatisfaction.

Lawson (2010) notes that the Engel–Blackwell–Miniard model (see Fig. 3.9) presents a comprehensive illustration of the variables influencing consumer behaviour and an appreciation of the flexible and dynamic nature of the consumer decision-making process.

The model shows how the decision-making process is influenced by external factors on the one hand, and the consumer's own memory on the other. Stimuli are processed by the person's mind and stored, rather than affecting action directly.

80 | Consumer Behaviour

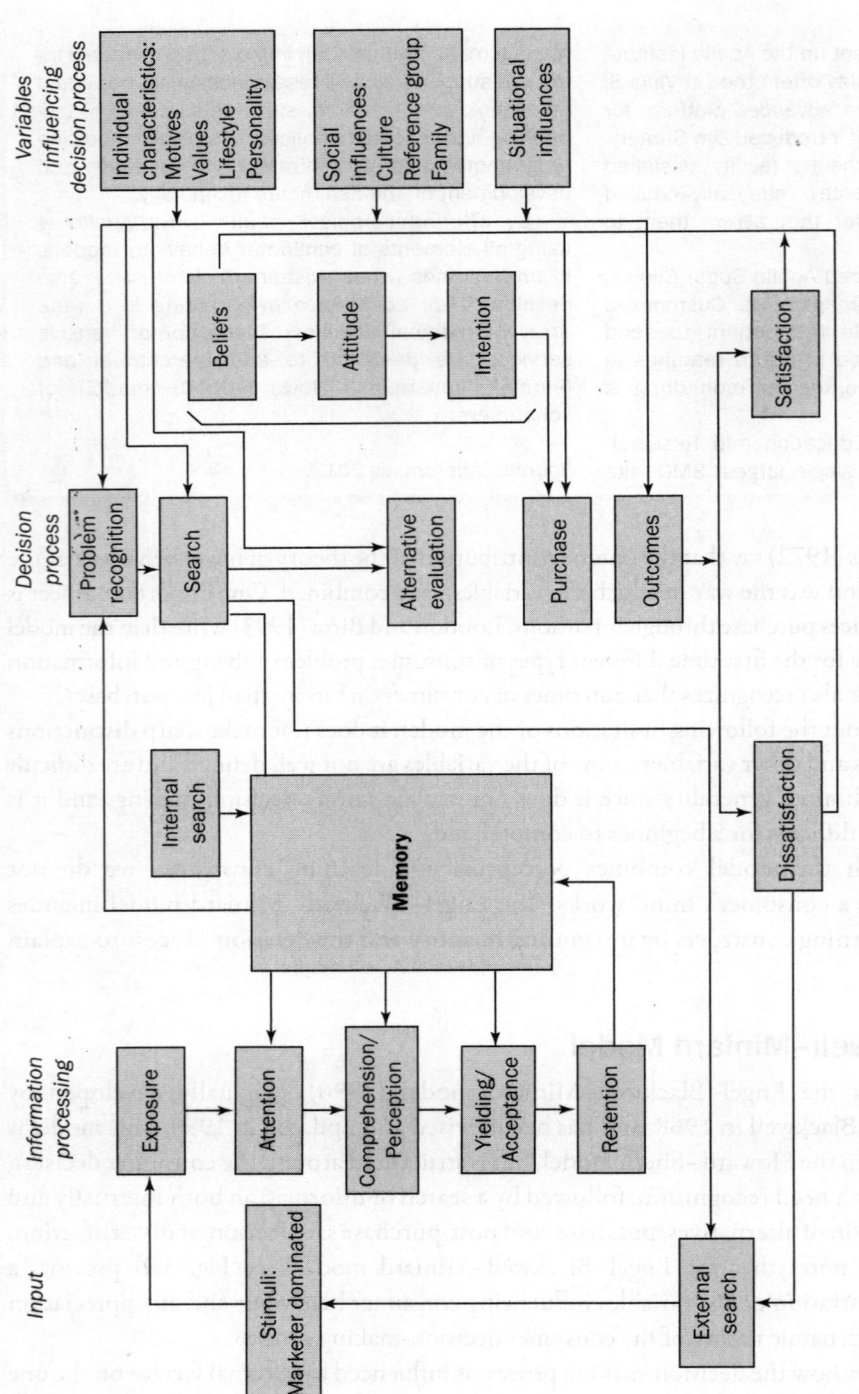

FIG. 3.9 Engel–Blackwell–Miniard model

Source: Adapted from Blackwell, Miniard, and Engel (2001)

The model shows the interactions of various factors. It is explained as follows: The starting point is in the third column, when the consumer recognizes a problem and searches for solutions. The decision process is shown in sequence in the third column ending with outcomes. The external environment is shown in the first column, from which the stimuli originate leading to consumer's exposure attention, comprehension, and acceptance. This is stored in memory, which in turn helps in problem recognition and related steps.

The variables influencing the decision process, consisting of individual characteristics, social influences, and situational influences are shown in the last column. These impact each stage of the decision process. These variables are connected by arrows to problem recognition, search, purchase and outcomes, which lead to internal search and memory.

Marketing and environmental stimuli are shown in the first column and as the customer is exposed to messages, he/she processes the information in steps of exposure, attention, comprehension, and retention, as shown in the second column. The output of the model is shown at the bottom, in terms of outcomes: customer satisfaction or dissatisfaction. This helps in future decision-making.

The model provides an understanding of how the variables affect the consumer decision process, which then becomes the basis of market segmentation. Two stages of problem-solving are recognized and are as follows:

Extended problem-solving (EPS)   It is characterized by high levels of consumer involvement and perceived risk. The consumer does a thorough evaluation and will search for information from various sources and various retail outlets. If satisfied, the consumer will build strong brand loyalty.

Limited problem-solving (LPS)   It is characterized by low involvement, risk, and motivation. The consumer does a casual search for information and alternative evaluation. The consumer is likely to display loyalty to the store where he/she likes to shop rather than to the brand.

The model is a comprehensive one, as it includes many variables that influence consumers. One of its key strengths is that it has evolved and been updated since it appeared in 1968, keeping pace with advances in the knowledge and theory of consumer behaviour. It is a clear depiction of consumption and is easy to understand. It incorporates several theories and includes information processing carried out in the consumer's brain.

However, the model has some limitations, as follows:

Environmental variables   These have been mentioned, but their interplay and impact are not very clear. Loudon and Bitta (2001) point out that the decision-making process is treated as somewhat mechanistic and therefore restrictive.

Complicated model   Such a complex model is unnecessary to describe a simple psychological phenomenon. Whether the brain actually functions in this sequential manner is not known.

Purchasing a social phenomenon   It considers purchasing decisions as essentially individual decisions. However, purchasing is as much a social as a psychological phenomenon.

Every individual is different   Individual differences may exert influence on how a consumer perceives marketing stimuli, and impacts on how these stimuli are received and processed.

Unfortunately, all the consumer behaviour models described suffer from shortcomings, which are discussed in the next section.

> **CB IN ACTION** Household Decision-making
>
> Select households with the following characteristics: (a) a couple with no children, (b) a family with two or more children, and (c) a joint family.
>
> Further, identify a product or service from the following: (a) purchase of a refrigerator, (b) going on a vacation, and (c) buying a house.
>
> Trace the entire process of decision-making in each household identifying factors and people involved, and drawing from the consumer behaviour models discussed in the chapter. Describe the decision-making process in each household identifying social, psychological, and marketing influences. In addition, study how each household engaged in evaluation of alternatives, purchase, and record post-purchase satisfaction or dissatisfaction.

Evaluation of Models

While models give a pictorial representation of the variables that interact with each other, they are at best a replica of the phenomena that they present. Some of the criticisms of the analytic consumer behaviour models are as follows:

Show an essentially psychological phenomenon As the interactions happen only in the mind, the models attempt to represent that. However, the human mind does not work like a neatly constructed flow diagram. Recent neurological research has shown that the mind is highly complex. It is not possible to explain the workings of the mind in a model.

Outdated The models were proposed at a time when media channels were limited. Further, the consumers themselves have evolved over time. The models do not take into account how the consumer has changed and how interactions with the company have also undergone a massive change over the years.

Assume that man is a rational decision-maker This basic assumption has been questioned. Studies have found that consumers often behave in an irrational and unpredictable manner. Neither the researcher nor indeed, the consumer himself, could not reason out their behaviour.

Ignore emotional buying or buying done for fun or their lifestyle needs Research has shown that consumers often buy on the basis of the lifestyles they aspire to have, or motivated by emotion and intuition. Shopping is often done for 'fun,' or for the joy of being with friends. Consumer behaviour models do not take into account such emotion and intuition.

Ignore consumers' tendency to act on fads and fashions that defy common sense Fads and fashions are not easily explained. Many researchers have found consumer behaviour in certain circumstances to be haphazard, disorderly, and opportunistic. Such behaviour does not comply with the well-structured models proposed.

Ignore the various types of decision-making The models fail to address the wide diversity of decision-making situations, product categories, and outcomes and could bias research in certain areas.

Are theories at best Another drawback is that these are conceptual models that cannot be checked for proof. Many variables are unobservable. So it is not possible to verify whether the models actually work in real life or have any predictive value.

Consumer behaviour these days is guided by a host of factors, and social influences have also become important. New communications technologies make interactions between consumers and companies more common. That is why a rethink is required on consumer behaviour models. The decision process may actually be seen as a journey that a consumer undertakes, moving seamlessly between the real and online world, communicating and interacting along the way.

MARKETING INSIGHT
Mobile Phones and Consumer Models

New technologies are changing consumer behaviour. Today, customers are changing the rules of marketing: they are in love with their mobile devices and that relationship is changing marketing. This is not to say that existing consumer models are outdated, but that the process of going through the stages of awareness, selection, purchase, and post-purchase is much faster than before.

Customers use their mobile devices for buying products in the following manner:

- They seek the opinions of others and call up their friends or relatives to ask them about the product they are considering. They also send an SMS to get others' opinions and send pictures of the products to their friends before buying.
- They can check product reviews, prices, and availability elsewhere immediately—even while they are in a store.
- They use their mobile phones to avail of coupons and special offers before buying.
- Finally, They purchase products using their mobile phones, placing orders even while they are on the move.

This behaviour upsets consumer behaviour models, and the best calculations of companies and retailers. The challenge for companies is how best they can use mobile devices to help people with their purchase decisions.

Companies and retailers are trying to use smartphones to influence consumer behaviour to:

- leverage their customers' mobile phones for personalized communication with them
- gain more real-time knowledge about the customers
- deliver tailor-made offers for individual customers in specific locales
- maintain ongoing relationships with customers

Clearly, to meet these consumers where they live, retailers need to go mobile. The question is, how do they do it? In a white paper published in 2010, Motorola has presented a model for mobile loyalty. Companies can follow five steps to use mobile devices in their marketing efforts.

- The company devises an app that provides information and offers to customers. Users opt for the company's marketing programme by downloading the app on their smartphones.
- This allows the company to capture customer data, such as name, address, and demographic data. Personal details such as birthday, brand/product preferences, and many other pieces of information that are stored on the phone, can be accessed by the company.
- A digital loyalty card is instantly transmitted to the customer's smartphone.
- Through the app, offers and coupons are immediately or periodically made available to the customer.
- All the customer has to do to use the saved coupons or discounts, is to swipe the bar code on their screens at the cash register. The process is much more convenient that cutting out and saving paper coupons. The app encourages repeat buying and customer loyalty.

Sources:

'How to bridge the gap between mobile advertising and consumer behaviour', *The Guardian*, 2013, http://www.theguardian.com/media-network/media-network-blog/2013/apr/25/mobile-advertising-consumer-behaviour, last accessed on 25 September 2013.

https://portal.motorolasolutions.com/web/Portal/resources/docs/ngem/pdf/Retail_Mobile_Loyalty_WP_0810-web.pdf, last accessed on 25 September 2013.

CONSUMER DECISION JOURNEY

Edelman (2010) writes about how the Internet has changed consumer behaviour. 'Today, consumers are promiscuous in their brand relationships', he writes. They connect with myriad brands and evaluate a shifting array of products. After a purchase, these consumers may remain aggressively engaged, publicly promoting or assailing products they have bought.

Watts and Hasker (2006) point to the social influence on consumer likings or purchases. They studied the entertainment industry and found that the greatest hits are not driven solely or primarily by intrinsic attributes such as sound, plot, style, or even star power. They found, on the other hand, that 'much of the success of entertainment products derives from social influence—the effect that consumers have on one another's decisions'.

The hyper-connected world of today, aided by social media and mobile phone technologies, makes the impact of social influence much greater than it ever was. Kumar (2012) writes that earlier the company tried to influence the consumer through advertisements and promotions, but could not influence the decision-making process. 'Now at each stage of the decision-making process, the customer can be approached by a different channel.' (Fig. 3.10).

For example, a female consumer becomes aware of products by watching television commercials, and again, when she visits the supermarket, or witnesses a demonstration by company-trained personnel. When she opens her Facebook page, she reads messages from her friends describing their experience, while an online merchant tries to catch her attention to persuade her to visit its site. She also discusses the brand with her friends at her kitty party or place of work, and companies send her SMS messages to lure her to buy the product.

It is rather unlikely that a model can describe such a complex phenomenon as purchase behaviour. The earlier models assume that companies advertise products and make an impression

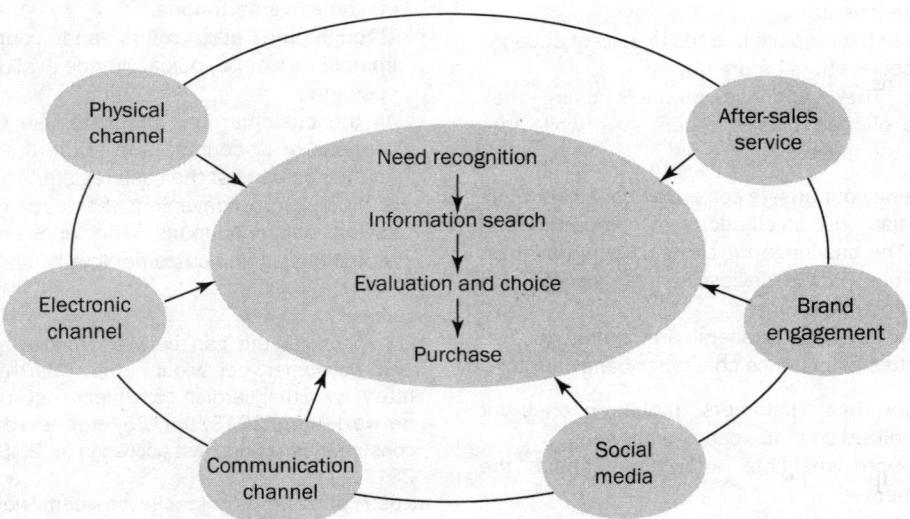

FIG. 3.10 Every stage of the consumer decision-making process is influenced by communications and electronic channels

Source: Kumar (2012)

CB IN ACTION Online Shopping

Select a group and analyse its attitudes to online shopping. Start with finding out the group members' beliefs about online shopping and how they evaluate those beliefs and consequences. Also analyse their beliefs about the perceptions of others. Through these, identify the attitude towards online purchasing and also subjective norms about the behaviour. Identify any other intervening factors as well that leads them to online purchase. After the survey, answer the following questions.

1. What are the attitudes of people belonging to different socio-economic strata towards online shopping?
2. What are the subjective norms that guide people for or against online shopping?

FIG. 3.11 Consumer decision funnel

Source: http://csi.mckinsey.com/en/Knowledge_by_topic/General/The_consumer_decision_journey.aspx, last accessed on 8 October 2011

on customers, and these factors come into play only when they buy products. However, now they may look for products from multiple sources, evaluate the alternatives and buy, and at each stage they interact with friends and media, sometimes even with companies themselves, as shown in Fig. 3.10. The decision-making process is thus more complex and can change at every stage.

As a consequence, the consumer decision-making process has become a circular journey with four primary phases: consider, evaluate, buy, and experience (see Fig. 16.6 in Chapter 16). Earlier it was thought of as a funnel-shaped process (see Fig. 3.11), where the customer started with a broad range of choices and gradually narrowed them down. Edelman further says that the new consumer decision journey is CEPEA—consider, evaluate, purchase, enjoy, and advocate. Companies have to build their strategy around consumer experience planning (CEP) that delivers the brand promise coherently and consistently along the touchpoints of the CEPEA journey.

In the next section, we discuss prescriptive cognitive models. These provide guidelines to structure consumer behaviour and provide the order in which elements appear. They also show the effect of the given factors.

PRESCRIPTIVE COGNITIVE MODELS

How beliefs and attitudes affect consumer buying behaviour are described in prescriptive cognitive models. Two theories are discussed—theory of reasoned action (TRA) and theory of planned behaviour (TPB).

Theory of Reasoned Action

This (Fig. 3.12) was developed by Fishbein and Ajzen (1975). It states that a person's behaviour is determined by the intention to perform it. This intention is itself determined by the person's attitudes and his/her subjective norms regarding the behaviour. Subjective norms are defined by the authors as 'the person's perception that most people who are important to him think he

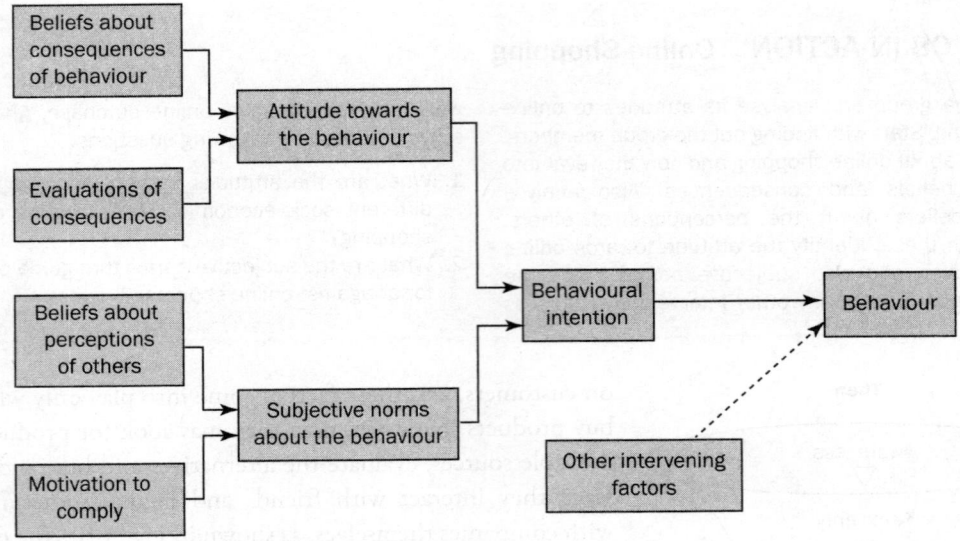

FIG. 3.12 Theory of reasoned action

Source: Fishbein, M. and I.Ajzen, *Belief, attitude, intention, and behaviour: An introduction to theory and research*, Addison-Wesley, 1975

should or should not perform the behaviour in question'. The theory can be summarized by the following equation:

$$\text{Behavioural intention} = \text{Attitude} + \text{Subjective norms}$$

In sum, a person's purchase behaviour derives from two sources: his/her own beliefs or evaluation of the purchase alternatives, and the opinions of others and the desire to adhere to what others say or think.

It adds a new dimension, the behavioural intention, which is derived from the consumer's attitude towards the product and subjective norms—the power of other people in influencing behaviour. People do worry about the thoughts of others and their behaviour is moderated by what others will think about what one buys or wears. The behavioural intention, along with other intervening factors shapes the final purchase decision.

A notable change in the TRA approach is that the act of buying is measured rather than considered as simply an attitude toward the object. This is important, as a consumer may have a favourable attitude toward a product, but may not purchase it. For instance, many people have a very favourable opinion about a high-end brand of laptop but when they actually visit the store, their decision is based on other considerations such as price, features, or durability.

Theory of Planned Behaviour

The theory of planned behaviour is an extension of the TRA. It tries to overcome the limitation of the TRA that depends on consumer's intentions to predict purchase behaviour. It adds another construct, 'perceived behavioural control' that is formed by combining the factors that may facilitate or impede purchase behaviour. These factors consist of the person's skills, resources, and

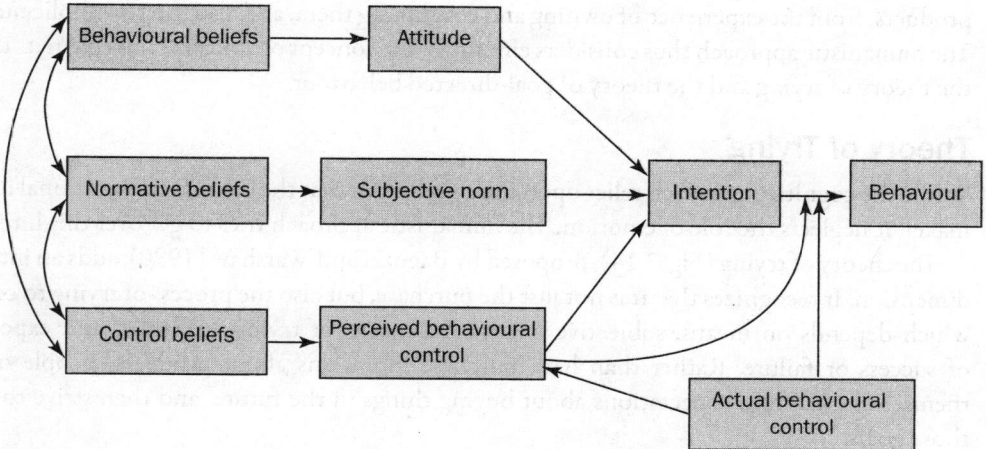

FIG. 3.13 Theory of planned behaviour

Source: Ajzen Icek, *The Theory of Planned Behaviour*, 1991

other conditions that are required to make a purchase. Perceived behavioural control is measured through questionnaires. Intention is controlled by a dynamic mix of attitudes, subjective norms, and perceived behavioural control variables. The actual behaviour is a result of behavioural intentions, but is controlled to some extent by perceived behavioural control (Fig. 3.13).

The TPB has been applied in a wide variety of behavioural domains. Tests have found that the TPB has significantly improved predictive ability over the TRA. The model has been modified by adding more variables such as ethical obligations, environmental obligations, and self-identity.

These models are easy to comprehend, and have found many applications. However, they depend on the ability of marketers to accurately identify and measure the attributes that are considered by consumers in forming their attitudes. This is not an easy task, since identifying such attributes is complex. Very often, subconscious elements come into play and people rely on thoughts that they are themselves not aware of, while buying products. Further, these models depend upon the assumption that the individual undertakes comprehensive cognitive processing prior to purchase behaviour. This is sometimes not correct, as emotions, spontaneity, habits, or strong desires, or cravings also play a role in the purchase act, as noted earlier.

HUMANISTIC MODELS

According to the humanistic perspective, the consumer is a coherent and rational being who is in control of his or her own experience and meaning. While the experience side of consumer behaviour depends on fantasies, feelings, and fun, the rational side constructs coherent and consistent representations of the world to make it more meaningful and predictable. These subjective maps are also inter-subjective, meaning that they are shared and understood by most people in society. The consumer therefore makes choices from the utility derived from buying products, from the experience of owning and consuming them, and also their symbolic meanings. The humanistic approach thus considers emotions, the concept of volition, and ego in its theories: the theory of trying and the theory of goal-directed behaviour.

Theory of Trying

While the cognitive approach relies upon the assumption that the consumer is a rational decision-maker, it neglects the role of emotion. The humanistic approach tries to get over this limitation.

The theory of trying (Fig. 3.14), proposed by Bagozzi and Warshaw (1990), adds an interesting dimension. It recognizes that it is not just the purchase, but also the process of trying to consume, which depends on means, subjective norms, the means of trying, attitudes, and expectations of success or failure. Rather than have purchase intentions about products, people often set themselves goals and expectations about buying things in the future, and then strive to achieve those goals.

The theory has two major elements: (a) It focuses on the individual's goals rather than on reasoned behaviour choices, and (b) It separates trying to achieve these goals from actual attainment of the goals. It thus focuses on an individual's aspiration or attitude towards trying to consume and attitude towards failing. The theory shows that past experiences of success and failure, along with attitudes and subjective norms, have a bearing upon intention to try. Much of today's advertising depends on the individual wanting and trying to buy goods.

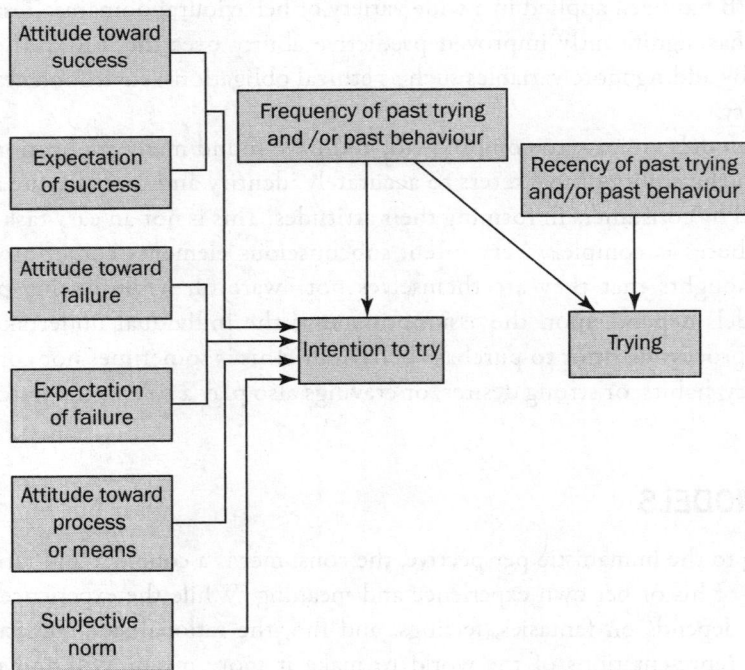

FIG. 3.14 Theory of trying

Source: Bagozzi and Warshaw, *Trying to Consume*, Journal of Consumer Research, The University of Chicago Press, Vol. 17, No. 2, 1990, pp. 127–140

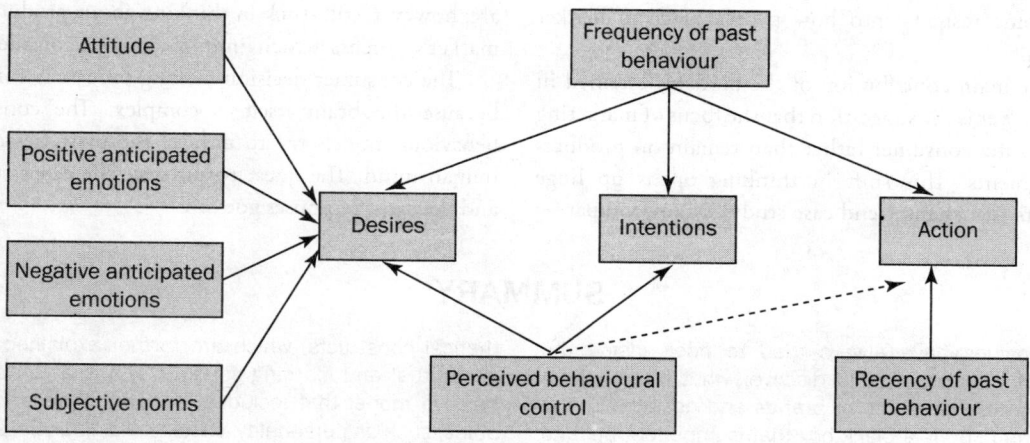

FIG. 3.15 Model of goal-directed behaviour

Source: Perugini, M. And R.P. Bagozzi, 'The role of desires and anticipated emotions in goal-directed behaviours: Broadening and deepening the theory of planned behaviour', *British Journal of Social Psychology*, Vol. 40, 2001, pp. 79–98

Goal-directed Behaviour

The model of goal-directed behaviour (Fig. 3.15) builds upon previous models and adds past behaviour and emotions, going on to desire and then intention to buy. When we consider purchase behaviour, we see that desire is often an over-riding feature that motivates consumers. Further, what others think, that is, subjective norms, are added to the model.

The model shows that a number of attitudes and emotions impact the desires and intentions of a person. These emotions and attitudes are a result of advertising messages and help from goals of consumption. Since everything cannot be bought immediately, behavioural control is applied. The person may buy the product depending on how strong the desires are and how quickly the resources for buying it can be collected. The model helps one understand how goals play a role in consumption. Companies increase the desirability of products and attach a personal value to purchase and ownership. If we look around, we see how this is done and how dreams are created with the consumption of certain products and services.

▪▪▪ CONCLUSION

Consumer decision models try to decipher the workings of the human mind and provide an understanding of the multiple factors that come into play while consumers make up their minds. The first decision models focused on the need of consumers to maximize the value they derive from their purchases. Later, social and individual attributes were added to these models.

Consumer behaviour models provide a framework to understand consumer buying variables and processes. This knowledge is used to nudge consumers towards desirable choices (see chapter-opening case study). However, consumer behaviour is less a matter of linear flow charts and more a complicated issue, especially since modern technologies allow companies and customers to interact at every stage of the buying decision. Thus a change in the models is required, which is suggested in the concept of the consumer decision journey. Scientists are also studying the brain, hoping that neurology will give some insights into how people react to market stimuli.

The main contribution of the models described in this chapter is the suggestion that the focus of marketing shift to the consumer rather than remain on products or segments. This shift in thinking opens up huge markets (see chapter-end case study). Many companies are, however, still stuck in thinking about product and market segments, which limits their scope considerably.

The consumer decision-making process is complex because the brain itself is complex. The consumer behaviour models try to unravel the mysteries of the human mind. The quest to discover the exact stimuli and the exact responses goes on.

SUMMARY

Companies have always tried to peek inside the minds of customers to discover what makes them buy certain products or brands and not others. The human mind is a black box that is impenetrable and very difficult to understand. Scientists attempt to figure out what goes on inside this black box. What they find in trying to decipher the human mind is very complicated indeed, and they have to take the help of consumer behaviour models.

The earliest attempt to decipher consumer behaviour was through Economics, which assumed that people were rational and tried to allocate their limited resources so as to derive the maximum utility from them. The assumption was that consumers were aware of the choices before them and logically weighed each one before arriving at a decision.

Such reasoning ignored the fact that humans are quite irrational, and many market decisions cannot be explained logically. The Nicosia model has four major fields. The first field connects the firm's marketing communications with consumer attitudes, both forming separate subfields. The second field is the customer's search and evaluation, leading to the third field, the act of purchase, which in turn leads to the fourth field, the feedback. The Nicosia model is more complex and is an improvement over the rationale offered by the idea of the economic man.

The Howard–Sheth model integrates social, psychological, and marketing influences on consumers. Consumers interpret marketing stimuli through hypothetical constructs, which are further explained as perceptual and learning constructs. It is a comprehensive model that includes many exogenous variables, such as personality, social class, financial status, and culture, which act as inhibitors.

The Engel–Blackwell–Miniard model is structured around the consumer decision process, starting with need recognition, followed by a search for information, evaluation of alternatives, purchase, and post-purchase satisfaction or dissatisfaction. The consumer's decision-making process is influenced by external factors on the one hand, and the consumer's own memory on the other.

Though these models show consumer behaviour as an interplay of many factors, they describe an essentially psychological phenomenon. The human mind does not function as a flow chart. They also do not take into account how the consumer has changed and how interactions with companies have also undergone a massive change over the years.

With the advent of the Internet, consumers have become promiscuous in their brand relationships, and they remain aggressively engaged, publicly promoting or assailing products they have bought. In fact, every stage of the consumer decision-making process is influenced by communications and electronic channels. Researchers suggest that the consumer decision-making process is a circular journey with four primary phases: consider, evaluate, buy, and experience.

KEY TERMS

AIDA model A model of communication that elaborates the steps of consumer involvement as attention, interest, desire, and action

Cognitive dissonance When there is a discrepancy between the decision-making process and the final choice of the brand, it is called cognitive dissonance

Consumer decision journey A theory stating that the consumer decision-making process is a circular journey with four primary phases: consider, evaluate, buy, and experience

Consumer decision-making process A process that explains the steps in purchase decision, namely, problem recognition, information search, alternative evaluation, purchase decision, and finally, post-purchase behaviour

Economic man The thinking that people take decisions based on economic rationale, that is, of maximizing utility while spending their limited resources

Engel–Blackwell–Miniard model The model shows how the decision-making process is influenced by external factors and the consumer's own memory

Howard–Sheth model The model integrates social, psychological, and marketing influences on consumers

Hypothetical constructs Factors affecting consumer decision-making as explained in the Howard–Sheth model, including perceptual and learning constructs

Marginal utility The utility or satisfaction derived from consuming an additional unit of a product, a declining function

Model of goal-directed behaviour This model adds past behaviour and emotions, going on to desire, then intention to buy

Nicosia model This model connects the firm's communication efforts and the consumers' attitudes. The firm's advertising affects consumers' attitudes and may lead to further action

Theory of planned behaviour This theory states that 'perceived behavioural control' which is formed by combining the factors that may facilitate or impede the purchase behaviour, plays a role in affecting consumer behaviour, along with other factors

Theory of reasoned action The theory states that a person's purchase behaviour derives from two sources: his/her own beliefs and evaluation of alternatives, and the opinions of others and the desire to adhere to what others say or think

Theory of trying This theory recognizes that it is not just the purchase, but also the process of trying to consume, which depends on means, subjective norms, the means of trying, attitudes, and expectations of success or failure

EXERCISES

Concept-review Questions

1. Explain the economic model of consumer behaviour. What are the assumptions it makes?
2. Describe the steps in the consumer decision-making process. Take up a purchase you made recently and explain how you proceeded.
3. Why is it important for companies to monitor post-purchase behaviour? What are the benefits that can be reaped by doing this?
4. Draw and explain the Howard–Sheth model. How is it different from the Nicosia model?
5. Compare the economic, cognitive, humanistic, and consumer decision models and describe how they add to the understanding of consumer behaviour.
6. Draw and explain the Nicosia model. Show its applicability in your purchase of a shampoo brand.
7. Evaluate the consumer behaviour models described in this chapter. How have they contributed to our understanding of consumer behaviour? What are their shortcomings?
8. Explain the concept of consumer decision journey and comment on whether it aids in understanding of modern consumers.
9. Explain and draw the cognitive theories, the TRA and the TPB. How have they contributed to the theory of consumer behaviour?
10. How have humanistic theories helped us understand consumer behaviour? What is their contribution?

Critical Thinking Questions

1. The economic model assumes that people are rational, but this assumption has been challenged. Do you think that most consumer decisions are rational? Mention examples of purchases made by your friends to explain.
2. 'The models and theories of consumer behaviour are attempting to describe the unexplainable—a psychological phenomenon.' How far do you agree or disagree with this statement? How can these models be further refined to include psychological variables?

3. Critically examine a purchase decision you made in the light of the consumer models described in this chapter. Which model would be most appropriate to explain your decision and why?

4. How do customers deal with cognitive dissonance? Does it actually happen or not? In what kind of cases is it likely to be more pronounced and what can companies do about it?

■■■ Projects and Assignments

1. Take up products such as (a) an expensive television, (b) a car, and (c) laptop and identify what influences their purchase decisions. Apply a model of consumer behaviour to these purchases.
2. Think of a product that you frequently consume, such as fast food or cosmetics. List the brands that constitute part of your evoked, inert, and inept sets. What are the reasons for some brands being unable to cross over to the evoked set? What are the factors that made you finally choose one brand?
3. Take a look at advertisements for different brands. Classify the ads based on their appeal to cognitive, emotional, or humanistic models.
4. Describe an activity that you recently undertook with your friends, such as watching a movie, going out to a party, or a shopping spree. Identify the needs and motivations for doing so. How would you market an event management company in the light of your findings?

■■■ REFERENCES

Ajzen, Icek, 'The theory of planned behavior', *Organizational Behavior and Human Decision Processes*, Vol. 50, 1991, pp. 179–211.

Bagozzi, Richard P. and Paul R. Warshaw, 'Trying to consume', *Journal of Consumer Research*, Vol. 17, No. 2, September 1990, pp. 127–140.

Blackwell, Roger D., Paul W. Miniard, and James F. Engel, *Consumer Behavior*, 10th Ed., Thomson South-Western, Mason, Ohio, 2006.

Fishbein, M., and I. Ajzen,. *Belief, attitude, intention, and behavior: An introduction to theory and research*, Addison-Wesley, Reading, MA, 1975.

Foxall, G., *Consumer Psychology in Behavioural Perspective*, Routledge, London, 1990.

Galbraith, John Kenneth, *The Affluent Society*, Penguin Books, London, Revised Edition, 1999.

Hackos, Joann T., *Information Development: Managing Your Documentation, Projects, Portfolio and People*, Wiley Publishing, Indiana, 2007, pp. 137–140.

Hollis, Martin and Edward J. Nell, *Rational Economic Man*, Cambridge University Press, Cambridge, 1975, pp. 52–55.

Howard, John A., and Jagdish Sheth, *The Theory of Buyer Behaviour*, John Wiley, 1969, pp. 467–487.

Kahneman, Daniel, *Thinking, Fast and Slow*, Allen Lane, London, 2011, pp. 377–390.

Kumar, Dinesh, *Marketing Channels*, Oxford University Press, New Delhi, 2012, p. 313.

Lawson, Rob, 'Consumer behaviour', in Baker, Michael John and Michael Saren, (Ed.), *Marketing Theory: A Student Text*, 2nd Ed., Sage Publishers, London, 2010, p. 268.

Loudon, David L. and Albert J. Della Bitta, *Consumer Behaviour*, 4th Ed., Tata McGraw Hill, New Delhi, 2002.

Nicosia, F., *Consumer Decision Processes, Marketing and Advertising Implications*, Prentice Hall, Englewood Cliffs, 1966.

Perugini, M., and Bagozzi, R. P., 'The role of desires and anticipated emotions in goal-directed behaviours: Broadening and deepening the theory of planned behaviour', *British Journal of Social Psychology*, Vol. 40, 2001, pp. 79–98.

Samuelson, Paul A., *Foundations of Economic Analysis*, Harvard University Press, Boston, 1947, (Enlarged Edition, 1983, p. 92.

Scitovsky, Tibor, *The Joyless Economy: The Psychology of Human Satisfaction*, Revised edition, Oxford University Press, Oxford, 1992.

Sen, Amartya K., 'Rational fools: A critique of the behavioral foundations of economic theory', Vol. 6, No. 4, *Philosophy and Public Affairs*, Summer 1977, pp. 317–344.

Tuck, Mary, *Essential Psychology—How do we Choose?*, Methuen & Co Ltd, London, 1976, pp. 25–26.

Watts Duncan J. and Steve Hasker, 'Marketing in an unpredictable world', *Harvard Business Review*, September 2006.

CASE STUDY
Why Customers Hire Milkshakes

The main contribution of consumer models is that they shift the focus to consumers rather than products. Indeed, understanding the customer is an important task for managers. It is not just about their needs, but how products are used by them to fulfil their needs. As Theodore Levitt used to tell his students, 'People don't want to buy a quarter-inch drill. They want a quarter-inch hole!'

This implies that customers have needs and they 'hire' products to fulfil those needs.

Christensen, et al. (2005) write in their article, *Marketing Malpractice*, that though managers agree with Levitt's insight, they continue to segment their markets by product types and price points. They measure the market share of drills, not holes; and they are more focused on features and functions of their drills, not on the service that the drill performs. In the process, they add improvements to their products that are irrelevant to their customers' needs.

Similarly, segmenting customers does not help in identifying customers. All that segmentation techniques do is to express a likelihood of purchase by a person in probabilistic terms. They write, 'the emphasis on products and not focusing on customer needs is the key reason that new product innovation has become a gamble in which the odds of winning are horrifyingly low'.

The task of marketing is to focus on customers, but companies are focused on products or markets. The manager's task, on the contrary, is to understand what jobs periodically arise in customers' lives for which they might hire products the company makes. Every job people want done has a social, a functional, and an emotional dimension. The job, not the customer, is the fundamental unit of analysis for a manager who hopes to develop products that customers will buy.

Successful businesses follow this route. E-bay was not launched as an 'auction psychographic,' but to help people sell personal items. Google was designed to help people find information, not as a 'search demographic.' Companies that design products to meet needs are more likely to be loved by customers as opposed to those who focus on products or segments.

A company selling milkshakes might focus on the quality of the product by making it thicker, smoother, or offering more flavours than its competitors. Instead of concentrating on improving the milkshakes, would it not be better to understand why consumers were 'hiring' the milkshakes and what needs they were fulfilling?

A researcher did exactly that. The first job was to gain insights and understand the jobs that customers were trying to get done when they hired a milkshake. When was each milk shake bought? What other products were purchased along with it? Were these consumers alone or with a group? Did they consume the shake on the premises or did they drive off with it? Consumers were observed and data collected to answer these questions.

It was discovered that 40 per cent of all milkshakes were purchased in the early morning. These customers were alone; they did not buy anything else; and they consumed their shakes in their cars. Customers were interviewed to find out what jobs they wanted done by buying the shake. This gave another valuable insight: the real reason that consumers bought milk shakes was to do something during their long, boring commute as they went to work. They needed something to make the drive more interesting. They were not hungry, but they wanted to consume something so that they would not feel hungry until noon. Most customers were in a hurry in the morning and they were carrying something, so that they had one hand free.

The 'job' that the milkshake was doing was to make the daily commute more interesting. It had a host of other advantages as well—it could be consumed with one hand, it was clean compared to other foods that left greasy fingers, and it took 20 minutes to consume.

Armed with these insights, it became clear to the company what changes it could make in the product or service to help customers do their jobs better. The following things stood out:

- The milk shake could be made thicker so that it would last longer and make the commute less boring
- Tiny chunks of fruit could be added to add unpredictability and anticipation as one consumed the milk shake, bringing delight to the morning commute
- As the customers were hard-pressed for time, the company could help them save time by moving the dispensing machine to the front of the counter, with a swipe machine to help them pay quickly
- Make the packaging spill-proof as it was to be used while travelling

Such insights helped the company gain a share, not only of the market for milkshakes produced by other chains, but against competing foods as well. Notice that knowing how to improve the product did not come from understanding the customer, but from understanding the job.

This case illustrates how serving needs will help get more customers than making innovations to the product alone that do not get any job done for the customer. That is, job-defined markets are much larger than product category-defined markets.

New markets are created when companies design innovative products that do jobs for customers. In fact, companies that have historically segmented and measured the size of their markets by product category, generally find that when they segment by job instead, their market is much larger than they had thought.

Questions for Discussion

1. Could the consumption of milkshakes be classified according to a consumer decision-making model? Analyse the various factors mentioned in the chapter as they relate to this case.
2. Select any other product and analyse how companies can gain insights into the way it is used. Can the company gain by shifting focus onto consumer jobs rather than products?
3. Develop a consumer decision-making model for milkshakes as described in this case.
4. Analyse why you and your friends go to a coffee house that is your favourite hangout. What are the products you hire for which jobs and why?

Source:
Christensen, Clayton M., Scott Cook, and Taddy Hall, 'Marketing malpractice: The cause and the cure', *Harvard Business Review*, December 2005.

CHAPTER FOUR

Business-to-business Buying Behaviour

LEARNING OBJECTIVES

A big chunk of all business transactions consists of business-to-business (B2B) buying and selling, in which the buyer does not buy goods for consumption, but for processing and selling to others. The chapter explains the buying behaviour of this large and important segment.

After studying this chapter, the reader would be able to

- understand the nature and structure of B2B buying and appreciate the differences between B2B and consumer buying
- analyse B2B transactions and segments, and understand the types and motives for B2B marketing
- learn about the B2B purchase process, types of customers, customer satisfaction, and B2B services
- understand and analyse B2B buying behaviour, B2B brands, and e-hubs
- analyse the role of relationships and understand the ethical issues in B2B buying

CASE STUDY

Rolls-Royce: The Long Arm of B2B Relationships

'The relationship between a seller and a buyer seldom ends when a sale is made. Increasingly, the relationship intensifies after the sale.' Theodore Levitt's words written in 1983 ring true in B2B situations, where suppliers and manufacturers are dependent on each other in a permanent bond. This is most evident in the airline industry. Each aircraft, regardless of the company making it, is a miracle of technology, dependable component manufacturers, and scientific and corporate daring.

Airlines buy planes from manufacturers such as Airbus, Boeing, Bombardier, and so on, who in turn buy components from their suppliers. A mistake anywhere down the line results in huge costs for the airlines, who are the customers flying the planes. Even the malfunctioning of a minor component could ground the fleet or have serious public safety repercussions. For instance, all the airlines using the Boeing 787, dubbed the 'Dreamliner' had to ground their fleets around the world in January 2013 following reports of battery malfunction. Such instances show the nature of interdependence in B2B situations.

One of the crucial components of a plane is the engine, which is supplied by leading manufacturers such as General Electric, Pratt & Whitney, and Rolls-Royce. Plane manufacturers and airlines don't just require properly fitted engines, they want service backup for them decades after the purchase.

Rolls-Royce realized this and decided to focus on service. Though the company had a great history, it nearly went under in the 1970s. The auto division was sold, and Rolls-Royce had a single-digit market share in the civil aerospace market. Since developing an airplane engine entails huge costs, the company made a strategic decision to develop risk- and revenue- sharing partnerships with other companies. Along with developing new technologies and risk sharing, Rolls-Royce decided to implement an in-flight system of monitoring its engines, which could warn airlines of problems before they happened.

Known as *engine condition monitoring*, the technology uses computers to check on how an engine is performing even when it is in mid-flight, tracking any signs of wear, as well as any malfunction. *The Telegraph* (2010) explains that vast amounts of data are transmitted to the company from flights taking off anywhere in the world, enabling a quick response to any engine problems. This means that if a problem is identified during any flight, details will be known to the airline's and manufacturer's engineers before the plane arrives at its destination. The system also helps in predicting engine trouble before it arises.

This was what its customers (manufacturers) and their customers (airlines) wanted, and it resulted in a dramatic turnaround for Rolls-Royce. From a bit player, that is from a single digit market share in the 1970s, the company has become a major presence in the aerospace market. Today, the company, along with General Electric, supplies engines for all three major new planes: the Boeing 787, the Airbus A380, and the Airbus A350.

Chief Equipment Health Manager of Rolls-Royce Nick Walters (2009) writes that around half of the civil engines fleet is covered by long-term service agreements, with 80 per cent of new business incorporating long-term support elements. Airlines outsource engineering and maintenance to the engine maker and concentrate on what they do best—flying the planes. Engine health management (EHM) reduces maintenance cost and avoids service disruption.

The company has its operations centres at several places. Each centre has a 'front desk' with a team of experienced engineers monitoring the worldwide fleet, tracking trends, and giving customers real-time advice 24/7, 365 days a year. The back-room team schedules engineering, repair, and overhaul. The system comprises five key stages:

Sense Measuring various parameters within the engine, permanently fitted with about 25 sensors, which are used to control the engine and provide data of engine operation to the pilot as well as the EHM system

Acquire Capturing this data at relevant periods during every flight, using the aircraft condition monitoring system (ACMS) to click snapshots during take-off, climb, and cruise as well as recording unusual engine conditions.

Transfer Transmitting data from the aircraft through digital datalink, via a very high frequency (VHF) radio or satellite link while the aircraft is in flight and a worldwide ground network then transfers this data to the intended destination

Analyse Normalizing data and detection of any unusual characteristics, subtle changes in condition from one flight to another, using automated algorithms based on neural networks, the multiple sensor information is used to provide the most sensitive detection capability

Act Providing advice so that corrective action can be taken

The strategy has helped Rolls-Royce, not only to get more engine orders, but also more service contracts. The service and maintenance businesses have better margins and are much more profitable than original engine sales. For airlines, maintenance is becoming an increasingly important component as passenger safety depends on it. Rolls-Royce has an arrangement with a concern called TotalCare, which assumes all the risks and costs of downtime and repairs. TotalCare charges a fee for every hour the engine is in operation.

Rolls-Royce is not alone in offering in-flight tracking of engine performance. Other engine makers like

GE have also developed live monitoring, but the system has helped Rolls-Royce get back into the aircraft business in a big way.

The case study shows the complex nature of B2B consumer needs and behaviour. Most B2B consumer needs are met in similar ways. It also shows the long-term nature of B2B transactions. Companies are not merely suppliers, but partners who can provide services that help them and their customers.

While reading this chapter, try to answer the following questions:

1. What is the nature of B2B transactions and what factors impact B2B behaviour?
2. What are the motives for B2B buying?
3. How is the buying process different and more complex in B2B than in business-to-consumer (B2C) transactions?
4. Do emotions also play a role in B2B buying, or is it a rational and logical buying process based on economic motives?

Sources:
http://www.businessweek.com/stories/2005-11-13/rolls-royce-at-your-service.
http://www.ingenia.org.uk/ingenia/articles.aspx?Index=552.
http://www.rolls-royce.com/services/index.jsp.
http://www.telegraph.co.uk/travel/travelnews/8111075/Live-monitoring-helps-engine-manufacturers-track-performance.html.
Waters, Nick, *Ingenia*, Issue 39, June 2009,
All websites last accessed on 10 July 2013.

INTRODUCTION

B2B, short for business-to-business, refers to commercial transactions between businesses. It is the selling of products, services, or information between two companies rather than companies selling to consumers.

Business-to-business transactions are defined as the buying of goods and services which are not meant to be consumed by the buyer, but are used by the buyer to further produce goods and services meant to be sold to consumers. For instance, if you buy flour to bake a cake for your family, it is a business-to-consumer (B2C) transaction, but if a bakery buys flour to make cakes and sell them, it becomes a B2B transaction. Business-to-business transactions keep the wheels of industry moving, enabling firms to buy raw materials, machinery, accessories, and services, using which they operate, process, produce, add value to raw materials, and resell them in the form of finished products that consumers are familiar with.

Business buying expectations are quite different from the purchase of consumer goods. Business-to-business purchases are more complex and require a more detailed prospecting effort, sales process, payment, and service delivery. The complex nature in B2B buying is often likened to a marriage. 'The sale merely consummates the courtship, at which point the marriage begins', writes Levitt (1983). He explains that buyers of automated machinery do not walk home like buyers at a flea market. They expect installation, application, parts, repair, and maintenance, and help to ensure the company remains competitive. The purchase decision is thus not to buy a particular item, but a decision to enter into a bonded relationship. For instance, as our chapter-opening case study shows, the decision to buy a particular aeroplane engine means entering into decades of contracted service and maintenance from the supplier.

Whether it is buying machinery, or entering into distribution or franchise agreements, or buying raw materials, B2B deals are characterized by complexity and longevity. Neither channel partners nor suppliers and contractors can be changed easily. No purchase manager wants to try out new suppliers, and the attendant risks of quality variation or supply disruption. Once B2B suppliers prove to be reliable and dependable, few companies want to change them unless there are serious problems. That is why B2B relationships are long-term and both sides have to invest in making their relationships work.

Unlike consumer marketing, where the purchase decision may change from time to time, companies have to treat their suppliers as equal partners. They have to ensure that their suppliers and dealers earn enough to keep them motivated. As Kumar (2012) points out in the book *Marketing Channels*, dealers of companies conduct business for many years, sometimes for generations. To understand B2B buying behaviour, we must answer two questions: (a) who buys the products, and (b) why they buy them. The first question is answered in the next section.

PLAYERS IN BUSINESS MARKET

Though B2B behaviour is distinct from consumer marketing, it is not homogenous behaviour, and has to be studied from different perspectives. Business-to-business transactions are quite different from one another. Business markets have two components, supply chain markets and business user markets.

Supply Chain Market

Supply chain users consist of manufacturers, suppliers, and service providers who keep stocks—whether of raw materials or finished goods—moving. Business users are those who consume or use the materials to produce goods that will be sold to consumers.

The following are some examples of supply chain markets:

- A small vendor who buys stocks from a wholesaler of a few brands of cigarettes and *paan masala* for display and sale in his shop
- Wholesalers or retailers taking delivery of goods produced by a manufacturer, which they will sell to consumers
- A company that enters into a franchise agreement with local parties for better reach
- An NGO that buys books or medicines to distribute among the poor
- B2B e-commerce portals that showcase products and help suppliers to find and meet buyers

Business User Markets

The following are a few examples of business user markets:

- A multinational like Kentucky Fried Chicken (KFC) buying raw chicken from a poultry farm to process and sell in its stores
- P&G hiring an advertising agency to create advertisements for its products and place them in newspapers and on television
- A software contractor who supplies software to a bank
- A transporter who buys Tata trucks, an airline that buys planes, or a company like Reliance that buys a jet for corporate travel
- A company taking a loan from a bank

As can be seen from these examples, there are many aspects of B2B behaviour, and it is not just a company buying products from its suppliers. The products have to be serviced and guaranteed to perform—any failure in the case of components supplied to a car or aircraft manufacturer, for instance, will have fatal consequences. Second, a company can be a B2B supplier as well as a customer. In the case of the airline industry, for example, manufacturers such as Boeing or Airbus buy many components from their suppliers and the finished product is sold to an airline, which is a business buyer. Such companies usually have very close relationships with their suppliers who must be dependable, and their customers as well, to whom training and support is provided.

A supplier must cater to the needs of the client in a variety of ways as given here.

- If supplying to wholesale and retail, the company must keep track of all outlets storing similar products and establish relationships with them. The supply schedule should be flexible so that it can be varied according to the demand.
- For a multinational food company like KFC that sources items from various suppliers, the latter must modify their manufacturing and packaging, and submit to quality checks, to meet the specific demands of the company. The suppliers must invest in and establish cold chains. Even a small error by the supplier will result in huge problems for the buying company.
- For service suppliers, it would be important to work closely with the company, often by deputing permanent representatives on their client's premises for the purpose. A software contractor employed by a bank, for instance, has to ensure that the system works properly at the bank's premises every single minute. A downtime of even a few minutes will result in chaos in the bank's branches.
- Suppliers of vehicles must keep track of how the vehicles are used and maintained by their buyers. Airline companies must ensure that they are able to respond to requests for advice, parts, and service by user airlines on a real-time basis (see chapter-opening case study).

CHARACTERISTICS OF B2B MARKETS

To understand B2B behaviour, it is important to understand how these markets operate. These characteristics determine the behavioural aspects of parties in the B2B marketing process (see Fig. 4.1).

Complex Decision-making Unit

Business-to-business marketing is quite different from consumer marketing because of the complexity of decision-making. In consumer marketing, most purchases are made by individuals or limited to family members. In B2B markets, the purchase of machinery or raw materials involves technical experts, purchasing experts, board members, production, finance, and safety experts. In studying B2B behaviour, we face the problem of whether to study the behaviour of the decision-makers or the organizational behaviour of the company. Identifying the target audience is therefore a major challenge.

Rational Buyers

We have discussed in Chapter 3 that individuals do not display rational behaviour. B2B situations are more rational since decisions are taken on technical and economic considerations. Consumer demand

FIG. 4.1 Characteristics of B2B markets

is based on wants while B2B demand is based on needs. Thus, identifying needs of organizations is easy and can be done on the basis of company size, volume purchased, and job function.

Customized Products

Consumers tend to take decisions based on simple criteria. For example, a car is bought on the basis of how it looks or how it is advertised. B2B products, on the other hand, have to be integrated into a larger system. There cannot be a standardized response and B2B suppliers have to tailor their offerings. A manufacturer supplying an electrical part to a car manufacturer has to ensure that its dimensions match perfectly so that it fits the assembly precisely; the performance and voltage has to be within specific parameters; it should have a specified life; and, there should never be a short circuit. Any malfunctioning of the part will have serious repercussions for the purchasing company.

Small Target Audiences

B2B markets adhere to the Pareto principle or 80:20 rule, where a small number of customers provide large sales volumes. This means suppliers have to cater to fewer clients but the orders are very large and long-term.

Importance of Personal Relationships

Since the customer base is small but regular, personal relationships and trust become very important in B2B markets. In many situations, B2B suppliers have a relationship with their client companies for years and sometimes generations. Most customers demand on-site service. Companies build relationships on the basis of trust; once the supplier is accepted, face-to-face visits are not required but orders can be placed over the phone.

Long-term Buyers

Companies stick with their suppliers for the long term. This is because suppliers invest in land or machinery to cater to the requirements of companies. While this results in stability, it also means that efforts have to be put in by both sides to build long-lasting relationships.

Drivers of Innovation

Business-to-business companies that innovate usually do so as a response to an innovation that has happened further upstream. For example, the shift from glass to plastic bottles for soft drink manufacturers is a gradual, long-drawn-out process. In contrast to FMCG companies, B2B suppliers have the comparative luxury of responding to trends rather than having to predict or even drive them. In other words, B2B companies have the time to continually re-evaluate their segments and value propositions and respond promptly to the evolving needs of their clients. However, they must respond to technical innovations in their industries or face the danger of getting outdated.

Fewer Behavioural Considerations

Consumer marketing is done mainly on behavioural factors, but B2B markets have far fewer behavioural considerations, simply because goods are bought and sold on technical and economic considerations. Business-to-business suppliers have to cater to and understand the behaviour and motives of the purchase committee members. There are many people involved and procedures have to be followed. Hence purchasing is not dictated by whims, fancies, and feelings, and extremes of behaviour do not really matter.

It is evident from the aforegiven discussion that B2B markets are quite different from B2C markets. A few differences between the two, are described in the next section.

DIFFERENCES BETWEEN B2B AND B2C

While consumer demand is directly generated by consumers buying goods, B2B transactions are a result of *derived demand*, that is, it follows consumer demand. Consumer demand is aggregated by companies and they make their production schedules accordingly. *Fluctuating demand* is another characteristic of B2B markets: a small change in demand by consumers can have a big effect throughout the chain of businesses. In the book, *Marketing Channels*, the author illustrates that a minor increase in consumer demand will have a huge impact in supply chains. *Joint demand* occurs when the demand for one product increases the demand for another. Most B2B demand is also *inelastic*, which means that it will not be affected with changes in price. This is because it depends on consumer demand.

Usually, marketing and consumer behaviour are thought of in the consumer context. The transactions are much larger; in terms of volume, B2B transactions are estimated to be 10 times the volume of B2C transactions in an economy. However, B2B and B2C marketing are quite different. Understanding these differences is the key to grasping B2B behaviour. The differences are summarized in Table 4.1.

The nature of B2B transactions is as follows:

Goods bought to aid further production The first characteristic of B2B buying is that goods are bought for further production. So the buyer is interested in the inherent qualities of the supplies, their contribution to cost, and wastage and efficiency parameters, rather than the physical attributes.

Bulk purchase and sale Business-to-business orders are placed in bulk so as to minimize transportation and stock-out costs. Companies prefer to place long-term buying contracts with their suppliers, which is quite unlike consumer markets. This places emphasis on complete understanding and trust between buyers and sellers.

TABLE 4.1 Differences in B2B and B2C buying

B2B marketing	B2C marketing
Goods are bought to aid further production	Goods are bought for consumption
Goods are bought and sold in bulk	Goods are sold in individual units
Orders are of high value	Low value, unit sales
Long-term, regular buying contracts	Consumers can switch loyalty at will
Few competitors, monolithic market	Many competitors, fragmented market
Complex buying process, involving several people	Single-step buying process, shorter sales cycle
Brand identity created through quality, delivery, and dependability	Brand identity created through repetition and imagery
Clusters of supplying and buying companies	Large and scattered market
Product demonstration or capability-based buying	Merchandising and point of purchase activities affect purchase decision
Buying decision on analysis, product specifications, and performance criteria	Emotional buying decision based on status, desire, or price
Buying risks are huge	Very little buying risk, limited to one purchase
High selling costs	High marketing costs

High-value orders Business-to-business contracts tend to be of high value. This implies that a number of people from different departments will be involved in the purchase, so the sales representative must be able to handle queries from them.

Long-term, regular buying contracts Companies seek long-term relationships with their suppliers so that disruption in supplies is avoided. They do not experiment with different suppliers as it will have an impact on the production process and on the entire business.

Monolithic market Suppliers of raw materials are few and companies know each other's capabilities. For instance, a car component with precise engineering can be supplied by just a few suppliers who have the requisite engineering skills.

Complex buying process, involving several people While consumer purchases are individual decisions or may involve some family members, B2B is a complex process that involves technical, financial, and purchasing professionals. The purchase is usually made by committees and each of the members may have different objectives. The decision-making process for B2B products is usually much longer than in B2C.

Brand identity created through quality, delivery, dependability Consumer brands create identity through advertising and imagery. B2B buying depends on the capability of the supplier and aspects such as quality, delivery, and dependability.

Suppliers and buyers form clusters Business-to-business suppliers usually exist in clusters, whereas consumer markets are large and scattered. For example, suppliers of raw materials are clustered around areas where mining is done.

Product demonstration or capability based buying A company buying photocopiers for its offices will seek product demonstrations and test the capability of the machines before buying. Salespersons have to be technically capable of handling queries.

Buying decision based on product specifications and performance criteria Buyers in B2B situations list the technical product specifications and performance criteria that must be met by suppliers. Testing will be done of each batch of raw materials before they are sent for production.

Huge buying risks Delays and discrepancies can hold up entire production lines. That is why buyer risks are huge and companies look for suppliers who are able to minimize those risks. A faulty car part sourced from a vendor, for example, will result in car recalls and a dent in the reputation of the company.

High selling cost Business-to-business selling involves high costs. Several meetings between buyers and sellers are held, prototypes are created, and testing is done at various stages.

These characteristics guide all buyer behaviour and helps us understand B2B transactions.

UNDERSTANDING B2B TRANSACTIONS

To understand B2B transactions, we must understand the buying drivers, types of products, motives for buying, and B2B segments. We will discuss these in the following sections:

B2B Buying Drivers

To understand B2B transactions, let us take the example of a company making bread and cakes. The bakery initially buys manufacturing equipments such as mixers, ovens, and other devices required for the purpose from their manufacturers. Then it buys raw materials such as flour, eggs, sugar, cream, and decorations from its vendors. These, along with packing materials, are purchased on a daily basis. The transactions of a bakery are shown in Fig. 4.2. We can infer from this figure that consumer transactions are just one aspect of any business.

The trucks delivering materials to the factory and the trucks transporting the finished bread and cakes from the factory to the wholesaler or retailer are providing B2B services. Any related services along the way would be classified as B2B because they are not consumed by the intermediaries but consumed to provide goods to end consumers.

The wholesaler will then sell the goods to bulk users such as hotels and institutional buyers or to retailers in a city to stock them. All these are B2B transactions. In Fig. 4.2, only the onward sales to the end consumers are called B2C transactions. The figure shows the complex nature of the transactions that take place at all stages to bring goods to the customer. We have not considered the production process and the many activities that take place in the factory, all of which are also B2B services. Any advertising done by the company to sell its products is also classified as B2B.

As can be inferred from the figure, only a small portion of business activity is B2C. The bulk of the operation is B2B. As a result, B2B revenues far exceed B2C revenues. Some estimates put the volumes of business and consumer transactions as 10:1. Most sales jobs involve selling to B2B customers rather than consumers.

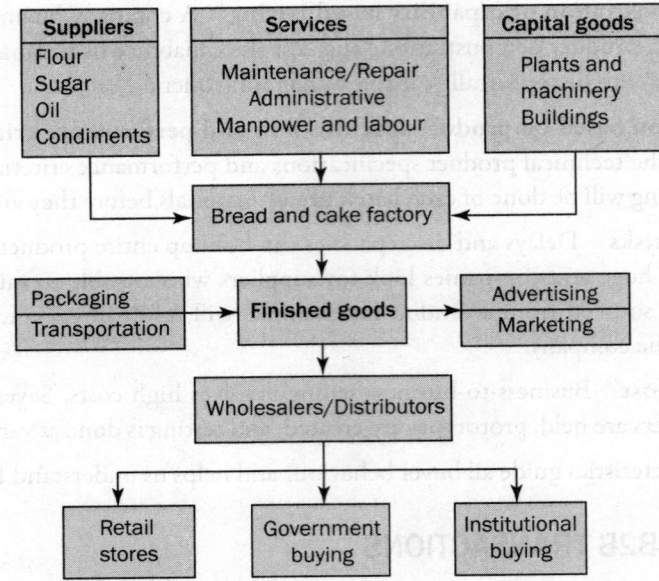

FIG. 4.2 B2B transactions of a bakery

In the preceding example, the supply of breads and cakes must be reliable, dependable, flexible, and transparent. If the bread reaches late or does not reach the shops on any given day, many customers will have to go without breakfast. Therefore, supplies have to be reliable and dependable. Flexibility and transparency are also required to adjust to the increase or decrease in consumer demand. Without these, the company will either experience too many returns or market shortages, causing consumers to shift to rival brands. The following are the B2B buying drivers (see Fig. 4.3):

Reliability An overriding concern in B2B transactions is reliability. Parts and products supplied must work according to specifications; even a small compromise on quality can result in great losses—as in the case of vehicle recalls if a part is defective, or the serving of spoiled food by restaurants if the supply chains are not reliable.

Dependability Both B2B suppliers and customers depend on each other. Both sides have to invest in each other: suppliers must invest in new plants, warehouses, or retail outlets, whereas companies must impart knowhow and invest in supply chains.

Flexibility As the marketplace is dynamic, companies and suppliers have to be flexible: an increase in demand must be met by matching supplies and adjustments to supply chains. Similarly, a decrease in demand means that production at supplying units slow down. Manufacturers look for flexible supply chains so that products can be modified or volumes can be varied according to demand. Ndubisi, et al. (2005) examined the impact of supplier selection and management strategies on manufacturing flexibility in manufacturing firms in the semiconductor industry in Malaysia. They found that the selection of suppliers based on technology is important for manufacturers who wanted product and launch flexibility.

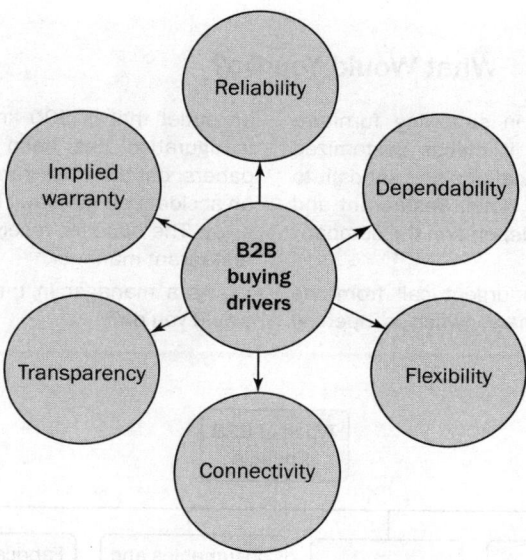

FIG. 4.3 B2B buying drivers

However, quality becomes important when the manufacturer wants volume flexibility. Further, inventory management and technology in supply chains have a great impact on manufacturing flexibility.

Connectivity Companies must have open systems of information with their dealers and suppliers. Kumar (2012) notes that this is often difficult, since information is not shared because of fear of loss of control. People tend to hide or modify information, leading to serious consequences, like the bullwhip effect—referring to the phenomenon of distortion in demand as information flows in supply chains. Small changes in demand get amplified as information flows up the channels, resulting in highly inflated figures when it reaches the manufacturer.

Transparency Though companies and their suppliers/dealers are independent units, both must be integrated with each other, share information, and be transparent in their approach. Even cost and pricing information is known. Both parties have to be concerned about each other's profitability.

Implied warranty Supplying companies have to behave as if they are part of the company they are supplying to. Sometimes products have to be reworked or modified, and this must be done as if these are covered under warranties.

Types of B2B Products

Business-to-business transactions also depend on the nature of goods to be purchased (see Fig. 4.4). The process for raw materials that are purchased regularly will be entirely different from the one-time purchase of capital equipment, for instance. B2B goods can be classified as follows:

CB IN ACTION   What Would You Do?

A company is a specialist in supplying furniture for restaurants and hotels. It makes customized furniture as per client specifications and sends it to the location specified by the hotel. Restaurant and hotel owners have begun to depend on the company for their requirements.

One day, it receives an urgent call from the manager of a restaurant chain, which is opening an outlet that is 500 km away from the city. The inauguration has been announced in the local papers, but the truck carrying the furniture has had an accident on the way. The opening is only two days away. The supplier receives a frantic call from the restaurant manager.

As a manager in the furniture company, what would you do?

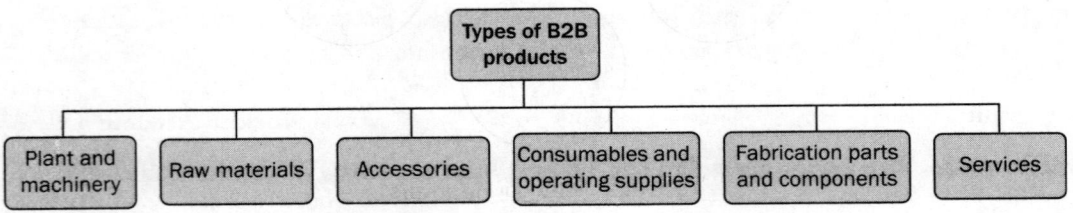

FIG. 4.4   Types of B2B products

Plant and machinery   Every manufacturing unit needs equipment in the form of plant and machinery. This is of the nature of capital expenditure, has high value, but a long decision-making lead time.

Raw materials   These are bought in raw form by manufacturing companies on a regular basis. They are ordered automatically as soon as the holding stock hits minimum levels. Such purchases can be classified as routine purchases.

Accessories   Supplementary material that may aid in production directly or indirectly, or in administration are called accessories. Office equipment such as computers and typewriters can be classified as accessories.

Consumables and operating supplies   Products such as oil and lubricants required for running machines and vehicles, as well as items such as paper reams and stationery items that are required for administration, but which do not form part of the finished product are termed consumables and operating supplies.

Fabrication parts and components   Parts and components, like one of the many parts required for automobile manufacture, take a lot of time for development. Suppliers will often seek help from their client companies to develop these parts.

Services   Advertising, transportation, airconditioning, and other support services are also an essential part of B2B buying. These are also required by manufacturing companies on a regular basis.

B2B Services

Businesses buy a variety of services, ranging from consultancy, financial services, data management, marketing for small and medium enterprises (SMEs), maintenance of installations, logistics, information technology (IT), travel, communications, and so on. It helps them to contract out activities in which they do not have expertise, and thus save time to concentrate on their core activities. Trade fairs and exhibitions are another form of service that provide an important means of communication between sellers and buyers. Geigenmuller and Bettis-Outland (2012) write that trade fairs are crucial to the development of relationships between buyers and sellers.

With the rise of business process outsourcing, B2B services have gained in importance and size. However, companies welcome not just service providers but those service suppliers who are able to solve problems. Han and Sung (2008) write that in business markets, the ability to solve client problems is a major source of economic success. They say that the supplier–buyer transaction performance is influenced by eight important factors, namely supplier competence, purchasing value, customer satisfaction, switching cost, brand trust and loyalty, relationship quality, commitment, and transactional performance. A service provider therefore must offer targeted solutions and must have the skills and knowledge for it. Service providers who are able to do so successfully thwart competition.

Marquardt, et al. (2011) set out the following three steps for B2B services marketing:

- Managers should first develop compelling and differentiated value propositions.
- They should then invest in communicating their brands' value to potential customers.
- Finally, they should commit resources to ensure consistent and favourable customer experiences with the brand.

The B2B purchase process has evolved in recent years. Earlier, companies floated tenders, got supplier data from trade magazines, or depended on their purchase departments to find suppliers of products and services. Salespeople did their best to get companies to try out their offerings. Today, because of the Internet, social media, and other online influences, purchase managers do independent research online, seeking advice from their peers and third parties.

As a consequence, companies do not approach prospective suppliers directly but do their own research first and refer to social networks for reviews. This is a challenging scenario because B2B sellers have to sell their wares like brands, so that they come into the evaluation shortlist of the buyer at the time of consideration.

B2B PURCHASE PROCESS

The B2B buying process is complex. The need is expressed by a user department or from the planning department, and an indent is raised. Based on the specifications demanded, the purchase department seeks suppliers and asks for quotations. For routine items, purchase orders are placed based on past supplier assessment, but for complex items a detailed process is followed. The process is explained in Fig. 4.5.

It is said that 90 per cent of the B2B buying process is done much before a prospect engages with the supplier. This is because buyers seek supplier information or reputation online.

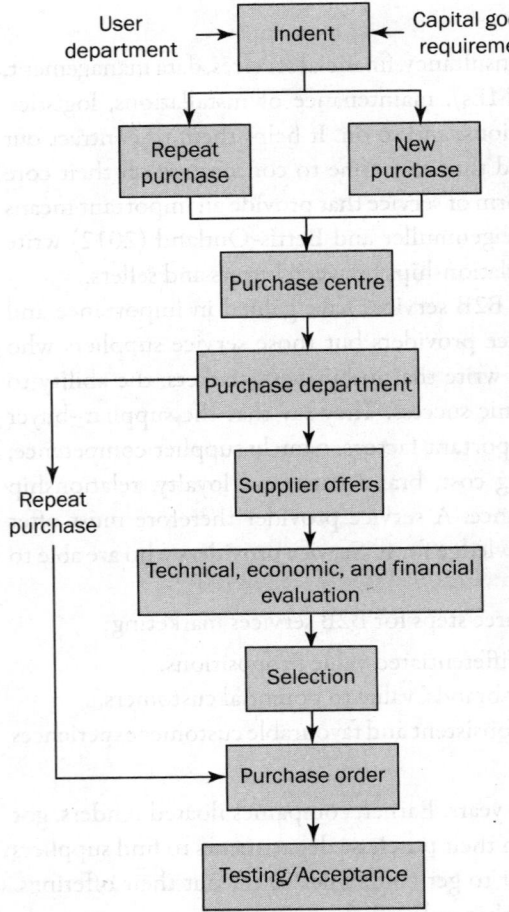

FIG. 4.5 Purchase process

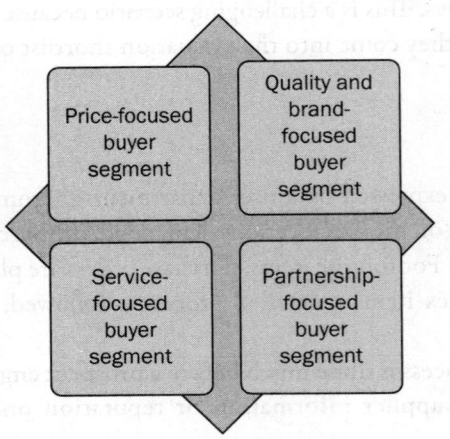

FIG. 4.6 Segments of B2B buyers

Often, buyers 'seek out' their suppliers rather than the other way round. Suppliers thus have to find ways of gaining the buyer's attention even before an indent is raised by the user department. News websites, social networks, and other means have to be used to reach the target audience both early and often, so that suppliers can influence prospective customers even before they are even thinking about buying.

B2B SEGMENTS

While consumer segments can be segmented on the basis of individual, society, or demographics, segmenting B2B markets is more complex. For one, differences in customers are not as observable as in consumer markets. The most obvious way to segment industrial markets is on the basis of size of customer. Companies assign different sales personnel to deal with large customers and with those who place smaller orders.

However, the task is much more complex. Companies can always segment industrial markets based on their knowledge of customers. Waaser, et al. (2004) write that 'meaningful improvements in sales come from doing three things: segmenting customers more thoughtfully, designing an organization that can serve the different segments more efficiently, and staffing that organization at the optimal level'.

Based on these motives, we can classify B2B sales as price-focused, quality-focused, service-focused, or partnership-focused (see Fig. 4.6). These behavioural segments are described here.

Price-focused Some B2B buyers look for the cheapest alternatives in raw materials and machinery. Such companies are likely to be in the government sector, and also in the small and medium enterprises (SME) category.

Quality and brand-focused Some companies look for quality and are willing to pay a high price for it. These companies are likely to be the owners of popular brands and have high margins. Since the raw materials will affect the quality of the finished product, brand owners do not compromise on quality. They will similarly pay high prices for quality-tested machinery as they are accountable for safety of their workers. Companies that look for quality are in the medium or large category, and place great importance on their products and services.

Service Companies in crucial sectors that cannot afford a disruption, such as transportation, food, defence, and so on, place high importance on quality and after-sales service. Such companies will place very high emphasis on equipment quality and quick rectification if something goes wrong, because a disruption would entail a crisis. Suppliers will have to place their engineers permanently on the site of their B2B partners to avoid these situations.

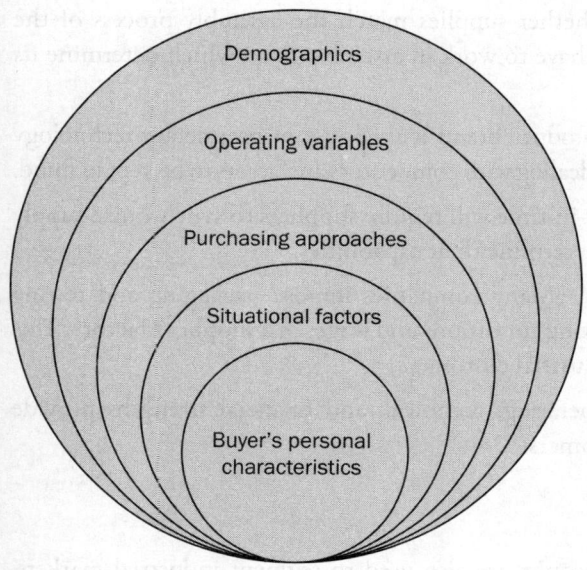

FIG. 4.7 Segmentation criteria for industrial markets

Partnership Many B2B situations depend on long-term partnerships. These consist of key accounts who seek trust and reliability and treat their suppliers as strategic partners. For instance, McDonalds seeks a long-term and dependable source of bread, fries, and patties from its suppliers who deliver on time every day of the year, and can adjust quickly to changes in demand. Car companies similarly seek long-term partnerships with their ancillaries.

Shapiro and Bonoma (1984) suggest five general segmentation criteria for industrial markets, arranged in a 'nested' hierarchy, like a set of boxes fitted into one another. Moving from the outer to the inner nests, the segmentation criteria consist of demographics, operating variables, customer purchasing approaches, situational factors, and personal characteristics of buyers (see Fig. 4.7).

Demographics

Demographics of industrial markets mean gathering information about the industry, company size, and location.

Industry Knowledge of the industry, purchase situations, and product and service needs is an important criterion.

Company size Another vital criterion is company and order size, and payment considerations.

Location Where customers are located or clustered, and proximity to plant as in the case of vehicle assemblies is also taken into account.

Operating Variables

Operating variables refer to segmentation criteria that enable more precise identification of customers within demographic categories. These include company technology, product and brand use status, safety stocks, packaging and testing standards, and customer capabilities.

Technology The supplier has to assess whether supplies match the assembly process of the customer, as precision-engineered products have to work in assembly lines, which determine its buying needs.

Product and brand use status How the product/brand is used, use of proprietary technology shared by the customer, and the restriction of dealing with competitors are factors to be kept in mind.

Safety stocks Customers operating on just-in-time will require suppliers to synchronize supply chains, inventory, and their lead times also determine their capabilities.

Packaging, labour, and testing standards Many companies impose packaging and testing standards, or even insist on monitoring working conditions and wages in a supplier's factory. This will also be another basis for segmenting industrial customers.

Customer capabilities The customer's operating, technical, and financial strengths provide further bases for segmenting industrial customers.

Purchasing Approaches

Purchasing approaches and company philosophy are also used to segment industrial markets. They strongly influence purchases; B2B buyers will prefer vendors who fit into their approach and philosophy. The factors for this segmentation nest are described here.

Purchasing function organization Whether the customer's buying organization is localized or central will determine selling approaches

Power structures Purchasing companies often have power structures, which dictate quality or price of incoming material. A seller can segment customers on this basis as well.

Payment policies Whether payments are made in time or extended, often dictate supplier selection criteria. If payments are delayed as a routine, a supplier might supply inferior goods and reserve his best produce for companies that pay well.

Agents and brokers Sometimes companies appoint agents and brokers as buying agents. Alternatively, as in the case of corrupt officials, companies may route all purchases from a broker who demands his own commission. A supplier will have different ways of dealing with such buying situations.

Buyer–seller relationships Companies are able to develop relations with their customer companies by virtue of long standing, consistent quality supplies, or other means. This forms another basis of segmenting customers.

General purchasing policies Companies have different purchasing policies. Some companies will prefer to lease rather than buy, others will want agreements based on supplier cost, others may prefer bidding and still others will support a tendering process. Supplier companies often have separate departments to deal with different buying methods.

Situational Factors

Situational factors resemble operating variables, but are temporary. Vendors have to be geared to special situations that influence B2B buying behaviour. Such factors necessitate close working between buyers and suppliers, and include order urgency, product application, and order size.

Urgency of order fulfilment   Routine or emergency nature of buying will determine the supplier's capability of meeting requirements.

Product application   How the product is to be used; for instance in the case of a critical component, customers will want guarantees from suppliers that it will be repaired or replaced within a specified time.

Size of order   Automated assembly lines have different requirements from manually-operated assembly lines.

Buyers' Personal Characteristics

Although B2B buying is done in organizational contexts, buying decisions are made by individuals working in them. That is why B2B vendors must keep into account the personal characteristics of those involved in the purchase process. These can form the basis of segmenting industrial markets.

People involved   Suppliers of industrial goods can often segment markets on the basis of individuals involved in the purchase process. Some buyers are risk averse and want reliable suppliers.

Cost versus quality   While some buyers are cost focused and try to save every rupee they can, others insist on buying high quality. Suppliers will be able to segment customers on this basis as well.

CB IN ACTION   What Would You Do?

As the purchase manager of a major apparel brand, you are in charge of sourcing materials and processes from around the world. The company looks for cost reduction and achieving economies. It wants to outsource the task of stitching clothes to factories in poor countries because it can get the job done at a fraction of the expense in its home country. After careful search, you zero in on some suppliers that have given very competitive offers. The samples that they have submitted are perfectly matched to your purchasing objectives. They have passed the technical and financial criteria set by the company.

At the same time, you are also aware that such suppliers have pathetic labour conditions and operate in dangerous buildings. On 24 April 2013, a factory in Bangladesh had collapsed, killing 1129 people. The factory was reported to be supplying goods to some of the best-known brands in the world. Though the brands had promised to make their sourcing safer, nothing much had happened on the ground. The suppliers assure you that nothing will happen, and that such conditions are common in that country. Further, any improvements in the work conditions will result in higher pricing for your firm.

You know that you and your company are protected by law. Since you neither own the factories nor employ the workers directly, you cannot be prosecuted.

1. As you are already under pressure by your company to reduce costs, what will you do under the circumstances? Do you face any danger?
2. How far can companies control the conditions at the factories owned by their suppliers? Can and should they do so?

UNDERSTANDING B2B BUYING BEHAVIOUR

As can be expected, B2B buying behaviour will depend on the segments, types of products, and the purchase process of each company. Further, an analysis of B2B buying behaviour will depend on two major determinants:

Individual determinants Motives of the people who are in the buying process

Organizational determinants Types of B2B customers, buying situations, and buying differences

Individual Determinants

While the B2B buying is more rational, methodical, and objective than consumer buying, the purchase process is handled by humans. Though emotions play less of a role and managers look for solving problems, individual psychology is also a factor to be considered. That is why it is important to study the motives of individual mangers. Some personal motives that affect the purchase manager are as follows:

- Fear of loss to the company if a purchase decision is bad
- Fear of losing the job and personal reputation
- Desire to reduce cost and contribute to profits of the company

On a personal level, the B2B buyer has a personal fear of loss of professional credibility and the desire to succeed and be recognized within his/her organization. The emotional process a B2B buyer goes through is very different from a B2C purchaser. Clearly, purchasing a pair of shoes has fewer consequences than buying a machine costing several lakh of rupees with the company's money.

Buying motives for industrial goods were described by Copeland (1924) after studying B2B advertisements in business publications. These motives, which are as follows, remain true even today.

Economy Every company seeks economy in the use of materials. One of the major buying motives of B2B goods is that the materials are economical in terms of saving time, eliminating wastage, as well as reducing operating expenses and maintenance costs. At the same time, the supplier should help in reducing inventory, and the purchase should also result in the economical use of space and power.

Protection against loss Companies look for suppliers who will help them avoid the embarrassment of things going wrong, simply because the market does not forgive mistakes. Lawsuits resulting from manufacturing faults or shortcomings have increased, so companies have a zero tolerance for supplier mistakes.

Productivity enhancement Most purchases for industrial machinery and equipments are done with a purpose of increasing productivity and efficiency. For instance, enhancing productivity is one of the chief buying motives for software and IT equipment. B2B sellers must therefore think from the point of view of buyers and help them boost productivity of their operations. Working closely with customers is thus an imperative in B2B situations.

Flexibility Since new product cycles have shortened, manufacturing companies do not want to be saddled with useless machinery. Thus, they look for flexible systems that can be used in a variety of products. Machines must be versatile and capable of being adapted to handle a variety of jobs, and supply chains should be flexible to match fluctuations in demand.

In addition, the B2B buyer also looks for dependability in supplies, as explained earlier, because disruptions in the supply chains are usually very costly for companies and will reflect badly on the purchase manager.

Whitney (2011) explains the behaviours of B2B buyers and sellers as 'doing more with less as a new normal'. Companies look for vendors who can take up tasks that are not their core competencies. 'Apart from zero tolerance for mistakes, companies also look for warranties that never end and vendors who lock in training or other support', he writes.

In a study of organizational buying behaviour in Nigeria, Ebitu, et al. (2012) found that the organizational buyer is largely rational in his choice and motivated by budgetary considerations such as profit goals, expense quotas, and cost–benefit guidelines. The buyer has to justify his purchases on the basis of measurable performance. The variables which influence the buyer's decision are quality, service, and price.

Organizational Determinants

As discussed, organizational determinants include types of B2B customers, buying situations, and buying differences.

Types of B2B Customers

Organizational determinants of B2B purchase behaviour vary with different types of customers. Broadly, there are three types of buyers—commercial, government, and institutions (see Fig. 4.8).

Commercial Enterprises

Commercial enterprises consist of companies buying plant and machineries, raw materials, and office supplies for their production process.

User An industrial user is a company that buys goods for its own use or to use in its manufacturing process. Industrial usage is marked by bulk consumption. The use of chemicals and oils by companies is in the category of industrial use. A paper manufacturer, for instance, may sell in bulk to printing companies, that are classified as industrial users. Users normally enter into long-term contracts with their suppliers.

Original equipment manufacturer An original equipment manufacturer (OEM) is a company that supplies equipment or parts to other companies to resell or build into another product, and sell it under the buying company's brand name. For instance, components such as bulbs, electrical, and mechanical parts will be bought by a car manufacturing company such as Maruti from OEMs and used in their cars. When consumers buy these parts, they will buy it under the brand name 'Maruti Genuine Parts' (www.mgp.co.in). Similarly, a company owning a well-known brand name may buy a complete television or refrigerator from an OEM and market it under its own name. Original equipment manufacturers must work closely with the companies they are supplying to and operate almost as if they were a branch of the company.

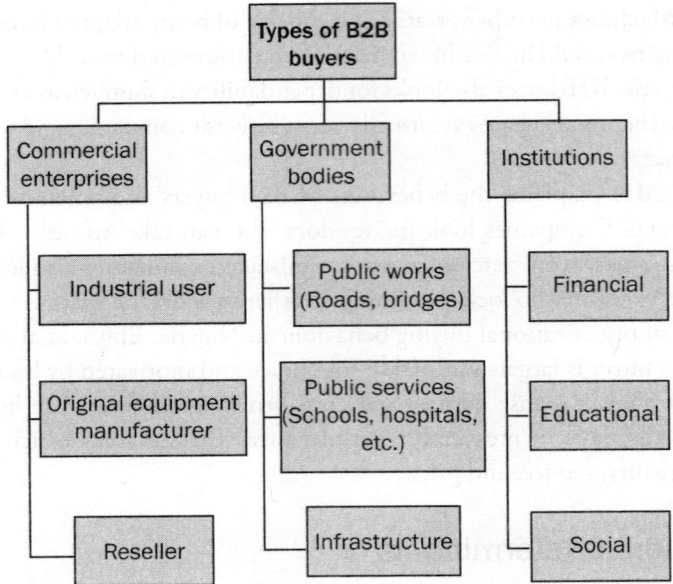

FIG. 4.8 Types of B2B buyers

Reseller A reseller is a company or individual that purchases goods or services with the intention of reselling them rather than consuming them or using them. There are two types of resellers: first, one who simply sells the goods without making any changes in them; and second, one who enhances the product by providing additional products or services. The latter is known as a value-added reseller (VAR), who buys the goods, adds value to them, and sells it again. For example, dealers of computers add value to the machines by loading the desired software, without which the machine would be worthless to the consumer. They also add value by bundling them with printers and power supplies, or by adding after-sales service. Resellers are independent agents who obtain materials from various sources and provide integrated services to their customers.

Government Bodies

The Government is a major B2B buyer for building and maintaining public works, providing public services, building infrastructure, and public sector buying.

Government bodies such as hospitals, schools, and services such as railways, public utilities, mining contracts, telecom contracts too, buy a wide variety of goods from companies. This is called business-to-government (B2G) buying. The process of purchase by governments is different in different countries, as it depends on a system of tendering.

Buying through Tenders

The government, or large public sector organizations invite companies to send offers, or tenders, through an open advertisement in a newspaper, website, or a notice circulated to them. Many companies are invited to participate in the tendering process after which the tenders are evaluated on some criteria and then one or more companies are selected for order placement.

The process starts when a requisition or an indent is received from the user department. This requirement is either advertised or sent to a panel of suppliers. They are asked to send their offers by a given date and time, which is called the tender opening date. Interested suppliers respond to the tender enquiry by giving their offers, mentioning quality, price, date of delivery, etc. Tenders received by the organization are opened on the tender opening date at the fixed time.

The tenders are then evaluated on the basis of financial and technical capability. Some tenders may be rejected at this stage if they do not meet the requirements on some parameters. Sometimes the suppliers may also be invited for negotiations. After this stage, the tenders found suitable are evaluated on the basis of price. The supplier who matches both the quality and price requirements is given the order. While some organizations lay great emphasis on quality, others place emphasis on lowest price. In many government organizations, price usually becomes the most important factor for placing orders.

Government tenders are available on various sites. The website http://tenders.gov.in/ has current and archived tenders, and http://tenders.indiamart.com/ has information on the latest tenders. Some other sites for tenders are http://www.tendertiger.com/ and http://www.tendersinfo.com/.

Tenders are of various kinds. A *global tender* is advertised to invite offers from suppliers situated anywhere in the world. It is raised when the requirement is very large, or when a wider choice of quality is sought for. Another reason for a global tender is to break a cartel among known vendors.

An *open tender* also invites offers from suppliers, but its reach is limited to within a country. Such tenders are printed in domestic newspapers or trade journals in a country.

E-tendering is uploading the tender online on a government website.

A *limited tender* is issued when the enquiry is limited to a selected few vendors. In this case, the vendors are well known to the purchaser. The purchasing organization maintains a list of approved suppliers to whom limited tenders are sent.

A *single tender enquiry* is made when the value of goods is small or in the case of proprietary goods, that is, where only one supplier exists. For example, maintaining of a machine can only be done by a vendor who is authorized by the original producer. In such cases, a single tender enquiry is issued.

Institutional Buying

Institutional sales are made in bulk to financial, educational, and social institutions.

Financial Institutional sales in the financial industry are made by large brokerage houses or mutual funds, such as private placements and initial public offerings of stock for companies. Institutional sales are usually reserved for high-net-worth clients and are not open to the average investor.

Educational Purchases made by schools, colleges, and universities are institutional sales. Such institutes buy books in bulk, photocopiers and other machines, food and related services, and place maintenance contracts. These sales are important for suppliers as they are in bulk and are long-term in nature.

Social Many non-profit social bodies and non-government organizations (NGOs) purchase supplies, food, educational materials, and so on, for distribution to the poor. They use a charity model and seek to build relationships and partnerships. This is also B2B buying but at the same time the parties try to inject social value into their buying decisions.

BUYING SITUATIONS AND BUYING BEHAVIOUR

Organizations exhibit different types of buyer behaviour, which depends on buying situations. Buying behaviour varies not only on the basis of how critical the goods are, but also how products and services are bought. Kaplan and Sawhney (2000) show that companies can either engage in systematic sourcing or in spot sourcing. *Systematic sourcing* involves long-term negotiated contracts with qualified suppliers. Such contracts depend on supplier reliability and develop into relationships. In *spot sourcing*, the company has an immediate need and looks for sources at the lowest possible cost. Commodity trading for oil, steel, and energy, exemplifies this approach. Spot transactions are done for commodities and do not involve long-term relationships.

Buying Situations

Buyer behaviour will also differ according to buying situations. Reeder, et al. (1991) describe three buying situations: new task buying, modified rebuy, and straight rebuy (see Fig. 4.9).

New Task Buying

The situation in which an organization buys something it has not bought before, is called a new task buying situation. This may happen if it wants to diversify, that is, add a new product line which requires new equipment, parts, or materials. In such a situation, the managers of the company lack experience and product knowledge to evaluate the goods to be purchased. They have to educate themselves about the new materials from various sources.

Modified Rebuy

In this situation, the buying organization makes modifications and improvements to existing materials and may continue to buy from an existing vendor or may commission another to supply them. According to Jobber and Lancaster (2000), modified rebuys often involve engineers, production managers, and purchasing officers with little involvement from the top management.

Straight Rebuy

This is the most common buying situation. In most scenarios, companies want the same raw materials to continue their production. Such purchases are routine or recurring, and usually little or no additional information is required by the purchaser. The suppliers have been evaluated and tested, and they simply have to be informed to make deliveries.

Hassan, et al. (2010) conducted a study in Malaysia to determine the factors affecting decision-making for purchase of industrial goods in a manufacturing company. They found that companies were satisfied with the supplies and there was a low intention to change the current suppliers. The results from the study indicate that in new task buying

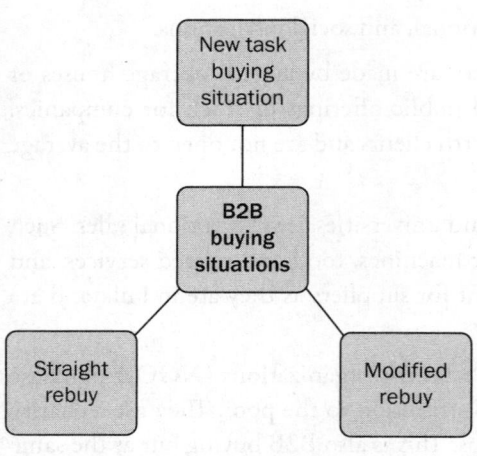

FIG. 4.9 B2B buying situations

and modified rebuy situations, the most significant reason for the buying decision was product performance. In a new task buying situation, product demonstration was the most important. In modified rebuy situations, the ability of sales representatives to convince buyers of the higher value provided by their offering, was the most significant strategy. The engineering team played the dominant influencer's role, both in product and supplier selection in the two buying situations.

Quayle (2001) found, interestingly enough, that the main factors that led to the switching of suppliers were continuity of supply, achieving price reduction, and security of supply. Items such as lead time, item price, competition, market protection, and purchasing power were not found to be significant.

Total cost of ownership (TCO) is the sum of total direct and indirect costs of a product or system. It includes cost of acquisition and operating costs of an asset. A TCO analysis is used to gauge the viability of any capital investment.

Buying Centre

A buying centre or a decision-making unit (DMU) is a group of employees of an organization or a formal committee responsible for making purchases. Unlike in consumer buying, where the consumer, alone or with an influencer makes his or her own purchase decisions, in business buying, a group is involved in purchase decisions. Business-to-business suppliers have to understand the purchase process of the company they are selling to, and the people involved. They have to understand the different committee members and their objectives. For instance, while the production manager looks for a machine that is easy to operate, the finance manager will look for efficiencies and savings.

Business-to-business purchases involve input from various parts of the organization, including technical, finance, purchasing, and senior management. Highly technical purchases, such as buying a new machine or software, require the involvement of senior management as well. For low-value items, senior management may not be involved. The buying centre is usually a formal group from different departments. The business buying centres have people who play the following roles:

Initiator The employee of the company who starts the purchase process by expressing a need is the initiator. For example, an operator working on a machine becomes an initiator when he/she expresses a requirement for a particular tool, or a photocopy attendant will become the initiator when he/she informs that the paper has run out.

Decider The person who exercises formal or informal power to select the supplier is the decider. In the previous example, the supervisor will have the power to decide which tool is required or the type of paper most suitable.

Decision-maker The person who makes or approves the final decision is the decision-maker. This could be the purchase or finance manager.

Gatekeeper People who control the flow of information to individuals in an organization are gatekeepers. These could be secretaries or managers who have had bad experiences with a supplier in the past.

Influencer People who define specifications and provide information for sourcing are influencers. Their inputs will determine what kind of vendor is selected. Influencers could be the company's own employees or outside consultants. They may include users, safety departments, store or finance managers, or even the wife of the boss.

Purchasing agent/buyer   The buyer is the person who makes the purchase order and contacts suppliers. A purchasing agent seeks bids, negotiates, and places orders.

Controller   The person who oversees the budget for the purchase is the controller.

User   People who will actually use the product or service in the organization are users.

Bonoma (1982) explains that each party in the buying process plays subtle roles. The B2B salesman must identify the people playing the aforementioned roles in an organization. Human psychology plays a role, because organizations do not buy, people do. In the purchase of a corporate jet, for example, it would be important to find the 'kid inside the CEO and excite him with the raw beauty of the plane'. The pilot, however, could stop the purchase by giving his opinion about plane safety and acts as the gatekeeper. Thus, the supplier's salesman must combine individual and group dynamics to predict and influence the DMU.

Influencing the people in the buying centre is easy if the B2B supplier is able to create a set of positive attributes and build a brand. Since customers look for dependability and reliability, B2B brands can be built around these and other attributes.

ROLE OF B2B BRANDS

Business-to-business brands such as IBM, Cisco, Oracle, and Intel have managed to build substantial equity and today feature amongst the most valuable brands globally. Bendixen, et al. (2004) found that B2B buyers are willing to pay a price premium for brands that offer high brand equity.

An analysis by Bondesson (2012) reveals that brand loyalty and price premium are determined by different brand image elements. He found that company reputation, service relationship, and business solutions mainly build brand loyalty, whereas price premium is built by dependability.

Kotler and Pfoertsch (2006) list the roles of brands in B2B situations.

Differentiation   Products that are undifferentiated can be 'de-commoditized' by B2B suppliers, which leads to better prices for sellers and dependability for buyers.

Long-term survival   Brands help to get future business and thereby make it easier for the company to survive. The writers give the example of Caterpillar and Komatsu. There were many companies in the heavy machinery category in Japan, but these were the only two that survived. Strong B2B brands help withstand crises.

Brand loyalty   Brands succeed in shifting transaction-based selling to relationship-based selling in B2B markets.

Barriers for competition   Brands create barriers for others who wish to enter. Buyers exhibit strong brand preference that serves as a barrier for others.

Price premium   Dependable suppliers can command a price premium for their products and services. By creating an in-flight monitoring system, for instance, Rolls-Royce was able to command a premium for its engines, as shown in the chapter-opening case study.

Creating B2B brands helps companies, as they are able to depend on their suppliers. The buyer increases sales and prevents others from entry, which leads to survival in the long run. It is a successful strategy, as several B2B brands find themselves in the 'Superbrands' category even in the steel industry (see Exhibit 4.1).

Business-to-business branding significantly reduces the consumer buying process. In order to create brands, B2B suppliers must think from very first point of engagement to the point the buyer becomes a customer. It is important to think in terms what the buyer needs, as was successfully

EXHIBIT 4.1 Steel Superbrands

Steel is a B2B commodity about which buyers are not particularly brand aware or loyal. This exhibit describes how Tata Steel was able to establish its own brands even in a strictly B2B market like steel. Starting with the signature line 'Tata Steel—Values Stronger Than Steel', the company tried to establish an image of assurance, reliability, and a superior brand experience. It also realigned operating strategy to enhance customer satisfaction and relationships. It took up the following initiatives to develop its brands:

- Tata Steel implemented its vehicle tracking system (VTS) in 2002 with about 1600 vehicles mounted with the global positioning system (GPS) deployed by transport partners. It was the largest implementation of a GPS-enabled fleet in the steel industry, fulfilling a customer need to track inventories and updates on delivery dates.
- A billboard was created online to track vehicles, again a first in India, to improve customer service.
- Infrastructure was developed at hubs and stock yards to reduce service claims.
- To create service differentiation, an auto-compliant hub was developed in Chennai.
- Standard operating procedures were introduced for receipt, storage, handling, and delivery of steel materials at all stock points.
- Transport parks in Jamshedpur were created to ease traffic flow and educate all drivers on safety and health concerns. About 2000 drivers undergo medical check-up at Tata Steel facilities every month (see Figs 4.10 and 4.11).

In an attempt to 'de-commoditize' steel, the company introduced several branded steel products. Dutt (2003) writes that Tata Steel's brands help shield it from radical price fluctuations. Even if spot

FIG. 4.10 Tata Tiscon steels
Courtesy: Superbrands

FIG. 4.11 Tata Steel Plant
Courtesy: Superbrands

prices soften, the brand can still sell at the same price. Moving from commodities to brands, Tata Steel has become the first company in the world to sell cold rolled (CR) strips under the brand name Tata Steelium. The brand established itself in a fragmented market in which a host of players caters to the needs of white goods manufacturers. Tata Steel has three generic brands and three product brands. The generic brands are Tata Bearings, Tata Pipes, and Tata Agrico. The product brands are Tata Shaktee sheets, Tata Tiscon rebars, and Tata Steelium strips. Tata Steel's other brands are as follows:

(Contd)

EXHIBIT 4.1 (Contd)

Astrum It is a brand in the hot-rolled products range for the SME segment. HR coils and sheets are used in the automotive, earth moving equipment, railways, fabrication, construction, and industrial machinery segments.

Galvano Galvanized plain steel used for products such as white goods, panels, and bus bodies is sold under the brand name Galvano.

Agrico Agricultural implements with brand name Tata Agrico, are used in agriculture, horticulture, maintenance of roads, dams, railway tracks, collieries, etc. The products are manufactured with ISO:9002 certification.

Bearings Tata Bearings is the brand for bearings and auto assemblies. It is one of the largest bearing manufacturers in India.

Pipes Tata Pipes is the flagship brand of the tubes division. Tata Pipes dominates in the plumbing, irrigation, industrial, and fire-fighting segments.

Shaktee The Tata Shaktee brand sells galvanized corrugated (GC) sheets. Stores called 'Shaktee Sansar' were opened to service B2B buyers in 2009–10 to sell the GC sheets.

Steelium A brand of the flat products division of Tata Steel, it assures the customer of the genuineness of the product. Exclusive retail stores of Tata Steelium CR coils and sheets called 'Steeliumzone' were opened and customer relationship-building programmes were undertaken to increase market share.

Structura Tata Structura hollow steel sections are used for structures and are preferred by architects in applications such as space frames, staircases, roofs, trusses, purlins, and portal frames.

Tiscon Tata Tiscon is used in residential and project construction. Tata Tiscon forms an unbreakable bond with cement, laying a strong foundation for building construction. It has been rated as a 'Superbrand'.

Wiron Steel wires are sold under the brand name Tata Wiron and used by industries such as automobile, infrastructure, power, and general engineering. The brand is established in the markets of Europe, USA, West Asia, Australasia, South Asia and the Far East.

Silicomag It is the country's first branded silico manganese for the steel sector.

Is it easier to create B2B brands than B2C brands? What are the differences between brands in these two buying situations?

Sources:
Dutt, Ishita Ayan, 'We also brand steel', http://www.rediff.com/money/2003/may/03spec1.htm.
http://www.tatashaktee.com/.
http://www.tatasteelindia.com/corporate/innovations/marketing-innovations-brands.asp.
http://www.tatatiscon.co.in/tata_steel.php.
'Tata Steel unveils brand to tap Rs 3,000 cr silico manganese market', *Business Standard*, 12 July 2013.
All websites last accessed on 10 July 2013.
Business Superbrands 2011.

done by Tata Steel branding, as shown in Exhibit 4.1. Having a short-term sales mindset ignores the buyer's needs and leaves the door wide open for competitors. Hitting a prospect with a sales pitch will simply alienate leads; purchasers tend to get put off by pushy marketing.

Suppliers must develop marketing materials for customers at each stage of the buying cycle and distribute them at the relevant time, through an automated marketing system. Not only is the B2B buying cycle longer, it is also more complex. It is not a linear process; instead B2B customers move back and forth in their decision cycle. This means marketers have to develop a marketing campaign that guides them through the buying cycle, helping with their buying decisions as much as possible.

Suppliers must keep track of requirements likely to arise and make their presence felt among purchase managers. They must anticipate the queries that are likely to be raised and provide valuable content that suits the technical, financial, and economic departments. Trade magazines, fairs and events, and online presence is essential. Above all, they must maintain a reputation of dependability in their industries because the purchase managers will seek testimonials from each other.

An important aspect is the close relationship that suppliers develop with their customers. They have to operate as if they are almost part of the companies they are supplying to. This aspect is discussed in the next section.

Customer Satisfaction in B2B Markets

Chakraborty, et al. (2007) conducted a survey of business customers of a manufacturer of hydraulic and pneumatic equipment and found reliability was the most important aspect in B2B purchases. They found that commercial aspects were important for respondents from the purchasing department, while for participants from engineering, maintenance, and production, product-related information was found to be more important than commercial aspects.

Bendixen, et al. (2004) found quality was the most desirable attribute in B2B transactions, followed by reliability, performance, after-sales service, ease of operation, ease of maintenance, price, supplier's reputation, and the relationship with the supplier's personnel.

Webster and Keller (2004) write that business-to-business buyers are different from consumer buyers in that they are profit motivated and budget constrained.

Rossomme (2003) writes that the following are the aspects of customer satisfaction that are important in B2B markets:

Information satisfaction This refers to the satisfaction of the buyer with respect to the information provided by the seller, that is, whether the sales literature was authentic and whether it helped in making the purchase decision.

EXHIBIT 4.2 Amadeus: Building a B2B Brand

Amadeus India Private Limited provides a global platform to the Indian Travel industry by enabling access to state of the art travel automation technology. The company was established with the objective of providing IT and software services, developing software products and automated tools, for the travel trade industry including customized software products for travel agents and travel service providers. With systems and software solutions to simplify travel management, Amadeus India provides complete IT-enabled services for the travel and tourism industry.

A B2B brand, Amadeus engages with Amadeus's stakeholders in multifarious ways. It works closely with internal stakeholders to ensure that up-to-date corporate information is packaged into brochures, presentations, multimedia channels, and other print materials for external public.

Besides traditional methods, the company targets its customers through the Internet, social networking sites, and mobile marketing initiatives. It also runs many collateral programmes like road shows to communicate with travel agents and corporations. Through these, it updates them on the company's latest products and offerings.

FIG. 4.12 Amadeus using mobile services
Courtesy: Superbrands

Television, national newspapers, trade magazines, financial newspapers, outdoors, exhibitions, websites, direct mailers, promotional films and videos, and other conventional as well as non-conventional media to reach out and touch its target audience. Please see Fig. 4.12.

Source: Superbrands 2012

Performance satisfaction   This occurs when the buyer is satisfied with the performance of the equipment or raw materials.

Attribute satisfaction   This is felt when the product attributes, for example, the method of handling of a raw material that affects the quality, texture, and feel of the finished product, meet the expectations of the buyer.

Personal satisfaction   This refers to the individual psychological judgments of the managers of the buying organization that helps in building relationships with the suppliers.

Please see Exhibit 4.2.

B2B E-MARKETPLACE

An e-marketplace is a location on the Internet where companies can obtain or disseminate information, engage in transactions, or work together in some way. Most of the e-marketplaces provide two basic functions: they allow companies to obtain new suppliers or buyers for company products, and aid in developing streamlined trading networks that make negotiating, settlement, and delivery more efficient. Currently e-marketplaces exist in many different industries.

E-marketplaces can be structured in several different ways. One structure of a marketplace is like that of eBay, where the market maker is neither a buyer or seller, but is a neutral third party. Other e-marketplaces are set up as a consortium of sellers that leverage their combined power to efficiently sell their products to buyers. Buyers can also set up a marketplace to reduce their costs and obtain better purchasing terms. An example of this type of marketplace is Covisant, run by the automobile industry. Moreover, large buyers can set up another type of marketplace, a private marketplace, for their supplier networks.

In order for a site to fall into the category of an e-marketplace, the site needs be open to multiple buyers and sellers and needs to provide one or more commerce-related functions. These functions include: forward or reverse auctions, vendor catalogues, fixed price ordering, trading exchange functionality, bulletin boards/wanted ads, and RFQ, RFI, or RFP capability. Successful e-marketplaces can deliver significant value to their users or members and are profitable.

For spot sourcing, where the need is immediate, e-commerce comes in useful. E-marketplaces aggregate goods from a number of sources and exhibit them on their websites. Industry-wise classification is done. The idea is to bring a number of buyers and sellers together.

Kaplan and Sawhney (2000) explain: 'Web markets expand the choices available to buyers, give sellers access to new customers, and reduce transaction costs for all the players'. The e-hubs not only list the products of suppliers, but also verify them and provide a guarantee to suppliers, for which they charge a commission. They can easily scale and grow their operations. Zhao, et al. (2010) also write that e-hubs create value by aggregating and matching buyers and sellers, creating marketplace liquidity, and reducing transaction costs.

B2B RELATIONSHIPS

As we have seen earlier, the B2B marketplace has few customers, but their requirements are large and regular. This implies that suppliers develop relationships over time with their client

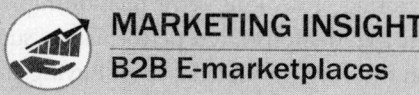

MARKETING INSIGHT
B2B E-marketplaces

E-marketplaces or B2B portals are companies that bring together businesses and provide valuable services like streamlined networks to enable companies to take buying decisions. They do not sell directly to customers, but are enablers of bulk buying.

Without these, in the past, buyers and sellers had great difficulty in locating suitable suppliers or buyers, sometimes located in different countries. They relied on trade fairs and trade publications, but the smaller suppliers could not be located through these methods. Apart from this, they had no way of knowing the credentials of distant suppliers except for travelling to those countries and meeting the suppliers themselves. Now B2B sites help in e-procurement that is, businesses sourcing bulk items from suppliers located anywhere in the world. Sites verify the credentials of registered suppliers and buyers, and both the offers as well as requirements are put up on the portal. This lowers communication as well as search costs. For small manufacturers, e-marketplaces lower marketing costs since they are a simple way of becoming known to potential buyers wherever they may exist.

Portals exist for sourcing electronics, chemicals, engineering goods, dairy and agricultural products, construction material, and practically anything and everything. They also help in increasing trade among countries (see Table 4.2).

B2B portals have simplified industrial sourcing of products and have helped exporters and importers in a very big way. Earlier buyers had no means of knowing about suppliers in other countries except for trade directories, but B2B portals like www.alibaba.com offer information about audited suppliers and also a host of services that aid in international trade.

How are B2B portals different from B2C portals? What extra services do they provide? Take a look at some e-marketplaces and describe their services.

TABLE 4.2 Some B2B e-marketplaces and the industries they serve

B2B e-market	Industry	Service	Special features
Made-from-india.com	All industries and products from India	Helps find buyers and sellers abroad	Large number of products and categories
Trade4goods.com	Most industries and products	Helps find buyers and sellers	Large number of products and categories
Indiabizclub.com	Furniture, plastics, jewellery, etc.	Alphabetical listing of products	Has city-wise business clubs
Tradeindia.com	All industries and products	Billed as 'India's largest B2B marketplace'	Buying and selling leads are posted regularly
Alibaba.com	All industries and products	'Global trade starts here'	Connects buyers and suppliers from all over the world

Source: Kumar (2012)

companies. Word-of-mouth publicity is very important in such situations and mass advertising does not work.

The B2B buying manager also does not disrupt the company's supply chains by experimenting with new suppliers. Companies thus want to enter into long-term contracts, which enhance the need for relationships. Ford, et al. (2002) found 88 per cent of B2B relationships to be greater than five years old.

Hutt and Speh (2010) write that developing and nurturing close, long-term relationships is an important goal for the business supplier. Built on trust and demonstrated performance, such strategic partnerships require open lines of communication between multiple layers of buying and selling organizations. The authors explain that B2B sourcing is increasingly emphasizing relationship management skills because these skills reside in people rather than in organizational structures.

The research conducted by Cater and Cater (2009) on customer–supplier relationships found that satisfaction and loyalty is negatively affected by price and positively by delivery performance, supplier know-how, and personal interaction.

Wilson and Mollar (2013) describe the relationships as based on commitment, satisfaction, and establishing social and structural bonds as follows:

- Commitment or dedication to the continuance of the relationship
- Satisfaction or degree of positive effect associated with a relationship
- Social bonds or the strength of the relationship between buyer and seller, including self-disclosure and concern for the welfare of the other
- Structural bonds or economic and social factors that develop during the relationship, creating contractual or investment barriers

Managing B2B Relationships

Relationship variables such as cooperation, trust, and long-term commitment are positively associated with business performance. Lambert and Knemeyer (2004) write that B2B relationships should have a sense of mutuality of shared purpose and perspective. 'It helps the organizations move beyond a zero-sum mentality and respect the spirit of partnership, even if the earnings of one partner are under pressure.' This will extend to a willingness to integrate systems or share financial information. The best partnership type, according to the authors, is when each company views the other as an extension of itself.

Narayandas (2005) writes that the benefits of customer loyalty are enormous in B2B markets. Companies benefit by entering into long-term, individual relationships with most customers in business markets. Consumer marketing solutions do not work since each customer uses machines and materials differently. Almost every B2B customer needs a customized product, quantity, or price. Each segment effectively consists of one customer. These 'segments of one' render mass marketing techniques expensive and ineffectual. Supplying companies have to communicate to each customer directly. The relationships are based on benefits that are delivered rather than attributes. The question that B2B suppliers answer is: How does our product helps solve your specific problems?', rather than commenting on the superiority of their products.

The following basics of good relationships apply in B2B markets:

Cooperation When independent parties work together, common objectives are achieved only if there is cooperation and coordination among them. Business-to-business buyers and suppliers are integrated systems, sharing information fully.

Trust The basis of all relationships is trust. Very often B2B partners make investments in technology, supply chains, storage, or IT, and partners will do so only if they believe they will not be exploited. The parties involved have to reduce opportunistic behaviour.

CB IN ACTION   What Would You Do?

Tata Motors had planned to set up the Tata Nano factory in Singur, West Bengal. A number of ancillary units of the company moved in along with the company and invested in land and buildings. Most of these 23 ancillary units had nearly completed the construction work on the project site. These units included Amtek Auto, JBM Auto, Bosch, Rasandik Engineering, Lucas TVS, Lumax Industries, Caparo Engineering, Rico Auto, Sona Kayo Steering, Tata Ryerson, Tata Toyo, Tata Johnson, Rane Madras, Sharda Motors, and Supreme Treves.

However, in October 2008 Tata Motors announced that it would relocate its Nano car project from Singur to Sanand in Gujarat over concerns of the continuing agitation by the Trinamool Congress. Not only did the company lose a huge amount of money, but the ancillary suppliers too, found their investment going waste. Some of these were small units, and the blow was severe.

1. What should the company have done in this situation?
2. How could the situation have been salvaged?

Power   Business-to-business partners often have power. Buyers can delay, or cancel their payments or purchase orders, while sellers can delay their supplies to exercise power. Responsible use of power will ensure good relationships.

Long-term orientation   As mentioned earlier, B2B relationships are long-term. It is not easy to change suppliers or vendors. Both buyers and suppliers must make long-term commitments with respect to each other.

Dependency   Relationships are marked by dependency: suppliers keep the production lines fed, while they in turn depend on timely payments. Dependence between the buyers and suppliers increases the level of commitment.

Bonding   Long-term relationships result in ties that bind. The ties are usually economic and strategic, but social bonds also result from a long-term association.

Lages, et al. (2008) have developed the B2B relationship performance (RELPERF) scale that reflects the performance of a buyer–supplier relationship marketing process at a specific point in time. This scale is composed of five dimensions: (a) relationship policies and practices, (b) trust, (c) relationship commitment, (d) mutual cooperation, and (e) relationship satisfaction. The authors write that these five dimensions are key ingredients of a relationship process and loyalty.

The relationships can be managed formally by customer relationship management (CRM), which is a system for managing a company's interactions with current and future customers, including methodologies, software, and Internet capabilities that help it to manage customer relationships. Rigby and Ledingham (2004) show that extending the CRM system in two directions—upstream links to suppliers and downstream links to customers—integrates the supply chain to match supply and demand.

While B2B encourages relationships, there are, however, dangers of such relationships becoming too cosy, to the detriment of both buying and supplying organizations. As deal sizes are very high, bribes and kickbacks are common. The bribes given to doctors by pharmaceutical companies to prescribe their pills to unsuspecting patients are described in the end-chapter case study. The ethical issues are discussed in the Ethical Insight box.

ETHICAL INSIGHT
Ethical Issues in B2B Buying

Ethical issues frequently crop up in B2B buying because companies sometimes use lobbying techniques or outright bribery to get business contracts.

Sarin (2012) writes that 90 per cent of the unaccounted money in India is generated from B2B buying and selling. This is reflected in hiring of transporters, petty civil contractors, imports of machinery and raw materials, the approval of suppliers, and the inspection of products before they are dispatched. No matter what the area of business, one finds 'ingenious ways and means used to give and take bribes. *India Today* (2013) reports that the money stashed in Swiss banks by Indian clients at the end of 2010 was 1.42 billion Swiss francs (about ₹9,000 crore).

Transparency International's 2011 Bribe Payers Survey reports that companies from China and Russia are perceived to be most likely to engage in bribery abroad. Some of the findings of the report are as follows:

- Clear evidence of bribery between private companies, and this is just as common as bribery between firms and public officials
- There has been no improvement since the Bribe Payers Index published in 2008
- The perceived likelihood of companies from a given country to bribe abroad is closely related to the level of business integrity at home, and the perceptions of corruption in the public sector of that country
- Bribery is perceived to occur in all business sectors, but is seen as most common in the public works contracts and construction sector

India has seen more than its share of scandals relating to B2B purchases. The government has been involved in coal and telecom scandals, and construction projects are routinely accompanied by allegations of corruption. In much of the government, construction work is done with the sole purpose of extracting government funds. Companies too are vulnerable. While multinational companies are controlled by strict laws at home, domestic companies in emerging markets and the public sector have no such controls and continue to accept and give bribes for B2B transactions. This works against consumer interest in terms of increased prices and substandard goods; in some cases as in medicines, people are made to consume medicines that they do not need (see end-chapter case study).

Countries have struggled to control corruption. Some have enacted strict laws and others have tried to control it through policing. Nevertheless, B2B fraud is here to stay, and better systems and ethical human beings are the only means of tackling it.

How can companies deal with the very real problem of corruption in B2B buying?

CB IN ACTION   What Would You Do?

You are the sales representative of a supplier of machine tools to manufacturing units. The company is a multinational that has headquarters in USA, which has strong anti-bribery laws.

In recent years, the company has faced stiff competition from local machine tool manufacturers. Though your products are recognized to be of good quality, you have lost a number of orders because the local manufacturers are able to supply the tools at a much cheaper price than your company. Both you and your sales manager are under pressure to increase sales. There are rumours of lay-offs in case the company cannot increase orders.

In one negotiation with a company, the purchase agent promises to give you the annual contract provided you pay for the holiday of some senior executives in the company. The contract is worth a large amount and the cost of the holiday is less than 1% of the contract value. You convey this to the sales manager who agrees to the arrangement provided the deal is kept under wraps because both of you could lose your jobs if found out.

What would you do in the present situation?

CONCLUSION

Though consumer marketing dominates most marketing thought, understanding B2B behaviour is important because it can result in huge savings for companies and also improve marketing efficiency. Describing the savings affected at Whirlpool, Slone (2004) writes that by integrating trade partners, the company was able to improve product availability and attain an order fill rate of over 96 per cent. Finished goods inventory went down, and freight and warehouse productivity also improved. Among other things, Whirlpool identified trade partner priorities and implemented system-to-system transactions, connecting the company and partners computers. Not only were the transactions streamlined, but partners could also check availability of stocks and place orders accordingly.

Companies indeed benefit when trade partners are able to predict demand better and share it with the company, and this information results in better manufacturing schedules, and less obsolete inventory write-offs. Indeed, if companies were able to understand partner psychology better, they could make their supply chains much more efficient. However, as Narayanan and Raman (2004) write, 'Engineers—not psychologists—build supply networks'. If companies want better B2B transactions leading to huge savings from manufacturing to manufacturing, they need to introduce psychology into their supply chains as well.

SUMMARY

Consumer marketing and B2B marketing—commercial transactions between businesses—are quite different. Business-to-business buying behaviour is not a homogenous behaviour and has to be studied from different perspectives. Business-to-business transactions are a result of derived demand, that is, it follows consumer demand.

Business-to-business buying drivers are reliability, dependability, flexibility, and transparency. The buying is done on technical and economic criteria, and seldom on emotions. A manager's motives in B2B transactions are fear of loss to the company, fear of loss of reputation, and desire to reduce cost and contribute to profits of the company. Managers will thus look for economy, protection against loss, and productivity enhancement. They also have zero tolerance for mistakes and look for never-ending warranties.

Business-to-business segments are classified as price-focused, quality-focused, service-focused or partnership-focused. Segmentation can also be done on the basis of demographics, operating variables, customer purchasing approaches, situational factors, and personal characteristics of buyers.

The B2B buying process is complex. Since buyers seek information and supplier information or reputation online, 90 per cent of the B2B buying process is done much before a prospect engages with the supplier. Since buyers 'seek out' their suppliers, the task of B2B marketing consists of coming to the buyer's attention. The B2B purchase process also varies with different types of customers: commercial, government, and institutions. Increasingly, B2B sellers have to sell their wares like brands, so that they come into the evaluation shortlist of the buyer at the time of consideration. Business-to-business branding helps in differentiation, long-term survival, building brand loyalty, and creating barriers for competition.

Businesses also buy a variety of services, ranging from consultancy, financial services, data management, marketing for small and medium enterprises (SMEs), maintenance of installations, logistics, IT, travel, communications, and so on.

Business-to-business marketing also depends on developing long-term relationships between buyers and suppliers. Built on trust and demonstrated performance, such strategic partnerships require open lines of communications and sharing of information. The basis of relationships are commitment, satisfaction, and establishing social and structural bonds. Relationship variables such as cooperation, trust, and a long-term commitment are also positively associated with business performance. However, close relationships often result in unethical behaviour like giving bribes to capture B2B contracts. These raise ethical issues, and must be addressed because the consequences can be severe.

KEY TERMS

Business-to-business (B2B) Commercial transactions between businesses and refers to the selling of products, services, or information between two companies rather than companies selling to consumers

Business-to-government (B2G) These transactions consist of government bodies such as hospitals, schools, and other services, who buy a wide variety of goods from companies

Buying centre or decision-making unit (DMU) A group of employees of an organization or a formal committee responsible for making purchases

Customer relationship management (CRM) A system for managing a company's interactions with current and future customers, including methodologies, software, and Internet capabilities that help it to manage customer relationships

Derived demand A demand arising out of and following consumer demand

Industrial user A company that buys goods for its own use or in its manufacturing process

Institutional sales Sales made in bulk to financial, educational, or social institutions

Original equipment manufacturer (OEM) A company that supplies equipment or parts to other companies to resell or build it into another product, and sell them using the buying company's brand name

Reseller A company or individual that purchases goods or services with the intention of reselling them with or without modification

Tender Offers sent by suppliers to large buyers like the government after being invited through an open advertisement in a newspaper, website, or a notice

Value added reseller (VAR) A company that buys the goods, adds value to them, and sells it further

EXERCISES

Concept-review Questions

1. What is B2B marketing? How is it different from consumer marketing in terms of buyer behaviour?
2. Explain the personal and organizational motives in B2B buying. How are they different from B2C buying situations?
3. What are the different types of B2B buyers and how does the purchase process differ among them?
4. Explain how B2G transactions take place. Describe the purchase process of government bodies.
5. What are tenders? Explain the different types of tenders and the situations in which they are used.
6. What are institutional sales? Explain the different types of institutional sales.
7. Discuss the role of brands in the B2B buying process. What benefits do they provide to (a) buyers and (b) sellers?
8. List all the kinds of B2B services. Analyse each, explaining how it would be sold and how service providers would add value in their offerings to companies.
9. Why is building relationships important in B2B situations? How do they benefit suppliers and their clients? What is the limit of such relationships?
10. Define market segments in industrial markets. On what basis can they be formed? Are they important?

Critical Thinking Questions

1. Implementing systems for satisfying needs of B2B buyers is hugely expensive, as in the case of Rolls-Royce discussed in this chapter. Given the high cost of capital, can companies really implement such systems? How can B2B suppliers look after customer needs if they do not wish to take risks?
2. Companies have to develop close relationships with their B2B partners and quite often, it leads to underhand dealings. Discuss the ethical implications of this. Can payment of bribes be justified to get business in a corrupt environment? Are there any limits?

3. Business-to-business systems have to be aligned between companies, their suppliers, and their dealers. This often means sharing of information. Given the human tendency not to share information, are such open systems really feasible? Would it not lead to leakage of company secrets? Will competitors not take advantage? How can a company resolve these issues?

4. Stock pile-ups with partners and increasing discounts for customers show that supply chain efficiencies have not worked in the favour of companies. It is said that psychologists should actually be involved in building supply chains. How can this be done? Is this feasible?

Projects and Assignments

1. Take up a company and study all its B2B relationships. Develop a chart to show its relations with suppliers, transporters, dealers, and so on. In addition, build in B2B services that the company buys.
2. Study a supermarket and analyse its B2B transactions. Follow the materials as they come into the stores till the time they are taken off the shelves by shoppers. How many B2B transactions are involved in the entire process? What can you say about the B2B relationships the supermarket has?
3. Talk to the purchase manager and purchasing staff of a manufacturing company. Understand their fears and motivations. Study the purchase process and comment on how they deal with their B2B partners.
4. Study an e-commerce portal and understand how it works. Apart from providing product and supplier information, how does the portal add value for B2B buyers and suppliers? Comment on the types of portals and the services they provide.

REFERENCES

Bendixen M., K.A. Bukasa, and R. Abratt, 'Brand equity in the business-to-business market', *Industrial Marketing Management*, Vol. 33, 2004, pp. 371–380.

Bondesson, Niklas, 'Brand image antecedents of loyalty and price premium in business markets', *Business and Management Research*, Vol. 1, No. 1, March 2012.

Bonoma, Thomas V., 'Major sales: Who really does the buying?' *Harvard Business Review*, May–June 1982.

'Bribe Payers' Index 2011', Transparency International, www.transparency.org, last accessed on 15 July 2013.

Cater, Barbara and Tomaž Cater, 'Relationship-value-based antecedents of customer satisfaction and loyalty in manufacturing', *Journal of Business & Industrial Marketing*, Vol. 24 Issue 8, 2009, pp. 585–597.

Chakraborty, Goutam, Prashant Srivastava, and Fred Marshall, 'Are drivers of customer satisfaction different for buyers/users from different functional areas?', *Journal of Business & Industrial Marketing*, Vol. 22 Issue 1, 2007, pp. 20–28.

Copeland, Melvin T., 'Buying motives for industrial goods', *Harvard Business Review*, January 1924, pp. 139–153.

Ebitu, Ezekiel, Tom Eyo, Emmanuel Essien, and Glory Basil, 'Price-quality dimensions of organizational buying behaviour in Cross River State, Nigeria', *International Journal of Marketing Studies*, Vol. 4, No. 4, 2012, pp. 78–82.

Ford D., P. Berthon, S. Brown, L.E. Gadde, H. Hakansson, P. Naude, T. Titter, and I. Snehota, *The Business Marketing Course*, Wiley, Chichester, 2002.

Geigenmuller, Anja and Harriette Bettis–Outland, 'Brand equity in B2B services and consequences for the trade show industry', *Journal of Business & Industrial Marketing*, Vol. 27, No. 6, 2012, pp. 428–435.

Han, S.L. and H.S. Sung, 'Industrial brand value and relationship performance in business markets—A general structural equation model', *Industrial Marketing Management*, Vol. 37 No. 7, 2008, pp. 807–18.

Hassan, Sallaudin, Abu Bakar, Abd Hamid, Nik Maheran, N. Muhammad, and N.M. Naziman Na Rahman, 'Factors affecting industrial goods buying decision making in a manufacturing company', *Journal of Marketing and Management*, Vol. 1, No. 1, November 2010, pp. 1–20.

Hutt, Michael D. and Thomas W. Speh, *Business Marketing Management: B2B*, 11th Ed., 2013, South-Western Cengage Learning, Ohio.

'Indians withdrawing their black money deposited in Swiss banks', *India Today*, 23 June 2013.

Kaplan, S. and M. Sawhney, 'E-hubs: The new B2B marketplaces', *Harvard Business Review*, May–June 2000, pp. 97–103.

Keller, K.L., *Strategic Brand Management: Building, Measuring, and Managing Brand Equity*, Prentice Hall, NJ, 2003.

Kotler, Philip and Waldemar Pfoertsch, *B2B Brand Management*, Springer Books, Berlin, 2006.

Kumar, Dinesh, *Marketing Channels*, Oxford University Press, New Delhi, 2012.

Lages, Luis Filipe, Andrew Lancastre, and Carmen Lages, 'The B2B-RELPERF scale and scorecard: Bringing relationship marketing theory into business-to-business practice', *Industrial Marketing Management*, Vol. 37, 2008, pp. 686–697.

Lambert, Douglas M. and Michael A. Knemeyer, 'We're in this together', *Harvard Business Review*, December 2004, pp. 48–55.

Levitt, Theodore, 'After the sale is over', *Harvard Business Review*, September–October 1983.

Marquardt, Adam J., Susan L. Golicic, and Donna F. Davis, 'B2B services branding in the logistics services industry', *Journal of Services Marketing*, Vol. 25, No. 1, 2011, pp. 47–57.

Narayanan, V.G. and Ananth Raman, 'Aligning incentives in supply chains', *Harvard Business Review*, November 2004.

Narayandas, Das, 'Building loyalty in business markets', *Harvard Business Review*, September 2005.

Ndubisi, Nelson Oly, Muhamad Jantan, Loo Cha Hing, and Mat Salleh Ayub, 'Supplier selection and management strategies and manufacturing flexibility', *Journal of Enterprise Information Management*, Vol. 18, Issue 3, 2005, pp. 330–349.

Rigby, Darrell K. and Dianne Ledingham, 'CRM done right', *Harvard Business Review*, November 2004.

Rossomme, Jeanne, 'Customer satisfaction measurement in a business-to-business context: A conceptual framework', *Journal of Business & Industrial Marketing*, Vol. 18, No. 2, 2003, pp. 179–195.

Sarin, Sharad, 'My years with B2B marketing in India: Reflections and learnings from a journey of 40 years', *Journal of Business & Industrial Marketing*, Vol. 27, No. 3, 2012, pp. 160–168.

Shapiro, Benson P and Thomas V. Bonoma, 'How to segment industrial markets', *Harvard Business Review*, May–June 1984.

Slone, Reuben E., 'Leading a supply chain turnaround', *Harvard Business Review*, October 2004.

Waaser, E., M. Dahneke, M. Pekkarinen, and M. Weissel, 'Smarter segmentation for your sales force', *Harvard Business Review*, March 2004.

Whitney, Mike, 'B2B selling', *Sales and Service Excellence*, August 2011.

Wilson, David T. and K.E. Kristan Moller, 'Buyer–Seller relationships: Alternative conceptualisations', in Stanley Paliwoda (ed.), *Perspectives on International Marketing*, Reissued 2013, Routledge Library Editions, Oxford.

Zhao, Xiaofeng, Hui Zhao, Jianrong Hou, 'B2B e-hubs and information integration in supply chain operations', *Management Research Review*, Vol. 33, No. 10, 2010, pp. 961–979.

CASE STUDY
Dark Side of B2B Selling Behaviour

Business-to-business selling depends on influencing the decision-maker. All too often, companies try to influence decision-makers through bribes and underhand dealings. Construction companies seek large contracts from the government, foreign companies seek to enter emerging market countries, and all companies buy raw materials and machinery regularly. It is easy to get these orders once bribes are paid. The logic is: 'Buy me a TV and get my business'. Unfortunately, the practice is widespread.

The marketing of medicines reveals this dark side of B2B marketing—companies bribe the doctors to prescribe their medicines, whether they are suitable for patients or not. This case study describes the situation when the B2B relationship gets too intimate to the extent that it ends up harming customers.

Though the practice has been discontinued in many developed nations, it is common for drug firms in emerging markets to offer perks to doctors to encourage them to prescribe their pills. Some of the biggest pharmaceutical companies are involved in this kind of questionable marketing.

The Economist (2012) reports that in China, Pfizer established a 'club' that provided 'high-prescribing' doctors with all kinds of entertainment under the guise of attending conferences. In Kazakhstan, the company awarded an exclusive distribution deal to a local that would help it secure government approval for its product.

However, laws in home countries do not allow such behaviour. Pfizer was found to have violated the Foreign Corrupt Practices Act (FCPA), a US law that punishes bribery abroad. Pfizer was fined about $60 million.

Pfizer was not alone. Johnson & Johnson had to pay $70 million for similar violations. *The Guardian* (2012) reports that GlaxoSmithKline (GSK) was fined $3 billion after admitting to bribing doctors and encouraging the prescription of unsuitable antidepressants to children. It is reported that eight of the world's ten biggest drug firms have warned of potential costs related to charges of corruption in markets abroad, which shows that such practices are normal for the industry.

Indeed, executives of medicine companies try to maintain relationships with doctors through various means. Free gifts and samples, parties, all-expenses-paid conferences, and so on, are industry practices to encourage doctors to prescribe medicines, often not needed by the patient. Another report in *The Economist* (2013) says that in 2012, pharmaceutical companies spent more than $24 billion marketing drugs to doctors; 35 per cent of doctors accept food, entertainment, or travel, while 16 per cent accept consulting or speaking fees. Companies also sponsor medical training required for further accreditation. Such practices are widespread in India and all the Asian countries. While multinational companies are fined for these in their home countries, domestic companies bear no such burden.

The US passed a Sunshine law in 1976 requiring openness in government to improve transparency in government buying. France passed a similar law in 2011. Firms in Britain are planning voluntary disclosures. Other countries may well follow suit.

However, developing countries do not have such strict laws and even if there are, do not enforce them strictly. In India, the Central Board of Direct Taxes (CBDT) had the benefits received by doctors from medical companies taxable and the government banned doctors from taking gifts and sponsorships from them. It now seems to be having second thoughts, and wants to legalize travel and hospitality sponsorship for doctors by pharmaceutical companies, according to a report in *The Times of India* (2013). The government wants to make amendments to the code of ethics to legalize drug companies' sponsorship of continuing medical education (CME) sessions, that is, conferences in India and abroad. This was revealed through an RTI application.

Pharmaceutical companies are a strong force to reckon with in emerging markets. And it is not just B2B selling. In many cases, doctors are encouraged to prescribe drugs that are not suitable for their patients. GSK was alleged to have encouraged sales reps in the US to mis-sell drugs to doctors and lavished hospitality and kickbacks on those who agreed to write extra prescriptions. The company paid for articles on its drugs to be published in medical journals. An antidepressant drug, Paxil, was promoted as suitable for children and teenagers by the company despite trials that showed it was ineffective. The company set up *Operation Hustle* to promote the drug to doctors, including trips to Jamaica, where speakers were paid up to $2500, earning far more than they did working in their surgeries.

Another drug, Advair, was sold as the ultimate answer for tackling asthma, though it had been approved only for treating severe cases. It is reported that the company's sales force bribed physicians to prescribe its products 'using every imaginable form of high-priced entertainment, from Hawaiian vacations and paying doctors millions of dollars to go on speaking tours, to tickets to Madonna concerts'.

A report in *Wall Street Journal* (2013) says that GSK was under probe in China for widespread bribery of doctors to prescribe drugs between 2004 and 2010. Chinese police questioned the company's employees in three cities as part of an investigation into 'economic crimes'.

Goldacre (2012) in his book, *Bad Pharma*, shows what is wrong with the way drugs are marketed. Companies use trials that make the drug look good, which are then published in medical journals. The bad results are simply hidden. Then companies pay doctors to speak highly of the drugs in conferences and create lobby groups to approve new drugs.

Due to these and many other instances, the drug industry is seen as 'a bunch of nefarious pushers who pay off vulnerable doctors to prescribe their latest expensive, mediocre product', writes Shaywitz (2013). The companies often work with doctors to produce life-saving medicines, but the relationship has extended to an unholy nexus that encourages doctors to prescribe unnecessary medicines for patients. While it is true that doctors and medicine companies play an important role and thrive on relationships, should this relationship extend to intimacy? The dark side of B2B needs to be controlled, but how?

Questions for Discussion

1. Describe the purchase process of medicines by institutional consumers such as hospitals and individual consumers. Illustrate the process by making a flow chart.
2. Since medicines must be prescribed by doctors, how can companies continue to influence them without violating laws? Is there a solution to this situation so that the consumers are not harmed?
3. Is it ethical to reward prescribing doctors? Comment on the ethical issues of the practice.
4. What can pharmaceutical companies do to improve their image, given the fact that they have to pay doctors to prescribe their drugs?

Sources:

Goldacre, Ben, *Bad Pharma: How Medicine is Broken, and How We Can Fix It*, Fourth Estate, London, 2012.

'Let the sunshine in: New efforts to reveal the ties between doctors and drug firms', *The Economist*, 2 March 2013.

Matthews, Christopher and Jessica Hodgson, 'GlaxoSmithKline probes bribe allegations in China', *The Wall Street Journal*, 12 June 2013.

Nagarajan, Rema, 'Bid to legalize pharma companies' sops for doctors?' *The Times of India*, 19 April 2013.

Neville, Simon, 'GlaxoSmithKline fined $3bn after bribing doctors to increase drugs sales', *The Guardian*, 3 July 2012.

'Pfizer: Taking its medicine', *The Economist*, 11 August 2012.

Shaywitz, David A., 'Getting to the right relationship between doctors and drug companies', *The Atlantic*, 7 May 2013, http://www.theatlantic.com/health/archive/2013/05/getting-to-the-right-relationship-between-doctors-and-drug-companies/275605/, last accessed on 10 July 2013.

PART TWO

Consumer as an Individual

CHAPTER 5:
Personality and the Consumer

CHAPTER 6:
Consumer Motivation

CHAPTER 7:
Consumer Perception

CHAPTER 8:
Consumer Learning

CHAPTER 9:
Consumer Attitudes and Change

CHAPTER FIVE

Personality and the Consumer

LEARNING OBJECTIVES

People respond to brands because of their personality: different brands appeal to different types of people. Consequently, companies try to impart the personality of their target market to their brands. This chapter examines the role of personality in consumer behaviour.

After studying this chapter, the reader would be able to
- learn about personality theories and how they apply to consumers and products
- examine how personality relates to consumer behaviour
- analyse how brand personality is created through personification and anthropomorphism
- examine the role of advertising elements, geography, gender, and colour in establishing brand personality
- learn about how human personality and brand personality interact through self-image, altering the self, and virtual personality

CASE STUDY

Woodland: Creating an Outdoors Personality

'Touch the earth. Breathe the wind. Taste the water. Feel the richness of the forest, the emptiness of the desert, the might of the rivers and the majesty of the mountains.' This is how the website of popular apparel and outdoor shoe brand Woodland invites people to love adventure. In doing so, it has built a brand that stands distinctly for the outdoors, for travel, and for adventure.

Woodland's parent company, Aero Group, was founded in Quebec, Canada. It has the distinct identity of being an outdoor shoe company. Since Canada experiences cold weather, the company began as a manufacturer of good quality protective winter clothing and accessories. It became one of the world's leading manufacturers of extreme weather outdoor gear and outerwear. Woodland today offers an extensive line of footwear, performance apparel, and outdoor gear.

In 1992, Aero Group launched Woodland, which catered to lovers of the outdoors with its rugged shoes and apparel. With a logo showing a tree, it conveyed not only its outdoor personality, but also its commitment to environment. Woodland uses pastel colours in shoes and apparel that help it stand out in the crowded apparel market. Aero Group has its own leather tanning units and production facilities in India, Sri Lanka, Bangladesh, China, Vietnam, Indonesia, Malaysia,

Philippines, Macau, and Canada. Woodland is now a global outdoor products brand, with a network of 350 exclusive stores worldwide and also has a presence in more than 3000 multi-brand outlets in a number of countries.

Product personality is not built by advertising alone. The company has used a multi-pronged approach consisting of product, production, logo, corporate social responsibility (CSR) activities, and advertising to convey its message and to create an image in the minds of the customer.

Products All Woodland products suggest adventure, be it rock climbing, trekking, or any other adventure sport. They appeal to the active man, woman, or kid. The company has also launched a yoga apparel collection.

Logo With a tree as its logo, Woodland conveys a sense of nature. The Woodland tree logo is synonymous with outdoor adventure.

Production The company states that everything, from the material used to the production techniques, is environment friendly. Its focus is on creating a sustainable environment. It says it tries to attain zero carbon emissions from its retail stores.

Proplanet Woodland launched a CSR initiative to protect earth called Proplanet. According to its website, the company undertakes many socio-environmental initiatives such as the Earth Hour, Spare Trees Campaign, and planting trees. Through Woodland Proplanet, the company tries to inculcate the message of environment conservation. It uses green technology and waste management systems. The company says its products are made from environment-friendly raw materials like organic cotton. The packaging utilizes recyclable materials. Product hangtags and company business cards are printed on recycled paper.

Advertising The brand has become synonymous with outdoor adventure and nature, evoking imagery of scenic landscapes and the wilds in its advertisements.

Brand personality Woodland's has an outdoorsy, rugged, stylish, and fashionable personality. It is defined by comfort, style, and versatility.

'Our goal is to substantially reduce the amount of materials used over time, and the energy consumed to manufacture and distribute those materials and products', says the company. It has partnered with several national and international organizations to take its environmental initiatives forward.

While reading the chapter, try to answer the following questions:

1. How do companies like Woodland acquire a distinct personality?
2. How do brands use theories of personality and knowledge of the subconscious to create an impression of personality in lifeless objects?
3. Do consumers really buy on personality traits, or does the purchase process remain a means of problem-solving?
4. Do consumer attributes such as ethnocentrism, cosmopolitism, innovation, and dogmatism affect buying decisions?

Sources:
http://woodlandworldwide.com/companyinfo.aspx.
http://www.thegoan.net/story_new.php?id=2950.
http://www.woodlandworldwide.com/proplanet/proplanet.html.
All websites were last accessed on 2 July 2013.

INTRODUCTION

The concept of personality arises from human differences. Each person has distinctive behaviour patterns that define their personality. Philosophers have tried to figure out what constitutes personality. The Greeks believed that the nature of a person depended on body fluids, called humours. However, personality remained a mystery. It was believed, for instance, that there was a little man who sat in the brain and made us do whatever we did. Dennett (2013) writes in his book, *Intuition Pumps and Other Tools for Thinking*, that 'the temptation is to imagine an inner agent, a little man—*homunculus* in Latin—who sits in the control room in the brain and does all the clever work'. This little man is personality itself.

Freud was the first thinker who converted the study of personality from philosophy to analysis. His theories influence thinking to this day. Later thinkers added to our understanding of personality.

Human qualities arose from differences in thought and Descartes realized this when he wrote, '*Cogito ergo sum*', Latin for 'I think, therefore I am'. Thanks to the materialistic way of life that modern civilization encourages, people do not see personality differences as differences in human qualities or differences in thinking, but in terms of how much they own. William James explained that 'self is the sum total of all that he can call his, clothes, house, lands, yacht and bank accounts'. Sartre echoed the same thought when he wrote, 'The totality of my possessions reflects the totality of my being'.

Though the thinking 'I am what I have' may appear too simplistic, this is what marketing and advertising exploits, imbuing qualities in objects that fit the needs of consumers' personalities. In the process, we give personality traits to objects as well, as this chapter will show.

Nature of Personality

Personality is defined as the distinctive and relatively enduring ways of thinking, feeling, and acting that characterize a person's responses to life situations.

In marketing, we are concerned with personality as it impacts on consuming and buying goods. There are different kinds of people and personalities, each having a different approach to products. While some people want to try out new products, others stick to their trusted brands. Consumers may also be differentiated on the basis of willingness to spend or wanting to save. Then again, while some people like to spend on luxuries others see this as a waste of money. These are some of the myriad behaviours linked to personality—different people respond to marketing communications differently. The job of marketing manager is to discover these differences and shape his/her marketing strategy such that the brand personality matches that of the target market.

Personality has three characteristics. First, it reflects individual differences. Since people are different by way of nature and outlook, their purchase patterns are also varied. Second, personality is consistent over time. We know, for instance, the kind of people our friends are and how they react in diverse circumstances. Finally, we see that personality can change. A person changes as he/she progresses in the family life cycle, from being single to being married, and then to the enhanced family stage. Personalities also change as people acquire more money, which changes their spending patterns.

To study personality, we need to understand the contributions made by several personality theories. These are discussed in the next section.

THEORIES OF PERSONALITY

Several theories of personality have been proposed. The most significant one is the one proposed by Freud, who saw personality as largely the product of a subconscious mind. Prior to Freud, the ancient Greeks believed that an individual's personality was dependent to a large extent on inherited 'humours' or fluids in the body. They classified personality into four descriptive terms—sanguine, melancholic, choleric, and phlegmatic. Plato (c. 390 BC) said that the human soul was the seat of personality, which consisted of three basic forces guiding human behaviour—reason, emotion, and appetite. Other philosophers stated that personality was a result of biological or social processes. It was Freud who described personality as a fascinating complex model of developmental stages, drives, and psychic structures. He made the study of personality interesting and started the process of serious research into personality.

Freudian Theory of Personality

Sigmund Freud (1856–1939) proposed a powerful theory of personality that influenced subsequent thinkers and gave birth to the field of psychoanalysis. Literature, art, philosophy, cultural studies, films, and many other subjects bear the stamp of Freud. In 1999, *Time* included him in the list of the 'century's greatest minds'. Indeed, his theory represents one of the major intellectual ideas of the modern world. Though not without critics, Freud's ideas have had a lasting and profound impact on the world.

The psychoanalytic theory of personality propounded by Freud starts with the unconscious. According to this theory, personality arises from a conflict between a person's desire to fulfil his conscious needs—needs which a person is aware of, such as food, shelter, sleep; and unconscious needs such as desires, intentions, aims, wishes, and thoughts, which do not operate in an open and logical manner but are instinctual. People suppress their needs so as not to go against societal norms, and this affects behaviour. Most behaviour is thus caused by thoughts, ideas, and wishes that exist in the subconscious. Personality, according to the psychoanalytic theory, is a reflection of the subconscious part of the mind.

The unconscious part of the mind is composed of three elements—the id, the ego, and the superego. The conflict between these elements creates the complex human personality.

Id

The id is about instant pleasure or about immediate gratification of all desires and needs. Id consists of our basic instincts and animalistic urges. Selfish and irrational, it aims to satisfy inherent biological urges and drives. Operating on the pleasure principle, it motivates one to satisfy feelings of hunger, thirst, sex, and other natural desires, aiming towards pleasurable things and away from painful experiences. Consequently, the id is the source of all psychic energy. If these basic needs are not satisfied immediately, a person experiences anxiety or tension.

It is easy to understand needs such as hunger and thirst, which must be met immediately. Even so, society imposes rules on our behaviour, which prevents us from grabbing things we want to satisfy our immediate needs. Certain psychological desires have to be similarly curbed as expressing them would be socially unacceptable.

Ego

Ego is the mind's mechanism for keeping in touch with reality. It helps the id get what it wants in realistic and socially acceptable ways.

The ego or the 'self' weighs the consequences of an action before deciding whether to satisfy desires or to suppress them. Working partly consciously and partly unconsciously, it regulates a person's behaviour. For example, if a person is hungry, the id will begin to imagine and dream about food. The ego will try to get some real food. So a very hungry person may want to grab the food that someone else is eating, but the ego causes the person to go to a restaurant and order food in a manner that is acceptable in the real world.

Superego

The superego is a person's conscience, a sense of right and wrong. It includes the moral ideas that a person learns within the family and society.

The superego is a kind of a regulator or a moral barometer, and creates feelings of pride or guilt according to his or her beliefs learnt from family and culture. It has two parts. The first includes the rules and standards for good behaviour. Obeying these rules leads to feelings of pride and accomplishment. The second part includes behaviour that is considered bad or unacceptable by the society. Such behaviour is forbidden and society imposes punishment for it. The superego will generate feelings of guilt and remorse if a person does something wrong.

The superego provides us with idealistic principles and guidelines for making judgments. It is a civilizing factor, suppressing the unacceptable urges of the id.

Interaction of Id, Ego, and Superego

It is easy to see that there is inherent conflict among these three elements. One part of us wants to fulfil our desires, but our mind and conscience pull us in the opposite direction. Another part of us tries to resolve that conflict.

We have all experienced this conflict at one time or another. When we visit a swanky shop displaying objects of desire, such as our favourite ice cream or the latest dress, in the window, our first reaction is to buy them. We do not care about the price and would just like to grab those beautiful objects. If we do not have enough money, we wish to steal, have the impulse to use a family member's credit card, or even borrow money from friends. That is the id operating.

However, we then start thinking about whether it is right to spend a large amount using somebody else's credit card. Our mind thinks logically and we wonder whether it would be better to wait for the time when we have our own savings. The superego will impose such feelings of right and wrong upon us.

Wait a little longer, and we start thinking of ways to acquire the object in an acceptable way. Our mind will work towards finding practical solutions. We remember some money we had put aside for emergencies. We think of covering the shortfall by earning a little more. The ego or the self finds acceptable ways of fulfilling desire by logical thinking.

This is how conflict is resolved among the id, ego, and superego. A normal, healthy person balances the id and the superego so that one of them does not become too dominant. As Hinrichs (2007) explains, a dominating or strong id makes one a psychopath, lacking a conscience, selfishly meeting one's needs without concern for others. An overly strong superego, on the other hand, makes one a worrier, so overwhelmed by guilt that it is difficult to get satisfaction. Many advertisements target id or instant gratification.

The psychoanalytic theory is not a scientific or empirical theory that can be tested. However, it demonstrates how the unconscious can influence our behaviour and personality. Events in childhood act as the seeds for adult personality development and traumatic happenings in childhood can have lasting effect on our personalities. The sexual drive also plays an important role in personality formation.

Freud had great influence, particularly early in the twentieth century, and he had many followers who developed their own theories of personality development, often contradicting his. These theories added to the understanding about personality. Some of the major ideas of some neo-Freudians are described in the subsequent sections.

Neo-Freudian Theory

Later thinkers disagreed with Freud that all personality traits were a result of the internal conflict between the id, ego, and superego. They believed that personality is the combination of individual characteristics as well as social learning. There were three main disagreements. The first was his belief that early childhood experiences were largely responsible for shaping personality. The second was Freud's failure to incorporate social and cultural influences on personality formation, and the third objection was to his reliance on dreams and emphasis on sexual needs and gratification as influencing personality.

Discussed in the next section are the contributions of major neo-Freudian theories, as proposed by Alfred Adler, Carl Jung, and Karen Horney.

Alfred Adler

Adler gave us the theory of 'Individual Psychology' that assigned three dimensions to personality. First, it assumed that we are motivated not so much by sexuality, as by our social urges. Second, Adler proposed the creative self, through which we interpret and find meaning in our experiences. Third and most important, Adler said that people suffer from inherent feelings of inferiority, called the *inferiority complex* and that the primary motivation of humans was a striving for superiority. This formed the basis of personality.

At its extremes, the inferiority or superiority complex is not normal. The inferiority feeling is developed in children, as they are small and weak. When they grow up, they strive to overcome this feeling by striving for perfection, security, conquest, and success. A normal person strives to overcome the feeling of inferiority by trying to become successful. Adler considered the striving for superiority to be the foremost drive in human beings. When this goes too far, a person develops a superiority complex, but the normal striving for superiority is, according to Adler, the driving force behind all human thoughts, emotions, and behaviours, which form personality.

Adler's theory finds constant application in ads. Almost all ads, whether of clothing, cosmetics, cars, real estate, and other products, address the consumer's inferiority complex by assuring that the consumption of such goods will help him/her look superior and appealing in the eyes of others. Please see Exhibit 5.1.

Carl Jung

Carl Jung disagreed with Freud's emphasis on the unconscious and on the sexual aspects of personality. He developed his own method of psychoanalysis, called *analytical psychology*.

EXHIBIT 5.1 Monte Carlo: Projecting a Young Brand

FIG. 5.1 Monte Carlo—A young brand

Courtesy: Superbrands

Monte Carlo epitomises superior quality and international styling at affordable prices. Its popularity stems from the inherent warmth and comfort exuded by its clothing. The personality and style are underpinned by the brand's core values: romance (the warmth, love and passion of wearing a top-of-the-line clothes range), joy (supreme happiness in living the good life) and quality (of design, fabric, cut and fit). Monte Carlo showcases a distinct image of its brand persona, characterising itself as young, cosmopolitan, cheerful, dynamic, loving and passionate—just the way its customers are.

And so using this brand would make customers more appealing. Please see Fig. 5.1.

Source: Superbrands 2012

Noting that the fears, behaviours, and thoughts of children and adults are remarkably similar across cultures (such as fear of the dark or of the devil), Jung proposed that the roots of personality go back to the dawn of human existence and reside in a *collective unconscious*. The collective unconscious contains primordial images or what we have inherited from past generations. Indeed, these are recurrent themes in folklore, art, and dreams across different cultures. He stated that this collective memory consists of *archetypes*, which are universally understood symbols, terms, statements, and patterns of behaviour.

Analytic psychology is concerned about how the collective unconscious influences personality. Advertisements frequently play out these archetypes as can be seen from the following examples:

- A mother's attachment to her children is exploited by manufacturers of health foods, soaps, instant noodles, and so on.
- The creative and rebellious nature of youth is captured in a large number of product ads, including those of liquor (see chapter-end case study).
- The apparel, cosmetics, jewellery, and other similar industries bank on our inherent drive to look better than others.

Delahousay (2013) writes that to be effective, advertisers must thoroughly research the motivators likely to be shared by its desired demographic. That is to say, they must address subconscious and conscious drives.

Mark and Pearson (2001) propose in their book *The Hero and The Outlaw* that advertisers use 12 archetypes to drive purchasing decisions. These are explained in Table 5.1, along with the core desires and goals they express, and examples of companies that use them.

Karen Horney

Karen Horney was another neo-Freudian. She emphasized the importance of socio-cultural factors in personality development. She wrote that anxious insecurity stems from inadequate

TABLE 5.1 Personality archetypes

Archetype	Core desire	Goal	Examples
The innocent	To experience paradise	To be happy	Coca-Cola, McDonald's, Bacardi
The explorer	To define one's self by exploring the world with freedom	To experience a better, more fulfilling life	Starbucks, Rockport
The sage	To discover the truth	To use intelligence and analysis to understand the world	Barnes & Noble, BBC, CNN
The hero	To prove one's worth through courageous action	To exert mastery in the world	Hero Motocorp, Nike, FedEx
The outlaw	To seek revenge or start a revolution	To destroy what is not working	Harley-Davidson, Diesel, Apple
The magician	Magical moments and transformational experiences	To make dreams come true	Chanel No. 5, Polaroid, Oil of Olay
The regular guy/girl	To form a connection with others	To belong, fit in	IKEA, Airtel, Bajaj
The lover	To attain intimacy and experience sensual pleasure	To be with people, and be in surroundings that one loves	Guess Jeans, Godiva, Jaguar
The jester	To live in the moment with full enjoyment	To have a great time and lighten up the world	Mentos, Fanta
The caregiver	To protect people from harm	To help others	Marriott, Johnson's Baby Shampoo, GE
The creator	To create something of enduring value	To give form to a vision	Lego, Apple
The ruler	To control	To create a prosperous and successful family, company or community	Microsoft, Mercedes, American Express

Source: Archetypes from Mark and Pearson (2001)

childrearing experiences and is the source of all personality conflicts. She differed with Freud as she felt that anxiety was a stronger motivating force than sexual drive or libido. She described the following three personality types: compliant, aggressive, and detached (CAD):

Compliant (*Moving toward people*) Such people have a desire to be loved, appreciated, and wanted; they are more likely to prefer branded products. Cosmetics and apparel ads frequently show people being complimented for their looks or style.

Aggressive (*Moving against people*) Such people desire to compete and win; they prefer brands with a strong masculine orientation such as sports goods, cars, and motorcycles.

Detached (*Moving away from people*) Such people are independent and self-reliant; they are less likely to be brand loyal and would like to try out new brands.

The development of neo-Freudian theories led to observational theories, which described personality as a set of traits. These theories were able to isolate the most important traits from the large number that humans possess, and suggest ways to measure them.

Trait Theory

Traits are defined as habitual patterns of behaviour, thought, and emotion. Passer and Smith (2007) define personality traits as relatively stable, cognitive, emotional, and behavioural characteristics of people that help establish their individual identities and distinguish them from others.

Human personality traits are based on individual behaviour, physical characteristics, attitudes, beliefs, and demography. The trait theory is based on these differences between individuals. The combination and interaction of various traits form a personality that is unique to each individual. When we describe the personality of a person, for example, we use a combination of words to describe traits such as agreeable, loyal, kind, shy, or outgoing. Allport and Odbert (1936) went through an English dictionary and found 17,953 words that could be used to describe human traits. Attempts have been made to condense this huge list into a usable form. Different methods have been proposed. Two are described here: the five-factor personality dimensions and 16 personality factors (16PF). Both of these are widely used in personality analysis.

Five-factor Model

The five-factor model, also called the 'big five' personality traits, suggests five dimensions of personality, which are universal to humans as these have been found to be common across different cultures. As John and Srivastava (2008) write, 'the big five taxonomy serves an integrative function because it can represent a diverse system of personality description in a common framework'.

The factors that characterize the emotional and motivational dispositions of an individual are openness, conscientiousness, extraversion, agreeableness, and neuroticism (OCEAN). According to the five-factor model, a person's personality can be captured by placing it at a specific point on each of these five dimensions by means of a test or observation. These dimensions are described here.

Openness Openness is associated with intellectual curiosity, appreciation of arts, and a sophisticated, modern outlook. People with this trait try out new products.

Conscientiousness Individuals with this personality trait tend to be fussy and tidy, follow plans, and spend more time planning.

Extraversion People with this trait are gregarious, take interest in interpersonal interaction, and are expressive. They tend to be cheerful and adventurous, and buy products that are bought by their peer group. Woodland uses this trait very successfully (see chapter-opening case study).

Agreeableness Individuals who are agreeable tend to avoid conflicts, are friendly, and seek positive social interaction. They are mild, co-operative people with a flexible disposition.

TABLE 5.2 Big five personality traits

Personality trait	Behavioural trait	Opposing trait	Marketing application
Openness	• Artistically sensitive • Intellectual • Polished • Imaginative	• Not aesthetic • Unreflective, narrow • Crude • Simple	• Well-designed, aesthetic, or simple products • Ads appealing to higher or basic dimensions
Conscientiousness	• Fussy and tidy • Responsible • Persevering	• Careless • Undependable • Fickle	• Loyal or fickle consumers
Extraversion	• Talkative, cheerful • Adventurous • Sociable	• Cautious • Reclusive • Serious • Silent	• Restaurants • Sports goods
Agreeableness	• Mild, gentle • Cooperative	• Headstrong • Jealous	• Luxury brands • Status and conspicuous consumption
Neuroticism	• Nervous • Excitable • Moody	• Calm • Composed • Stable	• Impulse purchases • Bright and attractive POP material

Neuroticism Subjects with a high degree of neuroticism tend to experience negative emotions more strongly, and are prone to anxiety and mood switches. Impulsive buying is a characteristic of this group.

The personality traits that are described by the five-factor model can also be used to predict a person's real-life behaviour. The relevance of these traits and behaviour for products and brands is summarized in Table 5.2.

Sedikides, et al. (2012) give another personality trait—narcissism—a trait that means self-love or self-obsession. They write that narcissists will buy symbolic products due to the high hedonic value of this type of consumerism. Freud argued that narcissists have a shaky inner self that they mask with a puffed-up persona. They boost their self-regard by giving the impression of themselves as successful, special, and superior. Since they seek to influence others, narcissistic individuals are primary drivers of social change.

Sixteen Personality Factors

While the five factors described in the previous section set out important features of personality, it is believed that the use of 16 factors would be better to capture nuances of human behaviour. The Sixteen personality factors (16PF) model proposed by Catell (1965) captures individual differences for each factor and provides a comprehensive description of personality. He was able to do this not only for individuals but also groups of people, which is of particular interest for marketing segmentation. By profiling a community or group, companies can work out effective segmentation and also develop products that meet the needs of these groups. A person's or group's personality can be plotted on 16 factors.

The 16PF model has wide marketing applications apart from those described here. The model has been used to map brand personalities as well. People are asked to answer questions about

Cattell's sixteen factors of personality (16PF)

	1	2	3	4	5	6	7	8	
Reserved									Outgoing
Less intelligent									More intelligent
Affected by feelings									Emotionally stable
Submissive									Dominant
Serious									Happy-go-lucky
Expedient									Conscientious
Timid									Venturesome
Tough-minded									Sensitive
Trusting									Suspicious
Practical									Imaginative
Forthright									Shrewd
Self-assured									Apprehensive
Conservative									Experimenting
Group dependent									Self-sufficient
Uncontrolled									Controlled
Relaxed									Tense

FIG. 5.2 16PF model

CB IN ACTION   Analysing Advertisements

- Go through newspapers, magazines, and web-sites and collect ads for diverse products. Find out
- whether they are targeted at id, ego, or superego, or convey the conflict among them
- whether they want one to overcome a feeling of inferiority
- whether they address any archetype, and if so, how
- whether they are targeted to compliant, aggressive, or detached personality types
- if the brand personality can be analysed on the basis of OCEAN or 16PF and carry out the analysis

brands based on each factor like, 'Do you think that brand X represents reserved or outgoing?' By plotting the impressions of consumers on the 16PF scale, a brand personality can be shown graphically (Fig. 5.2).

PERSONALITY AND CONSUMER BEHAVIOUR

Personality traits give indications about consumer behaviour, that is, how people will respond in the marketplace to new product offerings. Several aspects of consumer innovativeness, consumer dogmatism, social character, and cognitive personality factors are considered. These traits and the two extremes of consumption-related behaviour they give rise to, are summarized in Table 5.3 and are explained in this section.

TABLE 5.3 Personality traits and consumption behaviour

Personality trait	Extremes of consumption-related behaviour	
Open to new ideas	Innovativeness: Trying out new products	Dogmatism: Rigid in approach, customer loyalty
Need for stimulation	Excited by new products	Think of new products as marketing gimmicks
Curiosity	Novelty seeking: Look for the unusual	Low novelty seeking: Stick to habits
Independence	Assert their independence by choosing different products; don't want to be seen as dependent on family and friends	Look for parental or peer approval in their purchase decisions.
Uniqueness	Want to stand out, collect rare items and brands	Want to blend with the crowd, follow the fashion trends
Social character	Outer-directed: Look for social approval	Inner-directed: Depend on own values and beliefs
Need for cognition	High: Collect and analyse information	Low: Like fun, fantasy, music, jingles
Imagination	Visualizers: Are influenced by graphics, images, and videos	Verbalizers: Prefer written or verbal information

TABLE 5.4 Relationship between personality traits and brand personality

Personality trait	Brand personality	Examples
Extroversion	Excitement	Hedonic products
Agreeableness	Excitement, sincerity, competence	Peer group conformity
Conscientiousness	Competence, sophistication	Information-based buying
Neuroticism	Sophistication	Brand loyalty
Openness	Excitement, sophistication	New and innovative products

Consumer Personality and Brand Personality

Lin (2010) has explored the relationship between consumer personality traits and brand personality. He considered five personality traits: extroversion, agreeableness, conscientiousness, neuroticism, and openness, which are also referred to as the big five personality traits. These were matched with five brand personality traits: excitement, competence, peacefulness, sincerity, and sophistication (Table 5.4). He found that there was a positive relationship between these traits.

Matzler, et al. (2006) studied hedonic products such as sports shoes and mobile phones to investigate personality relationships. They showed that openness and extroversion have a positive influence on the loyalty to brands with hedonistic values.

Consumer Innovativeness

Consumer innovativeness, or the tendency to be attracted by new products, has been defined as 'consumption of newness' or the predisposition to try out and buy new products offered in the market more often, and more quickly than other people.

Consumer innovativeness is reflected in consumers' shopping approaches. Some consumers are among the first to check out new products as soon as they are launched. Others, however, dismiss them as marketing gimmicks and prefer to wait till they are convinced about them. Why do some consumers adopt new products and others resist them? Roehrich (2004) explains that it could be because of four needs:

Stimulation Some consumers are naturally curious and like to explore new products. They are excited by new and innovative products to maintain their inner stimulation. Companies have to maintain *optimal stimulation level* so that customers are willing to try out new products.

Novelty Humans are by nature novelty seeking and like to look for new things and find new information. Browsing web pages and looking for product information is a form of informative innovativeness. This may lead to adoption and use.

Independence Some consumers look for independence from others' communicated experience. For example, young people seek to assert their independence from their parents by adopting fashions that will find disapproval. Fashion-conscious women, too, will wear certain outfits only if their friends do not have similar dresses, as they want to be seen having independent views.

Uniqueness Some consumers also have a need to appear unique. New products satisfy their need for uniqueness. The need pushes them to distinguish themselves through the possession of rare items. They like to talk about their possessions and like to be praised by their friends for them.

Park, et al. (2010) distinguish between *sensory innovativeness* and *cognitive innovativeness*. Sensory innovators are attracted by colour, shape, design, and fashion. Cognitive innovators are attracted by factors such as quality and price. Products can be designed to appeal to both types of innovative consumers. They suggest that marketing communication and brand management should be based on the shopping styles of different types of innovative consumers.

Consumer Dogmatism

Consumer dogmatism is the opposite of consumer innovativeness. Dogmatism refers to the resistance to change of consumers, and represents the degree to which an individual's mindset is open or closed.

It explains the mental attitude of customers towards new ideas and products. People who are highly dogmatic are not open to new ideas and like to stick to their old consumption patterns. They tend to be closed minded and see new products with uncertainty. Companies marketing new products face the challenge of breaking this uncertainty. They encourage trials and low prices initially. Dogmatic customers are known to respond to figures of authority, so companies use celebrity endorsements and expert opinion to counter the resistance among such customers.

Examples of consumer dogmatism can be seen online. Whenever a new movie is released, people rush to comment about it on online forums. However, if anyone's comments are contrary to the views that have been generally expressed, other people post nasty and abusive counter-comments about it. Such behaviour is also seen in online comments on news articles and political views. This shows a high level of consumer dogmatism.

Consumers who are low in dogmatism are open-minded and prefer innovative products as opposed to established alternatives. They are not threatened by beliefs contrary to theirs. Informative ads stressing upon factual differences and benefits are also likely to appeal to such customers.

Since dogmatic customers are also loyal customers, this quality can be used by marketers to in the following ways:

- Devise marketing communications that would best appeal to the target group. For example, tradition and authority are highlighted for dogmatic customers
- Plan a word-of-mouth campaign using loyal customers. Loyal customers can be encouraged to be vocal as well as help launch such campaigns
- Continue to sell matured brands without any promotional effort. In other words, they can continue to sell certain products or brands that have become outdated or that are past the maturity stage in the product life cycle to the loyal customers, without much marketing effort, and thus continue to be profitable.

Social Character

Social character refers to whether consumers are *inner-directed* or *other-directed*. Inner-directed people are guided by their own values and beliefs in their approach towards new products. They

 EXHIBIT 5.2 Eurochamp: A Higher Calling

A vacuum cleaner in the India of the early 1980s was a product category that had market resistance written all over it. The ice-breaker was the Eurochamp who was able to bridge the chasm and develop a bond of trust with customers.

Over a period of time he came to be recognized as the 'friendly man' and his relationship became known as 'friends for life'. It was this special rapport that Euroclean leveraged in its communications. However, marketing cannot be all promise. On the ground, Euroclean fashioned a number of initiatives based on the feedback that was streaming in from the Eurochamp. This included educating consumers on how to get the most out of their vacuum cleaner; encouraging owners to allow domestic help to use their machines; and teach domestic help the correct method of using, cleaning, and storing the unit (see Fig. 5.3). It shows some of the print ads Euroclean used. These advertisements provides a lot of information aiming to educate customers.

As the endeavour took effect, communications shifted to fulfilling another objective: the task of creating awareness that a spotless home wasn't necessarily a healthy home. The company began to alert customers about the invisible threat posed by microscopic dust

FIG. 5.3 EuroCleaner print advertisements

Courtesy: Superbrands

mites. It developed literature in the form of an allergy booklet and sought endorsement from the Asthma and Allergy Resource Centre. Each of these further cemented its relationship with consumers. It did one more thing: it helped rechristen the Eurochamp as the dust and allergy controller. In its new *avatar*, the Eurochamp has graduated to a higher calling.

Source: Superbrands 2012

are more likely to have a positive attitude towards new products. Other-directed customers look for opinions of others in evaluating products.

Inner-directed consumers are attracted to ads that give product information and benefits. They have their own sense of values and standards, stick to their beliefs, and are less likely to be influenced by their friends and acquaintances. Please see Exhibit 5.2.

Other-directed consumers are likely to be influenced by ads that show social groups. They have a 'tribal outlook' and will most likely sport brands that their friends are wearing. Brand communities are helpful in involving other-directed consumers (see Marketing Insight). When people are receptive to social influence, they can be influenced about brands and products.

MARKETING INSIGHT
Other-Directed Influence

We are led by others' opinions. There are many ways of seeking opinion or approval. Friends going shopping seek each other's approval by asking, 'How do I look?' People post their pictures on social networking sites to gather 'likes', or approval from their friends. We often ask for recommendations from our friends before we go shopping.

Companies try to understand how a consumer segment responds to such influence in their buying behaviour. Three kinds of interpersonal influence have been identified.

Informational influence Informational influence is based on the desire to make informed decisions and optimize available choices. Consumers tend to rely on close friends and family members for information, and readily accept product recommendations. This gives rise to a powerful marketing tool: word-of-mouth. Product demonstrations and BTL campaigns generate buzz and get people talking to each other. There are several applications in marketing of this. First, companies use expert power and opinion leaders. Toothpaste ads featuring doctors or actors impersonating doctors serve as experts. Second, advertisements exhort people to 'Join the millions who trust brand X' trying to exert social pressure.

Value expressive influence When consumers seek social acceptance, compare themselves to others, and copy lifestyles so as to enhance their self-image or social standing, it is called the value expressive influence. Products are used for social status and acceptability within a certain social group. It is an 'identification process', in which people willingly make themselves similar to the group that they want to belong to. There are many examples of this. Pepsi builds the 'young generation' image hoping that consumers have accepted the values of this specific group. Children exhorting their parents to buy life insurance too play on this theme. Mobile phone manufacturers show famous celebrities or successful youngsters in their ads implying that people who use the same cell phone will have the same characteristics as the displayed group.

Utilitarian influence When people are conventional and yield to social pressure to gain approval or avoid punishment in the form of social ridicule, utilitarian influence is being exercised. It results from the influence of the consumer's own preferred social circle or family to satisfy expectations others have of her/him. It is a 'compliance process' in which an individual meets the group's expectations. An application of this is seen in a classroom when an individual, on getting a chance to cheat, changes answers to conform to the group answers, even changing the original right answers. Advertisements telling people that one may obtain social approval and acceptance by just using a certain brand, affects customers in the same way. Take a look at ads for personal care products in which consumers are seen to be ridiculed by friends for not using the anti-dandruff shampoo, deodorant, or mouthwash that is being advertised. TV advertisements ask people to 'watch the show everybody's talking about' so as to earn social approval.

How do companies use other-directed influence in their marketing campaigns?

COGNITIVE PERSONALITY FACTORS

Cognitive personality factors have a direct influence on consumer behaviour. People can be classified on the basis of whether they are influenced by images or information, called visualizers or verbalizers; and also as those who are thinkers or doers, which are classified as having high or low need for cognition. These are explained here.

Visualizers They are consumers who are influenced by graphics, images, and videos. Such consumers remember images and TV ads, or even the products themselves that have high visual appeal. They prefer the visual media or visual information rather than textual information.

Verbalizers They are consumers who prefer written or verbal information. They rely on what appears in newspapers or other print media and prefer products that have detailed information. Consumers with a high need for cognition are thinkers who collect information and deliberate upon it. Car customers who rely on technical specifications of the vehicle such as engine capacity, torque, mileage, length, and breadth, are in this category. Such customers need detailed product literature that they like to study and compare.

Consumers with a low need for *cognition* like messages that convey fun, fantasy, colours, music, jingles, etc. In our example of car customers, those with a low need for cognition, rely on the looks and style of the car while making their purchase decision. They will consider one or two factors such as mileage and resale value of the car and not go into technical details of the engine and the vehicle.

Consumers are also influenced by a larger trend in society, that of materialism. It means the importance a society places on worldly objects. While the extent of materialism will vary from person to person, modern marketing and advertising thrives on materialism—that is, people buying and displaying their material possessions. It is a tendency to consider material possessions and physical comfort as more important than spiritual values.

Materialism

When people place great importance in possessions, it is called *consumer materialism*. The opposite of materialism is spiritualism, when people do not place importance on things but on spiritual matters. Modern civilization, with an abundance of objects of desire backed by compulsive advertising, makes materialism a valued goal. Materialists

- want to own and show-off their possessions
- are self-centred and selfish
- take great pride in the things they own
- feel that their existence depends on their possessions
- do not have simple lifestyles
- have a consumption-oriented way of life

Readers will notice that these points describe modern societies to a large extent. Materialism gives rise to three behaviours: consumer fixation, impulsive, and compulsive behaviour.

CB IN ACTION   How Much Do We Need?

Graham Hill sold an Internet start-up in 1998 and with the money, bought a giant house crammed with stuff—electronics, furniture, cars, appliances, and gadgets. He writes in *The New York Times* (2013), 'Somehow this stuff ended up running my life, or a lot of it; the things I consumed ended up consuming me'.

He describes his experience: 'We live in a world of surfeit stuff, and people can deluge themselves with products. However, there isn't any indication that any of these things makes anyone any happier; in fact it seems the reverse may be true'.

Hill confesses that before long, he started to wonder why his upgraded life didn't feel very good. On the contrary, he felt more anxious than before. In this unnecessarily complicated life, thoughts about his personal identity started cropping up. 'Who had I become? My house and my things were my new employers for a job I had never applied for', he writes.

Modern life makes us fond of all kinds of goods and services. However, Hill asks a crucial question: Does this endless consumption result in measurably increased happiness? It took him a while to learn that 'the best stuff in life isn't stuff at all, and that relationships, experiences, and meaningful work are the staples of a happy life'.

Hill took a journey to simplify his life. He got rid of much of the stuff he collected. He concludes, 'My space is small. My life is big'.

1. Do the things you own define your personality?
2. Does consumer materialism add to happiness?
3. Is it important to have a lot of things or, like Hill, a simple life?

Source: http://www.nytimes.com/2013/03/10/opinion/sunday/living-with-less-a-lot-less.html?pagewanted=all&_r=0, last accessed on 11 March 2014.

Fixation, Impulsive, and Compulsive Consumption

Consumer fixation is the state in which an individual becomes obsessed or attached to a product or brand.

Fixated consumers have a passionate interest in a specific product category. They do not keep their objects or purchases of interest a secret, but frequently display them, and their involvement is openly shared with others who have a similar interest. They tend to be extremely loyal customers and actively support brands. Brand communities are examples of fixated consumers.

It is not necessary that fixated customers actually buy the products. People get fixated on some item they want to buy in the future and save for it over a long period of time. This is not considered as an abnormal behaviour.

Impulsive buying behaviour is when a consumer makes a sudden unplanned decision to buy a product or service, just before the purchase. It is a compelling, hedonic urge to buy something which the consumer gives in to without thinking.

Several factors cause impulse buying. Karbasivar and Yarahmadi (2011) found that window displays, credit cards, promotional activities such as discounts and freebies—can all lead to a consumer's impulse buying behaviour. With the growth of e-commerce and television shopping channels, consumers find that impulsive buying has become easy.

The four elements in impulse buying are as follows:

- A sudden desire or attraction
- A reduction in cognitive evaluation

- Lack of thinking of the consequences of the purchase
- A feeling that the purchase is a bargain or it will not be available again

Companies and retail stores adopt many methods to encourage impulsive buying, such as the following:

- Make displays so attractive that consumers end up buying
- Announce limited period offers or 'last day today' offers
- Present combo offers that are cheaper than buying individual items
- Set up bargain counters in shops offering low prices for goods

Most consumers admit to making impulse purchases at one time or another, and it is normal to be attracted to special displays. However, excessive impulsive buying behaviour can lead to spending on goods that a person does not really need. It is an easy way to acquire credit card debt.

Compulsive buying behaviour or compulsive shopping happens when people feel *compelled* to buy something; that is, they do not have control over their shopping. Such shopping is inwardly motivated. A compulsive shopper plans the shopping experience as a way to avoid or relieve uncomfortable internal feelings, like anxiety.

Shopping becomes a problem when people continue to do it even though it causes financial problems, disrupts work, family, and social life, or involves deceit, such as hiding bills and packages. Compulsive shoppers run into financial difficulties, have arguments with family members, and experience emotional confusion. However, they are unable to stop shopping becomes an addiction, so that they shop more and more to stave off stress and anxiety.

The Wall Street Journal (2011) writes that around six per cent of the US population suffers from compulsive buying behaviour. The Internet also encourages such behaviour because transactions move so quickly that it is hard to curb the buying urge. It lets people dissociate from reality and assume an alter ego fuelled by virtual cash. The stereotypical compulsive shoppers were traditionally women in their 30s, but the ease and speed of Internet shopping is luring more men young people. In a 2005 survey of 195 UK teenagers who grew up with the Internet, 44 per cent showed signs of compulsive shopping habits.

In a study of impulsive purchase behaviour, Shahjehan, et al. (2012) conducted a research in Pakistan and found that among the big five personality traits, both impulsive and compulsive buying were positively correlated with neuroticism, openness, and extraversion. Individuals who are moody, cultured, intelligent, and artistically sensitive are more likely to display impulsive buying behaviour. Increase in compulsive buying also occurs when individuals are gregarious, assertive, talkative, and active.

Consumer Ethnocentrism

Consumer ethnocentrism is a feeling of patriotism, and a resultant desire to accept or reject foreign-made products and brands. Ethnocentric consumers want to buy only goods made in their own country and feel that it is undesirable to prefer foreign products over indigenous ones.

The debate in India over the entry of foreign investment in retail is an example of consumer ethnocentrism. However, such feelings also exist in other parts of the world. Many countries look down upon big US brands as a sign of 'American imperialism'. For instance, research conducted by

CB IN ACTION   Consumer Ethnocentrism

Conduct a quick survey in your class about consumer ethnocentrism using the following scale:

What is your belief about foreign-made products?

1) Poor value for money	1 2 3 4 5 6 7	Good value for money
2) Technically backward	1 2 3 4 5 6 7	Technically advanced
3) Low quality	1 2 3 4 5 6 7	High quality
4) Unreliable	1 2 3 4 5 6 7	Reliable

1. Find out whether members of your class are ethnocentric or cosmopolitan.
2. Comment on the adoption or rejection of domestic and foreign brands by them.

Akdogan, et al. (2012) showed that both consumer ethnocentrism and animosity have a negative impact on repurchase intent toward US products in Turkey.

Shimp and Sharma (1987) have devised a 17-item, seven-point consumer ethnocentric tendencies scale (CETSCALE) that measures the level of ethnocentricity in consumers. The scale measures the acceptability of foreign goods and consumers' attitude towards multinational and domestic products and brands. Lindquist, et al. (2001) write that the 17 items of the CETSCALE are linked to the four consumers' beliefs that

- it hurts the domestic economy
- results in loss of jobs
- is unpatriotic
- is tied to product availability

Bawa (2004) conducted research and found that Indian university students have CETSCORES comparable not only to students in the Czech Republic, Estonia, and Poland but also to the US, which shows that consumer ethnocentrism is a worldwide phenomenon. She writes that the 'Made in India' label is not a liability for the country. Indian consumers will not lap up foreign goods merely because of their 'made in' tags. The opposite of consumer ethnocentrism is cosmopolitanism.

Cosmopolitanism

Cosmopolitanism refers to individuals who are oriented towards the outside world rather than their local community.

Originally coined by Merton (1957), the concept of cosmopolitanism relates to a 'world citizen', an individual whose orientation transcends any particular culture or setting. Cosmopolitan people view themselves as citizens of the world rather than the nation, a part of the broader, more heterogeneous cultural group. In marketing, cosmopolitanism is consumer orientation, which shows a positive orientation and openness to foreign cultures, internationalism, and world-mindedness. As the world has globalized, people have become more cosmopolitan. This trend is quite evident in Asia. Foreign fast food chains have made people cosmopolitan, and local populations have begun to expect global levels of service and efficiency even from domestic businesses.

Cannon and Yaprak (2001) propose the following four degrees of local–global outlook:

Parochial Consumers are restricted to their community and harbour parochial values and prejudices. They have little interest in or identification with local people or culture. They have strong loyalty to brands that cater to their community.

Local Consumers have parochial values but are not restricted to the community and see themselves as part of a city or town. Such consumers are open to trying out foreign brands.

Local cosmopolitan Consumers look broadly for standards of excellence and authenticity. Nevertheless, they feel personally attached to the local people and culture. They value their local relationships, culture, and sense of belonging. They see local roots as an expression of the 'extended self'. However, they are not ethnocentric and are not closed to foreign cultures. They transcend their local culture without abandoning it.

Cosmopolitan Consumers look broadly for standards of excellence and authenticity. They favour global cultures and connections. Such consumers will have global tastes in consumption.

The aforementioned degrees of local–global outlook also represent the level of openness in societies. This impacts marketing strategy as foreign brands will have to cater to these segments differently. For the first two categories, they will have to localize products, packaging, and promotion. Local cosmopolitans will be open to foreign brands, but the promotion will have to be according to domestic tastes. Finally, the cosmopolitans will look for imported products in their original packing and even respond to global ads.

Research conducted by Parts and Vida (2011) shows that cosmopolitan consumers have a stronger tendency to buy foreign rather than local products. It leads to better perception of foreign products, including their quality.

BRAND PERSONALITY

Aaker (1997) defines brand personality as the set of human characteristics associated with a brand. Companies try to build brand personality by endowing it with certain characteristics. The global brand Absolut Vodka, for instance, is presented in such a way that it is seen as a cool, hip, and contemporary personality (see chapter-opening case).

Aaker developed a framework of brand personality dimensions, reducing a large number of traits to five dimensions—sincerity, excitement, competence, sophistication, and ruggedness. The five dimensions, along with their traits and how they have been used by brands, is summarized in Table 5.5.

Brand personality is somewhat different from brand personification. In the personality dimensions, sincerity, excitement, and competence are part of human personality, but sophistication and ruggedness are dimensions that individuals aspire to but do not necessarily have (Exhibit 5.3). When brands start acquiring human-like qualities, it is known as brand personification, which is described in the next section.

Brand Personification

People attach human characteristics to products consciously or subconsciously. The process is aided through advertising. The most common way that this is done is to show certain kinds of

Personality and the Consumer | 155

TABLE 5.5 Aaker's brand personality dimensions

Brand personality dimension	Traits	Examples
Sincerity	Domestic, honest, wholesome, cheerful	Tide, Peter England, Indigo
Excitement	Daring, spirited, imaginative	Mountain Dew, Thums Up, Calvin Klein, Bacardi
Competence	Reliable, intelligent, responsible, successful, efficient	Citibank, Vim
Sophistication	Glamorous, charming, romantic, upper class	Lakme, Garnier, Raymonds, Mercedes, Dior
Ruggedness	Tough, strong, masculine	Harley Davidson, Scorpio, Woodland

Source: Adapted from Aaker, Jennifer L., 'Dimensions of brand personality', *Journal of Marketing Research*, Vol. 34, No. 3, 1997, pp. 347–356

EXHIBIT 5.3 Superbrands—Brands and Personality

A brand that uses all elements of personality is Barbie—a dashing young woman who has portrayed more than 130 careers, represented 50 nationalities, and collaborated with more than 70 different fashion designers across the planet. With one Barbie doll sold every three seconds somewhere in the world, Barbie remains the world's most popular doll and attracts girls of all ages.

Through the decades, the Barbie brand has evolved with girls, extending into entertainment, online, and more than 45 different consumer product categories. It has a large social media presence on Twitter, YouTube, and Facebook.

The brand is an aspirational role model for girls worldwide. The doll takes on new careers and roles from princess to popstar, showing that anything is possible for them. See Fig. 5.4. She engages young girls and, comes off as a best friend to them in unique ways.

The brand moves into the imagination of consumers in a variety of ways. In India, Barbie came

FIG. 5.5 Katrina Kaif promting Barbie

Courtesy: Superbrands

to life in the All Doll'd Up! fashion show at the Lakmé Fashion Week 10th year anniversary. Superstar Katrina Kaif graced the occasion by walking the ramp for Barbie. The company unveiled a one-of-a-kind doll in the likeness of Katrina Kaif—India's reigning Bollywood queen and a role model to millions of young girls. This doll was presented to Katrina at a special event, which helped to connect with Indian people. Mattel India launched the Barbie 'I Can Be a Movie Star' doll in 2011, with the message—'With Barbie®, if you can dream it, you can be it'. This was the first-ever Bollywood celebrity inspired doll made available for kids at retail; it proved to be a runaway success. Please see Fig. 5.5.

FIG. 5.4 Princess and Popstar

Courtesy: Superbrands

(Contd)

EXHIBIT 5.3 (Contd)

Barbie promotes Indian values and culture through the Barbie Indian Saree Doll range and the 'Expressions of India' Bridal Doll range. In these she carries the Indian look adorning the saree and the lehenga respectively.

Today, Barbie has become an icon and a celebrated friend to girls, inspiring them each day in hundreds of different ways. The key to her success is her ability to remain relevant across generations, being in sync with girls, their mothers and even cultural shifts as she travels from country to country and region to region. Barbie also understands the impact entertainment has on children. As such all Barbie movies have fun, engaging storylines rich in friendship, family values, bravery, honesty, and determination.

Various types of dolls or themes promote play patterns of young girls. Some famous themes are fashion and beauty dolls, princess and fairies and the 'I Can Be' series, which promotes knowledge of different careers via play. Barbie's house and family range ramps right up to the adult collectors' community as well.

Barbie is represented in over 45 product categories that, beyond dolls, appeal to girls. Some of the most popular themes revolve around apparel, accessories, personal care, back-to-school, home, publishing, sporting goods, and others that include do-it-yourself kits, puzzles, board games, and party products.

Source: Superbrands 2012

---

people in their ads. The US cigarette brand introduced the Marlboro man who, writes Connolly (2011) 'transformed the brand from a mild ladies' cigarette into a rugged, ultra-masculine accessory. The campaign was wildly successful—Marlboro sales increased 300 per cent in the two years after the ad debuted in 1955'.

McDonalds placing Ronald McDonald outside its stores is an example of brand personification. In India, the insurance company Bajaj Allianz uses the animated character of the Bajaj Allianz Super Agent (as face of the company) who promises to make things very easy for customers so that they can live without worries— *Jiyo Befikar*.

Celebrities too, help put a human face to brands. Faced with a scandal that threatened the chocolate brand Cadbury's when worms were found in its products, the company quickly signed on Amitabh Bachchan for its ads. Bachchan appeared in several ads of the company and soon became the face of the company.

Dumitrescu (2007) has proposed a model of product personality that includes 20 human dimensions. Respondents are asked to evaluate every dimension of product personality by providing a rating from 1 to 5 as shown in Table 5.6. By doing so, product personality can be mapped and personality features of a brand can be discovered. Since these dimensions are applicable to people as well, companies can map out the personality of the target segment as well.

Companies do this exercise for brands as well as for target segments. Brands with a personality map matching the personality map of the target market segment will do better than brands that are mismatched with their target segments. Woodland, for instance, matched its personality with the outdoor-loving consumer and established its personality (see chapter-opening case study). If differences are discovered between the two, companies can tweak their positioning strategy for better results. Thus, companies can follow the consumers' relationships with brands to successfully launch products.

TABLE 5.6 20-dimension personality model to measure product and brand personality

Dimension	Values						
Sense of self-worth	Vain	1	2	3	4	5	Modest
Brilliance	Brilliant	1	2	3	4	5	Dim
Complexity	Complex	1	2	3	4	5	Simple
Energy	Energetic	1	2	3	4	5	Passive
Sensitivity	Sensitive	1	2	3	4	5	Insensitive
Kindness	Violent	1	2	3	4	5	Gentle
Flexibility	Flexible	1	2	3	4	5	Inflexible
Politeness	Polite	1	2	3	4	5	Impertinent
Maturity	Mature	1	2	3	4	5	Childish
Openness	Open	1	2	3	4	5	Closed
Generosity	Generous	1	2	3	4	5	Selfish
Honesty	Honest	1	2	3	4	5	Dishonest
Seriousness	Serious	1	2	3	4	5	Light-hearted
Stability	Stable	1	2	3	4	5	Unstable
Tolerance	Authoritarian	1	2	3	4	5	Liberal
Morality	Principled	1	2	3	4	5	Opportunistic
Attitude	Naive	1	2	3	4	5	Cynical
Modernism	Conformist	1	2	3	4	5	Rebel
Outlook	Pessimistic	1	2	3	4	5	Optimistic
Closeness	Warm	1	2	3	4	5	Aloof

Source: Adapted from Dumitrescu (2007)

Once this exercise is done, companies can work out their communication and marketing strategy. They identify the advertising elements required for this, explained in the next section.

Advertising Elements

Batra, et al. (2009) give five key advertising elements that contribute to brand personality—endorser, user imagery, execution elements, symbols, and consistency.

Endorser The person who endorses the brand—celebrity, expert, or ordinary consumer—lends his or her own characteristics to the brand. People start associating the person's qualities with the brand, as with Cadbury's chocolate. Even people featured in an ad, like two young girls sharing each other's method of treating pimples, gives the brand a young, perky, feminine, and beautiful persona.

User imagery User imagery, or creating a distinct image in the consumer's mind, is a powerful tool to give a personality to a brand. Aaker (1997) defines user imagery as the set of human

CB IN ACTION — Find Out the Brand Personalities

Select your favourite brand. Then write the answers to the following questions about the brand:

1. If the brand was a car, what kind of car would it be? Think of the year, make, model, and colour when selecting the brand.
2. If the brand was a famous celebrity, who would it be and why?
3. If the brand was an animal, what kind of animal would it be, and why?
4. If the brand had a spokesperson, who would it be and why?
5. If the brand was a person, who would it be and why?
6. List some adjectives that describe the brand.
7. Select the archetype for the brand from Table 5.1.

Analyse your own personality and see whether the brand matches your personality and in what ways. Make this a presentation and explain reasons for your choices.

FIG. 5.6 Logo of LIC

Courtesy: Superbrands 2012

FIG. 5.7 Logo of Dainik Bhaskar

Courtesy: Superbrands 2012

characteristics associated with the typical user of a brand. For instance, to emphasize that its brand 'Happydent' was ideal for white teeth, Perfetti used images of people perched on lamp posts lighting up the dark street with their dazzling grins.

Execution elements By using advertising execution elements like colour, layout, labels, and typography, brands build their personality. Consider, for instance, the distinct font and colours used by Taj Hotels or Oracle in their logos, and notice how their consistent use lends a personality to the brand.

Symbols Symbols too give the brand a distinct personality. For example, the symbol of a keyhole for State Bank of India emphasizes the characteristics of safety and security. LIC shows protection within two hands in its logo, while Dainik Bhaskar uses the sun in its logo as a means of building their personalities (see Figs 5.6 and 5.7).

Consistency As brand personality is consistent, companies must develop it over a period of time. None of the personality elements should be changed. For instance, brands such as Lux and Pears have not changed their personality even though they have been relaunched a number of times.

Anthropomorphism

Advertising encourages consumers to view brands in human terms. Anthropomorphism is the process of ascribing human characteristics to non-human objects. In marketing, we are concerned with consumers assigning human traits to products, brands, and companies.

Puzakova, et al. (2009) write that anthropomorphized brands are perceived by consumers as actual human beings with various emotional states, mind, soul, and conscious behaviours that can act as social ties. In order for a brand to bond with consumers, a brand 'should possess multiple qualities of a human being, embracing emotionality, thoughtful behaviour, soul, and feelings,' they write.

Both brand personality and anthropomorphism have a humanizing effect on brands and products. They generate more favourable consumer attitudes and thus enhance brand performance. However, Puzakova, et al. (2013) note the negative consequences of brand humanization; that is, the anthropomorphism of a brand can negatively affect consumers' brand evaluations when the brand faces negative publicity caused by product wrongdoings. They conducted five experiments with products that had experienced negative publicity, or had failed in some way to live up to its advertising claim, or did not function based on consumer expectations. In every instance, participants reported that they had stronger negative reactions to the products that were given human characteristics. Clearly, brand anthropomorphism is a very powerful advertising tool, but companies need to be careful because when they imbue their products with human-like characteristics, the backlash when something goes wrong could be stronger.

Product Personality and Gender

Brands acquire male or female personalities by two means. First, the product or brand is specifically designed or modified to appeal to the stereotypical man or woman. Second, it is strongly associated with the masculine or feminine stereotype through advertising and promotion.

Companies try to assign a gender to brand personalities so as to

- precisely target the gender-specific segment
- expand the market to serve the neglected half
- build and manage lasting brand relationships with customers

Targeting Gender

Certain products are distinctly male or female. Most people think of pimple-removing creams, handbags, and other fashion accessories as feminine. Similarly, motorcycles, shirts, and leather jackets are thought of as male. Strong attitudes are associated with products considered as meant for the opposite sex. For example, males would not like to be seen with pink cell phones, as the colour pink is associated with women. Brands can exploit these differences to specifically target a gender.

Targeting Women

Silverstein and Sayre (2009) write that women represent a growth market bigger than China and India combined. However, even though they represent half of the market, women are underserved. 'Given those numbers, it would be foolish to ignore or underestimate the female consumer. And yet many companies do just that,' they write.

They give the example of the cosmetics industry, 'in which men make hit-or-miss guesses about what women want', as a result, women are dissatisfied. Instead, if companies identified and addressed the real needs of women, they would find a whole new range of commercial opportunities.

While targeting women, companies fall into the 'make it pink' mindset, hoping that by making superficial changes to the product, it will become attractive to women. HSBC Philippines offers a Red Mastercard which promises 'irresistible rewards for women' and HDFC Bank in India too offers a 'women's gold credit card', but when we read the terms and conditions of both, we find few differences between a normal credit card and a women's credit card. Laptops and many other products too are sold to women with the same mindset.

Targeting Men

Companies have targeted males on the basis of ruggedness. Anything strong or macho was considered to be male. However, as sexual roles changed due to the changing society, advertisers looked for the real male customer. Through faulty research, they came up with the idea of the 'metrosexual male' who, writes Byrnes in *Businessweek* (2006), 'seemed hip and urban. Women, it was said, loved him because he smelled good'. So companies cooked up lotions and potions for this new male, only to discover that the metrosexual male was in a minority. Most men, for instance, do not keep a separate soap or shampoo for themselves when these are easily available in the household.

Companies have targeted males with 'macho' or 'rugged' products. Yet, the bulk of the male market consists of the following three segments:

- Millions of dads, who shop for household goods because their wives are working. They shop for diapers, detergents and groceries, traditionally thought to be bought by women.
- An army of men in their 20s and 30s who care about their appearance but like macho activities as well
- A huge percentage of male teens, sophisticated consumers with web research skills to give them a say in family purchases

The challenge is to communicate to these men and move beyond the heavy focus on the fictionalized male. While targeting males, it is important to keep the real market segments in mind.

Making Brands Gender-neutral

A third challenge is to make a feminine brand acceptable to males and vice versa, with the objective of widening the market. Hair salons and beauty parlours now try to be gender-neutral so as to target both men and women. Apparel brands also try to include both sexes; Levi's Jeans successfully transformed the rugged, male brand to make it acceptable to women worldwide.

CB IN ACTION   Metrosexual Male

In the film, *Rab Ne Bana Di Jodi*, Shah Rukh Khan tries to project a macho image to impress his wife; the attempt fails. He is caught between two extremes, a shy do-gooder at one end and a macho dancing companion on the other. He discovers that his wife preferred the real hero who was somewhere in-between, part family man and part macho lover.

Are advertisers making the same mistake by targeting the metrosexual male? Does he exist? Who is the actual male customer and what does he want?

Observe shoppers at a supermarket and make notes to find answers to these questions.

1. What percentage of the shoppers are male?
2. What are the brands and products they buy?
3. What are the insights you got into the psyche of the male shopper?

Make a presentation to your class. It is sure to be a very interesting one!

Gender bending is the term used to show how brands target the opposite sex. There are inherent dangers in this, as we will see in Chapter 9. Male customers would not like to be seen using brands with a strong feminine orientation, and most women would not like to be seen buying male brands. Even so, companies try to make their brands gender neutral to expand their markets. Even a typically male brand like Axe woos women, while cosmetic brands try hard to make themselves acceptable to men (Exhibit 5.4).

Building and Managing Brand Relationships

The main problem in gender bending is moulding consumer attitudes, which leads to managing customer–brand relationships. If a product with a strong gender-bias tries to extend its reach to

EXHIBIT 5.4 How Brands Try to Extend Gender Usage

Companies in every sector try to extend brands with the objective of expanding market share and sales. They feel that the differences between male and female consumers, such as income, attitudes, and expenditure, are disappearing, so companies try to extend brands to make them acceptable to both men and women. Social trends show that women are earning more, spending more, and marrying later than before. Brands that have traditionally served men now try to make themselves attractive to women as well.

The Economic Times (2012) writes that by crossing gender lines companies are not doing a complete role reversal, but they are trying to extend brands to a large untapped market—the other half of the species—without abandoning the core proposition.

Unilever is extending its distinctively male brand Axe to women. Its website says that a limited edition version of Anarchy is the first fragrance from the Axe brand that has a female version packaged in a silver and pink canister with floral and fruity notes. Axe, known for its cheeky commercials, hopes to extend the boldness theme to females and thereby expand the market.

Bacardi woos women with Bacardi +, a ready-to-drink mixer, marking a clear shift in strategy as hard drink manufacturers have traditionally targeted men. The Bacardi Breezer has become popular with women in many parts of the world. *Mint* (2009) reports that electronic goods that traditionally targeted men are making their products friendly to females. Sony has a Vaio Pocket PC showing a young woman with a notebook tucked into her rear pocket, emphasizing how women use these products.

Allen Solly has reinvented itself to become a unisex brand. Traditionally a male brand, it now serves women as well. It tries to make its 'Friday Dressing' concept acceptable to women. Color Plus too, now has smart casuals for women. ICICI Prudential extended the insurance business with a very female-oriented advertisement, '*Jeete Raho.*'

Conversely, cosmetic brands have tried to shift from women to men. Nivea and Garnier have a men's range now. Gillette broke out of its male image and now offers shaving products for women. Marlboro cigarettes were initially targeted towards women and had the tagline 'Mild as May' but successfully changed the brand to the 'Marlboro Man.'

However, there have been failures. Nike, which is the name of the Greek goddess of victory, has tried to break into the female market for shoes and apparel for decades but without much success. The company, which has featured superstars such as Michael Jordan, Lance Armstrong, and Tiger Woods, found that women didn't respond to them like men did.

A slide show of gender-bending brands is available at http://images.businessweek.com/slideshows/20111013/gender-bending-a-brand

Sources:
Bapna, A., 'Gender Bender: Brands focused on men now wooing women customers', *The Economic Times*, 4 April 2012.
Chandran, Anushree, 'Brands try to cross traditional barriers, bridge gender divide', *Mint*, March 17 2009.
http://www.unilever.com/brands-in-action/detail/Axe-launches-its-first-fragrance-for-women/292067/, last accessed on 26 July 2013.

the other sex, it faces the danger of not only the targeted gender rejecting it, but also of alienating existing customers.

Jung and Lee (2006) write that gender bending of brands works if there is an image fit, that is, how well the brand accommodates the extension. Since the extension is in the same product category and shares the same features, the most critical aspect is a brand's perceived masculinity or femininity. For example, when a brand like Victoria's Secret extends into the male market, the key issue is whether men will accept the feminine image of the brand.

Product Personality and Geography

Many products have a strong association with the geographic area from where they originate. These geographical characteristics are referred to as geographical indications (GIs). It is believed that characteristics such as local raw materials, climate, soil quality, or other local factors influence the taste and quality of foods, or impart personality characteristics to them. Darjeeling tea, Parmigiano cheese, Bordeaux wine, Kobe beef, Idaho potatoes, Basmati rice, Jamaica Blue Mountain coffee, and Tequila are some of the popular products that are linked to their geography. They bear the unmistakable stamp of the region or place of origin which gives them competitive power. As Porter (1998) wrote, 'The enduring competitive advantages in a global economy lie increasingly in local things— knowledge, relationships, motivation—that distant rivals cannot match."

A report by International Trade Centre (2009) estimates the value for sales of GI products worldwide at well over US$ 50 billion. Over 10,000 legally-protected GIs exist globally. Together, developing countries have about 10 per cent of the total; many are recognized but not adequately protected.

The World Trade Organization (WTO) Agreement on Trade-Related Aspects of Intellectual Property Rights (TRIPS) defines GI as, 'Indications which identify a good as originating in the territory of a member, or a region or locality in that territory, where a given quality, reputation or other characteristic of the good is essentially attributable to its geographic origin.'

Geographic personality consisting of GIs are gaining in importance. They are valuable assets, like brands, that can play a vital role in marketing. The following factors contribute to geographic personality:

Uniqueness They should be differentiated from commodities usually in terms of both quality and price. The intrinsic distinctiveness should be recognizable by consumers and must have sufficient uniqueness to facilitate commercial promotion.

Local distinctiveness The personality should be distinctly local, and recognize the customary and value-adding traditions of the local people, their history and their relationship to a place.

Culture They should reflect a tangible culture to be shared and even traded with other cultures. The personality should represent globalization at its best by encouraging trade and also recognizing things that are intrinsically local in nature.

A product will have personality only where specific aspects of geography contribute to its uniqueness, often getting associated with the local culture and tradition of its place of origin.

Some GIs, such as Basmati (Indo–Pakistani rice) and Feta (cheese from Greece), may be from a particular place but do not use direct geographical names. It is different from labelling, like 'Made in Indonesia', which is not something that confers a personality trait. Watches and chocolates from Switzerland are notable exceptions. They illustrate that personality is gained when the country of origin is mentioned.

Personality and Colour

Labrecque and Milne (2012) demonstrate that colour has a relationship with brand personality, likability, and familiarity. They write that associations are triggered in memory through colour's referential meaning. As brands pair with colours, their association with the brand become linked in memory and this occurs without a person's conscious awareness or intention.

Many writers have commented on the link between colour and personality. Several quizzes are available online that helps analyse personality based on a person's favourite colour. Labrecque and Milne (2012) write that brands routinely use colour to stand out. Loud primary colours are used to attract the attention of drivers on highways. The colours of the national flag are often used in advertisement designs for companies that want to project patriotic feelings. Green is often associated with the environment, health, and hygiene sectors, and light blue or silver is often used to reflect diet foods. Fraser and Banks (2004) provide qualities and personality traits linked to brands.

- Black is the colour of sophistication, glamour, power, stateliness, and dignity. In fashion, black expresses status, elegance, richness, and dignity as seen in black limousines, black dresses, black tuxedos, suits, and ties.
- Blue is linked to competence, and with security, intelligence, communication, trust, efficiency, duty, and logic.
- Brown is related to seriousness, reliability, and support.
- Orange, along with other longer wavelength hues such as red and yellow, induce states of arousal and excitement. Orange is exciting, but less so than red. It is considered lively, energetic, extroverted, and sociable.
- Pink is considered nurturing, warm, and soft.
- Purple connotes luxury, authenticity, and quality. It is also a dignified and stately colour. Along with pink, purple also signifies sophistication as it is considered soft, feminine, and charming.
- Red is linked to excitement as it is considered an arousing, exciting, and vivacious colour. It is associated with activity, strength, and stimulation.
- White is associated with sincerity, purity, cleanness, simplicity, hygiene, clarity, and peace.
- Yellow is cheerful and sincere, as it elicits feelings of optimism, extraversion, friendliness, and happiness.

The personality traits represented by the various colours are summarized in Table 5.7.

Colour Differentiation

Brands can achieve differentiation by using colour combinations other than those used by the market leader. However, using similar colour and packaging as the leader offers benefits. Consumers have category associations and can recognize similar products. That is why sharing

TABLE 5.7 Colours representing personality traits

Personality trait	Colours representing it
Sincerity	White, yellow, and pink
Excitement	Red, orange, and yellow
Ruggedness	Brown and blue
Sophistication	Black, blue, purple, and pink
Competence	Blue and brown
Security	Blue and green

some visual aspects of the market leader helps new entrants gain the consumers' recognition, while also differentiating other attributes to signal a unique identity. Market entrants often adhere to the colour norms of the market leader.

Labrecque and Milne (2012) write that there is a risk if brands deviate from established market leaders and category norms. In low-risk categories, like consumer-packaged goods, deviations from category norms may be inconsequential for brand performance; for high-risk categories, category colour norms may allow the transfer of positive affect and reduce risk.

SELF AND SELF-IMAGE

People buy whatever they think fits with what they feel about themselves. This is the application of self-concept and self-image to marketing. People project their self-image through their clothes, the way they talk and walk, and the products they consume.

To illustrate, a young girl who sees herself as 'modern' will buy glamorous western dresses, but another who thinks of herself as traditional will stick to Indian wear. It is not that they would look bad if they wore each other's choices, but it is their self-image that guides their purchase behaviour. This reasoning can be extended to the purchase of many other products such as laptops, mobile phones, bags, accessories, and cosmetics. Indeed, many advertisements are targeted at the self-concept of consumers.

Rosenberg (1979) defined self-concept as 'the totality of the individual's thoughts and feelings having reference to himself as an object'. It can also be described as a cognitive appraisal of one's own attributes.

An understanding of self-concept and self-image thus guides the development of effective marketing programmes. Self-congruence suggests that the self-concept of consumers must match the user image of the brand or product. The *self-congruity theory*, proposed by Sirgy (1982), says that consumers prefer those products in which their self-concept is congruent with the product-user image of a product. In other words, people buy products if they see themselves as similar to the people that they think should be using them. Consumer behaviour will be directed toward furthering and enhancing a person's self-concept through the consumption and exhibition of goods as symbols of self-expression.

MARKETING INSIGHT
Turning Dreams into Reality

One of the major contributions of Freud has been to provide an understanding of the subconscious mind, a place where a person can imagine being what he/she is not. Aiding the subconscious are dreams, which help one to imagine oneself in various imagined selves. Freud suggested that dreams were a representation of unconscious desires, thoughts, and motivations. These thoughts are not consciously expressed and so are expressed in dreams. In his book, *The Interpretation of Dreams* (1900), Freud wrote that dreams are '...disguised fulfilments of repressed wishes'.

It is hardly a wonder that marketing and advertising are often referred to as dream factories. Advertising is called the 'dream industry', shopping malls are 'dream worlds', and catalogues are 'wish books'. They encourage the consumer to imagine and desire by allowing them into a world of anticipated consumption.

Freud's theory has been used in creating personality for products in more ways than we can imagine. Hogan (2013) explains in his book, *Invisible Influence* that advertisers create specific strategies for imbuing specific traits for the brand they are selling. They create scenarios that represent a person's alter ego, based on the hidden self deep within the unconscious. By projecting a dream-like sequence in which a person is more confident and sexy, they are able to create brand personalities that rub off on people.

Park and Young (2010) conducted studies that showed how this happens. In the first study, they asked female shoppers in a mall to carry a shopping bag for an hour during their shopping trip. Shoppers were allowed to use either a Victoria's Secret shopping bag or a plain pink shopping bag. After an hour, they were asked to rate themselves on a list of personality traits. It was found that shoppers who carried the Victoria's Secret bag perceived themselves as more feminine, glamorous, and good-looking than shoppers who carried the plain shopping bag.

Victoria's Secret advertising creates powerful imagery of women walking the ramp wearing lingerie and angel wings. Hogan (2013) explains that hypothetically, the brain sees the lingerie being worn by the self and this causes the glamorous feeling to increase. Appealing to the dream of a woman to appear glamorous and sexy, the brand creates a scenario in which a woman imagines wearing something flimsy and feeling good about herself. The dream-like sequence transforms the worst dream of a person (walking in the street with nothing but lingerie on) into a desired dream.

How do brands use the concept of multiple selves to help consumers identify with their brands? How are dreams and wish fulfilment used by advertisers? Study marketing communications in this perspective to find out what really happens in the minds of consumers.

Sources:
Hogan, Kevin, *Invisible Influence: The Power to Persuade Anyone, Anytime, Anywhere*, John Wiley and Sons, New Jersey, 2013.
Park, Ji Kyung and Deborah Roedder John, 'Got to get you into my life: Do brand personalities rub off on consumers?' *Journal of Consumer Research*, Vol. 37, December 2010, pp. 655–669.

The theory is extended to personality as well. The *personality congruence effect* states that people prefer those brands with which they share personality characteristics. These theories apply not only to what people actually are, but what they think of themselves, which gives rise to the concepts of multiple selves, extended self, and virtual reality.

Several studies have found empirical evidence of the congruence of brand personality with the consumer's personality. Research conducted by Aguirre-Rodriguez, Bosnjak, and Sirgy (2012) suggests that self-congruity effects are a function of the following:

Self-motive and degree of self-enhancement sought Self or internal motive consists of public self-motives that relate to one's social acceptance with usage of the brand, and private self-motives like internal standards of enhancement that one has set for oneself. Degree of self-enhancement sought concerns the social enhancement one feels on using the product.

Brand personality Brand personality refers to the brand as a person and whether the consumer feels 'friendly' towards it.

Brand's abstraction level Abstraction level refers to the ability of the consumers to imagine or retrieve from memory their interaction with the brand. For instance, consumers may think of a brand as fun, cool, and sophisticated whether they have experience with it or not.

Cognitive elaboration This refers to the cognitive evaluation of the brand, based on factors that are desirable to the consumer.

Impression formation Impression formation occurs as a result of either as a trait-by-trait evaluation of a brand, or as a holistic brand. In the first instance, consumers evaluate traits congruent with their personality and in the second, they consider whether the brand as a whole is congruent with their personality.

Khan and Bozzo (2012) studied the self-concept dimensions in Pakistan and examined the relationship of self-congruity with brand preference. The study found that people are more concerned about self-congruence for conspicuous products than for inconspicuous products.

Duarte and Raposo (2010) show that the social environment and the context in which the product is used influences the brand preference for mobile phones. The results stress the importance of brand identity and self-image of the consumer in brand preference, and that consumers tend to prefer mobile phone brands that are closer to their self-image.

The phenomenon is not limited to adult consumers alone. Rhee and Johnson's (2012) study of adolescents also confirmed that adolescents regard their favourite brand as being closely linked to their actual self-concept. Young consumers, too, aspire to the status and achievement they perceive to be symbolized by the brand. For example, a study by Park and Young (2010) found that students who used a pen with MIT embossed on it felt they were smarter than others.

FIG. 5.8 Multiple selves

One or Multiple Selves

People react in different ways according to the circumstances. That is to say, they have multiple selves, each one of which reveals itself as the situations and the individuals involved in them change (see Fig. 5.8). Multiple selves occur through the following:

Role identities How we act in our different roles, or in different components of the self

Social interaction How our relationships with other people play a part in forming the self, or by acting the way we assume others expect us to act

Looking-glass self   The process of imagining the reactions of others toward us—when we think of what others say

The multiple selves can be classified as follows:

Ideal self   How people would like to see themselves, or how a person would like to be

Actual self   How consumers see themselves. It is a person's realistic appraisal of the qualities he or she does and does not possess

Social self-image   Refers to how people are seen by others or how they imagine themselves to be seen by others

Fantasy self-image   A self-induced shift in consciousness through imagination. Fantasy appeals refer to advertising that encourage consumers to imagine themselves as their ideal selves

Extended Self

Extended self refers to products or brands that consumers consider a part of themselves. For instance, many people see their laptops as part of their extended self since they contain elements of their personality—pictures, movies, music they love, their work, and so on.

There are four levels of the extended self:

Individual level   Consists of personal possessions and products valued by the consumer

Family level   Consists of one's residence, furniture, and furnishings which reflect the personality of the owner

Community level   One's neighbourhood or town is part of the community self. Many consumers share personality traits of their community

Group level   Consists of social groups, friends, or clubs that one is a part of

Altering the Self

People alter their selves for self-improvement or getting accepted in their society. Our self can be altered in the following ways:

Getting an education   People alter their self, personality, and outlook by getting an education.

Changing clothes or accessories   Consumers alter themselves by buying different clothes or accessories and are able to express themselves and also report better levels of confidence as a result. Wearing a party dress, for example, puts one in a party mood.

Using self-altering products   Cosmetics, perfumes, sunglasses, and so on, help in altering the self. The manufacturers of such products rest on consumers' need for self-altering products.

Getting a makeover   Makeovers are of two kinds. One includes changes in appearance such as a new hair style or hair colour, wearing contact lenses, or other such products. The second is undergoing cosmetic surgery to alter a part of the body.

ETHICAL INSIGHT
Dark Marketing: Exploiting Negative Personality Traits

Marketing uses the study of personality to sell products and services to people. Very often, companies use the negative aspects of personality to appeal to customers. Take a look, for instance, at the numerous books written and movies made around death, torture, kidnappings, vampires, ghosts, and disasters, and you will realise that the use of dark marketing, described as 'the application or adaptation of marketing principles and practices to domains of death, destruction, and the ostensibly reprehensible', is widespread indeed.

Brown, McDonagh, and Shultz (2012) explain that 'thanatourism' has been around for a long time. To attract visitors, dark places are packaged, promoted, priced, and positioned, just like any other product or service. A British company, Historical Trips, for instance, organizes a tour of the concentration camps and torture chambers of Nazi Germany. Its website states, 'Our tour takes in the camp huts, gas chambers, and crematoria, as well as the memorials to those who died'.

Dark marketing encompasses the drugs trade, the sex trade, the sale of body parts, blood diamonds, surrogate children, and counterfeit goods, the funeral industry, the gaming industry, the private security industry, and aspects of the fashion industry. Although concerns are often expressed about the impact of violent or disturbing images, such experiences are marketed with impunity, based on the assumption that 'sick sells'.

Product advertising, too uses such images frequently. Business Insider (2012) reports that Dolce & Gabbana, for example, released an ad showing half-naked men standing around a lone woman, who's lying on the ground in a fairly suggestive position. Many people viewers thought it suggested gang rape.

Here are a few examples of the use of baser human instincts in marketing:

- Video games thrive on violent and grotesque images and people are required to cause murder and mayhem.
- Music performers like to shock audiences with grotesque costumes and obscene acts. The twerking of pop stars are now accepted practices in their effort to market their concerts.
- Fashion shows feature models wearing all kinds of grotesque material. Pop icon Lady Gaga wore a meat dress and kicked off the 'fashion food' spin. Designers are also experimenting with chocolate, meat, and vegetables, mainly to shock viewers, reports *The Times of India* (2012).
- Reality shows like Big Boss and the X Factor lets people gloat at the failures and foibles of others. The amateurish auditions, where couch potato viewers laugh at and mock the musically afflicted.

Critics point out that by appealing to the baser side of human personality, marketing uses the powerful technologies of advertising, promotion, public relations, and market research to take unfair advantage of the vanity, cupidity, stupidity, sloth, and other such human personality traits. Using modern technologies like neuroscience, marketing communications use subliminal manipulations to influence consumers towards harmful behaviour. As a consequence, it results in several negative behaviours among consumers, such as consumerism, shopaholism, and obesity.

Should companies use baser human instincts in their marketing? What are its ethical implications?

Sources:

Brown, Stephen, Pierre McDonagh, and Clifford Shultz, 'Dark marketing: Ghost in the machine or skeleton in the cupboard?', *European Business Review*, Vol. 24, No. 3, 2012, pp. 196–215.

http://www.businessinsider.com/13-brands-that-use-sex-to-sell-their-products-2012-2?op=1#ixzz2gXEbn3BZ, last accessed on 13 March 2014.

http://www.historicaltrips.com/faceofevil.html, last accessed on 13 March 2014.

Tahseen, Ismat, 'After meat, ready to wear octopus?' *The Times of India*, 10 January 2012.

Webster, Jason, 'I can see you're not neo-Nazis', *Financial Times*, 1 July 2011, http://www.ft.com/cms/s/2/47d18226-9e59-11e0-8e61-00144feabdc0.html#axzz2gL1jdqdg, last accessed on 13 March 2014.

A massive market exists for self-altering goods and services. Clothes, cosmetics, beauty services—a number of industries thrive on the individual's need for altering the self. Many sites help one create a virtual model of oneself and then one can try out different clothes using the model. Consumers can, in effect, design their own personality on such sites.

Another reason for altering the self is to portray oneself like other desirable people. Advertisements also project desirable images that consumers feel compelled to follow. People want to alter their self and change hairstyles to appear like celebrities or the people they see in advertisements. Young girls have harmed their health trying to attain a stick-thin figure like the models they see in advertisements. Many girls fall prey to anorexia trying to achieve a Barbie doll figure. Halliwell and Dittmar (2004) studied the impact of three types of advertisements—featuring thin models, average-sized models, or no models—on adult women's body-focused anxiety, and on advertising effectiveness. They found that exposure to thin models resulted in greater body-focused anxiety among women who internalize the thin ideal, than exposure to average-size models or no models. They also found that advertisements were equally effective, regardless of the model's size.

Virtual Personality

Online profiles of people help us in discovering real personalities. For instance, many people use *avatars* to describe themselves on social media and gaming sites. Avatars are alternative identities of individuals and help us discover their subconscious selves. Hemp (2006) writes that technology helps us have multiple identities and is very helpful for marketing communications: 'Advertising has always targeted a powerful consumer alter ego: that hip, attractive, incredibly popular person just waiting to emerge (with the help of the advertised product) from an all-too-normal self.'

People have always assumed alternative identities. Writers have pen-names and radio jockeys use evocative handles to describe themselves, say, 'Golmal Gagan'. As technology has expanded, people create multiple identities on social interaction sites and chat-rooms. Modern technology helps people realize a deep-seated desire to experience what it would feel like to be someone else. These avatars help us discover the real personalities of people. As explained in Chapter 6, they help us discover their real motivations.

Since avatars help us discover real personalities, they are useful in market research. Companies could collect profiles of those who might be likely buyers of products based on their psychological profile online.

Studying virtual personalities is a comparatively new area, but it is accompanied by big data—the data left behind by consumers as they browse the web. Companies are already allocating their budgets to study this new mine of data. *The Economist* (2013) reports that personality can be profiled from Twitter, from the words people tweet. In a fascinating study, Yarkoni (2010) recruited a group of bloggers and correlated the frequencies of certain words and categories of words that they used in their blogs with their personality traits. Software takes streams of 'tweets' and searches them for words that indicate a tweeter's personality, values, and needs. With such tools, it would be possible to build a personality profile of Twitter users that in turn would be linked to advertising and products designed for them. How this information is used, however, remains to be seen.

CONCLUSION

Personality theories reveal some valuable insights. One of the major contributions of personality theories to marketing has been the concept of brand personality and its matching with human personality to determine market segments. Many brands strive to develop personalities of their own and indeed, they succeed as well. It is common to hear the owner of an expensive car or mobile phone say that the product in question reflects the his/her personality. Descartes' famous quote 'I think, therefore I am', has been turned on its head by modern civilization. For much of the human race, it means, as in the famous artwork by Barbara Kruger, 'I shop, therefore I am'.

However, the assumption that people buy on the basis of deep-seated drives does not quite stand scrutiny since, as Assael (2005) explains, most consumer behaviour is a mundane, day-to-day affair. Further, since the focus of Freudian personality theories is on aberrant behaviour, to apply these theories to study a typical consumer will eventually lead us to general results.

Kassarjian, (1979) writes in his paper *Personality: The Longest Fad*, that personality by itself does not predict consumer behaviour and that only about ten per cent of it can be accounted for by personality variables. Personality researchers assume that if psychosis and the selection of a spouse, suicide, and child rearing can be accounted for by personality variables, so, too, it must be that the selection of Sunkist oranges over Florida oranges, preference for brands of canned peas, and so on, must be accounted for by personality.

Personality is a complex phenomenon. It can at best be used as an indication about consumer behaviour. It is not the focus of consumption but it does affect a person's responses to advertising.

SUMMARY

The study of personality is useful in marketing as it impacts on consuming and buying goods. Several theories have been proposed. Freud's psychoanalytic theory of personality states that personality arises from a conflict between a person's desire to fulfil his conscious and unconscious physical needs and also be acceptable in society at the same time. This unconscious part of the mind is composed of three elements—id (immediate gratification), ego (self-control), and superego (conscience).

Later thinkers disagreed with Freud and developed their own theories. Alfred Adler proposed that people are motivated by their social urges, and since we suffer from an inferiority complex, the primary motivation of humans was a striving for superiority.

Carl Jung proposed that the roots of personality are contained in our collective unconscious, inherited from our ancestors. He said this collective memory consisted of *archetypes*.

Karen Horney, another neo-Freudian, emphasized the importance of socio-cultural factors in personality development. She wrote that anxious insecurity stems from inadequate childrearing experiences and are the source of all personality conflicts. She described three personality types: compliant, aggressive, and detached (CAD).

Trait theory states that personality is based on individual behaviour, physical characteristics, attitudes, beliefs, and demography. Two methods based on trait theory are the five-factor personality dimensions and 16 personality factors (16PF).

Personality traits tell us about consumer behaviour, or how people will respond to new products in the marketplace. There are several aspects of consumer behaviour such as consumer innovativeness, consumer dogmatism, social character, and cognitive factors.

Consumer innovativeness is the predisposition to try and buy new products offered in the market. It includes need for stimulation, need for loyalty, need for independence, and need for uniqueness. The opposite of consumer innovativeness is consumer dogmatism, which refers to consumers' resistance to change, and represents the degree to which an individual's mindset is open or closed.

Social character refers to whether consumers are inner-directed or other-directed. Cognitive personality factors in consumers make them either visualizers or verbalizers, and reveal their need for cognition.

When people place great importance on buying and showing-off possessions, it is called consumer materialism. Materialism gives rise to three behaviours: consumer fixation, impulsive, and compulsive behaviour.

Consumer ethnocentrism is a feeling of patriotism, and a resultant desire to accept or reject foreign-made products and brands. Its opposite is cosmopolitanism, which refers to individuals who are oriented towards the outside world rather than their local community.

The concept of personality is extended to brands as well. Brands acquire personality when they are seen to possess a set of human characteristics. Anthropomorphism is the process of prescribing human characteristics to brands and products. Five brand personality dimensions have been proposed: sincerity, excitement, competence, sophistication, and ruggedness. Brand personality is different from brand personification: when brands start acquiring human-like qualities, it is known as brand personification. The advertising elements that contribute to brand personality are endorsement, user imagery, execution elements, symbols, and consistency. Companies also have to learn to sell masculine, feminine, or gender neutral products. Geography and colour, too, play a role in personality.

Finally, the concept of self-image was discussed. The huge industries of clothes, cosmetics, and accessories bank on people's desire to alter the self. Companies cater to the need of consumers to appear attractive and modern. They are also expanding into the virtual world, where they find people have made virtual personalities, which gives an indication of their true selves. Relying on big data, marketing to virtual personalities is the next big challenge.

KEY TERMS

16 personality factors model (16PF) Measures personality on 16 factors and captures individual differences for each factor to provide a comprehensive description of personality

Anthropomorphism The process of prescribing human characteristics to non-human objects

Brand personality The set of human characteristics associated with a brand

Brand personification When people attach human characteristics or qualities to products consciously or subconsciously, it is known as brand personification

Collective unconscious The primordial images and urges that we have inherited from our ancestors and that are contained in the collective unconscious

Compulsive buying behaviour Inwardly-motivated shopping behaviour, when consumers do not have control over their shopping, or shopping done as a means to avoid uncomfortable feelings

Consumer dogmatism The opposite of consumer innovativeness, it refers to consumers' resistance to change, and the degree to which an individual's mindset is open or closed

Consumer etcentric tendencies scale (CETSCALE) A seven-point scale that measures the level of ethnocentricity in consumers

Consumer ethnocentrism A feeling of patriotism, and a resultant desire to accept or reject foreign-made products and brands

Consumer fixation The state in which an individual becomes obsessed or attached to a product or brand

Consumer innovativeness The tendency to be attracted by new products, or the predisposition of some consumers to try and buy new products offered in the market more often and more quickly than other people

Cosmopolitism Refers to individuals who are oriented towards the outside world rather than their local community

Ego The mind's mechanism for keeping in touch with reality, it helps the id to get what it wants in realistic and socially-acceptable ways

Five-factor model Referred also as the 'big five' personality traits, it suggests five dimensions of personality: openness, conscientiousness, extraversion, agreeableness, and neuroticism

Freud's theory of personality Personality arises from a conflict between a person's desire to fulfil his conscious and unconscious physical needs and also be acceptable in society.

Geographical indications (GI) Indications which identify a good as originating in the territory, a region, or locality in that territory, where a given quality, reputation or other characteristic of the good is essentially attributable to its geographic origin

Id The urge for instant pleasure or immediate gratification of all desires and needs

Impulsive buying behaviour A consumer's sudden unplanned decision, made without thinking, to buy a product or service, just before a purchase.

Inferiority complex Alfred Adler proposed that human beings have feelings of inferiority, which they try to overcome, forming the basis of personality

Materialism When consumers place great importance on possessions

Personality The distinctive and relatively enduring ways of thinking, feeling, and acting that characterize a person's responses to life situations

Self-concept The totality of the individual's thoughts and feelings having reference to himself/herself as an object and can also be described as a cognitive appraisal of one's own attributes

Superego A person's conscience, a sense of right and wrong and includes the moral ideas that a person learns within the family and society

Traits Relatively stable cognitive, emotional, and behavioural characteristics of people that help establish their individual identities and distinguish them from others, establishing habitual patterns of behaviour, thought, and emotion

EXERCISES

Concept-review Questions

1. What is personality? Describe the psychoanalytical theory of personality.
2. Explain the contribution of neo-Freudian theorists to the development of personality theories and their application in marketing.
3. Describe the trait theory and how it led to the application of the concept of personality to brands.
4. Explain the role of personality in consumer behaviour. How do personality traits translate into consumption-related behaviour?
5. What is the difference between impulsive and compulsive buying?
6. Define consumer ethnocentrism and cosmopolitism. How do they impact consumption behaviour?
7. What is brand personality? How is it mapped?
8. What are the challenges faced when marketing to males and females? What difficulties are likely to be faced when products meant for males are sought to be marketed to females?
9. How does colour impact personality characteristics? Which colours are most likely to be used for banking and financial products companies?
10. What is the importance of studying self and self-image in consumer behaviour? How is virtual personality used by companies to market products?

Critical Thinking Questions

1. Personality is the sum total of qualities of an individual, but today it has come to mean the sum total of possessions of a person. Why is there a dichotomy? Which one is correct? Give reasons for your opinion.
2. Marketing products on the basis of personality means doing so on the basis of deep-rooted subconscious profiles of people. Do you think this is ethical? Should psychoanalysis, which was developed for curing personality disorders, be used in marketing?
3. Critically examine Freudian theory of personality and the later contributions made by neo-Freudian thinkers. Which of these seem far-fetched and which seem authentic? On the basis of these contributions,

select the most appropriate components to define personality in the modern context.
4. Should companies encourage impulsive and compulsive buying behaviour? Considering that such harmful behaviour is encouraged by subconscious research, can companies simply wash their hands of the issue and say that it is the consumers' problem? Should companies warn consumers about such behaviour?

Projects and Assignments

1. Choose an industry and collect the logos and/or advertisements of all the companies in it. Analyse their logos on the basis of colour and designs to see which elements are used by them to build their personality. Comment on which designs best reflect the personality of their companies and which ones do not. Which elements match and which don't?
2. Review the book *The Hero and The Outlaw* by Mark and Pearson and see how archetypes are used in advertising. Analyse brands according to these archetypes. Assess whether the brands succeeded on adopting these archetypes.
3. Examine the role of fixation, impulsive, and compulsive buying behaviour among your friends. List out the things that they bought as a result of such behaviour. Examine the reasons why they felt compelled to buy those things. Follow through with the consequences of such purchases. Were these harmful?
4. Examine the online profiles of your friends on social networking and gaming sites. How far do these virtual profiles match with the actual personalities of your friends? Do you discover any hidden qualities of your friends that you did not think they possessed? How can these virtual profiles be used to analyse human behaviour?

REFERENCES

Aaker, Jennifer L., 'Dimensions of brand personality', *Journal of Marketing Research*, Vol. 34, No. 3, 1997, pp. 347–356.

Aguirre-Rodriguez, Alexandra, Michael Bosnjak, and M. Joseph Sirgy, 'Moderators of the self-congruity effect on consumer decision-making: A meta-analysis', *Journal of Business Research*, Vol. 65, 2012, pp. 1179–1188.

Akdogan, M., S. Ozgener M. Kaplan, and A. Coskun, 'The effects of consumer ethnocentrism and consumer animosity on the re-purchase intent: The moderating role of consumer loyalty', *Emerging Markets Journal*, Vol. 2, January 2012.

Allport, G.W. and H.S. Odbert, 'Trait-names: A psycho-lexical study', *Psychological Monographs*, Vol. 47, 1936, Psychological Review Company, Princeton, NJ.

Assael, Henry, *Consumer Behavior: A Strategic Approach*, Indian Edition 2005, Bizantra, New Delhi.

Batra, Rajeev, John G. Myers, and David Aaker, *Advertising Management*, 5th Ed, 2009, Pearson Education, New Delhi.

Bawa, Anupam, 'Consumer ethnocentrism: CETSCALE validation and measurement of extent', *Vikalpa*, Vol. 29, No. 3, July–September 2004.

Beck, Melinda, 'Shop 'til you stop: How to treat compulsive spending', *The Wall Street Journal*, 6 December 2011.

Byrnes, Nanette, 'Secrets of the male shopper', *Businessweek*, 3 September 2006, http://www.businessweek.com/stories/2006-09-03/secrets-of-the-male-shopper, last accessed on 23 June 2013.

Cannon, Hugh M. and Attila Yaprak, 'Will the real world citizen please stand up! The many faces of cosmopolitan consumer behavior', *Journal of International Marketing*, Vol. 10, No. 4, 2002, pp. 30–52.

Connolly, Katie, 'Six ads that changed the way you think', *BBC News*, 3 January 2011, http://www.bbc.co.uk/news/world-us-canada-11963364, last accessed on 23 June 2013.

Delahousay, Jay, 'Use of archetypes in advertising', http://smallbusiness.chron.com/use-archetypes-advertising-38626.html, last accessed on 23 June 2013.

Dennett, Daniel C., *Intuition Pumps and Other Tools for Thinking*, WW Norton, New York, 2013.

Duarte, Paulo Alexandre O. and Mario Lino B. Raposo, 'A PLS model to study brand preference: An application to the mobile phone market', in Vincenzo Esposito Vinzi, Wynne W. Chin, Jörg Henseler, and Huiwen Wang (Ed.), *Handbook of Partial Least Squares*, Springer-Verlag, Berlin, 2010.

Dumitrescu, Andrei, 'Experiment for testing the concept of product personality', Polithenica University Bulletin, Series D, Vol. 69, No. 3, 2007.

Fraser, T. and A. Banks, *Designer's Color Manual: The Complete Guide to Color Theory and Application*, Chronicle Books, San Francisco, 2004.

Giovannucci, Daniele, Tim Josling, William Kerr, Bernard O'Connor, and May T. Yeung, *Guide To Geographical Indications: Linking Products And Their Origins*, International Trade Centre, Geneva, 2009.

Halliwell, Emma and Helga Dittmar, 'Does size matter? The impact of model's body size on women's body-focused anxiety and advertising effectiveness', *Journal of Social and Clinical Psychology*, Vol. 23, No. 1, 2004, pp. 104–122.

Hemp, Paul, 'Avatar-based marketing', *Harvard Business Review*, June 2006, pp. 48–57.

Hill Graham, 'Living with less. a lot less', *The New York Times*, 9 March 2013, http://www.nytimes.com/2013/03/10/opinion/sunday/living-with-less-a-lot-less.html?pagewanted=all&_r=0.

Hinrichs, Bruce, *Psychology: The Essence of a Science*, 1st Ed., Pearson Education, London, 2007.

http://www.arthistoryarchive.com/arthistory/feminist/Barbara-Kruger.html, last accessed on 26 March 2014.

Matzler, Kurt Sonja Bidmon, Sonja Grabner-Kräuter, (2006) 'Individual determinants of brand affect: the role of the personality traits of extraversion and openness to experience', *Journal of Product & Brand Management*, Vol. 15 Issue 7, pp. 427–434.

http://www.hdfcbank.com/personal/product/productdetails/womens-gold-credit-card/gts8miqf, last accessed on 26 March 2014.

http://www.hsbc.com.ph/1/2/personal/credit/redmc, last accessed on 26 March 2014.

John, Oliver P. and Sanjay Srivastava, 'The big five trait taxonomy: History, measurement and theoretical perspectives', in John, O. P., R.W. Robins, and L.A. Pervin (Ed.), *Handbook of personality: Theory and research*, 3rd Ed., 2008, Guilford, New York.

Jung, Kwon and Winston Lee, 'Cross-gender brand extensions: Effects of gender of the brand, gender of consumer, and product type on evaluation of cross-gender extensions', *Advances in Consumer Research*, 2006, Vol. 33, pp. 67–74.

Karbasivar, Alireza and Hasti Yarahmadi, 'Evaluating effective factors on consumer impulse buying behavior', *Asian Journal of Business Management Studies*, 2011, Vol. 2, No. 4, pp. 174–181.

Kassarjian, Harold H., 'Personality: The longest fad', in *Advances in Consumer Research*, Volume 6, Ed. William L. Wilkie, Ann Arbor Association for Consumer Research, Michigan, 1979, pp. 122–124.

Khan, Muhammad Asif and Cécile Bozzo, 'Connection between self concept and brand preference and the role of product usage', *International IJAS Conference for Academic Disciplines*, 13–16 March 2012, Las Vegas, USA.

Labrecque Lauren I. and George R. Milne, 'Exciting red and competent blue: the importance of color in marketing', *Journal of the Academy of Marketing Science*, 2012, Vol. 40, No. 5, pp. 711–727.

Labrecque Lauren I. and George R. Milne, 'To be or not to be different: Exploration of norms and journal of color differentiation in the marketplace', *Marketing Letters*, June 2013, Volume 24, Issue 2, pp. 165–176.

Lin, Long-Yi, 'The relationship of consumer personality trait, brand personality and brand loyalty: An empirical study of toys and video games buyers', *Journal of Product & Brand Management*, 2010, Vol. 19, Issue 1, pp. 4–17.

Lindquist, Jay D, Irena Vida, Richard E. Plank, and Ann Fairhurst, 'The modified CETSCALE: Validity tests in the Czech Republic, Hungary, and Poland', *International Business Review*, 2001, Vol. 10, No. 5, pp. 505–516.

Mark, Margaret and Carol Pearson, *The Hero and the Outlaw: Building Extraordinary Brands Through the Power of Archetypes*, 2001, McGraw Hill Professional, New York.

Merton, R. K., 'Patterns of Influence: local and cosmopolitan influential', in R.K. Merton (Ed.) *Social Theory and Social Structure*, 1957, The Free Press, New York, pp. 387–420.

Park, Ji Eun, Jun Yu, and Joyce Xin Zhou, 'Consumer innovativeness and shopping styles', *Journal of Consumer Marketing*, 2010, Vol. 27 No. 5, pp.437–446.

Parts, Oliver and Irena Vida, 'The effects of consumer cosmopolitanism on purchase behavior of foreign vs. domestic products', *Managing Global Transitions*, Vol. 9, Issue 4 (Winter 2011), pp. 355–370.

Passer, Michael W. and Ronald E. Smith, *Psychology: The Science of Mind and Behavior*, 3rd Ed., 2007, Tata McGraw Hill, New Delhi.

'Personality, social media, and marketing: No hiding place', *The Economist*, 25 May 2013.

Puzakova, Marina, Hyokjin Kwak, and Joseph F. Rocereto, 'Pushing the envelope of brand and personality: Antecedents and moderators of anthropomorphized brands', *Advances in Consumer Research*, 2009, Vol. 36, pp. 413–420.

Puzakova, Marina, Hyokjin Kwak, and Joseph F. Rocereto, 'When humanizing brands goes wrong: The detrimental effect of brand anthropomorphization amid product wrongdoings', *Journal of Marketing*, 2013, Vol. 77, No. 3, pp. 81–100.

Rhee, Jongeun and Kim K.P. Johnson, 'Predicting adolescents' apparel brand preferences', *Journal of Product & Brand Management*, 2012, Vol. 21, No. 4, pp. 255–264.

Roehrich, Gilles, 'Consumer innovativeness: Concepts and measurements', *Journal of Business Research*, 2004, Vol. 57, pp. 671–677.

Rosenberg, M., *Conceiving the Self*, 1979, Basic Books, New York.

Sedikides, C., S. Cisek, and C. M. Hart, 'Narcissism and brand name consumerism', in Campbell, Keith W. and Joshua D. Mille (Ed.), *The Handbook of Narcissism and Narcissistic Personality Disorder*, 2012, John Wiley and Sons, New Jersey.

Shahjehan, Asad, Jaweria Andleeb Qureshi, Faheem Zeb, and Kaleem Saifullah, 'The effect of personality on impulsive and compulsive buying behaviours', *African Journal of Business Management*, 2012, Vol. 6, No. 6, pp. 2187–2194.

Shimp, Terence A. and Subhash Sharma, 'Consumer ethnocentrism: Construction and validation of the CETSCALE', *Journal of Marketing Research*, Vol. 24, No. 3, (August 1987), pp. 280–289.

Silverstein Michael J. and Kate Sayre, 'The female economy', *Harvard Business Review*, September 2009.

Sirgy, M.J., 'Self-concept in consumer behavior: A critical review', *Journal of Consumer Research*, 1982, Vol. 9, No. 3, pp. 287–300.

'Time 100: The Century's Greatest Minds', *Time*, 29 March 1999.

Yarkoni, T., 'Personality in 100,000 words: A large-scale analysis of personality and word use among bloggers', *Journal of Research in Personality*, 2010, Vol. 44, pp. 363–373.

CASE STUDY

Getting High

There is a party and everybody is having fun. Then someone asks, 'What's your poison?' Little do you realize that your answer depends on the personality characteristics of the brand you choose and your own personality, or at least what you think of yourself. Liquor brands have successfully given personality to their brands and matched it with their target market. The result has been the spread of these brands among youth and women in Asian countries such as India, Malaysia, Thailand, and Indonesia, where drinking has traditionally been a male pastime. This case study examines the personalities of three popular brands, Absolut, Smirnoff, and Bacardi.

Absolut

When Absolut was launched in the US in 1979, one of the main characteristics of the brand was that it was 'cool'. The campaigns were designed by famous artists Andy Warhol and Keith Haring. They succeeded in establishing the idea that Absolut was more than vodka; drinking it got you involved with an idea, a culture, an ethos. Matching the spirit of the times, it gained a hip and cool personality.

The company gave personality to the product by employing two means: advertising that highlighted personality traits and bottle designs to match. Each ad had just a two-word copy, highlighting one trait: 'Absolut Perfection', 'Absolut Optimist', 'Absolut Profile', 'Absolut Subliminal', 'Absolut Manhattan', and so on. Each ad also featured the Absolut bottle, which was in itself a work of art. The campaign, with over 1500 ads, is one of the longest-ever advertising campaigns.

People treat the Absolut campaigns and bottle designs as works of art, and they have become collectors' items, often exhibited at art galleries and restaurants. The upper-class personality is also acquired by collaborating with famous fashion designers such as Jean-Paul Gaultier, Stella McCartney, and Gianni Versace.

The personality culture extends back into manufacturing. Operating on the motto *Onodigt Bra* or 'unnecesarily good', it instils pride among its employees. The company produces over 11 million cases vodka every year, which translates into producing 6,00,000 litres of vodka per day.

Keeping up with the times, it launched new products, sticking to its innovative personality. It launched Absolut Unique, an innovative bottling that put Absolut Vodka in individually numbered bottles each with their own design and pattern. Its other products are Absolut Elyx, Absolut Craft, and Absolut Amber.

Absolut Vodka is seen as a cool, American, creative personality. Indeed, the brand has been part of America's pop culture. It may come as a surprise that Absolut was till recently owned by the Swedish government and was acquired by a French wine company Pernod Ricard (http://pernod-ricard.com/) in 2008.

Smirnoff

Smirnoff conveys the personality of freedom, originality, fun, and versatility. Its slogan 'it leaves you breathless' was launched in 1952. The 'driest of the dry' campaign which followed, was a series of surrealistic images that captured the spirited character of the Smirnoff brand. Celebrities such as Woody Allen, Zsa Zsa Gabor, Marcel Marceau, Groucho Marx, and Buster Keaton endorsed Smirnoff, adding to the glamour of the brand.

Smirnoff promises to change your life. Its campaign, the 'effect is shattering' has this copy: 'Accountancy was my life until I discovered Smirnoff'. This established the personality of the Smirnoff drinker as individual, relaxed, rebellious, and mysterious. Continuing on this theme, it launched the 'pure thrill' campaign, which consisted of a series of distorted images viewed through a Smirnoff bottle. The campaign won many awards, including the Cannes Golden Lion.

Smirnoff has remained a premium product with personality traits of excitement and sophistication. Its personality consists of young people who like to party and socialize. It wants to be gender neutral and wants to include young, independent females who like to go out drinking and socializing with friends. Smirnoff wants to be an ideal component in cocktails as well.

In 2010, it launched the 'be there' campaign, inviting people 'to be inventive, to be extraordinary, to be able to say 'I was there'. This campaign gets consumers directly involved with the brand and incorporates Facebook and MTV partnerships as well. It also launched 'Mixhibit' a social film-making tool for people looking to remember the good times (www.mixhibit.com). Through the app, Smirnoff wants consumers to make their own short films. It takes selected photos from social networks, arranges them in an artful way, layers on a custom track, and lets the customers share the resulting creation with their friends.

Bacardi

Think of Bacardi and images of a tropical beach, seductive dancers, and a Latin way of life comes to mind. Through events and advertisement campaigns, the brand has tried to get the personality of young, carefree, party-lovers. Its advertisements used a catchy jingle, 'Be, what you wanna be/taking things the way, they come/nothing is as nice as finding paradise and/sippin' on Bacardi rum.'

In Thailand, a 'Bat Stage by Bacardi Breezer' was put up at bars and pubs, where trendy bands performed and a party atmosphere was created, to bring the brand personality to life.

In 2013, Bacardi launched a new campaign, 'Vivimos' (we live!). The campaign invited consumers to get insights on the brand's history through TV, digital, print, social, outdoor placements, and event marketing. It did so to add character to the brand personality. The company wanted to tap the need of the millennial consumer who looks for brands that have a history, provenance, heritage, and authenticity. By revealing its brand heritage and authenticity, the campaign drives consumer awareness and excitement while reinforcing the brand's heritage at a time when authenticity and masculinity are key themes among target consumers. The 'Bacardi Breezer' successfully acquired a female personality, conveying to traditional women that it was all right to have alcoholic drinks.

All three brands, Absolut, Smirnoff, and Bacardi, have managed to create unique personalities for themselves. Marketing on the basis of personality apparently has been very successful: the three brands remain in the world's top 10 biggest drink brands, according to World's Most Powerful Spirits & Wine Brands, 2013. People across the world identify with them as if the brands were an extension of their own personality.

Questions for Discussion

1. How did the brands discussed in the case use personality theories to acquire a personality of their own?
2. Which subconscious themes do these brands use to target the consumers' unarticulated desires?
3. Which personality traits do each of these brands have, other than those described in the case?
4. Profile the brands as if they were persons. Work out their age, sex, education, income, and lifestyles. Do these match with the actual consumers of these brands?

Sources:

http://images.businessweek.com/ss/10/08/0812_popularity_index/3.htm.
http://www.brandrepublic.com/news/159590/.
http://www.dmnews.com/bacardi-takes-a-shot-at-targeting-millennials/article/295399/#.
http://www.drinkspirits.com/vodka/absolut-scenes-absolut-vodka/#sthash.JRSkXpgG.dpuf.
http://www.drinkspowerbrands.com/top-10.html.
http://www.superbrandseastafrica.com/wp-content/uploads/file/Vol-1-Pdfs/142-smirnoff.pdf.
Kiick, Katy, *Absolute Utopia: Advertising the American Dream, in Utopian Images and Narratives in Advertising: Dreams for Sale*, edited by Manca, Luigi, Alessandra Manca, Gail W. Pieper, 2012, Lexington Books, UK.
All websites last accessed on 27 June 2013.

CHAPTER SIX

Consumer Motivation

LEARNING OBJECTIVES

Why does a person go to the market, select a product, and then part with money to buy it? This chapter uncovers the motivations of people as they buy products or adopt new ideas.

After studying this chapter, the reader would be able to

- understand needs, goals, motives, and how they impact consumer motivation
- analyse human needs and their marketing applications
- describe motives and how they are aroused
- learn about motivation research and how it is used in finding consumer motives
- analyse motives using various techniques

CASE STUDY

Handwashing—Motivating New Habit Formation

Washing hands with soap is an effective way of preventing infections among children in India and the developing world. Infections that cause diarrhoea and acute respiratory symptoms are often fatal for children and can be prevented by washing hands. However, teaching the handwashing habit is difficult—many people feel that merely washing hands with water or wiping them is enough. How can the habit of washing hands with soap be taught? Cultural and religious beliefs in some regions also make it difficult to motivate people to form the handwashing habit.

The *Global Handwashing Handbook* describes a marketing approach and says that the only way to change long-held habits related to handwashing is to understand the factors that drive and facilitate handwashing among the target consumers. The marketing approach focuses on the needs of the target audience and determines the nature and scope of the promotional activities based on perspective of the target audience. Changing behaviour requires the following three issues to be addressed:

Lowering environmental and cultural barriers Barriers in the environment include access to water, the high cost of soap, lack of handwashing facilities, and strong cultural prohibitions against washing on certain days in parts of Africa and Asia. These barriers have to be addressed while changing habits.

Transforming old habits The aim of handwashing promotion is not to achieve a single event, but to instil a new habit that is followed automatically after every contaminating event. Essentially, new habits have to be installed replacing old ones.

Finding motives and drivers Drivers are innate modules in the brain that motivate particular behaviours. They come in the form of emotions and the feelings. Discovering drivers and motivators is key to successfully promoting the handwashing habit.

The problem is not one of social marketing alone, as Chief Marketing and Communication Officer of Unilever, Keith Weed (2012) explains. He writes that his company is trying to reduce its environmental impact under the Unilever Sustainable Living Plan. Its challenge is to teach hygiene habits to children.

Weed writes that Unilever is well placed to influence customers as it engages directly with consumers through its brands. The Lifebuoy soap brand spearheads the company's efforts to reduce childhood mortality through the simple act of handwashing regularly. The Unilever website says that 'Lifebuoy is a good example of how brands that help to address social challenges can build brand equity and grow their business'.

The brand campaigned at the Kumbh Mela to raise awareness about good handwashing habits, partnering with more than 100 restaurants and cafés at the festival. For every food order placed, the first roti carried the branded message 'Lifebuoy *se haath dhoye kya?*' ('Did you wash your hands with Lifebuoy?'). The words were heat stamped onto the baked roti to draw attention at the time when handwashing is critical. More than 2.5 million branded rotis were consumed during the month-long campaign. Lifebuoy also placed soap in the toilets of each of the eateries to enable people to wash their hands with soap before eating.

The remarkable campaign can be viewed on YouTube at the following link: http://www.youtube.com/watch?v=e_2tQekUDy8.

Companies have to understand exactly how people use products, and what are the values, habits, or motivations required to be influenced to inculcate this habit. The company uses its 'Five Levers for Change' a set of principles that can change motivations among children to learn the habit of washing hands.

Make it understood People have to understand that the habit is good for them. Lifebuoy uses a 'glo-germ' demonstration that uses ultra-violet light to show children the invisible germs that cannot be washed out by plain water.

Make it easy The second lever is to make the habit convenient for people to adopt. To save water, for instance, the company holds live demonstrations to show that one bucket of water is enough for effective rinsing while washing clothes. Easy availability of Lifebuoy in low-income areas and the introduction of small packages that the poor can afford to buy, help in inculcating good handwashing habits.

Make it desirable One basic factor in motivation is to make the habit desirable. The company has to introduce people in poor localities who the residents can respect and emulate. Regular demonstrations by such people encourage the handwashing habit. Lifebuoy also taps into the desire of new mothers to be good mums, so that others can emulate them.

Make it rewarding People start following practices if they expect a reward. One such reward is demonstrating 'proof' and pay-off. The Rotary Club distributes free soap along with sweets to children in poor areas and gives demonstrations to motivate children to develop the habit of washing hands (Fig. 6.1).

FIG. 6.1 Handwashing demonstration

Make it a practice Habits are formed if people stick to their newly-acquired practice. The practice has to be repeated, reinforced, and remembered. Lifebuoy campaigns run for a minimum of 21 days and include quizzes, posters, and songs to encourage habit formation. As a reminder, the Global Handwashing Day is held on 15 October every year in over 100 countries.

While reading this chapter, try to answer the following questions:

1. How do motivation theories help in the process of changing habits of consumers?
2. How does marketing use the knowledge of needs, goals, and motives while designing advertisements or products?
3. Describe the process by which consumers are brought to higher needs through buying and using products.
4. How are motives aroused and consumers pushed towards desirable behaviour?

Sources:

http://www.unilever.com/brands-in-action/detail/Lifebuoy-creates-innovative-roti-reminder/346332/, last accessed on 18 July 2013.

http://www.unilever.com/sustainable-living/healthandhygiene/handwashing/, last accessed on 12 June 2013.

http://www.youtube.com/watch?v=e_2tQekUDy8, last accessed on 12 June 2013.

The Handwashing Handbook, The Global Public Private Partnership for Handwashing, Washington, DC; http://globalhandwashing.org/resources, last accessed on 12 June 2013.

Weed, Keith, 'Change Consumer Behavior with These Five Levers', HBR Blog Network, 6 November 2012; http://blogs.hbr.org/cs/2012/11/change_consumer_behavior_with.html, last accessed on 12 June 2013.

INTRODUCTION

The study of consumer motives is actually a study of 'what makes people buy products'. However, this has remained a neglected area as we remain focused on products and markets. Companies rely so much on data that they forget to focus on the real motives of consumers when they go out and part with their money. What Britt wrote in 1950 is true even today: 'We have available all kinds of facts and figures about markets, but we sometimes forget that these markets are made up of human beings. And we simply do not have enough information about the why's and wherefore's of their buying behaviour'. The result is that we do not know why we guzzle carbonated drinks, or why we buy automobiles, refrigerators, canned goods, and so on.

It is hardly a wonder that many new products fail even though they are backed by extensive market research. That is because discovering buyer motivation requires delving deep into a consumer's brain. It is like analysing an iceberg. Zaltman (2002) says that 95 per cent of all cognition, the thinking that drives our decisions and behaviours, occurs unconsciously.

So the problem really is to delve into the subconscious of consumers. Motivation research attempts to do that. Drawing on principles of Freudian psychoanalysis, motivation research became a discipline in its own right, for figuring out our real motivations in buying products. Motivation research dominates marketing to this day. As Samuel (2010) points out, the principles of psychoanalysis have become permanently ingrained in our cultural consciousness. Look at advertising messages and we find products are hardly sold on the power of their attributes but what they might do to us psychologically, appealing to some hidden motive in us.

Motivation research explains that the reason why some shoppers make a beeline for stores and buy things is that there is a discomfort in them, a pressing need, a thorn in their flesh. Many of us

> **MARKETING INSIGHT**
> **Motivating Women to Smoke**
>
> Edward L. Bernays, known as the father of public relations and nephew of Sigmund Freud, applied psychoanalytic principles to public relations and advertising. In his 1928 book, *Propaganda*, Bernays hypothesized that by understanding the group mind, it would be possible to manipulate people's behaviour without they even realizing it. To test this hypothesis, Bernays launched one of his most famous public relations campaigns: convincing women to smoke in public.
>
> In the 1920s, cigarettes were seen as symbolic of male power. It was taboo for women to smoke in public and the few who flouted convention were thought to be sexually permissive. The tobacco industry looked for ways to get over these formidable taboos to be able to expand the market by reaching out to women. Bernays, using public relations, helped the industry overcome one of the biggest social taboos of the time: women smoking in public.
>
> Equating smoking with challenging male power was the cornerstone of the 'Torches of Freedom' campaign, which debuted in New York on 1 April 1929. Bernays explained that women could contribute to the expansion of their rights by lighting up cigarettes and smoking them in public places. An event was organized and the press was warned beforehand. They couldn't resist the story. The 'Torches of Freedom Parade' was covered not only by the local papers, but also by newspapers nationwide and internationally. Bernays was convinced that linking products to emotions could cause people to change behaviour. In reality, of course, women were no freer for having taken up smoking, but linking smoking to women's rights fostered a feeling of independence.
>
> After this public event, women started lighting up more than ever before. Bernays made women smokers socially acceptable. The event was created as news, which, of course, it wasn't. Such events, when packaged as news, help in acquiring credibility in the consumers' minds and thereby motivate them to accept the behaviour. Even today, companies package advertising as news, thereby motivating thousands of unsuspecting consumers to adopt products and brands.
>
> How do companies use the power of public relations to motivate consumers to try out new products? Study the media and find out how unsuspecting consumers are sold products and ideas by this means.
>
> Sources:
>
> Axelrod, A., *Profiles of Folly: History's worst decisions and why they went wrong*, Sterling Publishing, New York, 2008.
>
> Bernays, E.L., *Crystallizing Public Opinion*, Boni and Liveright, New York, 1923.
>
> Bernays, E.L., *Propaganda*, H. Liveright, New York, 1928.
>
> Justman, S., 'Freud and his nephew', *Social Research*, Vol. 61, 1994, pp. 457–476.
>
> http://www.apa.org/monitor/2009/12/consumer.aspx, last accessed on 28 March 2014.

FIG. 6.2 Problem of converting unmotivated customers to buying customers.

experience this feeling either when we buy our daily groceries (if we don't do the chore, we will not get the dinner), or when we see a particularly desirable object (such as a car or an expensive smartphone that is owned by our neighbour). This discomfort or drive helps us to understand consumer motivation.

Consumer Motivation

Consumer motivation is defined as an internal state that drives people to identify and buy products or services that fulfil conscious and unconscious needs or desires.

It is the force that initiates, guides, and maintains goal-oriented behaviour: in marketing context, it is buying behaviour. It is what causes us to change from awareness stage to action or buying stage. Consumer motivation is the study of what pushes us into action, whether it is buying a cup of coffee, or changing our habits as the chapter-opening case study shows.

The problem is often to convert unmotivated customers into buying customers (Fig. 6.2). There are many factors that trigger motivation. Primary among them are felt needs, both physical and psychological. A study of needs is essential to understand what motivates us.

NEEDS, GOALS, AND MOTIVES

Needs are the starting point of marketing. They are seen as wants, desires, and motives. Human beings have needs and these needs get translated into wants that in turn result in motives. Managers hoping to garner a good market share for their brands must understand the needs, wants, motives, and drives leading to purchase behaviour. Please see Exhibit 6.1 to see how brands work towards it. The difference between *need* and *want* is that a need is a state of felt deprivation, whereas a want is a desire for a specific satisfier. A *motive* is an emotion, desire, physiological need, or similar impulse that acts as an incitement to action. A *drive* is a state of psychological tension that typically arises from a need. A *desire* is a strong feeling, or a sense of longing or craving for a thing.

 EXHIBIT 6.1 Fulfilling Needs

Cinthol

Today, the soap market in India is a deeply penetrated one with scores of brands vying for attention from crammed shelves—and a range of variants several times that number. There are now soaps that fulfil every conceivable need from disinfecting to creating a radiant, blemish free skin—and everything in between.

Cinthol Deo Soap, with the tagline Get Ready Get Close, hit the market in 2004. It addressed the need for effective body odour removal through the unique propositioning of a deodorant in soap. Cinthol extended this footprint into a deodorant talc and spray. The following year, with the addition of Cinthol Sport, the brand had reinforced its offering, strengthening it later with Cinthol Deo Musk in an exotic woody-musky fragrance.

To keep its hand on the pulse of the market, the company's specialized research team closely monitors consumer behaviour, changing attitudes and tweaks marketing and product strategies to suit up-and-coming needs (see Figure 6.3).

Tupperware

Tupperware's marketing strategy and approach has been a study in effective brand building in the

FIG. 6.3 Product line of Cinthol

Courtesy: Superbrands

kitchenware and direct selling segment. As a direct seller, the need was to put in place a robust brand and access plan.

Contributing to this high level of awareness is the proven quality of Tupperware products. Over the years the design teams at the company's research and development centres have perfected a system of studying local market needs and then developing products that best address them. Over the years Tupperware has won several awards for excellence in product design. This includes the prestigious 'Red

(Contd)

EXHIBIT 6.1 (Contd)

Dot Design Awards' that various Tupperware products have won more than 39 times. These products are not only aesthetically appealing but they are designed for functionality. Their innovative designs have come to revolutionize the way modern kitchens are thought of. Guinness Book of World Records included Tupperware in their edition of 'The Greatest Inventions of the 20th Century'. It's no surprise then, that many museums of modern art, across the world have included Tupperware products as works of art (see Figure 6.4).

FIG. 6.4 Range of Tupperware

Courtesy: Superbrands

Source: Superbrands 2012

Needs are primarily of two types:

Physiological These are also referred to as primary, biological, or biogenic needs, and comprise innate needs such as food, water, sleep, air, and shelter. All humans have these needs that are essential for survival.

Psychological Referred to as secondary or psychogenic needs, these needs arise out of sociology and psychology, such as the need for affiliation, power, recognition, esteem, and status. We acquire these needs during our socialization process, and they differ from person to person. These needs derive from culture and environment and motivate us to act as consumers.

Every marketing strategy must fulfil both these needs. As seen in the chapter-opening case study, addressing both needs resulted in the children changing their handwashing habits.

Needs are the consequence of instincts, incentives, drives, and arousal states. Human beings are guided by *instincts* that they have learnt through evolution. Our instincts for survival and self-preservation lead us to certain products. Psychologist William James (1890) had listed human instincts such as attachment, play, shame, anger, fear, shyness, modesty, and love.

People are also motivated to act because of *incentives*, that is, the expectation of rewards. Thus, buying behaviour can be moulded by offering discounts and incentives. Behavioural learning (described in Chapter 8) uses this to develop concepts such as association and reinforcement.

Human drives arise from unmet needs that create tensions. People are motivated to action to reduce this internal tension. While biological needs such as hunger or thirst create drives, the more powerful drives are psychological. Advertisers use this theory to create ads that create strong unmet needs to drive consumers to buy.

People are also driven to products depending on their *arousal* states—when we are psychologically aroused, say on seeing the picture of a creamy chocolate, we want to try it out. Companies use advertisements and enticing images to arouse consumers.

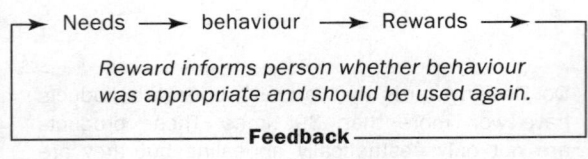

FIG. 6.5 Basic model of motivation

A basic model of motivation is shown in Fig. 6.5. Needs, both physiological and psychological, push consumers to action to fulfil those needs. They are rewarded with the satisfaction of consuming a product. If this reward is commensurate with their needs, it leads to positive feedback. When the need arises again, the consumer knows what products or brands to consume. When this loop is completed several times, brand loyalty or habitual consumption results.

Nature and Function of Goals

Consumers set goals for themselves arising from their needs. Some families may plan to buy a house or a car, or save for a foreign trip, or save to fulfil their goals. Individuals set goals related to their lifestyles. Goals represent the ideal state that a person desires. Goals are of two types: generic and product-specific.

Generic goals   Generic goals are those that satisfy consumer needs and wants. For instance, a consumer may want to buy a car.

Product-specific goals   These are for specifically branded products or services that the consumers desire to fulfil their generic goals. A consumer may, for instance, not want to buy any car but the Swift Dzire.

We can infer some of the qualities of needs and goals from the preceding discussion. These are the forces that operate on motivation.

Characteristics of Needs

Motivation results from our ever-changing and never-fulfilled needs and goals. As soon as one goal is fulfilled, we decide on new goals.

Needs display the following characteristics:

Multiplicity   Human beings exhibit a multiplicity of needs and wants. While physiological needs are few and universal, psychological needs are many and varied. A person may experience many needs and wants simultaneously.

 CB IN ACTION   **Difference between a Need and a Motive**

Observe two sets of shoppers at a mall. Both are exposed to several ads on any given day. They see the products displayed in shops that entice them with the best layouts and offers. The first set of shoppers pass the stores, see the products, but do not buy them. Maybe there is a desire in them and they also have the purchasing power, but they lack the force that pulls them into shops, select goods and pay for them.

At the same time, there are other shoppers who see the displays or remember the previous night's TV ads, shop and buy things, sometimes even those that they don't really need.

1. What is the difference between the first set of shoppers and the second set?
2. Why does the second set feel compelled to go into stores and buy the goods?
3. Are they propelled by felt needs—physical or psychological—or something else?
4. What would you do to convert the non-buyers into buyers?

Individual variation As individuals are different from each other in many ways, needs vary from person to person and within a person across situations.

Lack of satisfaction Wants are satisfied temporarily but needs are never fully satisfied. As soon as one need is satisfied, another need emerges, and this triggers desires and motives.

Grow, develop, and change Needs change in response to an individual and his/her environment. They grow, develop, and change.

Dormancy Needs may lie dormant in us and they may suddenly awaken owing to an event that happens around us. Physiological, social, or environmental factors may also trigger needs.

Success and Failure Influence Goals

A consumer's experience with brands also determines future goals. People feel upset if product claims in advertisements are not met in reality. Consumers who successfully achieve their goals will set newer and higher goals for themselves. *Substitute goals* arise when consumers are unable to achieve their primary goals and transfer their preference to alternatives. For instance, a consumer who is unable to buy an expensive watch will start liking a less expensive watch. *Frustration* arises when consumers are unable to accomplish their goals: for example, when certain products go out of stock. When this happens, consumers adopt defence mechanisms such as *rationalization*, *withdrawal*, and *identification*.

Maslow (1943) proposed a structure to understand needs—he wrote that basic goals are related to each other and are arranged in a hierarchy. While the lower-level needs are very powerful, once they are met, they are forgotten and new needs become more potent, leading to higher goals. Thus man is a perpetually desiring being, because as soon as a need is fairly well satisfied, the next need and goal emerges which then dominates the conscious life of the person.

Any person at any given time is often partially satisfied and partially unsatisfied. There are always unmet needs. Sometimes, the individual himself/herself does not know what those needs are. This becomes the central tenet of marketing—managers must present products that people are not yet aware of, and transform them into objects of desire. As Steve Jobs famously observed in an interview with *Businessweek* (1998): 'A lot of times, people don't know what they want until you show it to them. That's why a lot of people at Apple get paid a lot of money, because they're supposed to be on top of these things.'

Maslow proposed a hierarchy of needs that guide our actions.

MASLOW'S HIERARCHY OF NEEDS

According to Maslow (1943), there is a hierarchy of needs starting with lower-level or basic physiological needs, progressing to safety, love or belongingness, esteem, and finally culminating in self-actualization. Lower-level needs have different motivators and once they have been met, different cognitive needs arise and people get motivated differently. Table 6.1 describes Maslow's needs hierarchy, with the type of motivator and marketing applications.

Needs and goals are interdependent. Maslow (1943) wrote that 'there are at least five sets of goals, which we may call basic needs. These are physiological, safety, love, esteem, and self-

TABLE 6.1 Maslow's need hierarchy and its marketing applications

Type of need	Motivators	Marketing application
Self-actualization	Self-fulfilment	Clubs, spas Tourism and travel
Ego needs	Prestige, status, self-esteem	Upper end clothing brands Travel and travel accessories Cosmetics and beauty products Credit cards
Social needs	Attention, friendship, belonging	Telecom companies Travel companies Restaurants and cafes Fast-moving consumer goods (FMCG)
Safety and security needs	Protection, order, stability	Housing and real-estate companies Banks, insurance companies Financial services
Physiological needs	Food, water, air, shelter, sex	Public utilities Water bottles, Companies providing cheap housing

actualization'. He explained that people are motivated by the desire to achieve or maintain these basic satisfactions and by certain more intellectual desires. This has marketing implications, since all the levels of needs can be linked to different types of products (Table 6.1).

Marketing Applications of Need Hierarchy

Need hierarchy has straightforward applications in advertising. It is easy to spot advertisements that appeal to one of the need levels.

Maslow's hierarchy can be used to augment products. Price evaluations are higher when the product's advertising focuses on higher order needs. Maslow's hierarchy of needs offers a way to look at how consumers evaluate the core product and the augmented product. Herrington (1993) writes that

- the core product represents and fulfils basic physiological needs
- reliability and on-time product delivery are equated with safety needs
- customer interaction is related to belongingness
- matches innovations with esteem needs
- developing a supplier–customer partnership represents self-actualization needs

Maslow's hierarchy also helps us understand the motivations of people as they buy things. All products and services are intended to fulfil a need at some position in the hierarchy. Companies have to understand which needs their products serve and also the customer's motivation in buying them.

Products frequently move up the need hierarchy. For example, instead of selling a car based on specifications, car companies such as Maruti and Hyundai cater to our need for safety and thereby

GLOBAL INSIGHT
Luxury Goods in China

Sales of luxury goods are on a roll in China. With a turnover of over $35 billion, it is a luxury market second only to USA. Top luxury brands have continued to outperform even during the economic slowdown. The Chinese people have taken to heart Deng Xiaoping's advice that 'to be rich is glorious', as a motivation for buying expensive luxury items.

There are several reasons why luxury brands have become so popular in China, and some of them are as follows:

- Emerging from years of communism, and encouraged by liberal capitalist policies, people have developed a taste for the high life.
- The young love to own and display these brands—45 per cent of Chinese luxury consumers are between the ages of 18 and 34.
- China is already the largest Internet market in the world—513 million Internet users, according to McKinsey.
- The average Chinese millionaire is only 39, according to *The Economist*. The country already has 2.7 million of them.
- Women in China are willing to spend large amounts on handbags. China has its share of 'power women' who have their own spending money and a taste for edgier fashion content.
- Only two per cent of consumers bought top-end brands, so there is a great potential for growth of such brands.

The wide availability of luxury products, and shifting attitudes toward the display of wealth, have made Chinese consumers feel comfortable about buying luxury goods. As a result, China's love for them is moving down the economic ladder, that is, the market of luxury goods is not limited to the rich alone.

What motivates the Chinese to favour luxury brands? Luxury products have cultural connotations—owning them means to have a culture. There are three luxury consumer groups in China—the rich flaunting their fortune, the young people who derive a sense of satisfaction, and the bribe-givers for mutual collusion and showing-off their wealth to prove their self-esteem. The main motivations for buying luxury goods are to display one's status, to follow Western trends, gift-giving, and self-reward.

Graham and Lam (2003) explain some important values in Chinese culture.

Mianzi **(Face)** The concept of face, from traditional Confucian values, is analogous to one's reputation. Face is the prestige one has achieved in life, through success and ostentation, and is a function of one's social status. Face is obtained through personal qualities or derived from non-personal characteristics such as wealth, social connections, and authority.

Guanxi **(Interpersonal relations)** *Guanxi* is associated with one's network of relationships. Maintaining *guanxi* through building personal and professional connections is an important social value. A major aspect of managing interpersonal relations is doing favours or giving gifts. Chadha (2006) writes that in a business relationship, gifting reciprocation results in more expensive or exclusive gifts being given to maintain the moral superiority of the giver and indebtedness of the receiver.

Collectivism Face is collectivist in nature because one can gain or lose face on behalf of others. Chadha (2006) further explains, 'adorning yourself with visible symbols of success is not just for your own glory, but also for the greater glory of your family'. If luxury brands become the norm in a collectivistic culture via gift-giving, then it makes perfect sense to buy them. In the context of luxury consumption, gifting high-end goods can help maintain *guanxi* (social and business relationships) and preserve face.

Cultural and Social Motivations Due to the aforementioned factors, a rich person may lose face if he gives inexpensive gifts. Gifting luxury goods is a form of face-saving behaviour for the middle class and shows upward mobility. The obsession with Western brands is a motivating factor behind luxury purchases. For many consumers, luxury purchases are conspicuous and are made for the brand or price. Possessing luxury goods means climbing the social ladder. The wealthier one becomes, the more luxury goods one accumulates. People describe their luxury-owning friends as stylish, sophisticated, or having good taste. Owning luxury goods is an outward

(Contd)

GLOBAL INSIGHT (Contd)

display of one's status and connectedness to one's reference group. Luxury goods are also bought to display social status.

Are these values applicable to the rest of Asia too? What are the motivations of people when they buy over-priced goods?

Sources:

Chadha, Radha and Paul Husband, *The Cult of the Luxury Brand: Inside Asia's Love Affair with Luxury*. Nicholas Brealey, London, 2006.

Chen, George, 'Hotlines spring up for China VIPs to buy luxury goods amid anti-graft drive', *South China Morning Post*, http://www.scmp.com/business/china-business/article/1287960/hotlines-spring-china-vips-buy-luxury-goods-amid-anti-graft, last accessed on 29 March 2014.

Graham, John L. and Mark Lam, 'The Chinese negotiation', *Harvard Business Review*, October 2003.
http://www.businessinsider.com/china-future-luxury-goods-market-2012-7?op=1#ixzz2goQk5VWN, last accessed on 29 March 2014.
http://www.china.org.cn/opinion/2012-07/04/content_25803735.htm, last accessed on 29 March 2014.
'Luxury goods in China: Beyond bling', *The Economist*, 8 June 2013. 'Luxury without borders: China's new class of shoppers take on the world', http://www.mckinsey.com/insights/marketing_sales/tapping_chinas_luxury-goods_market, last accessed on 29 March 2014.
'Why Chinese people love luxury goods', *People's Daily*, 4 July 2012

---

to the next level of needs, our social needs. Car advertisements of these companies usually show families or couples going for drives together: a story about keeping one's family safe satisfies deep psychological needs.

Udell (1965) discussed how the hierarchy of needs is used in marketing. By analysing the buying motives of consumers for cosmetics, he found that while some minimum level of quality is important, the main motivations in buying cosmetics are the individuals' psychological interpretation of the product and the social prestige of the product. So the manufacturer will meet the minimum quality level but find it more profitable to invest marketing efforts in advertising and sales promotion. We see this approach in the marketing of modern products. While the quality requirements are met, companies spend most of their energy in advertising and creating an image for their products (Exhibit 6.2 shows how brands succeed in creating their image).

The study of motives helps us to answer some questions on marketing strategy. It helps to identify the target market based on different types of needs, in designing new product concepts that will appeal to the target market, and in formulating a marketing mix, including a promotion strategy. How the need hierarchy is used in product design and marketing is discussed in the next section. The CB in Action (Identifying real motivation for buying products) asks readers to identify the real motives behind buying a variety of products. The exercise will not only be an eye-opener, but will also show the reader how companies formulate their image-building strategies based on motives.

Product Design and Need Hierarchy

Maslow's hierarchy has been used in product design. Different levels of needs are identified with different design need hierarchy. The product design hierarchy matching with Maslow's hierarchy from low to high are functionality, reliability, usability, proficiency, and creativity as shown in Fig. 6.7.

EXHIBIT 6.2 Creating an Image

Blue Star

Blue Star's promotional activities include mass media advertising as well as field marketing. The advertising budget is invested primarily in television, print, hoardings and the Internet. The company's TV ads are placed on news and niche channels. In print, main line dailies are the preference. The markets targeted include metros and mini metros (see Figure 6.6).

FIG. 6.6 Print ad—Blue Star

Courtesy: Superbrands

Field marketing activities see the company investing substantially in customer meets, sponsorships of events organized by CII and other trade associations, participation in premium exhibitions and other on-ground events. Both the mass media and field marketing activities are aligned to the brand value proposition to ensure an integrated 360-degree brand communication.

Cinthol

At Cinthol, the communications process starts with a strategy that dove tails into the research conclusions. Bollywood superstar Hrithik Roshan was an easy enough choice. His boundless energy, macho image and passion to excel perfectly embodied Cinthol's brand ethos of invigorating products for people, who believe in an active life. The Cinthol 'Don't Stop' campaign featuring Hrithik captured the essence of this emerging Indian. The commercial featured Hrithik performing a series of high adrenaline stunts and participating in action-packed sports. From kayaking to bungee jumping, mountain climbing to cliff diving; this highly successful brand communication complemented Hrithik's macho and sporty image and invited viewers to emulate his 'Don't Stop' adventurous lifestyle.

Source: Superbrands 2012

Needs		Product requirements	Marketing applications
Creativity, morality	Self-actualization	Creativity	Company–Customer partnership (CRM) Elegance and efficiency
Confidence, respect	Esteem	Proficiency	Innovations, status
Friendship, family	Love/Belongingness	Usability	Customer interaction
Security	Safety needs	Reliability	Delivery, guarantee, service
Health, food, shelter	Physiological needs	Functionality	Core product, value

FIG. 6.7 Applications of Maslow's hierarchy to product requirements and marketing applications

Yalch and Brunel (1996) have applied Maslow's theory to marketing and product design, and demonstrate the relationship of a need hierarchy to consumer judgments. They gave consumers two electric shavers that were functionally equivalent but different in appearance, and found that consumers preferred the shaver with the more appealing appearance as it would better satisfy their higher order needs than the less attractive shaver. It was found that the 'European' styling of the fancy shaver appealed to consumers' self-actualization needs. Further, they were ready to pay more for it.

CB IN ACTION — Identifying Real Motivation for Buying Products

We have seen that products fulfil physical needs and psychological ones. Analyse the products that you own and discover your real motives for buying them. Complete the following table after analysing your thoughts.

Filling up the table will help you identify the real motivation for buying products. It will help you to understand how these products should be marketed.

Product/Brand	Physical needs	Psychological needs
Deodorant		
Visiting a cafe with friends		
Cosmetics		
Mobile Phone		
Apparel		
Going to the movies		
Chocolate		
Car		

Companies marketing luxury products are able to use this understanding by offering better-designed products at very high prices. The premium on price cannot be explained by product quality alone, but by the fact that the design or brand name appeals to higher-level needs. The design hierarchy of products is described as follows:

Functionality While all products must satisfy the functionality criterion, a design must be able to perform its function before anything else. For example, a website design must ensure that it loads quickly, otherwise consumers will be frustrated. Product design, however, has to go beyond functionality to appeal to higher needs.

Reliability After satisfying functional needs, the product must appeal to the next level in the design hierarchy, that is, reliability. The product design should offer reliable performance—it must work consistently. Many brands are able to build a USP on the basis of reliability.

Usability The next level is usability, that is, consumers should be able to use the product to accomplish basic tasks. Easy operation is part of usability. Manufacturers of the personal computer (PC) catered to this need and were able to move PCs to the public domain. They showed the world how it could be used to perform a variety of tasks.

Proficiency The next level of need that products cater to is proficiency, or empowering people to do more with them. Successful software makers not only help people to accomplish tasks easily but proficiently as well. Online retailer Amazon, for example, helps customers do more by recommending books and music to them on the basis of what they have bought in the past or what their friends have been reading. These applications help to cater to higher-level needs.

Creativity After meeting lower-level needs, product design moves to the self-actualization stage by satisfying creative needs. The product design helps the consumer to explore and create things.

> **CB IN ACTION** Choosing Target Market and Ad Campaign
>
> Maslow's hierarchy also helps us determine which market to target and how best to reach that market. The lower the tier is, the more basic is the need. The lower-level needs must be met (to a certain degree) before a person will move up the hierarchy. It helps to predict buying trends and target specific customers more accurately. Advertisements are a good indication of what needs are being met by the companies and the market segments that are being targeted by them.
>
> During an economic decline, many people drop to the lower tiers of the hierarchy. In times of economic slowdown, customers look for sustenance, safety, and the support of friends and family. For instance, to sell Coca-Cola in such an economic climate, the company will avoid campaigns that make the product look like a luxury product but instead create a commercial that portrays close family bonds and the warmth of friendship.
>
> Select advertisements of different categories of products and also collect videos of advertisements from YouTube.
>
> 1. Classify the advertisements on the basis of the needs that the company wants to fulfil.
> 2. Discover the target market for whom the advertisements of a company are catering to.
> 3. Describe how ads try to portray lower-level needs in times of economic slowdown and luxury needs in times of economic recovery.

A typical example is the iPhone that has various apps that help customers indulge in exploration and creativity. Creativity includes making the product look beautiful and distinctive, or by having functions that other products do not have. Creative designs cater to the highest-level needs and generate loyalty.

Karsak, et al. (2002) show how motives are used by companies to design products. They describe a planning matrix translating customer needs into measurable product technical requirements. The technique determines customer needs and translates them into product designs. It allows the company to allocate resources and to coordinate skills and functions based on customer needs, and these result in lower production costs by ignoring aspects meaning little or nothing to the customer. CB in Action (Choosing target market and ad campaign) helps the reader to understand how advertisements address our specific needs.

Maslow's theory has intuitive appeal, and the understanding of needs leads us to address them through our products and marketing communications. The self-determination theory (SDT) is a more recent theory that contributes to our understanding of motivation. The next section describes this theory.

Self-determination Theory

The SDT is a motivation theory proposed by Deci and Ryan (2000) and states that people are most fulfilled in their lives when they are able to satisfy three fundamental needs, namely competence, autonomy, and relatedness, which are explained here.

- Competence motivation reflects a human need to master new skills and challenges.
- Autonomy motivation represents an attempt to achieve freedom and regulation by the self, rather than external forces.
- Relatedness motivation reflects the desire of a person to form meaningful bonds with others.

Everyone is assumed to have these innate needs. According to the SDT, opportunities to satisfy these intrinsic needs will facilitate self-motivation. These needs create innate motives that are essential for on going psychological growth, integrity, and well-being. The theory is simply explained on its website www.selfdeterminationtheory.org/ as being 'concerned with supporting our natural or intrinsic tendencies to behave in effective and healthy ways'.

Deci and Ryan (2008) explain that SDT focuses on types, rather than amount of motivation.

It also addresses the social conditions that enhance these types of motivation, also examining people's life goals or aspirations on the basis of *intrinsic* and *extrinsic* life goals.

Intrinsic goals are those focused toward developing one's personal interests, values, and beliefs. They are congruent with the psychological needs for relatedness, autonomy, and competence. Most people buy products that satisfy intrinsic needs. People's life aspirations such as community contribution, social affiliation, health, and fitness are intrinsic goals.

Goals that are primarily characterized by having an 'outward' orientation that is related to external indicators such as some reward or social praise, are called extrinsic goals. These consist of characteristics such as wealth, fame, and appealing image. Financial success, appearance, popularity, power, and conformity have been categorized as extrinsic goals. Extrinsic goals do not stem from nor contribute to self-development. Intrinsic and extrinsic goals give rise to a feeling of well-being. Both are commonly exploited by advertisers— intrinsic motivation by using images and messages that convey a sense of happiness, fitness, and belongingness, and extrinsic motivation by ads that show wealth, power, and success.

These goals are found to be similar in all countries and cultures. In a study conducted by Grouzet, et al. (2005) across 15 countries, it was found that people organize their goals in essentially similar ways. It is hardly a wonder then that advertising across cultures stresses on essentially the same motivations.

Both the need hierarchy theory and the SDT show that needs give rise to powerful motives. The need hierarchy theory says that as a person progresses, his needs keep changing. The SDT gives three innate psychological needs for well-being and health. Both theories give an indication to marketing as to how to design and sell products. If we observe advertisements, we will see many products that appeal to our higher-level needs. Other products appeal to our self-determination needs: for example, cars are designed to impart a feeling of control. Sports utility vehicles (SUVs), for instance, appeal to the need for control and competence and are sold to people who have nothing to do with sports (see opening-case study in Chapter 7).

Needs lead us to motives, the force that pushes us into shops.

MOTIVES

A motive is defined as an emotion, desire, physiological need, or similar impulse that acts as an incitement to action.

To understand motivation, we must understand the different types of motives that cause people to buy things. Motivation in the marketplace could arise due to intrinsic or extrinsic needs, there could be rational or emotional motives for buying, and finally a person may be responding to positive or negative motives.

Extrinsic motives Extrinsic motivation depends on motivators external to the individual. They involve rewards such as monetary rewards, social recognition, or praise. Displays and point-of-purchase publicity try to create external motives for buying.

Intrinsic motives   Intrinsic motivation arises from within the individual, such as fulfilment of psychological needs, such as friendship, community, health, and so on. An individual's personality and thinking processes play a role in creating intrinsic motives.

Rational motives   Rational motives in buying behaviour are those resulting from evaluation of objective criteria such as price, quality, size, efficiency, and convenience.

Emotional motives   When purchases are made on subjective criteria such as liking for the ad, celebrity endorsement, or emotions such as happiness, envy, fashion, pride, and so on, they result from emotional motives. Appearance, colour, and aesthetics are all emotional motives.

Positive motives   Positive motivation occurs when the person is driven towards a product. It may occur because of rational or emotional motives.

Negative motives   Here, the person is driven away from a product or ad, with the consequence that purchase will not occur. Negative motivation occurs for a variety of reasons, such as a person not liking the message, or person featured in the ad, product quality, or bad past experiences. Credibility of the product is the main force to check negative motivation.

Motives are used to position brands. The chapter-closing case study shows how brands try to discover the real motives of consumers. Such techniques give new life to brands but must be applied after identifying consumer motivations.

Arousal of Motives

While most consumption motives lie dormant within us at any given time, they are aroused by various stimuli. Ads, or the sight of the product itself, or catchy slogans may arouse our motives. For example, in a restaurant, what people are having at the next table arouses our hunger. Such arousal is caused by internal stimuli, by our emotional or cognitive processes, or by external stimuli. People will make purchases when they experience a need and their motives are aroused. As our chapter-closing case study shows, retailers such as Reebok and Shoppers Stop try arousal techniques to attract customers and to ensure they spend time and money at the stores.

Berger (2011) writes that transmission of information is driven in part by arousal. Physiological arousal is characterized by activation of the autonomic nervous system, and the mobilization provided by this excitatory state may boost sharing. Further, emotions characterized by high arousal, such as anxiety or amusement, will boost sharing more than emotions characterized by low arousal, such as sadness or contentment.

As we have noted earlier, tensions arise because of unmet needs. If people can be made aware of these needs and tension created in their minds, then they would like to resolve that tension by buying products. Motivation levels can range from passion to inertia. One way of looking at motivation is to see what advertising does. The purpose of advertising is to remind customers of their unmet needs and create tension so that consumers go out and relieve their tensions by buying the products.

Internal needs and wants can be aroused through physiological, emotional, cognitive, or environmental arousal.

Physiological arousal Our bodies respond to stimuli like fear, happiness, or hunger. Similarly, we get physiologically aroused when we see something very attractive or very shocking. Ads often use this approach and succeed. Large lettering, very attractive or shocking visuals, headlines with double meanings, and tongue-in-cheek humour, are some of the ways in which physiological arousal is sought by companies. Feldman (2011) notes that for many people, the mere sight of the golden arches in front of McDonald's outlets makes them feel pangs of hunger and think about hamburgers. This shows that consumers often feel an urge to eat something when they see signs of a café or a popular fast food restaurant—a case of classical conditioning (see Chapter 8).

Emotional arousal Emotional arousal plays on latent desires and day-dreams. Ads play on such latent desires. Lifestyle or inspirational advertising uses this approach—consumers who imagine themselves in a particular income bracket are influenced to use the advertised products even though they are not that rich. An aspiring cricketer, for example, will identify himself with a major player like Sachin Tendulkar and use the products endorsed by him.

Cognitive arousal Sometimes random thoughts or a personal achievement can lead to a cognitive awareness of needs. Research conducted by Hyun, et al. (2011) in the restaurant industry shows that advertising has a significant impact on inducing emotional responses in customers. They found that cognitive factors like relevant news, stimulation, empathy, and familiarity in advertising positively influence patrons' perceived value. Further, it was found that the level of arousal induced by advertising plays a moderating function in the relationship between patrons' emotional responses and hedonic value. Advertisers have also used negative stereotypes and incongruent images to arouse viewers.

Environmental arousal The set of needs activated at a particular time are often determined by specific cues in the environment. Without these cues, the needs would remain dormant. For example, the sight or smell of freshly baked bread at a bakery will trigger a signal in the brain that you need bread. Environmental arousal occurs due to situational motivations that happen around the individual.

Companies have long known that motives can be aroused through advertising. How the elements of colour, sex, and music are used is explained in the Marketing Insight that follows.

Components of Motivation

How people make choices among alternatives is shown by the expectancy theory of motivation. It states that the desire to do something is a composite of the expected outcome of that action and the evaluation of that action. It explains that individuals develop a motivational force (MF) for each alternative while making decisions. The alternative with the highest MF is the choice made by the individual. There are three components of MF (Fig. 6.8).

Expectancy Expectancy is the belief that one's effort leads to fulfilment of desire. A cognitive component, it pushes people to action as they expect rewards. Either they buy products or they save for the future with the expectation that their spending will bring them satisfaction.

MARKETING INSIGHT
Arousal in Advertising

Arousal helps in spreading information. Indeed, we have seen that rumours flourish in times of panic. Positive emotion may also increase sharing of information, as when we recommend movies that we have liked to our friends. They impact our emotions and arouse us. The techniques used are discussed here.

Colour Colour is commonly used as a marketing tool. Brands are recognizable by their distinctive colours and may even arouse physiologically. Shi (2012) writes that colour can also influence mood or attitude towards a product. For example, we prefer brightly-coloured fruit and vegetables and regard them as fresh. Advertisers use colours to activate or arouse, as it will make the contents more attractive to readers. Apart from enabling more efficient processing of information, arousal can also enhance the storage of information.

Sex The use of sex in advertising is a popular technique to arouse viewers. It is sometimes used with unrelated products as well. Research shows that sex and nudity in advertising is likely to elicit psychophysiological reactions from the viewer. Belch, et al. (1982) showed that both nudity and suggestiveness in advertisements elicit strong physiological and cognitive reactions. Both opposite sex and same sex nude ads elicit strong physiological reactions, with appealing and offensive cognitive reactions respectively.

Music Music inspires and relaxes many people, and is an arousal technique when used in advertising. Indeed, some jingles become very popular and are even downloaded as caller tunes by consumers. Lantos and Craton (2012) write that simple, catchy lyrics can inspire deeper processing of ad music and improve recall of ad messages. Emotional appeals made through music can trigger emotional responses and influence the listener's attitude. Repeated exposure to music can create a positive response among low-affective-involvement consumers, although overkill can be damaging if a jingle becomes irritating. In another study by Dillman-Carpentier and Potter (2007), skin-conductance-level data showed that fast-paced music elicits greater activation in the skin than slow-paced music. Genre and faster tempo increased activation.

Should ads arouse desires or should they only inform and educate?

Sources:

Belch, Michael A., Barbro E. Holgerson, George E. Belch, and Jerry Koppman, 'Psychophysiological and cognitive responses to sex in advertising', in *Advances in Consumer Research*, Vol. 9, Ed. Andrew Mitchell, Ann Arbor, 1982, pp. 424–427.

Dillman-Carpentier, Francesca and Robert F. Potter, 'Effects of music on physiological arousal: Explorations into tempo and genre', *Media Psychology*, Vol. 10, No. 3, 2007, pp. 339–363.

Lantos, Geoffrey P. and Lincoln G. Craton, 'A model of consumer response to advertising music', *Journal of Consumer Marketing*, Vol. 29, No. 1, 2012, pp. 22–42.

Shi, Tommy, 'The use of color in marketing: Colors and their physiological and psychological implications', *Berkeley Scientific Journal*, Vol. 17, No. 1, Fall 2012.

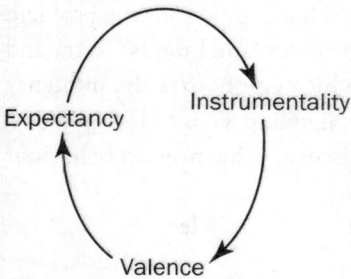

FIG. 6.8 Components of motivational force

Instrumentality Instrumentality is the belief that one's actions will lead to rewards. Motivation arises in individuals if they see outcomes associated with their behaviour.

Valence Valence represents an individual's preference for potential outcomes. For example, the value one places on price and benefits represents differences in valence for each outcome. Valence is a function of an individual's values.

Motivational force is a function of these three components and is expressed as

Motivational force (MF) = Expectancy × instrumentality × valence

DISCOVERING MOTIVES

The next step is to discover our real motivations in buying products. Think, for example, of the time you went for a cup of coffee to a café and the reason you did so.

We try to fulfil several utility needs when we buy consumer goods and services. For every consumption decision, we may try to fulfil one or several needs and have different motives. The different types of motives and needs that spur us to buy products are described in the next section.

Motivational Dimensions

Consumers compare products based on their ability to satisfy basic needs. These utility needs are the basic dimensions of motivation because consumers want to reach certain goal states and products are instrumental in reaching the goals. Sheth (1975) distinguishes five utility needs that products satisfy. I have added a sixth one, as hedonism too, plays a big role in consumer decision-making.

Functional motives Functional motives are related to the technical functions the product performs. The combination of product attributes forms the total functional utility of a product.

Aesthetic–emotional motives Aesthetic–emotional motives consider the style, design, luxury, and comfort provided by a product. People tend to select those products that match with their lifestyles and enable them to express their fundamental values.

Social motives Social motives are related to the impact that consumption makes on others. Status, prestige, and esteem are derived from the possession and usage of products and their conspicuous features. Some products are selected as they are 'conversation pieces'.

Situational motives Situational motives are those that trigger the purchase, such as easy availability and price discount.

Curiosity motives Curiosity motives prompt trials of new and innovative products. The consumer may try a new product; however, a repeat purchase may be independent of such trials.

Hedonic motives Very often, shopping is done for pleasure. When a consumer buys things just to feel good about himself or herself, hedonic motives are at play. Retail stores cater to hedonic motives by making shopping fun and easy through attractive displays and offers.

Though it is theoretically possible to classify utility needs and motives, identifying which needs are fulfilled by an individual is a different matter. It is difficult for a market researcher to discover the real motives of actions simply because they are psychological. What compounds the problem is that even consumers do not know their real motives in buying products and brands. To try and solve this problem marketing takes the help of psychoanalysis, which emphasizes the influence of the unconscious mind on human behaviour. Propounded by Sigmund Freud (1856–1939), motivation research(MR) delves deep into the human mind to discover influences on behaviour that are hidden in one's personality.

Motivation Research

It was psychologist Ernest Dichter (1907–1991) who applied the techniques of psychoanalysis to marketing and created a million-dollar business advising companies how best to sell products based on the real motives of customers. Dichter is referred to as the 'father of motivation research'. He used Freudian psychoanalysis to discover the hidden motivations of customers when they bought products such as cosmetics, cars, and cigarette lighters. Massey (2012) writes that his work was hugely popular—it gave birth to the very successful TV serial, *Mad Men*.

Motivation research is defined as the psychological or sociological investigation of consumer motives. It is a research process that employs projective techniques to tap into the consumers' subconscious to discover their real motivations for buying and using products. Let's discuss depth interviews and projective techniques.

Depth interviews In depth interviews, consumers are encouraged to talk freely in unstructured interviews and their hidden thoughts and motives are discovered from what they say. The reasoning is that people let their guard down when they are allowed to speak freely.

Projective techniques Consumers are given a situation, a picture, a cartoon, or a set of words and asked to project their thoughts and feelings about them. Another projective technique is to ask consumers to complete sentences such as: 'A person who buys brand X is _____', or fill up bubbles in cartoons to guess what the character in the cartoon would be saying. Consumers can also be asked to assess the personality of the brand or associate an animal with it. The images of the brand in a consumer's mind can be discovered in these ways.

Buying decisions, according to MR, are the result of emotions and subconscious feelings, and often have little to do with the product itself. Dichter (1957) explains in his book, *The Strategy of Desire* that 'Many of our daily decisions are governed by motivations over which we have no control and of which we are quite unaware'.

Motivation research using depth interviews was employed widely by advertising agencies. Turner (2012) explains that Dichter removed guilt and brought enjoyment to buying and consuming goods. He 'wanted to encourage people to shed their guilty feelings about self-indulgent pleasures and find erotic satisfaction in buying things' and created a 'living laboratory' where consumers interacted with products while researchers observed them and conducted depth interviews with them. The Barbie doll was one of the results of such research. Dichter was able to discover that little girls wanted someone sexy looking, someone they wanted to grow up to be like. His book, *The Psychology of Everyday Living* (1947) showed how the psychoanalytic approach could be applied to everyday things.

Although it made great contributions to advertising and consumer research, by the 1970s, motivation research had declined and Dichter's work was largely dismissed. Clancy and Krieg (2007) echo some of the criticism against motivational research: 'Great brand positioning is a combination of buyer motivation, perception of the brand, and the company's ability to deliver. Although psychoanalysis might help with the motivation part, it offers little in terms of competitive perception and feasibility'.

Some examples of products and the motives discovered by Dichter are summarized in Table 6.2.

Revival of Motivation Research Motivation research has seen a revival in recent times. *The Economist* (2011) writes that though Dichter's name has largely been forgotten, yet many of his ideas about the role of the unconscious in sales are now back in fashion. Companies try to discover psychological motivations not only through research but by engaging with customers

TABLE 6.2 Examples of Dichter's motivation research

Product	Motives for buying
Soap	Associated with sensuality, sexy, and refreshing
Cigarettes	Rewards for a job well done, or a break from a stressful work day
Cars (Convertibles)	Freedom, personal identity, youthful self-assertion, and sex Men associate them with freedom and the fantasy of having a mistress
Beer	Longing for acceptance and friendship, encouraged social relationships
Chewing gum	Relieving of tension and anxiety
Breakfast cereal	Satisfying a desire to overcome obstacles

online. Brain-scanning techniques are being used as well. Most advertising campaigns these days can best be described as psychological. Massey (2012) writes, 'Glance at the television or pass a billboard and you will recognize that the concepts pioneered by Dichter still dominate the advertising that surrounds us'.

Consultancies offer to find out subconscious desires for products. For example, Buyology Inc says on its website that it has developed proprietary web-based technology to help companies make better decisions on how to effectively connect with their current and prospective customers by accessing, measuring, and understanding consumers' non-conscious responses. It says that rigorously measuring the non-conscious provides clients with a huge competitive advantage.

Motivation research has today come full circle. The benefits of using the subconscious to create advertising messages and design products based on human needs are immense. Dichter knew that traditional marketing research would not yield much as people often did not know why they bought a product or chose a brand. These days, more than ever, economists are realizing that man is not a rational being. Marketing companies know that purchase decisions are driven by emotions and the subconscious (see Exhibit 6.3), and are often not based on product attributes. Dichter compared human motivation as an 'iceberg', with only one-third visible and two-thirds hidden from view.

What Dichter wrote in 1965 stays true even today. 'Advertisers will sell philosophy as well as their products, and often philosophy as being more important than the products themselves'. New techniques are now being formulated to discover motives.

Two methods of discovering psychological motives are also used in modern marketing, namely the analytical hierarchy process (AHP) and Zaltman metaphor elicitation technique (ZMET). Since it is difficult to comprehend people's psychology in the real world, online avatars help companies to match products to the subconscious. The techniques of motivational research are described here.

Analytic Hierarchy Process

The analytic hierarchy process (AHP) provides a basis for building a model of the way people differentiate multiple criteria. It provides an empirical basis for the comparison of objects by means of relative measurement and is a structured technique for organizing and analysing complex decisions.

EXHIBIT 6.3 Using Emotions

Given its brand name, it salutes the mother on Mother's Day by reminding people that she is the embodiment of love and affection and Mother's Recipe is her trusted lieutenant. On India's Independence Day Mother's Recipe runs a radio campaign asking its listeners to give their mothers freedom from the kitchen for this day. Let us look at its brand values.

Brand values Mother's Recipe epitomises mother's love. It's a brand that strives to bring home the true taste of homemade pickles by ensuring that only the freshest, purest fruits, vegetables and spices are used. There is another reason, too, for its pickiness. In a world that gives tradition a go-by it's hard to believe that a brand exists that, in truth, believes that when people who lust for the taste of home are spread across continents it's not right that they be given second shrift. It's for this reason that Mother's Recipe refuses to compromise and will spend endless months in perfecting its offerings (see Figure 6.9).

FIG. 6.9 Mother's Recipe: Keeping tradition alive

Courtesy: Superbrands

Source: Superbrands 2012

Saaty and Vargas (2012) describe several applications of the AHP. In particular, they apply the AHP to the design and evaluation of a marketing-driven business. The steps for resolving the problem of discovering motives of customers are summarized as follows:

- Structure the buying problem with a model and identify key needs and motivations.
- Elicit judgements that reflect knowledge, feelings, and emotions of customers.
- Represent these judgements with meaningful numbers.
- Use these numbers to calculate the priorities of the elements of the hierarchy.
- Synthesize the results to determine the overall outcome.
- Analyse sensitivity to changes in judgement.

Zaltman Metaphor Elicitation Technique

The unconscious reveals itself through metaphors—representations of one thing in terms of another. A metaphor is a figurative language used by poets in which a word or phrase that ordinarily designates one thing is used to designate another. An example is a line by Robert Burns, 'My love is a red, red rose', by which he means that she resembles a rose in beauty and fragrance. Zaltman (2011) explains that human beings use about six metaphors per minute of spoken language, establishing connections, helping us interpret the world, and making it intelligible.

The Zaltman metaphor elicitation technique (ZMET) is the process of analysing brands and products by analysing the consumers' unconscious thoughts through the use of metaphors. Zaltman's pioneering work brings together two different domains—a metaphor and a product or service. The metaphor helps consumers better understand the product or service. Secondly, when the metaphor and product interact, they sometimes create a new idea not inherent to either domain alone. 'Put simply, metaphors do more than help make a point; they can also shape what and how we think,' he writes.

Zaltman writes in his book, *How Customers Think* (2003) that companies benefit greatly by getting consumers to use metaphors about products. By bringing unconscious thoughts and feelings to the surface, they can find the real connections consumers see between products and their own lives. Market research techniques usually ask customers their opinions, but those are blunt instruments because more than nine-tenths of thought, emotion, and even learning, occur in the unconscious mind.

Coulter and Zaltman (1994) describe how ZMET is used. A set of about 25 consumers is recruited and asked to take photographs or collect pictures from magazines, newspapers, and other sources that indicate what the product means to them. After about a week or so, they are interviewed personally. Through depth interviews, customers describe products in terms of ten core steps as given here.

1. *Storytelling*: The customer describes the content of each picture
2. *Missed images*: The customer describes the pictures he or she was unable to obtain and explains their relevance
3. *Sorting*: The customer sorts the pictures into meaningful piles
4. *Construct elicitation*: The grid technique and the laddering technique are used to elicit basic constructs and their relationships
5. *Most representative picture*: The customer indicates the picture that is most representative
6. *Opposite images*: The customer describes pictures that represent the opposite of the task, for example, 'What is not Nike'
7. *Sensory images*: Consumers describe the taste, touch, smell, sound, colour, and emotion of the concept being explored
8. *Mental map*: Consumers create a mental map using the descriptors
9. *Summary image*: Customers create a summary image using digital imaging techniques
10. *Consensus map*: Researchers create a map or a model involving the most important points

The authors explain how a consumer actually described the detergent brand Tide using the ZMET. The images and metaphors used by customers are described in CB in Action (ZMET).

ZMET is a powerful technique that can help us discover inner motivations and perceptions (covered in Chapter 7). Effective metaphors in advertising strongly influence customers, by making their mind 'see' the information that is not actually there. When people express themselves online using alter-egos or avatars, it helps to see the metaphors in their mind by which they describe themselves. Managers are discovering that online identities too provide personality insights, as discussed in the next section.

Avatar-based Marketing

While ZMET helps uncover subconscious thoughts through metaphors, one problem faced by companies using survey techniques is that customers often give wrong answers, or answers that are acceptable but do not reflect their real intentions. In a conversation with *Harvard Business Review* (2002), Zaltman says, 'Consumers will say they will buy the product but then they don't',

CB IN ACTION   ZMET

Coulter and Zaltman (1994) show how the ZMET was used to understand what Tide meant to customers. Alice, a consumer, was asked to collect pictures that helped her describe the brand Tide. She divided the pictures into three things that the brand meant to her—comfort, freshness, and drudgery. Through interviews, the interviewer was able to reduce these to two constructs, namely unpleasantness and freshness; unpleasantness because doing the laundry was seen as a chore, and freshness because the clothes ended up being clean and smell nice.

The customer admitted during the interview that it 'makes me feel confident' and 'tells people what kind of person I am'. In Step 5, Alice indicated that the picture that most represented 'Tide' to her was her picture of a sunrise, since it meant to her freshness (the smell of her clothing after using Tide), brightness (the colours of her clothes after using Tide), calm or peacefulness (the product cleaned her clothes and put her at ease), and accomplishment (a new day to get things done).

Among other images that came to mind was that of a teddy bear or a kitten, representing how clothes felt after washing them with Tide. The smell was described as that of cool rain, not a perfume, the sound—a train whistle, the colour—orange, and the emotion—calm. By aggregating responses from other customers, researchers could come to an image that Tide inspired among users.

It is easy to see that eliciting metaphors becomes a powerful tool in advertising and in understanding consumer behaviour. Companies can comprehend what images to use in their advertising, and how best to pitch their brands.

You can try out this technique with another product, such as a carbonated beverage, mobile phone, or any other famous brand.

- Ask your friends to collect images that reflect the brand.
- Follow steps 1–10 described in the ZMET.
- Arrive at an advertising or promotion strategy using your findings.

---

adding that very often customers themselves are not aware of their intentions. As this is the cause of product failure, marketing needs a way to explore the real selves of people.

Help comes from technology. Today companies have huge amounts of information about customers. *The Economist* (2011) shows how personal data is generated. Every time people use a loyalty card, they surrender personal information. Every time they do a Google search or hit the 'like' button on Facebook, they surrender yet more. Google and Facebook sell generic information to advertisers. Professional dataminers use electronic data to create a detailed picture of what you have bought in the past ('history sniffing') and how you bought it ('behaviour sniffing').

Online profiles of people help us in discovering real personalities. For instance, many people use *avatars* to describe themselves on social media and gaming sites. Avatars are alternative identities of individuals and help us discover their subconscious selves. Hemp (2006) writes that technology enables us to have multiple identities and is very helpful. 'Advertising has always targeted a powerful consumer alter ego—that hip, attractive, incredibly popular person just waiting to emerge (with the help of the advertised product) from an all-too-normal self.' Marketing can use these alter egos to segment, reach, and influence customers directly. Since marketing depends on building people's dreams, companies can use the virtual world and target the potential customer—the avatar.

Suh, et al. (2011) also propose that avatars representing users' actual appearance may be helpful in experiencing and evaluating some business areas related to users' lives in the real world, such

RESEARCH INSIGHT
Examining Motivations for Online and Mobile Buying

The psychology of buying has been studied extensively in traditional settings, but the study of motivations of consumers while buying online or through mobile devices is still in its infancy. Consumers use their mobile phones not only for getting information and solving a problem, but also for having fun by using entertainment functions on their mobile phones. The impact of mobile technology and the spread of smartphones have changed retailers' interaction with customers. So what makes people buy online?

Joines, et al. (2003) found that motivational factors play a key role in online purchases. Economic motivations and transactional privacy concerns have significant influence. Online shopping activity is predicted by a range of motivations—information motivations, interactive control motivations, and socialization motivations.

Economic motivations People shop online to save money. However, privacy concerns have a detrimental effect on online shopping, especially related to credit card transactions and sharing of personal information. Security protocols have overcome these concerns to a great extent.

Informational motivations Customers can acquire information more efficiently and inexpensively on the Web, which helps them make better purchasing decisions.

Interactive control motivations People use the Web because it gives them greater control. They like components like individualized recommendations based on their previous purchases, the opportunity to review products, and make recommendations to friends or other customers.

Social motivations Online traders rely on strategies of building social relationships just like traditional retailers. Loyalty schemes and customer feedback are used to create a sense of community between companies and customers. The Web offers elaborate ways of creating a sense of pseudo-community among its customers.

Close and Kukar-Kinney (2010) investigate consumers' motivations using virtual cart use. Consumer attitudes and website personality are important determinants of online shopping. There are utilitarian and hedonic motives for using the Internet as well, such as usefulness, information seeking, convenience, and entertainment. Utilitarian and hedonic motivations help explain what drives shoppers to use their carts.

Utilitarian shopping motivation This refers to consumers looking at functional features of products, financial goals, and efficiency. Efficiency shopping refers to a consumer's need to save time such as saving a trip to the market and to be able to buy products quickly and easily. Online services are a boon for the time-pressed shopper, who will be willing to pay extra to save time. In mobile transactions, efficiency motivation for saving time and cost is significant—consumers can place orders while commuting, which are fulfilled by the time they return home. Mobile shopping is thus a medium for consumers to save time and costs of going to the retail store.

Hedonic shopping motivation Hedonic shopping motivation refers to the consumer's emotional feelings and psychological sensations while shopping. Six dimensions of hedonic motivation that influence consumer shopping activities are adventure, social, gratification, idea, role, and value. Since people shop to try out new things and new ideas, the experience of shopping is full of adventure and fun. This motivation is easily met by the smartphone. Since the mobile shopping channel is still a new medium for many people, consumers are interested in playing with their devices and discover services and features that are only available in mobile technology. Consumers not only have fun exploring shopping sites but are also able to buy on impulse, satisfying their hedonic motivation.

Social motivation Consumers use mobile shopping to get others' opinions on their mobile phones. The communication functions such as social networks and instant messaging enable consumers to fulfil their social needs while shopping online. This is another motive to shop by mobile phone. The Internet-enabled smartphone becomes a great platform for shopping and simultaneously connecting with others socially.

Yang and Kim's (2012) study of mobile shoppers' shopping motivations compared with those of non-mo-

(Contd)

RESEARCH INSIGHT (Contd)

bile shoppers shows that idea, efficiency, adventure, and gratification shopping are significant motives for mobile shoppers. *Gratification shopping* refers to shopping that evokes good feelings and brings special treats to the individual consumer. In mobile shopping, personalized services and promotions to each individual mobile phone user are provided as a personal treat. The entertainment features of mobile shopping applications relieve some of the consumer stress of shopping. *Idea shopping* occurs when the consumer collects information about new trends and fashion, and has fun searching for and receiving new information. *Value shopping* refers to the consumer focusing on bargain hunting and discounts. Consumers feel a sense of personal accomplishment when they get a bargain or discount. In mobile channels, consumers can acquire coupons instantly. Discussion forums enable the consumers to share discount information with others, giving them a sense of achievement.

Aljukhadar and Senecal (2011) show that online consumers form the following three global segments:

- Basic communicators or consumers who use the Internet mainly to communicate via e-mail
- Lurking shoppers or consumers who use the Internet to navigate and to shop
- Social thrivers or consumers who use the Internet to interact socially

Companies selling online can use these experience profiles to predict their consumers' online behaviour. Websites can have features tailored according to customer characteristics to improve outcomes.

These research studies try to explain the motivations of the online shopper. How can companies use these in making online selling strategies?

Sources:

Aljukhadar, Muhammad and Sylvain Senecal, 'Segmenting the online consumer market', *Marketing Intelligence & Planning*, Vol. 29, No. 4, 2011, pp. 421–435.

Close, Angeline G. and Monika Kukar-Kinney, 'Beyond buying: Motivations behind consumers' online shopping cart use', *Journal of Business Research*, Vol. 63, 2010, pp. 986–992.

Joines, Jessica L., Clifford W. Scherer, and Dietram A. Scheufele, 'Exploring motivations for consumer Web use and their implications for e-commerce', *Journal of Consumer Marketing*, Vol. 20, No. 2, 2003, pp. 90–108.

Kiely, T., 'The Internet: Fear and shopping in cyberspace', *Harvard Business Review*, 1997.

Yang, Kiseol and Hye-Young Kim, 'Mobile shopping motivation: An application of multiple discriminant analysis', *International Journal of Retail & Distribution Management*, Vol. 40, No. 10, 2012, pp. 778–789.

as virtual apparel shopping, matchmaking, plastic surgery, fitness clubs, and so on. Utilization of such avatars may be a new business opportunity likely to thrive in virtual worlds.

Maximum Difference Scaling

The challenge before companies is to identify the true motives of consumers when they buy products. Product development teams need a technique for identifying what features of products matter most to each market segment. The problem is that measuring something like consumer preference is not easy, and customers are also not forthcoming about their real desires. Almquist and Lee (2009) note that present-day market research techniques and copious customer data often cause companies to launch products suffering from 'feature creep' only to discover that customers want something completely different. A method is needed to discover customer preferences that even people are not aware of themselves.

The authors describe an application to discover and rank real needs called maximum difference scaling (MaxDiff). Pioneered in the early 1990s by Jordan Louviere, MaxDiff is an approach for obtaining preference scores for multiple items such as brand preferences, brand images, product features, advertising claims, and so on, and works on the principle of consumer trade-offs between product attributes. Starting with a list of product or brand attributes that represent potential benefits, consumers are presented with sets of four or so attributes at a time, asking them to select the attribute from each set that they prefer most and least. These rounds of groupings are repeated several times to identify the importance of each attribute relative to others on the basis of the number of times that customers select it as their most or least important consideration.

The method was used in evaluating a restaurant and to see why its promotional efforts were misfiring. When consumers were asked what they wanted in a restaurant, their answer was more healthful meal options and updated decor. However, when the restaurant was opened, all it could get was mediocre results. The company then asked customers to compare eight attributes using Maxdiff. The results showed that prompt service of hot meals and a convenient location were far more important to customers than healthful items and modern furnishings. The restaurant learnt that it had to improve kitchen service and select restaurant sites based on where customers worked.

CONCLUSION

The question: 'What makes people buy products?' is mysterious because much of our subconscious remains shrouded in fog. It takes us into the territory of psychoanalysis. Discovering the hidden motives of customers when they buy things, companies get to know how to project their brands to make them seductive, and as Turner (2012) writes, 'to ignite customers' desires, and make them buy things that they didn't really need or even know they wanted'.

Answering the question requires observing customers as they shop. When we do that, we see that shoppers who are exposed to soft music with a slow tempo tend to spend 18 per cent longer in the store and make 17 per cent more purchases than those who shop in silence.

Companies would do well to track shoppers around supermarkets and listen in on their conversations at the counter. How people examine products also shows what they want.

Though the techniques and findings of motivation research can be debated, it does provide valuable insights about people as they interact with brands. Today's hidden persuaders are much more sophisticated than those of the past as they are armed with personal data that people willingly surrender online. Successful companies always find ways to cater to our inner drives and motives, and that is why the study of consumer motivations remains vital in the field of marketing.

SUMMARY

The study of consumer motives is actually a study of 'what makes people buy products'. Motivation is what pushes consumers into stores and makes them buy goods. It is an internal state that drives people to identify and buy products or services that fulfil conscious and unconscious needs or desires. Managers hoping to garner a good market share for their brands must understand the needs, wants, motives, and drives leading to purchase behaviour. Needs are physiological or psychological, and arise because of instincts, incentives, drives, and arousal states of people. Human drives arise from the unmet needs which create tensions. Consumers set goals for themselves arising from their needs.

According to Maslow, there is a hierarchy of needs consisting of lower-level or basic physiological needs, progressing to safety, love or belongingness, esteem, and finally self-actualization needs. Needs and goals are interdependent and are used widely in marketing. They are used in product design and advertising. Better-designed products appeal to higher-level needs than functional ones. The design hierarchy corresponding to needs consists of functionality, reliability, usability, proficiency, and creativity.

The self-determination theory states that people are most fulfilled in their lives when they are able to satisfy three fundamental needs, namely competence, autonomy, and relatedness. It addresses the social conditions that enhance these types of motivation, also examining people's life goals or aspirations on the basis of intrinsic and extrinsic life goals.

Needs lead us to motives. These are emotions, desires, physiological needs, or similar impulses that act asincitement to action. Motives are aroused by various stimulilike advertising. Internal needs and wants can be awakened through physiological, emotional, cognitive, or environmental arousal. Advertisements make use of colour, sex, and music to arouse the latent desires of consumers.

The expectancy theory of motivation explains that individuals develop a motivational force for each alternative while making decisions. The three components of motivational force are expectancy, instrumentality, and valence.

Though it is theoretically possible to classify utility needs and motives, finding motives for purchase is difficult for a market researcher simply because they are psychological. To try and solve this problem, marketing takes the help of psychoanalysis, and motivation research delves deep into the human mind to discover influences on behaviour that are hidden in one's personality. Motivation research uses two methods, namely depth interviews and projective techniques. Buying decisions, according to motivation research, are the result of emotions and subconscious feelings, and often have little to do with the product itself. Though it saw a decline for some time, motivation research is witnessing a revival. Companies today try to discover psychological motivations not only through research but by engaging with customers online. Brain-scanning techniques are being used as well.

The methods of discovering psychological motives are the analytical hierarchy process (AHP) and the Zaltman Metaphor Elicitation Technique (ZMET). Online avatars of people help companies to match products to the subconscious. The Maxddiff technique helps us discover the importance of each motive and build a ranking to find out the most important one.

▪▪▪ KEY TERMS

Analytic hierarchy process (AHP) AHP provides a basis for modelling the way people differentiate multiple criteria

Avatar-based marketing Using online profiles of people as a marketing tool

Consumer motivation An internal state that drives people to identify and buy products or services that fulfil conscious and unconscious needs or desires

Desire A strong feeling, or a sense of longing, or craving for a thing

Drive An aroused state of psychological tension that typically arises from a need

Goals The ideal state that a person desires

Grid technique and the laddering technique The repertory grid technique is a method for eliciting personal constructs, or what people think about a given topic

Maslow's need hierarchy A hierarchy of needs progressing from lower-level or basic physiological needs, to safety, love or belongingness, esteem, and finally self-actualization needs

Maximum difference scaling (Maxdiff) An approach for obtaining preference scores for multiple items such as brand preferences, brand images, product features, advertising claims, and so on

Metaphor A figure of speech in which a word or phrase that ordinarily designates one thing is used to designate another

Motivation research (MR) The psychological or sociological investigation of consumer motives

Motive An emotion, desire, physiological need, or similar impulse that acts as an incitement to action

Need Needs are human requirements

Physiological needs Referred to as primary, biological, or biogenic needs, these consist of the innate need for food, water, sleep, air, and shelter

Psychological needs Referred to as secondary or psychogenic needs, they are needs for affiliation, power, recognition, esteem, and status

Self-determination theory (SDT) A motivation theory that states that people are most fulfilled in their lives when they are able to satisfy three fundamental needs, namely competence, autonomy, and relatedness

Zaltman metaphor elicitation technique (ZMET) The analysis of brands and products by analysing the consumers' unconscious through the use of metaphors

EXERCISES

Concept-review Questions

1. What is consumer motivation? Why is it important in the study of consumer behaviour?
2. Distinguish between needs, goals, motives, and desires. Show how these lead to drives that ultimately result in action.
3. Explain Maslow's hierarchy of needs and show its applicability to marketing. How are needs related to product design and advertising?
4. What are motives? Explain the different types of motives and how they are used to position brands.
5. How are motives aroused? How is the concept of arousal used in advertising?
6. What is motivation research? Explain the method by which it is able to uncover consumer motivation.
7. Critically examine the statement, 'Advertisers will sell philosophy as well as their products, and often as being more important than the products themselves'. How far is this true?
8. Explain ZMET and its importance in establishing brand positioning. Does the technique work in real life?
9. How does online availability of information and personal identities aid in marketing?
10. Analyse the concept of core and augmented product under various aspects of product design. Show how higher-level needs are addressed as the product is enhanced.

Critical Thinking Questions

1. 'Great brand positioning is a combination of buyer motivation, perception of the brand, and the company's ability to deliver. Although psychoanalysis might help with the motivation part, it offers little in terms of competitive perception and feasibility.' Analyse the concept of motivation research in the light of this statement and find out whether it actually helps to sell products.
2. Martin Lindstrom in his book, *Brandwashed: Tricks Companies use to Manipulate Our Minds and Persuade us to Buy*, makes the point that companies manipulate our thinking and target even the youngest of consumers. In the light of this criticism, comment on whether such techniques are ethical. How far should companies go to sell their products?
3. Marketing companies use arousal techniques to attract customers. Would it not result in people buying things that they don't really need? How far is this justified?
4. Comment on the statement made by Steve Jobs: 'A lot of times, people don't know what they want until you show it to them. That's why a lot of people at Apple get paid a lot of money, because they're supposed to be on top of these things'. How can companies cater to consumers when people themselves don't know what they want?

Projects and Assignments

1. Take up a piece of clothing. Try to discover the motivations of consumers in buying that piece. Devise promotional campaigns for clothing stressing on different levels of needs as specified by Maslow. Then compare your campaigns with campaigns of apparel companies to see if they are also doing a similar job.
2. Ask your friends to think of a time when they wanted something very badly. Then ask them to explain the reasons behind their desire. How far was the desire natural and how much of it was induced by advertising? Explain how companies are able to succeed in their objective by creating powerful needs and drives.
3. Take up an ordinary object such as a chocolate, cellphone, car, or anything consumed ordinarily by your friends. Now ask your friends to think of metaphors to describe the product. Ask them to use projective techniques like personification to find out the product personality.
4. Check out the online profiles of your friends on gaming or social networking sites. Study the pictures and messages posted by them. On the basis of this information, can you find out some facts about them that were previously hidden from you? Was there any discrepancy with their personalities?

REFERENCES

Almquist, Eric and Jason Lee, 'What do customers really want?', *Harvard Business Review*, April 2009.

Berger, Jonah, 'Arousal increases social transmission of information', *Psychological Science*, Vol. 22, No. 7, 2011, pp. 891–893.

Britt, S.H., 'The Strategy of Human Motivation', *The Journal of Marketing*, Vol. 14, No. 5, 1950, pp. 666–74.

BuyologyInc http//www.buyologyinc.com, last accessed on 11 June 2013.

Clancy, Kevin and Peter Krieg, *Your Gut is Still Not Smarter Than Your Head: How Disciplined, Fact-based Marketing Can Drive Extraordinary Growth and Profits*, John Wiley and Sons, New Jersey, 2007.

'Conversation with Gerald Zaltman: Hidden Minds', *Harvard Business Review*, June 2002, pp. 26–27.

Coulter, Robin Higie and Gerald Zaltman, 'Using the Zaltmanmetaphor elicitation technique to understand brand images', *Advances in Consumer Research*, Vol. 21, 1994, pp. 501–507.

Deci, Edward L. and Richard M. Ryan, 'Self-determination theory: A macro theory of human motivation, development, and health, *Canadian Psychology*, Vol. 49, No. 3, 2008, pp. 182–185.

Deci, Edward L. and Richard M. Ryan, 'The "what" and "why" of goal pursuits: Human needs and the self-determination of behavior', *Psychological Inquiry*, Vol. 11, No. 4, 2000, pp. 227–268.

Dichter, Ernest, 'Discovering the "inner Jones"', *Harvard Business Review*, May–June 1965, pp. 6–10.

Dichter, Ernest, *The Psychology of Everyday Living*, Barnes and Noble, New York, 1947.

Dichter, Ernest, *The Strategy of Desire*, Transaction Publishers, New Jersey, 2002.

Feldman, Robert S., *Understanding Psychology*, 10th Ed., Tata McGraw Hill, New Delhi, 2011.

Grouzet, F.M., T. Kasser, A. Ahuvia, J.M. Dols, Y. Kim, S. Lau, R. Ryan, S. Saunders, P. Schmuck, and K. Sheldon, 'The structure of goal contents across 15 cultures', *Journal of Personality and Social Psychology*, Vol. 89, 2005, pp. 800–816.

Hemp, Paul, 'Avatar-based marketing', *Harvard Business Review*, June 2006, pp. 48–57.

Herrington, Mike, 'What does the customer want?' *Across the Board*, April 1993, Vol. 30, p. 33.

Hyun, Sunghyup Sean, Wansoo Kim, and Myong Jae Lee, 'The impact of advertising on patrons' emotional responses, perceived value, and behavioral intentions in the chain restaurant industry: The moderating role of advertising-induced arousal', *International Journal of Hospitality Management*, Vol. 30, Issue 3, September 2011, pp. 689–700.

Karsak, Ertugrul E., Sevin Sozer, and S. Emre Alptekin, 'Product planning in quality function deployment using a combined analytic network process and goal programming approach', *Computers & Industrial Engineering*, Vol. 44, 2002, pp. 171–190.

Maslow, A. H., 'A Theory of Human Motivation', 1943, http://psychclassics.yorku.ca/Maslow/motivation.htm, last accessed on 7 June 2013.

Massey, Laura, 'The birth of mad men: Ernest Dichter, psychoanalysis and consumerism', 28 May 2012. http://www.peterharrington.co.uk/blog/the-birth-of-mad-men-ernest-dichter-psychoanalysis-and-consumerism/, last accessed on 11 June 2013.

'Retail therapy: How Ernest Dichter, an acolyte of Sigmund Freud, revolutionized marketing', *The Economist*, 17 December 2011.

Saaty, Thomas L. and Luis G. Vargas, *Models, Methods, Concepts & Applications of the Analytic Hierarchy Process*, 2nd Ed., Springer, New York, 2012.

Samuel, Lawrence R., *Freud on Madison Avenue: Motivation Research and Subliminal Advertising in America*, University of Pennsylvania Press, Philadelphia, 2010.

'Schumpeter: Hidden persuaders II', *The Economist*, 24 September 2011.

Self-determination theory, http://www.selfdeterminationtheory.org/, last accessed on 11 June 2013.

Sheth, J. N., 'A psychological model of travel mode selection', Bureau of Economic and Business Research of the University of Illinois, Urbana, Working Paper #291, November 1975.

Steve Jobs on Apple's resurgence: 'Not a one-man show', *Businessweek*, 1998, http://www.businessweek.com/bwdaily/dnflash/may1998/nf80512d.htm, last accessed on 7 June 2013.

Suh, Kil-Soo, Hongki Kim, and EungKyoSuh, 'What if your avatar looks like you? Dual congruity perspectives for avatar use', *MIS Quarterly*, Vol. 35 Issue 3, September 2011, pp. 711–730.

Turner, Christopher, 'The hidden persuader', *Cabinet Magazine*, Issue 44, Winter 2011–2012, pp. 28–32.

Udell, Jon G., 'A new approach to consumer motivation', *Journal of Retailing*, Winter 1964–65, Vol. 40, No. 4, pp. 6–10.

Yalch, Richard and Frederic Brunel, 'Need hierarchies in consumer judgments of product designs: Is it time to reconsider Maslow's theory?', in *Advances in Consumer Research*, Vol. 23, Eds. Corfman, Kim P. and John G. Lynch Jr., Provo, Utah : Association for Consumer Research, pp. 405–410.

Zaltman, Gerald, 'Co-creating: Harvesting the unconscious to create value for business and society', *Rottman Magazine*, Winter 2011, pp. 41–45.

Zaltman, Gerald, *How Customers Think: Essential Insights Into the Mind of the Market*, Harvard Business School Press, Boston, 2003.

CASE STUDY

Repositioning Brands to Match Real Motives

Why does a girl walk into a salon for a makeover? She may have felt that she has been sporting the 'same look,' or perhaps, her 'influencers' and 'stakeholders' may have advised her to do so. Rebranding is like the young girl's decision; it throws up an opportunity to junk its old values and adopt new ones that cater to the right motivations of customers to patronize the brand.

Many companies have to undertake rebranding exercises not just to acquire a new image, but to match the brands with real motivations of customers. As brands age and need change, consumers start patronizing competing brands. There is thus a need to realign brands with changed consumer needs.

Rebranding has been done by brands such as TajMahal Tea, Air India, Videocon, Airtel, Hero MotoCorp, Star Plus, and Vodafone. This case study looks at two brands that rebranded themselves to match customers' motivations of sporting them—Reebook and Shoppers Stop reinvented themselves to position themselves in line with what customers expected of them.

Reebok

While repositioning brands, companies must find out the actual motivation of consumers to buy them. The store concept, brand pitch, and advertising have to support the real motives of customers for visiting the brand store. An example is that of German sports goods maker Adidas. Its stores flaunted a sporty image, but the brand was not able to build a fitness image in India. The numerous stores around the country did not meet the company's objective. Then there was a financial scandal which caused the shutting down of hundreds of outlets in 2012, denting the image of the brand. Internationally too, Reebok sales had declined as clothing and shoe brands multiplied.

The company wanted to relaunch its stores. Kotler (1973) writes that shoes are sold not on utilitarian needs but by creating a fashion interest in them. He quotes a shoe executive as saying, 'Our business is selling excitement rather than shoes'. Once this view takes root, it spreads to the whole shoe-buying experience. 'The atmosphere of the store has to make the customer feel rich, special, important', writes Kotler, showing that motivations for buying shoes had changed completely.

Looking at the real motives for a customer who comes to the Reebok store, it decided to reposition the brand as a premium fitness brand. The stores, called 'Reebok Fit Hubs' would attract the fitness-minded customer and would immediately differentiate it from other apparel merchandisers. The company thus decided to build Reebok as a performance sports brand.

To fulfil customer needs and to differentiate itself from other stores, the company decided to have certified fitness trainers in these stores to advice customers on fitness-related matters. The product line was expanded to include categories such as yoga, dance, and others. Celebrities such as film stars and sports personalities were signed by the company to promote the stores. The company hoped that the exclusivity of such stores would enable it to sell premium products like shoes priced at ₹12,000 a pair.

The Fit Hub is an international concept used in Reebok stores across the world, including one in New York. With the repositioning, Reebok's logo was also altered with an additional element, the sign of a delta, added to it. In choosing the CrossFit delta with baremove+ technology that makes the wearer feel like they are naked when exercising, the company hoped to reap potential gains from exploiting a top-selling Reebok product. It introduced the motto 'Live with Fire', an attempt to be edgy and provocative as well as to match attitude with the modern consumer.

Shoppers Stop

Shoppers Stop took a rebranding decision in 2008 to reposition itself from its earlier image of a premium retailer. The store had started to lose market share as many other stores had opened up such as Globus, Westside, and Lifestyle, which catered essentially to the same customer segments. To differentiate the store, the company had to think of why people actually liked to visit it in the first place.

It decided to position itself as a 'bridge to luxury' as people associated the store with luxury. A new logo was introduced and the tagline changed from 'Shopping And Beyond' to 'Start Something New,' as people looked for new and innovative products to express themselves. It targeted affluent young adults. In keeping with its image, the store area was increased from 40,000–45,000 sq. feet to 75,000–85,000 sq. feet. It also set up trial rooms with day and night lighting options to help customers to check how the garments would look at night and in daylight.

Employees were trained to tackle customers with varied tastes, and a new dress code was introduced. A company anthem to motivate employees, an in-store radio station, as well as collectible shopping bags added to the shopping experience.

In rebranding the store, Shoppers Stop tried to satisfy three motives, namely, personal, social, and recreational. Personal motives refer to gratification, diversion, learning about new trends, physical activity, and sensory stimulation. Social motives represent the need to live out social experiences, to communicate with others, and to exist through status and authority. Recreational motivation refers to consumers engaged in shopping for experiences such as excitement. They want to enjoy the excitement during the shopping experience in a stimulating store environment. It positioned itself as a hedonic, luxury store. Lunardo (2010) writes that when consumers' motives are hedonic, they enjoy feeling arousal. In the retailing context, the shoppers' motives and their satisfaction by the retailer results in loyalty.

Questions for Discussion

1. Do you think that the brand positioning strategies of Reebok and Shoppers Stop are based on real motives? What motives were fulfilled by these two companies?
2. What motives were aroused by (a) Reebok and (b) Shoppers Stop and how did they cater to the needs of the hedonic shopper?
3. Analyse the needs addressed by these two companies. Did the repositioning succeed in satisfying consumer motives?
4. Analyse the components of motivation and how they were applied by Reebok and Shoppers Stop. In addition, analyse the needs fulfilled by them on the basis of Maslow's need hierarchy and the self-determination theory.

Sources:

Cruz, Julie, 'Adidas to make CrossFit Delta logo symbol for Reebok Fitness', *Businessweek*, 29 May 2013, http://www.businessweek.com/news/2013-05-29/adidas-to-make-crossfit-delta-logo-symbol-for-reebok-fitness, last accessed on 11 June 2013.

Joshi, Devina and Anushree Bhattacharyya, 'Rules of rebranding', *afaqs!*, 31 October 2011, http://www.afaqs.com/news/story/32015_Rules-of-Rebranding, last accessed on 11 June 2013.

Kotler, Philip, 'Atmospherics as a marketing tool', *Journal of Retailing*, Vol. 49, No. 4, 1973, pp. 48–64.

Lunardo, Renaud, 'A profile of shoppers based on in-store stimulation and motivational orientation', *Society for Marketing Advances Proceedings*, 2010, pp. 210–215.

'Reebok makes a comeback as a premium fitness brand', *The Economic Times*, 11 June 2013.

Shukla, Tanvi, 'New-look Shoppers Stop still black & white', *DNA*, 24 April 2008.

CHAPTER SEVEN

Consumer Perception

LEARNING OBJECTIVES

In this chapter, we learn of the ways in which people form perceptions about brands and products. As it is a psychological phenomenon, we delve into the subconscious and use a multi-sensory approach to understand what impacts the mind of the customer.

After studying this chapter, the reader would be able to

- define perception and understand how companies use sensory marketing to gain a favourable perceptual impression among customers.
- discuss hedonic consumption and multi-sensory approaches to marketing
- describe the four stages of perception, namely sensation, attention, interpretation, and retention and how they are used in marketing
- understand perceptual interpretation and inference, and their use in creating halos and favourable impressions
- learn about Gestalt psychology and the latest brain-scanning research which helps us to understand subliminal perception
- understand how to change perception by making perceptual maps

CASE STUDY
Selling a Mean Machine

In his book, *Buying In, What We Buy and Who We Are*, Rob Walker (2008) writes, 'Symbols can have meaning that transcends rational consumption patterns, partly because they help us solve the problem of balancing individuality and belonging'.

These two layers help us understand how a large number of people are able to connect with brands, and how brands are made more innovative and more remarkable or 'cool'—sometimes even when they are harmful. In the past, companies have made consumption of cigarettes and alcohol 'cool' making addicts out of millions of people.

Another product that has successfully bridged individuality and belonging to become a darling of consumers is the sports utility vehicle (SUV), which has fast caught on in popularity the world over. It is similar to the station wagon or an oversize jeep of the past, usually equipped with four-wheel drive. The SUV is a descendant from vehicles used in World War II as transporters of heavy equipment and men, but is today touted as a family car. It instils a feeling of arrogance in users, so that they can 'give their worst to other cars', creating a perception of superiority for the SUV driver.

How did a rugged military vehicle become so popular with suave city dwellers all over the world? Why did people start buying these oil guzzlers even as the world was becoming environmentally conscious, people who had nothing to do with sports or adventure?

Over the years, rising oil prices had led car manufacturers to make smaller, more fuel-efficient automobiles. However, companies make more money on bigger, more expensive vehicles and they wanted to find a way to sell big cars again. Here in lies the story of how public perception of SUVs was changed. Automobile companies projected the idea that SUVs were safe and rugged sports vehicles that took you through rough terrain, providing fun and adventure, even though most SUV owners neither went off-road, nor were remotely interested in sports.

Keith Bradsher (2002) has shown how SUVs became the fashion in his book, *High and Mighty, The World's Most Dangerous Vehicles and How They Got That Way*. He describes how perceptions were changed by companies to sell the arrogance that is the SUV.

Car manufacturers got past the emission norms that applied to cars in the US by labelling the outsized jeep as a 'light truck'. In India, the SUVs were a boon to manufacturers who wanted to cash in on cheaper running costs for cars as diesel prices were subsidized by the government.

Bradsher writes that the proliferation of SUVs has created huge problems. Their safe image is an illusion. As their centre of gravity is high, they roll over too easily, killing and injuring occupants at an alarming rate, and they are dangerous to other road users. He comments 'nor are they green' because they burn more fuel and contribute to pollution and points out that SUVs are not safe for its passengers *The New York Times* (2004) reported that people driving or riding in a sport utility vehicle were nearly 11 per cent more likely to die in an accident than people in other types of cars. The vehicles are dangerous for others as well, as the height and width of the typical SUV make it hard for car drivers behind it to see the road ahead. When they hit pedestrians, they inflict worse injuries than cars. Sports utility vehicle weigh half a ton more than cars and have longer stopping distances, and that explains why these vehicles are unable to stop in time before hitting an obstacle. Further, by consuming more fuel, these cars make a mockery of fuel efficiency standards prevalent worldwide.

Yet, they are perceived as 'cool'. They are especially popular with people who care about appearances, such as film stars and politicians. People buy these heavy vehicles as they are affected by advertising campaigns and vehicle designs that appeal to the dark half of human nature. It is hardly surprising that the SUV is the car of choice for the nation's most self-centred people. Bradsher quotes market research that shows SUV owners as 'insecure and vain. They are frequently nervous about their marriages and uncomfortable about parenthood. They often lack confidence in their driving skills'

To change the perception towards the vehicle, companies appealed to the 'reptilian' instincts of people who are attracted to SUVs not because of their perceived safety, but for their obvious aggressiveness—the vehicles are intentionally designed to resemble ferocious animals, with the front grill designed to look like the teeth of a monster. Constant advertising makes people believe they can be independent, tough, and sporty just by buying a SUV. In other words, SUV advertising has fed the negative side of human personality to push a product that is inherently harmful.

'As SUVs have multiplied in the US and beyond, they have fed a highway arms race that has made the world's roads less and less hospitable for car drivers, worsening a trend that hurts safety and the environment alike', writes Bradsher.

The success of SUVs shows how perceptions can be changed to make products seem fashionable. People start believing that using these products will somehow make them cool and smart, even when they are not.

Consumer Perception | 213

While reading this chapter, try to answer the following questions:

1. How can perceptions towards products be changed through compelling advertising?
2. Was the perception of SUVs changed by using subliminal advertising?
3. What elements of Gestalt psychology were used to changed perception of SUVs?
4. How were the concepts of perceptual interpretation used by companies in this case?

Sources:

Bradsher, Keith, *High and Mighty: SUVs: The World's Most Dangerous Vehicles and How They Got That Way*, Public Affairs, New York, 2002.

Hakim, Danny, 'Safety gap grows wider between SUV's and cars', *The New York Times*, 17 August 2004, http://www.nytimes.com/2004/08/17/business/safety-gap-grows-wider-between-suv-s-and-cars.html?pagewanted=all&src=pm, last accessed on 1 August 2014.

Walker, Rob, *Buying In, What We Buy and Who We Are*, Random House Trade Paperbacks, New York, 2008, p. 35.

INTRODUCTION

Companies send messages to consumers in various forms, intimating them how their products offer better quality or value for money. Advertisements play on emotions and psychological appeals. Every company tries to create space in the minds of the consumers and hopes that people think favourably about its products and services.

However, do customers think about companies and their offerings in the way that the company intends them to? Indeed, if we talk to different people, we will discover myriad impressions and preferences of brands and their messages. The same message is interpreted by some as favourable and rejected by others. It is almost as if impressions are made automatically and independently—sometimes quite opposite to what was intended by the advertiser.

For example, let's say that a company offers a 70 per cent discount on its products. How do people perceive it? The perceptions that will form in different people about the company are as follows:

- Some people will perceive it as a buying opportunity and hope to get bargains
- Others will suspect that such a hefty discount would come with some hidden conditions
- Still others will feel that the company's products are probably overpriced and are of low quality, so they are best avoided
- Another set of customers will feel that the discount is probably a gimmick

FIG. 7.1 Rotating snakes by Akiyosh Kitaoka

Source: http://visiome.neuroinf.jp/modules/xoonips/detail.php?item_id=6291, last accessed on 30 March 2014, reprinted with permission from Akiyoshi Kitaoka

The different perceptions are formed because the mind works on its own and people form independent impressions, as illustrated in Fig. 7.1. Readers will see that the picture gives the impression of movement even though nothing is moving in it. It is almost as if the mind is playing tricks.

The Economist (2009) reports that neuroscientists have found that subconscious processing in the brain starts much before the conscious: 'Simple decisions, such as when to move a finger, are made about three-tenths of a second before the brain's owner is aware of them, and subsequent work has found that the roots of such decisions can be seen up to ten seconds before they become conscious'.

The mind thus forms perceptions of goods and services on its own, and advertisers have to try hard to create favourable impressions.

PERCEPTION

Why and how does the mind operate and form perceptions? Our mind is always in overdrive, and it does not accept messages at their face value. If it did, the job of the advertiser would be very easy indeed—consumers would respond happily to all kinds of products and offers. The fact that some succeed and some do not shows that there are several factors at play in the mind. These factors shape perception in human beings.

Perception is defined as the process by which an individual selects, organizes, and interprets stimuli into a meaningful and coherent picture of the world. It involves organization and interpretation of sensory information to represent and understand the environment. Perception guides human behaviour even though it is based on individual impressions.

Perception determines how consumers view a company's product, service, or advertising. Very often people like companies because of the image of the company or brand in their minds. People choose products that match their personality or aspirations. The understanding of perception helps companies to target consumers so that they 'fit in' with their offerings.

Trampe, et al. (2011) show that advertisements do the reverse too—they trigger important self-processes. Advertisements of products that are related to physical attractiveness, like cosmetics, affect both the extent to which individuals think about the self and how they evaluate the self. That is, advertisements become a symbolic system that conveys meaning that goes beyond the physical features of the advertised products. Research found that an advertisement context can provide consumers with symbolic meaning, leading them to relate the advertisement to themselves, and changing their perception about themselves. Please see Exhibit 7.1.

▶ EXHIBIT 7.1 Barbie—Changing Perceptions

FIG. 7.2 Types of Dolls

Courtesy: Superbrands

Barbie® is an aspirational role model for girls worldwide. As she takes on new careers and roles she shows that anything is possible. She engages young girls and, in ways unique to each, she comes off as a best friend to them.

Various types of dolls or themes promote play patterns that appeal to young girls from three years of age to die-hard fans at twelve. Some famous themes that have captured little girls' imagination are fashion and beauty dolls, princess and fairies and the 'I Can Be' series which promotes knowledge of different careers via play. Figure 7.2 shows various models of Barbie.

Source: Superbrands 2012

Perception and Marketing

When different people are exposed to the same advertisements under the same conditions, they respond differently, because each person recognizes, selects, organizes, and interprets the information in a very personal manner. People respond to information according to their own values, personal experiences, and expectations. In her book, *Mapping the Mind*, Rita Carter (2000) explains that the mind does not store a faithful reflection of the world, 'rather it is a unique construction.'

To illustrate the fact that people look at objects in different ways, consider Fig. 7.3. Different people will see the glass as half-full, half-empty, containing medicine, and so on.

Perception has an important role to play in marketing. Consider these examples:

- The difference in price between a product costing ₹100 and one costing ₹99 is insignificant, but consumers treat it like a bargain.
- Customers who are fiercely loyal to a brand, like a soft drink, are often unable to spot the difference when offered other brands during blind tests.
- Consumers know that generic medicines are as good as branded medicines, but they prefer to pay a higher price for branded medicines.

FIG. 7.3 Differing perceptions

Zaltman (2003) writes that such instances call into question the notion that consumers are savvy, rational shoppers. Instead, many decisions are made in the subconscious mind. It's a place that companies must explore if they want to change perceptions and gain a competitive advantage.

Blijlevens, et al. (2009) write that companies that are able to communicate a meaning or prestige through the appearance of a product (Fig. 7.4), can create a competitive advantage in the market and increase the product's chance of success. When a product looks modern, consumers are motivated to assess it on its aesthetics. They perceive certain physical properties that together make up the design of the product (e.g., colour, shape, and texture). Certain combinations of colours, materials, and other physical aspects give the product a look that can be described by a certain appearance attribute. For example, a DVD-player that is angular, metallic-looking, and is made of a smooth material is perceived as modern.

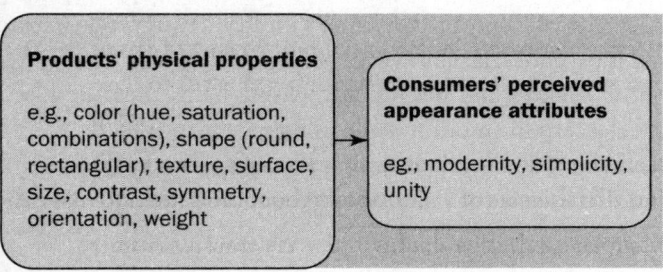

FIG. 7.4 Product properties and consumer perceptions

Source: Blijlevens, Creusen, and Schoormans (2009)

Advertising and Perception

Advertising uses different elements such as visual imagery and messages to change perceptions. You will notice that most advertisements do not stress on product attributes or sing praises about their wares. Advertising works in a very subtle way, changing impressions even without the active involvement of the viewer.

> ### CB IN ACTION Blind Tasting
>
> This experiment is to assess how brands affect our perception of quality. Buy one large bottle each of Coca Cola, Pepsi, and Thums Up. Make sure that they are cooled to the same temperature.
>
> Pour small quantities of these drinks in similar glasses. You may number the glasses by putting a small sticker at the bottom of each glass so as to identify which brand goes in which glass.
>
> Now ask your friends to taste the drink from two or three glasses and identify the brand in each. Ask them to write down the name of the brand that they have guessed against the number of the glass, as also their most preferred brand.
>
> Analyse the results to see how many people have identified the brand correctly.
>
> 1. What percentage of people was able to identify the drink correctly?
> 2. Considering that each brand has a probability of 33% if guessed randomly, find out which brand was guessed more than this percentage.
> 3. Was there a difference between their preferred brand and the brand they identified in the blind test? What was the perception of your friends regarding their preferred brand in the blind test?

For example, take a look at the Coca Cola commercials. The campaign is built around the theme of happiness—an attempt to change perceptions towards the brand. If people start connecting happiness with the brand, it results in positive associations and higher sales. Many people would buy the product when they are feeling happy, and conversely many people who want to be happy may also want to 'open happiness' even though it would be more logical to market the product as a drink or a thirst quencher.

Companies also try to influence perceptions about their products by using models, hoping that the consumers' perception about the model will rub off on the company

It is important to understand here that it would be extremely difficult to sell products on their attributes alone. That is why companies try to associate impressions and emotions with their brands, appealing to consumer tastes, desires, fantasies, and wants, as the chapter-opening case study on SUVs shows. Advertising tries to change a consumer's impression of products and brands. The perception thus generated is psychological but very real.

By playing on consumers' innermost feelings and desires, advertising helps them be like a certain person, look a certain way or feel a certain emotion while using specific products.

The idea is to make the consumer feel good about consuming products. This is the basis of *hedonic consumption* that is, employing all the senses of vision, smell, touch, and taste, to make the customer feel special about brands.

HEDONIC CONSUMPTION

People consume things for enjoyment. Sometimes shopping is done for the joy it gives. When things are bought or consumed for sheer happiness, it is called hedonic consumption. That is the reason people consume chocolates, buy big cars, go to fancy restaurants, and buy expensive clothes. The price paid for such things is likely to be much higher than compared to utilitarian goods, or goods bought to satisfy a need. Indeed, companies go all out to deliver enjoyable experiences through their goods or services, employing the senses of touch, taste, scent, and sound. Images and experiences are used to stimulate imagination and to produce emotional arousal.

Hirschman and Holbrook (1982) described hedonic consumption as 'those facets of consumer behaviour that relate to the multisensory, fantasy, and emotive aspects of one's experience with products', that is, consuming for enjoyment.

Retailers and companies understand that people look for pleasurable experiences. Stores are designed to deliver experiences that make shoppers feel special. Tifferet and Herstein (2012) studied gender differences in shopping behaviour and found that while women need the right atmosphere, space, and time to find just the right item, men want to just get the job done. They write that fashion retailers understand that for women in particular, shopping is not just about making the right purchase, but also about the experience.

With more couples shopping together, they design stores in a way that will serve men who do not enjoy shopping as well. Some retailers get around this conflict by including areas in their store where men can relax with a coffee, read magazines, or watch sports broadcasts, while their partners shop. This makes the shopping experience enjoyable for both men and women.

Brands that seek to be consumed for enjoyment or hedonic purposes use sights, smells, and images that help people to feel nice about consuming the products or services. This is done in a variety of ways. To understand how companies attach hedonic motives to consumption, we have to understand how people respond to imagery and other stimuli.

Imagery in Marketing

People respond to external stimuli by encoding the received messages, but also by generating multi-sensory images within themselves. For example, smelling a perfume causes the consumer not only to perceive and encode its scent but also to generate internal imagery containing sights, sounds, and sensations related to the smell. Many expensive perfumes associate themselves with the high fashion of France, lending a feeling of luxury to its user.

Cigarette companies have used imagery very effectively. Smokers enjoy imagining themselves as 'Marlboro men' while consuming the product. The cowboy theme succeeded in lending the cigarette and, hence its user, a masculine image. Many consumers generated a more literal image—that of an idealized cowboy. Smokers who had never been in the countryside imagined themselves to be in the Wild West just by smoking a cigarette. The internal images generated by consumers are of two types: historic and fantasy imagery.

Historic Imagery

This involves recalling an event from the past experience of the customer. The scent of a perfume, for example, can cause the consumer to remember an experience with one who wore that perfume. Many brands evoke old, traditional values, such as 'mother's cooking' or 'traditional cuisine'.

Fantasy Imagery

In fantasy imagery, the consumer responds by producing a multi-sensory image or sequence in his mind. Many products evoke such responses within customers—if the fantasy is good, customers will feel good using those products.

Imagery is also used for arousing consumers. People experience emotional arousal when they see certain images or slogans.

Emotional Arousal

In case of many products, the consumer's emotional desires override his/her utilitarian motives in consuming them. Brands create contexts in which emotions such as love, hate, or jealousy override consumers' economic decision rules. Emotive responses are both psychological and physiological, generating altered states in both the mind and body. Some products, such as novels, plays, and sporting events, evoke emotional responses. Emotional arousal is also tied to the consumption of products such as cigarettes, food, and clothing. Brands try to make people feel happy, proud, or superior by consuming those products.

Creation of Subjective Symbols

Consumers imbue a product with a subjective meaning that supplements its concrete attributes. Advertising contributes to creating subjective symbols that modify customer preference. As a result, products and brands come to be seen as subjectively superior symbols rather than as concrete objects.

Imaginary Constructs of Reality

Hedonic consumption is tied to imaginative constructions of reality by the consumer. Such consumption is based not on what consumers know to be real, but rather on what they desire reality to be. Fantasies are important determinants and consequences of hedonic consumption.

Brand Personality

Customers sometimes tend to think of brands as human. They assign life to their cell phones or cars, for instance, referring to them as living objects. Kapferer (2000) writes that the notion of brand identity goes beyond the surface identity or appearance of the product or brand. Apart from the physical qualities, brands also take on personality and culture. The way in which the brand is perceived shows what kind of person it would be if it were human. Many brands consciously do this by giving the brand a spokesperson or ambassador, like a celebrity, with which the brand is then associated.

In sum, hedonic consumption refers to consumers' multi-sensory images, fantasies, and emotional arousal in using products.

MARKETING INSIGHT
Brand Love

Companies seek to create fiercely loyal customers, those who are so enamoured of their products that they are willing to forsake personal resources to maintain an ongoing relationship with the brand. Park, et al. (2010) write that such consumers are willing to engage in difficult behaviours—those that require investments of time, money, energy, and reputation—to maintain or deepen a brand relationship. Brand love goes beyond loyalty and results in positive word of mouth (WOM), increased willingness to pay a price premium, and forgiveness of brand failures.

This happens when a person begins to identify himself/herself with a brand. Brand communities are an expression of this feeling of identification with products—people feel happy simply by being in the company of people with similar inclination. Self–brand connections are strengthened and the

(Contd)

MARKET INSIGHT (Contd)

individual develops a sense of natural comfort and fit with a brand, a feeling of emotional connectedness and bonding, a heightened level of desire and interaction, and a commitment to its long-term use. Brand love includes multiple emotions and goes beyond brand attachment.

Batra, et al. (2012) enumerate ten major components of brand love—high quality, linkages to strongly-held values, beliefs that the brand provides intrinsic rather than extrinsic rewards, use of the loved brand to express both current and desired self-identity, positive affect, a sense of rightness and a feeling of passion, an emotional bond, investments of time and money, frequent thought and use, and length of use.

Brand love can be seen in diverse products such as cars, mobile phones, motor cycles, cosmetics, schools, apparel, and food.

The authors describe five methods by which brand love can be developed.

Facilitate passion-driven behaviours Companies have to employ design and packaging techniques that have been shown to create a strong, hungry, visceral sense of desire. Red Bull, for instance, encourages passionate, outdoor behaviour through its events. Nike offers 'inspiration and innovation for every athlete in the world'.

Build brands that symbolize self–brand integration The brand has to not only express the consumers' actual and desired identities, but also to connect to life's deeper meanings and important values for the consumer. Apple products, for instance, have tried to match up with consumers' identities. Social networking sites achieve love through self–brand integration.

Create emotional connections with the brand Brands develop a sense of attachment with the customer, such as an 'old friend', or an 'everlasting bond' kind of an intuitive feeling. Some brands do this with a sense of authenticity from its origin and history, the vision of its founders, and its corporate culture so that the consumer feels a sense of kinship with it. The brands of Tata, whether it be steel or salt, are able to connect with the trust associated with the founder and the owners of the brand. The Raymonds brand too tries to connect with consumers by communicating a sense of history and emphasis on "the complete man". Its website invites consumers to follow its CMD, Mr Gautam Singhania on Twitter.

Become valued and trusted resources By becoming sources of expertise and advice, brands can induce a feeling of anticipated separation distress if the consumer does not have access to them. The Sunsilk 'Gang of Girls' is an attempt to create networking features, discuss the latest trends, give advice on hairstyle and fashion tips, and reveal the style secrets of celebrities. Similarly, Maggi offers advice on recipes under the banner, 'Taste Bhi, Health Bhi' in an attempt to become trusted resources for its consumers.

Build a sense of long-term relationship Companies develop consumer interactive marketing programmes for brands that are frequent and ongoing. Facebook pages for brands, such as those of Coca-Cola or P&G, are ongoing relationship programmes that help to build long-term relationships. Nike offers its 'Nike+ Running Community' through an app for long-term engagement with customers.

Roberts (2004), in his book, *Lovemarks: the Future Beyond Brands*, explains how brands can use these methods:

- Build on brand stories
- Use the company's past, present, and future
- Tap into dreams
- Nurture your myths and icons
- Build on inspiration

Sources:
Batra, Rajeev, Aaron Ahuvia, and Richard P. Bagozzi, 'Brand love', *Journal of Marketing*, Vol. 76, March 2012, pp. 1–16.
http://www.maggi.in.
http://www.nike.com.
http://www.raymondindia.in.
http://www.redbull.com.
http://www.sunsilk.in/.
Park, Whan C., Deborah J. MacInnis, Joseph Priester, Andreas B. Eisingerich, and Dawn Iacobucci, 'Brand Attachment and Brand Attitude Strength: Conceptual and Empirical Differentiation of Two Critical Brand Equity Drivers', *Journal of Marketing*, November 2010, Vol. 74, No.6, pp. 1–17.
Roberts, Kevin, *Lovemarks: the Future Beyond Brands*, Power House Books, New York, 2004.
All websites last accessed on 1 August 2014.

SENSORY MARKETING

Marketing that engages all the senses is called sensory marketing. Companies use the sight, smell, sound, taste, and feel of products to influence perception and thus consumer behaviour. How a product is presented—the touch, taste, smell, sound, and look of the products, affects emotions, memories, perceptions, preferences, choices, and consumption (Fig. 7.5).

Hultén, et al. (2009) explain how this happens through the example of Starbucks. By targeting all the five senses, the company delivers a sensory experience and creates a deeper and more personal relationship with its customers. It starts with an inspiring environment that makes customers comfortable: the green and yellow interior and pleasant lighting is supplemented by 'the sound of Starbucks'—the music played in the stores. A customer who enters a Starbucks coffee shop hears the sounds and smells the aroma of freshly ground coffee. In this way, Starbucks uses sensory marketing to create an atmosphere that is valued by customers.

Vision

A product's display and advertisement affect the chances of its being purchased. Companies take great care to design products so that they not only stand out, but are preferred by shoppers as well. Brands also project their logos using colour and visual appeal to help in customer recognition.

Creusen and Schoormans (2005) identify six different roles of visual appearance:

- Communication of aesthetics
- Symbolic role
- Categorization
- Ergonomic information
- Attention-drawing
- Functional information

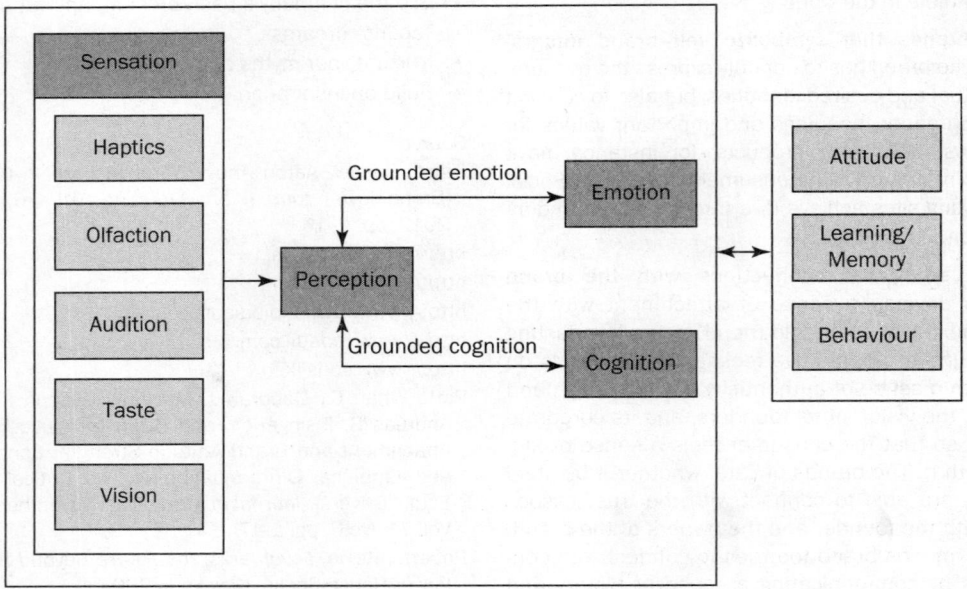

FIG. 7.5 Sensory marketing, perception, and consumer behaviour

Source: Krishna (2012)

TABLE 7.1 Colour and its impact on consumers

Yellow	Red	Blue	Green
Upbeat, happy, cheerful, youthful, and full of energy; used to grab attention of shoppers	Colour of energy and passion, and eye-catching; used to attract attention and create urgency	Signifies trust, security, stability, and tradition; often used by banks	Calming, refreshing, relaxing, and associated with the wealthy; used as a soothing tone in stores
Orange	**Pink**	**Black**	**Purple**
Aggressive and denotes urgency; used as a call for action	Romantic and feminine; used to market products to women, young girls, and babies	Colour of power and prestige, and denotes trust; used to market luxury products	Soothes and calms; often seen on beauty products

Intuitively, consumers associate darker colours with luxurious, formal, and respectable products. While reds are exciting and provocative, browns and blues are manly and pinks and lighter shades are preferred by women (see Table 7.1).

Geboy (1996) writes that colour helps communicate complex information by evoking emotional responses. While headlines and copy in an advertisement provide the rational information and emotional appeal, colour plays an important supporting role in communicating that message on a deeper level. Colour can be used to create a sense of personality for a brand, a positioning niche, or atmosphere for a service. Many companies have developed definitive graphic identity programmes that include strict parameters for colour.

Smell

Smells are symbols—they conjure up memories in people. Morean (2007) writes that though smell memories are personal in nature and thus variable, they are also subject to certain conditioning factors that may be cultural, individual, temporal, and contextual, but which provide the basis for the formation of a 'scent culture'.

Indeed, companies use smells not only to market soap, shampoos, and detergents but also food and drink. Retailers use smells to entice customers into shops and restaurants. They use perfume machines (See Fig. 7.6) that help in creating a pleasant smell in their premises and enhance sensory experience of customers.

Lindstrom (2009) explains how stores use the sensory experience effectively. As you go into an upmarket clothing store, you see the beautiful girls working there—as beautiful as the sinuous models on the billboard. 'You inhale that cloying, characteristic fragrance that lingers in your nostrils long after you've left the store…which produces a feeling in the brain that automatically links to the models outside, the fragrant and pervasive smell, and the late-night atmosphere of the store itself—and when you tuck that gorgeous bag under your arm, you're taking home a little bit of that popularity with you'.

However, it doesn't end there. Every time you walk the street, you are able to make out the familiar fragrance and you know that the brand's store is near. Again you remember the scantily-clad models and the beautiful people. Then 'irresistibly, as if yanked by a silver thread, you're drawn back inside to get another shot of pleasure and reward'.

FIG. 7.6 Perfume machines

The task of companies is to associate such sensory stimuli with memories, desire, and pleasure. Restaurants change consumer perceptions with their distinctive aromas—when exposed to the sights and smells of a restaurant, the person feels compelled to enter it for a snack.

Some companies try to create a *sensory signature*. Krishna (2010) gives the example of Singapore Airlines that used a signature aroma, Floridian waters, specially mixed for it. It is infused into hot towels, sprayed on planes, and worn by flight attendants. This special aroma affects perception, and makes flyers feel more comfortable, enhancing their flying experience and increasing their satisfaction.

Touch

Consumers like to touch and feel products. Companies provide opportunities for this experience. Apparel companies ensure that their products can be touched, felt, and tried on. A soft fabric, such as silk or velvet, imparts the feeling of luxury and feminine elegance. A rough texture, such as that of denim, conveys durability and ruggedness.

In India, supermarkets found that their sales were hampered by the fact that consumers could not feel products such as rice and lentils. Big Bazaar then placed bowls of the grain along with the packed material, so that people could feel the quality before buying. The classic, contoured Coca-Cola bottle was designed so that people could identify it even in the dark.

Online companies face a problem as some people hesitate to place orders before touching the products. Many people have a high 'need for touch' and are influenced by this. They like to touch products in stores and feel comfortable purchasing a product only after they have examined it by hand. To get over this shortcoming, they introduced 'cash-on-delivery' to reassure people. Some sites have also introduced the 'try and buy' facility, wherein consumers actually try out products when they are delivered.

Similarly, car companies organize exhibitions and below the line or BTL campaigns, during which they communicate with customers directly without the use of any media. Customers can touch the car, and they are encouraged to sit in it and feel the luxury of the interiors. Some cars are designed to make the user feel in command of the road, sitting tall and riding high, in a position from which he can look down on other vehicles. SUVs are sold on this proposition (see chapter-opening case study).

Similarly, perfume companies design their ads and bottles to impart the feeling of luxury—an elegantly sculpted glass bottle conveys a luxurious touch to consumers. The glamorous advertisement and the elegance of the bottle assure customers of the high quality of the perfume.

Taste

Taste also affects brand perceptions. Though many consumers are unable to identify brands during blind tests, when these are displayed with labels, they show a marked preference for one brand or another. Coca-Cola tried to change the taste of the product and developed a 'New Coke' that was perceived as superior in blind tests, but the company faced stiff resistance and had to bring back the original.

Ice cream companies and manufacturers of food items routinely give out free samples to encourage people to taste products. Food chains alter the taste of their products to match local tastes: in

India the food that one buys at international chains like McDonald's and KFC is spicier than that offered in European countries. *The Economist* (2012) reported that 'many Chinese find coffee too bitter for their liking, so Nestlé is offering Smoovlatte, a coffee drink that tastes like melted ice cream'.

Companies such as McDonald's try to balance nutrition with taste. It introduces new items cautiously, trying them in a few restaurants for a limited period. Only when sales of the products are satisfactory, are they introduced globally.

Sound

Music is a powerful tool to develop and change perceptions in all five functions of advertising—informing, persuading, reminding, adding value, and assisting other company efforts. It includes not only the song or background music, but also voice and sound effects that are instrumental in building the whole perception. Good music shapes attitudes towards advertisements and products.

Companies use music to make consumers aware of the product and create an enticing image of the brand. Consumers recall products when they are linked to catchy tunes that persuade them to try the advertised products.

Kubacki and Croft (2004) write that the response to well-known tunes is usually positive, but the awareness of the brand may not necessarily increase. Therefore, companies have to make efforts to connect the brand name with the song. Jingles and signature tunes are used to create positive associations with brands. Music is commonly used in promotions to activate different moods and stimulate the emotions of consumers. It is a powerful marketing stimuli and the skilful use of music and visuals in advertisements is memorable enough to become a lucid representation of a product and its attributes.

Elements such as pitch, tempo, rhythm, phrasing, and texture can be manipulated to evoke emotional expressions, and create behavioural responses in consumers. Companies also use customized music, specially created for a particular brand. Research conducted by Saulpaugh, et al. (2012) shows that brand personality dimensions can be conveyed through customized music. More importantly, while generic music improves the communication of brand personality, the use of customized music improves the strength of that communication.

Perhaps no other industry uses all the senses of touch, taste, smell, sound, and sight like the hospitality industry. Exhibit 7.2 looks at how Taj Hotels has been able to build consumer perception over the years.

EXHIBIT 7.2 Taj Hotels: More than a Luxury Brand

Taj Hotels, Resorts, and Palaces is the largest hotel brand in South Asia, with 109 hotels in 12 countries. The Taj is one of India's great iconic brands. This exhibit describes how The Taj maintains the perception that it is not just a luxury hotel, but reflects Indian heritage as well.

The perception of luxury that the hotel chain is able to impart comes from several physical and psychological values. It creates interpersonal aspects such as snobbery and conspicuousness, personal aspects such as hedonist and perfectionist motives, as well as situational conditions. This is achieved through a combination of exclusive products, services, and promotion. It is also done through HR systems that stress on values rather than profits.

(Contd)

EXHIBIT 7.2 (Contd)

The company's flagship brand is The Taj. The hotels in this category span world-renowned landmarks, business hotels, beach resorts, authentic Rajput palaces, and rustic safari lodges. The Taj attempts to reinterpret traditional Indian hospitality in all its properties and services, such as:

Taj Exotica The company's resort and spa brand

Taj safaris Wildlife lodges that allow travellers to experience the rustic beauty of the Indian forest

Premium hotels Full-service hotels and resorts catering to the new generation of travellers for work and pleasure

Gateway Hotel Upscale, mid-market full-service property

Taj Spa A spa brand offering Indian spa therapies inspired by the ancient wellness heritage of India

Taj Air An executive jet service for flying to any destination within a radius of five-and-a-half flying hours in India and abroad

Taj yachts Luxury boats equipped with a bar

Taj Hotels uses focused marketing activities and client relations management. Its in-house publication, Taj Magazine—Coffee Table and Spice covers new developments, product launches, events, and food festivals.

Deshpande and Rana (2011) describe the extraordinary commitment and heroism of Taj employees when the Mumbai hotel came under a terrorist attack on 26 November 2008. They write that employees' commitment is built through HR policies of recruitment and training. The Taj Group insists that employees must act as the customer's, not the company's, ambassadors. This creates an extreme customer-centric culture, which resulted in employees staying back to rescue guests instead of saving themselves. As they were not prescribed in any manual, the actions of the employees were all the more unique. According to the authors, some contextual factors could have helped, such as India's culture of hospitality that the chain prides itself in, the values of the House of Tata, and the Taj Mumbai's historical roots in the patriotic movement for a free India. An organizational culture that puts customers first, also led to employees helping the guests rather than themselves during the attack.

A combination of various factors has led to The Taj Group acquiring the perception of an exclusive hotel deeply rooted in India's culture. It is not just a luxury hotel chain in the minds of most people, but much more than that.

1. How do you perceive the personality of Taj Hotels?
2. How does the chain gain from historical and fantasy imagery in creating its perception?
3. How does the folklore surrounding the terrorist attacks create a special place for the Taj in the mind of the ordinary consumer?

Sources:
Deshpande, Rohit and Anjali Rana, 'The ordinary heroes of the Taj', *Harvard Business Review*, December 2011, pp. 101–106.
http://www.superbrandsindia.com/, last accessed on 7 October 2013.
http://www.tajhotels.com/About-Taj/Company-Information/Default.html, last accessed on 7 October 2013.

STAGES OF PERCEPTION

In this section, we discuss the stages of perception. Starting with stimulus and exposure, companies try to grab attention by influencing perception levels. Using principles of Gestalt psychology, they influence the organization of information in people's minds, thereby affecting interpretation and retention.

Four distinct stages of perception occur during consumer information processing: sensation, attention, interpretation, and retention.

Exposure

Any physical, visual, or verbal communication to customers is called stimulus. It is designed to influence customers' perception and finally the purchase decision.

People form perceptions when they are exposed to marketing stimuli. Consumers register cues through sight, sound, smell, taste, and feeling. All these then get associated with certain brands in the consumer's mind.

Walk into a store, for example, and one is exposed to its sights, sounds, and ambience. Some elements make an impression consciously while others are subconscious impressions. Marketing managers use all the stimuli carefully to make a positive impact.

The stimuli are of various kinds:

- *Visual*: When the customer sees an advertisement, a billboard or even the goods displayed
- *Olfactory*: The smell a person gets when he passes or enters a particular store
- *Audio*: The sounds or music that a person hears on a TV commercial or in a retail store
- *Taste*: Manufacturers of food products frequently allow sampling, so that customers can taste their offerings
- *Touch and temperature*: Apparel and shoes are best examined by hand. Air conditioning regulates the temperature of stores to provide pleasant stimuli to customers
- *Design*: The appearance of a product also influences consumer perception of functionalities, quality, and ease of use. Creusen, et al. (2010) show how preference for visual complexity and symmetry depends on the type of product value that is important to people
- *Emotions*: Happiness and fear appeals are persuasive messages designed to influence people into doing what the message recommends. Happy messages associate joy with consuming products, fear appeals depict the terrible consequences of non-compliance, and are frequently used in selling products such as insurance and in societal campaigns such as anti-smoking and prevention of drunken driving. Morales, et al. (2012) show that adding disgust to a fear appeal appreciably enhances message persuasion and compliance
- *Integrated sensory information*: Companies integrate some or all of the aforegiven elements to deliver a memorable brand experience

Companies use these cues through advertising, ambience in their retail stores, and through BTL campaigns. Cosmetics companies often use trials so that customers can touch, smell, and feel products before they make up their minds (Fig. 7.7).

FIG. 7.7 Cosmetics stores use sensory experiences to lure customers

Voluntary and Selective Exposure

Exposure occurs when a person comes across a stimulus. The stimulus could be an advertisement in a newspaper, TV, or Internet. Exposure also happens when consumers experience the sight, sound, and smell that they associate with certain brands.

Exposure is of two types, random or deliberate. The first is called *selective exposure* and the second *voluntary exposure*.

Selective exposure People do not notice all the stimuli they are exposed to. For instance, if you try to recall the advertisements that you saw on your recent visit to the mall or the ones you saw on television (TV)

last night, you will be able to recollect only a few, out of the hundreds you were exposed to. Further, people actively try to self-select media exposure in the following ways:

Zipping   Fast-forwarding of advertisements in recorded programmes through a remote control

Zapping   Switching channels during a commercial break

Muting   Pressing the volume mute button when commercials appear

Selective exposure also occurs psychologically—people only notice messages of products that they are interested in. If they are not interested in a product, its advertisements will not register in their minds. For instance, if you are not interested in buying a house, you will not notice advertisements of real-estate companies even when you are exposed to them.

To avoid this, companies use various techniques, such as dramatic visuals, and large and innovative billboards, buying the entire first page of a newspaper, or even using a catchy jingle, so that people just do not miss the commercial even if they want to.

Voluntary exposure   When people actively seek information about products or services, it is called voluntary exposure. This happens in the following ways:

Search engines   People actively seek information by searching the Internet. Search engines like Google place advertisements relating to the subject being searched right on top of the search results so that a person is inclined to visit those sites

Infomercials   The prospective customer watches infomercials, which are TV programmes dedicated to products, with a toll-free number through which an order can be placed. While popular channels broadcast these infomercials during less popular hours, dedicated channels like Homeshop 18 air them 24 hours

Seeking advice   Consumers seek active advice while buying products. This can be from friends or opinion leaders, or from websites that review products and services

Assisted search   People also seek help in their search by asking salesmen about their needs. When customers refer to a third party like Yellow Pages, it is called assisted search.

Using smartphones   Applications on smartphones like Google Maps help people in finding businesses or brands even while they are on the move.

Methods to Increase Exposure

Exposure can be increased in various ways. Some of them are as follows:

Road blocking   To get over the problem of people zapping TV commercials, advertisers buy a particular time slot across all channels. In this way, a viewer gets to see the same commercial no matter how many channels are changed. This process is called road blocking.

Repetition   Another way is to repeat the commercial so often that a viewer will get exposed to it at one time or another.

Wide presence   Companies have to ensure wide presence of commercials across all channels so that customers get to see it.

Interesting content   The ad is so interesting or has such engaging content that people themselves seek it, as a video on YouTube. Viral marketing increases exposure manifold.

Attention

Attention occurs when a person notices a product or brand. This is often quite difficult as a person is exposed to thousands of stimuli everyday in the form of numerous advertisements as also the products that are lined up on store shelves.

It is hardly surprising that everything that people are exposed to does not get their attention. Attention is selective, so the challenge before companies is to get their message or product noticed amidst the enormous clutter. They do this through powerful visuals, colour and movement, catchy tunes, distinctive smells, and attractive point-of-purchase publicity material.

Powerful visuals   Companies use dramatic visuals in their advertising to attract attention.

Size   Large billboards, full-page advertisements in print and long commercials on TV are likely to attract more attention than smaller ones.

Intensity   Repetition, loudness, and brightness of the message help attract attention of even the most disinterested consumer.

Position: The setting and positioning of the ad or product both in the media and in stores also impact attention, the reason why prime time ads and vantage positions in printed and outdoor media cost more, and luxury goods manufacturers don't display their products in supermarkets.

Colour and movement   Bright packaging and colours in products attract more attention. Similarly, if a person detects a movement in a shelf stocked with products, his eye will automatically focus on it, such as interactive point-of-purchase displays, blinking lights, moving fixtures on outdoor ads, and animated banner ads.

Catchy tunes   Jingles and catchy tunes attract attention even when the consumer is not watching. By associating certain tunes with brands, companies hope to catch the attention of consumers and remind them of their brand.

Distinctive smells   Aroma plays an important role in the selling of food products and people come to associate brands and retail stores with their distinctive smell

Point-of-purchase (POP) materials   Companies invest in POP materials such as large displays and flyers to catch the attention of shoppers and guide them to their brands

Size of stimulus   This refers to the size of the stimulus in relation to its surroundings. Products, packages, brand names, and other important ad elements should be relatively large.

Isolation   An object that is separated or stands out from other surrounding objects is more likely to be noticed.

Shapes   Unusual shapes stand out and are more likely to be noticed.

All these methods are meant to catch the attention of the customer. Such stimuli create sensation, but the next step is to ensure that the customer interprets the message as intended by the company.

CB IN ACTION   **Retail Perceptions**

Visit a supermarket or a store in your area and study it in terms of how it impacts your perception. Analyse the elements in the following table and see how they are used by the store to impact perception. Fill up the table as you go along.

Does the store succeed in its attempts?
Compare several stores on the basis of these perceptual elements to understand how they are used by the retail industry.

Element	How the store uses the element	Impact on your perception
Visuals		
Colour and movement		
Music		
Smell		
POP materials		
Size		
Isolation		
Shapes		

Perceptual Interpretation

Interpretation occurs when people assign meaning to stimuli. It is the process by which an individual selects, organizes, and interprets stimuli into a meaningful and coherent picture of the world.

Since people are different, they interpret messages in individual ways, based on their past experiences and mental make-up. Even when the stimulus is very clear, different people will interpret the messages in different ways. As such, the way messages are interpreted is not in the manufacturer's control. Pride and Ferrel (2010) explain how this happens. If an ad says, '35 per cent of people who use this toothpaste have fewer cavities', a customer may well infer that 65 per cent of the users have *more* cavities.

Perceptual interpretation is influenced by the following five factors:

Selective exposure   People tend to select specific aspects of information based on their perspectives, beliefs, attitudes, and decisions, selecting the favourable and ignoring the unfavourable.

Selective attention   Customers receive the information but perceive it differently, as shown in the aforementioned toothpaste example. The advertising has to be powerful enough to get past the consumer's attention into his memory. Selective perception means that consumers will tend to remember very simple messages that are consistent with their beliefs or aspirations.

Selective retention   Customers who perceive inputs to be inconsistent with prior beliefs are likely to forget the information quickly.

Perceptual defence People tend to ignore information that is offensive, unpleasant, or threatening. This psychological process by which certain stimuli are either not perceived or are distorted is called perceptual defence.

Perceptual blocking The subconscious act of 'screening out' of stimuli that are threatening or inconsistent with one's needs, values, beliefs, or attitudes is called perceptual blocking.

People do not assign meaning to stimuli in terms of words and language. In fact, they tend to assign images and metaphors to the messages they are exposed to and interpret them according to their culture. The chapter-opening case study shows how companies attached the metaphor of a cheetah to a SUV, which was a very effective use of metaphor.

Image
Consumers build images in their minds of brands, stores, and companies. While brands try to build their personality, stores try to add an aura of friendliness and convenience. Companies attempt to shore up their corporate image by being seen as environment friendly or socially responsible. Brand image is the total perception of the product or brand that consumers form. The image is formed by two methods: consumers draw inferences from external stimuli, including marketing and environmental stimuli. For instance, an advertisement will be interpreted in the backdrop of one's culture and aspirations. These help form an 'image' of the brand. Consumers draw inferences internally based on their experiences, dreams, desires, and fantasies. These help in adding psychological attributes to brands.

Metaphors
Zaltman (2003) writes that the unconscious reveals itself through *metaphors*, or the use of figurative language' (consisting of similes, analogies, allegories, and proverbs) for representing one thing in terms of another. Communicators benefit greatly by using metaphors, which can bring unconscious thoughts and feelings to the surface (see the use of the cheetah metaphor in the chapter-opening case study).

Metaphors reveal perception through literal language. They have a neurological basis since the brain uses imagery and metaphors to assign meaning. Thus, they are used to generate positioning and advertising images, and signal new product opportunities. For example, General Motors (GM) asked consumers to bring pictures of watches they found to be friendly and those they found to be fun. The subtle variations in design features on the watches showed them how small design differences in a car could make different statements.

Zaltman says that if recognized, metaphors can provide a keen insight into the mind.

The Zaltman Metaphor Elicitation Technique (ZMET) elicits and probes the metaphors that represent consumers' thoughts and feelings about a topic, and helps discover their perception, an abstract concept that is difficult to discover otherwise. It elicits both conscious and especially unconscious thoughts by exploring people's non-literal or metaphoric expressions. The method was explained in Chapter 6.

Cultural Backdrop
Perceptual interpretation is also influenced by a person's cultural background because people view messages in the context of their culture and upbringing. They interpret messages in the context

they understand. Banerjee (2008) writes that for brand marketing, cultural dimensions play a vital role in formulating imagery about the brand and help companies to communicate better.

Culture becomes an important issue due to globalization. As culture and values vary from country to country, a close insight about country-specific culture and core values is essential for a smooth sailing in any market. Messages that are well received in one culture may well be misinterpreted in another culture.

As explained in Chapter 11, Indian society faces two cultural influences: (a) a strong feeling of tradition and values, and (b) a society that is fast modernizing. These cultural categories create opportunities for new interpretations and for new products.

For example, Indian food has traditionally been prepared fresh everyday. However, with the modernizing of society, pre-cooked Indian dishes and *paranthas* are now available, catering to the modern, time-pressed customer.

PERCEPTUAL INFERENCE

The ability to fill in the gaps or assign meaning to incomplete information is called perceptual inference. For instance, when we hear a bark, we complete the information and assume that it is a dog. Similarly, when see a fast-moving object which we cannot recognize, we try to guess what it is, assigning meaning to it based on our past experiences. Inference is judgement, or the ability to assign meaning from past associations. Perceptual inference results in beliefs about objects and is personal and cultural.

Consumers tend to form images of brands, products, and companies, called imagery. They combine pictures and symbols to assign meaning to objects. The study of signs and symbols as elements of communicative behaviour, is called *semiotics*, that delves into how meaning is created in our minds.

Semiotics

Consumers tend to assign meaning to symbols. Brands must harness the following three components for brand signification:

- The object
- The symbol associated with the object
- The interpretation of the symbol

Companies use semiotics in their logos: the three-pointed star of Mercedes or the double arches of McDonald's convey distinct meaning to consumers.

Beasley and Danesi (2002) write that semiotics create recognizability of the product. The semiotics of advertising can be characterized as a study of the power of sound and light. In India, iconic brands such as Asian Paints and Amul used the character Gattu, and the image of a lovable little girl (created by Sylvester daCunha) respectively, to build their brands and Vodafone used the popular Zoozoos to establish a connection with customers.

Semiotics is used to develop a brand image. The image is the total perception about a product formed by consumers from different sources, built over a period of time.

Perceptual Distortion

Perceptual distortion occurs when consumers use their inherent impressions or biases in interpreting and forming images. This may be negative, if consumers think certain brands do not give value, or positive, as for example when certain brands acquire a green or socially responsible image in the minds of consumers. Perceptual distortions are used in marketing through stereotyping, the halo effect, using celebrities, and other methods.

Stereotyping

Stereotypes are generalizations about a group of people that people tend to assign to everyone in that group. These classifications can be positive or negative, such as when various nationalities are stereotyped as friendly or unfriendly. Advertisements use stereotypes, by showing a social group that people identify as their own group. Research carried out by Knoll and Eisend (2011) shows that female central figures in advertisements are more likely to be depicted as product users, are younger, are more likely to be depicted with domestic products, in a home setting and shown in dependent roles than males. On the other hand, male central figures are more likely to be depicted as authorities, as older, with products other than domestic products, and portrayed in locations other than at home, and in independent roles. The results support stereotyping of women and men, showing both genders in traditional roles where the professional opportunities of women are limited and traditional masculine ideals are upheld.

Advertisers also have to be careful about the imagery they use, simply because the images may be misinterpreted because of stereotyping by viewers. For example, an image of two handcuffed people used in a Benetton campaign had to be withdrawn because people protested that it showed a white man arresting a black man, even though there was no such indication in the image.

Halo Effect

First coined by Edward Thorndike, the halo effect describes the tendency to make specific inferences on the basis of a general impression. It describes the bias shown by customers towards certain products because of a favourable experience with other products made by the same company or because of a past favourable experience. Basically, the halo effect is driven by brand equity. For example, if you had a good experience with Dove soap, you would assume that Dove shampoo would also be equally good.

The halo effect used by companies by establishing strong brand names., through the celebrity effect, by which it is hoped that the positive feelings for a celebrity may be transferred to the product or brand. The term halo effect refers to two effects. The first one is the *similarity halo*, wherein a person tends to rate an object similarly across different dimensions. In the marketing context, this means that a consumer will use an observable attribute to infer an unobservable one. The second effect is the *general impression halo*, wherein an overall impression leads one to evaluate all aspects of performance.

Egan (2007) shows how the halo effect is used by companies as follows:

- Brand extension in which the halo of a brand is sought to be extended to other products
- Cause-related marketing where companies derive a favourable impression by associating with a cause or charity
- Sponsorship in which a favourable impression is derived by associating with a cause or event, like the World Cup

Umbrella Brand Name

An umbrella branding strategy is a marketing practice that involves selling many related products under a single brand name. Unlike individual product branding, which uses different brand names for different products, umbrella branding uses a single brand name, and in some cases logo, for different products. The marketing application of perceptual distortion in using umbrella branding is that by having a common name, the benefit of one product of the brand rubs off on all the products launched under that brand. Companies have powerful brands that are used to launch a number of products. The idea is that the favourable perception of consumers would help in selling other products as well. Please see Exhibits 7.3.

Celebrity Endorsements

The halo effect is also sought to be achieved by using celebrity endorsements. The idea is that the fame achieved by the celebrity should rub off the brand. The halo effect is seen from the marketing value gained by associating the product with the celebrity. Such an association can remain in the minds of many consumers even when a new celebrity is hired for a new marketing campaign.

Industry-wide Halo Effect

When a product becomes a phenomena, it can create a halo effect for all manufacturers within the industry. For example, when Toyota Prius, a hybrid vehicle was introduced and sold as environment friendly with great fuel efficiency, other companies also introduced their hybrid vehicles to ride on the popularity.

Price Perception

Price is seen by buyers as fair or unfair, high or low. It depends on many mental factors which have nothing to do with the actual product or service being offered. Price perception depends on four factors.

Past experience   What the customer paid in the past, and whether the experience was acceptable or not, determines price perception.

Price–quality relationship   While customers normally regard price as an indication of quality, in the case of standardized products, consumers see price as an indicator of cost.

Price reference point   When customers compare what others paid for the same or similar products, it becomes a price reference point.

Advertising   Recalled advertising, especially of price cuts, determines price perception. Customers prefer to wait for prices to be cut again rather than buy at full price.

Premium brand name perception   While some companies build brands on the promise of delivering value, others try hard to create a perception among consumers that their brand has premium or luxury attributes. The brand name perception will determine the price that customers are willing to pay.

Perceptual Categorization

Our brains tend to organize information based on some fundamental principles. When consumers categorize products into classes, it is known as perceptual categorization.

EXHIBIT 7.3 Umbrella Brands

MonteCarlo

Monte Carlo has pegged itself as high-quality fashion winter wear made from pure Australian Merino and lambs' wool, certified with the wool mark logo. While sweaters have been its mainstay, the brand has striven to ensure that it is always in sync with international fashion and trends. However, at the beginning of this decade, Monte Carlo reengineered itself emerging from the makeover as a complete fashion brand. In 1999, the company forayed into the summer casual segment with the addition of T-shirts to its portfolio.

To cater to denim fans, Monte Carlo offers a huge selection of basic denim in various tints and shades and includes accessories such as belts, metal buckles and coordinated rivets. Monte Carlo's range of shirts consists of linen shirts, trendy casual shirts and an innovative collection of washed formals.

The women's denim range has been styled in antique colours, using designer crystal buttons, rivets and embroideries. The collection has been named 'jewel in the crowd' and comprises linen shirts, tunics and printed cotton dresses. For the outdoorsy, there is a complete range of multi-pocket cargo and boxer shorts in linen and fine cotton. The entire group is topped by a collection of track suits available in value packs or as single sets. As part of its entry into the all-season, all-age market, Monte Carlo offers T-shirts and jackets for children in the 10–14 years age bracket. A recent addition to the adult range of offerings is called Outer Wear; this new line comprises tracksuits, jackets, sweatshirts and polo necks. Figure 7.8 shows different lines of Monte Carlo.

FIG. 7.8 Monte Carlo line of clothings

Courtesy: Superbrands

FIG. 7.9 Arrow introducing women wear

Courtesy: Superbrands

Arrow

Arrow stands for professional work wear. Being true to the philosophy of innovation though, Arrow has brought into corporate offices, new codes of formal wear. The New York Collection is the latest amongst these. With it the brand has redefined work wear with a line of slim fits. Right from jackets, blazers, trousers and shirts, the New York Collection is designed to articulate the trim look. With the Collection, also came ensembles. The impression ranged from the out and out professional, to the semi-casual look. Perfect for a younger target audience, the line, remains true to Arrow's legacy.

Arrow Woman was a refreshing change. Fashionably formal, the range was designed to enhance the beauty of a woman. While the cuts were fluid, the look was formal. See Figure 7.9.

Source: Superbrands 2012

Companies want consumers to recognize a brand as belonging to a product class. Within the product class, they want to ensure that the product is also seen as unique. Thus, for instance, all soaps will have more or less similar packing, so that they are recognizable as a product class by customers. At the same time, each pack of soap will also try to stand out in terms of perfume, colour, and alterations of shape, so that the product is seen as different from the competing brands.

Products and brands must be designed so that consumers should not be confused about which category each belongs to. At the same time, manufacturers do not want that their expensive offerings to be categorized with cheaper products, so they must differentiate as well. For example, manufacturers of phones ensure that smartphones are perceived differently from the general categories of mobile phones. People who have a need of status are at pains to show that they carry a smartphone, not just any phone. Physical appearances are thus important.

Physical Appearances

If goods have a similar physical appearance as established brands, they do not register in the consumer's mind as these goods are categorized accordingly. This is used by manufacturers of private brand labels, who ensure that their products look similar to national brands so that they fall in the same category, but then offer them at a low price so that consumers choose private labels. Nenycz-Thiel and Romaniuk (2009) compared the perceptual categorization of private label brands and national brands. They found that users of private label brands did not see them as being any less trustworthy than national brands. Private labels form a subgroup in consumers' memory, with low price and low quality as the main drivers of this categorization.

Categorization happens on two perceptual concepts: schema and subtyping.

Schema Clusters of thoughts, ideas, and symbols are known as schema. It has been found that people rely heavily on schema-like structures that are well established in memory. Assael (2005) gives the example of computers. In the 1950s, people would have categorized them as desk calculators or as business machines, but today they are seen more as laptops or mobile devices.

Subtyping When consumers develop a sub-category within a broader category, it is known as subtyping. When soft drink makers introduced fruit juices such as Slice and Minute Maid, such products were established in a subcategory within the category of soft drinks.

RETENTION

When a consumer remembers a brand or a product, it is called retention. Advertising attempts to create powerful stimuli so that consumers remember the brand when they see it in a store.

Carter (2000) explains: 'Stimuli enter the brain in a stream of electric pulses and for recognition to be complete, information is brought out from memory stores in the brain to flesh out stimulus with associations that give it meaning—perception is clothed with emotion.'

Further, we also see that people interpret messages and products in the following three ways:

Comparison The human mind compares products and pricing with a reference point. For example, consumers will tend to think of price of a particular product as lower when it is placed next to a more expensive product.

Subjective interpretation How consumers interpret messages is subjective and depends on individual factors. Companies thus have to care about the psychological meaning of their messages rather than being literally correct.

Coloured by emotion Consumers interpret messages through the lens of their emotions. This is known as *affective interpretation*, or the emotion or feeling that an advertisement evokes.

The purpose of all advertising and customer experience is to use these elements so that the product and its features are remembered. Customers form an image of the brand, which is the total perception of the object formed in a consumer's mind by processing information from various sources over time. The following three types of images can be formed:

Brand image This is the perception of the brand in the mind of the customer, either through processing external stimuli or through fantasies. Companies use brand positioning to establish a firm image in the minds of customers. Brand image impacts brand equity.

Store image Consumers develop a store image based on advertising, merchandising in the store, and shopping experiences. A positive store image will cause customers to repeat purchases. Stores are particular about delivering a memorable experience to customers. For instance, Ikea insisted that it be allowed to import its retail model to India in its entirety, after restrictions were placed upon it by the Indian government.

Corporate image Consumers also remember companies because of their corporate image. This is the way that companies hope to develop positive perceptions of their products and brands. Corporate image building is a huge and expensive task. Companies try to actively manage perceptions so that they are seen as ethical, moral, and respected. A survey by Fortune India found that Tata Steel, Hindustan Unilever, and Colgate Palmolive were the top three most respected companies in India (see Table 7.2). It is easy to see that people have a positive perception about

TABLE 7.2 The most admired companies in India and across the world

India's most admired companies, 2012	World's most admired companies, 2012
1. Tata Steel	1. Apple
2. Hindustan Unilever	2. Google
3. Colgate Palmolive	3. Amazon.com
4. Cadbury India	4. Coca-Cola
5. TCS	5. IBM
6. Tata Motors	6. FedEx
7. ITC	7. Berkshire Hathaway
8. Larsen & Toubro	8. Starbucks
9. IBM India	9. Procter & Gamble
10. Dell India	10. Southwest Airlines
11. Bosch	11. McDonald's
12. Infosys	12. Johnson & Johnson
13. Wipro	13. Walt Disney
14. GlaxoSmithKline Consumer	14. BMW
15. Raymond	15. General Electric
16. ONGC	16. American Express
17. Bharat Petroleum	17. Microsoft
18. Hewlett-Packard India	18. 3M
19. Indian Oil	19. Caterpillar
20. Hindustan Petroleum	20. Costco Wholesale

Sources: 'India's Most Admired Companies', Fortune India, March 2012; Fortune 500, Fortune, 19 March 2012.

their products as well. In the list of Fortune 500 companies, we see that the biggest companies of the world have brands that are also perceived well by customers.

PERCEPTION LEVELS

When we are exposed to stimuli, our body reacts automatically. We cringe when we see horrid images. Our eyes widen when we are surprised. This direct and immediate response of the body is called *sensation*.

Images, music, smells, taste, and feelings cause a change in energy in the environment that can be perceived by consumers. Companies use these experiences to their advantage. However, using these stimuli requires us to understand perception levels.

Absolute Threshold This is the lowest level of stimulus noticeable. For instance, a company may make so small a change in a package like reducing its weight that the customer does not notice that they are getting lesser quantity for the same price However, if consumers can detect that they are getting less for the same price, the difference is above the absolute threshold.

Differential Threshold The difference between two stimuli is called the differential threshold. It is involved in differentiating two different brands. The advertising and range of products of one brand should not be similar to that of another brand to enable consumers to differentiate.

Just noticeable difference Just noticeable difference (JND) is the minimum amount of stimulus needed for the consumer to tell the difference. Companies have to ensure that negative differences are not noticed whereas positive differences introduced by the brand are noticed well by customers. Instances of negative differences include decrease in quantity or quality, or small increase in price below the JND. Instances of positive differences include improvements in quality, packaging, and price decreases that are much above the JND.

Weber's Law

Weber's Law states that the stronger the initial stimulus, the greater the change must be for it to be noticed. It is the minimum amount of change required in the intensity of the stimulus to produce a noticeable variation in customer experience. It is a measurement of the percentage change needed before individuals can make out the difference. The stronger the initial stimulus, the greater is the stimulus needed subsequently to be noticed by customers.

For instance, if a brand uses a very strong stimulus initially, like the Axe effect, it must use a stronger stimulus subsequently to register with the customer. Otherwise, customers will simply not notice the messages. Similarly, price reductions have to be at least 20 per cent to be noticed by customers.

An interesting implication is that of messages that are targeted to the subconscious, that cannot be discerned by the conscious mind. These messages are much below the absolute threshold and invisibly guide consumers to action.

Subliminal Perception

Solomon (2009) explains that 'subliminal perception occurs when the stimulus is below the level of the consumer's awareness'. It consists of very weak stimuli that cannot be seen or heard, that is, which cannot be discerned consciously; if the person can see or hear it, it is *not* subliminal.

Can weak stimuli, which we cannot even discern, affect our behaviour? Vance Packard in his best-selling book, *The Hidden Persuaders* (1957) argued that it does, saying that big companies manipulated our minds through subliminal messages and the exploitation of embedded sexual images. Using these hidden images, advertising agencies tried hard to tap the irrational in the consumer mind, using applied psychology and sociology, selling not just brands but brand 'personalities'.

Galbraith (1969) echoed this view in his book, *The Affluent Society* saying that modern advertising and salesmanship does not depend on independently-determined desires, but instead manipulates them. He wrote 'wants can be synthesized by advertising, catalysed by salesmanship, and shaped by the discreet manipulations of the persuaders'.

The idea is that hidden images in advertisements affect the mind—for instance, a fleeting image in a movie or a tiny figure inserted into advertising. The idea took birth in the 1950s when single frames of messages such as 'Eat Popcorn' or 'Drink Coca-Cola' were inserted in a movie and projected for 1/3000th of a second. These messages were not noticeable and were well below the absolute threshold. It was reported that sales in the theatre increased as a result of these messages. There was, however, no proof that these efforts to manipulate the unconscious led to any benefits for companies. The experiment was later found to be a hoax.

In other instances, it has been reported that letters spelling out 'S-E-X' could be made out in popular ads or in certain scenes in movies, if one observed very carefully. Sexual imagery has been the favourite of subliminal advertising, and many ads do try to exploit it. However, the effectiveness of hidden messages was questioned, and the American Association of Advertising Agencies released an ad with the headline, 'People have been trying to find breasts in these ice cubes since 1957'. It added, 'Subliminal advertising doesn't exist...overactive imaginations do.'

The subject continued to interest popular imagination. Wilson Bryan Key (1973) rekindled interest on the subject with his book *Subliminal Seduction*, saying that subliminal sexual symbols or objects are often used to entice consumers to buy and use products and brands.

Brain Scanning

Many researchers have debunked subliminal perception. However, using machines to peer inside the brains of people, we are today able to see what affects the human brain and how. A brain scan can reveal our thoughts, moods, and memories; latest imaging technology allows us to see a person's brain registering a joke or experiencing a painful memory.

Neuroscientists attempt to find out what affects a human brain by using techniques like functional magnetic resonance imaging (fMRI) to measure changes in activity in parts of the brain, functional diffuse optical tomography (fDOT), electroencephalography (EEG) and steady state topography (SST) to measure brain response. The data obtained from these machines is accurate: as Wells (2003) writes 'unlike the people answering questionnaires or participating in focus groups, brain waves don't lie'.

Measuring Brain Activity

Several research methods have been used to measure reactions of people. These are as follows:

Implicit association measurement   Neurology measures reaction time of brand and advertising associations, and emotional responses to ideas.

Eye tracking   This involves monitoring people's eye movements as they see ads or marketing stimuli to see what captures visual attention, and how people navigate websites and communications.

Electro-encephalography   EEG and other biometrics such as heart rate and skin conductance look at people's immediate responses to marketing stimuli, without relying on self-report.

Automated facial coding   By continuously recording people's faces while they watch ads, and automatically coding their expressions (e.g. smiles, eyebrow raises, frowns, etc.), scientists have been able to understand people's emotional reactions to communications, on a moment-by-moment basis, and therefore pick up nuances that people are unable to report.

These methods add further understanding to marketing, and they also add predictive power to research, and help explain behaviour more effectively. For instance, eye-tracking has revealed that people do not look at or read whole areas of sites or ads, and glance at selective areas only.

Likewise, facial coding often reveals the negative emotional reactions that people, in order to be polite, are unwilling to reveal on surveys. Furthermore, implicit association or reaction time measures of emotional response to brands can help account for behaviour.

The fMRI is a brain scanning technique that measures the magnetic properties of haemoglobin in the body. The machine is able to pinpoint which parts of the brain get oxygenated blood when exposed to a stimulus. The machine is able to determine the activation level of about 20,000 three-dimensional regions, called *voxels*, in the brain. For instance, when a person thinks of an object such as an apple or a chair, only a part of the brain lights up with high oxygen levels. This shows the neural pattern that is unique for that particular word. Thus, by tracking the brain when exposed to a marketing stimulus, neuroscientists can determine what specific areas in the brain get activated by that stimulus.

Pradeep (2010) in his book, *The Buying Brain: Secrets for Selling to the Subconscious Mind* explains that companies are keen to learn about the interplay of the conscious and subconscious processes in the human brain and how this results in their buying and trying out new products. The task is difficult because consumers cannot tell why they do so; traditional marketing research that asks customers what they like or dislike, may lead us astray. The fMRI technique helps answer three questions:

- Do consumers notice us?
- Do consumers like us?
- Do consumers remember us?

In other words, fMRI helps find out consumer perception, by tracking the parts of the brain that light up due to a stimulus.

The fMRI has allowed researchers to go into the deepest recesses of the brain and companies to know how consumers respond to stimuli in ways that even they are not aware of. As Pradeep writes, it is difficult for people to describe in precise words the emotions that they experience when exposed to a stimulus, because the conscious mind cannot really verbalize what the subconscious mind recorded.

RESEARCH INSIGHT
Can Neuroscience Solve Brand Problems?

Neuroimaging is the study of brain scans, which helps us know which part of the brain lights up when people take decisions, shop online, or when they fall in love. Such techniques help us know consumers' reactions to brands or advertisements, as explained in this chapter. Several books explain the science. Van Praet (2012) writes in his book, *Unconscious Branding*, 'In order to improve the marketing process, we need to first shift the focus from within the walls of companies and unveil the process of behaviour change within the depths of the minds of people'.

Du Plessis (2011) in his book, *The Branded Mind* explains that neuroscience can figure out how people react to marketing stimuli. If consumers make decisions unconsciously, market research cannot uncover real motives for buying. For too long, we have been asking the wrong question: asking consumers directly will only get us wrong answers. Does neuroscience have the solution? Can we gauge consumers' real motives and perceptions through brain scans?

In their book, *Brainwashed: The Seductive Appeal of Mindless Neuroscience*, Satel and Lilienfeld (2013) offer a sceptical viewpoint. They question whether the human experience and behaviour can be explained from the exclusive perspective of the brain. In their opinion, neuroscience cannot be applied to commerce and other fields.

Though fMRI can look into our brains, 'neuromarketers' try to find out what drives us to buy one product rather than another. However, there's little proof that their methods work any better than surveys and focus groups. In any case, even if we know which parts of the brain are activated by a certain brand or image, can this information be used in marketing?

The authors explain that fMRI maps changes in oxygen levels in the brain through colourful splotches indicating the brain regions that become active when a person experiences something. 'Despite well-informed inferences, the greatest challenge of imaging is that it is very difficult for scientists to look at a fiery spot on a brain scan and conclude with certainty what is going on in the mind of the person', they write.

Some of the predictions are indeed quite off the mark. In 2006, a neuroscientist found that an ad by GoDaddy.com would be a flop since it failed to activate viewers' brains, but actually traffic to the site increased 16-fold. Similarly, *The New York Times* (2007) reported a study by a team of neuroscientists who had scanned the brains of undecided voters as they reacted to photos and video footage of the candidates for the US Presidential elections. The researchers translated the resultant brain activity into the voters' unspoken attitudes, and the scans taken while subjects viewed the photographs and videos of McCain and Obama 'indicated a notable lack of any powerful reactions, positive or negative'. These were the two 'boring' politicians who finally won the nomination for the election.

So while neuroscience can tell us what excites the brains of customers, what they do in reality still remains a mystery. Despite the elaborate brain scans, marketing managers still have to rely on their intuition. 'The fact of the matter is anyone can do neuromarketing without ever scanning a single brain', writes Van Praet. Knowledge about the human brain gives us the following insights into how marketing managers can form impressions in their customers' minds:

- Interrupt the pattern
- Create comfort
- Lead the imagination
- Shift the feeling
- Satisfy the critical mind
- Change the associations
- Take action

Do you think that brain-scanning technology can actually help marketing managers make better decisions? If so, how?

Sources:

Du Plessis, Erik, *The Branded Mind: What Neuroscience Really Tells Us About the Puzzle of the Brain and the Brand*, Kogan Page, London, 2011.

Satel Sally and Scott O. Lilienfeld, *Brainwashed: The Seductive Appeal of Mindless Neuroscience*, Basic Books, New York, 2013.

'This is your brain on politics', The New York Times, 11 November 2007, http://www.nytimes.com/2007/11/11/opinion/11freedman.html?pagewanted=all, last accessed on 14 October 2013.

Van Praet, Douglas, *Unconscious Branding: How Neuroscience Can Empower (and Inspire) Marketing*, Palgrave Macmillan, New York, 2012.

We cannot, however, place too much reliance on brain scans such as these as it is very difficult for scientists to look at a fiery spot on a brain scan and conclude with certainty what is going on in the mind of the person by obtaining measures of brain oxygen levels. They do show which regions of the brain are more active when a person is thinking, feeling, or, say, reading or calculating. However, it is a rather daring leap to draw confident conclusions from these patterns and deduce how people feel about political candidates or paying taxes, or what they experience in the throes of love, or what they end up buying.

Mirror Neurons

A research published in 1996 showed that the human brain has multiple 'mirror neuron systems' that specialize in understanding not just the actions of others but their intentions. *The New York Times* (2006) reported that mirror neurons allow us to form our perceptions by feeling, not by thinking. Lindstrom (2009) explains that everything we observe someone else doing, we do as well.

This finding leads us to understand perceptions about products, brands, and advertisements. If companies could find ways to fire up the mirror neurons, they could kindle desire even without advertising. Liquor and cigarette advertising is banned, but the companies try to kindle desire for their products by reminding customers of them even without mentioning the brand.

Lindstrom (2009) shows how this works. He writes that Philip Morris, the company that makes Marlboro cigarettes gives bar owners incentives to decorate their venues with colour schemes, specially designed furniture, ashtrays, and tiles similar to parts of the Marlboro logo, and other subtle symbols that convey the very essence of the brand. People get the message subconsciously, and feel the sudden urge to smoke a Marlboro in such settings even though they are not exposed to advertising. 'Thanks to worldwide bans on tobacco advertising, cigarette companies funnel a huge percentage of their marketing budget into subliminal brand exposure', he writes.

HOW CUSTOMERS THINK

Latest research has shown that the subconscious plays a very important part in consumer decisions. Gerald Zaltman, the author of *How Customers Think* (2003) believes that 95 per cent of decision-making is unconscious. Daniel Kahneman tells us that our intuitive system 'is more influential than your experience tells you, and is the secret author of many of the choices and judgments you make'.

Zaltman describes six ways in which customers think, highlighting the importance of the subconscious. Usually, managers focus on consumers' conscious thinking and apply their own conscious interpretations because it is easy, but they ignore the unconscious mind that drives most consumer behaviour. He explains as follows:

Consumers do not think in reasoned, logical, and linear ways Customers do not consciously assess product benefits and attributes to make their purchase decision. Instead, the selection process is largely affected by emotions, the unconscious, and social and physical contexts. For instance, emotions such as happiness and prestige play a bigger role.

Consumers cannot explain their thinking and behaviour rationally People use conscious thought to rationalize their purchases. In reality, 95 per cent of thinking takes place in our unconscious minds.

Consumers' minds, brains, bodies, and culture form one integrated whole Consumers' minds, brains, bodies, and culture cannot be studied independently of one another. The brain interacts with the external world and both help shape the other.

Consumers' memories are not reliable Memories do not accurately reflect consumers' experiences. Memory changes depending on the situation, and hence is unreliable to base interpretations.

Consumers do not think in words Brain scans suggest that only a small portion of the brain's neural activity is expressed in language.

Company messages cannot be injected and interpreted as companies intend Consumers do not passively absorb a company's intended messages, but constantly reinterpret them in terms of their experiences.

Since 95 per cent of the human mind is part of the cognitive unconscious, most thought processes, decisions, and opinion-formations happen in the unconscious.

Strahan, et al. (2002) show that subliminal messages affected people's behaviour when they were motivated. In thirst-related experiments, it was found that people's drinking behaviour was affected primarily when they were thirsty. The implication of this research is that companies should advertise and make available their products when people are most likely in need of a drink.

Consumer behaviour is also influenced by habits. Hodson (2003) says that habits, rather than subliminal messages, help to form our preferences and dispositions. Companies and institutions cause changes in habits of thought and behaviour, they constrain our behaviour, and develop our habits in specific ways. The framing, shifting, and constraining capacities of social institutions give rise to new perceptions and dispositions within individuals.

Perceptual Organization

Perceptual organization refers to the way in which human beings organize information in their minds and make sense of their environment. Our brains take in a variety of stimuli every day and organize the information on fundamental principles to be able to derive meaning relevant to us. Stimuli are thus interpreted in relation to other events, sensations, or experiences that already exist in the memory.

Assael (2005) explains that perceptual organization means that 'consumers group information from various sources into a meaningful whole to comprehend it better and to act on it'.

Gestalt Psychology

Gestalt psychology explains how people relate to their environment. People organize their life by attaching meaning to what is relevant to their individual needs or interests. People thus notice only relevant elements from their environment, assembling a Gestalt image from objective elements. The basic principle of Gestalt is integration, which means that consumers perceive various stimuli as an organized whole.

Coon and Mitterer (2011) define Gestalt as: 'A school of psychology emphasising the study of thinking, learning, and perception in whole units, not by analysis into parts.'

Gestalt means configuration or whole pattern. Humans and animals have a survival instinct, and because of this, they learn to make sense of the world around them. Young ones of animals learn quickly about their environment because their survival depends on it. Gestalt psychology shows how organisms relate to their environment, and how their brains are able to store information in patterns relating to individual needs or interests.

Carmer and Rouzer (1974) write, 'The basic premise of Gestalt psychology is that human nature is organized into patterns or wholes, that it is experienced by the individual in these terms, and that it can only be understood as a function of the patterns or wholes of which it is made'.

This has important implications for marketing strategy. People do not form impressions of products and brands taking each element of product, price, advertising, or distribution separately, but develop a brand image by interpreting all stimuli at once. As Solomon (2009) explains, 'the whole is greater than the sum of its parts.'

Since people develop a holistic impression of stimuli, ideally, the concept of 'whole configuration' must be applied to brands. Service providers such as hotels and beauty parlours use this concept. As such, the companies must try to deliver a brand experience rather than focus on individual attributes separately.

The use of Gestalt can be seen across a range of marketing concepts such as advertising, packaging, and merchandising. Gestalt principles and their marketing applications are as follows:

Proximity

Objects that are close together are perceived as a single object.

Using this principle, shops place complementary items near each other, suggesting that they go together. The following are some usages of proximity by marketers:

- Display mannequins show that the clothes they sport form one ensemble
- Combo meals in which all the items—a burger, fries, and cola—are perceived as one meal
- Products that are associated with common symbols, imagery, and endorsers
- Print advertisements, wherein similar objects are kept together, and white space and boxes are used to separate elements that are meant to be kept apart
- Retailers organize their stores based on usage

Similarity

Objects that are similar are perceived as a single object. Companies should design their various marketing communications so that customers perceive all of them as belonging to the same entity. For example, if a company wants to project that all its products have the same high quality it is known for, it will have a common 'quality' theme running through all its advertisements.

- Companies create campaigns so that the ads are similar, have common themes or slogans, models, graphic design elements, colours, formats, and convey the same overall 'look and feel'
- Department stores group similar items together to facilitate the shopping process
- Companies want to avoid the perception that their products are similar to other products. So they create packages and advertising that are quite different

Continuity

People categorize stimuli into smooth, uninterrupted, and continuous forms, rather than into discontinuous patterns.

This principle is used by companies in various ways:

- Companies prefer long-running, continuous ad campaigns so that people are able to recall their brands
- Retail stores are organized so that transition between sections is continuous
- Changes in visual marketing elements are usually made gradually because a sudden change would be too confusing and disruptive for consumers

Closure

People tend to perceive incomplete patterns as being complete, that is, they tend to 'fill in the blanks' in stimuli. Incomplete advertisements sometimes tend to increase attention and recall, as people try to guess what it might be

- Advertisers sometimes use headlines phrased as questions, encouraging audience participation
- Sometimes an object in an ad is cropped so that it appears ambiguous, encouraging consumers to guess what it is

Simplicity

The simplicity principle (pragnänz) suggests that people opt for simple perceptions even in complex situations. Thus every stimulus pattern is seen in such a way that the resulting structure is as simple as possible.

- Marketing communications follow the advice of 'keep it simple, stupid' (KISS). Advertisements are kept short and sweet—simple illustrations, uncomplicated language, and direct messages.
- Abstract concepts are explained through symbols like a heart shape for 'love'.
- Companies must use technology to guide customers seamlessly to buy. Spenner and Freeman (2012) write that the rising volume of marketing messages is overwhelming for customers. 'Rather than pulling customers into the fold, marketers are pushing them away with relentless and ill-conceived efforts to engage.'

Context

Principles of context relate to how perception of a stimulus is influenced by its surroundings. Two principles of context are figure and ground, and contrast.

Figure and ground This principle states that People interpret a stimulus in the context of its background. In advertisements, the most important stimuli, such as the product and selling theme, must stand out as the figure. Many ads fail as they choose a background to get consumers' attention such as a celebrity, humour, and sex. The message is often lost, as people notice the background but not the figure

Contrast A stimulus that stands out from its surroundings is more likely to be noticed. To be readily discerned, a sound must be much softer or louder, a colour brighter or paler, or an object larger or smaller than others near it. As a consequence, companies must 'differentiate or die'! They have to create unique brand names, packaging, and advertisements to be noticed by customers.

Experiential Marketing

Gestalt psychology shows that consumers make sense of their environment as a whole rather than evaluate individual stimuli. For instance, people do not evaluate a restaurant on the basis of individual elements such as colour, music, seating, and so on, but on the complete experience of being there. Advertisers use various techniques to send out their message. The idea is to use sensory principles and individual traits to deliver a sensation that is remembered by consumers.

Sensory evaluation   A science that tries to measure, analyse, and interpret levels of consumer reaction to a range of products. It is used in new product development and product upgrades and employs the five senses. It tries to work out what consumer perception and reaction might be to a range of possible new introductions. It is used to judge consumer reactions to consumer products before they are launched.

Sensory deprivation   When a person does not receive sensory inputs, such as when he/she is blindfolded, it is called sensory deprivation. Long used as a form of torture, it is used in marketing to make people feel deprived if they do not get the product immediately. Chocolates, cold drinks, beer, and a host of products are sold on this concept wherein advertising creates a feeling of deprivation among the consumers if they are not enjoying these products.

Sensory adaptation   Continuous exposure to similar stimuli will make people used to it and they will stop noticing it.

Ambush marketing   Advertising or any marketing activity that is done during popular events to imply that the company is associated with the event is called ambush marketing. For instance, if a company advertises heavily using cricket images during the World Cup, consumers will perceive it as being linked to the event.

In experiential marketing, three aspects need to be studied—individual characteristics, situational characteristics, and touch-point analysis.

Individual Characteristics

People process the same stimulus differently. This is because each individual categorizes and infers information differently. How perception will occur will depend on the following factors.

- *Traits*: Different people have different traits, and that is why they differ in their response to stimuli. While some people, for instance, respond emotionally, others are more logical in their approach.
- *Memories*: As people have different kinds of upbringing, their memories are also different. This affects how they perceive the world around them and their response to advertising stimuli is thus different as well.
- *Learning and knowledge*: This refers to the experiences and knowledge that individuals have acquired over their lifetime.
- *Expectations*: People approach products with certain expectations. These could arise out of advertising or from famous brand names.
- *Cultural backdrop*: Individuals operate in and are influenced by their culture. Brands use cultural contexts such as habits and beliefs to place their products.

Situational Characteristics

Another factor affecting interpretation is the situation in which the advertisement or the product is seen by the consumer. There are two aspects to this—the personal resources of the customer and the context in which he sees the product.

Price–Quality Consumers form impressions of products based on prices and quality, and their personal resources while a person of modest means will evaluate products on the value derived from them, a rich person will focus more on psychological benefits.

Products in certain settings Products displayed in certain settings, as in the homes of film stars or in other premium settings, are perceived as premium products. Manufacturers of luxury products (see chapter-end case study) take pains to be seen in elite surroundings to maintain their image.

Customer perception determines how much value customers associate with brands. It affects word of mouth publicity. If their experiences differ from their expectations, positive or negative publicity will be generated. Low expectations will result in customer delight, but high expectations must be matched by the real product offering. It is important to measure customer perceptions to manage customer expectations. This is done through surveys, customer touch-point analysis, and connecting with customers.

Surveys Consumer surveys help uncover perception, though straight questions are unlikely to yield meaningful results. However, metaphor elicitation techniques and other qualitative surveys help in identifying what is essentially abstract.

Touch-point analysis Touchpoints are interactions between the company and its customers, and can be used to influence perception. Each touchpoint must be analysed to find out the ways in which segments of the target market interact with the brand. This analysis provides a description of the relationship between a brand and its customers. It is further used to identify gaps or areas in which the company is not taking advantage of opportunities to communicate value.

Customer-connect The way that a brand connects with its customers also impacts perception. Apart from advertising, online customer interaction, ease, and after-sales service—all help in creating perceptions in the minds of customers.

All these elements come into play when companies try to change perceptions of customers towards their brands.

ALTERING PERCEPTIONS

All marketing is a battle of perception. Companies want to position their brands in such a way that customers remember them positively. This is a difficult task, as customers are bombarded with messages. The challenge is to make advertising so powerful that people are influenced by it.

Powerful advertising changes consumers' perceptions of products. Some popular attempts to change perceptions are as follows:

- Coca-Cola appealed to emotional perceptions of its product by incorporating happiness in its brand

- Maggi Noodles was able to promote perceptions about its noodles as a convenient 2-minute snack.
- Airtel used the bandwagon approach by highlighting friends and social media, trying to make customers feel they were 'missing out' or did not belong to a group if they didn't use its product

Consumer perception can be changed by understanding how individuals form opinions about companies and brands. Companies try to analyse consumer behaviour by describing motivations for buying particular brands or avoiding others, thereby helping to develop marketing and advertising strategies to retain current customers and attract new ones. This can be done in three ways, namely self perception, price perception, and benefit perception.

Self-perception It means how consumers see themselves, their values, and motivations. Through advertising, companies try to change self perception. For example, consumers who see themselves as rich and stylish tend to follow celebrities and lap up products endorsed by them. Similarly, consumers who consider themselves socially conscious tend to buy products that they perceive are environment friendly.

Price perception Whether logical or not, consumers tend to have a price perception, that is, an expensive item or a better-packaged one is seen as having better quality than its cheaper counterpart. In the case of perfume purchases for instance, people feel that the more expensive the product, the better it is.

Benefit perception People buy products based on what benefits they expect from them. Catering to this tendency, companies attach benefits to their products, some physical and others psychological, that customers feel they derive from brands. A customer may, for instance, buy an expensive moisturising cream and forego an equally good cheaper substitute not because of any additional physical attributes but because she feels using the product makes her feel smart and rich in her social circle. Food products highlight nutritional ingredients so that consumers start believing that they are better than what they would otherwise eat. Brands also get certification from respected bodies to change consumer perception about them.

The sum total of all types of perception is translated into customer-perceived value. Valuable brands have higher perceived value. This is explained in the next section.

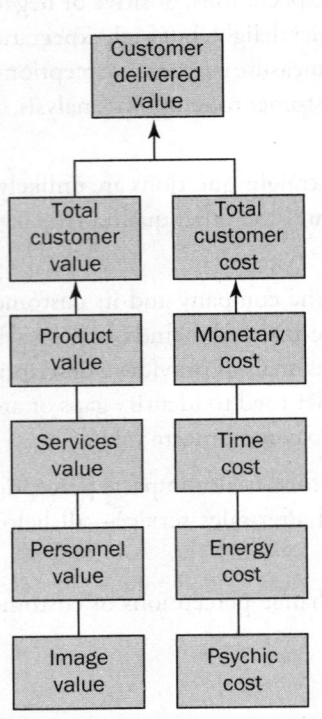

FIG. 7.10 Customer-perceived and delivered value

Customer-perceived Value

This Customer-perceived Value (CPV) is a sum of product, service, personnel, and image value (Fig. 7.10).

Customer-perceived value (CPV) is also defined as the difference between the prospective customer's evaluation of all the benefits and all the costs of an offering and the perceived alternatives.

Total customer value is the perceived monetary value of the bundle or economic, functional, and psychological benefits customers expect from a given market offering.

Total customer cost is the bundle of costs customers expect to incur in evaluating, obtaining, using, and disposing of the brand.

Let's take a customer who wants to buy a car. He looks around, collects information, and evaluates the models that are available in a price range. He assesses each model on reliability, efficiency, features, brand name, performance, show-off, and resale values. Customers will also evaluate delivery, after-sales service, and maintenance of the models.

It is quite possible that the customer rates some models higher, but settles for a lesser model because of cost. The expected value of the car is matched with its cost. At the moment of buying, the customer decides whether it is worthwhile to pay extra for the additional benefit he seeks.

Customer Perception and Product Strategy

Companies offer products that best meet customers' needs. They balance their offerings with the price they charge for it. Sometimes high prices are charged to enhance customer perception about value, and at others low prices are charged to increase customer value. Pricing and product strategy is an important role of for any successful company. While high-value products contribute to profits of a company, cheaper products keep the cash flowing.

In both cases, the company must have a way to measure consumer perceptions. A high perceived value must be matched by high prices. Thus, companies protect their brand names, logos, and symbols so that they continue to have the high customer-perceived value.

A product strategy helps companies to launch new products or modify existing ones. While devising new product offerings, companies work on not only the physical product attributes and quality, but also on the psychological value that the product will deliver.

When new products are launched, consumers evaluate them on several levels. They see the advertising and the packaging, and form an idea of the product value. They may then decide to buy or not to buy. Products are made more desirable by displays and promotion schemes. More than the tangible benefits, companies have to focus on augmented properties of products and brands. The use of celebrities as brand ambassadors can be understood in this context. Advertising helps to create augmented, psychological value.

Consumer perceptions change over a period. Products may do well for a time and then suddenly become outdated. Technological improvements and the product lifecycle have to be tracked by companies and product modifications undertaken accordingly. Continuous product development and improvement will help companies to better target their consumers and learn to react to their needs. A change in product strategy is necessitated by the following major factors.

Customer preferences Customer preferences change. A brand that did well in the past may flounder in present times for no other reason than that consumer preferences have changed with time. Many brands do not change with the times and soon other brands take over.

Technological advances Very often, technology renders products obsolete. A product with modern packaging will convey better perceived value to the consumer even though there is no intrinsic change in the product. Better technologies are continuously developed so the company has to keep track of product and packaging technologies to keep modifying products accordingly.

ETHICAL INSIGHT
Advertisements and the Self-perception of Women

Advertising loves women. They are used in ads not only to catch the viewer's attention but also to personify brands by beautiful women. These ads, called self-identity image ads, portray an image that people relate to or compare themselves with. They create an idealized image of a typical user of the product. The 'sex appeal' of advertisements is enhanced by using thin, flawless, beautiful women, who attempt to sell products based on its association with their beauty.

There is, of course, nothing wrong with this. Questions about ethics arise when the ideal of beauty is pushed too far. The images are usually enhanced using software like Photoshop that make it possible for the models to look picture-perfect, and their bodies slimmer. Many women relate to these images and see themselves as imperfect, and needing to be more like the women in the ads.

Trampe, et al. (2010) write that advertisements cause consumers to think about themselves in relation to the advertised product. The models portrayed in ads impart an identity to the brand and also make consumers identify with them. They start using the product hoping to get a similar personality. Aagerup (2011) writes that the self-identity transfers from the ad to the consumer. Consumers who thought of themselves as similar to the models had positive beliefs not only about the model, but also about the brand as well as to purchase intentions.

The fashion industry also promotes a skewed image of women's bodies and to such an extent that some young women aspire to achieve impossible figures, harming themselves in the process.

This creates a moral dilemma since women begin to compare themselves with manipulated or false images. Young girls associate themselves with these 'perfect' models and want to become like them. This is the purpose of 'self-identity image' advertising; to create a feeling of association with the ad, which causes a consumer to believe what is being presented. A woman might believe that if she uses the product, she too will fit this societal perception of 'beauty'.

It has been shown that these types of images have a negative effect on an individual's self-esteem and create a mental illusion that he or she must conform to the pressures implied in the advertisement. These images become implicated in afflictions such as anorexia and bulimia; and the use of tobacco and alcohol increases among young adolescents.

To achieve a fashionable body shape, young women starve themselves and their body mass index (BMI) becomes far lower than the recommended level for good health, leading to anorexia and loss of self-esteem. Consequently, they fail to reach their full potential in life.

Recognizing these ill-effects, many brands have moved to using 'real' women as against professional models in advertisements. Leading the pack is the Unilever brand, Dove. It launched the *Campaign for Real Beauty* in 2004. The campaign spearheaded the need for a wider definition of beauty after it was found that the definition of beauty had become limiting and unattainable. The study found that only 2 per cent of women around the world described themselves as beautiful. Dove advertisements challenged beauty stereotypes by including ordinary women instead of models in their ads. In 2010, Dove launched a campaign to make beauty a source of confidence, not anxiety, with its 'movement for self-esteem'. A research paper commissioned by Dove explains that it attempts to reclaim beauty and re-examine it from a 21st century point of view. The paper says 'It knows that beauty should not be reduced to a political or cultural problem but understood as a basic human pleasure.'

Should ads promote unrealistic images? What are the consequences of showing images of unattainable beauty ideals?

Sources:
Aagerup, Ulf, 'The influence of real women in advertising on mass market fashion brand perception', *Journal of Fashion Marketing and Management*, Vol. 15, Issue 4, 2011, pp. 486–502.

'The real truth about beauty: A global report', http://www.dove.us/Social-Mission/campaign-for-real-beauty.aspx, 2004, last accessed on 5 April 2014.

Trampe, Debra, Diederik A. Stapel and Frans W. Siero, 'The self-activation effect of advertisements: Ads can affect whether and how consumers think about the self', *Journal of Consumer Research*, April 2011.

Product lifecycles Many companies decide to alter, discontinue, or replace older products with newer models or more recent upgrades. These changes are usually made periodically, allowing existing products that reach maturity or decline to be phased out or modified, thus retaining their appeal.

PERCEPTUAL MAPPING

Perceptual maps help to illustrate graphically a brand's position in the minds of the customers relative to competing goods. Positioning is the set of perceptions, impressions, ideas, and feelings that consumers have for the product.

Perceptual maps can be made for brands, products, and for corporate positioning. Figure 7.11 depicts a perceptual map built on two dimensions. They are used to assess competition, discover new opportunities, and for building strategies for repositioning existing brands. Product perceptual maps are especially useful in identifying new, unexpected ways in which customer needs may be met. Corporate perceptual maps help companies build corporate images.

Modern technology allows perceptual maps, also called product-positioning maps, to be built on a large number of dimensions. The most common are developed on two dimensions for easy comparability and simplicity.

Benefits of Perceptual Mapping

Perception maps have many benefits for companies. Some of them are discussed as follows:

Building marketing or brand strategy Perceptual maps help understand and depict graphically what consumers think about a brand as also about competing brands. These inputs

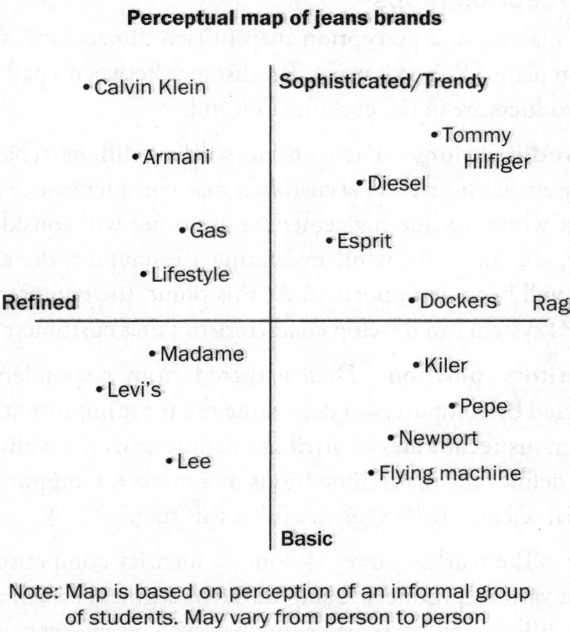

Perceptual map of jeans brands

```
                    Sophisticated/Trendy
   • Calvin Klein   |
                    |           • Tommy
   • Armani         |             Hilfiger
                    |      • Diesel
   • Gas            |
                    |      • Esprit
   • Lifestyle      |
Refined ————————————+———————————————— Ragged
                    |      • Dockers
   • Madame         |
   • Levi's         |      • Kiler
                    |      • Pepe
                    |      • Newport
   • Lee            |      • Flying machine
                    |
                    Basic
```

Note: Map is based on perception of an informal group of students. May vary from person to person

FIG. 7.11 Perceptual maps built on two dimensions

CB IN ACTION   Perceptual Maps

Perceptual mapping is a fun way to discover how brands are perceived by customers. Create perception maps for goods such as chocolates, cars, or cosmetics. First, assess which elements of perception you want to match. Next, get your friends together and assign values collectively to various brands on your selected elements. Map the brands on a X–Y plane.

1. Is there a cluster of brands in any quadrant?
2. Gaps in a quadrant will show opportunities to launch products.
3. Present your maps and discuss them in your class.

help companies discover the strengths and weaknesses of their brands, which can be useful in developing marketing strategy.

Communication strategy   Since perceptions are mostly built by communications, perception maps help work out communication strategies to counter those of competitors.

Differentiation   Perceptual maps show differentiation among products in the customer's mind.

Identify opportunities   Empty spaces in a perceptual map shows potential market opportunities. In this way, they help in identifying potential new products and segments. They not only help identify new product opportunities, but also aid in repositioning existing brands.

Market evolution   By comparing perceptual maps over time, companies can discover how the market is changing, find out about consumer expectations, as also whether the image of a brand has shifted. Important attributes may change as a result of changing habits and needs of customers.

Constructing Perception Maps

In this section, the making of a perception map in two dimensions is explained. These can be shown in a Euclidean plane (X, Y axis map). The distance between a pair of coordinates represents how far apart the products are in the consumer's mind.

Identify competitive dimensions   Each product will have different characteristics that are valued by customers. While evaluating a bank, a customer may consider ease of access, facilities, location, time saving, etc, but while considering cement, a customer will consider durability, availability, finish, brand image, etc. Similarly, while evaluating a restaurant, the ambience, service, quality of food, and so on, will become important. At this point, the company's customer relationship management (CRM) system can develop characteristics that customers have mentioned.

Determine competitors' position   Data gathered from respondents are organized into a matrix. This is analysed by computers to determine the most important competitive dimensions. One of the most famous techniques in attribute definition is the Kelly Grid (described later in the chapter) which defines the main dimensions of a market. Computer tools like the statistical package for the social sciences (SPSS) are useful at this stage.

Survey the market   The market survey is done to identify competitors, as well as to discover how consumers rate various products. Using different segments, such as male or female, old or young, can generate different characteristics and may even reveal some features that have not been thought of by managers.

Method of mapping There are several methods for drawing perceptual maps, and each one has its own advantages and disadvantages. Managers have to select the best method suited to their product and research needs.

Map the positions The positions of the brand and its competitors are plotted on an X–Y plane. The position of various brands is reflected and the size of the circle reflects its market share.

Interpret the map Perceptual maps reveal answers to many questions—whether consumer attitudes match what the company wants them to think about the brand, whether competitors are perceived highly, whether the company has brands positioned at required customer needs, and if there is a need for a new brand.

Changing marketing strategy Perception maps are useful in assessing the company's marketing strategy. If consumers do not see a brand favourably, the company needs to make changes. Sometimes they can reveal poor consumer attitudes despite the company's efforts to the contrary. This would reveal the need for a revamp. For instance, the Tata Nano, which was launched by the company as the world's cheapest car, found few takers as customers perceived it quite differently than intended by the company. Based on customer feedback, the company then decided to revamp the car with a more powerful engine and a change in image to change consumers' perception towards it.

Perceptual Mapping Methods

There are several methods for perceptual mapping. The main problem is to reduce a large number of product attributes to a few underlying factors. This is done through factor analysis, discriminant analysis, and multi-dimensional scaling.

Factor analysis Factor analysis is a data reduction technique in which the objective is to condense the original set of attributes into a smaller number of underlying factors.

Discriminant analysis Discriminant analysis too, reduces the number of attributes to a smaller number of underlying dimensions. However, it focuses on attributes which show differences between brands. Sets of observations represent different 'groups' and the analysis identifies those underlying dimensions, which are most useful in discriminating among groups.

Multi-dimensional scaling Through multi-dimensional scaling (MDS) method, the brands are mapped spatially, such that the relative positions reflect the degree of perceived similarity between the brands. Unlike the earlier methods, MDS asks respondents to rate brands on overall similarity, not individual attributes.

MEASURING BRAND IMAGE

Since brand image is an abstract concept, various methods are used to quantify the attitudes towards the brand.

Attitude scale The attitude scale consists of a set of statements concerning the subject's attitude towards a brand. The attitudes are measured through the Likert scale (Fig. 7.12) or a semantic differential scale.

```
Traditional semantic differential
                Brand 1
Clean :___:___:___:___:___:___: Dirty

Honest :___:___:___:___:___:___: Dishonest

                Brand 2
Clean :___:___:___:___:___:___: Dirty

Honest :___:___:___:___:___:___: Dishonest
```

FIG. 7.12 Example of a Likert scale

Q-sort An item set (Q-set) is defined describing all the important attributes for the brand evaluation (usually 30 and 60). Each attribute is printed on a separate card, and the whole card-set is presented to the respondents, who after a careful reading must classify all the cards progressively, from the most relevant to the least relevant, as to how well they describe the real brand, the ideal brand, its competitor, etc. Q-Sort can also be done using photos instead of cards.

Natural grouping In natural grouping, a large set of brand names (maximum 80) is presented to respondents, who are required to split up the whole set into two homogeneous subsets, explaining their motivation in doing so and describing the subsets in their own words. This task is repeated till the respondents cannot come up with any more meaningful subdivisions. The first subdivision represents the most crucial dimension in describing the features of the brand image that differentiates it from its major competitors. This method permits the analysis of the brand image through the categorization process. In this way, one can understand the brand image by observing the similar and different brands.

Kelly repertory grid In Kelly repestory gride (KRG), every element is compared with its opposite. Usually three brands are compared. Every brand name is written on a card and the interviewees are invited to indicate which two are the more similar ones. After every choice, the interviewees are asked: 'Which characteristics make these three brands similar or different?' Respondents are also asked to name the opposites of the qualities.

Laddering This is an interview technique used in semi-structured interviews to elicit the higher or lower level abstractions of the concepts that people use to organize their world. By using probing questions, interviewers 'peel back the layers' of meaning in the respondents' minds. It is used to elicit consumers' preferences towards certain products or services and categorized into three dimensions, namely attributes of a product or service, consequences, and values.

Means-end theory The means-end theory or MET is focused on the linkages between the brand attributes (the 'means'), the consequences derived by the attributes, and the consumer's personal values (the 'ends'). The technique is different from laddering as there is a dialogue with the respondents, who can be asked to spell out their reasons by answering the query, 'Why is this important for you?'

Benefit chain This method starts with a benefit or a brand characteristic provided as stimulus by the researcher. The participants have to indicate two other benefits. For every one of these two new benefits, the respondent has to indicate another two benefits. The evolution goes from the practical context to the emotive one. The respondents have to be stimulated as they go along, without manipulating or forcing the results.

Projective techniques The respondents can freely interpret and respond to ambiguous stimuli. They can 'project' their own unconscious feelings and motivations in their answers. Projective techniques are used not to measure, but to uncover feelings and motivations.

Association techniques The main association techniques are word association, pictures-and-words association, and the Photosort. These use the free association method, starting with an unstructured stimulus such as a word or an image. In word association, participants are asked to write the first word that comes into mind immediately after having seen or heard a brand or an adjective. The frequency with which any word is given as a response to a particular brand shows whether respondents associate the describing words with that brand. In Photosort, respondents assign to the brand those photographs which they think represent it. Instead of photographs, generic visuals can also be used.

Construction techniques   In *draw creation*, participants are invited to personify the brand by drawing it. In *cartoon tests*, some cartoons are shown referring to the specific brand context and respondents are asked to fill in the cartoon speech balloons with free text. This helps to visualize how customers think.

CONCLUSION

The study of consumer perception is about how people think. It is an exciting one as it delves into human consciousness. Companies use all the tools at their disposal to change the way people perceive their products and brands. The hope is that by understanding the human psyche, they can meet consumer needs faster and more efficiently.

In this chapter, we discovered how the messages to the conscious and the subconscious are designed to influence consumer behaviour. Science is aiding in this endeavour. Brain-scanning techniques promise to further add to our understanding of the human mind. These techniques peer inside the brain and delve into an area that has not been hitherto possible to study. It is possible that in the near future we may discover the 'buy button' in the brain that causes us to buy whenever companies want us to.

Coupled with the fact that companies are able to track our every online move, will this lead to an Orwellian future where our shopping instincts are held to ransom by corporations? How the future shapes, however, will depend on how we harness the information that future research may discover.

SUMMARY

This chapter examines how perception plays a role in buying behaviour. Companies try to create favourable perceptions of their products and brands through endearing ads that play on our emotions and other psychological processes. Companies are interested in the phenomenon as they want to create favourable impressions, yet perception is an individual construct. Since people notice stimuli from all senses, companies employ sensory marketing to deliver memorable experiences to customers to influence their perception.

Consumers often buy goods not because of rational motives but emotional ones. Shopping is also done for the sheer joy. This is called hedonic consumption, which creates historic and fantasy imagery to arouse latent desires in consumers. Companies use all the senses to influence the perception of consumers in sensory marketing—sight, touch, smell, music, and taste.

There are four stages of consumer perception, namely sensation, attention, interpretation, and retention. Sensation starts when we are exposed to stimuli. Since consumers zap commercials, the first step for companies is to increase the chances of people being exposed to their messages. Exposure must result in catching the attention of the consumer. After noticing, the customer assigns meaning to stimuli. Messages have to be created so that consumers create favourable perceptions in their minds. Advertisers use images and metaphors for perceptual interpretation. Perceptual interpretation is also influenced by a person's cultural background because people view messages in the context of their culture and upbringing.

The ability to fill in the gaps or assign meaning to incomplete information is called perceptual inference. Imagery and symbols (semiotics) create recognition of the product and brand image. However, companies have to be careful that messages are not misinterpreted through perceptual distortion and stereotyping. At the same time, this concept is used in the halo effect, umbrella branding, and the use of celebrities in advertising.

Consumers organize information in their minds on some fundamental organizational principles. This is called perceptual categorization, and this depends on physical appearance of products, and on two perceptual concepts, namely schema and subtyping.

The purpose of all communication is consumer retention, or remembering products and services when they go out shopping. Retention happens as consumers form an image of the brand, store, and company. The most-admired companies also have a number of products in their portfolio that have favourable images in customers' minds.

Advertising messages, or stimuli, must be such that they are noticed by customers. The lowest level of stimulus that a person can notice is called the absolute threshold. The difference between the two stimuli is called differential threshold, used in differentiating brands. These concepts are used in marketing by ensuring that negative changes are below the just noticeable difference (JND) level while the positive changes in products are above the JND. The application of Weber's law is also important, which states that the stronger the initial stimulus, the greater the change must be for it to be noticed. Companies must ensure that their advertising stimuli are stronger than initial stimuli to be noticed.

Subliminal perception occurs when the stimulus is below the level of the consumer's awareness. It consists of very weak stimuli that cannot be discerned, yet they impact consumer behaviour. Brain-scanning machines are able to detect activity and mirror neurons that show that the brain forms its perceptions even from stimuli that cannot be detected by the conscious mind.

The way that information is organized in our brains is called perceptual organization. Incomplete information is completed by the brain through Gestalt psychology. Principles of proximity, similarity, continuity, closure, simplicity, and context guide our brain into making meaningful patterns. Gestalt psychology plays a role in experiential marketing, which integrates sensory stimuli to deliver an holistic experience.

Perceptual mapping is a graphic way to show the position of a brand relative to its competitors in the minds of customers. Perceptual maps help identify competitive dimensions, opportunities, and in charting outs competitive strategy.

■■■ KEY TERMS

Absolute threshold The lowest level of stimulus that a person can notice

Attention The point when a person notices a product or brand

Below the line Campaigns consisting of direct contact with customers through non-media communications

Differential threshold The difference between two stimuli is called differential threshold

Gestalt psychology A school of psychology emphasizing the study of thinking, learning, and perception in whole units, not by analysis into parts

Hedonic consumption Those facets of consumer behaviour that relate to the multisensory, fantasy, and emotive aspects of one's experience with products, making the consumer feel happy about consuming products and services

Imagery The images consumers tend to form of brands, products, and companies in their minds

Just noticeable difference The minimum amount of stimulus needed for the consumer to tell the difference in a product

Kelly repertory grid A tool to measure brand image involving a grid, in which every element is compared with its opposite, and respondents indicate which two are the more similar ones

Perception It is the process by which an individual selects, organizes, and interprets stimuli into a meaningful and coherent picture of the world

Perceptual blocking The subconscious act of screening out stimuli that are threatening or inconsistent with one's needs, values, beliefs, or attitudes

Perceptual categorization The ability of humans to organize information in their minds, based on some fundamental organizational principles

Perceptual defence The psychological process by which certain stimuli that are offensive, unpleasant, or threatening are not perceived or are distorted

Perceptual inference The ability to fill in the gaps or assign meaning to incomplete information

Perceptual interpretation When people assign meaning to a stimulus

Perceptual mapping Helps to illustrate graphically a brand's position in the minds of the customers relative to competing goods

Perceptual organization Refers to the way in which human beings organize information in their minds and make sense of their environment

Retention When consumers remember a brand

Semiotics The study of signs and symbols as elements of communicative behaviour

Sensory marketing A type of marketing, which employs all human senses of vision, smell, hearing, touch, and taste

Stimulus Any physical, visual, or verbal communication to customers

Subliminal perception Occurs when the stimulus is below the level of the consumer's awareness. It consists of very weak stimuli that cannot be seen or heard, that is, which cannot be discerned consciously

Weber's law States that the stronger the initial stimulus, the greater the change must be for it to be noticed

Zaltman metaphor elicitation technique A technique developed by Gerald Zaltman that uses pictures and non-visual images gathered and/or generated by consumers to elicit and probe the metaphors that represent consumers' thoughts and feelings

EXERCISES

Concept-review Questions

1. What is perception? How do companies use consumer perception to create images and sell their products and services?
2. What is hedonic consumption? How is it used by companies?
3. Discuss the various elements of sensory marketing. What are its applications?
4. Discuss the four stages of perception. Describe what happens at these different stages.
5. What is semiotics? Discuss how semiotics is used by brands.
6. What is Gestalt psychology? How is it used in consumer perception?
7. Describe what is meant by subliminal perception. How does it work?
8. What is Weber's law? Discover some practical applications of this law.
9. Describe the process of perceptual mapping. What are the methods of perceptual mapping?
10. How does the brain organize information? Draw a perceptual organization for a product category like computers.

Critical Thinking Questions

1. The marketing of SUVs shows how product perceptions are changed by using the negative side of human personality. Do you think this is ethical? Should companies use such negative connotations to sell products? Give your opinion and also assess how this can lead to negative behaviour among consumers.
2. Study the applications of perception levels. Are there any practical applications of absolute threshold, differential threshold, and JND that you can find among brands?
3. Brain-scanning techniques are being used to discover the brain's reaction to stimuli. How will it help in resolving perception of brands? Do you think that these techniques can actually be useful in influencing the purchase decision?
4. Many people believe that subliminal advertising does not work. Yet, books continue to describe subliminal seduction of consumers. Critically examine the literature on the subject and give your views on whether subliminal seduction exists or not.

Projects and Assignments

1. Companies try to associate impressions and emotions with their brands, appealing to consumer tastes, desires, fantasies, and wants. Select a brand of your choice and collect information on how it uses desires, fantasies, and wants to create its brand image.
2. Perceptual distortion occurs when consumers use their biases to interpret information. By using ads of brands, conduct an experiment in your class and examine how perceptual distortion works. List down how people misinterpret messages and how messages can avoid being distorted.
3. Ask your friends to think of a product category such as cars or soaps, or an emotion such as joy or retrospection. Then ask them to bring a set of photographs that represent their thoughts and feelings about the product category. Do these pictures reveal metaphorical thinking? Are these important non-literal devices for uncovering deeply held, often unconscious, thoughts and feelings?
4. Make a list of all the restaurants that you and your friends like to visit. Ask them to list the reasons why they like to go there. Based on this, develop a perceptual map of restaurants on different dimensions.

REFERENCES

Assael, Henry, *Consumer Behavior: A Strategic Approach* (Indian Edition), Biztantra, New Delhi, 2005, p. 163.

Banerjee, Saikat, 'Dimensions of Indian culture, core cultural values and marketing implications: An analysis', *Cross Cultural Management: An International Journal*, Vol. 15, No. 4, 2008, pp. 367–378.

Beasley, Ron and Marcel Danesi, *Persuasive Signs: The Semiotics of Advertising*, Mouton de Gruyter, Berlin, 2002.

Bitner, M.J., 'Servicescapes: The impact of physical surroundings on customers and employees', *Journal of Marketing*, Vol. 54, 1992, pp. 69–82.

Blakeslee, Sandra, 'Cells that read minds', *The New York Times*, 10 January, 2006, http://www.nytimes.com/2006/01/10/science/10mirr.html?pagewanted=all, last accessed on 12 September 2012.

Blijlevens, J., M.E.H.Creusen, and J.P.L.Schoormans, 'How consumers perceive product appearance: The identification of three product appearance attributes', *International Journal of Design*, Vol. 3, No. 3, 2009, pp. 27–35.

Carmer, J.C. and D.L. Rouzer, D.L., 'Healthy functioning from the Gestalt perspective', *The Counselling Psychologist*, Vol. 4, No. 4, 1974, pp. 20–23.

Carter, Rita, *Mapping the Mind*, University of California Press, California, 2000.

Chaykin, Joan, 'Views on hues', *Wearables Business*, Vol. 11, Issue 3, March 2007, pp. 44–47.

Coon, Dennis and John O. Mitterer, *Psychology: A Journey*, 4th Ed., Wadsworth, Cengage Learning, Belmont, CA, 2011.

Creusen, Mariëlle E. H. and Jan P. L. Schoormans, 'The different roles of product appearance in consumer choice', *Journal of Product Innovation Management*, Vol. 22, 2005, pp. 63–81.

Creusen, Mariëlle E.H., Robert W. Veryzer, and Jan P.L. Schoormans, 'Product value importance and consumer preference for visual complexity and symmetry', *European Journal of Marketing*, Vol. 44, Issue 9, 2010, pp. 1437–1452

Egan, John, *Marketing Communications*, Thomson Learning, London, 2009, pp. 83–85.

'Food for Thought', *The Economist*, 15 December 2012.

Galbraith, John Kenneth, *The Affluent Society*, 40th Anniversary Edition, Penguin Books, London, 1999.

Geboy, Lyn Dally, 'Color makes a better message', *Journal of Health Care Marketing*, Vol. 16, No. 2, Summer 1996, pp. 52–54.

Hirschman, E.C. and M.B. Holbrook, 'Hedonic consumption: Emerging concepts, methods and propositions', *Journal of Marketing*, Vol. 46, No. 3, 1982, pp. 92–101.

Hodgson, Geoffrey M., 'The hidden persuaders: Institutions and individuals in economic theory', *Cambridge Journal of Economics*, 27(2), March 2003, pp. 159–75.

Hultén, Bertil, Niklas Broweus, and Marcus van Dijk, *Sensory Marketing*, Palgrave Macmillan, Hampshire, 2009.

'Incognito', *The Economist*, 18 April 2009.

Kahneman, Daniel *Thinking, Fast and Slow*, Penguin Books, New York, 2011.

Key, Wilson Bryan, *Subliminal Seduction: Ad Media's Manipulation of Not So Innocent America*, Prentice-Hall, Englewood Cliffs, NJ, 1973.

Knoll Silke and Martin Eisend, 'Gender roles in advertising', *International Journal of Advertising*, Vol. 30, 2011, No. 5, pp. 867–888.

Krishna, Aradhna, 'An integrative review of sensory marketing: Engaging the senses to affect perception, judgment and behaviour', *Journal of Consumer Psychology*, Vol. 22, Issue 3, July 2012, pp. 332–351.

Krishna, Aradhna, *Sensory Marketing: Research on the Sensuality of Products*, Routledge, New York, 2010.

Kubacki, Krzysztof and Robin Croft, 'Mass marketing, music, and morality', *Journal of Marketing Management*, No. 20, 2004, pp. 577–590.

Lindstrom, Martin, *Buyology*, Random House Business Books, New York, 2009.

Moeran, Brian, 'Leading marketers by the nose', *European Business Forum*, Issue 31, Winter 2007, pp. 8–9.

Morales, Andrea C., Eugenia C. Wu, and Gavan J. Fitzsimons, 'How disgust enhances the effectiveness of fear appeals', *Journal of Marketing Research*, Vol. XLIX, June 2012, pp. 383–393.

Namasivayam, K. and A.S. Mattila, 'Accounting for the joint effects of the servicescape and service exchange on consumers' satisfaction evaluations', *Journal of Hospitality and Tourism Research*, Vol. 31, No. 1, 2007, pp. 3–18.

Nenycz-Thiel, Magda and Jenni Romaniuk, 'Perceptual categorization of private labels and national brands', *Journal of Product & Brand Management*, Vol. 18, Issue 4, 2009, pp. 251–261.

Packard, Vance, *The Hidden Persuaders*, 50th Anniversary Edition, 2007, Ig Publishing, New York.

Pradeep, A. K., *The Buying Brain: Secrets for Selling to the Subconscious Mind*, John Wiley and Sons, New Jersey, 2010.

Pride, William, and O.C. Ferrel, *Marketing*, South-Western, Cengage Learning, Mason, Ohio, 2010, pp. 200–201.

Satel, Sally and Scott O. Lilienfeld, *Brainwashed: The Seductive Appeal of Mindless Neuroscience*, Basic Books, New York, 2013.

Saulpaugh, Casey, Tammy Huffman, and Mohammad Ahmadi, 'The effect of custom song compositions on brand personality: An empirical study', *International Journal of Business, Marketing and Decision Sciences*, Volume 5, Number 1, Winter 2012, pp. 150–163.

Solomon, Michael, *The Truth about What Customers Want and Why They Buy*, 1st Ed., Pearson Education, New Delhi, 2009, pp. 14–17.

Spenner, Patrick and Karen Freeman, 'To keep your customers, keep it simple, *Harvard Business Review*, May 2012.

Strahan, Erin J. Steven J. Spencer, and Mark P. Zanna, 'Subliminal priming and persuasion: Striking while the iron is hot', *Journal of Experimental Social Psychology*, Vol. 38, 2002, pp. 556–568.

Tifferet, Sigal and Ram Herstein, 'Gender differences in brand commitment, impulse buying, and hedonic consumption', *Journal of Product & Brand Management*, Vol. 21 No. 3, 2012, pp. 176–182.

Trampe, Debra, Diederik A. Stapel, and Frans W. Siero, 'The self-activation effect of advertisements: Ads can affect whether and how consumers think about the self', *Journal Of Consumer Research*, Vol. 37, April 2011, pp. 1030–1045.

Wells, Melanie, 'In search of the buy button', *Forbes*, January 2003.

Zaltman, Gerald, *How Customers Think: Essential Insights into the Mind of the Market*, Harvard Business School Press, Boston, 2003.

CASE STUDY

Dilemma of Luxury Brands

Thorstein Veblen's *The Theory of the Leisure Class*, originally published in 1899, sheds light on how people use wealth and goods to bolster their social position in society. People strive for status and to elevate their social position in the eyes of others through their belongings.

Veblen recognized that status did not automatically accrue to individuals who had wealth. Rather, status was obtained by putting their wealth on display. Although goods had practical value, Veblen recognized many goods were purchased because they were 'a mark of prowess and perquisite of human dignity'. Status was derived from being able to buy and show-off goods and services that were excessive and too expensive for others, giving rise to the phrase, 'conspicuous consumption'.

Many of Veblen's observations ring true even today. *The Economic Times* (2013) reports that expensive brands provide the super rich an identity and differentiates them from the rest. Many of them look for bizarre ways to differentiate themselves from others, or to get a psychological edge over others. Luxury goods often act as psychological armour, rather than just being status symbols.

A host of luxury brands help the super rich to spend their money. The luxury industry is a fascinating industry, since it uses perceptions to influence how people view their products, making them pay exorbitant prices for these, compared to similar goods that serve the same purpose. It depends on people who not only have money, but also feel good about spending it. They buy goods and services for showing-off, and for generating envy among the less fortunate.

Danziger (2005) writes that luxury taps into a consumer psychology that transcends the product being bought or consumed to reach a new level of enhanced experience, deeper meaning, richer enjoyment, and more profound feelings.

The challenge for luxury brands is to maintain 'brand integrity'—that indefinable aura that convinces consumers to pay a lot of money for something they could buy much more cheaply elsewhere.

Real luxury caters to the rarefied strata consisting of the very rich (Fig. 7.13), and it is much higher than the fashion and premium categories. Premium brands can be labelled as 'aspirational luxury'—to which common people aspire. However, the luxury brands are different—they consist of very highly priced, high quality goods whose cost is considered outrageous by ordinary people, for instance, brands such as Rolex, LVMH, Dior, and Armani.

However, that also poses a dilemma for manufacturers of luxury brands. Should they limit themselves to serving the extremely rich or should they extend their brands and serve the fashionable and premium customers? In doing so, they risk 'brand dilution', which is the price they have to pay for popularity. If too many people have a supposedly exclusive handbag or scarf, it is no longer exclusive, and therefore, in the customer's view, no longer worth its vertiginous price.

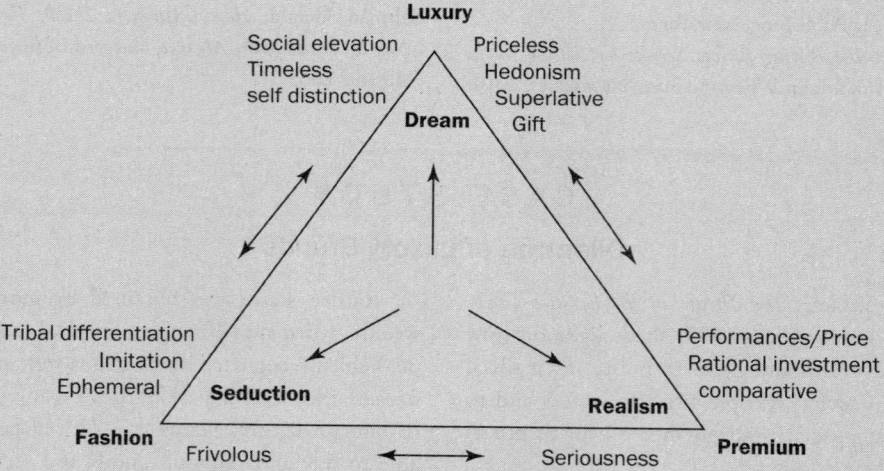

FIG. 7.13 The luxury market consists of fashion and premium brands but real luxury caters to dreams and self distinction

Source: Kapferer and Bastein (2009)

Growth will, however, come from expanding markets. Luxury brands recognize that they have to attract new customers in emerging economies. It is tempting to think that luxury goods are isolated from the broader economy, because customers are rich enough to ignore it. However, the industry's expansion into a broader 'aspirational' market, by selling its products to the merely affluent, makes it susceptible.

As consumers in these countries become rich, they can afford to buy international brands they have always aspired for. Radha Chadha and Paul Husband (2006) wrote that this socio-cultural phenomenon of 'luxeplosion' is reverberating throughout Asia. New money is upsetting old ways, allowing people to purchase their way up the status ladder. Selling in emerging economies poses some difficulties: for instance, how can luxury brands sell at Third World prices and still maintain that aura of exclusivity?

If luxury companies want to expand volumes, they have to reduce prices and adopt mass marketing. The danger is that the brand may get cheapened, like Christian Dior in 1984. *The Economist* (2012) writes that its founder had licensed his name to legions of firms, which slapped it on everything from sunglasses to nightgowns. The brand was cheapened. After taking it over, Moët Hennessy Louis Vuitton (LVMH) spent more than a decade buying back its 350 licences.

Such a strategy poses financial challenges. *The Economist* (2011) writes that the fashion industry's financial future is murky. A confusion of trends preoccupies the major brands—the rapid shift east of their customer base, a generational switch, as high earners get younger, and the challenge of making luxurious clothing accessible to new markets, including digital ones, while retaining the sense of exclusivity that makes people want to pay for them in the first place.

One of the main conundrums for the fashion industry concerns 'democratic luxury', that is, firms want to sell more, to make more money, but the more they sell, the harder it is to convince customers that they are buying something 'exclusive'. As the brands expand to emerging countries, they face the question as to whether snooty shoppers in the West want to own what thousands of Chinese people are wearing?

In the luxury business, perception is all. The industry's expansion into a broader 'aspirational' market, by selling to the merely affluent, makes it susceptible. *The Economist* (2007) notes that one problem is exchange rates—most of the industry's production is in the Eurozone. Converting European prices into local currencies make the products exorbitant. That is one reason why luxury brands have not been able to do well in the Indian market. According to a report in *The Economic Times* (2012), even Chanel and Christian Dior, among the best-known luxury brands in the world, have put lower price tags on select products. Chanel offers 30 off at sales of its ready-to-wear section twice a year while Dior offers discounts on items such as clutches and shoes.

Luxury companies could shift more of their production to countries with weaker currencies and cheap labour, but Asian customers want the elitism and craftsmanship associated with products manufactured in Europe.

Some people think that luxury makers need to follow Giorgio Armani and segment their customers more carefully with different product lines at different price ranges. Nevertheless, the danger of cheapening the brand remains.

Questions for Discussion

1. Why do people buy overpriced goods? How do companies create the perception of luxury in their offerings?
2. Take up a luxury brand of your choice and write down how it creates an ambience of exclusivity around it.
3. How can luxury brands expand into Asian countries without brand dilution? Should they extend their brands? Discuss.
4. What would be the impact on the brands if they expand into emerging economies as described towards the end of the case? Draw a perceptual map to show the existing and targeted position that the brands might achieve by entering emerging markets.

Sources:

Chadha, Radha and Paul Husband, *The Cult of the Luxury Brand: Inside Asia's Love Affair With Luxury*, Nicholas Brealy Publishing, London, 2006, pp. 252–54.

Danziger, Pamela N., *Let them Eat Cake: Marketing Luxury to the Masses as well as to the Classes*, Dearborn Trade Publishing, Chicago, 2005.

Kapferer, Jean-Noel and V. Bastien, *The Luxury Strategy: Break the Rules of Marketing to Build Luxury Brands*, Kogan Page Ltd, London, 2009, p. 35.

'Luxury goods: Less exuberant', *The Economist*, 6 December 2007.

'LVMH: The empire of desire', *The Economist*, 2 June 2012.

Rathore, Vijaya (2013), 'If you have a Louis Vuitton bag, here's a great idea!', *The Economic Times*, 2 January 2013.

Rathore, Vijaya, 'Global luxury brands like Chanel, Christian Dior, Burberry put up sale signs to woo first-time buyers', *The Economic Times*, 23 July 2012.

'The fashion industry: The glossy posse', *The Economist*, 1 October 2011.

Veblen, Thorstein, *The Theory of the Leisure Class*, 1899, http://www.gutenberg.org/files/833/833-h/833-h.htm#2HCH0004, last accessed on 3 January 2013.

CHAPTER EIGHT

Consumer Learning

LEARNING OBJECTIVES

Consumers learn to buy and utilize products. Marketing employs learning theories to achieve attitudinal and behavioural change towards products and brands. This chapter describes instrumental and classical conditioning, and how these are used to develop consumer loyalty and equity.

After studying this chapter, the reader would be able to
- analyze the elements of consumer learning such as motivation, cues, and response
- describe the relationships between consumer experience, learning, memory, and knowledge
- distinguish between the two behavioural learning theories, classical conditioning and instrumental conditioning, and cognitive learning theories
- learn about measures of consumer learning such as attitudinal and behavioural measures

CASE STUDY

Marketing a Stone

Marketing companies rely on techniques of consumer learning to sell a variety of products. Consumers are taught to buy and use new and innovative products through conditioning and to change attitudes towards products and brands. This chapter opening case study describes how attitudes of entire generations were changed towards a product. It describes how a stone with no intrinsic worth, became a symbol of love and romance and came to be valued by women the world over.

Edward Jay Epstein (1982) writes that until the late 19th century, diamonds were found only in a few river beds in India and in the jungles of Brazil. In 1870, however, huge diamond mines were discovered in South Africa, and the market was deluged with diamonds. Realizing that price of diamonds would fall because of the increased supply, investors in the diamond mines organized themselves to control production and perpetuate the illusion of scarcity of diamonds. In the process, they created marketing history by making a somewhat useless stone the heartthrob of women everywhere.

A single entity to control supply was created—De Beers Consolidated Mines Ltd—that became the most successful cartel in the annals of modern commerce. However, controlling supply was one aspect; the more important question was: Who would buy the stones? How could De Beers influence people to actually buy diamonds?

Through high-pressure campaigns and using elements of consumer learning, De Beers created an image for diamonds linked to love and romance.

As Epstein (1982) writes, it was 'a mechanism for converting tiny crystals of carbon into universally-recognized tokens of wealth, power, and romance'. The myth was created that the diamond was the ultimate token of affection. People had to learn that diamonds were an inseparable part of courtship and married life. The illusion had to be created that diamonds were symbol of commitment and permanence, and this was achieved by the famous tagline: 'a diamond is forever'. This meant that it should not be resold.

The advertising campaign was the brainchild N.W. Ayer a New York based advertising agency. It devised a well-orchestrated advertising and public-relations campaign to change social attitudes so that people would start buying expensive diamonds. The campaign linked diamonds with the idea of romance. It also had to appeal to men, since most engagement rings were bought by them. Diamonds were soon to become the gift of love. Young women were taught that diamonds were an integral part of any romance, and the image of romance was subtly changed. This was done by conditioning people through sensitive campaigns and placing diamonds in movies.

Movies The idea was to make diamonds an integral part of courtship, by placing them subtly in love stories. De Beers partnered with the film industry to promote diamonds in story lines, featured engagement rings in films, and placed diamonds in the hands of celebrities. For example, in the 1953 movie, *Gentlemen Prefer Blondes* for instance, Marilyn Monroe sang, 'Men grow cold as girls grow old, and we all lose our charms in the end…but square-cut or pear-shaped, these rocks don't lose their shape. Diamonds are a girl's best friend.'

Press A PR effort was undertaken. Stories were fed to magazines and newspapers to reinforce the link between diamonds and romance. They described celebrities presenting large diamonds to their lovers, and photographs showed the glittering stones on the hands of well-known women. The idea was to engage socialites so that the cultural desire for diamonds trickled down to the middle classes. Fashion designers talked on radio programmes about the 'trend towards diamonds'. The British royal family was also shown wearing diamonds; Queen Elizabeth accepted a diamond on a well-publicized trip to several South African diamond mines. For the middle class, these were role models. It caused millions of girls to dream of the day when they would be given a diamond.

Then, to increase demand, the idea was introduced that the gift of a second diamond, in later years of marriage, would reinforce the bond and be seen as a symbol of 'ever-growing love.'

Advertising N. W. Ayer created some of the most memorable and sensitive advertising ever seen, linking romance to diamonds. Four-colour advertisements were placed in magazines featuring reproductions of famous paintings by Picasso, Derain, Dali, and Dufy. The advertisements were intended to convey the idea that diamonds, like paintings, were unique works of art. The 'eternity ring' was introduced to sell smaller diamonds by attaching similar emotions to them as to the larger ones.

Lectures In the 1940s, lectures that revolved around the diamond engagement ring were organized to attract attention of girls in leading high schools.

Underlying messages The underlying message in all communications was that diamonds were essential to express love. De Beers insisted that each stone was unique, special, very exclusive, and hand crafted; an idea that appealed to young lovers who also believed that their romance was unique. Further, it stressed on conspicuous consumption. Diamonds were also portrayed as symbols of achievement. Celebrities flaunting diamonds reinforced this idea.

Information dissemination A 'diamond information centre' was set up which provided information on diamonds to publishing houses. An elaborate system of information dissemination enhanced the idea that diamonds were unique, with the underlying theme, 'a diamond is forever'.

The PR assault worked. Consumers were conditioned into believing that romance could best be expressed through diamonds. The next step was to expand the usage of diamonds. Goldfarb and Aster (2010) explained how this was done. The idea of a diamond potlatch was introduced. Potlatch is the anthropological custom where acts of generosity and giving gifts are sanctified as an aspect of culture, related to births, rites of passage, weddings, naming, and honouring the deceased.

After 20 years of the campaign, the younger generation was conditioned to believe that diamonds were indeed an integral part of courtship. A diamond engagement ring became a necessity, conveying the idea that true love could only be expressed through a diamond—the bigger the diamond, the greater the love. The subtle negative tone was that a girl who did not get diamonds from her lover was a little less loved.

As Gerstein (2012) writes, 'It's a lie that started less than a 100 years ago, and it's a lie the diamond industry has been banking on ever since'.

The case shows that people can be persuaded to learn to buy and consume products that were earlier ignored by them.

While reading this chapter, try to answer the following questions:

1. What is the importance of consumer learning in consumer behaviour? How can attitudes towards products and brands be changed through advertising?
2. What are the elements of consumer learning that were used by De Beers to attach emotions to a stone with no intrinsic worth?
3. How was behavioural learning used to teach consumers to buy diamonds?
4. How were the elements of motivation, cue, response, and reinforcement used to teach consumers the value of diamonds?

Sources:

Epstein, Edward Jay, 'Have you ever tried to sell a diamond?', *The Atlantic Monthly*, February 1982, http://www.theatlantic.com/magazine/archive/1982/02/have-you-ever-tried-to-sell-a-diamond/304575/7/, last accessed on 9 April 2013.

Gerstein, Julie, 'The diamond myth: How diamonds became a girl's best friend', *The Frisky*, February 2012, http://www.thefrisky.com/2012-02-09/the-diamond-myth-how-diamonds-became-a-girls-best-friend/, last accessed on 9 February 2013.

Goldfarb, M. and Howard Aster, *Beyond Branding*, Rupa Publications, New Delhi, 2010.

INTRODUCTION

New products require customers who learn how to use them. The most successful products are those that are easy to figure out how to operate and adopt. If innovations are successful, it is because consumers quickly realize the benefits of using new products.

Making consumers learn about products quickly has become important for companies because product life cycles have shortened. Marketing has become fast-paced. To be successful, customers must embrace new products as soon as they are introduced, or the innovation will languish, be forgotten, and disappear. Further, today's consumers are actively engaged in finding out information about products and communicate with each other. In other words, they are willing students. However, they also do not want to read lengthy manuals—they want user-friendly products. This has spawned a huge market for 'plug and play' products.

The question before managers is how to get consumers to learn to adapt to products. While one learning theory says that human beings are very advanced mammals that learn by a stimulus–response mechanism, other theorists maintain that human beings are cognitive creatures who use their brains to construct knowledge from the information received by the senses. This chapter examines the different approaches of consumer learning.

CONSUMER LEARNING

Consumer learning is *the process by which individuals acquire knowledge about products and brands, and use that knowledge and experience to know which brands are suitable for them and which ones are not.*

Companies use consumer learning techniques to change the preferences and liking of people towards their brands and products. The Indian market has witnessed big changes in recent times as companies have succeeded in changing customer habits and preferences. For example, traditional Indian foods made way for products such as burgers, pizzas, and noodles as consumers acquired new tastes. In the past, outings meant going to friends' homes or an occasional movie, but now a variety of cafés and malls are on the loyalty list of Indian consumers. Many activities such as watching cricket, consuming alcohol-based drinks, or smoking were almost exclusively male-dominated, but now women also have learnt to take part in these activities and to consume these products. Consumers in India have learnt to purchase online, overcoming their initial hesitation and concerns about security and privacy. E-commerce companies have used consumer learning to establish themselves.

These examples show that people learn how to consume new categories of products and also switch loyalties. This is of particular interest to marketing companies as they innovate and introduce new products to counter flagging sales of existing products or to extend product life cycles of others. To effectively market new products and brands, they have to understand the consumer learning process.

Nature of Learning

Learning theorists have provided us with a set of ideas about how people learn. These ideas have practical implications for studying or altering consumer behaviour. The underlying principles that provide a framework for consumer learning are as follows:

Role of the brain   Our brains process information as we interact with the world. It makes sense of visual, aural, verbal, or tactile information, and draws connections. The brain stores advertising information and product experiences which are used by it in subsequent purchases. To stimulate the brain, different media, such as sounds and pictures, that is, multimedia, is used by advertisers.

Environment   People also learn by making sense of the environment around them. Learning occurs in environments that are rich with stimuli and provide feedback in response to a learner's efforts. Learning is also enhanced when content is relevant, and when people have choices that are interesting to them. Companies try to place their products in environments that are familiar to consumers and to provide a variety of ways through which customers can be stimulated to learn.

Associations   The human brain learns by making connections or associations between new information and what is already known. The brain accepts, organizes, stores, and retrieves information whenever it is required. It stores a large body of product information and experiences.

New products and information is associated with existing knowledge. To aid in learning, companies must help people make connections with what they already know, and organize information to help consumers associate it with existing products.

Cultural and social contexts The way people make sense of information depends on what they encounter at home, in the community, and in the classroom, that is, learning occurs in cultural and social contexts. Advertisers thus have to communicate within social and cultural contexts. This aspect is covered in Chapter 11.

Learn different ways Since people learn in different ways, companies have to use multiple methods to get people to know about their products. They use advertising, peer influence, direct interactions, sampling, and so on, to cater to different people and different learning methods. In the case of making diamonds popular, product placement, advertising, press, lectures, and other devices like below-the-line (BTL) campaigns were used to help in the learning process (see chapter-opening case study).

Feelings matter Thoughts and emotions help learning. Advertisers portray positive emotions and help people feel good about it while buying products. Many brands make emotional appeals. Companies deliberately like to attach feelings and emotions to brands so that consumers learn to buy those products whenever they are feeling that way.

Learning Process

Consumer learning is a continuous process as people interact with new products either through experience or through learning about them from others. It takes place in a variety of ways:

- Most consumption behaviour is learnt through a process of consumer socialization involving family and peers (see Chapter 10).
- People experience products when they are given free samples or try out new products or when they make their first purchase. Figure 8.1 depicts how modern retailers ensure that people can try out their products and learn through experience.
- They see the products consumed by celebrities in movies and on television and want the same products and brands.
- Friends and acquaintances play an important role as they recommend products through word-of-mouth recommendations. People learn consumption through the 'mirror effect', when they see others consuming products, especially celebrities and role models.

Many people are strongly influenced to try out new products and services by watching advertisements.

People are fascinated by new products and packages, and it is a human tendency to want to try them out. That is why companies are always innovating.

The experience with the products is saved in the person's memory and serves as feedback. These memories provide the basis for future purchases. This is called the learning process.

FIG. 8.1 Learning through experience

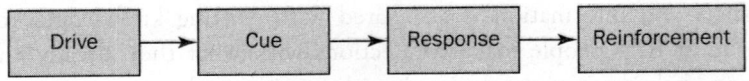

FIG. 8.2 Elements of consumer learning

Several learning models have been proposed. There are four basic elements in these models—motivation, cues, response, and reinforcement (Fig. 8.2). These are discussed in the next section.

Elements of Consumer Learning

The aforementioned four elements of consumer learning play out in our daily lives. By watching advertisements or the products themselves, a desire or motivation is kindled. Cues provide signals—like compelling point-of-sales offers—that cause consumers to let go of their inhibitions and buy the products, which is the response. Companies have to be careful that the products fulfil expectations, which results in satisfaction or reinforcement, which in turn will result in repeat purchases. These elements are explained in this section.

Motivation The driving force that impels consumers to try out new products is called motivation. When people see a new product or an advertisement, they become curious and want to try it out. Internal motivation occurs when unconscious needs or desires are fulfilled. External motivation occurs through advertising or other stimuli that encourage people to try out products by appealing to some consumer need. The experience in trying out the product results in learning. If the experience is good, the consumer learns to make a repeat purchase, but if the experience results in dissatisfaction, the consumer learns to avoid those products.

Cue A cue is a signal to a consumer to buy or consume a product or service. Cues act as stimuli and gives directions to motives. In theatre, a cue is a word or action that is a signal to the actor to begin a performance. In advertising, it is a word or signal that causes a person to consume something. For instance, an advertisement of food at the appropriate time may remind a customer that he needs a snack. The smell of coffee wafting out of a café also serves as a cue for customers to have a cup. Exhibit 8.1 describes educating customers by Vodafone.

Response The reaction of the consumer to the cue is called response. On seeing an advertisement, consumers may or may not immediately react, but they may keep it in their mind and buy the product when the need arises. Most advertising depends on a favourable response from customers.

Reinforcement When a customer is satisfied with the experience of consuming the product, reinforcement occurs. Consumer experiences are at the heart of consumer behaviour. When a product fulfils the expectations that a customer has, it results in positive reinforcement and learning takes place.

Different theories make use of the aforementioned elements in different ways. Three types of theories, namely behavioural learning, cognitive learning (information processing), and social learning, also called observational or vicarious learning will be explained.

EXHIBIT 8.1 Educating Customers

Vodafone is credited with opening up the predominantly postpaid-dominated BlackBerry services to a younger, youth-oriented market. Leveraging the benefits of BlackBerry chat, email and BlackBerry messenger, Vodafone gave the phone a whole new image supporting it with a 60-second television commercial (TVC). This resulted in stepped up interest in the brand. Mob activations in malls and Vodafone Blackberry Blast Smoothies, especially developed by Café Coffee Day, were the other spin-offs. The other Vodafone contribution is developing the 2G and 3G markets. Before the brand launched a broadside on this market, the penetration levels on a base of 500 million subscribers was an abysmal 9% and 3% respectively. It appeared that people weren't entirely convinced of the effectiveness of these formats.

Vodafone took it open itself to educate the consumer and help him shed his inhibitions. Before long, the markets surged forward and people on the periphery embraced these technologies. Vodafone Prepaid customers, too, were given the benefit of such services as Call-me-Back, Chhota Recharge, and Credit Transfer. In this way, conveniences available only to postpaid customers were made available to prepaid ones as well.

Vodafone did not leave behind even those who were not comfortable with mobile data. The brand made it easier for them to use and manage a wide variety of digital content by offering the services of 123—a simple number anyone could dial and get options for subscribing to recipes, astrology, or even matrimonial alerts (see Fig. 8.3).

Source: Superbrands 2012

FIG. 8.3 Promotion used by Vodafone

Courtesy: Superbrands

GETTING CONSUMERS INVOLVED

Educational psychologists have long known that involved students learn faster than uninvolved, bored students. Common sense also tells us that interested people learn things faster. This means that companies must get consumers involved in their products as also their promotional programmes if they are to succeed.

Most consumers, however, are passive. They collect information at random without being involved—this is called passive learning. Passive learning occurs when people do not actively engage in the learning process, but quietly absorb the information being presented. Consumers learn passively when they see billboards, read about products, watch TV or observe other people consuming products. Many people will see a hoarding, an online ad, or a TV commercial but will not seek information actively. The passive information stays in their mind and when they go shopping, recall may be triggered by the display and may result in impulse buying.

VLCC (Fig. 8.4) used For example, the testimonial-based 'before-after' print advertisement campaign, showing

FIG. 8.4 Logo used by VLCC

Source: Superbrands 2012

how its weight management solutions helped transform obese or overweight people to a beautiful, healthy, and fitter version of themselves. These advertisements have evolved over the years and, today, most other weight loss centres attempt to replicate the VLCC model of communication.

While passive learning is the mainstay of mass communications, companies are interested in methods for changing people from bored, passive consumers to involved, active consumers.

From Passive to Active Learning

People who are interested or motivated by their needs tend to notice advertising messages of products that fulfil their needs. Much of consumer learning takes place passively.

Krugman (1965) proposed the theory of passive learning that provides a perspective on low-involvement consumer behaviour. He noted that people watched television in a relaxed state and received information randomly without linking it to their needs or brand beliefs. They remembered the ads because of repetition so there was high recall, but it did nothing to change their brand attitudes. Watching television resulted in passive learning simply because the medium is low-involvement and does not actively involve the viewer. TV remains the most powerful means of passive learning today.

Krugman's theory of passive learning gives us some insights into consumer learning.

Consumers receive and process information at random   Consumer learning happens when they receive and process information at random through repetitive advertising.

Consumers are information catchers   People receive information passively and 'catch' bits as they are exposed to advertising.

Advertising remains a powerful tool   Since consumers receive information passively and may retain some parts of the message, advertising remains a powerful tool to aid consumer learning. As people go shopping, they remember what they saw in ads, which results in impulse or unplanned purchases.

Consumers seek acceptable levels of satisfaction   Most customers are happy when they get acceptable levels of satisfaction. They do not seek optimal levels of satisfaction and do not want to put in effort of looking and evaluating all brands to maximize satisfaction.

Consumer behaviour is not linked to lifestyle or personality   Most people buy products not as a function of self-beliefs and personality characteristics but to fulfil a certain need in a convenient manner.

Reference groups play a limited role   Reference groups play a limited role for passive consumers, since they fulfil their needs and do not look for social approval in everything.

Krugman's observations remain true for passive learners even today. However, online media has caused a major change to Krugman's theory. Consumers catch information, but they also seek it out and propagate it. Rayport (2013) writes that today, consumers are drowning in irrelevant messages delivered across media from the Web, TV, radio, print, and outdoor displays, to a proliferating array of mobile devices. Consumers fast forward TV ads, block pop-ups on their browsers, and opt out of banner ads. This has caused huge changes in the advertising strategy of companies.

Passive learning slows down product sales. The challenge is therefore to get consumers interested or involved with advertisements or products. This is easier said than done, so smart companies encourage consumer involvement.

Involvement is defined as the motivational state of an individual. This affects the person's response to a stimulus. Simply stated, it means that a person will notice something only if he is interested in it. The more involved a person is, the better will be the motivation to learn. For instance, a young girl who is conscious about her looks will notice the displayed product or advertisements of a shampoo that promises smooth, shiny hair. At the same time, a bald person will simply walk by without noticing the product even if the display is very attractive.

Laaksonen (1994) explains that involvement affects the cognitive, affective, and conative components—in low-involvement purchases, conative occurs before affective development and the opposite is true in high-involvement purchases. These components are explained in Chapter 9. Three stages of involvement, namely situational, enduring, and response are described here.

Situational involvement It focuses on the individual's concern with the purchase of a product. The purchase situation influences the buying decision, hence the importance of point-of-purchase publicity.

Enduring involvement It represents the individual's attachment to a product or advertisement. Products that cater to a person's ego state, such as cosmetics, clothes, and similar products are higher-order involvement purchases.

Response involvement It refers to a behavioural orientation, which involves information acquisition and decision processes. Expensive products such as cars and refrigerators, or products that affect a person's health and well-being would be categorized in higher-order information-seeking behaviour.

Michaelidou and Dibb (2008) write that involvement can be used to segment consumers into low-, moderate-, and high-involvement groups which can then be targeted with different promotional strategies. Involvement has been linked to a product class, a task, activity or event, a service, or advertising and promotions. It is also linked to channel choice as where people shop is linked to their level of involvement; many consumers often decide where to buy before they decide on the brand or product to purchase.

Zaichkowsky (1986) shows how antecedents and consequences of involvement are linked, covering products, advertisements, and purchase situations. Companies attempt to leverage consumer involvement with ads, product, and channels as shown in Table 8.1.

TABLE 8.1 Leveraging consumer involvement

Consumers' involvement	Application/Strategy	Examples
Involvement with advertisements	• Effectiveness of advertisements in terms of recall and inducement to purchase • Counter argument to competitor ads	• The axe effect • Raymonds: The complete man
Involvement with products	• Importance of the product to the consumer • Building perceived differences with competitors • Building preference and consumer loyalty	• Fairness creams • Brand X washes whiter than brand Y
Involvement with purchase decisions	• Channel decisions linked to why people buy • Helping in information search • Pricing decisions and brand choice • Inducing trials and testing of products	• Offers and discounts at stores • Free home delivery offered by stores • Loyalty rewards

Due to online channels, consumers' involvement, whether with advertisements, products, and purchase decisions, is getting linked. This is described in the consumer decision journey, explained in Chapter 16.

Central and Peripheral Routes

Involvement is described in the elaboration likelihood model (ELM), which states that consumer attitudes are changed by two 'routes to persuasion', namely a central route or a peripheral route (Chapter 9). It explains that learning occurs through a central route when people are interested in something, and through a peripheral route when they lack the motivation to pay close attention to products. This gives us two ways to market products. The first is by providing information to customers to satisfy their interest, whereas the second is to increase learning through the peripheral route—by encouraging trials and demonstrations so that even the disinterested consumer learns how to use products, as explained in Exhibit 8.1. Marketing to low-involvement customers is explained in Table 8.2.

TABLE 8.2 Marketing implications for high and low-involvement consumers

Marketing objective	Methods	Applications
Increase involvement for low-involvement products	• Link the product to an issue • Link the product to an activity	• Associating fairness cream with the issue of women's education • Linking a morning cup of coffee to happiness
Shift consumers from repetitive buying to cognitive learning	• Market leaders encourage habit forming • Lesser known brands encourage variety seeking	• Having a loyalty programme • Offering deals, discounts, and samples to encourage variety seeking
Segment markets by degree of involvement	Consumers are categorized as low, medium, or high-involvement	• Using different strategies for these segments

MARKETING INSIGHT
Consumer Learning at an Apple Showroom

FIG. 8.5 Apple Showroom

How do companies shift consumers from passive to active learning and get them involved with their products and brands? One way is to let them to touch and experience products and learn at their own pace. One company that does this successfully is Apple, which engineered its stores so that people would interact with products and employees (Fig. 8.5). Consumers were encouraged to learn about the products with no pressure to buy. So successful was the strategy that Apple Stores came to be ranked number one in sales per square foot in 2011 and 2012, earning twice as much as Tiffany's in 2012.

In an article in *The Wall Street Journal*, Kane and Sherr (2011) report that to learn how consumers

(Contd)

MARKETING INSIGHT (Contd)

interact in stores, the company created a prototype store in a warehouse near the Apple headquarters. The insight with which Apple worked was that the sale was less about the machine than what you could do with it. The store had to be designed so that people could experience and learn on the machines themselves.

In his book, *Punching In,* Frankel (2007) writes that traditional stores were organized by product category—that is, by how the company was organized internally, not by how a customer might actually want to buy things. So the stores were redesigned around the customer, including the human element. Frankel calls this strategy 'position, permission, probe.'

As Quelch and Jocz (2012) explain, Apple stores are now organized based on how customers use products by having 'product zones' and 'solution zones'. The 'placement of every object on the tables, from computers to power cords, to product information cards' is just the way that a customer wants them to be.

To learn more about their consumers, Apple asked a group of people, 'Tell us about the best service experience you've ever had'. Of the 18 people, 16 said it was in a hotel. The company tried to understand why this was so. It was because of the concierge desk, which was not selling anything; it was there to help. So the company decided to create a store that had the friendliness of a four seasons hotel.

Apple also decided to put a bar in its stores, but instead of dispensing alcohol, the company dispensed advice. People stopped by often to get a tutorial or advice at the Genius Bar.

The Apple Store concept debuted in 2001. The company replaced traditional paper signs with highly interactive and informative iPad smart signs. Apple placed emphasis on training its customers on how to utilize their technology. For example, each smart sign featured a 'specialist' button that allowed the customer to join the 'iQueue'.

The tables are uncluttered and the products are clean. In an Apple Store, the notebook screens are precisely angled to the same degree, using an app called 'simply angle'. This is to encourage customers to adjust the screen to their ideal viewing angle—in other words, to touch the computer. All the computers and iPads in the store are loaded with apps and software and connected to the Internet because the company wants customers to see the display and to experiment with apps and websites. Customers in an Apple Retail Store can spend all the time they want playing with the devices and using the Internet—nobody will pressure them to leave.

At an Apple Store, workers don't sell. And that encourages customers to learn at leisure. When employees become sharers of information, instead of sellers of products, customers respond. *Fortune* named Apple 'America's best retailer' in 2007.

Sources:

Apple store strategy: 'Position, permission, probe', http://counternotions.com/2007/10/21/apple-store-strategy/, last accessed on 8 April 2014.

Brownlee, John,' The Apple store's secret strategy to get you to touch (and buy) its laptops, cult of Mac, 15 June 2012, http://www.cultofmac.com/173993/the-apple-stores-secret-strategy-to-get-you-to-touch-and-buy-its-laptops/, last accessed on 8 May 2013.

Frankel, Alex, *Punching in: The Unauthorized Adventures of a Front-Line Employee*, Harper Collins Publishers, New York, 2007.

Kane, Iwatani Yukari and Ian Sherr, 'Secrets from Apple's genius bar: Full loyalty, no negativity', *The Wall Street Journal*, 15 June 2011.

La Vallee, Andrew, 'Apple's "Significant Store" Strategy', *The Wall Street Journal*, 12 November 2009, http://blogs.wsj.com/digits/2009/11/12/apples-significant-store-strategy/, last accessed on 8 May 2013.

Quelch, John and Katherine Jocz, *All Business is Local: Why Place Matters More than Ever in a Global, Virtual World*, Portfolio/Penguin, New York, 2012.

Companies are interested in using involvement to try and change passive learning to active learning. Marketing insight describes how Apple redesigned its retail stores to encourage active learning and became the most successful US retailer in 2007 as a result. The marketing objectives and how they are achieved for consumers with different levels of involvement are summarized in Table 8.2.

Online presence of consumers helps in increased involvement. Hemp (2006) writes that advertising tries to target the consumer's alter ego. People have an image of a hip, attractive, and incredibly popular person that emerges from ordinary people with the help of the advertised product. In virtual worlds, consumers adopt alter egos in public, so companies can segment, reach, and influence them directly.

Companies do not rely on passive learning alone while marketing products. As mentioned before, that is a slow process. As product life cycles have shortened, companies need faster ways of making consumers learn to adopt their products. For this, they use the principles of behavioural learning.

BEHAVIOURAL LEARNING

The behavioural learning approach was given by John Watson in the early 20th century. According to Watson, people enter the world as a 'blank slate', on which experiences are written through learning. Since people learn things from their environment and their experiences, they develop unique ways of behaving, which are the result of their unique learning experiences.

The behaviourist approach consists of two aspects that researchers can observe and measure, namely people's behaviour or responses and the environmental events that are the stimuli and reinforcement. Learning is viewed as a process of acquiring and modifying associations among stimuli and responses through a learner's direct interactions with the environment. Behaviourism is based on the belief that it is unnecessary to study internal mental processes when explaining behaviour; it is enough to know which stimuli elicit which responses, that is, people's psychology is based on observable behaviour.

This approach explains behaviour in two parts:

- The stimulus that causes a response
- The experience or learning of a person to respond to the stimulus in a particular way

According to this approach, a person learns to associate responses with some stimuli, and is hence called associative learning. It is the process by which an individual learns to associate a behaviour with a response. Behaviourism seeks to alter behaviour by arranging the environment to elicit successful changes. There are two forms of associative learning, namely classical and instrumental conditioning.

Classical Conditioning

In classical conditioning, people learn to associate two stimuli when they occur together, and eventually the response of one stimulus is transferred to another. This concept was originated by Ivan Pavlov in the late 19th century, who noticed that dogs kept in his lab would start salivating every time they saw the lab assistant who fed them, without even being shown any food—the dogs had learned to associate the assistant with food. In Pavlov's experiments with dogs, the food was accompanied by the ringing of a bell. The dogs learnt to associate the sound of the bell with food. After a while, when the bell was rung, the dogs started salivating even though no food was offered. In this experiment, the neutral stimulus was the ringing of the bell, which was accompanied by the unconditioned stimulus, food. The unconditioned response was the act of salivating.

People too learn in a similar way, through a process called conditioning two things are related. The process can be explained as follows:

If A represents food, B represents ringing of a bell, and C represents salivating, then
If A + B happens, then C results.
Therefore,
If A happens, C will result.
If B happens, C will result.
This can be represented as follows:

Unconditioned Stimulus (UCS) + Neutral Stimulus (NS) = Unconditioned Response (UCR)

After learning has occurred, the UCS or the NS happening independently will produce the UCR. This is achieved by classical conditioning.

Experiments conducted by Watson and Rayner (1920) showed that this type of conditioning works in humans as well. This paved the way for the application of classical conditioning in marketing. The question was whether companies can produce stimuli that cause urgent desires in consumers, equivalent to the salivating dogs of Pavlov's experiments.

They do so in various ways. Till and Priluck (2000) write that advertisers use classical conditioning techniques when they pair brands with pleasant images to evoke favourable responses or to attach meanings to brands. For example, Snuggles brand of fabric softener uses a teddy bear so that consumers will have positive feelings toward the brand and believe that the product makes clothing soft.

The following are some examples of classical conditioning in advertising:

- In a cold drink commercial, a consumer watching a cricket match finds that every time she opens a bottle, her team scores a boundary. The company tried to associate the opening of a bottle of cold drink with the performance of the home team
- Nescafe uses the jingle, *'ho shuru har din aise'*—start the day well—to associate the beginning of a happy day with its brand
- In the popular TV programme, *Kaun Banega Crorepati*, every time a contestant won a prize, the screen showed a Cadbury's chocolate with the message, *'khushiyon ka shubharambh'*—the commencement of happy times. The idea was to associate the start of anything special by consuming chocolates
- Bringing out the very core property of Rooh Afza as a refreshing drink, the television commercial details out the product's naturalness and emphasizes that the brand has no artificial flavours, no fat and no cholesterol—all pointers to the huge health qualities Rooh Afza possesses. Refer to a print advertisement in Figure 8.6.

FIG. 8.6 Print Advertisement: Rooh Afza

Source: Superbrands 2012

There are numerous examples of this kind, in which companies associate their brand or product with an event in the consumer's life. When that event occurs, the consumer finds himself wanting the product, similar in manner to Pavlov's salivating dogs.

The second type of conditioning is instrumental or operant conditioning, which is slightly different from classical conditioning in the sense that it also uses punishment.

Instrumental or Operant Conditioning

While response to a stimulus is learned in classical conditioning through reward, in instrumental conditioning, both positive and negative factors are used in the learning process. First described by B. F. Skinner (1904–1990), instrumental or operant conditioning uses reinforcement for a desired behaviour and punishment for an undesirable behaviour, to make consumers learn to behave in particular ways.

The actions of consumers is either reinforced or punished, which results in an altered behaviour. That is, a person learns from experience. Behaviour resulting in pleasant experiences is repeated while behaviour that causes pain is avoided. The difference is that operant conditioning uses reinforcement and punishment while classical conditioning focuses on stimulus–outcome association.

Operant conditioning works on the principle that an individual learns to seek out things that are rewarding and also learns to avoid those things that are painful or threatening. This approach was taken by Edward Thorndike (1932), who believed that all learning took place through trial and error, and actions that resulted in pleasure would be repeated while those resulting in pain would be avoided. 'When particular stimulus–response sequences are followed by pleasure, they tend to be "stamped in", responses followed by pain tend to be "stamped out",' he wrote. These ideas are used in marketing when consumers are rewarded for being loyal and whacked when they try to move away.

CB IN ACTION   Classical Conditioning

Classical conditioning—in which a positive outcome is attached to the buying of a product—is very common in marketing and advertising. Analyse advertisements (available on YouTube) and promotional efforts by companies (available in stores) to show how the process is used. Fill in the following table to identify the stimulus and response. The first one is done for you.

You may add more brands to this table.

Brand/Company	Unconditioned stimulus	Neutral stimulus	Unconditioned response
Tanishq	Formal or semi-formal occasion	Desire to look good	Desire to wear or buy jewellery
Cafe Coffee Day			
Facebook			
Cadbury			
Dove			
Wills Lifestyle			
Archies			

There are many applications of cognitive associative learning in marketing. One of the applications is learning through repetition or reinforcement; managers use the principles of consumer learning when they use repetition of advertisements, or reinforcement of consumption ideas.

Skinner defined a reinforcer as an experience that raises the frequency of a response associated with it. East, et al. (2008) explain that reinforcers may be rewards or reduction in cost, while punishers may be the withdrawal of the reward or charging of a higher price. This is called reinforcement theory of motivation and is based on 'law of effect', which simply means that behaviour with positive consequences will be repeated, while behaviour with negative consequences will be avoided. These two behaviours are positive and negative reinforcement.

Positive reinforcement A positive reinforcement is a stimulus that strengthens the desired consumer response and stimulates occurrence of a behaviour. An application of positive reinforcement is to reward consumers for buying a product or service, which reinforces the consumption. There are many examples of this type of operant conditioning.

- Manufacturers offer discount coupons for a product. Even when the discount is stopped, consumers will continue to buy the product, because they become conditioned to buying it.
- Car manufacturers send a letter of congratulations and offer services such as extended warranty and free pick-up of the vehicle so that customers feel happy about choosing that particular brand. Brand communities are also established for this purpose.
- Airlines offer free upgrades to frequent flyers or lounge facilities which serve as a positive reinforcer for the consumer who will continue to be loyal to the airline. Reward points offered by a host of firms are an instrument of positive reinforcement.

Negative reinforcement Negative reinforcement induces a desired reaction by removing an adverse stimulus. For instance, a medicine to remove headache or a cream to remove a skin condition uses negative reinforcement. It must be remembered that negative reinforcement is not the same as punishment. Lantos (2010) explains that whereas positive and negative reinforcement increase the probability of a response, either by offering something good or by removing something undesirable, punishment *decrease*s the probability of an undesirable response and is therefore avoided.

Punishment Punishment implies removing positive consequences so as to lower the probability of repeating undesirable behaviour in future. In other words, punishment means applying undesirable consequences for showing undesirable behaviour.

In *positive punishment*, a negative stimulus is administered for bad behaviour. For example, if you do not tip the waiter, you will not get good service. Some examples of punishing actions of companies are as follows:

- Loyalty schemes that reward customers for repeat business, but when customers move away, they lose the benefits of such schemes and accumulated points
- Insurance companies that punish customers by levying stiff charges if customers discontinue their policies
- Banks levying charges if monthly or quarterly balance falls below a certain level, so that consumers learn to maintain a balance

In *negative punishment*, a reward is removed as a result of undesirable behaviour. There are many applications of this in marketing such as the following:

- Some deals are time bound and a discount is withdrawn after a given period
- A free bag is denied if a customer does not order three perfumes at one time as part of an offer
- Advertisements that suggest punishment, such as embarrassment and ridicule, if the consumer does not purchase a particular brand. Deodorant manufacturers, for instance, often use social ridicule to sell their products.
- Mobile service providers charging higher call rates during peak hours. The idea is to divert traffic to off-peak hours by using a system of reward and punishment.
- Telemarketers calling at inconvenient times or using pressure tactics to sell products or services, with the hope that people will buy to avoid being pestered by sales people.
- The threat to void a warranty if the consumer does not sign up for an annual maintenance contract or spares bought directly from the company

Companies use positive and negative reinforcement to train customers to act in ways that are beneficial for them. A large part of our learning, however, happens while observing others. We copy what we see subconsciously. This is explained in observational or vicarious learning.

Observational or Vicarious Learning

When people imagine themselves doing something which someone else is doing, they are acting vicariously. The idea of vicarious learning was given by Albert Bandura (1986), who stated that people generally put themselves in the place of popular heroes or their friends and other influencers and pretend to be like them. It is an observational learning that occurs as a result of observing and copying others. There are four effects of vicarious learning.

Modelling effect People learn to duplicate consumption behaviour by modelling themselves on others. They learn new behaviour as a result of observing a model (see Fig. 8.7). Advertisers frequently use images of attractive models, celebrities, peer groups, groups to which one aspires to, and so on. People mentally act out the behaviour of the models and take to consuming the products advertised.

FIG. 8.7 Customers admiring a shop display—Most consumer learning happens through observation

Eliciting effect This occurs when a previously learned behaviour happens more frequently as a result of observing a model. Pear (2001) explains that the sound of creaking of a floor will generate fear in someone who has just watched a horror movie. Advertisers use this by placing their ads in the immediate context of other events. For example, when crime is reported frequently in a city, manufacturers of security systems increase their promotions in the hope of eliciting a favourable response from city residents.

Inhibitory effect The inhibitory effect refers to the strengthening of a behaviour as a result of observing a model being punished for not engaging in that behaviour. This is used in

MARKETING INSIGHT

Dove Soap and Consumer Learning

Traditional marketing is based on cognitive principles, that is, consumers must be made to learn about new products by using and experiencing them. Companies thus have to initiate one of the following in the customers:

- Communicating the product or service benefits effectively through the advertising and the selling proposition
- Creating a context within which the product or service is to be used
- Positioning the brand or product to emphasize how it is different from the competition, since the more distinct it is, the more will consumers feel tempted to buy

The aforementioned principles were employed in launching the Dove brand. Unilever launched Dove soap in India in 1993. It was priced at ₹30, which was about three times as expensive as other soaps at that time. For the price-conscious Indian consumer, this was a huge cost difference. To show that the product was indeed different enough to command a high price, the consumers had to be convinced to try it and learn how different it was from other soaps.

The company positioned the brand as distinct from the soap category, claiming that 'Dove is not a soap'. The claim was that it consisted of moisturizer rather than the harsh chemicals used in other soaps. The company launched a campaign which showed women who had used the brand being complimented for their beauty and soft skin. It did not use supermodels to endorse the brand but real women who used the product to give testimonials of their experience with the brand. The company identified some 50 women from upper-middle class households and handed them trial packs of Dove soap. After trying out the brand, their reactions were recorded and the most spontaneous responses were used in ads. The ads had an amateurish look as they captured women speaking naturally, seemingly without a script. What was the secret of their glowing skin? Was it love? The lady then beamed into the camera, saying, 'It's not love, it's Dove'. This was enough to send consumers scurrying to the market to try out the brand, which encouraged consumer learning.

The brand was the opposite of Lux, which was marketed as the beauty soap of film stars. In contrast, Dove advertisements showed beauty in ordinary people and the testimonials were critical for the success of the brand. The 'Dove campaign for real beauty' in fact, featured real women—wrinkles and all—in its ads. The idea was that ordinary people were beautiful, helped no doubt by Dove. Soon the gentle effect that Dove had on skin was being recommended for babies as well. The honesty in Dove testimonials struck a chord with its audience.

Dove launched its shampoo range in 2007 with a similar campaign that had a focus on consumer learning, highlighting their experience with the product. Camera crews in Mumbai, Delhi, and Bangalore asked women questions on hair care and recorded their responses. The video footage was uploaded on popular portals. This convinced consumers to try out the product.

Today Dove is a major brand for HUL. The brand has been extended to hair care products, body washes, creams, and lotions. The brand has a cult following, with 18,915,268 likes on its Facebook page as on October 2013. Consumers who use Dove display a fierce brand loyalty. From sales of ₹100 crore in 2007, it became a ₹1000 crore brand in 2012. It is the fastest growing brand for HUL, growing ten times in just over five years. It is also profitable as it is pushing consumers to try premium brands.

Can you think of other brands that have been built on consumer experience and learning? How were the consumers made to try out the brand to learn about it?

Sources:
Dove Facebook page: https://www.facebook.com/DoveIndia?brand_redir=1
Gordon, Ian, 'The marketer's challenge: How to teach customers new behaviours', http://www.iveybusinessjournal.com/topics/the-organization/the-marketers-challenge-how-to-teach-customers-new-behaviours#.UUEuMtZIP9Y, last accessed on 8 April 2014
HUL website: http://www.hul.co.in/brands-in-action/detail/Dove/303749
Malviya, Sagar, 'Hindustan Unilever's Rs 1,000 crore club swells; Dove, Pond's, Clinic Plus join in FY13', *The Economic Times*, 5 June 2013.
Sangameshwaran, Prasad, 'The secret of Dove's success', *The Economic Times*, 7 October 2009.

advertising messages in a number of ways. For instance, friends are shown ridiculing a person for not consuming or wearing a product.

Disinhibitory effect A disinhibitory effect occurs when one becomes lax in his or her belief systems as a result of observing others. That is, it occurs when a person who has previously avoided a certain behaviour engages in it after seeing a model perform the behaviour without any negative consequences. For instance, a girl who has never used cosmetics as a result of strict upbringing takes to using those products after seeing other girls using cosmetics without any negative consequence. The effect is also seen online, for instance, people who are hesitant to share their personal information online are encouraged to do so after seeing that their friends are doing it without any harm. Companies encourage trials of the product with the hope that consumers become disinhibited after using the product a few times.

Observational learning is powerful. Lindstrom (2008) explains that nearly 90 per cent of our purchase decisions take place at the unconscious level. He explains that 'mirror neurons' in the brain shed new light on consumer behaviour—for instance, why a smile from a salesperson can compel us to spend more money.

Mirror neurons help us adopt behaviour as the action is being performed by someone else. Explained as 'monkey see, monkey do' behaviour, it explains why people unwittingly imitate others' behaviour.

Lindstrom relates how mirror neurons work in marketing. One day in 2004, Steve Jobs (co-founder of Apple) was walking down Madison Avenue and noticed that everywhere people were sporting the white, signature earphones of the recently launched iPod. They were dangling from people's ears, hanging out of backpacks, and peeking out of pockets and purses. Jobs is quoted as saying, 'Oh, my God, it's starting to happen'. When consumers see an unusual product, their mirror neurons are triggered and they want to have that same cool-looking accessory too. That is how fashion spreads.

Indeed, many products and brands are able to project a cool image that strikes a chord with customers. As more and more people buy it, others are influenced just by watching others. What consumers notice is a matter of how involved they are, as we saw in the previous section. Cognitive learning theory provides further insights into how people process information and take decisions. This theory is explained in the next section.

COGNITIVE LEARNING—INFORMATION PROCESSING

While conditioning and observational learning explain how people learn to consume products as they get rewarded, it does not explain another aspect of consumer learning: that people are thinking beings and look for solutions in their everyday life. This is explained by the cognitive theory of learning. This theory explains human behaviour by trying to understand internal thought processes. It assumes that humans are logical beings and make consumption choices based on their thinking and reasoning, and are not merely dogs, which can be trained to salivate when they see desirable objects. Drawing a parallel to computers, the internal thought process is called information processing.

Cognitive learning rejects behaviourism as being too simple and based on cause and effect. Instead, it states that people learn by using their reason, intuition, and perception. These are in turn influenced by factors such as culture, upbringing, education, and motivation, which all form parts of cognition. People learn to like or dislike certain things through the following:

Response consequences By thinking about consequences of a certain action, people make their decisions.

Observation People learn from observation as it enables them to evaluate their decisions rather than make mistakes themselves. That is why peer influence and celebrity endorsements are strong influencers of consumption behaviour.

Symbolism People also learn by forming imaginary pictures and mentally acting out consumption and usage of certain products without actually consuming them.

The aforementioned factors contribute to learning by creating a learning loop that depends on storing experiences in memory. The response consequences exist in long-term memory so that consumers know how to obtain positive messages. Similarly, observation and symbols are also stored deep inside a person's brain. All this information is processed while buying and consuming. This is how the information-processing model explains the learning process.

Cognitive learning is explained by using the analogy of computers, that is, by likening the brain to an information-processing unit. Cognitive psychology assumes that the human mind receives information, stores and retains it, and retrieves it as and when required, just in the way that a computer functions.

RESEARCH INSIGHT
Learning to Consume Green Products

Concerns about environment destruction are on the rise all over the world, including India. All types of organizations are conducting green campaigns. School children are taught to be environmentally aware. Consumers are exhorted to turn greener. It is hardly surprising then that people are becoming more aware of the problems facing mankind and want to do their bit to reduce the burden on the planet. Indeed, many consumers the world over claim that they want to buy ecologically friendly products. However, when it comes to making a choice, they often choose the cheapest, most environment unfriendly product. Few people actually buy the more expensive green alternatives.

Bonini and Oppenheim (2008) describe how companies can do a lot more to help consumers turn green. They describe five barriers to learning to consume green products and how they can be overcome.

Lack of awareness While consumers know about climate change and want to do something about it, they do not know how to act on their greener impulses. Consumers are also confused about buying green products—attempts to label green products have been quite meaningless.

Negative perceptions Consumers have negative perceptions about green products. While some green products such as Toyota's Prius automobile that is available in the US and the globally-used compact fluorescent light bulbs (CFL)—have been successful, many environmentally friendly products perform worse than conventional goods. The Mahindra Reva electric car, for instance, never really picked up in India.

Distrust Consumers doubt the greenness of green products. Many companies resort to 'greenwashing', the act of misleading consumers and using green marketing deceptively to promote the perception that an organization's products are environmentally friendly. The Greenwashing Report (2010) mentions seven sins, such as making vague environmental claims on products, false labelling, and lack of certification.

(Contd)

RESEARCH INSIGHT (Contd)

High prices Green products are often more expensive, which becomes the biggest barrier to buying such products. For many green products, it takes years to recoup the investment made on them. For example, solar energy has failed to take off in India because consumers perceive its benefits to be small in the long term compared to the cost.

Low availability The final hurdle is that consumers can't find green alternatives easily. Consumers cannot use biofuel as it is not available. Supermarkets do not stock green products, since they are considered niche.

Knowing these barriers is only half the battle won. The next step is to close the gap between green thoughts and green acts. Can consumers be taught to act more responsibly towards the environment? Companies have to examine how people in different market segments make their purchasing decisions. They must break down these barriers for consumers to change their behaviour.

Educate consumers Companies have to be educators, not salespeople, and communicate to consumers as to how environmental protection can be increased by product choices. For instance, the power-saving guide for electrical appliances educates consumers about energy-efficient products which can help them reduce energy use, save money, and protect the environment.

Build better products Green products must be better than their conventional alternatives. Companies have to offer products that are indeed different from existing products. GE managed to motivate customers to switch to CFLs even though they were more expensive, by showing that they consumed less electricity and launched a 'change alight, change the world' campaign, increasing availability of the products. This increased awareness of CFLs and resulted consumers switching from bulbs to CFLs.

Another great success has been the Toyota Prius. The Prius was redesigned to meet performance and style preferences of consumers. The car was visibly different from other cars and became a style statement. It was promoted as 'quick, roomy, and economical' and consumers could see and feel the difference.

Be honest Many companies have resorted to 'greenwashing'. This has eroded public trust. To rebuild it, companies must inform the public about their true environmental impact, as well as about their attempts to reduce that impact. They must identify and address specific concerns about their products. Only then will consumers believe the company's environmental claims.

Offer more When consumers can track their savings from using a product, they are more willing to try new green products. Consumers, for instance, can track the electricity units consumed through the energy guide labelling. Such labels show the product's annual energy use in watts which consumers can compare with other products. Similarly, the Prius is successful because it has a unique and contemporary style, its dashboard communicates fuel consumption and energy efficiency, thereby broadcasting the car's environmental benefits.

Bring products to the people Many of today's green products are not widely available. Companies have to tie up with major retailers to make their products available. The government has to play a role in educating customers and helping them to switch to environment friendly products.

Green products and services are only a niche market today, but they are poised for strong growth. In general, many consumers are willing to pay a premium for green products. Green products can also improve companies' reputations and increase the value of brands. Further, companies can stay ahead of government regulations and standards for environmental compliance that are being introduced for many products.

How can companies make consumers learn to switch to environment friendly alternatives? Take a look at such products in the market and assess whether they address consumer needs.

Sources:
'Addressing consumer concerns about climate change', *McKinsey Quarterly,* March 2008, http://www.mckinsey.com/insights, last accessed on 8 October 2013.

Bonini, Sheila and Jeremy Oppenheim, 'Cultivating the green consumer', *Stanford Social Innovation Review*, 2008, http://www.ssireview.org/articles/entry/cultivating_the_green_consumer/last accessed on 9 April 2014.

'How companies think about climate change: A McKinsey global survey', The *McKinsey Quarterly,* December 2007.

http://sinsofgreenwashing.org/findings/the-seven-sins/index.html, last accessed on 9 April 2014.

Memory Stages

A simple model of cognitive learning is shown in Fig. 8.8. The brain receives a stimulus in the form of marketing communication that immediately impacts the senses. A picture, jingle, or a clip catches the attention of a person and this goes into sensory memory, also called a sensory store. This may be forgotten, or, with repetition or interest, may also be cached in the short-term or long-term memory stores. The brain preserves information in the short-term store first. Then, as the advertiser conditions the brain by repeating and rewarding, and by placing the information in context with previously stored information, called elaboration and coding, the information gets stored in the long-term memory.

Marketing companies use this theory and try to influence both short-term and long-term memories. The company hopes that consumers can remember information about its brand by repeat advertising and showing the same colour and graphics in various media. These are supplemented by delivering experiences and customer delight so that the information gets a longer lease of life in the brain. Companies also categorize information so that the brain stores the information along with similar experiences. For instance, an experience of a restaurant must be placed in context with experiences of other restaurants.

Using the analogy of a computer, the short-term memory may be referred to as random-access memory (RAM) that is wiped out when the computer is switched off, whereas the long-term memory may be referred to as read-only memory (ROM), which stays in the brain for a long time. Information is stored in sensory, short-term or long-term stores.

Sensory Store

The brain receives stimuli through the five senses. The stimuli create an immediate impact on the mind. Sensory memory is short-duration memory that helps individuals to remember the impact. It can be likened to watching a trail of light produced by a firecracker—when the light is fast enough, the brain can identify its trail as a continuous image. Blinking lights, for instance, create impressions of circles and other patterns. This is called the 'light trail' the fleeting image left in the mind. This effect is also called iconic memory. The challenge for marketing is to ensure that the initial impact of an advertising message is remembered by a person in a similar way.

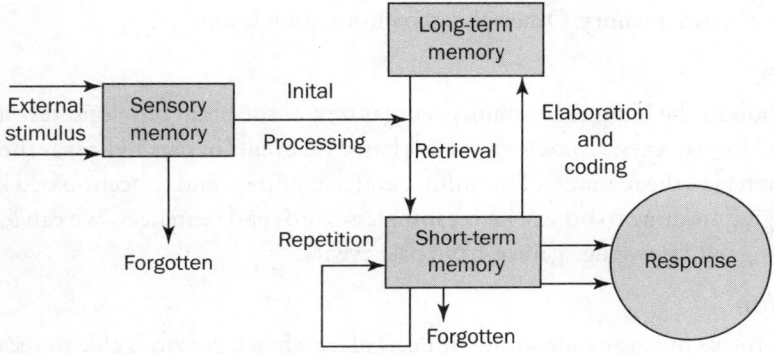

FIG. 8.8 Model of cognitive learning

TABLE 8.3 Impacting consumer memories

Memory stage	Actions taken by advertisers
Stimulus stage	• Gaining the consumer's attention • Catchy advertisements, jingles, and visuals
Short-term memory	• Repeat advertisements and use reminder techniques • Use the same graphics in print media, TV, and visual merchandising
Long-term memory	• Use the same advertising theme over time • Reward consumers by delighting them • Deliver experiences through BTL techniques • Placing information in the context of the consumer's previous experiences with other brands

Short-term store When people are able to remember things for a very short period, it is called short-term memory store. When we study something, only to be forgotten the next day, the information merely goes in the short-term store. In advertising, the task is to ensure people remember the messages, not just for a short while, but for a longer duration.

Long-term store When people are able to remember information over long periods of time, it means that the information is stored in their long-term memory store. Long-term positive memories result in customer loyalty.

The different memory stages and the actions taken by advertisers are summed up in Table 8.3. It shows how companies attempt to impact each memory stage in a consumer's mind.

It is thus important to know how people remember things or how memory works. There are three stages of memory, namely storage, retention, and retrieval.

Storage, Retention, and Retrieval

The brain stores information in neural networks. Brain research has shown that memories are formed by patterns of neural interconnections that are changing continuously. As the brain receives nerve messages from the eyes, ears, tongue, and skin, the stimulus is held for a fraction of a second in the sensory memory. It has been observed that a person must pay attention to the stimulus for about eight uninterrupted seconds if the information has to be encoded and stored in the short-term memory. Otherwise, the information is lost.

Storage
Information in the brain is constantly reorganized as the brain develops new links. Information is retained in two ways. *Episodic memory* is based on events or experiences as they occur. *Semantic memory* refers to the memory of meanings, understandings, and concept-based knowledge, which helps us give meaning to otherwise meaningless words and sentences. We can learn new concepts by applying our knowledge gained from past events.

Retention
It is the process of storing memories. It takes place when a person is able to recall, recognize, and relearn on the basis of stored memories.

Recall When information can be accessed without being cued, it is called *recall*. A retrieval cue is a signal that results in people remembering something stored in long-term memory. Recollection involves reconstructing memory from bits of information, using logical structures, partial memories, narratives, or clues. When people remember information on partial memories, it is recollection.

Recognize The purpose of recall is to *recognize* stimuli and place them in context. In marketing, it means that the customer recognizes that a particular visual or graphic is of a particular brand.

Relearn When information is reinforced from something that has been previously learned, it is called *relearning*.

Retrieval

The calling back of stored information in response to some cue for use in a process or activity is called retrieval. Recall and recognition are two ways in which information is *retrieved* from long-term memory.

Companies use an understanding of retrieval systems to place their messages in context of consumers' experiences so that they are able to remember the brands. Some of the techniques used are follows:

Sight and sound The sight and sounds of fresh coffee brewing as you go shopping reminds you of your need to have coffee

Combos Traditionally, movies have been associated with popcorn. Cinema theatres offer popcorn combos with tickets to make people relive the charm of going to the movies

Imitate real-life situation Companies frequently use 'slice of life' advertising which mimics a real-life situation. This helps consumers to apply the situation to their own lives making it relevant for them.

Cognitive Processes

Retention, retrieval, and recall are aided by cognitive processes such as rehearsal, encoding, visual memory, language processing, and grouping and chunking. All these help us understand how the mind really remembers.

Rehearsal The process by which people recall memories of stimuli and repeat them is called rehearsal. This happens when people think and talk about what they have seen and heard in advertisements. Rehearsal results in repetition or recycling of information in short-term memory to keep it active. It enables stimuli to be transferred to long-term memory. Companies try to ensure that consumers repeat the information they have seen in ads. When people talk about an ad, repeat its punch-line or hum the jingle, they are rehearsing, which helps transfer the information to the long-term memory store of the brain.

Encoding Encoding is the process concerned with getting information into memory—it is a method by which people remember things. They tend to associate a word or visual image with an object. Brands try to achieve this by using similar packaging or visuals as followed by the rest of the industry so that people place the products within the category. For instance, that all brands of detergent powders come in similar packages.

Visual memory Visual memory refers to our ability to remember what we have seen. We are able remember and recall objects, places, animals, or people in our minds. Advertisers try to manipulate our buying habits with sophisticated images. Companies spend millions each year on billboards, packaging, magazine ads, and television commercials. The images powerfully influence our behaviour. Attractive models and catchy lines, sometimes even shocking images, are used so that a person thinks about them and commits them to long-term memory. Hoffman (1998) explains that vision is not merely a matter of passive perception, but an intelligent process of active construction. The mind constructs its version of what it sees, which Hoffman terms as 'visual intelligence'. Our visual system intelligently constructs useful visual worlds based on images unconsciously. Visual images play an important role in persuasion; for example, in food products, it is said that the 'first taste is almost always with the eye'. Many products are sold on the basis of visual images and packaging rather than their intrinsic worth.

Language processing Human beings are able to communicate with each other through words. The way that words are stored in memory, used, and integrated with other words for meaningful communication, is called language processing. Advertisers try to use short phrases, as for instance '2-minute noodles', which are remembered and stick to brands. Such phrases increase the possibility of communication between consumers through word of mouth.

Grouping and chunking The process of organizing or grouping separate pieces of information together is called chunking. When information is grouped and placed in chunks, we can remember it easier. People tend to remember chunks of information better as compared to separate bits. The taste and experience of a chocolate brand, for instance, will be chunked together by the consumer and grouped with experiences of other brands of chocolates.

Cognitive Learning and Marketing Models

Cognitive learning is used in many marketing models. These models are described in Chapter 4. The assumption is that consumers look for solutions to their needs and take decisions through consumer learning. Most models explain consumer decision-making as a progression through different stages, from awareness, to evaluation, to buying. The consumer moves from awareness stage to gathering information, then tries out products and selects the best one.

Consumer Decision Models
Consumers make decisions moving from cognitive stages of awareness, acquiring knowledge, evaluating different products, making the purchase decision, post-purchase experience, and evaluation.

Some of these models are the AIDA Model, tri-component model, and innovation adoption model.

AIDA model The AIDA is used in promotion (Fig. 8.9). It states that consumers move from awareness to action as they look for products that suit their needs. Advertisers use this model the world over and try to create advertisements that

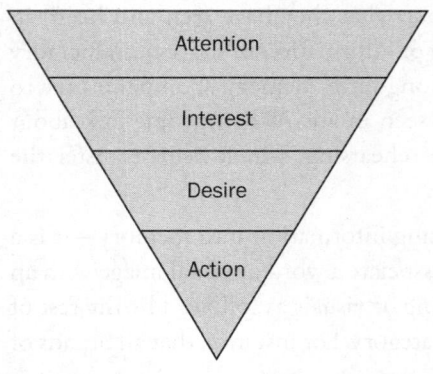

FIG. 8.9 Model of cognitive learning

attract, and then interest the consumer enough to read it, create a desire, and finally convince, so that it leads to a sale.

Tri-component model Described in detail in Chapter 9, it says that attitudes consist of three major components, namely cognitive, affective, and conative. The first component consists of a person's cognitions, that is, the knowledge and perceptions of the brands. The affective component is made up of the consumer's emotions or feelings about a particular product or brand. Conation, the final component of this model, is the actual behaviour itself. This component reflects the consumer's intention to buy.

Innovation adoption model The innovation adoption model describes five stages: awareness, interest, evaluation, trial, and adoption. The innovation decision model describes four stages, namely knowledge, persuasion, decision, and confirmation. The model is explained in detail in Chapter 12.

The cognitive learning theory is applicable for high-involvement purchases and consumers, who seek information actively and try to get the best alternatives.

MARKETING IMPLICATIONS OF BEHAVIOURAL LEARNING

Marketing companies use learning theories in many ways. Look closely at advertisements, and we see how subtly companies make us learn to buy and consume products. Very often, we see reinforcement and offers of rewards for purchase so that they strengthen the association between stimulus and response. Principles of reinforcement are applied in sales promotions and discounts. The reinforcement techniques used by marketing companies to influence behaviour are shaping, habits, repetition, and avoidance of advertising wear-out at the same time.

Shaping

Shaping is the process by which an existing response is gradually changed across successive trials towards a desired target behaviour by rewarding exact segments of behaviour. It implies gradual shifting of consumer behaviour through learning. For instance, a company may want customers to shift to more expensive models or those that have better margins, and this is achieved through shaping.

Examples of shaping are computers, cars, and mobile phones—we gradually seek the more expensive or sophisticated variety as we learn how to operate them. Manufacturers shape behaviour by introducing base models initially and then slowly encourage the consumer to go up the value chain. For instance, the Maruti 800 and the Zen models, once very popular in India, were discontinued by the company, Maruti Suzuki, as customers learnt to fancy more expensive models of cars. Similarly, people were happy to use simple cellphones, but now they want the latest smartphones. These are shaping techniques in action.

Habits

The outcome of reinforcement learning is that consumers should be locked into the habit of purchasing particular brands. Habit is defined as regularly exhibiting the same behaviour, sometimes even without thinking. Classical conditioning induces habits by using positive reinforcement—in the way that animals can be taught to press a lever and be rewarded with food. Soon this behaviour becomes a habit. Habits restrict experimentation and result in consumer loyalty. The challenge before marketing companies is to create strong habits, so that consumers ignore advertisements of rivals and do not even notice their discounts or offers. New brands, on the other hand, must try to disrupt habits and force consumers to try out the new offerings.

Repetition

Associative learning happens when people associate a stimulus with a behaviour. This requires constant repetition. The most common example is repeat ads. Announcement of discount sales by stores is repeated often; it is written in large letters all across the store and near individual items as well, making sure people get the message. Many advertisements do follow a similar method and famous brands such as Pears and Tide have reinforced the same idea over the years. Brand names and symbols have become household names because of constant repetition. For example, a symbol like the Nike 'swoosh' has become instantly recognizable and attached with meaning and the brand, because it has been repeatedly associated with certain images and messages over the years. Constant reinforcement is used in advertising. Positive reinforcement not only helps in learning, but also in developing a favourable image in the minds of customers. Advertising intended to reassure purchasers or to tell them that they have done the right thing in buying the particular product is called reinforcement advertising. For example, companies send letters of congratulations listing the benefits of the product to their customers, and explain how to get the best results from the product. The purpose of reinforcement advertising is to support consumer learning and make the link between stimulus and response stronger. The types of advertising that aid in reinforcement are described in the Marketing Insight that follows.

Consumers begin to recognize the brand and associate it with their lifestyles. In many cases, one finds that people start attaching the brand name to generic products—for instance, washing powders of all brands are referred to as 'Surf' by many customers of the older generation, after a very popular brand. At the same time, advertisers have to be careful that customers do not become so habituated to their messages that they stop noticing them. Companies have to guard against advertising wear-out, extinction and forgetting, stimulus generalization, and mindless line extensions.

Dangers of Repetition

Companies must know when to change their themes or stop their attempts to educate customers. People switch off if messages are repeated often. This section describes the dangers of 'over-learning' or exposing customers to the same learning experiences for a long period of time.

Advertising Wear-out

Overexposure to an advertisement results in *advertising wear-out*. When the same messages are repeated too long and too often, customers get used to them and they stop responding. That is why message execution, package design, logo, and other aspects of communications are changed from time to time. Companies have to determine the optimal level of exposure to a message for optimal results. This implies that overexposure to an advertisement may either cause people to stop noticing a message because it is seen as a permanent fixture, or they become bored with it and develop negative feelings towards the brand.

MARKETING INSIGHT
Advertising and Reinforcement

Skinner showed that reinforcement was the key to learning. The link between stimulus and response is established firmly only by repeating the process. Wright (2006) shows how this principle is used in advertising.

Burst advertising or flighting This is the practice of using heavy advertising in a short period of time, ensuring that people see the message. It is repeated after a gap, like a burst. Such advertising uses media concentration to reinforce the message and to remind consumers. It is usually used in chunks of four to six weeks, with the main focus being on achieving targets in a short period of time. Burst advertising is marked by a large audience and a small timeline.

Drip advertising Drip advertising is using an advertising campaign or the same theme a little at a time but stretched over a longer period. The idea is that constant and slow repetition will help consumers to remember the product and serve as reminder advertising. Established brands use drip advertising to reinforce their presence which serves as trigger during the purchase process.

Pulsating advertising It is used all round the year like a continuous pulse. Companies use low-intensity advertising during the off-season and increase the frequency during peak selling periods. Such advertising works by remaining in the consumers' memory for long periods.

Saturation advertising A strategy for achieving maximum impact by using various media and increased repetition to target consumers. It is referred to as *carpet bombing*, it ensures that everyone in the target audience gets exposed to the advertisement multiple times. It is an expensive method but achieves results in a short time.

Roadblock advertising An advertising method in which a commercial is broadcast simultaneously on several radio stations and/or television channels. The advertiser buys up all the advertising on a channel for a given period like a full day (vertical roadblock), or across a band of channels at a particular time, say an hour (horizontal roadblock), thus preventing any other advertiser from being present at those times. This ensures that viewers will see the ad no matter which channel they are watching.

Impact advertising Impact advertising is a form of advertising that has a lasting psychological effect on the audience. It is measured by the number of people who remember the advertisement. This is achieved by giving the audience something of value, in the form of entertainment or information that creates a positive association with the brand. The Airtel advertisement featuring friends or the Godrej advertisement with Aamir Khan dressed as a woman, are examples of advertisements that create tremendous impact.

Advertising wear-out This occurs when people fail to respond to the advertising stimulus. The same idea repeated over a long time, for instance, may fail to get audience attention or reaction.

Wear-out results in decreased effectiveness of advertising over a period of time. There are two types of wear-out. *Repetition wear-out* results from repeated exposure to the ad and *copy wear-out* results from the passage of time. Ads that try to overcome wear-out attempt to restore the original message and to get consumers interested again.

The number of exposures after which advertising wear-out happens is not known. Companies can figure it out when sales become stagnant. The relationship between advertising exposure and response displays an inverted U-shaped pattern, since initially the advertisement gets people's attention, then it peaks and declines quickly. Examples of advertising wear-out are seen in public service ads exhorting people to stop smoking or to save the environment. Repeated several times without reinforcement, such ads are mentally switched off by viewers whenever they appear. Such ads have failed to change behaviour of people because of advertising wear-out. Once wear-out happens, there is a further danger of extinction and forgetting.

Extinction and Forgetting

Extinction occurs when a previously established link between stimulus and response is broken, that is, when the effects of prior conditioning are reduced and finally disappear. It implies absence of reinforcements for purchase.

For example, in the case of a customer who used to get a positive outcome from a brand but has stopped getting it, the link between stimulus and response is broken. Extinction is different from forgetting because customers 'unlearn' the positive experience they used to have.

Brand ads repeated over a long period of time have the same effect. That is why companies change their marketing communications from time to time. Even when the selling proposition remains the same, advertisers change the visuals or the execution to attract their attention.

Another danger faced by companies is that of *stimulus generalization*, when consumers start mistaking a product with similar packaging for that of a popular brand.

Stimulus Generalization

When people transfer a response learned from one stimulus to a similar stimulus, it is called stimulus generalization. An example of this phenomenon is that if a child has been conditioned to fear a stuffed white rabbit, it will exhibit fear of objects similar to the toy, such as a stuffed white rat. John B. Watson and Rosalie Rayner (1920) conducted experiments that showed that a little boy, who was conditioned to fear a white rat, showed fear in response to similar stimuli including a dog, a rabbit, a fur coat, a white Santa Claus beard, and even Watson's own hair.

That is to say, people respond to things that look similar. Kapferer (2008) writes that imitation brands can be confused for the leading brand particularly when viewing time is brief. He gives four different types of brands.

Own brand   The own brand or private label is a distributor's brand that has its own name and does not generally refer to the company's name (see chapter-end case study).

Counter brand   Counter brand is created to divert clientele from a particular big brand, by slavishly imitating all its distinctive traits. The counter brand, with packaging similar in all respects, is placed next to the national brand on the shelf. Though the brand name is different, customers compare the products and often buy the counter brand as it offers matching quality at a lower price.

Positioning brand   This brand positions itself in the premium segment. A brand similar to, but not imitating the leading brand, piggybacks on the popularity of the main brand.

Counterfeit brands   Counterfeit or knock-off products are unauthorized products claiming to be well-known brands. They have the same brand names and packaging as the main brand with or without minor modifications. Customers are often fooled into buying these products assuming that they have the genuine product when in fact, they have a counterfeit product. The dangers of counterfeit products are discussed later in the chapter.

Marketing companies use stimulus generalization employing various methods such as brand and product line extensions, family branding, and licensing.

Product Line Extensions

An application of stimulus generalization is product line extension, in which a manufacturer extends use of an established brand name for a new item in the same product category. The idea is that a successful brand will evoke the same favourable response from consumers when it is applied to a variety of products. So a brand like Dove markets soap, shampoo, hair oil, and other products under the same umbrella brand. Please see Exhibit 8.2.

This strategy helps the company reduce the expenses of establishing a new brand name, and lowers the risk of launching new products, as customers are familiar with the brand name. Through stimulus generalization, they assume that the new variants will have the same quality as the existing brand. It is also a way to maintain customer loyalty. By launching products at different price points with an established brand name, customers will stick to the brand instead of buying a competitor's brand.

EXHIBIT 8.2 Good Knight's Line Extensions

GoodKnight is the country's dominant household insecticide brand and the world's largest selling electronic mosquito repellent. Available in all formats—coils, vaporisers, sprays, mats and personal application cream—GoodKnight has a market share of 30%.

The GoodKnight brand was launched by Transelektra Domestic Products Limited (TDPL) in 1984 when it introduced mats containing Allethrin, an active compound that was effective in combating the mosquito menace.

Godrej Hi Care took over TDPL in August 1994. A year later the new company had acquired and merged its other mosquito repellent brands like Jet and Banish. A strategic alliance with Sara Lee, a Fortune 500 consumer product giant, followed.

GoodKnight's strategy worked wonderfully till competition launched a coil containing Allethrin, the same active compound, as GoodKnight. With parity having been achieved and liquid vaporisers giving competition an edge, GoodKnight hit back by launching its own vaporiser. It deviated from competition by positioning it for total protection rather than just a mosquito repellent. This immediately struck the right cord and GoodKnight soon recaptured lost ground.

With the launch of its red coil variant in 1999, GoodKnight started consolidating its position. The immediate advantage the red coil offered was greater longevity – it burnt ten hours against the eight

FIG. 8.10 Product line—GoodKnight

Courtesy: Superbrands

competitors offered. Four years later, it introduced a twelve-hour coil and in the process became the manufacturer of the world's longest lasting coil. GoodKnight ensured that complacency didn't set in by recasting its role in the consumer's life. Figure 8.10 shows product line of GoodKnight.

GoodKnight was no longer just a relief from mosquitoes, it took on the mantle of a protector.

Source: Superbrands 2012

TABLE 8.4 Lure and pitfalls of line extensions

Lure of line extensions	Pitfalls of line proliferation
Line extension is seen as a low-cost, low-risk way of customer segmentation, to serve various market segments.	The line may expand to the point of over-segmentation, confusing customers and salespeople alike, called weak line logic.
Consumers like to try new products; line extensions help provide variety to satisfy customer desires while remaining loyal to the brand.	Brand extensions motivate customers to seek variety and hence to brand switching, lowering brand loyalty.
Companies can reap the advantage of pricing breadth by encouraging consumers to trade up from the brand to a more profitable premium extension.	Some product ideas are big enough to warrant a new brand, but the company leaves it unexploited by making it a sub-brand.
Excess capacity encourages line extensions that require only minor adaptations to existing products.	Line extensions do not increase demand: people do not consume more simply because more products are available.
It is a way to increase sales quickly and cheaply as compared to establishing new brands, leading to short-term gain.	Retailers cannot provide more shelf space simply because more line extensions are available, which is a cause of conflict with trade.
By increasing the overall category demand New line extensions are matched quickly by competitors, reducing profits and thus competitive intensity, they help in increasing sales and profits.	New line extensions are matched quickly by competitors, reducing profits.
Trade channels pressure companies to offer broad and varied product lines.	There will be increased costs of market research, packaging, product launches, and logistics as products proliferate.

However, there are dangers of wanton line extensions. Quelch and Kenny (1994) point out that unchecked product line expansion can weaken a brand's image, disturb trade relations, and disguise cost increases. Further, a company that extends its line risks undermining brand loyalty. Line extensions rarely expand category demand, and retailers can't provide more shelf space to a category just because there are more products. Most important, the costs of overextension can remain hidden. The advantages and disadvantages of product line extensions are summarized in Table 8.4.

Family Branding

Family branding, or umbrella branding, involves marketing and selling product lines using a single brand name. It allows brand leveraging through corporate and brand names, as a single name—the firm's name or the brand—is used on a host of products. The practice involves similar colours, packaging, and names on the firm's products. For example, Apple works under a family branding strategy by using its distinctive Apple logo on a host of products: computers, phones, accessories, music players, and tablets. Similarly, a company may tag all products with a line such as 'a quality product from Hindustan Unilever' to convey that all products of the company will have the same quality as the ones that have been tried by a consumer. The family branding strategy helps the company to capitalize on an established name and also to control costs because establishing a new logo and brand name is hugely expensive.

Licensing

Licensing is the permission or licence granted by the owner of a legally protected entity to an individual (the licensee), for a product, service or promotion, in exchange for a fee or royalty. The legally protected entity could be a brand name, logo, trademark, graphic design, or a combination of these elements. Manufacturers can expand their presence in unrepresented markets by granting a license to others to manufacture or sell products with their brand name. The licensor saves on making investments in new markets while a licensee gains marketing advantage.

For example, when a strong brand name like McDonald's opens a store in a city by giving a license to a local shop owner, the brand gets a foothold in the market by sharing the risks, whereas the shop owner is assured of a regular stream of customers who are attracted by the McDonald's name.

Licensing is a form of stimulus generalization. It helps the licensee get instant access to markets while the manufacturer gains through increased market coverage. Consumers too benefit as they get access to brands. However, the manufacturer risks leakage of know how from the licensee, who may develop similar products. Counterfeiting, or making and selling fake products, may result.

Counterfeit Products

Stimulus generalization is also used by manufacturers to employ copycat strategies and produce fake goods by making their brand names and packages similar to national brands. Customers can be forgiven if they buy a toothpaste brand called 'Colgate' thinking it is 'Colgate' if it is presented in the same colour and lettering as the well-known brand.

For manufacturers, dealing with counterfeit products is a headache. According to *The Times of India* (2012), such products are widespread in a wide variety of categories such as electronic items, automotive components, consumer durables, pharmaceuticals, herbal medicine, and cosmetics. Estimates made by the Associated Chambers of Commerce and Industry of India (ASSOCHAM) say that the market for counterfeited products is worth ₹55,000 crore. The report says that FMCG companies suffer a maximum loss up to 45 per cent and an average loss around 25 per cent of their market share of their well-known products. The most popular counterfeit market is for clothing, followed by shoes, watches, leather goods, and jewellery. Manufacturers have to find ways to educate consumers about genuine products and that is why stimulus discrimination becomes very important for them.

To counter such threats, companies have to ensure that consumers realize that similar-looking goods do not have the same pedigree. Consumers have to be educated about the need to differentiate products even if they have similar packaging and looks. This is called *stimulus discrimination*.

Stimulus Discrimination

In stimulus generalization, a person tends to transfer a response learned for a particular stimulus to another similar stimulus. How can companies ensure that consumers buy only their brands even when confronted with cheaper, look-alike brands and products?

Stimulus discrimination is attempted in various ways. Some companies use distinctive advertising and logos that are difficult to copy. Others use holograms and ask customers to look for them on products before buying them. Holograms are three-dimensional images, created with photographic projection. Since they cannot be copied, they are used on consumer products to assure people of their authenticity.

There are other ways of stimulus discrimination as well. Maruti, for example, encourages people to buy genuine spares from its own service centres by highlighting the dangers of using spurious spare parts.

The next section covers the measurement of learning.

MEASURING LEARNING

Companies spend billions of rupees in making their products and brands known. As Keller (2006) writes, brand knowledge is not knowing facts about a brand, but the real power of the brand lies in how much the consumer has learnt, that is, the thoughts, feelings, images, beliefs, attitudes, experiences, and so on, that exist in the mind of the customer. Brand image consists of consumer perceptions and preferences for a brand, as reflected in brand associations in a consumer's mind. The task before us is how to measure these.

Recognition and recall are the results of consumer learning and are ways to measure whether consumers remember the ads and the products. They test the memory for traces of last night's TV ad or this morning's print ads, and to what extent people remember what was contained in it. Recognition is the term for trying to access memory by prompting. An advertisement is shown and consumers are asked whether they have any memory of having seen it before, and whether they remember anything contained it. Recall has been discussed earlier in the chapter.

Du Plessis (2005) explains that both recognition and recall are memory-dredging techniques and can be measured by any of the following methods:

CB IN ACTION   Measuring Recall and Recognition

Conduct the following experiment with your classmates.

Collect ten advertisements of some famous and not-so-famous brands and make a slide show out of them. Make sure that different classes of products are covered—some consumer goods and some industrial goods. Set the slide show so that each ad is seen for 15 seconds. Next, give them a 3-minute distractor task, like analysing a film clip.

After this, give the respondents 10 minutes to write down everything they could remember about the advertisements they had viewed, in a sheet having separate boxes for each ad.

Next, give them a list of the 10 product classes they have already seen and ask them to fill in the brand names.

You are now prepared to measure the following:

Product class recall   The number of times that the respondents correctly mention the product class in the ad

Brand name recall   The number of times that the respondents correctly mention the brand name of the product

Copy attribute recall   The number of times the respondents correctly mention the product attribute conveyed in the copy

Additional copy recall   The number of times that respondents correctly mention specific copy information

This exercise will help you understand recall and recognition. A research paper can also be developed based on this study.

- Show respondents the advertisement and ask if they remember it
- Remove the branding from the commercial, show it to respondents and then ask them if they remember the brand
- Describe the commercial to the respondents without naming the brand, and then ask them if they have seen it, and what brand it is for
- Ask the respondents if they remember seeing a commercial for a particular brand
- Ask the respondents to describe the most recent commercial for a particular brand

Market research tries to measure recognition, recall, and brand image. Some of the techniques used are projective techniques, consisting of interpretation and completion tasks, comparison tasks, brand personality and relationships, observational techniques, and quantitative research techniques that measure recall, awareness, recognition, image, and brand associations. These methods are discussed in Chapter 14.

BRAND LOYALTY

Brand loyalty, or persuading a consumer stick to one brand, is the purpose of all consumer learning. Rowley (2005) writes that customers demonstrate loyalty in any one of a number of ways such as the following:

- They may choose to stay with a brand for a number of years
- They may increase the number of purchases or the frequency of their purchases of a brand
- They may become advocates of the brand by recommending it to others

Reichheld (2003) defines consumer loyalty as the willingness of a customer or company to make an investment or personal sacrifice in order to strengthen the relationship between them.

Loyal customers can be segmented into four categories, namely *captive consumers* who buy or use a product or service because they have no choice; *convenience seekers* who make routine, low-involvement purchases and buy the brand regularly; *contented consumers* who evaluate products, but are satisfied with the brand because of past experience; and *committed consumers* who are loyal buyers and do not consider other brands.

Companies strive for customer loyalty. It is said to offer many benefits.:

Pricing power Customer loyalty gives an organization 'pricing power', which means that loyal customers stick to a brand even when the company raises prices.

Reduced expenditure on attracting new customers The company spends less on acquiring new customers as it has loyal customers who stick to its brands and recommend them to other customers.

Improved profitability Reduced marketing expenditure results in better profitability.

However, brand loyalty is not easy either to measure or manage. Reinartz and Kumar (2002) question whether loyalty actually contributes to profits. They found in their research that there is no correlation between customers who purchased regularly from a company and profitability. Companies thus need to manage both—loyalty and profitability—rather than focus on loyalty alone.

CONCLUSION

Companies make great efforts to get consumers to learn about their products and brands. They use the techniques described in this chapter not only to increase awareness but to make sure that people remember their brands at the crucial moment when they are picking up products from retail shelves. Companies also try to build loyalty and word-of-mouth publicity, which can only come if people have the brand experiences stored in their long-term memory.

However, in their quest for achieving these goals, are some companies going too far? For instance, companies encourage the use of addictive products that have caused harm, not only to their users, but also to their families. Thanks to the use of emotions and compelling messages, many consumers learn to use harmful substances at an early age. The consumption of cigarettes and alcohol by young people have been attributed to advertising that uses consumer learning techniques a little too efficiently.

Similarly, companies may inadvertently be teaching wrong attitudes to consumers. The depiction of women in ads, for instance, has resulted in skewed thinking among populations and has done little to change societal attitudes towards them in emerging markets. Many commercial messages also encourage favourable attitudes towards violence, dishonesty, and socially undesirable behaviour.

Since consumers are part of society, what they learn from advertising messages impacts society directly. While using consumer learning techniques to build brand loyalty, perhaps companies need to keep this aspect firmly in focus so that they do not end up conveying the wrong messages to consumers.

SUMMARY

Consumer learning is an important tool in marketing as companies use it to sell new and innovative products. There are four basic elements in consumer learning models, namely motivation, cues, response, and reinforcement.

Learning theories are classified as behavioural or cognitive. According to the behavioural approach, a person learns from experience and environment and associates responses with some stimuli. There are two forms of associative learning, namely classical and operant conditioning.

In classical conditioning, people learn to associate two stimuli when they occur together, and eventually the response of one stimulus is transferred to another. Advertisements pair a pleasant image or experience with a product so that consumers think of that product or brand whenever they encounter that stimulus.

The second type of conditioning is instrumental or operant conditioning, which uses reinforcement and punishment to increase or decrease the occurrence of a behaviour. While behaviour resulting in pleasant experiences is repeated, behaviour that causes pain is avoided. Consumers learn to adopt behaviours that are rewarding and also to avoid behaviours that are painful. Companies reward customers by way of loyalty schemes and punish them by imposing charges to discourage undesirable behaviour.

By reinforcing these behaviours, companies are able to guide customers to more profitable products. While positive reinforcement is a stimulus that strengthens the desired consumer response, negative reinforcement induces a desired reaction by removing an adverse stimulus. This is different from punishment, which implies removing positive consequences so as to lower the probability of repetition of undesirable behaviour in future.

Principles of reinforcement are applied in sales promotions and discounts. The reinforcers used by marketing companies to influence behaviour are shaping, habits, repetition, and advertising wear out. Extinction and forgetting occurs when a previously established link between stimulus and response is broken.

Companies use stimulus generalization for brand and product line extensions, family branding, and licensing so that a successful brand evokes the same favourable response from consumers when it is applied to a variety of products. Unscrupulous manufacturers use the concept to sell look-alike or counterfeit products. To assure customers about genuine products, companies have to devise stimulus discrimination techniques.

The cognitive theory of learning explains human behaviour by trying to understand internal thought processes. It assumes that humans are logical beings and make consumption choices based on their thinking and reasoning. Cognitive learning is explained by using the analogy of computers, that is, by likening the brain to an information-processing unit. The human mind receives information, stores and retains it, and retrieves it as and when required, just in the way that a computer functions. Memory stages such as sensory, short-term, and long-term memory and how the brain stores information in memory, have important applications in marketing.

Consumers also learn passively, by watching ads or observing others. Krugman's theory of passive learning provides a perspective on low-involvement consumer behaviour. People also imagine themselves doing something that someone else is doing, which is called vicarious learning. Consumer involvement explains that effectiveness of learning depends on the mental state of consumers. Recognition, recall, and brand loyalty are measures of consumer learning.

KEY TERMS

Advertising wear-out A model of communication that elaborates the steps of consumer involvement as attention, interest, desire, and action

Associative learning The process by which an individual learns to associate a behaviour with a response

Classical conditioning A learning process that occurs when two stimuli are repeatedly paired so that a response that is at first elicited by the second stimulus is eventually elicited by the first stimulus alone

Cognitive theory of learning This theory explains human behaviour by trying to understand internal thought processes and assumes that humans are logical beings and make consumption choices based on their thinking and reasoning

Consumer involvement The motivational state of an individual, which affects the person's reaction to an environmental stimulus and aids in learning

Consumer learning The process by which individuals acquire knowledge about products and brands, and use that knowledge and experience to know which brands are suitable for them and which ones are not

Consumer loyalty The willingness of a customer or company to make an investment or personal sacrifice to strengthen the relationship between them

Cue A signal to a consumer to buy or consume a product or service

Extinction A phenomenon that occurs when a previously established link between stimulus and response is broken, or when the effects of prior conditioning are reduced and finally disappear

Family branding This is also known as umbrella branding and involves marketing and selling different product lines using a single brand name

Habit Regularly exhibiting the same behaviour, sometimes even without thinking

Licensing The permission granted by the owner of a legally protected entity to the license holder for use in conjunction with a product, service, or promotion, in exchange for a fee or royalty.

Motivation The driving force that impels consumers to try out new products.

Negative reinforcement The reward that induces a desired reaction by removing an adverse stimulus

Operant conditioning A type of learning in which an individual's behaviour is modified by the consequences of being either reinforced or punished

Passive learning The process by which people do not actively engage in learning, but absorb the information being presented—consumers learn passively by watching ads, reading, and watching TV or other people consuming products

Positive reinforcement A stimulus that strengthens the desired consumer response and stimulates re-occurrence of a behaviour

Product line extension An application of stimulus generalization in which a manufacturer extends use of an established brand name for a new item in the same product category

Punishment Removing positive consequences so as to lower the probability of the individual repeating undesirable behaviour in future

Recall An unaided technique that is used to find out if consumers remember any ad they have seen in a particular TV programme or a particular newspaper

Recognition The technique used to access memory by prompting to see whether consumers recognize an advertisement or not

Rehearsal The process by which people recall memories of stimuli and repeat them

Reinforcement This occurs when a customer is satisfied with the experience of consuming the product

Response The reaction of the consumer to a cue

Retrieval The process of accessing stored memories

Shaping The process by which an existing response is gradually changed across successive trials towards a desired target behaviour by rewarding exact segments of behaviour

Stimulus discrimination This occurs when consumers differentiate products even if they have similar packaging and looks

Stimulus generalization This occurs when people tend to transfer a response learned for one stimulus to a similar stimulus

Vicarious learning This occurs when people learn to do something by imagining themselves acting in the same way as someone else

EXERCISES

Concept-review Questions

1. What is consumer learning? Explain the consumer learning process.
2. Describe the elements of consumer learning and how they impact consumer experience.
3. Define and explain the process of classical conditioning. How is it used to modify consumer behaviour?
4. What is the difference between classical and operant conditioning? How do companies use both?
5. What is stimulus generalization? Explain its applicability in brand extension, family branding, and licensing.
6. Under what circumstances are product lines extended? What are the dangers that a company faces when undertaking line extensions?
7. Explain how vicarious learning happens. How do companies ensure consumers learn vicariously?
8. Describe the information-processing model of consumer learning. How does the brain store information and how can advertisements stay in the long-term memory of consumers?
9. How does consumer involvement play a role in learning? What are the strategies followed by companies to change passive learning to active learning?
10. Explain Krugman's theory of passive learning and the elaboration likelihood model.

Critical Thinking Questions

1. While behavioural learning assumes that people can be taught to consume products, cognitive thinking assumes that people are intelligent beings who solve their own problems. Which of these approaches is more applicable today? Consider the brands you consume and develop a case for one of these approaches.
2. Companies apply stimulus generalization to extend products and brands. Is this a good strategy? When private labels launch cheaper look-alike products, is it extending stimulus generalization too far? How can companies counter the threat from private labels?
3. Distinguish between high- and low-involvement purchases. Think of products that fall in these categories, and then suggest what strategies can be used to build brand loyalty among these.
4. Cognitive learning has been applied to several consumer models. Discuss each model and describe which aspects of learning theories are used by each of them. Illustrate with examples of recent advertising campaigns, the applicability of learning theories to these models.

Projects and Assignments

1. Ask your friends whether they have bought a mobile phone, a soft drink, or a breakfast cereal in the last six months. Analyse their purchase behaviour using a Likert scale, on the basis of involvement, importance, interest, usability, and convenience. On this basis, find out consumer loyalty, brand involvement, and reasons for purchase. Comment on brand learning from your findings.
2. Select a small group of students. Ask them about the products that they purchase as a matter of habit. Using interviews, determine how these habits were developed and the role of advertisements in developing these habits. Find out which habits were developed from family influence and which were developed from other influences. Determine ways in which these habits can be broken in favour of competing products.
3. Prepare a project on how companies enhance information given in advertisements by experience-oriented campaigns to help consumers remember their brands. Integrate the advertising message with information websites, BTL campaigns, and retail store experience and judge whether those activities are succeeding in making customers shift information in the ads to long-term memory.
4. Visit a supermarket and see how (a) a cosmetics company uses consumer learning to sell new products to customers, and (b) how a new product is introduced and how customers are encouraged to make a first purchase. Describe these processes and assess which elements of consumer learning are being followed by the brands. Make a detailed project analysing your experiences.

REFERENCES

Chandramouli, Rajesh, 'Fake products sale is likely to touch over ₹55,000 crore by 2013', *The Times of India*, 6 August 2012.

Du Plessis, Erik, *The Advertised Mind: Ground-Breaking Insights Into How Our Brains Respond To Advertising*, Millward Brown, London, 2005.

East, Robert, Malcolm Wright, and Marc Vanhuele, *Consumer Behaviour: Applications in Marketing*, Sage Publications Ltd, London, 2008.

Grant, Jeremy, 'P&G launches suit against private labels', *Financial Times*, 3 May 2006, http://www.ft.com/cms/s/0/6b90ff7a-da41-11da-b7de-0000779e2340.html#axzz2OLmVIuuf, last accessed on 22 March 2013.

Griffin, Jill, *Taming the Search-and-Switch Customer: Earning Customer Loyalty in a Compulsion-to-Compare World*, Jossey-Bass, A Wiley Imprint, San Francisco, 2009.

Hemp, Paul, 'Avatar-based marketing', *Harvard Business Review*, June 2006, pp. 48–57.

Hoffman, Donald D., *Visual Intelligence: How We Create What We See*, W. W. Norton & Co., New York, 1998.

Kapferer, Jean-Noël, *New strategic brand management: Creating and Sustaining Brand Equity Long Term*, 4th Ed., Kogan Page, London, 2008.

Keller, Kevin Lane, 'Measuring brand equity', in *The Handbook of Marketing Research: Uses, Misuses, and Future Advances* edited by Rajiv Grover and Marco Vriens, Sage Publications Inc, California, 2006.

Krugman, Herbert E., 'The impact of television advertising: Learning without involvement', *Public Opinion Quarterly*, Vol. 29, pp. 349–356.

Laaksonen, Pirjo, *Consumer Involvement: Concepts and Research*, Routledge, New York, 1994.

Lantos, Geoffrey Paul, *Consumer Behavior in Action: Real-Life Applications for Marketing Managers*, M.E. Sharp, New York, 2010.

Lindstrom, Martin, *Buyology: How Everything We Believe About Why We Buy is Wrong*, Random House Business Books, London, 2009.

McFadden, Daniel L., 'The new science of pleasure', NBER Working Paper Series, 2013, http://www.nber.org/papers/w18687, last accessed on 8 May 2013.

Michaelidou, Nina and Sally Dibb, 'Consumer involvement: A new perspective'. *Marketing Review*, Vol. 8(1), 2008, pp. 83–99.

Pear, Joseph, *The Science of Learning*, Psychology Press, Philadelphia, USA, 2001.

Quelch, John A. and David Kenny, 'Extend profits, not product lines', *Harvard Business Review*, September–October, 1994 pp. 153–160.

Rayport, Jeffrey F., 'Advertising's new medium: Human experience', *Harvard Business Review*, March 2013.

Reichheld, Fredrick F., 'The one number you need to grow', *Harvard Business Review*, December 2003.

Reinartz, Werner and V. Kumar, 'The mismanagement of customer loyalty', *Harvard Business Review*, July 2002.

Rowley, Jennifer, 'The four Cs of customer loyalty', *Marketing Intelligence & Planning*, Vol. 23, No. 6, 2005, pp. 574–581.

Till, Brian D. and Randi Lynn Priluck, 'Stimulus generalization in classical conditioning: An initial investigation and extension', *Psychology & Marketing*, January 2000, Vol. 17, No. 1, pp. 55–72.

Wright, Ray, *Consumer Behaviour*, Thomson Learning, London, 2006.

Zaichkowsky, J.L., 'Conceptualizing involvement', *Journal of Advertising*, 1986, Vol. 15, No. 2, pp. 4–14.

CASE STUDY

Private Labels—The Growing Trend

Private labels can be dubbed as 'alternative brands'. They are also referred to as store brands, private-label goods or private brands. They are brands owned by a retailer or supplier whose goods are made by a contract manufacturer. Consumers like them as they are cheaper than established brands, and sometimes are generic 'no-name' brands sold at retail stores. For stores, private labels earn higher margins than those given by national brands.

Private brands are nothing new; *kirana* shops in the country have traditionally ground spices and sold them in packs that carry the shop's name. This is a simple way of selling a private label. Now, large retail chains do the same thing and pack the goods in strikingly similar packages sold by brands owned by manufacturers. The goods are considerably cheaper than the well-known brands, which gives the private labels an advantage. When faced with similar product packages, one cheaper than the other, many consumers tend to pick up the cheaper brands. The goods have comparable quality, and there is also an implicit guarantee given by the seller. Sometimes grinding of food products is done in front of the customers, which reassures them of the quality and freshness.

Private label brands are popular in many grocery product categories. Retailers both large chains like Bharti Wal-Mart and small *kirana* stores—offer such packed goods. Some of the common private labels or generic goods that are available in India are *atta*, *dal*, soaps, snacks, biscuits, and noodles. Private-label products tend to mimic the packaging styles of leading national brands, for instance, the Tasty Treat sold at Big Bazaar is similar in packaging to Lays, and the Sudz brand of detergent has almost the same packaging as Surf. The colours, fonts, styles, and packaging materials mimic national brands. Such similarities cause consumers to try out the goods. If the quality is acceptable, consumers switch from national brands to private labels as they offer a substantial price advantage.

Sometimes retail chains get their private labels manufactured from the same manufacturers, who supply to the higher-priced well-known brands. The products are made by the same factories, with the same ingredients and quality, and the only difference is the label. Consumers learn that switching to a private label is an easy way to save 30 per cent or more. *Time* (2012) reports that by using the same branding tactics as that of consumer goods giants such as Procter & Gamble. and PepsiCo Inc., retail chains such as Safeway Inc. and Wal-Mart invest in their private labels, treating them as brands in themselves. They are expanding lines, adding new flavours and packaging, and finding ways to charge more.

Private labels also cater to local tastes. An article published by Wharton (2009) shows that private labels are able to cater to thinly divided market segments. It gives the example of Tasty Treat, which introduced *kasundi*, the pungent mustard paste that is part of the culinary tradition of West Bengal, as a private label. However, Big Bazaar does not sell this in all its stores, but stocks it only in markets with a Bengali population. Similarly, the Gujarati snacks *khakra* and *thepla* under the same brand name, are not sold in all its stores. The retail chain changes its product mix depending on local tastes and preferences. Many national brands are not able to cater to such segments.

Private labels are slowly emerging as brands themselves. They offer a price advantage as their expenses on product development and brand promotion are negligible. Most private brands are reverse-engineered copies of category leaders and they are only promoted within the store.

Private labels are not limited to groceries. Shoppers Stop sells apparel under its STOP label that became the first branded ethnic women's wear range. The Croma chain of electronics stores sells consumer electronics products under its own name. Its 'handpicked by Croma' brand is becoming popular and offers a wide range of products.

Big brands suffer when private labels, using principles of stimulus generalization, are able to garner market share. In their book, *Private Label Strategy: How to Meet the Store Brand Challenge*, Kumar and Steenkamp (2007) note that 'Brands are under attack from private labels'. Such products become popular during an economic slowdown as consumers shift to cheaper goods, but 'part of private label growth in a recession is permanent, caused by consumer learning. As consumers learn about the improved quality of private labels in recessions, a significant proportion of them remain loyal to private labels, even after the necessity to economize on expenditures is over'.

Companies frequently try to fight back. *Financial Times* (2006) reports that Procter & Gamble has periodically launched legal action against look-alike labels. In 2006, it took legal action against copycats of its famous brands Head & Shoulders, Old Spice, and Crest, filing separate lawsuits for trade dress infringement, trademark infringement, and 'unfair competition' in the US. The company website says, 'These look-alike products can confuse people and are a disservice to consumers. We are filing this lawsuit to put a stop to it'.

Whether such actions will be able to stop the growth of private labels remains to be seen. However, there is no easy way to stop look-alike products, as consumers seek value in their purchases.

Questions for Discussion

1. What elements of consumer learning are used by private label retailers in appealing to consumers?
2. How do private labels ensure that they get attention from consumers? What factors will consumers consider when they pick up a private label instead of their preferred brand?
3. How can manufacturers of national brands use stimulus discrimination to stop the preference for private brands?
4. How can manufacturers use positive and negative reinforcement techniques to make customers stick to their brands and not look for cheaper alternatives?

Sources:

http://news.pg.com/press-release/pg-corporate-announcements/procter-gamble-files-two-infringement-lawsuits, last accessed on 20 April 2013.

Kumar, Nirmalya and Jan-Benedict E. M. Steenkamp, *Private Label Strategy: How to Meet the Store Brand Challenge*, Harvard Business School Press, Boston, USA, 2007.

'More choices in store: India's retailers are stocking up on private-label brands', Knowledge@Wharton, 3 December 2009. http://knowledge.wharton.upenn.edu/india/article.cfm?articleid=4432, last accessed on 3 April 2013.

Tuttle, Brad, 'Brand names just don't mean as much anymore', *Time*, 1 November 2012, http://business.time.com/2012/11/01/brand-names-just-dont-mean-as-much-anymore/#ixzz2LnZHwvQq, last accessed on 3 April 2013.

CHAPTER NINE
Consumer Attitudes and Change

LEARNING OBJECTIVES

This chapter describes how consumer attitudes, or enduring beliefs towards products and brands are formed. Models of consumer attitude are explained as also attitude formation and change.

After studying this chapter, the reader should be able to

- define attitudes and understand the components of attitudes
- describe the nature and functions of attitudes
- understand various models of consumer attitude
- describe how attitude towards the product, ad, and store, affect consumer behaviour
- devise a strategy to change attitudes towards products and brands

CASE STUDY
Creating Brandtopias

One industry that relies heavily on attitude to market its products is the soft drink industry. If you take a look at how these products are sold, you will find that none of them are sold on product attributes but rate highly on attitude. Coca-Cola is the product for 'happiness', Pepsi reflects the attitudes of youth in its 'live for now' campaign, Mirinda has the *pagalpanti* (craziness) theme that encourages fun and pranks, while Sprite encourages 'seedhi baat' (straight talk), everything else being nonsense, of course! Thums Up wants you to 'taste the thunder,' no less. These brands are valued by customers not for what they do, but more for what they symbolize.

To build attitudes, companies have to do two things, namely create emotional benefits with the brand and link it to consumer personality. In his book, *How Brands Become Icons*, Holt (2004) writes that brands must create an identity mix and then extend that myth. If a right myth is created, he writes, 'consumers jump on board, using the brand to sate their identity desires. They begin to depend on the brand as an icon, remaining fiercely loyal'. Two brands—Mountain Dew and Red Bull—have done this very successfully by creating a unique identity and attitude of their own. The emotional benefits attached to these brands are exhilaration and excitement, while they create the personality traits of irreverence, daring, and fun.

Red Bull Red Bull is positioned as an energy drink. On its website you see the brand promise, 'Red Bull gives you wings', that is, it increases your performance, concentration, reaction speed, vigilance, and even well-being. You do not see the product at all, but pictures and videos of all sorts of outdoor activities such as surfing, motorsports, snowboarding, and the like.

Red Bull emphasizes on adventure and outdoor sports, by creating and getting involved in events across the world. The Red Bull Air Race is an international series of air races, the New York Red Bulls is a soccer team, and the company has invested in sporting facilities. Not all events are sponsored by the company—it gets enormous publicity because many outdoor events carry the Red Bull signage.

Red Bull Flugtag is a contest in which people are invited to build home-made, human-powered flying machines, take off from a 30-feet high deck and then land in the water. More than 35 Flugtags have been held around the world attracting up to 3,00,000 spectators per event.

Aaker (2012) writes that instead of using a few high-profile sponsorships, the company has created a large set of relatively inexpensive sponsorships that, because of the umbrella Red Bull brand, have a cumulative impact. They are effective because the message matches the brand and are so creative that they create buzz through the mainstream and digital media.

Mountain Dew Mountain Dew displays a smug attitude of 'done that'. Its ads show people attempting extreme sports, but the four 'Dew dudes' scoff at the stunts because they thrill doesn't compare to drinking Diet Dew. The campaign became hugely successful, as Laglace (2002) writes, becoming 'the irreverent bad boy of soda pop, deftly exploiting the emerging slacker and grunge rock scene of the time. Ever since, "Do the Dew" has managed to ride the adrenalized wave of youth culture like it was Vin Diesel in a can.'

In building the brand attitude, the company placed emphasis on youth-centred activities: music and sports. Its website features a number of adventure sports, such as skateboarding and mountain climbing. It also has a record label, Green Label Sound, to elevate independent artists. Green Label Sound allows music fans to download free music, watch videos, and discover new acts.

Holt (2004) explains that the difference between the nation's ideals and actual life produces a utopian desire. The 'Do the Dew' campaign resolved anxieties about masculine identity by providing an affirmative, if sassy, alternative. In doing so, the brand creates a utopia of its own, dubbed as 'brandtopia' that creates and sustains an imaginary world of attitude.

Both Red Bull and Mountain Dew have created brandtopias. The brands' outdoors attitude is shared by consumers. This helps the brands in two ways. First, people who share the attitude with the brand, become loyal customers. Second, the brands exhibit a unique attitude that helps them carve out sizeable markets on their own power.

While reading this chapter, try to answer the following questions:

1. How are attitudes formed and changed over a period of time?
2. How can companies build strong attitudes towards their brands?
3. What is the theoretical basis of understanding attitudes? What are its applications?
4. How do attitudes change behaviour in consumer markets?

Sources:
Aaker, 'How Red Bull creates brand buzz', http://blogs.hbr.org/cs/2012/12/how_red_bull_creates_brand_buzz.html.
Holt, Douglas B., *How Brands Become Icons: The Principles of Cultural Branding*, Harvard Business School Publishing Corporation, Boston, 2004.
http://mountaindew.com/.
http://www.redbull.com/en.
Lagace, Martha, 'Building "brandtopias"—how top brands tap into society', http://hbswk.hbs.edu/item/2985.html, 2002.
All last accessed on 25 July 2013.

INTRODUCTION

Attitude is a commonly-used term. Young people describe a peer's showing off as 'he/she has an attitude'. Attitude is also used to describe a person's likes and dislikes. The word is used to sell a wide range of products, from clothing and perfumes to cars and retail stores (see Fig. 9.1). Brands encourage you to 'show your attitude' and indeed many people wear clothes and perfumes to do precisely this, as shown in the chapter-end case study.

FIG. 9.1 Attitude is used to sell a host of products

Attitude is more than this. It is the way in which people make evaluative judgments, and this process is automatic. Social attitudes are built up during one's upbringing, and partly learnt by observing others. Since they are relatively stable ideas about whether something is good or bad, they exert powerful influences on people's evaluations of everything around them. In marketing, we are interested in knowing how consumers form evaluations about products and brands.

The study of attitudes goes much beyond likes and dislikes. They are deep rooted and very strong evaluations and prejudices.

It is now known that the human brain performs continuous evaluations: neuroscientists point to processing circuits in the brain that involve multiple neural regions. Cunningham and Zelazo (2007) explain that evaluations reflect a dynamic interaction between limbic and cortical structures. The brain processes information dynamically through feedback loops that progressively recruit additional regions of the cortex. Automatic evaluations are linked more to limbic processing, whereas reflective evaluations additionally recruit and use several cortical systems.

Frank (2009) writes of a fascinating study, the 'Pepsi Paradox'. In blind tests, Pepsi was the preferred cola. However, when people could see the labels, almost all of the respondents preferred Coca-Cola. They were convinced that the taste of Coca-Cola was far superior to Pepsi. Indeed, it is Coca-Cola that continues to be the absolute bestseller in the U.S. and the rest of the world. Why is this so? The difference in attitude is explained by neuroscience—the cerebral cortex intervened with its higher cognitive processes and triumphed over the immediate feeling of reward that was evoked by the taste impression.

Yet, attitudes do change, as the quick adoption of innovative products by people around the globe illustrates.

The question before marketing managers is how to affect these processes of the brain? This chapter examines how consumers form their evaluations about products and brands, and how these evaluations might be changed.

DEFINING ATTITUDE

An attitude is a state of mind relating to an object, fact, or situation.

Our attitudes are revealed through our behaviour—the way we behave lets others know our state of mind. An attitude is also a predisposition or a tendency to respond positively or negatively towards a certain idea, object, person, or situation. Allport (1935) defined an attitude as 'a mental and neural state of readiness, organized through experience, exerting a directive or dynamic influence upon an individual's response to all objects and situations with which it is related'.

Eagly and Chaiken (1998) define an attitude as 'a psychological tendency that is expressed by evaluating a particular entity with some degree of favour or disfavour'.

Attitude is an important concept in marketing. It is a mental state by which people structure their beliefs about things around them. Please see Exhibit 9.1. Attitudes are wired into our personalities—they are lasting evaluations of the social world that are stored in memory. They are organized through experience, exerting a dynamic influence upon how we respond to objects and situations. They are learned over time, creating a predisposition to behaviour, in a favourable or unfavourable manner with respect to a given object.

Attitudes are generally formed through an individual's subjective evaluation, influenced also by affective and emotional responses and related beliefs. Attitudes are built as a result of our evaluations of our environment. It would, for instance, be difficult to meet a person who is completely indifferent about his family, dog, job, choice of food, or religion. These influences begin to form in childhood and reflect in the individual's actions. Very often, they are a result of upbringing and that is why they are enduring. Some attitudes persist over one's lifetime.

In marketing, we are interested in how people acquire attitudes towards products, brands, and companies. It is not necessary for a consumer to have experienced the products; one is able to acquire beliefs based on advertisements and hearsay. Since attitudes become strong influencers, linking them with products results in very strong brand loyalty. Sometimes people acquire negative attitudes about brands, so companies have to know how attitudes can be changed.

 EXHIBIT 9.1 Blue Star: The Expert

Blue Star has developed a carefully researched positioning strategy. Its positioning statement is the result of a study that showed decision-makers, seeking peace of mind, preferred vendors competent in executing complex assignments. Given this insight, Blue Star zeroed in on the term 'expert'. The proposition that flowed from here—Experts in Cooling—became a strong corporate differentiator and positioned Blue Star several notches ahead of competitors.

This positioning worked equally well in the residential air-conditioning market where consumers appeared to believe that office cooling was superior to home cooling. Since Blue Star had established superiority in the office cooling segment, the proposition of bringing home an 'expert' blended in seamlessly, with the apt proposition of 'Get office-like cooling at home'. Here associating expert with the brand has worked successfully for it since people's attitude towards the term 'expert' is positive and on whom they can trust. Please see Figure 9.2.

FIG. 9.2 Blue Star 'from the experts'

Courtesy: Superbrands

Source: Superbrands 2012

Nature of Attitude

Attitude is an abstract concept and the term is used loosely to describe how a person behaves. However, understanding attitude provides us with a deep understanding of consumer behaviour. Allport (1935) had observed that attitude is the most distinctive and indispensable concept in social psychology. Understanding attitude allows us to understand not only the preferences and behaviour of individuals, but also provides insight into the actions of groups and cultures.

Albarracin and Patrick (2010) make several points to understand the nature of attitude in their paper in *Handbook of Social Psychology*, first published in 1935. They write that attitudes

- are evaluations, a basis for the likes and dislikes of individuals
- are held towards a variety of things—people, places, ideas, actions, and so on
- are complex and difficult to study
- may be measured and expressed in a variety of ways behaviourally, affectively, cognitively, implicitly, and explicitly are formed and changed in a variety of ways, with varying amounts of cognitive deliberation

We can further say that attitude is a hypothetical construct, not directly observable and can only be inferred from observable responses.

Attitudes can be studied from two perspectives. The structural approach, in which the psychological construct of attitudes in the brain is studied. The second is the functional approach, that is, a study of the functions that the attitude fulfils for an individual.

Functions of Attitudes

Why do people have attitudes? People hold attitudes because they serve some function. One function is that attitudes are a way of defining a society. Katz (1960), described four distinct functions of attitudes.

Instrumental The instrumental function helps the person to achieve rewards and gain approval from others, and is also known as adjustive or utilitarian function. People adjust or change their attitude as they expect to be rewarded. The most common form is when people are sent a message by a company to 'like' their page on Facebook, which would lead to a benefit or a discount coupon. Advertisements that highlight a benefit fall in this category.

Ego-defensive The ego-defensive function gives a perspective of the world that protects a person from harsh realities, supports their ego, and rewards them. Advertisements that bolster ego and help people feel good about themselves are appealing to the ego-defensive function. Examples of ego-defensive ads are fashion products that promise to instil confidence in a person as well as deodorant ads that promise to help people smell and feel better (see chapter-end case study).

Value-expressive Attitudes that appeal to a person's central values or self-concept fulfil a value-expressive function. A person forms an attitude towards a product because of what the product says about him or her as a person. Advertisements of mobile phones frequently use this function by stating that a mobile phone reflects one's true personality or by highlighting features that enhance value.

TABLE 9.1 Functions of attitudes and how they are used in advertising

Function of attitude	Types of ads
Instrumental	Promising reward
Ego-defensive	Help people feel good about themselves
Value-expressive	Appeal to a person's central values
Knowledge	Make the world more understandable

Knowledge Erwin (2001) explains that the core idea of the knowledge function is to make the world more understandable. It provides a frame of reference by ascribing meaning to things that happen to people or are encountered by them. Hand sanitizers harp on the knowledge function, by giving information on the dangers of dirty hands.

Applications in Marketing

The functions of attitudes are used widely in advertising and in developing promotional strategies. If we understand, for instance, that a particular brand is worn for style, our ads would highlight the style aspect rather than the comfort aspect. Table 9.1 summarizes the functions of attitudes and the types of ads that they are used in.

The second application is that effectiveness of advertising can be judged by measuring shifts in attitudes. If the campaign of a particular company is found to have resulted in a favourable attitudinal shift, we can assume that the campaign was effective. In contrast, if people simply recall the ad or like the ad but there has been no attitudinal shift, we can well say that the campaign has not succeeded.

Apart from advertising, attitudes are used in marketing strategy in the following ways:

Identifying benefit segments Marketing managers are able to identify and define market segments based on the benefits that customers want. In the car industry, for instance, different segments demand fuel economy, style, or powerful, stylish cars. The industry can identify these segments and offer products for them, as well as highlight these benefits in the advertising.

New product development Companies are able to identify vacant segments by focusing on attitudes. The instant snack industry, for instance, relied on potato chips for a long time. However, by identifying attitudes, the industry realized that the market wanted a more spicy Indian snack. While Pepsi developed Kurkure as a result, ITC came out with Mad Angles, moving away from the potato chips-dominated industry.

Co-branding When two or more brands enter into a partnership and jointly promote themselves, it is called co-branding. The idea is that brand attitudes are transferred between partners, giving them the synergetic benefits that would not have been possible individually.

MODELS OF CONSUMER ATTITUDES

In this section, we discuss structural models of consumer attitudes. These are the tri-component model, multi-attribute model, attitude towards the ad/store, theories of reasoned action, trying

MARKETING INSIGHT
Synergy through Co-branding

Companies look for partnerships for their brands hoping that the attitude of one will rub off on the other. This is done through co-branding, which occurs when two companies form an alliance to work together, creating marketing synergy. Since brands are judged by the company they keep, both brands gain as a result. Greenwald writes that innovative partnerships can make brands seem hipper, more modern, distinctive, interesting, and noteworthy.

One of the most popular examples of co-branding is the sticker saying 'Intel inside' on personal computers. Co-branding is now seen in cosmetics, hotels, restaurants, fashion wear, household products, and non-profit activities and is also known as brand or strategic partnership. If the partnerships are new and unexpected, they reinforce brand image and also increase awareness.

Co-branding is very popular in the retail and hospitality industry. The Ace Hotel in New York City, for example, has forged partnerships with shops and restaurants on its property. It also partners with local artists whose artwork is for sale in different hotel rooms if one likes the painting in the room, one can well buy it.

Many co-branding instances can be seen in the beverage industry. Designer Jack Spade has a collection of clothes and bags with Coca-Cola's most beloved advertising slogans, evoking nostalgia. Karl Lagerfeld designed a wine label to commemorate the 350th anniversary of a wine brand owned by Chanel. Such partnerships make the brands seem more contemporary and relevant, and both brands gain as a result.

The philosophy behind combining brands is that one plus one is greater than two. Innovative partnerships serve several strategic purposes by enhancing each other's images. The combined resources are greater than either could afford alone, resulting in synergy. For example, the endorsement of Ariel by Vimal helped the strategic interests of both brands through a perfect fit of apparel and washing powder. Interesting and surprising associations attract attention for a brand, breaking through the advertising clutter, attracting more press coverage and consumer buzz.

Brands have often forged partnerships with organizations undertaking social work. The association with a worthy cause helps the brand's image and increases the effectiveness of their ad campaigns. The charities get the advertising resources and awareness they could never have achieved on their own. The Aircel campaign for Save the Tigers had NDTV as a partner as well, and resulted in huge coverage. P&G co-branded with National Association for the Blind to start Project Drishti where for each pack of Whisper purchased by the customer, one rupee was donated by P&G to NAB for helping a blind female child.

Co-branding can be an effective strategy to survive down times and even grow. It can create new revenue streams, increase momentum, raise brand awareness, and reduce costs.

In India, co-branded credit cards are common. Some of these are Citibank and Jet Airways, State Bank of India and Indian Railways, Indian Oil and Citibank, and HDFC Bank and *The Times of India*. The cardholder gets extra points whenever the card is used to buy the co-branded service, and these points can redeemed for additional products or services from the merchant. In this way, it builds loyalty for both brands.

The 10 most popular co-branded campaigns are available on the *Businessweek* website. Analyse these campaigns and assess whether co-branding results in both brands gaining attitude. Name the successful co-branding campaigns and the not-so-successful ones.

Sources:
Greenwald, Michelle, 'The Secrets of Successful Co-brands', http://www.inc.com/michelle-greenwald/innovative-co-branding-and-creative-partnerships.html.
http://images.businessweek.com/ss/09/07/0710_cobranded/.
http://www.coolavenues.com/marketing-zone/co-branding?page=0,0.
http://www.forbes.com/2010/03/16/cold-stone-creamery-dan-beem-rocky-mountain-chocolate-cmo-network-co-branding.html..
All websites last accessed on 12 April 2014.

to consume, and planned action that were explained in Chapter 3. Two concepts are important to understand these models the attitude towards object (ATO) and attitude towards behaviour, which underlies all the models.

Attitude towards object Attitude towards an ad (A_{ad}) determines whether consumers associate themselves with the advertised product and have favourable feelings towards it, whereas attitude towards the store shows whether customers find the stores convenient or fun. Brands stocked in such stores will normally move off the shelves faster than in stores that customers do not like to visit.

A consumer's attitude towards an object is made up of a set of beliefs. The object refers to companies, products, brands, stores, advertisements and so on. Beliefs are acquired through experiences with the object. A consumer's beliefs of an object can be positive or negative, depending on their past experiences. ATO consists of three key elements beliefs, strength of the belief, and evaluation of attributes. A combination of these forms the overall ATO. For example, to measure the attitude towards a car brand, we could ask the consumer to rate several beliefs on a 7-point Likert scale ranging from extremely incorrect to extremely correct, with the centre value being neutral when the consumer is indifferent about that particular attribute. By asking a series of such questions about brands, we can come to know ATO for car brands. An example of one such question is:

Q. Do you think that the Maruti Swift has good sporty styling?

Totally agree	Moderately agree	Slightly agree	Neither Agree Nor disagree	Slightly disagree	Moderately disagree	Totally disagree
+3	+2	+1	0	−1	−2	−3

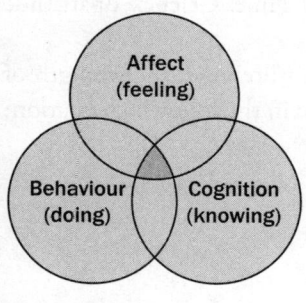

FIG. 9.3 ABC model of consumer attitude

Attitude towards behaviour Attitude towards behaviour implies what a person thinks about doing something, such as wearing a dress or eating an ice cream. According to the expectancy-value model, attitude towards a behaviour is determined by the beliefs linking the behaviour to outcomes and other attributes. Each belief is evaluated and the products are aggregated. An instance of attitude towards behaviour is when a person thinks, 'If I buy this product, what will people think of me?'

Tri-component Model of Attitudes

Solomon (2009) describes the ABC model of attitudes—affect, behaviour, and cognition (Fig. 9.3). It links feeling, knowing, and doing.

Affect is the feeling that an individual has towards an object. In the marketing context, affect represents the emotion or opinion about a product, service, or advertisement. This does not mean that people will buy products. While consumers may have

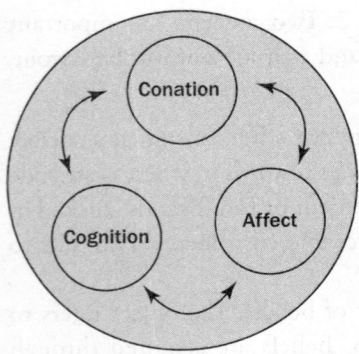

FIG. 9.4 Tri-component model of consumer attitudes

very positive feelings for expensive products such as Mercedes cars or Rolex watches, they may actually buy cheaper products.

Cognition is an individual's belief or knowledge about the product or advertisement.

Behaviour—also called the conative element—is the response of a consumer arising from affect and cognition. This may be intention to buy, talking about it, or even buying the product or service.

The ABC model is also known as the tri-component attitude model, which describes the three components as Affective, Cognitive, and Conative. All three elements interact with each other as shown in Fig. 9.4, that is, feelings, beliefs, and knowledge result in behaviour.

Though attitudes are described as an interplay between thoughts, emotions, and behavioural intentions, it is pertinent to note that all these are abstract elements which happen only in the mind. At times, behaviour may result from feelings, which in turn derive their strength from beliefs. The three are integrated and people have attitudes resulting from experience, upbringing, beliefs, and a host of other events. We study how attitudes are formed with the objective of identifying how they translate into preferences for products and brands. McGuire (1968) wrote that prior attitudes predict subsequent behaviour.

Multi-attribute Attitude Model

Attitude towards a product or brand is a function of the attributes and the evaluation of those attributes by the consumer. The model combines multiple attributes of an object, each one evaluated on two factors: how much the consumer likes or dislikes the attribute, and the level of importance that the consumer attaches to that attribute. Fishbein and Ajzen (1980) explain that the overall attitude is the summation of each individual attribute's likeableness in accordance with the importance placed on each of those attributes. The multi-attribute model is a method to quantify a person's attitude towards an object. The model has practical marketing applications. How it is used in real life is illustrated in Exhibit 9.2, which shows how Times Celebex, or attitude towards film stars, is quantified using this model.

Fishbein's multi-attribute model uses two aspects for attitude measurement, the strength of beliefs and the evaluation of those beliefs. The model can be expressed in the following equation:

$$A_o = \sum_{i=1}^{n} b_i e_i$$

where
A_o = attitude towards an object
b_i = the strength of the belief that the object has attribute i
e_i = the evaluation of attribute i
n = the number of salient beliefs about the object

In this model, attitude is calculated by multiplying the belief score with the evaluation score for each attribute and then summing up across the number of beliefs. A calculation example of this method is given in Annexure 9.1 at the end of this chapter.

EXHIBIT 9.2 Measuring Attitudes towards Film Stars

A practical application of the multi-attribute model is the Times Celebex index, which measures the ranking of film stars based on consumer attitudes. According to the website, it is the 'most definitive rating index of Bollywood stars and the power they wield over the masses'.

The company calculates the 'T Score' by rating the stars' popularity, performance, and visibility. The parameters used for calculating the T score are (b_i) as follows:

- Box-office returns
- Staying in the news across print and television (TV)
- Visibility through brand endorsements on print and TV
- Promotions of their upcoming movie releases on print and TV
- Popularity among fans across media including the Internet and social networking sites

These are given weight based on their evaluations (e_i) and the index calculated by multiplying and adding.

The Economic Times (2012) writes that data is sourced from credible external agencies that service the media industry, and collated from more than 200 publications, 250 TV channels, over 10,000 cinema halls, and millions of Internet users. It is calculated on a monthly basis and is a measure of a celebrity's power as opposed to other one-time annual reports.

The ratings give an indication of star power—as to how much a star charges for films and also product endorsements. The Times Celebex is a practical application of the multi-attribute attitude model.

Sources:
The Economic Times, 'How Times Celebex will measure the ups and downs of bollywood stars', 29 October 2012, last accessed on 27 May 2013.
www.timescelebex.com, last accessed on 27 May 2013.

The model is useful for companies to assess the strength of their brand relative to those of the competition. By determining how consumers evaluate brand alternatives on important attributes.

Theory of Reasoned Action

When people arrive at their intentions through a reasoned approach, they are showing rational behaviour. The theory of reasoned action states that behavioural intention is a function of two components:

- The consumer's attitude towards a certain behaviour, and
- The subjective norm with regard to what other people think.

This can be shown by a simple equation

$$BI = A + SN$$

in which behavioural intention (BI) is seen as a sum of attitude (A) and subjective norm (SN). In other words, a person's intentions depend on the person's attitude about the action itself and what other people would think about it. Readers will be well aware of such behaviour as we not only consider our purchases but often take the opinion of our friends or parents during our shopping.

These two determinants are then multiplied by their respective weights and summed up to calculate the attitude. According to this theory, a consumer weighs his own liking for the product as well as what others might think before buying it. While sometimes the first aspect will weigh more on a consumer's mind, at others, the second aspect will seem more important.

Both the aforementioned aspects result from consumers' beliefs about performing the behaviour. Beliefs provide the cognitive foundation from which attitudes, social norms, and intentions follow. Beliefs are influenced by cultural, personal, and situational factors. Different groups of people hold different beliefs, as they are affected by the physical and social environment, exposure to information, as well as values and prejudices. That is why groups of friends show similar attitudes, dress similarly, and hold similar values.

Theory of reasoned action (TRA) is based on the following assumptions:

- Intention immediately precedes actual behaviour.
- Intention is determined by the attitude towards the behaviour, subjective norms, and perceived behavioural control.
- Intention is determined by underlying behavioural, normative, and control beliefs.
- Beliefs vary, based on a wide range of background factors.

According to Fishbein and Ajzen (1975), a consumer's intention to do something is a predictor of actual behaviour. Attitudes influence a consumer's intention, which in turn influences their behaviour. They describe behavioural intention as 'the subjective probability that one will perform some behaviour'.

Attitude towards the Ad

People are influenced by ads. While some ads are well liked by viewers, others are not. The feelings that consumers have for advertisements is called attitude towards the ad and it in turn, impacts the buying decision.

Attitude towards an ad is an effort to understand the impact of advertising or promotions on consumer attitudes toward products or brands and purchase. Consumers form various feelings, judgments, and perception as a result of exposure to an advertisement. This affects the consumer's attitude towards the ad and attitude towards the brand.

Lutz (1985) defined attitude towards the ad as a predisposition to respond in a favourable or unfavourable manner to a particular advertising stimulus during a particular exposure occasion.

Several factors affect A_{ad}. A person's attitude towards advertising in general and attitude towards the company releasing the ad, tend to colour perceptions and beliefs: consumers' attitudes toward advertising affect advertising effectiveness. That is, people who have positive attitudes toward advertising are more likely to be persuaded by it. Along with these, some other factors too affect attitude towards advertising. These are a consumer's perception of the ad, its credibility, the consumer's mood and state of mind, and ad cognition.

Lutz, et al. (1983) describe the following five antecedents of A_{ad}:

Credibility of the ad Credibility of the ad refers to how truthful or believable the consumers perceive the assertions made about the brand to be. Many ads, for instance, are dismissed by consumers as 'over the top' and are not taken seriously by them. Credibility of the ad is further affected by the perceived claim discrepancy of the ad, the credibility of the advertiser, and the credibility of advertising in general as perceived by consumers.

Perceptions of the ad Attitude towards ads is clearly dependent on how a consumer perceives them. Ads are often described as annoying, enjoyable, informative, shocking, or offensive. Some ads make liberal use of emotions such as humour, sensuousness, fear, happiness, and even irritation. All these have a direct bearing on perception and attitude towards the ad.

Attitude towards the advertiser   Consumers develop perceptions about certain companies. Some companies are thought of as better than others. People tend to regard advertisements of these companies as better than those of companies that they do not like. Not only do the ads of admired company get noticed more, but people tend to talk about them more and also feel warmly towards them.

Attitude towards advertising in general   Some people develop distrust of advertising over a period of time, due to deceptive advertising. Darke and Ritchie (2007) show that deceptive advertising engenders distrust, which affects people's responses to advertising. This negative bias operates through a process of defensive stereotyping—the initial deception induces negative beliefs about advertising and marketing in general, thus undermining the credibility of further advertising. Citing a Nielsen study, *Inc* (2012) reports there was a 20–25 per cent drop in trust of television and print ads since 2009, from a survey of 28,000 online consumers in 56 countries in 2011.

Consumers' affective state or 'mood' while seeing the ad   People who are in a positive mood are more open to persuasion or acceptance of the ad than an average person. A viewer who has good feelings is in a positive frame of mind and thus open to what he/she views. Research conducted by Owolabi (2009) shows that there is a significant effect of mood on advertising effectiveness.

Subsequent studies have tested attitude towards the ad on four variables, namely entertainment, information, irritation, and credibility. Chowdhury, et al. (2006) tested the direct influence of these elements on consumer attitude towards mobile ads in Bangladesh. The results showed that only credibility showed a positive and significant influence on consumer attitude towards mobile ads and that people held negative attitudes with regard to entertainment and information. In a similar study conducted in Iran, Javid, et al. (2012) found that entertainment was the most effective factor. That is, people enjoyed receiving the advertisements and companies could increase acceptability of ads by making them entertaining.

Eze and Lee (2012) in a study in Malaysia tested six independent variables, namely consumer manipulation, product information, hedonic or pleasure, economic condition, social integration, and materialism on consumers' attitude towards advertising. The analysis reveals that consumer manipulation resulted in negative attitudes towards advertising. Social integration and attitude towards advertising was insignificant, but the other four variables, that is, product information, pleasure, economic conditions, and materialism had positive influence on attitude towards advertising.

Attitude towards the ad (A_{ad}) in itself is not enough to sell products. It can at best act as a moderator between brand attitude (A_b) and purchase intention (PI). Lutz, et al. (1983) give four dimensions of A_{ad}.

Ad cognitions   How a consumer perceives and understands the content of the ad

Brand cognitions   How a consumer perceives the brand being advertised

Attitude towards the ad   The consumer's affective reactions, that is, liking or disliking the ad

Attitude towards the brand   The consumer's reactions toward the advertised brand, that is, whether people have an attitude of desire toward purchasing the brand

Purchase intention   The likelihood that recipients will purchase the brand in the future

Further, advertising music too plays a role. Lantos and Craton (2012) have studied consumer response to music in broadcast commercials based on four variables, namely listening, situation, musical stimulus, and listener characteristics, and found that these affect the consumer's attitude towards advertising music (A_{am}). Music is easily remembered and gets associated with a brand. They also write that music suggests an image as well because of the perceived 'personality' of the music, such as sophisticated, sexy, or light-hearted. This creates a brand image. A brand personality can be moulded as music creates new associations or uses existing associations.

Ads succeed only if we take all these aspects into account. The following four alternative models of A_{ad} explain how outcomes are mediated by attitude towards advertising:

Affect transfer hypothesis   This hypothesis states that ads directly influence the attitude towards the brand. Influence operates through brand cognition because of the positive relationship between attitudes and acceptance of the ad claims.

Dual mediation hypothesis   The more favourable feeling toward the ad the consumers have, the more ad claims they remember. Therefore, there is a direct relationship between attitude towards the ad and brand cognition.

Reciprocal mediation hypothesis   If a consumer is exposed to an ad advocating a particular brand, the consumer will try to maintain a balanced view of the ad with two outcomes, namely (a) liking both the ad and the brand or (b) disliking both.

Independent influences hypothesis   This hypothesis assumes that attitudes towards the ad and towards the brand have no relationship, and both of them independently influence purchase intention. Thus, ads do not necessarily influence purchase even if they are liked.

Attitude towards the Store

Companies realize that their brands will move only if consumers like the shops they are available in. They go to great pains to create channels that are most convenient for the customer, design retail stores to create an ambience that attracts customers, makes them spend time in the stores, and also loosen their purse strings. Attitude towards the store suggests that the feelings of a customer towards a store, including design and atmospherics, have a direct influence on purchases from the store.

There are several factors that impact a customer's attitude towards a store. Ailawadi and Keller (2004) write that store image is a function of five factors:

• Access to the store	• Cross-category product or service assortment
• In-store atmosphere	• Within-category product or service assortment
• Price and promotion	

In addition, perceived value, comfort, ease of ordering, and billing add to consumers' attitude towards certain stores. Retailers try hard to position themselves in the consumer's mind on one or many of these factors. Many stores that are successful in imparting attitude and loyalty do so because they are able to differentiate themselves or exhibit some tangible, intangible, functional, or psychological attributes that consumer perceive.

CB IN ACTION Attitude towards Ad

A question that is often debated in advertising circles is whether ads should win awards or should they sell? Often there is a dichotomy between the two. Agencies come up with heart-warming, endearing ads that are much appreciated but fail to achieve sales. In this exercise, analyse attitude towards the ad by doing a quick survey and link it to purchase intention.

Choose some ads from YouTube and show them to a selected sample of people. Make sure that while some are very likeable ads, others are not. Ask them whether they like the ad. In addition, ask them whether they like the brand or company being advertised, and finally, whether they intend to purchase the brand. Tabulate the results.

What can you infer from the completed table? Is there a correlation between attitude towards ad and intention to purchase? How many companies succeed in creating ads that are both likeable and will lead to purchases? Which brands are rated as, likeable but do not result in intention to purchase? What do you conclude from this exercise?

Brand	Attitude towards the ad	Attitude towards the brand or company	Intention to purchase
X			
Y			
Z			
...			

Attitude towards the store directly affects how much people buy from there and also whether they buy the store's private labels, which are more profitable to the store than national brands (see chapter-end case study in Chapter 8). Research done by Collin–Dodd and Lindley (2003) shows a positive relationship between consumers' perceptions of store brands and the store's image of store brands in general.

Semeijn, et al. (2004) conclude that store image has a double effect: a direct and positive effect about goods and services, and an indirect one by reducing the functional, financial, and psychological risks. Further, De Wulf, et al. (2005) add that a favourable attitude towards the store will develop consumer loyalty and strengthen confidence in the store.

Rzem and Debabi (2012) conducted a survey of customers at a retail store and found that perceived risk and perceived value affected attitude towards the store. Perceived risk was classified on three factors:

Functional risk   It is related to potential loss if the product is defective and is also referred to as risk of performance or physical risk.

Social risk or psychological risk   It represents the symbolic aspect of the product, for example, whether the product purchased will reflect the status for which it is bought

Financial risk   It is the price paid for the product

Perceived value impacts attitude towards a store more than perceived risk because it takes into account price and quality. Customers are likely to patronize a store if they see psychological or real value in it.

Theory of Trying to Consume

In many cases, the consumer wishes to buy a certain product but is not able to do so because of the following reasons:

- There are financial limits as to how much a consumer can spend
- The product may have limited availability
- It requires great effort on the part of the consumer, like diet control for controlling weight

The theory of trying to consume is an attitude theory that accounts for cases where the outcome is not certain, but instead reflects the consumer's attempt to consume.

Rational behaviour assumes that once a positive attitude is made, no impediments stand in the way of consumption. However, consumers may have limitations, such as lack of money, environmental contingencies, or unconscious habits.

Bagozzi and Warshaw (1990) explain in their paper, *Trying to Consume*, that this theory tries to extend rational behaviour by pointing out impediments that arise when people cannot buy a product. They add further dimensions to understanding consumer attitudes:

- Success, failure, and the process of trying
- Incorporating self-efficacy judgments as expectations of success and failure
- Refinement of the model to reflect trying as the focal concept

At other times, consumers fail to see or are ignorant of their options, or they make a conscious effort not to consume, even though they have a positive attitude towards a product.

Theory of Planned Behaviour

The theory of planned behaviour is an extension of the theory of reasoned action. It shows that a person's intentions influence behaviour. They are indications of how hard people will try or how much effort they are planning to exert to buy something. The stronger the intention, the more likely it is that the person will buy the object of desire. This theory is discussed in Chapter 3.

ATTITUDE FORMATION

We have so far studied how attitudes impact on products and brands. Since attitudes play a great role in consumer choice and purchase decisions, marketing managers are interested to know how attitudes are formed and how they might be changed. They know that once consumer attitudes are developed in favour of particular brands, they result in strong loyalty that competitors will find difficult to dislodge. This section describes the crucial area of attitude formation and change.

Attitudes are formed primarily by observing other people, which is explained by 'mirror neurons' in the brain. People are likely to develop the same beliefs as their peer groups or someone they hold in high esteem. Children, for example, learn the attitudes of their parents and usually begin to demonstrate similar outlooks. In a direct application of this technique, the producers of diamonds placed the products in movies and on the hands of celebrities to develop a favourable attitude for the products (see chapter-opening case study in Chapter 8).

Apart from observing others, attitudes are also formed through personal experience, personality factors, and by the dictates of society and culture.

Role of Experience

Though attitudes are learned in a variety of ways, they form directly as a result of experience. That is why companies try to add an element of experience. This is done through the following means:

Sampling Manufacturers offer free samples of their products with the hope that consumers will use them and develop positive attitude towards them. For example, when short messaging service (SMS) was introduced, it was offered free to subscribers. When people used it, they developed a liking for it.

Below-the-line campaigns Below-the-line (BTL) campaigns encourage people to participate in contests and events and are organized so that the experience is remembered and positive associations built up with the brand.

Direct marketing When a salesman visits a consumer's home, the display of products or their demonstration is another method of imparting a memorable experience.

Internet Companies try to engage customers on the Internet through various methods, and engage them to take up activities so that they remember the brands when they go shopping.

Role of Personality

The role of personality in consumer behaviour is discussed in Chapter 5. How it affects attitude is explained here.

Much of attitude formation depends on the psychological make-up of a person, for the simple reason that attitudes themselves are psychological. Consumers with different personality traits have different feelings toward brands. A person's needs and cravings will define what affects him or her.

A further dimension is added by the concept of brand personality. People prefer brands that more closely match their own self-concept. In fact, human and brand personality mutually reinforce each other. As Karanika and Hogg (2013) write, products become part of consumers' extended selves, either before acquisition or afterwards. Thus, companies try to align brand personalities with people's personalities. Marketing managers have to understand consumers' evolving relationships and experiences with products throughout the consumption cycle. Successful brands, such as Apple and Samsung, are able to strike a chord with customers because they begin to see the brands as their own extended selves and affect consumer attitudes as a consequence.

Role of Society

Social roles and norms have a strong influence on attitudes. While social roles lay down expectations as to how people should behave in certain roles, social norms set out rules for appropriate behaviour. They also lay down what people should have and what they should consume.

The social judgement theory (SJT) given by Sherif and Hovland (1961) explained us how people process new information and form immediate opinions. The SJT states that people evaluate ideas by comparing them with their current attitudes, referred to as their *cognitive map*. We do this daily in our heads—when we hear of a new idea or come across an advertisement, we compare it with our present point of view, and accept or reject it. In other words, when we hear a message, we immediately judge it on our attitude scale in our minds. We judge messages as they are received. SJT is thus the subconscious sorting of ideas that happens the moment we come across things. Based on our ego-involvement, we see whether they fall within our latitude of acceptance.

The implication for marketing is that manufacturers should try and place their products within the cognitive map or frame of reference of consumers within a culture. As consumers start using products, their frame of reference become narrower resulting in the building up of habits and social attitudes.

Social attitudes, some dictated by culture, and others dictated by the community, are the strongest. Though the role of society and culture has been discussed in another chapter, how social attitudes are formed is summarized here.

Culture It imposes rules and restrictions on how people consume products. It includes knowledge, beliefs, morals, and customs received by members of that culture. Culture is a fundamental determinant of a person's wants and behaviour. A child growing up in a society learns basic values, perceptions, preferences, and behaviours through a process of socialization involving the family and other institutions.

Social class All human societies exhibit social stratification in the form of social classes. This builds attitudes in two ways. First, people within a social class tend to behave alike and share similar consumption habits. Second, people within a social class have similar occupation, income, wealth, education, and finally, the same values and attitudes.

Reference groups A person's behaviour is strongly influenced by reference groups. As we have seen earlier in the chapter, young people, for instance, dress alike and hold the same attitudes as their group members. Religious affiliations too exert a strong influence on attitudes.

Family It schools a person's attitude towards religious, politics, economics, personal ambitions, self-worth, and love. Even when the person no longer interacts with parents when he/she shifts out, their influence on the unconscious behaviour of the buyer is significant.

Role and status People also develop attitudes because of their role and status. People behave in a certain way sometimes 'to keep up appearances' in society. Advertisers use this very effectively by attaching products to status.

However, it is not always the case that attitudes lead to action. Very often attitudes lie in a latent state or people try to hide their attitudes, especially when they relate to socially unacceptable behaviour. It is important to consider the link between attitude and behaviour—when behaviour will result from attitudes and when it will not.

ATTITUDE AND BEHAVIOUR

As we have explained in the theory of trying to consume, attitudes do not necessarily result in purchase and consumption of any product. After all, we do not buy everything that we like. Social psychology has found that attitudes and actual behaviour are not always perfectly aligned. Examples abound. In India, we have seen that many people have a political alignment and support a particular candidate but more than half the population does not go out and vote. Similarly, a consumer may decide not to consume a product as it is bad for health, but buys it out of sheer force of habit.

As Myers (2013) explains, if people don't play the same game that they talk, attempts to change behaviour by changing attitudes often fail. He cites examples of warnings about the dangers of smoking that only minimally affect those who smoke. Similarly, people often talk of the harms of watching too much television but watch it more than ever.

People are more likely to behave according to their attitudes under certain conditions, when

- attitudes are the result of personal experience
- consumers are experts in the subject
- consumers expect a favourable outcome
- attitudes are repeatedly expressed
- consumers stand to win or lose something due to the issue

Very often it works the other way round. We do things and then find reasons for doing them. Attitudes may well follow behaviour, than lead it. As Festinger (1957) wrote, behaviour was very often the horse and our attitudes the cart. This poses a problem for companies. how can they change attitudes—should they target a person's thinking or behaviour? Wicker (1969) concluded from his research that marketing managers face a huge challenge in changing attitudes as people's expressed attitudes hardly predicted their buying behaviour. It has also been noted that in some cases, people actually alter their attitudes to better align them with their behaviour.

Though it is a difficult task, attitudes can be changed. Various methods are used to influence consumers' attitudes and behaviour.

CHANGING ATTITUDES

Attitudes are not set in stone. Attitudes can, and do, change. As described in Chapter 8, people learn new things and change their beliefs. Some classic examples of changing attitudes towards products are described here.

Mobile phones When mobile phones were first launched, people had the apprehension that it would be a burden to carry a device around, and further, that it would be a disturbance as people could reach them at any time of night or day. Today, people see it more as a necessity.

Jeans Indian women prefer traditional clothes and jeans were at one time seen as too 'modern'. Some Indian men still have problems with women wearing jeans—*India Today* (2012) reports that posters were put up in Ranchi saying, 'Any girl found wearing jeans and moving without *dupatta* will be attacked with acid'. Yet, it is now a common sight to see women wearing jeans in Indian cities.

Fast food Indians have always preferred traditional food. A meal was an incomplete thought without roti or rice. Slowly, attitudes towards fast food such as burgers and pizzas have changed and these are now accepted as full meals in themselves.

Attitudes are indeed viewed as means to change or modify behaviour. This is done through persuasion that is key to behavioural change. Attitude change has been described by three theories, namely learning, elaboration likelihood, and the cognitive dissonance theories. The ideal point method (IPM) is used to find out why people buy. These theories are described here.

Learning Theory
Attitudes change through learning. Classical and operant conditioning, as well as observational learning, can bring about attitudinal change. While classical conditioning creates positive attitudes towards a product or brand, operant conditioning strengthens desirable attitudes and weakens undesirable ones, as explained in Chapter 8. Advertisers use classical conditioning to influence attitude towards a particular product. Television commercials depict beautiful young people consuming products and having fun. Our attitude changes and the appealing imagery causes us to develop a positive association with those products. In operant conditioning, advertisers use fear appeals to change attitudes, for example, to discourage smoking.

Elaboration Likelihood Model
Bagozzi, et al. (2010) write that elaboration likelihood model (ELM) proposes that attitudes can be changed as a result of different psychological processes: the effortful elaboration, called the central route and non-thoughtful processes, called the peripheral route. This gives us two strategies for attitude change. First, consumers can be motivated to listen and think about the message, thus leading to an attitude shift. Or, they might be influenced by characteristics of the speaker, leading to a temporary or surface shift in attitude. Messages that are thought-provoking and that appeal to logic are more likely to lead to permanent changes in attitudes.

Cognitive Dissonance Theory
Festinger (1957) investigated cognitive dissonance and proposed the theory that we have an inner drive to keep our attitudes and beliefs in harmony and avoid disharmony or dissonance. Tension or cognitive dissonance results when opposing beliefs clash. To avoid the unpleasant feelings or the psychological distress, we try to reduce or eliminate them, and achieve consonance. People learn to change their attitudes, beliefs, or behaviour so as to reduce this tension.

Ideal Point Method
Ideal point method (IPM) is a mathematical method to solve multi-objective problems. Consumers assign different reasons for buying a product, by assigning psychological importance to attributes such as price, taste, and brand association. According to the ideal point method, a consumer buys a product based on how closely it fits with the consumer's single most preferred product attribute or the attitude of how the product 'should' be. The ideal point is defined as a combination of attributes and attribute-values describing the ideal choice of the consumer. Consumers often make decisions based on already formed preferences for a particular product and, if this product is available, they will buy it without making detailed evaluation of the other options. On some other occasions, however, consumers are undecided and they do not have a preferred option, or their preferred option is not available. In such cases, they assess their 'ideal point' based on what they think the product should be, and make a choice. Companies learn to shift the ideal point in the consumers' minds.

Strategies for Attitude Change

Companies are interested in how attitudes can be changed. Marketing strategy consists of changing attitudes towards products. The examples given in the previous section show that it would have been very difficult to sell mobile phones, fast food, jeans, and a host of products in India if attitudes towards them had not changed. While developing a positive attitude towards products creates customer loyalty, innovative products require societal change in attitudes.

The following are some of the methods by which attitudes can be changed:

- By changing the motivational function, that is, why people buy the brand
- Associating the product with an admired person, group or event, by introducing celebrities, social causes, or product placement
- Resolve conflicting attitudes by reducing negative attitudes about a product or highlighting attributes to take on the competition
- Altering components by adding attributes or changing brand beliefs
- Changing consumer beliefs about competitors

Changing the Motivational Function

Consumer attitudes toward a product or brand can be changed by highlighting particular needs. In the functional approach, attitudes are classified in terms of four functions, namely the utilitarian function, the ego-defensive function, the value-expressive function, and the knowledge function. By changing one of the elements in the product, we can change how consumers perceive products.

Utilitarian function Products fulfil certain utility functions. One way of changing attitudes in favour of a product is by highlighting a utilitarian function that people have considered.

Ego-defensive function People have a self-concept and want to protect this. They look for a sense of security and personal confidence. Ads for cosmetics and personal care products, by acknowledging this need, increase both their relevance to the consumer and the likelihood of a favourable attitude change by offering reassurance to the consumer's self-concept.

Value-expressive function People buy certain products to reflect their values, life styles, and outlook. For instance, people express themselves by owning the latest smartphone. It is common to see people in a public place displaying their iPhones and Galaxy mobiles. Apparel brands help display attitudes by placing their brand logos where they can be displayed by consumers (Fig. 9.5). Companies look for opportunities to serve customers and make products that help them reflect their values, lifestyle, or outlook.

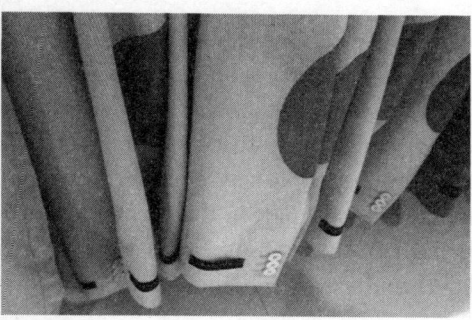

FIG. 9.5 Value-expressive function

Knowledge function People have a cognitive desire to know about the products they buy. This 'need to know' is used by companies to provide information about products that helps the consumer in placing the product on a higher need platform.

CB IN ACTION   Consumers and the Environment

It is said that consumer attitudes are changing, for instance, thanks to the ill-effects of pollution, people are becoming much more aware and concerned about environmental causes. However, when this is translated to consumer behaviour, we see quite a different picture.

- Given the choice between buying a small, cheap car that would consume less oil and a gas guzzler SUV, many people who otherwise are environmentally aware, prefer the latter
- Environment friendly products are now available in stores but they tend to cost more. Despite being environmentally aware, people often choose the cheaper product without any regard for the harm it may cause to the environment
- People often take part in rallies and programmes to keep their city clean, but throw garbage on the nearest open ground because it is easier to do so

1. How would you explain this behaviour?
2. What would you do to encourage environmental friendly purchases in the aformentioned instances?

Associating Products with a Cause or Event

People tend to think positively of a product or brand if it is connected to an event or cause which is close to their heart. Companies try to change consumer attitudes by sponsoring events or causes, event marketing, and product placement. Please see Exhibit 9.3.

Close, et al. (2006) writes that event marketing is a tool for experiential marketing. Events add sensory, emotional, cognitive, and behavioural aspects to a marketing programme. They show that people who attend the events are enthusiastic about them and get positively influenced by the sponsor's products. People who are more community-minded are appreciative of the sponsor as a result of their event experience and a better opinion of the sponsor contributes to increased intentions to purchase the sponsor's products.

To effectively use this method, events are coupled with promotional activities so that people can gain consumption experience. Events are also an opportunity to engage the consumer with a company and its brands. By raising the involvement level of those who attend, events cause consumers to be more receptive to marketing messages than they would be if exposed only to advertisements in the mass media. Sponsorship of events and sports marketing provide avenues to impart customer experience and thereby be better remembered by consumers.

Sponsorship

It is the acquisition of rights to associate a product or brand with an event or organization for mutual benefit. The brand gets promoted during the event while the organizing party gets paid. However, companies must choose events carefully for relatedness so that they change attitude towards the sponsoring company. *Relatedness* means that consumers must begin to relate the cause to the brand through the event. If the cause is very popular, people will remember the brand for a long time. However, if there is no relatedness, people will take part in the event and forget about the sponsoring company. Sponsorship must be done so that consumers develop positive mental association with the sponsors, which may spill over to their other brands. Companies may sponsor events or sports extravaganzas.

EXHIBIT 9.3 Companies with a Cause

Tata With the spirit of what comes from society should go back to society, Tata Chemicals has evolved an initiative it calls *Desh Ko Arpan*. Workers who work the salt beds are all migrants and lead a semi-nomadic life. Because of this, their children don't attend school. Under the *Desh Ko Arpan* programme the company fulfils an important corporate social responsibility: it supports non-government organizations which run hostels and crèches for these children and provide education to them. Over 45 villages have been supported over the last two years.

Tata Salt provides a variety of products. See Figure 9.6.

Dainik Bhaskar The share of consumption in key urban towns and the rest of urban India—excluding the six metros—had leapfrogged 70% (Source: An Ernst & Young study 2010). This substantiated Dainik Bhaskar's long-held belief that India's buoyant economic growth was not confined to a restricted geography but was, in fact, a movement sweeping regions even outside the metros. However, while economic gains were a reality in Bhaskar markets, water scarcity was identified by the group as an emerging problem. *Dainik Bhaskar* launched its Jal Satyagrah which highlighted the importance of conserving this resource and showed the many ways in which an individual could contribute. During *Holi*, for instance, it urged people to play with dry colours, thus also preventing contamination of otherwise clean water.

The Group also helped place Indore on the international map. At a *Dainik Bhaskar* event in collaboration with the Indian Tea Board and Tata Tea in February 2008, it created a Guinness World Record when it hosted the world's largest tea party, playing host to 32,681 people. It also helped the

FIG. 9.7 Print ad of Dainik Bhaskar

Courtesy: Superbrands

government cross-check its own implementation of the Jawaharlal Nehru National Urban Renewal Mission (JNNURM) initiative by conducting social audits across states.

On a less serious note, it surprised its readers on Holi in 2011 when it distributed the country's first perfumed newspaper to 4,168,889 readers of Dainik Bhaskar, Divya Bhaskar and Saurashtra Samachar. The kewra, or screw pine, scented newspaper not only became a talking point it also made it to the Limca Book of Records.

The promotions, that the newspaper does are much less about selling but a lot more about developing proactive suggestions that invite action, in turn, helping in community building. One such initiative, the *Zidd Karo Duniya Badlo* (insist on changing the world) call sought the involvement of its readers to aggressively take up causes they believed in. Going by its values, print ad of Dainik Bhaskar states that there are no paid news in it. Please see Fig. 9.7.

FIG. 9.6 Range of Tata Salt and spices

Courtesy: Superbrands

Source: Superbrands 2012

ETHICAL INSIGHT
Cause-related Marketing

Cause-related marketing refers to marketing that involves the cooperative efforts of a business and a non-profit organization for mutual benefit. Though the term is sometimes used to refer to any social marketing effort, cause-marketing differs from corporate social responsibility (CSR) or philanthropy, since it is a marketing relationship for a cause. Cause-related marketing links a company or a brand to a social cause.

In 1983, American Express first used 'cause-related marketing' when it launched a three-month programme for the Statue of Liberty Restoration Project. The objective was to increase card use and new card applications and at the same time to raise money and awareness for the non-profit Restoration Fund. American Express donated one cent for every card transaction and one dollar for every new card application to the fund. The effort was backed by a $4 million advertising campaign. It not only resulted in increase in card usage and new card application, but also helped the Restoration Fund raise over $1.7 million in three months.

The effort demonstrated that cause-marketing could achieve results by linking a company or brand to a cause and enabling its consumers to financially support a cause. Since then, cause-marketing programmes have evolved into sophisticated techniques in which companies achieve their goals while serving a social cause. This helps them achieve a better corporate image, since people begin to trust companies that support causes. It is a win-win situation as companies increase their sales, the NGO gets more funds, and the consumer feels happy that a part of the purchase is going for a good cause.

An Infosys white paper (2013) explains that cause-related marketing has the following impacts:

Brand loyalty By attracting customers and building long-term relationships with them, the company builds brand loyalty over the long term.

Market differentiation By creating an alternate and distinctive approach in advertising, companies can identify themselves better by linking themselves to community efforts.

Connect with stakeholders While external stakeholders feel that they are doing business with a good cause, internal stakeholders engage and bond with the company and participate in community efforts.

There are different types of cause-marketing campaigns. One of the most common types of the relationship is when the company donates a small amount such as ₹1 for each purchase made by the customer. However, many companies commit themselves to causes for the long term.

Infosys

The Infosys Foundation supports programmes and organizations devoted to the cause of the destitute, rural poor, mentally challenged, and economically disadvantaged sections of the society. It was established in 1996 with the objective *'Bahujana hithaya, bahujana sukhaya'*—for the benefit of many, for the happiness of many. It now works in several states such as Karnataka, Tamil Nadu, Andhra Pradesh, Maharashtra, Orissa, and Punjab. Its dedicated team identifies programmes in the areas of health care, education, culture, destitute care, and rural development.

The Infosys Foundation (see Fig. 9.8) partners with non-government organizations (NGOs) to support causes. Some of these are as follows:

- It partnered with local NGOs to construct homes across 18 villages in five districts under the state government's 'Aasare' scheme
- It constructed hospital wards and built *dharmashalas* (rest houses) at the National Institute of Mental Health and Neuro Sciences (NIMHANS)

Fig. 9.8 Infosys Foundation
Source: Infosys Foundation, reprinted with permission

(Contd)

ETHICAL INSIGHT (Contd)

in Bangalore. The Foundation also donates medicines and medical equipment to hospitals, and organizes health camps in rural India
- It partners with schools in rural India to enhance education and library facilities. Under the 'library for every rural school' project, it established more than 50,000 school libraries across Karnataka. It also donates books in Karnataka, Andhra Pradesh, Orissa, and Kerala, and has set up more than 10,150 libraries in rural government schools.

Reliance

Reliance Foundation focuses on five causes, namely rural transformation, education, health, urban renewal, and arts, culture, and heritage. It seeks to bring corporate systems and processes to the social sector.

Reliance Foundation launched the 'Bharat India Jodo' (BIJ) campaign which aims to bridge the gap between rural and urban India by strengthening sustainable agriculture practices amongst small and marginal farmers. Its information services programme provides advisories on climatic conditions, water- and weather-related risks, methods of handling new pests and diseases, sharing of best practices, and better farming methods. The Foundation:
- provides education to 15,000 children across 12 schools. A Reliance Institute of Technology in Jamnagar and Reliance Polytechnic in Dwarka add to the effort
- It has conducted over 10,000 cornea transplants across India since 2003 under Reliance Drishti, in association with National Association for the Blind (NAB). It launched India's first registered national Braille newspaper in Hindi in 2012.
- It has instituted the 'real heroes' to recognize ordinary Indians who are making a difference to people's lives.

Dr Reddy's Laboratories

Dr. Reddy's Foundation (DRF) is a non-profit partner of Dr. Reddy's Laboratories. It operates in two sectors, namely livelihoods and education. Through vocational training programmes, DRF addresses the issues of employability, income generation, and consequent improvement in quality of life. It also provides opportunities for learning to those who have never been to school, or have dropped out of it; in addition, it works to improve the quality of education in schools.

It has a unique livelihood advancement business school (LABS) project, which addresses the needs of youth aged 18–35 years who are constrained by low-income levels and inadequate skills. They are trained in livelihood and soft skills in tune with industry requirements. LABS programmes have been launched in association with several corporate partners such as the following:
- Michael & Susan Dell Foundation in 47 cities to provide employability skills to 36,000 youth and provide them suitable placements
- Accenture to give demand-driven livelihood training and placement assistance for 250 'below the poverty line' (BPL) youth in Chennai
- Ernst & Young for a programme of community engagement, education, entrepreneurship, and environmental sustainability.
- BlackRock to set up a livelihood advancement school linked with placements for youth from socially and economically challenged backgrounds at Loni in Delhi NCR region
- Confederation of Indian Industry (CII) to run LABS programmes in Pune and Mumbai, in association with CII-Young Indians
- Cisco to impart online e-learning under the aegis of the Cisco networking academy that conducts a globally certified 'IT essentials' course to provide training in basic hardware, software, and network operating systems to disadvantaged youth, enabling them to get good entry-level positions as technicians and hardware engineers, as well as in marketing, sales, and BPO services

Fair & Lovely Foundation

Since its inception in 2003, Fair & Lovely Foundation (FLF) has played a role in changing the lives of more than 1500 girls, by empowering them through education and career development. By providing scholarships, Fair & Lovely provides opportunities to girls across the country. Through FLF, Hindustan Unilever Limited (HUL) provides young women the means to avail higher education. The FLF scholarship of one lakh rupees helps academically brilliant girls from the lowest economic strata of the society fulfil their dreams of higher education.

(Contd)

ETHICAL INSIGHT (Contd)

Do these cause-related initiatives help companies acquire a socially responsible image?

Sources:
http://drreddysfoundation.org/index.html.
http://www.infosys.com/infosys-foundation/default.asp.
http://www.reliancefoundation.org/.
Infosys, Cause and effect: Modelling CRM to measure the impact of cause-related marketing, http://www.infosys.com/crm/idea-center/pages/index.aspx, 2013.
All websites last accessed on 18 October 2013.

Event marketing is defined as the practice of promoting the interests of a company and its brands by associating the organization with a specific event or activity. Event marketing also involves sponsorship, but this is not always the case. Sponsorship refers to the staging of an event wherein a company associates with another entity's event by paying a sponsorship fee. In event marketing, the sponsor blends its message and that engages consumers. This is most helpful in building attitudes.

For instance, a company may help stage a play on social causes by arranging a venue and in return the company's message is woven into the play. It can also engage consumers during and after the play. In this way consumers, start viewing the company's message as part of the event rather than as an advertising communication.

By ensuring that the brand is remembered and positive attitudes built around it, managers are able to increase the return on investment (ROI) on marketing spends. That is why events are an ideal way to supplement mass marketing activities. In a study conducted by Osterman Research (2009), it was found that in terms of ROI, face-to-face event marketing outperforms other forms of marketing activities. It found that events are a primary lead generation method, followed by telemarketing activities, webinars, and in-person seminars.

Sports marketing consist of sponsorships of individual athletes or an athletic event. Sports marketing have become very big in recent years. In India, the Indian Premier League (IPL) is one of the biggest sports marketing events. Since the matches are watched by millions of people both in stadia and on television, brand messages are received by these consumers when they watch a match. Companies get huge exposure through sports events and consumers remember the sponsors who promote the sporting events. Such activities favourably changes attitude towards the sponsoring brand.

Sports events provide a perfect fit to some advertisers because of two reasons: first, by getting a committed target audience, and second, by placing the product in the proper context. For instance, a soft drink company will be a perfect sponsor for a match as its product can be shown being served to players during breaks and viewers develop a positive image of the product. The fit helps boost brand recall. Earlier, image-building was the main objective of sponsoring sports events, but now advertisers want to see if their money is well spent. Measuring brand recall contributes to return on investment (ROI).

Product Placement

Product placement is a practice of placing brand name, logo, package, signage, and other trademarks in the content of mass media programming, mainly in movies and TV shows. It is aimed

MARKETING INSIGHT
Product Placements

One of the earliest product placements was done by the diamond industry (Chapter 8). Diamonds were placed in movies and on the hands of stars, which affected a generation of movie watchers. In 1982, the blockbuster movie *ET: The Extra Terrestrial* showed an alien creature that was lured from its hiding place with Reese's candy. De Gregorio and Sung (2010) write that brand sales increased by 65 per cent in just the three months following the movie's release. Some of the most successful product placements have been in James Bond movies, with the brands been shown in them gaining tremendous consumer attitude, mainly because of the way that they were presented. The Aston Martin, for instance, is part of the storyline and is therefore remembered as a 'Bond' brand. The most successful product placements happen when the products are an integral part of the plot. Otherwise they lurk in movie frames, hoping that someone will notice them.

Product placement has been done in Indian movies and television shows as well. One of the most successful product placements was in Raj Kapoor's film *Bobby* in which the protagonist Rishi Kapoor is seen riding a Rajdoot motor cycle in several scenes.

In the promo for the movie, *Zindagi Na Milegi Dobara*, one of the protagonists Farhan Akhtar is seen taking a swig of Mountain Dew before trying to do some gravity-defying adventure sports. Mountain Dew is associated with adventure and the movie was also about some friends embarking on an adventure trip. In another film, *Chalo Dilli*, Kellogg's is seen on the screen.

Another development is co-branded promotions. A hit song from the hit movie *Dabangg* made Emami's Zandu Balm suddenly popular. The company sued the producer of the film but later agreed for an out of court settlement as the brand actually rode to popularity on the song.

Television producers have also discovered that product placements can become revenue streams. Krishnamurthy (2011) writes that though product placement has been common since the 1980s in the US, Indian television viewers started seeing products as part of the programming content from the early 2000s. Products were placed unobtrusively in reality shows such as *Bigg Boss*, *Indian Idol*, *Sach Ka Samna*, and *Rakhi Ka Swayamvar*. Product placements during shows include branded coffee mugs, laptops, and branded premises. In Bigg Boss 3, Vodafone placed its logo inside the pool in the Bigg Boss house. In fiction serials, products were integrated in the storylines: serials like *Bade Acche Lagte Ho* had its characters talking about using Garnier products. Movies were also promoted in serials when the lead actors walked into certain episodes. However, how effective they were is not known.

The product placement market is worth over ₹1000 crore in India today. Khandelwal (2011) reports that brand integration with content (BIC) has moved from a mere passive saliency-driven approach to active audience engagement. Several agencies offer expertise in this. Among the established players are P9, part of the Percept Group, Limelight, part of Lintas, Mates of Madison, Group M's ESP, Mudra Max from Mudra, Showdiff Worldwide from Rediffusion Y&R, Ogilvy Live from Ogilvy India, and Leo Entertainment from Leo Burnett.

As these ads affect customers subconsciously, some countries are regulating them. Hackley (2012) writes that in the UK, viewers are prompted by a 'P' logo when they are seeing a product placement on their TV screens. Product placements are not allowed on children's shows.

Rezwana (2013) reports of many innovative methods of placing ads in unexpected places. In Japan, advertising stickers are placed on the leg, between the hem of a short skirt and the top of a long sock. This has for long attracted attention of young girls and manga (a Japanese form of comic strip) enthusiasts. DDB Auckland placed ads on the exposed thighs of people. FeelUnique.com, an online beauty products store, paid 10 men and women to apply temporary tattoos with the company's web address on their eyelids and then wink at strangers. Air New Zealand hired 30 individuals to carry the message 'Need a change? Head down to New Zealand' on their clean-shaven heads.

(Contd)

MARKETING INSIGHT (Contd)

> Do product placements work? Do people become motivated to buy products whose ads are seen at unexpected places? Look for other creative methods for product placements.
>
> Sources:
> Hackley, Chris, 'Unpaid product placement: The elephant in the room in UK TV's new paid for product placement market', *International Journal of Advertising*, Vol. 31, No. 4, 2012, pp. 703–718.
>
> Khandelwal, Payal, 'A smart serve', *Financial Express*, 12 July 2011.
>
> Krishnamurthy, Jagadeesh, 'TV product placement', 10 March 2011, http://www.campaignindia.in/Article/250811,all-about-tv-product-placement.aspx, last accessed on 13 April 2014.
>
> Manjur, Rezwana, 'LOOK do you really want your ads there?', http://marketing-interactive.com/news/41331, 2013, last accessed on 13 April 2014.

at influencing movie and television audiences, not by direct advertising but by showing the brands in the programming. The most successful product placement occurs when the brands are part of the story line. Dens, et al. (2012) show that while brand recognition scores are highest for brand placements that are both highly prominent and strongly plot connected, brand attitude is most positive when brands are strongly connected to the plot, but placed less prominently.

Audiences are influenced in three ways through product placement.

- They cannot skip the advertising as can be done in conventional advertising
- Seeing the brands in media programming affects the audiences both consciously and subconsciously and helps in building brand attitude
- They start imitating actors who are shown using the brands, through mirror neurons in the brain

Homer (2009) writes that the type of placement—subtle or prominent—and repetition interact to impact consumer judgments. She writes that for subtle cases of product placement, consumer attitudes are relatively positive. The findings of her research suggest that studios have to evaluate placement options carefully, as repetition of placements may lead to reduced effect.

Resolving Conflicting Attitudes

Conflicting attitudes arise among consumers as they interact with brands and consume them. Though there can be many attitudinal conflicts, three types of conflicting attitudes are commonly seen: one arising from globalization, second from conflict with self-identity, and the third relating to gender image.

Global and Local Culture Conflict

Very often, consumers feel a conflict between their culture and the culture brought along by globalization. Strizhakova, et al. (2012) mentions that globalization often requires consumers to make difficult trade-offs. The global and local consumer cultures can sometimes be in a conflicting relationship: in many countries including India, global consumer culture is often portrayed as being in conflict with traditional or religious values. Companies have to resolve the attitudes arising from conflicting cultures.

For instance, in India, a majority of people are strict vegetarians. To get over this attitude, fast food giants had to change their menu. *The Times of India* (2013) reports that global restaurant chains, such as Subway, Pizza Hut, and McDonalds, which are mainly known for their non-vegetarian fare, are offering vegetarian food and also Jain food in Gujarat. Another chain, KFC, not only introduced vegetarian meals, but also undertook a campaign to assure customers that vegetarian meals were made in separate areas and in separate utensils.

Conflict with Self-identity

Reed, et al. (2012) writes that each person has self identity, which is multidimensional and consists of role identity and social identity. Because both identities may be desirable to a person, the associations of one identity may interfere with the associations of another identity and may produce identity conflict. Consumption can often lead to identity conflict, or provide ways to resolve it. An example of identity conflict occurs when a person wants to buy a car. The efficiency of the car, that is, kilometres per litre of petrol, is of prime importance because of the high price of fuel. However, because of her social identity, she will consider buying a bigger, less efficient car. Companies have to resolve such identity conflicts to change attitudes.

Conflict with Gender-bending

Another type of conflict will arise if a product meant for one sex is extended to include the other sex: consumers face problems when masculine brands are extended to female versions, and vice versa. Avery (2012) describes this type of conflict. She studied the Porsche Cayenne SUV launch to analyse how men buying a 'male' brand respond to perceived brand gender contamination. She explains that Porsche owners stratify themselves along gender lines and create an in-group that is sharply defined by masculinity and an out-group that is defined by femininity. The company's attempt to gender-bend the masculine brand constitutes a threat to males who identify with the brand. Social barriers limit access to Porsche's meanings to those who achieve masculine ideals and cause the SUV owners to resort to hyper-masculine behaviours to combat exclusion. Conflict in attitudes arises if the firm tries to gender-bend the brand and can trigger a range of coping responses.

Altering Attitude Components

We have seen that in the multi-attribute model, consumer beliefs about brands and the evaluation of these beliefs influence the overall attitude towards the brand. We could change the beliefs about the product or attempt to change the evaluations by consumers. Assael (2005) gives four strategies than can be formulated for changing attitude components.

Change the values placed on product attributes In this strategy, companies try to convince consumers to reassess the value of a particular attribute.

Change brand beliefs This strategy uses advertising to change consumers' evaluations of products. Either existing product attributes are highlighted, or new product attributes are introduced.

Change brand attitudes In this strategy, companies use emotions and feelings to change attitude towards the brand. Some of the perceptions that brands are associated with are those of hedonism or luxury, status or fantasy.

Change behavioural intentions Companies try to induce customers by providing them discounts and offers. This is usually the case with new brands, the idea being to make customers buy the brand and having used it, wean customers away from the existing brands.

Changing Consumer Beliefs about Competitors

Companies also try to change consumer beliefs about competitors. A direct way is by publishing a comparison with a competing product. Or it can be done indirectly, by creating a perception such as 'washes whiter than any washing powder'. Comparative advertising attacking the USP of a competing brand is frequently used to change perceptions about competitor brands. *Business Today* (2013) reported the disputes between companies that had attempted to change the attitude towards each other's competing brands:

- Fortune rice bran cooking oil was advertised as healthier and cheaper than Marico's edible oils
- Reckitt Benkiser claimed that its Dettol dishwashing liquid was 100 times better than HUL's Vim brand. HUL retorted with an ad asking consumers to use the power of 100 lemons rather than use an antiseptic to clean utensils
- Pepsi's ad for Atom cola makes fun of the daredevil action that is used to advertise Coca-Cola's Thums Up brand

CONCLUSION

The relationship between consumers and products is a fascinating one. We have seen how people develop feelings and attitudes towards things, and discovering these attitudes towards products and brands is basic to marketing. To some extent, it is possible today for companies to make psychological profiles of customers based on their online activity, and match them with brands and products. This raises two issues. The first is the ethical issue of whether people are being manipulated into liking products and brands. Companies will have to wrestle with this issue sometime in the future.

The second issue is whether customers really want this. We have seen an explosion of activity designed to change our attitudes. *The Economist* (2013) writes that in America alone, $170 billion are spent on direct marketing attempts at improving relations with customers. Yet, only 3 per cent of the consumers bought anything at all. Online marketing is worse, with only a 0.1 per cent conversion rate. 'That means that about $165 billion was spent not on drumming up business, but on annoying people,' it concluded.

We also find that favourable attitudes do not necessarily result in change in behaviour. For example, often we find people have very positive attitudes towards green marketing and will also sign a pledge to save the environment. Yet when it comes to choosing products, they will usually pick up the cheapest ones. So the job of marketing managers does not merely end with changing attitudes.

The study of attitudes and consumer behaviour thus needs to be tempered with what consumers really want. Now, that is the hard part!

SUMMARY

Attitudes are evaluative judgements of people, formed during one's upbringing, and partly learnt by observing others. They are deep rooted, strong opinions and prejudices, yet they do change. In marketing, we are interested in how people acquire attitudes towards products, brands, and companies. The task is twofold: building brand attitudes resulting in strong brand loyalty, and second, to change attitudes if they are negative about certain products and brands.

People hold attitudes because they serve some function. These functions are instrumental, ego-defensive, value-expressive, and knowledge acquiring, and are widely used in advertising.

The tri-component or the ABC model of attitudes shows that attitudes are an interplay among three elements, namely affect, behaviour, and cognition. Affect is the feeling or emotion that an individual has towards an object. Cognition is an individual's belief or knowledge. Behaviour, or the conative element, results in responses of a consumer arising from affect and cognition.

Multi-attribute attitude models help quantify a person's attitude towards a product. They combine multiple attributes of an object, each one evaluated based on two factors: how much the consumer likes or dislikes the attribute, and the level of importance that the consumer attaches to that attribute.

The theory of reasoned action (TRA) states that a consumer weighs his own liking for the product as well as what others might think before buying it.

Attitude towards an ad is an effort to understand the impact of advertising or promotions on consumer attitudes toward products or brands and purchase. Several factors affect attitude towards an ad such as a person's attitude towards advertising in general, and attitude towards the company in the ad, tend to colour perceptions and attitudes. Other factors that affect attitude towards advertising are a consumer's perception of the ad, its credibility, the consumer's mood and state of mind, and ad cognition.

Attitude towards the store suggests that the feelings of a customer towards a store, including design and atmospherics, have a direct influence on purchases from the store. It directly affects how much people buy from there and also whether they buy the store's private labels.

The theory of trying to consume is an attitude theory that accounts for the cases where the outcome is not certain but instead reflects the consumer's attempt to consume. It highlights the importance of impediments to purchase and adds further dimensions to understanding consumer attitudes.

Attitudes are formed by observing others, as also through personal experience, personality factors, and by society and culture. Companies encourage experience through sampling, BTL campaigns, direct marketing, and engaging customers online. Personality traits such as extroversion, agreeableness, conscientiousness, neuroticism, and openness affect responses to ads and products.

Social roles and social norms have a strong influence on attitudes. The social judgement theory (SJT) states that people evaluate ideas by comparing them with their current attitudes, referred to as their cognitive map. It is a subconscious sorting of ideas that happen the moment we come across things. Social attitudes are dictated by culture, social class, reference groups, family, and status.

Attitudes can, and do, change as people learn new things and change their beliefs about products and brands. Attitude change is described in three theories: learning theory, elaboration likelihood theory, cognitive dissonance theory, and the ideal point method.

Attitudes can be changed by changing the motivational function, associating the product with an admired person, group or event, resolving conflicting attitudes, or altering competitor or brand beliefs.

KEY TERMS

Affect, behaviour, and cognition model Consists of affect, behaviour, and cognition (ABC); it links feeling, knowing, and doing and is called tri-component attitude model as well

Attitude A mental and neural state of readiness, organized through experience, exerting a directive or dynamic influence upon an individual's response to all objects and situations with which it is related.

Attitude towards the ad A predisposition to respond in a favourable or unfavourable manner to a particular advertising stimulus during a particular exposure occasion

Attitude towards the object As described by multi-attribute model, attitude towards a product or brand is a function of the attributes and the evaluation of those attributes by the consumer

Attiude towards the store The feelings of a customer towards a store, including design and atmospherics, have a direct influence on purchases from the store

Cognitive dissonance theory The theory, which states that we have an inner drive to hold our attitudes and beliefs in harmony and avoid disharmony or dissonance

Elaboration likelihood theory This theory proposes that attitudes can be changed as a result of different psychological processes—the effortful elaboration, called the central route and non-thoughtful processes, called the peripheral route

Event marketing The practice of promoting the interests of a company and its brands by associating the organization with a specific event or activity

Ideal point model The ideal point method states that a consumer buys a product based on how closely it fits with the consumer's single most preferred product attribute or the attitude of how the product 'should' be

Product placement The practice of placing brand name, logo, package, signage, and other trademarks in the content of mass media programming, mainly in movies and TV shows

Social judgement theory (SJT) The theory that states that people process new information and form immediate opinions by comparing them with their current attitudes, referred to as their cognitive map

Sponsorship The acquisition of rights to associate a product or brand with an event or organization for mutual benefit

Sports marketing Sponsorships to individual athletes or an athletic event

Theory of reasoned action (TRA) A theory, which states that the behavioural intention is a sum of attitude and subjective norms

Theory of trying to consume An attitude theory that accounts for the cases, which reflect the consumer's attempt to consume but the outcome or consumption is not certain.

Webinar A combination of web and seminar, it means a presentation, lecture, or workshop that is transmitted over the web

EXERCISES

Concept-review Questions

1. Define consumer attitude. How does it play a role in purchase and consumption decisions of individuals?
2. Describe the nature and functions of attitudes. How are these used by companies to create ads?
3. Describe the tri-component attitude model. Taking an example of your recent purchase, describe how the three components played a part in your purchase behaviour.
4. Explain how attitude is measured by using multi-attribute attitude models. Illustrate by using an example.
5. Define attitude towards the ad (A_{ad}). What are the factors that affect A_{ad}? Explain the different dimensions of A_{ad}.
6. Explain the theory of reasoned action and theory of trying. How do they affect consumer behaviour?
7. How are attitudes formed? What are the factors that affect attitudes?
8. Describe the different methods by which attitudes can be changed. Explain in the context of a new brand which is trying to grab customers from established companies.
9. How can companies deal with conflicting attitudes of consumers? What kinds of conflicts are likely to arise in consumer's minds and how can they be addressed?
10. What is sponsorship and product placement? What is the difference between sponsorship and associating the product with an admired person, group, or event?

Critical Thinking Questions

1. In which ways do attitudes affect brands? Considering that attitudes are psychological, does changing attitudes not amount to manipulation of the human mind? Evaluate your opinions and comment on the ethical issues that arise when we try to manipulate people.
2. Does attitude towards the ad affect your purchase behaviour? Consider the purchase of a recent product you purchased and assess how the advertisement affected your evaluation of competing brands and subsequently your purchase decision. Did you end

up buying the initial brand under consideration or did you change your loyalty because of the advertisement?
3. It is well known that soft drinks sell attitude. Assess the attitudes and brand personalities of two or three major brands of soft drinks. Using the big five personality traits, have your friends fill up a questionnaire about the image of the soft drink brands in their minds and determine how the companies have been able to attach attitude with a simple product like a soft drink.
4. Do sponsorships, event marketing, and sports marketing add to brand attitude? Take the sponsors of the last IPL matches and assess whether their brand image has improved after sponsorship. As a percentage, calculate how many of your friends remember the brands and how many of them actually switched brands after the matches.

Projects and Assignments

1. Take up a project to measure attitude towards the object by choosing various brands of mobile phones. First select a few attributes of the mobile phone, from things such as style, cost, looks, camera, music, video, and so on. Then ask your friends to evaluate each brand on the attributes selected, using a Likert scale. Calculate the attitude scores for each brand using the multi-attribute formula given in this chapter.
2. You are the manager of a non-vegetarian chain of hotels, but you discover that most of the population in your area of operation is vegetarian. How would you change the attitudes of the people towards non-vegetarian food? Chalk out a strategy of attracting people to your store, even though most of your menu is non-vegetarian.
3. Scan magazines and collect advertisements that are published in them. Classify these ads on the basis of elements of the tri-component model and assess which ones address the different motivational functions. Make a presentation to the class on the basis of what you have collected and discuss the reasons for your classification.
4. Visit different types of retail stores, from small *kirana* stores to large ones. Take pictures and analyse how they are designed to appeal to different classes of customers. Do you think these stores are segmented on the basis of consumer attitudes? Interview customers of these stores to determine how attitudes affect their preference of stores and how much they buy from these stores.

REFERENCES

Ailawadi, Kusum L. and Bari Harlam, 'An empirical analysis of the determinants of retail margins: The role of store–brand share', *Journal of Marketing*, Vol. 68, No. 1, 2004, pp. 147–165.

Ajzen, I., and M. Fishbein, 'The influence of attitudes on behaviour', in Albarracín D., B. T. Johnson, and M. P. Zanna (Eds.), *The Handbook of Attitudes*, Erlbaum, New Jersey, 2005, pp. 173–221.

Albarracin, Dolores and Patrick Vargas, 'From biology to social responses to persuasive intent', in *Handbook of Social Psychology*, Volume 1, edited by Fiske, Susan T, Daniel T. Gilbert, and Lindzey Gardner, 5th Ed., Wiley, New Jersey, 2010.

Allport, G. W., 'Attitudes', in C. M. Murchison (Ed.), *Handbook of Social Psychology*, Clark University Press, Winchester, Mass., 1935.

Assael, Henry, *Consumer Behavior and Marketing Action*, Bizantra, New Delhi, 2005.

Avery, Jill, 'Defending the markers of masculinity: Consumer resistance to brand gender-bending', *International Journal of Research in Marketing*, Vol. 29, Issue 4, December 2012, pp. 322–336.

Bagozzi, Richard P. and Paul R. Warshaw, 'Trying to consume', *Journal of Consumer Research*, 1990, Vol. 17, pp. 126–140.

Bagozzi, Richard, Zynep Gurhan-Canli and Joseph Priester, *The Social Psychology of Consumer Behaviour*, 2010, Tata McGraw Hill, New Delhi.

Chowdhury, Humayun Kabir, Nargis Parvin, Christian Weitenberner and Michael Becker, 'Consumer attitude toward mobile advertising in an emerging market: An empirical study', *International Journal of Mobile Marketing*, Vol. 1, No. 2, December 2006.

Close, Angeline G., R. Zachary Finney, Russell Z. Lacey and Julie Z. Sneath, 'Engaging the consumer through event marketing: Linking attendees with the sponsor, community, and brand', *Journal of Advertising Research*, December 2006, pp. 420–433.

Collins-Dodd C. and T. Lindley, 'Store brands and retail differentiation: the influence of store image and store brand attitude on store's own brand perceptions', *Journal of Retailing and Consumer Services*, Vol. 10, No. 6, November 2003, pp. 345–352.

'Consumers increasingly distrust traditional advertising', Inc Wire, 2012, http://wire.inc.com/2012/04/11/consumers-increasingly-distrust-traditional-advertising/, last accessed on 18 May 2013.

Cunningham, William A. and Philip David Zelazo, 'Attitudes and evaluations: A social cognitive neuroscience perspective', *Trends in Cognitive Sciences*, Vol. 11, No. 3, 2007, pp. 97–104.

Darke, Peter R. and Robin J.B. Ritchie, 'The defensive consumer: Advertising deception, defensive processing, and distrust'. *Journal of Marketing Research*, Vol. 44, No. 1, 2007, pp. 114–127.

De Gregorio, F. and Sung, Y., 'Understanding attitudes toward and behaviors in response to product placement', *Journal of Advertising*, Vol. 39, No. 1, 2010, pp. 83–96.

De Wulf, K., G. Odekerken-Schröder, and G. Van Ossel, 'Consumer perceptions of store brands versus national brands', *The Journal of Consumer Marketing*, Vol. 22, No. 4/5, 2005, pp. 223–232.

Dens, Nathalie, Patrick De Pelsmacker, Marijke Wouters, and Nathalia Purnawirawan, 'Do you like what you recognize?', *Journal of Advertising*, Vol. 41, No. 3, 2012, pp. 35–53.

Eagly, Alice H. and Shelly Chaiken, 'Attitude structure and function', in Gilbert, Daniel T., Susan T. Fiske, Lindzey Gardner (Eds.), *The Handbook of Social Psychology*, Vol. 1, 4th Ed.,, 1998, McGraw-Hill, New York, pp. 269–322.

Erwin, Phil, *Attitudes and Persuasion*, Psychology Press, East Sussex, 2001.

Eze, Uchenna Cyril and Chai Har Lee, 'Consumers' attitude towards advertising', *International Journal of Business and Management*, Vol. 7, No. 13, 2012.

Festinger, L., *A Theory of Cognitive Dissonance*, Stanford University Press, Stanford, California, 1957.

Frank, Lone, *Mindfield: How Brain Science is Changing Our World*, Oneworld Publications, London, 2009.

'Getting the most from your marketing events: The ROI of in-person seminars, trade shows and webinars', Osterman Research, 2009, http://www.gotomeeting.com/fec/images/pdf/GoToWebinar_Osterman_QLM_ROI_of_Webinars.pdf, last accessed on 20 May 2013.

Homer, Pamela Miles, 'Product placements: The impact of placement type and repetition on attitude', *Journal of Advertising*, Vol. 38, No. 3, Fall 2009, pp. 21–31.

http://indiatoday.intoday.in/video/posters-acid-attack-women-wearing-jeans-ranchi/1/212219.html, last accessed on 25 July 2013.

Javid, Morvarid Haghighi, Abolfazl Tajzadeh Namin, and Mahmoud Noorai, 'Prioritization of factors affecting consumers' attitudes toward mobile advertising', *Journal of Basic and Applied Scientific Research*, Vol. 2, No. 9, 2012.

Karanika, Katerina and Margaret K. Hogg, 'Trajectories across the lifespan of possession-self relationships', *Journal of Business Research*, Vol. 66, Issue 7, July 2013, pp. 910–916.

Katz, D., 'The functional approach to the study of attitudes', *Public Opinion Quarterly*, Vol. 24, 1960, pp. 163–204.

Lantos, Geoffrey P. and Lincoln G. Craton, 'A model of consumer response to advertising music', *Journal of Consumer Marketing*, Vol. 29, No. 1, 2012, pp. 22–42.

Lutz, R.J., 'Affective and cognitive antecedents of attitude towards the ad: A conceptual framework', in Alwitt, L.F. and A.A. Mitchell, (Eds.), *Psychological Processes and Advertising Effects: Theory, Research and Application*, Lawrence Erlbaum Associates, Hillsdale, NJ, 1985.

Lutz, Richard J., Scott B. MacKenzie, and George E. Belch, 'Attitude toward the ad as a mediator of advertising effectiveness: determinants and consequences', *Advances in Consumer Research*, 1983, Vol. 10, pp. 532–539.

McGuire, W.J., 'The nature of attitudes and attitude change'. in *The Handbook of Social Psychology*, Lindzey, G. and E. Aronson (Eds.), Vol.3, 1969, Addison–Wesley, Reading, MA, pp.136–314.

Myers David, *Social Psychology*, 11th Ed., McGraw Hill Higher Education, New York, 2013.

Owolabi, Ademola B., 'Effect of consumers mood on advertising effectiveness', *Europe's Journal of Psychology*, Vol. 4, 2009, pp. 118–127.

Pande, Shamni, 'Ad-ded rancour', *Business Today*, 9 June 2013.

Reed, Americus II, Mark Forehand, Stefano Puntoni, and Luk Warlop, 'Identity-based consumer behaviour', *International Journal of Research in Marketing*, Vol. 29, No. 4, 2012, pp. 310–321.

Rzem, Haifa and Mohsen Debabi, 'Store image as a moderator of store brand attitude', *Journal of Business Studies Quarterly*, Vol. 4, No. 1, 2012, pp. 130–148.

Semeijn J., A.C.R. Van Riel, and A.B. Ambrosini, 'Consumer evaluations of store brands: Effect of store image and product attributes', *Journal of Retailing and Consumer Services*, Vol. 11, No. 4, 2004, pp. 247–258.

Sherif, M., and C.I. Hovland, *Social Judgement*, Yale University Press, New Haven, CI, 1961.

Solomon, M., *Consumer Behavior: Buying, Having, and Being*, Pearson Education, New Delhi, 2009.

Strizhakova, Y., R.A. Coulter, and L.L. Price, 'The young adult cohort in emerging markets: Assessing their glocal cultural identity in a global marketplace', *International Journal of Research in Marketing*, Vol. 29, 2012, pp. 43–54.

Unnithan, Chitra, 'US food giants turn vegetarian in Gujarat', *The Times of India*, 6 March 2013.

Wicker Allan W., 'Attitudes versus actions: The relationship of verbal and overt behavioral responses to attitude objects', *Journal of Social Issues*, Vol, 25, No. 4, 1969, pp. 41–78.

CASE STUDY

Wearing Your Attitude

Attitude is a big business. Many industries rest on the assumption that positive attitudes towards brands can be made and maintained, and people buying these products do so for no other reason than to polish their egos and attitudes. Indeed, companies not only sell products that help create attitude but also those that have a good dose of attitude built into them (Fig. 9.9).

The apparel and perfume industries leave no stone unturned to sell attitude. Many exhort customers to 'wear your attitude'. The advertising, store design and displays, investments in brands, all of them weave meaning into a customer's life. Fashion magazines too talk of 'power dressing'. An article in *Esquire* (2007), describes dressing as the means to stand out, or making the subtle statement, 'I'm different'. *Esquire* describes the power of dress as 'the extra 10 per cent'. Over the years, many film stars and famous people have lent their name to apparel and perfume brands, hoping that their fame will rub off on the products as well.

Salman Khan introduced a line of clothing under the brand name *Being Human*. The star hopes that his celebrity status will attract shoppers. To add meaning to the brand, he has made public that royalties received on the sale of his fashion line will be utilized to support education and health care initiatives. Being Human stores have already been launched in many cities in India, France and several other European countries, and West Asia.

According to a report in *Business Today* (2013), the brand's clout comes from the Being Human Foundation, which provides affordable health care and primary education to underprivileged people across the country. The foundation was set up in 2007 and has teamed up with organizations like the Marrow Donors Registry India to help patients who suffer from diseases such as leukaemia and thalassemia.

The brand also tied up with Coca-Cola and NIIT to help a career development centre, which provides computer and electrical training to people from rural areas.

Being Human has an unusual revenue model. It is not donation based but raises its revenues from royalties on the sales of Being Human merchandise. Ten per cent of sales go to the foundation. The brand thus combines two powerful forces: star power and charity, and both are likely to appeal to shoppers. The front end is a lifestyle brand and the back end remains a philanthropic organization.

FIG. 9.9 Companies sell products that help create attitude

The idea is to make the brand iconic by drawing upon the popularity of Salman Khan. It attempts to create a build a community bound by the philanthropic cause. The foundation's website says that the attempt is to turn the brand into an inspiration, which in turn would increase footfalls to the stores and also encourage e-commerce sales. The website describes the charitable activities undertaken by Salman Khan and the foundation.

Another product that sells attitude is perfume. Horstman (2012) writes in the book, *The Scientific American Book of Love, Sex and the Brain*, that business knows the power of smell. She writes that the information that our brain obtains from our sense of smell defines our social, romantic, and sexual relationships.

Armani has a perfume named 'Attitude' that tells consumers to simply wear their attitude. Research suggests that perfumes are worn for other reasons than just to smell nice. Roberts, et al. (2009) conducted a study in collaboration with Unilever to see whether wearing a perfume has any effect on male behaviour. An interesting finding from their research was that when a man changes his natural body odour, it can alter his self-confidence to such an extent that it also changes how attractive women find him.

In their experiment, women were shown short, silent videos of volunteers who had sprayed themselves with a commercial formulation of fragrance and antimicrobial agents. The participants were not informed about the true purpose of the experiment but were filmed as they went about with their daily work. The women rated, just from watching the videos, that men wearing the deodorant were more attractive. This was surprising, since the women could only watch the men but not smell them. The findings suggested that the men's movement and bearing, and their confidence improved so much that women who could watch them but not smell them, noticed: it was movements, rather than their physical appearance, that was making the difference. In other words, the men's attitude had improved so much after wearing the perfume that women noticed them. The study showed that even wearing a perfume, even though it is invisible, changes our behaviour and attitude.

This insight gave birth to two Unilever products. The company plays up on the 'Axe effect' and the 'Lynx effect'—perfumes that are supposed to make men so self-confident that they become irresistibly attractive to women. The research suggests, however, that the advertised effect of the product may have nothing to do with smell, but with the psychological effect on the man wearing the perfume.

Karanika and Hogg (2013) use the life-story technique to study the sequence of respondents' experiences with their important possessions. They show that people value products and possessions for differentiating the self from others. People like products for recreation, security, nurturance, and transitions regarding loved ones. The relation of people with products often reflects life events and transitions in the consumer's life-story and do not necessarily reflect the object or product use-life.

What we wear affects our attitude, whether it is the visible part of our personality in clothes, or the invisible power of perfume.

Questions for Discussion

1. Explain how Being Human is using the tri-component attitude model to change people's attitudes towards the brand. Does it succeed?
2. How does Being Human integrate attitudes towards the object, store, advertising, and celebrity, to enhance its brand image?
3. Describe how an invisible entity like wearing a perfume would affect attitude. Does the choice of perfume match with human personality traits?
4. What would be better: Brands selling attitude or brands acquiring attitude of their own? Support your answer with examples and also comment as to which strategy is better at making an impression on customers.

Sources:
Granger, David, 'Why it's important to dress well', *Esquire*, 17 May 2007, http://www.esquire.com/dont-miss/useful-part/Whytodress0607, last accessed on 23 May 2013.

Horstman, Judith, *The Scientific American Book of Love, Sex and the Brain*, Scientific American, John Wiley and Sons, California, USA, 2012.

http://www.beinghumanfoundation.in, last accessed on 20 May 2013.

Karanika, Katerina and Margaret K. Hogg, 'Trajectories across the lifespan of possession-self relationships', *Journal of Business Research*, Vol. 66, Issue 7, July 2013, pp. 910–916.

'Perfume science: The scent of a man', *The Economist*, 18 December 2008.

Roberts, Craig S., A. C. Little, A. Lyndon, J. Roberts, J. Havlicek, and R. L. Wright, 'Manipulation of body odour alters men's self-confidence and judgements of their visual attractiveness by women', *International Journal of Cosmetic Science*, Vol. 31, Issue 1, February 2009, pp. 47–54.

'Salman Khan launches flagship Being Human store in India', *Business Standard*, 18 January 2013.

Shashidhar, Ajita, 'Branded for life', *Business Today*, 14 April 2013.

ANNEXURE 9.1

Measuring Attitude

The following is an example of consumer evaluations of three mobile phone brands. A consumer wanting to buy a cell phone rates it on the following attributes:

- Style
- Functions such as camera and multimedia.
- Ease of handling
- Cost

Using the following scale, each characteristic of mobile phones is evaluated.

Extremely Good	Moderately Good	Slightly Good	Neither Good nor bad	Slightly bad	Moderately bad	Extremely bad
+3	+2	+1	0	−1	−2	−3

Let's say the consumer gives the following responses, which represent the importance for each attribute, or evaluation of the attribute. In this case, the consumer rates style and functions in the mobile phone as extremely good (+3), ease of handling as moderately good (+2), and is not bothered too much about the cost (+1).

Attribute	Rating (e_i)
Style	+3
Functions	+3
Ease of handling	+2
Cost	+1

Next, we ask the consumer to rate three brands on whether he/she believes the brand possesses each attribute (the b_i), using the following scale. The data collected would be through a questionnaire so that each attribute can be rated by the consumer.

Extremely likely	Moderately likely	Slightly likely	Neither likely nor unlikely	Slightly unlikely	Moderately unlikely	Extremely unlikely
+3	+2	+1	0	−1	−2	−3

Let's say the consumer provides the following assessment of three brands.

Attribute	Nokia	Apple	Samsung
Style	+1	+4	+3
Functions	+3	+3	+2
Ease of handling	+2	+3	+3
Cost	+1	+3	+2

Next, we try to find the consumer's attitude. Using the Fishbein Attitude Model, we multiply the attribute evaluations time the brand's rating and sum for each brand:

$$A_o = \sum_{i=1}^{n} b_i e_i$$

Attribute	Rating (e_i)	Nokia	$b_i e_i$ for Nokia	Apple	$b_i e_i$ for Apple	Samsung (b_i)	$b_i e_i$ for Samsung
Style	+3	+3	9	+2	6	+2	6
Functions	+3	+2	6	+3	9	+2	6
Ease of Handling	+2	+3	6	+3	6	+2	+4
Cost	+1	+1	1	+3	3	+2	2
A_o =			22		24		18

The final scores reflect the attitudes towards the individual brands.

PART THREE
Influences on Consumer Behaviour

CHAPTER 10:
Family and Social Class

CHAPTER 11:
Culture and Consumer Behaviour

CHAPTER TEN

Family and Social Class

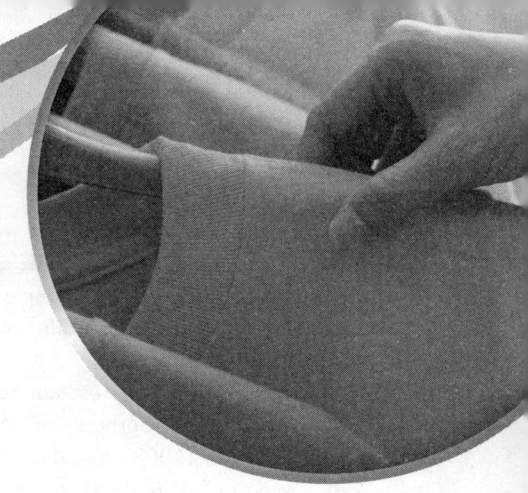

LEARNING OBJECTIVES

A person acquires his or her consumption habits from the family. These habits, in turn, depend on the family's socio-economic status. This chapter examines the two strongest influencers of consuming behaviour.

After studying this chapter, the reader would be able to
- learn about family buying behaviour and decision-making in the family
- understand the consumer socialization process and role of children as consumers
- analyse the family decision-making process at different stages of the family life cycle
- examine the role of social class and understand Indian social class segments
- learn methods of social class measurement and geodemographic clustering of markets

CASE STUDY
Tomorrow's Customers Today

People emulate the consumption behaviour of those around them. This means parents and immediate family members, and later friends, influence purchase behaviour. Family and social class imprints the consumption behaviour so strongly on a person's mind that it persists for an entire lifetime. Research confirms that this is indeed so. A study by Grier, et al. (2007) has found that children who develop particular habits and preferences in childhood tend to establish them as a lifelong pattern. Information, beliefs, and resources are transmitted from one generation to the next, and parents' brand preferences create comfort in children, they write.

Marketing companies use this knowledge to establish connections with consumers. One way they do it is by using one of the most endearing themes in marketing—the relationship between a mother and daughter. Huddleston and Minahan (2011) write that mothers and daughters often become lifelong shopping partners who ultimately influence one another. This bond can be seen repeatedly in advertisements: Pears uses the theme, 'Some complexions never grow up' and has established a connection with consumers for generations. Santoor had an ad in which a mother and daughter are mistaken for sisters. P&G ran a successful campaign, 'Thank you, Mom' and connects with families globally. Not surprisingly, these brands are firmly established in the Indian market.

The cultural ideals of motherhood and family bonding are used by companies to extend the bond to brands. The idea is to place products and brands in an environment that a customer finds most comfortable—her home. Since children reflect success of mothering practices and social and material status of their mothers, the brands are able to establish themselves in the minds of young consumers, who tend to consume the same brands even when they are away from their families.

Research shows how consumption habits are transmitted from mothers to their offspring. Scaglioni, et al. (2008) found that mothers who were preoccupied with their own weight and eating, reported restricting their daughters' intake, encouraging them to lose weight over time. This was linked to the daughters' restrained eating behaviour. Children of parents who consume fruits and vegetables were found to do the same.

It is interesting to see how mothers are targeted by companies. First, brands are shown as being responsible, that is, they are good for children. By using these brands, the duty of motherhood is realized through everyday consumption activities. Second, since a mother constructs and expresses her identity through her child, she is encouraged to express this identity by buying premium brands on behalf of the child, and try to impress others in her social network by reflecting her wealth. Third, a significant motive attached to brands is the desire to demonstrate to others how caring and devoted a parent she is. A caring mother must have immense knowledge of products, such as toys, food, and medicines so as to make the 'right' product choice for her children.

In today's consumption-oriented world, mother's love is expressed through brands. The mothering function requires the mother to be a very active consumer for addressing the development needs of a child and using products that express the ideals of motherhood. By targeting mothers, companies try and get tomorrow's customers today.

While reading this chapter, try to answer the following questions:

1. In what ways do family and social class affect consumer behaviour? How do companies try to change habits acquired in childhood?
2. How does decision-making take place in families?
3. How do mothers really influence their daughters' consumption habits?
4. In what ways does the social class of a family affect its buying habits? Do these change over time?

Sources:

Grier Sonya A., Janell Mensinger, Shirley H. Huang, Shiriki K. Kumanyika, and Nicolas Stettler, 'Fast food marketing and children's fast food consumption: Exploring parents' influences in an ethnically diverse sample', *Journal of Public Policy & Marketing*, Vol. 26, No. 2, Fall 2007, pp. 221–235.

Huddleston Patricia and Stella Minahan, *Consumer Behaviour: Women and Shopping*, Business Expert Press, New York, 2011.

Silvia Scaglioni, Michela Salvioni, and Cinzia Galimberti, 'Influence of parental attitudes in the development of children eating behaviour', *British Journal of Nutrition*, Vol. 99, Suppl. 1, 2008, pp. S22–S25.

INTRODUCTION

From the time that one is born, one is a consumer. As babies, we are fed and clothed by our parents and family members, and as we acquire knowledge of the world around us, we become aware of the wide variety of goods available for education and entertainment. What we end up getting depends on our family's wealth and the consumption beliefs held by the elders.

These two are the strongest influences on consumer behaviour. Children get socialized as consumers by learning from family members. The habits learnt as children stay with them for life.

Indian culture celebrates family traditions and the influence of family on buying behaviour is quite strong. Joint families are common even in big cities. In many families, grown-up sons do not move out of their family homes at all or return to their families once they have completed their education, to live with their parents. This contributes to the permanence of the joint family, popularly referred to as the 'great Indian family'. Television serials and movies are hits when they portray large, united families. Advertisements highlight the importance of family, too.

Families are also consumption units, and marketing managers are interested in finding out how they make purchase decisions. They put the family under the scanner to discover answers to questions such as, how the family buys things, how family members arrive at decisions regarding major purchases, how they select brands, who actually does the purchasing, and which members are the major influential forces in purchase decisions. Family buying behaviour is analysed using these parameters.

Family consumption behaviour varies depending on its economic status. While rich families tend to buy expensive goods that reflect their status, middle-class families look for value for money in their purchases. Poor families have to make do with cheaper brands or non-branded goods. Consumption is thus dictated by the family's social and economic class. The study of class becomes essential if one is to study buying behaviour of Indian consumers.

As Shukla (2012) writes in *The Economic Times*, 'The age old truism of success depending upon one's ability to understand the target audience is certainly valid for the heterogeneous and highly stratified Indian consumer landscape'.

This chapter discusses the influences of family and social class on consumer behaviour. The functions and roles of the family are examined in the next section.

ROLE OF FAMILY

A family is a group of two or more persons related by blood, marriage, or adoption who reside together.

The *nuclear family* consists of father, mother, and child/children living together. The *extended family* consists of the nuclear family plus other relatives, such as grandparents, uncles and aunts, cousins, and parents-in-law. The family into which one is born is called the *family of orientation*. A family established by marriage is called the *family of procreation*.

The family is a basic unit of human society. It has survived over millennia because it fulfils essential survival functions and plays certain roles. These are instrumental and affective roles. *Instrumental roles* involve provision of physical resources such as food, clothing, and shelter for family members, decision-making, and family management. *Affective roles* provide emotional support and encouragement to family members. Both sets of roles are essential for healthy family functioning. Some of the roles that the family fulfils are described here.

Provision of resources The family provides resources, such as money, food, clothing, and shelter, for all family members.

Nurturing and support The family provides inter-generational nurturing and supporting roles to its members. It provides comfort, warmth, and reassurance. For example, parents encourage and comfort children in times of distress, and family members come together and support one another after the death of a loved one.

Life skills development Children learn skills in their families. This includes physical, emotional, educational, etiquette, and social development of children and adults.

Maintenance and management Individuals learn leadership, decision-making, managing family finances, and assume other roles as they interact with family members, friends, and neighbours. They also learn shopping and consumption behaviour in this role.

Gender socialization and sexual needs Families instil sex-appropriate behaviour in their members and help fulfil sexual needs for couples. In India, families help find spouses for their younger members when they reach marriageable age.

Functions of Family

By fulfilling these roles, families provide important support to individuals. Children are nurtured so that they survive to become responsible adults. The functions of the family are economic, emotional, social, and imparting lifestyles.

Economic well being One of the basic functions of family is to provide financial means to its dependents. The family provides economic security and well being. In a nuclear family, traditionally, the husband is the sole breadwinner. Today women too, participate in earning. In a joint family, resources are pooled and managed by the head of the family. All the expenses of children are looked after by parents, and they often get pocket money as well. Earning children may decide to support the family.

Emotional support The family provides support and encouragement and assists its members in coping with personal or social problems. Children get affection, emotional support, and companionship as they grow up and learn. Many films and TV shows celebrate the emotional support that families provide. Companies take a cue from this and use family themes in their advertisements. The Everest: My mummy best advertisement is a very good example of this.

Imparting lifestyles Families impart standard of living and lifestyle to its members. Individuals get socio-economic status (SES) by being part of families. This in turn greatly influences consumption patterns. Companies track lifestyles and also try to influence them. For example, they associate the consumer's habit of visiting fast food restaurants with lifestyles and sell vacations so that family members can enjoy 'quality time' with each other.

Socialization functions The socialization of family members, especially young children, is a central family function. Social skills are imparted to members through instruction and observation. Children acquire communication and interaction skills through their families and get the social skills required to function as members of human society.

Indian Family Structures

In India, the patrilineal family is common, with the men of a family living together under one roof with their wives and families. This is referred to as the joint family and its members have a mutually beneficial social and economic relationship. A young bride moves into her husband's home, where she lives with his relatives. The joint family system has survived despite the impact of urbanization and westernization. *The Times of India* (2012) reports that Census 2011 data reveals that in urban India, the proportion of households with only one married couple has declined while the share of households with two and even three married couples staying together has increased since the last Census in 2001.

Large families are an advantage in the economic sense, because many Indians are underemployed and would find it expensive to run separate households. Economically weaker members of the family get looked after in this system. In rural areas and agricultural families, work is shared by family members, who get economic security in return. The joint family is also common in cities, with high cost of housing and economic hardship keeping people together. Kinship bonds help in getting jobs or business. Many business families live jointly and pool in resources.

Though the joint family has undergone some changes, it still thrives. For instance, even in nuclear families, it is seen that grown up children continue to live with their parents. When the family breaks up, it does not imply rejection of the joint family system. Even where the joint family gets disintegrated, clusters of relatives live very near each other. Strong networks of kinship ties remain. People of the same caste too maintain kinship ties and provide each other with economic and emotional support. In many towns, members of certain castes are clustered in their own localities.

Changing Indian Family

With growing urbanization and influence of Western ideals, families in India are in a state of flux. While the joint family is common, there is a trend towards smaller households as well. Census 2011 figures show that the median Indian household has just over four members. The figures show that there are 24.7 crore households in India. Of these, 49.7 per cent have four or less members. In rural India, the median household size is between four and five members. Uttar Pradesh (UP) is the only Indian state with a median household size above five. Large families however, remain a significant but not dominant component of Indian life. Close to 20 per cent of households have five members, and another 25 per cent have six to eight members, while 6.6 per cent have nine or more members. In UP, more than half of the households have six or more members (*The Times of India*, 2012).

Globally, family structures are undergoing changes as a result of increasing education and women's empowerment. An Organisation for Economic Cooperation and Development (OECD) report (2011) describes some powerful trends that affect family structures. These factors are also visible in India to some extent.

Fertility patterns Demographic trends point to low and declining fertility rates and increasing life expectancy rates in most countries including India, with the total fertility rate (TFR) dropping to below 3 children per woman. This leads to smaller families.

Postponement of family formation Another trend is the postponement of childbearing in many countries. As more and more men and women first want to establish themselves in their careers, they choose to postpone having children.

Childlessness The household childlessness rate is strongly linked to the education level of women. Women with tertiary education are more likely to be in a childless household than women with secondary education. As a consequence, there are many households without children.

Partnership patterns Both falling marriage rates and increasing divorce rates have contributed to the jump in single-parent families as well as 'reconstituted families'. On average across the OECD, marriage rates have fallen from 8.1 marriages per 1000 people in 1970 to 5.0 in 2009.

Indian families are also changing as these factors come into play. The slow shift changes buying behaviour to some extent, though families exhibit a few common traits. These are discussed in the next section.

Family Buying Behaviour in India

When we look at the buying behaviour in Indian families, we discover several interesting aspects. While families differ with regard to income, size, and age-groups of members, their buying behaviour varies. However, several buying habits of Indian families emerge.

Buying from the local grocer In many large households, the housewife makes a list of goods to be bought and conveys it to the local grocer either personally or on the telephone. To make the task easier for her, some grocers have printed shopping lists in which the items just have to be ticked. The supplies are sent on a handcart to the house, and payment is made subsequently by the housewife.

Role of servants In many upper-class households, purchasing is done by servants, who know which shops or brands are preferred by the family. When supplies are needed, the servants are sent to the market to pick up the stuff. They are common purchasers in large households and also in smaller households where both partners have regular jobs.

Nuclear households The purchasing pattern of nuclear households is somewhat individual. In homes where the woman is working, goods are purchased by either partner after work. Otherwise the housewife does the purchasing. Indian shops see heavy purchases in the first week of the month when salaries are disbursed. In the mornings, orders are fulfilled for households and markets are flooded with individual buyers in the evenings.

Emphasis on freshness Indian consumers like freshness. Vegetables and food items must be seen and felt before buying. As freshness is of prime importance, the concept of frozen foods has really not picked up in India so far.

Monthly or daily purchase of rations Larger households prefer to get a monthly supply of rations to save them the trouble of sending the servant to the market regularly. Small or poor households, however, prefer to buy more frequently.

Daily needs Daily needs such as bread, eggs, and milk are provided by a vendor who makes a home delivery. People who are not able to buy regularly pick up these products from neighbourhood shops.

Big-ticket purchases Expensive white goods and cars require family consultation in which members influence the purchase decision.

Indian household buying patterns are quite different from those in developed countries. This is one reason why the Western culture of supermarkets has not become popular in many areas. To cater to Indian households, some supermarkets have introduced free home delivery.

DECISION-MAKERS IN THE FAMILY

As part of families, individuals are part of a decision group, which influences purchases even though the actual buying is done by somebody else. The way that decisions are made in families is of interest to marketing managers. Members of a household play active roles as influencers,

TABLE 10.1 Consumer roles in families

Consumer role	Behavioural aspect	Who performs the role	What he/she does
Influencer	I want this brand/product	Everyone in the family	Able to influence what gets bought
Gatekeeper	You can't get this	Head of the family/Housewife	Able to stop consumption of certain things
Decider	We must use this product/brand	Head of the family or other elders	Has authority to decide about purchases
Buyer	I bought this	Housewife/Servant	One who goes out and buys stuff
Preparer	I made this	Housewife/Ladies/Servants	Cooks or converts raw goods to consumable goods
User	I used/consumed this	Everyone in the family	Actual consumers
Maintainer	I must get this repaired	Older male member	Looks after repairs and services
Disposer	'I sold this or threw it away'	Older members	Decides on what needs replacement

gatekeepers, deciders, users, maintainers, and disposers. These roles together with activities and behavioural aspects are summarized in Table 10.1. This section describes how individuals influence purchase decisions in families.

The roles played by family members in purchase decisions are explained with the example of the purchase of a water purifier.

In a joint family, the need for a water purifier is usually expressed by the lady of the house. Everyone in the family latches on and expresses an opinion about the best brand or technology. For example, while children want a brand that has a young actress posing for it, the young adults display their knowledge of technology. Older members, no doubt, have an opinion based on their past experiences of brands or their after-sales service. These are the *influencers*.

One of the older members points out how someone had trouble with a particular brand in the past—the company's call centre was unhelpful, the repairs were not done, and the engineer who came for the service was incompetent, and says, 'Buy any brand but this'. This is the *gatekeeper* function.

Based on everyone's opinions and the discussion among family members, the *decider*, usually the chief wage-earner, decides which brand to buy. The actual purchase may be done by a younger member who goes to the market and buys that brand, who in turn becomes the *buyer*.

The *preparer* in this case is not a family member, but the engineer who comes to install the machine.

The person who fills the water from the purifier, the housewife or the servant, is the *user*. After a while, the machine needs servicing. The chief wage earner or an adult member is told about it, who assesses the budget and calls the engineer, fulfilling the *maintainer* role. Finally, after a few years, the engineer says that the machine cannot be serviced anymore and needs replacement. As a result, a new machine is bought and the old one is sold as scrap. The family member who calls the scrap dealer and negotiates with him is the *disposer*.

This summarizes the roles undertaken by family members in the purchase and consumption process of a water purifier. How people acquire the skills to perform these roles reveals an interesting story of consumer socialization.

> **CB IN ACTION** **Analysing a Family Buying Decision**
>
> Suppose your family is buying a very expensive item like a motor car. Analyse how the decision would be taken. Identify the influencers, gatekeepers, deciders, users, maintainers, and disposers. Identify the influence wielded by each family member starting from the prime income earner to the children.
>
> Further, identify the sources that different family members will use to find information about various car models. What media are used by them and whose influence is the strongest?
>
> Draw a chart showing the following processes in different colours:
>
> - the decision-making process from information search to final purchase in black
> - the family decision roles in red
> - the information sources in green
> - highlight the most important person who contributes to the buying decision

Consumer Socialization

We have seen that family members influence the purchase decision. The influence exerted depends on the type of families, their size, and the age of family members. In this section, we look at family members who exercise influence and are instrumental in the buying process. The process by which young people develop consumer-related skills, knowledge, and attitudes is referred to as consumer socialization of family members.

Ward (1974) defined consumer socialization as 'the developmental process by which young people acquire the knowledge, attitudes, and skills relevant to their functioning in the marketplace'.

Consumer Socialization Process

The process of consumer socialization starts with children. How children learn and become socialized as consumers as they grow older is as follows:

Observation Children learn consumption by observing others consume. Since the prime reference point of a child is the family, consumption habits of parents and siblings are acquired simply by observing. Many studies have found that family background, social class, income, and education, mould the views of children and young people about consumption and advertising.

Experience Children express their feelings when they are fed, for instance. Over time, they learn to like certain foods and dislike others. Similarly, they learn to prefer products and brands as they grow older, though the influence of family and culture remains strong.

Peers Adolescents and young teenagers, called 'tweens' acquire consumption preferences by observing their peers. The tendency to be in conformity with friends, be acceptable socially, and a certain amount of envy—all add up to determine teenage consumer behaviour.

Advertising Children are exposed to advertising through various media. When they start demanding products from their parents by nagging or making a nuisance of themselves, it is called *pester power*. Advertisers rely on children to pester their parents and nag them to buy stuff which they would otherwise not buy. The idea is that children are able to influence the purchase decision. Many advertisements show children using certain brands.

TABLE 10.2 Consumer socialization of children

Age	Consumer experience	Stimuli observed	Stage of consumer socialization
3–6 years	• Observation • Feelings • Eating • Showing preferences	• One	• Cognitive perceptual
7–11 years	• Accompanying adults to markets • Influencing purchase • Building preferences	• Two or more	• Cognitive analytical
12–18 years	• Becoming independent buyers • Awareness of needs and wants • Awareness of self, personality, and brands • Exercising preferences	• Multiple	• Cognitive analytical and reflective

Shopping experiences When children accompany adults to market, it also adds to their consumer socialization process. Here they are able to see and touch products, and observe or take part in the actual buying.

Adult socialization When children become older, they are able to go out independently or with friends. They experience new products and services and learn to manage their money. Slowly children are absorbed into the consumer culture that surrounds them.

Online socialization Teenagers become web savvy in their mid- to late teens. However, whether they get socialized as consumers on the net, is questionable. Research reported in *The Economic Times* (2010), has found that 'they are insecure, unsure of their identity and, as is the defining characteristic of teenagers, often misunderstood'. We may conclude that children become aware of brands and become consumers only in their mid- to late teens. Exposure to big brands happens through television, rather than online.

Intergenerational socialization Brand preferences are transmitted down the generations. Woodson, Childers, and Winn (1976) found that intergenerational influences extended to brand and product choices. For instance, they found that about 32 per cent of their sample of men reported that the insurance company with which they dealt also supplied coverage to their fathers. Moore–Shay and Lutz (1988) found a similarity in buying styles as well as brand and product preferences among mothers and daughters.

The consumer socialization process from child to adult stage is shown in Table 10.2. It shows how a child experiences consumption, how preferences are developed, observation of stimuli and the stage of development, over the years.

Reverse Socialization

When parents mimic their children's consumption behaviour, it is called *reverse socialization*. Technology or fashion products, for instance, are adopted by parents by observing the younger generation. Ruvio, Gavish, and Shoham (2013) found that teenage girls have a strong influence on the products their mothers choose. Mothers have a much stronger tendency to mimic their daughters' consumption behaviour in products such as make-up or clothing. Reverse socialization suggests that the impact that adolescents have on their parents is much more profound than has been thought. This phenomenon has been referred to as the 'consumer doppelgänger' effect. A doppelgänger is the double of a living person. The research found that if a mother is young at heart, very fashion conscious, and views her daughter as a style expert, she will tend to become a doppelgänger of her daughter's consumption behaviour.

It is clear from the preceding section that children are important consumers for two reasons. First, as they learn about products and brands, they are able to exert influence on their families. Second, what they consume influences parents and peers as well. That is why children are a very important segment in marketing.

Children as Consumers

Children acquire skills as consumers by observing others. In the movie, *Home Alone*, a child shops and uses a credit card with ease, showing that these skills are acquired early in life. However, children influence shopping in a number of ways and advertisers use them unhesitatingly.

Paco Underhill in his book, *Why We Buy* (2009), writes about children as consumers and explains how retail stores and fast food companies make allies of children to sell products. 'It would be almost impossible for families to shop together if not for the advent of kid-friendly dining, and McDonald's, more than anyone, has prospered from this', he writes. 'The restaurants are part convenience, part bribery for the little citizens if only they'll behave through a morning at the mall.'

He further writes that stores realize that children like to touch things—they are exuberant participants in the world of objects. In fact, objects placed below a certain point will be touched *only* by children. Supermarkets thus have candy and gum racks near the cashiers, and smart booksellers place kids' books at a lower level, so that children can grab them.

Children are able to exert influence over purchases in two ways: (a) by exercising their pester power (Fig. 10.1), that is, by throwing tantrums till their object of desire is purchased, and (b) by becoming consumers themselves. McNeal (1999) tells us in his book, *The Kids Market—Myths and Realities*, that this happens in the same manner and at about the same age. Children observe the kind of products their parents buy, and the reasons for purchasing or not purchasing. 'All are typically standard elements in children's consumer education as a result of socialization by parents,' he writes. Companies look to children as a means of acquiring tomorrow's customers today.

FIG. 10.1 Children use pester power to influence purchases

There are several factors that encourage early consumer socialization of children.

Nuclear families Nuclear families go out more often and together. This increases children's exposure to the market.

Single parent homes Single parents are increasing in urban areas. They often take their children out shopping, and tend to give in to their children's whims more easily.

Increase in discretionary incomes With an increase in discretionary incomes, parents tend to indulge the children more than in the past. Some parents suffer from the affliction of more money, less time.

Culture of going out India is gradually developing the culture of going out. Families visit restaurants and malls together and more frequently.

Parents working late When parents work late, they try to overcome the guilt of neglecting their children by indulging them.

Keeping up appearances Parents often teach their children to show off brands when they want to enhance their own status in society.

Parental style Parental styles are more democratic now than in the past. Children thus have more say in family decision-making.

Peers Peer influence and pressure also help in consumer socialization of children.

Companies in India use consumer socialization of children to plug all kinds of products. *The Economic Times* (2012) reports that a number of companies including Panasonic, Sony, Bajaj, Disney, Piramal Healthcare, and Chicco are customizing televisions, ceiling fans, light fittings, washing machines, cologne, and even sunscreen lotion for children, to make the most of their worldly aspirations and pester power. It cites aspirations of children and their parents, together with the guilt factor of working parents, as encouraging this trend.

Gerbner, et al. (2002) have given the cultivation theory that examines the long-term effects of television. It states that the more time people spend watching television, the more likely they are to believe the social reality as portrayed on screen, leaving them with a misperception of the world. 'Television has become the primary common source of socialisation and everyday information,' they write, adding that the stories serve to define a world and legitimize a particular social order. Asserting that television shapes the way society thinks, Gerbner opines that television's major cultural function is to stabilize social patterns and to cultivate resistance to change.

There are great concerns about the effect on children of this trend. These are highlighted in several books and articles. Levin and Kilbourne in their book, *So Sexy, So Soon* (2009) write about the padded bras, risqué costumes, and sexy messages on T-shirts worn by children. Today's cultural environment bombards children with inappropriate and harmful messages. They write, 'Corporations capitalize on this disturbing trend, and without the emotional sophistication to understand what they are doing and seeing, kids are getting into increasing trouble emotionally and socially'. The ethical question of marketing to children and youngsters is discussed in Chapter 12.

The Times of India (2012) reports that today, girls are attaining puberty at the age of ten. It says that age of attaining sexual maturity among a girl, when she changes physically, hormonally and sexually has dipped, especially in urban India, to 10 years from 12–13 earlier. Companies see this as a marketing opportunity, selling cosmetics and fashion products to younger and younger audiences.

Marketing to Youth

Youth represents another segment that is targeted by marketing companies. Two trends have made this segment very lucrative: (a) a large part of India's population is young and (b) as young people enter the workforce, they also acquire considerable purchasing power.

Understanding the minds of the young is thus an important mission for manufacturers. Various surveys have discovered the purchasing habits of young people.

TABLE 10.3 Spending habits of young people

Expenditure	Male (%)	Female (%)	Overall (%)
Mobile phones	41.4	37.7	39.6
Eating out	22.9	22.4	22.6
Clothes	19.8	25.6	22.6
Movies	7.4	5.0	6.2
Gifts	1.0	2.1	1.5
Personal grooming	3.9	5.5	4.6
Liquor	1.0	0.4	0.7
Sports and gym	1.0	0.3	0.7

Source: HT Youth Survey (2012)

The Hindustan Times Youth Survey 2012 throws up some interesting findings about India's youth. 44.5 per cent of the respondents said that their source of happiness is parents and 21.1 per cent listed friends as their source of happiness. Ninety per cent believed in God. The survey covered 10,000 young people in the age-group of 18–25, consisting of mostly students.

To the question: 'What do you spend your money on?' 39.6 per cent of the youth said that they spent it on mobile phones, 22.6 per cent on eating out, and 22.6 per cent on clothes. Around 6.2 per cent of the youth said that they spent money on movies and 4.6 per cent on personal grooming. The percentage of young people spending money on liquor or sports was 1 per cent or less. The findings of the survey are summarized in Table 10.3.

Where the youth spends money That societal mores are changing is reflected in the fact that half of the respondents (50.5 per cent) felt that premarital sex is not an issue. Their consumption of music is mostly Indian, with film music dominating the preference (56.4 per cent). Asked what kind of dress they preferred wearing, 52.9 per cent of the girls replied that they preferred *salwar-kameez* while 31.3 per cent preferred Western attire. Some 90 per cent replied that they did not drink and 81.7 per cent of the youth said they did not smoke.

The conflicting winds of tradition and modernization create opportunities as well as challenges for manufacturers. They must cater to a society getting increasingly westernized, but at the same time must be careful of their methods and communications so that they are not seen as too bold. If this happens, companies face the danger of being taken to court for offending the sentiments of some community or the other.

Marketing to Couples and Adults

Couples and adults comprise the main market for consumer and household goods. How they shop is of particular importance to companies because a major chunk of purchasing power is held by adults. So far, companies have relied on their vague impressions of how couples and adults shop. *The Economic Times* (2013) reports of a study that separates the myths from the facts about shopping patterns of Indian consumers. The study, conducted by Indian Institute of Management, Ahmedabad, TNS, KiE Square, and Ogilvy Action, attempted to decode shopper behaviour in

MARKETING INSIGHT
Marketing to the Youth

Youth is the toast of marketing companies. They are enamoured of this new market, driven by figures that show India as a young country, they devise marketing strategies targeted at the young. Some campaigns follow the ads of the West, where the youth segment has been pitted against elders. Thanks to Woodstock, the Beatles, and protests against the US wars in other countries, youth have been shown as rebels. Even in India, adventure, music, and other symbols of 'cool' are used in youth-oriented brands.

Companies are targeting youth aggressively with messages and prices tailored to capture their attention. Some of the companies that have youth-oriented marketing campaigns and target the youth market aggressively are summarized in Table 10.4.

Despite these efforts, the youth pose a challenge for companies. Since the best friend of young people today is the cell phone, brands try to offer entertainment seamlessly fused with online experience. Any single medium does reach the youth today. MTV uses four zones to talk to them, namely TV, social media, digital, and real live space. Social media is treated as a hangout.

Red Bull utilized Formula 1 very effectively to connect with the youth. It launched Red Bull Speed Street with a Formula 1 show car running in front of India Gate. Nescafé has a very successful Facebook page 'Know Your Neighbours'.

PepsiCo launched Mountain Dew Xtreme Tour in India, to drive consumer engagement. Action sports matched with its positioning of 'Darr Ke Aage Jeet Hai', and also organized workshops and bike mobs in various colleges.

Channel V launched brand extensions such as the V Spot Café + Bar and Indiafest. Indiafest is a college festival to connect with the youth.

Reckitt Benckiser has come up with its Brand Me initiative, a social media experience aimed at helping graduates and students build a profile, just like marketers build brands.

In all this, it is difficult to figure out whether youth follow brands or whether brands chase the young. The trap with youth marketing is that companies end up treating youth as a different species. In popular ads, young people are shown as having tattoos all over their bodies, with multiple piercing and spiky hair. Young people are supposed to like music, hang around, and be disrespectful to authority. No doubt there are a few youngsters who match this description, but it would be a mistake to generalize youth on appearances.

While it is easy to rally youth around such points of difference, ads targeting the young make desperate attempts at humour and sometimes fall flat. In addition, they are in the danger of alienating the older audience.

In India, there is no history of rebellion against the system like in the West. India's post-Independence history is marked by scarcity and self-restraining values. When the economy opened up, people took to brands. Even the 25–45 year-olds behave more like teenagers. The same goes for the brands

TABLE 10.4 Brand campaigns targeting the youth market

Company/Brand	Youth-oriented campaign
Puma	'Puma loves vinyl' platform Original Puma social song
Pepsi	Uses the youth theme, 'Live for now'
Red Bull	Red Bull Speed Street with the Formula 1 show car
Mountain Dew	Mountain Dew Xtreme Tour: 'Darr Ke Aage Jeet Hai'
7UP	Dil bole I feel UP
Channel V	The V Spot Cafe + Bar and Indiafest
Airtel	'Har ek friend zaroori hota hai'

(Contd)

MARKETING INSIGHT (Contd)

as well—they too realized that being 'youthful' was the way to go.

However, when everybody feels young and all brands are youthful, real youth is the casualty.

Despite Pepsi's focus on the youth, it is seen as a family drink and Levi's is as much a brand for the intern as a chief executive officer (CEO). The youth of India have nothing that they can call their own. No wonder, in a country with a median age of 24 years and about 200 million people in the age band of 15–24 years, there are no mainstream youth brands.

Are companies chasing a mirage when they target the youth? Would it not be better to create family brands?

Sources:
Sinha, Dheeraj, 'Youth marketing: Choice of a new generation', *The Economic Times*, 3 June 2009.
Srivastava, Pallavi and Arshiya Khullar, 'How well do Indian marketers understand the Indian youth?', http://pitchonnet.com/blog/2012/08/21/how-well-do-indian-marketers-understand-the-indian-youth/, last accessed on 18 October 2013.

TABLE 10.5 Indian shoppers: Separating myth from fact

Myth	Fact
The shopper is a woman and she shops alone	One in two shoppers is a man; one in two shoppers has a companion
Women who shop with their spouses spend 30–50 per cent more than when they shop alone	The male spouse is brought along to play the role of a porter and driver. He is uninvolved and often no more than a trolley pusher inside the store
You've got three seconds to attract a shopper's attention. No one stands and reads product literature, announcements, or back-of-pack communications	On an average, shoppers spend 2 to 4 minutes in each category. Percentage of grab-and-go shoppers is below 10 per cent
The more you can get shoppers to browse, the more they'll buy	People who shop alone, browse the most and buy the least. Women who shop with their spouses browse the least and buy the most
Great navigation and neat on-shelf display reduces buying time and leads to a higher degree of product discovery	It almost seems that shoppers in India find comfort in chaos; most people familiar with urban India would not find this surprising
Affluent men with elastic wallets buy a lot on impulse	Price discount is the single largest factor that encourages impulse purchases
Impulse shopping is not an involved process. Shoppers are likely to spend the least amount of time in impulse categories	Shoppers spend the most amount of time in chocolate aisle. Categories are bought on impulse, not brands
Most brand advertising must talk to women; this ensures they're pre-decided on brands before entering the store	Men buy by brands and women buy by product format. Price is the second-most important criterion for men buying by brand. Men who buy by brands don't care much about the pack size or product format. All they care about is the brand. And if a small pack of their favourite brand is all they can afford, they'll go for it, even if another brand offers a larger pack size for the same price

Source: 'Eight myths busted about shopping', *The Economic Times Brand Equity*, 20 February 2013.

the hypermarket environment. Researchers observed the shopping patterns over nine FMCG categories in hypermarkets. The findings of the survey are summarized in Table 10.5.

FIG. 10.2 Indian customers feel comfortable shopping in chaos

The table gives an invaluable insight into how people actually shop and also shows some peculiarities in Indian shopping behaviour. For instance, it was found that Indian shoppers thrive on chaos. Women like to browse, so certain upmarket stores selling traditional apparel pile up the dresses so that customers can rummage through them and also provide a sitting area (Fig. 10.2). Given the preference for traditional wear among Indian girls, such stores are more popular than the neatly stacked stores selling branded apparel.

Seniors Market

India has a sizeable market of elderly people that is expanding as the younger generation ages. According to a report published by Wharton (2012), compared to the overall population of India, which is growing at 1.8 per cent per annum, the population of those who are aged 60 and older is growing at 3.8 per cent. Their number—which currently stands at 100 million—is expected to increase to 240 million by the year 2050. This group is a segment that manufacturers and service providers have begun to target. The report cites a study by global real estate services firm Jones Lang LaSalle (JLL), which points to the housing needs of senior citizens. Over the years, the notion of specialized homes for the elderly is gaining traction. The study says that the market for senior citizen housing is poised to take off in India. Seniors today are independent, financially stable, well-travelled, and socially connected. As a result, India provides an opportunity to developers, service providers, health-care players and operators to create solutions specific to India (see Exhibit 10.1).

However, treating senior citizens as an independent market segment is tricky because of affordability. In the absence of strong health insurance and social security measures, affluent older people will remain a very small segment. Earning capacity has not kept pace with longevity. Not

EXHIBIT 10.1 LIC for Senior Citizens

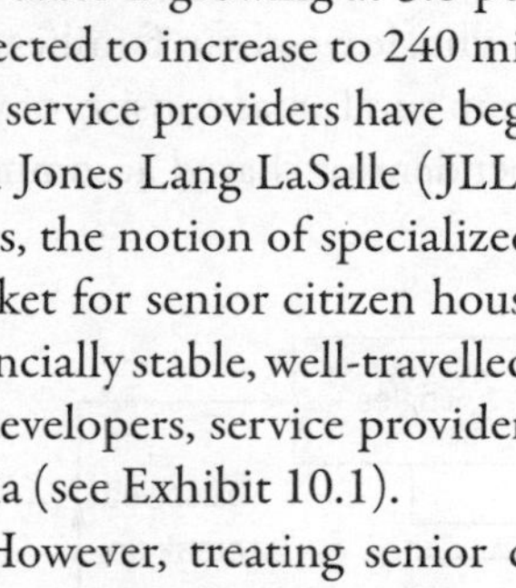

FIG. 10.3 Health plan for the family
Courtesy: Superbrands

LICs portfolio includes a wide array of life insurance and pension schemes to suit the differing needs of people. On offer is a vast smorgasbord of basic insurance plans, endowment assurance, money back plans, term assurance, health insurance plans, pension plans, children's plans and capital market-linked plans. Further, benefits such as the double accident benefit, critical illness riders, and the term rider provide a greater variety for the customer to choose from. Please see Fig. 10.3 that shows an LIC health plan for the entire family.

Source: Superbrands 2012

many senior citizens can independently afford the kind of lifestyle that they have had during their working life.

The report underlines the fact that there are rising numbers of seniors who spend their sunset years with companions of the same age and sharing facilities in settings of enablement and security.

The segments described exert a strong influence on consumption patterns. They dictate the kind of products that families consume, which depends on the age of the members. This is dependent on the life cycle stage of the family, which is described in the next section.

FAMILY LIFE CYCLE

The family life cycle is the composition of a family and the emotional and intellectual stages that a person passes through from childhood to retirement as a member of a family. Figure 10.4 shows us the size and composition of Indian families. In this figure, the stages of the life cycle are shown on the left and the types and progress of families are shown on the right. As families follow the path of growing and declining, they pass through several stages. The traditional family life cycle is as follows:

Bachelorhood People at this stage are young people who leave their families in search of education or jobs. Much of the urban migration in India from rural areas consists of young people who leave villages to find jobs in cities. They live in independent or shared accommodation and

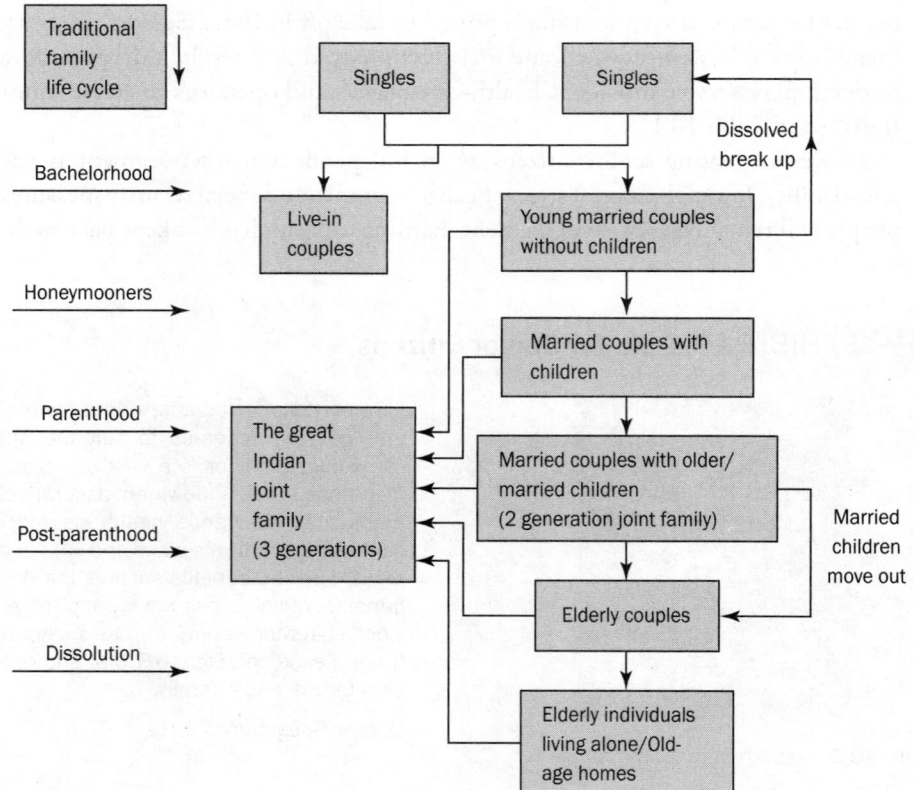

FIG. 10.4 Family life cycle in India households

have little social life. Migrants often send much of their earnings back home to their villages and lead a spartan life. However, students who get money from home, or young people who have better jobs, are able to have a better lifestyle than their peers who come for jobs. The singles make up a large market and companies see an opportunity in serving bachelors. For poor bachelors, there is a ready market for cheap goods and small packs of consumer goods. The well-off young people have a range of uppity retail outlets such as coffee shops, food courts, and malls to 'hang out' and companies offer products and services matching their carefree status.

Honeymooners   It is inevitable that singles will be drawn to each other and soon form couples, either getting married or else living together. This stage is called the honeymooners stage. It is a hedonistic, enjoyable time and marketing companies pitch in by providing products that are easily accepted by people in this stage. Gifts, clothes, electronic products, perfumes, and practically anything can be sold if romantic appeal is attached to it. It is also a time when people start building their homes, so there is a ready market for home products such as kitchen appliances, furniture, furnishings, and so on.

Parenthood   Soon children arrive. This is called the *full nest* stage. The character and needs of the family changes drastically. Families have to fulfil the needs of children. Expense on clothes, food, education, and toys must be balanced with saving for the future. Medical care for children is also in demand. Till the children become adults, they have special needs and parents provide for them. A host of companies provide for products and services needed by families at this stage. Clothing, cosmetics, and consumer goods are consumed in great quantities by such families. In India, the parenthood stage is an extended one, as grown-ups do not leave their parents' home, contributing to the size of the joint family.

Post-parenthood   As children grow up, they may leave home in search of education or jobs, leaving behind an *empty nest,* or there may be older couples without children. The shopping basket of such families is reduced. The family no longer consumes goods in great quantities, but a market opens up for travel, holidays, health care, entertainment, and restaurants. For couples who have not kept something for their old age, there is a need for old-age facilities and services.

Dissolution   When the grim reaper comes calling and a spouse dies, the wilting family faces the *dissolution stage*. It comes with declining consumption and the attendant problems of loneliness, health issues, and decreasing finances. A market for old-age homes, financial services, and health care is required at this stage.

Though families go through these stages, their purchase decisions will vary depending on whether it is a nuclear family or in a joint family. In the next section, the family decision-making at different stages of the life cycle is examined.

Family Decision-making

How families make decisions is of particular interest to marketing companies. Understanding family dynamics helps them better target the decision-maker with their marketing messages. Not only can the messages be suitably designed, but also placed in the appropriate media if we know who actually makes the buying decisions and how they are made. Research conducted by Ndubisi and Koo (2006) shows that there is a significant relationship between family type and joint purchase decisions. Decisions are examined at different stages of the life cycle in this section.

Young singles Young singles who move out of their family homes start buying things on their own. It is a time of exploration and trying out new brands. However, the influence of family is still strong, as they buy those brands that they consumed with their families. For expensive items, singles look for advice from their parents. Peer influence starts playing a role, as consumption is learnt by observing others and sometimes through peer pressure as well.

Young couples Power distance plays a role in purchase decisions by young couples. Among couples with traditional upbringing, men do all the purchasing and women are seldom consulted. While women buy only low-involvement articles such as food and vegetables, important decisions are taken by men. Among modern couples, especially in urban areas, joint decisions are made particularly in cases where the wife is working. Couples are much in marketing focus, and advertisers use images of happy couples to position products. Prestige uses this idea quite well in one of its promotions. Its most famous and unforgettable tag line has been *Jo Biwi Se Kare Pyaar, Woh Prestige Se Kaise Karen Inkaar*? (How can anybody who loves his wife refuse her a Prestige?).

Celebrity couples too, lend their muscle in marketing goods (see Marketing Insight).

Full nest In a full nest family, all members exert influence on the purchase decision (see Fig. 10.5), especially when buying big-ticket items. Children and young adults become important influencers in such families.

Joint family In joint families, while purchasing decisions for daily consumption goods are taken by the housewife, important purchasing decisions are taken by family elders. Other members exert influence, but the final decision rests with the head of the family. Family characteristics, individual characteristics, and situational factors play a role in the purchase decision, as shown in Fig. 10.5.

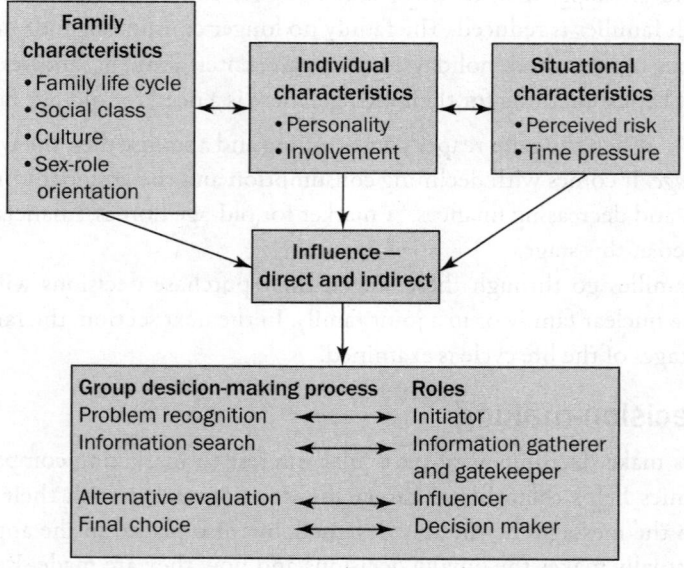

FIG. 10.5 Family purchase decision-making

Source: Levy and Lee (2004)

Empty nest For older couples, purchase decisions shift to one partner, usually the male. This becomes an important market for health care and vacations.

Older singles Consumption declines when one partner dies. The older single is brand loyal and relies on younger people or servants to help in the shopping. Purchase decisions are made by default for older singles and consumption declines.

Unconventional households and families are also part of the urban scenario. Companies need to know the trends of such families, as they form niche segments.

While family exerts a very strong influence on habits formed by young people, it is also natural to expect that the social setting in which the family exists dictates what kind of goods are consumed by the family members. Rich families will consume differently from middle class or poor families. Social class is thus a strong influencer and predictor of consumption behaviour. The next section describes social class and its influence on consumer behaviour.

MARKETING INSIGHT
Celebrity Couples Woo Indian Families

In urban India, among educated nuclear families, purchasing decisions are made jointly by husband and wife. High-ticket purchases are also joint decisions. Companies understand this and target young couples together, since both take part jointly in all three stages of the decision-making process, even for products and services that more associated with just one of the sexes.

To woo this segment, manufacturers of jewellery, home products, and consumer goods make ample use of celebrity couples. Superstar Amitabh Bachchan and his wife featured in Tanishq advertisements. Shah Rukh Khan and his wife Gauri Khan are seen in D'Decor advertisements. Earlier, Shahid Kapoor and Priyanka Chopra shared an interesting chemistry for the Bru advertisement. Another popular celebrity couple seen in endorsements is Saif Ali Khan and his wife, Kareena Kapoor in Airtel and other brands. Down south, Surya and Jyotika did a heart warming advertisement for Nescafé. The advertisement saw the couple together after their movie, *Perazhagan*. Cricketing couples too have been used in brand endorsements, but the major share in brand endorsements is held by cinema couples.

Using celebrity couples assures instant recognition for brands. However, companies face a danger as well: by piggybacking on the popularity of a celebrity couple, they may miss out on building a powerful brand image. The brand may be known for the couple and not establish an identity of its own.

It cannot be denied that a celebrity couple catches the consumers' attention instantly and also conveys a feeling of warmth to the brand, which benefits from their chemistry and also when the couple is featured in the press. Another advantage is instant segmentation. A company can target national or regional markets by choosing couples who are popular nationally or within a particular state.

The following are some couples frequently seen in advertisements:

- Amitabh Bachchan and Jaya Bachchan (Tanishq)
- Akshay Kumar and Twinkle (Micromax)
- Bipasha Basu and John Abraham (Head and Shoulders)
- Saif Ali Khan and Kareena Kapoor (Airtel)
- Kajol and Ajay Devgn (Whirlpool)
- Sharukh Khan and Gauri Khan (D'Decor)
- Shahid Kapoor and Priyanka Chopra (Bru)
- Dhoni and Sakshi (Star City)

Celebrity couples help products accelerate brand recognition. They give a wholesome meaning to the product, are visually appealing, and build brand image. They lend credibility to the brand and make the brand story more relatable. Consumers feel a thrill to see their favourite actors endorsing a brand.

Sources:
'Double bill', *The Telegraph*, 2 August 2011.
Rehna, K., 'Celeb couples, hot favourite of advertisers', *The Economic Times*, 24 September 2011.

GLOBAL INSIGHT
Unconventional Families

In recent times, following the Western trend, Indian society has seen the rise of unconventional families. Their numbers may not be large, but they do point to changing times. The family life cycle does not apply to them and their consumption patterns vary. These unconventional families have given rise to a number of epithets such as follows to describe them:

Singles Students or working people living alone. They live in small apartments, sometimes shared, and have limited incomes

Double income no kids (DINKs) Both partners are working and have no time or commitment for children

Young urban professionals (YUPPIES) Singles working in banks, call centres, and the like, have high disposable incomes, are materialistic, mobile, indulge in gadgets, and buy the fashionable vehicles

Middle-aged urban professionals (MUPPIES) When yuppies get older, they morph into muppies

No kids (NOKs) Couples with alternate sexuality or people who prefer not to have kids. Includes live-in couples and may or may not be DINKs

Single income, two kids, outrageous mortgage (SITCOMs) Divorced or widowed people with kids. Usually with financial encumbrances

Snot-nosed egoistical rude teenagers (SNERTs) When youngsters move in groups, they become aggressive and noisy, and are often referred to as SNERTs

Kids in parents' pockets (KIPPs) Children of rich parents. They have no income of their own but maintain a luxurious lifestyle living off their parents' incomes. Noisy and rude, they often get into fights and accidents, but have money to throw

Well-off older people (WOOPs) Retired, may or may not be widowed, but have plenty of purchasing power

Same-sex families Though same sex families are reported in many parts of the world, there is no data in India of such families. Consumer needs of such families, in any case, does not differ from other families

These unconventional families represent niche segments. Sometimes they have special needs, which can be met by marketing companies profitably.

Sources:
Foster, John, *Effective Writing Skills For Public Relations*, Kohan Page Ltd, London, 3rd Ed., 2005, pp. 40–42.
'Where are you now? DINK, SINK, SITCOM, nuclear family or other', http://www.adviserassistant.com/1/post/2011/4/where-are-you-now-dink-sink-sitcom-nuclear-family-or-other.html, last accessed on 19 February 2013.

SOCIAL CLASS

Social class refers to people having the same social, economic, or educational status. It refers to social stratification in which people are grouped into a set of hierarchical social categories, the most common being the upper, middle, and lower classes. Lenin (1919) described classes as large groups of people differing from each other by the place they occupy in a historically determined system of social production. Marxist theory assigns class according to a person's role in the production process: the *bourgeoisie* or the capitalists, who owned the means of production, the *proletariat*, or workers, who provided the labour and had to work for a living, and a transitional class known as the *petite bourgeoisie*. The structure was marked by high inequality and thus there was an inherent conflict between the two. There was no mobility among the classes, and there was no hope that a member of the working class could become a part of the privileged bourgeoisie.

In the modern context, class is not seen as a watertight compartment. Education and mobility of labour means that people can change their status. A working class person, for instance, can acquire skills and education and get a higher employment or even start a business. This is called

CB IN ACTION   History of Consumption in 10 Films

Interview your family members from the oldest to the youngest to get a snapshot of marketing and consumption in India over two or three generations. Ask them which brands they consume and how their consumption patterns were influenced by the media of their time. Ask them to identify a few films that impressed their generation.

Using the films as markers, develop a history of marketing and consumption in India in 10 films, over three generations. Foreign textbooks talk of the post-war generation and baby boomers, but as these are not applicable in India, divide your analysis into the following phases:

Socialist era   The post-Independence years guided by Nehru and Indira Gandhi, in which India was sought to be transformed into a socialist state, with public sector given pride of place

Swadeshi era   The period in which 'made in India' was considered supreme and foreign brands exited India

Awakening era   The period when the country tried to shed its socialist and swadeshi image and started looking towards foreign brands once again

Liberalization years   The era of opening up of the Indian economy in 1991 by the then Prime Minister Narasimha Rao and the subsequent impact on incomes and consumption

Social media era   The highly interconnected era in which mobile phones and the Internet started changing the way goods were marketed and consumed

Slowdown phase   The years when the economy slowed down, with slow growth, high unemployment, and high inflation, when people restricted their spending

What do you learn about your family consumption over the years?

upward mobility. At the same time, people also see erosion of their standards of living because of loss of employment or rising inflation. This is called *downward mobility*.

The social class forms segments that companies use to take decisions. How they do this is described in the next section.

Indian Social Class Segments

Indian households have been divided into five major segments according to their income by McKinsey Global Institute (2007). These are as follows:

Globals   The richest people in the country, with incomes of ₹10 lakh per annum or more—includes large business owners, politicians, top executives and professionals, and large agricultural land owners

Strivers   With incomes ranging from ₹5 to ₹10 lakh per annum, this group consists of business people, government officials, middle to senior executives, and professionals

Seekers   Often referred to as the middle class, with incomes between ₹2 to ₹5 lakh per annum, this is a varied group consisting of salaried people, traders, and small businessmen and middle- to junior-level executives

Aspirers   The group which earns between ₹90,000 to ₹2 lakh per annum, and consists of low-skilled workers, traders, small businessmen, farmers, and junior employees

Deprived   With incomes of less than ₹90,000 per annum, they are unskilled workers, people relying on odd jobs, sometimes without permanent employment, and live from day to day earnings

Consumer Behaviour

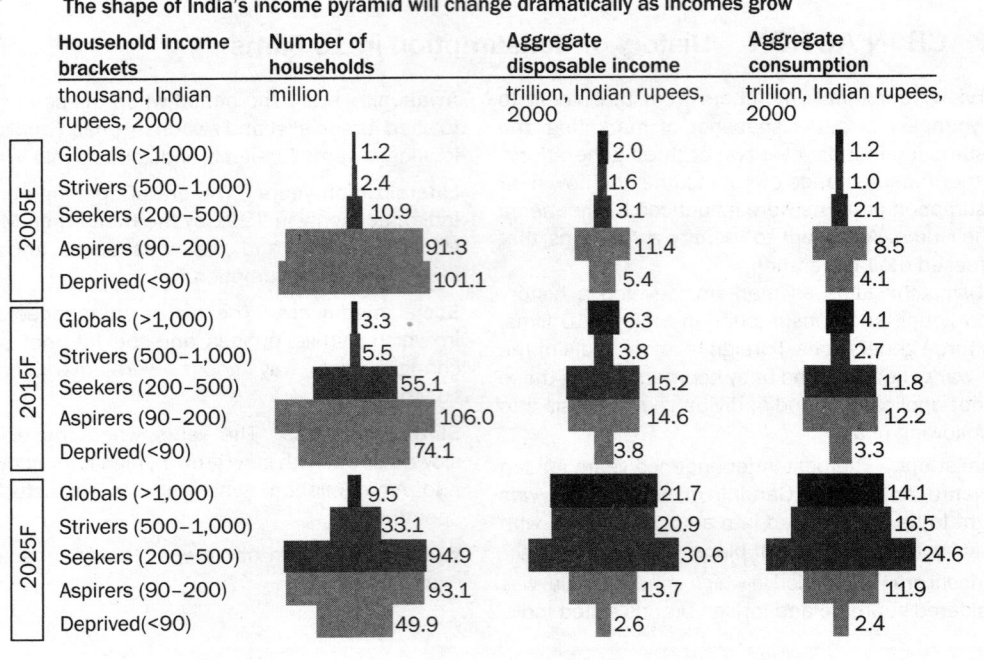

FIG. 10.6 Skewed income distribution in India

Source: *Bird of Gold*, McKinsey Global Institute (2007)

Estimates of the numbers in each class are shown in Fig. 10.6. The consuming class—that is people who have high disposable income—were a group with 14.5 million households in 2005. This represents just 7 per cent of the households. The majority of the population consists of aspirers and the deprived. Estimates of the future ignore the fact that growth rates have stalled and that inflation remains high, eroding the upward mobility of the classes: the numbers are, therefore, somewhat misleading. Companies have targeted the middle classes without realising that the middle class in India is quite different from the middle class in developed countries (see chapter-end case study).

Buying behaviour differs among classes. The deprived are poor and have to make ends meet. The aspirers look for value in their purchases. They are unlikely to pay a premium for branded products. The seekers, or the middle class, can be divided into two groups with distinct consumption preferences. The traditional middle class consist of families that are financially stable, but they neither educate their girls nor allow them to wear Western dresses. The boys are educated but encouraged to join the family business or look for careers and stay within the family. They are unlikely to buy branded goods but rely on traditional methods in their food and clothing habits.

The liberal middle class, though in the same income bracket, consists of families whose members are more educated and the principal wage earner is a salaried employee. Children of such families acquire education, are brand aware, and are also highly visible.

TABLE 10.6 Characteristics and consumption preferences of different classes in India

Class	Characteristics	Consumption preferences
Globals (Privileged class)	Chief wage earner is likely to be a businessman or holding a high-paying job. Such families are likely to be modern, educated, and outgoing.	Flashy lifestyle, conspicuous consumption, premium brands and products
Strivers (Upper class)	Consist of business people, government officials, middle to senior executives, and professionals	Highly brand conscious, have sizeable disposable income, visible in malls and premium outlets
Seekers (Middle class traditional)	Salaried people, traders and small businessmen, and middle to junior level executives	Traditional food and clothing preferences, look for value in their purchases.
Seekers (Middle class liberal)	Salaried people, middle to junior level executives, emphasis on educating their children	Likely to support Western consumption practices in food and clothing, brand aware
Aspirers	Chief wage earner not very educated and holds a low-paying or irregular job, low-skilled workers, traders, small businessmen, farmers, and junior employees	Unlikely to have disposable incomes, look for value in their purchases
Deprived	Families living in poverty	Unbranded products, live from month to month. They are referred to as 'bottom of the pyramid' market.

The characteristics and consumption patterns of the classes is summarized in Table 10.6.

The classes described show three kinds of consumption: status consumption, brand awareness, and value orientation.

Status Consumption

Status consumption, or *conspicuous consumption*, refers to the spending of money not to satisfy any physical need but for acquiring luxury goods and services for public display of economic power. It is extravagant and ostentatious expenditure to fulfil the psychological need for status or obtain the esteem of others.

The term was introduced by the economist and sociologist Thorstein Veblen. During the Industrial Revolution, a social class or the *nouveau riche* (new rich) emerged, who showed off their wealth as a mark of higher status. Conspicuous consumption characterized people who used the display of wealth to assert their social power and prestige.

Conspicuous consumption is seen among the rich in India with the privileged class supporting flashy lifestyles and showing off the latest cars, gadgets, and accessories.

Brand Awareness

People who acquire education tend to be more brand conscious. If they can afford the expensive brands, they flaunt them. However, if they cannot afford the brands, as a large section in India cannot, they look for something that can reflect their preference but at a lower cost. This need is fulfilled by counterfeit products or unbranded products, and India has a large market for such products.

The Economic Times (2012) citing a study conducted by the Associated Chambers of Commerce and Industry (ASSOCHAM), reports that the market size of counterfeit products sales was about ₹45,000 crore through illegal channels in 2011–12. It said that the sale of fake products caused a revenue loss of over ₹5000 crore to the government.

Products most likely to be counterfeited are electronics, automotive components, consumer durables, and pharmaceuticals. Spurious vegetable oils, ghee, spices, milk, and eatables are also sold under the label of popular brands. Other popular counterfeit products include clothes, shoes, watches, leather goods, and jewellery. Since fake products are cheaper than the original ones, people hope to get a bargain on popular brands by buying counterfeit products at discounted prices.

Value Orientation

Consumers in the middle class show a distinct value orientation. They look for products and brands that deliver benefits at low cost.

Many brands and retail chains found that Indian customers wait till they are able to get discounts. *The Economic Times* (2012) reported of a disturbing trend for many retailers: more and more Indians now withhold their purchases till the sales season.

Traditionally, sales are held twice a year, during December–January and July–August, when retailers offer deep discounts to clear their summer or winter inventory. Retailers of apparel such as Shoppers Stop, Landmark, and Pantaloons expect 20–30 per cent of their total revenues during end-of-season sales and discounts.

Many consumers are reluctant to pay a high price for branded products and prefer store brands, which are considerably cheaper. Store brands, or private labels, or private brands, are products labelled by retail shops and supermarket chains, and are available only in those outlets (see chapter-end case study of chapter 8). Since they do not have any marketing expenditure, they are less costly than national brands and provide better margins for the retailer. They are popular with consumers as they get comparable products at a lower price.

Consumers also look for unbranded goods as they are not willing to pay the premium by popular brands. Retail stores in India sell unbranded, locally packed goods or have their own store brands to cater to this preference for cheaper goods (Fig. 10.7).

FIG. 10.7 Low-priced non-branded *atta* displayed at a supermarket

MEASURING SOCIAL CLASS

We have seen that consumption depends on social class. Companies thus need to know how to measure social class. In this section, three methods of measuring social class are described: subjective, reputational, and objective.

Subjective Method

Subjective social status is an individual's self-perceived rank in society. In this method, researchers simply ask, 'Which category best describes your social class?'

The subjective social position is measured by the MacArthur Scale of Subjective Social Status, which asks respondents to use 10 rungs of a ladder to position themselves socio-economically relative to other people in their country and in their community. It presents a 'social ladder' and asks individuals to place an 'x' on the rung on which they feel they stand. There are two versions of the ladder, one linked to traditional socio-economic status indicators (SES ladder) and the second linked to standing in one's community (community ladder). This analysis helps to gain an understanding of how subjective assessments are formed.

The approach is direct and simple, but it has a number of flaws. Since it depends on subjective criteria, people may put themselves in a higher class than they actually are, according to their aspirations. Many people tend to consider themselves as middle class though they are not.

Reputational Method

In this method, the researcher asks people to classify others into social classes based on the reputation of these individuals. This method does not use subjective perception of their own lifestyles and assumes that people will tend to classify others more accurately based on the lifestyles they have observed. It is also based on the understanding of how people in a community perceive social divisions in their society. Reputational methods are, however, limited to small communities where people know one another.

Objective Method

The objective method uses a range of measures such as occupation, annual income, car ownership, employment, postal code, education, and so on, in determining social status. Respondents are asked factual questions about themselves, based on which social class is determined. Data on occupation, income, and education is collected through questionnaires and estimates of social class are arrived at. This data is coupled with geodemographic clustering, which is described in the next section.

The two most widely used measures are the Registrar General's Standard Occupation Classification (SC) and the Socio-economic Groups (SEG). The Registrar General's Standard Occupation Classification measurement has been employed in the Census since 1901. It is based on the occupation of the individual who is classified into one of six groups as shown in Table 10.7.

Companies make extensive use of such data. Socio-economic and market profiles are required to choose the media for advertising and to reach the target consumers efficiently. In doing so, they use single variable or composite variable indices.

TABLE 10.7 Classification of social class

Category		Description
I		Professional
II		Intermediate
III		Skilled
	III (NM)	Non-manual
	III (M)	Manual
IV		Partly skilled
V		Unskilled

Source: The Registrar General's Standard Occupation Classification measurement

CB IN ACTION — Measuring Social Class

Conduct an experiment with a friend to measure each other's social class.

First, ask each other the question, 'Which category best describes your social class?' Plot the answer on the SES ladder.

Next, using the reputational method, ask others the social class they perceive your friend to be in, based on his/her observed lifestyle. This step is based only on perception. Where in the SES ladder do others place your friend? A similar exercise is being done by your friend about you.

Finally, make your own assessment of your friend's social class based on objective criteria such as occupation of his/her parents, household income, educational status, and car owned by the family.

1. What were the differences between observations in the three methods?
2. Which method was the most accurate and of best use to companies?
3. Do you think your own social class was accurately measured? What do you have to say about the perception of others in the class about you?

Single variable indexes use just one variable to measure social class, such as occupation, education, or income.

Occupation What profession a person follows is one of the most common ways of estimating social class. We use it psychologically too, when tend to ask people we meet for the first time what they do. Companies tend to launch products aimed at people following particular occupations, since occupation reflects status as well.

Education Educated families tend to have a higher status in society than those with less education. A degree is seen in India as a passport to a good job and good standard of living.

Income Another variable that gives a good indication of social class is income. Companies dealing in real estate or leisure activities routinely target consumers based on the single index of income.

The danger of using a single variable index can result in major errors, as shown in our chapter-end case study. It shows that estimating the number of consumers merely on the basis of income resulted in many brands overestimating India's consuming class.

Composite variable indices combine two or more socio-economic factors to arrive at an estimation of social class. Often, single variable indices are not enough as they do not give an accurate measure of consumption. For instance, it is difficult to estimate the consumption of consumer goods based on occupation alone. Similarly, marketing messages will have to be different for a rich educated person and a rich uneducated person. A composite index that estimates the scores on a number of variables, can overcome these limitations. These multivariate indices help in building social class profiles.

SOCIAL CLASS PROFILES

Based on consumer data collected, companies build social class profiles of the population. A method that links socio-economic data with location-based geographic data is geodemographic clustering. It shows communities based on socio-economic status clustered in geographical areas like pin codes. This gives invaluable information for devising a company's marketing efforts, including targeting, communications, and direct marketing programmes.

Geodemographic Clustering of Markets

The combination of geographic and demographic consumer information is known as geodemographics. Geodemographic neighbourhood classification systems are used extensively in marketing. The principal tenet of these classification systems is that people with similar cultural backgrounds gravitate toward one another, illustrated by the saying, 'birds of a feather flock together'. They emulate their neighbours, adopt similar behaviour, tastes, and consumption patterns. This forms the basis for the development of classification systems such as Lifestyles, Prizm, Cluster Plus and Psyte, all of which classify US households into clusters or groups of neighbourhoods, based on their socio-economic and demographic composition. However, geodemographic cluster data is not available for India at present.

By using computer geomapping software in conjunction with sophisticated demographic databases, marketers are able to understand market diversity and target potentially attractive segments. Companies use cluster analysis to target families to influence their shopping habits through providing discount coupons or offering price cuts to encourage trial purchase.

Benefits of Geodemographic Clusters

Geodemographic clustering has a number of benefits: improving media plans, choosing retail sites, and predicting sales at new locations, introducing new products, planning merchandise mixes, and segmenting customer lists. For example, Sears uses geodemographic analysis by coding its credit card customer base to find its best customers and identify growth segments for targeting. It can also analyse which merchandise is best suited to an area's needs. The company has combined over 100 demographic, socio-economic, and housing characteristics in the US with consumer behaviour, that is, product purchase and media usage data, to define less than fifty kinds of homogeneous market segments, each consisting of consumers with a unique pattern of purchasing, consumption, media, and financial behaviour.

Discriminating Power

Cluster systems are superior to single variable measures such as age, sex, and income. These simplistic measures describe only one aspect of consumer behaviour. While cluster systems capture the different behavioural components of a product's user base, demographic measures homogenize consumer profiles into a simplistic caricature. To illustrate, if we take a look at the cluster profile of an expensive product, it will have a decidedly upmarket bias in buyer profiles, but when we look across clusters we find some penetration in the downmarket areas as well. In this way, we can discover the product's acceptability beyond the consumer profiles that we assume.

Integration

Geodemographic systems help in building targets matching customer or product profiles. Based on cluster targets, companies can use TV programs, time-of-the-day advertising, out-of-home media, and mailing lists. They can rank neighbourhoods and target retail distribution. In this way, clusters integrate all marketing information. When all media and point-of-purchase materials are used together, it is called *cluster bombing*. The real advantage of cluster approach is not in segmenting but in being able to hit the target and then concentrating all elements of the marketing mix on this target.

Measurability
The results of cluster targeting can be easily measured. Since the basic unit for geodemographic targeting is the postal code, companies can monitor the marketing effort by simply tracking the enquiries, sales, and deliveries by postal codes. They can determine the impact on sales in a particular cluster compared to the overall market, and can thus measure the success or failure of a marketing programme.

Longitudinal or Time Series Analysis
Through geodemographic cluster analysis, companies can analyse their sales over a period and see how the market has changed by cluster. It can help answer a number of questions important for marketing: for instance, when a company increased the price of a product two years ago, did it alter the demographics? If so, was the change uniform across all markets? What was the effect on customer profile when a new retailer entered the market six months ago?

Mappable Targets
Cluster-based targeting strategy can be mapped using a desktop Geographic Information Systems (GIS) mapping system, right down to individual localities. Cluster targets can be mapped, showing areas where sales are increasing or declining. Clusters can also be used in direct response marketing, in positioning and targeting new products, for media usage analysis, and for projecting future market penetration and share.

Though such data is not available for Indian cities, companies use geographic databases and information from available sources for targeting consumers. Dealers help in providing sales data and locality-wise sales can be tracked for this purpose. However, it is expected that in the future, such data will be available in India as well.

■■■ CONCLUSION

People inherit their consumption habits from their family and social class. The subject is of particular interest for marketing managers since consumers of different social classes and income groups will require separate marketing programmes—a one-size-fits-all strategy may not be as effective as a targeted strategy. Apart from advertising and communication, this enables manufacturers to create different product lines for different social classes.

Family and class are also used to create advertising messages that appeal to particular segments. In India, the family plays an important role, so film-makers and advertisers use family themes in their communications. Messages are also designed to appeal to social and income classes. For example, products targeting the upper classes must emphasize on status, style, taste, sophistication, and showing off. To emphasize on its common man appeal, the Tata Nano used campaigns that highlighted families buying their first car and youngsters going out with their friends. However, the list of products that are positioned on the basis of family and social class is endless.

SUMMARY

People live in families for several reasons: emotional support, economic well-being, and socialization. As a consequence, they learn about products and their consumption from their family members. Indian family buying behaviour is unique and distinct and guided by decision-makers in the family. Every family member plays a role in advising, influencing, or buying products. In India, the role of the family is quite strong, and is often exhibited in movies and advertisements.

Consumer socialization consists of children becoming aware of their role as consumers. They do so through observation, experience, friends' influence, exposure to advertising, and their shopping experience as they go out with parents. Companies, in fact, are particularly interested in children as they can influence and pester parents to buy. However, the emphasis on children as consumers raises questions about inappropriate messages targeted to them.

Consumption of families is also dependent on the life stage that the family members are in—bachelorhood, young couple stage, parenthood, post-parenthood, and dissolution. Young and single consumers buy products in small sizes, but when they get married and have children, their consumption patterns change. In later stages, when households become empty nests or start dissolving, consumption decreases dramatically.

Consumption also depends on the social class that families are a part of. The classes form distinct segments: globals, strivers, seekers, aspirers, and deprived. The rich acquire products for public display of their wealth. This is called conspicuous consumption. Other classes display consumer behaviour through brand awareness and value orientation.

Marketing companies measure social class with subjective, reputational, or objective methods. In doing so, they use single variable or composite variable indexes. Another important method is by using geodemographic clustering profiles that combines socio-economic profiles with geographic information.

■■■ KEY TERMS

Buyer The family member who actually goes and buys the products

Consumer socialization The developmental process by which young people develop consumer-related skills, knowledge, and attitudes

Decider The member of a family who has authority to decide about purchases

Extended family Consists of the nuclear family, plus other relatives, such as grandparents, uncles and aunts, cousins, and parents-in-law (when they live together, they are referred to as joint family)

Family A group of two or more persons related by blood, marriage, or adoption, who reside together

Family life cycle The composition of a family and the emotional and intellectual stages that a person passes through from childhood to retirement as a member of a family

Gatekeeper A member of a family who can prevent consumption of certain things considered harmful or undesirable relevant to their functioning in the marketplace

Geodemographic clustering The combination of geographic and demographic consumer information

Influencer A family member who influences the purchase decision

Maintainer The family member who looks after the repairs and services needed to keep products in working order

Nuclear family A family consisting of father, mother, and child/chidren living together

Pester power Exercised by children, it refers to their ability to affect their parents' purchase decisions, often through the use of nagging or pestering

Reverse socialization The process when parents learn about products from their children and mimic their children's consumption behaviour is called reverse socialization

Social class Refers to social stratification in which people are grouped into a set of hierarchical social categories, consisting of people having the same social, economic, or educational status

Status consumption Refers to the spending of money not to satisfy any physical need but for acquiring luxury goods and services for public display of economic power and is called conspicuous consumption

User The family member who actually uses or consumes a certain product

EXERCISES

▪▪▪ Concept-review Questions

1. Describe family buying behaviour in India. How does family influence consumption behaviour?
2. Describe the consumer socialization process. What marketing influences come into play at each stage of this process?
3. Describe the stages of a family life cycle and comment on the needs at each stage that must be fulfilled.
4. Comment on the role of decision-makers in the family. How do they influence family buying?
5. Describe the family buying behaviour for poor, middle-class, and rich families. What is the difference between the classes?
6. Explain how children influence the purchase decision in families. Is this a strong influence?
7. What is social class? What are the main social class segments in India?
8. Comment on the aspects of class consumption. What are the considerations of upper, middle, and lower classes in buying products?
9. Describe the methods of measuring social class. Discuss their relative advantages or disadvantages.
10. What is geodemographic clustering? How is it used in marketing?

▪▪▪ Critical Thinking Questions

1. Are companies doing legitimate marketing activity when they target children or are children losing their childhood because of constant media pressure? Should there be curbs on marketing messages to children? Is it ethical to sell products by hoping that parents will be pestered in their homes?
2. Many companies are targeting the youth market, hoping to cater to the large number of young people in India. Is this a proper strategy, considering that the real purchasing power is held by seniors in a family? Should the companies not target the decision-makers instead?
3. Critically examine the role of social class in consumption of clothes, financial services, and white goods. How are these goods purchased and who are the influencers in different social classes?
4. Comment on the process of reverse socialization. In what product categories does it work? Do parents actually try to follow the consumption habits of their children?

▪▪▪ Projects and Assignments

1. Conduct a survey of your classmates. Ask them to list out the brands that they like to buy. Then ask them to list why they prefer those brands. After the survey, find out how many brands are bought by them due to family or class influences and how many are their personal choices.
2. Visit different neighbourhoods of your city—upper, middle, and lower class. Ask the shopkeepers what brands they store. Try to answer the question as to whether there is a correlation between social class and consumption of brands.
3. Study the awareness and use of iconic youth brands in India among your classmates. Remind them of youth-targeted ads such as Mountain Dew, Airtel, or Cafe Coffee Day. Using the AIDA model, assess how many of them go beyond the awareness stage to interest, desire, and actual purchase. Try to find out whether these ads are actually working to lure new buyers.

4. Undertake an observational study of shoppers in your locality. Visit a supermarket and tabulate how many shoppers come alone for shopping, how many with children, family, or friends. Use this data to interpret buying behaviour of supermarket shoppers.

REFERENCES

'Bird of gold: The rise of India's consumer market', McKinsey Global Institute, 2007, http://www.mckinsey.com/locations/india/mckinseyonindia/pdf/India_Consumer_Market.pdf, last accessed on 25 July 2013.

'Can India's senior citizens be an attractive customer segment?' Knowledge@Wharton, 2012, http://knowledgetoday.wharton.upenn.edu/2012/01/can-indias-senior-citizens-be-an-attractive-customer-segment/, last accessed on 20 February 2012.

'Eight myths busted about shopping', *The Economic Times Brand Equity*, 20 February 2013.

Gerbner, G., L. Gross, M. Morgan, N. Signorielli, and J. Shanahan, 'Growing up with television: Cultivation processes', in Bryant, Jennings, and Dolf Zillmann (Eds.), *Media Effects: Advances in Theory and Research*, Lawrence Erlbaum Associates, New Jersey, 2002.

http://www.hindustantimes.com/Specials/coverage/YouthSurvey2012/YouthSociety.aspx, *Hindustan Times* Youth Survey 2012, last accessed on 20 February 2013.

Lenin, V. I., 'A great beginning: Heroism of the workers in the rear', *Collected Works*, Vol. 29, 1919, 4th English edition, Progress Publishers, Moscow, 1972, pp. 409–434.

Levin, Diane E. and Jean Kilbourne, *So Sexy So Soon: The New Sexualized Childhood and What Parents Can Do to Protect Their Kids*, Random House Publishing Group, New York, 2009.

Levy, Deborah S. and Christina Kwai-Choi Lee , 'The influence of family members on housing purchase decisions', *Journal of Property Investment & Finance*, Vol. 22, Issue 4, 2004, pp. 320–338.

Malviya, Sagar and Rasul Bailay, 'Retailers like Lifestyle, Shoppers Stop concerned as people hold back purchases for sale time', *The Economic Times*, 25 July 2012.

McNeal, James U., *The Kids Market, Myths and Realities*, Paramount Market Publishing, New York, 1999.

Moore-Shay, Elizabeth S. and Richard J. Lutz, 'Intergenerational influences in the formation of consumer attitudes and beliefs about the marketplace: Mothers and daughters', *Advances in Consumer Research*, Vol. 15, Michael J. Houston (Ed.), Association for Consumer Research, 1988, pp. 461–467.

'More than 1000 honour killings in India every year', PTI Report, *The Times of India*, 4 July 2010.

Mukherjee, Writankar and Sarah Jacob, 'Companies like Panasonic, Sony, Bajaj, Disney, custom-making TVs, fans, lights, cologne for children', *The Economic Times*, 27 April 2012.

Ndubisi, Nelson Oly and Jenny Koo, 'Family structure and joint purchase decisions: Two products analysis', *Management Research News*, Vol. 29 Issue 1, pp. 53–64.

OECD, 'Doing better for families', http://www.oecd.org/els/familiesandchildren/47701118.pdf, last accessed on 18 February 2013.

Rajagopal, Krishnadas, 'Living together a part of right to life, not an offence: SC', *Indian Express*, 24 March 2010.

Rehna, K., 'Celeb couples, hot favourite of advertisers', *The Times of India*, 24 September 2011.

Ruvio, Ayalla, Yossi Gavish, and Aviv Shoham, 'Consumer's doppelganger: A role model perspective on intentional consumer mimicry', *Journal of Consumer Behaviour*, Vol. 12, Issue 1, January/February 2013, pp. 60–69.

'Sale of fake items to touch ₹55,000 cr by 2013: Study', PTI report, *The Economic Times*, 6 August 2012.

Shrinivasan, Rukmini, 'Median household size drops below 4 in cities', *The Times of India*, 25 March 2012.

Shukla, Rajiv, India's elite: Retail giants like Walmart are vying for a piece of this multibillion dollar market, *The Economic Times*, February 6, 2012.

'The great Indian bazaar', McKinsey, 2008, http://www.mckinsey.com/locations/india/mckinseyonindia/pdf/The_Great_Indian_Bazaar.pdf, last accessed on 25 July 2013.

Underhill, Paco, *Why We Buy*, Simon and Schuster Paperbacks, New York, 2009.

Verma, S., 'Cities buck the trend, joint families are back', *The Times of India*, 8 April 2012.

Ward, Scott, 'Consumer Socialization', *Journal of Consumer Research*, September 1974, pp. 1–14.

Woodson, Larry G., Terry L. Childers, and Paul R. Winn, 'Intergenerational influences in the purchase of auto insurance', in *Marketing Looking Outward: 1976 Business Proceedings*, ed. W. Locander, American Marketing Association, Chicago, pp. 43–49.

CASE STUDY

Elusive Middle Class

Companies doing business in India bet on the middle and the upper classes—a set of consumers who have disposable incomes and can afford to splurge on branded apparel, nice cars, insurance policies, and expensive mobile phones. Indeed, India's demographic data holds a lot of promise. Of the 1.2 billion people, might not half of its population—about 600 million people—be in that category? If so, do they not represent an opportunity for companies to serve them?

This was the assumption of many companies which invested large amounts of money to woo the middle class. Cinema theatres were upgraded, great malls were built, and foreign brands started operations in India. However, apart from the numbers, no one knew who exactly constituted the middle class. Indeed, there is no official definition of the middle class. The National Sample Survey Organisation (NSSO) classifies Indian households into different income groups but does not specifically define the middle class. NCAER puts the Indian middle class as households with annual incomes ranging from ₹2–10 lakhs.

This was the class targeted by companies. Indian and Chinese middle-class consumers were supposedly the saviours of a troubled world. As growth slowed in the developed world, it was expected that the middle classes in developing countries would start buying and lead global growth. The expectation was that as more and more people were lifted out of poverty, they would become the new consumer class, pushing up sales of all kinds of branded goods.

Bird of Gold

Middle-class estimates were produced by a lot of banks and consulting firms. A Credit Suisse report says that India and China are going to be main growth drivers among the BRIC nations (Brazil, Russia, India, and China). It expects that continued expansion of the middle class in China and India will offset contraction in developed markets.

Such sentiments are echoed by a number of reports published by consulting agencies. A report titled 'Bird of Gold' published by McKinsey Global Institute (2007) said that the Indian market will undergo a major transformation. 'Income levels will triple,' it said, adding that as incomes rise, India's middle class would swell to 583 million. This was sizeable and a huge marketing opportunity for companies. They could meet the needs of this huge population, equivalent to the whole population of Australia. Ernst and Young's Attractiveness Survey (2012) writes that the high potential of the domestic market driven by an emerging middle class and other factors make India one of the most preferred destinations.

Depending on such calculations, a number of companies entered India hoping to participate in India's coming of age in the consumerist world. They brought foreign brands to India and invested in upmarket malls to cater to the ever-increasing numbers of India's middle class. Indeed, since 2005, there was a fourfold increase in the number of international brands entering the Indian market. It was expected that Indian consumers would love to buy the brands that they had only seen in advertisements or movies.

Gross Overestimation

It did not quite work out that way. *Outlook Business* (2013) quoting research done by Third Eyesight, reports that 'Since 2006–07, some 50-odd brands have either exited India or have restructured their operations in the country. Brands such as Versace and Alfred Dunhill are said to be eyeing the exit sign'.

People who built malls in the country to cater to the emerging middle class also found their projections gone awry. *The Times of India* (2013) citing a survey conducted by the Associated Chambers of Commerce and Industry of India (ASSOCHAM) has revealed that about half of the malls in the country are lying vacant. The figures in Delhi-NCR region show that 55 per cent of the malls lie vacant. In Hyderabad, 48 per cent of the malls are vacant.

A number of retail chains that had hoped to attract the middle classes, such as Subhiksha, Six Ten, More, Vishal Megamart, and Reliance either scaled down operations or completely shut down. *Business Standard* (2013) reported that even while car manufacturers were increasing capacity in India, their sales did not match expectations. Sales of most models remained tepid despite record discounts and introduction of new models. Insurance companies too found their plans biting dust. Many joint ventures broke down as a result.

Where did these companies go wrong? Where was the middle class that these companies wanted to cater to?

It was clear that these companies had grossly overestimated the number of people who would want to buy their brands. The mistakes were as follows:

- The middle class figures were estimated using a certain growth rate of the economy that would result in large numbers of people moving out of poverty. However, as inflation remained high and growth rates stalled, the size of the upper and middle classes in India showed only a nominal increase. That was just a fraction of the middle class size that was estimated by consultants.
- The second mistake was to assume the middle class as homogenous. Nothing could be farther from the truth. The middle class in India consists of some people who like to splurge but many others who seek value. They crowd into low-cost markets seeking bargains. They seek functional value rather than pay extra for fancy brand names.
- The third mistake was to overestimate the purchasing power of the middle class. With restricted incomes and no social security, a majority of Indians have a tough time making ends meet. It is hardly a wonder that they are not visiting malls regularly and opening their wallets

How steep the income pyramid!

Consumer class (Annual household income at FY02 prices)	Distribution or households (Mn) FY02	Distribution or households (Mn) FY10	Distribution or households (%) FY02	Distribution or households (%) FY10	Share of rural (%) FY02	Share of rural (%) FY10	Annual growth (%)
Deprived Below ₹90,000 (Below $2,000)	135.4 (731)	114.4 (618)	71.9	51.5	81.8	84.2	−2.1
Aspirers ₹90,000–200,000 ($2,000–4000)	41.3 (221)	75.3 (405)	21.9	33.9	48.5	61.2	7.8
Middle class ₹200,000–1,000,000 ($4,000–21,000)	10.7 (58)	28.4 (15.3)	5.7	12.8	35.2	33.4	12.9
Rich Over ₹1,000,0000 (Over $21,000)	(0.8) (4)	(3.8) (20)	0.4	1.7	22.9	22.2	21.4
Total	188.2 (1014)	221.9 (1195)	100	100	71.6	68.8	2.1

FIG. 10.8 Indian income pyramid

Source: *The Economic Times* (2012)

to buy the goods that foreign companies have lined up for them. Tapping India's middle class has therefore remained a challenge for most brands.

Estimates of Indian households based on their income are shown in Fig. 10.8. It shows that in 2010, the rich and the middle class constituted just 173 million people. The annual growth rate over 2002 to 2010 was estimated at 12.9 per cent. The majority of the population remained poor, with deprived consisting of 618 million people and another 405 million consisting of aspirers, with household income less than ₹2 lakh per annum.

While many companies thought they could target the middle class with their offerings, they soon discovered that this class was elusive. A majority of households in the country struggle to make ends meet. Hence, they like value in products rather than status. Companies found that the middle class could only be tackled by low prices. Fast food companies, mobile phone makers, and other companies have been reducing prices to achieve volumes and to sustain supply chains in India. Apparel companies find that offering discounts every season is the only way to achieve volumes. According to a report in *The Economic Times* (2012), a host of companies, including fast food companies, try to 'woo Indian consumers with rock bottom prices to drive volumes and higher sales in an inflationary economic environment'.

The figures show why the forecasts of companies had gone horribly wrong. While the number of deprived was decreasing, the rate of decrease was just 2.1 per cent, a result of a combination of economic data and bad policies of the Indian government. The thrust towards liberalization, which could result in better standard of living, has slowed down with coalition governments unwilling to take up reforms.

This implies that the real incomes of people have actually been eroded. Lifting the people out of poverty may well remain a challenge for India. Consequently, the estimates of the rise of the middle class were all wrong. The realistic scenario is that there will be only a marginal improvement in disposable incomes for the majority of the population.

As a result, many companies were not able to generate the volumes required for profitable operations. Many companies waited for the middle class to turn up in their shops, but the wait became very long. They had to face losses or had to shut down operations in the country. Other companies tried to appeal to consumers by lowering prices.

Questions for Discussion

1. Can class be a basis for assessing consumer behaviour? Was it right for companies to base their business model on projections of numbers of the middle class?
2. What other market indicators should have been considered by the companies before making investments in India?
3. Given the prevalent, scenario, how can companies survive in India? How can they encourage middle-class consumers to switch to branded goods?
4. What aspects other than income constitute middle-class consumer behaviour? If you were the country manager of a foreign brand, how would you estimate the size of your target market?

Sources:

'Bird of gold: The rise of India's consumer market', McKinsey Global Institute, 2007, www.mckinsey.com/locations/.../India_Consumer_Market.pdf, last accessed on 14 February 2013.

'Car sales end year with a sputter', *Business Standard*, 2 January 2013.

'Car sales set to decline in FY13, first time in a decade', *Business Standard*, 11 February 2013.

'India, China to be main growth drivers among BRIC: Report', *The Times of India* 2 December 2012.

Kulshrestha, T. 'Changing partners', *Outlook Business*, 16 February 2013, pp. 40–48.

Ray, Aparajita, 'Empty malls dampen shoppers' interest', *The Times of India*, 2 January 2013.

'Ready for the transition: Ernst & Young's 2012 attractiveness survey, India', Ernst & Young, http://emergingmarkets.ey.com/wp-content/uploads/downloads/2012/03/india-attractiveness-final-version1.pdf, last accessed on 14 February 2013.

CHAPTER ELEVEN

Culture and Consumer Behaviour

LEARNING OBJECTIVES

An individual's behaviour is guided by his or her cultural value system, and developed over time during the socialization process. It is influenced by society, global, national, and regional subcultures. This chapter examines how culture influences purchasing and consumption patterns and how companies make use of these elements in their marketing plans.

After studying this chapter, the reader would be able to

- appreciate the importance of culture in consumption
- learn about the impact of heroes, rituals, and religion in consumption
- analyse cultural dimensions and values of Indian customers
- examine the role of various subcultures that influence consumer behaviour
- appreciate the role of cross-cultural consumer behaviour
- learn about global influences on Indian consumers

CASE STUDY

Creating Madeleine Objects

People tend to attach meaning to objects. What kind of meaning it is depends on their background, culture, memories, and experience.

Marcel Proust in his work, *Remembrance of Things Past*, published in 1913, writes of the Celtic belief that the souls of those whom we have lost are held captive in some inferior being or in some inanimate object. That is, the past is hidden in some material objects.

He writes of his memory of his mother offering him tea and 'plump little cakes' called *petites Madeleine*. He recalls the times that he would raise 'to my lips a spoonful of the tea in which I had soaked a morsel of the cake' and in doing so, 'an exquisite pleasure had invaded my senses...at once the vicissitudes of life had become indifferent to me, its disasters innocuous, its brevity illusory. I had ceased now to feel mediocre, accidental, mortal.'

The taste of tea and Madeleine were also associated with memories of his Aunt Léonie, who 'used to give me, dipping it first in her own cup of real or of lime-flower tea.' The Madeleine brought the image, sight, and smells of his past.

The story illustrates that objects become a means to rekindle past memories, of growing up and of family. The smell and taste of things remain poised a long time, writes Proust, like souls, ready to remind us and bring back to us the vast structure of recollection.

McCracken (2005) shows that 'consumer goods are one of our most important templates for the self', saying further that consumer goods are an important medium of our culture. They are a place we keep our private and public meanings. Cars and clothing, for instance, come loaded with meanings, meanings we use to define ourselves. For instance, people buy SUVs because they think they are riding a wild animal (see chapter-opening case study in Chapter 7). We are constantly drawing meanings out of our possessions and using them to construct our domestic and public worlds.

The question arises as to whether companies can attach cultural and emotional meaning to products like Proust's Madeleine cakes. How can marketing companies create 'Madeleine objects' that evoke memories in people, memories of the sight and smell of pleasant bygone times, or cater to their cultural roots, so that they buy and value products? True, meanings are assigned through personal experiences, but companies try and attach similar experiences or cultural significance to goods, so that they become more than mere products and convey a larger meaning. This is done in two ways: either a company creates its own cult status, such as Harley Davidson or Absolut Vodka, or it attaches local culture and habits to a product, so that it conveys more significance to consumers. Some of the ways that memories can be attached to goods are as follows:

Gifts Gifts have special meaning for the receiver and companies attach meaning to them in various ways. Special occasions are sought to be associated with certain images so that the receiver feels special by associating with that image.

Festivals Companies attach meaning to traditional festivals. For instance, Cadbury tried to change consumer preferences by campaigning that chocolates were acceptable as Diwali gifts, rather than the traditional *mithai*.

Ceremonies Marriages, engagements, childbirth, and so on, are opportunities for companies to push their products. The 'great Indian wedding' is an opportunity to plug products, and advertisers use images of marriage liberally in their communications.

Occasions Opportunities to celebrate, such as birthdays, success in examinations, and going on dates, are also means to get into the lives of people. Products such as roses, chocolates, and other gifts, are imbued by the receiver with meaning that goes beyond the physical object.

Gifts, festivals, occasions, and ceremonies are an integral part of family and culture. Before attaching meaning to objects, companies need to understand family habits and cultural practices. Products are placed within the context of an individual's social and cultural environment, so that they too, attach Madeleine moments to brands.

While reading the chapter, try to answer the following questions:

1. How does culture influences purchase decisions of individuals?
2. Look at advertisements of popular products and find out how companies create memories so that people associate products with culture.
3. How do subcultures influence consumer behaviour?
4. How does culture interact with consumer behaviour?

Sources:

McCracken, Grant David, *Culture and Consumption II: Markets, Meaning, and Brand Management*, Indiana University Press, Bloomington, 2005, p. 3.

Proust, Marcel, 'Swann's Way', Vol. 1 of *Remembrance of Things Past*, 1913, E-book, 2009, http://ebooks.adelaide.edu.au/p/proust/marcel/p96s/, last accessed on 18 April 2012.

INTRODUCTION

Newborns of animals know what to eat, how to find and capture their food, and how to escape predators. This ability is what they are born with, and is called instinct. Humans too have instincts, which are further ingrained by culture as they grow up. This guides their behaviour and actions even when they are far removed from their culture. Ingrained and difficult to shake off, culture maintains a powerful influence on buying behaviour. Consumption is associated with childhood memories and traditions that an individual finds difficult to shake off, as described in the chapter-opening case study on Madeleine objects.

To illustrate, if you ask people who are vegetarian to eat meat, it will be extremely difficult for them to do so, showing the power of culture in our lives. Indians who go abroad tend to stick to their own communities and long for traditional food. It is, to use Adam Smith's phrase, an invisible hand that guides free market capitalism. As we saw in Chapter 10, it not only guides a person's actions but what to consume as well. How Indian consumers are guided by culture is evident from the following examples:

- Salons in India offer a discount on Tuesdays because people of some religions do not like to wash or cut their hair on this day. The Lakmé Salon, for instance, offers discounts on 'Trendy Tuesdays' to mitigate this cultural habit that keeps its salons empty on this day. .
- Subway had a scheme to offer vegetarian subs in India on Tuesdays and Saturdays, when many people avoid non-vegetarian food.
- Sales of cars and consumer durables plummet on Saturdays as it is considered inauspicious to buy metals on this day.

Cultural influences are indeed strong. Companies thus learn to operate in tune with a country's culture. However, they do attempt to change culture as well. Foreign food companies have successfully changed Indians' preference for culturally accepted foods to cornflakes, instant noodles, and burgers. The speed at which society is taking to Western habits shows that culture can indeed change.

This chapter examines the role of culture in consumer behaviour. Indian society is analysed according to its cultural and value dimensions. Global influences and the role of subcultures are also discussed. Managers have to understand these nuances to market their products and services.

MEANING OF CULTURE

Individuals exist within families, which in turn, are part of a larger culture. It describes people's 'way of life'. Different groups of people may have different cultures, which is passed on from one generation to the next. Culture is seen in people's writing, religion, music, clothes, cooking, and in what they do.

Hofstede (1991) explains that people carry within themselves, patterns of thinking, feeling, and potential acting that were learnt throughout their lifetime. Using the analogy of computers, he calls these patterns 'software of the mind', or culture. Hofstede formally defines culture as 'the collective programming of the mind, which distinguishes the members of one group or category of people from another.' It is also described as the glue that holds people together, consisting of shared values, beliefs, and attitudes. Companies try to attach cultural meanings and memories to their products, as seen in the chapter-opening case study, which describes how products and experiences conjure up memories in consumers.

For instance, Bata is a Czech brand but is considered an Indian brand because it has used Indian culture successfully in its campaigns.

Culture is also defined as the 'lens' through which all phenomena are seen, apprehended, and assimilated. Culture is the 'blueprint' of human activity. It determines the coordinates of social action and productive activity (McCracken, 1988).

Societies acquire cultural values by the following two methods:

Enculturation This means learning one's own culture, through observation or *informal learning*, when children learn by observing parents; through *formal learning* when people are taught norms of behaviour and by *technical learning* when children are taught cultural norms by teachers.

Acculturation This means learning of foreign cultures, through exposure to other lands in the media, word of mouth, or observation.

The first occurs in the family and the environment, as children observe what is acceptable and what is not. The second is learned people learn about the norms and values of other countries.

The process of enculturation and how it affects marketing strategy is covered in the next two sections.

Characteristics of Culture

Managers must figure out ways of positioning products within the system of values and beliefs. In some cases, companies try to change these beliefs so as to encourage people to buy products that otherwise look alien to them. We find that culture has the following qualities:

Guides our actions Like an invisible hand, culture guides our actions. This is reflected in the way people dress, their eating habits, and the way they behave. Through cultural norms, standards of behaviour are established. This is important for companies, because they would like to know how to position products in cultures. For example, many individuals follow the lifestyles of their families even when they move out. Girls follow the style of their mothers' cooking, whereas boys talk and behave like their fathers.

Satisfies needs The reason that people follow norms is that culture satisfies deep psychological needs. Individuals' need to relate with social groups and have an orderly social life are fulfilled by cultural norms. Culture guides habits as to what, when, and where to eat, and also builds beliefs in individuals about what is good or bad. Companies want to participate in this process to associate their products with these strongly felt needs.

Learned As children grow up, they are socialized and acquire culture (see Chapter 10). Both formal and informal learning are open to marketing influences. For example, people learn by looking at advertising. Further, as one grows up, the individual learns ways of dressing and behaving from peers. Wearing fashionable clothes is an example of consumer learning.

Dynamic Culture changes with the times. The process may be slow, but societies discard cultural practices (such as slavery and sexual discrimination in the West, and *sati* and traditional dresses like *dhotis* in India) and acquire new ones. In India, culture has changed over a period of time as the society was exposed to globalization. For example, while earlier cheaper eating places called *dhabas* were popular, now the preferences have shifted to branded food and hangouts. Companies operate within existing cultures but also try to change culture by making consumers switch their habits.

These characteristics are used by companies in designing their offerings and also in their communications. The next section describes the interaction of cultural value system with consumer behaviour through marketing communications.

Interaction of Culture and Consumer Behaviour

Luna and Gupta (2001) have given a model of the influence of culture on consumer behaviour and vice versa (Fig. 11.1). It shows that both the cultural value system and consumption behaviour affect each other. Companies attempt to influence both by the use of advertisements and marketing communications.

The model shows how companies attempt to transfer meanings or values from the culturally constituted world to consumer goods, so marketing communications in the model act as a moderator between culture and consumer behaviour. This is a two-way street, since people find it easier to identify with messages attuned with their culture, while at the same time learn from marketing communications and modify their behaviour as well. Some examples of products doing this are as follows:

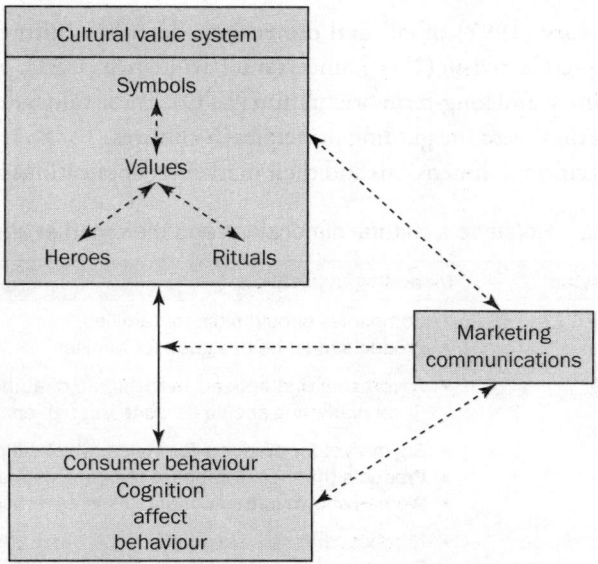

FIG. 11.1 Interaction of culture and consumer behaviour

Source: Luna and Gupta (2001)

FIG. 11.2 Model posing for Monte Carlo

Source: Superbrands 2012

- Fairness creams catered to the cultural need for fair skin and also affected behaviour of many people by creating in them a need for fair skin (see chapter-end case study).
- Maggi was able to change eating habits from *paranthas* to noodles by appealing to the time-pressed Indian housewife, who wanted to cook a tasty meal for her children quickly.
- Advertisements for apparel and fashion routinely show models that reinforce the value of being thin in Indian society that is then followed by millions of young girls, sometimes at risk to their health (see Fig. 11.2). The problem was so severe that the editors of *Vogue* banned skinny models and decided to project the image of healthy models, as reported in *India Today* (2012).
- Coffee lounges projected themselves as hangout destinations for youth and started a new culture. They became preferred places for youth to meet and spend time.

There is clearly an interaction between the cultural value system and consumer behaviour. Companies try to position their products so that they are culturally acceptable, while at the same time try to modify culture so that their products are acceptable in society.

This is done through the understanding of cultural values and dimensions. Hofstede described several cultural dimensions that are discussed with respect to Indian society in the next section.

HOFSTEDE'S CULTURAL DIMENSIONS

Hofstede's theory (1997) of cultural dimensions describes culture on five dimensions, namely individualism–collectivism (IDV), uncertainty avoidance (UAI), power distance (PDI), masculinity–femininity, and long-term orientation (LTO). These values describe behaviour of members of societies as they were the guiding principles in cultures.

Hofstede's cultural dimensions and their marketing applications are summarized in Table 11.1.

TABLE 11.1 Hofstede's cultural dimensions and their market applications in India

Cultural dimension	Marketing application
Individualism	• Companies should pitch for families • Products must be designed for families
Power distance	• Advertising that appeals to the figure of authority • Rural marketing should be done through communities
Masculinity	• Big market for products for males, which help them feel macho • Products that help symbolize feminine aspirations • Women shown in traditional roles in advertisements
Uncertainty avoidance	• Products that help save time • Brands that deliver quality and can be trusted
Long-term orientation	• Belief in karma makes society take a long-term view • Consumers want reliable and durable products

Culture and Consumer Behaviour | **381**

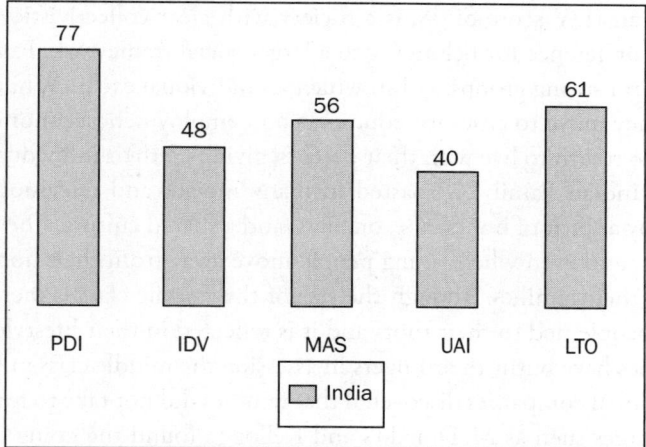

FIG. 11.3 Hofstede's scores for cultural dimensions of Indian society
Source: http://geert-hofstede.com/india.html, last accessed on 19 April 2012

Next, scores are assigned for these cultural dimensions for different cultures. These scores indicate the guiding principles for people in various countries and show which dimension is more powerful than others. The scores for India are given in Fig. 11.3 and are discussed with respect to cultural traditions in the country.

Individualism

Societies can be described as individualistic or collectivistic. Hofstede described collectivism as 'societies in which people from birth onwards are integrated into strong, cohesive in-groups, which throughout people's lifetimes continue to protect them in exchange for unquestioning loyalty.'

 CB IN ACTION   **Cultural Dimensions**

Collect advertisements of various products and analyse them with regard to each cultural dimension, that is, individualism, power distance, masculinity, uncertainty avoidance, and long-term orientation. Describe the elements that address each dimension.

Record your answers in the following table:
Do they match with the cultural dimensions of your society or do they project a culture from another country? Do the ads succeed? Why?

Brand/Product	Cultural dimension	Elements that address each cultural dimension	Which aspect of culture do they depict?
Advertisement 1			
Advertisement 2			
Advertisement 3			

India, with an IDV score of 48, is a society with clear collectivistic traits. This means that there is a high preference for belonging to a larger social framework. Family, community, caste, and religion form strong groups within which an individual exists. While many individuals live separately as they move to cities for education and employment, economic realities are pushing young people to return to live with their parents, giving up their individualism in the process.

The 'Great Indian Family' is toasted in many movies and television serials. The family is characterized by a spirit of bonhomie, oneness, and a shared culture. The joint family is still very strong in India, and even when young people move away from their homes, they still maintain close ties with their families. Though the size of the middle class is increasing, a strong shared culture keeps people tied to their roots and it is reflected in their lifestyle and food preferences. Many companies have burnt their fingers in assessing the middle class in India, for instance, and some multinational companies discovered that families did not take to foreign goods as they had hoped. Companies such as McDonald's and Kellogg's found the going difficult initially before they learnt to operate in Indian culture (see Global Insight).

GLOBAL INSIGHT
Multinationals and Indian Food

Multinational food companies find that adapting to local tastes is essential, if they want to succeed in markets like India. These companies entered India hoping that its large middle class would take to their products like a fish to water, but they burnt their fingers. They found their projections had gone wrong, as people wanted products to their tastes. This exhibit describes how such companies are catering to local tastes.

These companies discovered that the products and brands that they were selling so successfully in other countries would not succeed in India, unless they were modified to Indian tastes and culture. *The Economic Times* (2012) reports that Kellogg's India has localized its India portfolio for the second time, more than a decade after the launch of coconut and *elaichi* variants of its cornflakes met with a lukewarm response.

When it launched its oats range, it did so with variants such as *pudina*, tomato, and *garam masala*. The company is also looking to launch localized variants of its other products PepsiCo's Quaker Oats were similarly introduced in localized variants. Oats, an emerging food category, has been riding high on its health benefits that marketers such as PepsiCo, Marico, Kellogg's, GlaxoSmith-Kline, and Bagrrys are cashing on.

These companies followed the growing number of multinationals which have been forced to cater to Indian tastes rather than sell the same products that they sell in other countries. India is the only country where Yum Restaurants' owned KFC and Pizza Hut sell a 'thali' concept; McDonald's *aloo tikki* burger remains the chain's largest-selling product in India; and Subway India sells hot subs, even though in almost all other markets it sells its products cold.

To promote its Indian menu, McDonalds launched a campaign, *Life Banaye Chatpati @ ₹20 only*. Both the message and the price were Indian: nowhere else was anything priced at less than $1. Apart from *aloo tikki*, which is typically Indian, McDonald's offers *paneer* wraps and a menu that would be considered too spicy in its host country. PepsiCo's came up with another Indian brand, Nimbooz, cashing on the Indian preference for a *nimboo* drink in the hot summer months. It too, has made its products more acceptable to Indian taste buds. While Lay's potato chips come in variants such as 'Mango Mastana' and 'Magic Masala', Quaker Oats come in lemon, veggie, and *kesar* flavours.

These and a number of other companies see the breakfast segment as an opportunity. This market segment is estimated at ₹600 crore, growing at 18–20 per cent, with Kellogg's the leader with a roughly 55 per cent share. Others angling for a slice of this segment include PepsiCo, Marico, Bagrrys, Dr Oetker, Britannia, and McCain. While Britannia launched porridge and *poha* under its brand Healthy Start, McCain has frozen *idlis*.

(Contd)

GLOBAL INSIGHT (Contd)

In their book, *The $10 Trillion Prize*, Silverstein, et al. (2012) of Boston Consulting Group (BCG) stress the need for companies to adapt to local tastes—in terms of products and also how to sell them. They cite the case of Pepsico, which invented the spicy snack with an Indian name, 'Kurkure'. While Hermes sells French-made saris in India, Kraft has re-engineered the Oreo for Chinese taste buds. Such instances show the importance of local preferences and the need for companies to cater to local tastes if they have to succeed in emerging markets.

For multinational brands, a 'one taste suits all' strategy clearly does not work. They have to introduce flavours that appeal to local cultures. Going glocal is really the way to people's hearts and palates.

Do you think that the glocal products offered by multinational companies are pushing out Indian cultural traditions?

Sources:

Bhushan, Ratna, 'Kellogg's India to take a second shot at localising its India portfolio', *The Economic Times*, 19 October 2012.

http://www.mcdonaldsindia.com/ChatpataMcA-looTikkiTVC.pdf, 2009, last accessed on 15 January 2013.

Silverstein Michael J., Abheek Singhi, Carol Liao, and David Michael, *$10 Trillion Prize: Captivating the Newly Affluent in China and India*, Harvard Business Review Press, Boston, 2012.

Power Distance

Power distance is the extent to which the less powerful members of the family accept the power of other members of the family. India's score is 77, and this high score indicates high inequality. People show a high degree of dependency in families and offices, accept unequal rights, paternalistic culture, and so on, in exchange for loyalty.

In India, the inequality is endorsed by the family and is symbolized in the respect shown for older members. Male members exhibit more power than female members. Power is also held by caste, religious, and community leaders.

While India is seen to be modernizing at a fast rate, statistics do not support this belief. The Gender Inequality Index (GII), calculated by the United Nations Development Programme (UNDP), actually worsened between 2008 and 2011, according to a report in *The Times of India* (2011). According to UNDP figures, India now ranks 127 out of 147 countries on the GII in 2013, better only than Afghanistan in South Asia. Advertisements routinely project culturally assigned roles, for example, girls in the roles of housewives and men as ogling women on the road.

On the Human Development Index (HDI), India ranks 135 out of 187 countries in 2014. When inequality is factored in, it experiences a 30 per cent drop in its human development values, ranking 129 out of 146 nations.

The power distance plays itself out in several forms. Though the Constitution recognizes the principle of 'equal pay for equal work' for both men and women, working women continue to get lower wages in India. In agriculture, the hourly wage rates for women vary from 50 per cent to 75 per cent of male rates (*The Times of India*, 2011). According to the data provided by the World Economic Forum (WEF), the average annual income of a woman in corporate India was $1185, compared to a man's $3698 in 2010. Such findings point to a big imbalance in gender equality in India (see Marketing insight). According to the *Wall Street Journal* (2012), the majority of the female workforce in India is unskilled and has only a basic education. They often work in very poorly paid jobs with no security or benefits and in many cases below the minimum daily wage. An illiterate woman working in an occupation that doesn't require skills

MARKETING INSIGHT
Unempowered Indian Woman

Perhaps the greatest divergence between developed countries and India is in the composition of consumers and their influence in the purchase process. In developed countries, women have more power than their counterparts in India. Silverstein and Sayre (2009) write that women now drive the world economy, controlling about $20 trillion in annual consumer spending. Women represent a growth market bigger than China and India combined and companies would be ignoring their largest customer segment at their own risk.

The six key female consumer segments for women identified by them are as follows:

Fast tracker Women who are educated and in good jobs, or the economic and education elite

Pressure cooker Working married women with children, trying to balance home and work pressures

Relationship-focused Content and optimistic, usually housewives who are focused on managing the household

Managing on her own Single again, divorced, independent women

Fulfilled empty nester Older women whose children have moved out, focused on travel, exercise, and leisure

Making ends meet Poor women, making ends meet by working on low-paying jobs, no money for beauty or exercise

When we apply the above categorization to India, we find a huge anomaly. Women in India suffer immensely due to the power distance in its culture. The *Wall Street Journal* (2012) reports that women who have progressed beyond high school make up only about 6.5 per cent of Indian women of working age, between the ages of 15 and 59 years. It quotes National Sample Survey Office (NSSO) data: as of 2010, India had an estimated 112 million female workers. These figures included all workers doing a job for at least 30 days in the year.

First, 51.5 per cent of the households are in the deprived category. With 65 per cent of India's population living in rural areas, the deprived households form a staggering 84.2 per cent of the total. Companies thus cater to just 15.8 per cent of rural households or 48.5 per cent of households in India that are above the level of deprived.

The child sex ratio in India has dropped to 914 females against 1000 males—the lowest since Independence—in the provisional 2011 Census report (*The Economic Times*, 2011). This shows a continuing preference for boys in society, and the fact that females are not valued in India. Female mortality rates are high, and the share of the girl child in education is low. There are restrictions on what girls might wear (see chapter-end case study). Singh and Bhandari (2012) point out that in the case of married women, their access to money is limited as it is controlled by males, particularly in non-metropolitan households.

The Indian market is thus limited to girls and women in urban areas, who are independent, and can take financial decisions on their own. For the rest, day-to-day survival itself may be a problem, let alone buying cosmetics and clothes for themselves.

How can companies target women in societies where most decisions are taken by men?

Sources:

'Census of India 2011: Child sex ratio drops to lowest since Independence', PTI report, *The Economic Times*, 31 March 2011.

Chowdhury, Kavita, 'India is fourth most dangerous place in the world for women: poll', *India Today*, 16 June 2011.

Lahiri, Tripti, 'By the numbers: Where Indian women work', *The Wall Street Journal* Blogs, 14 November 2012, available at: http://blogs.wsj.com/indiarealtime/2012/11/14/by-the-numbers-where-indian-women-work/, last accessed on 15 January 2013.

Pai, Aditi and Deepika Khatri, 'She buys to conquer', *India Today*, 25 April 2008.

Silverstein, Michael J. and Kate Sayre, 'The female economy', *Harvard Business Review*, September 2009.

Singh, Supriya and Mala Bhandari, 'Money management and control in the Indian joint family across generations', *The Sociological Review*, Vol. 60, Issue 1, February 2012, pp. 46–67.

'Women in the workforce: The importance of sex', *The Economist*, 12 April 2006.

averages earnings of ₹85 rupees ($1.50) a day; an illiterate man doing such a job averages ₹177 ($3.20) a day.

Masculinity

The media likes to toast a class of women who are successful models or executives. Some women, indeed, have risen to great success in the country. However, the majority of the population struggles with discrimination. India scores 56 on the masculinity index pointing to a male-dominated society. Men resort to a visual display of success and power. 'The designer brand label, the flash and bling that goes with advertising one's success, is widely practiced', according to the Hofstede's website.

Masculinity is reflected in societal attitudes towards women, who are treated as a subordinate gender. Women continue to be shown in domestic roles in advertisements for better acceptability (see Fig. 11.4).

FIG. 11.4 Everest Tikhalal
Source: Superbrands 2012

There is no sign that such attitudes are changing. Even young people exhibit them. Interestingly, the Global Report Card on Adolescents 2012 published by the United Nations International Children's Fund (UNICEF) says that 57 per cent of adolescent boys in India think a husband is justified in hitting or beating his wife. Over half of the Indian adolescent girls, or around 53 per cent think that a husband is justified in beating his wife (*The Times of India*, 2012a).

This implies that while companies can cater to men's egos by providing 'macho' products, at the same time, there is a growing market for products that encourage the aspirations of downtrodden girls.

Uncertainty Avoidance

Uncertainty avoidance refers to the way that a society deals with unknown situations. It reflects anxiety about the future, which in turn affects the ability for risk-taking, there is more concern about security and less open-mindedness. Indians tend to be fatalistic, an attitude that stems from, and is reinforced by their religious beliefs.

India scores 40 on this dimension and is seen to have a medium to low preference for avoiding uncertainty. There is acceptance of imperfection, and traditionally, Indians are seen as patient and tolerant, which makes them settle into roles and routines easily. Rules are often circumvented and people rely on innovative methods to bypass the system. Indians 'adjust' to almost anything, and this attitude is both the cause of misery and paradoxically, empowerment.

Long-term Orientation

This dimension refers to society's search for virtue or whether it has a pragmatic future-oriented perspective. People with this orientation place greater value on investing in tomorrow and making plans for the future rather than instant gratification. Due to this, many Indians like to invest in property and gold and would rather eschew present comforts for a sense of security about the future.

India scores 61 on this dimension, which means that it has a long-term orientation. The philosophy of 'karma' traditionally dominates religious and philosophical thought. As a result of this thinking, Indians generally forgive lack of punctuality, and have a high acceptability of misfortune.

Hofstede's cultural dimensions provide insight into Indian culture on various parameters. Further understanding is provided by studying the cultural and value dimensions of Indian consumers, described in the next section.

VALUES

Rokeach (1973) defined 'a value as a centrally held, enduring belief which guides actions and judgments across specific situations and beyond immediate goals to more ultimate end-states of existence'.

A distinction is also made in *terminal values*, or the desired states of existence, and *instrumental values*, a set of values that helps individuals to achieve their desired states. For instance, 'becoming rich' is a terminal value, but young people have to achieve their ambitions to become rich.

Terminal and Instrumental Values

Values drive an individual's behaviour. Rokeach has given an inventory of values in two sets: one composed of 18 terminal values, or desired end states of existence, and the second consisting of 18 instrumental values, or preferable approaches to achieve the end states. A shortened list of these values most relevant to marketing is presented in Table 11.2. Marketing communications play on these values liberally.

Terminal values describe what one ultimately wants from life. To achieve this state, one has to follow instrumental values. The important point here is not whether people follow these values

TABLE 11.2 List of values relevant to marketing

Terminal values (Personal goals)	Instrumental values (Approach to reach terminal values)
Comfortable life	Ambitious
Exciting life	Broad-minded
Freedom	Capable
Happiness	Cheerful
Pleasure	Clean
Social recognition	Imaginative
Friendship	Loving
A world of beauty	Intellectual
Family security	Responsible
Self-respect	Logical

Source: Adapted from Rokeach (1973)

CB IN ACTION   Instrumental or Terminal

Make a list of all the products or brands that you own or like to use. This exercise requires you to study which of these brands are bought by you for instrumental (immediate result) or terminal values (final result), so it requires you to think deeply why you use them.

Enter the results as shown in Table 11.3. The first two entries are given as examples. For example, you would like to use soap for the immediate requirement of cleaning yourself, but you tend to use a brand that helps you feel beautiful. Similarly, you may buy a mobile brand because you want to be responsible by calling your mother everyday but ultimately you use it as a means of social recognition, as you show it off to your friends and send messages from it. Now, analyse all your other possessions or things that you like to use.

Discuss the results with your friends. What is the importance of doing such an exercise to marketing?

TABLE 11.3   Instrumental and terminal value of products or brands

Product/Brand	Instrumental value (Your immediate action)	Terminal value (What you want to achieve)
Soap brand	Clean	A world of beauty
Mobile brand	Responsible	Social recognition
...		

or not, but that they form a self-perception of having these values. Companies are thus able to project their products and services in the light of these values, so that they appeal to all. How companies use these is described in our discussion on Indian cultural and value dimensions.

Schwartz's Model of Universal Human Values

Schwartz (2012) has given a model that consists of 10 human value types. These are ordered along two major dimensions: openness to change versus conservation and self-enhancement versus self-transition (see Fig. 11.5). According to the theory, values form a circular structure that reflects their motivations. This circular structure captures the conflicts and compatibility among the ten values. Findings from 82 countries included in the Schwartz Value Survey show the validity of the theory across cultures.

The findings reveal substantial differences in the value priorities of individuals. The model also shows how values differ from attitudes, beliefs, norms, and traits.

According to Schwartz, the ten universal values are as follows:

Power   Social status and prestige, control or dominance over people and resources

Achievement   Personal success through demonstrating competence according to social standards

Hedonism   Pleasure and sensuous gratification

Stimulation   Excitement, novelty, and challenge in life

Self-direction   Independent thought and action

Universalism   Understanding, appreciation, tolerance, caring about humanity and nature

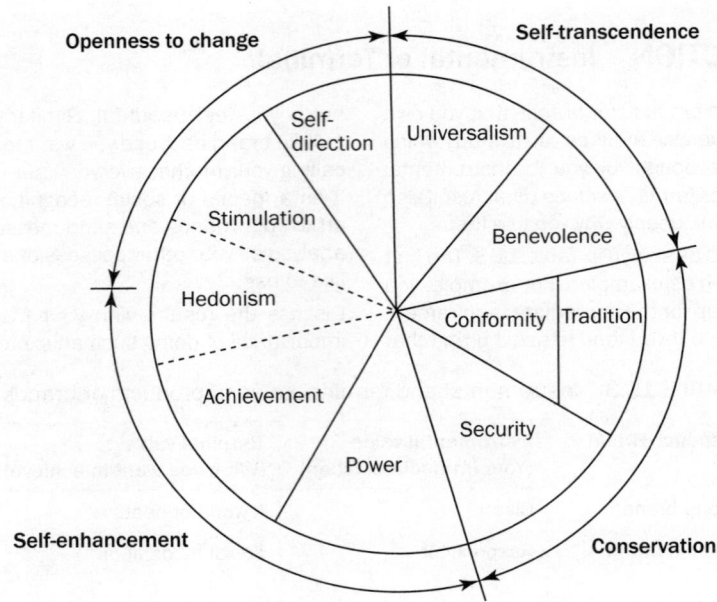

FIG. 11.5 Schwartz's model of universal human values

Source: Schwatrz (2012)

Benevolence Preserving and enhancing the welfare of loved ones, friends, and family

Conformity Restraint of actions, inclinations

Tradition Respect, commitment, and acceptance of the customs and ideas that traditional culture or religion provide the self

Security Safety, harmony, and stability of society, of relationships, and of self

If these values are placed in a two-dimensional space, they form a circumplex structure, with the values with similar motivational goals closer to each other, and the values with conflicting motivational goals further apart. For instance, self-direction is adjacent to stimulation, but farthest apart from tradition, conformity, and security values, because the latter are associated with restraint.

Indian Core Values

India has a rich tradition that defines its core values. These values are given by different religions, traditions, and practices. Some core values have been enshrined in the Indian Constitution, which defines the nation as a sovereign, socialist, secular, and democratic republic. Values such as justice, liberty, equality, freedom of expression and faith, fraternity, and unity are enshrined in the Constitution. The following are some more values that are mentioned in the list of fundamental duties:

- To uphold and protect the sovereignty, unity, and integrity of India
- To promote harmony and the spirit of common brotherhood

TABLE 11.4 Precepts of social and individual discipline as described in Indian culture

Yama: Precepts of social discipline	Niyama: Precepts of individual discipline
Ahimsa (Non-violence)	Shaucha (Cleanliness)
Satya (Truthfulness)	Santosha (Contentment)
Asteya (Non-stealing)	Tapas (Austerity)
Brahmacarya (Sexual responsibility)	Svadhyaya (Self-study)
Aparigraha (Abstention from greed)	Isvara pranidhana (Surrender of the self to God)

Source: Summarized from *The Study and Practice of Yoga*, http://www.swami-krishnananda.org/patanjali/raja_74.html, last accessed on 16 April 2012

- To renounce practices derogatory to the dignity of women
- To protect and improve the natural environment
- To develop a scientific temper, humanism, and the spirit of inquiry and reform
- To safeguard public property and to abjure violence
- To strive towards excellence in all spheres

Some basic values are also given by religion. Indian culture gives goals of human life to be followed by all as follows:

Dharma Obedience of ethical laws leading to righteousness, duty, and moral order

Artha Participation in economic activity, to generate wealth and prosperity, and to live an honest life

Kama Satisfaction of legitimate desires

Moksha Striving for and achieving salvation

Some more values are given by Indian traditions, like yoga, which enumerates the ethical precepts to be followed. They consist of moral training, called *Yama*, and individual discipline, called *Niyama*. These were given by Patanjali as rules required for the practice of yoga (Table 11.4). The *Yamas* give us a list of tendencies we need to control. The practice of the *niyamas* develops a more cultured nature.

These values are guiding principles for the population. However, many of these are not followed. As winds of globalization gather pace in the country, people are becoming more materialistic and less spiritual.

INDIAN CULTURAL AND VALUE DIMENSIONS

While the core values provide guidance to Indians, their consumption behaviour is dictated by cultural and value dimensions. The decisions and behaviour of the Indian consumer are guided by certain *value dimensions*, meaning their beliefs and judgments, and *cultural dimensions*, consisting of traditions and heritage. Banerjee (2008) offers a model of these dimensions of Indian consumers (see Fig. 11.6). It identifies six values dimensions: individual and family, modernity through conformity, success and growth, age and youthfulness, happiness and adaptability, religion, and spirituality.

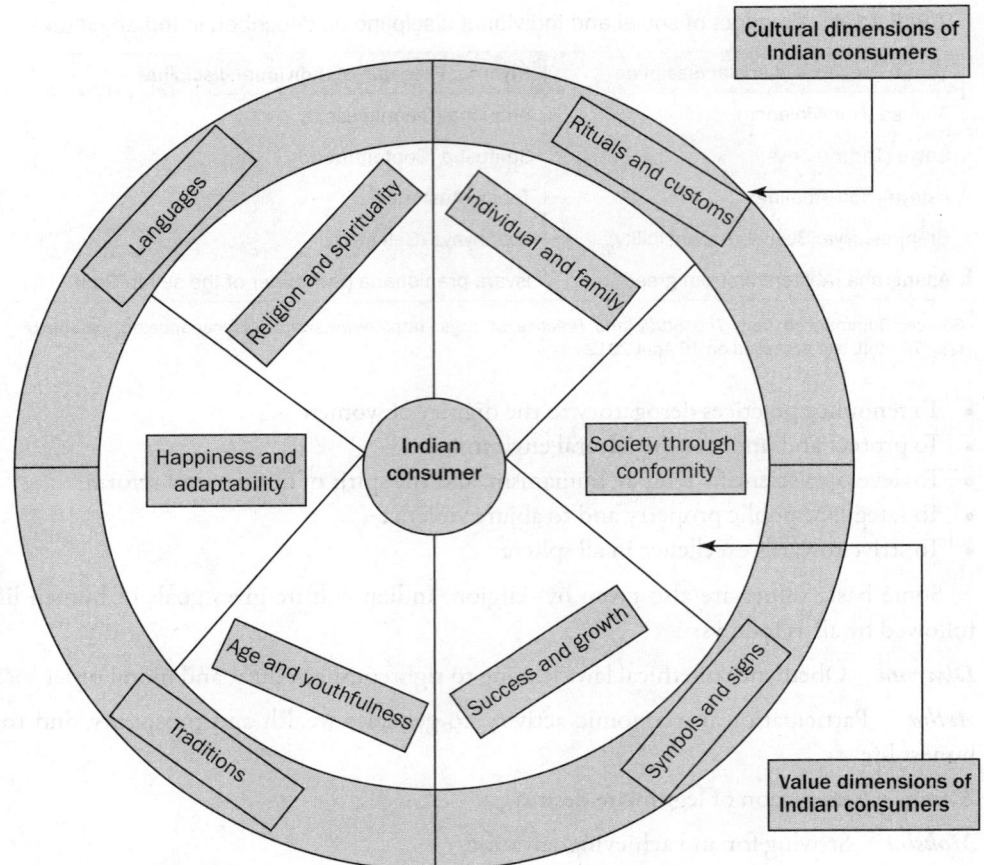

FIG. 11.6 Cultural and value dimensions of Indian consumers
Source: Banerjee (2008)

Cultural dimensions consists of four categories, namely traditions, symbols and signs, rituals and customs, and languages.

These ten dimensions are explained individually in this section.

Individual and Family

It has been assumed by sociologists that with increasing modernization and Western influences, the joint family would make way for nuclear families. However, according to a report in *The Times of India* (2012b), urban India has actually witnessed a rise in the number of joint families, a fact thrown up by Census 2011 data. It says that while the proportion of households with only one married couple has declined, the share of households with two and even three married couples staying together has increased since the last Census in 2001. This finding also matches with Hofstede's finding that Indian society is collectivist, showing the importance of family.

The share of nuclear family households is 70.1 per cent according to Census 2011, marginally down from 70.3 per cent in 2001. In rural areas, the share of one-married-couple households increased from 69.3 per cent to 69.6 per cent, but in urban areas, it dropped markedly from 73 per cent to 71.2 per cent. The average household size in India was 4.5 in 2008, according to NSSO data. The rural household size (4.7) was slightly higher than urban household size (4.2). A detailed discussion on family and social class is available in Chapter 10.

The marketing implications are as follows:

Large, economical packs Companies must provide large packs for most goods that are suitable for large families.

Price points As families look for value in their purchases, goods must be provided at various price points. For instance, Colgate has a range of products at different price points and also offers Colgate Cibaca at a much cheaper price point.

Quality and value Families seek quality and value. Products that deliver these have a high probability of succeeding than premium or foreign products that attract the attention of a selected audience. For instance, companies started offering *atta* (wheat) bread and *atta* noodles as they were considered healthier than ordinary white bread and noodles.

Modernity through Conformity

Indians are becoming modern, yet seek conformity. They adjust to the needs of others and seek harmony. Social hierarchies are very strong and people like to conform to traditions and customs, even though they adopt Western clothes and language. Standing out, in terms of clothes, appearance, or ideas, is looked down upon. Pellissery (2008) writes that hierarchical interaction does not allow scientific temper to prevail; rather, it is the power structure and persons near the top of the hierarchy, whose opinions are valued and respected.

Success and Growth

Banerjee (2008) writes that in Indian society, recognition, or social acceptability is valued more than individual achievement. Success is enjoyed from the perspective of a group than an individual.

FIG. 11.7 Lunch boxes by Tupperware

Source: Superbrands 2012

Though Indian culture has been marked by the *chalta hai* (take it easy) attitude, this is being questioned increasingly in society because people see it as a sign of mediocrity. This is the result of increasing education and the introduction of a multinational work culture. The attitude towards success and growth is slowly changing. The youth form a potent new market for fashioning India's newly globalized middle class. This generation oozes attitude and ambition, and young people see themselves as cool and confident. They do not carry social, political, or ideological baggage.

Tupperware understands this and has come out with more modern looking tiffin and carry boxes, which youngsters could carry to colleges and their offices (see Fig. 11.7).

Age and Youthfulness

India has one of the youngest populations in the world: 704 million people under the age of 30 in 2012, according to *Euromonitor* (2012). Basu (2007) writes that in 2020, the average age of an Indian is expected to be 29 years, compared to 37 for China and 48 for Japan. The young generation is often referred to as 'liberalization's children'. Lukose (2009) writes in her book by the same name that young people are caught both by powerful market forces that fashion them as consumers, and educational and political institutions that fashion them as citizens.

Though many millions in this group remain locked in a struggle with poverty, some 22 million belong to the urban middle class and are in a position to influence the economy dramatically as they grow older, writes *Businessweek* (1999). Another 100 million or so live in rural India. Even here, many young people are having their first taste of rising prosperity and expectations.

The impact of this is that India's youth are already having an enormous impact on the economy, on companies hoping to sell them products, on the media, and on culture. Companies try to cater to this generation by providing products and services, and advertisements are clearly focused on them. Many companies also offer places for them to hang out (see Exhibit 11.1).

EXHIBIT 11.1 Time out

Young people like to hang out with their friends. Catering to this need, a host of restaurants project themselves as not just mere providers of food, but places for young people to sit around and spend time with their friends. Many restaurants try to convey the impression that they are fashionable places to sit and enjoy, by providing facilities such as music, karaoke, indoor games, big screens, and a pleasing ambience.

Café Coffee Day (CCD) started advertising on television, debuting with its 'sit down' campaign, giving customers a purpose for hanging out at the café. Instead of standing up, it asks people to sit down and says that a lot of things can happen when you 'sit down'. It builds on youngsters' penchant for hanging out with friends at restaurants.

The commercial caters to the existing youth culture of hanging out with friends and tries to give a purpose to those youngsters who spend endless hours at Café Coffee Day. It tries to instil a sense of pride in them for doing something that a lot of people would say is a waste of time.

KFC also wants people to think of their restaurants as a place to take a break from work and enjoy a relaxing time. It moved away from promoting its 'finger licking' food offerings and has positioned itself as a place to hang out in its brand campaign.

The television commercial revolves around a young executive caught up with work and shows how the people around him help him get to a KFC outlet to unwind. It tries to focus on the KFC experience that extends beyond just food.

To make KFC a top-of-the-list hangout for young consumers, the company has also introduced Radio KFC, a branded channel that plays a mix of international music at KFC outlets. The music played is chosen to match the timing of the day and, by default, the mood of the consumers walking in.

Restaurants such as KFC, Café Coffee Day, and a host of others are trying to lure the young person by providing a place for them. Hopefully, these people will end up buying the food as well.

Given the fact that many young people like to sit around and not buy food in these outlets, are they following the right strategy as it would keep out paying customers?

Sources:
Gupte, Masoom, 'KFC: One more place to hang out', *Business Standard*, 9 April 2012.
'Largest Indian café brand Café Coffee Day's first campaign starts a new trend', *The Economic Times*, 12 December 2012.

The young generation also worships its heroes. Hofstede (1997) describes heroes as 'persons, alive or dead, real or imaginary, who possess characteristics which are highly prized in a culture, and who thus serve as models for behaviour'.

Heroes include reference groups and opinion leaders. Examples of heroes in Indian society are Amitabh Bachchan, Sachin Tendulkar, Katrina Kaif, and so on. They influence consumption of goods through their association with them. Marketing communications offer an obvious vehicle for this association and use heroes and celebrities liberally in campaigns. By and large, Indians are star-struck. Celebrities from films and cricket dominate the Indian psyche, and companies pay huge amounts to get endorsements from them.

Happiness and Adaptability

In India, materialistic gain is not considered the prime route to ensuring happiness. Seeking to attain the higher planes of existence is inherent to Indian culture. It is marked by adaptability, which makes the country relatively happy. India is ranked 32 out of 151 countries on the Happy Planet Index (HPI), which is a measure of average subjective life satisfaction, life expectancy at birth, and ecological footprint per capita. It shows mediocre life expectancy and well-being.

Religion and Spirituality

The religious composition of India's population is given in Table 11.5. Though Hinduism is the dominant religion, the Constitution has a secular nature and guarantees freedom of religion. Each religion adds its tradition and festivities to the rich cultural panorama that is India.

Religious beliefs work in two ways. The first way is by propagating the message. Dedicated television channels transmit religious messages round the clock. They also sell 'blessed products' to help ward off the evil eye and other ailments. Camps and ashrams are hugely popular, with holy products to match.

TABLE 11.5 Religious composition of Indian Population

Religion	Number	Percentage
Hindus	82,75,78,868	80.5
Muslims	13,81,88,240	13.4
Christians	24,080,016	2.3
Sikhs	19,215,730	1.9
Buddhists	79,55,207	0.8
Jains	42,25,053	0.4
Other religions	66,39,626	0.6
Religion not stated	7,27,588	0.1
Total	1,02,86,10,328	100.0

Source: Census of India, 2001, http://www.censusindia.gov.in/Census_Data_2001/India_at_glance/religion.aspx, last accessed on 3 September 2014

The second is to use culture by selling medicines and nature cure products. Anything with the word 'ayurveda' and 'yoga' attached to it conjures up images of Indian culture and people are quick to adopt them. Yoga too, has become a big business in India, with several resorts offering 'yoga vacations' to Indians and foreigners.

Rituals and Customs

Martin Lindstrom in his book, *Buyology* (2008) defines rituals and superstitions 'as not entirely rational actions and the belief that one can somehow manipulate the future by engaging in certain behaviours.' Ritual behaviour is dramatically scripted and acted out and is performed with formality, seriousness, and inner intensity.

Rituals are a set of actions practised in a society to follow cultural norms. They are mostly symbolic in nature. Sometimes they are handed down the generations, but people make their own rituals as well, as can be seen in some common ones. Table 11.6 gives some rituals that are practised globally, while local rituals and customs result in social bondage and gaining social acceptance. They have a beneficial effect as well, as some rituals make us feel good.

Rituals are enacted by members of the society. There are grooming rituals, romantic rituals, and feeding rituals. The challenge before managers is to place products within the rituals so that they are automatically consumed. Advertising plays an important part in modelling ritualistic behaviour and helping it spread. An example of using ritualistic behaviour is an advertisement that shows a young person watching a cricket match on TV. She thinks that every time she drinks a Coke, Sachin Tendulkar hits a four.

Religions also give different sets of rituals to their followers. The challenge before companies is to use these rituals to sell products. There are, in fact, many things that are common between religion and marketing. 'Spirituality and branding are inextricably linked', writes Lindstrom. He points out that brands that have rituals and superstitions associated with them are much 'stickier' than those that don't. Religion and brands also give us comfort.

Traditions

Companies also try to use traditions to position their products. The Indian tradition of offering sweets to celebrate occasions or festivals, for example, was used effectively by Cadbury Dairy Milk. The company came up with advertisements with the tagline *'Kuch meetha ho jaye'* (Let's have something sweet).

TABLE 11.6 Daily rituals and their effects

Everyday ritual	Effect on individual
Preparing for battle	How people start their day—Small acts that help them feel confident about the upcoming day, such as grooming and dressing
Feasting	Eating meals with others, resulting in bonding with other members of the group
Sexing it up	Primping and grooming, wearing clothes and cosmetics that help us look good and confident
Protecting yourself from the future	Acts performed that we consider as lucky, bed-time rituals, offerings in religious places, and so on

FIG. 11.8   Decorations in a mall

The tradition of using herbal remedies has resulted in many companies offering soaps, cosmetics, and medicines made with traditional Indian herbs. The Indian habit of hoarding gold was used effectively by Tanishq which showed heavily decked up ladies in its advertisements with the tagline, '*Parampara ki nayi kahani*' (a new story of tradition).

In India, because of the importance of festivals, malls are seen to be decked up for festivals (see Fig. 11.8). Consumer demand picks up greatly during festivals.

Festivals and special occasions are also very important traditions in Indian life. Companies keep track of such events because they know that great demand is generated during festivals and the marriages season and they must prime their supply chains accordingly. In India, manufacturers of consumer durables have discovered that most of the high-ticket purchases occur during festival days. *The Economic Times* (2010) reported that Maruti delivered 10,000 cars on some festival days against the daily

MARKETING INSIGHT
Wedding Market

Companies eye Indian weddings, which are shows of consumption, wealth, and status, reports *The Economic Times* (2013). Jewellery makers like Tanishq focus their campaigns on marriages. Weddings have witnessed a number of changes in the last few years, from clothing to jewellery, and the Tanishq website also offers an overview of the latest bridal trends across the country.

Fashion houses Dior, Gucci, and Christian Louboutin are among the brands that hope to get a slice of the Indian wedding market. Culturally, Indian weddings are opportunities for families to show off. In the process, they hope to corner a chunk of the share of luxury retail, which has still to pick up in the country. Foreign brands have realized that the wedding season is the peak selling period for most luxury brands, as the tradition of elaborate trousseaus and gifting is very much alive.

These brands look for tie-ups with wedding planners to create special lines for bulk orders, or offer discount on the retail pricing, to make customized goods for invitees. Return gifts are the new trend. These include accessories from a brand such as Dior, to sets of scarves and ties from premium brands, porcelain figurines by Lladro, and even imported food hampers and liquor. This trend offers hope for luxury brands, since large orders can be obtained during weddings.

While extravagance in Indian weddings is not new, it is being recognised by fashion houses as an opportunity to boost sales. French footwear and bags brand Christian Louboutin has launched a special bridal footwear range in the country. India's luxury market is expected to reach $14.73 billion by 2015, from an estimated $8.21 billion in 2013.

The brands are only too happy to cater to the ego of their super-rich clients. They provide saris and traditional wear like *lehengas* for women, with matching expensive accessories. The market has also opened for men's wear, since more awareness means that men would rather wear international branded suits and jackets for such occasions.

Which other brands have successfully tapped the wedding market?

Sources:
http://tanishq.co.in/control/viewContent?contentId=tanishq-trendspeak1&nodeTrailCsv=tanishq-trendspeak1, last accessed on 21 April 2014.
Rathore, Vijaya, 'Luxury goods makers like Dior, Gucci, others gatecrash big fat Indian weddings, luxury market to hit $14.73 billion', *The Economic Times*, 11 January 2013.

FIG. 11.9 A store offering prizes during Diwali festivities

average of 2,000–3,000 cars. Further, India celebrates not only its own religious festivals but has also assimilated festivals of other countries. For instance, Valentine's Day was unheard of in the country some years back but is today a big marketing opportunity.

Festivals are also the time when consumers are in the frame of mind to buy goods. Many employees of the public and private sector get bonus around the time of Diwali, which has also become a big marketing festival. Retail stores and malls offer many promotions during festivals (see Fig. 11.9). Some of the popular festivals that are celebrated in India are given in Table 11.7.

TABLE 11.7 Some popular festivals celebrated in India

Baisakhi	Dussehra	Janmashtami
Diwali	Onam	Karwa Chauth
Durga Puja	Holi	Maha Shivratri
Makar Sankranti	Naag Panchami	Ganesh Chaturthi
Navratri	Pongal	Ram Navami
Raksha Bandhan	Christmas	Easter
Good Friday	Guru Nanak Jayanti	Lohri
Eid ul-Adha	Eid ul-Fitr	Muharram
Thanksgiving	Valentine's Day	Children's Day
Gandhi Jayanti	Independence Day	Republic Day
Teacher's Day	Gahambars	Jamshedi Navroz
Khordad Sal	Zarthost No Deeso	Buddha Purnima
Hemis Gompa		

Languages

India is divided on a linguistic basis. There are many languages in India, and the Constitution lists 22 languages (together with the 92nd Amendment), given in Table 11.8.

The language in circulation, at least among the youth, is a mixture of English and Indian languages. *India Today* (2012) writes that language is no longer a homogenous entity but a mélange of words, slang, and dialect. Garbled English or Pidgin English is now used widely by companies in their communications. For instance, Pepsi tried to connect with the youth through the campaign, '*Youngistan ka wow*' and ITC has a snack called '*Tedhe medhe*'. SMS language has also entered the world of brands and advertisements.

Since advertisements must be comprehended by the target market, they should be in a language that people understand. More important, the advertisement copy can use the local dialect or word association to touch the mind of the consumer. This is not a rule, however, as some

TABLE 11.8 Languages of India

1. Assamese	7. Konkani	13. Punjabi	19. Bodo
2. Bengali	8. Malayalam	14. Sanskrit	20. Maithili
3. Gujarati	9. Manipuri	15. Sindhi	21. Dogri
4. Hindi	10. Marathi	16. Tamil	22. Santali
5. Kannada	11. Nepali	17. Telugu	
6. Kashmiri	12. Oriya	18. Urdu	

companies successfully use phrases such as 'Open happiness' and 'I'm loving it' across different cultures. Translating these phrases in a local language will lose the message in them. Similarly, it would be difficult to convey the meaning of an Indian usage 'Mind it' while translating into other languages.

The producers of Hollywood movies realized the importance of language. English movies generally find a small audience in India as many people do not understand the American accent. To reach a wider audience, dubbed versions are released which are shown in different regions of India. To cater to the English-educated crowd, original versions are also released, sometimes with subtitles. Foreign television programmes are also aired in India dubbed in local languages and have gained in popularity.

Mobile phone makers too, use culture to expand their markets. They introduced the Hindi SMS facility because they realized that a large section of the population was not familiar with English. Multinational companies frequently use Indian names to connect with Indian consumers, more so when they venture into rural markets, like LG's *Sampoorna* line of products.

Many companies also learnt that much of India used a kind of pidgin English, that is, a language that combined English words with a local language. National Geographic launched a series of programmes called *Mission Udaan*. Godrej introduced a small refrigerator named 'Chotukool', not only combining two languages but also using a popular word for better acceptability.

Symbols and Signs

Indian culture has a number of symbols that are endearing and help establish an instant connection with those who see them. For example, ICICI Prudential hit upon a brilliant idea when it used *sindoor* in its advertisements. By doing so, the company immediately struck a chord with the Indian customer and stood out in the clutter of insurance advertisements that harped on common themes such as security and benefits. Other symbols include movies, cricket, and food.

Movies and cricket Movies and cricket unify India culturally. Companies use their influence to create messages that are recognizable across the country. Certain movies like *Sholay* have entered Indian folklore and many advertisements imitate the style and situations from the movie. Others use old film songs in their advertisements. Similarly, cricket is often used in many advertising messages. Cricket matches, such as the World Cup, attract the highest spot rates.

Food A large proportion of the Indian population is vegetarian. Fresh vegetables are purchased and cooked daily. The preference is for foods made from whole grains. Recognizing this, Nestlé launched 'Atta Noodles'. Other companies cash in on the claim that they use real vegetables in

FIG. 11.10 'Ethnic' food served by restaurants is catching on

their products. Restaurants have started offering meals served in traditional style to lure customers (Fig. 11.10).

Though Indian values are guiding principles, marketing companies are happy to see that the principles of restraint and austerity (see Table 11.4), so lauded by Indian religion and tradition, are in reality not followed by many people. As their society is swept by the acquisitive and materialistic winds of modernization, Indians have taken to hedonism with a vengeance. This has worked in favour of companies, which would otherwise not have been able to market their products had people stuck to their original values. Many of the core values of India are observed only by their absence as consumers lap up products that would have been impossible to sell in a traditional culture (see chapter-end case study).

The cultural values of Indian consumers are based on language, rituals, and customs. These vary from region to region. Core values drive consumption. They dictate how people live and conduct their lives. Though many people adopt Western lifestyles, much of their behaviour is nevertheless influenced by core values. In the next section we see how culture can be measured and how the symbols and rituals can be used in marketing.

MEASURING CULTURE

Can an abstract concept like culture be measured? Researchers attempt to do this and classify cultures of different countries on various parameters. Some methods of measuring culture are described here:

Content analysis Through content analysis, companies try to discover cultural values of a society by studying a large number of advertisements, magazines, and movies. They try to find clues about a culture by the images and text being used by advertisers. By doing so, they can conclude whether the society is open or collectivist, as well as its attitudes to beauty, enjoyment, and consumption.

Market research Through *observational research*, researchers observe how consumers select and buy products. They observe customers in their natural environment, without telling them that they

---

 CB IN ACTION Rituals and Brand Loyalty

Rituals and customs are an important part of culture. If products and brands become part of these rituals and customs, they acquire brand loyalty.

Analyse the customs and rituals you follow in your life. Analyse the religious and personal rituals you follow and see which products or brands are attached to them. List the brands you associate with on the following occasions:

- Enjoying with friends, parties and get-togethers
- Traditions like birthdays and weddings in your family
- Your daily rituals like getting ready for college, taking a break, etc.

How can companies increase your brand loyalty so that you use those brands with your rituals?

are being watched. Researchers can discover what attributes of products are valued by people in a certain society while making their choices. Another method is *participatory research*, in which the researcher becomes part of the process, like a salesman in a store. Other companies employ *ghost shoppers*, who mingle with real shoppers, to discover what they think and how they buy.

Measuring instruments Survey instruments such as the Rokeach Value Survey and the Values and Lifestyles model (explained in Chapter 7) help classify societies.

When we use these techniques for India, we discover some contradictions in Indian culture, described in the next section.

CONTRADICTIONS IN INDIAN CULTURE

Apart from the cultural dimensions described in the previous section, the study of the Indian market would be incomplete without considering some more dimensions which point to contradictions in a changing society. A society facing an onslaught of consumerism makes reconciling with traditional values difficult. Such contradictions are evident in the attitudes towards women, treatment of old people, increasing consumerism, and contradictory traditional values.

Demographics

Population figures point to a very high proportion of young people in India. Advertisers have latched on quickly. Many companies use fresh young faces in their commercials and are busy launching products for the young. However, they ignore three facts: first, purchase decisions are often taken by parents; second, older people have more discretionary purchasing power; and third, the elderly population is increasing in India. A report in *Outlook* (2012) says that India has become a gerontic nation, as the number of our aged is growing rapidly. Official figures put 12 per cent (144 million) of India's population over 60 years, but estimates see India as having 250 million senior citizens very soon and the largest adult population by 2013.

Companies are also discovering that while the young are highly visible, the real purchasing power is held by older consumers. Channels targeted exclusively at the young, such as UTV Bindass or MTV cannot match the viewership or influence of general entertainment channels. Chains such as Cafe Coffee Day and Barista find that they have become popular meeting places but they are often crowded with non-paying customers. Many companies are now shifting their focus to older people (see Exhibit 3.1 in Chapter 3).

There is a demand for old age homes, creating a market opportunity for old age care. Far from respecting old age, the new generation does not hesitate to turn their old parents out on the streets. *India Today* (2012) cites a WHO report to say that anxiety, social security, and loneliness are some problems increasingly affecting the elderly. An *Outlook* (2012) report points out that old age homes across the country are occupied to capacity. However, this points to a market opportunity for products and services for the elderly. Real estate companies sell safe neighbourhoods and health care companies offer plans specially tailored for old people.

Modernity vs Traditionalism

Indian society prides itself on being modern and changing with the times. However, a large section of the population remains mired in outdated beliefs and ideas. Katju writes in *Indian*

Express (2012) that most Indians are fools, because 'the minds of 90 per cent Indians are full of casteism, communalism, superstition'. Even the young do not show signs of changing mindsets, which is evident from the increasing number of matrimonial sites and the caste or community bias they show openly. This conflict is often reflected in attitudes towards women.

Bling vs Spirituality

India has traditionally been a spiritual society. However, spiritualism has been taken over with a vengeance by bling culture, meaning a showy, flashy, ostentatious, and elaborate lifestyle. A large section of the population expresses itself through gaudy jewellery, tattoos, vehicles, and cell phones. Religious symbols are also popular (Fig. 11.11). Movies and advertisements encourage this trend.

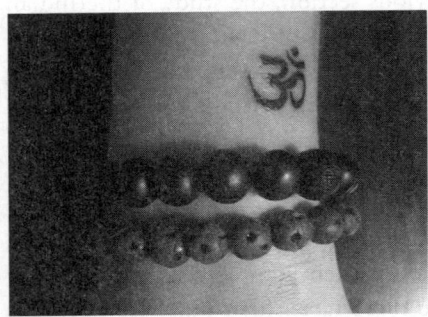

FIG. 11.11 Bling meets spiritual in Indian culture

Companies have jumped on this bandwagon. Mark Tully (2007) writes that though religion continues its hold on television channels, consumerism is mounting a formidable challenge to the spiritual fabric of India. 'There are even more advertisements on Indian television than there are on the British independent channels', he writes, showing how consumerism is taking hold in India. Consumerism has also resulted in manipulating popular sports and even cricket has not been spared from commercialization: 'Advertisers have invented the five-ball over, with advertisements often being shown before the sixth ball has been bowled'. This means that even TV programmes are cut short to accommodate advertisements.

Decency vs Obscenity

As the society opens up, advertisers and film makers are testing what is acceptable and what is not. Advertisers cock a snook at tradition and try to attract young consumers by creating messages bordering on the obscene. For example, the UTV Bindass used an obscene gesture to promote its brand before it was yanked off.

Violence vs Compassion

India was founded on principles of non-violence. Many people indeed show compassion to animals and their fellow beings. However, at the same time, the society is becoming increasingly brutal, as

---

 MARKETING INSIGHT
Two Indias or More

Contradictory trends in Indian culture suggest that there are actually 'two Indias'.

Toyama (2012) writes that the most widely noticed metamorphosis is economic. In the decade 2001–12, India's GDP has grown between 7–9 per cent per year, second only to China's sustained growth rates. However, India's governance resembles a feudal system in practice. Politicians and bureaucrats often act like dukes and barons with term limits, he writes. As a result, one part

(Contd)

MARKETING INSIGHT (Contd)

of society remains mired in poverty, superstitions, and social backwardness, while the other embraces capitalist lifestyles (see Fig. 11.12).

FIG. 11.12 Two Indias: Feudal society meets capitalist success

Suhel Seth (2010) writes, 'The fact is that there are two Indias and both shall remain for a long time to come. One that still experiences the ravages of poverty and poor infrastructure, while the other that sees luxury brands tempting the now-rich-and-arrived Indian'.

Companies have to learn to operate within this contradiction. Some brands have understood the power that both Indias possess. Seth further writes that companies are forced to adapt in three ways because of the contradictory nature of Indian culture:

Value for money Brands have to change the manner in which they present products before this market. The lowest common denominator in brand choice remains price with reasonable quality. There is the constant fear of being taken for a ride; hence the importance of the price-value equation.

Hoarders and re-users The Indian consumer is aspirational and sometimes it is peer pressure rather than genuine need that drives consumption. Indians are by nature hoarders and re-users. 'This is a trait that has now been built into the way brands create customer service and warranty programs; even a low-cost car like the Nano comes with a two-year warranty', writes Seth.

Prone to experiment Indian consumers do not have brand loyalty. They will try new and faddish products, a function perhaps of a desire to be acceptable in a group. Urban India has more restaurant closures than perhaps Manhattan and it is because the Indian consumer is an enduringly experimental animal.

What is the impact on marketing companies of these contradictions? How can they market products in a country that has a variety of subcultures?

Sources:
Seth, Suhel, 'From Gandhi to Gucci: A tale of two Indias', http://blogs.ft.com/economistsforum/2010/01/from-gandhi-to-gucci-a-tale-of-two-indias/#ixzz1sTs2b17i, 2010, last accessed on 19 April 2012.
Toyama, Kentaro, 'The two Indias: Astounding poverty in the backyard of amazing growth', http://www.theatlantic.com/international/archive/2012/02/the-two-indias-astounding-poverty-in-the-backyard-of-amazing-growth/253340/, 2012, last accessed on 26 January 2013.

seen from the number of horrific crimes reported in the country. Child labour is common. A report in *Outlook* (2012) describes how people routinely exploit and torture domestic servants, calling them the 'The New Slaves' adding that 'a nouveau riche middle class who seem to have no empathy with the poor'.

The contradictions in Indian culture result from a relentless exposure to the West. Marketing communications increasingly project Western values. In addition to the influence of foreign movies and TV shows, a part of the society aspires to modernity, but still seeks comfort in traditions, creating two Indias (see Fig. 11.13). Cross-cultural influences are indeed a catalyst for a changing society, and how these impact on consumer behaviour is described in the next section.

FIG. 11.13 Indian and Global cultures are becoming inter-twined in society

CROSS-CULTURAL CONSUMER BEHAVIOUR

India has slowly opened up its economy since 1991. As a result, a number of multinational companies are already operating in the country and more have sought to start operations here. However, its trade tariffs continue to be high when compared with other countries, and its investment norms are still restrictive.

Before 1991, India was a closed economy with average tariffs exceeding 200 per cent. Imports and foreign investment were restricted severely. The reforms process has been slow, as the government started liberalizing only under extreme necessity. At the same time, a number of Indian companies too ventured abroad, either buying out companies or entering into joint ventures with foreign companies. One of the major success stories has been the ability of Indian companies to get outsourcing business from foreign companies.

India is also part of trade agreements, including the WTO. It has signed regional and bilateral trade agreements such as the following:

- India–Sri Lanka Free Trade Agreement
- Trade Agreements with Bangladesh, Bhutan, Sri Lanka, Maldives, China, and South Korea
- India–Nepal Trade Treaty
- Comprehensive Economic Cooperation Agreement (CECA) with Singapore
- Framework Agreements with the Association of Southeast Asian Nations (ASEAN), Thailand, and Chile

As a result of regional and international trade agreements, trade is facilitated and the world is getting smaller every day. India is now connected to global economies, which are in turn interconnected. Businesses today seek to gain competitive advantage via international growth.

Strategic Decisions

To achieve competitive advantage, managers have to take certain decisions dictated by cultural differences. These include decisions about prices, communications, and products.

Prices

One of the first decisions to be taken by companies serving foreign consumers is the prices they are willing to pay. For example, a company selling a soft drink in the US for $2 will find it difficult to extract the same price from Indian consumers. In a hot country, people will be unwilling to pay a high price for a product that is used often. Companies have to adjust to different cultures and prices. McDonalds too, is selling a burger in India for ₹25, though it would be inconceivable to get anything for a price of $0.50 in the US. Indian companies selling abroad will similarly have to take into account local cultures and exchange rates. The profit projections will thus change in foreign markets.

Diversity

Companies take decisions within the cultural context of their home countries. However, when they have branches abroad, the cultural challenge is to be acceptable to consumers in those countries as well. Marketing strategies and decisions have to be taken that will be acceptable in different cultures (see Exhibit 11.2).

EXHIBIT 11.2 Star Network's Strategy

The Star Network was launched in India in 1991 but it could make an impact only when Star Plus was re-launched as a Hindi entertainment channel in the year 2000. Since then, the company has gone from strength to strength. Today, it telecasts 33 channels in eight languages reaching more than 400 million viewers each week.

Star Plus changed culture and redefined television in India with *Kaun Banega Crorepati* (Who wants to be a Millionaire?) with Amitabh Bachchan as host. The show made history and took Star Plus to the No.1 position overnight. *Satyamev Jayate* is another popular show on the channel (see Fig. 11.14). This was backed by a slew of daily soaps which went on to break viewership records. With a strong foothold already established in the Hindi belt, Star acquired a majority stake in Tamil Nadu's Vijay TV, following it with highly successful expansions into Maharashtra, West Bengal, Kerala, and Karnataka.

FIG. 11.14 Satyamev Jayate
Courtesy: Superbrands

In 2011, Star launched a new Hindi general entertainment channel called Life OK. In April 2012 Star acquired the rights from the Board of Control for Cricket in India (BCCI) to telecast all domestic and international cricket matches, firmly establishing itself as an 'Indian' brand.

Source: Superbrands 2012

Products

Another problem that multinational companies face is their limited ability to develop products suited for local markets. What is acceptable in some countries may well turn off consumers in another country. For instance, when food companies realised that selling pork products in India was just not acceptable, they had to localise menus and tastes. When companies try to market the same products globally, they face the risk of running contrary to the cultural norms of the people to whom they are attempting to sell them. Multinational companies face the challenge of developing and marketing products that have global appeal.

Communication

Some forms of communication have implied and understood meanings that only make sense within a culture's context. Brand names and advertisements will change meaning when translated into another language. Assael (2005) gives the example that 'Come alive with Pepsi' gets translated into 'Bring your ancestors back from the dead' in certain Asian languages. Similarly, GM's 'Nova' translated into 'Won't go'. This form of 'high context communication' requires knowledge and understanding of the local culture and traditions.

Symbols

Companies have to be careful in using colours and symbols in their communications. Certain colours are considered holy or lucky in some countries but not so in other countries. For instance, the colour of mourning in some countries is white, but black in others. Animals and symbols also have religious connotations or are associated with luck. An understanding of the country's culture will help companies determine what to use in ads and what to avoid.

Standard of Living

Different countries have different standards of living. This affects what products will be used and which will not. For example, many brands assumed that India's middle class was the same as the middle class in other countries and therefore would be willing to buy the same products that they sold elsewhere, but learnt to their dismay that people were not advanced enough to buy their products. Among those who faced rough weather was global brand Esprit, which found that Indians were not enamoured of its clothes. The brand shut shop in India in 2012 after reportedly making losses. While Dunhill had to close its stores in India, Corneliani too, faced rough weather in India. Earlier, Dockers, which had promised to bring a 'khaki revolution' to India had to exit the country in 2009. These are just some of the brands that overestimated the standard of living of the Indian middle class.

While companies have had to understand the cultural context of consumers in host countries, consumers too have been affected by global influences. Consumer culture too, has changed as a result of communications from developed countries. The global culture has percolated deep into Indian society.

Global Influences on Indian Consumers

As the economy has opened up, Indian consumers have been exposed to global influences. Thanks to satellite television and the Internet, people in India have learnt about foreign lifestyles and cultures. The process of acculturation is visible in their altered lifestyles. The consequences of these influences are summarised here.

Throwaway Society

Influenced by consumerism, a consequence of globalization, people are taking to use-and-throw products. Earlier some consumer goods and household appliances could be used time and again by repairing and recycling. Modern society encourages people to simply buy new products and throw away old ones. In many cities, for instance, one would be hard-pressed to find a repair service for old appliances. In the case of computers, mobile phones, and cars, consumers are encouraged to buy new models as soon as they are launched. One consequence of this is that Indian cities today resemble garbage dumps. However, the throwaway culture helps companies sell their products.

Glocalization

Thomas Friedman (2006) in his book, *The World is Flat*, terms the intermingling of cultures as glocalization: being open to other cultures while maintaining their own identities. He writes that the more a culture easily absorbs foreign ideas and best practices and melds those with its own traditions, the greater the advantage it will have in a flat world. Companies thus try to cater to all cultures.

Empowered Customers

Friedman writes that new technologies make consumers more powerful. Earlier companies were in control of consumers' behaviour but, thanks to new technologies, consumers are now in control of companies' behaviour. He explains that the Internet and other tools have created a means for every consumer to customize the price, experience, and service he or she wanted exactly.

He dubbed it the 'self-directed consumer'. Companies had to adapt their technology and business processes to empower this self-directed consumer. They create digital buffets for customers to serve themselves. This has impacted consumer behaviour in a very big way.

Global Communications

Indian consumers today have access to movies and television shows that the rest of the world is watching. Advertisements are also broadcast on a single theme globally. The influence of mass media affects culture and shapes the concepts of who we are, what is important to us, and how we live our lives. The change in people's attitudes due to this huge exposure is visible in the lifestyles of the people now. Consumers acquire 'global beliefs' and start following what they are exposed to.

Global Demographic Trends

As education and global trends catch on, the world is witnessing demographic trends that affect almost a majority of countries. These are as follows:

- An increasing number of working women in the economy
- A large number of single women; late marriages
- A large proportion of single-parent households
- Fewer children per household

India too, has seen these trends to some extent. This implies that consumers in most countries are becoming similar, and their behaviour will also be similar in some respects.

Materialistic Beliefs

The winds of liberalization have changed beliefs as well. Traditional Indian beliefs of contentment and spirituality are fast being replaced by materialism. People not only seek products to own and display, but also see them as part of their own personalities. Consumers love American products, such a Levi's jeans and Apple phones. Human relations are being replaced by relations with objects such as mobile phones and cars, and a cash economy replaces the traditional sense of community that existed earlier.

These cultural differences pose several political and economic challenges, but we discuss only the cultural challenges here. Companies venturing abroad must understand the country's social and cultural nuances. Kilachand (2012) says that in France it pays to take your counterparts to a trendy restaurant post-meeting, and in Argentina one might be expected to give a kiss on the cheek as opposed to a handshake. In some cultures, as in Japan, saying 'no' directly is not considered appropriate. Companies that venture outside their home countries find themselves adapting to different cultural norms in the global market. The cultural variations of consumer behaviour are discussed in the following section.

SUBCULTURAL INFLUENCES

Companies have to adjust to myriad cultural differences as they venture into other countries. In some markets, customers like to be assisted while shopping, in others they see assistance as an unnecessary intervention. International companies also learn the peculiar ways that culture affects marketing. *The Telegraph* (2011) reported how furniture chain IKEA discovered a peculiar phenomenon in China: its Shanghai store became a dating destination for large groups of middle-aged Chinese men and women, aged between 40 and 60. 'The singles parties take place every Tuesday and Thursday afternoons, when the Swedish furniture store offers free coffee to holders of its membership card. Ikea's enormous stores have become a second home to many Chinese, with families congregating at the weekend to nap on the display beds and eat in the cafe. In Beijing, traffic leading to Ikea often blocks the city's fourth ring road.' Couples occupied the store for such a long time, forcing Ikea to isolate an area for them. Sometimes the business for the store went down by 15 per cent on those days, showing that regular customers avoided the store. Such behaviour would be impossible to foresee in other cultures.

Clearly, companies have to discover how cultural differences affect consumer behaviour. While some aspects of culture can be predicted, others cannot. Companies marketing abroad have to discover the best ways of dealing with such aspects.

Each society has a number of subcultures within it. These subcultures exist because of religion, ethnicity, nationality, age, and demographics. In India, caste and religion form distinct subcultures. Companies find these groups important, as members of a subculture not only share common norms and values, but consume the same brands, shop at similar stores, and use similar media. Subcultures have the following characteristics:

Distinctive Members of a subculture are distinctive and maintain their separate identity. This could be in the way they dress or their common language. They tend to move in groups and find comfort in meeting in their clubs and associations.

Homogeneous Subcultures are homogeneous and exert influence on their members. There are common threads binding these homogeneous groups, such as religious ties, conservatism, male dominance, or a common language.

Exclusive Members of a subculture seek exclusivity. This exclusion helps them maintain their separate norms. For example, certain castes have sought to deny educational and job opportunities to members of other castes in India.

There are several global subcultures that can be identified. They are based on age, as teenage or young adults, referred to as Generation X, Y, or Z, or identified as geographic and religious subcultures. In India, generations follow a pattern similar to the Western model, but there are still major differences. In addition, people form perceptions based on the country from which the goods originate.

Country of Origin Effects

Consumers have a perception of goods depending on their country of origin. Wines from France, televisions from Japan, and cars from Germany are thought to be superior to those manufactured in other countries. Different countries are known for their skill in manufacturing high-quality goods, so consumers hold them in high esteem. Other countries, however, are associated with cheap and inferior goods.

Globalization of markets involves the growing interdependency among economies of the world. Sourcing, manufacturing, design, trading, and investment become multinational activities. Each of these create distinct *country of origin* (COO) affects.

Since global supply chains make it possible for companies to have goods manufactured anywhere in the world, consumers also have perceptions about the *country of manufacture* (COM). This is done to capitalize on low wages and costs in other countries, but it is not without its dangers. Nike faced a problem when it became known that it was having its products manufactured in China by exploiting workers.

The *country of design* (COD) concept is used by Apple and other countries. They mention that the product was designed in the US but manufactured elsewhere, and consumers accept it as a superior product.

The country of origin comes into play if countries take political decisions that create animosity in the host countries, that is, in countries where the products are sold. Issues such as French nuclear testing and the invasion of Iraq by US forces, for example, have created hostility towards products made in those countries and consumers have boycotted them in their host countries.

Age Subcultures

In India several age subcultures can be identified. Some of these are similar to global segments while others are distinct. For instance, many textbooks refer to 'baby boomers' and 'Hispanic cultures' but these segments are not relevant in India. The age subcultures that can be identified in India as having distinct lifestyles are described here.

Independence generation The generation that witnessed the Indian independence movement, that is, those born in the 1930s and 1940s were deeply nationalistic and patriotic. They were loyal to the new state and stuck to tradition. They lived through the socialistic state that was sought to be created by the founding fathers. As consumers they lived through a period of shortages, rationing, and state control, enduring much hardship.

Indian boomers The Indian 'boomers' are those born after independence and up to the early 1960s. The dream of this generation was to study and live abroad and they sought to escape the restrictive environment at home. Foreign goods were very popular at that time, and smuggling was rampant.

Generation X Born in the late 1960s up to 1980s, they were the 'post-Independence' generation. They were deeply unhappy with the way the Indian nation had shaped. They lived through events like the Emergency and saw institutions wither. The objective of this generation was to save and invest in the future through real estate and gold. Having lived through shortages and thriving black markets, this generation liked to scrimp and save, doing away with luxuries. Generation X has seen an improvement in India's economy and is comfortable with change. They are described as the 'mature market'.

Generation Y This term is used to describe the generation following Generation X. It is also called the millennial generation and includes those born from the early 1980s to the early 1990. According to *The Economic Times*, they're young, smart, brash, and ambitious. They like a casual look at the workplace and are fond of parties. Gen Y wants to achieve everything in a short span of time. They are willing to experiment with new products, show off their belongings, and spend on living life to the full.

Generation Z Consisting of the youth, they are the generation born during the satellite TV and Internet boom. Born after 1991, they have seen a rapidly changing India. They are often referred to by several names such as 'Facebook Generation', 'Generation Always On', 'Now Generation', 'Digital Natives', and so on. People in this group have seen an abundance of brands and consumer goods. They share a culture of consumerism and instant gratification.

Global teenager Youngsters are susceptible to influences of the global media, as they start imitating the dress and mannerisms of the actors in the movies and television shows they see. They share the same values and culture as their peers in developed countries. Consequently they wear identical brands, their tastes in music are alike, they enjoy the same soft drinks and hang out in similar places. Companies have started targeting the global teenager as a distinct segment, selling the same products with similar advertising all over the world. Foreign brands love this segment and target young people as they are more likely to adopt such products.

Geographic Subcultures

A geographic subculture is a region in any country whose residents share patterns of behaviour that are distinct from those of the remainder of the country. In India one can see distinct changes in lifestyles as one travels from North to South, or East to West. Geographic subcultures are characterised by two features. The first is the *physical landscape*, which is composed of the area's topography, climate, and resources. For example, people living in a warm climate will have consumption habits quite distinct from those living in a cold climate. The second is the *human landscape*, composed of the economic, population, historic, and legal structures of the area.

Religious Subcultures

Religions in India have their distinct subcultures. Apart from the main religions (see Table 11.5), there are several sects that have their own identities. A plethora of godmen adds to the variety of religious subcultures. Each of these exerts a strong influence on the values and norms followed by its members, and on their food and consumer goods consumption. Companies cater to these subcultures by providing specific goods for them. For example, KFC decided to supply *halal* food in some countries to suit religious subcultures. Its UK website notes, 'For some time, we have received requests to provide *halal* food in parts of the UK and as a result of this, we are running a *halal* trial within communities where we anticipate a strong demand for halal products'. The trial met with mixed success, but this shows how companies try to cater to religious subcultures.

Apart from understanding subcultures, companies also have to understand different international market segments (see Global Perspective). Though each country will have distinct segments, some characteristics would be common.

MULTINATIONAL STRATEGIES

Multinationals look beyond their home shores. They want to find new opportunities in foreign markets: very often they face bleak prospects in their home countries as the market is already saturated. Several trends are favourable for multinational companies such as follows:

GLOBAL PERSPECTIVE
International Market Segments

While venturing into international markets, companies have to decide which market segments they wish to serve. While consumers can be classified on various criteria, companies have to classify market segments on the basis of global and local customers for international markets.

Khanna and Palepu (2006) say that most product markets comprise four distinct segments:

Global customer segment A segment that wants products of global quality and with global features—that is, offerings with the same quality and attributes that goods in developed countries have—and is willing to pay global prices for them

'Glocal' segment A segment that demands products of global quality but with local features (and local soul) at less-than-global prices

Local segment A segment that wants local products with local features at local prices

Bottom-of-the-pyramid segment A segment, as C.K. Prahalad calls it, that can afford to buy only the most inexpensive products

The authors say that multinational companies often find it difficult to serve anything but the market's global tier. There are several reasons for this such as institutional gaps in developing countries, lack of market research, and paucity of distribution networks. These factors make it difficult for multinational companies to understand customers' tastes and deliver suitable products. Many companies do not succeed as they lack understanding of their varied customers. They must select multinational strategies that may mean being completely global or local in their approach.

- New market opportunities in the form of easing of global trade
- Emerging markets with millions of people who strive for higher standards of living
- Internet and integrated banking technologies, enabling sales anywhere in the world
- Foreign travel, making people aware of international brands
- Consumers who seek variety and are eager to try out foreign products

The process of acculturation is used in two ways. First, companies must be familiar with the culture, values, and traditions of host countries to be able to position their brands within those cultures so that they find easy acceptability. Second, in the case of new products, companies try to change culture by encouraging people to break away from their traditions to try out new things. They follow three types of strategies to achieve their objectives, namely global, local, and glocal.

Global Strategy

When companies decide to sell the same product in different countries and cultures without any modification, it is called a global strategy. The advertising is also universal: one message is beamed in all countries. The advantage is that people identify with the brand no matter where they are and become brand loyal to it. Companies such as Coca-Cola, McDonalds, and Levi's follow this strategy and their brands are instantly recognizable anywhere in the world. However, even these companies make minor adjustments in different countries. The advertising is tweaked to have local models speaking local languages even while the message remains the same. For example, Pepsi appeals to the new generation in all countries using local celebrities and heroes in their campaigns.

A global strategy is advantageous because the company does not need to change products and campaigns in all the countries it operates in, and can exercise full control. However, it has some limitations as well as given here.

- The advertising messages may be misunderstood or misinterpreted in different cultures.
- The products may not be acceptable in different cultures.
- Since the company ignores local tastes, it will not be able to succeed against local manufacturers.
- The company may face a backlash if consumers dislike its country of origin. For example, American companies face protests when the US government takes a decision that is unfavourable to the host countries they operate in.

GLOBAL PERSPECTIVE
Wal-Mart's German Fiasco

When operating in different countries, companies have to consider many variables, including the culture and management styles of the host countries, way of doing business, and available infrastructure. Many companies ambitions to become 'global players' in foreign markets have been thwarted by their inability to fully understand and to adapt to consumer behaviours in other countries. This case shows that a successful company in one country need not succeed in another country, showing lack of understanding of inter-cultural skills.

Kai and Lewis (2013) write in their book, *Fish Can't See Water: How National Cultures Can Make or Break Your Corporate Strategy* that companies cannot see the water that they are swimming in. National culture, they write, has a powerful but invisible impact on the success of global companies. Wal-Mart's experience in Germany shows how this happens. The company bought two German chains and immediately began Americanising them. Employees greeted customers at the door and wished the shoppers a good day and smiled at them. The result was a disaster and eventually it had to exit Germany.

Wal-Mart was founded in 1962. The company was incorporated as Wal-Mart Stores, Inc., on 31 October 1969. Wal-Mart serves customers and members more than 200 million times per week at more than 9759 retail units under 60 different banners in 28 countries. With fiscal year 2010 sales of $405 billion, Wal-Mart employs 2.1 million associates worldwide. It is the biggest retailing company in the world.

Wal-Mart moved into Germany in 1998, hoping to repeat its phenomenal US success in Europe's biggest economy. However, it didn't turn out that way. Wal-Mart found its American approach to business did not quite translate into German and had to close its operations in Germany with a loss of about $1 billion. In a paper that analysed Wal-Mart's mistakes, Knorr and Arndt (2003) wrote: 'Wal-Mart's attempt to apply the company's proven US success formula in an unmodified manner to the German market turned out to be nothing short of a fiasco.'

The CEO of Wal-Mart admitted that 'If you want to be successful in a foreign market, you have to know what your customers want... It does no good to force a business model onto another country's market just because it works well somewhere else.'

For instance, the company found that American pillowcases were a different size than German ones. Wal-Mart Germany ended up with a huge pile of pillowcases, which they couldn't sell to the German customers.

An endless string of amazing blunders plagued Wal-Mart's German operation from the very start. Wal-Mart's principal mistakes were as follows:

- Lack of understanding of the behaviour of the German consumer
- Not recognizing difference in management styles
- Failure to deliver on its legendary promises such as we sell for less—always', 'everyday low prices' and 'excellent service'
- Bad publicity due to its repeated infringement of some important German laws and regulations

Instead of growing organically, Wal-Mart entered Germany with acquisitions. In doing so, it also acquired a work culture that was so firmly entrenched that it was difficult to replace it with the 'Wal-Mart' way of doing things. The company was unable to upgrade most of these stores and implement a uniform design to build brand recognition.

Wal-Mart appointed a boss for Germany who spoke no German. Not only that, he insisted that his managers use English. The next boss, an Englishman, tried to run the show from England. It appointed four chief executive officers (CEOs) during its first four years of operations.

(Contd)

GLOBAL PERSPECTIVE (Contd)

Wal-Mart promises 'every day low price' to consumers. This strategy backfired in Germany, as all affected German competitors matched Wal-Mart's price cuts. The company was not able to live up to its promise, and its assortment was not cheaper than other retailers' offerings. Further, the company misunderstood the customers. German shoppers like to hunt for bargains on their own, without smiling assistants at their elbows, which was a US-centred view. German consumers have been accustomed to shopping in self-service formats and considered the assistance offered to them as harassment. Other surprises for Wal-Mart were Germany's short shopping hours, including almost no Sunday trading.

Wal-Mart exited Germany in 2006. Its failure presents many lessons for companies venturing abroad. Instead of shaking up the extremely competitive German retailing sector with an innovative approach to doing business, Wal-Mart's Germany experience shows the pitfalls that companies face when they venture into unknown foreign markets.

Sources:
Hammerich, Kai and Richard Lewis, *Fish Can't See Water: How National Cultures Can Make or Break Your Corporate Strategy*, Wiley, 2013.
http://walmartstores.com/AboutUs/, last accessed on 20 October 2013.
Knorr, Andreas and Andreas Arndt, 'Why did Wal-Mart fail in Germany?' Institute for World Economics and International Management, 2003. http://www.iwim.uni-bremen.de/publikationen/pdf/w024.pdf, last accessed on 20 October 2013.
Schaefer Louisa, 'World's biggest retailer Wal-Mart closes up shop in Germany', July 28, 2006, http://www.dw-world.de/dw/article/0,,2112746,00.html, last accessed on October 20, 2013.
The Economist, 'Heading for the exit', 3 August 2006.

Local Strategy

Many companies either prefer a local approach or are forced to modify their global approach because their products are not accepted because of local tastes or customs. Kellogg's, McDonald's, and Nestlé are some of the companies that have adopted local strategies to gain the favour of consumers (see Global Perspective).

A local strategy has the advantage of creating products and advertising that are acceptable in local cultures and therefore appeals to a large number of consumers. This however, means that companies should know the local cultures and nuances. They would also face the danger that if a local product fails, the companies would find it difficult to market their main brands in those countries.

Another disadvantage of local strategies is that they are expensive. Khanna and Palepu (2006) write that multinational companies find it costly and cumbersome to modify their products, services, and communications to suit local tastes, especially since the opportunities in developing countries tend to be relatively small and risky. Further, their organizational processes and cost structures make it difficult for them to sell products and services at optimal price points in emerging markets; and they often end up occupying small, super-premium niches. This is now changing for many global companies.

Glocal Strategy

Many companies adopt a middle-of-the-road approach by combining global and local strategies to form a glocal strategy. While the overall marketing remains the same globally, the companies modify products and advertising in different countries to serve local tastes better. These companies launch products that are country-specific and even the advertising captures local moods and traditions. For example, Domino's Pizza has successfully localized its marketing strategy. It varies its pizzas by using 'cultural toppings' according to the country it operates in, and its advertising is also localized.

The advantage of a glocal approach is that while companies become more capable of serving local tastes, they maintain their global identity as well. It is a flexible approach. However, it also means that the parent company will have to give up some control in favour of local managers.

CONCLUSION

As the winds of globalization blow into each country, consumer behaviour is influenced in myriad ways. Consumers are exposed to and adopt new products and their culture also gets affected. The advantage is that consumers get more choice and acquire higher standards of living. They also start following higher standards of hygiene and service delivery. At any given time, culture is dynamic, as people get exposed to the ways of the world.

However, as companies try to change culture in an attempt to sell their products, the variety in local products is slowly but surely vanishing. Everywhere one goes, one can find the same packets of potato chips, the same bottles of soft drinks, and the same advertisements to accompany the products. The smart packaging ends up dirtying the countryside and clogging our waterways. This is the downside of the global consumer culture: we start consuming the same goods and are weighed down by the enormous amount of garbage that this lifestyle churns out.

Society has to learn to manage this trash as much as it wants to enjoy the fruits of modernization. As we move to acquire the global culture, perhaps we need to give a thought as to what we are doing to the planet as a result of our lifestyles.

SUMMARY

Culture is the shared beliefs and values among a group. Our consuming patterns are guided by it. Companies try to position brands and products within cultural contexts for easy acceptability. Societies acquire culture through *enculturation*, or learning one's own culture, and *acculturation*, that is, learning of foreign cultures.

Culture has four characteristics, namely it guides our day-to-day actions, it satisfies needs, it can be learned and it is dynamic. Marketing communications must be within cultural contexts, but also attempt to change culture and encourage people to buy things that are from other cultures.

Hofstede describes culture on the basis of several dimensions, namely individualism–collectivism, uncertainty avoidance, power distance, masculinity–femininity, and long-term orientation. Indian society shows collectivist traits, has high power distance, is male-dominated, has medium uncertainty avoidance traits, and high long-term orientation. Advertisers use these traits to position goods within the Indian cultural context.

The inventory of values is given by Rokeach. These are *terminal values*, or the desired states of existence, and *instrumental values*, a set of values that helps individuals to achieve their desired states. Indian culture is examined on six value dimensions: individual and family, society through conformity, success and growth, age and youthfulness, happiness and adaptability, and religion and spirituality. The cultural dimension consists of four categories: traditions, symbols and signs, rituals and customs, and languages..

Culture can be measured by content analysis, market research studies, and measurement instruments. A better indication of culture for marketing purposes can be had by studying heroes, rituals, and values of Indian society.

Indian society can also be understood using Hofstede's cultural dimensions. Contradictions in Indian culture mean that companies have to tread carefully while designing marketing communications. Such challenges are examined by multinational companies in cross-cultural consumer behaviour. Trade agreements have opened up trade for both multinational companies to enter India and for Indian companies to venture abroad. The strategic decisions to be taken by them relate to prices, offering products to culturally diverse consumers, modifying products, designing communications, using symbols, and catering to different standards of living in different countries.

Indian consumers are also influenced by global trends such as the throwaway society, glocalization, empowered consumers, global communications, global demographic trends, and moving towards materialistic beliefs. Subcultures are also examined on country of origin affects. Age subcultures also play a role, and these are applied to Indian markets. Multinational companies can follow global, local, or glocal strategies in different cultures.

KEY TERMS

Acculturation The process of learning of foreign cultures

Buyer The person who does the physical act of purchasing goods

Content analysis Learning about cultural values of a society by studying images and text being used in advertisements, magazines, and movies

Country of origin (COO) The country from which goods are supplied—this will affect consumer perception

Cultural dimensions Traditions and heritage of a society

Culture The collective programming of the mind that distinguishes the members of one group or category of people from another

Enculturation The process of learning one's own culture and cultural values

Generation X Those born in the late 1960s and 1980s, or the 'post-Independence' generation

Generation Y Those born in the early 1980s and the early 1990s

Generation Z Consisting of the people born after 1991, when satellite TV and Internet was easily available

Ghost shoppers Researchers who mingle with shoppers, to discover what shoppers think and how they buy

Glocalization The intermingling of cultures: companies are open to other cultures while maintaining their own identities

Heroes Persons, alive or dead, real or imaginary, who possess characteristics, which are highly prized in a culture, and who thus serve as models for behaviour

Hofstede's cultural dimensions theory A systematic framework for assessing and differentiating national cultures on the basis of individualism, power distance, masculinity, uncertainty avoidance, and long-term orientation.

Instrumental values A set of values that helps individuals to achieve their desired states

Madeleine objects Things that are associated with past memories and experiences

Observational research Consists of observing customers in their natural environment, without telling them that they are being watched

Participatory research The researcher becomes part of the process, like a salesman in a store

Ritual A religious or solemn ceremony consisting of a series of actions performed according to a prescribed order

Subcultures Groups within a larger culture, which exist because of religion, ethnicity, nationality, age, and demographics and whose members share common norms and values

Superstitions Not entirely rational action and belief that one can somehow manipulate the future by engaging in certain behaviours

Terminal values Desired state of existence

Value dimensions Beliefs and judgements of people

Values Centrally held, enduring beliefs in a society which guide actions and judgments across specific situations

EXERCISES

Concept-review Questions

1. Why is it important to study the role of culture in consumer behaviour? How is it relevant to marketing managers?
2. What is culture? How does the cultural value system of a person impact consuming behaviour?
3. Discuss India's core values and modern values. How do they impact consumption of goods?
4. Explain Hofstede's cultural dimensions as applied to Indian culture. What insights do they provide of Indian culture?
5. Describe some contradictions in Indian culture and how they may pose a difficulty for companies. How can these be overcome?
6. Discuss the female market segments used by marketing. Are they applicable to India?
7. In what ways does religion impact on consumption? Explain how religion is similar to marketing.
8. Discuss the importance of subcultures in consumer behaviour. What are the different subcultures that impact consumption?
9. How do global influences affect consumer behaviour? Discuss the various global segments and see if they are applicable to India.
10. Discuss the strategies of multinationals when they venture abroad. What are the advantages and disadvantages of each?

Critical Thinking Questions

1. Do you think that advertisements reflect society's values or do they distort them? Is Indian culture getting distorted by modern-day advertisements? Are Indians forgetting their core values?
2. State whether culture can be measured? If yes, discuss whether this should be measured? What are the benefits or disadvantages of measuring culture, or should they be left to observation by practitioners of marketing?
3. Discuss whether companies should attempt to change a country's culture? In what ways has the culture of your country changed due to marketing communications? Do you think they are normal changes or have they been triggered by multinational companies?
4. Comment on the viewpoint that multinational companies are able to tap only the premium segment in any country. How can they go beyond this segment and target the mass market as well?

Projects and Assignments

1. Collect advertisements to illustrate Rokeach values. Explain how companies use these values to promote goods and services.
2. Make a list of products/brands that you like to consume. Then think of why you consume those particular brands. What are the cultural factors that have pushed you towards those brands? Describe the memories that are aroused in your mind as you see or consume them.
3. Companies often try to introduce consumption rituals so that they can influence purchase. Can you spot such rituals in current advertisements? Make a project to illustrate how companies portray rituals.
4. Collect advertisements that portray women in different situations. Identify how many of them really require the presence of women and how many are sexist in their approach?

REFERENCES

Assael, H. *Consumer Behavior: A Strategic Approach*, Bizantra, New Delhi. 2005.

Bakshi, A. B., 'Grey Cells', *Outlook*, 23 April 2012.

Banerjee, Saikat, 'Dimensions of Indian culture', *Cross Cultural Management: An International Journal*, Vol. 15, No. 4, 2008, pp. 367–378.

Bashford, Suzy, 'Marketers need to understand teen consumers', *The Economic Times*, 16 June 2010.

Basu, Kaushik, 'India's demographic dividend', http://news.bbc.co.uk/2/hi/south_asia/6911544.stm, last accessed on 15 January 2013.

Doval, P., 'Dhanteras: Mad rush to drive home new cars', *The Economic Times*, 4 November 2011.

Friedman, Thomas L., *The World is Flat: A Brief History of the Twenty-first Century*, Farrar, Straus, and Giroux, New York, 2006.

'Generation Y: The future of India Inc', *The Economic Times*, http://economictimes.indiatimes.com/features/slideshows/ gen-y-the-future-of-india-inc/generation-y-the-future-of-india-inc/quickiearticleshow/3359765.cms, last accessed on 21 January 2013.

Hofstede, G., *Cultures and Organizations: Software of the Mind*, McGraw-Hill, London, 1991.

'India's youth: They're capitalist-minded—and they're changing the nation forever', *Businessweek*, 1999, http://www.businessweek.com/1999/99_41/b3650015.htm, last accessed on 15 January 2013.

Katju, Markandey, 'The 90%', *Indian Express*, 9 April 2012.

Khanna, Tarun and Palepu, K.G., 'Emerging giants—building world-class companies in developing countries', *Harvard Business Review*, Vol. 84, No. 10, October 2006, pp. 60–69.

Kilachand, Sean, 'Pitfalls to watch for when conducting business abroad', http://www.forbes.com/sites/seankilac hand/2012/03/24/pitfalls-to-watch-for-when-conducting-business-abroad/, last accessed on 18 January 2013.

Lindstrom, Martin, *Buyology*, Random House Business Books, London, 2008.

Lukose, Ritty A., *Liberalization's Children: Gender, Youth, and Consumer Citizenship in India*, Duke University Press, Durham, 2009.

Luna, David and Susan Forquer Gupta, 'An integrative framework for cross-cultural consumer behaviour', *International Marketing Review*, 2001, Vol. 18, No. 1, pp. 45–69.

McCracken, G., *Culture and Consumption: New Approaches to the Symbolic Character of Consumer Goods and Activities*, Indiana University Press, Bloomington, 1988, p. 73.

Moore, Malcolm, 'Love is brewing in Shanghai's Ikea', *The Telegraph*, 2 September, 2011.

Nagrajan, Rema, 'Unequal pay for equal work dogs working women in India: Study', *The Times of India*, 9 March 2011.

Pai, Aditi, 'OMG, hve u heard d way ppl tlk?;)', *India Today*, 23 April 2012.

Pellissery, Sony, 'Social hierarchies, economic inequalities and interpersonal relationships: An overview from India', *Interpersona*, Vol. 2, No. 2, 2008, pp. 243–259.

Press note on 'Employment and unemployment situation in India', 2007–08, National Sample Survey Office, http://mospi.gov.in/NSS_Press_note_531_25may10.pdf, last accessed on 19 April 2012.

Rokeach, M., 'A theory of organization and change in value-attitude systems', *Journal of Social Issues*, 1968, Vol. 24, No. 2.

Rokeach, M., *The Nature of Human Values*, New York: Free Press, 1973.

Schwartz, S. H., 'An overview of the Schwartz theory of basic values, online readings in psychology and culture', 2012, 2(1), http://dx.doi.org/10.9707/2307-0919.1116, last accessed on 23 April 2014.

'Sedentary lifestyles affecting health of India's elderly', http://indiatoday.intoday.in/story/world-health-day-healthy-ageing-sedentary-lifestyle/1/183278.html, last accessed on 17 April 2012.

Shrinivasan, Rukmini, 'Gender bias: Only Afghanistan fares worse than India in South Asia', *The Times of India*, 3 November 2011.

Shukla, Rajesh, 'India's elite: Retail giants like Walmart are vying for a piece of this multibillion dollar market', *The Economic Times*, 6 February 2012.

Sinha, Kounteya, '57% of boys, 53% of girls think wife beating is justified', *The Times of India*, 25 April 2012a.

Sinha, Kounteya, 'Now, girls hit puberty at 10', *The Times of India*, 26 April 2012b.

'The world's youngest populations', Euromonitor Special Report: http://blog.euromonitor.com/2012/02/special-report-the-worlds-youngest-populations-.html, last accessed on 15 January 2013.

'Thin no longer in: *Vogue* bans too-skinny models', *India Today*, 4 May 2012.

Tully, Mark, *India's Unending Journey*, Rider Publishing, London, 2007, p. 122.

Website of Geert Hofstede: http://geert-hofstede.com/india.html, last accessed on 19 April 2012.

Youth Survey 2012, *The Hindustan Times*, 7 February 2012.

CASE STUDY
Satisfying Needs or Encouraging Racial Bias?

Human skin comes in many hues. It is genetic in origin and is explained as a geographical phenomenon—that a substance called melanin in the skin protects against skin cancer by absorbing UV light—people living in or near the tropics need dark skin to protect themselves from the sun's rays.

However, the prejudice against dark skin is cultural. Nanda and Warms (2010) write that racial class, based on skin colour, has been a 'compelling fact of human society for at least the past 500 years. On the basis of the colour of their skin, some people have been enslaved, oppressed and subjected to public scorn and humiliation'. This fact illustrates that people tend to create symbolic, cultural meaning around simple, biological aspects.

The cultural prejudice against dark skin is deep-rooted and global. Kowner and Demel (2012) write that the use of skin colour for status and ethnic distinction was common in pre-modern times. Ancient tribes in many cultures, many with little contact with the West, too have this prejudice. Native Africans associate positive values such as wisdom, purity, and luck with lighter hues and negative ones such as evil and death with black ones. Within Japanese society too, negative attitudes towards dark skin were common well before the first encounter with black people.

The documentary, *Dark Girls* explores the prejudices that dark-skinned women face throughout the world. Viglione, et al. (2011) report how perceived skin tone is related to the prison sentence and time served for a sample of over 12,158 black women in US. They found that women deemed to have light skin are sentenced to approximately 12 per cent less time behind bars than their darker-skinned counterparts. The results also show that having light skin reduces the actual time served by approximately 11 per cent. In Indian culture too, fair skin is preferred, as is evident from the countless matrimonial advertisements published in newspapers.

Fairness products address this deep-rooted cultural prejudice against a dark skin. Families in India encourage their sons and daughters to use fairness creams. Indeed, *Business Today* (2011) reports that the market for fairness creams and bleaches is a huge ₹2000 crore, with fairness creams accounting for approximately ₹1800 crore, while the rest consists of bleaches.

Critics go into fits about the use of fairness creams. They say that such products are racist and encourage bias against dark skin. Karnani (2008) in his case study 'Doing well but not doing good' says that Hindustan Unilever (HUL) is doing something unethical by marketing its popular brand, Fair and Lovely. Such thinking ignores the cultural drivers of using such products and the fact that all cosmetics manufacturers, from a multinational like Revlon to an ayurvedic company Dabur, sell fairness products. *The Guardian* (2011) reports, 'Avon, L'Oreal, Ponds, and The Body Shop—all sell skin whiteners'. Some products also offer a 'Fairness Meter', an index card that helps consumers to track how fair they are becoming.

The market is not limited to women. CNN (2010) reported that Vaseline launched a skin-lightening application for Facebook users in India that invited Indian men to download their profile photos and drag a line across the screen to digitally 'lighten my skin.' The app was to promote Vaseline Men UV Whitening Body Lotion.

Manufacturers are slowly expanding the market. Nivea teamed up with MTV to promote a fairness cream for underarms and started a Facebook campaign asking women to 'shed your sleeves' and submit their photos in sleeveless dresses, terming it as 'the biggest freedom movement for women'. Pictures of many sleeveless girls on the site showed that they had indeed done so.

However, marketing companies must live with the cultural contradiction that is associated with the product. While a huge market exists, fairness products also invite the charge of racism and encouraging bias against dark skin. They must provide products and services that the society demands, but must tread carefully in their advertising and sales so that they do not offend communities and groups. How can companies reconcile this contradiction? The answers are not easy.

Questions for Discussion

1. How can companies reconcile the contradiction described in the case study that people demand fairness products but they are also seen as encouraging racism?
2. Is it unethical to supply fairness products? Are companies encouraging the bias against dark skin by selling fairness products?
3. Do companies have the right to fulfil the latent cultural needs of society, even if those needs are not accepted culturally in it?
4. How do fairness products fit into a society's cultural and value dimensions explained in the chapter? Draw a diagram to illustrate.

Sources:

Karnani, Aneel, 'Unilever's fair and lovely whitening cream: Doing well but not doing good', in Mike W Peng (ed.), *Global Strategy* (2nd Ed.), South-Western Cengage Learning, Mason, Ohio, 2008, pp. 411–418.

Kowner, Rotem and Walter Demel, *Race and Racism in Modern East Asia: Western and Eastern Constructions*, Koninklijke Brill NV, Leiden, The Netherlands, 2012.

Nanda, Serena and Richard L. Warms, *Cultural Anthropology*, Wadsworth Cengage Learning, 10th Ed., Belmont, CA, 2010.

Rath, Nishi, 'Market for fairness creams, bleaches touch ₹2k cr', *Business Today*, 28 July 2011.

'Vaseline skin-lightening app stirs debate', CNN World, 16 July 2010, http://articles.cnn.com/2010-07-16/world/facebook.skin.lightening.app_1_skin-lightening-creams-indian-government?_s=PM:WORLD, last accessed on 26 April 2012.

Viglione, Jill, Lance Hannon, and Robert DeFina, 'The impact of light skin on prison time for black female offenders', *The Social Science Journal*, Vol. 48, 2011, pp. 250–258.

Westhead Rick, 'The promise of fair and lovely armpits', *The Sunday Guardian*, 3 July 2011.

PART FOUR
Modifying Consumer Behaviour

CHAPTER 12:
Consumer Influence and Diffusion of Innovation

CHAPTER 13:
Communications and Consumer Behaviour

CHAPTER TWELVE

Consumer Influence and Diffusion of Innovation

LEARNING OBJECTIVES

New products are the engine of marketing. Consumers crave for new products and companies invest huge amounts in research and development (R&D) to satisfy customer needs better. This chapter describes the innovation process, its adoption, and the spread of new ideas and products.

After studying the chapter, the reader would be able to:
- appreciate the importance of innovation for companies and consumers
- learn about innovation, types of innovation, and the innovation value chain
- analyse how innovations are diffused in a social system
- know about the innovation adoption process and diffusion models
- learn about reasons for rejection of new products and how to overcome them

CASE STUDY

P&G—Creativity of Edison and Speed of Ford

Chief executive officers (CEOs) across industries and countries struggle to find ways of sustained and steady top-line growth. At a time when product life cycles have become short, they look for a pipeline of innovative products that will contribute to the sales of their companies. Managing this is not easy, because there is no way of knowing which new product will be accepted by customers and which one will not. Yet, product development cannot be left to chance. The challenge is to 'marry the creativity of Edison's lab with the speed and reliability of Ford's factory', as Brown and Anthony (2011) write. They describe how Procter & Gamble (P&G) developed a programme of innovation that helped the company to capitalize on the same and launch successful products.

Using the disruptive–innovation theory, P&G has been able to drive growth by making products 'that are simpler, more convenient, easier to access, and more affordable', explain the authors. For example, P&G introduced Tide Naturals, keeping in mind the need in emerging markets to provide greater benefit at lower cost, significantly increasing Tide's share in India. In the US, it introduced a quick and easy way to clean clothes, Swash which offered a 'good enough' alternative between washes, and developed a new business model called Tide Dry Cleaners.

An article written by P&G's Vice-president for Innovation Larry Huston and the company's Senior Vice-president for Corporate Research Nabil Sakkab (2006) describes the pressures on the company to create a system for innovation. They write that most companies rely on their internal R&D departments but by 2000, the company realized that this model could not generate growth—the innovation success rate was down to 35 per cent and the company's stock slid from $118 to $52 a share, eroding half of its market value. Clearly, the company required a new strategy that could create products that gave the company sustained growth.

The result was the creation of P&G's *connect and develop* (C+D) innovation model—'with a clear sense of consumers' needs, we could identify promising ideas throughout the world and apply our own R&D, manufacturing, marketing, and purchasing capabilities to them to create better and cheaper products, faster'.

The C+D model aims to find good ideas from anywhere in the world and then modify them to enhance internal capabilities. Six C+D hubs were created in different countries that would capitalize on the knowledge of their host country; China, for instance, was strong in low-cost manufacturing, whereas India was strong in computer modelling. Technology entrepreneurs mine scientific literature and other data sources with physical prospecting for ideas, such as scouring shelves in local stores and combing trade fairs. The company also created a secure platform to share technology briefs with suppliers, 'co-creating' products with them. To facilitate C+D activities, the company created networks as follows:

Open Networks

These networks were created to connect with researchers and scientists globally. Some of these are as follows:

NineSigma It creates a technology brief and sends it to its network of thousands of possible solution providers worldwide, who submit proposals that are transmitted to the contracting company. If the solution works, NineSigma connects the company and solver, and the project is commercially developed.

Innocentive It brokers solutions to narrowly defined scientific problems. The problems are put to 75,000 contract scientists who then suggest solutions, creating a quick and easy way to solve technical issues.

YouEncore It connects high-performing retired scientists and engineers from 150 companies. P&G is thus able to bring people with deep experience and new ways of thinking from other organizations and industries like Boeing, and introduce cross-disciplinary approaches to problem-solving.

Yet2com It is an online marketplace for intellectual property exchange for companies, universities, and government labs, started by a group of Fortune 100 companies. Clients post their briefs describing the technology that they're seeking or offering, and network members can get introduced to relevant clients.

So effective was the model that at P&G, the R&D productivity increased by 60 per cent, the innovation success rate doubled and the cost of innovation fell. 'We believe that connect and develop will become the dominant innovation model in the twenty-first century,' write the authors.

While reading this chapter, try to answer the following questions:

1. Why is it necessary for companies to have an innovation strategy? What are the steps in the innovation and diffusion process?
2. What are the different types of innovation and how can companies utilize the innovation chain concept?
3. What are the elements in the diffusion of innovation process?
4. What are the stages of adoption and how can knowledge of adopter categories be used to diffuse ideas?

Sources:

Brown, Bruce and Scott D. Anthony, 'How P&G tripled its innovation success rate', *Harvard Business Review*, June 2011.

Huston, Larry and Nabil Sakkab, 'Connect and develop: Inside Procter & Gamble's new model for innovation', *Harvard Business Review*, March 2006.

INTRODUCTION

In 1954, Peter Drucker wrote that organizations have only two basic functions, marketing and innovation, 'because the purpose of business is to create a customer, the business enterprise has two—and only two—basic functions: marketing and innovation'.

Marketing thrives on new products. Companies manufacture products to fulfil existing and latent needs and constantly invent products and reinvent existing ones to catch the fancy of customers. Some of these catch on, while others are not able to sustain themselves and soon get forgotten. Ralph Waldo Emerson's famous quote, 'Make a better mousetrap, and the world will beat a path to your door' is true only if customers get to know about the invention and also see the product as offering better value than existing ones. New products also have to get over long-held habits and the inherent resistance people have to change them.

Innovations drive markets. Consumer tastes, their likes, and dislikes are constantly shifting. People also look for new things and are excited by them. As tastes and fashions change, companies must keep up and offer new products, but innovation is risky and costly. While many new products do not make it to the market, those that are launched end up with very high failure rates.

In the past, product innovation was based on what manufacturers could provide. In India, innovation was stifled by the protective policies followed by the government since independence. For example, outdated car models continued to be sold in the country after they had been discontinued for decades in the rest of the world. It was only when the country opened up in 1991 that Indian companies adopted varying degrees of innovation. New products and brands using new technologies were launched. The economy saw growing competition: simply making and supplying products, as companies had done in the post-independence years, became insufficient to maintain a position in the market. Consumer needs and innovative products came into focus.

This chapter explains two processes: innovation and its diffusion. In the first part, innovation and its types, its importance, and need is discussed. In the second part, the diffusion process, product adoption, and the means of spread of products is explained in detail.

Innovation and its Sources

In common parlance, an innovation refers to any new product or process, any changes in existing shape, size, and other attributes of products, or anything perceived as being new. Fashion houses are quick to discard last year's style as outdated and launch new collections every year. Mobile phone makers and car manufacturers introduce new models regularly. Many products are packaged or designed in different ways and re-launched when the market for previous looks and packages becomes lukewarm.

Innovation is no doubt all of these things, but it has a larger purpose. Drucker (2002) defines innovation as 'The effort to create purposeful, focused change in an enterprise's economic or social potential.' It is, he writes, the specific function of entrepreneurship, the means by which wealth is produced.

Though innovation may sometimes occur in a flash of inspiration, companies invest in R&D or implement other methods so that they always have new products in the pipeline. The sources of innovation, as described by Drucker, are as follows:

Unexpected occurrences Markets spring unexpected surprises, and with that, unexpected opportunities. Companies have to be alert to look out for such changes.

Incongruities Incongruities between economic conditions, between expectations and results, and between assumptions and realities, give rise to innovative products and practices.

Industry and market changes Industries and markets can change overnight. When this happens, industry leaders are sometimes caught napping. Entrepreneurs cash in on the opportunity to build businesses; in fact many companies have been built when gaps were exposed during industry changes.

Demographic changes The innovation opportunities made possible by demographics, such as age distribution, education, occupations, and geographic locations, are among the most rewarding of business activities, according to Drucker.

Changes in perception When the 'mood' of the population changes, market opportunities arise. For instance, when economic conditions are good, people like to spend on luxuries and value-added services but avoid them when there is an economic slowdown.

New knowledge As scientific knowledge advances, opportunities for new products open up. Computers, laptops, and mobile phones opened up vast new markets. So did better materials and better methods of doing things that served customer needs in more efficient ways.

Companies need to have innovation strategies to meet rising market opportunities. The need for innovation arises not from a desire for novelty alone, but is necessary for business survival.

Need for Innovation

Customers demand new products as old products go out of fashion. They seek new and improved products as their lifestyles improve. Companies need to keep up with consumer tastes and thus need a pipeline of new products that can be launched as their old products reach the decline stage in the product life cycle. The need for innovation and to develop new products is becoming increasingly important because of the following:

Competition As more companies compete for the same market and new entrants enter the industry, consumers have more incentives to shift loyalty. Companies must launch new products just to keep up with the competition.

Knowledgeable customers Thanks to information technology, consumers today have great access to information. While earlier innovations took time to become known, they now spread almost instantly across the globe as and when they are launched anywhere in the world.

Rapid change in technology Rapid changes in technology mean new products and new ways of doing things are introduced faster than ever before. As a result, companies face the threat of obsolescence of their products and brands faster than ever before.

Globalization With globalization, consumers have access to international products and brands that puts a great deal of pressure on domestic companies to innovate.

Shorter life cycles Products have much shorter life cycles than before. Tastes change quickly, making it imperative for companies keep launching new products from time to time.

Consumers crave for change Finally, consumers too want change. They get bored with what they have and seek new ways to express themselves. They like to buy and own new products.

Coping with these changes is a major function of innovation. Bower and Christensen (1995) write, 'One of the most consistent patterns in business is the failure of leading companies to stay at the top of their industries when technologies or markets change.' Companies and brands that are the darlings of customers lose track and let others take over their markets. History is replete with such instances as discussed here.

- Sony was once at the cutting edge of consumer electronics. Its innovations, such as the Walkman, Compact Disc, PlayStation, and BluRay are legendary. It earned a great reputation for quality and reliability, but lately it has entered a slow but consistent decline, losing out on many new markets.
- Nokia was once a market leader in mobile phones, but let its dominance erode as other nimble-footed mobile phone makers took over its market.
- Apple has dominated the markets for iPads and iPhones and became the most valued company at one time, but its market value has since eroded. Its ability to churn out innovative products is under severe strain as competitors offer similar and cheaper products.
- Microsoft dominated the world in software for personal computers, but has struggled to launch subsequent products.

GLOBAL INSIGHT
Century of Innovation

Founded in 1902, the 3M Company, formerly known as the Minnesota Mining and Manufacturing Company, is the third most frequently cited innovation leader, right behind Apple and Google. Innovation is in the company's DNA, and perhaps its reason for being a leading multinational for over 100 years. Its products range from the ubiquitous Post-it notes and materials for car care, to construction, and dental care equipment. It would be difficult to imagine a world without 3M; its products are everywhere.

- Its optical films are used to enhance the performance of electronic displays in cell phones and large LCD display monitors and televisions.
- Its Post-it notes are found in offices, on car windscreens, on refrigerators, and serve as reminders for tasks. Post-It Picture Paper allows consumers to print pictures and stick them on any surface without damaging it.
- Scotch tape was invented by Richard Drew, a 3M engineer.

Govindarajan and Srinivas (2013) analyse how the company has been able to keep up with its innovation strategy to hold its place every year in *Fortune*'s annual survey, 'America's most admired corporations'. Some of the elements of 3M's focus are as follows:

Employees 3M gives opportunities and support to promising employees, and watches them learn and thrive. A pool of practical ideas is created through forums, which are then nurtured into opportunities. Encouraging a cross-disciplinary approach, scientists go out and observe customers, while customers visit the company's innovation centres. These centres have been set up to explore possibilities, solve problems, and generate product ideas.

(Contd)

GLOBAL INSIGHT (Contd)

Present and future The company focuses on present and future concerns. Called 'and thinking' it employs the thirty per cent rule—30 per cent of each division's revenues must come from products introduced in the last four years. Employee bonuses are based on achievement of this goal. The company also has a three-tiered research structure: the first, with a focus on near-term products, the second, with 3–10 year time horizons, and the last, on basic research with a time horizon of as long as 20 years.

Systems and structures The company has also created several systems and structures that encourage innovation.

Seed capital 3M provides seed capital to its employees to develop fresh ideas. Inventors can also apply for corporate funding for research that is given in the form of a Genesis Grant, worth as much as $1,00,000.

New venture formation Inventors recruit their own teams through networking forums. However, even if the product fails, no one loses his or her job.

Dual-career ladder Scientists can continue to move up the ladder without becoming managers, getting the same prestige and compensation as corporate management. As a result, good scientists and engineers are not compelled to become poor managers, a common problem in the manufacturing sector.

Measurement and reward 3M has created measurement and reward systems that tolerate mistakes and encourage success. It rewards successful innovators through various awards.

Culture 3M also has a rich tradition of sharing the stories of famous failures that subsequently created breakthrough products like the Post-it note, to ensure a culture that stays innovative and risks failure for unexpected rewards. It has published a book *A Century of Innovation* (2002), which helps spread the stories of inventions made by its employees. Its website details the company's latest initiatives.

Arndt (2006) gives some additional insights into the company's innovation orientation. The commitment, from the chief executive, is reflected in its budget: it spends an unusual 6 per cent of its revenue on R&D. It allows researchers to apply ideas across disciplines and encourages them to 'talk, talk, talk', both through formal and informal networking. Apart from an annual technical forum, labs also host their own conferences and webcasts. Scientists come to know whom to call for advice or to team up with on a project. Many innovations have resulted from a strong customer focus.

William McKnight, the long-term CEO of 3M, has given some interesting directions to encourage innovation, including: 'Encourage experimental doodling. If you put fences around people, you get sheep. Give people the room they need'. 3M engineers and scientists can spend up to 15 per cent of their time pursuing projects of their own choice, are free to look for the unexpected, and for breakthrough innovations that have the potential to expand the pie. For example, some employees in the infection-prevention division used their '15 per cent time' to pursue wirelessly connected electronic stethoscopes. The result: in 2012, 3M introduced the first electronic stethoscope with Bluetooth technology that allows doctors to listen to patients' heart and lung sounds as they go on rounds, seamlessly transferring the data to software programs for deeper analysis.

Usually companies are focused on growth and expanding their markets. What can they learn from 3M?

Sources:
'A century of innovation'. The 3M story, 2002, http://solutions.3m.com/wps/portal/3M/en_WW/History/3M/Company/century-innovation/, last accessed on 15 December 2013.

Arndt, Michael, '3M's seven pillars of innovation', *Bloomberg Businessweek*, 9 May 2006, http://www.businessweek.com/stories/2006-05-09/3ms-seven-pillars-of-innovation,

Govindarajan, Vijay and Srikanth Srinivas, 'The innovation mindset in action: 3M Corporation', HBR Blog Network, 6 August 2013, http://blogs.hbr.org/2013/08/the-innovation-mindset-in-acti-3/, last accessed on 15 December 2013.

http://solutions.3m.com/innovation/en_US/, last accessed on 15 December 2013.

Von Hippel, Eric, Stefan Thomke, and Mary Sonnack, 'Creating breakthroughs at 3M', *Harvard Business Review*, September–October 1999.

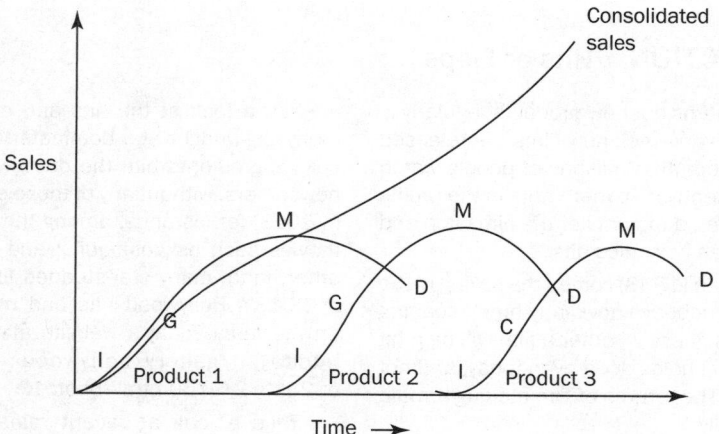

FIG. 12.1 Series of new product launches pushes up sales

Businesses thus have to keep changing just to retain their market. Drucker sums it up succinctly: 'Within five years, if you're in the same business you are in now, you're going to be out of business.'

Importance of New Products

The examples in the previous section show why it is important for companies to change with the times. Not only products, but processes too must change to retain the competitive edge. Charles Darwin's observation about nature applies to businesses as well: 'It is not the strongest of the species that survive, nor the most intelligent, but the ones most responsive to change'.

New products are a company's lifeline to long-term survival. It is natural to expect that fashions and technologies change over time. Every successful product faces extinction as competitors crowd the market. Companies thus have to match up to consumers' expectations by launching new products. The importance of new product development is explained here.

Managing the product life cycle The product life cycle shows that products go through four main stages, namely introduction, growth, maturity, and decline. This means that products eventually enter a phase when sales and profitability start declining. When this happens, companies must have new products to take the place of declining products or risk getting outdated altogether (see Fig. 12.1).

FIG. 12.2 Archies showroom

Competitive advantage New products provide a competitive advantage to companies. Companies that continue to tweak products and launch new products are able to stay a step ahead of their competitors. For instance, Archies has been successful in creating a niche market and bringing in concepts such as Valentine's Day, Father's Day, and Mother's Day, which are celebrated globally but were not celebrated in India traditionally (see Fig. 12.2).

CB IN ACTION Hits or Flops

An industry that churns out new products regularly is the film industry. Every week new films are released and film makers hope that millions of people watch them and consequently help them rake in the profits at the box office. Yet, a majority of the films flop and only a few end up as box-office hits.

William Goldman (1983) coined the saying in the film industry, that 'nobody knows anything' meaning that it is anybody's guess whether a film will be a hit or a flop. The saying holds good even today, and not only in Hollywood. The returns of film-making remain dismally low globally.

This exercise requires you to analyse the ingredients required to make a hit film. It is generally assumed that a film would do well if it has the following:

- A big budget and an impressive star cast
- Slick production values that appeal to young audiences
- Item songs, a dose of sex, and violence to spice it up

Yet, a look at the hits and misses shows that many big-budget star-dominated films with all the spicy ingredients bite the dust, whereas films with newcomers, without any of those elements succeed. In 2013, for instance, among the hits were unlikely movies such as *Aashiqui 2* and *Jolly LLB*. On the other hand, many star-studded films flopped. A list of 2013's Bollywood hits and misses is available on the *India Today*'s website at: http://indiatoday.intoday.in/gallery/bollywoods-hits-and-misses-of-2013/3/9750.html#photo1.

Take a look at recent releases and analyse their success or failure on whether they were made with the innovation principles discussed in this chapter. Were the movies important in some way, unique in their approach, sustainable, and marketable? Did these principles help in the success of the films? On the basis of your study, can you predict which movies are going to be hits or flops? Or does the famous quote 'nobody knows anything' apply to development of all new products, including movies?

Corporate image   New products help in building the image of the company. Since consumers are attracted to new products, companies that keep launching new products become darlings of consumers.

Reduction of risk   Launching new products is a way to diversify and reduce risk. If a company has a large number of product and brand portfolios, the risk is spread and they tend to be more stable in the long-run.

McGahan (2004) writes that industries must have an innovation strategy as they face two types of threats of obsolescence—the threat to the industry's core activities that have historically generated profits for the industry, and a threat to the industry's core assets consisting of the resources, knowledge, and its brand capital. When this happens, industries have to go in for *radical change* for survival. Rather than wait for this to happen, companies must adopt *progressive change*, that is, invest in research and development and create new products as old ones die out.

A third type of change is the *creative change* when an industry's core assets are under threat but core activities are stable. In this situation, companies must restore their assets while protecting customer and supplier relationships. Film studios follow the strategy of creative change and are continually restoring their assets. The *intermediating change* occurs when core activities are threatened with obsolescence. Companies have to define which change trajectory they are on, assess the threats to their core assets and activities, and develop an innovation strategy for their long-term survival. Industries do not shift their trajectories often, nor can they do so. Keeping track of how change will occur in the industry will help a company within it to determine how to exploit change as it occurs. This is explained in the next section.

TYPES OF INNOVATION

To keep up with innovation, companies must know and understand different types of innovation. There are six main types of innovations.

Firm-oriented Innovation

When a company launches a new product in its portfolio, it is a firm-oriented innovation.

It is seen as an innovation from only the company's perspective: the product may already exist in the market but it is considered new when the company starts manufacturing it. Even if a company copies products made by others, it is considered new from the point of view of the firm, even though technically it is not so. Thus, a company launching a new product line, a brand extension, or a product not previously in its portfolio, are firm-oriented innovations.

Market-oriented Innovation

Analysing innovation from the point of view of the market, a market-oriented innovation is a measure of how new the product is in the market.

When companies launch products that have been developed or available elsewhere in new markets, it is considered a market-oriented innovation. Market gaps and unmet consumer needs can be discovered through a strong market orientation. Using this perspective, companies identify new markets and find out how they can be better served. Interaction between technological and marketing capabilities of a company is required, so that the company's technological base and innovations are market oriented. Table 12.1 shows how innovation has affected different marketing areas when the company considers innovation from the market point of view. Note that each of the marketing areas is geared to identifying and discovering new trends rather than merely tracking consumer purchases or behaviour.

TABLE 12.1 Effects of market-oriented innovation on marketing areas

Marketing area	Effect of innovation
Marketing research	• Identifying new market and product opportunities • Finding new ways of tracking customers and analysing data
Segmentation and targeting	• Identifying segments and markets and their purchase • Using technology to manage customer relationships and better response to customer needs
Product	• Initiating product launch and modifications that are most needed by the market • Developing products that best suit individual needs
Promotion	• Matching messages to individual activity and personalized promotion • Developing two-way communication with customers
Distribution	• Using e-commerce for distribution and transaction, making it easier for customers to buy. • Allowing more control over inventory management and real-time shipment monitoring
Pricing	• Ensuring better pricing for customers • Using dynamic pricing methods

Product-oriented Innovation

When a completely new product is launched, or there is a change in its shape or size, or in functional elements that makes it easy to use, such innovations are called product innovations.

Product-oriented innovation considers innovation from the perspective of features of the product. There are three types of product innovations. A *continuous innovation* occurs when the company makes small, incremental changes to the product with the passage of time. The product is modified rather than re-invented, which causes little disruption in manufacture, marketing, or distribution. A *dynamically continuous innovation* is a major change of an existing product. Such a change is disruptive but does not alter existing consumer behaviour. A *discontinuous innovation* is one in which consumer behaviour changes considerably when consumers adopt that product. Digital cameras, social media sites, and online ticketing are discontinuous innovations that have changed consumer behaviour considerably.

For example, Cello's innovations include the dispensation of ink flow for 0.5 mm tips. It's R&D department focuses on continuous innovation. It employs a low pressure-high volume technology that ensures that a uniform flow of ink is released even when pressure applied is reduced. A special range of gel pens—Maxriter, Pinpoint, Technotip, and Technotip XS—have been developed with special performance tips and long lasting ink (see Fig. 12.3).

A successful product innovation must meet four criteria.

Important A new product must offer benefits that will be perceived as important by customers.

Unique The new product must be seen as unique and differentiated from other products to be noticed by customers.

Sustainable Since product attributes can be quickly copied by competitors, new products must be able to sustain competitive advantage over the long run.

Marketable The new product must be marketable, that is, it must be produced at a price the customer can afford and be distributed widely.

New product development helps a business to remain competitive, stable, and succeed in the long run. It includes conceptualizing of new ideas and developing new lines of products, or upgrading existing products. The development of new products is an essential part of business strategy.

Booz, Allen, and Hamilton (1982) have suggested the following six main types of product development.

New-to-the-world products These are products that are completely new to the company and the market

New product lines New products are launched by a firm to enter a market for the first time, or when the products are new to the company, not to the market

Additions to existing product lines New products are launched to supplement a company's established products lines, launching new package sizes. or flavours, and so on

FIG. 12.3 Types of Cello pen

Source: Superbrands 2012

Improvements and modifications of existing products   Modifications are made to existing products to provide better performance or greater perceived value

Cost reductions   Companies attempt to provide new products that give similar performance at lower cost

Repositioning   Existing products are repositioned so that they are targeted to new markets or market segments

Kim and Mauborgne (2005) suggest a new way of looking at product innovations. In their book, *Blue Ocean Strategy*, they say that companies should position their products not against the competition, but search for uncontested market spaces. Called blue oceans, they represent untapped market space, demand creation, and the opportunity for profitable growth. Traditionally, business strategy treats markets as red oceans, representing industry boundaries that are well defined and accepted, with known competitive rules. In this scenario, companies try to grab market share from competing companies. This, say the authors, has led to ignoring the more lucrative aspects of strategy. Identifying blue oceans makes the competition irrelevant by creating new market spaces where there are no competitors.

Service Innovation

A new or significantly improved service concept is called service innovation.

It is not limited only to service companies. Manufacturing companies too, invest in service processes, infrastructure to provide goods and services, customer interface, delivery systems, and so on. A cosmetics company, for instance, may provide trained personnel at retail counters to assist shoppers, which is a service innovation. These and other hybrid forms of providing goods and services are a result of service innovation. Miles (2005) explains that 'innovation in services extends beyond the service sectors to affect service activities in all sectors of the economy'.

Very often, service innovation leads to the creation of systems that lead to competitive edge, like when the innovation cannot be copied by others. Dell and McDonalds, for instance, created delivery systems that offer them the competitive edge. Such innovation leads to disruption in traditional marketing channels and business practices to enhance customer experience in significant ways.

Hertog (2000) has given a four-dimensional model of service innovation that has the following inter-connected dimensions.

Service concept   A service concept is new to the market, such as a new service, a new value proposition, and new solutions to consumer problems. Examples of innovative service concepts include a new type of bank account, an information service, a new retail format or introduction of call centres that provide services to customers without them having to visit the company's offices.

Client interface   Very often companies introduce innovations in the interface between the company and the customers. Technology is helping create responsive client interfaces. Customer portals, automated voice response, and electronic data interchange (EDI) allows a wide range of interactions to be partially automated. Automated teller machines (ATMs) have changed the client interface with banks considerably.

Service delivery system The service delivery system refers to the internal organization that allows service workers to perform their job properly, and to offer innovative services. Frontline employees have to be empowered, so that they can perform their jobs and deliver service products adequately. Such employees also have to be trained to enhance their personal capabilities and skills to deliver the level of service required by the company. For instance, the pizza delivery system has witnessed innovations in production, transport, and packaging, so that hot pizzas are delivered within 30 minutes to hungry customers. E-commerce too has evolved through innovations in the service delivery system.

Technological options New information technology allows for greater efficiency in serving customers. Credit cards, customer loyalty cards, and 'smart' RFID cards for transactions, are some of the technological innovations that are part of service innovation.

Service innovations should meet the following three imperatives as provided by Bradt (2013):

Core purpose The innovation must be aligned with the company's *core purpose*—a restaurant, for instance, must be focused on its core services, that is, really good food served by genuinely nice people in a friendly, welcoming place. All innovations for the restaurant must be centred only around these three areas.

Meet a future consumer need Innovation is forward-looking and is about knowing *future consumer needs*. The company creates a picture of the future innovation, then inspires and motivates people, and establishes clear behaviours that are required to get there.

Develop organizational capabilities Companies must achieve the doable and *develop organizational capabilities* to meet the service innovation being developed.

Process Innovation

When a company identifies better ways of making existing products or significantly improves production or delivery methods, it is called process innovation.

Many innovations depend not on new products, but on determining better ways of making existing products. As Davenport (1993) explains, a process is a structured, measured set of activities designed to produce a specified output for a particular customer or market. Changing this set of activities for better efficiency is the basis of process innovation.

The objectives of process innovation could be time reduction, price reduction, or better products. When banks reduced the waiting period for sanctioning loans, it was an example of time reduction. Wal-Mart is able to offer low prices by adopting practices of continuous replenishment, shelf management, and simplified communications. Price reduction has also been tried by the Indian retail industry by implementing 'farm-to-fork' supply chains and thereby reducing prices. Japanese cars were made using different processes than Indian or American cars, and resulted in better products that consumers in both countries liked. More examples of product, service, and process innovations are given in Table 12.2.

Disruptive Innovation

Disruptive innovation, described by Clayton Christensen in his book, *The Innovator's Dilemma* (2000), is the process by which a simple product or service takes root at the bottom of a market

TABLE 12.2 Types of innovation

Type of innovation	Examples	Company
Product innovation	• Walkman • iPod, iPhone • Mobile phone	• Sony • Apple • Motorola
Service innovation	• Credit card • Internet bookstore • Airline reservation system	• Diner's Club • Amazon • IBM
Process innovation	• Assembly line • Made-to-order laptops • Low retail prices	• Ford • Dell • Wal-Mart

CB IN ACTION   Impact of Innovation

Take a look at the ads that are currently being aired on TV. Make a list of all the new products that the companies are launching.

Now analyse the products on the basis of what we have learnt about innovation so far. First, classify the products on the basis of types of innovation. How many of these are firm-oriented, market-oriented or product-oriented? How many of these are service or process innovations? Do some of them qualify as being disruptive innovations? How many of them are absolutely new products and how many are due to improvements, cost reductions, or repositioning?

Second, analyse the new products on the basis of their importance, uniqueness, sustainability, or marketability.

On the basis of your analysis, what can you say about the state of innovation in your country? Does it impact the competitive abilities of the companies you have analysed?

and then moves up, displacing established competitors. He writes that new technologies that evolved were not better or more advanced, but the new products generated were cheaper and easier to use. As a result, people or companies started using the products, leading to their rapid spread. These low-end innovations are called 'disruptive technologies' since they disrupted established practices.

Disruptive technologies are usually inferior to mainstream technologies but help in performance, which is most important to mainstream customers. Subsequently, it is developed further, which raises the performance of the disruptive technology still further. Market disruption occurs when, despite its inferior performance, the new product displaces the mainstream product in the market.

The objective of all these innovations is to add value for the customer and for the company. How such value is created and added is described in the next section.

INNOVATION VALUE CHAIN

Hansen and Birkinshaw (2007) give the concept of the innovation value chain, which views innovation as a sequential, three-phase process that involves idea generation, idea development, and diffusion (see Fig. 12.4). Across these phases, companies have to perform six critical tasks: sourcing—internal, external, and cross-unit sourcing, selection and development, and finally

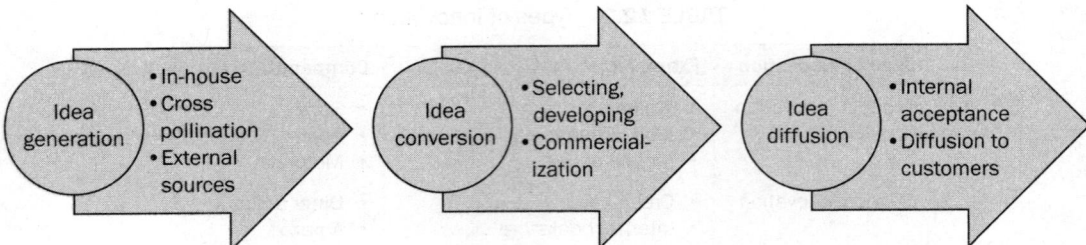

FIG. 12.4 Innovation value chain

spreading of the idea throughout the company. Each is a link in the value chain. While some links or capabilities may be weak, others may be strong. The value chain views the process as an integrated flow, rather than a series of disconnected steps.

Idea generation Bigger ideas are discovered when fragments of ideas come together or globally through external sources (see chapter-opening case study). This means that cross-unit collaboration is required. The company should also be open to ideas from outside. Thomke and von Hippel (2002) write that the company should co-opt customers as idea generators, which would save the need for understanding consumer needs and secondly, to avoid the trial-and-error cycles involved in testing products.

Idea conversion Idea conversion consists of selecting the ideas and developing them commercially. In many companies, tight budgets, conventional thinking, and strict funding criteria combine to shut down most novel ideas. Ideas can be converted easily if organizations get over such constraints.

Idea diffusion Making ideas spread is the next step in the value chain. Ideas have to be accepted internally by relevant departments and then by customer groups. Companies must have marketing systems that help ideas diffuse quickly and easily.

By viewing innovation as a chain, companies can avoid becoming

- an idea-poor company, which spends a lot of time and money on mediocre ideas and products
- a conversion-poor company, which has a lot of good ideas but is unable to develop and convert them. Budget problems and a lack of imagination keeps the company from developing novel ideas
- a diffusion-poor company, that is unable to commercially market good products

The value chain offers a systematic way to assess a company's innovation performance. Such a view of innovation helps companies unleash a wave of innovation. A look at the weakest links can help companies overcome these shortcomings.

Having good ideas and converting them is only half of the story. The second major part of the innovation story is to get it accepted by consumers. The next section discusses the diffusion process in detail.

DIFFUSION PROCESS

The spread of an innovation in a market is termed 'diffusion'. Rogers (2003) defines the diffusion process as 'the spread of a new idea from its source of invention or creation to its ultimate users or adopters'.

The speed with which a new product is adopted depends on several factors, they are as follows:
- The *relative advantage* that the product has over existing ones
- The degree to which the new product is *compatible with existing operations and attitudes*
- The degree to which the new product is simple to use
- The degree to which the new *product performs* on a limited trial basis
- The degree to which the product is *observable*

Diffusion of innovations explains how new products are taken up by a population. To understand the process of diffusion, we have to study the underlying causes that help ideas to spread. The diffusion process depends on understanding the qualities of the innovation that lead to its widespread use, the product, social, and people characteristics, and its achieving critical mass.

Spread of Innovations

In his book *Diffusion of Innovation*, Everett Rogers (2003) defines diffusion as the process by which an innovation is communicated over time among the members of a social system. Markets consist of groups of customers who differ in their readiness and willingness to adopt new products. While some people like to explore new products and try them out quickly, others wait till they hear positive reviews from their friends, and still others stick to their habits and will only buy them once the products gain widespread popularity. That is why innovative products spread through markets not in one straight line but in a series of successive, overlapping waves.

There are four key elements in the diffusion process, namely innovation, channels of communication, time, and social system. *Innovation* is a product or idea that is perceived as new by members of a social system. *Communication channels* are the means by which information is transmitted or shared in the social system. Mass media channels communicate the idea to millions of people at a time, whereas interpersonal communication refers to people communicating with each other. *Time* refers to the rate at which the innovation spreads or is adopted by members of the social system. The *social system* refers to individuals, organizations, or informal groups (real or virtual) who share a common culture.

Instead of focusing on persuading people to change, diffusion implies that change is a natural evolution of products and services, so that they become better fits for the needs of individuals and groups.

Product Characteristics

The success of an innovation can be attributed to five product characteristics, known as Roger's five factors.

Relative advantage It is the degree to which an innovation is perceived as better than existing products, or how improved it is over what people have been using before. Relative advantage is also reflected in the economic benefit, social prestige, convenience, and satisfaction that is perceived as being obtained from the innovation, and measured by consumers. If the perceived relative advantage of an innovation is higher, then its rate of adoption will be rapid.

Compatibility Compatibility refers to whether the new product can be assimilated into the consumer's life with little effort. The degree to which an innovation is perceived as being consistent with the existing values, past experiences, and needs of potential customers will impact on the speed at which it is adopted. An idea that is incompatible with values, norms, or practices of customers will not be adopted as rapidly as an innovation that is compatible.

Simplicity and ease of use New ideas that are simpler to understand are adopted more rapidly than innovations that require the adopter to develop new skills and understanding.

Trialability The degree to which an innovation can be experimented with also impacts customers. Consumers who are able to test a product are more likely to adopt it, as it reduces their uncertainty.

Observability This refers to 'the degree to which the results of an innovation are visible to others'. It refers to whether the product can be seen by others; the more visible the product, the more communication it can provoke between the individual's peers and in his/her personal networks. Role modelling or peer observation is the key motivational factor in the adoption and diffusion of innovations. The easier it is for individuals to see the results of an innovation, the more likely they are to adopt it. Visible results lower uncertainty and also stimulate peer discussion of a new idea, as friends and neighbours of an adopter often request information about it.

Social Characteristics

The rate of adoption of a new product or the relative speed at which an innovation is adopted. It depends on the number of individuals who adopt a new idea in a specified period. Generally speaking, open and affluent societies will tend to try out new products faster than traditional or poor societies.

The rate of adoption is explained by the following four intrinsic social characteristics of innovations that influence an individual's decision to adopt or reject an innovation:

Decision-making Unit

When a single individual has to make a decision about buying a new product, it is adopted faster than when more persons are involved in the buying process. Three types of innovation decisions have been identified within diffusion of innovations.

Optional innovation decision A decision that is made by an individual who is distinguished from others in a social system, or is held in high esteem

Collective innovation decision It is a decision made by all the individuals of a social system through a collective process

Authority innovation decision A decision that is made for the entire social system by a few individuals who are in positions of influence or power

Such behavioural approaches to innovations can be seen in many societies and families. It is how society is structured that gives it an open or closed approach to new products. Various other social factors too, affect the rate of adoption process.

Personal Communication

How people adopt products depends on the level of personal communication between them. While mass media channels succeed in building awareness, they do not provide a trigger for consumers to buy a new product. This comes through witnessing others and hearing their recommendations. This is often not easy, as people may be scattered over large areas, as in rural India, or there are social taboos about communicating directly with people, especially the womenfolk (see chapter-end case study).

Nature of Social System

Social systems play an important role in the spread of innovations. The social system, the degree to which it is interconnected, and the openness in it, impact the new product adoption process. Traditional or closed societies do not take to new products easily and in fact view them with suspicion. Open social systems, on the other hand, encourage people to learn from others because adaptability is easy.

Change Agents' Efforts

Change agents, or people held in high esteem by the society, also help in product adoption. Such agents could be experts or religious leaders in traditional societies and celebrities and sports persons in modern societies. When opinion leaders adopt and recommend, followers are quick to adopt new products. Change agents are also found online: people review products, which has a direct impact on those who read and trust those reviews. Once a critical mass of adopters is reached, the role of such leaders decreases.

Apart from societal factors, personal factors too play a role in new product adoption. Consumers go through their own personal journeys of discovering and trying out new products, which is explained in the next section.

Characteristics of People

Rogers (2003) explains that a person goes through five stages while adopting a new product. These are awareness, interest, evaluation, trial, and adoption.

This can be explained by taking the example of a television advertisement. People who see it become *aware* of the product. At this stage, they are exposed to the product but do not have complete information about it. When people seek information and begin to think that the product is suitable for them, they show *interest*. At the *evaluation* stage, the individual considers alternatives and applies the innovation to the present and anticipated future situation. At this stage, the person decides whether or not to buy it. Assuming that the product is bought, the next is the *trial* stage when the consumer uses the product. If the experience at the trial stage is good, the consumer will *adopt* the product. At the adoption stage, the consumer decides to continue using the product.

The important factor to observe here is that advertisements succeed in imparting information and may also generate a desire for products, but the conviction to buy often comes from friends talking about them. That is why advertising campaigns are usually accompanied by promotions and BTL activities to push consumers from one stage to the next.

The rate at which diffusion takes place depends on the speed at which these five stages are traversed. This, in turn, depends on the nature of people. People are different: While some people like to try out new things as soon as they are launched, some wait for others to try them out before they buy them. We can understand the nature of adoption by dividing people into adopter categories.

Adopter Categories

In the 1940s, Ryan and Gross studied the diffusion of hybrid seed among Iowa farmers and found that there were five segments of farmers or adopter categories, which they labelled as innovators, early adopters, early majority, late majority, and laggards.

Innovators

Innovators are the first individuals to adopt an innovation. Innovators are willing to take risks, are young, have the highest social class, have great financial liquidity, are very social, and have the closest contact with scientific sources and interaction with other innovators. The first farmers, who adopted the hybrid seeds were described as cosmopolites, frequent travellers, and of higher socio-economic status than later adopters. These farmers required a shorter adoption period than any other category. Innovators have the following characteristics:

- Venturesome, have a desire for bold decisions, the daring, and the risky
- Rich so as to absorb possible loss from an unprofitable innovation
- Educated so as to understand and apply complex technical knowledge
- Able to cope with a high degree of uncertainty about an innovation

Early Adopters

This is the category of individuals that is next-fastest to adopt an innovation. These individuals have the highest degree of opinion leadership among the other adopter categories. Early adopters are typically young, have a higher than upper-class social status, have more financial liquidity, advanced education, and are more socially forward than late adopters. The early adopters display the following characteristics:

- High degree of opinion leadership
- Serve as role models for others
- Respected by peers
- Successful in their fields

Early Majority

Individuals in this category adopt an innovation after varying amounts of time. The time of adoption is significantly longer than the innovators and early adopters. The early majority tend to be slower in the adoption process and display the following characteristics:

- Interact frequently with peers
- Do not hold positions of opinion leadership
- Constitute approximately one-third of the population, making them the largest category of consumers
- Think before adopting a new idea

Late Majority

Individuals in this category adopt an innovation after the average members of the society have done so. These individuals approach an innovation with a high degree of scepticism and after the majority of society has adopted the innovation. They display the following characteristics:

- Constitute a large group, consisting of one-third of the population
- Susceptible to pressure from peers
- See the innovations as economic necessity
- Sceptical and cautious

Laggards

Individuals in this category are the last to adopt an innovation. Unlike some of the previous categories, they show little or no opinion leadership. The laggards are the last to adopt an innovation. They display the following characteristics:

- Not opinion leaders
- Isolates
- Like to think of the past
- Suspicious of innovations
- Take a long time to decide
- Possess limited resources

These five adopter categories have become the accepted terminology in marketing. Figure 12.5 shows the distribution of new product adoption among the five categories: first, only a small number of people try out new things, represented by 2.5 per cent of the total customers. They are followed by early adopters, who influence others in the early and late majority (68 per cent). Laggards, or people who adopt products last constitute about one-sixth, or 16 per cent of the customers.

The specific characteristics described by Rogers are used by advertisers to influence different segments of the population. Efforts to target each group are important if critical mass of customers is to be reached.

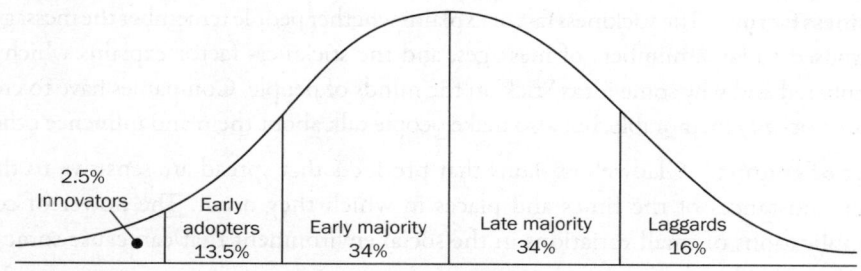

FIG. 12.5 New product adoption curve

CB IN ACTION Adopter Categories

With respect to new products, people are classified as innovators, early adopters, early majority, late majority and finally, laggards. Conduct an experiment to analyse your classmates and estimate the percentage of people falling in these categories.

This is how the experiment is done. Introduce a new product, such as a candy bar or a writing instrument, to the class and display the product to them. Tell them the price and ask them to buy the product from you. Keep a tally of the number of people who buy the product from you everyday, making sure to see how many new customers you are adding everyday.

Plot the findings on a curve. Does it resemble the S-shape curve?

Next, plot the number of customers on a normal distribution graph and see how many people fall in each of the adopter categories.

Importance of Critical Mass

To be successful, new products must be adopted by a large number of consumers. Critical mass is the volume where a product acquires self sustaining viability. Many products fizzle out before reaching this volume. So the challenge for marketing is to reach across to all categories of adopters and increase the numbers in each category.

Delre, et al. (2010) demonstrate through their study that social influences can have either a positive effect on the diffusion of the innovation when a given critical mass is reached or a negative effect, when the critical mass is not reached. That is, if the innovation does not reach the critical mass, consumers do not adopt it because their neighbours did not do so.

Gladwell (2000) in his book, *The Tipping Point*, explains the moment when an idea or trend crosses a threshold and spreads like wildfire. He identifies three key factors—the law of the few, the stickiness factor, and the power of context—that play a role in this mysterious phenomenon that determines whether a particular trend will 'tip' into wide-scale popularity or fade into oblivion.

Law of the few Using the Pareto principle, which states that in any situation 80 per cent of the work done is contributed by 20 per cent of the participants, Gladwell explains that a small percentage of people are responsible for popularizing trends. These are usually in the category of early adopters. The challenge is to identify these 20 per cent and cause them to spread the innovation. He calls them connectors, mavens, and salesmen. *Connectors* are people who are well-connected and have a large following. *Mavens* are experts or knowledgeable people whose advice is sought by others. *Salesmen* are people who persuade others to adopt new products.

Stickiness factor The stickiness factor explains whether people remember the message. Consumers are exposed to large numbers of messages, and the stickiness factor explains which messages are remembered and why some ideas 'stick' in the minds of people. Companies have to create messages that are not only memorable, but also make people talk about them and influence others.

Power of context Gladwell explains that products that spread are sensitive to the conditions and circumstances of the times and places in which they occur. The power of context shows the implications of small variations in the social environment that can cause some new ideas to become epidemics.

There is a distinction between the adoption process and the diffusion process. Adoption is an individual process while diffusion occurs within a society or population. It is a mental process that occurs when an individual first hears about an innovation, leading to buying and final adoption.

The diffusion of innovation can be explained by various models, which are described in the next section.

MODELS OF INNOVATION DIFFUSION

If a company introduces a new product, how should it estimate the level of sales it can reach? This obviously depends on the number of people who are willing to try out and adopt the innovation. The original diffusion research was done by the French sociologist Gabriel Tarde (1903) who

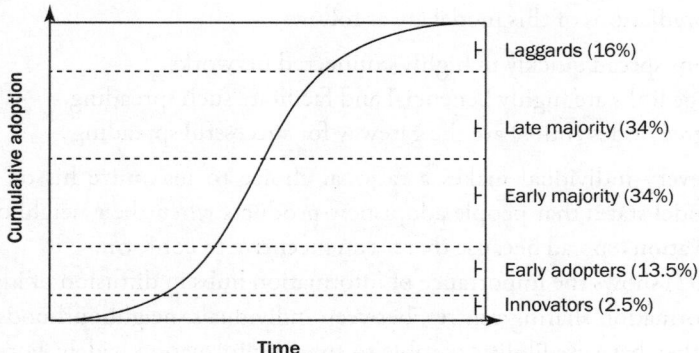

FIG. 12.6 S-shaped curve displaying the rate at which innovations are adopted by a social system

showed that diffusion of a new product followed an S-shaped curve. Most innovations follow this S-shaped rate of adoption, the difference lying in the slope of the curve (Fig. 12.6). Some products are adopted quickly creating a steep S-curve; other innovations have a slower rate of adoption, in which case the slope of the S-curve is gradual. The S-curve provides a basic understanding as to how innovations spread.

This approach assumes that sales will continually grow throughout the product's life cycle. Various qualitative and quantitative methods have been proposed as described here.

Bass Model

Bass (1969) developed a model for diffusion that describes how new products get adopted in a population. It allows us to forecast adoption of innovations, even when no data exists. The model explains that adopters are of two kinds: innovators or imitators. The rate at which adoption spreads depends on how innovative the product is and the rate of imitation among adopters. The Bass model consists of a simple differential equation and states that the probability that an individual will adopt the innovation is linear with respect to the number of previous adopters. New adopters are affected by two types of influences: external influences, such as advertising and other communications, and internal influences like the individual adopting products based on what they see or hear from prior adopters.

The model is expressed as a linear function of M, the total potential market, p, the coefficient of innovation (external influence), and q, the coefficient of imitation:

$$P(t) = p + q/M \, (N(t))$$

where $N(t)$ is the cumulative number of customers who have already adopted the innovation.

Epidemic or Cascade Model

The underlying assumption of this model is that people adopt new products when they come in contact with others who have already adopted them. That is, innovations spread like epidemics once a sizeable number of people adopt products.

The key predictions of this model are as follows:
- Innovations spread quickly in highly-connected networks
- Long-range links are highly beneficial and facilitate such spreading
- High-degree nodes (hubs) are the gateway for successful spreading

Though every individual makes a rational choice to maximize his or her satisfaction, the epidemic model states that people adopt new products when their neighbours have adopted it; that is, innovations spread because there is an incentive to conform.

Peck (2002) shows the importance of information hubs in diffusion of ideas. Communication hubs are information sharing centres, between individuals, neighbourhoods, and agencies. Such hubs, when they have credibility, are able to spread information widely. For example, The Oprah Winfrey Show is such a hub. In 1996, it launched the campaign, 'Get the country reading again' and was able to influence a large number of people and got them reading. The campaign also resulted in a series of best-selling books as they were recommended by Oprah on her television show.

A similar effect is seen when brands are endorsed by famous persons, who are the hubs of the communication network because consumers know them and are influenced by them. In the pharmaceutical market, the hubs are the doctors who prescribe the medicines to patients, and hence advertising and promotional activities are directed to them.

Social Percolation Model

The social percolation model shows people in a social structure represented in a regular lattice G consisting of L × L cells. Each person or group can be shown as adopting an innovation and is shown as (1) activated or not, shown as (0) not activated. The fraction of activated cells depends on the value of r, where r is the probability of activation in the system. When neighbours have one side in common, clusters begin to develop. Percolation occurs in G when a cluster of cells is big enough to touch at least one cell of each row and each column of G. A percolation threshold is defined as the minimum value of r for which a percolation in G is observed. A simple illustration of the model is given in Fig. 12.7 which represents a 3 × 3 lattice with a neighbour N getting influenced to use the product, and thus forming clusters. (1) represents product adoption and (0) represents non-adoption. N represents the neighbour to get influenced.

0	1	1
1	N	0
0	0	0

FIG. 12.7 Simple representation of the social percolation model

The models show the importance of friends and neighbours in the new product adoption process. Companies encourage this by using reference groups, brand communities, tribes, and social movements, which are discussed in the next section.

REFERENCE GROUPS

Innovations spread when people not only come to know about them but feel convinced to try out the new product offerings. A large part of the conviction comes by observing others. We are influenced by friends and family, and seek out people who have similar interests and tastes. We are motivated to buy or use products to conform to what other people do. Advertising does its best to show role models whom we like and people similar to the targeted audience enjoying products, which also has a great influence on us. In this section, the importance of reference groups, word-of-mouth publicity, viral marketing, and the use of social platform is discussed.

A reference group consists of people who influence an individual's affective responses, cognitions, and behaviour. It is a group or category of people to which individuals believe they belong, whether or not they actually do. Buying behaviour is influenced because of their relationship to the reference group: for example, a person will buy a more expensive car than he normally would because others in the group have expensive cars. The reference group is used by an individual as a benchmark for evaluating his/her own beliefs and attitudes. One need not be a member of that group; it is simply what one aspires to. The psychology of status, a concept coined by Herbert Hyman in 1942, explains that people use reference groups to determine their rank in status, as well as to determine a point of reference for their future status. Hyman explains that an individual sees the group as a 'point of reference' in determining his or her own judgments, preferences, beliefs, and behaviour.

Reference groups have the following characteristics:

- They are conceptual, and not the actual groups to which an individual thinks that he belongs.
- Individuals take on the values and lifestyles of the group to which they would like to belong.
- People change their reference groups as they take on different roles.
- They are very important in modern societies as people like to conform and be accepted by their group members.
- People relate to the other members of groups and adopt their values and standards.
- In collectivist cultures, there is emotional dependence on groups.

McFerran, et al. (2010) study the social influence of food consumption and find that our food choices depend on what other consumers choose. Their studies show that consumers are often influenced by what they see others eating and that they choose a quantity similar to what others are having, adjusting it for their own body type.

Zhou (2011) examined the determinants of online community user participation from a social influence perspective and found that both social identity and group norms have significant effects on user participation. In addition, group norms affect social identity.

Reference groups exercise three types of influence on people: informational, utilitarian, and value-expressive.

Informational influence The consumer seeks information about products and services consumed by others in the group, experts, or celebrities.

Utilitarian influence The consumer decides to purchase goods based on the experience or preferences of others in the group, and products are purchased on the basis of how useful they are for consumers.

Value-expressive influence Products are purchased to enhance the image of the user in the eyes of group members. Consumers identify with the models in the advertisements, and feel they are being admired for using those products.

By exercising the aforegiven influences, groups exhibit several types of power. The fact that people make consumption decisions based on what others think of them shows their *social power*. When people imitate someone in the group, it is called *referent power*, and companies indeed use such powers to help innovations to be adopted by groups. *Legitimate power* is used when the leader of the group or a person in authority endorses a product. Sometimes experts—such as models dressed as doctors—are used by companies as they utilize *expert power*, the assumption being that consumers get influenced by experts in their fields.

Reference groups may be classified as *aspirational*, those against whom one would like to compare oneself, or *associative*, that includes peers and people who represent the individuals' current equals, or dissociative, which includes people that the individual would not like to be like.

Some examples of how reference groups work are as follows:

- A child asks his mother to buy him a particular kind of school bag because all other kids carry a similar bag
- A lady buys diamonds because she wants to be admired by her group
- A person buys a smartphone because all his friends have one

Reference groups are used in marketing to exert influence and power on consumers, and thereby help products and ideas to spread. There are several ways that reference groups are organized, from the virtual group that consumers think they belong to, to actual groups engineered by companies or consumers themselves. Some of these types of reference groups are described here.

Brand Communities

A brand community is an ideal vehicle for the spread of new ideas. It is a group of consumers that shares social relationships based on usage or interest in a product. It is based on attachment to a brand; the stronger the brand, the stronger is the brand community. It is not limited by geography since brand loyalists are not concentrated in any one area. Events are organized around the brand so that consumers can bond with people who share their enthusiasm for the brand. Such events are called *brandfests*.

Brand communities are powerful diffusion tools. Fournier and Lee (2009) write that brand communities become popular in times of slow economic growth: 'In today's turbulent world, people are hungry for a sense of connection; and in lean economic times, every company needs new ways to do more with what it already has'. A strong brand community, they write, increases customer loyalty, lowers marketing costs, authenticates brand meanings, and yields an influx of ideas to grow the business. Companies that can create strong brand communities will not reap the rewards of loyalty but also better returns through commitment, engagement, and support.

McWilliam (2000) writes that such communities have to be handled with care because the brand community is not just another communications vehicle. A successful brand community requires that the company promotes interplay among community members, which helps in the spread of new products, and should not be seen as pushing for sales.

Social Movements

Goldman and Howard (2013) write that companies have a lot to learn from social movements as these are able to mobilize communities towards collective action. Since social movements are able to diffuse ideas across a population, companies are now considering using the intersection of social movements and business strategy. Brand communities are attempts to make brands and products tap into such movements. Collective action is woven directly into the brand experience, and in so doing, spreads the movements to a broader public. 'When an organization is genuinely committed to serving the authentic passions of a particular community, "movement strategies" can dramatically increase performance', they write. An example of how social movements work is described in the chapter-end case study. However, movements cannot be manufactured for every product, if a movement is seen as a quick marketing fix, it is highly unlikely to succeed.

Tribes and Tribal Marketing

A tribe consists of families or communities linked by social, economic, religious, or blood ties, with a common culture and dialect. In the marketing context, a tribe is defined as a heterogeneous group that is linked by the shared passion or emotion towards a brand. Joeri Van den Bergh and Mattias Behrer (2013) explain in their book, *How Cool Brands Stay Hot* that its members are advocates and since they meet each other both in real life and virtually, they are capable of collective actions. Tribal marketing is about supporting brands that keep youngsters together as a group of enthusiasts. For companies, knowing and recognizing the different crowds in a youth market is more useful in identifying tribes because adolescents tend to adapt their consumption and concrete brand choice to a crowd's reference behaviour. The authors describe how products tie up with movies: a company introduced a lipstick called 'Twilight Venom' to cash in on the craze for the popular vampire movie, *Twilight*, in 2009. 'This product should be shaken before use to represent the blending of the human and vampire worlds', says its packaging. Another company launched nail polish brands to coincide with another fantasy movie in 2010, *Alice in Wonderland*. The brands, named 'Off with her Red', 'Thanks so Muchness', 'Absolutely Alice' and 'Mad as a Hatter' were instantly adopted by teenage girls, showing the power of tribal marketing.

Tribes are fuzzy societal sparkles rather than socio-economic realities—members of lifestyle tribes signal their membership through symbolic choices. Members of a tribe can be identified through their choice of fashion styles, hairstyles, shoes, favourite hangouts, and their choice of music. By using brands explicitly, they try to establish an identity for themselves.

Young people look for brands that reflect their self-identity. Cova, et al. (2007) write, 'Active and enthusiastic in their consumption, sometimes in the extreme, tribes produce a range of identities, practices, rituals, meanings, and even material culture itself.' They explain that consumer tribes do not act as mere consumers, but add meaning to the brand, do things, and make brands 'cool'.

Making Brands 'Cool'

Diffusion of new products is faster if products are accepted by consumers as being 'cool'. And because it is so important in acceptance of innovations, companies 'will need to track what cool means right here, right now (and preferably tomorrow too)', write Nancarrow and Nancarrow (2007).

Consumption tribes help make products cool as they consume products in public places, showing off the labels, and thereby making the brands fashionable. Consumption communities give the consumer a sense of identity and belonging to some larger group or purpose. These

ETHICAL INSIGHT
Is Marketing of Cool Ethical?

In his book *BrandChild*, Lindstrom (2004) advises that companies must deeply engage with the unique emotions of childhood and adolescence to succeed in marketing their products. Indeed, companies do so by creating 'cool products' that immediately catch the imagination of children and young adults all over the world.

The marketing of cool requires building of an idyllic fantasy world. It is a world in which life is perfect, parents are understanding, everybody is beautiful and is a friend, there is enough money, and nobody worries about sex. It's a world that any youngster would like to be a part of. It is also a fictional world built by advertisers by delving deep into child and youth psychology.

Using motivation research, companies are able to find out about the fears and hopes of youngsters. For example, deodorants have become 'cool' building on the vulnerability of teenagers and young males. They are exposed to sexually suggestive images that lead them on with the false hope of attracting and seducing girls. Deodorant ads use increasingly overt sexualized marketing to sell to the young.

Television programmes are created in order to sell merchandise. The cultural creativity of the youth is completely dominated by advertisements and movies. For instance, children in India routinely imitate 'item numbers'—sexually suggestive movie songs—in their school programmes and social functions. The culture of the country is defined by the latest hit song with all its vulgar moves. However, that is the marketing of cool.

Advertising targeted to children too, exploit children's innocence. *The Economist* (2013) reports that Michelle Obama has joined the fight against childhood obesity. Children's preferences 'are being shaped by the marketing campaigns you all create', she told executives of companies, 'And that's where the problem comes in'.

Video games too pitch in by selling images of sex and violence. *The Guardian* (2013) describes Nickelodeon's popular online game, 'Boneless Girl', which encourages players to smash an apparently unconscious, naked woman against various-sized spherical objects, and to squeeze her through impossibly narrow gaps, causing her limp body to be crushed and contorted. 'Poke and pull this scantily clad babe all over bubble-land' the site exclaims. 'You'll be amazed by the small spaces she can fit through, and throwing her across the screen never gets old'. It is a matter of debate as to whether sexual stereotypes are being reinforced by such games.

It is invasive marketing that no longer shocks. The kids do not behave 'naturally' but follow the ideal imposed on them by media. Companies put together the image for the teens that becomes acceptable for them to follow. The youth market is the ideal market. It is a burgeoning market in India as they have the disposable income and the time to spend it. Advertisers have started a market exclusively for people aged 16–24. Our media, our music, our forms of popular entertainment are blaring out the message: 'This is the greatest time in your life; you can mock at authority and act in ways that would not have been considered decent a few years back'.

This raises several questions:

1. Is it ethical to delve deep into a child's or a young person's psychology and then create ads that play on their vulnerabilities?
2. Are we creating a generation of zombies who are incapable of behaving naturally but follow the mannerisms of the latest TV serial or the latest movie in their day-to-day behaviour?
3. Is the marketing of cool making us culturally bankrupt?
4. Should advertising to children be banned?

Sources:

Bakan, Joel, 'Exploiting children's emotions for profit at odds with Nickelodeon's CSR', *The Guardian,* 4 April 2013, http://www.theguardian.com/sustainable-business/exploiting-children-for-profit-nickelodeon-csr, last accessed on 7 December 2013.

'Cookie monster crumbles', *The Economist,* 23 November 2013.

Lindström, Martin and Patricia B. Seybold, *Brandchild: Remarkable Insights into the Minds of Today's Global Kids And Their Relationships With Brands*, Kogan Page, London, 2004.

www.bonelessgirl.net/, last accessed on 7 December 2013.

community linkages become important in modern societies in which loneliness is pandemic and an average consumer desperately needs something to hang on to or to identify with.

Lindstrom (2012) describes cool personalities as 'socially skilled, popular, smart, and talented people' and of course, good-looking. When applied to brands, coolness is achieved through good looks, a dose of humour, and a splash of social awareness. However, since coolness is defined by the consumer, it is not necessary that brands that try to achieve coolness will always do so. A list of the coolest brands of the world is given in Table 12.3.

TABLE 12.3 20 coolest brands in the world in 2013

Rank	Brand	Rank	Brand	Rank	Brand
1	Apple	8	Twitter	15	Adidas
2	Aston Martin	9	Virgin Atlantic	16	BBC iPlayer
3	Rolex	10	Ray-Ban	17	Sony
4	Nike	11	Mercedes-Benz	18	Sony Music
5	Glastonbury	12	Bang & Olufsen	19	Alexander McQueen
6	YouTube	13	Chanel	20	Spotify
7	Media	14	Prada		

Source: http://www.coolbrands.uk.com/about, last accessed on 7 December 2013

The marketing of cool is not without its critics, who say that young people have taken to beer, soft drinks, fast food, chewing gum, and expensive shoes simply because they are seen as cool. In her book, *No Logo*, Naomi Klein (2010) writes, 'Peer pressure became a powerful marketing tool—companies discovered that if you sell to one, you sell to everyone in their school'. Klein points out that cool is 'riddled with self-doubt', therefore the brand has a stake in the self-doubt of teenagers. The purpose of marketing cool to young adults is to perpetuate the ideal that through the right purchasing, one can reach that just out-of-reach untapped well of cool. Klein discusses the morality of this type of marketing as selling to insecure teenagers. Marketing is defining the ideal of beauty with the motivation of profit; and this is being done to a demographic which needs no encouragement to be insecure, she writes. Thus, we see that youngsters pursue lifestyles and adopt brands that their parents can ill afford. She writes of the 'peculiar cachet of working-class kids acquiring status by adopting the gear of prohibitively costly leisure activities such as skiing, golf, or sailing'.

Kitty Parties

A major tool that helps spread innovative products in India is the kitty party. These parties are popular among housewives and office-goers. The kitty party is built around the concept of savings and thrift, and is organized at home or in a restaurant. It is also a platform to spread new products—companies make presentations at such parties and demonstrate or sell products. Direct marketing companies such as Tupperware and Amway make use of such parties to spread awareness about their products.

Aspiration Groups

An aspiration group is a reference group that an individual has no contact with but has a positive attraction towards it. Purchases are often made based on what the person thinks that the aspiration group would recommend.

A company will try to be part of a group that exerts influence and thought leadership on its members about products or services. Consumers do not buy products merely to satisfy basic needs, but to express and build their own self-concept. They often purchase brands when there is a match between the brand image and their self-concept. Thus, a person will buy, or desire to buy an expensive brand to feel richer or more glamorous than he or she is.

Companies appeal to symbolic aspirations by using celebrities in their advertisements. For example, when Lux uses a film star in its ads, it is with the hope that consumers will associate the soap with the beauty to which they aspire.

Negative Reference Groups

A negative reference group is one that an individual disapproves of and avoids. For instance, a person may want to avoid being labelled as a 'nerd' or 'fresher' and will avoid using anything that will identify him as belonging that group.

Anti-brand communities are built around the common theme that brand names exploit people and even harm them. The idea is to publicize unethical marketing tactics and harmful corporate actions, informing the public about them, and trying to construct a new collective identity free from brands and corporate influence. Companies are seen as oppressive, exploiting, destructive, and unethical.

Such communities form because

- the members feel morally motivated to join with similar-minded people and express disapproval of brand practices
- sometimes disgruntled employees form anti-brand or anti-company communities to expose some malpractices
- anti-brand communities are formed to provide information, publicize wrongdoings, and create a platform for taking action

Various consumer groups form to support each other in their efforts to resist marketplace practices and globalized consumption patterns. Klein rues the fact that logos are everywhere, staring at you during your most private moments; invading once clearly delineated public spaces like schools. In a 'branded world', taste, cultural standards, and even values are defined by megabrands, she writes. The Nike swoosh has become the centrepiece of athletic and cultural spectacles, and has come to represent athletic style. Its slogan, 'Just Do It' identified Nike with the assertion of individuality. The anti-brand movement sees this as exploitative and manipulative.

Hollenbeck and Zinkhan (2010) write that anti-brand communities consist of members who have a common detestation for a brand. The anti-brand members' focus is to enhance social justice. Yet, despite large numbers of consumers joining together to voice their disapproval of corporate actions, brands continue to thrive. In the years since *No Logo*, the power of brands has increased, rather than declined.

Consumer Activism on the Internet

The Internet helps to build communities for a common cause. The virtual space allows various conversations and publicizing of the wrongs by corporations as seen by the group's members. Though the groups are not geographically united, they have the characteristics of community such as reliance upon one another, sharing information, and being united for a common cause.

This has led to the rise of *virtual communities*. A virtual community is a community of people sharing common interests, ideas, and feelings over the Internet or other collaborative networks. Virtual communities are also called online communities and some of the common examples are the fan clubs of popular film stars, like Amitabh Bachchan. Brands too form virtual communities in which consumers can post about the brand and also talk to the company through it.

DIFFUSION THROUGH WORD OF MOUTH

Word-of-mouth (WOM) communication is the passing of information from person to person by oral communication. Perhaps the fastest way to spread ideas and products with a great degree of credibility is through this method. People believe what they hear, especially from someone close to them; this is the stuff of gossip and rumours. Companies realize that using WOM is indeed a powerful way of diffusing information about new products.

Sernovitz (2012) defines word-of-mouth marketing as (a) giving people a reason to talk about you and, (b) making it easier for the conversation to take place.

WOM refers to C2C conversations in which consumers talk about products and brands to their friends, relatives, other consumers, and so on, and is therefore a powerful diffusion tool. It reaches where advertisements cannot. It forces companies to focus on their products and services, since people talk about the products that delight them.

Since consumers talk about the products and brands themselves, companies must understand why they should talk about them at all. The reasons why people talk about products or companies are summarized in Table 12.4.

Reichheld (2001) notes that if growth is what a company is after, it cannot learn much from complex measurements of customer satisfaction or retention. You simply need to know what your customers tell their friends about you, highlighting the power of WOM in spreading use of products.

The converse is also true: an account of a bad experience relayed by word of mouth has a very strong negative influence on purchase. Consumers tend to tell more people about a bad experience than they do about a good one. For the diffusion process, WOM and buzz (discussed in the next section) are powerful tools.

Importance of Buzz

Buzz refers to the low humming sound that is discernible when people are talking to each other in a room. In marketing, buzz refers to people talking about brands, making recommendations, and describing their experiences about products and brands to each other.

TABLE 12.4 Why people talk about companies

Reason 1: They like the company or brand.	When consumers like the company or brand, they feel emotionally connected. So they talk to friends, because they are driven to share things they like, so their friends can enjoy them too
	Focus: Companies should create great products and services to get people talking
	Strategy: Be likeable. Make great stuff. Provide great service
Reason 2: Talking makes them feel good	People talk about brands because it makes them feel special, smart, connected, in the know, and important. People also feel good when they can help others find what they need or solve problems
	Focus: Provide information and give people something to talk about
	Strategy: Provide reasons for people to talk about the brand. Make the talkers feel smart and special
Reason 3: They feel connected to the group	Talking about a company and being passionate about it makes consumers feel like part of a family. They talk about it because they feel included on the team
	Focus: Give consumers reasons to love the brand
	Strategy: Rally the team. Give them shirts, private discussion groups, special events, and public recognition

Source: Adapted from Sernovitz (2012)

Marketing buzz has always existed as people ask their friends for suggestions and learn from each other. With online methods, such conversations have increased manifold over the years, adding to product and brand buzz. The Nielsen Global Trust in Advertising Survey (2012) says that a majority of the people trust word of mouth opinions: 92 per cent of consumers around the world say they trust earned media such as word of mouth and recommendations from friends and family, above all other forms of advertising. It adds that online consumer reviews are the second-most trusted form of advertising.

Mitchell and Khazanchi (2010) write that word of mouth is perceived by consumers as being more credible, more accessible through social networks, and more influential on consumer behaviour. They found that online sales increased with the addition of online word of mouth. They also found that the volume of online word of mouth significantly affected product sales. Buzz, or people talking about brands, helps the diffusion process dramatically.

Social Networking

Using existing social networks to spread marketing messages is called social media marketing.

Social networking has always existed: people have shared their experiences as they interact through clubs, communities, and groups. Now, with online social networking sites, this process has been made easy and quick. People not only share pictures and experiences with products and brands, but they also start following brands and celebrities on sites such as Twitter and Facebook. Other methods of sharing information are through blogs, online reviews, wikis, and other sites.

Companies have long taken note of this phenomenon, but few have been able to come up with strategies for social marketing. Many are limited to attracting 'likes' on their pages or garnering the number of hits of their videos, but this can hardly be termed as marketing. However, social media is a method by which products and ideas can spread quickly.

Guerrilla Marketing

Guerrilla marketing is a strategy in which low-cost unconventional means are used to promote a product or a brand. The term derives from guerrilla warfare, which uses methods such as ambushes, sabotage, raids, petty warfare, and hit-and-run tactics to surprise and shock the enemy. In marketing, the tactics used are graffiti (messages written illicitly on a public wall), sticker bombing (providing stickers to consumers to display on their vehicles), flash mobs, and hijacking campaigns of competitors. Guerrilla marketing campaigns are unexpected and unconventional and consumers are targeted in unexpected places. Because of this, such campaigns generate a lot of buzz.

The term was coined by Jay Conrad Levinson in his book *Guerrilla Marketing* (1984) and is described as 'achieving conventional goals, such as profits and joy, with unconventional methods, such as investing energy instead of money'.

Guerrilla marketing helps in spreading ideas by engaging people in unique and thought-provoking concepts and, since people talk about their experiences, it generates buzz. Since guerrilla campaigns are highly creative, they are able to generate tremendous WOM and consequently turn viral.

Viral Marketing

Viral marketing refers to marketing techniques that use existing social networks to produce increase in brand awareness or sales through self-replicating viral processes. The process is similar to the spread of biological or computer viruses.

Viral marketing is done through video clips, interactive games, e-books, software, images, text, and email messages. The idea is that the content appeals to users so that they share with friends and it spreads like a contagion.

Seth Godin (2008) defines viral marketing as an idea that spreads, and while it spreads, it actually helps a company to increase its market.

It is important to note here that anything on the Internet becoming viral is not the same as viral marketing. For instance, if a person posts a video and a lot of people see it, it is not marketing as it does not market the product or the business in a tangible or useful way. Companies often fall in the trap that they create content that goes viral but it does not do any marketing at all. In an effort to get people talking and sharing, companies create content that is outlandish or funny. The content does succeed in going viral but does not add to brand building or sales.

Examples of viral marketing include Hotmail and YouTube: the more people used the product, the more it spread. These ideas replicated themselves and therefore became viral.

Role of Opinion leaders

Opinion leaders are individuals whose ideas and behaviour serve as a model to others. People follow what opinion leaders do and consume, and so they have the power to influence trials and sales of products and brands. Companies direct their communications to opinion leaders to speed the acceptance of the product itself or the advertising message. They are often used in advertising to give testimonials, which influence consumers.

Opinion leaders have the ability to influence others, such as doctors, beauty experts, sports stars, leaders, and even housewives. They are used very often to spread awareness about products and brands. They exercise influence online as well, through reviews and spreading ideas on social media. Patterson, et al. (2008) write that it is important for companies to harness peer pressure and to enlist social support. Describing the process in their book, *Influencer: The Power to Change Anything*, they say that opinion leaders should have four qualities: they must be knowledgeable, trustworthy, respected, and connected.

Since people pay heed to opinions leaders, they are a valuable means of spreading new ideas and innovations to others.

HURDLES IN DIFFUSION

Diffusion of innovation is not a smooth process. Many factors prevent customers from trying out and buying new products. Even if the innovation is useful and desirable, consumers consider aspects such as pricing, promotion, and availability. Emotional and psychological hurdles also have to be overcome.

Resistance to new products can be overcome by adopting some of the following methods:

- Allow consumers a free trial of the new product.
- Do not withdraw the old product so that customers can go back to it at any time.
- Offer a money-back guarantee to encourage trials.
- Provide services that give them additional benefits such as access to quick support and advice.
- Defer payment and offer money-back guarantees.
- Publicize positive adoption stories.

Gourville (2006) has developed a behavioural framework to explain why a majority of new products fail. Resistance to innovative products occurs because consumers find it difficult to give up their old habits and some of the benefits that they derive from the products they already use. 'They assess innovations in terms of what they gain and lose relative to existing products', he writes, adding that the products which have a greater chance of succeeding are those that require least behavioural change.

However, it is not always that gains and losses account for product failure. For example, the Tata Nano was an idea that spread widely—it was seen as an example of frugal engineering. Consumers could gain a lot by switching to a Nano—it was a perfect car for modern times, considering the rising cost of fuel and lack of parking space in cities. Yet it did not do well as it could not get over the hurdles in the minds of consumers. Coca-Cola has tried to launch variants of Coke, such as the New Coke and Vanilla Coke, but had to quickly withdraw them as there was a backlash from consumers. It is therefore, not necessary that a good product and wide diffusion are guarantees of success. More important, companies should make sure that people buy it at different stages of the adoption process.

One problem is that the company looks at its innovation and attaches a premium to its idea and begins to see it in a multiple of 3x. Customers too, see innovations from their point of view and value them by a factor of 3x, resulting in a mismatch of 9x. Only when the innovation crosses the threshold of 9x, do customers begin to take notice.

Crossing the Chasm

Diffusion is thus a complex process and many hurdles prevent customers from buying products. In his book, *Crossing the Chasm*, Geoffrey Moore (1999) demonstrates that there are cracks in the adoption curve, between each phase of the cycle—innovator, early adopter, early and late majority, and laggards (see Fig. 12.8). The figure shows that gaps between each stage of the adoption cycle are sometimes difficult to bridge.

The gaps represent a disassociation between two groups. The largest crack, so large it can be considered a chasm, is between the early adopters and the early majority. Discontinuance occurs if the consumer is not satisfied with use of the product. This will happen after the first trial or if the consumer finds a better experience with another product. Rogers (2003) identifies two types of discontinuance: a decision to reject an idea as a result of dissatisfaction with its performance is called *disenchantment discontinuance*. The other is *replacement discontinuance* when the consumer rejects an idea in order to adopt a better idea. Companies should focus on the product, 'by thinking through your customer's problems— and solutions—in their entirety'. Successful innovation depends on the ability of a company to combine a wide range of capabilities, from technological capacity to finance, understanding market needs, recruiting high-skilled staff, and establishing effective communications.

Joan Schneider and Julie Hall (2011) explain that numerous factors can cause new products to fail, but the biggest problem they encountered was lack of preparation. Companies were so focused on designing and manufacturing new products that they postponed the hard work of getting ready to market them until too late in the game. They list the following five other frequent, and frequently fatal, flaws:

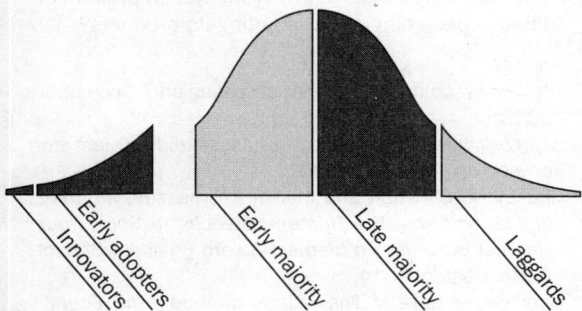

FIG. 12.8 Gaps in the adoption cycle are difficult to bridge

Source: Moore (1999)

- The company has no plans to support swift growth
- The product falls short of its claims, so consumers avoid it
- The new item exists in 'product limbo', that is, the product does not have differences that will sway buyers
- The product defines a new category and requires substantial consumer education— but doesn't provide it
- The product is revolutionary, but there's no market for it since the company was not able to answer the basic questions: 'Who will buy this and at what price?'

GLOBAL INSIGHT
Unconventional Approach of Adidas

Over the years, Adidas has kept ahead of the growth curve in sports accessories. *The Economist* (2013) writes that ten years ago, sportswear-makers in general were cramming ever more features and futuristic designs into their products. But in 2004, the company decided to go against that tide and focus more on the customer. Since then, Adidas's sales have grown steadily, and its shares have given above-average returns.

Founded by Adi Dassler, from whom it gets its name, Adidas takes a quieter approach than Nike, spending less of its revenues on marketing and depends more on customers. Working with a consultancy, ReD, it creates fashionable products that go viral as American rappers mention them in their lyrics. The unconventional approach of ReD is to hire ex-academics, anthropologists, and ethnologists to study customers' motivations intimately. It trained a group of Adidas design staff, and sent each of them to spend 24 hours with a customer.

Madsbjerg and Rasmussen (2014) explain the thinking at ReD. It uses 'human sciences to investigate the invisible background—the layered nuance behind what we perceive'. Using this approach, they found that 'well-being, not competition, is the main motivating factor for many people participating in sport'. This led to a complete change of approach for Adidas marketing.

ReD began working for Adidas when they wanted to shift their focus from a pro athlete-inspired audience to one that directly targeted fitness for the masses. ReD studied why people in different countries exercised in order to understand Adidas' customers better. It recommended that Adidas use colours and materials that were softer and less agitating. It also helped Adidas focus more on the women's market.

ReD created a kids' strategy to encourage children to participate in sports. The strategy blends a digital and community-based initiative with Adidas' miCoach interactive fitness monitor. The miCoach is an innovative running watch that monitors continuous heart rate, and contains GPS, Bluetooth 4.0, wireless music player, WLAN, and a colour touch screen.

In another project, ReD mailed dozens of customers a disposable camera, asking them to photograph something that made them work out. Surprisingly, of 30 women who responded, 25 sent a picture of a little black dress. This turned the company's belief upside down: it had assumed that customers wanted to be good at specific sports; but actually for many customers, fitness itself was their 'sport'.

In another unconventional approach, its researchers spent time with the Bayern Munich football club to find out what would determine the success of a footballer. They learned that the crucial element that could not be taught was speed. This insight led Adidas to adapt one of its track shoes into an exceptionally light football boot, which when released in 2010 became an instant hit.

Intimate studies of customers have influenced design too. For the London Olympics, Adidas and ReD told designer Stella McCartney, to think 'untraditionally British'. She used the unconventional approach of putting the Union Jack's red only on shoes, socks, and trim, while making elements of the flag so big that on some shirts they were unrecognisable. Despite some initial criticism, it was a commercial hit.

For the Football World Cup uniforms, the company interviewed Russians to find out what made them proud. It found Russians were proud of Dostoevsky, the Second World War, and winning the space race. So Russia's uniforms feature a curve representing Yuri Gagarin's view from orbit.

What can companies learn from the approach of Adidas in designing and marketing its products?

Sources:
http://www.adidas.co.in/, last accessed on 7 December 2013.
http://www.redassociates.com/cases/adidas/, last accessed on 7 December 2013.
Madsbjerg, Christian and Mikkel Rasmussen, *Moment of Clarity: Using the Human Sciences to Solve Your Hardest Business Problems*, Harvard Business School Press, Boston, 2014.
'Sportswear-makers: The Adidas method', *The Economist*, 24 August 2013

CONSUMER INFLUENCE

With communication technologies making it easy for companies to interact with customers, companies seek to collaborate with them not only for getting feedback, but also in helping in new product development and diffusion process. Customers are involved in the innovation process within companies in a number of different ways:

New ideas New market opportunities emerge as a result of changes in customer needs. By articulating these needs and helping companies develop relevant products, consumer needs become drivers of innovation for companies. Consumers play a significant role in the development of new products and services.

Refining and evaluating ideas Customers assist in new product development by testing out prototypes and giving feedback to companies. Ideas are refined and evaluated in this way and many of the product flaws can be removed through customer feedback.

Detailed design of new products and services Many business-to-business (B2B) suppliers engage customers in detailed design. User experience design (UXD) is used to address all aspects of a product or service as perceived by users.

Test marketing By giving prototypes of products to customers and then analysing the feedback as to how they were used, companies conduct test marketing and modify products to better meet customer needs.

Market launch plans By interacting with customers and sometimes involving them, companies are able to devise and modify their launch plans.

Continuous communication with the customer not only gives valuable insights to companies, but also helps them improve their profitability. This is explained in the four gears model in the next section.

Four Gears Model

Geoffrey Moore (1999) has given the four gears model(see Fig. 12.9), which provides a framework for adapting to today's social marketplace. The idea of the model is that in order to drive viral growth, business strategy needs four gears moving together as follows:

Acquisition It is the starter gear that provides awareness and interest, which enables companies to attract new consumers. It is a mechanism that enables companies to attract and capture new consumers.

Engagement It is the power gear, which engages customers, nurtures prospects, and cultivates long term loyalty.

Enlistment The engagement gear moves the enlistment gear that enables customers to participate in the business by exercising their influence, helping acquire new customers, and generating new product ideas.

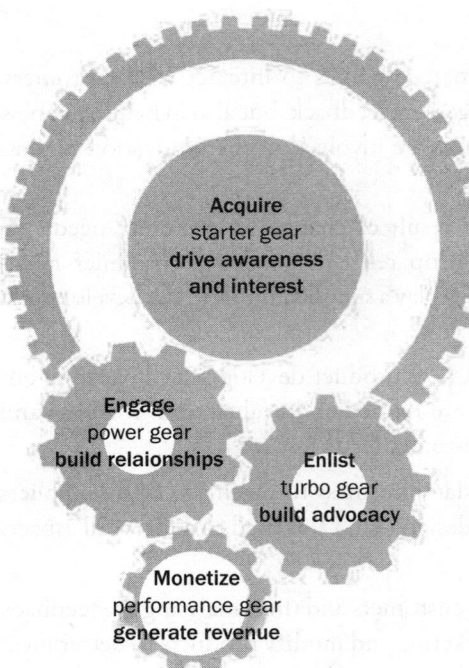

FIG. 12.9 Four gears model

Monetization This gear helps to convert customers. E-commerce and CRM systems are integrated to monetize relationships.

Each gear in this system helps drive the next gear. Companies want to acquire new consumers at a high rate, engage them in experiences to create and enlist fans, and monetize them. All four gears should move in concert to get the viral loop spinning persistently over the long-term. Done right, companies get customers who are not only willing to participate, help to create content, buy more, but also pay a premium for products, stay loyal longer, and recruit other customers.

Wu (2012) explains that if companies focus on acquisition and monetization gears alone, it will not be sustainable. 'The traditional model simply misses everything that social engagement offers and demands. You need four gears to win on customer experience in the long run', he explains.

More and more companies involve their customers in making and experimenting with new products. Increasingly, innovations are being sourced or modified using customers as co-creators.

Consumers as Innovators

Thomke and von Hippel (2002) write that new product development is traditionally a costly trial-and-error cycle that makes prototypes go back and forth from the company to customers and back, where the suggested changes are incorporated. By making customers an integral part of the design process, this error-prone cycle can be avoided.

The process is explained in Fig. 12.10. Usually companies test products with customers and keep going back and forth as changes are suggested (see Fig. 12.10a). In the new social strategy, customers are made part of the development team, so that the trial-and-error changes for product development are now carried out only by the customer (see Fig. 12.10b). 'The result is greatly increased speed and effectiveness,' write the authors.

They describe five steps for turning customers into innovators.

User-friendly tool-kit for customers Equip customers with tools to design and develop their own products, ranging from minor modifications to major innovations, such as computer simulation and rapid prototyping.

Flexible production processes With customers taking over design, companies must focus on providing best custom manufacturing, so that fast, low-cost production of designs can take place.

Select the first customers First customers should be those who have a strong need for the custom products and have skilled engineers who can help in debugging the design when required.

Consumer Influence and Diffusion of Innovation | **457**

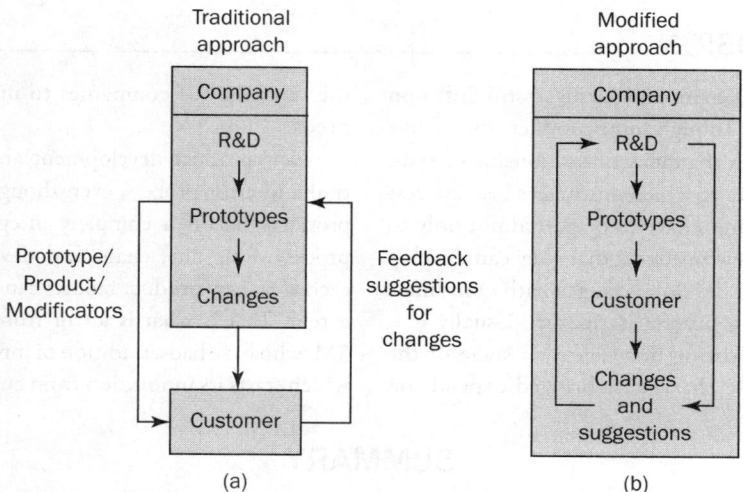

FIG. 12.10 New product development with consumers as innovators (a) Traditional approach (b) Modified approach

Evolve the tools to engage leading customers   As customers interact with the company, the tools used to engage them should evolve for better meeting production needs.

Adapt business practices   Outsourcing product development requires revamping of business models, to cater to the change in relationships with customers.

GLOBAL INSIGHT
Going Social with Starbucks

Starbucks is a company that has re-invented the coffee experience globally, but it does not rest on its laurels. It keeps introducing new flavours regularly, and many of these are inspired by customers and employees. In 2012, it introduced the Frappuccino using a unique social strategy. Customers can visit the website www.Frappuccino.com, and create their own Frappuccino remix—a new way to create their own music tracks. They can customize their personal soundboard, load the audio and video clips inspired by Frappuccino beverages, and then create and share their personal remix. The site also encourages customers to 'share your sip-face' and to 'create your own drink'.

The company introduced the new 'Mocha Cookie Crumble Frappuccino' that was one of the most requested new flavours. Using social media, customers could create their preferred Frappuccino, and then personalize and share their experiences through the remix. Bringing back the 'Happy Hour', Starbucks encourages customers to sample the 'Mocha Cookie Crumble Frappuccino' and personalize it with additional flavours for half the price.

Further, customers can connect with Starbucks and build their personalized Frappuccino blended beverage on the website and share it on Facebook and Twitter. They can tag their 'Happy Hour' photos on Instagram and Twitter 'with #Frappuccino Happy Hour to win prizes. Each day of the challenge has a theme to inspire Frappuccino fans to post their top beverage-inspired photos. The top 10 pictures of the day make it into the daily photo album on the Frappuccino Facebook page.

Study other companies that are using social media to make customers innovators.

Sources:
http://news.starbucks.com/news/starbucks-introduces-new-frappuccino-blended-beverage-flavors-invites-custo
http://www.frappuccino.com/en-us/drink-builder
Both last accessed on 1 January 2014.

CONCLUSION

New product development and its successful diffusion is a difficult process. Though some products spread like contagions and catch the fancy of fashionable crowds, there are many stages at which customers lose interest in products. Companies have to be geared not only to have a pipeline of new products that they can develop and launch, but also develop linkages with consumers so that the adoption process is smooth. Usually it is not so, with gaps existing between each stage of the adoption. How these chasms are bridged depends on the capability of companies to understand consumer needs.

New product development and diffusion is not a trial-and-error process, even though a majority of new products fail. If a company integrates its innovation process in a value chain and develops capabilities in each area, new product failures can be reduced to a great extent. That is what is learnt from companies such as 3M, who have had a tradition of innovation, and Adidas, which starts its innovation from customer needs.

SUMMARY

This chapter covers innovation and its diffusion among the targeted population. Companies need to launch new products regularly to meet the expectations of consumers and also to counter the competition. Rapid changes in lifestyles and technology have shortened product life cycles so that companies have to keep re-inventing themselves to remain the darlings of consumers.

Different types of innovation have been described. A *firm-oriented* innovation is when a company launches a new product in its portfolio; a *market-oriented* innovation is based on how new the product is in the market; a *product-oriented* innovation is one when a new product is launched, or an old product with modifications is introduced in the market. A *service innovation* is a new or significantly improved service concept, while a *process innovation* occurs when a company finds better ways of making existing products. *Disruptive innovation* occurs when a simple product or service takes root at the bottom of a market and then moves up, displacing established competitors.

The *innovation value chain* views innovation as a sequential, three-phase process that involves idea generation, idea development, and diffusion. By seeing innovation as a chain, managers can identify the weakest links so as to get over their shortcomings.

Having built a unique new product, the next step is to make it known to prospective customers. This is called the diffusion process, and it includes (a) the number of people to be reached, and (b) the speed at which the idea is accepted by the audience. There are four key elements in the diffusion process: innovation, channels of communication, time, and the nature of the social system. Product characteristics too, play a role in how they spread. These characteristics are relative advantage, compatibility, simplicity, trialability, and ease of use. The social characteristics that help diffusion are the social decision-making unit, personal communication, nature of the social system, and change agents' efforts. People can be characterised by how quickly they adopt innovations. *Innovators* are the first individuals to adopt an innovation; the second-fastest category of individuals who adopt an innovation are called *early adopters*; *early majority* and *late majority* are people who wait till others have adopted the new products. *Laggards* are the last to adopt the innovation.

At the same time, achieving a critical mass of customers so that they are sustainable and profitable for the company is important. The *tipping point* is the moment when an idea or trend crosses a threshold and spreads like wildfire.

Several models of innovation diffusion were discussed in the chapter: the Bass model, the epidemic or cascade model, and the social percolation model.

Innovations spread when people not only come to know about them, but feel convinced to try them out, and this conviction comes by observing others. People are influenced by friends and family, and seek out people who have similar interests and tastes. That is why reference groups are a powerful tool in the diffusion process. A brand community is a group of consumers who share social relationships on the basis of usage or interest in a product, based on attachment to a brand. Brand communities are powerful diffusion tools. Social movements such as these are able to mobilize communities towards collective action.

Tribal marketing is about supporting brands that keep youngsters together as a group of enthusiasts. For companies, knowing and recognizing the different crowds in a youth market is more useful in identifying tribes because adolescents tend to adapt their consumption and concrete brand choice to a crowd's reference behaviour. Diffusion of new products is faster if products are accepted by consumers as being cool.

Companies also use kitty parties and aspiration groups for diffusion of innovation. The fastest way to spread ideas and products with credibility is through word-of-mouth (WOM) communication. People believe what they hear, especially from someone close to them. Companies realise that using WOM is indeed a powerful way of diffusing information about new products. Social networking, the creation of buzz, using guerrilla methods, and viral marketing, too, spread ideas quickly. Opinion leaders are respected members of society and are used to spread ideas among the followers.

KEY TERMS

Anti-brand communities Formed around the common theme that brand names exploit people and even harm them

Aspiration group A reference group that an individual has no contact with but has a positive attraction towards it

Blue ocean strategy When companies try to position their products not against the competition, but in uncontested market spaces

Brand community A group of consumers who share social relationships based on usage or interest in a product

Brandfest An event organized around a particular brand

Cool Achieved through looks, a dose of humour, and a splash of social awareness

Creative change When an industry's core assets are under threat but core activities are stable, companies restore their assets while protecting customer and supplier relationships, for example, film studios

Diffusion The spread of a new idea from its source of invention or creation to its ultimate users or adopters

Disruptive innovation When a simple product or service takes root at the bottom of a market and then moves up, displacing established competitors

Early adopters The consumers who adopt a new product after some time and are more discreet in adoption choices than innovators

Early majority Individuals in this category tend to be slower in the adoption process and adopt an innovation after a varying degree of time, significantly longer than innovators and early adopters

Firm-oriented innovation When a company launches a new product that it was not making earlier, even though the product may already exist in the market

Guerrilla marketing A strategy in which low-cost unconventional means are used to promote a product or a brand

Innovation The effort to create purposeful, focused change in an enterprise's economic or social potential

Innovation value chain Views innovation as a sequential, three-phase process that involves idea generation, idea development, and diffusion

Innovators The first individuals to adopt a new product or service

Intermediating change Occurs when core activities are threatened with obsolescence, forcing companies to change trajectory

Laggards Individuals in this category are the last to adopt an innovation and show little to no opinion leadership unlike those in some of the previous categories

Late majority These individuals approach an innovation with a high degree of scepticism and adopt it after the majority of society has adopted it

Market-oriented Innovation A product that is new in the market

Negative reference group One that an individual disapproves of and sees as something to avoid

Opinion leaders Individuals whose ideas and behaviour serve as a model to others

Process innovation When a company finds better ways of making existing products, or significantly improves production or delivery methods

Product-oriented innovation When a completely new product is launched, or a change in its shape or size, or in functional elements that makes it easy to use

Progressive change Occurs when companies invest in research and development and create new products as old ones die out

Radical change What a company undergoes when it perceives a threat to the core activities that have historically generated profits for the industry

Reference groups Consist of people who influence an individual's affective responses, cognitions, and behaviour

Service innovation A new or significantly improved service concept

Social movements Mobilize communities towards collective action

Stages of adoption These are awareness, interest, evaluation, trial, and adoption

Tribe Consists of families or communities linked by social, economic, religious, or blood ties, with a common culture and dialect

Viral marketing Marketing techniques that use social networks to increase brand awareness or sales through self-replicating viral processes

Virtual community A virtual community is a community of people sharing common interests, ideas, and feelings over the Internet or other collaborative networks

Word of mouth (WOM) The passing of information from person to person by oral communication

Word-of-mouth marketing Giving people a reason to talk about you, and making it easier for the conversation to take place

EXERCISES

Concept-review Questions

1. Why is it necessary for companies to invest in innovation and to have a pipeline of new products? What is the importance of innovation?
2. Explain the different types of innovations with the help of examples.
3. What is innovation value chain? How do companies use this concept in developing new products?
4. What is meant by diffusion of innovation? What are the means by which innovations get diffused in society?
5. Explain the four key elements in the diffusion process and explain how do they impact diffusion.
6. What are the different adopter categories? What are their characteristics?
7. What are the five stages of new product adoption? What is the consumer's state of mind at each of these stages?
8. What are reference groups? What is their importance?
9. Why is it important to study social movements? What can business enterprises learn from social movements?
10. What is meant by 'cool'? How do brands acquire coolness? Explain with the help of examples.

Critical Thinking Questions

1. Analyse the statement that a business enterprise has only two basic functions: marketing and innovation. Do you agree with the statement? What roles do functions such as consumer behaviour, sales, pricing, and promotion play in the working of a business enterprise?
2. Consider the cases of Tata Nano and Vanilla Coke. Both these products were innovations and the idea was also diffused globally: almost everyone knew about these products. Yet, they flopped. What do these examples teach you about innovations and their diffusion?
3. The song 'Kolaveri di' is often cited as an example of viral marketing. However, it merely represents the number of people who watched the video on YouTube. Is this really marketing? What was sold and bought?
4. Do you agree with Naomi Klein's view that marketing exploits the vulnerable groups such as teenagers and children by preying on their fears? Is our entire culture being usurped by marketing companies?

Projects and Assignments

1. Study the launch of any innovative product in recent times. Analyse the product in terms of innovation and how the company achieved large-scale diffusion.
2. Analyse Peter Drucker's statement that a business has only two objectives: marketing and innovation. Compare companies in the developing and the

developed world and see where they stand on these two objectives. Take up companies such as Tata, Infosys, and Reliance on the one hand and 3M, Google, and P&G on the other. What do you find when you compare these companies on the variables of marketing and innovation?
3. Conduct an experiment in your class. Think of an absolutely new product and develop an advertisement for it. Then ask your classmates whether they would like to buy the product. Calculate what percentage of people is willing to buy it and how many are resisting. Then ask some of your friends to talk about the product and speak about how nice the experience was. Work out the calculation again. Is it different from the earlier percentage? What is your conclusion regarding word-of-mouth communication after doing this exercise?
4. Explore the sites of some brand communities. Analyse what these communities do. How are they creating conversations? Do you agree with the statement that companies should keep their intervention in such communities to the minimum? Can they be left to consumers?

REFERENCES

Bass, Frank, 'A new product growth model for consumer durables', *Management Science*, Vol. 15, No. 5, 1969, pp. 215–227.

Bower Joseph L. and Clayton M. Christensen, 'Disruptive technologies: Catching the wave', *Harvard Business Review*, January–February 1995.

Bradt, George, 'Three imperatives for service innovation', http://www.forbes.com/sites/georgebradt/2013/02/20/three-imperatives-for-service-innovation/, 2013, last accessed on 21 October 2013.

Candice R. Hollenbeck and George M. Zinkhan, 'Anti-brand communities, negotiation of brand meaning, and the learning process: The case of Wal-Mart', *Consumption Markets & Culture*, Vol. 13, No. 3, September 2010, pp. 325–345.

Christensen, Clayton, *The Innovator's Dilemma: When New Technologies Cause Great Firms to Fail*, Harvard Business Review Press, Boston, 2000.

Cova, Bernard, Robert Kozinets, and Avi Shankar, 'Tribes Inc., the new world of tribalism', in Cova, Kozinets, and Shankar (Eds.), *Consumer Tribes*, Butterworth-Heinemann, Oxford, 2007.

Davenport, Thomas H., *Process Innovation: Reengineering Work Through Information Technology*, Harvard Business School Press, Boston, 1993.

Delre, Sebastiano A., Wander Jager, Tammo H. A. Bijmolt, and Marco A. Janssen, 'Will it spread or not? The effects of social influences and network topology on innovation diffusion', *Journal of Product Innovation Management*, Vol. 27, 2010, pp. 267–282.

Den Hertog, P. (2000). Knowledge-intensive business services as co-producers of innovation, *International Journal of Innovation Management*, pp.491–528.

Drucker, Peter, 'The discipline of innovation', *Harvard Business Review*, August 2002.

Drucker, Peter, *The Practice of Management*, Harper & Row Publishers, New York, 1954.

'Even now, nobody knows anything', *The Economist*, 20 December 2013.

Fournier, Susan and Lara Lee, 'Getting brand communities right', *Harvard Business Review*, April 2009.

Gladwell, Malcolm, *The Tipping Point: How Little Things Can Make a Big Difference*, Little, Brown and Company, London, 2000.

'Global consumers' trust in "earned" advertising grows in importance', Nielsen 2012, http://www.nielsen.com/us/en/press-room/2012/nielsen-global-consumers-trust-in-earned-advertising-grows.html, last accessed on 9 December 2013.

Godin, Seth, 'What is viral marketing?', http://sethgodin.typepad.com/seths_blog/2008/12/what-is-viral-m.html, 2008, last accessed on 14 December 2013.

Goldman and Howard, 'To tweet or not to tweet: What business can learn from social movements', *Rotman Magazine*, Spring 2013.

Goldman, William, *Adventures in the Screen Trade*, Warner Books, New York, 1983.

Gourville, John T., 'Eager sellers and stony buyers: Understanding the psychology of new-product adoption', *Harvard Business Review* Vol. 84, No. 6, June 2006.

Hansen Morten T. and Julian Birkinshaw, 'The innovation value chain', *Harvard Business Review*, June 2007.

Kim W. Chan and Renée Mauborgne, *Blue Ocean Strategy: How to Create Uncontested Market Space and Make the Competition Irrelevant*, Harvard Business School Publishing Corporation, Boston, 2005.

Klein, Naomi, *No Logo*, 10th ed., Knopf, Canada, 2010.

Levinson, Jay Conrad, *Guerilla Marketing: Easy and Inexpensive Strategies for Making Big Profits from Your Small Business*, Houghton Mifflin Company, New York, 2007

Lindstrom, Martin, 'Fast company for brands being cool is as hot as sex', http://www.martinlindstrom.com/fast-company-for-brands-being-cool-is-as-hot-as-sex/, 2012, last accessed on 7 December 2013.

McFerran, Brent, Darren W. Dahl, Gavan J. Fitzsimons, and Andrea C. Morales, 'I'll have what she's having: Effects of social influence and body type on the food choices of others', *Journal of Consumer Research*, Vol. 36, No. 6, April 2010.

McGahan, Anita M., 'How industries change', *Harvard Business Review*, October 2004.

McWilliam, Gil, 'Building stronger brands through online communities', *MIT Sloan Management Review*, Spring 2000.

Miles, Ian, 'Innovation in services', in *The Oxford Handbook of Innovation* edited by Jan Fagerberg, David C. Mowery, and Richard R. Nelson, Oxford University Press, New York, 2005.

Mitchell, A. and Deepak Khazanchi, 'The importance of buzz', *Market Research*, Summer 2010.

Moore, Geoffrey A., *Crossing the Chasm, Marketing and Selling High-Tech Products to Mainstream Customer* (revised edition), HarperCollins Publishers, New York, 1999.

Nancarrow, Clive and Pamela Nancarrow, 'Hunting for cool tribes, in Cova, Kozinets, and Shankar (Eds.), *Consumer Tribes*, Butterworth-Heinemann, Oxford, 2007.

'New business models: The golden age of consumer influence', *The Economist* Group, 9 July 2013, http://www.economistgroup.com/leanback/new-business-models/the-golden-age-of-consumer-influence/, last accessed on 5 September 2013.

New Products Management for the 1980s, Booz, Allen & Hamilton, New York, 1982.

Patterson, Kerry, Joseph Grenny, David Maxfield, Ron McMillan, and Al Switzler, *Influencer: The Power to Change Anything*, Tata McGraw Hill, New Delhi, 2008.

Peck, J., 'The Oprah effect: Texts, readers, and the dialectic of significance', *Communication Review*, Vol. 5, No. 2, 2002, pp. 143–78.

Reichheld Frederick F., 'The one number you need to grow', *Harvard Business Review*, December 2001.

Rogers, Everett M., *Diffusion of Innovations*, 5th Ed., The Free Press, New York, 2003.

Schneider, Joan and Julie Hall, 'Why most product launches fail', *Harvard Business Review*, Apri 2011.

Sernovitz, Andy, *Word of Mouth Marketing: How Smart Companies Get People Talking*, Greenleaf Book Group Press, Austin, 2012.

Thomke, Stefan and Eric von Hippel, 'Customers as innovators: A new way to create value', *Harvard Business Review*, April 2002.

Van den Bergh, Joeri and Mattias Behrer, *How Cool Brands Stay Hot: Branding to Generation Y*, 2nd Ed., Kogan Page, Philadelphia, 2013.

Wu, Michael, *The Science of Social 2*, Lithium Technologies, San Francisco, 2013.

Zhou, Tao, 'Understanding online community user participation: A social influence perspective', *Internet Research*, 2011, Vol. 21, Issue 1, pp.67–81.

CASE STUDY

Spread of Social Movements—Grameen Bank and BRAC

Readers of this book will be familiar with the terms 'microcredit' and 'microfinance'. They describe the process of giving of micro loans (sometimes as low as ₹2000) to people who living in extreme poverty. These people do not have access to formal sources of finance, and above all, have nothing to offer as collateral against which to raise loans.

It took a professor, Muhammad Yunus, to turn conventional banking on its head by inventing the concept of micro-loans and the Grameen Bank Project was born in 1976. Returning to Bangladesh in the seventies, Dr Yunus was horrified to discover that just outside his academic compound, thousands of people were dying of starvation. He writes in his book, *Banker to the Poor* (2007), 'That night I lay in bed ashamed that I was part of a society which could not provide $27 to forty-two able-bodied, hard-working, skilled persons to make a living for themselves'.

This thought was to turn into an innovation in banking which changed the lives of millions of poor, not only in his country, but across the world. The Grameen Bank, which he founded, has reversed the conventional banking wisdom by removing collateral requirement and created a banking system which is based on mutual trust, strict supervision, accountability, participation, and creativity.

Rizvi (2006) writes, 'The power of the idea and the magnitude of the impact of micro-credit are quite staggering'. According to its website, the Grameen bank has 8.35 million borrowers, 97 per cent of whom are women. With 2,565 branches, it provides services in 81,379 villages, covering more than 97 per cent of the total number of villages in Bangladesh as on October 2011. In Bangladesh alone, the three largest micro-credit institutions—the Grameen Bank, the Bangladesh Rural Advancement Committee (BRAC), and the Association for Social Advance—had cumulatively disbursed nearly $10 billion, and had loan recovery rates in excess of 95 per cent.

In the quarter of a century since the launch of Grameen Bank, microcredit has become a near global movement. It is estimated that more than $20 billion is being disbursed to nearly 100 million households in over fifty countries today, including the US. Grameen America helps women who live in poverty to build small businesses to create better lives for their families. Dr Yunus won the Nobel Peace Prize in 2006 for his pioneering work in microcredit.

This case study shows how the banking innovation spread. As explained in this chapter, the four key elements in the diffusion process are innovation, channels of communication, time, and social system.

How these elements were utilised in the creation of Grameen Bank is described here.

Innovation

The innovation arose from the needs of the poor. Conventional banking gives loans to rich borrowers—those who can provide collateral or security for the loans. The poor have no security or guarantee, are unbankable, and do not even have access to banking services. Banks do not know how to deal with the poor, nor do they have the capability or reach to track millions of microloans. Dr Yunus invented a system to provide the poorest of the poor small loans without any collateral by using social capital. He was able to understand the nature of poverty and tailor the loans to the requirements of the target population.

Time

As social habits were required to be changed, the innovation could not be rushed through. Dr Yunus had to get over social norms—in Bangladesh society, even talking to women was taboo. As described in *Banker to the Poor*, it was a long and patient process: 'Because of the rules of *purdah*, we never dared enter women's houses in the villages we visited. So when I went to meet village women, I never knocked on their doors. Instead, I would stand in a clearing between several houses, so that everyone could see me and observe my behaviour. I usually brought one of my female students with me. This go-between would enter the house, introduce me, and speak on my behalf. She would then bring back any questions the women might have. I would answer the questions, and back the girl would go. Sometimes she would shuttle back and forth for over an hour. We wasted a lot of time. Often the young girl would not catch all my ideas or the women's questions would get jumbled. It was an inefficient system'.

Channels of Communication

How does one communicate with the poorest of the poor? The traditional methods of advertising just would not work: Dr Yunus was faced with a seemingly insurmountable problem: 'How would we find women borrowers in a country where most poor women had never even seen a bank and where 85 per cent could not read our billboards or advertisements?'

Gawande (2013) writes, 'Though we yearn for technological solutions, people talking to people is still the way that habits change'.

He gives the example of saving children suffering from dysentery: in 1980, BRAC tried to get oral rehydration therapy adopted nationwide. Chowdhury and Cash (1996) in their book, *A Simple Solution* write that the organization attacked the problem in a way that is routinely dismissed as impractical and inefficient: by going door-to-door, person by person, and just talking.

It started with a pilot project that set out to reach some 60,000 women in 600 villages. Teams of 14 young women, a cook, and a male supervisor were organized. They travelled on foot, pitched camp near each village, fanned out door to door, and stayed until they had talked to women in every hut. A salary system was devised to pay each worker according to how many of the messages the mothers retained. The field workers realized that having the mothers make the solution themselves was more effective than just showing them. 'Later, BRAC and the Bangladeshi government took the program nationwide. They hired, trained, and deployed thousands of workers region by region. By going door-to-door through more than 75,000 villages, they showed 12 million families how to save their children. The program was stunningly successful. Use of oral rehydration therapy skyrocketed. The knowledge became self-propagating. The program had changed the norms,' writes Gawande.

Social System

Through peer groups and social pressure, it used word-of-mouth and communities to propagate the idea. Hossain (2013) shows how Dr Yunus used social capital in their microcredit program and helped in reducing poverty of Bangladesh. Initially giving money from his own pocket, he found that it created an emotional counter response from the people who got the money. He continued giving loans and 'was pleasantly surprised to see that it was working perfectly. I continued to expand the program'. In 1983, this was transformed into a formal bank.

Using the concept of *propinquity*, loans are provided to women in groups of five, signing for each other's loans, so that they could support one another. Each borrower has to commit to 16 'decisions' including educating children, hygiene, planting seedlings, and stopping the practice of dowry. The last of these decisions encourage social activity: 'We shall take part in all social activities collectively.'

Peer groups were also utilized. By demanding that no one worked alone, Dr Yunus ensured that the microcredit clients always worked in teams. One unique feature is the use of peer pressure as a substitute collateral, since there is a joint responsibility for repayment.

Questions for Discussion

1. What can businesses learn from the methods used by Grameen Bank and BRAC to accomplish their goals? How did the ideas spread and become huge successes?
2. Discuss the importance of direct communication and using personal contact to spread ideas and innovations.
3. 'Companies are now considering the intersection of social movements and business strategy. Companies that successfully create brand communities are able to make their brands and products tap into such movements'. Discuss this statement with reference to the social movements described here.
4. Given the huge logistical challenge to reach consumers directly, would it really be feasible for companies to adopt the tactics of social movements?

Sources:

Chowdhury A. Mushtaque R. and Richard A. Cash, *A Simple Solution—Teaching Millions to Treat Diarrhoea at Home*, The University Press Limited, Dhaka, 1996.

Gawande, Atul, 'Annals of medicine', *The New Yorker*, 29 July 29 2013, http://www.newyorker.com/reporting/2013/07/29/130729fa_fact_gawande?currentPage=all, last accessed on 7 December 2013.

Hossain, Dewan Mahboob, 'Social capital and microfinance: The case of Grameen Bank, Bangladesh', *Middle East Journal of Business*, Vol. 8, No. 4, October 2013.

http://grameenamerica.org/, last accessed on 7 December 2013.

Rizvi, Gowher, 'Muhammad Yunus: The transformative power of an idea', 2006, http://www.hks.harvard.edu/news-events/news/news-archive/muhammad-yunus-the-transformative-power-of-an-idea, last accessed on 24 April 2014.

Yunus, Muhammad and Alan Jolis, *Banker to the Poor: Micro-lending and the Battle Against World Poverty*, 3rd Ed., Public Affairs, New York, 2007.

Yunus, Muhammad and Karl Weber, *Building Social Business: The New Kind of Capitalism That Serves Humanity's Most Pressing Needs*, Public Affairs, New York, 2010.

CHAPTER THIRTEEN

Communications and Consumer Behaviour

LEARNING OBJECTIVES

Communications are an important part of any marketing strategy. Companies have to reach out to customers to inform them about their products, but more than that, to create desires and dreams. This chapter examines how this can be done.

After studying this chapter, the reader would be able to:
- understand the importance and role of marketing communications
- learn about communication models and how they work
- analyse how communications strategies are made and persuasive messages designed
- analyse the message strategies, celebrity endorsements, and emotional techniques
- learn about different types of media and analyse media strategies
- understand the importance of word-of-mouth communication and modern technologies that connect people

CASE STUDY

Nokia's Communication Strategy

How does a well-known company that is browbeaten by competitors, regain lost ground? Nokia, lost to rivals like Samsung in the Indian mobile phone market and faced the problem of winning back customers, even as the brand almost looked like it was history. It did so by devising an innovative communications strategy to reached the target customers so effectively that they were willing to buy the product on the spot. This impossible task is the dream of any manager, to leap over the AIDA steps of awareness, interest, desire, straight to action (discussed later in Section 'AIDA model').

Nokia realized that any communication strategy to reach people in India was incomplete if it did not reach the villages. While media is available to cover urban areas, villages are another matter altogether. They are out of reach of FM channels, newspapers are delivered late, if at all, and satellite television is still to make inroads. The absence of electricity compounds the problem—long power cuts are the norm. Many villages in developing countries are 'media dark', meaning that media does not reach them at all.

Further, as people were already aware of the brand, the communications strategy had to go beyond the awareness stage and had to grab customers as they came. Nokia used out-of-the-box communication to start a buzz around their launch of dual-SIM mobile phones in smaller towns, thereby cornering a sizeable market share in this category.

Nokia was under attack from rivals such as Samsung and Micromax. It found its market share slipping by over half in 2011, from a dominating 70 per cent market share in 2007. It faced stiff competition from low-cost local and Chinese handset makers. The company also made a huge mistake in delaying the launch of dual-SIM handsets that were the current flavour of the market.

Though Nokia launched its first dual-SIM handset two-and-a-half years after competitors, in less than a year, it dethroned the first movers. A CyberMedia Research report cited by *The Times of India* showed that the Finnish handset maker had a 30.7 per cent slice of the market followed by Samsung with 14.9 per cent and Micromax with 5 per cent in the period January–November, 2011. It launched the Asha brand with smartphone features at lower prices, to catch customers in small towns and encourage first-time data users on mobile devices.

Nokia realized the importance of reaching out to the villages and communicating with its customers. In doing so, it retained its dominance over cheaper phones, and regained lost ground with its dual-SIM phones. It did so by following a unique communications strategy.

Nokia blue brigade rally The company hired large groups of 200 bikers in blue-coloured uniforms waving blue flags. They would descend on the main market streets in villages in the manner of a political rally. The bikers would be accompanied by crackers and *dhols* (drums), along with a group of *bhangra* dancers. The rallies immediately aroused interest in the sleepy villages and succeeded in generating a buzz in the small towns of Punjab, Rajasthan, Himachal Pradesh, Uttar Pradesh, and Uttarakhand. The blue brigade rallies announced the launch of Nokia's dual-SIM handsets.

Nukkad naatak To encourage consumer engagement, Nokia relied on street plays and torch rallies at night. The company undertook a massive street play activity in 575 towns and villages across six states. In Chhattisgarh, local artistes from Lok Kala Sanstha were hired to perform *nukkad naataks* in local languages. They would enter a crowded market area and enact a play that smartly wove the benefits of dual-SIM handsets into the script. This was followed by demonstrations of the device and prizes for those who purchased on the spot. In rural Maharashtra, it spread awareness using torch rallies, with 75–100 people participating.

These activities had a huge response: the company claims that it reached more than three lakh people, and sold over 5300 dual-SIM handsets on the spot.

Digital and radio campaigns For cities such as Delhi, Jaipur, Lucknow, and Bhopal, the company ran digital and radio campaigns, inviting twins to launch C2-00 and X1-01 dual SIM phones. They became Nokia's brand ambassadors for a day. In Delhi, the Nokia's *Twins Day Out* festival saw 63 pairs of twins come together. The festival highlighted the 'twin power' of dual SIM. Nokia claims to have entered the Limca Book of Records for organizing the largest gathering of twins in India at a single venue.

Viral campaign Nokia launched an aggressive viral campaign called 'Blown away by Lumia' comparing its Lumia with rivals like Samsung Galaxy. The YouTube campaign showed short clips of Lumia representatives challenging consumers with rival smartphones, mostly that of Samsung, at malls and pubs in terms of Internet and social networking speed and experience. When Lumia won, the other consumer held aloft a banner that said, 'My phone just got blown away by the Nokia Lumia'. The campaign had been inspired by a similar recent global campaign 'Smoked by Windows Phone' by Microsoft that helped demonstrate the benefits of Nokia Windows phones. Such comparisons were difficult with conventional advertising. Samsung said that the campaign was unethical. Nokia's campaign helped consumers compare their phones in social networking and Internet capabilities that were the most important factors for younger consumers. The YouTube videos were popular and attracted more than 1.5 lakh views.

While reading the chapter, try to relate this real-life situation to the ideas and concepts in the chapter and answer the following questions:

1. How did Nokia decide on its message and media strategy? Do you think it was ideal? Why were BTL methods used and what was their impact?
2. Nokia relied on BTL methods. What are BTL methods and what advantage do they have over ATL campaigns?
3. What communications could Samsung have used to counter Nokia's onslaught?
4. How does communications strategy integrate with the overall marketing strategy of a company?

The case shows how an understanding of consumer behaviour is essential to create precise communications that can, in a coordinated manner, affect purchase behaviour. Ultimately, the task of all communications is to influence the consumer. This case study shows that several activities, taken together, can achieve great results.

Sources:

Mukherjee, Writankar, 'Nokia's "smart" viral campaign attack leaves Samsung fuming', *The Economic Times*, 11 April 2012.

'Nokia No.1 in Indian mobile market: Study', PTI report, *The Times of India*, 2 March 2012.

'Nokia tops smartphone sales in India', PTI report, *The Economic Times*, 24 January 2012.

Sen, Sunny, 'Sucker punch', *Business Today*, 27 May 2012.

Singh, Rajiv, 'Double or quits', *The Economic Times Brand Equity*, 11 April 2012.

INTRODUCTION

Every day and every moment, we receive communications from companies wanting to sell us something or the other. We are confronted with bright and beautiful faces while reading newspapers or watching television who make us believe that happiness is the latest model of a car or a mobile phone. If we go out on a drive, we see huge billboards with images of young people who seem to have achieved *nirvana* by eating the latest chocolate or by buying a new car. Our mobile phone can break our deepest thoughts by ringing at any moment with a call from an insurance company selling us instant security. When we open our e-mail or social networking account, and some advertisements pop up offering us an easy way to get married or to earn extra income.

Communications are indeed the backbone of marketing. How else is the customer to know about the latest products, or having known about them, how is he to feel a deep desire so that he goes to the shop and places his money on the counter? The chapter-opening case study illustrates that this is very much possible. Indeed, this is the challenge for modern communications: companies cannot force people to buy something, so the task is to push customers by appealing to all their senses by discovering what is obvious and what is not.

Very often, they succeed. This chapter examines the principles of communication and how they are used by companies to make powerful messages that people simply cannot ignore. Companies must figure out how and where advertisements must be placed, how best an appeal is to be delivered, and how best to approach the customer. Sometimes lifelike qualities are sought to be attached to products, so that they become part of the personality of the consumer.

MARKETING COMMUNICATION

Companies communicate to customers: they tell them about product offerings, the benefits that may be obtained from using those products, and establish a rapport with their customers. On a subtle level, they create space in the consumer's mind by attaching psychological and cultural tags. Featherstone (2007) explains the success of marketing communications thus: 'Advertising in particular is able to exploit this and attach images of romance, exotica, desire, beauty, fulfilment, communality, scientific progress, and the good life to mundane consumer goods such as soap, washing machines, motor cars, and alcoholic drinks.'

Marketing communications strike deep in the mind, so that consumers start linking products to their own personalities or start attaching lifelike qualities to inanimate objects. Consider statements such as 'I can't live without my iPhone', or look at the ways that people take care of their cars and other belongings, and we discover that consumers place much more importance in their possessions than can be rationally justified.

Why does this happen? Through powerful communications, companies are able to attach meaning to their brands that goes much beyond the products themselves. This is done by treating the brand as a semiotic system—a system of signs and symbols—that appeals to the consumers' imagination.

Semiotic System

A brand can be described as a combination of product, price, promotion, and place, but it is much more than that. If we look closely, we see that brands consist of a system of signs, symbols, and people that engages consumers on a psychological plane rather than the rational. Oswald (2012) writes that a brand can be defined as a system of signs and symbols that engages the consumer in an imaginary/symbolic process that contributes tangible value to a product offering. The mind places brands in a complex system of images, signs, and symbols.

Morris (1971) writes that semiotics consists of *syntactics* or the study of the methods by which signs may be combined to form compound signs, *semantics* or the study of conditions under which the sign denotes something, and *pragmatics* or the study of the origins, uses, and effects of signs.

All three are used by companies in various ways. Note the signage, packaging, colours, and trademarks of successful brands and you will see how semiotics is used to create distinct personalities (see Chapter 7). It is no coincidence that certain brands get attached to colours; for instance Coca-Cola's red colour or Apple's white are part of the semiotic environment.

Colours, images, messages, and subtle hints contribute to the brand experience that is sometimes vicarious. They help to build relationship with consumers, or to fulfil psychological needs. Brand communication has to be essentially symbolic to create an impression in the mind of the customer. For instance, Pears soap is perceived as much more than soap and has a distinct personality, because its advertisements and communications have been highlighting the relationship between mother and daughter for years. This symbol has endeared the brand to consumers over the years.

Evidence of brands as semiotic comes from brain-scanning techniques developed by neuroscientists. A.K. Pradeep (2010) in his book, *The Buying Brain: Secrets for Selling to the Subconscious Mind,* gives us an understanding about peoples' brains using fMRI scans, and their implications for communication strategies for companies. The findings reveal the following about the brain:

Has limited processing ability   The marketing interaction should be quick, clear, and interesting; simple 'Zen'-like packaging appeals to the brain

Likes to be rewarded   When the brain comes across a rewarding behaviour, it increases the level of dopamine transmission in the brain. The implication is to motivate customers to buy brands by activating their pleasure–reward circuits

Likes to be stimulated   Companies must make the communication riveting by using interesting people, puzzles, and humour

Has restricted focused attention   The interaction should be quick, clear, and interesting

Understands by making neural connections   Companies must use direct and active verbs in their communications to guide the brain

Indeed, it is the brand image that ultimately creates differences between brands, write Van den Bergh and Mattias Behrer (2013). The brand image is more than the desired positioning of the brand—it is the collection of all brand associations held in consumer memory.

The task of conveying all that the brand stands for—tangible as well as intangible—is the purpose of marketing communications. To create powerful associations, we have to understand the communications process. This is understood with the help of communication models.

COMMUNICATION MODELS

Models of communication help us to understand the elements that need to be controlled to communicate effectively with consumers. Some of the questions that face a marketing communicator are as follows:

- How should the message be formulated? What should it emphasize?
- Who are the people who will communicate the message?
- What are the types of media to be used?
- How should the message be packaged to be acceptable to the target consumers?
- Will they understand the message in the manner it is intended?

Communication models help us to answer these questions formally. Some of these are discussed in the next section.

Shannon–Weaver Model of Communication

The first major model for communication was proposed by Shannon and Weaver (1949), which explains the process of sending and receiving messages from one person to another (see Fig. 13.1). It breaks up the communications process into six components:

Source   The point from which the message originates is the source. In marketing communications, the source will be the company that advertises its products.

Encoding   The objectives are encoded in the form of a message or presentation that is easy to communicate to the target audience.

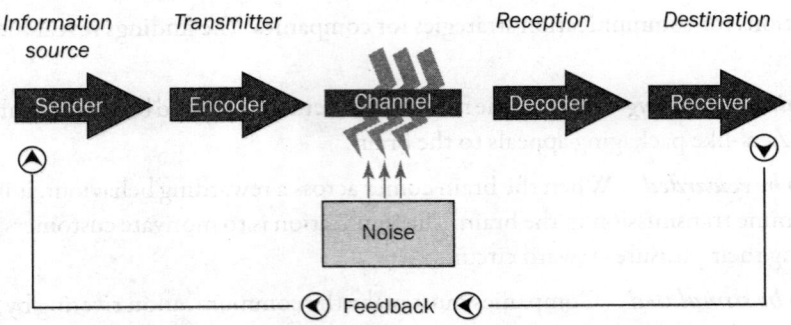

Shannon–Weaver's model of communication

FIG. 13.1 Simple communication model

Source: http://communicationtheory.org/shannon-and-weaver-model-of-communication/, last accessed on 5 May 2012.

Channel Messages have to be sent through a channel, which may involve mass media, word-of-mouth communications, direct mail, or social messages.

Decoding Consumers interpret the message on the basis of their own understanding or perception, and this process is known as decoding. Companies have to ensure that the message is interpreted and remembered as it was intended to, and also that the product or company is viewed positively by the consumers.

Receiver In our context, the receiver is the consumer. A concern for the communicator is whether the message is received without interference.

Feedback How consumers respond to advertising messages is conveyed through feedback. Companies have to track whether the ads are liked and whether they are strong enough to encourage a purchase.

The model also shows another element, *noise*, which is a dysfunctional factor: any interference with the message travelling along the channel. This could be a technical glitch—if the electronic signal is distorted so that the message is garbled; or a psychological disturbance—a distraction that prevents the consumer from getting the message. A consumer may be busy with something else when the message is sent, or in a different mode of thought. Noise could also be personal perception—something that colours the message, preventing it from being received the way it is intended to. For example, a company may say it has the best products in the world, but the customer thinks of it as exaggeration or hype.

The model points to several barriers to effective communication at each of these stages, which is labelled as 'noise'. Companies have to be careful about these barriers as they distort messages, and in some cases convey quite the opposite of what was intended. These barriers can be as follows:

At source Companies are not able to define their objectives, resulting in a poor focus on product benefits, and advertising that is out of sync with consumer needs.

In encoding Companies create advertisements that are very attractive, but fail to convey consumer benefits. The claims may also be deceptive or misleading so as to convey a wrong impression to the audience.

TABLE 13.1 Ads that did not work

Brand	Ad theme	Why it did not work
Maruti Swift	The brand's attempt to attract the young, hip, and cool loosely translated into a haphazard and rather random series of shots of five- to twenty-five year olds swinging and splashing about	*Barriers at source and encoding*: Did not gel with the brand being advertised
Eno	To make it appealing to young people, the ad had the story of two best friends who fell in love with the same girl. However, the boy who drank Eno got the girl, and they lived happily ever after	*Barriers in decoding*: Unconvincing script, desperate attempt at humour
Electrolux	To counter Hema Malini featured in a water purifier ad, Electrolux roped in Shilpa Shetty who makes a wholly unconvincing pitch about her water purifier	*Barriers at source and decoding*: Copycat advertising, unconvincing
Everyuth	Shows a girl with flawless skin, despite assaults by rain, sun and grime	*Barriers in transmission*: Repeated, tired formula; does nothing for the brand

Source: Ten hits & misses: Best &; Bekaar ads of 2013, *The Economic Times Brand Equity*, 25 December 2013

In transmission   Choice of wrong media or placing ads in highly cluttered environments are barriers in transmission. Messages tend to be forgotten and fail to register with consumers.

In decoding   When consumers misinterpret the message or ignore it or think it lacks credibility, it usually arises from barriers in decoding.

Companies have to guard against these barriers if the message is to succeed. With increased media cost, multiplication of media channels and increased clutter, it is imperative that messages overcome these barriers. Examples of advertisements that did not work and the reasons for them, according to *The Economic Times Brand Equity*, are given in Table 13.1.

Because barriers to communication result in ads being forgotten or misunderstood, messages have to be designed so that they achieve three distinct objectives—people see them, they remember and like them, and they buy the goods that are advertised.

That is why ads must be *repeated* often, have a high *contrast* or dramatic image that helps break through the *clutter*, or try to attract attention through some other method. The use of sex in advertising is also sometimes justified for these reasons.

AIDA Model

The objective of marketing communications and its impact on consumer behaviour is also understood through the AIDA model (see Fig. 13.2). The model describes four stages of consumer behaviour that result when people are exposed to communications.

Attention   The communication must grab the customer's *attention* or it is lost. Dramatic images or words such as 'free', 'new', 'special', and 'limited period' are likely to get the customers' attention.

Interest   Consumers should be *interested* in the offering. It should help the customers in some way or solve some problem.

Desire   The communication should generate a *desire* in the customer to buy.

Action   The last stage is *action* when the consumer should go out and and buy the advertised product.

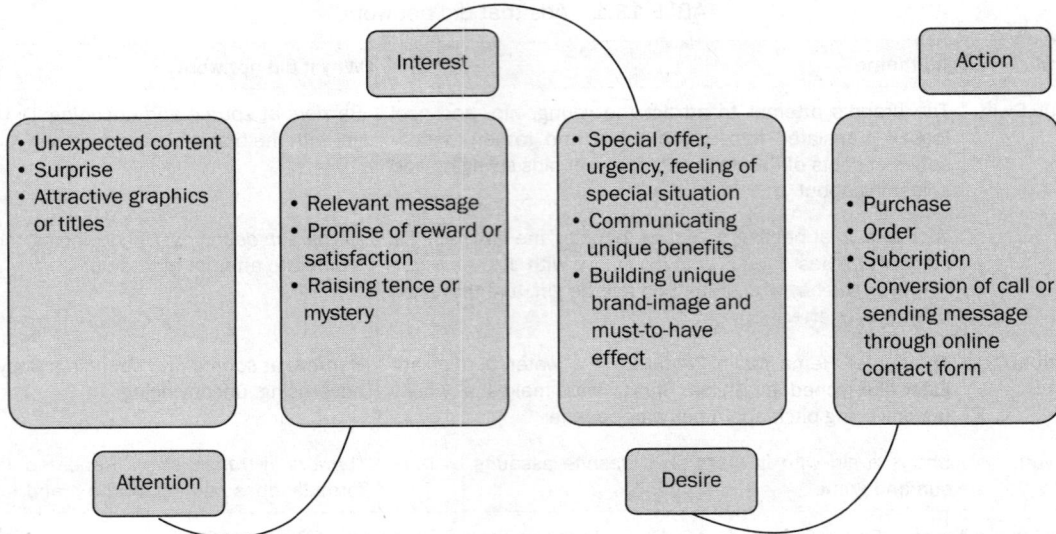

FIG. 13.2 AIDA model

Source: http://www.guerrillaonline.com/cs/Guerrilla-Marketing-Principles-54.htm, last accessed on 5 May 2012

Understanding the models of communication helps us to draw up a communications strategy, that is, the use of language, signs, and images in meeting the company's objectives.

Fogg's Behaviour Model for Persuasive Design

Fogg (2009) has given a behaviour model which shows three elements that must exist in all communications to persuade consumers. It says that for a person to perform a behaviour (like making a purchase), the following three must occur simultaneously:

- *Motivation*: The consumer must be sufficiently motivated
- *Ability*: He or she must have the ability to perform the behaviour
- *Trigger*: There must be a trigger to perform the behaviour

We see from this that marketing communications must address the elements of motivation, ability, and provide a trigger for making the purchase. If a consumer does not buy, at least one of those three elements is missing. Every person has a behaviour activation threshold and the threshold can only be crossed when all three factors work together. These are explained in this section.

Motivation

The goal in motivation is to move to a higher position so that action is initiated. That is, people who have low motivation need to be converted, so that they cross the *behaviour activation threshold*. Fogg describes three core motivators, each with two characteristics.

Pleasure/Pain Advertisers stress on pleasure when people buy goods and also on avoidance of pain. Both become powerful motivators. The pleasure theme is exploited in advertisements for products ranging from chocolates to cars; on the other hand, companies also advise people to stock pain relievers like Moov ointment in their homes to go from 'Ah to Aha'.

Hope/Fear Advertisements inspire hope or fear. They are able to link hope with an anticipation of something good happening. Many advertisements also seek to invoke fear such as anticipation of loss and motivate people towards products. The fear appeal is used effectively in insurance and health products. Pictures of sick people or horrible accidents discourage people to take up bad habits such as smoking or driving after drinking.

Social acceptance/Rejection It is easy to see that people are motivated to do things that win them social acceptance and importantly, to avoid being socially rejected. People adopt clothes, music, and language in order to be accepted in their group. Many interactions on Facebook, for example, are driven by the desire to be socially accepted.

Ability

Ability is not about teaching people to do new things. Since consumers do not like anything that requires effort, companies must try to increase a user's ability by making things easier to do. Persuasive design in advertising thus relies heavily on the power of simplicity. For example, the one-click shopping at Amazon makes it easy to buy things, so people buy more. Apple too, made it easy for consumers to use their products by eliminating manuals and instead made the product itself easy to use and adapt. There are six elements related to ability, which a communicator must realize.

Time Companies have to respect the time of customers. Interactions must be kept short and crisp. For instance, lengthy survey forms or long waiting times turn people away. Websites, for instance, make it easy and secure to pay, saving time for customers.

Money While communications are targeted to people who have the purchasing power, aspirational products target people who may not afford them at present but may do so at a future time.

Physical effort Some responses require effort on the part of the consumer, like going to the market to buy products. Stores may help out with home deliveries in order to reduce physical effort.

Thinking Some communications will cause people to think. Social campaigns seek action by making people think. Social initiatives undertaken by companies such as Reliance and Infosys have been covered in a separate chapter.

Social deviance Some customers are rebels and want to be seen as standing out of the crowd. Companies promote products that help such customers to express their individuality.

Habits People form habits resulting in brand loyalty. Communications should encourage habits among people but also try to break habits.

Triggers

Triggers or cues complete the buying behaviour expected from communications. There are three kinds of triggers.

Spark Communications should provide a trigger that pushes consumers towards buying. Examples of sparks include announcements such as 'limited period offer' and 'limited stocks'.

CB IN ACTION — Analyse the Communication Model

We have learnt about communications models. This exercise will help you learn whether they have any practical application or are just theories never to be applied in real life.

Select a company of your choice. Collect all its communications to you, whether they are ads, mailers, e-mails, SMS, social media pages, web pages, etc.

1. Analyse the Shannon–Weaver model with respect to these communications and see how the messages were devised and transmitted. Was there any noise or barriers to communication?
2. At what stage of AIDA were the company's communications? What could it do so that the action stage was reached earlier?
3. What are the Fogg's motivators used in the communications? Did they address motivation, ability, or trigger? If no, how can the company apply the model to its communications?

Facilitator Some customers have high motivation but lack the desire or ability. A facilitator helps speed up the decision. For instance, e-commerce sites offer cash on delivery (COD) facility to assuage customer fears of using credit cards online.

Signal A reminder is called a signal that will trigger the appropriate action. It is like providing a green light to perform an action.

After understanding what pushes a customer towards action, the next step is to find out how consumers can be motivated to act voluntarily. This is done by understanding the customer in his environment, and includes not only his purchasing behaviour, but also the scenarios in which he exists and his needs.

The next step is to use our learning of communication models to make a powerful communications strategy.

COMMUNICATIONS STRATEGY

In earlier days, communications strategy consisted of devising advertisements that were released in the mass media. With new technologies that encourage interaction and communication, companies cannot rely on mass campaigns alone and hope that people will react the way that the company wants them to. It requires a paradigm shift in thinking about the way that companies communicate.

Today's technology allows consumers also to communicate with companies or influence purchase decisions through online interactions. The role of communications has thus expanded from a one way business-to-consumer (B2C) interaction through mass media to an interactive two way business-to-consumer-to-business (B2C2B) interaction. Another element that has been added is consumer-to-consumer (C2C) communication, where consumers interact with their friends or acquaintances without any intervention from companies, or person-to-person (P2P) where people who are not customers interact with each other and talk about their impressions of brands or companies. This is done via social networks and blogs, and as these can turn out to be influential in making or marring reputations, companies have to keep tab on the online chatter about their products and brands.

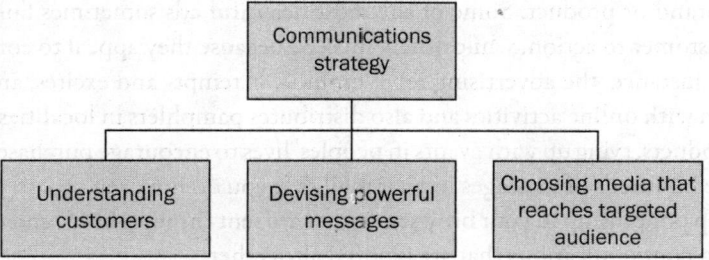

FIG. 13.3 Marketing communications strategy has three major interlinked components

A successful communications strategy has three components (Fig. 13.3). These are: identifying and understanding customers, working out a strategy to frame the message such that it appeals to consumers, as also the kinds of media to be used to reach consumers when they are most open to receiving marketing messages.

It is easy to see that these elements are interlinked. Very often companies make errors in one or the other component. First, sometimes companies say what they want to say, but the communication does not fulfil customer needs. People simply ignore such messages. A successful communication must start from the consumer. Second, communicators make messages that do not appeal to consumers, like the many advertisements that you simply ignore or that turn you off. Third, even though the message is good, it is released in media that consumers do not use—a channel that is not viewed by the targeted audience, a newspaper that is not read by them, or as pop-up messages every time they visit a site, or the useless SMS messages that are sent daily. Mistakes in any of these components mean return on marketing spends is significantly reduced.

A communications strategy of a company can be defined as a method of communicating the company's marketing messages to consumers so that they are the most effective.

While building a communications strategy, it is important to understand people, brands, and their interaction on a psychological and physical plane.

To decide on the best communications strategy, companies have to figure out answers to the following questions:

- *Audience*: Who must be reached?
- *Message:* What must be told to the target audience?
- *Proposition:* What is the promise of the product or brand?
- *Style:* Is the message and execution relevant to the target audience?
- *How:* What is the best way to reach customers?

The starting point of all communications is the customer; therefore understanding him/her is of crucial importance.

UNDERSTANDING CUSTOMERS

Good communications succeed because they are able to reach the customers when they are most comfortable, open to ideas, and able to understand the message. It is then easy to persuade them to try the brand or product. Some of the most beautiful ads sometimes fail, as they just do not push the customer to action, while others succeed because they appeal to consumers.

Take for instance, the advertising for Domino's. It tempts and excites, and the company uses social media with online activities and also distributes pamphlets in localities encouraging people to try its products, tying up with events in peoples' lives to encourage purchase. On the other hand, think of the hundreds of messages in your mail that you do not even care to read, or the irritating ads that keep popping up in your browser, or that are sent through SMS, and one witnesses wasted resources on communications that are ignored altogether.

Customers are People

All communications strategies start with the customer. Not only must the target customers be identified, but their needs and aspirations must also be understood. However, many companies don't carry out this exercise, as they are enamoured of their own products and advertising. Quite often companies make the mistake of indulging in marketing warfare, which puts them in a combative mode rather than understanding mode.

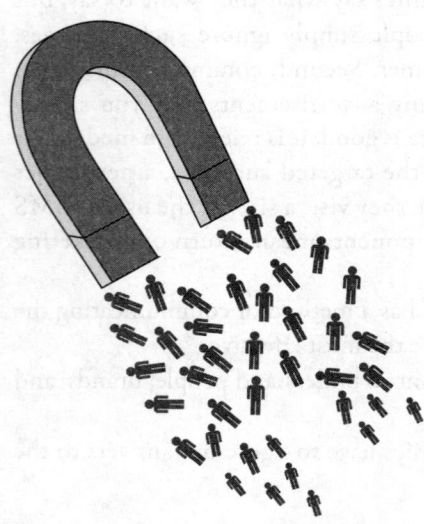

FIG. 13.4 Are customers creatures meant for stucking on magnets?

Gobe (2001) writes that marketing vocabulary draws on warfare and conflict. Words such as campaigns, target, market domination, ambush, and market penetration show that communications are stuck in the past. 'In communication circles, the consumer is often approached as the "enemy" whom we must attack. It is us against them,' he writes. In marketing literature, we often find images showing customers getting stuck on fishhooks or stuck to a magnet (see Fig. 13.4). This creates unnecessary animosity.

Phillips, et al. (2010) say that this should be a wake-up call. People are not fish, whom companies are out to hook. Nor do people want to be hooked, or stuck, or attacked. 'When we begin to change our vocabulary, we begin to change the way we think. Customers know that they're "targets", and nobody wants to be a target. They'll even go out of their way to avoid your message,' they write.

Instead, companies must try to create a win-win partnership with customers based on a relationship of mutual trust. Instead of being in combat mode, they should focus on creating something that is so compelling that people start talking about it. In other words, they should create consumer movements so that customers recommend the products themselves, creating a buzz. The advertisements of companies must seek to ignite desire and passion, and focus on feelings and connections.

To understand customers, we have to peep into their minds to see how they think and understand the scenarios in which they buy products.

Understanding Customer Scenarios

The importance of understanding the consumer has been stressed in marketing literature. Companies do so by finding out who the customer is, by analysing demographic, socio-economic, and other data. However, to really understand the customer, companies have to understand how customers select, buy, and use products and services. This is called 'customer scenario' by Seybold (2001) in her article, *Get Inside the Lives of Your Customers*. She outlines some basic steps to develop customer scenarios.

Select the target set   Customers must be studied in the context in which they are buying.

Select a goal that the customer wants to fulfil   Companies should select a goal desired by customers and make it easy to fulfil it. For example, supermarkets can provide a customizable list of groceries and inform customers where these are located in the store.

Envision a situation for the customer   Companies must envision the situation in which customers use products. For instance, they must explain how the product or brand is useful: a refrigerator serving a large family will be used in different situations than one required by a small family.

Determine a start and end point for the scenario   Companies should visualize how consumers start consuming and how they finish the task.

Map out many variations of each scenario   Mentally walk through each step the consumer takes while consuming.

Map out individual activities the customer performs and work out every step   Can the company support these activities?

Integrate marketing, distribution, and service channels   Sales force, website, and call centre should be streamlined to help the consumer at every step.

The practical application of this approach is described in the chapter-end case study of National Semiconductors in Chapter 3. The next step is to understand the customer and his or her interactions with various media.

 EXHIBIT 13.1 Communication Strategy of Axe

After the day's work, you watch some television before going to sleep. Half-awake, you see—but hardly notice—advertisements tucked inside your favourite programmes. One of them is for a deodorant that you would never buy. It shows a hunk who sprays himself with it, and then suddenly all hell breaks loose: beautiful girls forget what they were doing and make a beeline for the hunk. There are accidents on the roads, boyfriends are abandoned, and shopping is forgotten.

You wake up the next day feeling that something is missing. It is a nagging feeling, and you feel incomplete without it. This feeling—a strong urge sometimes—stays with you till you buy what you saw the previous night.

Strange as it may sound, this feeling was induced in millions of people as they watched the television commercial and they felt that just had to start buying the product. The company, Unilever, dubbed this 'the AXE effect'.

Lindstrom (2011) writes, 'How Unilever created this now-legendary Axe campaign isn't just another demonstration of the power of sex in advertising; it's also a fascinating example of just how deeply companies and marketers probe the depths of our inner psyches—our hopes, dreams, and daydreams—in the service of crafting the kinds of provocative, scandalously sexual, and smashingly successful campaigns that push the very limits of advertising as we know it.'

Unilever was faced with a huge challenge of establishing a brand and cutting through the clutter, in what is essentially an add-on grooming product. In

(Contd)

EXHIBIT 13.1 (Contd)

the past, advertisements have highlighted the need for smelling good, but this was not a compelling reason for purchase. How should the company create a need so powerful that customers would buy Axe and not any other deodorant?

The communications of the company had to address four major objectives: (a) communicate the social and emotional benefits of using a fragrance, (b) excite consumers about a somewhat unexciting antiperspirant or deodorant, (c) adapt consumer behaviour to encourage use of deodorants, and (d) educate consumer usage of body sprays—all over the body.

An effective communications had to be backed by customer habits. In-depth, pre-launch research in the U.S. among the target (men aged 18–24) showed that product education was key to increasing purchase motivation. The strategy was: excite and educate! Unilever's Axe marketing team wanted consumers to be excited about something new; to see, hear, and interact with Axe everywhere.

How was this Communications Strategy Created?

First, the company learnt about the consumer. It studied 100 males and observed them in action. The company then identified six psychological profiles of the potential Axe user: the predator, the natural talent, the marriage-material guy, always the friend, the insecure novice, and the enthusiastic novice. On this basis, it identified three segments to target—the insecure novice, followed by the enthusiastic novice, and then the natural talent. The first two could be persuaded to buy Axe to increase their chances with girls, while the third would include the product as a finishing touch to his grooming.

Next, 30 second advertisements were made based on what the research had revealed to be the ultimate male fantasy. The ads were not subtle and directly confronted male and female sexuality.

The brand used social media to spread the message. A buzz was created with pictures of parties that allowed users to tag their own pictures. A graphic novel and pictures of activities increased engagement of the brand. Other Facebook pages include an Axe University and an Axe Angels Club. The risqué messages kept the interest alive in the brand.

Television programmes like 'Axe your ex' on Channel [V] supplemented the communications of the company.

The advertisements used tongue-in-cheek humour and showed the emotional and social benefits of smelling good. Non-traditional methods were used to build excitement around the brand. Consumers just could not miss the message: in movie theatres, on social networking websites, on radio, and on television. Some of the most risqué messages were created, which brought a smile on the faces of consumers.

Though the advertisements were often seen as 'stupid' by youngsters and several complaints of obscenity were filed, but it did touch an emotional chord and became a huge success.

Axe has been wildly successful all over the world. It has established itself as a cool, iconic, youth brand. Research shows that the brand awareness of Axe has continued to grow. The humour served another purpose: it encouraged online involvement of young people, with many ads going viral.

So powerful has been the Axe communications that many people have started associating deodorants with Axe. Though similar new products have been launched in the men's deodorant category, many would be hard pressed to remember their names. Importantly, most advertisements by competitors are following the Axe storyline that consumers find hard to differentiate. The Axe communications have firmly established the brand in the minds of customers.

The case shows why companies must understand consumer psyche before designing their communications. It also shows how the mass media is used to project the brand, while an online presence will multiply the mass media effect. Both should form the core of companies' communications strategy.

Should companies use direct messages? Are the complaints against the Axe advertisements justified?

The case mentions that competing products have been unable to get brand recall. If you were a competitor, how would you design your communications to counter the Axe effect?

Sources:
Kamra, Diksha, 'Deo ads face the Axe effect', *The Times of India*, 27 May 2011.
Lindstrom, Martin, *Brandwashed*, Crown Publishing Group, New York, 2011.
Lindstrom, Martin, 'Can a commercial be too sexy for its own good? Ask Axe', *The Atlantic Monthly*, 24 October 2011. http://www.theatlantic.com/business/archive/2011/10/can-a-commercial-be-too-sexy-for-its-own-good-ask-axe/246863/, last accessed on 9 May 2012.

Integrating Customer Experience

As the consumer is exposed to various media, there is need to understand consumers' interaction across different media and then draw them into an integrated experience. Sugiyama and Andree in their book, *The Dentsu Way* (2010) describe how this can be achieved. They advocate creating customer scenarios to move them through calibrated contact points. This approach is called the 'cross switch (CS)' and is described as 'flipping a switch in the consumer's mind.'

Cross switch employs a variety of methods across media which repeatedly push the consumer towards new levels of engagement. There are four elements of CS.

Target and media insight Instead of defining customers in terms of demographic characteristics, this approach emphasizes the combined insight of customers and media. That is, it tries to find out what consumers are thinking and what they want, their lifestyle and media behaviour, and discover the details of how they view and react to information—in combination.

Breadth and depth Cross communication approach tries to link messages with consumer behaviour, so that consumers are motivated to take action of their own accord. While breadth is the array or variety of information, depth is the amount of information available on each topic. The goal of communication is to strike a balance with both the breadth and depth of information in marketing communications.

Communications scenario The 'communication scenario' is the action path that helps draw target consumers outside of their information barriers, so that they voluntarily move towards products or brands.

Contact point planning The focus of contact points is to link the consumer with the brand. A customer may have contact with the brand through various points, such as television commercials, magazine articles, websites, and point of sale (POS) promotions. These media are integrated at all levels of consumer experience.

It is therefore essential that all channels—communication, sales, and marketing—be integrated into one strategy. Many companies make mistakes by outsourcing different activities. For example, many companies swear by customer relationship management (CRM) and claim in commercials that they are customer-focused, but if customers call the helpline numbers provided by the company, they enter an endless loop of automated options, and are made to press buttons put on infinite hold.

Shimp (2010) describes the synergistic effect of combining multiple communication tools. Used in conjunction with one another, they can 'produce greater results than tools used individually and in an uncoordinated fashion,' he writes. Research has shown that using print, TV, and online tools in an integrated fashion produces combined effects that are greater than the individual effects of each medium.

Synergy is also achieved through identifying and integrating all forms of touchpoints to achieve 360-degree branding. A touchpoint, also called 'moment of truth', is the point of contact of the product, brand, or service with customers. 360-degree branding refers to well-integrated marketing activities, so that the brand is presented similarly at all points of consumer contact.

All touchpoints must be treated as potential delivery channels. Companies use this by surrounding customers and potential customers at every possible opportunity and allowing them to interact with the company and use information. Shimp (2010) identifies four key features of the strategy.

- The consumer must represent the starting point of all communications.
- Use any or all marketing communication tools that can meet the objectives.
- Multiple messages must speak with a single voice.
- Build relationships rather than engage in one-time sales.

These steps not only help in branding but help establish message credibility.

Consumer Processing and Evaluation

Consumers have their own way of processing marketing communications. A major issue is whether consumers find that the communications are trustworthy and credible. Credibility refers to a person's perception of the truth of a piece of information. Due to the hard-sell that many companies employ, an element of distrust has been introduced in whatever companies say. Hoyer and MacInnis (2010) write, 'Consumers tend to perceive information through marketing sources as being less credible, more biased, and manipulative.' On the other hand, non-marketing sources, such as friends, relatives, and independent reviewers, are seen as more credible. That is, any person or group that does not have a personal stake will be seen as more credible than someone who does.

There are three aspects of credibility: *message credibility, channel credibility,* and *source credibility.*

Message Credibility

Message credibility is defined as a consumer's perception of the truthfulness and believability of the message. The way the message is crafted conveys a good deal to a consumer. Metzger, et al. (2008) mention three factors that impact message credibility: message structure, message content, and message delivery or presentation style.

Message structure It refers to the way that the message is organized: well-designed and well-organized messages are perceived as more credible than unorganized ones.

Message content It refers to information quality, language intensity, and message discrepancy. Well-written, interesting, and error-free messages with the use of high quality evidence from a qualified source are seen as credible. Consumers use five dimensions to assess quality of information: accuracy, comprehensiveness, currency, reliability, and validity.

Message delivery It is the way in which a message is presented. The delivery factors that impact credibility are the speaker's language, style, and speed—moderately fast speakers are seen as more credible than slow speakers.

Channel Credibility

Channel or media credibility refers to whether consumers perceive the channel of information to be credible. State-owned media are generally seen as less credible than independent media houses. The credibility of newspapers, magazines, and TV channels also depends on how established they

TABLE 13.2 Different types of channels and their credibility factor

Channel control	Type of channel	Credibility factor
Independent control	Radio	Variable, depending on the channel
	TV	Variable, depending on the channel
	Newspapers	Big branded newspapers—high
		Local newspapers/Tabloids—low
	Magazines	Specialist magazines—high
		General magazines—low
	Independent industry reports	High
Company controlled	Company press releases/ Communications	Low
	Company spokesperson	Low
	Company/Product advertising	Low
Consumer controlled	Conversations and word of mouth	Conversations between friends—high
	Wikipedia	High
	Online forums/Blogs	Variable, depending on reputation of the blog
	Social networking	High

are. Bigger brand names in media are generally seen as more credible than local channels. The channel credibility of different media and how consumers perceive them is shown in Table 13.2.

Source Credibility

Source credibility is the believability of a communicator—the person shown in the ad—as perceived by the consumer. Companies try to use credible spokespersons in their communications, since source credibility improves its persuasive impact. For example, housewives are shown speaking for a company where children's health is the issue, while trusted celebrities are shown where public trust is sought to be earned.

Eisend (2006) has studied source credibility based on factor analysis. He identifies three dimensions on which it depends and companies should be aware of them when striving for credibility.

Inclination toward truth Whether the consumer perceives that the source will tell the truth

Potential of truth Whether the consumer perceives that the source actually knows the truth

Presentation dimension Whether the consumer perceives that the presentation made by the company is based on facts

An expressive or exciting presentation intensifies the perception of truth inclination and potential, and a source would not be perceived as having an extreme inclination toward truth or potential of truth when the presentation is unexciting and inexpressive.

Eisend also examines credibility on the basis of three sources, namely company, salesperson, and spokesperson.

Company credibility The factors that impact company's credibility are trustworthiness, competence, and dynamism.

Salesperson's credibility Salespersons get their credibility from trustworthiness, competence, and attraction.

> **CB IN ACTION**   **Evaluating Advertisements**
>
> We have seen that consumers see marketing communications with a pinch of salt—they do not see the communications from companies as entirely credible.
>
> This exercise will help you find out the credibility of various companies and advertisements. Select five advertisements of different products and show them to a group of volunteers. Then ask them to rate the visuals on a five-point scale ranging from 'highly trustworthy' and 'highly untrustworthy'. A simple plotting of the percentages of the responses will show you which companies/advertisements are seen as trustworthy and which ones are not.
>
> If you have access to SPSS software, you can also analyse the reasons why respondents think the way they do. Develop a questionnaire listing the reasons such as sincerity, fairness, closeness to reality, objectivity, dynamism, and so on. Ask the respondents to rate the communications on each of these factors. Run the data on SPSS and identify which factors are most significant in establishing credibility of advertising messages.

Spokesperson's credibility   Company spokesmen must display sincerity and professionalism in addition to attraction.

Advertisers have to be careful that their claims do not look too outlandish. In India, the Advertising Standards Council of India (ASCI) promotes responsible advertising and acts on complaints. The ASCI code is given in Annexure 13.1.

MESSAGE STRATEGY

In Greek mythology, the Sirens were beautiful creatures, who sang such enchanting songs that sailors were lured to their deaths. Advertising messages try to do something similar: they lure people into buying things, while forgetting everything else. A message strategy consists of making such powerful messages.

Messages have to rise above the clutter and leave an impact on the consumer. However, advertising agencies sometimes resort to creating dramatic messages with an overdose of sex, humour, or by using grotesque images. Such techniques arouse curiosity for a while but do nothing for the brand. Effective communications, on the other hand, try first to understand consumer scenarios and then create messages that will appeal to the target customers.

The communications strategy of a company lays the foundation for designing a message that works. The company has to be clear about what it wants to say and how. As a first step in designing a message, companies have to decide how best they want to communicate with customers. They can use impersonal or interpersonal messages. How the messages are visualized and scripted will depend on which media are chosen.

Impersonal communications   Communications are impersonal when they are sent through a medium. Communications through mass media such as radio, newspapers, or television are impersonal, in the sense that they do not have direct contact with customers. Advertising agencies, media companies, and public relations companies deliver messages to the target audience in exchange for a fee.

Interpersonal communications When the message is delivered by personal interaction, such as by employing a salesman, interacting with customers through events or direct marketing methods, it is called interpersonal communication. Communication through peers, friends, and social groups are informal methods of interpersonal communication.

Usually companies use a combination of mass media and personal communication to reach target audiences. The advantage of mass media is that it is able to reach a large number of people, which is difficult through interpersonal communication. As Exhibit 13.1 on Axe shows, an impact was created through the use of mass communication. The same impact could not have been achieved using any direct media.

However, not all advertisements are as powerful. People may see a TV commercial and like it, but all it does is stay in the memory. As explained in Fogg's model, though mass media may create awareness, sometimes campaigns lack a trigger that makes customers go to a retail shop and buy. Interpersonal communications provide that trigger that affects purchase. So companies inform through mass media and provide a trigger by sending their salesmen, organize events, provide coupons and discounts for a purchase, and so on. The idea is that if you have seen something on television last night, here is an opportunity to try it out.

A model that is helpful to understand message strategy is the Elaboration Likelihood Model (ELM) that demonstrates how people get persuaded. It is described in the next section.

Elaboration Likelihood Model

Should the message be direct or indirect? The ELM shows when messages should be direct or indirect. Developed by Petty and Cacioppo (1986), it states that there are two routes through which persuasive messages are processed:

- The central route a straightforward route, is one where a person considers an idea relevant or interesting and so pays attention to the message. Consumers will actively consider the arguments presented by the advertiser and form attitudes and beliefs.
- The peripheral route is taken when consumers are not interested or motivated to think about the message. In such situations, companies employ means such as catchy tunes, colours, and celebrity endorsements, so that a person uses pre-existing ideas and superficial qualities to be persuaded.

How this works is shown in Fig. 13.5.

The ELM is useful for creating advertising messages. Messages sent through the central route must be straightforward and factual, and depend on thoughtful consideration of ideas and content. The consumer reads the message, scrutinizes the content, and evaluates the idea. Messages using the central route have a high level of consumer involvement; they care about the subject and thus will evaluate the message. Every word will be read and analysed, so consumers are directly affected by the message.

The peripheral route of persuasion is used for products with low receiver involvement. The consumer does not process the messages cognitively but is likely to be persuaded by factors that have nothing to do with the product. For example, candy is a low-involvement purchase since one

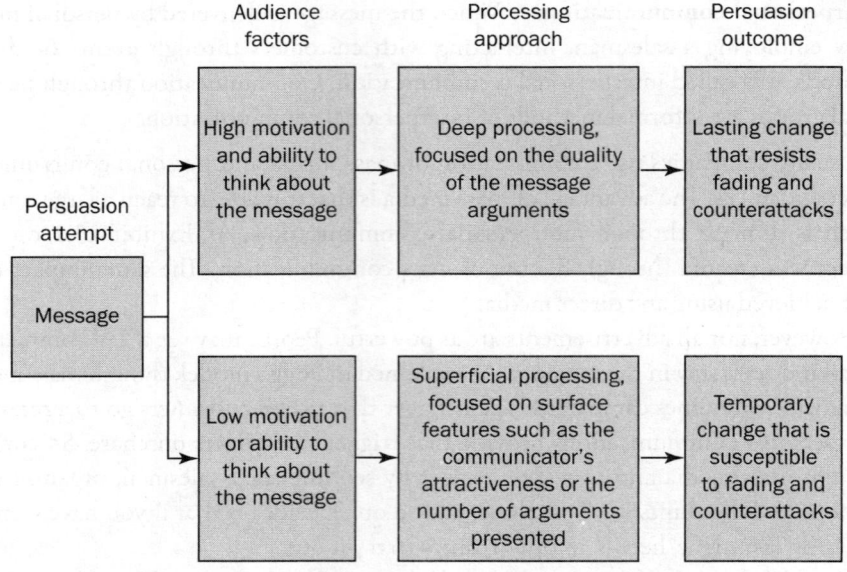

FIG. 13.5 Elaboration Likelihood Model

Source: Kenrick, Neuberg, and Cialdini (2002)

brand of candy is almost the same as that of any competitor. Advertisers use the peripheral route for such products. They try to grab attention by evoking positive feelings in consumers and hope that they will get attached to the product.

Advertising appeals are created after understanding which route the company wants to take in the ELM model. A careful understanding is important because using a peripheral route for a high-involvement purchase might trivialize the brand itself, while using a central route for a low-involvement purchase will be seen as puffery.

Types of Messages

Devising persuasive messages is a complex task simply because it is difficult to know beforehand what appeals to consumers and what does not. A company has to answer several questions for devising powerful messages.

- Should it stress on a unique benefit or a host of product benefits?
- Should the message be in words or pictures? What type of pictures must be used?
- Should the product be compared to competing products directly or indirectly?
- Should it present a conclusion or leave it for the consumer to decide?
- Should a famous celebrity be used or should the ad show slice-of-life?
- Should the message have sex, humour, or fear appeal?

Answering these and other questions will result in creating powerful communications that do not get lost in the clutter. Advertisements use different types of messages to get their ideas across to consumers.

Visual Messages

Pictures are a powerful means employed in ads as they make an immediate impact. They are easily remembered, and result in changing beliefs and attitudes about products and companies. Consider the example of a powerful brand, Benetton (see chapter-end case study), the ads for which were created using such powerful images that they created advertising history. Factual information, however, has to be conveyed in words, which are used in high-involvement purchases. Normally, advertisers use *framed ads*, in which a visual is accompanied by text.

One or Two-sided Messages

One-sided messages are those in which product superiority is claimed on all attributes. Most advertising messages are one-sided and are suitable for loyal consumers who are favourably disposed towards the product or brand. Such customers will not like to hear anything against the product. A two-sided message, on the other hand, is one in which the advertiser recognizes attributes where the product may not be superior. Studies have indicated that two-sided messages tend to elicit more favourable ad attitudes than one-sided messages. Domino's went against conventional wisdom and launched truthful ads that criticized its own products and found that its sales increased.

GLOBAL INSIGHT
Does Truth in Advertising Work?

How truthful should companies be in their advertising messages? Usually advertising agencies resort to conventional wisdom that consumers perceive 'what is beautiful is good'. Models are air-brushed to make them look better than they are, pictures of food items show them to be more attractive than they actually are, and the world of advertising is populated by perfect objects and perfect human beings, even if they are fictional.

Gregory (2011) describes how Domino's used the two-sided messages to its advantage in the US. It launched a 'just tell it like it is' campaign, asking people to write what they thought of the product. Taking a page from Wikileaks, it wanted to be more transparent and truthful, not using photographic tricks to make their pizzas look better than the actual product. Reflecting consumer dissatisfaction with its products, the company used words written by unhappy customers to describe its products such as 'cardboard' and 'mass produced, boring, bland' in its advertising in 2009.

It was rather a bold move. Sauer (2010) wondered, 'Is this level of openness admirable? Sure. Is it stupid? Perhaps.'

However, the bold approach paid off. The company used the advertisements for its launch of a new pizza recipe in 2009-10, sending a simple message: 'We admit we made a mistake. We're trying to improve. Give our pizza another chance.' It was a risk the company took to criticize its own product.

The messages worked, showing that honesty sells. By doing this, Domino's engineered one of the more impressive turnarounds in the restaurant industry. In 2010, U.S. same-store sales rose 9.9 per cent, in a market in which 1 per cent to 3 per cent growth is the norm.

The honest advertising led to people believing the chain and trying out the new pizzas. Instead of hearing, 'It's new and improved', a statement that customers are accustomed to hearing all the time, the company admitted that there were problems, and the honesty worked with customers.

The Domino's example offers lessons for companies. One-sided campaigns result in companies talking at customers rather than with them, and such messages tend to be ignored. The lesson is that great brands are built by engaging customers and that is how two-sided communications work.

(Contd)

GLOBAL INSIGHT (Contd)

Domino's let consumers post feedback—good and bad—on its Facebook page and posted all Twitter comments about the new pizza on the company website. Along with the strong advertising, the company delivered a new pizza recipe with a better sauce and richer crust.

Traditional marketing says that companies should always focus on good aspects and differentiate. Domino's USP had been, 'We'll deliver our pizza to you very quickly and reliably' for 49 years even if the pizza was average in taste. The company was able to resolve the conflict between not only delivering quickly but also in making a better pizza.

How far should companies be truthful in their advertising? Was the Domino's campaign an exception?

Sources:
Gregory Sean, 'Domino's new recipe: (Brutal) truth in advertising, *Time*, May 2011.
Sauer Abe, 'Domino's to pizza-lovers: Can you handle the truth?, *Brand Channel*, 8 July 2010, http://www.brandchannel.com/home/post/2010/07/08/Dominos-Gets-Real.aspx, last accessed on 7 January 2014.

Comparative Advertising

When a company compares its brand with a competing brand to claim superiority of its product over others by direct comparison, it is called comparative advertising. There are two types of comparative advertising: indirect comparative advertising (ICA), which does not name any particular rival brand, and compares it with 'Brand x'. Direct comparative advertising (DCA) occurs when an advertisement cites a well-known brand and makes a direct comparison. The idea is that consumers will be influenced when two brands are compared side by side. In India, such advertising has been seen in Tide versus Rin and Pepsodent versus Colgate. Comparison also generates perceived similarity among brands and is a means by which brands can get associated with the market leader.

Research shows that naming competing brands works. Dianoux, et al. (2013) show that a comparative ads that cites the name of a competing leader or high-market-share brand, along with price information, increases purchase intentions toward the sponsored brand, more than when the name of the brand is not shown and replaced with 'Brand x'. Naming the brand increases the probability of message processing, with a higher probability that consumers perceive the ad content as compelling. However, competitors do not like to be shown in a derogatory manner and law suits often result from blatant comparisons among brands.

Repetition

Companies repeat their advertising messages because it increases exposure to the brand and, up to a certain point, leads to better recall and favourable impressions of the brand. Repetition has to be used with care. While repeated ads result in brand familiarity, it can also result in *advertising wear-out*—the declining effectiveness of the advertisement due to increased exposure since consumers get bored seeing the same thing over and over again. Consumers get so used to seeing an advertisement that they stop paying attention to it. Campbell and Keller (2003) find that processing of ads is different with repetition depending on the familiarity with the brands, and that brand familiarity influenced repetition effectiveness. Repetition of advertising of an unfamiliar brand showed decreased effectiveness as opposed to a known, familiar brand.

Berlyne's (1970) two-factor theory states that repetition increases familiarity but over time, boredom increases with each exposure. The first phase, called 'wear-in' is when the consumer learns about the product. In this phase, there may be some hostility or uncertainty about a new message. Message repetition increases positive feelings and reduces negative responses. The second phase is when continued repetition results in tedium so that the message decreases in effectiveness and results in 'wear-out'.

Message Appeals

Advertising or message appeals are a way of persuading people to identify with products. They are designed to create a positive image of consumers who use those products. Companies use different types of advertising appeals to influence the purchasing decisions of people. An advertising or message appeal is the primary claim used in an advertisement. Most advertisements have one major appeal designed for consumers, which has little to do with the merits of the product itself. Instead, advertising appeals to the emotions such as happiness or fear, or other aspects of their consumer's lives. Words, images, and music are used to show how owning a brand will increase one's social standing, happiness, attractiveness, or security.

While creating persuasive messages, it is important to find out what sells. Some of the common advertising appeals are described in this section (see Exhibit 13.2), along with their intended impact.

Fear

Fear appeals are commonly used in marketing communications. Insurance, health products, and certain toilet products are sold on the premise of protecting users from unforeseen events or infections, which may or may not exist. The basic message in fear appeals is: 'If you don't buy/vote for/believe/support/learn this, a very bad thing will happen to you.' The negative results of not using a product are highlighted. Fear appeals are also used to discourage people from following certain behaviour, such as smoking or drinking alcohol.

On the other hand, fear appeals are sometimes used to encourage use of these products.

Humour

There are two points of view regarding use of humour in advertisements. The first is that since advertisements are salesmen for brands, and people do not buy from clowns. The opposing point of view is that humour increases the likeability of the brand and improves recall.

> ### EXHIBIT 13.2 Message Appeals According to Ogilvy
>
>
>
> David Ogilvy lists ten kinds of commercial appeals which are above average in their ability to change brand preference. These are as follows:
>
> - Humour
> - Slice of life
> - Testimonials
> - Demonstrations
> - Problem solution
> - Talking heads
> - Characters
> - Reason why
> - News
> - Emotion
>
> *Source*: Ogilvy, David *Ogilvy on Advertising*, Prion Books, London, 1983, pp. 14–15.

In India, the usual form of humour is imitation of film stars and of scenes of certain movies like *Sholay*. Radio ads frequently use such imitations. Highlighting linguistic or regional lifestyles or accents provide some more sources of mirth.

While it is true that a good joke will help the advertisements stand out of the clutter, some advertisers make the mistake of using humour for its own sake. The result is that people enjoy the humour but the advertisement does nothing to increase sales. Tuttle (2012) writes that though funny ads grab viewers' attention, they are not effective in steering viewers buy the product that is advertised. Citing research conducted by Ace Metrix, he says that funny ads are 'more appealing and more memorable than their unfunny counterparts', but they are 'less likely to increase desire or intent to purchase than commercials that played it straight.'

Another study by Millward Brown (2013) finds a strong relationship between humour and impact because humour drives involvement and is therefore memorable. However, it adds that humour does not aid persuasion, as humorous ads are seen as a little less credible and relevant. The way to use humour is to make humorous ads that are persuasive as well.

Sex

Advertisers often resort to using sexual images in advertisements in an effort to stand out. Images of glamorous women are used even when they have nothing to do with the advertised product. For instance, images of scantily-dressed women are frequently used in launches of cars. One advertisement for cement displays a glamorous girl and sometimes even a bikini-clad girl. Double entendres are used in ads for candy and other unrelated products.

Even if it does not relate to the product, explicit sexual imagery is used to attract attention, in which it succeeds. However, Hawes (2010) writes that it has also been shown in multiple studies that most people respond negatively to advertising in which the sexual image has little relevance to the advertised product. Sengupta and Dahl (2008) found men often reported positive attitudes towards sexually explicit ads while women on average exhibited a marked negative reaction to them. This indicates that for almost half the population, the cliché 'sex sells' may not hold.

Emotion

Happy families, attractive couples deep in love, a girl running to a cricket field and doing a dance, chuckling babies, friends singing a song in a classroom—these are images that arouse positive emotions among us. Advertisers love to use them. Erik Du Plessis in his book, *The Advertised Mind* (2005) writes, 'Emotion is critical to advertising because it is critical to all human thought. It plays a critical role in guiding our instinctive reaction to events happening around us.'

Mehta and Purvis (2006) explain that consumers do not make brand purchase choices at the time of advertising exposure; rather, it is the memory of the advertising messages that influences consumers. Advances in neurology show that it is emotion rather than cognitive/rational response that guides our attention. Emotions are therefore powerful tools. Studies have shown that advertisements evoking a positive emotional response are remembered more.

However, there are two questions that managers have to answer while using emotional communications. First, are the emotions understood and interpreted in the way the advertiser wants them to be? Second, while they are remembered, do they succeed in selling products?

In their research, Williams and Aaker (2000) found that emotional messages are interpreted differently by different groups of people. For instance, a young girl sharing a chocolate with a boy in a chocolate commercial will be interpreted differently across age-groups, and also by males and females. Youngsters may feel that doing so is all right, but an older person may feel that the girl is stupid as she may be 'falling' for the boy. Such storylines are also interpreted differently in different cultures.

To the question whether emotions sell products, the answer is ambiguous because some campaigns selling emotions are phenomenally successful, while others are not, despite the fact that they are memorable.

Slice of Life

Slice of life is an advertising technique where a real-life situation is dramatized and a product is shown as the solution to a common problem. In these ads, a real-life experience is represented realistically with the hope that it convinces ordinary people. Made famous by Procter and Gamble in the 1950s, it was used in the early days of television advertising to reach millions of people in their homes. The slice of life communication usually has four components: encounter, problem, interaction, and finally the solution.

O'Guinn and Allen (2009) give the reasoning of such communications—they say that brands placed in social settings gain meaning by association. By embedding the idea in everyday life, consumers are able to associate their own lives with the depiction and thus they have fewer questions about the product. One of the most successful uses of slice-of-life method has been the commercial by ICICI Prudential in which a lady uses *sindoor* to emphasize the security and bonding of marriage.

However, advertisers have to be careful while presenting slice-of-life commercials. If not done well, the picture will ring false and will be rejected by the audience. For instance a commercial of a chocolate company showing ragging taking place in a college took a drubbing on online posts and was criticized by professionals. Rangaswami (2012) wrote, 'Ragging doesn't make me feel warm and fuzzy. This is not a *Shubh* anything. The commercial shows a few students being ragged at their college. It shows bullies and the bullied. And, tragically, it shows the "clever" victim bribing his way out of trouble.'

In India, slice-of-life commercials are frequently used. A little too frequently, as Shatrujeet (2003) has pointed out. 'A consensus emerging from within the industry is that slice of life, as a genre, is being done to death.' Too much use of a technique results in viewer fatigue, that is, people start disbelieving such commercials or turn away from them.

Hedonic and Utilitarian Appeals

Advertisements can either appeal to emotions of consumers or can inform about product attributes and features. Emotional ads usually outperform rational ones in terms of the attitude towards the ad and the brand. These two opposing appeals are called hedonic and utilitarian.

Hedonic appeals Hedonic appeals place emphasis on the image or the value-expressive function. They involve building a personality for the product, from which consumers may project images, values, and lifestyles of product users. Hedonic appeals are characterized by their focus on promoting attractive user portrayals. Emotional advertising is important for low-involvement products. For example, ads for Maggi noodles—a low-involvement purchase—stress on children, families, and joyful emotions. Its advertising line in 2013–14 (https://www.maggi.in/default.aspx) was '*2 minute mein khushiyan*', meaning 'happiness in 2 minutes'.

Utilitarian appeals Such appeals cater to functional aspects of the product. The utilitarian appeal addresses product attributes or focuses on product quality claims. Utilitarian products often use a rational, message-oriented appeal. For high-involvement products—expensive products that are purchased only after long and careful consideration, such as a car, refrigerator, or home—there is emphasis on product differentiation, not appeals to the emotions. For example, in the mobile phone industry, brands such as Samsung, Nokia, and Apple base their communication on their phone's key features, which helps them differentiate on clear rational benefits.

Apart from hedonic and utilitarian message appeals, companies use several more advertising appeals that complete the communications arsenal. Their application, intention, and impact, are summarized in Table 13.3.

TABLE 13.3 Persuasive techniques

Advertising appeal	Application	Explanation and intention	Impact
Bait and switch	'Up to 60 per cent off!'	Advertisement or salesperson lures customers by offering bargains	Consumers end up buying more expensive goods
Bandwagon	'You don't have a mobile with a double SIM card, Uncle?'	'Everybody else' buys these products	Consumers want to conform, so buy the products. Assumption is that if others buy it, the product must be good
Celebrities	'Boost is the secret of my energy.'	Celebrity or star endorses a product	Feelings for the celebrity or star transferred to the product
Comparison	'My shirt is whiter than yours.'	Compares a product with the 'inferior' competition	Consumers believe the product is better
Demonstration	'The health drink made my child grow taller.'	Shows how product is used or effects of consuming a product	Customers get convinced about the efficacy of products
Emotional appeals	'Happiness in 2 minutes.'	Make viewers feel happy, excited, or fearful, family and group appeals	Consumers transfer emotion to the product
Humour	'Teeth so white you don't need a bulb.'	Used to make audiences laugh	Results in high recall. Products seen as unique, stylish, or cool
Loaded language Double entendre	'Everyone wants it.'	Uses words with double meanings in ads, attempt to run down a competitor	Intended to generate negative feelings for competitors
Name-calling	'Bujhaiye sirf pyaas, baaki sab bakwaas.'	Shows people or groups in poor light to discredit their products	Companies hope that controversy will help get publicity for the brand
Noble causes	'Be a green consumer.'	Highlight valued beliefs, such as patriotism, peace, freedom, or green concerns	Influences like-minded consumers even though claim may not be correct
Problem-solving	'Seven days to fairer skin.'	Attempts to solve a problem that a consumer has	Customers with similar problems are attracted

(Contd)

TABLE 13.3 (Contd)

Advertising appeal	Application	Explanation and intention	Impact
Slice of life	'Good for my family.'	Shows ordinary people using or supporting a product	Consumers trust the product because it's good enough for ordinary people
Testimonials	'I couldn't walk, but now I run everyday.'	Narrates experience of others	Customers get convinced to use products by watching others

Message as Art Form

Marshall McLuhan mentioned in an interview in 1969 that advertising is the greatest art form of the twentieth century. Though it is a form of communication, it attracts, convinces, persuades, and affects us deeply. Many companies create ads that are beautiful to behold and affect us in similar ways that art does. Indeed, the ads of many companies are seen displayed in museums and restaurants all over the world. Some companies are known for their collaboration with artists. Pop artist Andy Warhol turned the Campbell's soup can into art; artists design bottles, labels, packages, and ads. Benetton hired award-winning photographer Oliviero Toscani who created some of the most memorable advertising for the company (see chapter-end case study).

However, ads and art must seek a balance. Ultimately, companies seek to sell products through advertising. In his book, *Ogilvy on Advertising* (1985), David Ogilvy wrote, 'I do not regard advertising as entertainment or art form, but as a medium of information. When I write an advertisement, I don't want you to tell me that you find it "creative". I want you to find it so interesting that you buy the product.'

Once the message has been formulated, companies have to figure out where to place the messages. The idea is to reach consumers through media that they find most credible, and also to reach them when they are most conducive to product suggestions. These questions are answered by media strategy.

MEDIA STRATEGY

In reaching the target customers, companies have to figure out what media to use. The media strategy is concerned with how messages are delivered to consumers. Messages should be precisely targeted so that customers get them, at a time when they are open to receiving marketing messages. Companies often spend huge amounts only to find that their advertising has been lost. Media strategy involves identifying customers, analysing which media they use, understanding media characteristics, and finally selecting the proper media for message delivery. Several types of media are explained in the next section.

Types of Media

There are two types of media: *mass media*, consisting of television, newspapers and radio, and *interactive methods* such as direct selling, direct mail, organizing events, and online interactions.

Usually a combination of media must be used. For instance, if a company relies only on television, it may succeed in making customers aware, but unless a trigger is provided through direct sales and promotions, customers may not feel motivated enough to actually go to a shop and buy the product. On the other hand, if a company relies only on online media, it may lose out on the mass market. How a company mixes media forms the basis of marketing strategy.

There is a variety of media available for companies to use. These are given in Table 13.4.

TABLE 13.4 Types of media available for marketing communications

Mass media	Media available	
Mass media	• Newspapers • Magazines • Television	• Radio • In-movie product placements
Direct response media	• Interactive television (ITV) • Testimonials • Trade shows, samples, coupons • Event marketing, parties, gatherings	• Advertorials, infomercials • Tele-calling
Place advertising	• Out-of-home media (OOH) • Store signage, point-of-purchase displays (POP) • Billboards	• Posters and pamphlets • Cinema ads
Interactive media	• Online media—Websites • Online media—Social networking sites • E-commerce and online merchants	• Word-of-mouth (WOM) and viral marketing • Brand communities • Opinion leaders, reference groups
Mobile media	• SMS	• E-commerce

Combining the different types of media is the basis of media mix strategy. Companies do not want to throw money at the media without results. They want to achieve results, so reach, cost, credibility, efficiency, and measurability should always be the focus of managers. The media used should answer the following questions:

- Does it have the ability to *reach* the customers intended?
- How expensive is it? What is the rupee *cost* per customer?
- Does the media chosen have *credibility*?
- Can it reach consumers fast and convert them into customers *efficiently*?
- Are analytics available to *measure* results?
- Does it *engage* customers?

A comparison of media on the aforegiven parameters is in Table 13.5. What media a company uses depends on its objectives; a mix is usually chosen since different media vary on their efficiencies. Developing a media mix is a difficult task because not only is media becoming increasingly expensive, but also it is becoming fragmented. This aspect is discussed next.

Fragmentation of Media

Joachimsthaler and Aaker (1997) write that though mass media has been the cornerstone of all brand-building efforts, that norm is threatening to become obsolete. 'Fragmentation and rising

TABLE 13.5 Comparison of various media

Parameter	Newspapers	Magazines	Television	Radio	Internet
Reach	Very large, in all languages, high readership	Specialized, segmented audience	Very large, mass medium	FM stations provide regional and local reach	Penetration about 10%, but increasing Large number of SEC A households
Cost	Very high	Very high	Very high during prime time	Comparatively cheap	Very cheap per click rates
Credibility	High	High	Message-dependent	Low	Variable
Efficiency	High clutter, messages can be changed for different regions and languages	High quality printing, but high clutter, long life as some magazines are preserved	Short-duration, multimedia messages, great impact but short recall, high clutter	Ideal for local business, messages in regional languages	Targeted advertising, dependent on individuals, high clutter, ads, e-mails likely to be missed
Measurability	Dependent on figures provided by National Readership Survey (NRS)	Dependent on figures provided by NRS	Dependent on television rating points (TRPs)	Low	Very high
Engagement	Somewhat—easy to distribute coupons	Somewhat—delayed	None—viewers change channels during commercials	Little—viewers likely to change channels or forget	Very high

costs are already inhibiting marketing through traditional mass media like television. New communication channels, which, in some cases, allow individuals to bypass advertising—are already in use,' they write.

BBC (2012) reports that India has more than 70,000 newspapers and over 500 satellite channels with more than 80 news channels as on December 2011, and is the biggest newspaper market in the world with over 100 million copies being sold each day.

Similarly, there are 1,400 television stations as of 2009 according to Wikipedia, and the country ranks fourth in the list of countries by number of television broadcast stations.

Companies face a big dilemma as to which newspapers or channels to choose to broadcast their message. Choosing TV channels or newspapers becomes a difficult task because of the number of options. Because of this, advertisers have to be very careful in devising mass media strategies in order to reach their target audience. Though data and TRPs about the reach of various media are available, multiplicity in each category adds to the confusion.

Websites too have a problem of fragmentation. Companies have their own websites but the problem often is how to drive traffic to these sites. E-commerce sites depend on the number of visitors but advertising for customers is an expensive proposition (see Chapter 16). Due to this, many companies prefer to host their products on the sites of e-merchants rather than sell themselves. For example, Sony has its own website but does not sell on it, even though its products are available on a host of e-commerce sites. Regarding social media, companies have to track C2C conversations on a number of sites, which is again a difficult task.

Cost is another inhibiting factor. A newspaper like *The Times of India* charged ₹3925 per square cm for its Mumbai edition in 2012. A *single* ad of 4 cm × 4 cm (one column) in that edition cost ₹62,800. Channels too charge high rates: Colors charged ₹1.5–₹1.75 lakh for 10 seconds for its Bigg Boss 4 programme. For weekends, the rate went up to ₹2.5 lakh per ten seconds (*The Economic Times*, 18 November 2010).

With media costs going up by the day, an intelligent media mix becomes more important. For a national campaign, with multiple slots and repeat advertising, the cost can go through the roof. Designing persuasive communications and choosing the appropriate media therefore become crucial.

Different media have their own advantages and disadvantages. These are summed up in Table 13.6.

TABLE 13.6 Advantages and disadvantages of different media channels

Medium	Advantages	Disadvantages
Newspapers	• Geographic selectivity and flexibility • Short-term commitment, quick results	• Little demographic selectivity • Expensive • Declining readership
Magazines	• Good colour reproduction • Targeted audience • High pass along rate	• Long-term commitment • Lack of urgency • Long lead time
Radio	• Low cost • Immediacy of message • Can be done on short notice • No seasonal change in audience • Short term	• Lacks visual treatment • Short message life • High frequency required to generate retention • Clutter
Television	• Wide audience • Low cost/thousand • Audio and visual messages, demonstrations are easy • Immediate results • Entertainment carryover	• Short life • Growing consumer skepticism, remote for skipping ads • High cost • Long production time • Clutter
Outdoor	• Moderate cost • Flexibility • Placement selectivity • Local Reach	• Short message • Lack of demographic selectivity
Internet	• Micro-targeted messages • Short lead time • Moderate cost	• Difficult to convert visitors • Exposure relies on click through rates • Requires Internet access

Sometimes companies try to blend into the editorial matter of newspapers by creating an advertisement that looks like a news story. These are called *advertorials*. Though an advertorial should have a declaration saying that it is an advertisement and should have a different font than that of the newspaper, yet some people do believe that it is the view of the newspaper and thus has more credibility.

CB IN ACTION Analysing Messages

We have seen that marketing communications must start with the customer, build persuasive messages, and choose the media that reaches the target market. This exercise requires you to analyse current advertisements and see whether the aforementioned objectives are met or not.

Select about ten advertisements and watch them with your friends. After watching each commercial, answer the following questions relating to it. Tabulate the answers as shown here. On the basis of answers received, assess whether the company is using all the elements of consumer behaviour and communications correctly. What would you advise the company about their message and media strategy?

	Respondent 1	Respondent 2	Respondent 3	Respondent 4
What is the main message you get from this ad?				
What does the advertiser want you to know, believe, or do?				
Will you undertake the implied action after watching this ad?				
What works well in the ad and what works poorly?				
How does the ad make you feel?				
In which media and where would you be most likely to notice the ad and pay attention to it?				

Direct-response advertising comes in two ways: distributing leaflets which carry discount coupons and 'infomercials' that are aired on television. Infomercials are long-format television commercials, typically five minutes or longer. They are also known as paid programming or teleshopping, and are shown outside of peak hours; they also include a phone number or website so that people can place direct orders.

In terms of credibility, *testimonials* and *word-of-mouth* publicity have more credibility in the minds of consumers. For example, after seeing a doctor recommending a miracle cure for short height or cavities for a child, people tend to believe that it is actually recommended by doctors. Similarly, if a friend or a trusted person recommends a product, people will tend to believe the recommendation more than an advertisement.

Above- and below-the-line campaigns

The combination of media that a company uses for its marketing communications is referred to as its media mix. It is helpful to understand the media mix in terms of above the line or below the line. The 'line' refers to the accounting term used to describe current or capital expenditure.

Above the line Above the line (ATL) communications refer to mass media campaigns, using television, out-of-home media (OOH), magazines, cinema, newspapers, and radio. In terms of the AIDA model described earlier in the Chapter, ATL refers to awareness or attention stage.

Above the line is long-term brand building, so it is in the nature of capital expenditure, whereas below the line is a current expenditure.

Below the line Below the line (BTL) communications refer to activities that provide incentive to purchase, using promotional methods such as catalogues, trade fairs and direct marketing activities. It consists of short duration campaigns and promotions, consisting of direct mail, sampling, and sales promotion activities, including organizing events. Activities such as telemarketing, road shows, promotions, in-shop, shop front activities, and display units are also part of BTL campaigns. The results are immediate or short term, so the expenditure incurred on BTL campaigns is classified as current or revenue expenditure. BTL encourages 'touch and feel' of products. If celebrities and stars are used or if the promotion is otherwise unusual or dramatic, it will also result in very high brand recall. This kind of campaign encourages Interest + Desire in the AIDA model.

Through the line Through the line (TTL) uses both ATL and BTL communications, that is, mass communications and direct marketing activities. It is necessary to do so, because it is important to first inform, and then engage with customers at various levels. Emergence of social media allows person to person (P2P) communications, which may affect brands. Thus, mass media needs to be supplemented by BTL campaigns. However, smaller companies wanting to avoid high mass media spends will consider using only BTL communications but their mass reach will be limited.

The chapter-opening case study illustrates how BTL campaigns are used effectively by companies, especially in India where reaching villages through the mass media is a hard task. Increasingly, companies are using such techniques to reach the interiors, as well as to counter the high cost of mass media.

The characteristics of ATL and BTL campaigns are summarized in Table 13.7.

TABLE 13.7 Comparison of ATL and BTL communication strategies

Parameter	ATL campaigns	BTL campaigns
Reach	• Mass audience	• Targets individuals or groups • Addresses specific needs
Cost	• High campaign cost	• Low campaign cost
Credibility	• High, especially in established media	• Varies with the event
Efficiency	• Highly efficient—can communicate to large numbers at the same time	• Caters to groups of people, hence not very efficient
Measurability	• Metrics are available	• Number of people contacted can be measured
Engagement	• Low	• High
Action	• Establishes brands, identities, and brand personality • Promotes emotional concepts of brands	• Encourages direct engagement, sampling, or discounts • Results in high recall
Customer response	• May not drive customer response	• Drives customer response • Immediate sales may result
Impact on customer relations	• Very little or none	• Establishes one-to-one relationships with consumers

MARKETING INSIGHT
Below-the-line Promotional Techniques

Direct communications, consisting of mailers, brochures, road shows, sampling, events, phone calls, emails, and digital contacts, are being favoured by advertisers as a cost-effective, measurable medium in these times. One-to-one communications market is estimated at ₹1000 crore-plus yearly as in 2012, with likely annual growth of 15–20 per cent.

BTL campaigns involve non-media communication such as group events in which the brand is promoted. These are also becoming important in the marketing mix of many companies and some companies are spending large amounts on such events. Advertising agencies have started separate divisions to offer below-the-line promotion solutions to companies. The Mudra Group started Celsius, a division offering integrated event solutions, in 2008. It offers integrated communications planning and implementation services within and outside the country. The division is able to provide its clients a range of services including designing branded experiences, creating thematic programs, and maximizing the impact of brand communications.

One memorable campaign undertaken by the company was the launch of Slim Can by Pepsi. It enlisted Bollywood actor John Abraham for the 20-day promotion in which he performed mass workouts with people in malls and multiplexes across Mumbai, New Delhi, and Bangalore. The event, which had a budget of around ₹1.5 crore, resulted in Pepsi getting 40,000 calls asking about the mass workouts. However, these techniques are suited for companies who want to create awareness through need engagement, not just with consumers, but also with intermediaries such as dealers and distributors. Some other innovative BTL campaigns are as follows:

UTV Bindass Youth channel UTV Bindass too, took the BTL route to promote its new fiction show for youngsters, *Meri Toh Lag Gayi...Naukri!* The activity, conceptualized by Mudra Concrea, was executed across colleges in various cities. The aim was to capture the attention of the youth, but as many of them were busy with exams, the activities were designed to bring relief to such students. The channel identified places that youngsters frequent, one of them being shops photocopying services.

To involve the students, the channel initiated a free photocopy campaign outside various colleges. Each photocopied sheet carried a Bindass message 'Do not get stressed out' at the end.

This campaign was supplemented by another on-ground initiative outside examination halls—a facility to provide comfort to stressed-out students. UTV Bindass placed 'comforters' outside such centres, to soothe students coming out of the examination halls. The centres offered students wipes to beat the summer heat, and gave them tips such as 'take a chill pill' and 'don't get stressed' to remain calm during exams.

Reliance Mutual Fund Ogilvy One Worldwide created a campaign for Reliance Mutual Fund's Systematic Investment Plan (SIP). Breaking from the tradition of targeting investment promotions for men only, the company wanted to woo housewives too. OgilvyOne placed boxes that resembled detergent cartons in supermarket shopping aisles. Each box contained a booklet and information on the Reliance SIP. In all, 10,000 packs were put up. They generated 3,000 leads, and 1,000 investors in the SIPs. Of these, 600 were women investors. The campaign cost was ₹1.5 lakh but its success was phenomenal.

Brufen Softra Lodestar's campaign for Abbot Pharmaceuticals was another innovative campaign. A contest for doctors was planned, where doctors had to write Brufen Softra in three different calligraphic styles. This was done in 58 cities, with the help of 45 key field managers; 9000 doctors were contacted. This generated 8605 responses from the doctors. ORG-MARG figures stated that Brufen Softra saw a 35 per cent increase in prescription presence, with an average of 65,000 prescriptions each month. More than 5200 doctors started writing the word, Softra.

Asian Paints Asian Paints wanted to promote its glow in the dark paints to children. Ogilvy & Mather created a glow-in-the-dark Cinderella storybook, and at the end of the book, there was a message that said, 'Make the magical glow of these come alive on your walls.' The books were given out to children in 13 cities at malls and bookstores. Glow-in-the-dark bookmarks and pencils were also given away. Soon

(Contd)

MARKETING INSIGHT (Contd)

after this innovation, Asian Paints had about 278 homes painted.

Sources:
Chandran, Anushree, 'Direct marketing is the new ad mantra', *Mint*, 1 July 2009.
Das, Nandana, 'UTV Bindass comforts students during exams', afaqs! New Delhi, 25 March 2011: http://www.afaqs.com/media/story.html?sid=30059, last accessed on 13 September 2011.
Sayal, Surina, 'Emvies 2008: Direct marketing saw innovations galore', afaqs!, 23 July 2008 http://www.afaqs.com/news/story.html?sid=21725_%3Cfont+color=#CC0033>Emvies+2008: +Direct+marketing+saw+innovations+galore, last accessed on 13 September 2011.

These steps not only help in branding but help establish message credibility as well. Since the secret is consumer engagement, companies must use WOM techniques in their strategy. The methods are described in Chapter 12. In this chapter, we see how these techniques are used by companies.

WOM Techniques

Companies try to build credibility through various means by encouraging people-to-people interactions. The idea is that if people talk about brands, credibility will be higher because they are obtaining the information from friends and from those whom they trust. The methods used are as follows:

Using Opinion Leaders

Companies create or use *opinion leaders*—a doctor, teacher, religious leader, or a housewife—people who are held in regard by others and who recommend goods or brands to them. Direct marketing companies such as Amway and Tupperware too, operate through the organizers of kitty parties, for example, to put up an exhibition and sale of their products. Figure 13.6 shows products by Tupperware. The idea is that if sold by friends, people will not doubt the quality of the products. Opinion leaders also are very active online.

FIG. 13.6 Stylish Products by Tupperware

Source: Superbrands 2012

Building Brand Communities

Companies also create *brand communities*—the brand is connected to various activities to create a cultural setting for it. Brand communities are both offline and online. People are able to interact with the brands and communicate with companies and also buy branded merchandise. Fournier and Lee (2009) say that inspired by Harley Davidson, which has created a highly successful brand community, companies dealing in packaged goods and industrial equipment are trying to build communities around their own brands. They say that people are hungry for a sense of connection. However, companies often misunderstand the concept and try to make brand communities serve the business. A successful brand community should exist to serve the people in it and the benefit to the brand should be incidental. If there is too much focus on the brand without meeting the needs of the people, they will turn away.

Creating Reference Groups

A *reference group* is any group to which one refers when making purchase decisions. It consists of people whose attitudes, behaviour, beliefs, opinions, preferences, and values are used by an individual as the basis for his or her judgement. These are conceptual groups, that is, they do not exist physically, but influence people in that category. For example, a young girl adopts the speech, style, and mannerisms of a popular TV programme because she uses the people in the programme as a reference group.

The idea of reference suggests that for some people, behaviour is influenced by their judgement of members of groups to which they belong or aspire to belong. Barnett (1969) writes that identifying a reference group is very difficult because it is psychological. For example, if a product such as a colour television set is seen by the bulk of middle-class families as a symbol of upward mobility, portraying it in working-class surroundings will prove disastrous. According to the reference group hypothesis, it would be more effective to display the product in an obviously upper-class setting.

The use of reference groups and their types are discussed in Chapter 12.

Using Buzz

Creating *buzz* is to get people talking positively about a product or brand, encouraging people-to-people (P2P) conversations. Movies rely on reviews and music to get people to spread the message. Every time a person hums a song or uses it as a caller tune, for instance, it adds to the buzz. Companies sometimes do the unusual to get attention. The Benetton campaigns (see chapter-end case study) succeeded because they the audacious images resulted in people talking about them. *The Telegraph* (2012) reported that Benetton launched the 'Unemployee of the Year' campaign in 2012, with an online contest to identify 100 creative projects submitted by those aged 18 to 30 years old and who were out of work. This was a way of generating buzz on what was uppermost in peoples' mind in a downsized world: unemployment. Dye (2000) writes that many products are buzz worthy. Toys, sporting goods, movies, and fashion are largely driven by buzz, while financial services, hotels, electronics, cars, and so on, are partially driven by buzz. She gives two criteria for buzz worthy products: first, that the product should be unique in some way, and second, the products should be highly visible. Internet chat groups and social networking sites are tools to encourage buzz.

Using Viral Marketing

Viral marketing refers to a self-replicating process in which an idea spreads rapidly among large number of people, like an infectious disease. Such strategies take advantage of rapid multiplication of the message to millions of people. Successful viral messages include the song, *Why this kolaveri di*, that millions of people viewed on YouTube. Watts and Peretti (2007) call it 'the ultimate free lunch: pick some small number of people to seed your idea, product, or message; get it to go viral; and then watch while it spreads effortlessly to reach millions.' Yet it is not simple, because nobody knows what gets people to spread messages. For every success like *Kolaveri di*, there are thousands of desperate attempts to build traffic on websites or songs, which never take off. Like some disease outbreaks, many viruses burn out without affecting a sizeable number of people.

CONSUMER IMAGERY AND BRAND PERSONALITY

Consumers often create an 'image' for the brand in their minds, which is *brand personality*. A brand acquires personality when consumers start attaching human traits to brands.

David Ogilvy (1983) wrote, 'Every advertisement should be thought of as a contribution to the brand image.' Successful brands design their communications to project the same image, over time. For example, consider the advertisements for Lux, Pears, and other powerful brands. Like an individual's personality, these images have remained similar over the years.

Brand personality is also sought to be achieved through celebrity endorsements. By attaching a famous name to a brand, such as a film star or a sportsperson, the personality of the celebrity is sought to be attached to the brand. Companies use this technique quite often. According to a report in *Hindustan Times* (2011), film stars dominate celebrity advertising in India, followed by sports personalities.

Though signing celebrities is expensive, it is a short-cut method of building brand personality, since celebrities are instantly recognizable. The brand piggybacks on their popularity. More important, the brand tends to acquire the personality of the star. For instance, by attaching a peppy actress to a vehicle, the brand gets a peppy image for itself. Establishing such an image without the celebrity would take the brand a longer time.

However, celebrity advertising also carries risk. Using a film star may work for a while, but if some of his films flop, the brand itself would lose value. Similarly, a sports star may lose a few matches and the brand suffers as a result. More seriously, some celebrities gain notoriety by their actions. The negative publicity associated with Michael Jackson and Tiger Woods for instance, had the potential to flatten the brands they endorsed. Such brands are quick to dissociate themselves from such celebrities after such instances.

It is quite evident that celebrities affect ordinary people. Several apps are available that compare a person's image and inform them which celebrity they look like (http://celebrity.myheritage.com/celebrity-look-alikes). Facebook has an app that answers the question: 'Which celebrity do you look like' that is very popular among users. A celebrity similarity test is available at http://psych.wfu.edu/woodlab/celebrity/celebritytest.pl. Several sites promise to tell you which celebrity you most resemble.

Several cosmetic brands too, build on this and promise to make you look like celebrities. The Revlon Facebook page says: 'Get the chance to star in your own celebrity-style photo-shoot with ace photographer Anushka Menon. Simply visit the Revlon Celebrity You app to join.'

Communications and Brand Srategy

Our discussion of communications and its impact on consumer behaviour will be incomplete without mentioning the fact that any communications strategy must dovetail with brand strategy. Very often, companies try to create advertising or online conversations without considering what their brand stands for. They create, for instance, cheeky content that might get a lot of likes on social media sites, but do nothing for sales. This happens because companies usually outsource their online conversations, which then happen without considering the key asset of the company—the brand.

Joachimsthaler and Aaker (1996) point to precisely this problem. Successful companies, on the other hand, 'actively make brand building part of their strategic plans and, as a result, integrate their alternative approaches to brand building into their overall concept of the brand'. Thus, activities are not taken up to get people talking, but activities related to the brand are followed passionately, which in turn generate buzz.

They give the example of The Body Shop, a company that 'walks the walk' in terms of developing programmes that reflect its core identity. 'We're different because of our values,' says its website. It is not just a cosmetics company but promotes 'Beauty with heart'. Its campaigns—on sex trafficking, HIV, and stopping violence at home—are not activities taken up to encourage buzz or viral marketing, but are integral to the brand.

All of this helped the company establish a firm image in the minds of customers before the death of its founder, Anita Roddick, in 2007. The Body Shop still has a distinct brand image compared to other cosmetics brands. It is part of the L'Oreal group today.

Michael Porter (2001) points to the obsession managers have about new technologies. He says that we have to move away from rhetoric and 'see the Internet for what it is: an enabling technology—a powerful set of tools that can be used, wisely or unwisely, in almost any industry and as part of any strategy.' He further says that virtual activities must supplement physical activities.

New technologies have the potential to create a 'groundswell', which refers to gathering people for a cause. It is also the name of a book by Li and Bernoff (2008), who write that the biggest challenge is not mastering technology but 'accomplishing a useful business goal'. They identify five primary objectives that companies can pursue in the groundswell.

Listening It implies gaining consumer insights by following comments and remarks made online.

Talking It implies use of technology to spread messages about the company.

Energizing It implies identifying the most enthusiastic customers and supercharge the power of their word of mouth.

Supporting It implies setting up of tools to help customers support each other.

Embracing It implies integrating customers in the way the business works.

In short, companies must learn to use technology to support business, and not the other way round.

Dealing with Negative Publicity

Negative publicity can occur at any time, and companies must respond as it causes immense harm to brands. Product or service deficiencies, employee misbehaviour, and accidents are reported widely. Such occurrences can happen in any company. Consumers too can post comments or videos that become quickly viral, affecting a large number of people. Companies can deal with it in the following ways.

Track negative instances First, companies must know if any negative material is posted about their brands. This often means tracking online reviews, social sites, and the media. A response can be prepared after knowing about the negative threads.

Be prepared Companies have to be prepared for the worst-case scenario. An emergency procedure must be worked out and drilled. Employees who deal directly with customers have to be trained for emergencies.

Respond quickly Once the company knows something negative is going on, the response must be quick and direct. For instance, if a customer posts a critical review, immediate contact should be made. In the case of critical blogs and forums, companies must proactively insert themselves into the conversation. This will show consumers that the company is rectifying the situation. Two things that must be avoided are: pretending that everything is all right, and secondly, criticizing or censoring negative comments.

Be proactive Companies should not wait for complaints to arise. Instead, a newsletter to customers and sharing information will convince customers that the company is taking steps to contain the damage.

EXHIBIT 13.3 Cadbury's—Handling Negative Publicity

Cadbury India is a fully owned subsidy of Kraft Foods Inc. It is the world's second-largest food company and operates in over 70 countries. Cadbury began operations in India in 1948 by importing chocolates. The company's core purpose is to 'make today delicious' and it operates in four categories, namely chocolate confectionery, milk food drinks, candy, and gum. The company has maintained its market leadership over the years. Some of the key brands in India are Cadbury Dairy Milk, 5 Star, Perk, Éclairs, and Celebrations.

In 2003, Cadbury India faced a crisis. Just before the festive season, the media reported that the government was receiving complaints about infestation of worms in Cadbury milk chocolates. Sales decreased amid intense negative publicity, and consumers avoided Cadbury chocolates. The company's credibility and reputation were at stake. As SMS jokes circulated, trade confidence in the brand, including the morale of the sales team, took a hit. Traditionally, the festive season in India sees a high demand for all kinds of sweets and chocolates and retailers order huge stocks. However, the Diwali season did not start with a happy note for the company.

Cadbury issued a statement that their manufacturing process was foolproof and worms could not possibly get into the chocolates at that stage. It said that the most likely cause was poor storage at the retail level. This did not cut much ice with consumers, since storage and display is also part of a company's responsibility. The company could not simply transfer responsibility to the retailers and continue to sell damaged chocolates.

The problems identified were as follows:

Storage The chocolates were stored in warehouses and the Indian summer, which lasted over 6 months, ensured that the chocolates melted at the distribution and retail points, where the counters were without refrigeration.

Packaging The packaging—chocolates wrapped in foil covered with a paper wraparound that was not sealed—was defective.

No-returns policy With a no-returns policy, retailers pushed their stock to the customers, no matter what state the chocolates were in. Very often, the chocolates sold had melted several times over and were in a sorry condition, especially if bought from smaller retailers who did not have refrigerators.

While these problems could be rectified, the company faced a tremendous challenge—how to change the perception of consumers who thought that there was something wrong with the company and its manufacturing process. There was a media onslaught that brought the issue to front pages of newspapers and prime time on television.

It was a disaster. The damage to Cadbury's public image was severe and its reputation was at stake.

(Contd)

EXHIBIT 13.3 (Contd)

Keegan (2011) writes that the challenge was to restore the confidence of the consumers, trade, and the media, and it had to be done directly and quickly.

A case study written by Bharat Puri, Senior Vice-president of Kraft Foods, and Sarah Clark (2012) describes how the company dealt with the problem. The company's first response was to identify core principles that would guide their actions moving forward: place the consumer first; always tell the truth; and dare greatly, act quickly.

The company responded internally and externally. Internally, letters from the Managing Director were sent out to all the employees. The doubts in the minds of the sales team were removed by asking them to go into their markets, buy chocolates worth up to ₹1000 and see for themselves if any bars were infested. A series of town hall meetings were held with the senior managers and employees to ensure the employees were kept informed of the steps being taken by the company. Regular email updates were also used to communicate the management's point of view and to ensure consistency of messaging.

Cadbury's external response to the crisis included changing the packaging, launching a media campaign, and reaching out to retailers and consumers. It also launched Project Vishwas to win back the confidence of the consumer. A press advertisement, 'Facts about Cadbury' was released nationally, which highlighted corrective steps being taken by the company.

Cadbury then signed up Amitabh Bachchan as its brand ambassador because he was seen as one of the most credible people in India. He spoke straight into the camera and described how he visited the Cadbury factory to first convince himself of the quality of Cadbury chocolates before agreeing to become a spokesperson. A second TV advertisement showed Bachchan playing with his granddaughter, who is wary of eating the chocolate he offers her, stating she has heard there is 'something in it'. Bachchan assures her of the safety of the product. In both the communications, the issue was faced directly and there was no attempt to skirt the issue.

As a result of these actions, consumers started believing the company. By June 2004, consumer confidence returned.

Negative publicity is a part of the risk that companies face. However, if companies ignore the problem or do not face it head on, the problem can escalate out of control. Cadbury was able to win back consumer confidence as it faced the issue directly, used a media strategy involving a trusted brand ambassador, and acted quickly.

What do you learn from Cadbury's media response?

Sources:

Keegan, Warren J. and Naval L. Bhargava, *Global Marketing Management*, 7th Ed., Pearson Education, New Delhi, 2011.

Puri, Bharat and Sarah E. Clark, 'How to transform consumer opinion when disaster strikes: The 2003 Cadbury India worm infestation', The Fletcher School, 2012, http://fletcher.tufts.edu/CEME/publications/~/media/Fletcher/Microsites/CEME/pubs/reflections/Cadbury%20Case%20Final%202012.pdf, last accessed on 14 January 2014.

'Worms found in Cadbury Cashew Magic', http://timesofindia.indiatimes.com/city/bangalore/Worms-found-in-Cadbury-Cashew-Magic/articleshow/259825.cms, *The Times of India*, 2003, last accessed on 31 October 2013.

CONCLUSION

Marketing communication is a powerful means of reaching customers. A powerful message made with an understanding of the consumer and placed in appropriate media, can help build brands and impact consumers around the globe. Yet, these tasks are more difficult than they look. Consider this: Nobel (2011) writes that according to Harvard Business School professor Clayton Christensen, each year 30,000 new consumer products are launched—and 95 per cent of them fail. The reasons are many, but the most obvious one is that companies think in terms of products and segments while consumers think in terms of what job a product will do for them. So there is often a mismatch of communication.

Companies often limit their marketing effort by showing the targeted audience in their advertisements and hope that people like them and will buy the product. In India, it is common to see young people in advertisements for almost any product. However, 'the fact that you're 18 to 35 years old, with a college degree, does not cause you to buy a product,' Christensen says. A communications strategy therefore has to go much beyond guessing the type of customers for a company's products.

The secret of powerful communications is that they address a need of the customer. Discovering that need is the secret of how a company may develop its communications strategy. Can companies 'crawl into the skin of the customer'? Successful companies do precisely that and so succeed on a deeply psychological plane.

SUMMARY

Marketing messages are sent from company to consumer through a channel or medium, and the consumer's action serves as feedback. Consumers also respond to communications as described by the AIDA model, that is, they generate attention, interest, desire, and action.

Communications strategy has three aspects: understanding customers, having a message strategy, and a media strategy. Understanding consumers means finding out how they perceive brands. They do so in a combination of language, signs, and symbols, which is called a semiotic system. Fogg's Behaviour Model shows that three elements, namely a) motivation, b) ability, and c) trigger, must converge at the same moment for a behaviour to occur: Even if one is missing, the communication will not be successful.

To understand customers, it is important to understand the scenarios in which they use products and solve their problems. Companies that do are able to develop a deep understanding of their markets and brands. Customer scenarios are also studied with respect to customers and their interaction with the media.

The message strategy consists of creating powerful messages that persuade customers. The elaboration likelihood model (ELM) shows how attitudes are formed and changed. The human mind uses two routes through which persuasive messages are processed: the central route, which provides complete information and is straightforward, and the peripheral route, which uses means such as catchy tunes, colours, and celebrity endorsements, in which a person uses pre-existing ideas and superficial qualities to be persuaded. Advertising appeals can be formulated based on these.

Some of the common appeals used in advertising are fear, humour, sex, emotion, and slice of life. Strong, persuasive communications result in positioning of the brand in a consumer's mind. Ultimately, this helps in creating a brand image. Sometimes people also attach human qualities to brands, which is referred to as brand personality. Brand personality is also sought to be achieved through celebrity endorsements. Celebrities are in great demand to endorse brands and charge heavily to do so.

Media strategy consists of deciding which media to use. The task is very difficult because of fragmentation of the media and the existence of a large number of newspapers and television channels. It is also complicated by the high media cost. Companies have to decide whether to use mass media or interactive methods. They do this on the basis of reach, cost credibility, efficiency, and measurability. They can also decide whether to use above- or below-the-line campaigns. However, it is crucial to integrate various media to deliver a unified brand experience to customers.

Credibility depends on the message, which should be believable, and the source, where the message will be seen. Word-of-mouth publicity, which people do of their own accord, is generally more credible than advertising. Companies try to encourage this through opinion leaders, reference groups, and employing viral marketing techniques, which encourage people to talk about products and brands, creating a buzz. Finally, communications strategy must dovetail with the brand strategy. Instead of devising strategies for new technologies, companies must build brands on their beliefs and core values, which then become the source of buzz.

KEY TERMS

360-degree branding Marketing activities, which are well integrated to present the brand similarly at all points of consumer contact

Above the line (ATL) Communications through mass media campaigns, using television, out-of-home media (OOH), magazines, cinema, newspapers, and radio

Ad zapping The practice of switching channels by consumers when commercials are shown

Advertising appeal A distinctive message used by companies in their advertising to influence the way consumers view themselves and conveying how buying certain products can prove to be beneficial for them

Advertising Standards Council of India (ASCI) A body that promotes responsible advertising and acts on complaints about false advertising

Advertorial An advertisement in the form of an editorial

Attention, interest, desire and action (AIDA) model A communication model that explains the steps that a consumer's mind goes through on seeing an advertisement.

Behaviour activation threshold When the combination of motivation and ability triggers the target behaviour in a person. If a person is below this threshold, then a trigger will not lead to the target behaviour

Below the line (BTL) Communications that refer to direct marketing activities that provide incentive to purchase, including promotions, events, coupons, and discounts

Brand communities The brand is connected to various activities to create a cultural setting for it and both offline and online communities are present

Brand personality The image of a brand that develops in the mind of the consumer that associates human personality traits with particular brands

Buzz or P2P conversations Creating buzz is to get people talking positively about a product or brand

Clutter Numerous advertisements in media placed together or shown at the same time, and are easily missed by consumers

Communications model A basic model that explains how communications take place, from sender to receiver through a medium

Communications strategy A method of communicating the company's marketing messages to consumers so that they are the most effective

Consumer imagery The images or symbols that a consumer associates with a particular brand

Credibility Refers to whether the marketing communications is believed by consumers and consists of message credibility and source credibility

Cross switch A method used by Dentsu that advocates creating customer scenarios to move them through calibrated contact points and is described as 'flipping a switch in the consumer's mind'

Customer referral value (CRV) A way of quantifying the value of referrals made by a customer—the present value of his/her referrals plus the present value of customers who would have joined anyway

Customer scenario An understanding that customers select, buy, and use products and services for better customer experience

Elaboration likelihood model (ELM) A model that shows how attitudes are formed and changed in consumers

Fogg's behaviour model It shows that three elements, namely motivation, ability, and trigger, must converge at the same moment for a behaviour to occur

Impersonal communications Communications are impersonal when they are sent through a medium

Infomercials Long duration direct response television commercials

Interpersonal communications When the message is delivered by personal interaction, as by employing a salesman or any direct marketing methods, it is called interpersonal communication

Media strategy A combination of media (newspapers, television, radio, Internet) that a company uses to spread its message

Message strategy A strategy that determines what a company wants to say to consumers and how it wants to say it

Noise Obstructions in receiving and interpreting messages by consumers

Opinion leaders People who are held in great regard by others and who recommend goods or brands to them

Positioning A brand strategy that aims to capture a special place in the mind of the customer that is distinct from other brands

Reference group A reference group is any group to which one refers when making purchase decisions

Semiotic Study of signs and symbols that engages consumers in an imaginary or symbolic process that contributes tangible value to it

Slice of life An advertising technique where a real-life situation is dramatized and a product is shown as the solution to a common problem

Synergistic effect Combining multiple communication tools so that they can produce greater results than tools used individually and in an uncoordinated fashion

Through the line (TTL) Communications that use a combination of ATL and BTL techniques

Touchpoint The point of contact of the product, brand, or service with customers and is known as moment of truth

Viral marketing A marketing technique that uses existing social networking services and other technologies to produce an increase in brand awareness or sales through self-replicating viral processes

Word of mouth The passing of information from person to person by oral communication

Word-of-mouth marketing (WOMM) The passing of marketing information from person to person by oral communication

EXERCISES

Concept-review Questions

1. Describe communications models and explain how they are used to reach customers.
2. What does a marketing communications strategy consist of?
3. Explain how Fogg's Behaviour Model works in marketing communications.
4. What is meant by customer scenarios? Why is it important to study customer scenarios while designing a company's communications?
5. List down the various advertising appeals and explain how they work in influencing customers.
6. What is slice of life advertising? Explain how it works. Give examples to show how slice of life works in reality.
7. How is consumer imagery used to establish brands?
8. Explain the different types of media. In what circumstances are either types used?
9. What is word-of-mouth and viral marketing? How are they used by companies?
10. What is customer referral value and how is it calculated?

Critical Thinking Questions

1. As the cost of advertising in mass media goes up, companies are increasingly opting for BTL campaigns. How effective are they? Do they succeed in achieving what mass media is able to achieve?
2. Classify the type of advertising appeals that would work for different types of products. In which cases would the appeals be most effective?
3. A communications strategy starts with understanding the customer, but many ads do not attempt this at all. Why do you think this happens?
4. It is said that the primary purpose of the advertisement is to sell. Do you agree with this statement? Is brand building also important?
5. Internet marketing is said to be the next big thing that will lead to a paradigm shift in communications. Give your opinions on the subject.

Projects and Assignments

1. Read and analyse a range of persuasive advertisements and identify key features. Distinguish between advertisements which try to persuade and those that simply inform. Make a list of words or images that recur in these advertisements.
2. Take up a popular brand and study its communications strategy. Discover its message strategy and the media used by the company. Further, comment whether it is effective. What are the changes you would make in the communications strategy and why?
3. Take a look at the online engagement undertaken by a brand such as Coca-Cola or Axe. Comment on how effective it is in engaging customers. In addition, assess if the engagements will lead to increased sales for the brand.
4. Study some campaigns that use celebrities to promote brands. Do a recall test with your friends to see how many remember the brand the celebrity is associated with. On the basis of this research, state your findings on whether celebrity advertising is effective or not.

REFERENCES

Barnett, Norman L., 'Beyond market segmentation', *Harvard Business Review*, Vol. 47, No. 1, January–February 1969, pp. 152–166.

Berlyne, Donald E., 'Novelty, complexity, and hedonic value', *Perception and Psychophysics*, Vol. 8, 1970, pp. 279–286.

Campbell, Margaret C. and Kevin Lane Keller, 'Brand Familiarity and Advertising Repetition Effects', *Journal of Consumer Research*, Vol. 30, 2003, pp. 292–304.

Dianoux, Christian, Jean-Luc Herrmann, and Helen Zeitoun, 'Comparative advertising: Citing or not the leading brand and its price', *Journal of Consumer Marketing*, Vol. 30, No. 4, 2013, pp. 345–354.

Du Plessis, Erik, *The Advertised Mind: Ground-Breaking Insights into How Our Brains Respond to Advertising*, Millward Brown, London, 2005.

Dye, Renee, 'The buzz on buzz', *Harvard Business Review*, November–December 2000, pp. 139–146.

Eisend Martin, 'Source credibility dimensions in marketing communication—A generalized solution', *Journal of Empirical Generalisations in Marketing Science*, Vol. 10. pp. 1–33.

Featherstone, Mike, *Consumer Culture and Postmodernism*, 2nd Ed., Sage Publications, London, 2007, pp. 10–14.

Fogg, B., 'A behaviour model for persuasive design', http://bjfogg.com/fbm_files/page4_1.pdf, last accessed on 9 May 2012.

Fournier, Susan and Lara Lee, 'Getting brand communities right', *Harvard Business Review*, April 2009.

'Global communication channel credibility: How are citizen-consumers getting information about your organization?', IPSOS Public Affairs, 2010, http://www.ipsos.com/public-affairs/sites/www.ipsos.com.public-affairs/files/files/INT%20Global%20Comm%20Channel%20Credibility%20Summer%202010_0.pdf, http://www.ipsos.com/public-affairs/sites/www.ipsos.com.public-affairs/files/files/INT%20Global%20Comm%20Channel%20Credibility%20Summer%202010_0.pdf, last accessed on 4 January 2014.

Gobe, Marc, *Emotional Branding*, Allworth Press, New York, 2001.

Hawes, Daniel R., 'Care for some sexy toilet paper? Sex in advertising', *Psychology Today*, 15 January 2010, http://www.psychologytoday.com/blog/evolved-primate/201001/care-some-sexy-toilet-paper-sex-in-advertising, last accessed on 10 May 2012.

Hoyer, Wayne D. and Deborah J. MacInnis, *Consumer Behaviour*, 5th Ed., South-West Cengage Learning, Mason, Ohio, 2010.

http://en.wikipedia.org/wiki/Media_of_India, last accessed on 17 September 2012.

Joachimsthaler, E., and D.A. Aaker, 'Building brands without mass media', *Harvard Business Review*, January–February, 1997, Vol. 75, No. 1, pp. 39–50.

Kotaro Sugiyama and Tim Andree, *The Dentsu Way: Secrets of Cross Switch Marketing from the World's Most Innovative Agency*, McGraw-Hill Professional, New York, 2010.

Li, Charlene and Josh Bernoff, *Groundswell: Winning in a World Transformed by Social Technologies*, Harvard Business Press, Boston, Mass., 2008.

Mehta, A., and S.C. Purvis, 'Reconsidering recall and emotion in advertising', *Journal of Advertising Research*, March 2006, pp. 49–56.

Metzger, M.J., A.J. Flanagin, K. Eyal, D.R. Lemus, and R.M. McCann, 'Credibility for the 21st Century: Integrating perspectives on source, message, and media credibility', in Kalbfleisch, Pamela J. (Ed.), *Communication Yearbook*, 27, Taylor and Francis, 2008.

Millward Brown, 'Does humour make ads more effective?', 2013, http://millwardbrownsweden.wordpress.com/2013/10/08/should-i-use-humour-in-advertising/, last accessed on 14 January 2014.

Morris, Charles William, *Writings on the General Theory of Signs*, Mouton, The Hague, 1971.

Nobel, Carmen, 'Clay Christensen's milkshake marketing', HBS Working Knowledge, 14 February 2011, http://hbswk.hbs.edu/item/6496.html, last accessed on 15 May 2012.

Ogilvy, David, *Ogilvy on Advertising*, 1983, Prion Books, London, pp. 14–15.

O'Guinn, Thomas C., Chris T. Allen, and Richard J. Semenik, *Advertising and Integrated Brand Promotion*, 5th Ed., South-Western Cengage Learning, Mason, Ohio, USA, 2009.

Oswald, Laura R., *Marketing Semiotics: Signs, Strategies and Brand Value*, Oxford University Press, Oxford, 2012.

Petty, R. E. and J. T. Cacioppo, 'The elaboration likelihood model of persuasion', in L. Berkowitz (Ed.), *Advances in Experimental Social Psychology*, 1986, Academic Press, San Diego, Vol. 19, pp. 123–205.

Phillips, Robbin, Greg Cordell, Geno Church, and Spike Jones, *Brains on Fire: Igniting Powerful, Sustainable, Word of Mouth Movements*, John Wiley & Sons, Inc., New Jersey, 2010.

Porter, Michael, 'Strategy and the Internet', *Harvard Business Review*, March 2001, pp. 63–78.

Pradeep, A. K., *The Buying Brain: Secrets for Selling to the Subconscious Mind*, John Wiley and Sons, New Jersey, 2010.

Ries, Al and Jack Trout, *Positioning: The Battle For Your Mind*, McGraw Hill Professional, New York, 20th Anniversary Edition, 2001.

Sengupta, Jaideep and Darren W. Dahl, 'Gender-related reactions to gratuitous sex appeals in advertising', *Journal of Consumer Psychology*, Vol. 18, No. 1, pp. 62–78.

Seybold, Patricia B., 'Get inside the lives of your customers', *Harvard Business Review*, May 2001, pp. 81–89.

Shannon C. E. (1948), A mathematical theory of communication, *The Bell System Technical Journal*, October, 1948.

Shatrujeet, N., 'Slice-of-life: Advertising idea or executional trap?' 2 September 2003. http://www.afaqs.com/news/story.html?sid=6978_Slice-of-life:+Advertising+idea+or+executional+trap?+-+Part+II, last accessed on 11 May 2012.

Shimp, Terence A., *Advertising, Promotion, and Other Aspects of Integrated Marketing Communications*, 8th Ed., South-West Cengage Learning, Mason, Ohio, 2010.

'Ten hits & misses: Best & bekaar ads of 2013', *The Economic Times Brand Equity*, 25 December 2013.

The Playboy Interview: Marshall McLuhan (1969), *Playboy Magazine*, March 1969.

Tuttle, Brad, 'Ha! Ads that make you laugh don't really make you buy', *Time*, 18 July 2012, http://business.time.com/2012/07/18/ha-ads-that-make-you-laugh-dont-really-make-you-buy/#ixzz2phtrh7mn, last accessed on 14 January 2014.

Van den Bergh, Joeri and Mattias Behrer, *How Cool Brands Stay Hot: Branding to Generation Y*, 2nd Ed., Kogan Page, Philadelphia, 2013.

Watts, Duncan J. and Jonah Peretti, 'Viral marketing for the real world', *Harvard Business Review*, May 2007.

Williams, Patti A., and Jennifer L. Aaker, 'The peaceful co-existence of conflicting emotions: Examining differential responses to mixed emotional appeals', September 2000, http://knowledge.emory.edu/papers/981.pdf, last accessed on 11 May 2012.

CASE STUDY
Making of Brand Benetton

Think of Benetton and what comes to mind are brightly coloured clothes displayed in distinctive, spacious stores. It is a well-recognized global brand with sales of over €2 billion in 2011. However, what is most memorable about the brand are its audacious advertisements that helped create presence in the minds of millions of people around the world. This case describes how the company used a unique communications and media strategy to establish an international brand.

The communications of the company are built around dramatic images 'with the young eyes of the future: always at the cutting edge—with colour, with the revolution of the point of sale, with an absolutely unique production and commercial network, and with a universal form of communication', says its website.

The strategy helped establish the brand firmly all over the world. Giroux (1994) writes that Benetton's advertising campaigns have been instrumental in its success in the fashion world. The advertising 'is important not merely as a means for assessing Benetton commercial success in extending its name recognition; it is crucial for understanding how the philosophy of the company has attempted to re-inscribe its image within a broader set of political and cultural concerns', he writes.

The company was started as Fratelli Benetton in 1965 by the Benetton family headed by Luciano Benetton, near Treviso, Italy. It originally made colourful sweaters. The business is now a fashion empire with over 7000 franchise stores in more than 100 countries.

The brand started changing colour in 1984, when it hired Oliviero Toscani, an award-winning photographer, to head its advertising campaign. He was given a free hand, which resulted in his creating some of the most memorable advertising in history, transforming the brand in the process.

Early advertisements show playful, bright, culturally diverse young people dressed in eye-catching colours. The campaign linked the apparel colours to the diversity of colours in the human race, highlighting the theme of racial harmony, world peace, and unity. As a consequence, the brand was transformed and became 'United Colors of Benetton' in 1985. Benetton is perhaps the only brand to have changed itself because of its marketing communications.

As Liz Wells writes in the case study, *Benetton, Toscani and the Limits of Advertising* (2009), the effects of this advertising were phenomenal. In 1978, Benetton was exporting 26 per cent of its sales, but by 1981, this figure had zoomed to 40 per cent. By 1983, its export sales exceeded domestic sales. During the mid-1980s, the company changed from being an Italian family brand to become an international player.

So far, the images used were in the genre of fashion studio photography. The advertisements showed bright, happy, and colourful children of diverse races frolicking in a kind of a 'fashion heaven' in the words of Giroux. They portrayed racial harmony that appeared banal, make-believe, and sterile.

In a dramatic masterstroke, in 1991, Toscani removed Benetton apparel from the firm's advertising, and started using controversial and disturbing photographs. The images were so compelling and provocative that no one could ignore them. The advertisements are remembered to this day: blown-up condoms of different colours floating in the air, a nun kissing a priest, a row of test tubes filled with blood, and a newborn baby girl covered in blood and still attached to her umbilical cord. Giroux writes that the switch to controversial photojournalistic images showed that Benetton wanted to redefine its corporate image as a company concerned with social change in a world fraught with famine, violence, and war.

Racist imagery and history were evoked. One advertisement showed a black woman's body nursing a white baby, evoking images of slavery when black slave mothers nursed white children. This created a storm in the US, and for a while Benetton's sales fell but recovered soon. 'Controversy eventually seemed to increase sales,' writes Wells.

The next phase is described as 'pseudo documentary'. Toscani started using a series of highly charged, photojournalistic images in advertisements, with the green Benetton logo. It was a stark contrast to the genteel images of fashion photography. A person dying of AIDS, a black soldier holding a human bone, and so on. Many editors cringed at publishing these controversial ads.

The media strategy was also unique. The advertisements were placed as double spreads in fashion magazines and in huge billboards. Predictably, there was unease among publishers, so the artworks were delivered late so that they could not be dropped. *Elle* magazine accused the company of sending advertisements just before the printing deadlines. In one incident, the magazine was forced to leave two pages blank because the Benetton ad did not reach it in time for publication. This, however, gave Benetton more publicity.

The advertisements are remembered not only for their shock value, but also for generating hot public debate. A 'buzz' was created much before the word was associated with marketing, and increased word-of-mouth publicity, resulting in higher sales and profits.

Morris (2005) writes that the Benetton communications strategy is a fine example of the power drawn from interpretability. The images left people to interpret what was portrayed—usually war, famine, and disease. In doing so, it forced people to *think* and that helped establish the brand.

The campaigns, including the 2011 'Unhate' campaign that showed world leaders lip-locking, kicked up massive controversies. In many cases, the Benetton ads were either banned from particular countries or refused by publications. All this worked for the company. The Benetton brand is well-recognized now, and is part of advertising folklore.

All along, Benetton supported the campaigns. It aggressively defended its advertising and used the debate to establish its social responsibility. Benetton also used the controversy to build a culture around the brand, in the form of books, magazines, talks, interviews, and articles. It publishes a magazine, *Colors*, and has its own design institute, Fabrica.

As one company document puts it, 'Benetton believes that it is important for companies to take a stance in the real world instead of using their advertising budget to perpetuate the myth that they can make consumers happy through the mere purchase of their product. The company has opted for a communication strategy in which issues, and not clothes, play the lead part. The company has decided to devote some of its advertising budget to communicate on themes relevant to young and old people worldwide.'

Some part of the communications strategy needs refurbishing, as growth in Benetton seems to have stalled. *Time* (2009) reports, 'Upstart brands such as Zara and H&M are stealing the headlines—and the allegiance of many younger shoppers—as they storm the world from Moscow to Manila...the ads for United Colors of Benetton stores are tamer and its growth less stellar.'

Questions for Discussion

1. Comment on the communications strategy of Benetton. How did the shocking images help establish the brand?
2. Look at the Benetton advertisements available online at www.benetton.com. List your reactions on seeing the images. How would it impact you as a consumer?
3. As growth of the company is stalled and other brands are stealing the headlines, what communication strategy should Benetton follow to establish itself as a leader again?
4. Does the advertising of the company establish the social responsibility of the company or has it left the brand besmirched, as critics say? Give reasons for your answer.

Sources:

Bergin, Olivia, 'Benetton launch "unemployee of the year" campaign', *The Telegraph*, 19 September 2012.

Giroux Henry A., 'Benetton's "World without borders": Buying social change', in Carol Becker, Ed., *The Subversive Imagination: Artists, Society, and Social Responsibility* (Routledge, New York, 1994), pp. 187–207.

Gumbel, Peter, 'Benetton's bold strategy', *Time*, 26 October 2009.

http://www.benettongroup.com/archive/2011-annual-report, last accessed on 30th October 2014.

http://www.benettongroup.com/the-group, last accessed on 30th October 2014.

http://www.csus.edu/indiv/o/obriene/art7/readings/benetton.htm, last accessed on 30th October 2014.

Morris, Martin, 'Interpretability and social power, or, why postmodern advertising works', *Media, Culture & Society*, September 2005, Vol. 27, No. 5, pp. 697–718, http://mcs.sagepub.com/cgi/content/abstract/27/5/697, last accessed on 5 May 2012.

Wells, Liz (ed.), *Toscani and the Limits of Advertising in Photography: A Critical Introduction*, 4th Ed., Routledge, London, 2009, pp. 239–246.

ANNEXURE 13.1

ASCI Code The Code for self-regulation in advertising: Pertinent extracts

Advertising Standards Council of India (ASCI) is a self-regulatory voluntary organization of the advertising industry. Established in 1985, it is committed to the cause of self-regulation in Advertising, ensuring the protection of the interests of consumers. Its main objective is to promote responsible advertising.

Definition
An advertisement is defined as a paid-for communication, addressed to the public or a section of it, the purpose of which is to influence the opinions or behaviour of those to whom it is addressed.

Declaration of Fundamental Principles
The Code for Self-Regulation for fair advertising practices in the best interests of the ultimate consumer has the following provisions:
- To ensure the truthfulness and honesty of representations and claims made by advertisements and to safeguard against misleading advertisements.
- To ensure that advertisements are not offensive to generally accepted standards of public decency. Advertisements should contain nothing indecent, vulgar or repulsive which is likely, in the light of generally prevailing standards of decency and propriety, to cause grave or widespread offence.
- To safeguard against the indiscriminate use of advertising in situations or of the promotion of products which are regarded as hazardous or harmful to society or to individuals, particularly minors, to a degree or of a type which is unacceptable to society at large.
- To ensure that advertisements observe fairness in competition so that the consumers need to be informed on choices in the market-place and the canons of generally accepted competitive behaviour in business are both served. Both the general public and an advertiser's competitors have an equal right to expect the content of advertisements to be presented fairly, intelligibly and responsibly. The Code applies to advertisers, advertising agencies and media.

Responsibility for the Observance of this Code
The responsibility for the observance of this Code for Self-Regulation in Advertising lies with all who commission, create, place or publish any advertisement or assist in the creation or publishing of any advertisement. All advertisers, advertising agencies and media are expected not to commission, create, place or publish any advertisement which is in contravention of this Code. This is a self-imposed discipline required under this Code for Self-Regulation in Advertising from all involved in the commissioning, creation, placement or publishing of advertisements. This Code applies to advertisements read, heard or viewed in India even if they originate or are published abroad so long as they are directed to consumers in India or are exposed to significant number of consumers in India.

Source: http://www.ascionline.org/index.php/asci-codes, last accessed on 15 May 2012.

PART FIVE

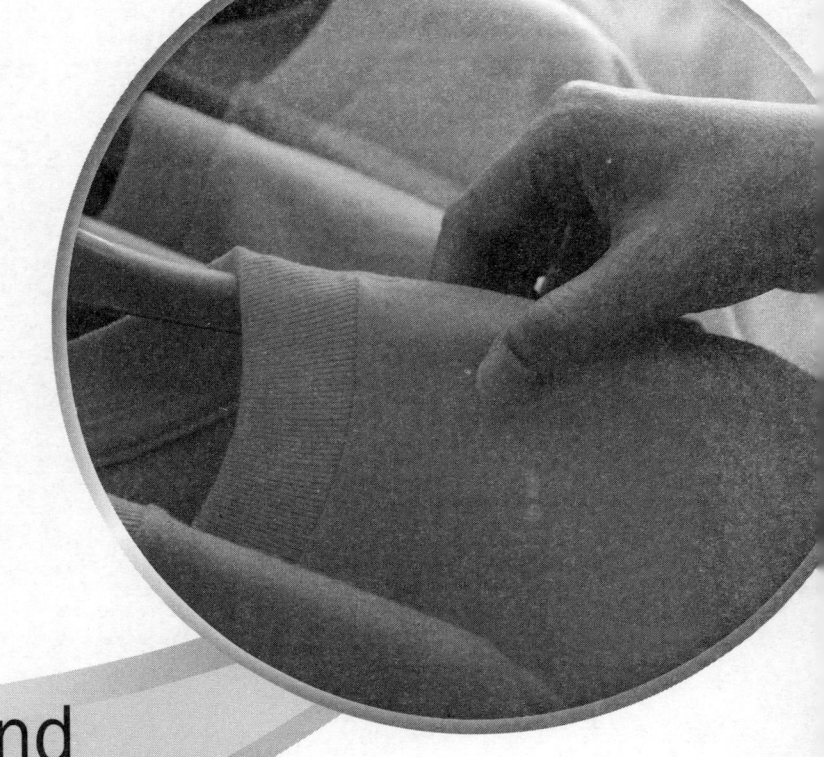

Measuring and Analysing Consumer Behaviour

CHAPTER 14:
Consumer Research Process

CHAPTER 15:
Consumption and Post-purchase Behaviour

CHAPTER FOURTEEN
Consumer Research Process

LEARNING OBJECTIVES

Consumer behaviour is the basis of marketing decisions: companies have to know what motivates and moves customers and how they take their decisions. This formidable task is accomplished through consumer research. This chapter describes consumer research techniques and how they are used by companies.

After studying this chapter, the reader will be able to

- understand the process and importance of consumer research for companies, brands, and consumers
- analyse the steps in consumer research process
- examine the different types of research processes and methods to conduct them
- comprehend qualitative and quantitative research methodology
- learn about sources of primary and secondary data, sampling, and questioning techniques
- scrutinize methods of measuring aspects of human behaviour through scaling techniques
- learn about the future of marketing research through data analytics

CASE STUDY

Tommy Hilfiger—Using Market Research for Higher Margins

Tommy Hilfiger is a global designer lifestyle brand, which inspires the 'classic American cool' spirit with its preppy designs. With more than 1200 stores and distribution in 90 countries, Tommy Hilfiger has a strong global brand awareness and recognition. As per the company's website, the global retail sales of Tommy Hilfiger brands were approximately $6 billion in 2012.

The brand's portfolio includes three lines. Each line targets a different core customer in terms of styling, category offering, price points, and channels of distribution. The Tommy Hilfiger brand is considered to be 'preppy with a twist', and focuses on consumers aged between 25 and 45 years. Hilfiger Denim is a fashion forward brand, targeting 25 to 30 year-old men and women, with premium denim offerings, including footwear, bags, accessories, eyewear, and fragrance. Tommy Girl focuses on ladies in the age group of 12 to 18 years, and offers youthful and spirited apparel such as denim, casual tops, sweaters, dresses, skirts, and accessories.

The fashion market is complex as there is a plethora of brands facing intense competition. The growth of private label brands of retailers poses a challenge to established brands. As a result, there has been a pressure on prices, reduction in margins, and flat growth. Consumers, on the other hand, are spoilt for choice and show a reduced brand loyalty.

As their tastes change fast, the industry has to cater to reduced time-to-market cycles. In addition, most consumers look for value for money, chasing deals, reduction sales, and online sales.

In this situation, the company had to opt for a method to select the most profitable customers and build targeted marketing strategies around them. This case study describes how this was achieved through market research. As most organizations only have a limited view of their customers using basic demographics and buying behaviour, the task was to ferret out as much information about customers as possible.

Through a comprehensive market research undertaken by Ernst and Young, Tommy Hilfiger changed its mindset from a traditional product-centric thinking to a more customer-centric one. This strategy helped the company to market its products at higher price points, in higher-end distribution channels and to different consumer groups. As a result, the company was able to optimize its marketing spend, launch-tailored customer relationship management (CRM) activities, and increased its sales margins and revenue.

The first task was to identify customers with the highest present and potential value. An in-depth understanding of the underlying motives and values that drive customer behaviour was needed. The segmentation chosen was based on the following factors:

- Buying behaviour and customer economics
- Customer needs and attitudes
- Customer experience and brand relationship
- Social demographics and lifestyle

Primary market research was taken up across Tommy Hilfiger's key markets in Europe, comprising nearly 6000 consumers in Belgium, Germany, Italy, Spain, and the United Kingdom. A brand pyramid for each segment was made, that represented the five main stages that customers go through—from awareness, brand proximity (feeling a bond with the brand), purchase intention (visiting a store to buy the brand), first-time buyers, and finally, loyal buyers. This helped in revealing significant differences in conversion ratios. It also revealed the leakages or the loss of customers at each stage of the brand pyramid, while moving up from one stage to another. The segments with the highest conversion ratios were qualified as primary segments.

For each segment, key drivers and personality traits were identified, along with their buying behaviour and customer economics, needs and attitudes, customer experience and brand relationship, and socio-demographics and lifestyle. A quantitative description of the segments was provided and communicated through booklets and workshops to different departments and key decision-makers.

The company then selected the most profitable customer segments, and optimized product management, channel management, and communication. It understood the unique characteristics of each segment and the potential ways to address the segments' needs. A targeted marketing strategy was built around three primary segments:

Conversion ratio Ratio of customers who knew about the brand to those who bought it. The company had to continually improve the conversion ratio in its target market.

Average annual customer spend The average annual sales revenue per customer was calculated. It differed significantly across segments. The highest contributors to revenue were identified.

Brand fit Through quantitative and qualitative assessment, the Tommy Hilfiger brand personality was mapped with the characteristics of each of the segments. The primary segments identified had the strongest fit with the Tommy Hilfiger brand, and they possessed the characteristics and growth potential for each segment.

The research had a bearing across the company in the following areas:

Product management The brand was able to link market segmentation as the guiding principle for future product design. This helped the transformation from product-centric to consumer-centric thinking. Product categories and collections were attuned to specific segments. It was also able to optimize allocation of product categories and product lines across channels to optimize the reach of primary segments. Each primary segment was analysed in terms of its attitude towards fashion, product categories bought, its reasons for buying, and its usage of sales channels. This helped to identify opportunities for attracting more customers from the primary segments in the target market.

Channel management Sales margin and revenue improvements were achieved by steering segments towards higher margin sales channels—from indirect to direct channels. The margins improved by moving customers from lower margin indirect channels to higher margin direct channels. In addition, the company got the necessary information on which CRM had to be based. The Tommy Hilfiger loyalty programme was designed to send customers to the direct channel by means of targeted initiatives such as personal sales and service propositions.

Marketing communication The company switched to segmentation-based communication. The shift from a generic marketing approach to a highly segmented and personalized communication helped optimize marketing spends through increased conversion ratios and sales revenue. The average annual sales revenue per customer increased significantly. The performance differences between segments increased over time, indicating the added value of targeting the primary segments. Building a long-term relationship helped to create revenue growth for the brand.

Customer life-time Value Tommy Hilfiger launched its first loyalty programme to increase the customer life-time value (CLV) by means of targeted communication. A CRM programme with segmentation-based communication strengthened its relationship with primary segments. With data from customers who signed up for the loyalty programme, Tommy Hilfiger was able to implement large-scale segmented marketing campaigns. Using the segments' profile and the analysis of individual customer's buying patterns, the brand approached individual customers. They used personalized communication such as tailored sales and service offerings. Each customer in the database was tagged with a segment label, based on an algorithm built for each segment and country separately. This was based on a subset of questions from the original market segmentation study, which are used in interactions with customers when they purchase products online. The CLV was increased through the following means:

- Improved margin by steering customers to the direct channel
- Increased revenue by stimulating cross- and up-selling
- Increase customer profitability by strengthening brand loyalty

While reading this chapter, try to answer the following questions:

1. In what ways can consumer research help companies?
2. What are the different types of research and what benefits do companies gain from it?
3. How is quantitative and qualitative research conducted? Mention the situations in which they are suitably employed.
4. How can companies ensure that the research is unbiased and free from errors?

Sources:

Gelsumino, Angelo, Bob van der Beek, and Kasia Blicharz, *How Tommy Hilfiger capitalizes on its most profitable customers*, Ernst & Young, Netherlands, 2010, http://performance.ey.com/2010/11/12/how-tommy-hilfiger-capitalizes-on-its-most-profitable-customers/, last accessed on 15 January 2014.

http://www.pvh.com/brands_tommy_hilfiger.aspx, last accessed on January 20 2014.

Malhotra, Naresh K., and S. Dash, *Marketing Research: An Applied Orientation*, 6/e, Pearson Education, New Delhi, 2011.

INTRODUCTION

Marketing is an interplay between companies and customers. Companies must not only make products that consumers want, but they must know how much quantity to make, how and where to deliver, and how best to reach their customers. This is a daunting task, as knowing what consumers want implies going into the complex world of people's minds, knowing how much to make means they must know how many people will actually pay for the products. If companies manufacture in excess, they will be flooded with returns and refund claims; if they manufacture too less, consumers will simply buy the next easily available product.

Moreover, markets change constantly. Yesterday's customers may have moved on, and yesterday's products may suddenly start looking dowdy. Companies, therefore, need a way to get information on a regular basis about consumers, markets, and the economic environment (see Fig. 14.1). Market research helps in obtaining this information.

Traditional methods of market research, such as customer interviews, surveys, and focus groups rely on direct questions. Customers are asked what features they would like in future products or are questioned about their reaction to current offerings. Ethnographic research follows a 'fly on the wall' approach—the researcher observes people in their own environment to find out how people use products. Both these approaches are quite opposite to the intuitive approach, or the gut feeling of managers and entrepreneurs, that has resulted in some hugely successful products in the past.

In this chapter, we discuss methods of measuring aspects of consumer behaviour that are described in the previous chapters. Discovering consumer needs and wants is a complex process; however, it is a skill greatly demanded by companies all over the world.

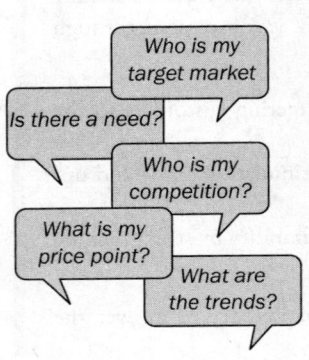

FIG. 14.1 Information obtained through market research

Importance of Consumer Research

The main purpose of market research is to provide businesses with a comprehensive view of consumers. As the amount of money involved in marketing is huge, it is no longer enough to make decisions by relying on the intuitive feelings of managers. Decisions need to be backed by data. Market research helps to support the process by significantly reducing the level of financial risk attached with investment decisions.

The earliest attempts to understand consumer behaviour were through the utility theory. Richarme (2005) explains that the theory assumed people to be rational beings, maximizing what they got out of their expenditure. This was followed by the satisficing model given by Herbert Simon that described consumers as looking for alternatives and stopping when they found a 'good enough' choice. In 1979, Daniel Kahneman and Amos Tversky developed the prospect theory, which added two elements—value that customers perceived, and endowment, in which a product becomes more precious if someone else owns it. Both these concepts are in the realm of psychology but are crucial to understand and measure consumer behaviour.

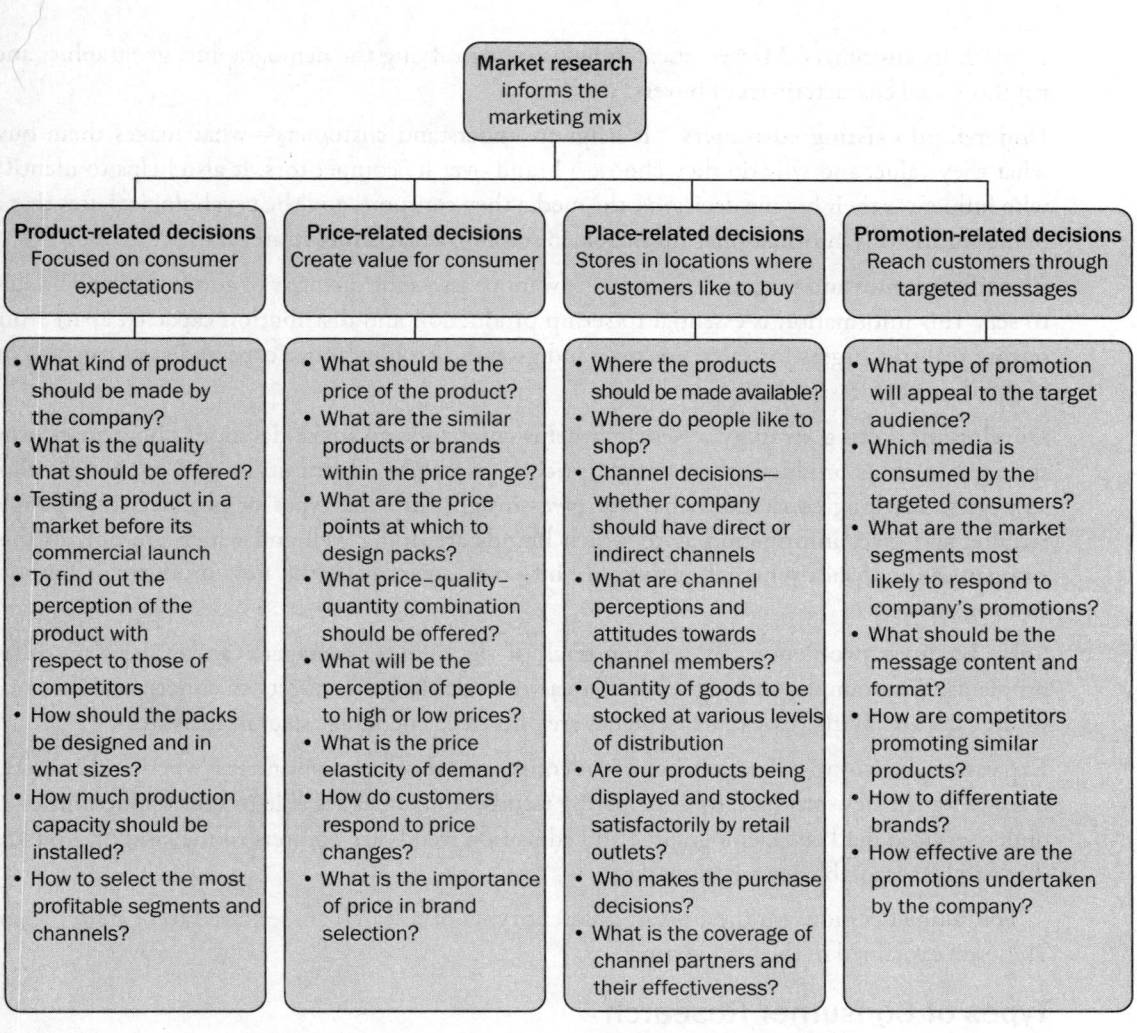

FIG. 14.2 Market-related decisions facilitated by market research

Market research can answer questions relating to analysis of consumers, competitors, and market trends. This enables companies to assess the level of demand for its products accurately. It also influences decisions to target capital investment on projects that will offer the best return on that investment, such as opening a new store or entering a new market.

Consumer research helps in all aspects of a marketing strategy. For each element, managers require data for taking decisions. The kind of decisions for which data can be gathered through research is shown in Fig. 14.2. It can be inferred that market research helps companies in the following ways:

Identify potential customers and segments Companies can identify buyers for its products by understanding customer needs in order to devise effective campaigns and to decide on channels to reach its customers. Market research helps in identifying the demographic, geographic, and psycho-social characteristics of buyers.

Understand existing customers It helps to understand customers—what makes them buy, what they value, and why do they choose a brand over its competitors. It also helps to identify who influences their buying decisions, the media they consume, and the psychological uses that a brand fulfils. This information is invaluable in framing a marketing strategy.

Identify volumes and targets Companies want to assess the quantity of goods they will be able to sell. This information is essential to set up production and distribution capacity, apart from setting realistic targets for sales, revenue, and growth. An idea about expected sales can also be assessed through research.

Develop marketing strategy Research helps companies to make decisions about marketing strategies such as products, their design, pricing, packaging, distribution, and communication strategies. Tracking consumer behaviour gives insight into the types of products that people require, and gives information as to which brands are doing well and which are not, so that companies can decide whether to diversify into new areas, or launch new products or support existing ones.

Solve business problems By keeping track of the market, managers can resolve day-to-day problems. For example, keeping track of area-wise sales helps managers to concentrate on areas where sales are falling. Consumer schemes are offered to encourage sales in such areas.

Expansion decisions Research helps to identify areas for expansion and test whether the market is ready for the new product. By anticipating trends, companies are able to spot opportunities or under-serviced markets. Demographic and education trends are pointers to the kind of products that will be acceptable for target markets.

For taking decisions on these areas, different types of research are required to be undertaken. These are explained in the next section.

Types of Consumer Research

It becomes clear from the previous section that information inputs are required at all stages of a business operation. All decisions are linked—how much consumers will buy at a given price has an impact all the way back to setting up of production capacity to suppliers of raw materials. Managers have to decide which type of research is the best suited for a given situation. Several types of consumer research provide vital inputs for decision-making and are explained here.

- Market research and consumer behaviour research
- Primary research and secondary research
- Qualitative and quantitative research

Market research and consumer behaviour research

Companies are keen to know how their communication messages and products will be received by consumers, whether their products will be accepted or not, and whether people will buy them in expected quantities. This can be done in two ways—market research and consumer behaviour research.

Market research is a systematic collection, analysis, and interpretation of data related to the market and the surrounding environment. It consists of research in marketing strategies, marketing channels, and marketing institutions. The stages are described as follows:

Marketing strategies   These refer to the research into price, product, promotion, and place decisions.

Marketing channels   These involve finding out where people like to shop, based on the image and positioning of the product. High-end luxury products, for instance, cannot be sold through agents and in normal retail channels because people expect a high-class store and service along with the products.

Marketing institutions   Marketing institutions, such as associations of producers, common marketing initiatives, unions, auctions, and so on are rich sources of market information and research.

Consumer behaviour research, on the other hand, is the study of preferences, motivations, and buying behaviour of targeted customers through direct observation, mail surveys, telephone or face-to-face interviews, and from published sources. In this type of research, the objective is to know the consumers, understand their decision-making influences and processes, their buying and consumption behaviour, and their thinking as well. Consumer research focuses on how companies can anticipate and respond to what people are thinking.

Understanding consumer behaviour is the driver behind a firm's marketing strategy. It shapes new marketing strategies, provides the necessary information about product development, the nature of promotions to be done, and how to place products at places where consumers like to shop.

The differences between market research and consumer research are summed up in Table 14.1.

TABLE 14.1   Differences between marketing and consumer research

	Marketing research	Consumer research
Focus	Marketing environment	Customers
What is researched	Market trends, opportunities, and risks	Individual motives and drivers
End result	Market potential	Consumption behaviour and trends

Primary research and secondary research

Primary research is collected first-hand for a specific purpose. Secondary research consists of data that has already been gathered and recorded by someone else for purposes other than the current project. Sources for secondary research include internal records of a company, or information taken from a book, database, or journals.

Primary research involves finding out new information, answers to specific questions, or solution for a specific problem. For instance, a company may undertake primary research to find out why sales in a particular segment are declining. Such research may take the form of direct questioning, surveys, questionnaires, telephone interviews, or focus groups. These methods are explained later in this chapter.

Secondary research is cheaper and faster, as it uses information that has already been collected for some other purpose. For example, a company's internal records that includes sales bills made at the time of the sale can yield precious information about location of customers, how much they bought over a period of time, what kind of products they bought, and provide information for sales forecasting. Similarly, published data about industry or consumer trends becomes very useful for companies seeking to understand segments and targeting.

Qualitative and quantitative research

Quantitative research involves variables that can be measured or quantified. It involves questioning a large number of respondents. The measurement must be objective, quantitative, and statistically valid. The sample size selected is based on formulae that indicate how much is needed from a given population in order to attain the findings with an acceptable degree of accuracy. Companies generally seek findings with at least 95 per cent confidence interval; therefore, if the survey is repeated 100 times, then it would yield the same response 95 times, with an error margin of plus or minus five percentage points.

Qualitative research is based on information that is not measurable, such as feelings, concepts, definitions, characteristics, attitudes, and so on. These include the following:

- How people feel about products and services
- What they like or do not like
- What they would want from a new product

Qualitative research is subjective, exploratory, and open-ended. In-depth interview is conducted for a small number of people or a focus group is formed. The moderator probes and explores the responses to find out about people's perceptions, opinions, and feelings. Quantitative research, on the contrary, is objective, and measures what it assumes to be a static reality.

The differences between qualitative and quantitative research are summarized in Table 14.2.

TABLE 14.2 Differences between quantitative and qualitative research

Elements	Qualitative research	Quantitative research
Purpose	• To discover underlying reasons and motivations • To find out insights into a problem, or generating ideas • To discover trends in thought and opinion • To discover new product ideas, positioning, and other strategies	• To measure or quantify markets or consumers • To generalize results from a sample for the entire population • To describe the size of a market, segments and other characteristics of markets and consumers
Objectives	• To explore phenomenon and describe variations • To describe and explain relationships	• To confirm hypothesis and quantify variation • To quantify markets • To predict causal relationships
Sample	• Usually a small number of non-representative cases • Non-probability sampling methods	• Usually a large sample representing the population. Probability sampling. • Results are extrapolated to the entire population
Question format	Open-ended	Close-ended
Data format	Textual	Numerical

(Contd)

TABLE 14.2 (Contd)

Elements	Qualitative research	Quantitative research
Research methods	Observation, individual depth interviews or group interaction; subjective	Structured techniques such as questionnaires, surveys, experimentation, interviews; objective
Data collection	• Unstructured or semi-structured techniques • Open-ended questions • Probing by researcher and disguised questions	• Usually closed-ended questions with given response choices • Direct questions that require no probing
Analysis	• Non-statistical, analysis of verbal responses to identify themes • Conducted by behavioural science experts	• Statistical data analysis based on standard testing methods. • Findings are conclusive

Qualitative research methods are explained later in the chapter.

OVERVIEW OF THE CONSUMER RESEARCH PROCESS

When a company decides to undertake research, it follows eight steps as follows:

- Define the research problem and objectives
- Develop a research plan
- Search for and evaluate secondary data
- Design a primary research study
- Select a sample
- Collect primary data
- Analyse the data
- Use the findings to make marketing decisions

These steps are explained here.

Defining the Research Problem and Objectives of Research

The research objective is the specific query that is sought to be answered by the research. It examines what must be questioned, sets the parameters of the project, and suggests the methods for data collection. This stage, also called problem definition, involves stating the problem and identifying the components that are required to be studied.

Clarity about why the research is to be done is the first and the most difficult step in the consumer research process. At this stage, the company must clarify what is to be achieved by undertaking the research. Questions such as 'What is the purpose of the research? What is the problem that is hoped to be solved?', help in defining the objectives of research.

A carefully designed statement can help in determining the type and level of information needed, the kind of research that should be undertaken, and the kind of data required. Sometimes, to determine the direction of research, a small exploratory research is carried out before conducting a full-scale study. This is done to explore the main issues and to help define the research process.

Developing a Research Plan

The research plan consists of identifying the kind of questions that need to be asked, whom to ask those questions, and what methods have to be used for analysing the data so obtained. It involves testing of hypotheses, making a plan to draw a representative sample, and deciding the methodology to collect data from the sample.

Searching for and Evaluating Secondary Data

After the problem has been defined, the next step is to see what data is available within the company. Such data is called secondary data. Usually, companies have much data available with them, including studies undertaken earlier or sales data, that have information on sales and payments that can yield insight into market share and market coverage. Such information sometimes does away the need for primary research.

There are two types of secondary data—internal and external.

Internal Secondary Data

Data that is already available in the company and which was collected for some other purpose is called internal secondary data. Such data is available in the company in the accounts department, in sales reports, pending order analysis, or customer complaint reports. Though these reports were collected for some other purpose, they can provide inputs for marketing research and analysis.

For example, for making a sales forecast, the researcher needs to collate data from the past sales reports that are already available in the company. The advantage of using internal records is that the internal data available is available easily and is organized in a way that is consistent with the company's products and brands. Moreover, the data is available with suitable geographic and business heads so as to support marketing-related decisions. Current data is also available from external secondary sources.

External Secondary Data

External sources for secondary data consist of published data available with the following:

Government departments Government departments usually have a lot of data pertaining to their area. These include data on transport, schools, public health, and so on, and are collected by the government regularly.

Census records Population figures are available with the census department.

Trade associations Associations such as the Federation of Indian Chambers of Commerce and Industry (FICCI), the Confederation of Indian Industry (CII), and those relating to particular industries collect data regularly and commission reports relating to their area of operation.

Media Newspapers and magazines, directories, and trade and research journals are a great source of secondary data. The Internet is also a huge resource of secondary data.

Professional research companies Several professional research agencies such as Nielsen, IMRB, McKinsey, Ernst and Young, and others undertake research, and publish industry reports. They also publish reports pertaining to a variety of issues relating to marketing.

Computer databases Computer databases are available on a variety of data subjects. Data about population, projections, and trends, for example, are available on computer databases.

Internet Websites, blogs, and social media comments are also a source of secondary data, especially to research consumer sentiment.

Secondary data has several advantages as follows:

Less expensive It is much cheaper than conducting a field study and collecting data.

Quick It is faster to obtain. Published data has no lead time, unlike field studies in which data has to be collected, collated, and analysed.

Helps primary research It is used in designing primary research. For example, sample sizes can be estimated by studying census data, and can also indicate the questions that should be asked and the ways to conduct research.

Indicates macro trends It helps unravel macro trends and gives the larger picture. Such research is usually outside the scope and means of companies. Studying the education trends from published data, for instance, gives an indication as to the kinds of products that will be consumed in the future.

While secondary data has several advantages, it needs to be used with caution. Such data tends to be outdated, as it was collected for some other purpose earlier. It may also not be relevant to a company's business. Most important, credibility of data that is easily available will always be in question.

Designing a Primary Research Study

Primary research is undertaken to collect specific information relating to the current problem. While secondary research provides a basis for research, to address a specific problem, more relevant information is needed. Primary research is conducted when detailed information on consumers' purchasing patterns or product usage is needed. At this stage, the method of collecting primary data is decided—survey, interview, or observation. Questionnaires are designed and tested, samples are finalized, and the methodology is worked out.

Sampling Methods

As it is not possible to talk to or survey every consumer or non-consumer, companies decide that they can select some people and question them, with the hope that the findings from these people will be applicable to all the population. Selecting these few people out of the total population is called sampling. The selection has to be unbiased and be representative of the total population as possible. An unbiased sample is, thus, an accurate representation of the entire population and can help draw conclusions about the entire population. This is a crucial task; managers tend to think out of their own experiences. It is common, for instance, to hear generalizations like 'my children are very smart with computers, so the entire younger generation is smart these days.' Such observations will lead to wrong results.

In an unbiased sample, each member of the population (consumer, respondent, or product) should have an equal chance of being chosen. To ensure that we get an accurate representative sample, we need methods that can remove our inherent bias. These sampling methods are summarized in Fig. 14.3, and are categorized into two types—probability sampling and non-probability sampling.

Probability Sampling Methods

Probability methods rely on random selection. This means that they follow a procedure in which each unit in the population has an equal chance of being chosen. This method has been put to

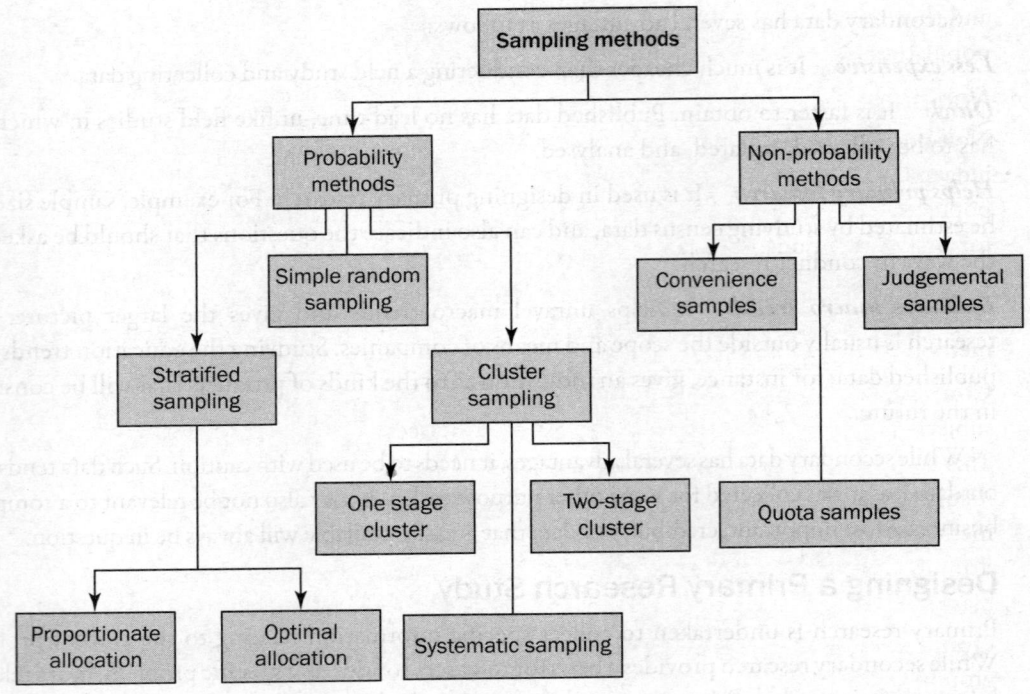

FIG. 14.3 Sampling methods

use for several years in areas such as picking a name out of a hat at a party. To select entities from a larger population, computers are used for generating random numbers. Probability sampling can be of various types—simple random, stratified, systematic, and cluster.

Simple random sampling A selection drawn on a random process, either using a random number generator or a random number table, so that each person in the population has the same probability of being selected, is called simple random sampling.

Stratified sampling All people are not the same and sub-populations vary in terms of characteristics. Choosing only one group will result in faulty findings; hence, companies require taking a sample from each sub-population. Stratification is the process of dividing members of the population into homogeneous subgroups. Simple random sampling or systematic sampling is then applied within each sub-group. For example, a company may like to choose a sample from upper, middle, and lower classes to find out consumer behaviour across the entire population and divide the population into three strata.

Systematic sampling Systematic sampling is a statistical method for selecting elements from an ordered sampling frame, like a list. The sampling starts by selecting an element from the list at random and then every kth element is selected, where k is the sampling interval. For example, if we want to study customers in a shop, we may decide to interview every 10th person checking out and ask the questions. This is an example of systematic sampling.

Cluster sampling In this technique, the total population is divided into clusters, and random samples from the groups are selected. For example, to survey a city, we may divide it in areas and then take random samples from each of the areas chosen. This is an example of dividing the population into clusters.

Non-probability Sampling

Non-probability sampling occurs when researchers select samples based on their subjective judgement rather than random selection. Thus, in this sampling technique, all the elements in the population do not have an equal chance of being selected. Non-probability sampling is often done for practical reasons; sometimes companies lack the time or resources to conduct full-fledged surveys. In such situations, managers perform quick surveys based on samples they can access conveniently, such as their friends or the company's own employees. There are three common methods in non-probability sampling—convenience, quota, and judgemental.

Convenience sampling Convenience sampling is a non-probability sampling technique where subjects are selected because of their convenient accessibility and proximity to the researcher. This could mean surveying friends, students, or colleagues that the researcher has access to, or it could mean stopping people in a street corner, or asking questions to passers-by in a mall. The method, though quick, may not give reliable results. For example, if a researcher wants to study drinking habits of young people and asks people attending a party, the results would be highly biased.

Quota sampling In quota sampling, the population is segmented into mutually exclusive subgroups, and entities are selected from each segment based on a specified proportion. For example, a company may wish to survey young people, but wants to ensure 200 females and 200 males are interviewed in each college. A quota is thus established and the researcher will have to ensure that such numbers are interviewed in each area.

Judgemental sampling When a researcher or an expert uses his judgement in selecting the entities from the population, it is called judgement sampling. This method is used if the population to be studied is difficult to locate or if some members are thought to be more appropriate than others for the survey. For instance, if a company wants to survey its wholesalers, a manager will be able to recommend who should be interviewed and who could be left out. They may do so on the basis of the size and knowledge of wholesalers.

Collecting Primary Data

Once the research study has been designed and the samples have been defined, data has to be collected. For this, the researchers need to go out and meet the selected respondents and conduct interviews or administer surveys, and record the responses.

There are three common ways of conducting primary research—surveys, interviews, and observations.

Surveys Surveys involve asking participants about their opinions and behaviour through a pre-determined questionnaire. Surveys may be conducted through personal interviews, asking questions over a telephone and filling up survey forms, sending questionnaires by mail or e-mail, or undertaking an online survey.

Interviews Interviews are conducted by asking participants questions in a one-on-one or a small group setting.

Observation In observation, the research does not ask questions, but is involved in watching, counting involves observing and measuring markets and consumers, such as finding out how many people visit a store.

Analysing Data

The responses collected in the previous stage are collected and the data is tabulated. The task at this stage is to make sense of the data collected. Statistical tests are applied to check the reliability and validity of data. The statistical methods used for data analysis are as follows:

Correlation Correlation is a statistical measure that indicates the extent to which two or more variables are related to each other in the sense that they vary together over a period. A positive correlation indicates that these variables increase or decrease in parallel; a negative correlation indicates the extent to which one variable increases as the other decreases.

Regression Regression is a procedure used to estimate how the value of a dependent variable changes as the values of a number of independent variables change. For example, companies may want to find out how sales revenue (the dependent variable) changes in relation to expenditures on advertising, placement of ads, and timing of ads (independent variables).

Discriminant analysis This statistical technique is used to assign data to one of two or more groups. For example, this technique would be used if a company wants to find out which advertising would be most effective for different types of products.

Factor analysis Factor analysis is used to determine the strongest underlying components from a larger set of variables; it identifies a small number of factors that explain most of the relationship in a larger number of variables. Thus, factor analysis is about data reduction. Factor analysis is used where many variables are correlated and identifies which relations are the strongest. For example, factor analysis can be used to determine the key attributes from a larger set of attributes that influence consumer choice.

Cluster analysis Cluster analysis is used to separate objects into a specific number of groups that are homogenous and mutually exclusive. This process is used in market segmentation where segments are established on the basis of similarities among consumers.

Conjoint analysis This statistical method is used to determine the relative importance consumers attach to attributes in the consumer choice process. It is used to measure preferences for product features, to learn how changes to price affect demand for products or service, and to forecast the likely acceptance of a product if brought to market. See CB in Action (Using conjoint analysis).

Multidimensional scaling Multidimensional scaling (MDS) represents a class of techniques to represent perceptions and preferences of consumers through a visual chart. It is used to make perceptual or spatial maps of competing brands or products. Brands are shown in a space of attributes in which distance between the brands represents dissimilarity. Malhotra and Dash (2011) explain that this technique is used for image measurement, market segmentation, new product development, attitude scale construction, channel decisions, advertising, and pricing analysis.

CB IN ACTION Using Conjoint Analysis

Conjoint or trade-off analysis is one of the most widely-used quantitative methods in marketing research. This exercise helps understand conjoint analysis by doing an exercise that measures preferences for product features and to forecast the likely acceptance of a product if brought to the market.

First, get the attributes of a number of laptops. Then answer the following question:

How likely are you to buy this laptop on this attribute?

Use a scale from 0 to 100, where 0 = not likely at all to 100 = definitely would purchase. The total scores give the likelihood of purchase of that particular product.

Readers can take sample conjoint analysis surveys at http://www.sawtoothsoftware.com/index.php?option=com_content&view=article&id=887&catid=80#trial-version, last accessed on 30 September 2014.

Brand	Toshiba Satellite	Score	Dell Vostro	Score	Lenovo Essential	Score
Processor	3rd Gen PDC		Core i3		Core i5	
RAM	2GB		4GB		8GB	
Hard disk capacity	500GB		500GB		500GB	
Looks	Premium glossy black		Grey		White	
Operating system	No OS		Windows 8		Windows 8	
Price	₹22,850		₹33,000		₹45,000	
Total score	–		–		–	

Presenting Findings

Finally, the researcher has to present the findings or suggest what action can and should be taken to solve the problem being researched. Report presentation is the final step of the research process. The report contains what the researcher started out to do, the objectives of the study, research methodology, review of secondary data, analysis of primary data, findings, and recommendations. The report should also mention the limitations of the study.

Management decisions are guided by the recommendations made by the researcher. Since this is the tangible result of the research process, the findings must be written or presented in a way that is easy to read and visualize. Tables, graphs, bar charts, and pictographs must be used to make the report more acceptable and comprehensible for the management. The oral presentation must be lively and use visual aids. Malhotra and Dash (2011) mention two principles that are used at this stage:

Tell 'em principle The 'tell 'em' principle is a presentation technique that creates anticipation at the start and helps the audience remember the key points at the end. It uses repetition to hammer home the key points, but without appearing to be coercive or boring. The principle states the following:

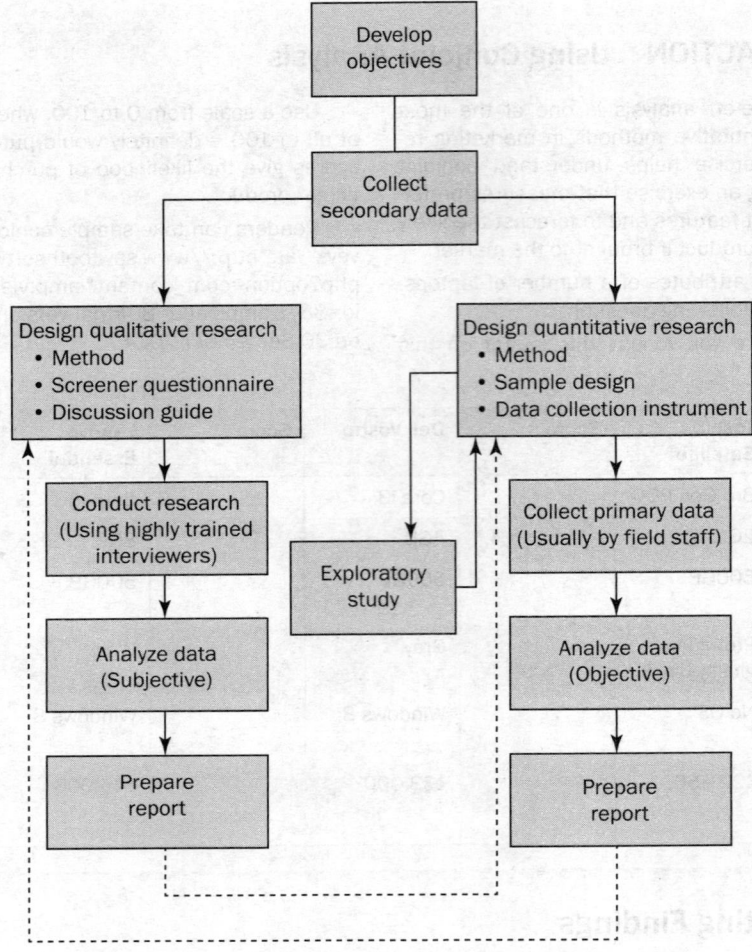

FIG. 14.4 Research process

Tell 'em what you are going to tell 'em Summarize what is ahead, and build anticipation and excitement.

Tell 'em Tell them in detail what you want to tell them. This is the main body of the presentation.

Tell 'em what you told 'em Summarize what has been said, highlighting key points and important messages.

KISS 'em principle This principle states that the presenter must keep it simple and straightforward (KISS).

The research process is shown as a flow chart in Fig. 14.4.

QUALITATIVE RESEARCH

Understanding consumers and their psychology requires delving into the human mind. Qualitative research is used when there is need for deep understanding of human behaviour and analysis of

CB IN ACTION   Identifying Consumers and Market Size

Suppose you are representing a company that wants to market a new brand of chocolates in your locality. You want to cover the maximum consumers of your locality. Your task is to identify consumers, quantify them, assess the market size, and develop a marketing mix for them.

- Identify the secondary sources of data that you would use.
- Would you need a primary study? If so, what kind of study would you propose to conduct?
- Develop a research plan for assessing the market in your locality.
- How would you ensure that the data you collect is free from bias and is correct?

the underlying reasons for the behaviour. It helps study behaviours, beliefs, and attitudes that are difficult to quantify. It answers the why and how of decision-making, by providing information about the human side of buying, that often contains contradictory behaviour, beliefs, opinions, emotions, and relationships. Such qualitative methods are effective in identifying intangible factors such as social norms, socio-economic status, gender roles, ethnicity, and religion, whose role in consumer decision-making have been discussed in previous chapters. Thus, qualitative research is especially effective in obtaining culturally-specific information about values, opinions, behaviour, and social contexts of people.

Qualitative research uses various techniques such as narratology, storytelling, classical ethnography, projective techniques, and metaphor analysis. These methods are used to

- analyse opinions, feelings, attitudes, and experiences
- describe consumer behaviour as it occurs naturally—no attempt is made to manipulate the situation
- take a holistic perspective, rather than looking at a set of variables
- help to discover underlying causes that can help develop concepts and theories

Qualitative data collected through direct encounters—through interview or observation—is rather time-consuming. Some of the methods used are described here.

Discovering Hidden Needs

The main challenge in consumer research is to discover hidden needs. Goffin, Lemke, and Koners (2011) describe the hidden needs analysis in their book, *Identifying Hidden Needs*, which helps to find out about consumer needs that may not be stated or described, and hence, requires a deeper probing than traditional market research. Direct questions are inadequate because customers, sometimes, are unable to describe their requirements and are able to merely express their ideas about improvements to existing products. The authors mention that traditional market research traps companies into developing incremental and me-too products. To get over this trend, companies use sophisticated methods from psychology and anthropology to uncover customers' hidden needs—needs that they are unable to articulate or have not even recognized themselves.

The main methods of hidden needs analysis are repertory grid analysis and lead user groups. Along with ethnographic research, these techniques have major advantages when compared with traditional market research tools and, when used in combination, are very effective at uncovering customers' hidden needs.

Repertory Grid Analysis

Repertory grid analysis helps to understand how individuals think and uncover their cognitive maps. This technique is ideal for developing new product ideas. It uses indirect questions and stimulates users to compare and contrast their experiences of existing products. Through the process of comparing and contrasting, customers' hidden needs can be revealed. Many companies have used repertory grid analysis in their market research.

The process is a semi-structured interview in which the respondent is confronted with a triad of elements and is asked to specify some important way in which two of the elements are alike and thereby different from the third element. The characteristic that the respondent uses to distinguish between the elements is called the construct. Often, the constructs most important to the participant are surprising, and is the key aspect of the exercise—to uncover what is important to the participant.

After discovering a construct, the participant names its polar opposites, and is asked to rate it on a scale. Then, the interviewer moves on to the next triad of options. Typically, these steps are repeated until the respondent mentions no new constructs anymore. The key is to elicit as many constructs as possible, without any suggestions from the researcher.

Lead Users

Lead users are customers who use products under extremely demanding conditions, such as war zones, space probes, or places where there is high human traffic. For example, 3M studied the requirements of field hospitals in war zones when it was developing hygiene-related products for the operating room. In demanding situations like wars, users often have to modify products as they work, and the company could obtain ideas for product improvements by looking at how products were being used in those conditions.

Hidden needs techniques are most effective when applied together. The unique insights obtained from each technique can be studied in contrast to gain a deeper market understanding. However, organizational barriers need to be overcome if new methods of market research are to be adopted, because managers are mostly trained in traditional research methods and are reluctant to adopt hidden needs approaches, as they go against traditional methods.

Observational or Ethnographic Research

Hidden needs are also discovered by observational or ethnographic research. This method consists of simply watching people as they come across products or advertisements, make purchase decisions, use products, and so on. It is based on the assumption, 'You can observe a lot just by watching.' It is a systematic market research that involves observing customers in their own environment using products and services.

Ethnography is a branch of anthropology. Anthropological researchers visit consumers in their homes or offices to observe and listen in a non-directed way, following a 'fly on the wall' approach. By mere observation, companies learn about the context in which customers use a product, the meaning that the product might hold in their lives and spot opportunities for breakthrough innovations as well. Systematic observation allows market researchers to understand the role products or services play in people's lives. Cohort, cross sectional, and case studies are part of observational techniques because the researcher simply observes and makes no intervention. This is an important research technique because many questions can be answered simply by observing people. Moreover, it is a non-intrusive method that does not depend on judgement of the consumers, which may often be wrong.

The advantage of observational research is that companies come to know how people really interact with products, displays, and promotions. For example, the case study in Chapter 12 shows, to learn how consumers behave in stores, Apple created a prototype store in a warehouse near its headquarters and simply observed people as they came and interacted with the products. The insights from this observational research led to Apple's store design in which people could experience and learn on the machines themselves. The stores were an instant hit across the world.

The key characteristics of ethnographic market research are as follows:

Visits to customers' locations   The researcher visits customers in their homes and collects qualitative data such as videos of product usage and contextual interviews. Some prepared and some spontaneous questions are also asked. The analysis is done by identifying key issues in qualitative data, looking for contradictions when a customer says one thing and does another, and identifying the cultural characteristics of the customer. By observing customers as they naturally use products, companies gain powerful insights into product requirements.

Audio or visual recordings   A common approach in observational research is to film customers using existing products, or their interviews, and then conducting an analysis of what was observed.

Often, valuable insights are obtained while observing the contradictions between what consumers say and what they do. For example, Panasonic used ethnographic market research to probe into requirements for an electric shaver for women. By recording the grooming behaviour of women and talking to them, the company was able to develop an ergonomic design with the right colours and style to fit the market. The product, named Lady Shaver, was significantly different from shavers available in the market. The company found that the Japanese market required high-gloss white shavers that was associated with quality. American women, on the other hand, preferred pastel colours with a rubberized finish. Another example of such research is given in Exhibit 14.1.

Product and consumer photos   Photographs of consumers taken discreetly can show product purchase patterns. They can show when and where consumers are stimulated, and this knowledge can be used to create new product designs. Close-up pictures of consumers' eyes, for example, show the size of their iris—when stimulated with product promotions or packaging, the iris expands involuntarily.

Store displays   The effect of store displays on consumer behaviour can be seen in videos and photographs, and is much better than asking people about them. In supermarkets, researchers can correlate their effect on sales, and also assess how the design of point-of-purchase promotions influences whether consumers put the products in their shopping carts.

Consumer traffic patterns   Videos of store layouts reveal how people move in stores, where they pause, and what is the order of their purchases. This helps in designing displays, product placement, and store ambiance.

Ethnographic research is gaining popularity in consumer research. Anderson (2009) writes, 'Corporate ethnography isn't just for innovation anymore. It's central to gaining a full understanding of your customers and the business itself.' Ethnography has been increasingly used in popular companies such as Xerox, Intel, Procter & Gamble, Steelcase, and Microsoft. These companies employ ethnographers to help them design better products or explore new market opportunities.

Though ethnographic research is the only technique that really allows companies to know how people use products, it is both labour-intensive and expensive. If the researcher is not experienced, certain cultural behaviours can easily be overlooked.

 EXHIBIT 14.1 Using Ethnographic Research—A PC for Students and Teachers

Ethnography has wide applications, ranging from product design to developing marketing strategy.

The design of Intel's new Classmate PC with its full touch-screen support is based on observations and research collected about the way computers are used in real-world classroom settings. This case study describes how the Classmate PC was developed using ethnographic research.

'Yes, Intel employs an anthropologist. Her name is Genevieve Bell. Her mission is to understand how people are using today's technology so we can create better technology for tomorrow,' says the Intel website.

The Classmate PC is Intel's entry into the market for low-cost and child-friendly notebook computer for children in the developing world. It met with phenomenal success, selling more than two million units. Anthropologist Genevieve Bell and her team used ethnographic research to help design the computer. Bell used observational research to watch how children used computers, interviewed them, and asked them unstructured questions. Intel used ethnography to understand how children actually learn in the classroom environment—what were classrooms like? What were the learning and teaching processes and how does one develop a product to fit a classroom in Uganda as well as one in Buenos Aires?

In a video published by Intel on its YouTube channel, the company describes the background research conducted for the design of Classmate PC. By observing how students collaborate and move around in classroom environments, Intel introduced micro-mobility, or the ability to move computers by students. The company realized that children should have the ability to carry around Classmate PCs in the same way that they carry around paper and pencil. The computer also had to be rugged to be able to bear everyday use.

The result was a small and inexpensive computer, with a solid and semi-rugged construction that could bear rough handling. According to a review posted on www.cnet.com, the Classmate PC looks 'more like a toy than a laptop computer, with a thick, plastic chassis with rounded corners suitable for children. The keyboard is water resistant, and the entire body felt solid and unyielding. Even the back of the lid, which is covered with a thin, flimsy piece of plastic on many laptops, felt rugged. The system has a removable snap-on cover, made of thick leather, which doubles as a handle.'

The teacher's needs were also observed and kept into account. The Classmate PC was designed so that the teacher could control and direct students. From the teacher's laptop, the students' work can be monitored, text messages can be directly sent to the student's PCs, work could be transferred to screens of the students, or PCs could be remotely 'silenced' by turning off their screens.

Can you find other product breakthroughs using ethnographic research?

Sources:
Intel Classmate PC review http://reviews.cnet.co.uk/netbooks/intel-classmate-pc-review-49296097/, last accessed on 26 January 2014.
Intel sponsors of tomorrow–A minute with Genevieve Bell, http://www.intel.com/content/www/us/en/sponsors-of-tomorrow/sot-genevieve-bell-60-video.html, last accessed on 26 January 2014.
Intel website, http://www.intel.com/content/www/us/en/corporate-responsibility/better-future/intel-anthropologist-geneieve-bell.html, last accessed on 26 January 2014.
Knowledge@Australian School of Business (2011), The rise of ethnography: How market research has gone gonzo http://knowledge.asb.unsw.edu.au/article.cfm?articleid=1499, last accessed on 20 January 2014.

Depth Interviews

Depth interview is an open-ended and in-depth conversation with an individual, conducted by a trained researcher. The purpose of the interview is to deeply explore the participant's points of view, feelings, attitudes, or perspectives. Such interviews are wide ranging and probe into the issues in detail. They are semi-structured—though the issues are probed, the interview does not involve asking a set of predetermined questions; instead, they encourage people to speak and express their views at length.

Conducted telephonically or face-to-face, in-depth interviews help understand individual motivations about products and brands. However, they are time-consuming, expensive, and require skilled researchers as responses can sometimes be difficult to interpret. Companies also have to guard against interviewer bias.

Laddering

Laddering is an interview probing technique that helps elicit ideas and concepts that people use to organize their world. The interviewer probes or 'peels the layers' of the participant's experience by asking probing questions. The technique helps in understanding people's core values and beliefs, and attempts to understand the way in which the respondent sees the world. Often used in psychology, it is used in marketing to describe the link between customers' values and their purchasing behaviour. Laddering uses the means–end chain model to understand how consumers perceive outcomes of product use and consumption. According to the theory, there is a hierarchy of consumer perceptions and product knowledge that ranges from attributes (A) to consumption consequences (C) to personal values (V), as follows:

Attributes Individuals recognize the attributes of a product easily. For example, 'I like this car, because it has a powerful engine.'

Consequences Attributes have consequences for the individual, for example, the car makes its driver feel young and free. Each attribute may have one or more consequences for any individual.

Values Finally, each consequence is linked to a core value of the person's life. For example, for a young driver, the sense of youth used in the marketing campaign of the car makes that driver feel youthful.

The A-C-V sequence forms a chain or ladder, that indicates the relationship between a product's attribute and a core value. We can collect all the ladders to form a hierarchical value map that illustrates all the means–end connections, and describes the linkages between customers' values and their purchasing behaviour. This theory provides a framework for capturing laddering research data and a model for assessing consumer values and behaviour.

Laddering shows the connection between consumer and product through consequences linked with product use and, finally, consumers' values. Since product attributes are means through which consumers achieve their ultimate values, in the means–end chain model, products are not chosen and purchased for themselves or their characteristics, but rather for the meaning they engender in the minds of people. A means–end chain is a conceptual structure linking product attributes and consumer values.

Focus Groups

A focus group is a form of qualitative research in which a group of people are asked about their perceptions, opinions, beliefs, and attitudes towards a product. Such a group usually comprises eight to 12 members, led by a moderator who uses the group interaction to gain information about a specific issue. The interview is conducted in an informal manner where respondents are free to give views on any aspect.

Focus groups are used in the early stages of product development, and are used to get feedback regarding new products before they are commercially launched. They are used to develop, package, name, or test the market for a new product. This can help companies know whether the product will be accepted in the market.

There are online focus groups as well, where selected respondents are required to log in at a fixed time to take part in an online discussion. The moderator guides the discussion as respondents interact with each other as well as the moderator on a real-time basis. The advantage is that respondents from all over the world can take part in the discussion. Often, respondents open up more online than they would in person. Similar to in-person focus groups, online groups are usually limited to eight to 10 participants.

Through online groups, travel time and costs are avoided, as they are faster than traditional groups. The group can be drawn from a wide geographical area. However, as with in-person groups, the skill of the moderator, the quality of the respondents, and the ability to draw results are critical.

Online groups are also useful to judge reactions when respondents are required to interact with a website or a prototype, view online ads or concepts, videos, commercials, and so on. As the participant is viewing the screen, the webcam starts recording his/her face. After the task is completed, the participant is questioned about the message or performance. This type of research can yield real insight when people interact with online ads or websites and help improve the online experience.

Projective Techniques

Projective techniques are unstructured and indirect methods that encourage participants to project their feelings, beliefs, and attitudes to the product or brand. They are asked to project their own thoughts to situations and to interpret them. In doing so, they reveal their own prejudices and beliefs. Sometimes, the situations are vague and ambiguous, that cause respondents to project their own emotions into them, revealing the way their minds work. In projective techniques, the purpose of the research is disguised and direct questions are not asked, as in other types of research. Consumers can also express themselves through stories, photographs, drawings, and collages.

Projective techniques are especially useful because it is difficult for consumers to express their deep feelings and views regarding brand images. These techniques attempt to capture all relevant associations that consumers have with a particular brand using pre-structured questionnaires. Such techniques allow participants to express their feelings without requiring them to put them into words. Another advantage is that projective techniques allow participants to provide their opinions intuitively—when assigning photographs or metaphors to brands, participants do not

> **MARKETING INSIGHT**
> **Success Story of GoodKnight**
>
> The GoodKnight Mat is the product of extensive research. This resulted in the formulation of the GoodKnight Advanced range comprising its flagship GoodKnight Advanced Activ+, the GoodKnight Advanced Low Smoke Coil, and the top-end GoodKnight Advanced Mosquito Spray. Figure 14.5 shows a promotion of low-smoke coil.
>
> GoodKnight is consistently researching and trying to ascertain how the homemaker is evolving, what her latest needs are and how best GoodKnight can fulfil them.
>
> It is research that distinguishes a Godrej-driven brand from everyone else. Indeed, every creative brief starts with insights into the Indian family and how its needs are evolving. This helps develop solutions that are deeply rooted in consumer psyche and play out favourably on the stage of real life. The brand has won international acclaim for communications that are sharply focused even as they are creatively poignant.
>
>
>
> **FIG. 14.5** Low-smoke coil
>
> *Courtsey*: Superbrands
>
> *Source*: Superbrands 2012

have to be concerned with explaining their meanings of motivations. Sometimes, these are the only methods of research available, for instance, when responses are required from children. The techniques used in projective research are discussed here.

Associative Techniques

These techniques discover what a person associates a stimulus with in his/her mind. This stimulus could be a brand, product, or company. Such research is ideal for measuring consumers' perceptions of products and their loyalty to brand names. Associative methods are useful to find out brand positioning and imagery that comes to respondents' minds when they are asked to think of a brand. The basic premise is that thoughts immediately brought to mind by the stimulus constitute consumer imagery and spontaneous emotions, and provide clues of what consumers actually think of brands or products.

Word Association

In word association, consumers are shown a brand and asked to say the first word that comes to their mind on seeing it. Such an exercise reveals a person's subconscious mind as it shows what things are linked together. Alternatively, a list is prepared in advance and shown to consumers, who are free to say whether that attribute matches well or not with the brand. Another variation is that the words and brands are written separately and respondents are asked to match the words with the brands. This reveals associations with the subject being discussed at a spontaneous level. The answers provide the researcher with a variety of 'consumer vocabulary' associated with brands or products that is useful in discovering a brand image.

Word association is used in market research, for example, to find out whether proper message is conveyed by a company's promotion. There are many variations of the technique, such as user imagery, brand personification, and obituary.

In user imagery, respondents draw pictures of their perceptions of particular brands and these are compared to the people who use them. The perceived image of the user in contrast to the non-user of the brand or product helps to understand the effectiveness of communications.

In brand personification, participants answer questions like 'if the brand was a person, who would that be?' As a variation to this, respondents are asked to choose from given words and pictures that they associate with a brand or product and to explain their choice. Answers to such questions help companies to know the emotional importance, the brand image in the mind of the respondents, and its importance in their lives.

Similarly, writing a brand obituary, as if the brand was a person who just died, helps discover the good and bad points of the brand in consumers' minds. There are many more variations of such associative techniques that companies modify for their specific objectives.

Narration and Story Telling

Building brand stories is another projective technique that helps to build a culture around a brand. Such stories can transform a company's market outlook. Cayla and Arnould (2013) write that narratives focus on the rich details of human experience; their explanatory power comes from highlighting the importance of brands in peoples' lives. Researchers can understand consumers by listening to stories that consumers recount about brands and their market experiences.

Zaltman (2003) writes that leading companies like Procter & Gamble recognize the critical role of storytelling as a consumer research instrument. Storytelling is also used as a way to communicate more effectively with consumers.

Brand Mapping

Brand mapping is a technique in which respondents are asked to group together brands according to a given characteristic. It is an invaluable technique for understanding competitors and is used for visualizing the relationships between brands, the key factors that differentiate one brand for another, identifying opportunities to introduce and position new products, and repositioning existing products. Consumer mapping is done in three stages.

The first is the elicitation stage, in which important brand associations are elicited from consumers. Respondents are asked to write down the brand in a circle in the centre of a blank sheet of paper.

In the second stage, consumers map these elicited associations to show how they are connected to one another. They are then given a few minutes during which they write down everything they can think of the brand, working from the centre and creating branches of thoughts and feelings, taking each branch as far as they can. When completed, the respondents circle the branch most significant to them. Participants then share and discuss their mind maps with the group, making additional connections and associations.

In the third stage, researchers aggregate these individual brand maps and associated data to produce a consensus brand map. The completed mind maps show satisfaction, frustrations, pain points, and unmet wants and needs with regard to the brand.

Deborah Roedder John and her colleagues (2006) have given a new consumer mapping approach, called brand concept maps (BCM) that shows the network of salient brand associations that underlie consumer perceptions of brands. They describe the following three basic steps involved in making BCMs:

Elicitation stage At this stage, researchers identify salient associations for the brand based on a survey consisting of open-ended questions. The most frequently mentioned brand associations are selected, that is, those that are mentioned by at least 50 per cent of respondents.

Aggregation stage Individual brand maps are combined to obtain a consensus map for the brand. Frequencies are used to construct a consensus map, showing the most salient brand associations and their interconnections.

Mapping stage The consensus map is now built by identifying which core brand associations should be linked directly to the brand. Next, the remaining core brand associations are mapped, with a link to at least one of the first-order brand associations. Links between core and non-core brand associations are also shown on the consensus map by means of lines. Non-core brand associations are shown with dotted lines and the core brand associations are shown with thick lines. The intensity of the connection between associations is shown with single, double, or triple lines. For each link, the mean number of lines is computed and rounded to the nearest integer to determine how many lines to use on the consensus brand map.

There are several other associative methods that are used. Pictorial methods are used to discover what cannot be expressed in words. Sometimes, respondents are given cameras to photograph anything that reminds them of a brand. This method helps uncover the imagery in consumers' minds about a particular brand. The mood-board approach consists of asking participants to clip photographs from magazines of celebrities or whatever seems appropriate to them and make a collage to represent a brand. When they use pictures of people, it helps to understand brand personification. Similarly, job-sorting is a task in which participants connect jobs to different brands.

In construction, the respondents are asked to construct a story or a picture from a stimulus. They are given a picture or a series of pictures in which consumers and products are the primary topics. One or more persons are depicted in ambiguous situations. Participants tell what the person is thinking, saying and doing, and to build a story around each picture, what led to it and what may happen in future. In speech bubbles or cartoon tests, respondents are required to fill in the bubbles of the characters in cartoons or pictures describing what they are thinking or doing. In completion, respondents are given an incomplete sentence, story, argument, or conversation, and are asked to finish it.

Metaphor Analysis

A metaphor is a method of description, using language or symbols that likens one thing to another. Metaphors are used commonly for marketing communications, as explained in Chapter 9—Attitudes. Examples of metaphors include *'resham si twacha'* (smooth as silk complexion) and impart linguistic, visual, and symbolic meaning to the brand. Brand names such as Scorpio, Attitude, and Tide use metaphors as their names. Visual or symbolic metaphors are used such as showing a tiger in the ad of an SUV or a film star in the ad of a soap for brand imagery.

Respondents are asked to list the metaphors that come to their minds with relation to a certain brand. The most common metaphors are identified, which helps understand how people think of brands.

Metaphors achieve the following objectives in marketing communications:

- They gain consumer attention and help them to remember a brand by association.
- They evoke imagery.
- They provoke comparisons.
- They explain a complex or technical product through comparison with an unrelated image.
- They influence consumer beliefs and attitudes.

The Zaltman metaphor elicitation technique (ZMET) and the way in which metaphors are used in consumer motivation is described in Chapter 6.

Mystery Shopping

Mystery shopping consists of persons deputed by a company to visit retail stores, posing as shoppers, to collect information about the stores' display, prices, and the sales experience. Retailers cannot make out whether these are company deputed people, so an accurate observation of the retail environment is obtained. It is a tool for observing and measuring consumer reactions, customer service, displays, product quality, and the environment of the retail establishment.

Mystery shoppers consist either of company personnel or people from agencies that provide such services. They are told about making specific observations during their visits and serve as the eyes and ears for companies getting first-hand feedback of customer experience. The information gathered during mystery shopping programmes is used to improve training programmes, displays, or service standards, and the ways in which companies interact with their customers.

QUANTITATIVE RESEARCH

Quantitative methods try to measure not only the market size, market share, penetration, and market growth rates, but gauge consumer behaviour as well, quantifying things that otherwise cannot be measured such as attitudes, satisfaction, and commitment. They can also be used to measure customer awareness and to understand customer behaviour in a market. This method involves collecting data to obtain knowledge about customers' needs.

At the heart of all quantitative research is the statistical sample. Since it would be very costly and time-consuming to collect data from the entire population of a market, extensive use is made of sampling from which, through careful design and analysis, researchers can draw inferences that holds true for all consumers. Great care has to be taken in selecting the sample as well as in designing questions to derive meaningful information.

Quantitative Data Collection Methods

Collecting data requires some procedures and a structured format so that the researcher knows what to ask. A questionnaire, also called a schedule or an interview form, is a series of written questions a researcher has to ask subjects and record their responses. While sometimes, the

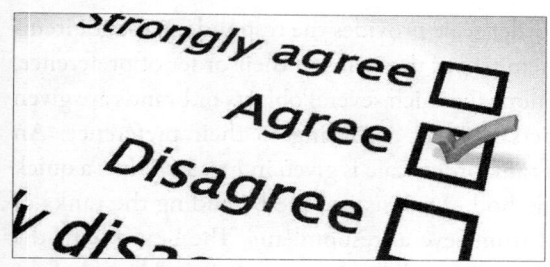

FIG. 14.6 Options in a close-ended questionnaire

questionnaire is to be filled by respondents themselves, at other times the researcher asks the questions and records the answers. The way the data is to be analysed influences the layout of the questionnaire. For example, close-ended questions (see Fig. 14.6) provide boxes for the respondent to tick that gives easily coded information, but open-ended questions provide a blank for the respondent to write answers, and gives more freedom of information, but is difficult to code.

Questions have to be suitably framed to get valid responses. For example, the question—'Do you like Pears, Lux, or Dove?' will give wrong responses because it does not give enough choices for the respondent. Another trap is not to define the terms. The question, 'Are you in the young or the middle-aged category?' is faulty because the terms 'young and middle-aged' have not been defined. Similarly, 'Do you attend dances frequently?' will give meaningless answers because the word 'frequently' is not defined. Hence, care must be taken to use direct and ordinary words, remove biased questions, and avoid implicit assumptions.

The first task is to devise a method to quantify feelings and reactions of consumers. This is done through measurement scales that allow people to express otherwise abstract concepts.

Measurement Scales

Scaling is a technique used to measure human judgment. Liking, loyalty, or satisfaction are psychological concepts, and are, therefore, difficult to measure. Measurement scales have been devised to get over this problem as numbers are assigned to characteristics and consumers are asked to rate objects according to their perceptions. In this way, psychological constructs such as attitudes, liking, and preferences can be measured. This section describes various scales that are used in consumer research.

Liking or disliking is measured on product attributes or benefits. Customer satisfaction is influenced by the perceived quality of product and expectations that the consumer has of the product. Companies must define and develop measures for each attribute that impacts customer satisfaction. Cognition or judgment is measured by asking whether the product was useful or not and whether consumer expectations were met. Questions on one attribute at a time are asked of consumers, such as—How well do you like the taste of the drink? In which colour would you like to buy the product? When these are rated on numbers, the measurement is conducive to statistical analysis. Several methods have been developed which are used to scale persons, stimuli, or both.

Comparative scales

Comparative scales are used when there is a direct comparison between objects or stimuli. Paired comparison is done when the consumers are required to choose between two products at a time according to their preferences. For example, two objects are presented at a time (say, Colgate and Pepsodent) and the consumer selects one. Assuming the respondent selects the first one, the selected object is paired with another brand (Colgate and Close-up), and so on, till the final preference is arrived at.

Rank order scale Instructions		
Rank the various brands of shampoos according to your preference. The brand most preferred by you will be ranked 1, the next preferred brand 2, and so on, till the brand least preferred by you will be ranked 10. The same rank should not be given to two brands.		
S.no.	Brand	Rank
1.	Sunsilk	_____
2.	L'Oreal	_____
3.	Garnier	_____
4.	Dove	_____
5.	Lux	_____
6.	Pantene	_____
7.	Dabur	_____
8.	Axe	_____
9.	Johnson's	_____
10.	Head and Shoulders	_____

FIG. 14.7 An example of a rank order scale

A rank order scale provides the respondent a set of items and asks them to put the items in their order of preference. It is a technique in which several objects or brands are given to consumers to rank according to their preference. An example of rank order scale is given in Fig. 14.7. It is a quick and easy method. Analysis is done by adding the ranks of each brand from several respondents. The brand with the least aggregate score will be the most preferred brand of the sample.

The constant sum scaling technique is similar to rank order scale, except that instead of assigning ranks, respondents are asked to assign 100 points to stimulus objects such as product attributes, according to their importance. Thus, if the price of a soap has more importance for a respondent than its perfume, more points will be assigned to price and less to perfume, and the total points across all attributes will total 100.

Non-comparative Scaling

In comparative scaling, the items are directly compared with each other. Each item is scaled independently from the others. Respondents rate products or their attributes on a continuous rating scale, also called the graphic rating scale, by placing a mark on a line which shows two extreme responses, such as the best and the worst at each end. Sometimes, numbers or scale points, are shown under the line (see Fig. 14.8). Sometimes, visual aids are shown that makes it easy for respondents to answer the question.

Rating scales are used to measure consumer attitudes such as perceptions, product preferences, purchase intentions, and service satisfaction. Continuous scales are easy to construct and use. Respondents can simply move their cursors on computer screens towards the scale to record their responses. They are also used to measure perception; for instance, respondents can record their emotions about seeing a TV commercial quickly through a continuous scale. The perception analyser is an instrument that is used in consumer research, through which consumers can instantly record their emotions, perceptions, and reactions on coming across marketing stimuli.

Itemized rating scales have numbers or brief descriptions on them. The commonly used rating scales are Likert, semantic difference, and Stapel scales. The Likert scale is a subject-centred approach as only subjects receive scale scores. Thurstone scaling is a method to evaluate the stimuli with respect to some designated attributes. It is the stimuli rather than the persons that are scaled. Guttman scaling is an approach in which both subjects and stimuli can be assigned scale values.

Likert Scales

Likert scales can be used to determine attitudes, views, and experiences of consumers. It is a method of ascribing quantitative value to qualitative data. These scales have become one of the dominant methods of measuring social and political attitudes.

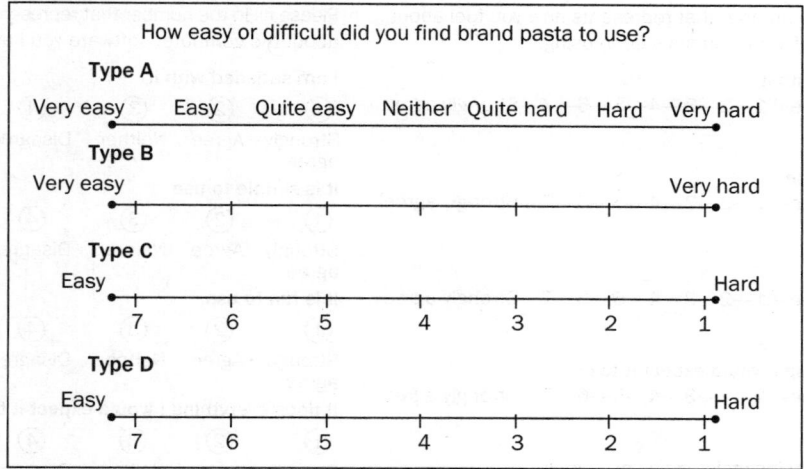

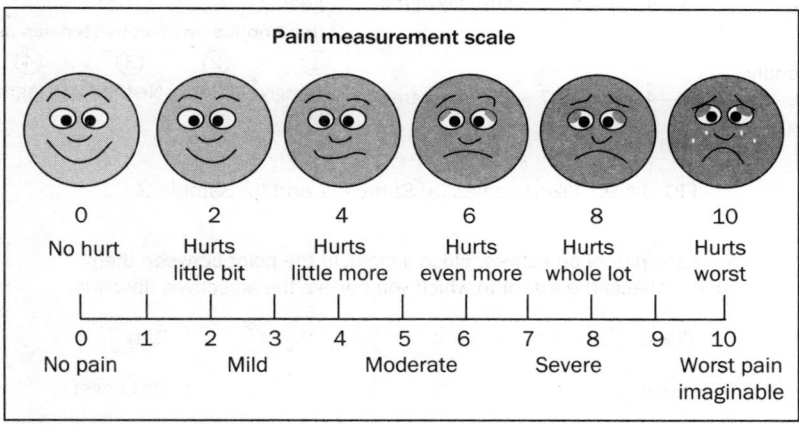

FIG. 14.8 Examples of continuous rating scales

This scale was developed by Rensis Likert in 1932. Respondents tick their decision about an issue on their level of agreement, generally on a five-point scale consisting of strongly agree, agree, neither agree nor disagree, disagree, and strongly disagree (Fig. 14.9). The results are analysed by looking at each item separately or by summing up the item responses to create a score for a group of items. Hence, Likert scales are often called summative scales. For instance, if a research is undertaken to find out perceptions towards a new product, each attribute can be scored by respondents. Those having the highest score have the most favourable perception about the product.

Thurstone Scales

Thurstone scaling is 'based on the law of comparative judgment'. It requires the individual to either agree or disagree with a large number of statements about an issue or object. Thurstone scales typically present the reader with a number of statements to which they have to respond, usually by ticking a true or false box, or agree or disagree—a choice of two possible responses.

Please circle the number that represents how you feel about the computer software you have been using.

I am satisfied with it
Strongly disagree—1—2—3—4—5—6—7—Strongly agree

It is simple to use
Strongly disagree—1—2—3—4—5—6—7—Strongly agree

It is fun to use
Strongly disagree—1—2—3—4—5—6—7—Strongly agree

It does everything I would expect it to do
Strongly disagree—1—2—3—4—5—6—7—Strongly agree

I don't notice any inconsistencies as I use it
Strongly disagree—1—2—3—4—5—6—7—Strongly agree

It is very user friendly
Strongly disagree—1—2—3—4—5—6—7—Strongly agree

(a)

Please fill in the number that represents how you feel about the computer software you have been using.

I am satisfied with it
① ② ③ ④ ⑤
Strongly   Agree   Neither   Disagree   Strongly
agree   disagree

It is simple to use
① ② ③ ④ ⑤
Strongly   Agree   Neither   Disagree   Strongly
agree   disagree

It is fun to use
① ② ③ ④ ⑤
Strongly   Agree   Neither   Disagree   Strongly
agree   disagree

It does everything I would expect it to do
① ② ③ ④ ⑤
Strongly   Agree   Neither   Disagree   Strongly
agree   disagree

I don't notice any inconsistencies as I use it
① ② ③ ④ ⑤
Strongly   Agree   Neither   Disagree   Strongly
agree   disagree

(b)

FIG. 14.9 Likert scales (a) Sample 1 and (b) Sample 2

For each pair of adjectives, place a cross at the point between them which reflects the extent to which you believe the adjectives describe.

Clean   : : : : : : : Dirty
Honest   : : : : : : : Dishonest
Kind   : : : : : : : Cruel
Helpful   : : : : : : : Unhelpful
Fair   : : : : : : : Biased
Strong   : : : : : : : Weak
Foolish   : : : : : : : Wise
Energetic : : : : : : : Lazy
Unreliable : : : : : : : Reliable

FIG. 14.10 Semantic differential scale

Guttman Scale

The Guttman scale is used to determine if a relationship exists within a group of items. The items are ordered from low to high, according to difficulty so that approving the last item implies approval or success for all prior ones. The respondent selects an item that best applies in the situation. The list contains items that are cumulative, so the respondent either agrees or disagrees with them.

Semantic Differential Scaling

The semantic differential is used to discover meaning and perception of brands. It is a seven-point scale with polar adjectives (opposite-meaning terms) at each end. Respondents mark the blank space that best describes their description of the brand or object being rated. A semantic differential scale helps understand the perception of consumers towards brands as shown in Fig. 14.10. When measured for brands such as Jaguar or Huggies, for instance, the researcher is bound to discover the opposite perceptions held by consumers for these brands. This scale is used to measure self-concept, person concept, and product concept.

The semantic differential scale is a versatile scale and has many applications in consumer research. A company's advertising images, packaging, and product attributes can be measured by this scale.

Three main factors can be measured by using the semantic differential scale as follows:

- The evaluative factor (good–bad, pleasant–unpleasant, kind–cruel)
- The potency factor (strong–weak, thick–thin, hard–soft)
- The activity factor (active–passive, slow–fast, hot–cold)

Stapel Scale

The Stapel scale is a unipolar ten-point rating scale. It ranges from +5 to −5 and has no neutral zero point. Used to measure attitudes, it is a slight modification of semantic differential scale. The scale consists of a single adjective in the middle and respondents are asked to indicate how accurately each statement describes the object of interest by selecting a number on the scale. The data obtained by using a Stapel scale can be analysed in the same way as semantic differential data. An example of Stapel scale is shown in Fig. 14.11.

Stapel scale instructions
Evaluate each word or phrase that describes the following brands. The more accurately that you think the word describes the brand, the larger plus number should be chosen. If the word does not accurately describe the brand, choose a negative number. Thus, +5 represents very accurate and −5 represents very inaccurate.

Brand X		
+5	+5	+5
+4	+4	+4
+3	+3	+3
+2	+2	+2
+1	+1	+1
Pleasant Perfume	**Luxury**	**Freshness**
−1	−1	−1
−2	−2	−2
−3	−3	−3
−4	4	−4
−5	−5	−5

FIG. 14.11 Example of the Stapel scale

Observation

A common method of quantitative research is observation that involves recording of people, objects, and events in a systematic manner. Examples of such methods are recording the number of visitors to a retail store, number of vehicles crossing a toll bridge, or the number of items stacked on a shelf. Observation can be mechanical, if it is recorded by sensors; or personal, if a researcher records it. For example, just by counting the number of visitors to a restaurant or a store can give an idea of demand.

Observational methods have several advantages. First, they are cheap and fast. Second, observation is an objective criterion, that is, it does not have researcher bias. Third, it is the only method available for certain consumers, for instance, companies can study behaviour of consumers in a store only by observation.

Surveys

A survey is used to gather information from individuals through questions asked from a representative sample. It is used to collect information on thoughts, opinions, and feelings by using scales. The answers are quantified and inferences can be drawn from them. Surveys may be conducted in the following three ways:

Direct questioning The researcher meets the respondent or connects by telephone and asks questions directly from a questionnaire, recording the responses on a form. Personal in-home interviews may be conducted or consumers may be intercepted at shopping outlets.

Written responses The questionnaire is given or sent to the respondent by mail and the respondent is asked to fill up the responses and return it to the researcher.

Online surveys A questionnaire is sent through e-mail or it is created online and a link sent to respondents. They are asked to respond to the questions in the online form that is saved and stored for analysis.

The survey method is commonly used to get consumer responses. It is a common sight to see researchers questioning respondents in malls and other shopping areas. Sometimes, they are conducted by the company itself or are contracted to professional market research agencies. Surveys are quick and easy to administer. They are fairly accurate as consumers usually have to tick from fixed choices that reduces variability. The fixed choices, usually represented by a number, are easy to code and analyse.

Surveys also measure customer loyalty and satisfaction. To measure overall satisfaction, consumers are asked questions such as 'Overall, how satisfied are you with Brand X?' The question can be asked on three aspects of customer experience and the customer is required to answer on a rating scale as follows:

- How satisfied are you with the overall quality of the brand?
- How reliable do you perceive the brand is?
- To what extent does the brand fulfil your needs?

Loyalty is the tendency to buy a brand or visit a store repeatedly as a matter of habit. It is measured by asking whether a consumer buys the brand, visits the store again, or recommends it to family and friends. Such questions show whether the customer's experience is satisfactory or not, the assumption being that a loyal customer will want to visit the store repeatedly. Customer satisfaction is a major predictor of repurchase and is also guided by product performance, quality, and value.

As loyalty is measured as a function of three factors—overall satisfaction, wanting to buy again, and willingness to recommend the brand to a friend, it can be calculated as the sum of scores for the following three questions:

- How satisfied are you with the brand or product?
- How likely are you repurchase the brand?
- Would you like to recommend the brand to a friend or family member?

Surveys, however, call for skilled interviewers. People are reluctant to spare time to give answers, and sometimes are not able to answer questions as they are not even aware of their motives while buying products. They may also perceive the questioning as an intrusion on their privacy.

Experimentation

Experimental research is a systematic method in which the researcher manipulates one or more variables, and checks for or measures change in other variables, if any. Experiments help in testing the actual consumer behaviour when a condition or two changes. For example, a company may conduct an experiment to see how consumers react to price changes; the same product with different prices is placed in different stores to see if there is an impact on demand. Consumers may be offered choices under different circumstances, to see how they react to different displays or promotions. The main advantage of experimentation is that it helps companies to know what consumers will do with changed circumstances, not what they say they will do. Companies can test one feature at a time to assess its suitability for the target market. However, micro experiments conducted in controlled conditions may not work the same way in the real world; hence, the technique has to be used with care.

When a company wants to establish a cause and effect relationship in consumer behaviour, it will conduct experimentation. The effect of a planned advertising campaign, the response of consumers to future price changes or sales promotion schemes, or the impact on trade partners of a proposed policy change can be measured by conducting an experiment on a selected sample of respondents.

Test marketing is a replication of a planned marketing strategy in a selected market. The company can modify any element of the marketing mix to see how the selected consumers respond, before launching it on a large scale. Controlled test marketing occurs when it is done on a limited scale and involves all functions of warehousing to selling products at retail. In simulated test marketing, pre-selected respondents are exposed to products in a real-life situation and then interviewed or observed about their reactions.

Davenport (2009) lists down six steps for conducting a successful experiment:

Create or refine a hypothesis The hypothesized relationships should be untested and yield useful economic value, leading to an actual decision or action.

Design test The test must have sufficient statistical significance. Sometimes, control groups have to be created and statistical analysis techniques must be finalized.

Execute test The test must be executed and things that might go wrong must be predicted and catered for. People must be trained to conduct the test.

Analyse test The test results are analysed and the need for further testing is determined. Site attributes are examined to see how key variables interact.

Plan roll-out If the test has been successful, it can be rolled out and implemented in markets.

Roll-out The implementation can be staggered by continuous analysis of early-adopting sites. If the results are not acceptable, the approach can be modified for other sites.

Moskowitz and Saguy (2013) write that experimentation contributes to open innovation principles and drives consumer-centric innovation. It results in a different way of working, leading to new management roles and cultures. It leads to an innovative consumer research process and changes the marketing approach.

MODERN RESEARCH

Consumer research has evolved over time mainly because consumers have changed as well. While it was difficult to get people to answer questionnaires or give personal information earlier, nowadays, they happily share their most intimate details on social networking sites. Companies can also track consumers on a real-time because people carry smartphones. There is huge data available because people use their connected devices and it becomes a resource for consumer research. Companies have sophisticated tools such as data mining and data analytics to conduct research (see chapter-end case study).

Data Mining

Companies are now mining huge amounts of data that consumers leave behind as they browse and search for products online. Data mining, sometimes called knowledge discovery, is the process of analysing data from different perspectives and summarizing it into useful information about consumer behaviour, or to increase revenue, cuts costs, or both.

Nicols (2013) explains that seismic shifts in both technology and consumer behaviour during the past decade produced a virtually infinite record of every action consumers take online. There is a huge amount of data from digital set-top boxes, retail checkouts, credit card transactions, call centre logs, and other sources. There is an unimaginable trove of information that companies can make use of.

McAfee and Brynjolfsson (2012) explain how this data is used in the context of online retailers who can track not only what customers buy, but also what else they look at; how they navigate through the site; how much they were influenced by promotions, reviews, and page layouts; and similarities across individuals and groups. Using this information, they developed algorithms that could predict what books individual customers would like to read next. As the algorithms became better, they could predict consumer behaviour accurately. 'It's no wonder that Amazon has put so many brick-and-mortar bookstores out of business,' they write.

The power of big data lies in powerful analytics. 'We can measure and, therefore, manage more precisely than ever before. We can make better predictions and smarter decisions. We can target more-effective interventions, and can do so in areas that so far was dominated by gut and intuition rather than by data and rigor,' write McAfee and Brynjolfsson.

Day (2011) highlights the power of new 'analytical and knowledge-sharing technologies' such as 'deep analytics' that harness technological advances to foster vigilant and adaptive market learning. These efforts to mine market data for customer insight are consistent with an information-processing perspective, in which an organization gains competitive advantage by sourcing and analysing market information more rapidly and effectively than its competitors.

Data Analytics

Data analytics comprise a set of capabilities that can go through terabytes of data and hundreds of variables in real time. Enabled by advances in computing power, this job has become the powerhouse of modern marketing.

Barton and Court (2012) write that data analytics provide companies 'the ability to see what was previously invisible improves operations, customer experiences, and strategies.' They explain how companies use data mining and data analytics. For instance, a bank can improve the efficiency of its customer-service through a 360-degree view by combining information from banking touchpoints such as ATM transactions, online queries, customer complaints, and so on. However, this is not all. If we add the streams of data flowing in from other sources like local demographics to weather forecasts, we can develop predictive systems that can significantly improve customer service and experience.

Davenport (2013) writes that the new methods which he calls 'Analytics 3.0', consist of a new resolve to apply powerful data-gathering and analysis methods 'not just to a company's operations but also to its offerings—to embed data smartness into the products and services customers buy.' Data from every device, shipment, and consumer can be used for the benefit of customers and markets, as companies now have the ability to embed analytics and optimization into every business decision made at the front lines of operations.

Real-time Experience Tracking

Macdonald et al (2012) explain the method of real-time experience tracking (RET) that can capture customer reactions immediately, is non-intrusive, reduces bias, and can be applied to customers in large numbers.

It tracks the four most important things about each customer encounter—the brand, the type of touchpoint, the consumer's assessment about the experience, and how persuasive it was. It is based on a quick SMS-based micro-survey that customers can take on their mobile phones every time they encounter a brand—whether in making a transaction, seeing an advertisement, or even in informal conversations with other people. Consumers have to input only a four-character text message every time they encounter a brand. It builds on people's habit of texting and tweeting about their experiences all the time.

In an experimental research, a few hundred consumers were recruited and completed four phases of research.

First, they filled out an online questionnaire and agreed to provide information to the company. They agreed to text a four-character message whenever they came across any of the brands, and wrote an online diary in which they expanded on their encounters with brands and how they felt about them. At the close of the project, they completed a modified version of the first questionnaire to see whether their attitudes toward the brands had shifted.

Through this research method, companies could uncover the following:

Key drivers Companies can discover which touchpoints are most closely related with certain behaviour, like making the actual purchase, by applying simple regression analysis to the RET data. People who were exposed to the product in a friend's house, For example, were three times more likely to buy it as people who did not see it at all.

Competitive analysis Companies can also see how effective their touchpoints are relative to those of competitors, through a touchpoint impact matrix that compares the performance of various touchpoints across selected parameters.

Chains of touchpoints Customers' reactions to each touchpoint are affected by their previous interactions with a brand. The decision to go into a store, for instance, is a result of getting a recommendation from a friend, seeing the window display, or something else. These are touchpoint chains. RET data can indicate where such chains might be broken.

Advertising Analytics

It is often said 'I know half of my advertising budget is wasted; I just don't know which half.' Traditional market research tries to find out the effectiveness of media by taking up surveys and asking people about which ads they remember and which ones influence them. With data analytics, companies can gain new insights into the effect of advertising and marketing activities on revenue. Nicols (2013) writes that this function involves three broad activities as follows:

Attribution As a first step, the company quantifies the contribution of each element of advertising using advanced analytics. At this step, data across five broad categories—market conditions, competitive activities, marketing actions, consumer response, and business outcomes is integrated. Analytics can reveal the impact of marketing activities across channels; for example, between two media—television and social media.

Optimization Optimization occurs by using predictive-analytics tools to run scenarios for business planning. Using such tools, companies can find out, for instance, what will happen to revenue if outdoor display advertising for a certain product line is cut by 10 per cent in a town; or if 15 per cent TV ad spending is shifted to online search and display. This step is called 'war gaming' that uses actual elasticities of business drivers to run hundreds or thousands of scenarios within minutes.

Allocation Allocation involves real-time redistribution of resources across marketing activities. This is quite flexible; companies can adjust or allocate advertising quickly. By analysing hundreds of variables, companies can quantify the precise combination of ads that are most effective, and reallocate resources between channels. By shifting between off-line and online spending, for instance, companies can improve effectiveness of their marketing efforts.

When businesses have multiple sales channels and geographies, analytics can become complex. However, as Nicols mentions, the challenge is organizational; marketing is becoming a war of knowledge, insight, and asymmetric advantage gained through analytics. 'Companies that don't adopt next-generation analytics will be overtaken by those that do,' he writes.

Social Media Analysis

As people have become very active on social media, companies are looking at social media analytics as a powerful tool for uncovering customers' sentiments across countless online sources. This flood of information is a resource for market intelligence. Analysis of social media data can be used to improve customer satisfaction, identify patterns and trends, and make smarter decisions about marketing strategy.

According to the IBM website, social media analytics help in the following ways:

Consumer Research Process | 551

- Capture consumer data from social media to understand attitudes, opinions, trends, and manage online reputation. Candid conversations on social media are key to useful insights on consumer wants and needs, and brand and product perceptions.
- Predict customer behaviour and improve customer satisfaction by recommending next best actions
- Create customized campaigns and promotions that resonate with social media participants

GLOBAL INSIGHT
IBM Watson—Using Online Chatter to Decipher Consumer Behaviour

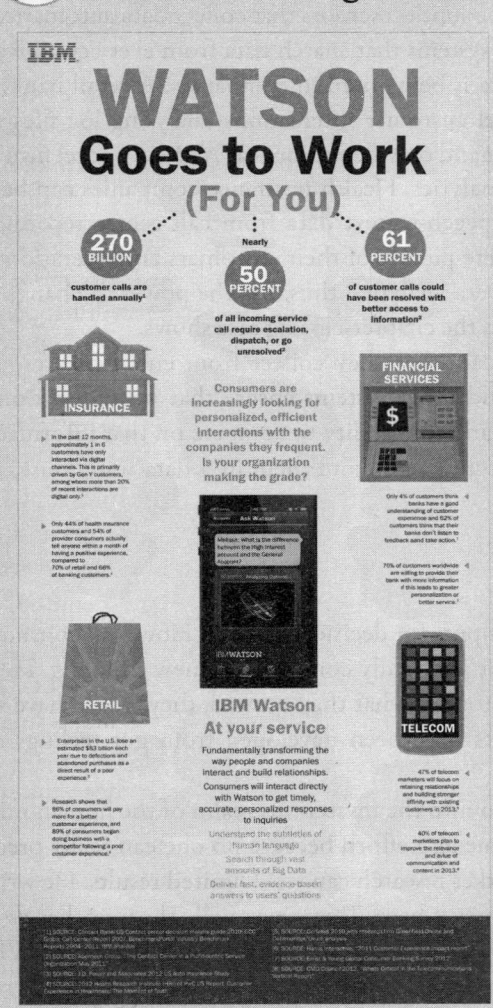

FIG. 14.12   IBM Watson

Courtesy of International Business Machines Corporation. © International Business Machines Corporation. Reprinted with permission from IBM Corporation.

IBM Watson has the unique ability of making sense of the huge amount of natural language that is written daily by users of the Internet. Blogs, Facebook comments, and almost everything posted anywhere on the net can now be analysed, thanks to Watson. Through this analysis, companies get to know the mood and concerns of consumers, their activities, needs, and what they may be needing next. IBM Watson uses natural language processing and analytics, and processes information the way that people think. Through this ability, companies can analyse and respond to big data.

This ability of using and combining information that consumers are willingly sharing on social and other sites is a boon to understand consumer behaviour. Using this data with predictive models will give fresh insights into what customers need at a precise moment in time, and thereby produce highly effective products and advertising. Barton and Court (2013) write, 'Companies that inject big data and analytics into their operations show productivity rates and profitability that are 5% to 6% higher than those of their peers.'

IBM Watson now gives companies to perform the following (see Fig. 14.12):

- Predict consumer trends and changing tastes
- Predict which advertising will be the most effective
- Predict how new products will fare in the market
- Analyse social conversations and generate leads

Sources:
AdAge, http://adage.com/article/datadriven-marketng/nielsen-taps-ibm-s-watson-measurement-planning/241631/, 2013

Forbes, http://www.forbes.com/sites/markfidelman/2013/09/04/ibms-watson-set-to-revolutionize-marketing/, 2013

IBM, http://www-03.ibm.com/press/us/en/presskit/27297.wss

All websites last accessed on 3 October 2014.

Traditional market research methods rely on surveys and questionnaires to understand their target market. With social media analysis tools, researchers can get to know everything about their target audience—from demographics to consumer opinions and sentiments. One advantage is that it is real-time analysis; one does not have to wait for the results of market surveys to know the market trends.

Due to the emergence of data analytics, the ways of conducting a consumer survey have changed. The next section describes how analytics are used.

Uses of Big Data

Big data refers to the huge amount of data that is being generated from diverse sources—consumers, supermarket checkout counters, and countless sensors that collect data automatically. Companies have invested millions of dollars in systems that snatch data from every conceivable source. Davenport (2014) explains how big data is being used in companies. A retail bank, for example, can get a handle on its multi-channel customer interactions analysing log files and combining customer interactions on the Internet and on video records at ATMs. A hotel firm can analyse customer lines with the help of video analytics. Health insurance companies can better predict customer dissatisfaction by analysing speech-to-text data from call centre recordings. These companies can have a much more complete picture of their customers and operations by combining unstructured and structured data. Data analytics, thus, has the power to change the very face of marketing and marketing research, as the chapter-closing case shows.

Indeed, companies have huge amounts of data that they collect from enterprise resource planning programmes, CRM, points-of-sale, and other systems ensure that no transaction or significant exchange occurs without leaving a mark. The ability to compete on that information requires using data from different formats, integrate and store them in a data warehouse, and make them easily accessible to all.

LIMITATIONS OF CONSUMER RESEARCH

We have seen that consumer research provides inputs for decision-making. However, consumers respond from their own frames of reference that are hardly conducive to new thinking. Henry Ford had once remarked, 'If I had asked my customers what they wanted, they would have said a faster horse.' Historically, innovative products have been developed from gut feelings and intuitions of entrepreneurs.

To be meaningful, consumer research must go into the mysterious realm of the human mind. Many researchers suggest that it is a waste of time and effort, because no one can really predict human behaviour. Brown (2011) writes that market research can yield limited results. He writes, 'Consumers do not know what they want. They never have. They never will. The wretches *do not* even know what they do not want.' Graves (2010) writes in his book, *Consumerology*, 'When market research wanders into the realm of the future, it is inherently reckless.'

In recent years, there has been overemphasis on quantitative methods and data. Although data analytics represent compelling advances in sorting vast amount of information, there are lingering questions about the suitability of such techniques for dealing with the complexity of human emotions and motivations. Quantitative processes sap the creativity of organizations, ignoring

CB IN ACTION   Quantitative Analysis or Intuition?

Conduct a debate in your class about the method to be used for consumer research. Should companies depend on quantitative analysis or intuition? As there are examples on both sides, search the Internet to get information on market breakthroughs that have resulted from intuition of the entrepreneur and also from quantitative analysis. What are the dangers of relying too heavily on the first method or the second? In which circumstances would you rely on analysis or intuition? Which holds more dangers?

These are issues that form the basis of an interesting debate. These are also issues confronting companies. Clearly, no company would like to wager huge sums of money solely on a person's gut feeling. However, is the overemphasis on analytics sapping the creativity of organizations, as explained in the text?

If you were the marketing manager of a large company, what strategy would you adopt?

gut feeling or intuition that have given several innovations to the world. Marketing successes, 'have proceeded from a deeper understanding of what people want than would ever emerge from the bowels of a data mine,' writes Brown.

Therefore, companies are rethinking about the efficacies of consumer research. 'Research must change,' was the theme of the presentation made by Stan Sthanunathan, Vice-President, Marketing Strategy and Insights of the Coca-Cola Company, at the Advertising Research Foundation Re:Think Convention in New York in 2011. He emphasized that conventional market research had failed to inspire executives and stimulate organizational creativity. Consumer insight departments would have to radically change their work practices. Their role was to 'provide provocation and inspiration that drive transformation and actions that generate growth inspiration.'

There are indeed rumbles on the territory of market research. On one side, it is becoming an increasingly data-driven activity, and on the other, managers feel the need for more creativity and inspiration. How this shapes out in the future remains to be seen.

CONCLUSION

Though measuring consumer psychology is not easy, managers rely on consumer research to give them direction in their decision-making. If conducted well, research helps consumers to connect with brands on a deep psychological level as brands such as Apple and Axe have done. It also helps in identifying profitable segments as explained in the chapter-opening case study of Tommy Hilfiger. However, consumer research also follows the principle of 'garbage in, garbage out.' If the research problem and the research plan are not designed well, or if the plan is not executed well, it will almost certainly provide wrong conclusions.

Making a questionnaire and conducting a survey is not market research, as many students tend to believe. Each stage has to be well-thought of and each question must be framed so that it contributes to the research problem in a meaningful way. Sometimes, companies and researchers fall in the trap of collecting data for its own sake that has been reflected in demands for changing the approach of traditional market research. The criticism is reflected in Brown's (2001) comment of research as 'CRM inspired tactic, which are tantamount to stalking.' Indeed, no customer likes to be stalked.

The role of intuition or gut feeling cannot be ignored. Though intuition too results from observing people and deciphering their needs, it can also lead to costly errors. There is a need to refine the consumer research process so that it can yield useful and creative results.

Ultimately, it all boils down to understanding people and that is what consumer research aims at.

SUMMARY

Businesses require a comprehensive view of consumers and this is provided by consumer research. Knowing about consumer habits helps us make better decisions about the kind of products to make, how much to price them, their availability, and finally, which media to use for promotions and how to devise the campaigns. Starting with research objectives, companies have to decide on the kind of research to be undertaken, sampling, research techniques, and finally, collecting and analysing data.

Secondary data is published data and is easy to find. It helps in designing primary research. Primary data is collected through surveys, interviews, and observation. Analysis of data consists of techniques such as correlation and regression, factor, cluster, and conjoint analysis, and multidimensional scaling (MDS).

Qualitative research is used when we require a deep understanding of human behaviour the underlying reasons for the same. Hidden needs analysis uses repertory grid analysis and lead user groups to delve deep into the human mind. Observational or ethnographic research consists of observing people as they come across products or advertisements, make purchase decisions, or use products. The advantage of observational research is that companies come to know how people really interact with products, displays, and promotions. Laddering helps in understanding people's core values and beliefs, and thus to understand the way in which the respondent sees the world through analysing attributes, consequences, and values. Focus groups, used in product development and testing new concepts, consist of a group of people who are asked about their perceptions, opinions, beliefs, and attitudes towards a product. Projective techniques that are unstructured and indirect methods to encourage consumers to project their feelings, beliefs and attitudes to the product or brand, reveal prejudices and beliefs of people. They consist of associative techniques, word association, narration, storytelling, and brand mapping.

Metaphors are commonly used in marketing communications. Researchers use unrelated language or symbols to impart meaning to brands. Mystery shopping helps to uncover customer experience and consists of selected people deputed by a company to visit retail stores, posing as shoppers.

Quantitative methods try to measure not only market size, market share, penetration and market growth rates, but about consumer behaviour as well. It involves the collecting data to obtain knowledge about customer's needs. Questionnaires are used to ask questions and record the responses of consumers. Scaling is used to measure human judgment and psychological concepts such as liking, loyalty, or satisfaction. Some of the commonly used methods are Likert scale, semantic difference scale, and the Stapel scale.

Observation and surveys are quantitative methods to collect information from respondents in a systematic manner. Another method is experimentation that helps in testing consumer behaviour when one or more variables change.

The chapter also describes modern research methods that consist of data mining and data analytics. A real-time experience tracking (RET) system helps uncover key drivers, competitive analysis, and chains of touchpoints. Companies are also increasingly using social media analysis. Finally, the limitations of consumer research is discussed, as it is increasingly felt that conventional market research has failed to inspire executives and stimulate organizational creativity.

KEY TERMS

Consumer behaviour research The study of preferences, motivations, and buying behaviour of targeted customers

Data analytics A set of capabilities that can go through terabytes of data and hundreds of variables in real time

Data Mining The process of analysing data from different perspectives and summarizing it into useful information

Depth interview An open-ended and in-depth conversation with an individual conducted by a trained researcher

Ethnographic research Anthropological research that consists of simply observing people as they come across products or advertisements, make purchase decisions, or use products

Experimental research A method in which the researcher manipulates one or more variables, and measures any change in other variables

Focus groups A form of qualitative research in which a group of people are asked by a moderator about their perceptions, opinions, beliefs, and attitudes towards a product

Laddering An interview probing technique that helps elicit the ideas and concepts that people use to organize their world

Lead users Customers who use products under extremely demanding conditions

Likert scale Scale used to determine attitudes, views, and experiences of consumers and is a method of ascribing quantitative value to qualitative data

Market research A systematic collection, analysis, and interpretation of data related to the market and the surrounding environment

Metaphor analysis A method in which consumers use unrelated language or symbols to impart linguistic, visual, and symbolic meaning to the brand

Mystery shopping A method in which selected people are deputed by a company to visit retail stores, posing as shoppers, to collect information about the stores' display, prices, and the sales experience

Observation A method of quantitative research which involves recording of people, objects, and events in a systematic manner

Primary research Research that is collected firsthand for a specific purpose

Projective techniques Unstructured and indirect methods that encourage participants to project their feelings, beliefs, and attitudes to a product or a brand

Qualitative research Research used when a deep understanding of human behaviour is required and the underlying reasons for it

Quantitative research Research involving variables that can be measured or quantified

Questionnaire A series of written questions a researcher has to ask subjects, recording their responses

Repertory grid analysis A process is a semi-structured interview in which the respondents compare and contrast their experiences of existing products, thus revealing their hidden needs

Scaling A technique used to measure human judgment, for example, psychological concepts such as liking, loyalty, or satisfaction that are difficult to measure can be quantified by using scaling techniques

Secondary research Research consisting of data that has already been gathered and recorded for purposes other than the current project

Semantic differential scaling Scaling used to discover meaning and perception of brands, it is a seven-point scale with polar adjectives (opposite-meaning terms) at each end and respondents mark the point that best describes their description of the brand or object being rated

Stapel scale A unipolar ten-point rating scale ranging from +5 to −5 and has no neutral zero point

Survey A method used to gather information from individuals through questions asked from a representative sample

EXERCISES

▪▪▪ Concept-review Questions

1. Define consumer research. How is it different from market research?
2. Explain the importance of market research in managerial decision-making. In what kind of decisions can it help managers?
3. List and explain the steps involved in the consumer research process.
4. What is sampling? Explain the methods of selecting samples.
5. What are focus groups? In what situations are focus groups helpful?
6. Explain different kinds of projective techniques and discuss how they are useful in understanding consumer psychology.
7. Describe and explain the importance of observational or ethnographic research. What are its advantages?
8. Why is it important to use scaling techniques in consumer research? Discuss the various scaling techniques and their efficacy.
9. What is data mining? How can it help in finding out information helpful to market researchers? Which companies use data mining techniques?
10. What is social media? How can social media sites be used for market research activities?

Critical Thinking Questions

1. Discuss the importance of qualitative techniques in consumer research. Which methods would be suitable in different kinds of consumer research? As qualitative data is hard to analyse, what are the skills needed in qualitative research?
2. It is often said that some of the biggest breakthrough products have been developed by intuition and not through market research. Should companies thus be spending huge amounts on research? Should they rely on intuition of managers instead?
3. There is a feeling in the industry that overdependence on data is leading to stifling of creativity of managers. What is your take on this? Should companies depend on data mining and analytics or should they encourage their employees to be creative? If you agree with the statement that 'research must change,' in what ways would you like to change the orientation of market research?
4. Social media is increasingly becoming important in market research. How can companies engage in social networks? Do consumers see real value in such interventions or are they seen as irritating intrusions? Does it amount to stalking customers? Analyse social media interventions by companies on these questions and decide in what ways companies should use such media.

Projects and Assignments

1. Conduct a survey among your friends to find out their preferences and reasons for visiting coffee shops. Develop ranking scales for three coffee brands—Barista, Cafe Coffee Day, and Starbucks—for ambience, quality of service, and pricing. Collect the data through a questionnaire and analyse it. What are your findings?
2. Develop a study to find out the perceptions and preferences of consumers towards two job searching portals—naukri.com and monster.com. Compare what they think about quality and relevance of jobs posted, ease of navigation, and how helpful these sites are in helping people to find jobs.
3. Search the Internet for market research agencies in the country. Make a table of your findings regarding services offered, skills and expertise, location and projects conducted. Which agencies have global affiliations? Which agencies specialize in consumer research as opposed to market research? What kind of reports do they publish?
4. Visit the website of the Census of India. What kind of secondary information is available that would be of use to a company marketing to young and elderly segments? If you are thinking of opening stores for cosmetics and health care, which states would you most like to enter?

REFERENCES

Anderson Ken, 'Ethnographic research: A key to strategy', *Harvard Business Review*, March, 2009.

Barton, Dominic and David Court, 'Making advanced analytics work for you', *Harvard Business Review*, October 2012, pp. 78–83.s

Brown, Stephen, 'Torment your customers (They'll Love It)', *Harvard Business Review*, October 2001.

Cayla Julien and Eric Arnould, 'Ethnographic stories for market learning', *Journal of Marketing*, Vol. 77, July 2013, pp. 1–16.

Davenport Thomas H., 'How to design smart business experiments', *Harvard Business Review*, February 2009, pp. 67–76.

Davenport, Thomas H., 'Analytics 3.0', *Harvard Business Review*, December 2013.

Davenport, Thomas H., *Big Data at Work: Dispelling the Myths, Uncovering the Opportunities*, Harvard Business Press Books, Boston, 2014.

Davenport, Thomas H., Leandro Dalle and Mule, and John Lucker, 'Know what your customers want before they do', *Harvard Business Review*, December 2011.

Day, George S., 'Closing the marketing capabilities gap', *Journal of Marketing*, 75 July 2011, pp. 183–95.

Goffin, Keith, Claus J. Varnes, Chris van der Hoven, and Ursula Koners, 'Beyond the voice of the customer: Ethnographic market research', *Research-Technology Management*, July-August 2012.

Goffin, Keith, Fred Lemke, and Ursula Koners, *Identifying Hidden Needs: Creating Breakthrough Products*, Palgrave, Basingstoke, UK, 2011.

Graves, Philip, *Consumerology*, Nicholas Brealy, London, 2010.

http://www-01.ibm.com/software/in/analytics/solutions/customer-analytics/social-media-analytics/, last accessed on 12 March 2014.

Kahneman, D and Amos Tversky, 'Prospect theory: An analysis of decision under Risk', *Econometrica*, 47, 2nd edition, 1979, pp. 263–291.

Kelly, George A., *The Psychology of Personal Constructs*, Vols. I and II, Norton, New York, 1955.

Macdonald, Emma K., Hugh N. Wilson, and Umut Konus, 'Consumer insight – In real time', *Harvard Business Review*, September 2012.

McAfee, Andrew and Erik Brynjolfsson, 'Big data: The management revolution', *Harvard Business Review*, October 2012, pp. 59–68.

Moskowitz Howard R., and I. Sam Saguy, 'Reinventing the role of consumer research in today's open innovation ecosystem', *Critical Reviews in Food Science and Nutrition*, Volume 53, Issue 7, 2013.

Nicols, Wes, 'Advertising analytics 2.0', *Harvard Business Review*, March, pp. 60-68, 2013.

Richarme, Michael, 'Consumer decision-making models, strategies, and theories, Oh My!' *Decision Analyst*, www.bj.decisionanalyst.com/Downloads/ConsumerDecisionMaking.pdf, last accessed on 15 February 2014.

Roedder John, Deborah, Barbara Loken, Kyeongheui Kim, and Alokparna Basu Monga, 'Brand concept maps: A methodology for identifying brand association networks', *Journal of Marketing Research*, Vol. XLIII, pp. 549–563, 2006.

Sthanunathan, Stan, 'Research must change,' keynote address to the Advertising Research Foundation Re:Think Convention, New York, March 20–23, 2011.

Zaltman, Gerald, *How Customers Think: Essential Insights into the Mind of the Market*, Harvard Business School Press, Boston, 2003.

CASE STUDY
Future of Market Research

Traditional market research arms researchers with questionnaires and sends them in search of people who would be kind enough to spare their time and effort to answer their queries. It has to deal with sampling and interviewing errors as well as bias of interviewers and respondents. Even so, the results may be faulty as the answers received may not be correct because respondents simply cannot articulate their own needs and desires.

Researchers would indeed have wondered how nice it would be if data were available easily and voluntarily without tedious surveys involving asking the same questions repeatedly.

Today, customers disclose their most personal information on various websites willingly. Sensors collect data from them automatically and in real time. Critical data like feelings expressed through facial expressions, may miss a researcher but not the video recording of customers in a store or at an ATM. Data from diverse sources about consumers, combined with other data, like local weather conditions that affect consumer behaviour, can now be used to focus on consumers and to design offers for them, without ever asking a single question or conducting a single survey. Therefore, the face of marketing research is changing like never before.

The shift towards data driven decision-making has changed the way managers must approach market research studies. Davenport, et al (2011) list down the abilities required for modern organizations to use big data. They write that 'using increasingly granular data, from detailed demographics and psychographics to consumers' click-streams on the web, businesses are starting to create highly customized offers that steer consumers to the 'right' merchandise or services—at the right moment, at the right price, and in the right channel.' Called 'next best offers' (NBOs), they are based on the consumer' attributes and behaviour, and are targeted precisely.

Building the next best offer involves three steps. First, the company decides the specific goals and objectives it wishes to achieve, such as attracting new customers or increasing sales, loyalty, or share of wallet. In the second step, NBOs are tailor-made for consumers; so companies need to have their demographics and psychographics, purchase history, social, mobile, and location information, preferred channel, and buying habits. Finally, using statistical analysis, predictive modelling, and other tools, it matches customers with offers. Each offer is then analysed and the data on customers' responses is included in follow-on offers. This helps in designing new offers based on the performance of previous ones.

The task is not easy; there are multiple types of data, as explained by Davenport in his book, *Big Data at Work* (2014). Organizations have to integrate data from internal and external sources in structured and unstructured formats to yield new insights in predictive and prescriptive models. For instance, consumer data has to be combined with data from social media and also from countless automatic sensors that provide information about the context of purchasing. Companies have started harnessing technologies and methods of analysis to focus on customers better.

Examples of the use of data analytics are abound. LinkedIn combines data to recommend to users to 'people you may know,' 'groups you may like,' 'jobs you may be interested in,' and so on. GE uses big data for improving services to optimize service contracts and maintenance intervals for industrial products. Google processes huge amounts of data to refine its core search and ad-serving algorithms. Kaplan, a testing firm, uses data analytics to advise customers on effective learning and test-preparation strategies. These companies use big data to directly focus on products, services, and customers. This directly impacts on how companies organize their marketing activities, how they use big data and the processes and pace of new product development.

Some of the findings help companies in a variety of ways. *The Economist* (2010) mentions some of the interesting findings from analysing data. Credit-card companies, for example, are able to monitor every purchase and can identify fraudulent ones with a high degree of accuracy, using rules derived by crunching data. They found that stolen credit cards are more likely to be used to buy hard liquor than wine, providing important insights to controlling credit card fraud. Insurance firms use data analysis to spot suspicious claims. They found that fraudulent claims are more likely to be made on a Monday than a Tuesday, 'since policyholders who stage accidents tend to assemble friends as false witnesses over the weekend.' Mobile-phone companies analyse subscribers' calling patterns to determine whom they are calling on rival networks. If that rival network is offering an attractive promotion that might cause the subscriber to defect, the company can then be offered an incentive to stay. Retailers use data analysis to tailor promotions to particular customers as well.

Analysing big data is not only helping companies gain insights into consumer behaviour, but contributing to profitability as well. McAfee and Brynjolfsson (2012) find that data driven companies performed better on financial and operational results. 'Companies in the top third of their industry in the use of data driven decision making were, on average, 5% more productive and 6% more profitable than their competitors,' they write.

Big data, however, comes with a word of caution. Ross, et al (2013) write, 'big data has been hyped so heavily that companies are expecting it to deliver more value than it actually can. Moreover, turning insights from data analytics into competitive advantage requires changes that businesses may be incapable of making.'

This idea is echoed by several other writers. Stikeleather (2013) writes, 'Machines don't make the essential and important connections among data and they don't create information. Humans do.' Since data is just a tool, it can only be an enabler, facilitator, accelerator, and magnifier of human capability, not its replacement. In the words of software architect Grady Booch, 'A fool with a tool is still a fool.' Lee and Sobol (2013) explain that data cannot decipher human emotions. They write, 'Human behaviour is nuanced and complex, and no matter how robust it is, data can provide only part of the story. Desire and motivation are influenced by psychological, social, and cultural factors that require context and conversation in order to decode.'

Davenport (2013) too writes that even while using data, intuition has an important role to play. 'One might even say that developing the right mix of intuition and data-driven analysis is the ultimate key to success with this movement. Neither an all-intuition nor an all-analytics approach will get you to the promised land,' he writes.

As data technologies become sharper, is it possible that market research based on questionnaires and surveys becomes redundant? As much of what is required is available in streams of data flowing into the companies, will the future researcher simply be a data scientist? Furthermore, will marketing itself change?

Questions for Discussion

1. Data analytics is being used in a variety of ways to predict consumer behaviour. Which other companies are using such analysis?
2. Do you agree that the face of market research may change as data analytics become more popular?
3. How effective are consumer offers derived from analysis likely to be? Is it likely to be seen as stalking as some writers have suggested? Will consumers turn away from this sharply focused marketing?
4. If surveys continue to be used in the future, in what situations will they be used? Do you think data analytics will replace surveys and questionnaires?

Sources:

Davenport, 'Big data and the role of intuition', HBR Blogs, 2013 http://blogs.hbr.org/2013/12/big-data-and-the-role-of-intuition/, last accessed on 12 March 2014.

Davenport, Thomas H., *Big Data at Work: Dispelling the Myths, Uncovering the Opportunities*, Harvard Business Press Books, Boston, 2014. 2.

Davis, Jim, 'Is big data over hyped?', 2012, http://www.sas.com/knowledge-exchange/business-analytics/featured/is-big-data-over-hyped, last accessed on 11 March 2014.

Lee, Lara and Daniel Sobol, 'What data can't tell you about customers', HBR Blogs, 2012, http://blogs.hbr.org/2012/08/what-data-cant-tell-you-about/, last accessed on 12 March 2014.

Ross, Jeanne W., Cynthia M. Beath, and Anne Quaadgras, 'You may not need big data after all', *Harvard Business Review*, December 2013.

Stikeleather, Jim, 'Big data's human component', HBR Blogs, 2013, http://blogs.hbr.org/2012/09/big-datas-human-component/, last accessed on 12 March 2014.

The Economist, 'The data deluge: Businesses, governments and society are only starting to tap its vast potential', 25 February 2010.

CHAPTER FIFTEEN

Consumption and Post-purchase Behaviour

LEARNING OBJECTIVES

The purpose of studying behaviour is not merely to sell goods, but to build customer satisfaction and long-term loyalty.

After studying this chapter, the reader will be able to

- differentiate products for enhancing them, from generic to branded products
- understand the basis of consumer satisfaction and the various theories explaining it
- learn about the techniques and models of measuring satisfaction for formulating better strategies
- analyse the use of experience to improve customer loyalty
- learn about the methods of measuring loyalty and develop strategies to improve loyalty
- understand the link between loyalty and profits, and create loyalty programmes for building loyalty beyond reason

CASE STUDY

Loyalty Beyond Reason

The purpose of all marketing is not to sell once, but create long-term loyalty among customers. Yet, despite the introduction of consumer loyalty programmes by many companies, few of them have succeeded in building real loyalty. Many companies have adopted improvement programmes ad hoc, however the results have not been very satisfactory. Building a highly loyal customer base must be integral to a company's basic business strategy, writes Reichheld (1993). 'The economic benefits of high customer loyalty are considerable and, in many industries, explain the differences in profitability among competitors,' he writes.

However, developing a loyalty programme is easier said than done, because many such programmes are based on giving rewards. As Evanschitzky et al. (2012) find, loyalty programmes do not automatically lead customers to be loyal to the company. 'In order to gain long-term benefits from their relationship marketing efforts, managers must consider delivering both emotional and economic benefits to the customer. Providers offering loyalty reward programmes devoid of emotional benefits run the risk of losing their customers in the long run,' they write.

The answer is to develop emotion and passion in customers. Kevin Roberts, the CEO of Saatchi and Saatchi, says in his book, *Lovemarks* (2007) that if they wanted to survive, great brands needed to create 'loyalty beyond reason' and that this was the only way to differentiate themselves in the future. The secret to this differentiation is a passionate commitment to three powerful concepts in everything the brand does and represents—mystery, sensuality, and intimacy.

Mystery Great stories of the past, present, and future, dreams, myths, icons, and inspirations

Sensuality Sounds, vision, touch, taste, and aroma

Intimacy Commitment, empathy, and compassion

Roberts writes that there is a new currency—companies have to compete for attention. Once attention is gained, they have to prove that they deserve it. However, advertising merely focuses on attention. Marketing needs to go beyond getting attention and develop the relationship with customers. Viral marketing, guerrilla marketing, and experience marketing can grab attention if done well, but once they have it, customers may not want to buy the products. The captivating marketing moves and tricks can only help if there is an emotional connection with the consumer. The next step is to build and add value. As people look for emotional connections, they have higher expectations. To put it bluntly, they are looking for love, writes Roberts. The difference between brands and loyalty beyond reason is given in Table 15.1.

Some of the brands that inspire intense loyalty and love are Harry Potter, Barbie, Harley Davidson, Levis, Amazon, Chanel, IKEA, Apple, Calvin Klein, Coca-Cola, Porsche, Gillette, Twinings, Nokia, LEGO, Nickelodeon, Red Bull, Nike, Playstation, Corona, Virgin, and Google. Some of these brands have been described in various chapters in this book.

Roberts describes the principles on which loyalty beyond reason can be based. These are given here.

Introduce passion in marketing Companies have to be passionate about their marketing efforts. Managers must love their brands, because if they are not in love with their business, consumers will not love them either.

Involve customers Customers want to be involved with the brands they like. They must be involved from product design to marketing.

TABLE 15.1 Differences between brands and lovemarks

Brands	Lovemarks
Information	Relationship
Recognized by consumers	Loved by people
Presents a narrative	Creates a love story
Promise of quality	Touch of sensuality
Symbolic	Iconic
Statement	Story
Defined attributes	Wrapped in mystery
Values	Spirit

Source: *Lovemarks*, Kevin Roberts (2007)

Celebrate loyalty Both partners must be willing participants. Once loyalty is established, companies have to make efforts to build on it, by celebrating activities and moments of experience.

Find, tell, and retell great stories *Lovemarks* is infused with powerful stories that can become legends in their own time. Many companies describe their brand histories on their websites. These must be built upon and brand stories must be told and retold.

Be prepared Once consumers become loyal, intense feelings are generated. Companies have to be prepared for this stage and build on it.

Many studies have emphasized the importance of developing emotion and passion with brands. Batra et al. (2012) write that brand love can be achieved by introducing passion driven behaviours, self-brand integration, creating positive emotional connections, and a sense of long-term relationship.

While reading this chapter, try to answer the following questions:

1. How do companies achieve customer satisfaction and loyalty? What are the theoretical models used?
2. How can companies achieve loyalty in the era of the connected consumer, where all information is easily available?

3. Can social media be used effectively to provide integrated customer experience across touchpoints?
4. What are the benefits of customer loyalty? How can loyalty be linked to profits?

Sources:

Batra, Rajeev, Aaron Ahuvia, and Richard P. Bagozzi, 'Brand love', *Journal of Marketing*, Vol. 76, pp. 1–16, 2012.

Evanschitzky, Heiner, B. Ramaseshan, David M. Woisetschläger, Verena Richelsen, Markus Blut, and Christof Backhaus, 'Consequences of customer loyalty to the loyalty program and to the company', *Journal of the Academy of Marketing Science*, Vol. 40, pp. 625–638, 2012.

Reichheld Frederick F., 'Loyalty-based management', *Harvard Business Review*, March, 1993.

Roberts, Kevin, *Lovemarks: The Future Beyond Brands*, Powerhouse Books, New York, 2007.

INTRODUCTION

Customer satisfaction and loyalty are the holy grail of all marketing activities. It is a known fact that loyal customers drive volumes and profits. If the customer finds value in a brand or a company's offerings, it is likely that he/she will keep coming back to the company. Peters and Waterman (2004) found that, 'Excellent companies really are close to their customers. Other companies talk about it, but excellent companies do it.'

Most companies, on the other hand, focus on short-term, transaction-oriented activities, and term it as 'marketing.' Driven by the need to meet targets, they are unable or unwilling to invest in deep relationships with their customers. Consequently, most marketing activities are defined by acquiring new customers and then discarding them through sloppy service and bad customer experience. As proof of this trend, we have to look no further than a host of struggling industries in India—financial services, telecom companies, and so on, (see chapter-end case study). Most of these industries make sizeable investments in customer services equipment such as automated response systems, 24 × 7 call centres, and heavy back-end expenditure, but the actual customer experience imparted is despicable.

No amount of technology can really improve the situation as long as companies are set up to market products rather than cultivate customers. To compete in this aggressively interactive environment, companies must shift their focus from driving transactions to maximizing customer lifetime value. This means making products and brands subservient to long-term customer relationships. In order to achieve long-term relationships, companies have to change strategy and structure across the organization—and reinvent the marketing department altogether.

TYPES OF PURCHASE DECISIONS

Companies are interested to find out how much time and effort consumers put into a purchase decision. This is of importance to managers, who use their knowledge of purchase decisions to devise campaigns and marketing activities to reach their target market. For example, a company making toys for children attempts to know how toys are purchased; sometimes, consumers are influenced by the child, or may buy it as a gift or a reward. After observing the decision-making process, a company will be able to see that parents typically have little or no time in deciding about toys to buy for their kids.

Armed with this information, the company would hardly like to spend its advertising budget on highlighting technical details but instead would like to design ads for time-pressed parents. Such ads would contain information appealing to parents such as safety of the product, the age group for which it is suitable, and its educational value.

Companies craft strategies that are most effective for the target market by knowing how people make purchase decisions and the steps that consumers go through before making a purchase. The following are types of purchase behaviour:

Habitual purchasing behaviour For low involvement and products used as part of everyday routine such as bread, eggs, or snacks, people buy out of habit. As significant brand differences are absent and the products are inexpensive, consumers do not spend time in comparing or thinking about their purchase. Consumers may also purchase certain brands because they are familiar with them and do not wish to risk trying out alternatives. This is also called routine decision-making behaviour. Habitual consumer behaviour is also called inertia.

Variety-seeking purchasing behaviour When there are significant brand differences even when the involvement is low, customers do great deal of brand switching for the sake of variety. Such behaviour is shown in the case of fast foods, restaurants, different flavours of ice creams, and so on.

Impulsive decision-making When people buy in unplanned actions, on the spur of the moment and without much deliberation, it is called an impulse purchase.

Complex purchasing behaviour Complex purchase behaviour occurs when products are expensive, seldom bought, and involve risk. Cars, homes, furniture, and electronics are things for which consumers will spend considerable time in making the purchase decision, saving up for them, asking opinions of others, and searching for alternatives. Complex purchase behaviour is shown when consumers are highly involved in a purchase, and are aware of significant differences among brands.

Dissonance-reducing behaviour When consumers are highly involved in the purchase, but believe that there are few differences between the brands, they will try to select the best product that reduces dissonance in their minds. Refrigerators and white goods, for instance, are more or less same across brands. The buyer looks at alternatives and selects the one which would not psychologically dissatisfy him.

Brand loyal behaviour Brand loyalty is exhibited when a consumer buys products of the same brand or from the same manufacturer repeatedly, showing a marked preference for it over others. Brand loyalty is not simply repurchasing, because sometimes people re-buy a brand due to easy availability and lack of alternatives. Such loyalty is called spurious loyalty as the customer will start buying the preferred brand if its availability improves. Brand loyalty is said to be true if customers exhibit a strong liking for a brand that they can bear some inconvenience to get it. Extreme loyalty is called brand love; companies strive for brand love as it gives them pricing power.

Purchase Continuum

As there are different shades of consumer decisions, it is easier to think of the decision types as points on a continuum, ranging from high to low involvement (Fig. 15.1). Consumer behaviour

	Routine	Limited	Extensive
Involvement	Low	Low to moderate	High
Time	Short	Short to moderate	Long
Cost	Low	Low to moderate	High
Information search	Internal only	Mostly internal	Internal and external
Number of alternatives	One	Few	Many

FIG. 15.1 Purchase involvement continuum

is classified into three categories on the basis of involvement. Post-purchase behaviour also varies with product categories—while high involvement products are displayed and are taken care of (such as an expensive dress or a car), low involvement products are forgotten almost as soon as they are bought (bread, eggs, and other small items).

Low Involvement

Habitual and routine behaviour are at the low involvement end of the continuum. At this end, the time spent by the consumer and the product cost is low, and only one alternative is considered. It is also called nominal decision-making, in which people are least involved in their purchase. They realize that they have a need and make a repeat purchase based on habit or on past experience. The only time nominal decision-making moves into a more evaluative state is when the product fails to meet expectations. It is possible that the consumer has initially sought different alternatives and gone through an extensive decision-making process before choosing one particular brand but after using it for some time, it becomes a habit.

For new products, companies find it difficult to break long-entrenched habits. Free samples, coupons, and elaborate point-of-purchase displays have to be used to draw consumers and make them break out of their habits. Alternately, low-involvement products have to be converted up the product continuum to high-involvement products by building brands and attaching psychological and emotional value to them.

High Involvement

At the high end of the continuum, the time spent by the customer in searching and evaluating alternatives is high and the cost of the products also tends to be high. Brand differentiation is very high. High-involvement purchasing is called extended decision-making, and occurs when people think of buying a house or a car. Such purchases are at the high end of the involvement scale, requiring extensive evaluation of alternatives. Consumers seek opinions, read articles, search on the Internet, talk to friends and relatives, and spend considerable time in evaluating the alternatives. In such decision-making, the post-purchase evaluation is the most extensive; people are more likely to keep evaluating alternatives even after making their purchase decisions.

In such decision-making, companies have to invest in the most extensive marketing activity— they must make sure their advertising is forceful so that their product is considered in the decision-making process. The advertising has to provide detailed information and links to other sources such as websites and product forums to aid the external research phase. Lastly, they must make sure they follow-up with customers after a purchase is made to reassure them of their decision and to avoid post-purchase dissonance.

Limited Involvement

In the middle of the continuum is the limited decision-making type, where consumers consider alternatives and briefly evaluate them. For example, a consumer will look at a display of products on a shelf and evaluate them on price and packaging, selecting the one that is found to be most suitable. Products that do not impact on health are usually chosen through limited decisions. For such products, companies have to use market research to find out which decision rules are used for that purchase—whether price is the deciding factor, or quality, product availability, style, or something else is. With this information, they can focus promotional activities on accentuating the benefits of their product when compared to competitors.

Companies with strong brands try to be at the right extreme of the purchase continuum. Even with daily use products, they try to create loyalty and make them high-involvement type. This is the basis of customer satisfaction and loyalty, will be discussed in detail in this chapter.

Marketing tries to move products from the low end of the continuum to the high end. Companies constantly try to differentiate their products from products of other competitors.

For example, Tata Salt moved an extremely low-involvement product, salt, up the continuum. It created emotional and psychological value by releasing high impact ads highlighting the salt as *desh ka namak* (the salt of the nation). This strategy created brand equity and consumers started asking for salt by its brand name. Other manufacturers too link emotions or status to low-value products and attempt to move up the involvement scale.

As Levitt (1980) writes, 'there is no such thing as a commodity. All goods and services are differentiable.' This is seen in products such as salt, groceries, and metals. While the generic product is undifferentiated, the offered product claims distinction on various parameters. Some products claim to be different on product features, some are visually identifiable, some others are only cosmetically implied, and some claim on the basis of real or hidden attributes that help the product to be perceived differently from offerings by competitors. These distinctions—real or implied—help the product move from a customer's routine decision-making to a more extensive decision-making.

Each difference is intended to produce some amount of consumer satisfaction and loyalty. Satisfaction and loyalty remain the objectives of all marketing activities. Such activities try to add value to commodities and convert them into brands.

CONSUMER SATISFACTION

Satisfaction can be determined by subjective factors such as customer needs and emotions, and by objective factors such as product and service features. Oliver (2010) defines satisfaction as the consumer's fulfilment response, a judgement that a product, a service, or its features provide a pleasurable level—that is, something that increases pleasure or reduces pain—of consumption-related fulfilment.

Consumer satisfaction is a psychological construct that is a combination of five elements of experience—the product's physical properties, its beneficial properties, its expressive properties, its image properties, and capacity for emotional fulfilment.

- *Physical properties*: As consumers derive satisfaction by consuming products, satisfaction is a function of expectations and product characteristics.
- *Beneficial properties*: Products provide benefits to customers, or, companies 'hire' products to solve their problems. Sometimes, these benefits are not even intended by producers. These are properties that depend on the outcome or the result that arise from owning or consuming products.
- *Emotional properties*: Consumption satisfies deep emotions. Satisfaction is a cognitive or emotional response as a result of owning and using products.
- *Expressive and intrinsic properties*: Consumers like to use some products to express their personalities, make fashion statements, or show off their premium products. These products become part of the lifestyles of customers.
- *Image properties* Consumers think of enhancing their image by owning products. Expensive cars and watches are bought hoping that others will think highly about the person wearing a particular brand or product and this is a source of satisfaction.

Companies strive for consumer satisfaction. Thus, the authors contend that the future growth of a company depends on consumer satisfaction.

Theories of Customer Satisfaction

Several theories have been proposed that help understand the nature of consumer satisfaction. These are related to people's expectations of the products that they want to purchase and then performance levels. If the expectations and performance do not match, the consumer experiences a degree of tension. Some approaches of customer satisfaction are described here.

The assimilation theory considers post-usage evaluation by the consumer. It states that, sometimes, customers learn to assimilate certain products that they would like to use even when they are not completely satisfied with them. For example, if a washing machine is making a small noise which it should not, consumers learn to live with it and be satisfied with it. Therefore, consumers seek to avoid dissonance by adjusting perceptions about a given product to bring it more in line with their expectations. People tend to reduce the tension resulting from a discrepancy between expectations and product performance either by reducing expectations or by raising the level of their satisfaction.

The contrast theory takes into account that people tend to compare products with what is shown in advertisements. The theory explains the tendency to magnify the discrepancy between one's attitudes and previously held expectations about products because of advertising or other factors. If these expectations are high, and if a customer's experience is only slightly less than promised, the product or service would be rejected as totally unsatisfactory. Conversely, under-promising in advertising and over-delivering causes high satisfaction. While the assimilation theory states that consumers seek to minimize the discrepancy between expectation and performance, the contrast theory points to the discrepancy being magnified or exaggerated due to prior expectations.

The assimilation–contrast theory takes the magnitude of the discrepancy into account. It suggests that if a product's performance is within a customer's range of acceptance, the discrepancy will be disregarded even though it may fall short of expectations. Here, the consumer tends to assimilate the product and its performance, and will deem it as acceptable. However, if performance does not fall within the range of acceptance, contrast will prevail and the difference will be exaggerated so as to make the produce/service totally unacceptable.

The negativity theory states that when expectations are strongly held as in highly loyal customers, there will be a negative response to any disconfirmation. Even a small discrepancy of performance from expectations will disrupt the individual, producing 'negative energy'. This theory accounts for most bad publicity generated for brands.

Cognitive dissonance is an uncomfortable feeling caused by holding two contradictory ideas simultaneously. The theory of cognitive dissonance states that people tend to reduce dissonance by justifying or rationalizing it. The theory helps in explaining the state of discomfort that buyers often feel after they make a purchase. This happens for a variety of reasons—the consumer starts feeling that the money spent was too much, feels that the product is not worthwhile, may get swayed by somebody's opinion, or discover better alternatives after the purchase has been made.

Festinger, et al. (1956) explain that dissonance produces discomfort, and takes three forms. The consumer may try to reduce or eliminate the dissonance by changing one or more beliefs or opinions involved in the dissonance; or will try to acquire new information that will increase the existing consonance and reduce dissonance; or will try to forget or reduce the thoughts that caused the dissonance. For example, a cigarette smoker feels dissonance because he/she knows that smoking is bad for his/her health. He/She will try to reduce the dissonance by either giving up smoking, or justifying in his mind that the bad effects will not happen to him. Rationalization can reduce dissonance to a certain extent. The consumer will seek support from others to make the rationalization seem correct.

The equity concept states that the ratio of benefits to inputs should be constant for both participants in an exchange. Hence, satisfaction is deemed to exist when customers believe that their benefits to input ratio is equal to that of the seller.

These theories help provide a conceptual understanding of consumer satisfaction. They explain some of consumers' thoughts as they buy products.

Measuring Satisfaction

Customer satisfaction has always been a primary objective of business. As global economies slow down, companies realize that they must keep their customers satisfied and loyal. Griffin, et al. (1995) write that companies should try and make a larger selection of products and services available to the same set of buyers. Rather than chase new customers aggressively through large marketing spends, companies must adopt defensive strategies or maintain their customers because, on average, approximately 70 per cent of all sales are derived from repeat purchases.

Measuring customer satisfaction is, therefore, necessary and important. Usually, customer satisfaction is measured during customer-interaction functions such as services and repairs. It is easy to measure satisfaction in these areas by getting comments from customers, and improvements are easy to implement.

Satisfaction in Services—SERVQUAL Model

The key strategy for the success and survival of any business is to deliver quality services to customers, which, in turn impacts on customer satisfaction and loyalty. A technique to measure

MARKETING INSIGHT
Lessons for Marketing Managers

The study of consumer satisfaction has several lessons for marketing managers, which can be explained as follows:

- After people buy durables like white goods, companies should help them assimilate the products by highlighting the functions. If they are not completely satisfied, consumers should be helped by teaching them adjusting their usage. This helps build relationships and results in consumer loyalty. For example, if a consumer is not completely happy with the cleaning done by a washing machine, company representatives can teach customers how to set it at a higher cleaning capacity or how it can be used for soaking clothes.
- The contrast theory holds important lessons for advertising and service industries. Usually, companies make tall claims in their advertisements that create dissatisfaction among consumers when the same are not met. Customer delight, however, remains hidden in under-promising and over-delivering. Paul Hemp (2002) writes about his experiences at the Ritz hotel, 'Always bring more than you think people need.' This is how the service industry delivers consumer delight.
- Loyal customers must be made to feel important and representatives are assigned to deal with each individually so that all expectations are met. This has more relevance for the service industry, where even a small discrepancy in service results in negative energy among customers.
- To reduce cognitive dissonance, company representatives must not hide any limitations of the products they sell. They should facilitate comparison with competitive products. After selling the product, customers should be given additional information that increases consonance or reduces dissonance. This is especially true for companies selling expensive and durable goods.

service quality and satisfaction is the SERVQUAL model, which is based on five dimensions of service—empathy, tangibility, responsiveness, reliability, and assurance.

Tangibility refers to physical facilities, equipment, and appearance of personnel, and serves to increase customer satisfaction. Responsiveness is willingness of employees to assist and provide prompt services to customers. Reliability implies that customers can depend on the service provider to deliver a standard of service. Assurance is the degree of trust and confidence that customers feel about the services, which again has a positive influence on customer satisfaction. Finally, empathy, or the personal service provided to the customer has a positive impact on satisfaction.

Kano Model

Kano, et al. (1996) gave a model of customer satisfaction that classifies attributes based on how they are perceived by customers and their effect on customer satisfaction. The Kano model is a popular model to identify those product or service features that represent key drivers of customer satisfaction and dissatisfaction. The model divides product attributes into three categories—threshold, performance, and excitement.

The Kano model measures satisfaction against customer perceptions of attribute performance, grades the customer's requirements, and determines the levels of satisfaction. The underlying assumption behind this method is that customer satisfaction is not always proportional to how fully functional the product or service is. That is, higher quality does not necessarily lead to higher satisfaction. Kano distinguishes among three types of basic requirements that influence customer satisfaction as follows:

Threshold attributes—must-be requirements Threshold includes the basic attributes that a product must have. These do not provide any product differentiation because all brands in the category must have those attributes. The absence or poor performance of these attributes will result in customer dissatisfaction. For example, a car must move and a soap must clean.

Performance attributes—one-dimensional requirement Performance attributes are those that are explicitly demanded by the customer—the higher the level of fulfilment, the higher the customer's satisfaction and vice versa. For example, fuel efficiency is a performance attribute that one looks for in a car.

Excitement attributes—attractive requirement These attributes add excitement to the brand and result in high levels of customer satisfaction; however, their absence does not lead to dissatisfaction. They fulfil a customer's latent needs, or those needs of which customers are unaware. For example, Red Bull and Wooldlands associate themselves with the outdoors and adventure, which adds excitement to the brand.

The Kano model has become a popular tool to identify attributes that contribute to consumer satisfaction. It helps identify and understand the attributes in product or service design that have a great influence on customer satisfaction. By classifying product attributes, companies are able to classify and figure out the ways in which they must be highlighted. The must-be attributes must have the highest priority in the development of a product or a service. They are the encompassing functions of the offering. If these are already fulfilled, companies will not find it useful to invest in improving them further. The results can also be used as the basis for market segmentation—products and services can be differentiated according to the utility expectations of different customer segments.

Customer Satisfaction Index Models

Many countries have built the customer satisfaction index (CSI) showing the industry-wise and company-wise satisfaction index. This score ranks companies within an industry and also shows rankings across industries. The index serves to help companies compare their customer satisfaction efforts with others and also gives the state of customer service within industries and within an economy. Fornell, et al. (1992) helped build the first nation-level measurement system of customer satisfaction called the Swedish Customer Satisfaction Barometer (SCSB). The SCSB became a uniform, cross-company, and cross-industry national measurement instrument of customer satisfaction and perceptions of quality offered by companies.

Later, the American Customer Satisfaction Index (ACSI) was launched (Fornell, 1996).

The ACSI is based on consumer interviews of about 80,000 people annually about their satisfaction with the goods and services they have consumed on a scale of 1–10, with 10 indicating very satisfied and 1, indicating very dissatisfied. The variables used are overall satisfaction, expectancy, and comparison with the ideal.

The CSI is recognized by governments and companies as a good instrument to gauge not only a company's quality of products and services, but also of the nation as a whole, contributing to its competitive ability. Now, CSIs have been developed and are being used by many countries as mentioned here:

- Swedish Customer Satisfaction Barometer (SCSB)
- American Customer Satisfaction Index (ACSI)
- European Customer Satisfaction Index (ECSI)
- National Consumer Satisfaction UK
- Norwegian Customer Satisfaction Barometer (NCSB)
- German Barometer
- Swiss Index of Customer satisfaction (SWICS)
- Korean Customer Satisfaction Index (KCSI)
- Malaysian Customer Satisfaction Index (MCSI)

In addition, Brazil, Argentina, Mexico, Canada, Australia, Hong Kong, Turkey, Puerto Rico, and Taiwan are developing their CSI systems.

The CSI model is a structural equation model that links customer satisfaction to its determinants—perceived quality, customer expectations, perceived value, and, to its consequences—customer loyalty and complaints (Fig. 15.2). These indicators are calculated based on surveys and customer interviews. The scores obtained through consumer interviews are multiplied by the weights to get composite index.

Vavra (1997) writes that the ACSI initiative helps in meeting three primary objectives as follows:

- **Measurement** It helps to measure economic output on the basis of consumer preferences.
- **Contribution** It provides a conceptual framework for understanding how service and product quality relate to economic indicators.
- **Forecasting** It provides an indicator of future economic variability by measuring the intangible value of the buyer–seller relationship.

The CSI models not only help to compare satisfaction levels between companies but also indicate as to how to devise strategies to increase satisfaction. The way brands make strategies for achieving customer satisfaction is discussed in the next section.

Strategies for Satisfaction

Sometimes, there is a discrepancy between satisfaction and the consumer's first choice. In surveys, customers consistently rate some brands as their first choice. However, they often end up buying

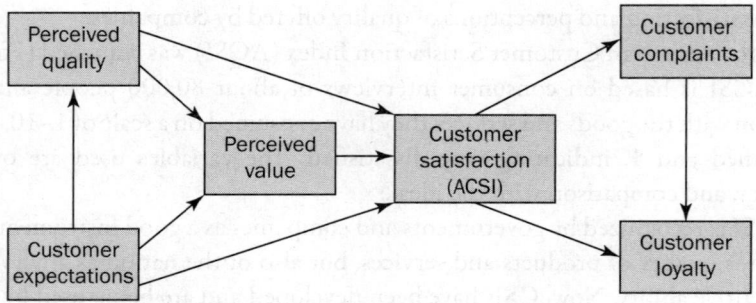

FIG. 15.2 CSI model

another brand out of convenience or habit, with which they are a little less satisfied but find easy to buy the latter. For example, if the preferred brand is not available easily, customers make do with an alternative brand that is easily available. This gives some direction about strategies to market products.

For customers who are both highly satisfied with a brand and prefer it above all others, the company has to continue to delight them. In case of brands that are low in satisfaction, the company has to maintain unique items or to find ways to erect market barriers that make access to a preferred brand difficult for them. For customers where satisfaction is high but first choice is low, high satisfaction levels mask customers' real perceptions of the brand. Managers typically tout the fact that customers are highly satisfied, but the reality is that the brand is one among several others that the customer uses and views as being basically equivalent. Therefore, we refer to them as parity brands. The strategy for these brands must be differentiated from core competitors; in other words, you must give customers a reason to believe your brand is better.

Despite low satisfaction, there are also brands that still represent customers' first choice. These low-service category brands compete successfully either through price leadership or because the category has few competitors. Some stores of Wal-Mart, for instance, have lowest satisfaction levels yet many customers rank it their first-choice grocer. The company has developed systems that serve as barriers for competitors, such as its buying and logistics superiority.

There are also lessons for lesser known brands that do not figure in consumer preference surveys. Such brands need to spend on marketing activities but concentrate on their distribution. If such brands are placed in convenience or neighbourhood stores, customers will tend to buy them. Instead of competing with the bigger brands, it would be advisable to make their availability easier.

No company can last for long without satisfied customers. Companies have to make efforts to increase satisfaction levels, even though there will always be some dissatisfied customers. At the very least, dissatisfaction should not be encouraged by companies, which they unwittingly do, as is seen in complaints posted online. Long waiting times caused by use of technology such as automated voice response and unhelpful employees at call centres add to, rather than mitigate, consumer dissatisfaction.

Unhappy Customers and Decreasing Satisfaction

Grainer, et al. (2014) write that despite companies having invested in technology to provide better customer service, they are finding it more difficult to create satisfied and loyal customers today. Among the problems are a rise in customer expectations, complaint-handling policies, and easy ways to voice complaints through social media and word of mouth.

The 2013 National Customer Rage in the US showed complainant satisfaction is lower today than in 1976. Such surveys point to the fact that many customers are unhappy today. Today's customer has a tendency to get extremely upset. More than two-thirds of customers surveyed felt that they were either 'extremely' or very upset, while 36 per cent said they had 'yelled or raised (their) voice' in connection with most problems. Companies are failing in their efforts to create one-stop complaint resolutions with technology and people dedicated to resolving customer problems. Customers report that they typically needed to make four or more contacts with a company before achieving a resolution to their problem.

Companies ignore what they know about their customers—people today are extremely time-pressed. Failure to resolve complaints during the initial contact leads to customer rage as well as decreased satisfaction and brand loyalty. Despite this, companies forward customer complaints to different employees within an organization without resolution. Frontline employees are not empowered to solve customer complaints as they come.

The widespread use of social networking means that the details of the customer's problem will be shared widely. Online social networking and other communication tools have raised the stakes drastically in the area of customer satisfaction. While earlier, disgruntled customers may have expressed their dissatisfaction to 10 friends and family, the modern and socially-connected consumers reach an average of 280 others each time they post their queries on social networking sites. This has the potential for echo effects through 'retweeting' and other viral activity on sites like YouTube. The share of customers reporting problems has also grown. About half of consumers surveyed reported having experienced a problem with products or services during 2013. This has serious implications for the choices companies make when handling customer complaints.

So what can companies do to improve the level of customer satisfaction in complaining situations? The authors suggest adopting a broad and an open approach to resolve customer complaints—one that takes into account the fact that many interactions between companies and customers will be shared with a broad network and will, therefore, influence future purchases. This new approach is called the community lifetime value of problem resolutions, suggesting the need for more liberal guidelines and discretion for frontline service representatives.

Solicit complaints and solve them The mere act of complaining had a positive effect on customers and seemed to be enough to improve their level of brand loyalty, regardless of the outcome. Thus, it is in their interest to solicit complaints. However, futile complaint-handling experiences result in reduced brand loyalty. Today, customers having complaints expect companies to solve them quickly and flawlessly. Simply having a complaint department or providing an email address without following up with high-quality resolution can do more harm than good.

Measure return on investment (ROI) of complaint resolution investments Though companies invest huge amount in technology and systems to resolve complaints, they do not see how these investments are helping to achieve customer loyalty. For example, call centres are expensive to set up and run, but if agents are not adequately empowered, customers have to experience long wait times or wrestle with complicated automated response systems. In such scenarios, there will be hardly any returns on investment of these complaint management systems.

Recognize that technology has limits Even today, a majority of customers use the telephone to make complaints in the hope of having them resolved quickly. However, they are made to wrestle with automated options without resolution of their problems. Therefore, technology itself does not solve problems; people do.

Viral potential of social media Since dissatisfied customers tell more people about their experiences than satisfied ones, complaints have to be managed more interactively than ever before. The consumer rage survey found that prospective buyers are more influenced by positive

CB IN ACTION   Unhappy Customers

Visit some websites meant for making consumer complaints and analyse the complaints that are posted on it. Make a list showing the following:
- Which are the most featured companies?
- Are these companies doing well in terms of stock market returns?
- What percentage of complaints is related to product, service, employees, or systems?
- What are companies doing to rectify consumer complaints posted online?
- Which companies are the most active and which companies do not respond to complaints?

posts than negative comments and that users of social networking sites were more likely to post information about their good experiences than their bad experiences. These findings suggest that companies should be just as interested in developing channels for customers to broadcast their positive experiences as they are in removing negative postings from the website.

Complaints are not about freebies   There is a belief among managers that many customers who complain are really just looking for freebies, such as refunds, free products, or services. Research shows that only 26 per cent of respondents wanted financial compensation for their lost time, inconvenience, or injury. The largest number, 92 per cent, wanted to be treated with dignity. Others wanted an assurance that the problem would not be repeated (76%); an explanation (74%); a thank you (72%); an opportunity to vent (63%); and/or an apology (62%). These non-financial remedies can have a major influence on continued brand loyalty.

Simply throwing money at complaint-handling remedies does not make much sense. A smarter and a more effective approach involves a combination of actions, including hiring better personnel, providing appropriate training, and using soft skills such as flexible language, empathy, and adaptive responses to address the issues.

CUSTOMER LOYALTY

Customer loyalty is generally understood as consisting of customers who periodically buy from a company. Reichheld (2003) defines loyalty as the willingness of a customer to make an investment or a personal sacrifice in order to strengthen the relationship with a brand or a company. This means that a customer prefers to stick to a brand or a store even though he/she may not get the best price.

Companies, therefore, have to manage customer experience and drive loyalty at each touchpoint—the point of interaction between a customer and a brand.

Integrated Experience across Touchpoints

Opportunities for customer interaction with companies have increased over the years. Companies have to deliver a consistent experience across all these brand touchpoints. Touchpoints are the critical moments when customers interact with companies in some way or the other. A customer will see an advertisement for a brand on television, check out information on a website, seek a friend's opinion, see the brand displayed at a store, read about the brand online—all these

>
>
> ### EXHIBIT 15.1 LIC Offers Integrated Experiences
>
> Today, LIC has one of the country's largest wide area networks linking its offices to a central server. The Corporation has also simultaneously implemented an Enterprise Document Management System for digitization of all policy records. This has created one of the world's largest corporate active data warehouses and has enabled the Corporation to use advanced online analytical/monthly income statement tools for predictive modelling and enhancing client relationship management initiatives.
>
> To bring service to the customers' doorstep, the Corporation offers a number of options for receiving information and making payments. Customer zones have been conceptualized as a one-stop shop for all phone-in and walk-in customers. Figure 15.3 shows the options that LIC provides for its customers to pay their premiums.
>
> **FIG. 15.3** LIC's paying options
>
> *Courtesy*: Superbrands
>
> *Source*: Superbrands 2012

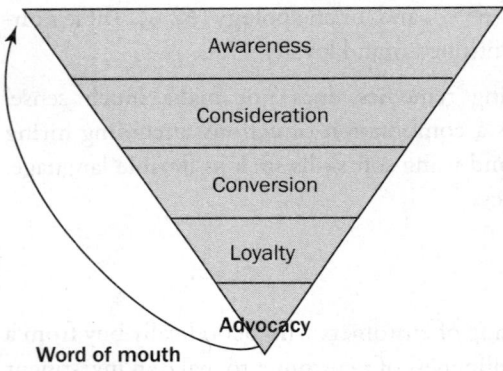

FIG. 15.4 Marketing funnel

experiences across physical and communication channels, constitute touchpoints. Please see Exhibit 15.1.

Edelman (2010) explains that earlier, buyers would methodically look for product choices and then evaluate them on the basis of needs, eliminating the unsuitable brands until they arrived at the one that best met their criteria. The process is illustrated by the marketing funnel (Fig. 15.4), showing that the numbers decrease as customers proceed from awareness to purchase and loyalty. Edelman says 'But today, consumers are promiscuous in their brand relationships: They connect with myriad brands—through new media channels beyond the manufacturer's and the retailer's control or even knowledge—and evaluate a shifting array of them, often expanding the pool before narrowing it.' The funnel metaphor, thus, no longer describes this relationship. Instead, companies have to manage the various touchpoints they have with their customers.

Touchpoints have changed both in number and nature. While earlier marketing strategies consisted of building brand awareness through advertising, now companies have to figure out at what touchpoints consumers are most open to getting influenced, and how they can interact with them at those points. Thus, instead of focusing on how to allocate resources across different media—which is an outdated strategy, companies have to target stages of consumer decision-making to deliver an integrated customer experience.

Enhancing Customer Experience

Customer loyalty is built by combining the physical, emotional, and value elements of customer experience. Customer experience management helps drive customer satisfaction, retention, and loyalty. Enhancing customer experience is an effective way to differentiate products and services with those of competitors. When customers are engaged on an emotional and intellectual level with a brand or company, it is beneficial for the brand. Customers too gain by being loyal as they do not have to search for alternatives and can also avail discounts and offers that companies are able to direct to them.

Rawson, Duncan, and Jones (2013) write that focusing on touchpoints alone can create a distorted picture. For instance, if a customer calls up a company repeatedly, he/she may express satisfaction with each encounter and his immediate problem is solved satisfactorily. However, it hides the overall dissatisfaction about the product for which he has to call up repeatedly. Therefore, instead of analysing touchpoints only, companies need to impart service at every level, that is, on the cumulative experiences across multiple touchpoints and multiple channels. For this, customer journeys must be embedded in operating models of companies in four ways as follows:

- Identify the journeys to excel
- Measure how they are performing
- Build cross-functional processes to support journeys
- Institute cultural change for continuous improvement

Companies have to focus on the entire journey and measure end-to-end success instead of focusing solely on touchpoints. Many companies use regression models to ascertain which journeys have the greatest impact on customer satisfaction and business outcomes, and attempt to redesign customer experience and engage the front-line employees in delivering that experience. This entails modifying the entire organization to deliver excellent consumer journeys and creating metrics and incentives to support journeys, not just touchpoints. Successful companies are able to enhance the experience so much that fierce loyalty results, and are able to reap its benefits.

Benefits of Consumer Loyalty

There are many benefits of cultivating consumer loyalty. Loyal customers ensure sales, are less likely to be influenced by competitor advertising, and will not mind paying a premium for the company's brands or services. They also reduce costs of marketing if they become net promoters for the company's brands. Benefits of consumer loyalty are explained here.

Retaining Customers is Cheaper

Companies have to spend heavily to acquire new customers. Acquiring new customers cost more than retaining existing ones. This cost can be recovered only if customers are retained over a period of time. When customers become loyal and buy repeatedly from a company, they add economic value to the firm, helping it to recover the initial investment and subsequently make profits. The net return on the first transaction is minimal or even negative because of very high marketing costs. However, as the relationship continues, the customer becomes profitable to the seller, simply because repeat customers do not require acquisition costs. Some services, for example, traditional life insurance, only reach break-even point after five years such that if any customers leave before that, they generate a loss. Life insurance policies are profitable only over the long term. In credit-card finance business, the break-even time for a new customer is more than six years because of high marketing and bad debt costs. The longer the relationship, the lower the amortized cost of acquisition. New account set-up, credit searches, and promotional expenses to sell to a new customer can add huge costs. Therefore, retaining a customer makes economic sense.

Loyal Customers are Less Deal Prone
Loyal customers do not look elsewhere for deals but tend to buy more products and services from the firm. This gives the companies competitive advantage. Since customers have many choices and do not exhibit single brand loyalty, companies do well to retain them. Companies have to find ways of enhancing their value proposition so that customers become less likely to shift to competitors. Customers in long-term relationships with banks, for instance, are unlikely to switch banks even if better deals are offered by competitors. Many customers who have a friendly and a personal relationship with their banks or service providers do not consider alternatives and are willing to override price or convenience attributes.

Word-of-mouth Publicity and Referrals
Loyalty leads to referrals. As loyal customers are happy customers, they speak well about their experience to others and serve as ambassadors for the company. This saves the company money by way of reduced customer acquisition costs. In the hotel industry, for instance, guests who were delighted and felt loyal to a specific hotel tend to narrate the experience and make positive comments about it. Loyal hotel customers make business referrals, and provide references and publicity.

Selling Additional Products with Less Marketing Effort
Loyal customers tend to place a greater share of their business with the firm, even to the extent of single sourcing. Companies can always pitch in and offer additional products to a loyal customer. For example, regular users of Dove will not hesitate to try other products under the same brand name. Additionally, loyal customers are more receptive to new service offerings by their regular vendors.

Cost Savings
Regular customers are easier to serve because they understand the service provider's operation and therefore make fewer demands on employee time. As they do not carry acquisition costs, they are more profitable to serve. When companies retain customers, they reduce investments in customer replacement.

Customer Loyalty Leads to Employee Loyalty
Improved customer retention leads to greater employee retention because employees are familiar and take pride in serving their regular customers. Long-term customers like familiar faces and build good working relationships with loyal employees. Increased employee retention, in turn, leads to improved customer retention because employees develop a sense of warmth for the

workplace and their customers. Knowing their customers' likes and dislikes, employees deliver friendly service to them. This leads to efficient service and substantial cost savings.

Goodwill Factor

Loyal customers provide organizations with a goodwill or credibility factor that encourages customer tolerance in the event of a service failure. For example, a customer will attribute service failures, like excessive waiting time, to factors beyond the service provider's control.

Better Prices

Customer loyalty is associated with lower price elasticity. This means that customers do not mind paying higher prices, resulting in higher margins for the company. Companies with a following of loyal customers have pricing power, or the ability to raise prices without affecting demand.

Customer loyalty, thus, generates a higher return over the life of the relationship. The revenues are estimated over their lifetimes, and arrive at the customer lifetime value (CLV). To achieve this, managers have to understand the different types of loyalty.

Types of Loyalty

Companies need to understand the different types of loyalty to understand its nature. There are four types of loyalties, each with its own benefits, risks, and measurement.

Contractual When a customer purchases from a company through a formal agreement, it is called contractual loyalty. This is common in B2B situations; however, companies bind customers through contracts in B2C situations as well. These include subscriptions for newspapers, magazines, cable, telephone, and broadband services, along with service and warranty contracts. Contractual loyalty can be very profitable for companies, but sometimes result in dissatisfaction when customers feel trapped, for example, if a cheaper option becomes available. Companies also become vulnerable when contracts come up for renegotiation and competitors try to steal customers.

Transactional Repeat purchasing without any contracts is called transactional loyalty. This type of loyalty is based on factors such as price, value perception, and convenience. Customers have the freedom to switch at any time, for example, when they find a cheaper or better option. Transactional loyalty can be stimulated with promotions or rewards programmes, but is difficult to sustain. Companies use a system of rewards and punishments to achieve transactional loyalty. Increasing switching costs is one way of erecting barriers which customers find difficult to cross. For example, consumers will face difficulty when they want to switch banks in return for marginally better service.

Functional When a customer buys repeatedly from one company because the company's products are perceived as superior, it is called functional loyalty. In the case of telecom companies, if a customer perceives better network availability of a service provider than another, he/she has functional loyalty. Similarly, if a company's products are perceived as more suitable than those of another, customers will stick to it because they associate a functional benefit by sticking to it. Functional loyalty is achieved through differentiation. If a company provides customers something that is either perceptually or tangibly superior to competitors, it can achieve functional loyalty.

CB IN ACTION   Which is Real Loyalty?

- Suzuki is the leading manufacturer of cars in India. It buys tyres from several companies under a master purchasing agreement for its car models. The company receives volume-pricing discounts from suppliers. Suzuki represents a sizeable revenue and repeat business for the tyre companies. Is Suzuki a loyal customer?
- Pharmaceutical companies rely on doctors to prescribe their medicines. These companies offer incentives such as conferences and paid trips to Goa to doctors who complete a certain number of prescriptions for the company's brands. Doctors say that, all other things being equal, they would prescribe the company's brands as they look forward to a free holiday with their families. Are the doctors exhibiting loyalty?
- A restaurant offers a loyalty card on which it offers one free meal after a customer has had four meals. Many customers tend to eat more frequently at the restaurant, especially when they are nearing their fourth meal, so that they get a free meal. Is this genuine loyalty?
- A customer does not cook and frequently orders food at home. Most of the time, he/she orders food from a nearby restaurant even though he/she does not like it very much, simply because it is near and the service is quick. Does this customer exhibit loyalty?
- A frequent traveller can buy coffee anywhere but seeks out Starbucks in whichever city he or she is travelling to. Customers like the familiar ambience and service, and know that they can unwind there. Can such customers who seek out Starbucks said to be loyal?
- A fashion-conscious young lady gives Shoppers' Stop high customer-satisfaction scores for breadth of merchandise, good pricing, and friendly service. She also carries the Shoppers Stop rewards card. Can we say that this customer is loyal?
- A young student mentions that Mercedes is his most preferred brand and rates it highly in satisfaction among all car manufacturers. When asked which would be the car that he would like to buy, he mentions 'Mercedes'. However, he also mentions that he does not have money to buy the brand. Is this customer satisfied and loyal?
- Nike is positioned for sports lovers and many sports people prefer the brand. It also has high repurchase rates among athletes who find Nike shoes a better fit for wide feet. Are these buyers loyal to the Nike brand?

In each of the situations described here, assess whether it depicts consumer loyalty and specify which type of loyalty is being described. Which of these is the best type of loyalty that companies should strive for?

Emotional   When a customer develops preferences for products or services based on their appeal to the individual's values, ego, sensibilities, or other intangibles, it is called emotional loyalty. Emotional loyalty caters to the feelings of customers and tends to identify the brand with some non-functional benefits such as experience or status. Emotional loyalty is often sought by companies because it is hard to break; emotionally loyal customers stick to the brand and tend to forgive minor errors in their experience and maintain the relationship. This kind of loyalty is also used to earn price premiums.

Measuring Loyalty

It is clear from the definition of loyalty that it is difficult to quantify. Companies use either behavioural or attitudinal measures of consumer loyalty. While behavioural methods measure actual purchases made over a specific time period, attitudinal methods measure stated preferences, commitment, or purchase intentions of customers. Both methods suffer from drawbacks. Behavioural methods tend to ignore why purchases are occurring—it may be because of shortage of an alternative brand. Attitudinal measures are likewise faulty because they venture into psychological and qualitative areas, which are not only impossible to measure but also change from time to time.

Customer loyalty can be measured through a number of methods. Four methods—the RFM, share of the wallet, NPS, and VOC techniques are described here.

Recency, Frequency, and Monetary Value Model

One way of measuring customer loyalty is by using the recency, frequency, and monetary value (RFM) of customer purchases. The technique can also be used for market segmentation and analysing consumer behaviour.

The model identifies customer behaviour and loyalty on three variables:

Recency How recently did the customer purchase? It refers to the interval between latest customer purchase and the time the analysis is being done.

Frequency How often does the customer purchase? It refers to the number of transactions in a particular period.

Monetary value How much did the customer spend? This is calculated by adding up the amount spent by a customer in a particular period.

RFM can be computed in two ways. In the first method, customer data is sorted based on RFM criteria and grouping it in equal quintiles. Alternately, relative weights for R, F, and M are assigned using regression techniques and then the combined score of RFM is calculated. The RFM score is thus the sum of the weighted recency, frequency, and monetary value scores for a customer.

Steps in calculating RFM score An illustration of the RFM calculation is shown in Table 15.2 and explained here. The calculation is done on the following basis:

Recency = Number of months that have passed since the customer last purchased
Frequency = Number of purchases in the last 12 months
Monetary = Value of the highest order from a given customer (maximum value: ₹10,000)

Assign recency scores The first step is to assign scores based on company requirements. In recency, we assign scores based on the customer's last purchase date and sort them into newest to the oldest buyers. Customers who have purchased from the company recently, say in the last three months of a given year, are assigned a score of 5, whereas those who have last bought 11–12 months ago are assigned a score of 1. Sometimes, a scale of 1–10 is used, with 10 assigned to those making the most recent purchase.

TABLE 15.2 Table showing assigning of scores for each of R, F, M for a company

Recency by months	Score	Frequency (Number of purchases)	Score	Monetary value (₹)	Score
0–3	5	10+	5	10,000	5
3–5	4	7–9	4	7500–9999	4
6–8	3	5–6	3	5000–7499	3
9–10	2	3–4	2	2500–4999	2
11–12	1	1–2	1	0–2499	1

Assign frequency scores Frequency scores are based on the number of purchases made by the customer in the past year. Customers who purchased most frequently—ten or more orders every year are assigned a score of 5, whereas those buying least frequently, with just 1–2 orders during the entire year, are assigned a score of 1.

Assign monetary scores Monetary scores are assigned on the basis of size of the order in rupee terms. Customers who place high value orders (in this case, we have taken ₹10,000 or above) are assigned a score of 5 while those placing least value orders are assigned a score of 1.

Calculate RFM scores To get to the composite RFM score, separate scores or R, F, M for each customers are added up. While customers scoring 5 + 5 + 5 are classified as most loyal, those with 1 + 1 + 1 scores are considered to be least loyal.

The assigning of scores is shown in Table 15.2, in which a scale of 1 to 5 to calculate RFM scores is used.

Plotting these scores on a grid gives us a classification of customers who are most loyal (555) to least loyal (111) and all those in between. After identifying customers in this way, a company can use strategies to move the least loyal customers up the ladder to become more loyal, or the least in monetary value to buy some more stuff from the company. The numbers of customers in each category indicates whether the company has a majority of loyal customers or not.

The RFM approach has a few limitations. It ignores time between purchases; a customer may not have purchased recently but may buy after long gaps, for instance, making him/her a loyal customer, so companies can misjudge buying patterns. It also measures monetary values and, thus, ignores profitability. It ignores customers who buy small quantities of low margin orders. Therefore, a customer may score high in recency and frequency, but only for those products on which the company makes very little profit. In effect, such customers may actually be causing a loss to the company since they buy only discounted items. An example will help understanding this better.

As explained in *Marketing Channels* (2012), small retailers are the first to enter supermarkets in certain areas and pick up all the discounted goods and those with special offers that the supermarket actually sells at a loss to entice retail customers. The retailers pick up these products to get better margins by selling them in their shops, but in the process stymie the efforts of the store to lure the genuine customer who comes later and finds no special deals on offer.

Share of Wallet

Writing that traditional measures of loyalty are not enough, Keiningham, et al. (2011) gave the concept of the share of the wallet. This concept refers to the percentage of a customer's spending of a brand within a category of products. This is done to get over the problem where customers may say they are very satisfied with a company or brand, but may prefer to buy an alternative brand instead. They give the example of Wal-Mart, which found that customers said they were very satisfied with the stores but sales entered the longest decline in the company's history. Even as satisfaction increased, the share of the wallet fell.

Based on a longitudinal study of 17,000 customers, they suggest the wallet allocation rule that correlates the rank that consumers assign to a brand with a share of the wallet. This is explained here.

TABLE 15.3 Ranking brands

Customer	Brand 1	Brand 2	Brand 3
A	3	1	2
B	3	2	1
C	3	1	2

Wallet allocation rule Let us say that there are three brands and consumers rank them as shown in Table 15.3.

$$\text{Share of the wallet} = 1 - \frac{\text{Rank}}{\text{No. of brands} + 1} \times \frac{2}{\text{No. of brands}}$$

Using this formula, we get Brand 1's share of the wallet as $(1 - \tfrac{3}{4}) \times 2/3 = 17\%$ approximately. This is calculated for all the three brands to get a share of the wallet as in Table 15.4.

TABLE 15.4 Share of wallet

Customer	Brand 1	Brand 2	Brand 3
A	17%	50%	33%
B	17%	33%	50%
C	17%	44%	39%

The rule is used by companies to make strategies to gather more customers spending in a category. Through this approach, companies can ascertain why customers are ranking one brand over another and then modify their offerings to move up the ranking ladder.

Net Promoter Score

Another model to measure customer loyalty is the net promoter score (NPS) method. Reichheld (2003) studied several questions that could be asked to customers to measure loyalty and concluded that detailed questionnaires do not serve the purpose. His research showed that companies use the wrong yardsticks to measure customer loyalty.

According to him, customer loyalty can be measured by just one question— 'How likely is it that you would recommend a product or company to a friend or colleague?' He writes, 'an individual's propensity for recommending a company to friends or colleagues may be the most direct gauge of customer loyalty and ultimately, financial success.' He describes the NPS as a measure that both reflects 'the emotional and the rational dimensions' of the relationship between the customer and the company. The NPS is a simple but powerful tool to measure consumer satisfaction with just one single question, and is an indication of the growth potential of the company or product.

On the basis of responses to this question, Reichheld (2006) proposed the NPS. The customer responds by rating the answer on a scale of 0 to 10, with 0 labelled 'not at all likely', 5 labelled 'neutral', and 10 labelled 'extremely likely'. The responses are then aggregated and transformed into a single score, called the NPS. A company's NPS is the difference between the proportion of customers placing themselves at points 9 or 10, called 'promoters', and the proportion of customers scoring between 0 and 6, called 'detractors' (Fig. 15.5).

Using the NPS, a company's customers can be divided into three categories—promoters, passives, and detractors.

Promoters—score 9–10 Loyal enthusiasts who will keep buying and refer others, fuelling growth.

Passives—score 7–8 Satisfied but unenthusiastic customers who are vulnerable to competitive offerings.

Detractors—score 0–6 Unhappy customers who can damage the brand and impede growth through negative word of mouth.

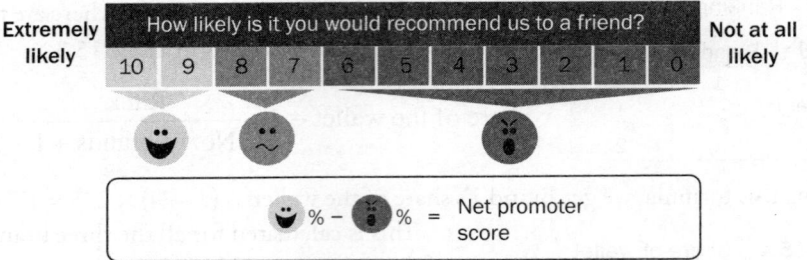

FIG. 15.5 Calculation of net promoter score

Voice of the Customer Approach

The voice of the customer (VOC) approach describes customers' feedback about their experiences and expectations of products or services. It gathers multi-source information to find customer needs, expectations, and product improvement. It is based on the knowledge that customers are far more inclined to get involved in the marketplace and start conversations about brands and products online. Social media provides ample opportunity to post comments and interact with others about their experiences of using products and services. This information can be tapped by organizations, dynamically, continually, directly, and indirectly.

Direct information flows when customers make calls, send emails, and complete surveys. Indirect information flows when they talk among themselves online in blogs, product forums, and social media. They are quick to like and dislike and share experiences liberally. They also have suggestions for better features. This huge information—referred to as big data—flows to different groups within an organization. While some information may come to the marketing department directly, other information flows are limited to the service department. Feedback posted online goes to website administrators. Moreover, this big data consists of unstructured prose and not really data, and contains valuable insights for companies, if they care to listen.

Such data is increasing exponentially faster than structured data; it is estimated that seven million web pages are published every day. Social media channels such as blogs, forums, wikis, and other spaces are also not controlled and often even monitored by the company. That is why information from customers is not used at all. The unstructured data requires humans to read and understand it. This is a huge task.

Some companies provide analytics software to analyse consumer information. One example is the Infosys HIMI Voice of Customer Analytics, which is an end-to-end solution that enables enterprises to process customer sentiments and opinions in unstructured text. The Infosys website says that the HIMI VOC Analytics presents actionable insights in a business dashboard. It has a comprehensive approach to analyse data from various formal and informal sources of touchpoints and correlate the analysis with enterprise-structured data to generate inferences for decision-making. It combines text processing algorithms with a natural language processing (NLP) approach, dashboards designed for business users, and easy approach for modelling.

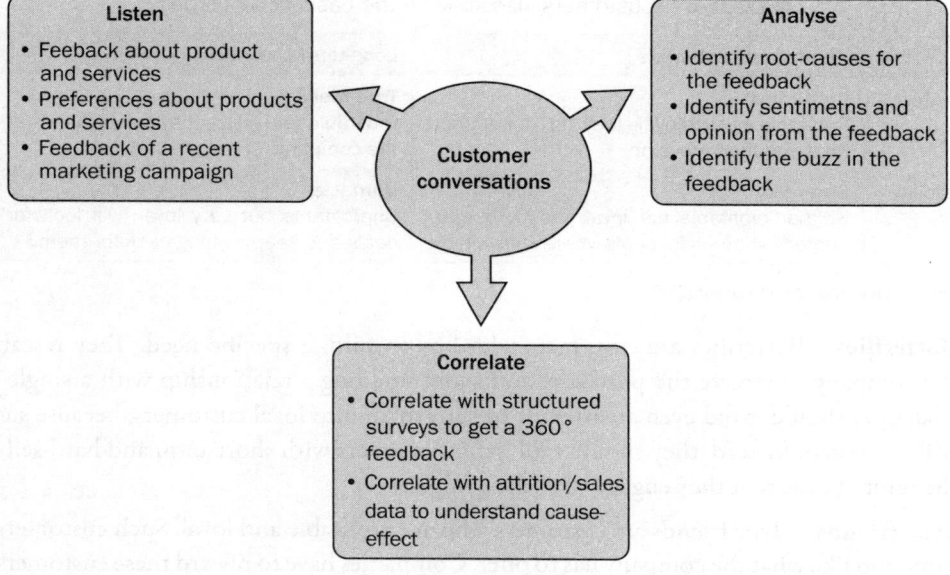

FIG. 15.6 VOC approach

The VOC approach gives deeper insights into customer preferences, feedback on new product launches, analyses trends and early warnings from social media and network conversations, provides better root cause analysis of issues by exploiting unstructured text in CRM systems, and granular analysis of customer preferences at various sources. Figure 15.6 shows a framework of VOC approach.

Measuring loyalty leads to using the information to develop strategies to develop and enhance it. The next section discusses these strategies and how to use them.

LOYALTY STRATEGY

Creating a loyalty strategy is of great importance to companies because, as Kapferer (2005) writes, brand loyalty is in decline today. Consumers are more versatile and less loyal today than they ever have been. When contemplating their next purchase, satisfied consumers do not automatically buy the same brand of car or television set. This new situation is described as 'choice repertoire.' A consumer can no longer be identified by a brand, but rather by a set of brands he will choose, with a specific probability, within the same product category. Instead of brand loyalty, companies know they have to live with 'shared loyalties,' 'divided loyalties,' or even 'multiple loyalties'.

A successful loyalty strategy has to consider loyalty and profitability at the same time. Customers can be classified on the basis of low and high profitability and whether they are short or long-term customers as shown in Table 15.5.

Reinartz and Kumar (2002) question the assumption that loyal customers drive profits. 'Instead on focusing on loyalty alone, companies will have to find ways to measure the relationship between loyalty and profitability,' they write. The ways to approach these customers are described here.

TABLE 15.5 Customers classified on the basis of profitability

	Short-term customers	Long-term customers
High profitability	**Butterflies** Profitable but disloyal—they buy for a short time and then move on.	**True friends** Profitable and loyal—they buy regularly and stick to the company
Low profitability	**Strangers** Neither profitable nor loyal; mostly bargain hunters who look for deals wherever available	**Barnacles** Unprofitable but very loyal; will look for the best deals and keep coming back for them.

Source: Adapted from Reinartz and Kumar (2002)

Butterflies Butterflies are customers who buy to fulfil a specific need. They research about the company, complete the purchase, and avoid building a relationship with a single provider. Managers should avoid even an attempt to turn them into loyal customers, because such efforts will be wasted. Instead, they should milk such customers with short-term and hard-sell offers for the limited time that they engage with the company.

True friends True friends are customers who are profitable and loyal. Such customers look for value and like what the company has to offer. Companies have to reward these customers for their loyalty not only through promotions but granting them access to special events. Such activities help make customers feel special and build a bond with them.

Strangers Strangers are short-term customers who are also not profitable. They are bargain hunters who look for deals where available and are not loyal to one store or brand. The strategy to be followed with such customers is to invest nothing on them.

Barnacles Barnacles are unprofitable customers but are loyal. They stick to the best deals that a company has to offer. Managers have to deal with different types of customers differently, by identifying their share of the wallet.

Reducing Customer Effort

Managers often assume that more satisfied the customers are, the more loyal they will be. However, there is little relationship between satisfaction and loyalty. For example, one may be very satisfied with an expensive restaurant, but will prefer a cheaper or more accessible restaurant for regular eating or for ordering food at home.

Dixon, et al. (2010) report that delighting customers does not build loyalty but reducing their effort does. Rather than great service and ambience, loyalty has a lot more to do with how well companies deliver on their basic promises. This advice flies in the face of conventional business practices, where companies make it difficult for customers to solve their queries and are, instead, forced to press buttons on automated voice response systems while playing out useless information over the phone.

Using this insight to modify customer service helps to reduce service costs, and results in more loyal customers. They write that companies would do well to 'make it easy' for customers. This can be done by reducing obstacles or bottlenecks that customers resent. Some of these bottlenecks are as follows:

- Customers do not like to contact the company repeatedly
- They do not like having to repeat information
- They do not like switching from one service channel to another.

A majority of customers report such difficulties when dealing with companies. This issue can be measured by the customer effort score (CES). Through this, customers can rate how much effort they spent in resolving their problem on a scale of 1 to 5, with 5 representing very high effort. They suggest the following methods for improving the CES:

Implement first-contact-resolution The biggest cause of excessive customer effort is when the representative is unable to resolve the issue and the customer has to call back. Many companies get over this issue by measuring first-contact-resolution (FCR) scores. Companies can, by mining their customer interaction data, understand the relationship among various customer issues, called event clusters. These clusters give an indication to company representatives not only to resolve the customer's primary issue but also to anticipate and address related issues, so that the customer does not have to call back. For instance, customers who buy a software will most likely call back to get instructions on using it and resolving common glitches. By giving a quick tutorial to customers about the key aspects of the software before hanging up, companies can reduce repeat calls by customers. For complex or recurring issues, the company can send e-mails, explaining the features and resolution steps.

Connect with customers emotionally Repeat calls have to be made because of the emotional disconnect between customers and representatives. For example, the customer may not trust the representative's information or does not like the answer given. To get over this, representatives are trained to listen for clues to a customer's personality type and classify them as a controller, a thinker, a feeler, or an entertainer. Responses are then tailored accordingly, offering the customer the details in the appropriate manner for the personality type diagnosed. Basic training in language also helps in this regard. For example, instead of saying, 'We don't have that item in stock,' a representative might explain, 'We'll have stock availability for that item in two weeks.' Such interactions can greatly reduce repeat calls by customers and increase CES scores.

Minimize channel switching Most customers visit the company's website first and call the company only if they are unable to find a solution on it. However, many companies do not make problem resolution easier on their websites and resist making improvements. Technology upgrades are usually counterproductive and expensive; instead, all possible customer issues should be addressed on company websites.

Talk to disgruntled or struggling customers Companies should seek feedback from customers who are facing difficulties or have a grudge against them. Service improvements resulting from such feedback help future interactions with customers.

Empower the front line Many companies spend huge amounts of money in creating infrastructure but neglect front-line employees, who are often paid less and lack motivation to deliver great service. They are also pressed for speed, since most customer service organizations emphasize metrics like average handle time when assessing representative performance. Instead, the focus should be on making the customer's experience easy.

Some companies make low customer effort the cornerstone of their service. South Africa's Nedbank, for instance, instituted an AskOnce promise, which guarantees that the representative who picks up the phone will own the customer's issue from start to finish.

LOYALTY PROGRAMMES

Loyalty programmes are schemes offered by companies to customers who frequent a brand or store, in which they are rewarded for making purchases. Such programmes are used to provide advanced access to new products, special sales coupons, or free merchandise. Customers are asked to register their personal information with the company and are given an ID or membership card that is used to give reward points to customers. These can be redeemed after a period of time.

Loyalty programmes can generate as much as 20 per cent of a company's profits, according to a study, *Loyalty: is it really working for you?* by McKinsey and Company (2011). However, the study found out that a good loyalty programme is surprisingly rare. Many companies implement 'me too' programmes, consisting of awarding points but the rewards do little to drive value. Most loyalty programmes are modelled on airline reward point structure—the more you buy the more points you earn, which, after a while, can be redeemed for gifts. Such schemes do not make use of either the latest technologies available, or indeed consumer loyalty. The companies usually forget the system once it is in place without measuring their impact on real loyalty. Very often, companies with loyalty programmes posted lower sales increases than those without any loyalty programmes.

Most so-called loyalty programmes or loyalty cards are, defacto, based on consumers' self-interest. They are, in fact, retention programmes. They follow Skinner's theory of learning, that is, reinforce repeat behaviour by rewards. Loyalty cards merely serve to track frequency. Companies hope that, through time, repeated behaviour will turn into habits. Later, these habits will be psychologically internalized to produce a positive attitude to a brand.

The McKinsey analysis goes on to say that as the loyalty programmes are not focused, some of the best customers may not even be members since companies fail to focus on their most loyal customers. The reward points end up creating liabilities without catering to their most loyal customers. 'To succeed today, it is clear to us that companies need to embrace new digital tactics, re-examine old systems, and move beyond just points and rewards,' says the report.

To design a loyalty programme that impacts high-value, high-potential, or at-risk customers, for maximum value, the following three steps are suggested:

Clarity about objectives As a first step, companies need to be clear as to what the loyalty programme should do—is the objective to increase wallet share, to rewards repeat purchases, or to cater to the most loyal customers? Concrete objectives help to design the right benefits, focus on the right metrics, and to serve their most loyal customers.

Get granular information Standard metrics for loyalty programmes like those purchasing frequently do not identify high value customers who may be purchasing infrequently. As a result, companies invest resources in the wrong customers. Instead, companies must get granular information about customer buying habits, not only how frequently they buy but how profitable they are to the company.

Build a programme that generates value There are two kinds of loyalty programmes—published and unpublished. Published or visible programmes motivate and appeal to a broad audience, generate excitement, and build scale. Such programmes must be implemented on levels of service offered such as platinum, gold, or silver, or on the value and/or potential of customer groups, such as their life stages or needs, that is, for families, students, or older people, so that augmented offerings can be made to specific segments based on their needs.

Unpublished rewards are only given to selected customers and not known to the average consumer. They have surprise and delight elements, and are executed through invitation-only programmes.

These rewards convey an exclusive status and are generally very useful in increasing share of wallet of those most profitable customers, and are harder to be duplicated. A combination of published and unpublished reward system creates a matrix of loyalty efforts that surrounds the company's most desirable customers.

A carefully built loyalty programme results in converting customers into loyal ones, motivating them to buy more, and also in focusing on the most profitable customers (see box on Global Insight). A blind implementation of a system offering loyalty reward points does not result in increasing sales or profits.

GLOBAL INSIGHT
Amazon's Loyalty Programme

Customer loyalty programmes usually follow a standard pattern—offer reward points on the amount of purchases made by a customer. Collect enough reward points and customers are entitled to redeem them for free gifts. Such programmes follow the frequent flyer schemes offered by airlines—reward points are added whenever tickets are purchased. In general, hotels, credit card companies, retail shops, and the like offer reward points programmes. Most of these programmes are free and are designed to motivate customers to continue using their loyalty cards by buying more, in their attempt to get enough reward points for a free gift.

Amazon decided to do things differently. Instead of launching a common reward point programme, Amazon used breakthrough thinking to design a programme to convert customers into die-hard fans. Its programme was not free; people had to pay $79 annually to join the programme. They got free two-day shipping on millions of items on the Amazon site with no limitation of minimum-order size. This ingenious approach immediately benefited frequent buyers, because it removed the two big barriers to online purchasing—shipping charges and lengthy delivery times. Amazon Prime was launched in 2005. By 2009, it had two million members, and according to some estimates this number tripled to six million members by 2010.

The Amazon Prime Program was very successful to convert occasional shoppers into hard-core Amazon addicts. Estimates say that about 20 million consumers currently have Prime memberships, and they spend about twice as much in a year as non-Prime customers. The programme is innovative in its approach; it offers immediate benefits to customers and does away with reward point accumulation. The features of Amazon Prime are as follows:

Basic benefits Unlimited free two-day shipping; one-day shipping for $4.

Perks Unlimited free streaming from Amazon instant video, featuring 5000-plus movies and TV shows; penalty-free cancellation if the programme is not used; can add up to four household members.

Additions Book lending was added for Kindle owners.

Apart from the offer of free shipping, Amazon has been turning Prime into an online incentive for digital

(Contd)

GLOBAL INSIGHT (Contd)

media. It added movie and TV streaming to the Prime membership, cleverly bridging the gap between hard goods with free two-day shipping, and digital goods with unlimited instant videos and free eBooks. It also added the Kindle owners lending library, which gently encourages Prime members to purchase a Kindle, so as to gain access to eBooks on loan.

Amazon Prime eliminates the complexity of points, which involves collection, tracking, and redemption. Instead, it offers benefits that relate directly to preferential service. Therefore, Amazon Prime redefines the basic premise of a customer loyalty programme.

Customers with a Prime membership use Amazon like a utility—they tend to check at Amazon first and end up buying, knowing that the item will arrive before they can buy it from the local store. Prime customers have the 'Amazon first' mentality, where it becomes the default shopping option for them. As the delivery time is two days, this saves a trip to the retail store. The ease of purchasing, the giant selection, coupled with quick delivery, encourages customers to shop at Amazon often, even though it does not give any rewards points or discounts.

The loyalty programme is also profitable. According to Consumer Intelligence Research Partners, the average Prime customer spent about $1340 in 2013. With Amazon's 26.5 per cent gross margin, the company made $355 from each customer. Shipping losses are easily covered with this margin. The company is not worried about short-term profit, instead, it has been building a long-term programme, aimed at taking a larger share of the wallet from customers.

Bloomberg Businessweek (2010) describes Amazon Prime as 'the most ingenious and effective customer loyalty programme in all of e-commerce, if not retail in general.' The programme resulted in the best customers increasing purchases on the site by 150 per cent. It converts casual shoppers into Amazon addicts. Prime is one of the reasons that Amazon's sales grew 30 per cent during the recession (2008–2010).

Amazon exploits the wide range of its distribution system, while cashing in on the need to maximize the benefits of a loyalty scheme.

The scheme is promoted widely, with free offers of Prime trials to students and parents. It is estimated that Prime members increase their purchases on the site by about 150 per cent after they join. Amazon stores details of what customers have ordered before, and its 'subscribe and save' programme automatically re-ships items on a regular schedule. Now, the company is considering increasing the membership fee to about $119 per annum.

Amazon Prime provides an ongoing revenue stream for Amazon. More importantly, it encourages consumer loyalty, which is the prime objective of loyalty programmes. In this case, customers are willing to pay to get a value-added service and express a willingness to continue to shop with Amazon. It has since built on the Prime base to create two new segment-specific offerings—Amazon Student and Amazon Mom.

With Prime, Amazon continues the company's transition from an online retailer of books to an Internet megamall that sells almost everything sourced from various companies, to a seller of digital goods and even its own devices, like the Kindle Fire tablet computer.

Sources:

http://www.forbes.com/sites/markrogowsky/2014/02/02/prime-factors-should-amazon-really-mess-with-the-best-loyalty-program-in-retail/, last accessed on 9 October 2014.

Stone, Brad, What's in Amazon's Box? Instant Gratification, *Bloomberg Businessweek*, November 24, 2010, http://www.businessweek.com/magazine/content/10_49/b4206039292096.htm, last accessed on 12 November 2014.

Woo, Stu, http://online.wsj.com/news/articles/SB10001424052970203503204577036102353359784, November 14, 2011, last accessed on 9 October 2014.

Consumer Loyalty and Profits

We have seen that consumer satisfaction and loyalty result in long-term customers, and, hence better growth and profitability. However, companies are also looking at the types of customers who come back—are they profitable to the company or are they just bargain seekers? In this section, we analyse two important relationships—between loyalty and satisfaction, and between loyalty and profitability.

In his book, *The Loyalty Effect*, Reichheld (1996) lays out the 'economics of loyalty' that links loyalty and learning to cash flows and profits. Reichheld writes that this connection is invaluable for improving a company's performance through increasing the loyalty of customers, investors, and employees. He shows that loyalty drives profits in direct and quantifiable ways through increased growth, learning, and productivity. 'In addition, loyalty generates a spiritual energy that powers the value creation process that is at the heart of sustained business success. In many industries, loyalty explains the differences in profitability among competitors more effectively than scale, market share, unit costs, or most other factors usually associated with competitive advantage,' he writes.

Latest findings show that these findings are now being challenged. Research published in *MIT Sloan Management Review* (2014) shows that satisfaction explains only one per cent variation in a company's market return. *Bloomberg Businessweek* (2013) reports similar findings—'There's no statistical relationship between customer-service scores and stock-market returns.' Research found that companies that customers hate perform better than those that are rated highly by customers. It makes a startling finding, 'If anything, it might hurt company profits to spend money making customers happy.'

Analysis conducted by Rego, et al. (2013) on extensive time series of data indicates a significant negative association between market share and customer satisfaction. They also found that the effect of a firm's customer satisfaction on its future market share is strengthened by benchmarking it as being relative to the firm's nearest rival and considering the firm's customers' switching costs. Gupta, et al. (2012) conducted analysis of Groupon offers and revealed that cheap coupons were very popular and were, often, money losers for merchants. However, because of their high customer satisfaction, they generated a huge demand and contributed most to Groupon volume.

These findings go against conventional wisdom and numerous findings that consumer satisfaction leads to increased share of wallet and referrals that should subsequently result in better stock market performance. This leads to the question whether spending to increase customer satisfaction is actually a waste of money. Though customer satisfaction can be increased by lowering prices, should companies actually do so? As companies reward employees for higher customer satisfaction levels, and managers tend to devise schemes to improve satisfaction, managers face a difficult choice—should they increase volumes and customer satisfaction by selling things that are unprofitable? The answer is that they must understand the profit impact of improved customer satisfaction.

MIT's (2014) research on more than 1,00,000 consumers covering more than 300 brands found three critical issues that have a strong negative impact on translating customer satisfaction into positive business outcomes.

Money-losing delighters Low price is a major driver of customer satisfaction; however, satisfaction and price are almost always inversely related. For instance, a financial services company was found to have highly satisfied customers. A closer analysis revealed that over two-thirds of these highly satisfied customers were also unprofitable to the company. The high satisfaction levels were a result of getting great deals and cheap services, which were often priced below cost. Customers bought these in large quantities. These customers were not only unprofitable, but also large in numbers and size. Further, they also expected other services from the company, such as free delivery and preferential treatment that is offered to high value customers.

Smaller equals happier The second major finding is that there is little relationship between satisfaction and market share; in fact, research finds that high satisfaction is a strong negative predictor of future market share. The broader a company's market appeal relative to the offerings of competitors, the lower the level of satisfaction tends to be. The reason for this is that market share typically comes from attracting customers whose needs are not completely aligned with the company's core target market. As a result, smaller niche companies are better able to serve their customers. Companies with a large market share, on the other hand, must by their very nature serve a more diverse set of customers. Therefore, consumer satisfaction index as measured by ACSI for two famous companies—McDonald's and Wal-Mart—consistently rank behind their competitors. However, these companies have by far the largest market shares in their respective industries.

Importance of being number 1 Companies tend to believe that higher satisfaction scores result in a greater share of a customer's wallet. Research shows that knowing a customer's satisfaction level reveals almost nothing about the purchase decision among different brands. This is because consumers these days are loyal to multiple brands. They are likely to look at all options, a preferred brand and as well as its competitors, and spread their spending than completely defect from a business or brand. Thus, companies have to focus on improving customers' share of spending with their brand than to improve customer retention.

Deloitte's (2013) study of the hotel industry found that, on an average, approximately 50 per cent of hotel guests' spending is not with their preferred hotel brand. Such findings pose a unique problem—if highly satisfied customers do not shop with the company or brand, what must a company to do to increase share of their customers' spending?

These three findings show that it is easy for customer satisfaction and profitability to become misaligned. In the light of these findings, managers should focus on what companies can do to manage consumer satisfaction and grow their market share.

E-loyalty

Loyalty on the Internet may not seem very relevant, as customers can shift from one site to another with a mere click of a mouse. However, Reichheld and Schefter (2000) write, 'the Web is actually a very sticky place in both the B2C and B2B spheres.' Indeed, customers like to consolidate their purchases with one primary supplier, so that the supplier's site becomes part of their daily routine.

They write that good e-commerce sites understand that cultivating loyalty is an economic necessity because acquiring customers on the Internet is very expensive. Such businesses can be profitable only when they cultivate loyal customers who spend on the site regularly. E-loyalty can be generated by earning the trust of customers and delivering 'such a consistently superior experience that they will want to do all their business with you.'

The way to acquire loyalty on the web is by building trust and enduring relationships. Many companies such as Amazon and eBay have indeed achieved them. Customers rate sellers on these sites and the ratings are available for all to see. eBay holds payments made by customers in an escrow account until the customer is satisfied with the purchase. This transparent system has helped build trust among millions of customers.

CONCLUSION

While conducting aggressive marketing campaigns to try to influence new customers and to wrench them from competitors, we often forget the importance of retaining existing customers. Such customers, if satisfied, are more profitable for companies than new customers. Hence, companies try to build satisfaction and loyalty among them, especially among those who contribute to profitability. This goal can be achieved by business processes that lead to customer retention.

However, anyone who has wrestled with automated voice response machines to contact the customer service departments knows that companies are not serious about reinforcing satisfaction or loyalty. The problem is that each satisfaction system is treated as separate and distinct from all others. Thus, customer relationship programme is not integrated with customer service, while technologies acquire their own objectives. Loyalty programmes are also implemented with little thought and remain stand-alone programmes that do nothing to contribute to loyalty or profitability.

The challenge is then to integrate all customer experience points to deliver one message and one level of satisfaction. This challenge cannot be met because managers like to think of each activity as a separate and hierarchal department. This is ironic, because today we have powerful technologies to collect and integrate customer data like never before.

The need of the hour is to reinvent the marketing department, as Rust, Moorman, and Bhalla (2010) write, to make it a 'customer department.' It is time to replace the chief marketing officer with a chief customer officer (CCO), as many forward-looking companies have done, to 'make the conventional organization more customer-centric.' The idea is to promote a customer-oriented culture and remove obstacles for customer service throughout the organization. The advice is extremely valuable—'Organizational structures that block information must be torn down.' Whether companies will be able to break out of their silo mentality however, remains to be seen.

SUMMARY

Consumer decision-making ranges from routine and habitual behaviour to more involved and complex behaviour. The purpose of marketing is to shift such behaviour to brand loyalty, in which customers exhibit a strong liking for a brand that they can bear some inconvenience to attain the product. This is done by building satisfaction, in which some pleasurable feelings are induced when consumers buy or consumer products. Brand loyalty gives pricing power to companies.

Several theories provide the conceptual understanding of consumer satisfaction. They explain some thoughts of consumers as they buy products. Marketing strategies must focus on customer experience so that there is satisfaction, which, in turn induces loyalty.

There are several methods to measure satisfaction. Satisfaction in services is measured by SERVQUAL method, which is based on five dimensions of service—empathy, tangibility, responsiveness, reliability, and assurance. The Kano model of customer satisfaction classifies attributes based on consumer perception. The model divides product attributes into three categories—threshold, performance, and excitement. Customer satisfaction index (CSI) models are used by many countries that show industry-wise and company-wise satisfaction indices. These indices help companies compare their customer satisfaction efforts with others and also reveal the state of customer service within industries and within an economy. The scores also help companies to draft their strategies for increasing customer satisfaction.

Despite satisfaction measures, surveys show that consumer satisfaction has decreased over the years. The widespread use of social networking means that the details of the customer's problem will be shared widely. Companies, therefore, have to be customer-oriented and measure ROI of their customer service investments.

Customer loyalty is the willingness of a customer to make an investment or a personal sacrifice in order to strengthen the relationship with a brand or a company. Companies have to deliver consistent experience across all brand touchpoints because loyalty is built by combining physical, emotional, and value elements of customer experience. There are four types of loyalty—contractual, transactional, functional, and emotional. Of these, the emotional loyalty is the most important as there are several benefits that companies can reap due to increased loyalty. Loyalty is measured by four methods—the RFM, share of the wallet, NPS, and VOC techniques.

All these initiatives help in framing a loyalty strategy. A successful strategy has to consider loyalty and profitability at the same time, and should focus on reducing customer effort and enhancing customer experience. Many companies implement 'me too' loyalty programmes, consisting of awarding points but the rewards do little to drive value. To survive, great brands need to create 'loyalty beyond reason' and to differentiate themselves in the future. The secret to this differentiation is a passionate commitment to three powerful concepts in everything the brand does and represents—mystery, sensuality, and intimacy.

KEY TERMS

American Customer Satisfaction Index (ACSI) An index representing consumer satisfaction in the US, which ranks companies within an industry and also shows rankings across industries

Customer loyalty The willingness of a customer to make an investment or personal sacrifice to strengthen a relationship

Customer satisfaction The consumer's fulfilment response or judgement that a product, service, or its features provide a pleasurable level—that is, something that increases pleasure or reduces pain—of consumption-related fulfilment

Kano model A model of customer satisfaction that classifies attributes based on how they are perceived by customers and their effect on customer satisfaction, and divides product attributes into three categories—threshold, performance, and excitement

Loyalty programmes Loyalty programmes are schemes offered by companies to customers who frequent a brand or store, in which they are rewarded for making purchases

Net promoter score (NPS) A simple but powerful tool to measure consumer satisfaction with just one single question, and is an indication of the growth potential of the company or product

Purchase continuum A diagram that represents different shades of consumer decisions, from high to low involvement

RFM Model A model for measuring customer loyalty is by using the recency, frequency, and monetary value (RFM) of customer purchases

SERVQUAL A technique to measure service quality and satisfaction, based on five dimensions of service—empathy, tangibility, responsiveness, reliability, and assurance

Share of the wallet The percentage of a customer's spending of a brand within a category of products

Voice of the customer (VOC) A term that describes the customer's feedback about their experiences with and expectations for products or services and gathers multi-source information tool to find customer needs, expectations, and product improvement

EXERCISES

Concept-review Questions

1. Describe the types of purchase decisions and show them in a continuum with their qualities.
2. What is customer satisfaction? Explain the various theories of customer satisfaction.
3. What is customer satisfaction index (CSI)? How is it calculated?
4. Define customer loyalty. Explain the benefits of maintaining customer loyalty.
5. What steps can be taken to improve quality of customer experience and loyalty in a company?
6. Explain the methods of measuring loyalty. Which method is the best and why?

7. Describe the benefits of customer loyalty. What are the benefits of loyalty to a company and to a customer?
8. What steps can be undertaken by a company to reduce customer effort? Why is this necessary?
9. Explain the importance of loyalty programmes. How are these administered?
10. What is meant by lovemarks? Explain the concept and its principles.

Critical Thinking Questions

1. Though technologies have improved over the years, customer satisfaction has declined. How do you explain this contradiction? How can companies use the latest technologies to improve customer experience and satisfaction?
2. Not all loyal customers are profitable for a company. How would you identify such customers in a retail set-up? Having identified them, what steps would you take to either make them more profitable, or get rid of them?
3. How would you explain the contradiction in the statement that companies hated by customers do well in terms of stock market returns? As there is no statistical relationship between customer-service scores and stock-market returns, how much importance would you place on customer service in your company?
4. Loyalty programmes are meant to encourage loyalty but end up as imitations of competitors while they create liabilities for rewarding customers. How should companies create loyalty programmes that actually promote loyalty? Think in terms of airlines and retail stores and suggest a true loyalty programme for them.

Projects and Assignments

1. Call up the customer helpline of three banks and seek help regarding issuance of a credit card. Explain the process that you were put through. Assess your experience with the helplines on parameters such as waiting time, quality of response, and assistance regarding resolution of your query. What suggestions would you make for improving customer experience by these banks? How would you rate your experience on the basis of customer effort score?
2. Study the loyalty programmes of five companies, some online and some physical stores. Make a comparison of their loyalty schemes. Which companies generate real loyalty and which ones are me-too schemes? How should companies modify their me-too schemes to make them really worthwhile for a company?
3. Conduct a survey among your friends who buy online to see whether they are loyal to particular e-commerce sites or not. Do they tend to buy from their preferred sites or do they conduct a broader search before placing orders? In case they are loyal to some sites, ascertain the reasons why they are loyal, especially since it is easy to search the Web for bargains and deals.
4. While physical stores can create customer experience, how do e-commerce sites create customer experience? Look at three popular sites and write a report on how these sites create and deliver unique experience to their customers.

REFERENCES

American consumer satisfaction Index website http://www.theacsi.org/the-american-customer-satisfaction-index, last accessed on 8 May 2014.

Chemi, Eric, 'Proof that it pays to be America's most-hated companies', *Bloomberg Businessweek*, 17 December 2013.

Consumer Rage Study 2013, http://www.customercaremc.com/the-2013-customer-rage-study/, last accessed on 28 April 2014.

Edelman, David C., 'Branding in the digital age: You're spending your money in all the wrong places', *Harvard Business Review*, December 2010.

Festinger, Leon, Henry W. Riecken, and Stanley Schachter, *When Prophecy Fails*, Harper and Row, New York, pp. 27, 28, 1956.

Fornell C., 'A national customer satisfaction barometer: The Swedish experience', *Journal of Marketing*, Vol. 6, No.1, pp. 6–21, January 1992.

Fornell C., M.D. Johnson, E.W. Anderson, J. Cha., and B.E. Bryant, 'The American customer satisfaction index: Nature, purpose, and findings', *Journal of Marketing*, Vol. 60, No.4, pp. 7–18, October 1996.

Fornell, Claes, Roland T. Rust, and Dekimpe G. Marnik, 'The effect of customer satisfaction on consumer spending growth', *Journal of Marketing Research*, Volume 47, Number 1, February 2010.

Grainer, Marc, Charles H. Noble, Mary Jo Bitner, and Scott M. Broetzmann, 'What unhappy customers want', *MIT Sloan Management Review*, Spring 2014.

Griffin, Abbie, Greg Gleason, Rick Preiss, and Dave Shevenaugh, 'Best practice for customer satisfaction in manufacturing firms', *MIT Sloan Management Review*, Winter, 1995.

Gupta, Sunil, Timothy Keiningham, Ray Weaver, and Luke Williams, 'Are daily deals good for merchants?' *Harvard Business School Background Note*, pp. 513–559, December 2012.

Heskett, James L., Thomas O. Jones, Gary W. Loveman, W. Earl Sasser, Jr., and Leonard A. Schlesinger, 'Putting the service–profit chain to work', *Harvard Business Review*, July, 2008.

Infosys HIMI website http://www.infosys.com/SiteCollectionImages/voc-approach.jpg, last accessed on 8 May 2014.

Kano, N., N. Seraku, F. Takahashi, and S. Tsuji, 'Attractive quality and must-be quality', *The Journal of the Japanese Society for Quality Control*, April 1984.

Kapferer, J. 'The roots of brand loyalty decline: An international comparison', *Ivey Business Journal*, Vol. 69, No. 4, March/April 2005.

Keiningham, Timothy L., Lerzan Aksoy, Alexander Buoye, and Bruce Cooil, 'Customer loyalty isn't enough. Grow your share of wallet', *Harvard Business Review*, October 2011.

Keiningham, Timothy, Sunil Gupta, Lerzan Aksoy, and Alexander Buoye 'The high price of customer satisfaction', *MIT Sloan Management Review*, Spring 2014.

L. Gentry and M. Kalliny, 'Consumer loyalty—A synthesis, conceptual framework, and research propositions', *Journal of American Business Review*, Cambridge 1, No. 1 pp. 119–127, December 2012.

Levitt, Theodore, 'Marketing success through differentiation—of Anything', *Harvard Business Review*, January–February 1980.

Loyalty: Is it really working for you? McKinsey and Company Chief Marketing and Sales Officer Forum, December 2011: http://cmsoforum.mckinsey.com, last accessed on 7 October 2014.

Oliver, Richard L., *Satisfaction: A Behavioral Perspective on the Consumer*, 2/e, M.E. Sharp, New York, 2010.

Peters, Thomas J. and Robert H. Waterman, *In Search of Excellence: Lessons from America's best-run companies*, Collins Business Essentials Edition, New York, 2006.

Rawson, Alex, Ewan Duncan, and Conor Jones, 'The truth about customer experience', Harvard Business Review, September 2013.

Rego, Lopo L., Neil A. Morgan, and Claes Fornell, 'Reexamining the market share—Customer satisfaction relationship,' *Journal of Marketing*, Vol. 77, No. 5, September 2013.

Reichheld, Frederick F., 'The Loyalty Effect: The Hidden Force Behind Growth, Profits, and Lasting Value', Harvard Business Press, Boston, 1996.

Reichheld, Frederick F. and Phil Schefter, 'E-Loyalty: Your secret weapon on the web', *Harvard Business Review*, July–August 2000.

Reichheld, Fredrick F., 'The one number you need to grow', *Harvard Business Review*, pp. 46-54, December 2003.

Reichheld, Fredrick F., *The Ultimate Question. Driving Good Profits and True Growth*, Harvard Business School Press, Boston 2006.

Reinartz, Werner and V. Kumar, 'The mismanagement of customer loyalty', *Harvard Business Review*, July, 2002.

Roberts, Kevin, *Lovemarks: The Future Beyond Brands*, Powerhouse Books, New York, 2007.

Rust, Roland T., Christine Moorman, and Gaurav Bhalla, 'Rethinking marketing', *Harvard Business Review*, January 2010.

Vavra, Terry G., *Improving Your Measurement of Customer Satisfaction*, American Society for Quality, Wisconsin, 1997.

Weissenberg A., A. Katz, and A. Narula, 'A restoration in hotel loyalty: Developing a blueprint for reinventing loyalty programs,' Deloitte, 2013.

CASE STUDY
Loyalty or Profits?

While companies swear that they are committed to great customer service, they often follow practices to profit from customers. Instead of increasing loyalty and satisfaction, this results in dissatisfaction and complaints. Companies find that they can increase profits if they withhold information or encourage customers to make wrong choices so that they end up paying more. McGovern and Moon (2007) write that telecom, banking, credit card, and a host of other industries create systems to profit unfairly from customers. Using rules about minimum use, minimum balances, overdrafts, credit limits, or payment deadlines, these industries succeed in vexing customers. They use opaque, company-centric strategies for punishing customers who fail to understand or follow these conditions. Although this approach may work for a while, such companies are vulnerable to the pent-up hostility of their customers, facing bad publicity, lawsuits, and defection.

The decision to use fees and penalties to cover costs and to discourage undesirable customer behaviour is legitimate, but it results in erosion of competitive advantage. A company is less likely to keep customers if it squeezes customers to generate more profits. Customers retaliate against them and post their bad experiences on the Internet. Such practices also increase churn, so companies have to invest in heavy advertising to keep attracting new customers.

Companies also profit from customers' bad decisions by relying on penalties and fees. Such charges are conceived as a way to deter undesirable customer behaviour and offset the costs that businesses incur as a result of that behaviour. Penalties for bouncing a cheque, for example, were originally designed to discourage banking customers from spending more than they had and to recoup administrative costs. The practice was, therefore, fair to company and customer alike. However, firms who profit from penalties have an incentive to encourage their customers to incur them. Many credit card issuers, for example, choose not to deny a transaction that would put the cardholder over his or her credit limit; it is more profitable to let the customer overspend and then impose penalties.

Therefore, penalties are profitable; they at least contribute to short-term profits as companies are willing to compromise on consumer satisfaction and loyalty to be able to make more money from their customers. Some of such practices that companies follow are described here.

Mobile Phone Service Industry

Mobile phone customers typically choose a pricing plan from among several offers ranging from low-priced plans with a limited talk-time to high-priced plans with unlimited calling. If customers cannot predict which plan is suitable for them, or if their usage changes, companies benefit from the scenario—customers are penalized either for using too much time or for not using enough. It is estimated that as much as 50 per cent of income of US telecom companies comes from overage and underage fees—what the industry refers to as 'breakage.'

These tactics may be profitable, but they also fuel discontent and discourage loyalty. There are scores of consumer complaints against mobile phone companies every year. Customers retaliate by posting blogs and creating pages on Facebook such as 'I Hate Airtel' or 'I Hate Vodafone.' Company-specific hate sites have proliferated and earn bad publicity for the company. People switch their operators, and this is reflected in high percentages of customer churn. It is hardly surprising that telecom companies must engage in aggressive customer acquisition, including very high levels of spending on advertising.

Retail Banking

When people open accounts with banks, they are usually asked to keep a minimum balance. If the balance falls below that level, banks merrily slap steep penalties and service charges. On the other hand, if their balances climb over the minimum, they are stuck with high service charges linked to accounts with lower balance stipulations. Banks gain as customers make bad account selections. For people who do not check their accounts regularly, a visit to the bank may bring a nasty surprise, when they find that their balances have vanished as the bank had deducted a penalty every quarter for not maintaining adequate balance.

As banks have discovered the profit potential of fees and penalties, they have gradually adjusted their tactics to take advantage of customers. When making entries in accounts, for instance, the debits get priority over credits and the biggest debits appear first. This increases the chance of bouncing other cheques in the queue, for which penalties are levied. Similarly, banks provide quick overdrafts against fixed deposits, encouraging customers to do so, and thus, increase their earnings from customers who avail of the facility. Many banks also charge customers by default to send them alerts for their transactions.

Milking consumers for fees would seem to be an effective business strategy. Profits for banks have increased greatly over the past ten years. Stock prices and revenues have also risen for the largest banks. Therefore, banks began relying on high fees. As in the case of the mobile phone industry, customer frustration has become acute in the banking sector as well. Consumer complaints have become so pervasive that in 2014, the RBI stepped in and advised banks to stop charging minimum balance charges. *The Times of India* (2014) reported that the RBI had proposed to frame consumer protection regulations based on domestic experience and global best practices. 'Banks should not take undue advantage of customer difficulty or inattention. Instead of levying penal charges for non-maintenance of minimum balance in ordinary savings bank accounts, banks should limit services available on such accounts to those available to basic savings bank deposit accounts and restore the services when the balances improve to the minimum required level,' the RBI said.

Credit Card Industry

The credit card industry sells its products on the basis of convenience, status, and privilege. However, consumers' complaints about credit cards are common. *NDTV Profit* (2013), citing information submitted to the Lok Sabha, reports that the government received complaints about practices related to credit cards such as undue penal charges, late payment charges, issue of unsolicited cards, and harassing telephone calls. A total of 7744 such complaints were received in 2012–13, which shows that such complaints are common, under the RBI's banking ombudsman scheme.

Credit cards charge extremely high interest or finance costs if customers do not clear their full dues. Interest rates are levied by credit card companies on the outstanding amount if it is not paid before the expiry of the due date. Interest rates are mentioned as between 2.5 per cent and 4 per cent per month that hides the actual annual interest rate that customers pay. Many customers do not realize that they end up paying interest of more than 50 per cent annually on their outstanding amounts—if they keep paying minimum amount due every month, they would forever be in credit card debt.

The charges for easy credit make customers wince. If customers make a late payment, they are whacked with charges over and above the interest rate charged. HDFC Bank, for instance, charges ₹100–₹700 as late payment charges, depending on the amount outstanding. Cash withdrawals on credit cards attract charges as a certain percentage of the transaction value or a fixed sum. For some banks, this charge is 2.5 per cent of the transaction value subject to a minimum of ₹300. Should customers spend more than their limit, they are charged 2.5 per cent of the overdrawn limit, subject to a minimum of ₹300–₹600, depending on different banks. Foreign currency transactions attract 3.5 per cent of the transaction, subject to a minimum of ₹250 and a higher conversion rate than offered on traveller's cheques. Petrol transactions, railway ticket purchases, and payments of insurance attract fees at 2.5 per cent of transaction value, subject to a minimum amount that varies from bank to bank. There are further penalties for depositing outstation cheques and for return of electronic clearing service (ECS). On all these charges, a service tax of 12.36 per cent is also levied.

Customers do not see the fine print before signing the credit card agreement, which then results in dissatisfaction and complaints thereafter.

Questions for Discussion

1. Should companies strive for helping customers and improve satisfaction and loyalty or should they pursue profits, as described by the case? What are the pros and cons of the strategy?
2. Conventional marketing wisdom says that companies should improve service and satisfaction levels. This case, however, describes how profits take a priority over conventional wisdom. If you were a manager, how would you reconcile between these two conflicting objectives?
3. What are the long-term effects of following such strategies? Do you think that customers can do anything apart from complaining and bearing the penalties?
4. Since companies follow their industry practices—which leaves little incentive for customers to change their service providers—what can customers do to save themselves from unnecessary penalties?

Sources:

McGovern, Gail and Youngme Moon, 'Companies and the customers who hate them', *Harvard Business Review*, June, 2007.

NDTV Profit, 3,673 credit card complaints against banks: minister, December 13, 2013, http://profit.ndtv.com/news/industries/article-3-673-credit-card-complaints-against-banks-minister-374822, last accessed on 5 May 2014.

The Times of India, 'No penalty for bank balance below minimum limit: RBI to banks', 1 April 2014.

PART SIX

Modern Consumer

CHAPTER 16:
Online Buying Behaviour

CHAPTER 17:
Consumer Engagement and Equity

CHAPTER 18:
Ethics and Social Responsibility

CHAPTER SIXTEEN

Online Buying Behaviour

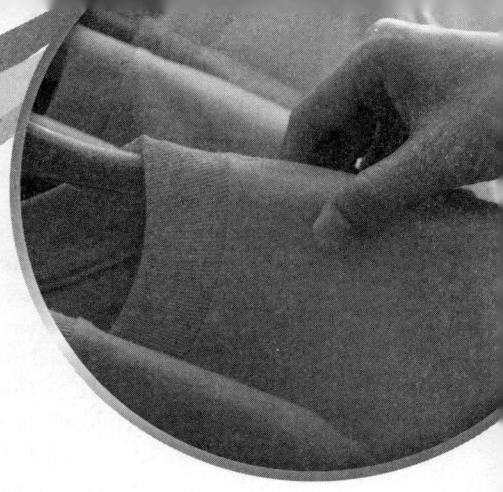

LEARNING OBJECTIVES

As people shop online through their laptops and mobile devices, consumer behaviour is changing like never before. This chapter provides an understanding of online buying behaviour.

After reading the chapter, you will be able to

- understand the tectonic changes taking place in consumer behaviour
- learn about e-commerce in India and online behaviour of Indian customers
- describe the consumer decision journey and consumer touchpoints
- analyse a framework for online consumer behaviour
- learn about digital value creation and web equity

CASE STUDY

Is Traditional Marketing Dead?

As more people connect to each other through mobile devices, traditional marketing faces a challenge in trying to understand consumer behaviour in the era of digital marketing. Lee (2012) writes that traditional marketing—including advertising, public relations, branding, and corporate communications—is dead, simply because consumer habits have changed.

There are several reasons for this change. With people spending more time on mobile devices, traditional media is losing out. Studies show that in the 'buyer's decision journey', traditional marketing communications are not relevant anymore. Buyers check out product and service information in a variety of ways, often through the Internet, and from sources outside the firm such as word-of-mouth or customer reviews. Therefore, companies increasingly question whether their mass media spends are actually delivering results or not.

Lee also says that traditional marketing and sales do not work because a company hires people who do not come from the buyer's world and whose interests are not necessarily aligned with the company. These people are expected to persuade the buyer to spend his money on products which they are not convinced about either. 'When you try to extend traditional marketing logic into the world of social media, it simply doesn't work,' he writes.

So what takes the place of traditional marketing? Goodson (2012) writes that traditional marketing has indeed given way to 'movement marketing'. Movement marketing, or cultural movement marketing, is a marketing model that starts with an idea in culture, and then ties that back to the brand, creating communities and fan-based organizations that are supportive of the movement. Movements begin with an idea rather than the product. Scott

Goodson, the founder of StrawberryFrog, writes that brands can 'identify, crystallize, curate, and sponsor movements, accelerating their rise.' StrawberryFrog, the world's first cultural movement agency, invented the movement marketing model in 1999, for brands such as Smart Car and IKEA. This model can provide a way for business to connect more deeply with culture, address social issues, get close to customers and their deepest interests, and maybe even be part of something worthwhile and important.

The new marketing model tries to involve consumers and includes 'tribe-building', an idea formulated by Seth Godin (2008). It involves collecting a unique group of fans, friends, and followers who resonate with the company's worldview, or creating a community of people who want to hear from it. Tribe-building is done through messages that are personal, relevant, and anticipated. The meaning of marketing in the digital era has changed in two profound ways:

- Marketing is about participating in a dialogue with consumers.
- Marketing is no longer about generating transactions, but about building relationships.

Lee gives three tips for the new marketing and how tribes can be built up.

Community-oriented marketing Using social media is similar to the experience of consumers buying in their local and physical communities. For instance, when contemplating on a major purchase, consumers talk to people they know, such as relatives, neighbours, or friends, or search websites for information. Social media efforts should replicate this community-oriented buying experience as much as possible.

Finding customer influencers Companies should find and cultivate customer influencers. This requires a new concept of customer value that goes way beyond customer lifetime value that is based only on purchases. There are many other measures of a customer's potential value, like customer's networks and how they are used to advocate products.

Help consumers build social capital Traditional marketing often tries to encourage customer advocacy with cash rewards, discounts, or other untoward inducements. The new marketing helps advocates and influencers create social capital—it helps them build their networks, increase their reputation, and provides them access to new knowledge. The idea is to get customer advocates involved in the solutions.

By doing so, companies are able to create customers by tapping the best source of buyer motivation—peer influence. New possibilities of peer influence-based and community-oriented marketing hold greater promise for creating sustained growth.

The new rules of marketing demand that companies stop talking about themselves and their products. Instead, companies have to start listening to what people are talking about. They also need to figure out what people need, to really build movements, and help them in fulfilling their needs. This new model of marketing is primarily built around listening, sharing, and facilitating the consumer. If companies do that, people will trust them enough to let them be a part of their cultural movement. However, traditional advertising cannot accomplish the same. Goodson concludes, 'increasingly, in the future, the movement will be the medium.'

While reading the chapter, try and answer the following questions:

- Do you agree that traditional marketing is dead?
- In what ways is changing consumer behaviour impacting traditional marketing?
- How can companies start movements rather than depend on traditional media?
- How will companies market in the future?

Sources:

Goodson, Scott, 'Marketing is dead. Now what?', *Forbes*, http://www.forbes.com/sites/marketshare/2012/08/13/marketing-is-dead-now-what/, last accessed on 11 October 2012.

Lee, Bill, 'Marketing is dead', *HBR Blog Network*, http://blogs.hbr.org/cs/2012/08/marketing_is_dead.html, last accessed on 11 October 2012.

INTRODUCTION

Mobile communication and computing devices are becoming ubiquitous. They are no longer just means of personal communication; they are virtual malls in consumers' hands, through which people get product information, visit stores, and view products. They are also payment devices. Thanks to technology, today, it is possible for people to search for just about anything no matter where they are, seek online reviews and help, and place orders in a matter of seconds. Consumer behaviour is changing like never before.

Earlier, companies could study consumers as they did their shopping in stores. They could try to decipher consumer motivations and behaviour by observing them or asking questions to them in the physical world. Online shopping consists of an individual with his laptop, tablet, or mobile phone, interacting with brands not only through company sponsored advertisements and websites, but also learning about the opinions of others through blogs, reviews, and social media sites.

The splintering of the media has made the task of studying online consumer behaviour more complex. For years, companies have depended on mass marketing through mass media. They communicated through newspapers and television, and consumers responded to these messages. In the connected world, media is splintered right up to the individual, who chooses the medium himself or herself. In the developed world, mass media's role has been declining as more people prefer individual media on their devices.

The job of companies is to understand consumers as they browse and interact online. Existing consumer models no longer work; these models study consumer behaviour as the effect of marketing stimuli provided by companies on consumers. In the online world, marketing stimuli are no longer in control of companies. Consumers now interact with brands through a variety of commercial and personal channels.

Online consumer behaviour is a new area of study. People check out the Internet almost compulsively (see chapter-end case study) and companies are interested in ascertaining how this affects buying behaviour, how the online experience can be used to plug their products, or how products can be made more relevant to customers. Digital strategies have to ensure that companies are where the consumer is, that is, on their mobile devices and show up on search engines. As people do not like intrusive ads popping up on their devices, companies look for ways to leverage social media presence, or provide interesting applications or content that makes the customer want to engage with the brand.

Understanding online consumer behaviour involves understanding the following:

- What is consumer browsing?
- What type of channel does the consumer prefer?
- What type of products appeal to consumers?
- What drives consumers online and what are their habits?
- What are the factors affecting online purchases?

If the experience is good and consumers get some value in terms of variety, low prices, or after-sales services, they will talk about it and share their experience with others. As more and more people get connected, many purchase paths usually begin with an online search, and companies look to setting up digital interactions right from the stage of intention to purchase.

Internet penetration also plays a key role. Strauss and Frost (2012) report that 76 per cent of US consumers use the Internet and similar figures were reported in many other countries. This has changed the e-commerce scenario in a big way. India has a long way to catch up with respect to the Internet penetration; however, already people are displaying a penchant for online shopping. As technology helps more people to connect and as it penetrates deep into rural areas, online buying—or the online influence on purchases in the physical world—is expected to increase in the future.

Online Shopping in India

Online shopping is catching up rapidly in India. Customers can now choose from a number of websites for goods ranging from beauty and fashion products, and B2B portals for industrial buying. Going by the growth of online buying, Indian consumers are taking to the habit of buying through the Internet. *Business Standard* quoting Internet and Mobile Association of India (IAMAI) data reports that online purchases were estimated to be ₹46,520 crore at the end of 2011. According to IAMAI, the digital commerce market grew by 33 per cent to ₹62,967 crore in 2013 as against ₹47,349 crore during the corresponding period of 2012. Of the total digital commerce business in 2013, travel business accounted for 71 per cent, valued at ₹44,907 crore. The growth of e-commerce in India is shown in Fig. 16.1. Many factors have contributed to the growth of e-commerce. Some of them are as follows:

These factors are explained in detail.

Population In terms of population, India has one of the youngest population in the world. Every year, it adds around two million college graduates to the workforce. The younger generation has been described as tech savvy, which means that they can use e-commerce with ease.

Telecom and growth of Internet usage The government had opened the telecom sector and private investment rushed in. Due to increased competition, companies offer technology and services to users that can be compared to the best in the world. *DNA India* (2012) cites figures of

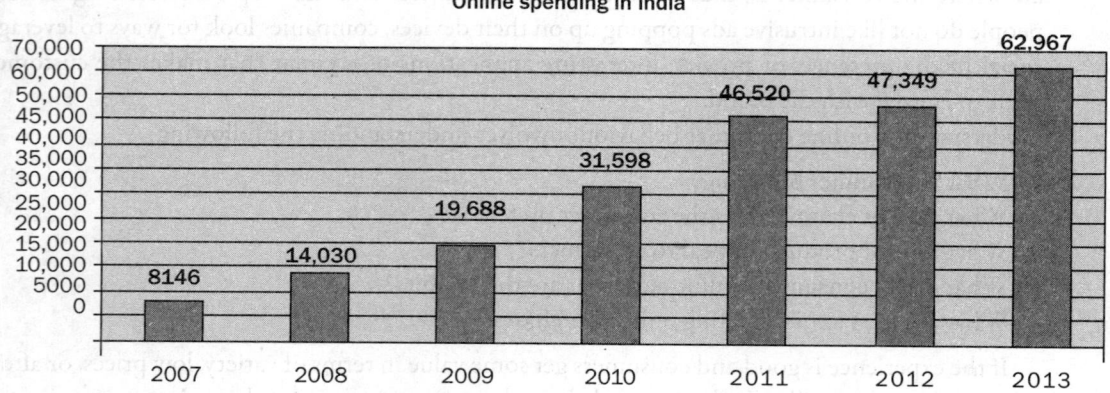

FIG. 16.1 Growth of e-commerce in India (Figures in ₹ crore as on December of every year)

Source: Internet and Mobile Association of India (IAMAI) data

the IAMAI and reported that the number of rural Internet users reached 38 million at the end of June 2012. The penetration of Internet users in rural India grew from 2.6 per cent in 2010 to 4.6 per cent in 2012. Though this represents a compounded annual growth rate of 73 per cent, the figures point to a growing opportunity and a huge growth potential in the Indian market. Companies are starting online portals and are betting on continuing growth of e-commerce in the coming years. At the end of December 2011, the total Internet subscriber base in India stood at 121 million, which represents a penetration of about 10 per cent, according to IAMAI data. These figures are likely to increase in the future.

Inflow of venture capital In 2011, venture capitalists invested US$187 million in e-commerce in India, according to the Forrester report, *Trends in India's E-commerce Market* (2012). This initiative gave a boost to websites. The online consumer, who is largely upper and middle class, is now comfortable with online shopping. Venture capital expects that consumers in both urban and non-urban areas get ready to shop online. Companies are also diversifying to include retail sectors such as women's lingerie, perfumes, deodorants, condoms, and gifts that can be ordered to be delivered in any Indian city.

Online grocery shopping is catching up Purchase of grocery, vegetables, and fruits is starting to move online in metropolitan India. The Nielsen Global Survey of Digital's Influence (2012) found that 25 per cent of people surveyed in India claimed they would buy food and beverages online that were long sold only offline. For the customer, home delivery saves them the bother of traffic jams and parking problems, apart from time. This comes as a boon for the time-pressed families in which both partners are working.

Expansion into non-metro areas Online retailers are expanding to the people living outside metro areas in India. Online retail chains are already seeing demand for their products outside the metros. Heavy investments are being made in delivery and payment infrastructure, by introducing cash on delivery facility for the unbanked or those unwilling to pay in advance.

Offline retailers are going online Brick-and-mortar retail chains offer online sales as well. Stores such as Croma, Shoppers' Stop, Landmark, and Westside have started online retail chains, along with their physical stores. Global retailers like Wal-Mart are restricted by India's FDI laws but may start online sales once the law permits them. However, smaller stores operating locally in cities and towns are establishing online ordering channels.

Social media helps online adoption India has close to one billion wireless subscribers—social media and mobiles have caught on in India in a big way. India is ranked as Facebook's third-largest audience in the world after the US and Brazil. Such sites play an important role in driving consumers online and subsequently to engage with brands.

Electronic payments The use of credit and debit cards in India is steadily increasing, thanks to a large earning population with growing disposable incomes. A PTI report (2012) citing RBI data says that at the end of June 2012, there were a total of 1.8 crore credit cards in the country. The number of debit cards stood at over 29 crore as on 30 June 2012. During 2011–12, the total amount spent through credit cards was ₹96,614 crore, with an average transaction size of ₹54,738 per card in a year. In comparison, debit cards were used for transactions worth ₹53,432 crore in 2011–12, leading to an average transaction size of ₹1920 on every card in a year.

Net commerce market size from 2007 to 2011 (Figures in crores. Percentages indicate share of the overall market size)				
Year	Dec. 2007	Dec. 2008	Dec. 2009	Dec. 2010+
Total market size	8,146	14,030	19,688	31,598
Online travel industry	6,250 (77%)	10,500 (75%)	14,953 (76%)	25,258 (80%)
Online non-travel industry	1,896 (23%)	3,530 (25%)	4,735 (24%)	6,340 (20%)
– eTailing	978	1,120	1,550	2,050
– Digital downloads or paid content subscription	238	290	435	680
– Financial services*		1,200	1,540	2,000
– Other online services (incl. online classifieds)	680	920	1,210	1,610

*:Financial services were not calculated in the years prior 2008 +:Estimated figures

FIG. 16.2 Online business is huge in India

Source: Shah (2011)

Card payment and electronic transactions accounted for only six per cent of total online payment transactions in India. These figures point towards low penetration and usage, with scope for substantial growth potential in terms of penetration of electronic payments systems as well as to increase spending per card issued. To get over the problem of low availability of electronic cards and the fear of using them online, many online companies now offer cash on delivery (COD) to encourage users to place orders.

According to Forrester research (2012), shoppers in metropolitan India are driving e-commerce by making travel reservations, and buying consumer electronics and books online. Though spending per online buyer remains low, the habit is catching on. Consumers in non-metro areas will also help fuel growth as they are more likely to shop online for goods that are unavailable at local stores.

Composition of India's E-commerce

Figures of e-commerce in India (Fig. 16.2) show that though the market was dominated by online travel business with 80 per cent share, e-tailing or selling of goods and services over the Internet, has more than doubled in value from 2007 to 2011. The habit of online buying, thus, appears to be catching on in India. As Internet penetration increases, these figures are expected to rise further in the future.

According to the Internet Economy Watch data collected from e-commerce sites released by IAMAI, there was a huge spurt in e-tailing of branded apparels as well, with sites registering five million visits in April 2012 as compared to 2.54 million visits in April 2011 (Table 16.1), showing a 100 per cent annual growth. Categories of footwear, designer labels, jewellery, spas, and restaurants also showed an increase of online sales. Online recruitment portals too witnessed growth, with 2.05 million uploads in April 2012. The number of profile uploads on matrimonial websites increased from 1.35 million in April 2011 to 2.74 million in April 2012.

TABLE 16.1 Figures showing increasing popularity of online activities of Indian consumers

Activity	April 2012 (₹ in millions)	April 2011 (₹ in millions)
Branded apparel (number of visitors)	5.0	2.54
Profile uploads on recruitment sites	2.05	1.82
Profile uploads on matrimonial sites	2.74	1.35
Railway tickets bookings	5.56	2.26
Airline tickets bookings	1.92	1.01

Source: IAMAI data

It has also been seen that travel-related spending dominated online spending. E-ticketing done on irctc.com showed 5.56 million bookings in April 2012 as compared to 2.26 million bookings in April 2011. Airlines recorded 1.92 million bookings in April 2012, as compared to 1.01 million bookings in April 2011.

The data shows that the Indian consumer is latching on to the online habit very fast.

With this trend catching up, there is need to understand the habits and behaviour of the shopper. The Indian shopper is, in many ways, similar to shoppers elsewhere in the world; however, in many ways he exhibits distinct tendencies as well. The next section describes the online shopper in terms of segmentation and motivation.

UNDERSTANDING THE ONLINE SHOPPER

With online transactions increasing and customers getting connected and using mobile devices become common, there is a need to understand online consumer behaviour. It is disruptive, in the sense that it has the potential to change the existing marketing theory. Companies are spending huge amounts to track and understand the online shopper. The online shopper exhibits certain characteristics. This section helps understand some of them.

Age and Online Buying

Sorce, et al. (2005) conducted research to study the shopping and buying behaviour of younger and older online shoppers, and their attitudes toward Internet shopping. They found that, while older online shoppers search for significantly fewer products than their younger counterparts, they actually purchase as much as the younger consumers do. Therefore, though older consumers were less likely to search for a product online, once they had done so, they were more likely to buy it online than younger shoppers. Goal-oriented shoppers have four objectives for online shopping:

- Convenience
- Information access
- Selection
- Ability to control the shopping experience

Online Segmentation

Aljukhadar and Senecal (2011) have provided a basis for segmentation of online customers. Their study reveals that online consumers form three global segments:

Basic communicators They are consumers who mainly use e-mail to communicate, and consist of mostly highly educated people and older people.

Lurking shoppers They are consumers who employ the Internet to navigate and to heavily shop, consisting of highly educated males or females who belong mainly to the higher income and age groups.

Social thrivers They consist of consumers who use the Internet to socially interact by chatting, blogging, video streaming, and downloading information. Social thrivers belong to the youngest age group (less than 35 years old) and fall in the lowest income bracket.

Companies can use segmentation to allocate their marketing expenditure effectively. Marketing and advertising strategies can be developed according to the customer's online segment.

Profile of the Online Shopper

A Pew research report (2005) points out that men are more intense Internet users than women, even though women are catching up. It says that men are online more often and more frequently than women.

Men go online in greater numbers than women for a vast number of activities. Women outpace men for a small number of activities, including areas such as health, medicine, and religion. Men are more likely to use the Internet to check the weather, get news, get do-it-yourself information, check for sports, political and financial information, do job-related searches, download software, listen to music, rate a product, person, or service through an online reputation system, download music files, use a webcam, and take a class. Women are more likely to use the Internet to send and receive emails, get maps and directions, look for health and medical information, browse websites to get support for health or personal problems, and get religious information.

Reasons for Buying Online

Consumers are discovering several reasons for placing orders online. Some of the factors that make people prefer online shopping are given here:

- **Ease and convenience** The primary reason of shopping online is ease and convenience, coupled with quick home delivery. People save time and effort of going out, and avoid hassles of traffic and parking.

Better prices With a plethora of e-commerce sites each vying to notch up customers through deals and discounts, customers are able to get better prices than they would in retail shops. This is a major boost for online sites.

Availability Many products and brands sold online are sometimes not available in shops. In case of electronic goods, the variety and number of brands cannot be found in one store. Online stores give variety to shoppers.

Better information Detailed specifications and information about products is displayed online. Consumers can also check reviews of other buyers.

Avoiding pesky salespersons The real world is full of pesky salespersons who try to convince buyers. Enquiries by shoppers are followed up by phone calls and messages. To avoid unnecessary sales messages, people often prefer the virtual world.

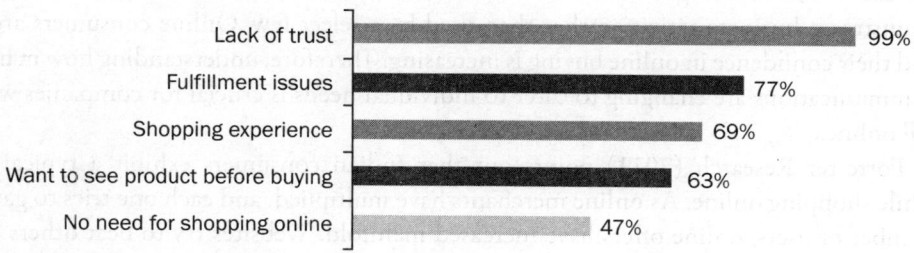

FIG. 16.3 Reasons for not buying on the Internet

Source: Shah (2011)

Payment terms Many websites and banks offer instant instalment plans and easy payment terms. Customers are tempted to buy products because of these facilities that are sometimes not available in stores.

A study by White and Manning (1998) showed that in case of food products, retail shopping was much preferred to either mail order or online purchases. Results also showed that in the case of food products, high age or income individuals are more likely than low age or income individuals to purchase from an online site.

Reasons for Not Buying Online

It is important to know why people do not buy online. Several things hold people back—security issues, product not as per expectations, privacy, and so on. The major factors identified by a report, *Ecommerce in India—Statistics, Trends & Insights* (2011), are given in Fig. 16.3.

Though the data shows that Indian consumers are taking to online activities in a very big way, many consumers are still averse to the idea of online shopping. The reasons, based on a survey of 6.1 million Internet users, are summarized in Fig. 16.3.

In addition to the reasons mentioned here, a look at complaints posted online shows that many consumers face problems due to the following issues:

Delivery of low quality products Sometimes, consumers expect better products than what is delivered to them. Many complain that they got products that were not of high quality, or were not the same that they had ordered, or were not from the same company, were damaged in transit, or were defective.

Difficulty in returning products Customers face difficulty in returning defective products. While they can easily approach stores in case of problems, returning products to the website office in another city, often causes a problem.

Lack of after-sales service Customers complain that many sites have non-existent after-sales service. The customer care numbers are not available. If they are available, customers interact with automated menus that make registering of complaints almost impossible.

Lack of ability to see and touch products Very often, customers do not buy online because they want to see and touch products before buying.

Expectations of Online Shoppers

As more consumers get access to the Internet, e-commerce is being transformed into a mainstream business activity rather than used by a select few. Online consumers are maturing and their confidence in online buying is increasing. Therefore, understanding how marketing and communications are changing to cater to individual needs is crucial for companies who look to sell online.

Forrester Research (2011) points out that Indian consumers exhibit a typical behaviour while shopping online. As online merchants have multiplied, and each one tries to gather a large number of users, online offers have increased manifold. Websites try to beat others by offering lower prices. This has led Indian consumers to expect a number of benefits:

Inflated expectations Indian consumers have inflated expectations from online commerce as e-commerce sites are doing whatever it takes to drive customers to their sites. Customers have learnt to expect freebies and discounts, as well as deals from banks as they shop on particular sites. For instance, websites of banks as ING-Vysya Bank and HDFC Bank offer additional discounts if their cards are used to shop on certain sites.

Product returns Consumers expect a high level of service, including product returns. Some online retailers offer easy product returns using reverse logistics, despite high costs, in order to build consumer confidence.

Free shipping Consumers expect free shipping and quick delivery of online orders. Even though this adds to cost, websites have to offer this facility in order to compete in the given situation.

Low prices Easy availability of information makes consumers search for low prices. Websites offer low prices along with deals and offers that make consumers expect discounted prices. Whether this is sustainable in the long run is doubtful; many entrants have already shut shop as they found low prices and high costs of free delivery unsustainable.

Companies have to understand the motivation of consumers to buy online as well. Gehrt, et al. (2012) have empirically investigated dominant behaviours in online buying of Indian consumers. These are as follows:

Value singularity This refers to people who are positively motivated by issues related to value—they look for cheaper prices on the Internet. People in this category tend to be older, value website security, and use the web to pay utility bills, buy air or rail tickets, books, and CDs.

Quality at any price People look for known brands or products that are exclusive with high quality. Young professionals who have sizeable incomes but are hard pressed for time are likely to fall in this category. Price is relatively unimportant for them. They like to purchase utilities and consumer electronics online and visit travel websites online.

Recreational orientation People with recreational orientation enjoy shopping and like looking for new products. They like to browse online stores and explore websites and products, and sometimes end up making a purchase.

In addition to these online shopping orientations, Indian consumers also explore online shopping sites for recreation, quality, convenience, variety, and ease of shopping. Indeed, many websites in India cater to these needs. Discounts, promise of low prices, quality branded products, and quick deliveries have become the selling propositions of various online stores.

The Financial Express (2009) reports that there is evidence that the economic slowdown that the country has faced since 2008 encourages online shopping as Indian shoppers are motivated to compare prices online. Online ticketing offered by the Indian Railways has helped online purchase habits as millions of passengers prefer to transact ticket purchases online instead of waiting in queues. In small towns and villages, e-commerce sites like ITC's e-chaupal provide the latest goods, helping companies to penetrate to areas where traditional distribution channels do not reach.

Indian consumers are discovering the transition from mass marketing to individual marketing. This is changing media consumption as well, a trend that is described in the next section.

MEDIA CONSUMPTION

Indian consumers have taken to online buying similar to their counterparts in developed countries. In this scenario, traditional marketing faces a challenge as markets and media have become fragmented. As people have changed their media consumption and buying habits, marketing and communications are changing in several ways. These tectonic shifts in consumer behaviour are changing companies as well. The new media and how it is used is summarized in Table 16.2.

Chaffey (2003) mentions six ways in which consumption of media has changed and how companies can adapt to these changing consumer behaviour patterns.

From push to pull Traditional media are essentially push media, where information flows mostly in one direction from the company to the consumer. In contrast, the web is a pull medium, where consumers decide what they want to see. This aspect is both a strength and a weakness. It is a strength as customers only visit the company's website when they want to do so. They are proactive and self-selecting. This is also a weakness as companies have less control in communications as to who will see their message and when they see it.

From monologue to dialogue The new media enables companies to enter into a dialogue with customers. These dialogues can enhance customer service, deepen relationships and trust, and build loyalty. They have both advantages and disadvantages as follows:

TABLE 16.2 Splintered media—Online execution of different communications tools

Communications tool	Online execution
Advertising	Banner ads, search engine registration
Selling	Virtual sales staff
Sales promotion	Online incentives, rewards, loyalty schemes
Public relations	Online editorials, e-zines, newsletters, discussion groups
Sponsorship	Sponsoring on-line events, site or service
Direct mail	E-mail and web response
Exhibitions	Virtual exhibitions
Merchandising	Shopping malls, e-tailing, online interface
Packaging	Real packaging is displayed online
Word of mouth	Viral, affiliate marketing, e-mail, links, social media

- The advantage is that digital dialogues help companies to collect intelligence about customers, and in turn, they help companies in refining products and offers.
- At the same time, companies have to ensure that they are not wasting time by entering into a dialogue with people who have no intention to buy. An example is of companies that collect online fans and likes but have no real interest in the company or its brands.

From one-to-many to one-to-some and one-to-one Traditional communications are one-to-many, with the same message delivered to different segments. The new media enables one-to-some communication, reaching particular niches, or one-to-one communications where personalized messages are delivered to individual customers.

From one-to-many to many-to-many communication Today, customers can interact with other customers. This is called many-to-many communications, or C2C communications. In terms of e-commerce, online auction sites and online classified advertising show the power of many-to-many communications. However, this becomes a threat as well, as it is difficult to control negative communication about a company.

From 'lean-back' to 'lean-forward' Earlier, companies spent on mass media and could 'lean-back' and wait for customers to come. Now, customers lean-forward to get information. The website gets a visitor's undivided attention. However, if visitors do not find what they are looking for immediately, they will move on, to probably never to return. Companies have to learn to 'lean-forward' to meet customer expectations.

Integration of media Although new media is ubiquitous and has many advantages, this does not mean that companies can ignore traditional media. Many online companies are discovering that advertising in traditional media is important to build traffic to their websites. Companies should, therefore, try to achieve synergy in the use of media. This kind of integration is important because consumers interact with companies at each stage of the buying process through numerous touchpoints. This is explained in the next section.

Media Usage—Interactions During the Purchase Process

In the highly connected digital world, the interaction of consumers with brands is not limited to media and stores. Starting from the need recognition, a consumer can interact with multiple channels during all through the purchase processes (Fig. 16.4). For instance, consumers look for products online as well as in stores. Information search and evaluation of products is done with continuous interaction with physical stores, traditional media, online search, as well as interaction with social groups. Customers also look for reviews and interact with other consumers through rating websites.

At every stage, positive word-of-mouth recommendations are a trigger for other customers to look into the company's website. Many consumers now use non-traditional aids such as blogs, social media websites, customer-generated reviews, or e-word of mouth to explore issues. Companies must try to use the power of these tools to generate social influence to encourage customers for repeat purchases. They can use them for meeting the needs of the customer in the following ways:

Identify customer needs Companies can find out about customer's needs through comments, enquiries, requests and complaints, bulletin boards, and chat rooms. Further, they can use secondary

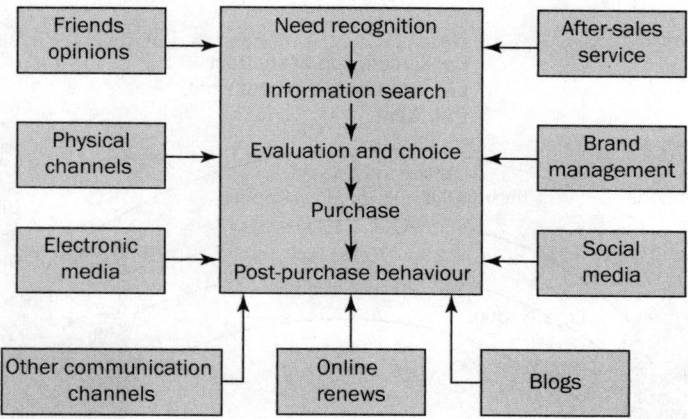

FIG. 16.4 Consumers interact with multiple channels at each stage of the purchase decision

Source: Adapted from Kumar (2012)

sources of data that provide free and in-depth insight into customer needs. This data is called 'data exhaust', and is left behind by people when they do online searches and can be accessed through search patterns, pages visited, and time spent on them.

Anticipate needs Companies can find out future customer needs by having a dialogue with customers. Profiling techniques based on data mining allows companies to discover and anticipate buyer's needs. Cookies are pieces of code sent to the visitor's computer. They recognize the computer, and record the sites a person visits; these help target advertisements to individual systems.

Satisfy needs Companies employ the technology to serve customers with prompt responses, order status updates, reminders, after-sales services, and better communication.

Build customer relationships Information technology helps improve service quality and analyse data, adding to memory of the company to help maintain customer relationships.

The idea is to use technology to help improve interactions with customers at every touchpoint. It is important to integrate the online experience with offline brand existence. For instance, after performing search and evaluation, the purchase may well be made either online or through a retail store. Companies, therefore, have the means to interact with customers at every stage of the consumer buying process. The challenge before companies is to manage all the possible touchpoints that consumers have with brands—in physical and virtual worlds. They do so by analysing the consumer's decision journey that shows how consumer behaviour has changed due to the increased touchpoints.

Consumer Decision Journey

Edelman (2010) writes that the consumer decision-making process is a circular journey with four phases, namely consider, evaluate, buy, and experience. These are explained as follows:

Consider The products in the consumer's consideration set

614 Consumer Behaviour

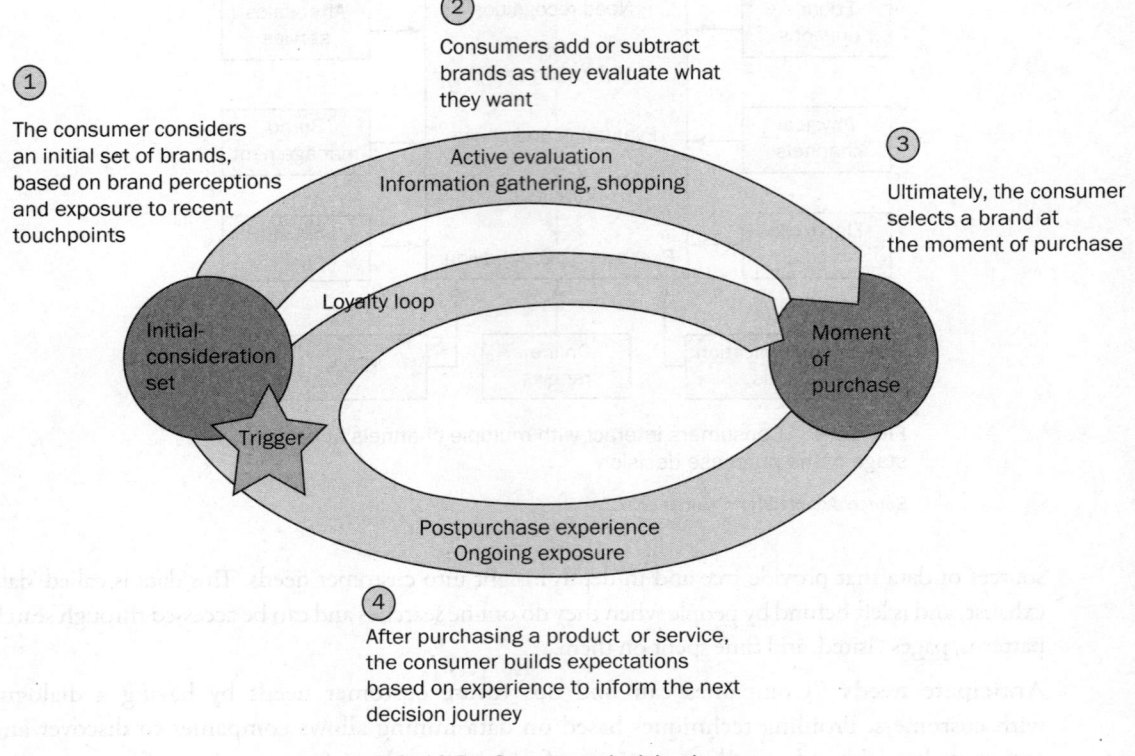

FIG. 16.5 Consumer decision journey

Source: McKinsey & Company, 2009, reprinted with permission

Evaluate Consumers evaluate brands by interacting with friends online and offline

Buy The purchase is done after checking products and information from various sources

Experience At this stage, people like to enjoy, advocate, and bond by sharing brand experiences and post reviews about the product. Please see Fig. 16.5

Therefore, instead of using the marketing funnel metaphor in which customers interact with several brands during the search stage and then narrow down their choices as they go through the purchase decision, companies need to manage several touchpoints of the consumer and the brand. The process of brand building requires managing these touchpoints that have changed in number and nature. The marketing strategy, therefore, has to be realigned to where consumers are actually spending their time.

The goal of mapping out a customer's journey or lifecycle is to establish the digital touchpoints that can be used to address consumer issues on the path to purchase. The resulting digital strategy must include a consumer value proposition. Along with a roadmap of actions, this provide a framework encompassing the entire decision cycle.

FRAMEWORK FOR ONLINE CONSUMER BEHAVIOUR

Deciphering consumer behaviour is a difficult task. When consumers interact with brands remotely and through numerous touchpoints, understanding their behaviour becomes all the more complex.

A framework for online consumer behaviour has been developed by Cheung, et al. (2003). This model consists of the following parts:

A framework for online consumer behaviour given by Cheung et al. (2003) framework considers the influence of five variables on three key elements of consumers' intention, adoption, and continuance in online purchase (Fig. 16.6):

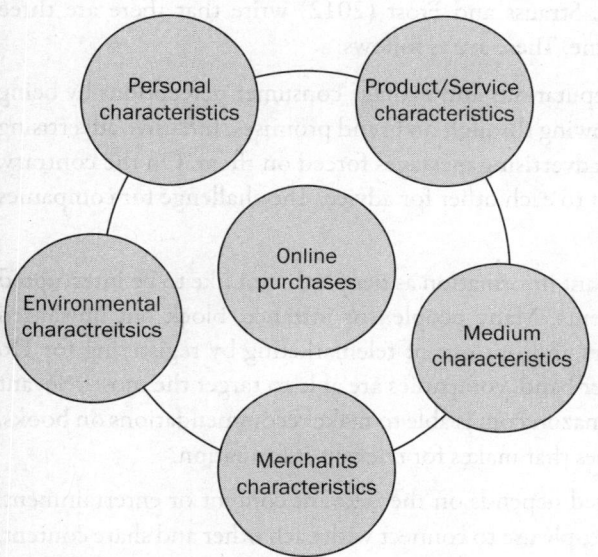

FIG. 16.6 Factors affecting online purchases

Consumer characteristics These consist of consumer's lifestyle, motivation, and confidence of buying online

Environmental influences These consist of peer group influence, education, payment systems, security, and financial issues

Product/Service characteristics The type of product, its price, quality, frequency of purchase, conducive to online buying

Medium characteristics These consist of web design, ease of navigation, ease of placing order, and reliability

Characteristics of online merchants and intermediaries These consist of service quality, delivery, reputation, and after-sales service

These factors interact continuously at each stage of consumer buying process.

Figure 16.6 helps in connecting the factors that affect how consumers use and adopt websites. The framework shows that all the variables interact with consumers at every stage of their intention, adoption, and continuance processes. As a result, the number of touchpoints between the brand and the customer has increased with online technologies. Companies have to understand these interactions at every stage to decipher online consumer behaviour. The purchase process involves customer–company interactions at each stage.

Consumer and Environmental Characteristics

Consumer characteristics refer to the factors specific to the consumer such as demographics, personality, value, lifestyle, attitude, consumer resources, consumer's psychological factors, behavioural characteristics, motivation, and experience. In online marketing, consumers are in control of the information they receive.

Kotler (2002) notes that 'Internet users, in general, place greater value on information and tend to respond negatively to messages aimed only at selling. They want to decide what marketing information they will receive about which products and services and under what conditions. In online marketing, it is the consumer, not the marketer, who gives permission and controls the interaction.'

Companies that are able to establish significant online volumes have to integrate their activities that match the motivations for web use. Otherwise, their advertising will be seen as intrusive and customers will turn away from it.

The idea is to dovetail these individual motivations with commercial activities. To do so, companies must operate within the social and cultural contexts of consumers. Many companies have indeed learnt to involve customers. Strauss and Frost (2012) write that there are three cornerstones for attracting customers online. These are as follows:

Reputation Companies build online reputations and manage consumer perceptions by being honest, making authentic claims, and following through on brand promises. Intrusive advertising does not work as people tend to distrust advertising messages forced on them. On the contrary, they bond and share experiences, and turn to each other for advice. The challenge for companies is to join online conversations.

Relevance Brands have to provide relevant information as people do not like to be interrupted with irrelevant and intrusive advertisements. Many people, for instance, block out unwanted e-mails by directing them to spam folders and opt out of telemarketing by registering for Do Not Disturb (DND) service. On the other hand, companies are able to target the most relevant information to customers. For example, amazon.com is able to make recommendations on books, depending on the customer's past purchases that makes for relevant information.

Engagement Keeping customers engaged depends on the relevant content or entertainment. One way is to use social media sites that people use to connect with each other and share content. Consumers can, thus, build personal associations with brands by uploading their pictures and sharing them with friends.

Other environmental factors consist of the consumer's education, status, peer group influence, and financial issues

Product or Service Characteristics

The Internet helps in building and disseminating knowledge about the product, product type, frequency of purchase, tangibility, differentiation, and price.

Technology offers increased customer benefits in a number of ways. The most important approach is the mode in which products are offered through mass customization. Consumers can customize products automatically and pay the lowest prices. The simplest example is the way in which people can customize their travel plans by searching information and choose modes of travel or hotels based on their personal choices.

Another benefit is through personalizing products. Online companies are able to offer products to consumers based on their past purchases or by showing them what their friends have bought. Many sites also allow users to add products to 'wish lists' that helps in offering them products similar to what they have added.

In addition, companies must offer a clear value proposition to the consumer, consisting of product attributes, branding, support services, and labelling.

Product Attributes

Offline brand presence and product attributes have a significant impact on online sales. Gulati and Garino (2000) write that the distinction between online and physical stores is rapidly fading. As customers do not distinguish between offline brands and online purchases, companies have recognized that 'success in the new economy will go to those who can execute clicks-and-mortar strategies that bridge the physical and the virtual worlds.'

Through the Internet, consumers can combine the attributes that they seek. Retail stores offer augmented products, which are a combination of product attributes and benefits. This can be done online by the consumer with ease. People are able to combine various product attributes they seek and order accordingly. Fashion sites, for example, offer combinations of clothes and accessories that consumers can mix, match, and order. Such sites are trying to combine offline experiences with their online trade to enhance the shopping experience, as shown in see Exhibit 16.1

Offering cheap products and services is another way of attracting consumers to buy online. Indian websites offer cheap mobile phones and electronic items with offers that are sometimes not available in retail shops. Sites such as indiatimes.com and homeshop18, for example, offer a variety of cheap products bundled with offers from credit card companies that are not available in stores. This has lured many people to online buying, overcoming their initial fears.

Branding

A challenge for companies is to create online brands with the promise of quality, security, and after sales service. As customers never get to see the physical stores and live in towns away from the online trading company, this becomes a difficult task indeed.

Branding is achieved by companies by providing offline stores and services. Yatra.com, for instance, started as an online portal but later added physical stores in order to build its brand and make it easier for consumers to experience the services it offered. Similarly, indiatimes.com gets branding benefits from its parent brand, *The Times of India*.

Companies, thus, have to combine their online activities with offline brand building. A study of young adults by Kim and Park (2005) showed that creating and enhancing consumer attitude toward the offline store positively influences attitude toward the online store. Store image and service consistency are beneficial for retailers to enhance consumer's attitude towards the online store. The existing image and reputation of the traditional retail store is transferred to the online format. Thus, click and mortars perform better than click-only retailers, possibly because they have already established the stable segment of target customers and have built retailer trust.

At the same time, brands use online activities to build brand relationships and equity. By building online brand communities and holding conversations with customers, brands extend their offline presence to online activities.

Support Services

Customer support is crucial for online companies, mainly because customers can share experiences and write reviews immediately. Physical distance between the company and the customer is often a hindrance. The customer has to communicate through e-mail or telephone, and if this is not

EXHIBIT 16.1 Adding Tangibility to Online Trades

Online players find that they must integrate their online offerings with real-world commerce. Many such sites are now not only simulating offline buying experiences to provide touch-and-feel comfort to consumers; they are also opening physical outlets to woo potential buyers and tackle negative perceptions about online shopping.

CNBC (2014) reports that despite the shift towards online shopping, a number of brands have turned the tables—first, by developing their virtual presence, and later, by moving into the physical space. Pure-play online retailers find that growth comes from multiple channels. Many brands have realized that to build volume and scale, they need to have offline presence as well. Physical stores bring them opportunity to expose their brands.

Zivame.com, a pure-play online retailer of bras, panties, and thongs, is conducting lingerie fitting workshops for female customers. The company realized that as women are used to buying offline, it needs to talk to them in the language and environment they are comfortable with. This activity not only spreads awareness about the brand, but also gives the brand a face and credibility.

Travel portal, yatra.com, opened physical stores to aid online buying to reach out to people looking for additional information or offering tailor-made travel plans. Yatra holiday lounges can now be seen in many cities and towns of India.

Another online company, Zovi, an apparel retailer that sells in-house designed labels, had to differentiate itself from a number of online retailers. It decided to roll out a virtual trial room to enable its buyers to check out how selected merchandise looked on them via an interactive webcam. To back up those efforts, the online retailer rolled out a brand awareness campaign, including a television commercial, and displayed its range of merchandise at kiosks at malls and high-footfall sites. The company realized that having an offline presence gave them credibility and also took them closer to their customers who could touch and feel the product offerings.

Multi-brand online fashion retailer Myntra (taken over by Flipkart) has been advertising on television and has now rolled out a style studio, which is a virtual dressing room aimed at making online shopping more interactive. The style studio enables users to click their pictures using a web-camera, select a product they want to try, and see how it looks on them. It also enables users to share their look with friends on Facebook and Twitter.

Myntra also offers a 'Try & Buy' service in which consumers shop for a product online, get it delivered at their home, try it out, and then decide about buying it. This enables customers to get over their reservations about looks and style of the apparels they are buying. Fashionara, a multibrand online fashion retailer, has online stylists, much like shop-floor assistants, to guide buyers through certain fits and categories.

Sources:
From clicks to bricks, *The Economic Times*, 15 November, 2012.
http://www.cnbc.com/id/101573601, last accessed on 10 May 2014.

---

handled well, it will lead to frustrations. A study of comments made on a third party consumer forum website conducted by Goetzinger, et al. (2006) found that the ease of ordering, speed of shipping, packaging, and customer service were critical for the online transaction to be a success. The most common complaints were related to issues dealing with credit cards, e-mail correspondence, and receipts.

A look at the complaints posted on online review sites also shows mishandling of communications by companies. Some of the common complaints posted on such sites include the following:

- E-mails not answered
- Telephone numbers provided by websites do not exist or put the customer in automated loops by interactive voice response (IVR) instead of taking complaints
- Customers do not know how and where the defective goods are to be sent.

These issues tend to put off the online shopper.

Labelling

Labels and instruction manuals help customers in learning about products and also to know their sources. Proper labelling helps in product recognition and delivers an unwritten warranty for the consumer. This becomes all the more important for products that are ordered online. Software products come with online support and many popular brands do have detailed labelling and instructions.

However, cheaper products bought online come without proper labelling and with defective operating manuals, leading to complaints. Often, these products are imported or sourced from small manufacturers and carry no guarantees. The absence of proper labelling leads to decreasing the value proposition and does not build long-term trust among buyers.

MEDIUM CHARACTERISTICS

Constantinides (2004) writes that the primary means of delivering the web experience to customers is the corporate website. 'Sites delivering superb web experience are designed in a way not only addressing the client's product needs and expectations but also assisting the customers through the steps of the buying process,' he writes. Websites must be seen, therefore, as vital instruments of customer service and persuasion rather than simply as online brochures or catalogues of the company's products, through the following factors:

Functionality factors Websites enhance the online experience by good functioning, ease of navigation, and by operating in a fast and interactive manner. Functionality includes usability and interactivity elements (Fig. 16.7), such as convenience, site navigation, ability to be found in search engines, speed, and the payment process. Online sites must allow functionality in order to succeed.

Psychological factors Websites should be able to persuade customers to stop, explore, and interact online. Companies have to overcome psychological factors such as fears of fraud and doubts as to the trustworthiness of the website and the vendor. The psychological factors affecting online trust are security, transparent ordering and refund processes, guarantees, and uncertainty reducing elements. Further, since people like to see and touch products before buying, websites offer 'try and buy' functions.

Content factors Content factors refer to the marketing mix related elements of the website. They are divided in two subcategories—aesthetics and marketing mix. They involve the look and feel of the website that influence customer behaviour. Communication, fulfilment, price, and promotion are part of the marketing mix elements that will influence consumer behaviour.

Online atmospherics Dailey (2004) defines online atmospherics as the 'conscious designing of web environments to create positive affect and/or cognitions in surfers in order to develop positive consumer responses.'

FIG. 16.7 Online sites try to provide the same functionalities that consumers experience during physical buying

Hunter and Mukerji (2011) describe attempts by websites to create online atmospherics, and found that atmospheric cues have the potential to influence change in consumer goals. Therefore, companies should provide the information and environmental cues that target consumer expectations. 'Overall, online atmospherics play as significant a role as atmospherics offline,' they conclude. 'It is necessary to consider the target market and the relative content when developing a website because, although atmospherics may be thought of only as aesthetic in nature, they can have significant effects on the consumer and consumer purchase intentions.'

For instance, stimuli such as overcrowding and loud music reduce consumer interaction and browsing time. If a consumer experiences a retail atmosphere that decreases the experience of shopping, it will have a negative impact on buyers. As online interface in which the consumer purchases products still has atmospheric qualities, consumers' experience of an online shopping site is likely to produce similar cognitive and emotional responses that a physical store would.

Online Merchants

Factors such as service quality, security issues, reputation, price, delivery, and after sales service play an important role in the purchase decision. The organisation for Economic Co-operation and Development, that is, OECD (2010) defines Internet intermediaries as those parties that bring together or facilitate transactions between third parties on the Internet. They give access to, host, transmit, and index content, products, and services originated by third parties on the Internet or provide Internet-based services to third parties. The functions of online intermediaries go beyond the functions of trade intermediaries in the sense that they have to provide information and services at various touchpoints of consumer experience such as the following:

- Provide the infrastructure
- Collect, organize, and evaluate dispersed information
- Facilitate social communication and information exchange
- Aggregate supply and demand
- Facilitate market processes
- Provide trust
- Take into account the needs of buyers and sellers or users and customers

To encourage B2C or B2B trade on their sites, merchants have to provide all the aforementioned. As a matter of fact, online merchants and intermediaries face the same issues of trust and reliability that mail order businesses face. However, sometimes, there is tension between these functions; for example, tension between preserving identity and privacy while personalizing products and services in ways that benefit users. A customer would be willing to send money in advance to a supplier only if there is confidence that the promise of quality goods and warranties would be fulfilled and that privacy would be maintained. Online merchants have to build this confidence through the following ways:

Security Online payments must be secure and refunds policy must be strictly adhered to. Further, websites have to ensure that the data on their sites is not given to third parties or open for hacking. Passwords, credit card details, telephone numbers, and addresses must be secure with the merchants.

After sales service One doubt that consumers have is regarding after sales service for goods purchased online. Online intermediaries have to ensure that such services are provided at consumers' sites through third parties. Further, in case of complaints, a quick system to respond must be firmly established.

Trust Trust is built over a period of time through quick deliveries, response to customer queries, and being sensitive to customer needs.

Deliveries Online merchants depend on courier companies for deliveries. Delays and product damages may occur in certain cases. In some cases, multiple delivery attempts are required and this adds to costs. Referred to as the 'last mile problem,' online merchants struggle to solve this issue. Some portals have set up their own distribution centres to get over the last mile problem.

These issues have been found to be determinants in consumer buying in several studies. A study by Al-hawari and Mouakket (2012) found that customers tend to continue to use online services of those organizations they perceive as unique, reliable, caring, and highly respected compared to competitors. Employee-based service quality not only builds trust, but drives consumers to online channels as well. Thus, retailers with a good organizational image can capitalize on it when they go online. Building a strong image is not only important in triggering customers' intentions to use online services, but also achieves marketing loyalty as well.

Reichheld and Schefter (2000) stress the importance of loyalty and trust in online customer behaviour. In online portals, business is conducted at a distance and consumers feel greater risks and uncertainties. They have to rely on images and promises, and trust is an important element when they place orders. Research conducted by the authors showed that when asked to name the most important attribute for online shopping, the answer was 'a website I know and trust.' All other attributes, including lowest cost and broadest selection, lagged far behind. This is very true as people tend to buy from websites that offer ease of operation, security, and quality products.

DIGITAL VALUE CREATION—INFINITE POSSIBILITY

Consumer behaviour is changing in several ways due to mobile devices that allow people to search and order products anywhere and at any time. Consumers now move seamlessly from the virtual to the real world and this enables them to switch channels easily for both information and purchase. The Closing case study describes how people are using mobile devices in the purchase process.

In their book, *Infinite Possibility: Creating Customer Value on the Digital Frontier*, Pine and Korn (2011) describe a multiverse which reshapes the landscape by altering three dimensions—time, no-space, and no-matter. Technology extends each of these dimensions for value creation:

Time Technology is able to enact autonomous events that engage people through nonlinear and asynchronous methods that today's digitally savvy customers prefer. People interact with companies when it fits their own schedule, like banking at an ATM in off-hours rather than having to match a company's priorities.

No space Digital technology enables companies to construct offerings in virtual places rather than in the real places. Companies can interact with customers on websites, via social media, in virtual worlds, on whatever device best meets their individual needs.

No matter Offerings need no longer be comprised merely of material substances but can also be formed from digital substances.

Companies fuse the real and the virtual worlds the same way that customers have done. They do this in various ways; courier companies let customers track packages through their websites. Restaurants enhance their real places with Wi-Fi access. Apparel retailers help people try out new clothes on a virtual model and help them select what suits them best.

These are ways of creating digital value. Some companies do so by offering online services, such as Google and Facebook. Others use the Internet as a distribution channel, selling software and music. Many other companies use it as an electronic store. However, companies can create value for the customer using tools and technologies that are available easily. The Internet offers a way to talk to and track customers as one-to-one marketing evolves.

One-to-one marketing is the ability to personalize communications and products so as to make a unique product offering for each customer. Peppers, et al. (1999) write that one-to-one marketing, also called relationship marketing or personalized marketing, means being willing and able to change a company's behaviour toward an individual customer based on customer feedback. In an online context, it means to identify, track, and interact with an individual customer and then reconfigure products or services to meet that customer's needs. These developments have the potential to affect every company's relationship with its customers. The ways in which online consumer behaviour affects marketing strategy are explained in Table 16.3.

As the Table 16.3 shows, online consumer expectations are reshaping marketing strategy. These are discussed with reference to the 7Ps of service marketing.

TABLE 16.3 How online consumer behaviour affects marketing strategy

Elements	Marketing strategy
Product	• Augmented products • Exclusive products not available in physical stores
Price	• Low prices, cash on delivery • Deals and discounts • Guarantees, refund policies
Place	• Interacting with a virtual shop front • Free or low cost delivery • Try and buy facilities • Delivery efficiency and tracking • Online service delivery
Promotion	• Internet value proposition (IVP) • Individualized messages can be delivered • Integration of online and offline messages
Physical evidence	• Consistent website design • On site assurance, refund policies • Independent reviews, 'try and buy' facilities • Physical stores augmenting online experience
Process	• Transactional and internal communications • Integration of business processes

Product To differentiate product offerings, websites offer augmented products. For example, electronic goods come complete with batteries, memory cards, and carrying cases, which a consumer would otherwise have to buy separately.

Price Consumers learn to expect low prices, deals, and discounts on the Internet. While expensive items do sell, many people like to look for deals and discounts. At the same time, shoppers are concerned with guarantees and returns, in case the product does not live up to their expectations.

Place Consumers buy from the comfort of their homes or while they are on the move and are becoming comfortable with virtual shops. They also expect free and quick delivery of their purchases. This adds to convenience, as in the case of buying groceries or vegetables. Products that can be digitized– such as books, music, and videos—are delivered instantly through online delivery.

Promotion Companies integrate online and offline promotion. They exploit opportunities not available earlier such as online virtual exhibitions, product demos or seminars. Customers are targeted on individual basis through personalized messages, and to create and deliver an Internet value proposition (IVP) or the online value proposition (OVP). This is the unique benefit that an online company offers to the consumer as a means of obtaining competitive advantage.

People In an online context, 'people' means how customer service is delivered, either as customer self-service or through interaction with staff at all levels. This implies that online updates and service information must be on a streaming basis. Many websites offer virtual assistants and frequently asked questions (FAQs) to enhance their service.

Physical evidence Customers look for physical evidence to reassure them. In the online environment, the physical evidence is digital. Online reviews and interactions with other users is part of the evidence. Guarantees, security icons, endorsements, well-known brand names, trade body memberships, customer lists and independent reviews also enhance physical evidence. 'Try and buy' facilities offered by websites are also part of this step.

Process Consumers expect seamless buying and communication processes. These processes are not visible, but menus, shopping baskets, and interactions are the visible part of processes, based on which customers will judge service.

Every aspect of service marketing is a means of creating and adding digital value creation in the minds of the consumers. Many websites integrate the elements to offer customer value. Adding up, they are able to create web equity, which is described in the next section.

Web Equity

Brand equity relates to consumer awareness and perceptions about a brand. Page and Lepkowska-White (2002) define web equity as consumer awareness and perception about an online company's website which builds loyalty of customers towards the company. As there are many online retailers selling similar products and services, web equity refers to the likelihood that the consumer thinks of a particular site first.

Web image is a function of two variables—site related and non-site related. The former refers to how the website looks and operates, while the latter refers to product and service characteristics.

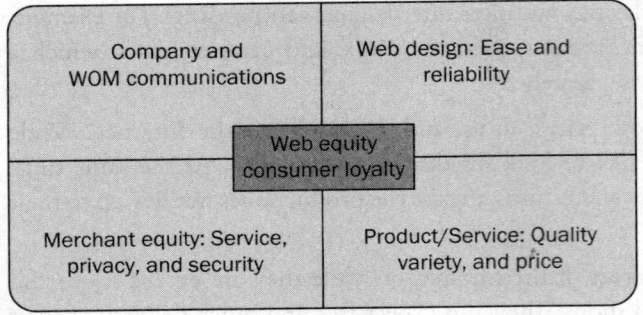

FIG. 16.8 Web equity determinants

Thus, websites have to take into account the ease of navigation, ordering, concern for security, and other site issues with delivery, after-sales service, number, types, and quality of products offered.

Websites have to generate positive perceptions of vendors such as being trustworthy, accessible, and caring about privacy and security issues. These are vital to the image of online companies. At the same time, consumers' experience with the site determines their opinion about their site and also intentions to visit the site again. Web equity goes beyond brand equity in the types of associations needed to build a positive image and consumer value.

The task of an online company is to build loyalty. Loyal customers are less likely to switch to other online stores, are also typically less price sensitive, and contribute to positive word-of-mouth referrals. These create entry barriers to competition as well as reduce marketing costs.

The factors that affect web equity are shown in Fig. 16.8, and are described here.

Company communications Consumer awareness is built through offline and online communications. Many online companies use print, television, and outdoor advertising to encourage people to visit their sites. This is aimed to build web equity. This strategy is expensive and creates only short spikes of attention rather than long-term equity. Mass media is a powerful tool to create brand equity, but has to be used well; many campaigns for online companies are misconceived and ill-executed, which generates traffic to the website in the short term but does not result in sales or long-term interest of the visitors. Online company communications have a well-defined objective, and integrated with all other marketing communication tools.'

A word of caution is sounded by Michael Porter (2001), who wrote that Internet brands have proved difficult to build, despite advertising campaigns. He explains that despite huge ad spends, price discounts, and incentives, 'dot-com brands have not approached the power of established brands, achieving only a modest impact on loyalty and barriers to entry.'

Online advertising fares worse. Banner advertising and e-mails are largely seen as intrusive and many consumers block such communications. Click-through rates are not encouraging globally, and while they drive traffic, converting the clicks into paying customers has remained a big challenge.

Non-company communication Word-of-mouth communications remains a powerful communication tool as it helps people to overcome the uncertainties of online buying. Consumers who are new to online buying are likely to be influenced by experiences of their friends and acquaintances. Therefore, many dot-com companies reward their customers with rewards and incentives for referring their friends to the site.

Both company and customer communications should be used to build an image and a unique identity for the online company. This is achieved by associating the dot-com company with a particular source, a unique message, an event, and so on. Such associations help develop a preliminary image of the company.

Web design features A more durable web image is formed when customers actually experience the site. The website design, look and feel, ease of operation, security and reliability issues, transparency, and quality of information, will play a more important role.

Many websites enable customers to build their personal profiles and save information about their sizes and preferences. While customers who do so are likely to be more loyal, companies can tailor make offers based on individual profiles, to serve customers better. Other companies make websites with content that is interactive and fun.

Merchant characteristics Consumers are influenced by facilities such as cash on delivery, try and buy offers, prices, and so on. The purchase experience—delivery, quality, and after sales service –determine whether the purchase remains a one-off or whether it will be repeated.

Product or service characteristics Once the products are delivered, the experience with the products helps in building the brand. Good quality and long-lasting products will result in repeat buying and buzz. If, however, the products do not turn out well in terms of features or performance, the website will lose its equity.

Christodoulides and Chernatony (2004) give ten factors contributing to the web interaction contributing to web equity.

Online brand experience The online brand experience includes all points of online interaction between the customer and the brand. Companies can deliver experiential marketing through the Internet.

Interactivity The Internet allows interactivity, or communications from consumer to company. The degree and nature of interactivity have a significant effect on the perceived quality of corporate web sites.

Customization Brands are not rigid offerings from companies; consumers look for customization. Companies can collect personal information about their customers and offer not only personalized communications but also personalized products.

Relevance Companies have to create relevance in a world where brands need to meet individual needs.

Site design Web design is not just about visual appeal but encompasses a number of functional parameters that need to be in place to underpin the online brand experience. Ease of navigation and ease of use are important considerations when designing a web site.

Customer service Customer service can be enhanced through providing product, security and shipping information, providing links to inventory to determine if products are available, sending automatic order confirmations, responding to customers quickly, providing alternative means of contact, and using individuals to support automated functions.

Order fulfilment Since most service failures of online trade occur during delivery, online companies have to invest heavily in delivery infrastructure. If items delivered do not match the order or if there is a delay in delivery, customer complaints will follow. Similarly, if the offline consumption of a physical product does not meet customer expectations, then no matter how good the online experience is, it will not result in web equity.

Quality of brand relationships Individuals value their relationships with brands. The quality of brand relationships is enhanced by providing interesting and relevant content, deals and offers. Brand trust is even more pertinent in an online context because of customers' concerns about data privacy and transaction security. Relationships with customers have become one of the key differentiating factors of websites, because of the enormous choice customers have online.

Communities Internet technologies allow companies to build online brand communities. Such communities integrate customer-to-customer interaction. Successful online communities help build customer loyalty and advocacy.

Website logs Each time a user accesses a Web page, a variety of information is recorded on the server logs. Server logs contain what pages were accessed, date and time of access, and the computer's IP address. This data is a key to understand online consumer behaviour. Web log metrics that can be related with brand equity include number of hits, the number of revisits, and view time per page. This data can be incorporated into a holistic brand equity measurement system.

USING SOCIAL MEDIA

Social media is the online interaction of people through which they create, share, and exchange content among themselves in virtual communities and networks. Many studies have stressed on the importance of engaging customers on social media. As people spend more time on this, companies look for ways that they can plug into the experience and thereby create brand equity. Many research papers have been written stating that fan pages are excellent tools for companies to communicate with customers. Today, companies have dedicated departments to create content for such interactions, but still struggle to convert these fans into paying customers.

While social media is where consumers are, using it for commercial purposes remains a mystery. All but a few companies have managed to make a success of this media. Many companies started 'me-too' pages on popular social sites and even managed to collect a number of fans, but converting them into paying customers remained an uphill task.

According to a report in *Businessworld* (2010), most companies struggle to achieve success in the social media space. The reason is that they only have a half-baked knowledge on its commercial use. 'On one side are advertising and marketing professionals who understand the finer aspects of branding, but are clueless about how to effectively use social media. On the other end of the spectrum are the young-and-able social media wizards who know everything about technology and the rules of social media, but are completely lost when it comes to brand management skills,' says the report. This is quite correct—companies want people who are good in information technology and who understand the business in order to make full use of today's considerably changed marketing environment.

Social Behaviour of Consumers

Social media strategies will fail, unless social behaviour of customers is tied to e-commerce. Piskorski (2011) writes that most companies do not succeed on online social platforms. Though

MARKETING INSIGHT
Most Successful Social Media Campaigns

Some of the most successful social media campaigns are given as follows:

Samsung's Oscars Tweet with Ellen DeGeneres

During the Oscars, the host, Ellen DeGeneres walked into the audience and took a selfie with some of the most famous stars. This extremely happy picture went viral across the globe. The Times of India (2014) reported that Samsung, the main sponsor for the Oscars, succeeded in executing a great social media moment with DeGeneres' picture, which had the major stars in it. The tweet, which was done from a Galaxy Note 3, broke the retweeting record and Twitter itself went down for 20 minutes as it was unable to the surge of traffic. The picture can be viewed on https://twitter.com/TheEllenShow/status/440322224407314432/photo/1

Dunkin Donuts Coolatta

In June 2009, Dunkin Donuts released another new product: Coolatta. The product was promoted with a Facebook campaign called 'Dunkin Donuts' Facebook Campaign Turns Your Profile Pic into Prizes.' Combining it with its Twitter account, @dunkindonuts, it sent customers a discount coupon to try a Coolatta for $1.99, get a picture taken of them consuming the product by their friends, post the picture on the Facebook page, and make it their profile picture, which would them entitle them to win prizes. The successful campaign resulted in a large number of entries and also succeeded in involving friends of users. As a result of the campaign, Dukin Donuts' number of Twitter followers increased from around 23,000 followers to almost 43,000 followers. People also posted comments on the update with around 500 clicks on the like button.

Domino's UK Campaign for Cheap Pizza

Domino's UK ran a Twitter campaign through which customers could reduce the price of the star pizza depending on how many people tweeted it in time for lunch. They could get a £15.99 pizza for £7.74. People had to include the hashtag "#letsdolunch" in their tweets to help reduce the price of a large pepperoni pizza.

The campaign was a success and a large number of people included the hash tag to get the promised discount.

WATERisLIFE Campaign

WATERisLIFE, a non-profit organization, wanted to raise awareness and support for its cause. Instead of trying to get followers and likes, it asked people to post their problems on the hashtag: '#firstworldproblems'. People responded by posting their silly complaints like, 'I hate it when my phone charger won't reach my bed' or 'I hate when my leather seats aren't heated.'

WATERisLIFE then made a documentary of people in Haiti reading the hashtagged tweets. The video showed these people in real settings, where they lived in poverty and strife. The tweeted problems seemed so flippant compared to the problems that the poor had. The contrast the problems of people in rich countries as simply ridiculous. The video ended with the message, 'First world problems...aren't problems.'

The video went viral and became a great success. In just four days, the video got over one million views. The campaign generated a huge response and people donated to get the clean water project going for poor communities.

Sources:

Domino's UK Use Tweets to Knock Down the Price of Pizza: http://www.simplyzesty.com/Blog/Article/March-2012/Domino-s-UK-Use-Tweets-to-Knock-Down-the-Price-of-Pizza, last accessed on 10 October 2014.

Dunkin Donuts' Facebook Campaign Turns Your Profile Pic into Prizes; http://mashable.com/2009/06/03/dunkin-donuts-facebook-campaign/, last accessed on 10 October 2014.

http://www.exacttarget.com/blog/the-30-most-brilliant-social-media-campaigns-of-2014-so-far/, last accessed on 10 October 2014.

The Times of India, Oscars host Ellen DeGeneres endorses, Samsung, tweets via iPhone, dated 3 March 2014.

they try to use social media, 'only [a] few of those companies succeed in generating profits on social platforms, despite collecting lots of 'friends' and 'followers,' he writes. His research shows why this happens: people use social media to connect with other people, not with companies. Thus, importing digital strategies to social environments just does not work.

Instead, companies should understand consumers and their activities on social media platforms before engaging with them. How do people use social media? Li and Bernoff (2009) in their book, *Groundswell*, identify six categories of people using social media:

Creators   Those who produce and share online content such as blogs, web sites, articles, and videos.

Critics   People who post comments, ratings, and reviews of products and services on blogs and forums.

Collectors   Those who collect information and vote for web sites online

Joiners   Those who maintain a social networking profile and visit other sites.

Spectators   Those who read blogs, listen to podcasts, watch videos, and generally consume media.

Inactives   Those who do none of these things.

By understanding the activities of people as they interact online, companies must help people to connect and then they will be open to engage with companies. They can

- reduce costs by helping people to meet and strengthen relationships
- increase willingness to pay by helping people meet and strengthen relationships

Digital strategies have to be developed to use social behaviour of customers for e-commerce. Successful companies help personalize and integrate value-added content to improve user experience. A Nielsen report, *How Digital Influences How We Shop Around the World* (2012) describes how consumer behaviour can be harnessed with marketing strategy as follows:

Focus on the right shopper   Since not everyone is going to use digital, companies can focus on the first four categories described above. Nielsen found that about 25% of shoppers can be considered as 'Trendsetters,' or people who love to keep ahead, try new things and tell others about them. Comprising the younger lot, they have children in the household and are more affluent compared to the general population.

Engage shoppers with the right message   Companies have to create messages that will attract the active users. They have to determine activities that are important to core shoppers and customize their messages. For example, if shoppers are deal-centric, deals and coupon promotions can be send via social media.

Connect with shoppers via the right medium   Consumers have a wide array of choices—online, mobile, social, or in-store; hence, companies have to focus on the medium that provides the best return on investment. They have to pair mobility with the need and create apps that make it easier for shopping.

Companies cannot limit themselves by medium since people move between media seamlessly. To engage with customers and to connect with them, all channels have to be integrated in one experience.

Omnichannel Marketing

Customers find integrated channels easy and convenient. Suppose a customer is looking for a laptop that is found on a website that also lists the addresses of physical stores. An order can be placed online and the delivery is made in three to seven days. However, if it is needed urgently, the customer can simply drive down to the nearest store and pick it up. Integration of channels and customer service thus complements the brand with the online shopping benefits. Brands should thus extend naturally to the Internet.

The importance of integration is also highlighted by Michael Porter (2001). He writes that consumers will 'value a combination of online services, personal services, and physical locations over stand-alone web distribution. They will want a choice of channels, delivery options and ways of dealing with options.' Companies thus have to integrate traditional and online methods of doing business.

Giamanco and Gregoire (2012) write that buyers today typically complete most of the purchase journey before having any contact with sales. Social media offers a peer-to-peer environment that holds promise for candid referrals—and warnings. They write 'social media's greatest potential is at the front end of the sales cycle—during the prospecting, opportunity qualification, and pre-sales-call research that leads up to a face-to-face meeting. But social platforms also offer a means of maintaining customer relationships and building brand loyalty throughout.'

E-commerce is now integrating with social media clout, according to a report in *The Economic Times* (2011). Deals on e-commerce site get shared and re-tweeted on social media platforms, generating buzz, and this triggers social commerce across categories. Travel websites depend on social media fans to reach out to the online target consumers. Brick-and-mortar stores too add their presence on social media. E-commerce sites acquire social 'skin' and social sites are seen extending into the e-commerce space to utilize individual influence and micro-networks.

A new trend is that e-commerce, travel, and social media platforms are intruding into each other's playing ground. E-commerce sites try to collect a large number of users by offering incentives for people who add their friends. Sites such as fashionandyou, snapdeal, and others try to mobilize a new category of e-shoppers through referrals. At the same time, social media add e-commerce platforms to their sites, hoping to get a share of online buying through their well-established users.

In an effort to be more attractive, websites offer several deals to consumers such as discounts, cashbacks, and a multitude of deals and packages. About 25 per cent of the buzz on online retailing is garnered by discount sites or 'deal-tailers,' showing consumers' penchant for searching and getting discounts and deals (Table 16.4). With a greater share of conversations being captured by deal and discount sites, 'deal-tailing' indicates where consumer interest moves. The deal and discount sites differentiate on the basis of daily and limited period deals.

It remains to be seen which sites remain in business and which do not. As it is, the online buying space is highly crowded, with many players dishing out the same fare without much differentiation. That is why building loyalty is of prime importance in e-commerce.

Building Customer Loyalty

Companies also have to unravel the mystery of customer loyalty on the web. If customers buy from a website once, how does one ensure that they come back to the same site? Traditionally,

TABLE 16.4 Top five websites on Indian social media

E-tailers	Deal-tailers	Travel sites
1. Infibeam	1. FashionAndYou	1. Yatra
2. Book My Show	2. Snapdeal	2. Cleartrip
3. Shoppers Stop	3. Deals and you	3. Ixigo
4. eBay India	4. Tradus India	4. Make My Trip
5. Flipkart	5. City offers	5. Trip Advisor

Source: The Economic Times (2011)

companies create brands or customer experience to build loyalty. However, when one can use a search engine to locate the cheapest offerings or when numerous online sites offer the same products, how does a website develop loyalty for itself?

The problem is acute in online selling, as the cost of acquiring customers on the Internet is huge, a fact that is often overlooked by online traders. Hoffman and Novak (2000) say that many e-tailers average more than $100 to acquire a new customer and some are spending upwards of $500. They cite the case of CDnow, a popular music company at one time: it was the fourth most visited shopping site in 1999, with 7,00,000 visitors and five million page hits every day. However, by March 2000, it ran into financial difficulties. Its mistake was to acquire new users at a very high cost: though ad rates may appear low per 1000 clicks, when combined with a one per cent click-through rate and a one per cent conversion rate, acquiring customers is indeed expensive.

Instead of relying wholly on media or click-through ads, a successful online strategy consists of building a strong social presence and even building online communities, which makes users bond with each other and also with the brand.

Online Communities

Fournier and Lee (2009) write that strong brand communities are built when companies understand the individual and social needs of members and do everything possible to support and engage them. The company should not try to control the community; rather it should be guided by it. By managing and sustaining their communities, firms can build fierce customer loyalty and enhance their brands.

It is important to understand why people join online brand communities. They do not boost sales but are means of helping people meet their needs. Most consumers do not want to gain status through brand affiliation, but participate in communities to find emotional support and encouragement, to explore ways to contribute to the greater good, and to cultivate interests and skills.

Online communities can be built around any of the following:

Pools People have strong associations with a shared activity or goal, or shared values, and loose associations with one another. This becomes the key to community affiliation. An example of a pool is the community of Apple fans, and they see the brand as a common link between themselves.

Webs People have strong one-to-one relationships with others who have similar or complementary needs. Online relationships form the basis of community affiliation. Facebook users, for instance, form webs communities.

Hubs People have strong connections to a central figure and weaker associations with one another. A charismatic figure binds such communities. The community formed by Virgin group is an example, and its chief executive, Mr Richard Branson acts as a hub around which the community is built.

Data Mining and Analytics

When customers browse online, or when they use their loyalty cards, they leave behind a wealth of data that companies can analyse and use to improve loyalty. Data mining has become an important tool to study consumer behaviour.

Data mining refers to the extraction of hidden predictive information from large databases. It is a powerful new technology that can predict future trends and behaviours based on past history and data of a customer's online search and behaviour.

The understanding of consumer behaviour is helped a great deal by the data left behind by customers as they browse the web. As they shop, consumers leave behind a trail of information that is of interest to companies.

- Cookies reveal where consumers have been browsing
- Cookies on their social site profiles reveal their income bracket, age and sex
- The Internet address can often be matched to their physical address
- Clicking on the homepage also reveals customer behaviour: someone clicking too quickly to checkout means that the consumer has already decided to buy, so no discounts may be offered.

Analysing this data, companies can figure out consumer habits and preferences. Data analytics is the process of inspecting, cleaning, transforming, and modelling data with the purpose of discovering patterns and drawing conclusions. As Davenport (2006) writes, 'they know what products their customers want, but they also know what prices those customers will pay, and how many items each will buy in a lifetime, and what triggers will people buy more.' Using sophisticated analytical techniques, they can identify the most profitable customers, increase the likelihood that products will be liked and increase customer loyalty.

Loveman (2003) explains that customer loyalty is built in a company by 'mining our customer data deeply, running market experiments, and using the results to develop and implement finely tuned marketing and service delivery strategies that keep our customers coming back.'

Dubbing it a 'future diamond mine,' millions of individual transactions are tracked and used to study consumer preferences. Customer activity is tracked at various touchpoints, which is combined with personal information and spending preferences are built. The information is then sliced and diced finely to generate marketing ideas. For instance, data might show the promotional efforts that customers responded to. By evaluating customer value, the company can create marketing interventions that would increase customer interaction with the brand.

Increasingly, companies are combining the internal data generated by companies with data from other sources to connect better with customers. Called big data, it uses all data from the Internet, with automatic sensors in various devices, audio and video recordings, and so on. These data are then used to develop predictive and prescriptive models. Known as Analytics 3.0, the new capabilities 'adapt operational, product development and decision processes,' writes Davenport (2013).

MARKETING INSIGHT
How Companies Use Data to Decipher Consumer Behaviour

Data mining is big business, mainly because consumer behaviour is hidden in it. As consumers connect online, they leave behind a trail of data. Companies use this data to profile their customers and offer personalized products and messages pinpointed to customers. This exhibit shows how three companies—Apple, Google, and eBay, use data to understand consumer behaviour.

Apple

Apple's iAd service allows the company to analyse the behaviour pattern of its 160 million customers in iTunes and the AppStore. Retail users are analysed in terms of the following:

- Website preferences
- Internet usage behaviour
- App preferences
- Music, TV, and audiobook genre preferences
- Locations and devices
- Demographics
- Network

By using this data, Apple knows its customer's preferences and needs. Based on data analysis, Apple targets customers for advertisements within its own app ecosystem. Apple integrated these functions in a user-friendly way, creating a unique customer experience.

Each ad is shown only to the audience it wants to. The pinpoint target can leverage demographic data, as well as people's unique interests and preference data that are relevant for particular brands.

Using this service, companies can create ads that are of interest to their audience, within their favourite apps. iAd is built into iOS, the operating system of the iPhone, iPad, and iPod, enabling interactive experiences in ads. Users can download content, add reminders, create shopping lists, compose and send emails, save coupons and barcodes, and also find nearby stores.

Google

Google collects, analyses and interprets vast amounts of customer data. Its philosophy, as explained on its website, is to 'focus on the user and all else will follow.'

The company uses data mining on a grand scale—it gathers IP addresses, search terms, and browser types every time a person searches for something. For users who sign up for individual services, their data is analysed in detail and Google is able to build a precise picture of the customer.

Some of the ways that Google uses data are as follows:

- iGoogle provides data about place of living with a built-in weather forecast
- Google collects data about music and video preferences via YouTube
- Google Maps provides information on possible travel destinations

Data is analysed by complex recognition algorithms or by just comparing all available data records. Google applies its data mining know-how to its product development process. For example, on Google Labs, one can test ideas and beta versions of new software while the company evaluates their usage patterns, gaining insight as to how these products will be used.

eBay

eBay developed a holistic view of its buyers and sellers. According to John Donahoe, CEO of eBay, 'We are very focused on capitalizing on this period of dynamic change in how consumers behave.'

The company stores more than 10 petabytes of data in its central data warehouse, and this is continuously growing. The company uses its holistic and integrated customer view to quickly generate innovations.

All in-house departments can use the data through sand boxes. They can then compare it against additional external data by means of a web interface and start experimenting. The scalability, consistency, and speed of customer data analysis allow eBay to act fast and on a low overall cost base.

Sources:
http://advertising.apple.com/brands/.
http://hbr.org/2011/03/the-hbr-interview-how-ebay-developed-a-culture-of-experimentation/ar/1.
http://www.google.co.in/about/company/philosophy/.
http://www.jac-conference.org/jac/system/application/views/images_ce/Customers.pdf.
All last accessed on 10 May 2014.

Barton and Court (2012) explain three steps how data analytics is used for analysing consumer behaviour:

Source data from multiple sources Companies must be able to identify, combine, and manage multiple sources of data as the consumer experiences various touchpoints.

Prediction and optimization models Companies must develop capability to build advanced analytics models for predicting and optimizing outcomes.

Organizational transformation Organizations must be transformed so that the data and models actually yield better decisions.

As consumers become more comfortable with online shopping and companies analyse them with complex data tools, businesses themselves will be transformed in the future. They have to remodel themselves keeping into account changing consumer behaviour.

TRANSFORMING THE BUSINESS

Berman (2012) writes that due to digital revolution, businesses in every industry are under intense pressure to rethink their customer value propositions and operations. They have to consider the following:

- Reshaping customer value propositions
- Remodelling their business operations to deliver new customer value propositions effectively, efficiently, and in innovative ways
- Doing both of the aforementioned at the same time, leading to broad industry transformation

Companies have to reshape customer value propositions and transform their operations using digital technologies for greater customer interaction and collaboration. New capabilities have to be built to survive in the future. See Table 16.5.

Kanter (2001) writes that a transformation is essential. 'Even the most successful company cannot buy its way to change by applying a little lipstick and altering its appearance with a website. It must be willing to change more fundamental aspects of its way of life.'

Online buying poses a great threat to traditional companies. Companies are changing themselves to keep pace with changing technologies. Will this change the ways that we do business in future?

Future of Online Consumer Behaviour

The manner in which consumer behaviour evolves as a result of online habit remains to be seen. We are already seeing some changes (see Closing case) where people compulsively check their phones and feel deprived if Internet access is not available. As these trends spread, it is possible that the way retailing is done may well go through huge changes.

Trends such as showrooming and smartphonatics are already impacting the retail industry (see Closing case). Another trend is that people will use physical shopping as a way to socialize and hang out, and real purchasing might be done online. Retail stores will feel the pinch and it is possible that many will start downsizing as they lose business to the Internet. Will the retail store of the future be an empty room where consumers see and feel products on 3-D imaging

TABLE 16.5 Transforming businesss

Business model	Focus on customer value rather than on products
Customer focus	Build customer centricity, use social networking, and involve customers in making products
Channels	Integrate all touchpoints across the consumer decision journey (CDJ)
Using data	Develop data analytics abilities, collect, and integrate data from all possible sources
People	Break silos, get the whole workforce focused on delivering customer experience

technology instead of physical products? If they like what they experience, they could place orders for the products to be delivered to their homes.

Audi has already opened a store in a similar format in London. The company's website says, 'Audi City is a new digital car showroom format that uses state-of-the-art technology to make clever use of precious city space. Visitors can experience every possible combination of the Audi range.' The company attempts to help consumers experience the brand digitally. It does not display actual cars but uses digital presentations to present the car.

Huge screens display models of cars. One can check out the interior and exterior, listen to the sounds of exhaust, and opening and shutting of doors. The store also has paint, wood, and leather samples that can be viewed and touched personally. The huge digital walls are also controlled by tablets on which customers can create a car and view their configuration of the big digital screens.

Such stores save on real estate costs and allow the brand to test new markets where it does not have dealers. It also helps to cut down inventory and vehicle maintenance costs.

However, another possibility that online companies are discovering is that delivering products to individual customers is too uneconomical and might force them to shut shop. Should that happen, companies will use websites to deliver information and guide customers to the nearest retail stores, instead of taking online orders.

Both these trends are visible today. The evolution of the retail phenomenon will depend on new technologies such as 3-D printing that may well change the course of business in the future.

3D printing refers to the making of parts and products using a computer-driven, additive process, with one layer at a time. It can build plastic and metal parts directly from computeraided design (CAD) drawings that have been cross sectioned into thousands of layers. It is possible to print out an object using these drawings in just the same way as we use printers. Such printers may help mass customization of consumer goods in the future.

Mass customization is the use of flexible computer-aided manufacturing systems to produce custom output, combining the low unit costs of mass production processes with the flexibility of individual customization. According to *The Economist* (2011), 'Three-dimensional printing makes it as cheap to create single items as it is to produce thousands and thus undermines economies of scale. It may have as profound an impact on the world as the coming of the factory did.'

Technology is indeed changing many aspects of business. *The Economist* (2012) reports of price discrimination software that helps companies use consumer information to price their products, especially those products whose pricing is complex, variable, and therefore, unpredictable to buyers. These include insurance, air travel, mobile-phone plans, and hotel rooms.

Another aspect of online purchases is that companies cannot pressurize people into buying something. Negra and Mzoughi (2012) researched online procrastinators and found that people deliberately postpone decisions so as to maximize the likelihood of having the best deal. When consumers delay decisions, they can look for better offers and additional information, which could result in the purchase being abandoned.

Easy availability of information, coupled with technological advancement, is the ultimate consumer democracy. The information will be used in a myriad of ways in the near future.

CONCLUSION

Consumers are changing like never before. This is a tectonic change that promises to change the business scenario of the future. It is bringing about a change in the way consumers browse for products and buy them, forcing companies to change their business models. This change is not limited merely of switching to e-commerce. It may well change the way goods are advertised and sold, causing some to remark that 'traditional marketing is dead'.

Indeed, many companies are changing their value propositions, supply chains, promotions and delivery to suit the digitally connected consumer. As Internet penetration increases, more people will latch on. The tectonic changes in consumer behaviour described in this chapter pose a threat to traditional retail, and stores are already feeling the threat. As websites offer more facilities and better customer service, they may well become the preferred choice of buying for the modern, time-pressed shopper. However, e-commerce sites have still to address many issues, including high cost of delivery of products and after sales service. Many sites have found that these issues make the whole business unviable, and have been forced to shut shop.

How businesses change remains to be seen. One possibility is that future stores will not carry inventories of products. They may become places where consumers experience products using 3D technology and once they decide to buy, the stores can simply 'print' out the product for them using 3D printing technology.

Another possibility is that as more people buy online using showrooming (see closing case), large store formats may become unviable and small stores may well see a comeback. The real challenge today is how companies adapt to the behaviour of consumers in the digital age, which has already dawned upon us.

SUMMARY

The penetration of the Internet and mobile technologies are changing consumer behaviour like never before. As customers interact with brands and also buy online, businesses try to respond to new purchase patterns. Online business has seen an expansion in India as well, where small towns and rural areas are latching on to online buying along with the urban buyer. Even groceries and vegetables, which were earlier in the offline domain, are bought online. While the lion's share of online buying in India is that of travel bookings, fashion and jewellery purchases also show an exponential increase.

There are several reasons why consumers are taking to e-commerce. It offers complete information, ease and convenience to the modern customer. At the same time, lack of security and trust hinders some people from making online purchases. Online companies are trying to get over inhibitions against online purchases. But there is no denying that consumer behaviour is changing as smart devices spread and access to the Internet increases.

Instead of the traditional model of consumer behaviour using the funnel metaphor, consumers now go through decision journeys, interacting with brands in a myriad of ways. There are four stages in consumer decision journey: consider, evaluate, buy, and enjoy, advocate and bond. Companies have to manage the digital touchpoints that can be used to address consumer issues on the path to purchase.

A framework of online consumer behaviour shows that five variables, consumer characteristics, environmental influences, product/service characteristics, medium characteristics and online merchants and intermediaries characteristics on three key elements of consumers' intention, adoption and continuance in online purchase. Companies have to manage the numerous touchpoints created by these interactions at every stage.

Digital value is created by a combination of time, no-space and no-matter offered by virtual spaces. Consumer interactions are thus changing marketing strategy as each of the 7Ps of service marketing go through a transformation.

Web Equity, or the consumer awareness and perception about an online company driving loyalty and repeat purchases, is how companies create positive awareness and image about their websites. To this end, companies use social media and social behaviour of consumers to build web equity. The challenge is to focus on the right shopper, engage shoppers with the right message and connect with shoppers using the right medium.

This is possible only through integration of marketing and communication channels. Social media helps in this integration and companies are trying to dovetail social media with e-commerce. It also helps in managing customer relationships and building online loyalty. Online communities are also created for this purpose.

Consumer behaviour is also studied through data mining and analytics. Gradually, as more and more companies use these new technologies, businesses themselves will be transformed. While 3D printing enables mass customization, a host of technologies will change the very ways in which we do business and deliver customer value.

KEY TERMS

Consumer decision journey A theory that states that consumer decision- making process is a circular journey with four stages of consumer behaviour, namely consider, evaluate, buy and enjoy, and advocate and bond

Data analytics Process of inspecting, cleaning, transforming, and modelling data with the purpose of discovering patterns and drawing conclusions for optimal decision making

Data mining Data mining refers to the extraction of hidden predictive information from large databases

Deal-tailing Discount sites, or retailers whose USP is discounts and offers

E-tailing Selling of retail goods over the Internet

Internet value proposition (IVP) The unique benefits, also called online value proposition (OVP) that an online company offers to the consumer as a means of obtaining competitive advantage

Mass customization The use of flexible computer-aided manufacturing systems to produce custom output, combining the low unit costs of mass production processes with the flexibility of individual customization

Movement marketing A marketing model, also called cultural movement marketing that starts with an idea in culture, and then ties that back to the brand, creating communities and fan-based organizations that are supportive of the movement

One-to-one marketing The ability to make a unique message or product offering for each individual customer. Also called personalized marketing or relationship marketing

Showrooming A practice when shoppers go to brick-and-mortar stores to check out products only to buy them later online after surfing for the best deal

Smartphonatics Consumers who change their shopping, banking and payment behaviour after switching to a smartphone are called smartphonatics

Social media The interaction of people online through which they create, share and exchange contents among themselves in virtual communities and net-works

Touchpoints Interaction points between the customer and the brand

Tribe-building Collecting a unique group of fans, friends, and followers who resonate with the company's worldview, or creating a community of people who want to hear from it

Web equity Consumer awareness and perception about an online company's website, which builds loyalty of customers towards the company

EXERCISES

Concept-review Questions

1. How is online consumer behaviour different from consumer behaviour in the real world shopping? Why is it important to study online consumer behaviour?
2. Discuss the behaviour of Indian consumers for online buying. How has it impacted growth of online shopping in India?
3. Explain five reasons why online buying is picking up. Further, discuss the reason why people are still inhibited about online purchases.
4. How has changing media consumption changed buying habits? How can companies adapt to these changing consumer behaviour patterns?
5. Explain the consumer decision journey. What is its importance?
6. Describe the framework for online consumer behaviour. How are elements of consumers' intention, adoption and continuance affected in each stage?
7. What are the building blocks of web experience? How do companies add tangibility to what is essentially a virtual experience?
8. In what ways does online consumer behaviour affect marketing strategy of companies? What will companies have to do to cater to changing behaviour?
9. What is web equity? What are the factors that influence web equity?
10. What is data mining and data analytics? How can they help in the study of consumer behaviour?

Critical Thinking Questions

1. In what ways will marketing change as e-commerce introduces tectonic changes in consumer behaviour? Do you think that traditional marketing will become extinct or will it evolve? How do companies implement movement marketing?
2. Analyse the consumer touchpoints for an online customer and answer the following questions. How do companies influence each touchpoint? Is value added at each interaction? Do you think that integration of various channels add digital value?
3. How does website design influence consumer behaviour and web equity? Describe the various medium characteristics and how they affect consumers in their buying decisions.
4. Critically examine the framework for online consumer behaviour given in this chapter. Do you think it adequately describes online consumer behaviour? In what ways can the framework be modified, in view of your own experience of online purchases? Can you develop a new model for online consumer behaviour?

Projects and Assignments

1. Companies use the infinite possibilities created by time, no-space and no-matter for digital value creation. Study the websites of an online company, a brick-and-mortar store and a fashion company to explain how value is created digitally by them.
2. Despite acquiring many fans, many companies do not succeed on social platforms. Study the social media use by P&G, Coca Cola, Starbucks, and HUL to find out whether these companies succeed or not. Discover how people use social platforms and suggest what should be the response of companies.
3. Take a look at online communities created by brands, like the one created by Harley Davidson. Make a project report of at least three brand communities. High-light how consumers are using these communities and also assess their importance to the brand.
4. Study the online buying behaviour of members of your class. Find out what they have been buying and how they have gone about in their purchase process. Discover the touchpoints between the company and the consumers.

REFERENCES

Al-hawari, Mohammad Ahmad and Samar Mouakket, (2012), 'Do offline factors trigger customers' appetite for online continual usage?: A study of online reservation in the airline industry', *Asia Pacific Journal of Marketing and Logistics*, Vol. 24 Issue 4 pp. 640–657.

Aljukhadar, Muhammad and Sylvain Senecal (2011), 'Segmenting the online consumer market', *Marketing Intelligence & Planning*, Vol. 29 Issue 4 pp. 421–435.

Barton, Dominic and David Court (2012), 'Making advanced analytics work for you', *Harvard Business Review*, October, 2012, pp. 79–83.

Berman, Saul J. (2012), 'Digital transformation: opportunities to create new business models', *Strategy & Leadership*, Vol. 40 Issue 2 pp. 18–24.

Chaffey, Dave (2003), *E-marketing* in Michael J. Baker (Ed.) *The Marketing Book*, 5/e, Butterworth-Heineman, Oxford, pp. 637–668.

Cheung, Christy M. K., Lei Zhu, Timothy Kwong, Gloria W.W. Chan and MoezLimayem (2003), 'Online consumer behavior: A review and agenda for future research', 18th Bled eCommerce Conference, Bled, Slovenia, June 9–11, 2003.

Christodoulides, George and Leslie de Chernatony, (2004), 'Dimensionalising on- and offline brands' composite equity', *Journal of Product & Brand Management*, Vol. 13 No. 3 pp. 168–189.

Constantinides, Efthymios (2004), 'Influencing the online consumer's behavior: the Web experience', *Internet Research*, Vol. 14 Issue 2 pp. 111–126.

Dailey, L. (2004) 'Navigational web atmospherics: Explaining the influence of restrictive navigation cues', *Journal of Business Research*, Vol. 57 No. 7, pp. 795–803.

Davenport Thomas H. (2006), 'Competing on Analytics', *Harvard Business Review*, January, 2006.

Davenport, Thomas H (2013), 'Analytics 3.0', *Harvard Business Review*, December, 2013.

Demangeot, Catherine and Amanda J. Broderick, (2007), 'Conceptualising consumer behaviour in online shopping environments', *International Journal of Retail & Distribution Management*, Vol. 35 Issue 11, pp. 878–894.

Edelman, David C. (2010), 'Branding in the Digital Age', *Harvard Business Review*, December, 2010.

Fournier, Susan and Lara Lee (2009), 'Getting Brand Communities Right', *Harvard Business Review,* April, 2009, pp. 105–111.

Gehrt, Kenneth C., Mahesh N. Rajan, G. Shainesh, David Czerwinski and Matthew O'Brien, (2012), 'Emergence of online shopping in India: shopping orientation segments', *International Journal of Retail & Distribution Management*, Vol. 40 Issue 10 pp. 742–758.

Giamanco, Barbara and Kent Gregoire (2012), 'Tweet me, friend me, make me buy', *Harvard Business Review*, July–August, 2012.

Godin, Seth (2008), *Tribes*, Portfolio Books, New York.

Goetzinger, Lynn and Jung Kun Park, Richard Widdows, (2006), 'E-customers' third party complaining and complimenting behavior', *International Journal of Service Industry Management*, Vol. 18 Issue 2 pp. 193–206.

Gulati, Ranjay and Jason Garino (2000), 'Get the right mix of bricks and clicks', *Harvard Business Review*, May–June, 2000.

Hoffman, D.L. and T.P. Novak, 'How to acquire customers on the web', *Harvard Business Review*, Vol. 78, Issue no. 3, May–June 2000.

Hunter, Rory and Bhasker Mukerji (2011), 'The role of atmospherics in influencing consumer behaviour in the online environment', *International Journal of Business and Social Science,* Vol. 2 No. 9, Special issue May 2011.

'IAMAI Releases Internet economy watch report; Branded apparels register 100% Y-o-Y growth with over 5 million visits', May 30, 2012, http://www.iamwire.com/2012/05/iamai-releases-internet-economy-watch-report-branded-apparels-register-100-y-o-y-growth-with-over-5-million-visits/, last accessed on 27 September 2012.

Kanter, Rosabeth Moss (2001), 'The ten deadly mistakes of wanna-dots', *Harvard Business Review*, January 2001, pp. 91–100.

Kim, Jihyun and Jihye Park, (2005), 'A consumer shopping channel extension model: attitude shift toward the online store', *Journal of Fashion Marketing and Management*, Vol. 9, Issue 1, pp. 106–121.

Korgaonkar, P. and Wolin, L. (1999), 'A multivariate analysis of web usage', *Journal of Advertising Research*, Vol. 38 No. 1, pp. 7–21.

Kotler, P (2002), *Marketing Management*, 13/e. Prentice Hall, New Jersey, pp. 325.

Kumar, Dinesh (2012), *Marketing Channels*, Oxford University Press, New Delhi, pp. 312–313.

Lee, P.M. (2002), 'Behavioral model of online purchasers in e-commerce environment', *Electronic Commerce Research*, Vol. 2, pp. 75–85.

Li, Charlene and Josh Bernoff (2009), *Groundswell*, Harvard Business Press, Boston.

Loveman, Gary (2011), 'Diamonds in the Data Mine, in Increasing Customer Value', Harvard Business Press, Boston, pp. 151–166.

Menezes, Beryl (2012), 'Rural Internet usage grows faster than urban', *DNA India*, 31 August, 2012.

Negra, Anissa and Mohamed Nabil Mzoughi, (2012), 'How wise are online procrastinators? A scale development', *Internet Research*, Vol. 22, Issue 4, pp. 426–442.

OECD (2010), The economic and social role of Internet intermediaries, OECD Paris, http://www.oecd.org/sti/interneteconomy/44949023.pdf, last accessed on 13 November, 2012.

Page, Christine and Elzbieta Lepkowska-White, (2002), 'Web equity: A framework for building consumer value in online companies', *Journal of Consumer Marketing*, Vol. 19, No. 3, pp. 231–248.

Park, Chung-Hoon and Young-Gul Kim, (2003), 'Identifying key factors affecting consumer purchase behavior in an online shopping context', *International Journal of Retail & Distribution Management*, Vol. 31, Issue 1, pp. 17–29.

Peppers, Don, Martha Rogers, and Bob Dorf (1999), 'Is Your Company Ready for One-to-one Marketing', *Harvard Business Review*, January-February, 1999, pp. 151–170.

Pew Internet and American Life Project Survey (2005), 'How women and men use the Internet', http://www.pewinternet.org/~/media/Files/Reports/2005/PIP_Women_and_Men_online.pdf.pdf, last accessed on 14 October, 2012.

Pine B. Joseph and Kim C. Korn (2011), *Infinite Possibility: Creating Customer Value on the Digital Frontier*, 1st edn, Berrett-Koehler Publishers, Inc., San Fransisco, California.

Piskorski, Mikołaj Jan (2011), 'Social strategies that work', *Harvard Business Review*, November, 2011.

Porter, Michael (2001), 'Strategy and the Internet', *Harvard Business Review*, March 2001, pp. 63–78.

PTI report (2012), 'Credit card usage 30 times of debit card payments in a year', *Business Standard*, 6 September, 2012

Ravichandran, R. (2009), 'Online shopping is recession proof in India', *Financial Express*, May 21, 2009, www.financialexpress.com/news/online-shopping-is-recessionproof-in-india/463054/, last accessed on 11 October 2012.

Reichheld Frederick F. and Phil Schefter (2000), 'E-Loyalty: Your secret weapon on the web', *Harvard Business Review*, July-August, 2000.

Sangameshwaran, Prasad (2010), 'Social media: Choosing for Mr right', *Businessworld*, 19 July 2010.

Saraswathy, M (2011), 'Rising online sales make e-commerce sites confident', *Business Standard*, 9 December, 2011.

Shah, Sahil, 'Ecommerce in India—Statistics, trends & insights', 2 May 2011. Source: http://www.imediaconnection.in/article/91/Digital/Internet/ecommerce-in-india-statistics-trends-and-insights.html, accessed 27 September 2012.

Singh, Rajiv (2012), 'Online retailers like Zovi, Myntra offer simulating 'Touch & Feel' comfort to consumers', *The Economic Times*, 14 November, 2012.

Sorce, Patricia Victor Perotti, and Stanley Widrick, (2005), 'Attitude and age differences in online buying''', *International Journal of Retail & Distribution Man-agement*, Vol. 33 Issue 2 pp. 122–132.

Strauss, Judy and Raymond Frost (2012), *E-Marketing*, 6/e, PHI Learning Pvt Ltd, New Delhi, pp. 153–155.

The Economist (2011), 'Print me a Stradivarius', 10 February, 2011.

The Economist (2012), 'Caveat emptor.com', 30 June 2012.

The Nielsen Company (2012), 'How digital influences how we shop around the world', August 2012, http://es.nielsen.com/site/documents/NielsenGlobalDigitalShoppingReportAugust2012.pdf, accessed 20 November, 2012.

Time (2014), 'Nowhere to hide', March 31, 2014.

White, Gregory K. and Barbara J. Manning, (1998), 'Commercial WWW site appeal: how does it affect online food and drink consumers' purchasing behavior?', *Internet Research*, Vol. 8, Issue 1, pp. 32–38.

Wigder, Zia Daniell and Manish Bahl (2011), 'Trends in India's eCommerce market: How online retail in India is evolving differently from other major markets', Forrester Research, Cambridge, USA, http://www.assocham.org/arb/general/Forrester_Trends_In_Indias_eCommerc.pdf, accessed 20 November 2012.

CASE STUDY
How Online Behaviour Changes Everything

The Internet has become an integral part of the lives of people. As people use their mobile devices and computers to interact among themselves and with companies, the behaviour is impacting consumer behaviour in numerous ways. This case study describes two such ways that e-commerce is changing how people look for and buy products, causing real world retailers to change strategy. Two trends are described in this case—showrooming and smartphonatics.

The first trend is the spread of smartphones has changed how people interact and also e-commerce. Consumers who change their shopping, banking, and payment behaviour after switching to a smartphone are dubbed as the "smartphonatics."

The second is showrooming. *The Economic Times* reported a trend that became visible in India during the festive season in 2012. It was noticed that consumers came in stores and spotted deals offered, but then went home and ordered them online. Consumers walked into stores, looked at the gadgets, requested for a demonstration, sought the best price and then walked out. Are retail stores becoming a victim of *showrooming*: where shoppers go to brick-and-mortar stores to check out products only to buy them later online after surfing for the best deal? How real is the threat? Are we looking at a huge change in consumer buying behaviour that may well change the landscape of tomorrow?

Smartphonatics

Smartphones not only help people keep in touch but also influence how people shop and manage their money. Smartphones help people in conducting their banking and mobile payment transactions. Such uses are driving widespread change in the banking and retailing industries. The percentage of smartphonatics in the U.S. is 20 per cent, which lags countries like India, where 60 per cent of phone users can be put in that category.

Smartphonatics refers to consumers who aggressively change the way they shop based on ownership of a smartphone. They use their devices to check out prices and order even as they are on the move. For example, smartphones are used to photograph objects or bar codes and the consumer can have all information about the product, its availability, prices and order deliveries.

FIG. 16.9 College students exhibit high levels of smartphone addiction, reflecting change in the experience of human interaction.

Smartphones are seen as essentials by users and many people are addicted to them. See Fig. 16.9. Some 73 per cent people admit to feeling panicky if they misplace their phone. Many users develop compulsive behaviour in which they feel the urge to check up their phones every few minutes. Such behaviour is easily seen in India, where people have no hesitation in using their phones in public places and even while they are driving, without any consideration for others. In fact, about 25 per cent mobile phone users admit to checking their phones while driving. Smartphones are changing human behaviour in many ways. Kadlec (2012) writes that they are changing the way people live and interact with others:

- Nearly 60% of smartphone owners don't go an hour without checking their phones.
- Some 54% check their phones while in bed—before they go to sleep, after they wake up or in the middle of the night. And 1 in 5 checks immediately after sex.
- Nearly 40% check their phones while on the toilet.
- Some 30% check their phones during a meal with others, and 9% check their phones during religious services.

Retailers realize that they have to change with the changing aspects of human behaviour. They are trying to modify themselves due to the aforementioned compulsive behaviour. In many cases, retailers bring their stores closer to the consumer by creating remote store-fronts at subway stations or any other location that people frequent. People use these store fronts to scan QR codes with their smartphones and have the products delivered to their homes, sometimes on the same day. Smartphones are also going to play an increasing role in helping make consumers aware of discounts or special deals and connecting them with additional product information that will help them make purchase decisions.

Showrooming

The practice of consumers who check out merchandise in a physical store and then buy it at a cheaper price online is called showrooming. This is a real a threat to traditional retailers. Some shoppers use a smartphone to check online prices even when they are inside the store and physically check out products. Showrooming is described as an Achilles' heel for the electronics retailers. Retailers wonder how can such habits be discouraged and sales steered back to retail shops?

Showrooming has set the alarm bells ringing: the fear is that if offline stores do not upgrade or change strategy, they would push consumers online. Online retailers selling gadgets, such as Flipkart, Indiatimes, Indiaplaza and a host of others, are fast weaning away customers from physical stores. It is feared that this change has the potential to wreck physical stores.

Some brick-and-mortar stores are responding to the threat in a variety of ways. Some have shut down loss-making stores, while others try to serve customers by improving customer service, integrating offline and digital formats and imparting technical training to staff.

Reliance Digital offers potential shoppers of TVs a visit by trained staff to their home to have a look at the room in which they plan to install the TV. A staff member then accordingly suggests best suitable TV models. The idea is that skilled and knowledgeable in-store sales associates make for superior customer service experiences.

Other retailers such as Next Retail and Digiworld try to capitalize on the touch-and-feel factor. Since in India, shopping for expensive gadgets is a family affair, they try to improve customer experience and get families into stores. Videocon is focusing on enhancing in-store ambience with a bright and rich display of products, imparting technical training to its staff and integrating the digital and offline worlds. The MobileStore also works on a similar strategy and has launched its MobileStore Lounges, in which customers interact with trained sales staff-or 'tech buddies', who are armed with tablets to help customers. Spice Hotspot integrated its online and offline stores and started offering consumers the option to shop online and collect from any of its offline stores.

On the other hand are online companies like Indiatimes which offer enhanced online experience because the touch and feel confuses people more when buying gadgets, since the salesmen sometimes give incorrect information or are too pushy. Online companies, by contrast, give complete information and consumers are free of pushy salesmen while they make up their minds.

While showrooming is catching up in India, in other countries it is a major trend. Retailers are now introducing apps, mobile-shopping tools, and online features that mimic showrooming. Wal-Mart has added its 'In-store mode' to its iPhone app. Consumers who launch the app in a Wal-Mart store can scan bar codes for price checks, customer reviews, and information about the product. The app also helps consumers in accessing the latest ads, discounts, and QR codes, which help lower the prices listed in the store.

Similarly, Target shoppers can use the 'Shopkick' app, through which consumers earn points, or 'kicks', by scanning merchandise in the store.

The kicks can be redeemed for things like gift cards and iTunes downloads. Target hopes that people who scan the goods will be more likely to buy those goods in the store.

Another retail chain, Best Buy allows customers to shop online in stores even if they do not have mobile devices. Salespeople equipped with tablets and other devices help shoppers find more detail on products and look up reviews while in the Best Buy store. The chain hopes to build store loyalty through this.

The grocery chain Safeway introduced the 'Just 4 U' digital savings program at its stores, which sends personalized deals to shoppers when they're in the store. Such deals make customers buy from the store immediately rather than waiting to compare prices elsewhere.

Questions for discussion

1. How can companies use the behaviour described in the case study smartphonatics and showrooming to serve modern, connected consumers?
2. In what other ways is consumer behaviour changing because of smartphones and mobile devices? What can companies or retailers do integrate their real and virtual marketing strategies?
3. Refer to the opening case in which it was mentioned that marketing is dead. What is your opinion after reading the above case on this? Do you think that real world companies or retailers can survive online buying behaviour?
4. Take a look at physical retailers and assess how they are responding to e-commerce and enhancing their offerings.

Sources:

Kadlec, Dan (2012), 'How smart phones are changing the way we bank, drive, have sex and go to the bathroom', *Time*, June 22, 2012, http://business.time.com/2012/06/22/how-smart-phones-are-changing-the-way-we-bank-and-drive/#ixzz2CXJ1HOQt, last accessed 19 November 2012.

Singh, Rajiv (2012), 'Consumers spot deals in stores, close them online', *The Economic Times*, 30 November 2012.

Tuttle, Brad (2012), 'The impact of smart phones on people and retail stores', June 27, 2012, http://business.time.com/2012/06/27/why-everyone-should-be-shopping-online-while-in-actual-stores/#ixzz2CXIaLebS, last accessed 19 November 2012.

CHAPTER SEVENTEEN

Consumer Engagement and Equity

LEARNING OBJECTIVES

Consumer behaviour is changing due to omni-channel retail. This chapter describes the changes taking place across markets and how companies must reorient themselves to customer experience and engagement for greater equity.

After studying this chapter, the reader will be able to

- analyse the huge changes taking place in consumer behaviour due to omni-channel experience
- learn about the drivers of customer equity and calculate brand equity
- analyse some important trends taking place in the world of marketing and how they impact consumer behaviour
- understand the importance of consumer engagement and build consumer experience across channels

CASE STUDY
Future of Shopping

At eight in the morning, Neha catches the subway to go to her office. As she hurries to the station, she remembers the time she had to stand in the queue to buy the train ticket. Today in 2020, she has a bar code on her watch which she touches to a sensor at the turnstile. The gate whirs open. An app tells her that the balance on her subway card is reducing, and she has to replenish it by debiting her bank account. Neha presses yes, and instantaneously gets a message from her bank that the amount has been credited to her subway card. She smiles as she recalls her father talk about the past when he had to remember a variety of passwords for different sites. Now, she logs on to bank automated teller machines (ATMs) and websites immediately by merely pressing her fingerprint. Passwords have become history. Figure 17.1 shows an automated subway station in Japan.

She has several more things on her mind. Groceries have to be purchased in the evening; she needs a new dress for a party during the weekend. She is reminded of the upcoming birthday of a friend.

She settles down in her seat on the subway and turns to her smartphone to check up on her friends on a social site, and simultaneously opens a site on which she buys groceries. She looks at the virtual shopping list that the site has recommended for

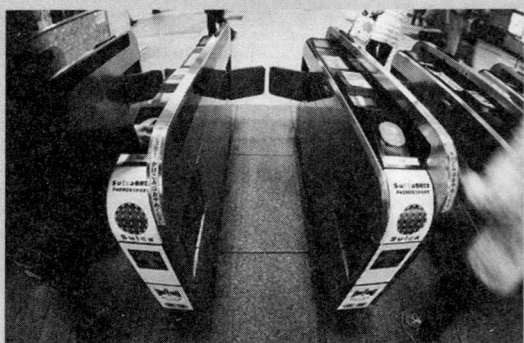

FIG. 17.1 Subway stations are automated for handling large crowds. Watch-scanning facility will be added soon

Source: Photos by InoAoi, Japan, reprinted with permission

her, based on her previous purchase patterns. She makes a few modifications, adding and deleting a few items, and places her order. She wants them to be delivered in the evening when she has reached home.

When she gets off the train, she grabs a cup of coffee from a kiosk. Near the kiosk is a screen that connects with her through an app on her phone and immediately personalizes the display for her, showing her dresses suited for her. One of them catches her eye and she saves its bar code on her phone.

There is also a giant display in the corridor like a shop's window showing various items, but there is no shop. The display changes every few minutes, showing different items that catches the interest of several shoppers. Passers-by slow down and look at the displays, often taking pictures of anything that appeals to them. Quick response (QR) codes are embedded in each display that help people to guide them to the website offering those products through their devices. Some people merely turn their eyes towards the display and tap their spectacles to save the displays which they can later access on their laptops. A dress worn by a model catches Neha's attention and she captures it by pressing a button on her watch.

On reaching office, she has a busy morning. When she is a little free, she checks out some dresses on the Internet on her laptop, using the bar codes that she has earlier saved through the watch. The codes are automatically available on all her devices, and she tries them on her virtual avatar that she has created earlier. However, she is still not sure. She sends the picture of her avatar to her friends and immediately gets their feedback. One of them suggests it should be a little shorter; another suggests a different colour. She connects to the store and starts chatting with an expert who sends her some more suggestions. While chatting, she also checks out another dress offered by a different supplier. She checks the online reputation of the retailer, and finding a number of negative comments, drops the idea of changing her supplier.

After office, she goes to the store to try out her dress. The moment she walks in, she gets a message on her phone welcoming her with a coupon code that offers 15 per cent discount. She is greeted by name by the store manager who mentions the discount to her. This makes her happy as she calculates that she would be saving a good amount that day.

As she is trying out her dress, her best friend walks in the store. 'My phone told me you were nearby in this store, so I came,' she says. This was a treat for Neha, as she trusts her friend. They discuss several dresses together, selecting one, and asking the store to make some shorter. The store manager pulls his tablet and shows accessories to go with the dress. The girls choose an earring and a belt as well. The store manager promises to deliver the dress along with the chosen accessories to her home the next day.

The two friends then have coffee together and bid goodbye to each other. Neha catches her train, noting that the displays at the station have turned to restaurants in the area. Some people are touching interactive screens to make reservations. There is also a computer terminal owned by Amazon on which people were making their orders. Near the terminal, there were some lockers that customers were accessing through codes they received from the company. Neha thought that they were very convenient because she knew that people who did not want to get disturbed at home had the goods delivered to the locker, conveniently located at the subway station. Some customers were placing orders on the terminal and they would find the products in the locker the next day.

She reaches home, after which the groceries that she had ordered are delivered. The chores were accomplished without much effort, she watches television, has dinner that has been delivered from a restaurant, and then falls asleep.

Little does she know that, even as she sleeps, companies are analysing the data that she has left on various websites throughout the day. They could also analyse which media Neha likes to use, and could modify their strategies easing the customer in the following ways:

- Shop for products through a subway display and having them delivered at a convenient time at home or placed in a locker.
- Use digital store exteriors at shopping malls
- Check prices and alternatives through tablets that salespersons carry, by which they can track every customer's history and preferences
- 'Magic mirrors' in stores that show customers how something will look on them
- Digital mannequins that change according to trends, weather, or customers
- Displays provide product information and choice, and are linked to inventories held anywhere
- Digital signage to guide customers and call salespeople when needed
- Computers at stores with artificial intelligence and natural language abilities that outperform sales associates
- Customers scan displays with their phones and receive ideas on how to combine it with other items
- Customers see an item, take a picture of it, and search for the lowest price
- Engaging consumers to vote on the products
- Real-time offers to customers during the shopping process for relevant items
- Creating small stores that serve as delivery hubs

While reading this chapter, try to answer the following questions:

1. How is consumer behaviour changing in the modern era? What are the major changes taking place?
2. How are companies offering a great experience and engaging their customers?
3. What is the ideal relationship that companies can build with their customers across touchpoints?
4. What is customer lifetime value and customer equity? How are these concepts used in marketing?

Sources:

Kantar Retail, 'The future shoppper', http://www.kantar-retail.com/The_Future_Shopper.html, last accessed on 20 May 2014.

Rigby, Darrell, 'The future of shopping', *Harvard Business Review*, December 2011.

INTRODUCTION

It is generally believed that the purpose of all marketing is to sell goods, and the purpose of studying consumer behaviour is to make people buy more. However, as Theodore Levitt had explained in his classic article, the real job of disciplines of marketing and consumer behaviour begins after sale. In his book, *After the Sale is Over* (1983), he writes, 'The sale merely consummates the courtship, at which point the marriage begins. The quality of marriage determines whether there will be continued or expanded business, or troubles and divorce.'

Levitt made some very important observations that underline all learning of marketing and consumer behaviour:

- The relationship between a seller and buyer seldom ends when a sale is made, but intensifies after the sale.
- The purchase decision is not a decision to buy an item (to have a casual affair) but a decision to enter a bonded relationship (to get married).
- Instead of trying to get buyers for what the seller has, the seller must try to have what the consumers want.

These may sound strange to many students and practitioners of marketing who are trained to sell aggressively in order to meet their targets. Companies instruct their managers to 'sell, or else,' merrily discarding customers the moment the sale is made, pushing them to automated voice response systems should they wish to contact the company later on. The salesman who promised product performance and made the sale vanishes, and the customer is left to deal with service centres that have their own targets and are least bothered about building relationships or fulfilling customer needs. It is hardly surprising that companies have to perpetually incur heavy advertising and marketing spends to recruit new customers all the time, simply because those recruited earlier have abandoned them. This phenomenon can hardly sustain any business model.

This chapter addresses a crucial need of today's organizations—the need to retain their customers and become customer-centric. This is an art that lies beyond decision-making. As consumers become spoilt for choice and as their level of interaction increases, this art will determine which companies prosper and which companies continue struggling for business.

MARKETING INSIGHT
Gift-giving Behaviour

Gift-giving is an important social norm in most societies (Fig. 17.2). It is a way of cementing relationships, to express a feeling of empathy with friends, family, co-workers, and others. Gifts are commonly given during birthdays. Different cultures use festivals to exchange gifts, such as on Christmas, New Year's Day, Diwali, Valentine's Day, and so on. Special occasions such as weddings, graduation, and achievements also call for sharing joy by giving gifts. Some gifts are given from the heart when a person feels happy or wants to appreciate another, but others are given as a formality, as when a subordinate gives a gift to a senior. Sometimes, gifts are given as bribes—companies give expensive gifts to government officials and people from whom they expect some sort of benefit.

Whatever be the motive, gift-giving is a common behaviour. Several companies such as Archies and Hallmarks cater to the growing market for gifts.

FIG. 17.2 Gift-giving is an important social norm in most societies

Online gifting is also becoming popular, with sites such as fernsnpetals, archiesonline, pepperfry, and

(Contd)

MARKETING INSIGHT (Contd)

indiangiftsportal, offering a wide variety and quick delivery of gifts.

Another aspect of gift-giving behaviour is when people buy something for themselves. This is known as self-gifting. When people are feeling good about a personal accomplishment or on the contrary, when one feels down in the dumps, one tends to let go by buying something expensive as a personal reward. Kauppinen-Räisänen, et al. (2014) show that luxury brands are often purchased for personal reasons. Companies, therefore, have to cater to the luxury experience of shopping that becomes more important than the brand. Ward and Tran (2007) suggest that as consumers frequently combine a gifting situation with the opportunity for self-gifting, advertising could encourage, 'One for them, one for you' promotional appeals.

'Buy one, get one free' offers are on the rise and salespersons are trained to encourage shoppers to incorporate self-gifts in conjunction with interpersonal gift purchases.

How many times have you given gifts in the past year? How many of these were given sincerely and how many as a formality or a bribe?

In what ways can companies use this behaviour to enhance sales?

Sources:
Kauppinen-Räisänen, Hannele, Johanna Gummerus, Catharina von Koskull, ÅkeFinne, Anu Helkkula, Christian Kowalkowski, and Anne Rindell, 'Am I worth it? Gifting myself with luxury', *Journal of Fashion Marketing and Management*, Vol. 18, Issue 2, 2014.

Ward Cheryl B. and Thuhang Tran, 'Consumer gifting behaviors: One for you, one for me?' *Services Marketing Quarterly*, Vol. 29(2), 2007.

Evolving Consumer Behaviour

As e-commerce gets integrated into traditional commerce, consumer behaviour is changing like never before. Rigby (2011) writes that soon it will be hard even to define e-commerce, let alone measure it, as it is rapidly becoming part of commerce. We already see instances of this integration as in the following examples:

- A customer goes to a store but the product is out of stock. He immediately orders it on the company's store or an in-store terminal to have it sent to his home
- A customer likes a dress in one store, then uses her smartphone to find a lower price online, and instantly orders it for delivery or store pickup
- A customer looks for something online, selects it, and then goes to the local retailer to buy it
- A customer orders a dress for her niece online but it does not fit. She exchanges it at a physical store that the company has set up in the city

This is why digital retailing is quickly acquiring a new name—omni-channel retailing. This means that companies interact with customers through countless channels—websites, physical stores, kiosks, direct mail and catalogues, call centres, social media, mobile devices, television, networked appliances, and so on. Companies will have to integrate these disparate channels into a single and seamless omni-channel experience. The era of consumer engagement is here.

Era of Consumer Engagement

To understand how consumers interact with various channels, we have to see how they interact with the brands. Schmitt (2012) describes a model that distinguishes three levels of consumer engagement—object-centred, self-centred, and social. The model also distinguishes five brand-related processes—identifying, experiencing, integrating, signifying, and connecting with the brand.

FIG. 17.3 The challenge before companies is to engage the customers who are always connected, on the move, and engrossed in their mobile devices

Source: Photo by InoAoi, reprinted with permission

In the first stage, a consumer identifies the brand and its category, forms associations, and compares it with other brands. Following this, the consumer has a sensory and a participatory experience with the brand. The next process—integrating—refers to combining brand information into an overall brand concept and personality. Once the brand is used as an informational cue, identity signal, and cultural symbol, it is called signifying. Finally, the consumer connects with the brand, including forming an attitude towards it, becoming personally attached to it, and connecting with its brand community. These processes are not necessarily linear but may occur in different sequences.

Joachimsthaler and Aaker (1997) had also stressed on the impact of customers' personal experiences that help in creating a relationship beyond the loyalty generated by methods like advertising. They advise companies to involve the customer into the brand-building experience that results in a larger experience when using a product.

Companies now have means to involve the customer into the brand-building experience. A report published by the McKinsey CMSO Forum (2012), describes the new rules of consumer engagement (Fig. 17.3). It says that to truly engage customers, companies must do more beyond the confines of the traditional marketing organization. Customers no longer separate marketing activities from the product, or from their in-store or online experiences; they consider the experience they get no matter who they interact with. 'In the era of engagement, marketing is the company,' says the report.

Marketing faces digital disruption. Frelin (2013) writes, 'digital has resulted in profound shifts in the business of marketing, with innovation dramatically increasing the ability to target and engage with consumers.' As navigation apps are improving all the time, customers and companies have better ways to interact with each other.

Downes and Nunes (2013) recognize this move as 'big bang disruption,' which has already resulted in mature products being wiped out by new technologies and shorter product life cycles, but now 'entire product lines and whole markets are being created or destroyed overnight.' This has created a knowledge gap, because 'digital marketing is a fast-moving target,' says Frelin. Companies know that they need to adapt faster, but do not know how to.

This great change in consumer behaviour means that companies have to engage customers whenever and wherever they interact with a company—in a store, on the phone, responding to an e-mail, a blog post, or an online review. This can only happen if marketing pervades the entire organization so that there is a shift of focus around all interactions of customer touchpoints.

This kind of thinking means that traditional ways of marketing have to change. In traditional organizational structures, companies divide various consumer functions into silos. For instance, marketing is concerned with brands, whereas sales is assigned to a different department. Customer relationship management (CRM) is yet another separate silo, whereas physical consumer experience is farmed out to retailers. This system is becoming defunct. Companies have

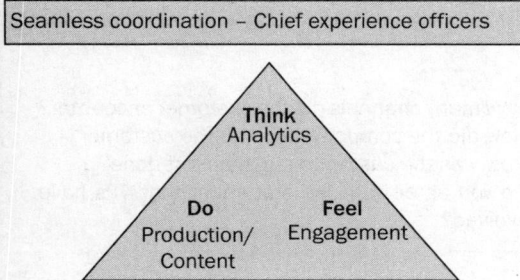

FIG. 17.4 Marketing organization of the future will integrate three consumer functions—think, feel, and do

Source: Marketing2020

to stop viewing customer engagement as a series of discrete interactions. Instead, they have to think about it from the viewpoint of customers, as a set of related interactions that emanate from customer experience.

A report, *Marketing 2020* (2013), published by Effective Brands, describes the marketing organization of the future to be highly integrated, such as hub-and-spoke structures whereby the chief marketing officer (CMO) is placed in the middle, and managers for product, advertising, public relations (PR), market-research, and promotion are connected as spokes to the centre. Functional departments of silos are broken, while the integrated departments ensure the delivery of customer experience. The CMO also functions as the 'chief experience officer', who integrates three functions—'think' (analytics), 'feel' (engagement), and 'do' (production or content Fig. 17.4). This kind of marketing organization has also led to rethinking of the 4Ps of marketing.

Rethinking the 4Ps

Ettenson, Conrado, and Knowles (2013) have modified the 4Ps of marketing, which could well serve the needs of the future. Their model shifts the emphasis from products to solutions, place to access, price to value, and promotion to education (SAVE). The focus of marketing as given by this model is summed up as follows:

From product to solution Instead of focusing on products, their features, functions, and technological superiority, companies have to focus on solutions. They have to take a customer-centric approach and see why consumers use a particular product and which problem is solved by it.

From place to access Instead of focusing on individual purchases at a location, companies need to develop an integrated omni-channel presence that consumers can access, based on the entire purchase journey of the consumer.

From price to value Instead of focusing on price as related to production and distribution costs, profits and competitor prices, companies must learn to associate benefits that consumers get relative to the price. They must think of ways to deliver value to their customers.

From promotion to education Traditionally, companies have relied on advertising, PR, and personal selling. In the new orientation, they have to provide specific information at each stage of the consumer decision journey. Instead of promoting products, companies have to focus on information and education.

Such a shift in thinking is required to enhance customer engagement across channels.

Customer Engagement

Customer engagement (CE) consists of establishing a strong and enduring bond between a brand and consumers, based on consumer interaction, shared values, experiential contents, and rewards. Vivek, Beatty, and Morgan (2012) write that CE is the intensity of an individual's participation

> **CB IN ACTION** **Purchase Journey**
>
> Follow the purchase journey of a friend while buying an item like a mobile phone. Find out how the need was identified, how the information search was done, and how the purchase decision was finally taken. Then answer the following questions:
>
> - How many channels did the customer encounter?
> - How did the company focus on the customer?
> - How was the customer engagement done?
> - Do you agree with the statement that 4Ps have evolved?

in and connection with an organization's offerings and/or organizational activities. These are initiated either by the customer or the organization. It is composed of cognitive, emotional, behavioural, and social elements. As explained earlier in this chapter, modern marketing has evolved into a new wave of customer interactions and interface. Van Doorn, et al (2010) write, 'Customer engagement behaviours go beyond transactions and may be specifically defined as a customer's behavioural manifestations that may have a brand or firm focus, beyond purchase, resulting from motivational drivers' (see Fig. 17.5).

Gambetti and Graffigna (2010) write that consumer engagement plays a key role in the new customer-centric marketing approach for the evolving individual and social dynamics of post-modern consumer behaviour. Three factors have emphasized the role of consumer engagement in building and maintaining strong customer–brand relationships:

- Customer-related factors
- Media-related factors
- Company-related factors

Customer-related factors These factors highlight the importance of consumption and its hedonistic and experiential aspects by individuals. This means that today customers satisfy composite needs through consumption, which has both cognitive and emotional dimensions. Products have a symbolic value and an ability to elicit pleasure and fun, engage with emotions and fantasies, and customers tend to identify with them.

FIG. 17.5 Malls combine the cognitive, emotional, behavioural, and social elements of the shopping experience, thereby engaging customers completely

Consumers also want to play a more active role in the consumption process. They want to co-create brand content and add value to the brands they love, express themselves creatively, socialize with other consumers, and enjoy experiences. Companies are trying to engage customers through interaction, participation, and entertainment. The consumer is now at the heart of the marketing process.

Media-related factors Changes to media are forcing companies to rethink on how they should plan their media. These are called media-related factors. Rapid advances in media technology are boosting cross-sector convergence. Fragmentation of audience makes it increasingly difficult to reach a large number of consumers using traditional media. Further, media preferences are also changing. Today, people prefer to use media on their phones rather than switch to television or read the newspaper.

Company-related factors Company-related factors relate to changes in corporate behaviour brought about by evolving consumer profiles and attitudes to consumption. As mentioned earlier, companies are forced to break functional silos and change organization structures to focus on the connected consumers. Competitive strategies centre on the company's ability to build strong and distinctive brands, combining the principles of market proximity and customer experience management.

Thus, the new marketing approach is based on anticipation of customers' needs and desires through cool-hunting. They have to co-create an experience with customers that can boost their brand attachment and loyalty, building context clues rather than performance clues. Customer satisfaction and product differentiation are gained by creating a unique and positive experience of the product and the brand.

French, LaBerge, and Magill (2012) explain that consumer behaviour is changing rapidly; they check prices at a keystroke, form impressions from every encounter, and immediately post online reviews. The biggest change that this entails is that 'all of us have become marketers—the critical moments of interaction, or touchpoints, between companies and customers are increasingly spread across different parts of the organization, so customer engagement is now everyone's responsibility.' Companies have to widen the lens to view customer-engagement needs, enabling more rapid responses, and building internal lines of communication. These steps create nimbler organizations with more pervasive marketing. The following steps have been suggested:

Customer-engagement summit While companies hold conferences for planning and financial results, a few of them undertake a similar process to discuss how to engage with the lifeblood of all companies—customers. A customer engagement summit should be held, in which all internal departments and external channel partners coordinate the activities required to reach and engage customers across the full range of touchpoints, thereby creating a customer-engagement ecosystem. In this way, all functions that are usually managed independently within silos, are given one focus. The result is a coordinated plan. For example, the customer experience in a call centre can be coordinated with physical stores and touchpoints.

Create a customer-engagement council A customer-engagement council is an ongoing forum for focusing on engagement, the purpose of which is to bring together all primary forms of engagement—marketing, communications, service, sales, product management. Customer-engagement councils play a critical role in breaking the silo mind-set that diminishes the effectiveness of customer engagement in many organizations.

Appoint a 'chief content officer' It is necessary to create a supply chain of sophisticated and interactive content for consumers, and to manage the content that consumers generate on their own. This calls for appointing a chief content officer (CCO). Many companies are adopting a journalistic approach through this position so as to recognize hot issues and shape emerging sentiment by delivering content that forges stronger emotional bond with consumers. The CCO develops and manages all aspects of creating content, and sourcing it from external or internal agents. Designing and executing a content strategy requires coordination with all business areas.

Create a 'listening centre' Social and other media interactions are often centres that start viral fires. In this environment, companies should establish listening centres that monitor what is being said about their organizations, products, and services on social media, blogs, and other online forums. Such monitoring should help to shorten response times, complement internal metrics and traditional research, and serve as a platform for testing customer reactions. Nestle's Digital Acceleration Centre, in Vevey, Switzerland is one such listening centre, which tracks consumer comments and sentiments in real time.

Rework the customer-engagement budget Companies can now communicate with customers through digital and social channels that are radically cheaper and, sometimes, more effective than traditional media communications or face-to-face sales visits. Large amount of money can be freed from traditional channels for framing a digital strategy. The efforts made by customer service centre to resolve a crisis—say, a lost credit card on a honeymoon or a major machine failure on a critical production run—may build more lifetime loyalty than years of traditional loyalty campaigns.

By adding up spends on customer engagement—in areas such as sales, service, operations, product management, and marketing, companies can identify cheaper approaches. Trade-offs are analysed across functions—for example, among investments in store renovations, revamped e-commerce sites, higher ad spending, changes in sales force coverage, or improved customer service centres. It is important to determine the elements that should be prioritized and the order in which they should be done. Such decisions should be made not just on the projected financial returns but also on how customer expectations are evolving, and where the company has distinctive capabilities that could help it win through superior customer engagement.

Enhancing Customer Experience

Omni-channel means that companies have to devise different ways of wooing customers, by identifying the unique paths and pain points for each segment, and creating tailored solutions for them. Disney, for example, is changing its stores to become entertainment hubs with interactive displays that make customers visit more often and stay longer in the store.

The omni-channel approach is used to satisfy modern customers by integrating digital and physical worlds. Digital world has unique advantages such as a limitless selection, price transparency, and ease of transactions while physical stores have advantages of touch and feel, interaction with experts, trying out products, as well as offering the social experience of shopping. All of these are integrated through the omni-channel approach.

Digital technology enhances customer experience by replacing lifeless storefront windows with vibrant interactive screens that change with the weather or time of the day. They will soon be able to recognize faces of regular customers and will instantaneously generate personal

MARKETING INSIGHT
Customer Engagements in Banks

Customer engagement is being pursued by companies in diverse fields. It is more evident in the banking industry that has the potential to engage customers, send targeted offers, and deliver services online. A study conducted by Standard Chartered Bank (2012) says that the world's wealthiest are much more likely to use the Internet, mobile applications, and other digital media communication tools to create, manage, spend, and invest their money.

Digital modes of communication are fast becoming a hygiene factor (basic expected service) in banking. Private banks that are able to utilize online and offline solutions can differentiate themselves from the competition.

Many banks in India are also utilizing the growing power of social networking sites to engage customers through them, writes Mukerjee (2013). HDFC Bank, for instance, uses its Facebook page to communicate discounts on a host of stores for customers using the bank's credit or debit card. ICICI Bank offers its online tool, 'My Money', for electronic transactions. The bank's new Facebook application, 'Pockets by ICICI Bank', allows users to log in to their accounts through Facebook and book movie tickets or transfer funds. Other banks also make similar offers on Facebook and Twitter.

Apps offered by banks and financial services agencies (see Fig. 17.6) also make it easier for customers to interact with them.

Standard Chartered Bank works with Facebook for its marketing campaigns, which helps to target and reach out to the right consumers. The bank offers discount schemes on purchases through Flipkart and Ezone on its Facebook page. Several banks have tied up with e-commerce companies and offer discounts and cash back offers on social networking sites. Social media helps consumers to make an informed choice of products and services, and banks use this platform to be within their consideration set and at every point. Banks promote various products such as education loans and youth accounts, as well as mobile banking and debit card initiatives.

Banks exploit social media networks to reach out to new and existing customers, as they realize that social media offers an invaluable opportunity

FIG. 17.6 HDFC's Mobile App

Courtesy: Superbrands 2012

to reach target audience. Social media also get consumers talk about their banks. People can communicate with the banks as it is an interactive process. Customers find that customer care numbers and emails are slow to respond, but a tweet will get them the desired response in a faster way.

Another way to engage customers is through videos that educate people about financial services. Many banks upload videos on YouTube. HDFC Bank has 'Money Talk', discussing financial matters such as change in the RBI's monetary policy and interest rates, or about GDP growth and how it impacts the common man. Citibank emphasizes concerns regarding information security and fraud.

There are several challenges while connecting with clients via social media. Banks have to ensure prompt and relevant replies.

An Accenture report, Banking 2016, says that banks will have to change their approaches. From the present model in which they optimize their branch network and contact centres with enhanced

(Contd)

MARKETING INSIGHT (Contd)

digital channels, they have to build a new model that centres around multichannel experiences, leverage social media interactions, and use the power of mobile technology.

The 'intelligent multichannel' bank One that builds on enhanced multichannel experiences to engage customers and meet their financial needs effectively with the strategic application of analytics

The 'socially engaging' bank Banks have to leverage social media interactions to increase customer intimacy. The key components of these banks are use of social media to engage customers, and react to issues; social digital marketing with the best content for individual customer profiles; social CRM, enriching customer data with social media data, and facilitate effective propositions.

The 'financial/non-financial digital ecosystem' bank Banks have to be at the centre of an ecosystem, selling financial and non-financial services, leveraging the power of mobile technology in particular.

A report by McKinsey (2012) describes four areas that help form a customer-centric company:

Vision and positioning Create an institution that customers want to bank with and employees feel proud of

Customer engagement model Design a bank that delivers exceptional customer service where customers expect it, and excites them where they do not

Development agenda Define an integrated development agenda to drive short-term gains and long-term growth

Organization, capabilities, and insights Build the insights engine, organizational capabilities, and governance needed to sustain momentum

Sources:
Accenture (2012), 'Banking', http://www.accenture.com/in-en/Pages/insight-banking-2016-next-generation-banking-summary.aspx
McKinsey and Co, 'Banking on customer centricity', http://www.mckinsey.com/insights/financial_services/navigating_the_new_era_of_asian_retail_banking
Mukherjee, Arpita, 'Socially Aware', *Business Today*, 8 December 2013
Standard Chartered Bank, 'Digital media the key to engaging the world's wealthiest', 28 December 2012 https://www.sc.com/en/news-and-media/news/global/2012-11-28-digital-media-key-to-engaging-worlds-wealthiest.html
All last accessed on May 29, 2014.

recommendations or advertisements. When the physical store is closed, customers can still scan bar codes and order products online (see Fig. 17.7).

Payments are also made seamless. Mobile money is already being used, and is being integrated into the customer's social media behaviour. For example, Mahindra Comviva has launched its mobiquity wallet, a digital wallet platform that supports near-field communication (NFC), QR codes, and bluetooth low energy (BLE), and works on multiple connected devices. It offers security and ease of use to bank customers, telecom operators, and retailers. The platform helps to develop an ecosystem, increase revenues from existing customers, and boost customer acquisitions. It also bundles location-based promotions, automated coupon redemption, and loyalty card selection during checkout, enabling single click payments. It integrates into the merchant's enterprise resource planning (ERP) and the existing mobile application or web portal, and enables companies to leverage the potential of social media and data analytics

FIG. 17.7 Customers interact with companies using multiple channels

for word-of-mouth advertising and one-on-one marketing, following the customer's path to purchase, from discovery and payments to inducements and loyalty.

A similar rethink is required about brands and branding as well, which have, over a period of time, squeezed dry and no longer appeal to consumers, as explained in the next section.

Brands Squeezed Dry

Consumer social media taken a toll on brands. Kevin Roberts, CEO of Saatchi and Saatchi, writes in his book, *Lovemarks* (2007) that brands are failing to standout in the marketplace and connect with people. 'Brands are out of juice,' he says, due to the following reasons:

Worn from overuse   Brands have been overused. As customers have an increasing number of options, people are becoming less brand loyal. Brands are, thus, becoming 'blands'. Instead of investing heavily in branding, companies should be paying personal attention to consumers.

No longer mysterious   Today's consumers are savvy; they know how brands are intended to work on them. The information age means that brands are a part of the public domain, in which hidden agendas, subliminal messages, or tricky marketing activities do not work. Brands have lost their mysterious air and now belong very much to the consumers.

Not connected with new consumers   The new customer is better informed, critical, less loyal, and harder to predict. This is the new population—multi-generational, multi-ethnic, and multinational. Companies do not understand them.

Struggle with competition   The more brands there are, the less customers remember them. Take a look, for instance, at the number of clothing brands that are present in a mall. Consumers will be hard pressed to remember more than just a few.

Taken over by formula   Companies follow the same rules of branding, and the result is a sea of clones. Roberts says that brands cannot be different by following the same formula for differentiation as everybody else. Nor do formulas deal with human emotions.

Smothered by creeping conservatism   Instead of being different and inspirational, brands have become boring and conservative, and have gone from daring to dull. Great brands are a result of more than a rational attachment, but occupy a special place in the heart of consumers. Achieving this status would make them *Lovemarks*.

Traditional marketing and branding no longer work with today's hyper-connected customer. Brands and the marketing function have to be reinvented so as to become customer-centric.

Becoming Customer-centric

The multiplicity of channels and touchpoints pose great challenges for modern organizations. How does a company ensure that every customer has a tailored communication and experience? Robinson and Brown (2012) write that in a survey of more than 140 North American companies, only three per cent were identified as 'customer-centric organizations,' while one-third were found to be 'customer-oblivious.'

Failure to deliver a high-quality customer experience can result in erosion of a company's customer base—a loss of as much as 50 per cent over a five-year period. This happens because of outdated ideas on management; most companies operate by forming departments which think of themselves as silos, unable or unwilling to share information, having independent processes. For the customer, however, such distinctions are meaningless; all touchpoints are seen as a single company: a bad experience with one department reflects poorly on the whole company.

An Accenture report (2012), 'How to make your company think like a customer,' says that consumers compare their experiences with a company not only with its competitors but to their experiences with companies in general. Such customers expect attention and instant gratification. The traditional shopper has been joined by the digitally oriented and multichannel customer; as a result, operating models must accommodate both types. A growing base of digital customers tends to be more open with data. For them, online and offline experiences mean the same thing and they look for products that combine both aspects.

Nike followed exactly the same approach with its Nike + iPod Sport Kit, partnering with Apple to change its running shoes. The company modified its shoes to include a sensor that sends workout data wirelessly to an iPod. The sensor tracks distance, time, pace, and calories burned. Nike's online portal allows consumers to compare with their best performances, and also to compare and compete with others. Companies today must reinvent themselves as markets evolve and get over the obstacles for integrating shopper experiences, described as follows:

Make a customer experience blueprint The blueprint helps to make objectives clear to employees and helps them navigate the experience path in a step-by-step manner. Achieving customer-centricity requires rethinking the way business is done, by following a holistic approach that encompasses everything from analytics and insights to strategy and customer experience. The operating model design, execution, and governance have to be integrated.

Respond to negative feedback Social media sites and online reviews accelerate word-of-mouth publicity. Companies need to have a strategy to address negative feedback hitting the Web in real time.

Integrate the back office The trend of outsourcing creates discrete processes and separates teams to deal with one or a few functions of the purchase process, breaking up the customer experience. The silos thus created handle their own operations efficiently, but prevent companies from coordinating customer experiences. Few companies took pains to understand what happens when a customer moves from one interaction to another. For instance, the journey from purchase to after-sales service departments is often littered with customer dissatisfaction, but some of the best companies followed this process. However, it is necessary to connect the customer-facing and non-customer-facing functions if satisfaction and loyalty have to be achieved. Nowadays, an increasing number of companies are getting rid of the back-office mentality. They are connecting internal data and analytics to enable contact points to drive interactions based on real-time customer insight. A customer-centric operating model requires collaborative planning and integration across functions and units.

Gather customer reactions Since a poor customer experience with one channel is often communicated through another, the ability to gather and organize customer reactions will enhance customer experience. For example, in hotels, reservations are made online or by phone, but the physical experience is delivered by different employees. Customer reactions from all touchpoints must be gathered because a bad experience at one point will turn the customer away, even if the experience at other points is satisfactory. Hence, not only must functions be linked, but the shortcomings in each area must be gathered and removed.

Conduct a customer experience audit The customer experience audit is done to assess the effectiveness of customer-facing and internal capabilities to deliver the intended customer experience. During such an audit, companies follow customer's interactions from his/her perspective. This helps managers understand what happens at the points of contact and identify awkward transitions. For example, the customer experience audit studies what happens when the customer moves from online browsing to purchase and then delivery to service, shifting between online and physical interactions. It determines whether the right information is imparted at all those points. The customer experience audit helps to get insights to move from vision to execution, and to integrate all processes and functions to become customer-centric.

Analytics for a 360-degree view Analytics are used to get a 360-degree view of customer interactions, leading to a customer-centric organization. Predictive modelling can help anticipate a customer's needs. This information is then used to direct messages or offers. Analytics help distinguish a company from its competition.

Customer centricity leads to higher customer engagement. It is a relatively new way of looking at the non-transactional side of customer relationships. People are happy to engage with companies by offering suggestions and spreading positive word-of-mouth publicity. Companies are using a combination of CRM activities to engage customers.

CUSTOMER ENGAGEMENT VALUE

Companies are discovering the importance of customer engagement. A study by Villaneuva, Yoo, and Hanssens (2008) of customers of an Internet firm during a 70-week observation period reveals that marketing-induced customers add more short-term value, in contrast to word-of-mouth customers who added nearly twice as much long-term value to the firm. Garnefeld, Helm, and Eggert (2011) found a strong positive relationship between word of mouth and loyalty.

Kumar, et al. (2010) have given the concept of customer engagement value (CEV), and describe four key areas. The following concepts are explained later in the chapter:

- Customer lifetime value
- Customer referral value (CRV)
- Customers' influencer value (how customers' influence other customers that increases acquisition, retention, and share-of-wallet through word of mouth of existing customers as well as prospects)—CIV
- Customer knowledge value (the value added to the firm by feedback from the customer)—CKV

Brodie, et al. (2011) combine these concepts by examining it from the viewpoints of the marketing, sociological, political, psychological, and organizational behaviour. They write that companies must attempt to manage and measure customer assets through a combination of word of mouth, share-of-wallet, and customer engagement strategies.

Brand Engagement

Gambetti, Graffigna, and Biraghi (2012) write that customer brand engagement combines the elements of attention, dialogue, interaction, emotions, sensorial pleasure, and immediate activation. Going beyond traditional cognitive, emotional, and conative dimensions, customer brand engagement is based on experiential and social dimensions. The experiential dimension encompasses multisensory elements of the brand encounter that dominates the relationship between the brand and the consumer.

The social dimension comprises interaction and attempts of the brand aimed at taking customers onboard, and letting them participate in brand building. The brand's effort to frame a social creation platform for its consumers builds avenues for brand enacting. *Brand enacting* means that consumers help to put the brand into action, participating in its world. When the brand is enacted, it gets embedded in the consumer's life, becoming a kind of a 'life mate' for them. This process is marked by an increasing level of affinity, intimacy, mutual commitment, and reciprocal trust. To build the social dimension, the brand leaves its desk, and goes into the streets to meet consumers, and finally goes to their homes too, as if it were a human being. This marks a shift in marketing focus, from a brand-centric to a consumer-centric perspective.

Gambetti and Graffigna (2010) found that companies have not yet turned their attention to long-term engagement initiatives and strategic vision. The emphasis is on tactical approaches and tools aimed at achieving short-term results. They suggest that a more strategic approach could help arrive at a broader understanding of the drivers and consequences of engagement. This would prevent engagement from being seen as just another new marketing 'trick' to reawaken consumer attention and revitalize the media market in the short term.

Customers engage with brands on various levels. Schmitt (2012) distinguishes five brand-related processes—identifying, experiencing, integrating, signalling, and connecting with the brand. The consumer identifies the brand and its category, forms associations, and compares the relations between brands. Then, he experiences it through sensory, affective, and participatory experiences that a consumer has with a brand. Next, the consumer integrates brand information into an overall brand concept, personality, and relationship with the brand. Using the brand as an informational cue, the consumer then uses it as a cultural symbol, which is signalling. Finally, the consumer forms an attitude toward the brand, becoming personally attached to it and connecting with the brand in a brand community. These steps are used to build consumer equity.

Customer Equity Management

Customer equity management (CEM) seeks to maximize customer equity by managing the customer asset base. The shift toward CEM, which is a method for evaluating the worth of a customer to the firm, has been driven by three changes in the market place as follows:

- Data availability across consumer touchpoints and the ability to analyse and crunch data and use these key assets
- Huge investments in CRM technologies
- Advances in the concept of customer lifetime value (CLV) and practices

    CEM is a function of three elements—value equity, brand equity, and relationship equity.

Value equity Value equity is the consumers' assessment of a brand, based on costs and benefits—what is given up for what is received. If consumers think they get something additional in terms of value on buying a brand in comparison to other brands, they will continue to buy it. It depends on a customer's switching propensity. It is a measure of satisfaction and loyalty, and is said to be the first driver of loyalty. It can be understood as the ratio between what consumers perceive as getting from a brand to what they have sacrificed. Value equity is a function of three drivers—quality, price, and convenience.

Brand equity According to Keller (2000), brand equity is the subjective estimation of a customer's choice. Brand equity is defined as an assessment of the price premium that a customer is willing to pay in comparison to other brands. It is reflected in strong brands that customers love. When the brand name is extended to new products, consumers tend to attach the same premium to those products even without trying them out. Brands having strong equity have a resilience to survive crisis situations and attacks from competitors, and survive shifts in consumer tastes. Brand equity is a function of the following drivers—customer brand awareness, customer's attitude towards the brand, and customer perception.

Relationship equity Relationship equity is a customer's tendency to stick with the brand beyond its objective and subjective assessment. Consumers feel a bond with the company or brand, and therefore, like to stick with it, even amidst stiff competition or price cuts offered by competitors. They feel well-treated by the company, are highly satisfied, and recommend it to others. Many brands, for instance, are consumed by families for generations. Companies spend a lot of effort in building relationship equity through CRM programmes. It results from the following drivers—loyalty, special recognition and treatment programmes, affinity or community activities, and knowledge building programmes.

Wu and Batmunkh (2010) conducted a study in a petrochemicals firm in Mongolia and found that all three independent variables—value equity, brand equity, relationship equity—have a direct and significant influence on customer satisfaction.

GLOBAL INSIGHT
Integrating Channels—CNN and its Flight 370 Coverage

Companies have to integrate their channels and learn to listen to the customer. This is true for broadcasters as well, who need to know what their viewers want to watch. The method of getting viewer feedback is executed by means of television rating points (TRPs) calculated by marketing research agencies. However, the figures are released after a period of time. This case study shows how CNN modifies its programming by listening to customers across different channels in real time.

On 8 March 2014, Malaysian Airlines Flight 370 from Kuala Lumpur to Beijing lost contact with air traffic control, less than an hour after take-off. The aircraft, a Boeing 777-200ER, was carrying 12 Malaysian crew members and 227 passengers from 14 nations. No flight debris and no crash site have been found.

As CNN reported the story, it noted that mobile page views and video views both shot up more than 150 per cent. Real-time analytics showed that the story outperformed other articles in the same spot on CNN's homepage. The story went off news networks after a few days of reporting the futile search effort; however, CNN's data showed that people had not grown tired of the story; they wanted more news. That led CNN to dedicate more resources, attention, and time to the story, leading to better viewership than other news networks.

(Contd)

GLOBAL INSIGHT (Contd)

Writing on the CNN website, Kohn (2014) explains that the missing plane made a gripping story for most consumers. 'There's something about death in sudden, large numbers that grabs our attention,' she writes. The idea that a large group of people are harmed suddenly makes for compelling viewing, and the mystery surrounding it made for real-life detective story.

People were left wondering how a plane could suddenly and unpredictably drop out of the sky, without any reason. Explaining that it ruptured our need for control, the story also showed that people followed the story because they wanted to know this would not happen to them.

CNN used data to track the viewership of consumers online and on television, and this helped it to know that people wanted to know about the missing airliner. Research showed that people were turning to CNN for the latest updates, and this helped the network to keep the story on air longer than news producers of other channels.

This could only happen by integration of channels. The newsroom was once split between digital and television; the company integrated the editorial side of the network and its online properties. Using data analysis, the network changed its programming more in tune with what customers wanted. Popular celebrities have shows in spots once occupied by traditional news programmes. This has helped CNN to become a network more focused on customer needs. It is the first 24-hour news network that no longer shows news 24*7. Since news does not keep breaking all the time, CNN has replaced it with what people like to watch—human interest programmes such as one that that visits unique individuals and shows what they are doing, and another that investigates international criminal investigations.

This change was significant. The company that was most synonymous with news embraced data to help understand not just what to say and how to say it, but where to say it and when to stop saying it.

CNN used digital resources to understand what viewers wanted, and started using data as an editorial tool. As per it website, data forms nearly every part of CNN's editorial decisions. By tracking consumption patterns and trends across the web, mobile, social media, videos, and on third-party sites, it takes decisions about programme offerings for all platforms.

Among the tools used by CNN Digital are Dataminr, which combs Twitter to help journalists find stories as they happen. Outbrain analyses real-time mobile consumption, Chartbeat monitors how each story performs, content is tested with Optimizely, Moat maps the performances of stories on CNN sites in real time as well as help with ads, and Omniture, an Adobe-owned analytics company, is also being used.

Taken together, these tools make a potent combination that tells the network what to cover and how to cover the same. Editorial judgment is now augmented with a deeper understanding of what the audience wants. The data tells the producers which stories must be followed vigorously or not.

Data from three different analytics systems, combined with overnight TV ratings, told CNN to double down on the missing airliner. The intense coverage paid off. Embracing data and pushing the MH370 story beyond conventional limits has helped the company reap better television rating and online traffic, even though many have criticized the method. CNN responds by pointing out that numbers, not critics, are the measure of success.

The emergence of analytics in digital media has given consumers a much-needed voice in journalism. It also shows a lesson to other businesses—CNN's changes are regarded as a shrewd move to update an old model, to position itself with modern consumers. That is what brands have to do—reinvent themselves in this new age, in which the brand is fully customized, personalized, and revolves around the customer's needs.

Sources:
Abbruzzese, Jason Y, 'Why CNN is obsessed with flight 370: 'The audience has spoken', 9 May 2014, http://mashable.com/2014/05/09/cnn-obsessed-malaysia-mh370-zucker/
Kohn, Sally, 'Why are we so obsessed with Flight 370?' http://edition.cnn.com/2014/03/19/opinion/kohn-flight-370-obsession/
Both last accessed on 25 May 2014.

Customer Value

Customer Value (CV) is the quantification of the perceived value of the product or service from a customer's point of view. It can be understood as the difference between what a customer gets from a product and what he or she has to give in order to get it. It is related to quality and satisfaction and concerns the interaction between products or services with the user. CV is considered to be a better predictor of customer behaviour than quality as it encompasses sacrifices apart from benefits.

Klanac (2013) presents a comprehensive and practical approach to study value from the customer's point of view. It builds on three approaches—the benefit–sacrifice, the means–end, and the experiential.

The benefit–sacrifice approach is the most common one, and considers gains and losses that a customer considers while buying a product. The approach defines CV as a trade-off between benefits and sacrifices perceived by customers to a seller's offering.

The means–end approach defines value as a customer-perceived preference for, and evaluation of those product attributes and performance of the product. The approach distinguishes three levels as follows:

- Characteristics of an object—the product attributes and performance
- Consequences—the results of using the object
- Desired end-states—final reasons of using the object.

The experiential approach treats customers as thinkers, feelers, and doers. The approach maintains that the essence of value proposition is in the customer's resulting experiences, arguing that value is the one in customer's experience not in the product or service. Steenkamp and Geyskens (2006) write that it is not emotions but rather the pursuit of pleasure that is more important in judgement formation in individualistic societies. The utilitarian experience is more important in collectivist societies.

Helkkula, and Kelleher, (2010) show that the customer service experience–perceived value process is not a linear value chain but rather it emerges as a dynamic and interrelating process of experiencing and conditioning value perceptions. They write that it is not possible for companies to fully understand customer service experience and customer perceived value in isolation of the customer's other lived experiences recalled within his or her phenomenological frame of reference.

For example, one may buy books from various websites. Basic features that one may look at before selecting a website are availability, price, and delivery. Together, these features provide a combined experience which contributes to building a perceived value.

CUSTOMER LIFETIME VALUE

The value that a brand represents is called brand equity. Keller (2003) writes that brand equity is the added value endowed to a product in the thoughts, words, and actions of consumers. Quantitatively, it means the total combined customer lifetime values of all customers of a company. We estimate the expected contribution of customers over their expected life. Then, we discount the values to a net present value and sum them up. It is shown mathematically as follows:

$$CLV = \sum_{t=0}^{T} \frac{(p_t - c_t)r_t - AC}{(1+i)^t}$$

p_t = price paid by customer
c_t = cost of servicing customer; r = retention rate
i = discount rate; AC = acquisition cost; t = time period

Keller explains that brand equity has two important components—brand awareness and brand image. Brand awareness refers to whether the brand can be recognized or recalled, and the variety of purchase and consumption situations in which the brand comes to mind. Brand image is defined as consumer perceptions and brand associations held in consumers' memory.

Brand equity can be measured by finding out about consumer mindset or brand knowledge. Brand awareness can be assessed through aided and unaided memory measures to test brand recall and recognition; brand image can be assessed through qualitative and quantitative techniques. While quantitative methods measure recall, recognition, and awareness, qualitative research techniques consist of free association, projective techniques, etc.

Free association   Free association is a technique in which consumers are asked about the brand. This is accomplished by asking questions like, 'What comes to your mind when you think of Brand X? What do you like about the brand? What do you think is unique to the brand?'

Projective techniques   These consist of completion and interpretation tasks, such as asking consumers to interpret a picture, or comparison tasks by asking questions like, 'If Nike were a car, which one would it be?'

Measuring brand personality   Sometimes, consumers think of brands as persons. In this technique, we try to find out what kind of person is associated with a brand, by asking questions such as, 'If the brand were to come alive as a person, what would it be like, what would it do, where would it live, what would it wear, who would it talk to if it went to a party?' Many other techniques for measuring brand personality are available.

Ethnographic and observational approaches   Consumers are unobtrusively observed as they shop or as they consume products. Some companies take consumers' permission to spend time with them in their homes to see how they actually use and experience products.

These techniques are explained in detail in Chapter 14 (Consumer Research).

It is important to influence customers to buy more and also to refer new customers. If people start referring their friends and acquaintances to brands, the cost of acquisition of new customers goes down considerably. Thus, it is important to calculate the customer referral value (CRV), which is described in the next section.

CUSTOMER REFERRAL VALUE

Word-of-mouth marketing (WOM) is encouraged by creating a buzz about products and brands through publicity activities, and communications from consumer-to-consumer and consumer-to-marketer. Apart from events organized by companies, these include a good amount of online interaction. Blogs, viral campaigns, interactions through social media sites such as Facebook and Twitter, form the arsenal of WOM. For example, Wills LifeStyle has more than 4,00,000 fans on Facebook. Barbie has more than 300 dedicated Facebook pages and more than 1000 YouTube channels.

However, these activities ignore the real purpose of WOM—to create delighted customers who are motivated enough to speak well of the brand. Reichheld in his classic article, 'The one number you need to grow' (2003) writes that a company should aim at getting its loyal customers to become, in effect, its marketing department. Favourable WOM is created when a customer sticks with a supplier 'who treats him well and gives good value in the long term even if the supplier does not offer the best price in a particular transaction.'

Reichheld further writes that companies tend to use the wrong yardsticks of loyalty such as measuring customer satisfaction or retention. Complex algorithms based on customer surveys also do not yield proper results. Instead, accurate indications can be obtained by asking a simple question, 'How likely is that you would recommend [the product] to a friend or a colleague?' Research cited in Reichheld's article found that there was a strong correlation between a company's growth rate and the percentage of customers who were extremely likely to recommend the company to a friend or colleague. It is also possible to quantify the value of customer's recommendations through customer referral value—the value obtained by the company through referral of new customers by existing customers.

Kumar, Peterson, and Leone (2007) go a step further from WOM. Taking the concept of CLV, they calculate the CRV to measure the value of the referrals made by a satisfied customer. First, they estimate the average number of successful referrals a customer makes to a company after an incentive has been offered to him, and also value of the referrals. It is calculated as follows:

$$CRV_i = \frac{\text{Value of customers who joined because of referral}}{\text{Discount rate}}$$

$$CRV_i = \sum_{n=1}^{T} \frac{N_n R_n - AC_n MC_n}{(1=r)^n}$$

where

T = number of periods (years, for example) that will be predicted into the future
N_n = number of referred customers
R_n = revenue generated per referred customer
AC_n = acquisition cost of the referred customers
MC_n = marketing cost needed to retain the referred customers

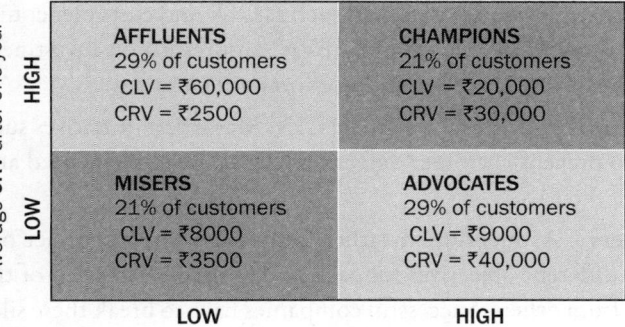

FIG. 17.8 Customer value matrix shows the relation between CLV and CRV

Source: Adapted from Kumar, Peterson, and Leone (2007)

An interesting finding is that a high CLV is not a good predictor of CRV. This is explained in the customer value matrix (Fig. 17.8), which clubs customers on the basis of their lifetime and referral value. Customers high on both measures are named champions, those who buy a lot but do not refer friends are called affluents, those who buy lesser quantities and also refer few friends are misers, and those who may buy less but are strong advocates of the company are referred to as advocates. The figure demonstrates that many low-CLV customers are valuable to the company as their referral value is high.

TABLE 17.1 Segments and strategies to lure customers

Segment	Strategy
Affluents	Make them into champions by encouraging them to refer more customers and also keep buying the company's products
Advocates	Making them buy more products while also maintaining their referral habit
Misers	Persuading them to buy more and also refer new customers.
Champions	Nurturing champions and reinforcing loyalty with them so that they are not influenced by the competition

Source: Adapted from Kumar, Peterson, and Leone (2007)

Based on this, the company can think of a strategy of increasing the effectiveness of WOM. It can ask the affluents to refer new customers, try to convert the advocates into better purchasers, and persuade the misers to buy more and refer more. The strategy is summarized in Table 17.1.

Building Customer Equity

As managers seek to embrace the customer equity philosophy and implement it within their own organizations, they will be faced with several challenges. Bell, et al (2002) describe the following six action items required for customer equity management:

Assemble customer data Some companies accumulate customer data as part of their business. These are subscription service providers, insurance providers, credit card issuers and banks, and membership organizations. Other companies have to incur costs to assemble customer data. This group includes manufacturers who sell through retail stores, providers of services such as entertainment and fast-food restaurants; and in general, those who serve a broad, shallow customer base with little potential for repeat business. The risk facing this group is that competitors with customer-specific data stand to learn more about customer needs than those without the data.

Track ROI of marketing efforts Customers are assets who are acquired at a cost that is justified or not by a flow of income into the future, just as are the fixed assets of the firm. However, customer assets are not accounted for in balance sheets. Though brand assets are accounted for in financial statements in certain countries, in others customer asset metrics such as CLV and customer equity are used. Financial measures, such as economic value analysis (EVA) and return on investment (ROI) must be used to track and assess the impact of marketing efforts of a company.

Maximize CLV Companies have to make efforts to maximize CLV. Marketing initiatives such as loyalty programmes and schemes to prevent customer defection have to be implemented and measured.

Orient the organization to customers As mentioned earlier, companies often contract out their sales and service functions with different objectives for each one of them. Each step of the customer purchase journey is isolated from others. Successful companies have to break these silos and structures to focus on the customer and embed CRM processes into the entire organization.

Deal with privacy concerns Customer's entitlement to privacy has become a serious issue. Companies wish to collect their customers' personal data but it can be misused or stolen at times.

Companies have to assure customers that data with them is safe and build systems to prevent leakage.

Dialogue Marketing

Kalyanam and Zweben (2005) provide the concept of dialogue marketing. Many companies in today's times are guilty of overcommunicating—sending unnecessary and unwanted e-mail and SMS messages. This turns people off, resulting in irritation or anger. Instead, if companies can figure out the right moment to contact their customers and then send a relevant message, people will not be irritated. Figuring out the right moment is done by a computer-based model called dialogue marketing.

Dialogue marketing describes the efforts made by companies to engage consumers in an ongoing dialogue to create lasting relationships. Collecting data at touchpoints, companies use it to customize their marketing messages and personalize the experience for their consumers. It is also a means to offer discounts, tips, and free trials exactly when the customer wants it, and avoids sending unnecessary messages as it is wait and respond approach. It is completely interactive, and uses all communication channels to track every nuance of a customer's interaction with a company. Kalyanam and Zweben explain that dialogue marketing, responds to each change in the relationship as it occurs.

Rayport (2013) writes that standard ad messaging and conventional creative executions are becoming outmoded. Advertising has to talk less to its targets but stress more on what it does for them. As a result, advertising becomes a sustained and rewarding presence in consumers' lives.

Therefore, television spots and display ads must be supplemented by adding customer experience. Companies such as Demand Media, Skyword, and BuzzFeed are providing native content, creating both text and video that complement commercial messaging. This encourages consumers to engage with it because it relates to their lives. Such advertising content engages through relevance and value. The days of yelling louder are over, instead human experience is fast becoming a medium for advertising.

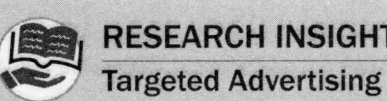

RESEARCH INSIGHT
Targeted Advertising

Digital marketing is believed to be consisting of banner ads, affiliates links and search campaigns. If a consumer searches a website about a boat, it means that he is looking to buy a boat. Therefore, boat dealers would buy ad space on websites about boats. This was similar to buying an ad in a magazine—ads should be placed in the context of buying.

With the evolution in technology, marketing has evolved remarkably as consumers use the Internet for a variety of purposes, such as communicating with others, and searching for information and entertainment as well as buying stuff. Placing ads in the context of buying becomes, outdated. Instead, the need is to target ads individually to customers based on their personality and interaction.

This was the basis of emergence of audience-based buying or programmatic ads. Changing the concept of contextual ads, companies link real-time data to ads based on the specific person seeing the space. These ads are placed through real-time bidding (RTB) on an exchange—an advertising inventory auction platform—to show one specific ad to one consumer in a specific context. This hyper-targeted

(Contd)

RESEARCH INSIGHT (Contd)

strategy is the new face of marketing that results in gains in the quality of users and reduction in cost.

This is how programmatic marketing platform works. A publisher or website is integrated with an SSP (supply-side platform) and the advertiser operates on a DSP (demand-side platform). When a user visits the website, the SSP attempts to fill the ad request created by the user. The SSP sends the request to the RTB exchange with the pertinent information about the user, obtained from devices such as browser, cookies, device, URL, content type, and so on.

The RTB exchange distributes the request to multiple DSPs, of which most will have a cookie on the user's browser. The DSP uses a data management platform to obtain knowledge about the user from his/her browsing history, activity on other sites, purchase history, as well as obtain third-party data such as credit card data, household income, and purchase patterns. All these user data trigger the ad request. Based on DSP algorithms, a maximum bid is calculated and a matching creative sent to the exchange. On completion of the auction, the winning creative is selected. Based on user history, this could have pre-populated fields, like how a user previously looked at the boat. The page is served to the user and any engagement and behaviour is recorded. All these steps take less than a second.

Programmatic buying allows managers to pay only for the impressions they want. It enables them to show relevant ads to the right audience, in the right place at the right time, and at a price they are willing to pay.

Trends suggest that by 2015, all search and media buying will be largely executed as audience-based programmatic buying, and touch all channels and platforms.

Compared to online display ads, programmatic delivers significantly greater sales compared to conventional online ad spend. Using highly segmented data, brands can bid for ad impressions that target specific consumers at the most appropriate time, place, and point in the consumer decision journey, across a variety of media platforms.

Virgin Media splits programmatic spend into retargeting ads and prospecting ads. The company has set caps on frequency to avoid over exposure on all types of ad spend. It splits its programmatic spend into retargeting ads tailored for people who have used or researched a service and prospecting ads, aimed at new consumers.

Programmatic buying allows companies to make use of their customers' varied online activity, instead of restricting ad spend to a narrow set of websites considered a fit for the brand. The advantage is that companies can place ads where the customers are, instead of where the brand presumes them to be.

Having good audience data is key to programmatic buying. Instead of deploying all the data, companies have to learn to identify the right data that is unique to the business or campaign. They also have to think about their most important data segments in new ways. Using targeted third-party data, they can build predictive and lookalike modelling that identifies consumers, and incorporates time, geographic and frequency optimization to increase return on investment of marketing spends.

National Rail Enquiries (NRE) uses PubMatic technology to ensure that ads against the 68 million monthly page impressions on its website are served smoothly to their target audiences. This technology delivers the message to millions of likely users in five seconds. This one-to-one relationship is afforded by programmatic technology. Its ability to deliver campaign analytics in real time also allows marketers to adjust targeting mid-campaign.

CONCLUSION

This chapter describes rapid and tectonic changes in consumer behaviour, as a consequence of omni-channel marketing. Though crystal gazing cannot be done, there are certain trends that threaten to disrupt the world of brands and marketing as we know it. One major development is the advent of 3D printing. Presently used to print prototypes, it is surely a matter of time before it spreads and is used to print diverse things like electronics, clothes and so on. Consumers can have the styles they want, in their size, and as per their taste, in a matter of minutes. This might lead to a revolution in consumer purchasing—the speed of consumer gratification will increase manifold. 3D printing promises to change all the rules by revolutionising the manufacturing process.

The second major trend is slowing growth rates in both developing and developed countries as a result of ageing population. *The Economist* (2014) reports that the world is on the cusp of a staggering rise in the number of old people. Over the next 20 years, the global population of those aged 65 or more will almost double, from 600 million to 1.1 billion. This shift will lead to slower economic growth and secular stagnation. The world of marketing cannot remain isolated from this stage. While companies rely on young people to sell fashion and premium brands presently, the slowing growth rates and ageing population may well see a shift in engagement strategies.

This brings us to the third trend—the rise of private labels. Organized retail is pushing private labels like never before. These products are much cheaper than established brands but are almost equal in quality to them. In many cases, the products are made by the same contract manufacturers of big brands. Chains such as Big Bazaar, Reliance Retail, Wal-Mart, and others, sell a variety of products from spices to fashion garments under their own labels,

posing a threat to big brands. This might lead to decline of big brands in the future.

Yet another trend that is becoming evident is that people are getting tired of being online. Mobile usage may well hit a peak as people realize they are getting cut-off from social experiences. Many people already show a mobile usage syndrome. Further, as companies track every move on consumers, people feel stalked. There is a rise of privacy concerns as well. In 2014, the European Union court made a landmark judgement, which gave people the 'right to be forgotten'. Such trends could well culminate in people switching off their connected devices. Will the world move full circle and come back to the wise, old world of traditional retail?

The world is witnessing huge changes and not all of them economic changes. Scientists have predicted global upheavals due to a looming threat—global warming. As weather patterns change, so will consumption patterns. The nature and extent of these changes can only be imagined. The future is another country.

SUMMARY

Consumer behaviour is changing like never before, thanks to wireless handheld devices that people use all the time. Companies interact with customers through countless channels—websites, physical stores, kiosks, direct mail and catalogues, call centres, social media, mobile devices, television, networked appliances, and so on. The ways in which companies retain their customers and become customer-centric in this changed scenario have been discussed in this chapter.

E-commerce is rapidly becoming a part of commerce, and digital retailing is quickly becoming omni-channel retailing. In this era of consumer engagement, companies have to integrate disparate channels into a single seamless omni-channel experience. There are three levels of consumer engagement—object-centred, self-centred, and social; there are five brand-related processes—identifying, experiencing, integrating, signifying, and connecting with the brand. Marketing faces digital disruption; to engage customers, it has to pervade the entire organization so that there is a shift of focus around all interactions of customer touchpoints. A new model for the digital age shifts the emphasis from products to solutions, place to access, price to value, and promotion to education (SAVE).

Companies have to become oriented towards customer engagement. They can achieve this goal by holding customer engagement summits, forming customer engagement councils, appointing chief content officers, creating a listening centre, and reworking the customer engagement budget.

Omni-channel approach is used to satisfy modern customers by integrating both the digital and physical worlds. However, most companies operate by forming departments which think of themselves as silos, unable or unwilling to share information, having independent processes. This has to change by getting rid of the back office mentality and developing analytics for a 360-degree view of customers as they interact with brands. This helps in building customer equity, which is a function of three elements—value equity, brand equity, and relationship equity.

Customer value (CV) is the quantification of the perceived value of the product or service from a customer's point of view. It is the difference between what a customer gets from a product and what he or she has to give in order to get it. It builds on three approaches: the benefit–sacrifice, the means–end, and the experiential. Customer lifetime value (CLV) is the total combined customer lifetime values of all of a company's customers.

Customer equity is built through several steps: assembling consumer data, tracking marketing ROI, CLV, and by orienting the organization towards customers. Dialogue marketing describes the efforts made by companies to engage consumers in an ongoing dialogue to create lasting relationships. Consequently, advertising is also poised to change.

KEY TERMS

Brand equity The subjective estimation of a customer's choice and is defined as an assessment of the price premium that a customer is willing to pay in comparison with other brands

Customer engagement Establishing a strong and enduring bond between brand and consumers based on consumer interaction, shared values, experiential contents, and rewards

Customer equity management An approach to marketing that seeks to maximize customer equity by managing the customer asset base

Customer lifetime value Total combined customer lifetime values of all customers of a company

Customer value The quantification of the perceived value of the product or service from a customer's point of view, or the difference between what a customer gets from a product and what he or she has to give in order to get it

Dialogue marketing Efforts made by companies to engage consumers in an ongoing dialogue to create lasting relationship

Omni-channel retailing When companies interact with customers through countless channels—websites, physical stores, kiosks, direct mail and catalogues, call centres, social media, mobile devices, television, and networked appliances, it is called omni-channel retailing

Relationship equity A customer's tendency to stick with the brand beyond its objective and subjective assessment

Value equity The consumers' assessment of a brand based on costs and benefits—the ratio between what consumers perceive as getting from a brand to what they have sacrificed

EXERCISES

Concept-review Questions

1. Summarize the changes that are taking place in consumer behaviour. How do digital technologies impact consumer behaviour?
2. What is omni-channel retailing? What does it consist of?
3. What is consumer engagement? Why is it important for companies to engage customers?
4. Customer experience should be same across all channels. Explain how different channels can deliver a uniform experience to customers.
5. How can companies increase engagement with their customers? Describe the steps that they have to go through.
6. What is customer equity? What does it consist of?
7. What is customer lifetime value (CLV)? What is its importance and how is it calculated?
8. Explain how companies can build customer equity?
9. What is dialogue marketing? What is its importance?
10. What is customer relationship management (CRM)? What are the steps required to build an effective CRM in a company?

Critical Thinking Questions

1. Write a paper on consumer behaviour of the future. In what ways will marketing and consumer behaviour change? How will organizations respond to the changes? How will the marketing department's organizational structure look like in the future?

2. Many companies are not customer-centric, as shown by several surveys on consumer satisfaction. Why do you think this happens? How can companies get out of this trap and become customer-oriented?
3. Efforts by many companies to engage customers such as sending them e-mails, collecting their personal data, and posting on their social networking pages are seen by some as stalking. It has raised questions about consumer privacy and many people have complained about unwanted commercial attention. Is this real? How can companies avoid this charge, while pursuing their consumer interests as well?
4. It has been suggested that the 4Ps of marketing should be modified to solutions, place to access, price to value, and promotion to education (SAVE). What does this shift reveal about consumer behaviour? What is the difference in the two approaches? How should companies adjust to this change?

Projects and Assignments

1. Interview your parents and your friends' parents. Ask them how they used to buy products and how they interacted with companies or retailers. Compare it with your own interactions with companies and retailers. In what way was their experience same or different from yours? How did companies or retailers build brand equity or relationships with them? What do you think will change in the future?
2. Follow some friends as they go shopping. Make a list of all the touchpoints between your friends and companies associated with them. How many channels did they encounter and what factors culminated in the purchase decision?
3. Make a list of all the brands that you have 'liked' on Facebook and all the brands that you follow on twitter. Assess your level of engagement with these brands. Which brands are more active than others? With which of these brands do you really like to engage?
4. Interview the marketing managers of a few companies. Ask them their views about the nature of their job. What part of their jobs goes in making and implementing strategy and what part goes in managing customer experience? Ask them their views on engaging customers online and the efforts made by them to enhance customer experience.

REFERENCES

Bell, David, John Deighton, Werner J. Reinartz, Roland T. Rust, and Gordon Swartz, 'Seven barriers to customer equity management', *Journal of Service Research*, Volume 5, No. 1, August 2002.

Brodie, R., Hollebeek, L., Juric, B., and Llic, A., 'Customer engagement: Conceptual domain, Fundamental propositions and implications for research', *Journal of Service Research*, 14 (3), pp. 252–271, 2011.

Downes, Larry and Paul F. Nunes, 'Big-bang disruption', *Harvard Business Review*, March 2013.

Ettenson, Richard, Eduardo Conrado, and Jonathan Knowles, 'Rethinking the 4 P's', *Harvard Business Review*, January 2013.

Flatters, Paul and Michael Willmott, 'Understanding the postrecession consumer', *Harvard Business Review*, July, 2009.

Frelin, Johanna, 'The digital disruption of marketing and the executive knowledge gap', *Bloomberg Businessweek*, 7 October 2013.

French, Tom, Laura LaBerge, and Paul Magill, 'Five 'no regrets' moves for superior consumer engagement', *McKinsey Quarterly*, July 2012.

Gambetti Rossella C, Guendalina Graffigna, and Silvia Biraghi, 'The grounded theory approach to consumer-brand engagement: The practitioner's standpoint', *International Journal of Market Research*, Vol. 54, Issue 5, 2012.

Gambetti, Rossella C and Guendalina Graffigna, 'The concept of engagement: A systematic analysis of the ongoing marketing debate', *International Journal of Market Research*, Vol. 52, Issue 6, 2010.

Garnefeld, I., Helm, S., and Eggert, A., 'Walk your talk: An experimental investigation of the relationship between word-of-mouth and communicator's loyalty', *Journal of Service Research*, Vol. 14, pp. 93–107, 2011.

Helkkula, A. and Kelleher, C., 'Circularity of customer service experience and customer perceived value', *Journal of Customer Behaviour*, 9 (1), pp. 37–53, 2010.

Joachimsthaler, Erich and David A. Aaker, 'Building brands without mass media', *Harvard Business Review*, January 1997.

Kalyanam, Kirthi and Monte Zweben, 'The perfect message at the perfect moment', *Harvard Business Review*, November 2005.

Klanac, Nataša Golik, 'An integrated approach to customer value: A comprehensive-practical approach', *Journal of Business Marketing Management*, Vol. 6, pp. 22–37, 2013.

Kumar, V., Aksoy, L., Donkers, B., Venkatesan, R., Wiesel, T. and Tillmans, S., 'Undervalued or overvalued Customers: Capturing total customer engagement value', *Journal of Service Research*, 13(3), pp. 297–310, 2010.

Kumar, V., Venkatesan, R. and Reinartz, W., 'Knowing what to sell when to whom?', *Harvard Business Review*, pp. 131–137, March 2006.

Levitt, Theodore, 'After the sale is over', *Harvard Business Review*, September–October 1983.

Marketing2020, http://effectivebrands.com/index.php?/global-marketing/global-marketing-2020, report published by *Effective Brands*, last accessed on 20 May 2014.

McKinsey and Co., 'The marketing organization of the future', December 2012, http://mckinseyonmarketingandsales.com/the-marketing-organization-of-the-future, last accessed on 15 May 2014.

Rayport, Jeffrey F., 'Advertising's new medium: Human experience', *Harvard Business Review*, March 2013.

Rigby, Darrell, 'The future of shopping', *Harvard Business Review*, December 2011.

Roberts, Kevin, *Lovemarks: The Future Beyond Brands*, Powerhouse Books, New York, 2007.

Robinson, Floren and Justin M. Brown, 'How to make your company think like a customer', Accenture Outlook, http://www.accenture.com/us-en/outlook/Pages/outlook-journal-2012-make-company-think-like-customer.aspx, last accessed on 25 May 2014.

Schmitt, Bernd, 'The consumer psychology of brands', *Journal of Consumer Psychology*, Vol. 22, pp. 7–17, 2012.

Steenkamp, J.E.M., and Geyskens, I., 'How country characteristics affect the perceived value of web Sites', *Journal of Marketing*, 70 (July), pp. 136–150, 2006.

Van Doorn, J., Lemon, K., Mittal, V., Nass, S., Pick, D., Pirner, P., and Verhoef, P., 'Customer engagement behaviour: Theoretical foundations and research directions', *Journal of Service Research*, 13 (3), pp. 253–266, 2010.

Villanueva, J., Yoo, S. and Hanssens, M., 'The impact of marketing-induced versus word-of-mouth customer acquisition on customer equity growth', *Journal of Marketing Research*, Vol. 45, No. 1, pp. 48–59, 2008.

Vivek, Shiri D., Sharon E. Beatty, and Robert M. Morgan, 'Customer engagement: Exploring customer relationships beyond purchase', *Journal of Marketing Theory and Practice*, Vol. 20, No. 2, Spring 2012.

Wu, Tain-Fung and Munkh-Ulzii Batmunkh, 'Equity and satisfaction: An empirical study of Mongolian gas station channels', *International Journal of Trade, Economics and Finance*, Vol. 1, No. 2, August 2010.

CASE STUDY

Optimizing Customer Equity at Celtel

Companies spend huge amount of money to acquire new customers. Lowering acquisition costs per customer can reduce 'payback' time of investments, that is, the time for customers tend to become profitable. This case study illustrates the use of a loyalty programme to generate goodwill among the customer base and to create a halo effect among the potential customer base, resulting in easier acquisition of new and high-value customers.

Zambia's mobile market is considered to be one of the major growth markets in Africa, where mobile penetration has been increasing over the years. Celtel is Zambia's dominant GSM service provider. By bundling value-added services and innovative tariff structures, it has emerged as Zambia's most popular service provider. The operator has gained 70 per cent market share.

In 2005, Celtel Zambia registered 100 per cent growth in net subscriber additions and crossed over 15,00,000 users, the bulk of whom were prepaid customers. However, an accompanying drop in mobile tariffs in the region has increased the payback time for each customer. Consequently, maximizing returns on customer investment is directly dependent on the subscriber's lifetime value—a product of the average lifespan on the network as well as the value of customer spends. Industry consensus indicate that extending the length of a customer relationship by one year increases the potential of revenue earnings by 45 per cent. Consequently, for Celtel, retaining and treating customers as a lifetime stream of revenues was of paramount importance.

Celtel Zambia deployed Bharti Telesoft's loyalty management system to identify, retain, and grow its profitable customers. The highlights of the loyalty system are summarized here:

- Omni-channel enrolment methods through interactive voice response (IVR), short message service (SMS), and wireless application protocol (WAP)
- Flexible framework that enables operators to define rewards based on usage, age on network, subscriber profile, category, and region
- Simplifies all aspects of campaign execution and administration
- Provides 360-degree view of the customer to tailor marketing offers to individual user or segments
- Comprehensive metrics to monitor customers' average spend, responsiveness, and award redemption
- Highly scalable hardware and software to handle multiple currencies and multiple languages
- Multiple deployment options, spanning provisioning and customer service

As the customers were predominantly prepaid who could change network and services at will, they had to be engaged for the long-term so as to ensure consistent returns on investment. Additionally, a majority of the customers used mobile phones mainly for basic voice and text services. These services are poorly differentiated, and can be easily substituted, making them increasingly vulnerable to attack from the competition.

To build on customer retention, the company needed information about the distinct demographic and economic attributes of different customers over their lifetime so as to profit from existing customer relationships. However, the prepaid model is non-contractual in nature and does not foster any CRM activities or insight into individual customer value drivers. The ability to identity profitable customers to provide a differentiated customer experience is instrumental in protecting and extending the lifetime value of various customer segments.

Rewarding Profitable Behaviour

Bharti Telesoft's loyalty management system was used to manage the loyalty campaign lifecycle from planning and execution, to monitoring and assessment, with the following components:

Subscriber profiler Subscriber profiles were used to identify and, consequently, leverage customer-specific value levers. To support promotional activities, data relating to a customer's use of mobile network services was captured and retained. The system collected event-related data from all sources that was used to create and manage groups of customers such as silver and gold to achieve program attractiveness.

Campaign manager Using an intuitive graphical user interface (GUI)-based business rule framework, information related to campaign-associated activities were collected and integrated by the company. These include enrolment, accrual, and redemption parameters. The system is used to quickly create and execute a variety of promotions.

Communication manager The communication manager is used to send messages to targeted customers to introduce the loyalty scheme and to administer campaigns.

Rewards manager The rewards manager uses automated workflows to monitor members' transactions in real time, compute credit points, and manage awards.

Business manager The business manager generates a set of historical and real-time reports regarding demographic and transaction profiles of specific subscriber segments that are enrolled and non-enrolled. Identification of customers' lifecycle phases helps in enhancing existing segmentation and optimizes planning of campaign sequences per segment.

Customer relationship manager The GUI-based CRM module provides customer-facing agents with tools and information to resolve customer requests and situations in a time-bound manner.

In January 2005, Celtel Zambia became the first operator in the region to launch a customer loyalty programme. Branded 'Reward Yourself', the programme was intended for prepaid customers and was designed to incentivize service usage. The programme offered rewards at different usage levels that can be redeemed every month. Customers who used 10 units of airtime in a month were awarded bonus airtime, automatically credited to their respective accounts in the first week of the following month. The number of bonus minutes earned was directly proportionate to the specific usage patterns of the customer. For high-value customers—users who consume 300+ units per month in one year—a mobile handset valued at 10 per cent of their total spend was offered.

Measurable Impact

The loyalty programme gained instant traction. On the first day of the launch, it enrolled approximately 3000 users and crossed over 20,000 participants in the first 30 days.

Incremental sales units used per month	Bonus minutes
10	5 minutes
20	10 minutes
50	25 minutes
1000+	500 minutes

Posters were distributed to retail and dealer outlets, and radio advertisements in seven local languages were used to publicize the programme. Live call-in question and answer sessions during sponsored radio time explained the easy enrolment and redemption process. Online advertisements explained the product functionality. Experiential marketing was also used; these included drama groups, onsite customer care support, and brand ambassadors across all 72 districts of Zambia.

The loyalty programme created a stable revenue base of existing customers. The rewards have lowered the perceived cost barriers associated with the tariff schemes and positively influenced consumption-oriented behaviour. On average, the monthly minutes of usage per member is over 100 minutes, and the average revenue per user (ARPU) earned from participants is 10 per cent higher as compared to non-members. Overall, the participants contributed over 70 per cent to Celtel's revenues. Some of the features of the loyalty programme are as follows:

Profitability drivers The company identified the profitability drivers and the underlying factors that drive customer behaviour related to these profitability drivers.

Corporate buy-in All departments were geared to the objective of increasing customer loyalty.

Segment members Customers were segmented based on value.

Loyalty analytics Leverage data for the design and management of the loyalty management programme were executed.

Incentive structure WIIFM (What's-In-It-For-Me) is a key element in driving customer participation; rewards must be relevant and attainable.

The loyalty programme has helped Celtel to strengthen relationships with existing customers. The attrition rate among enrolled members is 50 per cent of average monthly churn rate for all subscribers. For customers, the opportunity to earn awards every month ensures that they feel esteemed and appreciated. It also helped in differentiation from the competition as it instilled a perception of higher value in the continued consumption of Celtel's services.

The enrolment process encourages consumers to voluntarily share personal information in order to receive full programme benefits. This allows Celtel to match customer transaction data (what prepaid denomination was bought, when, at what outlet) with customers' demographic and psychographic profiles (birth dates, gender, and preferences) and optimally model marketing.

Questions for Discussion

1. Describe the elements of omni-channel integration as used by Celtel Zambia.
2. Discuss the efforts of the company in building customer equity and reducing the payback period of customer acquisition investments.
3. How does customer's demographic data help the company in building a loyalty programme?
4. How did the activities undertaken by the company help in increasing customer lifetime value?

Sources:

http://www.comviva.com/newsletter/Bharti%20Telesoft_Newsletter_Qtr1.htm

http://www.kiwanja.net/database/project/project_mobiquity.pdf

http://www.mahindracomviva.com/media/Computer.com%20%20Bharti%20Telesoft1.pdf

All last accessed on 27 March, 2014

CHAPTER EIGHTEEN

Ethics and Social Responsibility

LEARNING OBJECTIVES

Business has the legitimate objective of selling goods and thereby making profits. However, at the same time they have a responsibility towards society. This chapter describes the ethical considerations that companies must keep in focus as they use consumer behaviour in their marketing

After studying this chapter, the reader will be able to

- understand the importance of ethics and issues that arise in marketing
- learn to reduce the intended and unintended consequences of marketing activities
- appreciate the need to reduce consumer's carbon footprint and increased ethical consumption
- understand how globalization affects ethical considerations and learn to avoid the sins of greenwashing
- learn the concept of corporate social responsibility and understand how companies use it

CASE STUDY

Hunger Games

In the book, *The Hunger Games*, Collins (2008) has created a dystopia set in Panem, whose name means 'bread and circuses'. It is a country consisting of very wealthy residents and all they have to do is entertain themselves. It has 12 very poor districts in which people struggle for everyday existence, from which young people are drawn every year to participate in a game of death.

Panem is fictional; however, the society described in it is increasingly real in many countries. Consider this—every third poor person and every second malnourished child in the world is an Indian, reports *Business Standard* (2013), citing the International Monetary Fund (IMF). The country also adds 7.5 million babies with low-birth weight annually, which is the highest figure anywhere in the world. In 2011, India ranked 73 out of 88 countries listed in the annual Global Hunger Index, six places down from the previous year. Eight Indian states account for more poor people (421 million) than in the 26 poorest African countries (410 million) taken together.

At the same time, according to Christine Lagarde (2014), Managing Director, IMF, 'In India, the net worth of the billionaire community increased 12-fold in 15 years, enough to eliminate absolute poverty in this country twice over.'

Evidently, the society is getting divided into haves and have-nots. The have-nots are not considered by most marketing efforts; after all, its objective is to serve customer needs and make a profit. Companies cater to the needs of the rich, learning about consumer behaviour of the rich, and love to serve the rich, many of whom are hard pressed to find avenues to spend.

One manifestation of this focus is the attention to children as consumers. The adults have their cars and high fashion, so can the market be expanded to sell to the children of the extraordinary rich?

The Economic Times (2014) reports that kids-only products and services that were once bought by and for adults are the hottest new market trend in India. A host of such products have been launched by companies targeting the age group of five to 10 years. Assisting the marketing efforts are elite schools, which are asking children to apply things like sunscreen lotions. Peer pressure is also sought to be built up. For parents who are both rich and aware, such products find easy acceptability.

Following the success of its sunscreen for kids, Lotus Herbals plans to market a line of products, such as mosquito repellents and other lotions for children. Swati Piramal's Jungle Magic perfumes are available in green apple, strawberries, and chocolate variants. Jungle Magic will soon be a ₹100-crore brand as sales are doubling every year, according to Ms Piramal. The annual growth of these products ranges from 15%–20%.

Other companies have entered the market as well. Phillips has joined Disney to launch hair clippers and a lighting range for children up to seven years. Shahnaz Hussain has a kids-only range of cleansers, dusting powders, and skin treatment cream. It will not be long perhaps before children get their own beauty parlours in India.

In the US, Club Libby Lu was one such store for girls aged between five and 12. Founded in 2000, the store chain operated 98 stores before closing in 2009 when the economy collapsed. Children would sit in front of pink, heart-shaped mirrors, listening to hip music, and were transformed into rock stars, princesses, and favourite celebrities including Miley Cyrus and Ashley Tisdale. A makeover costs $25–$60, and included hair styling, decorating nails, and applying makeup. The club's 'Very Important Princesses' had counsellors, who would help them avail special services like the 'potion bar' where they could make their own lotion, perfume, or lip gloss, and a Pooch Parlor, where the guest could adopt a stuffed animal of their choice.

Children get affected by such relentless marketing. One of the consequences is that they become sexually mature very early. Levin and Kilbourne (2009), in their book, *So Sexy So Soon*, write, 'Children become involved in and learn about sexual issues and behaviour that they do not yet have the intellectual or emotional ability to understand and that can confuse and harm them.' However, this is perhaps of no consequence for the super-rich.

It is a scenario described in *The Hunger Games*. While rich children spent their time in looking and feeling good, the poor live in horrible conditions, where everyday survival is a challenge. *The Hunger Games* does not seem fiction anymore.

Questions for Discussion

1. Should companies consider the after-effects of marketing on society, and in particular, on children such as sexualizing them so early in life, when they market products specifically for them?
2. Is it ethical for companies to market to young children products that are generally perceived to be not required by them?
3. Is it ethical to exploit children belonging to the rich category simply because they have purchasing power? Is the pursuit of profits so deadly that companies are willing to sacrifice the future of individuals for their own benefit?
4. This question concerns personal ethics. What will be your position if you are working in a company that markets products or follows marketing practices that you may not agree to? What would be your reaction if your children wanted to look sexy at a tender age?

Sources:
Business Standard, 'India has a problem with inequality, and it won't be solved easily', 25 May 2013.
Club Libby Lu, http://en.wikipedia.org/wiki/Club_Libby_Lu, last accessed on 26 July, 2014.
Collins, Suzanne, *The Hunger Games*, Scholastic Press, New York, 2008.
Lagarde, Christine, *A New Multilateralism for the 21st Century: the Richard Dimbleby Lecture*, 3 February 2014, https://www.imf.org/external/np/speeches/2014/020314.htm, last accessed on 26 July 2014.
Levin, Diane E. and Jean Kilbourne, *So Sexy So Soon: The New Sexualized Childhood and What Parents Can Do to Protect Their Kids*, Ballantine Books, New York, 2009.
The Economic Times, 'Companies customising grown-up products for consumers of age group 5–10', 28 July 2014.
The Times of India, 'Income inequality on the rise in countries like India: IMF', 4 February 2014.

INTRODUCTION

Consider the following situations:

- You buy a swanky T-shirt of a famous brand. Do you think how it was made, whether the workers were paid fair wages, whether they worked in safe and hygienic surroundings, or whether the production process involved any harmful processes?
- You buy a shampoo that does not cause eye irritation. Do you worry about whether the manufacturer tested it on animals, dripping concentrated shampoo, for instance, in monkeys' eyes to see whether it would cause them pain and blindness before launching the final product?
- You buy a car. Do you consider whether you actually need a big car which causes more emissions than a smaller car that would serve your purpose equally well? Do you think about the consequences of your choice on the environment?
- You are going on a picnic with your friends. Food and drinks are passed around. Do you think about the empty food packets, bottles, and cans that you leave behind? After consuming any eatable, do you think twice before tossing the empty packet out of your car window?
- You have many gadgets in your home. They are all on standby mode, ready to come to life when you press the remote. Do you think of the electricity consumed by them to be in that mode day and night? Do you think about the consequences of your lifestyle on others?

FIG. 18.1 When people buy dresses or products, they rarely think of how and where the products were made

Most people think of themselves as generally ethical. However, many of us are guilty of not thinking about and doing something about the harm that our consuming decisions cause.

Consumers may well argue that they do not know about the production processes and cannot be responsible over something that they do not control. Yet, knowingly or otherwise, people make choices that have ethical consequences. Marketing is concerned with encouraging the consumption of goods but not about encouraging ethical choices among them. We explore the larger question in this chapter—do companies and consumers have an ethical responsibility that goes beyond consumption? See Fig. 18.1. People rarely think of how and where the products were made. Ethical considerations involve taking into account the consequences of consumption.

ETHICS

Ethics is a branch of philosophy that deals with morals and values. Aristotle referred to character, which he called 'ethos', as the most potent means of persuasion. He also identified elements of virtue as 'justice, courage, temperance, magnificence, magnanimity, liberality, gentleness, prudence, and wisdom'. Ethics was incorporated into the legal system during the Roman Empire which also educated lawyers concerning ethics, morality, and law. Napoleon established a code of thirty-six statutes based on the concept that all citizens, regardless of circumstances of birth or social stature, should be treated fairly and equally. Utilitarianism in ethics considers how moral actions produce the greatest overall good for all.

There is a distinction to be made between legality and ethics. Very often, people and companies think that if they are following the law, they are also being ethical. However, the ethical consideration consists of going much beyond the law and doing what is right, as the Ethical Insight shows.

Ethics consist of principles of conduct that guide the decisions that companies and consumers make. Ethics in marketing means applying standards of fairness, or moral rights and wrongs, to marketing decision-making, actions, and practices.

Marketing ethics concerns principles and values behind the operation and regulation of marketing. It refers to the principles that govern companies as they promote, distribute, and sell products or services to consumers. It also concerns consumers because the choices made by them have consequences that go much beyond mere consumption.

The study of marketing ethics involves many areas. Ethics of advertising and promotion overlap with media ethics. Ethics of consumption overlap with personal ethics. As we are dealing with influencing people, ethics of society and the impact of marketing on culture get overlapped. Finally, as we deal with individual psychology, we must question whether we should manipulate the minds of people, imposing our own values and culture on impressionable minds.

ETHICAL INSIGHT
Legal, But Not Ethical?

In 2012, there were reports that Starbucks had paid just £8.6 million in corporation tax in the UK in 14 years and no tax in the past three years. The American coffee giant, at that time, was valued at £25 billion and had generated more than £3 billion of sales in the UK since 1998. That is, it had paid less than one per cent as tax during the period. However, the company had complied with the law and said that it has paid its 'fair share of taxes' in full compliance with the law of the land and no authority had suggested otherwise.

Reuters (2012) reported that Starbucks had been able to cut its tax liability by paying fees to other parts of its global business, like royalty payments for use of the brand. In effect, Starbucks UK was making a loss in the country and, thus, did not have to pay tax. It had not broken any law. The reduction in tax liability was a part of its tax planning, which every company does and is a legitimate activity.

The company, however, faced the wrath of people and politicians. There were calls for Starbucks to be boycotted over its non-payment of tax. The practice was seen as unfair and against the interests of the countries where such companies operate.

Companies and individuals the world seek to minimize their tax liability through tax planning. By making the most of the tools and mechanisms available in tax laws, they use allowances, deductions, rebates, and exemptions to claim deductions. This is a legitimate activity, but is seen as too aggressive

(Contd)

ETHICAL INSIGHT (Contd)

when it uses the provisions not intended as, or anticipated by governments.

In case of Starbucks, the company paid no income tax on sales of £1.2 billion in the UK. Yet, transcripts of investor and analyst calls over 12 years show how Starbucks officials regularly talked about the UK business as being 'profitable'. They said that they were very pleased with it, and even cited it as an example to follow for operations back home in the United States.

Starbucks was complying with the law; but was it ethical?

This is a difficult question to answer. If a company follows all provisions of the law in a country and gets benefit from skilfully managing laws, is it also not being ethical? The public was angry that the government was cutting spending; in such an environment, systematic tax avoidance by rich individuals and companies struck a particularly ugly note. Avoiding tax was seen as avoiding social obligation. The company was accused of greed and selfishness, damaging its reputation, and destroying the public's trust. Other companies such as Google and Amazon also faced public anger as they were also paying very little taxes in the UK.

Paying a fair amount of tax in the countries where the companies operate is seen as being socially responsible. Taxes provide funds for public services such as healthcare, education, and infrastructure. These are public services which companies benefit from either directly or indirectly. Tax avoidance has been branded by some as an immoral and unethical practice that undermines the very integrity of the tax system.

Companies argue that their responsibility is to maximize value for their shareholders and that includes keeping tax costs to a minimum through legal means. Companies, however, can avoid taxes by showing excessive expenses and reporting losses on their operations. It is quite plausible that a company that has high sales but pays no tax may be making no profit. The General Anti-Avoidance Rule (GAAR) provides some clarity around what is tax avoidance, but legislation that centres on ideas of what is 'reasonable' behaviour is too subjective to define. What businesses most want out of a tax system is certainty; they want to know what their tax bills will be so they can plan their strategy and investments accordingly.

Though there was no suggestion that Starbucks had broken any law, faced with mounting criticism, Starbucks caved in to public pressure and agreed to pay £10 million in 2013–14, despite incurring losses. The company said that it would not claim tax deductions for royalties, coffee purchases, interest on inter-company loans, or capital allowances, and would not carry forward tax losses. It said the resulting payments would be above those required by the law.

Several questions arise about tax avoidance. If a company reduces its tax liability legally, should it still pay additional taxes because people think it is paying too less? If so, how much additional burden should they bear? At the same time, government and business should ensure that corporate tax contributions are a demonstrably fair return to society.

This case illustrates that avoiding taxes may be legal, but it raises ethical questions. Rather than hiding behind tax avoidance, companies need to be transparent about their tax planning. This would restore public trust and bring more certainty for business.

Global firms such as Starbucks, Google, and Amazon have come under fire for avoiding paying tax on their British sales. There seems to be a growing culture of naming and shaming companies. Should companies worry?

Questions for Discussion

1. If a company follows all laws, can it still be ethical?
2. What is the difference between legality and ethics?
3. What exactly is ethics?
4. Do consumers really bother about companies behaving ethically or are they simply interested in making profits?

Sources:
BBC News Magazine, http://www.bbc.com/news/magazine-20560359, 21 May 2013, last accessed on 26 July 2014.
Reuters, http://www.reuters.com/article/2012/10/15/us-britain-starbucks-tax-idUSBRE89E0EX20121015, 15 October 2012, last accessed on 26 July 2014.
The Guardian, http://www.theguardian.com/sustainable-business/avoiding-tax-legal-but-ever-ethical, 23 April 2013, last accessed on 26 July 2014
The Financial Times, http://www.ft.com/cms/s/0/ac97bb1e-3fa5-11e2-b0ce-00144feabdc0.html#axzz36NQKk3Lg, 6 December 2012, last accessed on 26 July 2014.

Pursuit of Low Prices and Ethical Considerations

At heart of the issue of marketing ethics is the one factor that most consumers want—low prices. However, they do not consider how low prices can be offered without exploiting either human or environmental resources. Moreover, ethical choices often come with a cost—a company will do everything ethically and lawfully, but will have to sell goods at higher prices than those offered by competitors who are not so ethical. This leads them to a disadvantage, as consumers are not prepared to pay a premium for more ethical goods and services.

Ethical behaviour in the marketplace has two sides—companies who would like to reduce costs even while disregarding some ethical consideration, and the consumers who clamour for low prices.

In a free market economy, a company acts in its own interests. The purpose of marketing is to create competitive advantage. A company achieves this purpose when it does a better job than its competitors in meeting customers' needs at a lower cost. There are no pressing considerations to focus on ethical values because the job of the company is to simply make and supply products and services better than others, and thereby make a profit. The focus on ethics comes into play because of the following two reasons:

1. First, it is assumed that if a company behaves ethically, customers would develop a positive attitude towards it, its products, and services. If a company does not employ ethical marketing practices, it may lead to dissatisfied customers, bad publicity, a lack of trust, loss of business, and sometimes, legal action as well. As the risk is very high, most companies try to look ethical so that consumers develop and maintain positive feelings towards them.

2. Second, though it is recognized that companies must make a profit, there is a moral and a social responsibility on them to behave ethically. There is also pressure from social and government organizations. Consumer interest groups, professional associations, NGOs, and the media exert considerable influence on a company's activities. Companies must adhere to a wide range of laws and regulations that aim to protect consumer rights and the environment, provide safe products, and adhere to guarantees and fairness in trade.

ETHICAL INSIGHT
Recent Bribery Scandals

Some of the famous business scandals that have hit the headlines show grave ethical gaps in the way that companies are managed.

- Walmart de Mexico, a highly successful business for Walmart (one-fifth of Walmart's stores worldwide are in Mexico), systematically bribed Mexican government officials for years. The bribes, which may have totalled more than $24 million, were paid to win permission to open new stores more quickly than would have been possible had the company adhered to Mexican laws.
- The largest corporate foreign corruption case to date is Siemens AG's (SIEGn.DE) $1.6 billion settlement with the Justice Department and other authorities in 2008 over an alleged bribery scheme in Argentina.
- Hewlett-Packard (HP) was fined $108 million to settle a corruption scandal involving employees at subsidiaries in three countries, who were charged

(Contd)

ETHICAL INSIGHT (Contd)

with bribing government officials to win and retain lucrative public contracts. Corruption was unearthed in contracts to install IT equipment at the national police headquarters in Poland, €35 million of work for government prosecutors in Russia, and a deal to supply Mexico's state-owned petroleum company.

- GSK's former head of operations in China was arrested on charges of bribery on a widespread scale. Officials arrested four senior managers from GSK's China business while investigating RMB3bn (£320m) in potential bribes to individuals at every level of the health-care system, from doctors to government officials in order to win market share and agree to higher prices.
- Aluminium producer, Alcoa reached a settlement with the US Securities and Exchange Commission and the Department of Justice over charges of bribing Bahraini officials. From 1989 until 2009, Alcoa had Aluminium Bahrain B.S.C. (Alba), a company that is one of the largest aluminium smelters in the world, as one of its largest customers. An SEC investigation found that Alcoa made more than $110 million payments to Bahraini officials who had influence over contract negotiations between Alcoa and the government-operated aluminium plant.

Discuss these scandals with your friends. Additional information can be obtained from the Internet. In each of these scandals, decide as to what went wrong. Could they have been avoided? How?

Sources:
'Alcoa reaches settlement with SEC and DOJ over Bahraini bribery scandal', Forbes, 2014, http://www.forbes.com/sites/maggiemcgrath/2014/01/09/alcoa-reaches-settlement-with-sec-and-doj-over-bahraini-bribery-scandal/.
'GSK bribery scandal could cause 'irreparable damage', says China', The Telegraph, 16 May 2014.
'Hewlett-Packard to pay $108m to settle scandal over bribery of public officials', The Guardian, 9 April 2014.
'Wal-Mart pays lawyer fees for dozens of executives in bribery probe', Reuters, 2013, http://www.reuters.com/article/2013/12/04/us-walmart-bribery-lawyers-idUSBRE9B305W20131204.
All last accessed on 19 October 2014.

ETHICAL ISSUES IN MARKETING

Marketing managers have to ensure that goods are available in markets and that they make a profit from their activities. Often, their objective is 'to get the job done' rather than think about the consequences of their actions. This gives rise to several ethical issues that have been reported in the various scandals involving companies that have erupted in the past. These scandals relate to the following:

Gifts and bribes Gifts and bribes are often demanded by buyers and offered by sellers for better orders or for protection in markets. In economies that are not open, government officials can stall competitors, hold up permissions, or provide protection for certain companies in exchange for a consideration. In institutional buying, bribes in cash and kind are often given to consumers for larger or long-term orders. In India, companies spend huge amounts in giving gifts to their large customers during the Diwali season, hoping for benefits in return. When such scandals are reported in the press, it results in regulatory action and consumer backlash (see Ethical Insight—Recent Bribery Scandals).

Price discrimination and unfair pricing Consumers complain if they are charged more or find that they got a raw deal from companies. There have been cases where companies have been fined for price discrimination or for charging unfair prices. For instance, products come marked with a maximum retail price (MRP) in India. The law stipulates that any retailer charging more than MRP is liable to a fine up to ₹5000 or serve a prison term of five years with a fine.

Discriminatory and dishonest advertising Very often companies make false claims or resort to discriminatory advertising to increase sales. Many countries have enacted laws to prevent these practices. Advertising is also sometimes accused of showing violence, sex, and profanity. Sexual innuendo is common in advertising. Further, advertising of certain products may strongly offend some people. Some examples include feminine hygiene products, illnesses such as haemorrhoids and constipation, obesity, cultural mistakes, and so on. Some companies have actually marketed themselves on the basis of controversial advertising. Negative advertising techniques, such as attack ads, or highlighting the disadvantages of competitors is also considered unethical. In this context, liberation marketing is a strategy whereby a product masquerades behind an image that appeals to a range of values, including ethical values related to lifestyle and anti-consumerism.

Unfair competitive practices Unfair competition is defined as any fraudulent, deceptive, or dishonest trade practice that is prohibited by statute or regulation. Laws have been enacted by countries to protect consumers and businesses alike against deceptive business practices, such as trademark infringements, trade defamation, and misappropriation of business trade secrets. Competition laws are designed to prevent unfair pricing strategies, restricting monopolies, and false or misleading representations.

Cheating customers and unfair selling practices Companies often make false claims and promises while selling their products. They are also able to sell cheaper goods by avoiding local taxes. Laws make such practices illegal; this also includes selling under-weight products, goods which are beyond their expiry dates, and making promises that are not kept. Another fraudulent selling practice consists of pyramid schemes that promise to make money by recruiting people for direct selling of products. These are also called 'Ponzi' schemes, and they work by asking new participants to make a payment to join, who then get a commission, based on the number of people they further recruit.

Price collusion Sometimes companies join hands to keep the price of a product or service at a higher level so as to overcharge customers and make huge profits. Price collusion is also done to chase out competitors by pricing products at a lower level. Among the practices in pricing that are considered unethical are price fixing, price skimming and price discrimination, variable pricing, predatory pricing, bid rigging, and dumping.

Dishonesty in making or keeping a contract Companies sometimes renege on contracts. For instance, selling a house but not completing it on time, or under-delivering of goods. They also tend to give guarantees and warrantees on their products but later fail to honour their contracts. Customers often have to take recourse to legal action to get these contracts enforced. Going by the number of consumer complaints in consumer courts, many companies appear to follow this unethical practice.

Unfairness to employees While treatment of employees does not strictly fall under marketing activities, it reflects badly upon the company and affects consumer behaviour. As our closing case shows, an accident in a factory in Bangladesh resulted in consumer boycott of the brands in England. Nike, too, faced consumer backlash in the 1990s when a report—documenting low wages and poor working conditions in its manufacturing unit in Indonesia—was published. A Nike subcontractor was paying 14 cents an hour to workers, less than minimum wages, and other kinds of abuse that were meted out were documented. There were protests against the company at the Barcelona Olympics in 1992. Such bad publicity and consumer backlash has to be avoided at all costs.

Targeting vulnerable sections of the population Companies are often accused of targeting vulnerable sections of the population such as children and young people, obese people, the elderly, and so on. Making psychological and fear appeals, such people are conned into buying things they never needed, often doing harm to themselves. Such practices are considered unethical.

Portraying certain sections in poor light Advertisements frequently portray certain sections of the society in poor light. Questions have been raised, for instance, on the portrayal of dark skin in ads. People who do not know or do not use a certain product are depicted as backward. Ads also depict people making fun of others who use other products.

Denying after-sales service Salesmen often convince customers that their company will provide excellent after-sales service for the products sold. Yet, when people call up company helplines, they are put in endless loops of automated voice response systems. If at all they get through to talk to a representative, they are given excuses so as to avoid providing service. In many cases, companies ask their customers to ship the product to the factory for repairs which is cumbersome for many people.

Tax avoidance Tax planning, by means of using provisions of tax laws, is a perfectly legitimate activity followed by companies. Strictly speaking, it does not affect consumers. Yet, if they perceive that the company is avoiding its responsibility by paying less tax, it can have serious repercussions. As our chapter-opening case study shows, Starbucks faced consumer anger in the UK when it was reported that the company had paid very little taxes in that country despite high sales.

It is seen from the aforementioned instances that everything that a company does is liable to affect its consumers. Companies, therefore, have to focus on all aspects of their business, from manufacturing to hiring to subcontracting, if they are to avoid consumer backlash and loss of reputation. Both intended and unintended consequences of manufacturing and selling have to be kept in mind at all times.

Marketing ethics can be examined on two aspects:

Intended consequences If a company deliberately misleads the consumer by giving wrong information or deliberately disregards harm done by it in manufacturing, distributing, or selling its products

Unintended consequences If some harm is done unintentionally to the consumer or community as a result of activities of a company

Intended Consequences

It is difficult to differentiate between intended and unintended consequences of marketing activities. For instance, when a tobacco or alcohol industry advertises, is it intended that people may become habitual to their products and fall ill? Or, if a fast food company advertises cheaper combo meals, is it intended that people become obese as a result of consuming something that they do not need?

Nevertheless, companies can introduce checks and balances so that they do not intentionally commit acts that may be considered unethical. The theory of due care describes how unethical intended consequences can be avoided.

Theory of Due Care

The theory of due care helps specify what companies and organizations owe to their customers. Companies have the moral responsibility for their products and services to

- meet safety standards warranted by the product
- accept responsibility for accidents resulting from faulty functioning
- monitor the manufacturing process so that defective products are not sold
- issue adequate safety warnings about products
- respond to and investigate consumer complaints

Fleckenstein (2008) explains that a consumer expects that a product purchased is as safe as possible. The 'due care' approach is based on the assumption that the manufacturer has greater knowledge, and thus, has the moral duty to deliver a product that is safe and lives up to its claims. The due care theory involves the following elements:

Design Companies have a responsibility to design products that are safe, meet all governmental regulations, and specifications, and should be reasonably durable. The design should incorporate safety devices and mechanisms.

Materials The materials used in the manufacture should be safe and durable, and meet governmental regulations.

Production The products should be without defects, the production processes should be safe for workers, and companies should break any laws relating to hiring and compensation. Cutting corners on quality without informing customers is considered unethical. The product's quality should be such that product performance meets expectations with regard to reliability, service life, maintainability, and safety.

Quality control Products must be inspected regularly for quality, so that defective products do not find their way into people's homes.

Packaging Products should be safely packed and carry proper labelling and warnings. They should have clear, easily understood directions for use, including a clear description of hazards.

Recall Companies should have a system to recall products that have defects that cause them to be dangerous.

Business methods Companies have to follow business methods that are not exploitative. For instance, pharmaceutical companies often bribe doctors to prescribe their brands to patients, sometimes unnecessarily, in order to meet targets. Such practices invite government wrath and consumer complaints.

Unintended Consequences

Marketing, with its emphasis on consumption, has a number of unintended consequences. Traditionally, values of thrift and savings have been taught to children; today, the consumer society wants to fulfil needs 'here and now', because progress is measured by ever-rising consumption. It does not matter if people become fat or poor in the process. Some of the after effects of the consumer society are obesity, rise in consumer debt, and degradation of the environment. Sove and Warde (2002) write that the modern consumer culture has been admonished because of the following:

- Large sections of the world population are excluded
- Material prosperity fails to bring happiness
- Leads to wastage of resources
- Materialism compromises spiritual values
- Culture is vulgarized

Other causes for admonishing the consumer culture and unbridled consumption include the following:

- Epidemic of obesity in the modern world
- Rise in consumer debt
- Horrifying environmental impact

We discuss these unintended consequences in this section.

Exclusion of the poor The meaning of life has been reduced to consuming goods and services. To consume is the surest route to happiness, social status, and national economic growth. However, this thinking ignores millions of people who cannot afford new products. A large section of the population, which cannot afford market offerings cannot assimilate the new culture, and this leads to alienation and isolation. It leads to denial of resources, goods and services, and eventually, to social inequality and tension.

Elusive search for happiness Consumers are stimulated to buy and, therefore, marketing attempts to create unfulfilled needs at all times. Consequently, people are dissatisfied with what they have or who they are, leading to unnecessary tension in their lives. It is said that modern progress produces human unhappiness as it produces only material wealth. The consumer culture manipulates people. Vulnerable groups are targeted and addictions developed. Availability of easy credit and playing on emotions traps consumers endlessly.

Wastage of resources Products are made psychologically obsolete long before they physically wear out, leading to waste of resources. Chronic purchasing of new goods and services with little attention to their true need, durability, working conditions, or environmental impact encourages waste.

Compromise of spiritual values The religion of the market replaces humanity and spirituality. It seeks fulfilment through materialism. Technology has left us isolated with no sense of belonging. You are what you own and the more you own, the happier you will be. All problems have a material or monetary solution. People use spending and materialism as a way to build their ego or become a new person by buying products, which support their self-image. As opposed to spiritual values, things are given meaning, identities, and personality. Everybody is a walking advertisement. Spiritual values are ignored.

Culture gets vulgarized Consumerism brings in a culture of vulgarity. There is widespread lack of moral discipline; marketing encourages glorification of greed and material accumulation, leading to breakdown in family and community, inequality, rise of lawlessness and disorder, racism and bigotry, and priority of personal interests over those of the country and humanity.

In the culture of consumerism, our language is becoming increasingly coarse, we do not flinch at images of nudity and violence, and the lyrics of our songs are degenerating.

Siegel (2013) explains that the 'explicit sexual innuendo and nakedly explicit violence come fast and furious. Old and young, high and low, the idiom is the same. Everything goes.' Leisure is organized around consumption, which becomes the basis for social relationships. Many people have no interests or activities other than consuming things. The culture of consumption dominates and replaces traditional culture. Social relations are stripped of any social–historical context. There is loss of cultural diversity through cultural homogenization—everything is covered with a blanket of sameness of consumption.

Obesity   One-third of people on this planet are overweight, according to a study published in *The Lancet*. There has been a startling increase in rates of obesity and overweight in both adults (28 per cent increase) and children (up by 47 per cent) in the past 33 years. The number of overweight and obese people has risen from 857 million in 1980 to 2.1 billion in 2013, reports *The Times of India* (2014).

Consumer debt   Reserve Bank of India (RBI) data shows that financial liabilities of Indian households have gone up sharply and stand at ₹2.74 lakh crore in 2012. The decade saw two major trends leading to a sharp rise in consumption expenditure. Home loans have now become popular with no stigma attached any more. The age bar of people opting for home loans has come down from those in mid-forties to early thirties. Moreover, the very young have got addicted to credit card spending, leaving them with very little to save.

Environmental degradation   As mentioned earlier, the consumer society places emphasis on consumption. Durning (1992) explains that in the process, it has been stunningly effective in harming the environment. At the same time, it has failed to provide humanity with a sense of fulfilment. 'Consumerism has hoodwinked us into gorging on material things because we suffer from social, psychological, and spiritual hungers,' he writes. It has also led to environmental degradation worldwide. Poor people are forced to clear forest lands to plough, the oceans suffer from over-fishing, and the mineral wealth of the planet has been eroded. At the same time, the by-products of consumerism—emissions that have led to global warming, large swathes of industrial and consumer wastes, and the environment becoming toxic—threaten our very existence.

CB IN ACTION   Excessive Consumerism

Excessive consumerism leads to pollution, hazardous wastes, exhausted resources, irreversible environmental damage, spiritual withdrawal, and an increased gap and rising inequalities, as described in this chapter. Short-term satisfaction is encouraged rather than long-term health of the planet and its people.

Consumer choices, taste and style, are seen to be indicators of who they are as a person and of their status of class, prestige, status, and hierarchy. Human values matter less and less in the consumer society.

The consumer is the centre of the society which, through choices, exercises power over economic institutions. Usually the choices made are quick, convenient, or cheap, without taking a long-term view on the health of the planet. There is commercialization of leisure and mechanization of the home so that there are more things to buy. Social activities and emotions are turned into economic activities.

Do you think that the consumer society has given us more benefits or will it eventually lead us to our doom? Is humanity short-sighted?

> **MARKETING INSIGHT**
> **Dumb and Dumber**
>
> One of the major consequences of marketing and advertising, as perceived by many people, is that it is making the society progressively dumb. Research conducted by a team from Stanford University shows that we are indeed losing our intellectual and emotional capabilities because the mutations in genes contributing to brain power is not being selected among people because we no longer need intelligence to survive.
>
> That is because marketing reduces everything to a matter of consumption. Heart break? Have a chocolate. Want to turn environment-friendly? Have a soft drink in a green bottle. A pimple on your chin? Apply a cream. Everything in life has been reduced to simple acts of consuming.
>
> Dumbing down is described as the deliberate diminution of the intellectual level of society. It is used to describe the invasion of 'pop' culture propagated by advertising to wipe out high culture in which activities relating to the classical arts were held in the high regard by society. Popular culture, which was once considered ephemeral, commercial, and thus inferior, has invaded all levels of society today. The repercussions are visible in many areas of endeavour.
>
> **Education** Short-term courses and online education promises to make people experts without much effort. Online education claims that you can 'earn your college degree in your pajamas'.
>
> **Literature** Serious writing takes a back-seat as the market is flooded with easy to read short novels that can be read in a few hours. Ask your friends whether they have read *Brave New World* or *Crime and Punishment*, and few will answer in the affirmative.
>
> **Medicine** Many people trust modern medicine, thinking that it is easy to solve medical problems. Hospitals, too, sell knee replacements, heart bypass procedures, hip, and other body part replacements as 'plug and play' procedures.
>
> **Cinema and TV** Gone are the days when plays and movies were made on classic literature. Today's cinema is not made for social causes but for quick consumption.
>
> **News** News is presented to catch the viewer's attention. Crime and local politics are presented as 'breaking news' while serious issues are pushed down in priority.
>
> This has led to the charge that advertising has contributed to the dumbing down of society. Products are reduced to messages of a few seconds, so everything has to be presented in a simple style.
>
> Debate on the issue with your friends and classmates. Do you agree that advertising is making us dumb? Or, is the combination of technology and advertising making us smart?

As a result of the negative impact on the society, people think of ways to reduce the impact of their consumption. This awareness has slowly been dawning on humanity. The developed countries are on the forefront of this awareness but the poor countries are still plundering their environment. One way is to follow ethical consumption, but even in this there are sizeable roadblocks. These are described in the next section.

ETHICAL CONSUMPTION

When consumers become aware and prefer buying products, which are ethically produced and/or which are not harmful to the environment and society, it is called ethical consumption. The Institute of Grocery Distribution (IGD) defines ethical consumerism as 'the practice of purchasing products and services produced in a way that minimizes social and/or environmental damage, while avoiding products and services deemed to have a negative impact on society or the environment.'

The concept of becoming ethical consumers arises from the fact that every human activity—from breathing to commuting to eating—produces carbon dioxide. A person's (or organizations') carbon footprint is the sum of all emissions of greenhouse gases like carbon dioxide, induced by activities in a given time frame. Readers can calculate their carbon footprint at http://www.carbonfootprint.com/calculator.aspx and at http://footprint.wwf.org.uk/. Our lifestyle and consumption make up the size of our carbon footprint. Consumers who are aware try to reduce their carbon footprint through ethical consumption.

There are many manifestations of ethical consumerism such as follows:

Buying local produce   When we buy goods transported across large distances, we indirectly contribute to excess energy consumed for the transportation. Buying local produce from a farmers' market helps us minimize 'food miles', or the energy spent on getting the food to us.

Boycotting goods produced by child labour   This includes buying goods from factories that have not used child labour or exploited workers contributes towards fair trade practices.

Buying organic products   Organic products are those that have not used industrial fertilizers and pesticides. By buying organic products, consumers contribute to environment-friendly practices.

Buying energy-efficient lighting   By using energy efficient lighting devices, people can reduce electricity consumption and thereby, their carbon footprint. Similarly, using renewable energy and recycled products helps in becoming ethical consumers.

The assumption underlying ethical consumption is that consumers vote with their purchasing power—if large numbers of consumers start following such practices, it would affect manufacturing processes and trade practices. Getting customers to change, however, is a difficult task.

Factors Impeding Ethical Consumption

Though many people agree that ethical consumption can help reduce the burden on the environment, it is difficult to implement it. Carrigan and Attalla (2001) found that most consumers did not bother about ethical considerations in their purchase decision-making behaviour. Evidence provided by them suggests that the emphasis on social responsibility and marketing ethics is misplaced because the link between social responsibility and consumer purchase behaviour remained unproven.

A study conducted by Bray, Johns, and Kilburn (2011) found that the key factors that impede consumers from consuming ethical goods are price, which was an oft-repeated factor, followed respectively by experience, ethical obligation, lack of information, quality perception, inertia, cynicism, and suppressing their guilt. These are discussed here.

Price sensitivity   The study reported that participants often mentioned price, suggesting that they cared more about financial than ethical values, particularly with reference to food and other frequently purchased items. When they purchased an ethical alternative, people seemed to experience post-purchase dissonance as soon as they noticed that the price was higher. In some cases, this resulted in the future avoidance of ethical products. Participants said that they did care about ethical issues and were willing to pay slightly more; however, they were reluctant to pay more than a few pence extra for goods for which they saw no significant tangible reward.

Personal experience   McDevitt, et al. (2007) write that people do not recognize the ethical consequences of their purchasing choices. Consumers are receptive to changes in their purchasing when a particular news story forces them to think about an ethical issue or when they were personally affected. Recent negative news stories generated more interest than positive stories.

Gap between thought and action   Though consumers expressed support for ethical purchasing, there were contradictions between rhetoric and action. Although consumers spoke of an obligation to 'do one's bit', they gave various reasons why it was 'too difficult' to consume on a purely ethical basis.

Lack of information   Very often, consumers felt that they did not have enough knowledge to make ethical decisions. Avoiding unethical products or companies that had received bad press was more important. However, even negative stories did not encourage ethical consumption as people tended to be turned off from the unethical ones but this did not necessarily push them towards ethical choices.

Quality perception   Consumers also felt that ethical products were poorer in quality. Carrigan and Attalla (2001) note that consumers have an 'unhealthy scepticism' that there is little to choose between companies. Since the perceived quality of ethical goods was not good, consumers just bought what was easily available.

Inertia in purchasing behaviour   Habit is another factor preventing people from switching to ethical consumption. Purchasing inertia prevented any change, or even consideration of change, in consumption patterns. Brand loyalty also made them less likely to move towards an ethical option.

Cynicism   There was also cynicism about ethical claims of products. It was felt that claims were just a means to charge higher prices. Companies were not seen as sincere. Many consumers also feel that when companies collect donations for social causes, the money did not reach the proper beneficiaries.

Suppressing guilt   Though consumers have a sense of guilt, it was not a part of the decision-making process. Consumers tended to suppress their feelings of guilt by expressing doubt that their purchase would have actually not made a difference.

Due to these very powerful factors that impede ethical consumption, companies could well ask, 'Do Ethics Matter?' Carrigan and Attalla (2001) question whether ethics really matter in purchase behaviour. They question the assumption that an ethical company would attract customers whereas an unethical company would have consumers boycotting its products. This is especially true in poor countries, where people are very price-conscious because of low incomes. Smaller manufacturing units provide cheaper products than large companies by disregarding taxes or making investments in environment-friendly practices. For instance, a large hospital may have installed a means of waste disposal and thereby become more expensive, but smaller clinics simply throw it out in the open.

Many companies feel that there may be very little commercial reward in terms of consumer purchases to be gained by behaving ethically. Therefore, some companies are guilty of trying to hoodwink customers into believing that their products are ethical and environment-friendly when they are not. Some companies merely change the label on their products to appear ethical. This is discussed in the next section.

Sins of Greenwashing

Greenwashing is defined as disinformation disseminated by an organization so as to present an environmentally responsible public image. It includes the practice of misleading customers about the ethical or environmental benefits of a product through false advertising.

Forbes (2012) described some examples of greenwashing—a water bottler claimed that its bottles were 'biodegradable' and 'recyclable,' when actually they were not. No reliable scientific evidence that the product would decompose in a reasonably short-time frame was provided. A soft drink manufacturer claimed that its bottles were 'environmentally friendly and superior'. It was found that the company's overall manufacturing, distribution, and packaging of the water caused as much, if not more, of an adverse environmental impact when compared to similar bottled water, and hence, the claim was disputed.

Some more examples of greenwashing are given here:
- The tag 'biodegradable' is misleading. A host of products are termed biodegradable as ultimately they will break down—it could take a year, ten years, or ten thousand years.
- 'Green tourism' is being promoted by a host of resorts. Yet, these very resorts dump their kitchen wastes and untreated sewerage on hills and in lakes.
- When you use 'whole grain bread' check out the percentage of whole grain in it. When you buy 'fat-free' and 'low salt' products, do check out the actual fat and salt content on these packs. Some claims like 'high fibre' cannot simply be checked by consumers. These are common examples of greenwashing.

Terrachoice (2010) has described seven sins of greenwashing. According to its website, http://sinsofgreenwashing.org/, more than 95 per cent of the products claiming to be green were found to commit at least one of the sins listed as follows:

Sin of the hidden trade-off   Such a sin is committed by suggesting that a product is 'green', based on a narrow set of attributes. Recycled paper, for example, is not necessarily environmentally-preferable; other important environmental issues in the paper-making process, including energy, greenhouse gas emissions, and water and air pollution, may be equally or more significant.

Sin of no proof   Companies often make an environmental claim that cannot be substantiated. In the absence of third-party certification, it is difficult to verify the claims made. For instance, there is no way of ascertaining whether a product claiming to be green was actually grown on an organic farm.

Sin of vagueness   Very often, claims are made on product labels and advertisements that is so poorly defined that its real meaning is not clear. For instance, the line 'made from natural extracts' and 'all natural' is quite misleading, because everything can be labelled as natural. Arsenic, uranium, mercury, and formaldehyde are all naturally occurring, but also poisonous. Such a claim is not necessarily green and is misleading.

Sin of irrelevance   Another method of misguiding is to make a claim that may be correct but is unimportant or irrelevant. For example, the claim 'CFC-free' is correct, but since chlorofluorocarbons (CFCs) are banned, it is merely stating the legal position.

Sin of lesser of two evils   When a claim is made that may be true, but distracts the consumer from the greater environmental impacts of the product category, it is referred to as sin of lesser of two evils. For example, an SUV advertised as 'the most fuel-efficient SUV' may be true in its product class, but other hides the fact that better fuel efficient vehicles exist.

Sin of fibbing In this category, the company makes environmental claims that are simply false. Products are merely given labels even though no changes are made to them.

Sin of worshiping false labels Some companies give the impression, through words or images, that a third party has endorsed the product even where no such endorsement actually exists.

Ogilvy Earth (2010) in its report, *From Greenwashing to Great*, advises companies on how to avoid the charge of greenwashing. Among other things, it says that companies should focus on fundamentals, make honesty a priority, find strength in humility, show and do not tell, and commit for the long term.

As the world globalizes, new ethical issues emerge. Global supply chains are built, for instance, on the premise of low cost. Yet, countries which offer low costs also are notorious for their abuse of the environmental and human resources. The cheap prices that consumers pay for their favourite brands, in fact, hide many ethical problems.

ETHICAL INSIGHT
Controversial Marketing Methods

Some marketing methods are considered unethical, but are so common that readers can easily spot them. Companies indulge in the following practices:

Bait and switch The practice in which the customers are first provided a 'bait;—some extremely cheap items, through advertising, but when customers visit the store, they discover that the advertised goods are not available. They are convinced by sales people to 'switch' to, or buy similar but higher priced items. 'Breakfast at one rupee' is one such example, because the cheap breakfast can only be availed with a ₹5000 per night hotel room.

Pyramid schemes Generally used by direct marketing companies, these schemes charge people to become members who, in turn, recruit more members. The higher the level that you join, the more commissions you make. The money collected is given as commissions to the recruiters. However, these commissions are not sustainable and ultimately, such schemes collapse.

Scarcity and planned obsolescence Sometimes, companies create artificial shortage of goods by supplying less to their distributors. Planned obsolescence is the policy of planning or designing a product with a limited useful life, so that it will become obsolete after a certain period of time. To remain fashionable, customers have to continue buying new products. Thus, companies are able to sell new products at higher prices. Such practices are seen commonly in technology marketing, where new versions of products and upgrades are launched regularly so that a person has to keep buying new ones.

Vendor lock-in It is a situation in which a customer using a product or service cannot easily change to a competitor. This happens because of proprietary technologies that are incompatible with others.

Viral marketing This refers to marketing techniques that use existing social networking and other technologies to try to produce increases in brand awareness through self-replicating viral processes. The idea is to get people talking and posting on social networking sites about brands and companies. People are persuaded to buy not on product attributes but because something funny or stupid has been posted about it.

Guerilla marketing This refers to low-cost, unconventional marketing tactics, which include ambushes, sabotage, raids, and elements of surprise. The aim of guerrilla marketing is to surprise the customer, make an impression, which, in turn, spreads viral messages. For example, in events like the World Cup, guerrilla tactics are unethical because they are is unfair to the company that has paid a huge sum for legitimate marketing rights.

(Contd)

ETHICAL INSIGHT (Contd)

Anti-competition practices Anti-competitive practices are such practices that prevent or reduce competition in a market. These include dumping, exclusive dealing, price fixing, and a host of similar practices.

Search engine optimization Search engine optimization (SEO) is the process of affecting the visibility of a website or a web page in a search engine's natural search results. The more commonly searched words that a search engine can pick up, the higher ranked will be the website. Very often, customers are directed to useless sites through SEO tactics when they are looking for genuine products.

Spamdexing Spamdexing is the practice of including certain words in a web page so that search engines can index it and improve its ranking. Consequently, consumers are guided to illegitimate sites. It is also called overstuffing—including a key word dozens or even hundreds of times on a web page so that a search engine ranks it higher.

Embrace, extend, and extinguish A strategy for entering product categories involving widely used standards, extending those standards with proprietary capabilities, and then using those differences to disadvantage its competitors. This strategy was first used by Microsoft.

Spyware and adware Spyware is a means of making money by giving free software to customers. However, the free software has banner ads embedded in the products from which the developer makes money. It is another term for advertising supported software (Adware). While the consumer does not have to pay for the software, the developers are still making money. The annoying banners can only be removed by paying a license fee. The companies also install additional tracking software on your system, which continuously send statistical data to the company about you and your surfing habits to a remote location without your consent.

Classify the methods discussed into unethical and ethical. Give reasons for your answer. Apply the fundamentals given in the *Ogilvy Earth* report discussed in the text and then decide whether they meet the required criteria or not.

GLOBALIZATION AND ETHICS

Globalization has made a deep impact on social responsibility and ethics. As people become aware of practices in other countries, they become more demanding at home.

The World Trade Organization (WTO) is primarily responsible for policing the world trading system and making sure that nation states adhere to the rules laid down in trade treaties signed by member states. Due to the globalization, international companies have to deal with ethical issues in cross-cultural settings. They are often criticized for ethical misconduct as they operate in different values and ethical norms. They face this dilemma—which ethical position should a company assume in a foreign culture? Should they follow the ethical standards back home or the ethical standards of host countries? For example, giving business gifts of high value to customers, for example, is generally condemned in the US, but in many countries including India, gifts are not only accepted but also expected. It would be impossible to do business in countries that are rated high on the corruption index without giving bribes, yet such practices when exposed cause many problems.

Some of the ethical problems faced in international markets are as follows:

Traditional small-scale bribery This involves payment of small sums of money to government officials to speed up routine actions. When goods are transported across India, small sums are demanded by policemen just to let a truck pass.

Large-scale bribery Large bribes are paid to allow a violation of the law or to influence government policy. Political contributions are also demanded from companies.

Gifts, favours, and entertainment Gifts and opportunities for personal travel at the company's expense, favours and expensive entertainment are some of the ways that customers or officials are sought to be influenced. These are common in B2B transactions.

Pricing Many unethical issues arise in pricing, such as unfair differential pricing, or manipulating invoices, where the buyer requests a written invoice showing a price other than the actual price paid, pricing to force out local competition, dumping products at prices well below that in the home country, and following pricing practices that are illegal in the home country but legal in the host country.

Products or technology Products and technology banned in the home country are exported as no laws exist in the host country. Very often, polluting or outdated technologies are exported to less developed countries where such laws do not exist or are lax.

Tax evasion practices Transfer pricing, where prices paid between affiliates and the parent company are adjusted to avoid showing profits and thereby avoid taxes, the use of tax havens, adjusted interest payments on intra-firm loans, charging management, and service fees between affiliates and the parent company are some of the tax evasion practices followed by industry.

Illegal or immoral activities Illegal practices such as polluting the environment, maintaining unsafe working conditions, copying of product or technology, short-weighting overseas shipments, and so on.

Questionable commissions to channel members Channel members such as agents and distributors are paid large amounts so that they may hinder the distribution of rival products.

Involvement in political affairs Sometimes, multinational companies interfere in political affairs of host countries. Such practices turn away generations of consumers, as is evident in the boycott of US goods in many countries of the Middle East.

DeGeorge (2000) proposes five guidelines that will help international companies:

- Do not do intentional harm.
- Do more good than harm for the host country.
- Respect the rights of employees and of all others affected by the company's actions or policies.
- To the extent consistent with ethical norms, respect the local culture and work with and not against it.
- Multinationals should pay their fair share of taxes.

CONSUMER PROTECTION

The government tries to protect consumers through legislation and has enacted laws for this purpose. It requires businesses to disclose detailed information about products, particularly in areas where safety or public health is involved, like food.

Consumer protection laws, enacted in various countries, regulate relationships between consumers and companies. It covers a wide range of topics including product liability, privacy rights, unfair business practices, fraud, misrepresentation, and other consumer or business interactions.

In India, the Consumer Protection Act, 1986, has given recognition to consumer rights. A three-tier grievance redressal machinery has been introduced, at the district, state, and national level. The Act protects the interests of consumers to prevent being exploited by traders and manufacturers. However, it does not include a person who obtains goods for resale or for commercial purpose.

Consumers now have recourse to dead phones, malfunctioning television sets, delayed liquefied petroleum gas (LPG) connections, losses due to negligence in banks and hospitals, medical malpractices, and a host of promises not met by manufacturers and service providers. The Act enshrines the following rights:

- The right to be protected against the marketing of goods, which are hazardous to life and property
- The right to be informed about the quality, quantity, potency, purity, standard, and price of goods so as to protect the consumer against unfair trade practices
- The right to be assured, wherever possible, access to variety of goods at competitive prices
- The right to be heard
- The right to seek redressal against unfair trade practices or unscrupulous exploitation of consumer
- The right to consumer education

The Act has created consumer courts and empowered them. It provides for a three-tier consumer grievance redressal machinery with the district forums at the base, the State Commission at the middle level, and the National Commission at the apex level. The state and national-level bodies also function as appellate authorities. Any verdict given by the National Commission can be challenged in the Supreme Court. No court fee is charged, which gives easy access to services of the court.

The Act also covers complaints relating to unfair trade practices, which include food adulteration, short weighing, and overcharging. Complaints can also be made against charging in excess of the maximum retail price printed on packs.

The Act also provides for the formation of consumer protection councils in every State. These councils do not have any legal authority but are meant to promote the cause of consumer protection relating to six consumer rights—right to safety, to be informed, to choose, to be heard, to redress, and to consumer education.

While behaving ethically earns companies points with consumers and helps build a good image, corporate social responsibility is what companies contribute willingly to society. This concept is discussed in the next section.

CORPORATE SOCIAL RESPONSIBILITY—THE BASIS

The purpose of business has traditionally been to make profits as described famously by the Nobel Prize winning economist, Dr Milton Friedman. In an article in *The New York Times Magazine* in 1970 he wrote, 'The social responsibility of business is to increase its profits.' Indeed, this thinking has guided managers across the world as they manage business corporations. It may well be argued that social responsibility is being fulfilled by the government; therefore business should be free to pursue profits relentlessly.

This argument is uncontested because the sole purpose of any corporation is to increase value for its stakeholders. Public disclosure of quarterly results put the spotlight on these functions of companies. Managers can be forgiven for their focus on values creation.

The idea of CSR was first mentioned in 1953 in HR Bowen's 'Social Responsibilities of the Business.' Since then, businesses have become aware that unrestricted greed for profits, while adding value for the short term, can lead to disastrous consequences. It has led to great misery, as exemplified by the financial crisis that occurred in 2008. The collapse of investment banks in the US led to huge problems across the world. Investors lost their wealth, old people found that their savings had evaporated and stock markets the world over crashed. In India the stock market lost almost two-thirds of its value. Subsequent growth rates in emerging markets have plunged. Banks ranging from Iceland to Mexico and China suddenly found they were stressed. The need for social responsibility of business arose once again. If business can lead to harm, should it not serve as a force for social good?

Peter Drucker was one of the first thinkers to realize that 'profit is not the purpose of business and the concept of profit maximization is not only meaningless, but dangerous.' The reason for such thinking is that business has a larger responsibility than to merely earn profits. Porter and Kramer (2006) say that corporate social responsibility (CSR) has four appeals, namely moral obligation, sustainability, license to operate, and reputation.

Definition and Scope

The United Nations Industrial Development Organization (UNIDO) defines CSR as 'a management concept whereby companies integrate social and environmental concerns in their business operations and interactions with their stakeholders.'

According to UNIDO, CSR is the way through which a company achieves a balance of economic, environmental, and social imperatives, called the 'triple-bottom-line approach', while at the same time, meeting the expectations of shareholders. There is a difference between CSR, which is a strategic business management concept, and charity, which includes sponsorships or philanthropy. The concept of CSR goes much beyond merely giving money for charity or social causes.

The basis of CSR is that a corporation is also a citizen as it enjoys the same legal insights and responsibilities as an individual. While companies use natural resources to make a profit, they also have the responsibility of caring about how their activities are impacting society. Therefore, corporations must integrate social, environmental, ethical, and consumer concerns into their business operations and strategy, simply because they do not act in isolation.

The pursuit of profit thus must be linked to 'improving the quality of life of the workforce, their families as well as of the community and society at large,' according to a report by the World Business Council for Sustainable Development (WBSD).

In India, CSR is still seen and conducted as a philanthropic activity. Though there have been attempts to provide schools and hospitals in backward areas, and many community development programmes have also been undertaken by companies, any philanthropic or charitable activity is viewed as CSR.

Corporate social responsibility, however, links companies to the goal of sustainable development by thinking beyond profits. The triple bottom line perspective takes the view that sustainable growth must have three elements:

- First, that the company must be financially secure
- Second, while pursuing profits, it should minimize or eliminate negative environmental impact, and
- Third, the company must act in conformity with societal expectations

Corporate social responsibility integrates all these objectives. Pfitzer, Bockstette, and Stamp (2013) write that companies must solve social problems because these represent daunting constraints to their operation and to opportunities for growth. 'Leaders of companies that are making significant progress in building large scale social enterprises consider solving major social problems in profitable ways to be *a* , if not *the*, raison d'etre,' they write. This idea has its origin in the work of Dr C. K Prahlad, who outlined business with a social cause in his book, *Fortune at the Bottom of the Pyramid*.

All these factors make CSR a wide and strategic tool that encompasses environmental and societal expectations. It also includes the following:

Eco-efficiency   Reducing harm to the environment including the company's carbon footprint

Responsible sourcing   Getting raw materials from places that do not exploit the environment or human resources

Labour standards   Giving people at least minimum wages, not employing child labour

Working conditions   Ensuring safe working conditions not only for its employees but at factories of sub-contractors as well

Employee and community relations   Undertaking activities that involve and improve employees and community

Achieving social equity   Companies should strive towards achieving the same status for people within a specific society or groups

Gender balance   Promoting equal participation of women and men in decision-making positions, no discrimination based on gender, unless there is a sound biological reason for different treatment

Human rights   Moral principles or norms that describe standards of human behaviour, and are regularly protected as legal rights in national and international law

Good governance   How companies and public institutions conduct public affairs and manage public resources.

Anti-corruption measures   Companies must institute practices that do not require the giving and taking of bribes.

It can be seen from this discussion that CSR is much more than a philanthropic tool. It becomes more a way of conducting business than throwing money at charitable causes. 'Creating shared value entails embedding a social mission in the corporate culture and channelling resources to the development of innovations that can help solve social problems,' explain Pfitzer, Bockstette, and Stamp.

Table 18.1 gives a list of a few CSR initiatives carried out in India.

Legal Provisions Relating to CSR in India

CSR has been made mandatory in India under clause 135 of the Companies Act, 2013. The law mandates that all companies, including foreign firms, with a minimum net worth of ₹500 crore, turnover of ₹1000 crore, and net profit of at least ₹5 crore, spend at least two percent of their profit on

TABLE 18.1 Some CSR initiatives in India

Company	Areas of operation	Initiative
Amul	Inclusive growth through work with dairy farmers	Amul Relief Trust, tree plantations, providing animal husbandry inputs to farmers
Bajaj Auto	Community development—education, health, women empowerment, self-reliance, rural development, environment, and natural resources	Trust undertakes long-term projects in rural areas
Castrol	Community service—Castrol drive for safety initiative	Rehabilitation of earthquake affected victims in Gujarat
Mahindra & Mahindra	Education, environment, health, culture, and sports	Operates through KC Mahindra Education Trust, Mahindra Foundation, Tech Mahindra Foundation
Infosys	Support and encourages underprivileged sections	Infosys Foundation provides medical facilities to remote rural areas, organizes pension schemes, a library for every school, Human Capital Education index for its employees
ITC	Empowering farmers	Watershed development programme, greening wastelands, e-choupal, organizing farmers, primary education, livestock development, social forestry, integrated watershed development
L&T	Community service and environment protection	Create awareness on HIV/AIDS
Dabur	Overall socio-economic development of the rural and urban poor, ecological regeneration and protection of endangered plant species, health, and hygiene	Sustainable Development Society (SUNDESH)

CSR. As a result of this provision, around 8000 companies fall into the ambit of the CSR provisions. It is expected that this would lead companies spending $1.95 billion to $2.44 billion on CSR activities. With this law, India became the only country that has made a legislation for CSR spending.

The Act lists out a set of activities eligible under CSR. These include the following:

- Eradicating extreme hunger and poverty
- Promotion of education
- Promoting gender equality and empowering women
- Reducing child mortality and improving maternal health
- Combating HIV, AIDS, malaria, and other diseases
- Ensuring environmental sustainability
- Imparting employment enhancing vocational skills
- Social business projects
- Contribution to certain funds

Under the law, a company has to give preference to local areas and also take local conditions into account while formulating CSR activities. It can implement CSR activities through the following methods:

CB IN ACTION   Mandatory CSR?

Debate in your class whether mandatory CSR can help social causes in India. After all, charity comes from the heart, not by diktat. Yet, the law makes a provision that companies with a certain turnover and profits must spend two per cent of their average profits on CSR activities.

Would this not amount to companies throwing money at NGOs just to meet their CSR requirements? After all, many NGOs in India do not have very high credibility. Many are set up just to siphon off government and foreign funds and are, in fact, run by politicians. Would it not be better to leave CSR to the conscience of companies rather than impose a fixed limit? Would it not limit companies?

Further, as we have seen in the chapter, strategic CSR is much more than merely spending on social causes. It gets built into the DNA of a company. What about a company which continues to pollute, exploits its manpower and other resources, does not maintain labour standards, but still contributes two per cent of profits to CSR? Does that make it a socially responsible company?

Address these questions in the debate. What conclusions do you reach?

- Directly on its own
- Through its own non-profit foundation to facilitate this initiative
- Through independently registered non-profit organizations that have a record of at least three years in similar related activities
- Collaborating or pooling their resources with other companies

All CSR funds must be spent in India. The Act excludes money spent on activities that are part of the normal course of the company's business or on projects for the exclusive benefit of employees or their family members. Contributions to political parties are not permitted under CSR activities. However, companies are allowed to contribute their CSR funds to support development projects initiated by the prime minister or central government. A company is required to set-up a CSR committee to oversee the implementation of the activities.

CONCLUSION

Marketing managers will, at some time or the other, face a dilemma whether to do what they think is right or whether they should just 'get the job done.' Ethical questions are bound to arise, such as not disclosing all information about a product which could make the customer turn away, or hiding the side effects of consuming certain things, or manipulating consumer psychology to create a need for certain brands.

Both individual and organizational ethics come into play when we consider such questions. For many people, getting the job done becomes important than worrying about what is right and what is wrong. Perhaps, that is why we see many consequences of unrestrained consumption around us.

However, it is the ethical consideration that makes us human. Consideration about others and providing the basis of good life for all separates us from other life forms. In business, it is the ethical company that gains long-term success; unethical concerns fall quickly when hit by gusts of bad publicity. Perhaps, it is time to implement Aristotle's principles back in our lives.

SUMMARY

Most people think of themselves as generally ethical. However, they cannot escape the responsibility for consequences that they cause, knowingly or not, by their consuming decisions. Companies, too, are in the business of influencing people; hence, ethics of society and the impact of marketing on culture too get overlapped. Ethical behaviour in the marketplace has two sides—companies who would like to reduce costs even while disregarding some ethical consideration, and the consumers who clamour for low prices.

Some of the ethical issues that arise in marketing are payment of gifts and bribes, price discrimination, dishonest advertising, cheating, unfair competitive practices, not meeting contractual obligations, unfairness to employees, targeting vulnerable sections or portraying others in poor light, and tax avoidance. Even though some of these are not related to marketing, consumers get affected by bad publicity when accidents happen. Companies have to focus on all aspects of their business, from manufacturing to hiring to sub-contracting to avoid consumer backlash and loss of reputation. Both intended and unintended consequences of marketing actions have to be kept in mind.

The theory of due care to customers is based on the assumption that the manufacturer has greater knowledge, and thus, has the moral duty to deliver a product that is safe and lives up to its claims. It has the following elements—design, materials, production, quality control, packaging, notification, and business methods.

When consumers become aware and prefer buying products which are ethically produced and/or which are not harmful to the environment and society. It includes buying local produce, boycotting goods produced by child labour, buying organic products, and using energy-efficient lighting. The key factors that impede consumers from consuming ethical goods are price, experience, ethical obligation, lack of information, quality perception, inertia, cynicism, and suppressing their guilt.

Companies also resort to greenwashing—the disinformation disseminated by them so as to present an environmentally responsible public image. It includes the practice of misleading customers about the ethical or environmental benefits of a product through false advertising.

The consumer protection law regulates relationships between consumers and companies. It covers a wide range of topics including product liability, privacy rights, unfair business practices, fraud, misrepresentation, and other consumer or business interactions.

KEY TERMS

Carbon footprint The sum of all emissions of greenhouse gases such as carbon dioxide, induced by activities of a person or organization in a given time frame

Consumer protection Law to regulate relationships between consumers and companies, covering product liability, privacy rights, unfair business practices, fraud, misrepresentation, and other consumer or business interactions

Corporate social responsibility A management concept whereby companies integrate social and environmental concerns in their business operations and interactions with their stakeholders

Ethical consumerism The practice of purchasing products and services produced in a way that minimizes social and/or environmental damage, while avoiding products and services deemed to have a negative impact on society or the environment

Ethics A branch of philosophy that studies morals and values

Greenwashing Disinformation disseminated by an organization so as to present an environmentally responsible public image, including the practice of misleading customers about the ethical or environmental benefits of a product through false advertising

Marketing ethics Applying standards of fairness, or moral rights and wrongs, to marketing decision-making, actions, and practice

Theory of due care The theory is based on the assumption that the manufacturer has greater knowledge, and thus, has the moral duty to deliver a product that is safe and lives up to its claims

EXERCISES

Concept-review Questions

1. What is ethics? Why is it necessary to study ethics in consumer behaviour?
2. What is the difference between legal requirements and ethical requirements? Can they be reconciled?
3. Describe the ethical issues in marketing. Give examples to support your answer.
4. Distinguish between intended and unintended consequences of consumption.
5. Explain the theory of due care and the elements included in it.
6. Describe some of the unintended consequences of marketing.
7. Explain the concept of ethical consumption. What are the factors impeding ethical consumption?
8. What is greenwashing? How do companies greenwash?
9. Describe how globalization affects ethics.
10. Describe consumer protection. What are the salient features of the Consumer Protection Act?

Critical Thinking Questions

1. 'Ethical behaviour in the marketplace has two sides: companies who would like to reduce costs even while disregarding some ethical consideration, and the consumers who clamour for low prices.' Can these two conflicting behaviours be reconciled? How?
2. 'A company cannot be responsible for unintended consequences of its actions.' How far is this statement true? Can companies really do something about unintended consequences of marketing activities?
3. 'Marketing vulgarizes spiritual values and culture.' Critically examine this statement by taking arguments on both sides. What is your take on this?
4. Do you think that ethical consumption will really make a difference to the environment? Does it not amount to encouraging inefficient, small-scale local producers who may not even keep the safety standards into account?

Projects and Assignments

1. Take any product that you use. Study the company and follow its supply chain from manufacturing to marketing. Is this product totally ethical? What are the gaps that you could observe while studying its supply chains?
2. Conduct an experiment. Show your friends pictures of some people in their social environment and ask your friends what they think of them. How many gave their impression about the people by considering what they owned? What does this experiment show?
3. Visit a local supermarket. Check out the section where they display the organic foods. How are these foods different from others? Is there a real difference or stated difference? Find out from the manufacturer whether the claims made are actually true.
4. Visit the site of consumer court. Find out what type of complaints are filed by consumers and the judgements delivered. What can you conclude about ethics of the companies mentioned in the complaints?

REFERENCES

Bray, Jeffery, Nick Johns, and David Kilburn, 'An exploratory study into the factors impeding ethical consumption', *Journal of Business Ethics*, February 2011, Vol. 98, Issue 4, pp. 597–608, 2011.

Carrigan, Marylyn and Ahmad Attalla, 'The myth of the ethical consumer—Do ethics matter in purchase behaviour?', *Journal of Consumer Marketing*, Vol. 18, Issue 7, pp. 560–578, 2001.

DeGeorge, R.T., 'Ethics in international business—A contradiction in terms?, *Business Credit*, September 2000, Vol. 102, Issue 8, 2000.

Durning, Alan Thein, *How Much Is Enough?: The Consumer Society and the Future of the Earth*, Worldwatch Environmental Alert Series, W. W. Norton and Co., New York, 1992.

Fleckenstein, M., 'Due care theory' in R. Kolb (Ed.), *Encyclopedia of business ethics and society*, SAGE Publications, Thousand Oaks, CA, pp. 622–624, 2008.

http://164.100.47.134/intranet/CorporateSociaResponsbility.pdf, last accessed on 21 October 2014.

http://rbi.org.in/scripts/PublicationsView.aspx?id=14367, last accessed 25 July 2014.

http://www.unido.org/en/what-we-do/trade/csr/what-is-csr.html, last accessed on 21 October 2014.

Institute of Grocery Distribution (IGD), http://www.igd.com/our-expertise/Sustainability/Ethical-social-issues/3429/Ethical-Consumerism/, last accessed on 25 July 2014.

Kewalramani, Devika and Richard, J. Sobelsohn, 'Greenwashing: Deceptive business claims of eco-friendliness', http://www.forbes.com/sites/realspin/2012/03/20/greenwashing-deceptive-business-claims-of-eco-friendliness/, last accessed on 25 July 2014.

McDevitt, R. Giapponi, C. and C. Tromley, 'A model of ethical decision-making: The integration of process and content', *Journal of Business Ethics*, Vol. 73 No. 2, pp. 219–229, 2007.

'Obesity rates climbing worldwide', *The Times of India*, 30 May 2014.

Ogilvy Earth, 'From greenwash to great', https://assets.ogilvy.com/truffles_email/ogilvyearth/Greenwash_Digital.pdf, last accessed on 25 July 2014.

Pfitzer, Marc, Valerie Bockstette, and Mike Stamp, 'Innovating for shared value', *Harvard Business Review*, September 2013.

Porter, Michael E. and Mark R. Kramer, 'Strategy and society: The link between competitive advantage and corporate social responsibility, *Harvard Business Review*, December, 2006.

Price Waterhouse and Co., *Handbook on Corporate Social Responsibility in India*, www.pwc.in/.../handbook-on-corporate-social-responsibility-in-india.pdf, last accessed on 21 October 2014.

Siegel, Lee, 'America the vulgar', *The Wall Street Journal*, 6 December 2013: http://online.wsj.com/news/articles/SB10001424052702304451904579238140379017148, last accessed on 25 July 2014.

Sove, Elizabeth and Alan Warde, 'Inconspicuous consumption: The sociology of consumption, lifestyles and the environment', in Dunlap, et al. (Ed.), *Sociological Theory and the Environment: Classical Foundations, Contemporary Insights*, Rowman and Littlefield Publishers, Oxford, 2002.

Terrachoice, 'The sins of greenwashing', http://sinsofgreenwashing.org/index35c6.pdf, last accessed on 25 July 2014.

World Business Council for Sustainable Development CSR: Meeting changing expectations, http://www.wbcsd.org/pages/edocument/edocumentdetails.aspx?id=82&nosearchcontextkey=true, last accessed on 21 October 2014.

CASE STUDY
Rana Plaza Disaster

Companies build their supply chains across the length and breadth of the globe, trying to leverage lower costs wherever they are available. Unfortunately, this is done very often by ignoring some aspect of the human or environmental cost in other countries.

Till the supply chain works well, everybody is happy—consumers get cheap products, companies make their profits, and poor workers get some money that they otherwise would not. However, when accidents occur, the horrific conditions of work are exposed, public perception about the brands take a beating, consumers start boycotting the brands involved, and the industry is forced to do something about the factories.

This case study is about the garment industry in Bangladesh, which has boomed into a $19 billion dollar industry, according to Accord Foundation. Its website says, 'The Bangladeshi textile and garment manufacturing sector is fuelled by young, urbanizing workers, many of whom are women. With the majority of production destined for US and European markets, Bangladesh's ready-made garment industry now accounts for approximately 78 per cent of total exports, second only to China as the world's largest apparel exporter.' The factories churn out clothes for brands such as Benetton, Bonmarché, the Children's Place, El Corte Inglés, Joe Fresh, Monsoon Accessorize, Mango, Matalan, Primark, and Wal-Mart.

How these factories operate is a different matter altogether. Their unsafe conditions have been highlighted by several fires and building collapses, and was once again brought into media focus on 24 April 2013, when an eight-story building—Rana Plaza in Bangladesh—collapsed. The building housed five clothing factories, making clothes for well-known brands. There were 1129 casualties and 2515 people were rescued. It was one of the worst industrial accidents of modern times.

The accident was avoidable. A day prior to the accident, a TV channel recorded footage showing cracks in the Rana Plaza building and the building had been evacuated. Cracks had appeared; while the shops and the bank in the building were immediately closed, the owner stressed it was safe for others. The workers were ordered to work after being threatened that they would not be paid for the entire month. The rush was because suppliers were penalized and five percent was deducted for each week of delay from the payment, as reported by *The Guardian* (2014). It was also revealed that the top four floors had been built without a permit, and that the building was made to house only shops and offices. The structure was not strong enough to bear the weight and vibration of heavy machinery. Most victims were women, along with a number of their children, who were in nursery facilities within the building.

There was widespread condemnation of the accident. BBC reported (2013) that Pope Francis denounced the 'slave labour' and said he had been shocked by reports that some of the labourers had been paid just 38 euros a month. 'Today in the world this slavery is being committed against something beautiful that God has given us—the capacity to create, to work, to have dignity,' the Pope said at a private Mass. 'Not paying a fair wage, not giving a job because you are only looking at balance sheets, only looking to make a profit, that goes against God,' he was quoted as saying by Vatican radio.

Consumers revolted as well and there were protests in England outside Primark stores. In the US, people were agitated, unleashing their anger at retailers who did not have any connections to Rana Plaza, but sourced their manufacturing to Bangladesh. There was anger for the fact that had the brands accepted their responsibility towards those workers, or had they imposed safety standards as per the norms in their home countries, no one would have died.

Several organizations have become active to improve the conditions of workers. The Clean Clothes Campaign makes a pledge for consumers on its website, 'I want the women and men who stitch my clothes to earn enough to feed their family, pay their rent and live a decent life. A living wage is a human right, for all people all over the world. I say it's time to pay a living wage to all garment workers.' Financial support was promised; yet, compensation is far away. A year after the collapse, just one-third of the funds needed have been contributed and only half of all brands associated with factories in the collapsed building have made any contribution. The legal position is that the workers were not employees of the brands; they were employees of contractors so the brands could not be forced to pay.

However, the very purpose of international outsourcing is low cost; it is unlikely that these low costs can be achieved if safety and compensation standards as applied in the West are applied in poor countries as well.

Questions for Discussion

1. Are consumers—constantly demanding low prices—to be blamed for companies paying less to their contract staff?
2. What should be the ethical position of big brands that get work done in poor countries at a low cost?
3. How do reports of accidents as the Rana Plaza impact consumers? Do you think there are long-

term impacts or, since public memory is short, companies should not bother about the bad publicity?
4. How should companies balance out demands for low cost on one hand and ethical dealings on the other? Can a balance ever be reached?

Sources:

BBC (2013), 'Bangladesh "slave labour" condemned by Pope', 1 May 2013: http://www.bbc.com/news/world-asia-22370487.

Burke, Jason, 'Rana Plaza: One year on from the Bangladesh factory disaster', *The Guardian*, 19 April 2014: http://www.theguardian.com/world/2014/apr/19/rana-plaza-bangladesh-one-year-on.

http://en.wikipedia.org/wiki/2013_Savar_building_collapse 2014.

http://www.bangladeshaccord.org/bangladesh/.

http://www.cleanclothes.org/.

All last accessed on 25 July 2014.

Index

4Ps 649

Adopter categories 438
Advertising 215
Advertising analytics 550
Advertising and reinforcement 287
Advertising wear-out 286
Age subcultures 407
Analytic hierarchy process 198
Attitude 302, 304
   and behaviour 316
   Towards the ad 310
   Towards the store 312
   Functions 304
   Nature 304
Attitude formation 314
Attitude model 308
   Multi-attribute 308
   Tri-component 307
Avatar-based marketing 200

B2B brands 118
B2B buying behaviour 112
   Individual determinants 112
   Institutional buying 115
   Organizational determinants 113
B2B e-marketplace 122
B2B markets 99
   Characteristics 99
B2B relationships 122
B2B transactions 103
   Buying drivers 103
   Ethical issues 126
   Products 105
   Purchase process 107
   Segments 108
   Services 107
Bata 32
Behavioural learning 272
   Classical conditioning 272
   Instrumental 274
Brain scanning 237
   Mirror neurons 240

Brand communities 444
Brand engagement 658
Brand love 218
Brand loyalty 293
Brand personality 218
Brand personality 154
   Anthropomorphism 158
   Brand personification 154
Brands squeezed dry 655
Business market 98
   Business user markets 98
   Supply chain market 98
Buying centre 117
Buying situations 116
   Modified rebuy 116
   New task buying 116
   Straight rebuy 116

Central and peripheral routes 270
Changing attitudes 317
   Cognitive dissonance theory 318
   Elaboration likelihood model 318
   Ideal point method 318
   Learning theory 318
Children as consumers 350
Cognitive learning 278
   and marketing models 284
   Cognitive processes 283
Cognitive personality factors 150
   Compulsive consumption 151
   Consumer ethnocentrism 152
   Cosmopolitanism 153
   Fixation 151
   Impulsive 151
   Materialism 150
Communication models 469
   AIDA model 471
   Fogg's behaviour model 472
Communications strategy 474
Comparative advertising 486
Consumer behaviour 18
   Economic uncertainty 18
   Future 21

Consumer culture 5
Consumer decision journey 84, 613
Consumer decision-making 65
   Cognitive models 65
   Economic models 65
Consumer decision-making process 68
   Alternative evaluation 71
   Purchase decision 71
   Recognizing the problem 68
   Search for information 70
Consumer dogmatism 147
Consumer engagement 647
Consumer imagery 500
Consumer influence 455
Consumer innovativeness 146
Consumer learning 264
   Elements 266
Consumer motivation 181
Consumer protection 692
Consumer psychology 15
Consumer psychology 17
   Limitations 17
Consumer research 518
   Primary research 521
   Process 523
   Secondary research 521
   Types 520
Consumers as innovators 456
Consumer satisfaction 565
   Customer satisfaction index 569
   Kano model 568
   Measuring 567
   Servqual model 567
   Theories 566
Consumer socialization 348
Corporate social responsibility 693
Counter-segmentation 52
Critical mass 440
Culture 377
   Characteristics 378
   Measuring 398
Customer engagement 649, 657
   Value 657
Customer equity 664
Customer equity management 658
Customer loyalty 573
   Benefits 575
   Loyalty programmes 586
   Measuring 578
Customer-perceived value 246
Customer value 660
   Lifetime value 661
   Referral value 662

Dark marketing 168
Data analytics 548, 631
Data mining 548, 631
De-massifying markets 30
Depth interviews 535
Dialogue marketing 665
Differences between B2B and B2C 101
Diffusion process 434
   Buzz 449
   Word of mouth 449
Digital value 621

Economic man 68
Elaboration likelihood model 483
Ethical consumption 686
Ethnographic research 532
Experiential marketing 244

Family 343, 356, 357
   Decision-making 357
   Life cycle 356

Globalization and ethics 691
Goal-directed behaviour 89
Goals 182, 184
   Nature and function 184
Greenwashing 689
Guerrilla marketing 451

Happiness and adaptability 393
Hedonic consumption 216
Hofstede's cultural dimensions 380

Imagery in marketing 217
Indian core values 388
Indian family 345
Innovation 423
   Disruptive 432
   Firm-oriented 429
   Market-oriented 429
   Process 432

Product-oriented   430
Service   431
Innovation value chain   433

Laddering   535
L'oréal   27

Making brands 'cool'   445
Marketing   8, 351
  Seniors   355
  Youth   351
Measuring brand image   251
Measuring learning   292
Media strategy   491
Message appeals   487
  Hedonic and utilitarian   489
  Slice of life   489
Models of consumer behaviour   72
  Engel–Blackwell–Miniard   79
  Howard–Sheth   76
  Nicosia   73
Models of innovation diffusion   440
Motivational dimensions   196
Motivation research   196
Motives   182, 192
Multinational strategies   408
  Global   409
  Glocal   411
  Local   411

Needs   182, 184
  Characteristics   184
  Maslow's hierarchy of   185
Negative publicity   501
Neo-Freudian theory   140
  Alfred Adler   140
  Carl Jung   140
  Karen Horney   141
Net promoter score   581

Online buying   607
Online merchants   620
Online segmentation   607

Passive to active learning   268
Perception   214, 215
  Altering perceptions   245
  Exposure   224

Perception levels   236
  Subliminal   236
Perceptual categorization   232
Perceptual inference   230
  Celebrity endorsements   232
  Halo effect   231
  Perceptual distortion   231
  Price perception   232
  Semiotics   230
  Stereotyping   231
  Umbrella brand name   232
Perceptual interpretation   228
Perceptual mapping   249
Perceptual organization   241
  Gestalt psychology   241
Personality   137
  Freudian theory   138
  Nature   137
  Theories   137
Post-purchase behaviour   71
  Cognitive dissonance   71
  Customer equity   71
Private labels   298
Product personality   159
  and colour   163
  and geography   162
Product placement   324
Purchase continuum   563
  High involvement   564
  Limited involvement   565
  Low involvement   564
Purchase decisions   562
  Brand loyal   563
  Complex   563
  Dissonance-reducing   563
  Habitual   563
  Impulsive   563
  Variety-seeking   563

Real-time experience tracking   549
Recency, frequency, and monetary value model   579
Reference groups   442, 499
Retention   234
Reverse socialization   349
Rolls-royce   95

Schwartz's model   387
Segmentation   30, 34–38, 40–42

Bases   34
Benefit   40
Demographic   36
Geographic   35
Hybrid   42
Psychographic   38
Psychological   41
Sociocultural   37
Use-related   42
Self and self-image   164
Self-determination theory   191
Sensory marketing   220
Share of wallet   580
Social class   360
   Indian social class segments   361
   Measuring   364
   Status consumption   363
Social class profiles   366
   Geodemographic clustering   367
Social media   626
   Omnichannel marketing   629
   Online communities   630
   Social behaviour of consumers   626
Social media analysis   550
Social movements   444
Social networking   450
Society   10
   McDonaldization   10
Stimulus discrimination   291
Stimulus generalization   288
   Counterfeit products   291
   Family branding   290
   Licensing   291
   Product line extensions   289

Symbols and signs   397

Theory of planned behaviour   86, 314
Theory of reasoned action   85, 309
Theory of trying   88
Theory of trying to consume   314
Trait theory   143
   Five-factor model   143
   Sixteen personality factors   144
Tribes and tribal marketing   445
Types of loyalty   577
   Contractual   577
   Emotional   578
   Functional   577
   Transactional   577

Uncertainty avoidance   385

Values   386
   Instrumental   386
   Terminal   386
Vicarious learning   276
Viral marketing   451, 499

Web equity   623
Weber's law   236
WOM techniques   498
   Buzz   499
   Reference groups   499

Yankelovich mindbase   48

Zaltman metaphor elicitation technique   199

About the Author

Dinesh Kumar, PhD, formerly Associate Professor (Marketing) at Birla Institute of Management Technology (BIMTECH), Greater Noida, has over 16 years of experience in academia, wherein he taught at management institutions such as FORE School of Management and University Business School, Panjab University, Chandigarh. He has also been awarded fellowships twice for teaching in Norway. Dr Kumar currently resides and teaches in Chandigarh.

His industry experience of 15 years includes stints as Director at Mastermind Consultants, Business Manager at US Embassy in New Delhi, and Associate Director at the Centre for Science and Environment.

He has presented and published many papers and has a large number of articles to his credit.

He is the author of *Marketing Channels* (OUP, 2012).

Related Titles

Marketing (9780198079446)
Baines, Cranfield University, **Fill,** University of Portsmouth, **Page,** Cardiff Business School, and **Sinha,** IIM Ahmedabad

Marketing is an exciting new textbook packed with learning features, combining authority with a lively and engaging writing style; and a diverse range of resources available online.

Key Features
- Provides separate chapters on digital marketing, relationship marketing, not-for-profit marketing, postmodern marketing, and marketing, sustainability, and ethics
- Numerous case insights, market insights, and research insights have been included along with contemporary marketing practices with relevant examples drawn from international as well as Asian markets to help readers understand and apply marketing theory
- Includes well-integrated online resource centre for lecturers and students

Sales And Distribution Management, 2/e (9780198077046) **Tapan K. Panda,** Great Lakes Institute of Management Studies, Chennai and **Sunil Sahadev,** University of Sheffield, UK

The second edition of *Sales and Distribution Management* is a comprehensive textbook, which has been updated and enlarged with new chapters. Specially designed to meet the requirements of management students specializing in sales and marketing, it gives a balanced presentation of the concepts of sales and distribution through examples and cases.

Key Features
- Contains classroom-tested cases from Indian as also international business organizations
- Includes examples and boxed exhibits in key areas of sales and distribution management
- Includes online resource centre encompassing resources to support the faculty using this text

Brand Management (9780198069867)
Kirti Dutta, Bhartiya Vidya Bhavan's Usha and Lakshmi Mittal Institute of Management, New Delhi

Brand Management–Principles and Practices is a comprehensive textbook designed for students of postgraduate management programmes specializing in marketing. It explores the core concepts of branding and illustrates them through numerous examples, exhibits, figures, images, case studies, and videos.

Key Features
- Provides rich learning from brand practices of Indian brands such as Kingfisher, Maggi, Airtel, Aircel, Micromax, ITC, and LIC
- Discusses practices of global and Indian companies such as Singapore Airlines, Lux, Amul, and Tata Group, and includes exhibits with marketing insights from industry
- Includes exclusive chapters on creating a brand, understanding organizational culture, consumer behaviour, e-branding, and managing brand architecture

Advertisement Management, 2/e (9780198074120)
Jaishri Jethwaney, Professor at the Indian Institute of Mass Communication (IIMC), New Delhi and **Shruti Jain,** Chief Communications Officer and Global Head- CSR, EXL Service

The second edition of *Advertising Management* is a comprehensive textbook tailored to meet the syllabi requirements of management students, mass media, and stand-alone courses on advertising. Interspersed with examples, exhibits, and real-life cases, the book provides an in-depth coverage of the key components, namely advertising and promotions, media strategy and planning, and agency relationships.

Key Features
- Discusses new topics such as measurement of brand equity, positioning platforms, media scheduling, and sales-force sales promotion in detail
- Examines the advertising strategies followed by business organizations using numerous cases and examples
- Explores the emerging issues in advertising management from an Indian perspective

---

Also by the same Author: Dinesh Kumar   *Marketing Channels* (9780198077091)

Other Related Titles

9780198062929	Rajneesh Krishna: *Consumer Behaviour*	9780198072027	Pradip Kumar Mallik: *Sales Management*
9780195676969	Sunanda Easwaran & Sharmila J. Singh: *Marketing Research*	9780195667585	Govind Apte: *Services Marketing*
9780198069843	Parag Kulkarni, Sunita Jahirabadkar & Pradip Chande, *e-Business*	9780195689082	Vinnie Jauhari: *Services: Marketing, Operations and Management*
9780198077022	Rakesh Mohan Joshi: *International Marketing, 2/e*	9780198061151	Chetan Bajaj, Rajnish Tuli & Nidhi Varma Srivastava *Retail Management, 2/e*
9780198089407	Justin Paul & Rajiv Aserkar: *Export Import Management, 2/e*	9780198075943	Piyush Kumar Sinha & Dwarika Prasad Uniyal: *Managing Retailing, 2/e*
		9780195677942	P. K. Ghosh: *Industrial Marketing*

Visit us at www.oup.co.in and www.oupinheonline.com